For Students

MEANINGFUL HELP AND FEEDBACK

- Personalized interactive learning aids are available for point-of-use help and immediate feedback. These learning aids include:
  - Help Me Solve This walks students through solving an algorithmic version of the questions they are working, with additional detailed tutorial reminders. These informational cues assist the students and help them understand concepts and mechanics.
  - eText links students directly to the concept covered in the problem they are completing.
  - Homework and practice exercises with additional algorithmically generated problems are available for further practice and mastery.
  - NEW! Worked Out Solutions—now available to students when they are reviewing their submitted and graded homework. The Worked Out Solutions provide step-by-step explanations on how to solve select problems using the exact numbers and data that were presented to the student in the problem.
- NEW! Dynamic Study Modules—Using a highly personalized, algorithmically driven process, Dynamic Study Modules continuously assess students' performance and provide additional practice in the areas where they struggle the most.

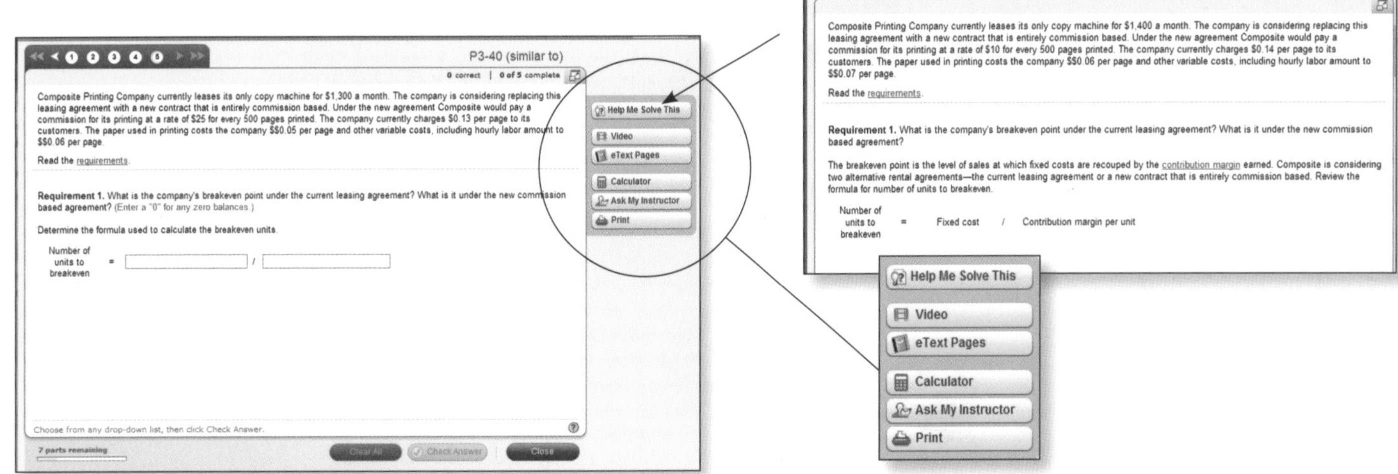

PERSONALIZED AND ADAPTIVE STUDY PATH

- Assist students in monitoring their own progress by offering them a customized study plan powered by Knewton, based on Homework, Quiz, and Test results.
- Regenerated exercises offer unlimited practice and the opportunity to prove mastery through Quizzes on recommended learning objectives.

Cost Accounting

A Managerial Emphasis

Fifteenth Edition

Charles T. Horngren
Stanford University

Srikant M. Datar
Harvard University

Madhav V. Rajan
Stanford University

PEARSON

Boston Columbus Indianapolis New York San Francisco Upper Saddle River
Amsterdam Cape Town Dubai London Madrid Milan Munich Paris Montréal Toronto
Delhi Mexico City São Paulo Sydney Hong Kong Seoul Singapore Taipei Tokyo

Editor in Chief: Donna Battista
Acquisitions Editor: Ellen Geary
Editorial Project Manager: Nicole Sam
Editorial Assistant: Christine Donovan
Marketing Manager: Alison Haskins
Managing Editor: Jeff Holcomb
Project Manager: Roberta Sherman
Manufacturing Buyer: Carol Melville
Senior Art Director: Anthony Gemmellaro
Cover Designer: Liz Harasymczuk
Manager, Rights and Permissions: Samantha Graham
Cover Photo: © JOHN KELLERMAN/Alamy
Editorial Media Project Manager: James Bateman
Production Media Project Manager: John Cassar
Full-Service Project Management and Composition: Integra
Printer/Binder: Courier/Kendallville
Cover Printer: Lehigh-Phoenix Color/Hagerstown
Text Font: 10/12 Sabon

Credits and acknowledgments borrowed from other sources and reproduced, with permission, in this textbook appear on appropriate page within text (or on page 938).

Library of Congress Cataloging-in-Publication Data
Horngren, Charles T.
Cost accounting: a managerial emphasis/Charles T. Horngren, Stanford University, Srikant M. Datar, Harvard University, Madhav V. Rajan, Stanford University.—Fifteenth edition.
pages cm
Includes bibliographical references and index.
ISBN 978-0-13-342870-4
1. Cost accounting. I. Datar, Srikant M. II. Rajan, Madhav V. III. Title.
HF5686.C8H59 2015
658.15'11—dc23

2013047266

10 9 8 7 6 5 4 3 2 1

ISBN-10: 0-13-342870-2
ISBN-13: 978-0-13-342870-4

Brief Contents

Contents

About the Authors

Charles T. Horngren was the Edmund W. Littlefield Professor of Accounting, Emeritus, at Stanford University. A Graduate of Marquette University, he received his MBA from Harvard University and his PhD from the University of Chicago. He was also the recipient of honorary doctorates from Marquette University and DePaul University.

A certified public accountant, Horngren served on the Accounting Principles Board for six years, the Financial Accounting Standards Board Advisory Council for five years, and the Council of the American Institute of Certified Public Accountants for three years. For six years, he served as a trustee of the Financial Accounting Foundation, which oversees the Financial Accounting Standards Board and the Government Accounting Standards Board. Horngren was a member of the Accounting Hall of Fame.

A member of the American Accounting Association, Horngren had been its president and its director of research. He received its first Outstanding Accounting Educator Award. The California Certified Public Accountants Foundation gave Horngren its Faculty Excellence Award and its Distinguished Professor Award. He was the first person to have received both awards.

The American Institute of Certified Public Accountants presented its first Outstanding Educator Award to Horngren. Horngren was named Accountant of the Year, Education, by the national professional accounting fraternity, Beta Alpha Psi. Professor Horngren was also a member of the Institute of Management Accountants, from whom he received its Distinguished Service Award. He was also a member of the Institutes' Board of Regents, which administers the Certified Management Accountant examinations.

Horngren is the author of other accounting books published by Pearson Education: *Introduction to Management Accounting*, 15th ed. (2011, with Sundem, and Stratton); *Introduction to Financial Accounting*, 10th ed. (2011, with Sundem and Elliott); *Accounting*, 8th ed. (2010, with Harrison and Bamber); and *Financial Accounting*, 8th ed. (2010, with Harrison).

Horngren was the Consulting Editor for the Charles T. Horngren Series in Accounting.

Srikant M. Datar is the Arthur Lowes Dickinson Professor at the Harvard Business School. He served as Senior Associate Dean from 2000 to 2010. A graduate with distinction from the University of Bombay, he received gold medals upon graduation from the Indian Institute of Management, Ahmedabad, and the Institute of Cost and Works Accountants of India. A chartered accountant, he holds two master's degrees and a PhD from Stanford University.

Datar has published his research in leading accounting, marketing, and operations management journals, including *The Accounting Review, Contemporary Accounting Research, Journal of Accounting, Auditing and Finance, Journal of Accounting and Economics, Journal of Accounting Research,* and *Management Science.* He has served as an associate editor and on the editorial board of several journals and has presented his research to corporate executives and academic audiences in North America, South America, Asia, Africa, Australia, and Europe. He is a coauthor of three other books: *Managerial Accounting: Making Decisions and Motivating Performance, Rethinking the MBA: Business Education at a Crossroads*, and *Rethinking Graduate Management Education in Latin America.*

Cited by his students as a dedicated and innovative teacher, Datar received the George Leland Bach Award for Excellence in the Classroom at Carnegie Mellon University and the Distinguished Teaching Award at Stanford University.

Datar is a member of the board of directors of Novartis A.G., ICF International, T-Mobile US, and Stryker Corporation and has worked with many organizations, including Apple Computer, Boeing, DuPont, Ford, General Motors, Morgan Stanley, PepsiCo, Visa, and the World Bank. He is a member of the American Accounting Association and the Institute of Management Accountants.

Madhav V. Rajan is the Robert K. Jaedicke Professor of Accounting and Senior Associate Dean for Academic Affairs at Stanford University's Graduate School of Business. He is also Professor of Law (by courtesy) at Stanford Law School. Rajan oversees the MBA and MSx programs as well as the Marketing and Organizational Behavior faculty areas at the GSB.

Rajan received his undergraduate degree in commerce from the University of Madras, India, and his MS in accounting, MBA, and PhD degrees from Carnegie Mellon University. In 1990, his dissertation won the Alexander Henderson Award for Excellence in Economic Theory.

Rajan's primary area of research interest is the economics-based analysis of management accounting issues, especially as they relate to internal control, capital budgeting, quality management, supply chain and performance systems in firms. He has published his research in a variety of leading journals, including *The Accounting Review, Journal of Accounting Research, Management Science*, and *Review of Financial Studies*. In 2004, he received the Notable Contribution to Management Accounting Literature award. He is a coauthor of *Managerial Accounting: Making Decisions and Motivating Performance*.

Rajan has served as the Departmental Editor for Accounting at *Management Science* as well as associate editor for both the accounting and operations areas. From 2002 to 2008, Rajan served as an editor of *The Accounting Review*. Rajan has twice been a plenary speaker at the AAA Management Accounting Conference.

Rajan has received several teaching honors at Wharton and Stanford, including the David W. Hauck Award, the highest undergraduate teaching award at Wharton. He has taught in a variety of executive education programs, including the Stanford Executive Program and the National Football League Program for Managers, as well as custom programs for firms, including Genentech, Hewlett-Packard, and nVidia.

Rajan is a director of Cavium, Inc., and iShares, Inc., and a trustee of the iShares Trust.

Preface

Studying Cost Accounting is one of the best business investments a student can make. Why? Because success in any organization—from the smallest corner store to the largest multinational corporation—requires the use of cost accounting concepts and practices. Cost accounting provides key data to managers for planning and controlling, as well as costing products, services, even customers. This book focuses on how cost accounting helps managers make better decisions, as cost accountants are increasingly becoming integral members of their company's decision-making teams. In order to emphasize this prominence in decision making, we use the "different costs for different purposes" theme throughout this book. By focusing on basic concepts, analyses, uses, and procedures instead of procedures alone, we recognize cost accounting as a managerial tool for business strategy and implementation.

We also prepare students for the rewards and challenges they face in the professional cost accounting world of today and tomorrow. For example, we emphasize both the development of analytical skills such as Excel to leverage available information technology and the values and behaviors that make cost accountants effective in the workplace.

New to This Edition

Deeper Consideration of Global Issues

Businesses today have no choice but to integrate into an increasingly global ecosystem. Virtually all aspects, including supply chains, product markets, and the market for managerial talent, have become more international in their outlook. To illustrate this, we incorporate global considerations into many of the chapters. For example, Chapter 6 talks about the special challenges of budgeting in multinational companies while Chapter 23 discusses the challenges of evaluating the performance of divisions located in different countries. The opener for Chapter 17 highlights the differences in the way process flows are accounted for under U.S. and international accounting rules and the impact of these differences on companies' margins and after-tax income. Chapter 22 examines the importance of transfer pricing in minimizing the tax burden faced by multinational companies. Several new examples of management accounting applications in companies are drawn from international settings.

Increased Focus on Merchandising and Service Sectors

In keeping with the shifts in the U.S. and world economy, this edition makes greater use of merchandising and service sector examples, with corresponding de-emphasis of traditional manufacturing settings. For example, Chapter 10 illustrates linear cost functions in the context of payments for cloud computing services. Chapter 20 highlights inventory management in retail organizations and has a revised example based on a seller of sunglasses. Chapter 21 now incorporates a new running example that looks at capital budgeting in the context of a transportation company. Several Concepts in Action boxes focus on the merchandising and service sectors, including the use of activity-based costing to reduce the costs of health care delivery (Chapter 5), the structure of SGA costs at Nordstrom (Chapter 2), and an analysis of the operating income performance of Best Buy (Chapter 12).

Greater Emphasis on Sustainability

This edition places significant emphasis on sustainability as one of the critical managerial challenges of the coming decades. Many managers are promoting the development and implementation of strategies to achieve long-term financial, social, and environmental performance as key imperatives. We highlight this in Chapter 1 and return to the theme in several subsequent chapters. Chapter 12 discusses the benefits to companies from measuring social and environmental performance and how such measures can be incorporated in a balanced scorecard. Chapter 23 provides several examples of companies that mandate disclosures and evaluate managers on environmental and social metrics. A variety of chapters, including Chapters 4, 10, and 15, contain vignettes that stress themes of energy independence, using cost analysis to reduce environmental footprints, and constructing "green" homes in a cost-effective manner.

New Cutting-Edge Topics

The pace of change in organizations continues to be rapid. The fifteenth edition of *Cost Accounting* reflects changes occurring in the role of cost accounting in organizations.

- We have introduced sustainability strategies and the methods companies use to implement sustainability with business goals.
- We have added ideas based on academic research regarding the weights to be placed on performance measures in a balanced scorecard.
- We have provided details on the transfer pricing strategies used by multinational technology firms such as Apple and Google to minimize income taxes.
- We discuss current trends in the regulation of executive compensation.
- We describe the evolution of enterprise resource planning systems and newer simplified costing systems that practice lean accounting.
- We discuss the role of accounting concepts and systems in fostering and supporting innovation and entrepreneurial activities in firms.

Opening Vignettes

Each chapter opens with a vignette on a real company situation. The vignettes engage the reader in a business situation or dilemma, illustrating why and how the concepts in the chapter are relevant in business. For example, Chapter 2 describes how Hostess Brands, the maker of Twinkies, was driven into liquidation by the relatively high proportion of fixed costs in its operations. Chapter 4 explains the importance of job costing for "green" homebuilders such as KB Home. Chapter 8 examines Tesla Motors' understanding of fixed and variable overhead costs for planning and control purposes. Chapter 12 shows how Volkswagen's Brazilian subsidiary used the balanced scorecard to guide its journey out of the global financial crisis. Chapter 15 shows the impact of two alternative methods of cost allocation considered by the U.S. government for charging customers for the costs of developing "Smart Grids" for power. Chapter 23 describes the historical misalignment between performance measurement and pay at AIG and the recent changes to the compensation plans for its executives.

Concepts in Action Boxes

Found in every chapter, these boxes cover real-world cost accounting issues across a variety of industries, including automobile racing, defense contracting, entertainment, manufacturing, and retailing. New examples include:

- Cost–Volume–Profit Analysis Makes Megabus a Mega-Success (Chapter 3)
- Flexible Budgets at Corning (Chapter 7)
- What Does It Cost AT&T to Send a Text Message (Chapter 10)
- Are Charitable Organizations Allocating Joint Costs in a Misleading Way? (Chapter 16)
- Avoiding Performance-Measurement Silos at Staples (Chapter 23)

Streamlined Presentation

We continue to try to simplify and streamline our presentation of various topics to make it as easy as possible for students to learn the concepts, tools, and frameworks introduced in different chapters. A major change in this edition is the reorganization of Chapters 12 and 13. Chapter 13 in the fourteenth edition, "Strategy, Balanced Scorecard, and Strategic Profitability Analysis," has been moved to Chapter 12, and Chapter 12 in the fourteenth edition, "Pricing Decisions and Cost Management," has been moved to Chapter 13. As a result of the switch, Chapter 13 is the first of four chapters on cost allocation. We introduce the purposes of cost allocation in Chapter 13 and discuss cost allocation for long-run product costing and pricing. Continuing the same example, Chapter 14 discusses cost allocation for customer costing. Chapter 15 builds on the Chapter 4 example to discuss cost-allocation for support departments. Chapter 16 discusses joint cost allocation. As a result of the reorganization, we have also made major revisions in the structure and writing of each of these chapters as we discuss in detail in the next section.

Other examples of more streamlined presentations can be found in:

- Chapter 2 on the discussion of fundamental cost concepts and the managerial framework for decision making.
- Chapter 6, which has a revised appendix that ties together the chapter example and the cash budget.
- Chapter 8, which has a comprehensive chart that lays out all of the variances described in Chapters 7 and 8.
- Chapter 9, which uses a single two-period example to illustrate the impact of various inventory costing methods and denominator level choices.

Selected Chapter-by-Chapter Content Changes

Thank you for your continued support of* Cost Accounting. *In every new edition, we strive to update this text thoroughly. To ease your transition from the fourteenth edition, here are selected highlights of chapter changes for the fifteenth edition.

Chapter 1 has been rewritten to include greater discussion of sustainability and why this issue has become increasingly critical for managers. It also includes more material on the importance of ethics, values, and behaviors as well as the role of the Sarbanes–Oxley act in improving the quality of financial reporting.

Chapter 2 has been updated and revised to make it easier for students to understand core cost concepts and to provide a framework for how cost accounting and cost management help managers make decisions.

Chapter 3 now includes greater managerial content, using examples from real companies to illustrate the value of cost–volume–profit analysis in managerial decision making.

Chapter 4 has been revised with the addition of substantial new material to the section discussing end-of-period adjustments for the difference between Manufacturing Overhead Control and Manufacturing Overhead Allocated. The chapter also now discusses criteria for allocating costs and relates them to real examples to highlight why managers need allocated cost information to make decisions.

Chapter 5 has been reorganized with a new section on first-stage allocation to help students understand how costs from the standard accounting classifications (salaries, depreciation, rent, and so on) are allocated to activity-cost pools. The discussion of behavioral considerations in implementing activity-based costing has been moved to a new section and integrated with other material in the chapter. There is also new material on the tradeoffs related to allocating facility-sustaining costs to products or not allocating them at all because these costs do not have good cost drivers.

Chapter 6 has been significantly rewritten with the addition of more managerial content. In addition, the appendix has been completely reworked to tie together the chapter example and the cash budget.

In Chapter 7, the appendix on market-share and market-size variances has been replaced with one on mix and yield variances, which provide a natural extension of efficiency variances to settings with substitutable inputs. Chapter 8 now provides a revised comprehensive summary of the variances in both Chapters 7 and 8 via an innovative new exhibit.

Chapter 9 has been simplified substantially by a change in the integrated example from three to two periods. This retains the pedagogical value of the example while making it much easier for students to read and understand. Exhibit 9-4 and the material around it have been simplified further, and the self-study problem has also been revised.

Chapter 10 provides a practical guide to the use of various cost estimation techniques with many illustrative examples. The opening vignette has been revised, and we include a new discussion of the difference between correlation and causation, as well as a more streamlined description of inference and hypothesis testing when using regression analysis.

Chapter 11 has been revised substantially; the material on "Theory of Constraints and Throughput Contribution Margin" from Chapter 19 has now been incorporated into a new section in this chapter. The text and numbers have been rewritten to link with the Power Recreation problem already in Chapter 11 (and the chapter appendix). The chapter has been made easier for students to follow by replacing paragraphs with tables. Throughout, there is greater emphasis on understanding why relevant costs and revenues are important when making decisions.

The new Chapter 12 (on the balanced scorecard) has been rewritten with a completely new section on using the balanced scorecard to achieve environmental and social goals. This section describes the motivations for companies to focus on sustainability goals (such as the concept of shared value), sustainability strategies, and the methods companies use to implement sustainability with business goals. There is also a new exhibit extending the Chipset balanced scorecard to include environmental and social objectives and measures.

The new Chapter 13 focuses on cost allocation for long-run pricing decisions. The material on short-run costing and pricing (from Chapter 12 in the fourteenth edition) has been moved to Chapter 11.

Chapter 14 has been completely rewritten. It continues the same example of Astel Computers from Chapter 13 but switches the context from cost allocation for pricing to cost allocation for customer profitability. The order of presentation, the content, the examples, and the exhibits are all new. The chapter now starts with customer profitability based on customer-level costs and discusses the hierarchical operating income statement. It then motivates why corporate, division, and distribution channel costs need to be allocated and the criteria that can be used to allocate them. The chapter closes with sales variances and market-share and market-size variances (moved here from Chapter 7). The example is new and builds on the Astel Computers example that is used throughout Chapters 13 and 14.

Chapter 15 is also heavily revised, with new content, examples, and exhibits. It continues the example of Robinson Company from Chapter 4 but adds more issues around cost allocation—single rate, dual rate, and support-department cost allocations using direct, step-down, and reciprocal methods. Using the same example helps link and integrate normal costing and support department cost allocation.

Chapter 16 now provides an in-depth discussion of the rationale for joint-cost allocation and the merits and demerits of various joint-cost allocation methods. It also uses real-world examples to highlight the preferred method of joint-cost allocation in various settings.

Chapters 17 and 18 present actual costing with the material on standard costing discussed in the appendix. We have added a discussion of managerial issues when estimating equivalent units and choosing between the FIFO and weighted-average costing methods. Chapter 18 emphasizes the importance of reducing spoilage and scrap and more generally the theme of striving for a sustainable production and service environment.

As a result of moving material on the theory of constraints to Chapter 11, Chapter 19 now focuses on quality and time. We use the same Photon example throughout the chapter to discuss both quality and time-based competition. This helps to integrate and streamline the chapter.

Chapter 20 contains revised content and presentation comparing traditional and just-in-time purchasing (and a changed Exhibit 20-5). The sections on supplier evaluation, relevant costs of quality, and timely deliveries have also been rewritten, as well as the material on enterprise resource planning systems and lean accounting.

Chapter 21 has been completely redone with an entirely new example and a set of revised (and clearer) exhibits. The focus has shifted from a manufacturing setting to a transportation firm evaluating the purchase of a new hybrid-engine bus.

Chapter 22 has been significantly revised to reflect the latest developments in the controversial use of transfer prices for tax minimization by multinational corporations, with several real-world examples. The revision also highlights the costs and benefits of decentralization and the tradeoffs involved in setting a transfer pricing policy.

Chapter 23 includes a description of the use of environmental, social, and ethical objectives by companies as part of top management's pay structures. It discusses the new SEC regulations on disclosure of executive compensation and the Dodd-Frank "say on pay" rules. The chapter also incorporates research findings on the relative weight to be placed on different measures of the balanced scorecard.

Hallmark Features of *Cost Accounting*

- Exceptionally strong emphasis on managerial uses of cost information
- Clarity and understandability of the text
- Excellent balance in integrating modern topics with traditional coverage
- Emphasis on human behavior aspects
- Extensive use of real-world examples
- Ability to teach chapters in different sequences
- Excellent quantity, quality, and range of assignment material

The first thirteen chapters provide the essence of a one-term (quarter or semester) course. There is ample text and assignment material in the book's twenty-three chapters for a two-term course. This book can be used immediately after the student has had an introductory course in financial accounting. Alternatively, this book can build on an introductory course in managerial accounting.

Deciding on the sequence of chapters in a textbook is a challenge. Because every instructor has a unique way of organizing his or her course, we utilize a modular, flexible organization that permits a course to be custom tailored. *This organization facilitates diverse approaches to teaching and learning.*

As an example of the book's flexibility, consider our treatment of process costing. Process costing is described in Chapters 17 and 18. Instructors interested in filling out a student's perspective of costing systems can move directly from job-order costing described in Chapter 4 to Chapter 17 without interruption in the flow of material. Other instructors may want their students to delve into activity-based costing and budgeting and more decision-oriented topics early in the course. These instructors may prefer to postpone discussion of process costing.

Resources

In addition to this textbook and MyAccountingLab, a companion website is available for students at www.pearsonhighered.com/horngren.

The following resources are available for instructors in MyAccountingLab and on the Instructors Rescource Center at www.pearsonhighered.com/horngren.

- Solutions Manual
- Test Bank in word and TestGen, including algorithmic questions
- Instructors Manual
- PowerPoint Presentations
- Image Library

Acknowledgments

We are indebted to many people for their ideas and assistance. Our primary thanks go to the many academics and practitioners who have advanced our knowledge of cost accounting. The package of teaching materials we present is the work of skillful and valued team members developing some excellent end-of-chapter assignment material. Tommy Goodwin and Tola Lawal provided outstanding research assistance on technical issues and current developments. We would also like to thank the dedicated and hard-working supplement author team and Integra.The book is much better because of the efforts of these colleagues.

In shaping this edition, we would like to thank a group of colleagues who worked closely with us and the editorial team. This group provided detailed feedback and participated in focus groups that guided the direction of this edition:

Wagdy Abdallah
Seton Hall University

David Alldredge
Salt Lake Community College

Felicia Baldwin
Richard J. Daley College

Molly Brown
James Madison University

Shannon Charles
Brigham Young University

David Franz
San Francisco State University

Anna Jensen
Indiana University

Donna McGovern
Custom Business Results, Inc.

Cindy Nye
Bellevue University

Glenn Pate
Florida Atlantic University

Kelly Pope
DePaul University

Jenice Prather-Kinsey
University of Missouri

Melvin Roush
Pittsburgh State University

Karen Shastri
Pittsburgh University

Frank Stangota
Rutgers University

Patrick Stegman
College of Lake County

We would also like to extend our thanks to those professors who provided detailed written reviews or comments on drafts. These professors include the following:

Robyn Alcock
Central Queensland University

Robert Alford
DePaul University

T. S. Amer
Northern Arizona University

David S. Baglia
Grove City College

Charles Bailey
University of Central Florida

Robert Bauman
Allan Hancock Joint Community College

David Bilker
University of Maryland, University College

Marvin Bouillon
Iowa State University

Laurie Burney
Mississippi State University

Dennis Caplan
Columbia University

A. J. Cataldo II
West Chester University

Karl E. Dahlberg
Rutgers University

Kenneth Danko
San Francisco State University

Kreag Danvers
Clarion University of Pennsylvania

Jennifer Dosch
Metro State University

Joe Dowd
Eastern Washington University

Michael Eames
Santa Clara University

Thomas D. Fields
Washington University in St. Louis

Patrick J. Fiorelli
Columbus State Community College

Michael Flores
Wichita University

Ralph Greenberg
Temple University

Donald W. Gribbin
Southern Illinois University

Ronald N. Guymon
Georgia State University

Rosalie Hallbauer
Florida International University

Robert Hartman
University of Iowa

John Haverty
St. Joseph's University

Jean Hawkins
William Jewell College

Rodger Holland
Francis Marion University

Jiunn C. Huang
San Francisco State University

Constance Hylton
George Mason University

Zafar U. Khan
Eastern Michigan University

Larry N. Killough
Virginia Polytechnic Institute & State University

Keith Kramer
Southern Oregon University

Leslie Kren
University of Wisconsin–Madison

Benjamin Lansford
Penn State University

Jay Law
Central Washington University

Sandra Lazzarini
University of Queensland

Gary J. Mann
University of Texas at El Paso

Ronald Marshall
Michigan State University

Maureen Mascha
Marquette University

Michele Matherly
Xavier University

Pam Meyer
University of Louisiana at Lafayette

Mike Morris
Notre Dame University

Cinthia Nye
Bellevue University

Marjorie Platt
Northeastern University

Roy W. Regel
University of Montana

Diane Satin
California State University East Bay

Karen Schoenebeck
Southwestern College

Pradyot K. Sen
University of Cincinnati

Gim S. Seow
University of Connecticut

Margaret Shackell-Dowel
Notre Dame University

Rebekah A. Sheely
Northeastern University

Robert J. Shepherd
University of California, Santa Cruz

Kenneth Sinclair
Lehigh University

John Stancil
Florida Southern College

Vic Stanton
California State University, Hayward

Carolyn Streuly
Marquette University

Diane L. Tanner
University of North Florida

Gerald Thalmann
North Central College

Paul Warrick
Westwood College

James Williamson
San Diego State University

Peter D. Woodlock
Youngstown State University

Sung-Soo Yoon
UCLA at Los Angeles

We also would like to thank our colleagues who helped us greatly by accuracy checking the text and supplements, including Molly Brown, Barbara Durham, Anna Jensen, and Sandra Cereola.

We thank the people at Pearson for their hard work and dedication, including Donna Battista, Ellen Geary, Nicole Sam, Roberta Sherman, Christine Donovan, and Martha LaChance. We extend special thanks to Lena Buonanno and Amy Ray, the development editors on this edition, who took charge of this project and directed it across the finish line. This book would not have been possible without their dedication and skill. Amanda Zagnoli at Integra expertly managed the production aspects of the manuscript's preparation with superb skill and tremendous dedication. We are deeply appreciative of their good spirits, loyalty, and ability to stay calm in the most hectic of times.

Appreciation also goes to the American Institute of Certified Public Accountants, the Institute of Management Accountants, the Society of Management Accountants of Canada, the Certified General Accountants Association of Canada, the Financial Executive Institute of America, and many other publishers and companies for their generous permission to quote from their publications. Problems from the Uniform CPA examinations are designated (CPA); problems from the Certified Management Accountant examination are designated (CMA); problems from the Canadian examinations administered by the Society of Management Accountants are designated (SMA); and problems from the Certified General Accountants Association are designated (CGA). Many of these problems are adapted to highlight particular points. We are grateful to the professors who contributed assignment material for this edition. Their names are indicated in parentheses at the start of their specific problems. Comments from users are welcome.

SRIKANT M. DATAR
MADHAV V. RAJAN

In memory of Charles T. Horngren 1926–2011

Chuck Horngren revolutionized cost and management accounting. He loved new ideas and introduced many new concepts. He had the unique gift of explaining these concepts in simple and creative ways. He epitomized excellence and never tired of details, whether it was finding exactly the right word or working and reworking assignment materials.

He combined his great intellect with genuine humility and warmth and a human touch that inspired others to do their best. He taught us many lessons about life through his amazing discipline, his ability to make everyone feel welcome, and his love of family.

It was a great privilege, pleasure, and honor to have known Chuck Horngren. Few individuals will have the enormous influence that Chuck had on the accounting profession. Fewer still will be able to do it with the class and style that was his hallmark. He was unique, special, and amazing in many, many ways and, at once, a role model, teacher, mentor, and friend.

He will be deeply missed.

Srikant M. Datar
Harvard University

Madhav V. Rajan
Stanford University

To Our Families

Swati, Radhika, Gayatri, Sidharth (SD)

Gayathri, Sanjana, Anupama (MVR)

Cost Accounting

A Managerial Emphasis

1 The Manager and Management Accounting

Learning Objectives

1. Distinguish financial accounting from management accounting
2. Understand how management accountants help firms make strategic decisions
3. Describe the set of business functions in the value chain and identify the dimensions of performance that customers are expecting of companies
4. Explain the five-step decision-making process and its role in management accounting
5. Describe three guidelines management accountants follow in supporting managers
6. Understand how management accounting fits into an organization's structure
7. Understand what professional ethics mean to management accountants

All businesses are concerned about revenues and costs.

Managers at companies small and large must understand how revenues and costs behave or risk losing control of the performance of their firms. Managers use cost accounting information to make decisions about research and development, budgeting, production planning, pricing, and the products or services to offer customers. Sometimes these decisions involve tradeoffs. The following article shows how companies like Apple make those tradeoffs to increase their profits.

iTunes Variable Pricing: Downloads Are Down, but Profits Are Up[1]

Can selling less of something be more profitable than selling more of it? In 2009, Apple changed the pricing structure for songs sold through iTunes from a flat fee of $0.99 to a three-tier price point system of $0.69, $0.99, and $1.29. The top 200 songs in any given week make up more than one-sixth of digital music sales. Apple began charging the highest price ($1.29) for these songs—songs by artists like Adele and Carly Rae Jepsen.

Six months after Apple implemented the new pricing model, the downloads of the top 200 tracks were down by about 6%. But although the number of downloads dropped, the higher prices generated more revenue than the old pricing structure. Because Apple's iTunes costs—wholesale song costs, network and transaction fees, and other operating costs—do not vary based on the price of each download, the profits from the 30% price increase more than made up for the losses from the 6% decrease in volume.

Apple has also applied this new pricing structure to movies available through iTunes, which range from $14.99 for new releases to $9.99 for most other films.

To increase profits beyond those created by higher prices, Apple also began to manage iTunes' costs. Transaction costs (what Apple pays credit-card processors like Visa and MasterCard) have decreased, and Apple has also reduced the number of people working in the iTunes store.

---

[1] *Sources:* Bruno, Anthony and Glenn Peoples Variable iTunes pricing a moneymaker for artists. Reuters, (June 21, 2009); http://www.reuters.com/article/idUSTRE55K0DJ20090621" The long tale? *Billboard* (November 14, 2009); http://www.billboard.biz/bbbiz/content_display/magazine/features/e3i35ed869fbd929ccd cca52ed7fd 9262d3?imw=Y" Savitz, Eric,Apple Turns Out, iTunes Makes Money Pacific Crest Says (2007); Subscription Services Seems Inevitable. Barron's "Tech Trader Daily" blog, April 23. http://blogs.barrons.com/techtrader-daily/2007/04/23/apple-turns-out-itunes-makes-money-pacific-crest-says-subscription-service-seems-inevitable/ Apple, Inc. "Frequently Asked Questions (FAQ) for Purchased Movies. Accessed May 1, 2013; Nekesa Mumbi Moody, "Adele, Carly Rae Jepsen Top iTunes' Year-End Sales," *Billboard* (December 13, 2012).

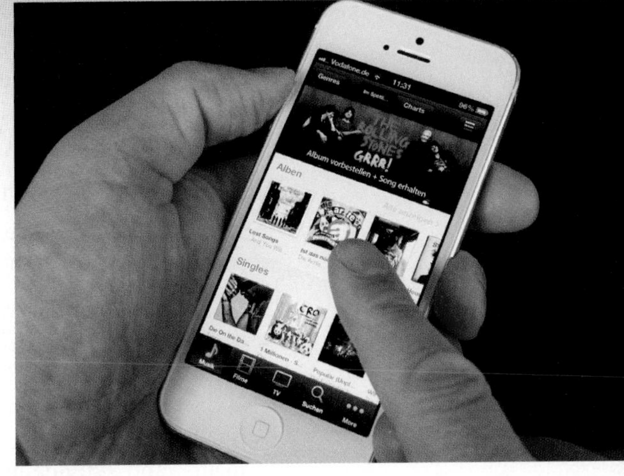

By studying cost accounting, you will learn how successful managers and accountants run their businesses and prepare yourself for leadership roles in the firms you work for. Many large companies, including Nike and the Pittsburgh Steelers, have senior executives with accounting backgrounds.

Financial Accounting, Management Accounting, and Cost Accounting

Learning Objective 1

Distinguish financial accounting

...reporting on past performance to external users

from management accounting

...helping managers make decisions

As many of you have already learned in your financial accounting class, accounting systems are used to record economic events and transactions, such as sales and materials purchases, and process the data into information helpful to managers, sales representatives, production supervisors, and others. Processing any economic transaction means collecting, categorizing, summarizing, and analyzing. For example, costs are collected by category, such as materials, labor, and shipping. These costs are then summarized to determine a firm's total costs by month, quarter, or year. Accountants analyze the results and together with managers evaluate, say, how costs have changed relative to revenues from one period to the next. Accounting systems also provide the information found in a firm's income statement, balance sheet, statement of cash flow, and performance reports, such as the cost of serving customers or running an advertising campaign. Managers use this information to make decisions about the activities, businesses, or functional areas they oversee. For example, a report that shows an increase in sales of laptops and iPads at an Apple store may prompt Apple to hire more salespeople at that location. Understanding accounting information is essential for managers to do their jobs.

Individual managers often require the information in an accounting system to be presented or reported differently. Consider, for example, sales order information. A sales manager at Porsche may be interested in the total dollar amount of sales to determine the commissions paid to salespeople. A distribution manager at Porsche may be interested in the sales order quantities by geographic region and by customer-requested delivery dates to ensure vehicles get delivered to customers on time. A manufacturing manager at Porsche may be interested in the quantities of various products and their desired delivery dates so that he or she can develop an effective production schedule.

To simultaneously serve the needs of all three managers, Porsche creates a database, sometimes called a data warehouse or infobarn, consisting of small, detailed bits of information that can be used for multiple purposes. For instance, the sales order database will contain detailed information about a product, its selling price, quantity ordered, and delivery details (place and date) for each sales order. The database stores information in a way that allows different managers to access the information they need. Many companies are building their own enterprise resource planning (ERP) systems. An ERP system is a single database that collects data and feeds them into applications that support a company's business activities, such as purchasing, production, distribution, and sales.

Financial accounting and management accounting have different goals. As you know, **financial accounting** focuses on reporting financial information to external parties such as investors, government agencies, banks, and suppliers based on Generally Accepted Accounting Principles (GAAP). The most important way financial accounting information affects managers' decisions and actions is through compensation, which is often, in part, based on numbers in financial statements.

Management accounting is the process of measuring, analyzing, and reporting financial and nonfinancial information that helps managers make decisions to fulfill the goals of an organization. Managers use management accounting information to:

1. Develop, communicate, and implement strategies
2. Coordinate product design, production, and marketing decisions and evaluate a company's performance

Management accounting information and reports do not have to follow set principles or rules. The key questions are always (1) how will this information help managers do their jobs better, and (2) do the benefits of producing this information exceed the costs?

Exhibit 1-1 summarizes the major differences between management accounting and financial accounting. Note, however, that reports such as balance sheets, income statements, and statements of cash flows are common to both management accounting and financial accounting.

Cost accounting provides information for both management accounting and financial accounting professionals. **Cost accounting** is the process of measuring, analyzing, and reporting financial and nonfinancial information related to the costs of acquiring or using resources in an organization. For example, calculating the cost of a product is a cost accounting function that meets both the financial accountant's inventory-valuation needs and the management accountant's decision-making needs (such as deciding how to price products and choosing which products to promote). However, today most accounting professionals take the perspective that cost information is part of the management accounting information collected to make management decisions. Thus, the distinction between management accounting and cost accounting is not so clear-cut, and we often use these terms interchangeably in the book.

Businesspeople frequently use the term *cost management*. Unfortunately, the term does not have an exact definition. In this book we use **cost management** to describe the activities managers undertake to use resources in a way that increases a product's value

Exhibit 1-1 Major Differences Between Management and Financial Accounting

	Management Accounting	Financial Accounting
Purpose of information	Help managers make decisions to fulfill an organization's goals	Communicate an organization's financial position to investors, banks, regulators, and other outside parties
Primary users	Managers of the organization	External users such as investors, banks, regulators, and suppliers
Focus and emphasis	Future-oriented (budget for 2014 prepared in 2013)	Past-oriented (reports on 2013 performance prepared in 2014)
Rules of measurement and reporting	Internal measures and reports do not have to follow GAAP but are based on cost-benefit analysis	Financial statements must be prepared in accordance with GAAP and be certified by external, independent auditors
Time span and type of reports	Varies from hourly information to 15 to 20 years, with financial and nonfinancial reports on products, departments, territories, and strategies	Annual and quarterly financial reports, primarily on the company as a whole
Behavioral implications	Designed to influence the behavior of managers and other employees	Primarily reports economic events but also influences behavior because manager's compensation is often based on reported financial results

to customers and achieves an organization's goals. In other words, cost management is not only about reducing costs. Cost management also includes making decisions to incur additional costs—for example, to improve customer satisfaction and quality and to develop new products—with the goal of enhancing revenues and profits. Whether or not to enter new markets, implement new organizational processes, and change product designs are also cost management decisions. Information from accounting systems helps managers to manage costs, but the information and the accounting systems themselves are not cost management.

Decision Point

How is financial accounting different from management accounting?

Strategic Decisions and the Management Accountant

Learning Objective 2

Understand how management accountants help firms make strategic decisions

...they provide information about the sources of competitive advantage

A company's **strategy** specifies how the organization matches its own capabilities with the opportunities in the marketplace. In other words, strategy describes how an organization will compete and the opportunities its managers should seek and pursue. Businesses follow one of two broad strategies. Some companies, such as Southwest Airlines and Vanguard (the mutual fund company), follow a cost leadership strategy. They have been profitable and have grown over the years by providing quality products or services at low prices and by judiciously managing their costs. Other companies such as Apple and the pharmaceutical giant Johnson & Johnson follow a product differentiation strategy. They generate their profits and growth because they offer differentiated or unique products or services that appeal to their customers and are often priced higher than the less-popular products or services of their competitors.

Deciding between these strategies is a critical part of what managers do. Management accountants work closely with managers in various departments to formulate strategies by providing information about the sources of competitive advantage, such as (1) the company's cost, productivity, or efficiency advantage relative to competitors or (2) the premium prices a company can charge relative to the costs of adding features that make its products or services distinctive. **Strategic cost management** describes cost management that specifically focuses on strategic issues.

Management accounting information helps managers formulate strategy by answering questions such as the following:

- *Who are our most important customers, and how can we be competitive and deliver value to them?* After Amazon.com's success selling books online, management accountants at Barnes & Noble outlined the costs and benefits of several alternative approaches for enhancing the company's information technology infrastructure and developing the capability to sell books online. A similar cost–benefit analysis led Toyota to build flexible computer-integrated manufacturing plants that enable it to use the same equipment efficiently to produce a variety of cars in response to changing customer tastes.
- *What substitute products exist in the marketplace, and how do they differ from our product in terms of features, price, cost, and quality?* Hewlett-Packard, for example, designs, costs, and prices new printers after comparing the functionality and quality of its printers to other printers available in the marketplace.
- *What is our most critical capability? Is it technology, production, or marketing? How can we leverage it for new strategic initiatives?* Kellogg Company, for example, uses the reputation of its brand to introduce new types of cereals with high profit margins.
- *Will adequate cash be available to fund the strategy, or will additional funds need to be raised?* Procter & Gamble, for example, issued new debt and equity to fund its strategic acquisition of Gillette, a maker of shaving products.

The best-designed strategies and the best-developed capabilities are useless unless they are effectively executed. In the next section, we describe how management accountants help managers take actions that create value for their customers.

Decision Point

How do management accountants support strategic decisions?

Learning Objective 3

Describe the set of business functions in the value chain and identify the dimensions of performance that customers are expecting of companies

. . . R&D, design, production, marketing, distribution, and customer service supported by administration to achieve cost and efficiency, quality, time, and innovation

Value-Chain and Supply-Chain Analysis and Key Success Factors

Customers demand much more than just a fair price; they expect quality products (goods or services) delivered in a timely way. The entire customer experience determines the value a customer derives from a product. In this section, we explore how a company goes about creating this value.

Value-Chain Analysis

The **value chain** is the sequence of business functions by which a product is made progressively more useful to customers. Exhibit 1-2 shows six primary business functions: research and development (R&D), design of products and processes, production, marketing, distribution, and customer service. We illustrate these business functions with Sony Corporation's television division.

1. **Research and development (R&D)**—generating and experimenting with ideas related to new products, services, or processes. At Sony, this function includes research on alternative television signal transmission and on the picture quality of different shapes and thicknesses of television screens.
2. **Design of products and processes**—detailed planning, engineering, and testing of products and processes. Design at Sony includes deciding on the number of component parts in a television set and determining the effect alternative product designs will have on the set's quality and manufacturing costs. Some representations of the value chain collectively refer to the first two steps as technology development.[2]
3. **Production**—procuring, transporting, and storing ("inbound logistics") and coordinating and assembling ("operations") resources to produce a product or deliver a service. The production of a Sony television set includes the procurement and assembly of the electronic parts, the cabinet, and the packaging used for shipping.
4. **Marketing (including sales)**—promoting and selling products or services to customers or prospective customers. Sony markets its televisions at tradeshows, via advertisements in newspapers and magazines, on the Internet, and through its sales force.
5. **Distribution**—processing orders and shipping products or services to customers ("outbound logistics"). Distribution for Sony includes shipping to retail outlets, catalog vendors, direct sales via the Internet, and other channels through which customers purchase new televisions.
6. **Customer service**—providing after-sales service to customers. Sony provides customer service on its televisions in the form of customer-help telephone lines, support on the Internet, and warranty repair work.

In addition to the six primary business functions, Exhibit 1-2 shows an administration function, which includes accounting and finance, human resource management, and information technology and supports the six primary business functions. When discussing the value chain in subsequent chapters of the book, we include the administration

Exhibit 1-2 Different Parts of the Value Chain

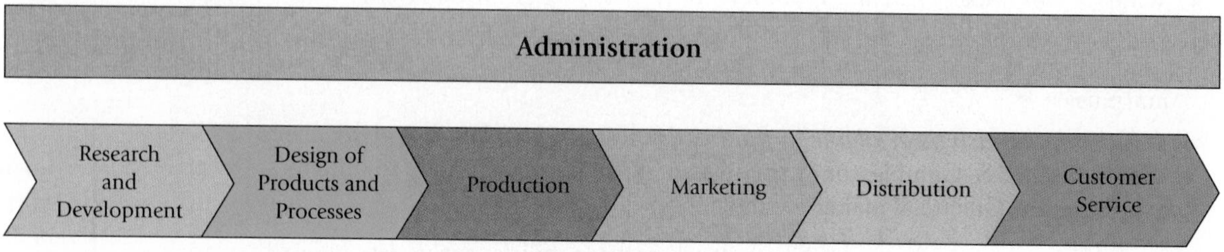

Administration

Research and Development → Design of Products and Processes → Production → Marketing → Distribution → Customer Service

[2] M. Porter, *Competitive Advantage* (New York: Free Press, 1998).

function within the primary functions. For example, included in the marketing function is the function of analyzing, reporting, and accounting for resources spent in different marketing channels, whereas the production function includes the human resource management function of training frontline workers. Each of these business functions is essential to companies satisfying their customers and keeping them satisfied (and loyal) over time.

To implement their corporate strategies, companies such as Sony and Procter & Gamble use **customer relationship management (CRM)**, a strategy that integrates people and technology in all business functions to deepen relationships with customers, partners, and distributors. CRM initiatives use technology to coordinate all customer-facing activities (such as marketing, sales calls, distribution, and after-sales support) and the design and production activities necessary to get products to customers.

Different companies create value in different ways. Lowe's (the home-improvement retailer) does so by focusing on cost and efficiency. Toyota Motor Company does so by focusing on quality. Fast response times at eBay create quality for the online auction giant's customers, whereas innovation is primarily what creates value for the customers of the biotech company Roche-Genentech. The Italian apparel company Gucci creates value for its customers by building a prestigious brand. As a result, at different times and in different industries, one or more of these functions is more critical than others. For example, a company such as Roche-Genentech will emphasize R&D and the design of products and processes. In contrast, a company such as Gucci will focus on marketing, distribution, and customer service to build its brand.

Exhibit 1-2 depicts the usual order in which different business-function activities physically occur. Do not, however, interpret Exhibit 1-2 to mean that managers should proceed sequentially through the value chain when planning and managing their activities. Companies gain (in terms of cost, quality, and the speed with which new products are developed) if two or more of the individual business functions of the value chain work concurrently as a team. For example, a company's production, marketing, distribution, and customer service personnel can often reduce a company's total costs by providing input for design decisions.

Managers track the costs incurred in each value-chain category. Their goal is to reduce costs and to improve efficiency. Management accounting information helps managers make cost–benefit tradeoffs. For example, is it cheaper to buy products from a vendor or produce them in-house? How does investing resources in design and manufacturing reduce costs of marketing and customer service?

Supply-Chain Analysis

The parts of the value chain associated with producing and delivering a product or service—production and distribution—are referred to as the *supply chain*. The **supply chain** describes the flow of goods, services, and information from the initial sources of materials and services to the delivery of products to consumers, regardless of whether those activities occur in one organization or in multiple organizations. Consider Coke and Pepsi: Many companies play a role in bringing these products to consumers as the supply chain in Exhibit 1-3 shows. Part of cost management emphasizes integrating and coordinating activities across all companies in the supply chain to improve their

Exhibit 1-3 Supply Chain for a Cola Bottling Company

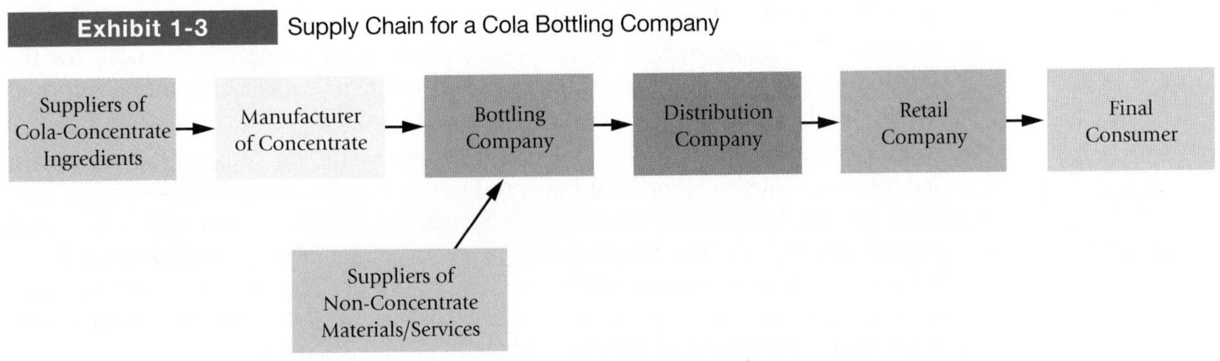

performance and reduce costs. For example, to reduce materials-handling costs, both the Coca-Cola Company and Pepsi Bottling Group require their suppliers (such as plastic and aluminum companies and sugar refiners) to frequently deliver small quantities of materials directly to their production floors. Similarly, to reduce inventory levels in the supply chain, Walmart requires its suppliers, such as Coca-Cola, to directly manage its inventory of products to ensure the right amount of them are in its stores at all times.

Key Success Factors

Customers want companies to use the value chain and supply chain to deliver ever-improving levels of performance when it comes to several (or even all) of the following:

- **Cost and efficiency**—Companies face continuous pressure to reduce the cost of the products they sell. To calculate and manage the cost of products, managers must first understand the activities (such as setting up machines or distributing products) that cause costs to arise as well as monitor the marketplace to determine the prices customers are willing to pay for products or services. Management accounting information helps managers calculate a target cost for a product by subtracting from the "target price" the operating income per unit of product that the company wants to earn. To achieve the target cost, managers eliminate some activities (such as rework) and reduce the costs of performing activities in all value-chain functions—from initial R&D to customer service (see Concepts in Action: Trader Joe's Recipe for Cost Leadership). Many U.S. companies have cut costs by outsourcing some of their business functions. Nike, for example, has moved its manufacturing operations to China and Mexico, and Microsoft and IBM are increasingly doing their software development in Spain, Eastern Europe, and India.
- **Quality**—Customers expect high levels of quality. **Total quality management (TQM)** is an integrative philosophy of management for continuously improving the quality of products and processes. Managers who implement TQM believe that each and every person in the value chain is responsible for delivering products and services that exceed customers' expectations. Using TQM, companies design products or services to meet customer needs and wants, to make these products with zero (or very few) defects and waste, and to minimize inventories. Managers use management accounting information to evaluate the costs and revenue benefits of TQM initiatives.
- **Time**—Time has many dimensions. Two of the most important dimensions are new-product development time and customer-response time. New-product development time is the time it takes for companies to create new products and bring them to market. The increasing pace of technological innovation has led to shorter product life cycles and more rapid introduction of new products. To make new-product development decisions, managers need to understand the costs and benefits of a product over its life cycle.

  Customer-response time describes the speed at which an organization responds to customer requests. To increase the satisfaction of their customers, organizations need to meet their promised delivery dates as well as reduce their delivery times. Bottlenecks are the primary cause of delays. For example, a bottleneck can occur when the work to be performed on a machine exceeds its available capacity. To deliver the product on time, managers need to increase the capacity of the machine to produce more output. Management accounting information can help managers quantify the costs and benefits of doing so.
- **Innovation**—A constant flow of innovative products or services is the basis for the ongoing success of a company. Managers rely on management accounting information to evaluate alternative investment and R&D decisions.
- **Sustainability**—Companies are increasingly applying the key success factors of cost and efficiency, quality, time, and innovation to promote **sustainability**—the development and implementation of strategies to achieve long-term financial, social, and environmental goals. The sustainability efforts of the Japanese copier company Ricoh include energy conservation, resource conservation, product recycling, and pollution prevention. By designing products that can be easily recycled, Ricoh simultaneously improves its efficiency and the cost and quality of its products.

Concepts in Action

Trader Joe's Recipe for Cost Leadership

Trader Joe's has a special recipe for cost leadership: delivering unique products at reasonable prices. The grocery store chain stocks its shelves with low-cost, high-end staples (cage-free eggs and sustainably harvested seafood) and exotic, affordable luxuries (Ethiopian Peaberry coffee and Thai lime-and-chili cashews) that are distinct from what traditional supermarkets offer. Trader Joe's can offer these items at everyday low prices by judiciously managing its costs.

At Trader Joe's, customers swap selection for value. The company has relatively small stores with a carefully selected, constantly changing mix of items. While typical grocery stores carry 50,000 items, Trader Joe's sells only about 4,000 items. Recently, it has been removing non-sustainable products from its shelves, including genetically modified items. About 80% of the stock bears the Trader Joe's brand, and management seeks to minimize costs of these items. The company purchases directly from manufacturers, which ship their items straight to Trader Joe's warehouses to avoid third-party distribution costs. With small stores and limited storage space, Trader Joe's trucks leave the warehouse centers daily. This encourages precise, just-in-time ordering and a relentless focus on frequent merchandise turnover.

This winning combination of quality products and low prices has turned Trader Joe's into one of the hottest retailers in the United States. Its stores sell an estimated $8 billion annually, or $1,750 in merchandise per square foot, which is more than double Whole Foods, its top competitor.

Sources: Based on Beth Kowitt, "Inside the Secret World of Trader Joe's," *Fortune* (August 23, 2010); Christopher Palmeri, "Trader Joe's Recipe for Success," *Businessweek* (February 21, 2008); Mark Mallinger and Gerry Rossy, "The Trader Joe's Experience: The Impact of Corporate Culture on Business Strategy," *Graziadio Business Review* (2007, Volume 10, Issue 2); and Allessandra Ram, "Teach Us, Trader Joe: Demading Socially Responsible Food," *The Atlantic* (August 7, 2012).

The interest in sustainability appears to be intensifying among companies. General Electric, Poland Springs (a bottled-water manufacturer), and Hewlett-Packard are among the many companies incorporating sustainability into their decision making. Sustainability is important to these companies for several reasons:

- More and more investors care about sustainability. These investors make investment decisions based on a company's financial, social, and environmental performance and raise questions about sustainability at shareholder meetings.
- Companies that emphasize sustainability find that sustainability goals attract and inspire employees.
- Customers prefer the products of companies with good sustainability records and boycott companies with poor sustainability records.
- Society and activist nongovernmental organizations, in particular, monitor the sustainability performance of firms and take legal action against those that violate environmental laws. Countries with fast-growing economies, such as China and India, are now either requiring or encouraging companies to develop and report on their sustainability initiatives.

Management accountants help managers track the key success factors of their firms as well as those of their competitors. Competitive information such as this serves as a *benchmark* managers use to continuously improve their operations. Examples of continuous improvement include Southwest Airlines' efforts to increase the number of its flights that arrive on time, eBay's efforts to improve the access its customers have to online auctions, and Lowe's efforts to continuously reduce the cost of its home-improvement products. Sometimes, more fundamental changes in operations, such as redesigning a manufacturing process to reduce costs, may be necessary. To successfully implement their strategies, firms have to do more than analyze their value chains and supply chains and execute key success factors. They also have to have good decision-making processes.

Decision Point

How do companies add value, and what are the dimensions of performance that customers are expecting of companies?

Learning Objective 4

Explain the five-step decision-making process

...identify the problem and uncertainties; obtain information; make predictions about the future; make decisions by choosing among alternatives; implement the decision, evaluate performance, and learn

and its role in management accounting

...planning and control of operations and activities

Decision Making, Planning, and Control: The Five-Step Decision-Making Process

We illustrate a five-step decision-making process using the example of the *Daily News,* a newspaper in Boulder, Colorado. Subsequent chapters of the book describe how managers use this five-step decision-making process to make many different types of decisions.

The *Daily News* differentiates itself from its competitors by using (1) highly respected journalists who write well-researched news articles, (2) color to enhance attractiveness to readers and advertisers, and (3) a Web site that delivers up-to-the-minute news, interviews, and analyses. The newspaper has the following resources to deliver on this strategy: an automated, computer-integrated, state-of-the-art printing facility; a Web-based information technology infrastructure; and a distribution network that is one of the best in the newspaper industry.

To keep up with steadily increasing production costs, Naomi Crawford, manager of the *Daily News,* needs to increase the company's revenues. To decide what she should do, Naomi works through the five-step decision-making process.

1. **Identify the problem and uncertainties.** Naomi has two main choices:

   a. increase the selling price of the newspaper or
   b. increase the rate per page charged to advertisers.

   The key uncertainty is the effect any increase in prices or rates will have on demand. A decrease in demand could offset the price or rate increases and lead to lower rather than higher revenues.

2. **Obtain information.** Gathering information before making a decision helps managers gain a better understanding of uncertainties. Naomi asks her marketing manager to talk to some representative readers to gauge their reaction to an increase in the newspaper's selling price. She asks her advertising sales manager to talk to current and potential advertisers to assess demand for advertising. She also reviews the effect that past price increases had on readership. Ramon Sandoval, management accountant at the *Daily News,* presents information about the effect of past increases or decreases in advertising rates on advertising revenues. He also collects and analyzes information on advertising rates competing newspapers and other media outlets charge.

3. **Make predictions about the future.** Based on this information, Naomi makes predictions about the future. She concludes that increasing prices would upset readers and decrease readership. She has a different view about advertising rates. She expects a marketwide increase in advertising rates and believes that increasing rates will have little effect on the number of advertising pages sold.

   Naomi recognizes that making predictions requires judgment. She looks for biases in her thinking. Has she correctly judged reader sentiment or is the negative publicity of a price increase overly influencing her decision making? How sure is she that competitors will increase their advertising rates? Is her thinking in this respect biased by how competitors have responded in the past? Have circumstances changed? How confident is she that her sales representatives can convince advertisers to pay higher rates? After retesting her assumptions and reviewing her thinking, Naomi feels comfortable with her predictions and judgments.

4. **Make decisions by choosing among alternatives.** When making decisions, a company's strategy serves as a vital guidepost for the many individuals in different parts of the organization making decisions at different times. Consistent strategies provide a common purpose for these disparate decisions. Only if these decisions can be aligned with its strategy will an organization achieve its goals. Without this alignment, the company's decisions will be uncoordinated, pull the organization in different directions, and produce inconsistent results.

   Consistent with a product differentiation strategy, Naomi decides to increase advertising rates by 4% to $5,200 per page in March 2014, but not increase the selling price of the newspaper. She is confident that the *Daily News*'s distinctive style and Web presence will increase readership, creating value for advertisers. She communicates the new advertising rate schedule to the sales department. Ramon estimates advertising revenues of $4,160,000 ($5,200 per page × 800 pages predicted to be sold in March 2014).

Steps 1 through 4 are collectively referred to as *planning*. **Planning** consists of selecting an organization's goals and strategies, predicting results under various alternative ways of achieving those goals, deciding how to attain the desired goals, and communicating the goals and how to achieve them to the entire organization. Management accountants serve as business partners in these planning activities because they understand the key success factors and what creates value.

The most important planning tool when implementing strategy is a *budget*. A **budget** is the quantitative expression of a proposed plan of action by management and is an aid to coordinating what needs to be done to execute that plan. For March 2014, the budgeted advertising revenue of the *Daily News* equals $4,160,000. The full budget for March 2014 includes budgeted circulation revenue and the production, distribution, and customer-service costs to achieve the company's sales goals; the anticipated cash flows; and the potential financing needs. Because multiple departments help prepare the budget, personnel throughout the organization have to coordinate and communicate with one another as well as with the company's suppliers and customers.

5. **Implement the decision, evaluate performance, and learn.** Managers at the *Daily News* take action to implement the March 2014 budget. The firm's management accountants then collect information on how the company's actual performance compares to planned or budgeted performance (also referred to as scorekeeping). The information on the actual results is different from the *predecision* planning information Naomi collected in Step 2, which enabled her to better understand uncertainties, to make predictions, and to make a decision. Allowing managers to compare actual performance to budgeted performance is the *control* or *postdecision* role of information. **Control** comprises taking actions that implement the planning decisions, evaluating past performance, and providing feedback and learning to help future decision making.

   Measuring actual performance informs managers how well they and their subunits are doing. Linking rewards to performance helps motivate managers. These rewards are both intrinsic (recognition for a job well done) and extrinsic (salary, bonuses, and promotions linked to performance). We discuss this in more detail in a later chapter (Chapter 23). A budget serves as much as a control tool as a planning tool. Why? Because a budget is a benchmark against which actual performance can be compared.

Consider performance evaluation at the *Daily News*. During March 2014, the newspaper sold advertising, issued invoices, and received payments. The accounting system recorded these invoices and receipts. Exhibit 1-4 shows the *Daily News*'s advertising revenues for March 2014. This performance report indicates that 760 pages of advertising (40 pages fewer than the budgeted 800 pages) were sold. The average rate per page was $5,080, compared with the budgeted $5,200 rate, yielding actual advertising revenues of $3,860,800. The actual advertising revenues were $299,200 less than the budgeted $4,160,000. Observe how managers use both financial and nonfinancial information, such as pages of advertising, to evaluate performance.

Exhibit 1-4 Performance Report of Advertising Revenues at the *Daily News* for March 2014

	Actual Result (1)	Budgeted Amount (2)	Difference: (Actual Result – Budgeted Amount) (3) = (1) – (2)	Difference as a Percentage of Budgeted Amount (4) = (3) ÷ (2)
Advertising pages sold	760 pages	800 pages	40 pages Unfavorable	5.0% Unfavorable
Average rate per page	$5,080	$5,200	$120 Unfavorable	2.3% Unfavorable
Advertising revenues	$3,860,800	$4,160,000	$299,200 Unfavorable	7.2% Unfavorable

The performance report in Exhibit 1-4 spurs investigation and **learning,** which involves examining past performance (the control function) and systematically exploring alternative ways to make better-informed decisions and plans in the future. Learning can lead to changes in goals, strategies, the ways decision alternatives are identified, and the range of information collected when making predictions and sometimes can lead to changes in managers.

The performance report in Exhibit 1-4 would prompt the management accountant to raise several questions directing the attention of managers to problems and opportunities. Is the strategy of differentiating the *Daily News* from other newspapers attracting more readers? Did the marketing and sales department make sufficient efforts to convince advertisers that, even at the higher rate of $5,200 per page, advertising in the *Daily News* was a good buy? Why was the actual average rate per page ($5,080) less than the budgeted rate ($5,200)? Did some sales representatives offer discounted rates? Did economic conditions cause the decline in advertising revenues? Are revenues falling because editorial and production standards have declined? Are more readers getting their news online?

Answers to these questions could prompt the newspaper's publisher to take subsequent actions, including, for example, adding more sales personnel, making changes in editorial policy, or putting more resources into expanding its presence online and on mobile devices. Good implementation requires the marketing, editorial, and production departments to work together and coordinate their actions.

The management accountant could go further by identifying the specific advertisers that cut back or stopped advertising after the rate increase went into effect. Managers could then decide when and how sales representatives should follow up with these advertisers.

Planning and control activities must be flexible enough so that managers can seize opportunities unforeseen at the time the plan was formulated. In no case should control mean that managers cling to a plan when unfolding events (such as a sensational

Exhibit 1-5

How Accounting Aids Decision Making, Planning, and Control at the *Daily News*

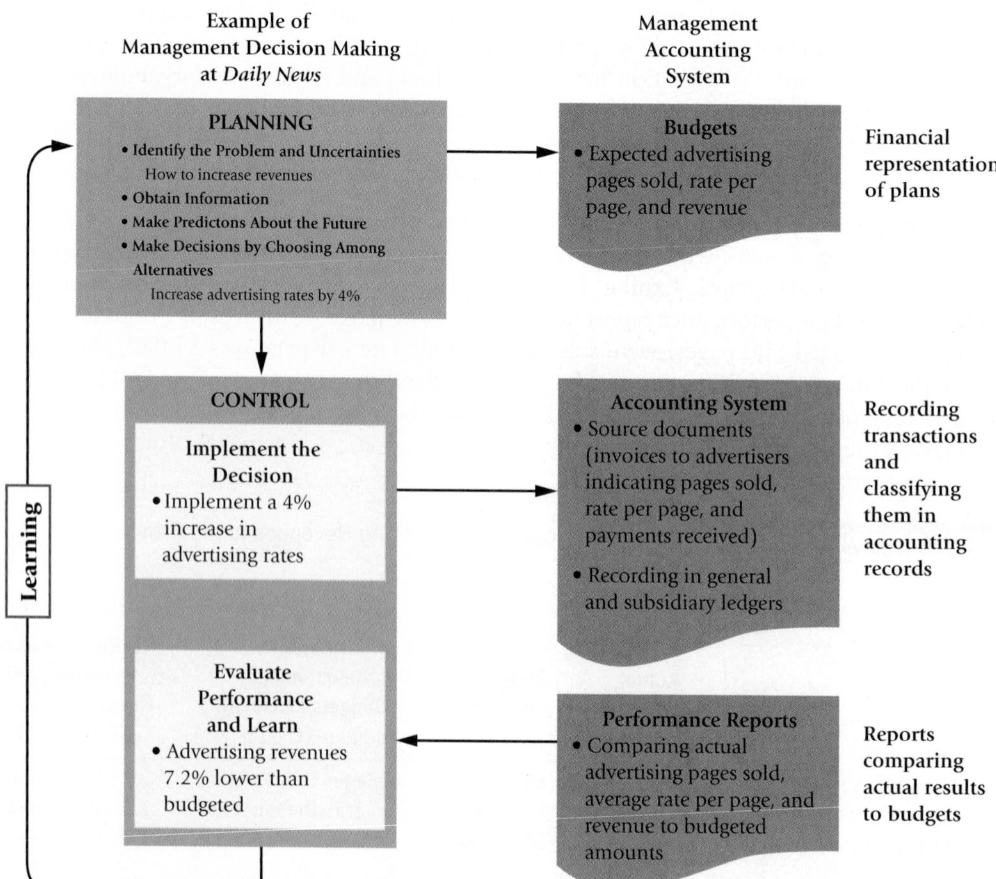

news story) indicate that actions not encompassed by that plan (such as spending more money to cover the story) would offer better results for the company (from higher newspaper sales).

The left side of Exhibit 1-5 provides an overview of the decision-making processes at the *Daily News*. The right side of the exhibit highlights how the management accounting system aids in decision making.

Decision Point

How do managers make decisions to implement strategy?

Key Management Accounting Guidelines

Learning Objective 5

Describe three guidelines management accountants follow in supporting managers

. . . employing a cost–benefit approach, recognizing behavioral as well as technical considerations, and calculating different costs for different purposes

Three guidelines help management accountants provide the most value to the strategic and operational decision making of their companies: (1) employ a cost–benefit approach, (2) give full recognition to behavioral and technical considerations, and (3) use different costs for different purposes.

Cost–Benefit Approach

Managers continually face resource-allocation decisions, such as whether to purchase a new software package or hire a new employee. They use a **cost–benefit approach** when making these decisions. Managers should spend resources if the expected benefits to the company exceed the expected costs. Managers rely on management accounting information to quantify expected benefits and expected costs (although all benefits and costs are not easy to quantify).

Consider the installation of a consulting company's first budgeting system. Previously, the company used historical recordkeeping and little formal planning. A major benefit of installing a budgeting system is that it compels managers to plan ahead, compare actual to budgeted information, learn, and take corrective action. Although the system leads to better decisions and consequently better company performance, the exact benefits are not easy to measure. On the cost side, some costs, such as investments in software and training, are easier to quantify. Others, such as the time spent by managers on the budgeting process, are more difficult to quantify. Regardless, senior managers compare expected benefits and expected costs, exercise judgment, and reach a decision, in this case to install the budgeting system.

Behavioral and Technical Considerations

When utilizing the cost–benefit approach, managers need to keep in mind a number of technical and behavioral considerations. The technical considerations help managers make wise economic decisions by providing them with the desired information (for example, costs in various value-chain categories) in an appropriate format (for example, actual results versus budgeted amounts) and at the preferred frequency (for example, weekly or quarterly). However, management is not confined to technical matters. Management is primarily a human activity that should focus on encouraging individuals to do their jobs better. Budgets have a behavioral effect by motivating and rewarding employees for achieving an organization's goals. So, when workers underperform, for example, behavioral considerations suggest that managers need to discuss ways to improve their performance with them rather than just sending them a report highlighting their underperformance.

Different Costs for Different Purposes

This book emphasizes that managers use alternative ways to compute costs in different decision-making situations because there are different costs for different purposes. A cost concept used for the purposes of external reporting may not be appropriate for internal, routine reporting.

Consider the advertising costs associated with Microsoft Corporation's launch of a product with a useful life of several years. For external reporting to shareholders, Generally Accepted Accounting Principles (GAAP) require television advertising costs for this product to be fully expensed in the income statement in the year they are incurred. However, the television advertising costs could be capitalized and then amortized or written off as expenses over several years if Microsoft's management team believed that doing so would more accurately and fairly measure the performance of the managers that launched the new product.

Decision Point
What guidelines do management accountants use?

We now discuss the relationships and reporting responsibilities among managers and management accountants within a company's organization structure.

Learning Objective 6
Understand how management accounting fits into an organization's structure
...for example, the responsibilities of the controller

Organization Structure and the Management Accountant

We focus first on broad management functions and then look at how the management accounting and finance functions support managers.

Line and Staff Relationships

Organizations distinguish between line management and staff management. **Line management,** such as production, marketing, and distribution management, is directly responsible for achieving the goals of the organization. For example, managers of manufacturing divisions are responsible for meeting particular levels of budgeted operating income, product quality and safety, and compliance with environmental laws. Similarly, the pediatrics department in a hospital is responsible for quality of service, costs, and patient billings. **Staff management,** such as management accountants and information technology and human-resources management, provides advice, support, and assistance to line management. A plant manager (a line function) may be responsible for investing in new equipment. A management accountant (a staff function) works as a business partner of the plant manager by preparing detailed operating-cost comparisons of alternative pieces of equipment.

Increasingly, organizations such as Honda and Dell are using teams to achieve their objectives. These teams include both line and staff management so that all inputs into a decision are available simultaneously.

The Chief Financial Officer and the Controller

The **chief financial officer** (CFO)—also called the **finance director** in many countries—is the executive responsible for overseeing the financial operations of an organization. The responsibilities of the CFO vary among organizations, but they usually include the following areas:

- **Controllership**—provides financial information for reports to managers and shareholders and oversees the overall operations of the accounting system.
- **Treasury**—oversees banking and short- and long-term financing, investments, and cash management.
- **Risk management**—manages the financial risk of interest-rate and exchange-rate changes and derivatives management.
- **Taxation**—plans income taxes, sales taxes, and international taxes.
- **Investor relations**—communicates with, responds to, and interacts with shareholders.
- **Strategic planning**—defining strategy and allocating resources to implement strategy.

An independent internal audit function reviews and analyzes financial and other records to attest to the integrity of the organization's financial reports and to adherence to its policies and procedures.

The **controller** (also called the *chief accounting officer*) is the financial executive primarily responsible for management accounting and financial accounting. This book focuses on the controller as the chief management accounting executive. Modern controllers have no line authority except over their own departments. Yet the controller exercises control over the entire organization in a special way. By reporting and interpreting relevant data, the controller influences the behavior of all employees and helps line managers make better decisions.

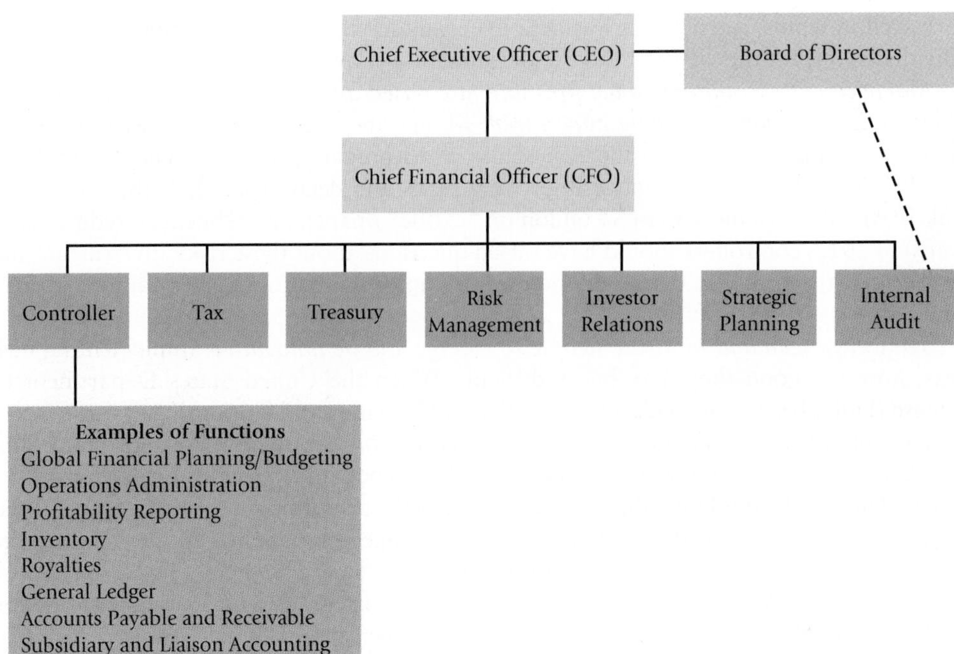

Exhibit 1-6

Nike: Reporting Relationship for the CFO and the Corporate Controller

Exhibit 1-6 shows an organization chart of the CFO and the corporate controller at Nike, the leading footwear and sports apparel company. The CFO is a staff manager who reports to and supports the chief executive officer (CEO). As in most organizations, the corporate controller at Nike reports to the CFO. Nike also has regional controllers who support regional managers in the major geographic regions in which the company operates, such as the United States, Asia Pacific, Latin America, and Europe. Because they support the activities of the regional manager, for example, by managing budgets and analyzing costs, regional controllers report to the regional manager rather than the corporate controller. At the same time, to align accounting policies and practices for the whole organization, regional controllers have a functional (often called a dotted-line) responsibility to the corporate controller. Individual countries sometimes have a country controller.

Organization charts such as the one in Exhibit 1-6 show formal reporting relationships. In most organizations, there also are informal relationships that must be understood when managers attempt to implement their decisions. Examples of informal relationships are friendships among managers (friendships of a professional or personal kind) and the personal preferences of top management about the managers they rely on when making decisions.

Think about what managers do to design and implement strategies and the organization structures within which they operate. Then think about the management accountants' and controllers' roles. It should be clear that the successful management accountant must have technical and analytical competence *as well as* behavioral and interpersonal skills.

Management Accounting Beyond the Numbers[3]

To people outside the profession, it may seem like accountants are just "numbers people." It is true that most accountants are adept financial managers, yet their skills do not stop there. The successful management accountant possesses several skills and characteristics that reach well beyond basic analytical abilities.

Management accountants must work well in cross-functional teams and as a business partner. In addition to being technically competent, the best management accountants

[3] United States Senate Permanent Subcommittee on Investigations. *JPMorgan Chase Whale Trades: A Case History of Derivatives Risks and Abuses*. Washington, DC: Government Printing Office, March 15, 2013; Wendy Garling, "Winning the Transformation Battle at the Defense Finance and Accounting Service," Balanced Scorecard Report, May–June 2007; Nixon, Bill, Burns, John, and Mostafa Jazayeri. The role of management accounting in new product design and development decisions. Volume 9, Issue 1. London: Chartered Institute of Management Accountants, November 2011; and Ben Worthen, "H-P Says It Was Duped, Takes $8.8 Billion Charge," The Wall Street Journal (November 12, 2012).

work well in teams, learn about business issues, understand the motivations of different individuals, respect the views of their colleagues, and show empathy and trust.

Management accountants must promote fact-based analysis and make tough-minded, critical judgments without being adversarial. Management accountants must raise tough questions for managers to consider, especially when preparing budgets. They must do so thoughtfully and with the intent of improving plans and decisions. Before the investment bank JP Morgan lost more than $6 billion on "exotic" financial investments (credit-default swaps) in 2012, controllers should have raised questions about these risky investments and the fact that the firm was essentially betting that improving economic conditions abroad would earn it a large profit.

They must lead and motivate people to change and be innovative. Implementing new ideas, however good they may be, is difficult. When the United States Department of Defense (DoD) began consolidating more than 320 finance and accounting systems into a common platform, the accounting services director and his team of management accountants held meetings to make sure everyone in the agency understood the goal for such a change. Ultimately, the DoD aligned each individual's performance with the transformative change and introduced incentive pay to encourage personnel to adopt the platform and drive innovation within this new framework.

They must communicate clearly, openly, and candidly. Communicating information is a large part of a management accountant's job. When premium car companies such as Rolls Royce and Porsche design new models, management accountants work closely with engineers to ensure that each new car supports a carefully defined balance of commercial, engineering, and financial criteria. These efforts are successful because management accountants clearly communicate the information that multi-disciplinary teams need to deliver new innovations profitably.

They must have a strong sense of integrity. Management accountants must never succumb to pressure from managers to manipulate financial information. They must always remember that their primary commitment is to the organization and its shareholders. In 2012, Hewlett-Packard wrote down $8.8 billion on the value of British software maker Autonomy, which it acquired in 2010, due to serious accounting problems. Hewlett-Packard has accused senior managers at Autonomy of "serious accounting improprieties" and "outright misrepresentations" by mischaracterizing some sales of low-margin hardware as software and recognizing some deals with partners as revenue, even when a customer never bought the product. These actions inflated Autonomy's revenue and profitability, which made the company a more attractive acquisition target.

Decision Point

Where does the management accounting function fit into an organization's structure?

Learning Objective 7

Understand what professional ethics mean to management accountants

...for example, management accountants must maintain integrity and credibility in every aspect of their job

Professional Ethics

At no time has the focus on ethical conduct been sharper than it is today. Corporate scandals at Arthur Andersen, a public accounting firm; Countrywide Financial, a home mortgage company; Enron, an oil and gas company; Lehman Brothers, an investment bank; Olympus, a Japanese optical equipment company; and Bernie Madoff Investment Securities have seriously eroded the public's confidence in corporations. All employees in a company must comply with the organization's—and more broadly, society's—expectations of ethical standards.

Ethics are the foundation of a well-functioning economy. When ethics are weak, suppliers bribe executives to win supply contracts rather than invest in improving quality or lowering costs. Because customers have very little confidence in the quality of products produced, they can become reluctant to buy them, causing markets to fail. Costs are higher because of higher prices paid to suppliers and fewer products being produced and sold. Investors are unsure about the integrity of financial reports, affecting their ability to make investment decisions, resulting in a reluctance to invest and a misallocation of resources. The scandals at Ahold, an international supermarket operator, and Tyco International, a diversified global manufacturing company, and others make clear that value is quickly destroyed by unethical behavior.

Institutional Support

Accountants have special ethical obligations, given that they are responsible for the integrity of the financial information provided to internal and external parties. The Sarbanes–Oxley legislation in the United States was passed in 2002 in response to a series of corporate scandals. The act focused on improving internal control, corporate governance, monitoring of managers, and disclosure practices of public corporations. These regulations impose tough ethical standards and criminal penalties on managers and accountants who don't meet the standards. The regulations also delineate a process for employees to report violations of illegal and unethical acts (these employees are called whistleblowers).

As part of the Sarbanes–Oxley Act, CEOs and CFOs must certify that the financial statements of their firms fairly represent the results of their operations. In order to increase the independence of auditors, the act empowers the audit committee of a company's board of directors (which is composed exclusively of independent directors) to hire, compensate, and terminate the public accounting firm to audit a company. To reduce their financial dependency on their individual clients and increase their independence, the act limits auditing firms from providing consulting, tax, and other advisory services to the companies they are auditing. The act also authorizes the Public Company Accounting Oversight Board to oversee, review, and investigate the work of the auditors.

Professional accounting organizations, which represent management accountants in many countries, offer certification programs indicating that those who have completed them have management accounting and financial management technical knowledge and expertise. These organizations also advocate high ethical standards. In the United States, the Institute of Management Accountants (IMA) has also issued ethical guidelines. Exhibit 1-7 presents the IMA's guidance on issues relating to competence, confidentiality, integrity, and credibility. To provide support to its members to act ethically at all times, the IMA runs an ethics hotline service. Members can call professional counselors at the IMA's Ethics Counseling Service to discuss their ethical dilemmas. The counselors help identify the key ethical issues and possible alternative ways of resolving them, and confidentiality is guaranteed. The IMA is just one of many institutions that help navigate management accountants through what could be turbulent ethical waters.

Typical Ethical Challenges

Ethical issues can confront management accountants in many ways. Here are two examples:

- **Case A:** A management accountant is concerned about the commercial potential of a software product for which development costs are currently being capitalized as an asset rather than being shown as an expense for internal reporting purposes. The firm's division manager, whose bonus is based, in part, on the division's profits, argues that showing development costs as an asset is justified because the new product will generate profits. However, he presents little evidence to support his argument. The last two products from the division have been unsuccessful. The management accountant wants to make the right decision while avoiding a difficult personal confrontation with his boss, the division manager.
- **Case B:** A packaging supplier, bidding for a new contract, offers a management accountant of the purchasing company an all-expenses-paid weekend to the Super Bowl. The supplier does not mention the new contract when extending the invitation. The management accountant is not a personal friend of the supplier. He knows cost issues are critical when it comes to approving the new contract and is concerned that the supplier will ask for details about the bids placed by competing packaging companies.

In each case, the management accountant is faced with an ethical dilemma. Ethical issues are not always clear-cut. Case A involves competence, credibility, and integrity. The management accountant should request that the division manager provide credible evidence that the new product is commercially viable. If the manager does not provide such evidence, expensing development costs in the current period is appropriate.

Exhibit 1-7

Ethical Behavior for Practitioners of Management Accounting and Financial Management

Practitioners of management accounting and financial management have an obligation to the public, their profession, the organizations they serve, and themselves to maintain the highest standards of ethical conduct. In recognition of this obligation, the Institute of Management Accountants has promulgated the following standards of ethical professional practice. Adherence to these standards, both domestically and internationally, is integral to achieving the Objectives of Management Accounting. Practitioners of management accounting and financial management shall not commit acts contrary to these standards nor shall they condone the commission of such acts by others within their organizations.

IMA STATEMENT OF ETHICAL PROFESSIONAL PRACTICE

Practitioners of management accounting and financial management shall behave ethically. A commitment to ethical professional practice includes overarching principles that express our values and standards that guide our conduct.

PRINCIPLES

IMA's overarching ethical principles include: Honesty, Fairness, Objectivity, and Responsibility. Practitioners shall act in accordance with these principles and shall encourage others within their organizations to adhere to them.

STANDARDS

A practitioner's failure to comply with the following standards may result in disciplinary action.

COMPETENCE

Each practitioner has a responsibility to:

1. Maintain an appropriate level of professional expertise by continually developing knowledge and skills.
2. Perform professional duties in accordance with relevant laws, regulations, and technical standards.
3. Provide decision support information and recommendations that are accurate, clear, concise, and timely.
4. Recognize and communicate professional limitations or other constraints that would preclude responsible judgment or successful performance of an activity.

CONFIDENTIALITY

Each practitioner has a responsibility to:

1. Keep information confidential except when disclosure is authorized or legally required.
2. Inform all relevant parties regarding appropriate use of confidential information. Monitor subordinates' activities to ensure compliance.
3. Refrain from using confidential information for unethical or illegal advantage.

INTEGRITY

Each practitioner has a responsibility to:

1. Mitigate actual conflicts of interest. Regularly communicate with business associates to avoid apparent conflicts of interest. Advise all parties of any potential conflicts.
2. Refrain from engaging in any conduct that would prejudice carrying out duties ethically.
3. Abstain from engaging in or supporting any activity that might discredit the profession.

CREDIBILITY

Each practitioner has a responsibility to:

1. Communicate information fairly and objectively.
2. Disclose all relevant information that could reasonably be expected to influence an intended user's understanding of the reports, analyses, or recommendations.
3. Disclose delays or deficiencies in information, timeliness, processing, or internal controls in conformance with organization policy and/or applicable law.

Source: IMA Statement of Ethical Professional Practice, 2005. Montvale, NJ: Institute of Management Accountants. Reprinted with permission from the Institute of Management Accountants, Montvale, NJ, www.imanet.org.

Exhibit 1-8

Resolution of Ethical Conflict

In applying the Standards of Ethical Professional Practice, you may encounter problems identifying unethical behavior or resolving an ethical conflict. When faced with ethical issues, you should follow your organization's established policies on the resolution of such conflict. If these policies do not resolve the ethical conflict, you should consider the following courses of action:

1. Discuss the issue with your immediate supervisor except when it appears that the supervisor is involved. In that case, present the issue to the next level. If you cannot achieve a satisfactory resolution, submit the issue to the next management level. If your immediate superior is the chief executive officer or equivalent, the acceptable reviewing authority may be a group such as the audit committee, executive committee, board of directors, board of trustees, or owners. Contact with levels above the immediate superior should be initiated only with your superior's knowledge, assuming he or she is not involved. Communication of such problems to authorities or individuals not employed or engaged by the organization is not considered appropriate, unless you believe there is a clear violation of the law.
2. Clarify relevant ethical issues by initiating a confidential discussion with an IMA Ethics Counselor or other impartial advisor to obtain a better understanding of possible courses of action.
3. Consult your own attorney as to legal obligations and rights concerning the ethical conflict.

Source: IMA Statement of Ethical Professional Practice, 2005. Montvale, NJ: Institute of Management Accountants. Reprinted with permission from the Institute of Management Accountants, Montvale, NJ, www.imanet.org.

Case B involves confidentiality and integrity. The supplier in Case B may have no intention of asking questions about competitors' bids. However, the appearance of a conflict of interest in Case B is sufficient for many companies to prohibit employees from accepting "favors" from suppliers. Exhibit 1-8 presents the IMA's guidance on "Resolution of Ethical Conflict." The accountant in Case B should discuss the invitation with his or her immediate supervisor. If the visit is approved, the accountant should inform the supplier that the invitation has been officially approved subject to following corporate policy (which includes not disclosing confidential company information).

Most professional accounting organizations around the globe issue statements about professional ethics. These statements include many of the same issues discussed by the IMA in Exhibits 1-7 and 1-8. For example, the Chartered Institute of Management Accountants (CIMA) in the United Kingdom advocates the same four ethical principles shown in Exhibit 1-7: competency, confidentiality, integrity, and credibility.

Decision Point

What are the ethical responsibilities of management accountants?

Problem for Self-Study

Campbell Soup Company incurs the following costs:

a. Purchase of tomatoes by a canning plant for Campbell's tomato soup products
b. Materials purchased for redesigning Pepperidge Farm biscuit containers to make biscuits stay fresh longer
c. Payment to Backer, Spielvogel, & Bates, the advertising agency, for advertising work on the Healthy Request line of soup products
d. Salaries of food technologists researching feasibility of a Prego pizza sauce that has minimal calories
e. Payment to Safeway for redeeming coupons on Campbell's food products
f. Cost of a toll-free telephone line used for customer inquiries about using Campbell's soup products
g. Cost of gloves used by line operators on the Swanson Fiesta breakfast-food production line
h. Cost of handheld computers used by Pepperidge Farm delivery staff serving major supermarket accounts

Classify each cost item (a–h) as one of the business functions in the value chain in Exhibit 1-2 (page 6).

Solution

a. Production
b. Design of products and processes
c. Marketing
d. Research and development
e. Marketing
f. Customer service
g. Production
h. Distribution

▶ Decision Points

The following question-and-answer format summarizes the chapter's learning objectives. Each decision presents a key question related to a learning objective. The guidelines are the answer to that question.

Decision	Guidelines
1. How is financial accounting different from management accounting?	Financial accounting is used to develop reports for external users on past financial performance using GAAP. Management accounting is used to provide future-oriented information to help managers (internal users) make decisions and achieve an organization's goals.
2. How do management accountants support strategic decisions?	Management accountants contribute to strategic decisions by providing information about the sources of competitive advantage.
3. How do companies add value, and what are the dimensions of performance that customers are expecting of companies?	Companies add value through research and development (R&D), design of products and processes, production, marketing, distribution, and customer service. Customers want companies to deliver performance through cost and efficiency, quality, timeliness, and innovation.
4. How do managers make decisions to implement strategy?	Managers use a five-step decision-making process to implement a strategy: (1) identify the problem and uncertainties; (2) obtain information; (3) make predictions about the future; (4) make decisions by choosing among alternatives; and (5) implement the decision, evaluate performance, and learn. The first four steps are planning decisions. They include deciding on an organization's goals, predicting results under various alternative ways of achieving those goals, and deciding how to attain the desired goals. Step 5 is the control decision, which includes taking actions to implement the planning decisions, evaluating past performance, and providing feedback that will help future decision making.
5. What guidelines do management accountants use?	Three guidelines that help management accountants increase their value to managers are (a) employing a cost–benefit approach, (b) recognizing behavioral as well as technical considerations, and (c) identifying different costs for different purposes.
6. Where does the management accounting function fit into an organization's structure?	Management accounting is an integral part of the controller's function. In most organizations, the controller reports to the chief financial officer, who is a key member of the top management team.
7. What are the ethical responsibilities of management accountants?	Management accountants have ethical responsibilities that relate to competence, confidentiality, integrity, and credibility.

Terms to Learn

Each chapter will include this section. Like all technical terms, accounting terms have precise meanings. Learn the definitions of new terms when you initially encounter them. The meaning of each of the following terms is given in this chapter and in the Glossary at the end of this book.

budget **(p. 11)**
chief financial officer (CFO) **(p. 14)**
control **(p. 11)**
controller **(p. 14)**
cost accounting **(p. 4)**
cost–benefit approach **(p. 13)**
cost management **(p. 4)**
customer relationship management (CRM) **(p. 7)**
customer service **(p. 6)**
design of products and processes **(p. 6)**
distribution **(p. 6)**
finance director **(p. 14)**
financial accounting **(p. 3)**
learning **(p. 12)**
line management **(p. 14)**
management accounting **(p. 4)**
marketing **(p. 6)**
planning **(p. 11)**
production **(p. 6)**
research and development (R&D) **(p. 6)**
staff management **(p. 14)**
strategic cost management **(p. 5)**
strategy **(p. 5)**
supply chain **(p. 7)**
sustainability **(p. 8)**
total quality management (TQM) **(p. 8)**
value chain **(p. 6)**

Assignment Material

Questions

MyAccountingLab

1-1 How does management accounting differ from financial accounting?

1-2 "Management accounting should not fit the straitjacket of financial accounting." Explain and give an example.

1-3 How can a management accountant help formulate strategy?

1-4 Describe the business functions in the value chain.

1-5 Explain the term *supply chain* and its importance to cost management.

1-6 "Management accounting deals only with costs." Do you agree? Explain.

1-7 How can management accountants help improve quality and achieve timely product deliveries?

1-8 Describe the five-step decision-making process.

1-9 Distinguish planning decisions from control decisions.

1-10 What three guidelines help management accountants provide the most value to managers?

1-11 "Knowledge of technical issues such as computer technology is a necessary but not sufficient condition to becoming a successful management accountant." Do you agree? Why?

1-12 As a new controller, reply to this comment by a plant manager: "As I see it, our accountants may be needed to keep records for shareholders and Uncle Sam, but I don't want them sticking their noses in my day-to-day operations. I do the best I know how. No bean counter knows enough about my responsibilities to be of any use to me."

1-13 Where does the management accounting function fit into an organization's structure?

1-14 Name the four areas in which standards of ethical conduct exist for management accountants in the United States. What organization sets forth these standards?

1-15 What steps should a management accountant take if established written policies provide insufficient guidance on how to handle an ethical conflict?

Exercises

MyAccountingLab

1-16 Value chain and classification of costs, computer company. Compaq Computer incurs the following costs:

a. Electricity costs for the plant assembling the Presario computer line of products
b. Transportation costs for shipping the Presario line of products to a retail chain
c. Payment to David Kelley Designs for design of the Armada Notebook
d. Salary of computer scientist working on the next generation of minicomputers
e. Cost of Compaq employees' visit to a major customer to demonstrate Compaq's ability to interconnect with other computers
f. Purchase of competitors' products for testing against potential Compaq products

g. Payment to television network for running Compaq advertisements
h. Cost of cables purchased from outside supplier to be used with Compaq printers

Required

Classify each of the cost items (**a–h**) into one of the business functions of the value chain shown in Exhibit 1-2 (page 6).

1-17 Value chain and classification of costs, pharmaceutical company. Pfizer, a pharmaceutical company, incurs the following costs:

a. Payment of booth registration fee at a medical conference to promote new products to physicians
b. Cost of redesigning an insulin syringe to make it less painful
c. Cost of a toll-free telephone line used for customer inquiries about drug usage, side effects of drugs, and so on
d. Equipment purchased to conduct experiments on drugs yet to be approved by the government
e. Sponsorship of a professional golfer
f. Labor costs of workers in the packaging area of a production facility
g. Bonus paid to a salesperson for exceeding a monthly sales quota
h. Cost of FedEx courier service to deliver drugs to hospitals

Required

Classify each of the cost items (**a–h**) as one of the business functions of the value chain shown in Exhibit 1-2 (page 6).

1-18 Value chain and classification of costs, fast food restaurant. Burger King, a hamburger fast food restaurant, incurs the following costs:

a. Cost of oil for the deep fryer
b. Wages of the counter help who give customers the food they order
c. Cost of the costume for the King on the Burger King television commercials
d. Cost of children's toys given away free with kids' meals
e. Cost of the posters indicating the special "two cheeseburgers for $2.50"
f. Costs of frozen onion rings and French fries
g. Salaries of the food specialists who create new sandwiches for the restaurant chain
h. Cost of "to-go" bags requested by customers who could not finish their meals in the restaurant

Required

Classify each of the cost items (**a–h**) as one of the business functions of the value chain shown in Exhibit 1-2 (page 6).

1-19 Key success factors. Dominic Consulting has issued a report recommending changes for its newest manufacturing client, Casper Engines. Casper Engines currently manufactures a single product, which is sold and distributed nationally. The report contains the following suggestions for enhancing business performance:

a. Develop a hybrid engine to stay ahead of competitors
b. Increase training hours of assembly-line personnel to decrease the currently high volumes of scrap and waste.
c. Reduce lead times (time from customer order of product to customer receipt of product) by 20% in order to increase customer retention.
d. Negotiate faster response times with direct material suppliers to allow for lower material inventory levels
e. Benchmark the company's gross margin percentages against its major competitors.

Required

Link each of these changes to the key success factors that are important to managers.

1-20 Key success factors. Morten Construction Company provides construction services for major projects. Managers at the company believe that construction is a people-management business, and they list the following as factors critical to their success:

a. Provide tools to simplify and complete construction sooner.
b. Foster cooperative relationships with suppliers that allow for more frequent deliveries as and when products are needed.
c. Integrate tools and techniques that reduce errors in construction projects.
d. Provide continuous training for employees on new tools and equipment.
e. Benchmark the company's gross margin percentages against its major competitors.

Required

Match each of the above factors to the key success factors that are important to managers.

1-21 Planning and control decisions. Conner Company makes and sells brooms and mops. It takes the following actions, not necessarily in the order given. For each action (**a–e**) state whether it is a planning decision or a control decision.

a. Conner asks its marketing team to consider ways to get back market share from its newest competitor, Swiffer.

b. Conner calculates market share after introducing its newest product.
c. Conner compares costs it actually incurred with costs it expected to incur for the production of the new product.
d. Conner's design team proposes a new product to compete directly with the Swiffer.
e. Conner estimates the costs it will incur to sell 30,000 units of the new product in the first quarter of next fiscal year.

1-22 Planning and control decisions. Ed Sykes is the president of Valley Tree Service. He takes the following actions, not necessarily in the order given. For each action (**a–e**) state whether it is a planning decision or a control decision.

a. Sykes decides to expand service offerings into an adjacent market.
b. Sykes calculates the profitability of a job recently performed for the state arboretum.
c. Sykes weighs the purchase of an expensive new wood-chipping machine proposed by field managers.
d. Sykes estimates the hourly cost of providing emergency services next year to the local power company.
e. Sykes compares actual fuel costs for operating the company's equipment to budgeted costs.

1-23 Five-step decision-making process, manufacturing. Tadeski Foods makes frozen dinners that it sells through grocery stores. Typical products include turkey, pot roast, fried chicken, and meatloaf. The managers at Tadeski have recently proposed a line of frozen chicken pies. They take the following actions to help decide whether to launch the line.

a. Tadeski's test kitchen prepares a number of possible recipes for a consumer focus group.
b. Sales managers estimate they will sell more chicken pies in their northern sales territory than in their southern sales territory.
c. Managers discuss the possibility of introducing a new chicken pie.
d. Managers compare actual costs of making chicken pies with their budgeted costs.
e. Costs for making chicken pies are budgeted.
f. The company decides to introduce a new chicken pie.
g. To help decide whether to introduce a new chicken pie, the company researches the costs of potential ingredients.

Required

Classify each of the actions (**a–g**) as a step in the five-step decision-making process (identify the problem and uncertainties; obtain information; make predictions about the future; make decisions by choosing among alternatives; implement the decision, evaluate performance, and learn). The actions are not listed in the order they are performed.

1-24 Five-step decision-making process, service firm. Brook Exteriors is a firm that provides house-painting services. Richard Brook, the owner, is trying to find new ways to increase revenues. Mr. Brook performs the following actions, not in the order listed.

a. Mr. Brook decides to buy the paint sprayers rather than hire additional painters.
b. Mr. Brook discusses with his employees the possibility of using paint sprayers instead of hand painting to increase productivity and thus profits.
c. Mr. Brook learns of a large potential job that is about to go out for bids.
d. Mr. Brook compares the expected cost of buying sprayers to the expected cost of hiring more workers who paint by hand and estimates profits from both alternatives.
e. Mr. Brook estimates that using sprayers will reduce painting time by 20%.
f. Mr. Brook researches the price of paint sprayers online.

Required

Classify each of the actions (**a–f**) according to its step in the five-step decision-making process (identify the problem and uncertainties; obtain information; make predictions about the future; make decisions by choosing among alternatives; implement the decision, evaluate performance, and learn).

1-25 Professional ethics and reporting division performance. Maria Mendez is division controller and James Dalton is division manager of the Hestor Shoe Company. Mendez has line responsibility to Dalton, but she also has staff responsibility to the company controller.

Dalton is under severe pressure to achieve the budgeted division income for the year. He has asked Mendez to book $200,000 of revenues on December 31. The customers' orders are firm, but the shoes are still in the production process. They will be shipped on or around January 4. Dalton says to Mendez, "The key event is getting the sales order, not shipping the shoes. You should support me, not obstruct my reaching division goals."

Required

1. Describe Mendez's ethical responsibilities.
2. What should Mendez do if Dalton gives her a direct order to book the sales?

1-26 Professional ethics and reporting division performance. Joshua Wilson is the controller of Apex Picture Frame Mouldings, a division of Garman Enterprises. As the division is preparing to count year-end inventory, Wilson is approached by Doug Leonard, the division's president. A selection of inventory previously valued at $150,000 had been identified as flawed earlier that month and as a result was determined to be unfit for sale. Leonard tells Wilson that he has decided to count the selected items as regular inventory and that he will "deal with it when things settle down after the first of the year. After all," Leonard adds, "the auditors don't know good picture frame moulding from bad. We've had a rough year, and things are looking up for next year. Our division needs all the profits we can get this year. It's just a matter of timing the write-off." Leonard is Wilson's direct supervisor.

Required

1. Describe Wilson's ethical dilemma.
2. What should Wilson do if Leonard gives him a direct order to include the inventory?

MyAccountingLab

Problems

Required

1-27 Planning and control decisions, Internet company. PostNews.com offers its subscribers several services, such as an annotated TV guide and local-area information on weather, restaurants, and movie theaters. Its main revenue sources are fees for banner advertisements and fees from subscribers. Recent data are as follows:

Month/Year	Advertising Revenues	Actual Number of Subscribers	Monthly Fee per Subscriber
June 2011	$ 415,972	29,745	$15.50
December 2011	867,246	55,223	20.50
June 2012	892,134	59,641	20.50
December 2012	1,517,950	87,674	20.50
June 2013	2,976,538	147,921	20.50

The following decisions were made from June through October 2013:

a. June 2013: Raised subscription fee to $25.50 per month from July 2013 onward. The budgeted number of subscribers for this monthly fee is shown in the following table.
b. June 2013: Informed existing subscribers that from July onward, monthly fee would be $25.50.
c. July 2013: Offered e-mail service to subscribers and upgraded other online services.
d. October 2013: Dismissed the vice president of marketing after significant slowdown in subscribers and subscription revenues, based on July through September 2013 data in the following table.
e. October 2013: Reduced subscription fee to $22.50 per month from November 2013 onward.

Results for July–September 2013 are as follows:

Month/Year	Budgeted Number of Subscribers	Actual Number of Subscribers	Monthly Fee per Subscriber
July 2013	145,000	129,250	$25.50
August 2013	155,000	142,726	25.50
September 2013	165,000	145,643	25.50

Required

1. Classify each of the decisions (**a–e**) as a planning or a control decision.
2. Give two examples of other planning decisions and two examples of other control decisions that may be made at PostNews.com.

1-28 Strategic decisions and management accounting. Consider the following series of independent situations in which a firm is about to make a strategic decision.

Decisions

a. Pedro Phones is about to decide whether to launch production and sale of a cell phone with standard features.
b. Flash Computers is trying to decide whether to produce and sell a new home computer software package that includes the ability to interface with a sewing machine and a vacuum cleaner. There is no such software currently on the market.
c. Celine Cosmetics has been asked to provide a "store brand" lip gloss that will be sold at discount retail stores.
d. Nicholus Meats is considering developing a special line of gourmet bologna made with sun-dried tomatoes, pine nuts, and artichoke hearts.

Required

1. For each decision, state whether the company is following a cost leadership or a product differentiation strategy.
2. For each decision, discuss what information the management accountant can provide about the source of competitive advantage for these firms.

1-29 Strategic decisions and management accounting. Consider the following series of independent situations in which a firm is about to make a strategic decision.

Decisions

a. A popular restaurant is considering hiring and training inexperienced cooks. The restaurant will no longer hire experienced chefs.
b. An office supply store is considering adding a delivery service that its competitors do not have.
c. A regional airline is deciding whether to install technology that will allow passengers to check themselves in. This technology will reduce the number of desk clerks required inside the airport.
d. A local florist is considering hiring a horticulture specialist to help customers with gardening questions.

Required

1. For each decision, state whether the company is following a cost leadership or a product differentiation strategy.
2. For each decision, discuss what information the managerial accountant can provide about the source of competitive advantage for these firms.

1-30 Management accounting guidelines. For each of the following items, identify which of the management accounting guidelines applies: cost–benefit approach, behavioral and technical considerations, or different costs for different purposes.

1. Analyzing whether to keep the billing function within an organization or outsource it.
2. Deciding to give bonuses for superior performance to the employees in a Japanese subsidiary and extra vacation time to the employees in a Swedish subsidiary.
3. Including costs of all the value-chain functions before deciding to launch a new product, but including only its manufacturing costs in determining its inventory valuation.
4. Considering the desirability of hiring an additional salesperson.
5. Giving each salesperson the compensation option of choosing either a low salary and a high-percentage sales commission or a high salary and a low-percentage sales commission.
6. Selecting the costlier computer system after considering two systems.
7. Installing a participatory budgeting system in which managers set their own performance targets, instead of top management imposing performance targets on managers.
8. Recording research costs as an expense for financial reporting purposes (as required by U.S. GAAP) but capitalizing and expensing them over a longer period for management performance-evaluation purposes.
9. Introducing a profit-sharing plan for employees.

1-31 Management accounting guidelines. For each of the following items, identify which of the management accounting guidelines applies: cost–benefit approach, behavioral and technical considerations, or different costs for different purposes.

1. Analyzing whether to produce a component needed for the end product or to outsource it.
2. Deciding whether to compensate the sales force by straight commission or by salary.
3. Including costs related to administrative function to evaluate the financial performance of a division, but including only controllable costs in evaluating the manager's performance.
4. Considering the desirability of purchasing new technology.
5. Basing bonus calculations on financial measures such as return on investment or basing bonus calculations on delivery time to customer.
6. Deciding whether to buy or lease an existing production facility to increase capacity.
7. Determining the loss in future business because of poor quality but including only estimated scrap and waste as potential loss on the budgeted financial statements.

1-32 Role of controller, role of chief financial officer. George Jimenez is the controller at Balkin Electronics, a manufacturer of devices for the computer industry. The company may promote him to chief financial officer.

Required

1. In this table, indicate which executive is *primarily* responsible for each activity.

Activity	Controller	CFO
Managing the company's long-term investments		
Presenting the financial statements to the board of directors		
Strategic review of different lines of businesses		
Budgeting funds for a plant upgrade		
Managing accounts receivable		
Negotiating fees with auditors		
Assessing profitability of various products		
Evaluating the costs and benefits of a new product design		

2. Based on this table and your understanding of the two roles, what types of training or experience will George find most useful for the CFO position?

1-33 Budgeting, ethics, pharmaceutical company. Chris Jackson was recently promoted to Controller of Research and Development (R&D) for BrisCor, a *Fortune* 500 pharmaceutical company that manufactures prescription drugs and nutritional supplements. The company's total R&D cost for 2013 was expected (budgeted) to be $5 billion. During the company's midyear budget review, Chris realized that current R&D expenditures were already at $3.5 billion, nearly 40% above the midyear target. At this current rate of expenditure, the R&D division was on track to exceed its total year-end budget by $2 billion!

In a meeting with CFO Ronald Meece later that day, Jackson delivered the bad news. Meece was both shocked and outraged that the R&D spending had gotten out of control. Meece wasn't any more understanding when Jackson revealed that the excess cost was entirely related to research and development of a new drug, Vyacon, which was expected to go to market next year. The new drug would result in large profits for BrisCor, if the product could be approved by year-end.

Meece had already announced his expectations of third-quarter earnings to Wall Street analysts. If the R&D expenditures weren't reduced by the end of the third quarter, Meece was certain that the targets he had announced publicly would be missed and the company's stock price would tumble. Meece instructed Jackson to make up the budget shortfall by the end of the third quarter using "whatever means necessary."

Jackson was new to the controller's position and wanted to make sure that Meece's orders were followed. Jackson came up with the following ideas for making the third-quarter budgeted targets:

a. Stop all research and development efforts on the drug Vyacon until after year-end. This change would delay the drug going to market by at least 6 months. It is possible that in the meantime a BrisCor competitor could make it to market with a similar drug.
b. Sell off rights to the drug Martek. The company had not planned on doing this because, under current market conditions, it would get less than fair value. It would, however, result in a one-time gain that could offset the budget shortfall. Of course, all future profits from Martek would be lost.
c. Capitalize some of the company's R&D expenditures, reducing R&D expense on the income statement. This transaction would not be in accordance with GAAP, but Jackson thought it was justifiable because the Vyacon drug was going to market early next year. Jackson would argue that capitalizing R&D costs this year and expensing them next year would better match revenues and expenses.

Required

1. Referring to the "Standards of Ethical Behavior for Practitioners of Management Accounting and Financial Management," Exhibit 1-7 (page 18), which of the preceding items (**a–c**) are acceptable to use? Which are unacceptable?
2. What would you recommend Jackson do?

1-34 Professional ethics and end-of-year actions. Linda Butler is the new division controller of the snack-foods division of Daniel Foods. Daniel Foods has reported a minimum 15% growth in annual earnings for each of the past 5 years. The snack-foods division has reported annual earnings growth of more than 20% each year in this same period. During the current year, the economy went into a recession. The corporate controller estimates a 10% annual earnings growth rate for Daniel Foods this year. One month before the December 31 fiscal year-end of the current year, Butler estimates the snack-foods division will report an annual earnings growth of only 8%. Rex Ray, the snack-foods division president, is not happy, but he notes that the "end-of-year actions" still need to be taken.

Butler makes some inquiries and is able to compile the following list of end-of-year actions that were more or less accepted by the previous division controller:

a. Deferring December's routine monthly maintenance on packaging equipment by an independent contractor until January of next year.
b. Extending the close of the current fiscal year beyond December 31 so that some sales of next year are included in the current year.
c. Altering dates of shipping documents of next January's sales to record them as sales in December of the current year.
d. Giving salespeople a double bonus to exceed December sales targets.
e. Deferring the current period's advertising by reducing the number of television spots run in December and running more than planned in January of next year.
f. Deferring the current period's reported advertising costs by having Daniel Foods' outside advertising agency delay billing December advertisements until January of next year or by having the agency alter invoices to conceal the December date.
g. Persuading carriers to accept merchandise for shipment in December of the current year even though they normally would not have done so.

Required

1. Why might the snack-foods division president want to take these end-of-year actions?
2. Butler is deeply troubled and reads the "Standards of Ethical Behavior for Practitioners of Management Accounting and Financial Management" in Exhibit 1-7 (page 18). Classify each of the end-of-year actions (**a–g**) as acceptable or unacceptable according to that document.
3. What should Butler do if Ray suggests that these end-of-year actions are taken in every division of Daniel Foods and that she will greatly harm the snack-foods division if she does not cooperate and paint the rosiest picture possible of the division's results?

1-35 Professional ethics and end-of-year actions. Macon Publishing House produces consumer magazines. The house and home division, which sells home-improvement and home-decorating magazines, has seen a 20% reduction in operating income over the past 9 months, primarily due to an economic recession and a depressed consumer housing market. The division's controller, Rhett Gable, has felt pressure from the CFO to improve his division's operating results by the end of the year. Gable is considering the following options for improving the division's performance by year-end:

a. Cancelling two of the division's least profitable magazines, resulting in the layoff of 25 employees.
b. Selling the new printing equipment that was purchased in January and replacing it with discarded equipment from one of the company's other divisions. The previously discarded equipment no longer meets current safety standards.
c. Recognizing unearned subscription revenue (cash received in advance for magazines that will be delivered in the future) as revenue when cash is received in the current month (just before fiscal year-end) instead of showing it as a liability.
d. Reducing the division's Allowance for Bad Debt Expense. This transaction alone would increase operating income by 5%.
e. Recognizing advertising revenues that relate to January in December.
f. Switching from declining balance to straight-line depreciation to reduce depreciation expense in the current year.

Required

1. What are the motivations for Gable to improve the division's year-end operating earnings?
2. From the point of view of the "Standards of Ethical Behavior for Practitioners of Management Accounting and Financial Management," Exhibit 1-7 (page 18), which of the preceding items (**a–f**) are acceptable? Which are unacceptable?
3. What should Gable do about the pressure to improve performance?

1-36 Ethical challenges, global company. Andahl Logistics, a U.S. shipping company, has just begun distributing goods across the Atlantic to Norway. The company began operations in 2011, transporting goods to South America. The company's earnings are currently trailing behind its competitors and Andahl's investors are becoming anxious. Some of the company's largest investors are even talking of selling their interest in the shipping newcomer. Andahl's CEO, Max Chang, calls an emergency meeting with his executive team. Chang needs a plan before his upcoming conference call with uneasy investors. Andahl's executive staff make the following suggestions for salvaging the company's short-term operating results:

a. Stop all transatlantic shipping efforts. The startup costs for the new operations are hurting current profit margins.
b. Make deep cuts in pricing through the end of the year to generate additional revenue.
c. Pressure current customers to take early delivery of goods before the end of the year so that more revenue can be reported in this year's financial statements.
d. Sell off distribution equipment prior to year-end. The sale would result in one-time gains that could offset the company's lagging profits. The owned equipment could be replaced with leased equipment at a lower cost in the current year.
e. Record executive year-end bonus compensation for the current year in the next year when it is paid after the December fiscal year-end.
f. Recognize sales revenues on orders received but not shipped as of the end of the year.
g. Establish corporate headquarters in Ireland before the end of the year, lowering the company's corporate tax rate from 28% to 12.5%.

Required

1. As the management accountant for Andahl, evaluate each of the preceding items (**a–g**) in the context of the "Standards of Ethical Behavior for Practitioners of Management Accounting and Financial Management," Exhibit 1-7 (page 18). Which of the items are in violation of these ethics standards and which are acceptable?
2. What should the management accountant do with regard to those items that are in violation of the ethical standards for management accountants?

2

An Introduction to Cost Terms and Purposes

Learning Objectives

1. Define and illustrate a cost object
2. Distinguish between direct costs and indirect costs
3. Explain variable costs and fixed costs
4. Interpret unit costs cautiously
5. Distinguish inventoriable costs from period costs
6. Illustrate the flow of inventoriable and period costs
7. Explain why product costs are computed in different ways for different purposes
8. Describe a framework for cost accounting and cost management

What does the word *cost* mean to you?

Is it the price you pay for something of value, like a cell phone? A cash outflow, like monthly rent? Something that affects profitability, like salaries? Organizations, like individuals, deal with different types of costs. At different times organizations put more or less emphasis on these costs. When times are good, companies often focus on selling as much as they can, with costs taking a backseat. But when times get tough, companies shift their emphasis from selling to cutting costs. Unfortunately, when times are really bad, companies may find that they are unable to cut costs fast enough, leading to Chapter 11 bankruptcy, as was the case with Hostess Brands.

High Fixed Costs Bankrupt Twinkie Maker[1]

In 2012, Hostess Brands—owner of the iconic Twinkies lunchbox snack—announced it would go out of business and liquidate its assets. Declining sales and trends toward healthier snacking crippled the company given its high fixed costs—costs that did not decrease as the number of Twinkies and Ho Hos sold declined.

After emerging from bankruptcy in 2009, Hostess management tried to turn around the company's fortunes through innovation and workplace efficiency. Despite initial progress reducing its variable costs, the prices of the commodities that Hostess relied on—corn, sugar, and flour—increased during the recession. Unfortunately for Hostess, the remaining large percentage of its operating costs were fixed because union contracts made it difficult to close facilities, consolidate distribution routes, or reduce pensions owed to retired workers.

By the second half of 2011, Hostess was losing $2 million per week. With a stifling debt burden, the company filed for bankruptcy protection again in January 2012. Further cost reductions proved elusive and controversial negotiations with unions resulted in thousands of employees striking that November. Within days, Hostess collapsed under the weight of its fixed costs and filed to liquidate its assets. The wind down resulted in the closure of 33 bakeries, 565 distribution centers, about 5,500 delivery routes, and 570 bakery outlet stores and the loss of 18,500 jobs.

As the story of Hostess Brands illustrates, managers must understand their firms' costs and closely manage them. Organizations as varied as the United Way, the Mayo

---

[1] *Sources:* David A. Kaplan, "Hostess is Bankrupt... Again," *Fortune* (July 26, 2012); Rachel Feintzing, Mike Spector, and Julie Jargon, "Twinkie Maker Hostess to Close," *The Wall Street Journal* (November 16, 2012); "Hostess Brands Obtains Court Authority to Wind Down All Operations, Liquidate Assets, Hostess Brands press release (Irving, TX, November 21, 2012).

Clinic, and Sony generate reports containing a variety of cost concepts and terms managers need to understand to effectively use the reports to run their businesses. This chapter discusses cost concepts and terms that are the basis of accounting information used for internal and external reporting.

Costs and Cost Terminology

Learning Objective 1

Define and illustrate a cost object

...examples of cost objects are products, services, activities, processes, and customers

A **cost** is a resource sacrificed or forgone to achieve a specific objective. A cost (such as the cost of labor or advertising) is usually measured as the monetary amount that must be paid to acquire goods or services. An **actual cost** is the cost incurred (a historical or past cost), as distinguished from a **budgeted cost,** which is a predicted, or forecasted, cost (a future cost).

When you think of a cost, you invariably think of it in the context of putting a price on a particular thing. We call this "thing" a **cost object,** which is anything for which a cost measurement is desired. Suppose you're a manager at BMW's automotive manufacturing plant in Spartanburg, South Carolina. Can you identify some of the plant's cost objects? Now look at Exhibit 2-1.

You will see that BMW managers not only want to know the cost of various products, such as the BMW X6 sports activity vehicle, but they also want to know the costs of services, projects, customers, activities, and departments. Managers use their knowledge of these costs to guide decisions about, for example, product innovation, quality, and customer service.

Now think about whether a manager at BMW might want to know the *budgeted cost* or the *actual cost* of a cost object. Managers almost always need to know both types of costs when making decisions. For example, comparing budgeted costs to actual costs helps managers evaluate how well they did controlling costs and learn about how they can do better in the future.

How does a cost system determine the costs of various cost objects? Typically in two stages: accumulation followed by assignment. **Cost accumulation** is the collection of cost data in some organized way by means of an accounting system. For example, at its Spartanburg plant, BMW collects (accumulates) in various categories the costs of different types of materials, different classifications of labor, the costs incurred for supervision, and so on. The accumulated costs are then *assigned* to designated cost objects, such as the different models of cars that BMW manufactures at the plant. BMW managers use this cost information in two main ways: (1) when *making* decisions, for instance, about how to price different models of cars or how much to invest in R&D and marketing and (2) for *implementing* decisions, by influencing and motivating employees to act, for example, by providing bonuses to employees for reducing costs.

Now that we know why it is useful for management accountants to assign costs, we turn our attention to some concepts that will help us do it. Again, think of the different types of costs that we just discussed—materials, labor, and supervision. You are probably thinking that some costs, such as the costs of materials, are easier to assign to a cost object than others, such as the costs of supervision. As you will learn, this is indeed the case.

Decision Point

What is the cost object?

Exhibit 2-1 Examples of Cost Objects at BMW

Cost Object	Illustration
Product	A BMW X6 sports activity vehicle
Service	Telephone hotline providing information and assistance to BMW dealers
Project	R&D project on enhancing the DVD system in BMW cars
Customer	Herb Chambers Motors, the BMW dealer that purchases a broad range of BMW vehicles
Activity	Setting up machines for production or maintaining production equipment
Department	Environmental, health, and safety department

Learning Objective 2

Distinguish between direct costs

...costs that are traced to the cost object

and indirect costs

...costs that are allocated to the cost object

Direct Costs and Indirect Costs

We now describe how costs are classified as direct and indirect costs and the methods used to assign these costs to cost objects.

- **Direct costs of a cost object** are related to the particular cost object and can be traced to it in an economically feasible (cost-effective) way. For example, the cost of steel or tires is a direct cost of BMW X6s. The cost of the steel or tires can be easily traced to or identified with the BMW X6. The workers on the BMW X6 line request materials from the warehouse, and the material requisition document identifies the cost of the materials supplied to the X6. Similarly, individual workers record on their time sheets the hours and minutes they spend working on the X6. The cost of this labor can easily be traced to the X6 and is another example of a direct cost. The term **cost tracing** is used to describe the assignment of direct costs to a particular cost object.
- **Indirect costs of a cost object** are related to the particular cost object but cannot be traced to it in an economically feasible (cost-effective) way. For example, the salaries of plant administrators (including the plant manager) who oversee production of the many different types of cars produced at the Spartanburg plant are an indirect cost of the X6s. Plant administration costs are related to the cost object (X6s) because plant administration is necessary for managing the production of these vehicles. Plant administration costs are indirect costs because plant administrators also oversee the production of other products, such as the Z4 Roadster. Unlike steel or tires, there is no specific request made by supervisors of the X6 production line for plant administration services, and it is virtually impossible to trace plant administration costs to the X6 line.

  The term **cost allocation** is used to describe the assignment of indirect costs to a particular cost object. **Cost assignment** is a general term that encompasses both (1) tracing direct costs to a cost object and (2) allocating indirect costs to a cost object. Exhibit 2-2 depicts direct costs and indirect costs and both forms of cost assignment—cost tracing and cost allocation—using the BMW X6 as an example.

Exhibit 2-2

Cost Assignment to a Cost Object

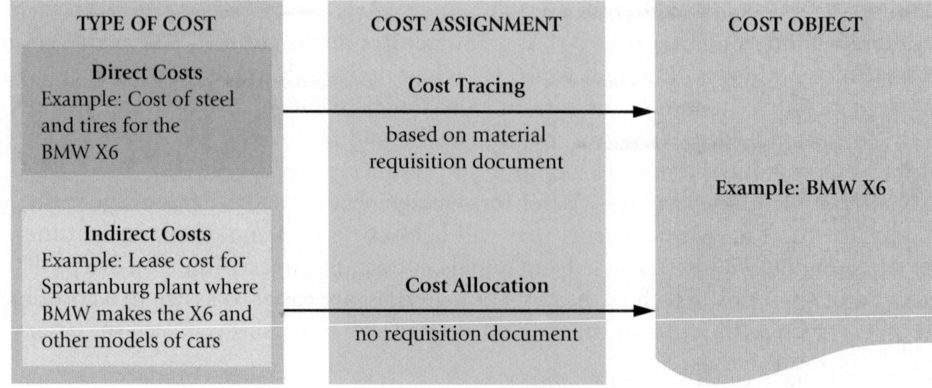

Cost Allocation Challenges

Managers want to assign costs accurately to cost objects because inaccurate product costs will mislead managers about the profitability of different products. This, for example, could result in the managers unknowingly working harder to promote less-profitable products instead of more-profitable products. Generally, managers are more confident about the accuracy of the direct costs of cost objects, such as the cost of steel and tires of the X6.

Consider the cost to lease the Spartanburg plant. This cost is an indirect cost of the X6—there is no separate lease agreement for the area of the plant where the X6 is made. Nonetheless, BMW *allocates* to the X6 a part of the lease cost of the building—for example, on the basis of an estimate of the percentage of the building's floor space occupied for the production of the X6 relative to the total floor space used to produce all models of cars. This approach measures the building resources used by each car model reasonably and accurately. The more floor space a car model occupies, the greater the lease costs assigned to it. Accurately allocating other indirect costs, such as plant administration, to the X6, however, is more difficult. For example, should these costs be allocated on the basis of the number of employees working on each car model or the number of cars produced of each model? Measuring the share of plant administration used by each car model is not clear-cut.

Factors Affecting Direct/Indirect Cost Classifications

Several factors affect whether a cost is classified as direct or indirect:

- **The materiality of the cost in question.** The smaller the amount of a cost—that is, the more immaterial the cost is—the less likely it is economically feasible to trace it to a particular cost object. Consider a mail-order catalog company such as Lands' End. It would be economically feasible to trace the courier charge for delivering a package to an individual customer as a direct cost. In contrast, the cost of the invoice paper included in the package would be classified as an indirect cost. Why? Although the cost of the paper can be traced to each customer, it is not cost-effective to do so. The benefits of knowing that, say, exactly 0.5¢ worth of paper is included in each package do not exceed the data processing and administrative costs of tracing the cost to each package. The time of the sales administrator, who earns a salary of $45,000 a year, is better spent organizing customer information to help with a company's marketing efforts than tracking the cost of paper.
- **Available information-gathering technology.** Improvements in information-gathering technology make it possible to consider more and more costs as direct costs. Bar codes, for example, allow manufacturing plants to treat certain low-cost materials such as clips and screws, which were previously classified as indirect costs, as direct costs of products. At Dell, component parts such as the computer chip and the DVD drive display a bar code that can be scanned at every point in the production process. Bar codes can be read into a manufacturing cost file by waving a "wand" in the same quick and efficient way supermarket checkout clerks enter the cost of each item purchased by a customer.
- **Design of operations.** Classifying a cost as direct is easier if a company's facility (or some part of it) is used exclusively for a specific cost object, such as a specific product or a particular customer. For example, General Chemicals classifies the cost of its facility dedicated to manufacturing soda ash (sodium carbonate) as a direct cost of soda ash.

Be aware that a specific cost may be both a direct cost of one cost object and an indirect cost of another cost object. *That is, the direct/indirect classification depends on the choice of the cost object.* For example, the salary of an assembly department supervisor at BMW is a direct cost if the cost object is the assembly department. However, because the assembly department assembles many different models, the supervisor's salary is an indirect cost if the cost object is a product such as the BMW X6 sports activity vehicle. A useful rule to remember is that the broader the cost object definition is—the assembly department rather than the X6—the higher the proportion direct costs are of total costs and the more confident a manager will be about the accuracy of the resulting cost amounts.

Decision Point

How do managers decide whether a cost is a direct or an indirect cost?

Learning Objective 3

Explain variable costs and fixed costs

...the two basic ways in which costs behave

Cost-Behavior Patterns: Variable Costs and Fixed Costs

Costing systems record the cost of resources acquired, such as materials, labor, and equipment, and track how those resources are used to produce and sell products or services. Recording the costs of resources acquired and used allows managers to see how costs behave. Consider two basic types of cost-behavior patterns found in many accounting systems. A **variable cost** changes *in total* in proportion to changes in the related level of total activity or volume of output produced. A **fixed cost** remains unchanged *in total* for a given time period, despite wide changes in the related level of total activity or volume of output produced. Costs are defined as variable or fixed for *a specific activity* and for *a given time period.* Identifying a cost as variable or fixed provides valuable information for making many management decisions and is an important input when evaluating performance. To illustrate these two basic types of costs, again consider the costs at BMW's Spartanburg, South Carolina, plant.

1. **Variable costs.** If BMW buys a steering wheel at $600 for each of its BMW X6 vehicles, then the total cost of steering wheels is $600 times the number of vehicles produced, as the following table illustrates.

Number of X6s Produced (1)	Variable Cost per Steering Wheel (2)	Total Variable Cost of Steering Wheels (3) = (1) × (2)
1	$600	$ 600
1,000	600	600,000
3,000	600	1,800,000

The steering wheel cost is an example of a variable cost because *total cost* changes in proportion to changes in the number of vehicles produced. However, the cost per unit of a variable cost is constant. For example, the variable cost per steering wheel in column 2 is the same regardless of whether 1,000 or 3,000 X6s are produced. As a result, the total variable cost of steering wheels in column 3 changes proportionately with the number of X6s produced in column 1. So, when considering how variable costs behave, always focus on *total* costs.

Panel A in Exhibit 2-3 shows a graph of the total variable cost of steering wheels. The cost is represented by a straight line that climbs from left to right. The phrases "strictly variable" and "proportionately variable" are sometimes used to describe the variable cost behavior shown in this panel.

Now consider an example of a variable cost for a different activity—the $20 hourly wage paid each worker to set up machines at the Spartanburg plant. The setup labor cost is a variable cost for setup hours because setup cost changes in total in proportion to the number of setup hours used.

Exhibit 2-3

Graphs of Variable and Fixed Costs

PANEL A: Variable Cost of Steering Wheels at $600 per BMW X6 Assembled

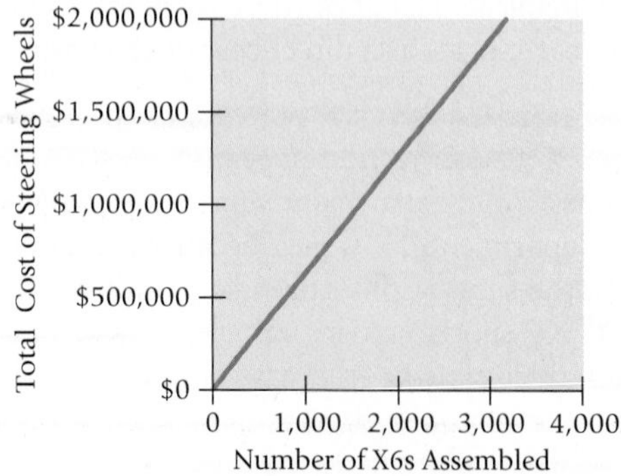

PANEL B: Supervision Costs for the BMW X6 assembly line (in millions)

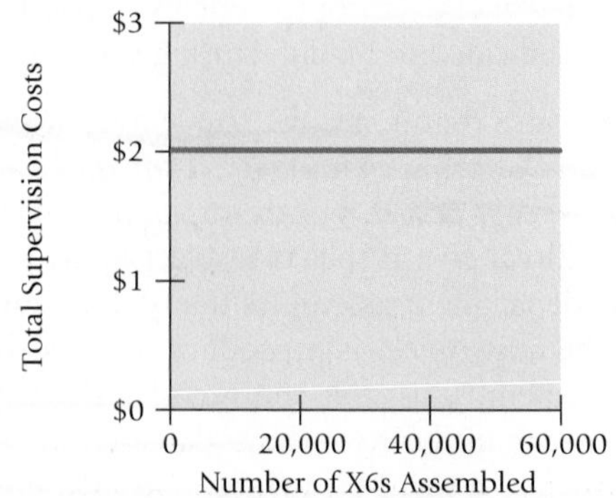

2. **Fixed costs.** Suppose BMW incurs a total cost of $2,000,000 per year for supervisors who work exclusively on the X6 line. These costs are unchanged in total over a designated range of vehicles produced during a given time span (see Exhibit 2-3, Panel B). Fixed costs become smaller and smaller on a per-unit basis as the number of vehicles assembled increases, as the following table shows.

Annual Total Fixed Supervision Costs for BMW X6 Assembly Line (1)	Number of X6s Produced (2)	Fixed Supervision Cost per X6 (3) = (1) ÷ (2)
$2,000,000	10,000	$200
$2,000,000	25,000	80
$2,000,000	50,000	40

It is precisely because *total* line supervision costs are fixed at $2,000,000 that fixed supervision cost per X6 decreases as the number of X6s produced increases; the same fixed cost is spread over a larger number of X6s. Do not be misled by the change in fixed cost per unit. Just as in the case of variable costs, when considering fixed costs, always focus on *total costs*. Costs are fixed when total costs remain unchanged despite significant changes in the level of total activity or volume.

Why are some costs variable and other costs fixed? Recall that a cost is usually measured as the amount of money that must be paid to acquire goods and services. The total cost of steering wheels is a variable cost because BMW buys the steering wheels only when they are needed. As more X6s are produced, proportionately more steering wheels are acquired and proportionately more costs are incurred.

Contrast the plant's variable costs with the $2,000,000 of fixed costs per year incurred for the supervision of the X6 assembly line. This level of supervision is acquired and put in place well before BMW uses it to produce X6s and before BMW even knows how many X6s it will produce. Suppose that BMW puts in place supervisors capable of supervising the production of 60,000 X6s each year. If the demand is for only 55,000 X6s, there will be idle capacity. Supervisors on the X6 line could have supervised the production of 60,000 X6s but will supervise only 55,000 X6s because of the lower demand. However, BMW must pay for the unused line supervision capacity because the cost of supervision cannot be reduced in the short run. If demand is even lower—say only 50,000 X6s are demanded—the plant's line supervision costs will still be $2,000,000, and its idle capacity will increase.

Unlike variable costs, fixed costs of resources (such as for line supervision) cannot be quickly and easily changed to match the resources needed or used. Over time, however, managers can take action to reduce a company's fixed costs. For example, if the X6 line needs to be run for fewer hours because the demand for the vehicles falls, BMW may lay off supervisors or move them to another production line. Unlike variable costs that go away automatically if the resources are not used, reducing fixed costs requires active intervention on the part of managers.

Do not assume that individual cost items are inherently variable or fixed. Consider labor costs. Labor costs can be purely variable for units produced when workers are paid on a piece-unit basis (for each unit they make). For example, some companies pay garment workers on a per-shirt-sewed basis, so the firms' labor costs are variable. That is, the costs depend on how many shirts each worker makes. In contrast, other companies negotiate labor union agreements with set annual salaries that contain no-layoff clauses for workers. At a company such as this, the salaries would appropriately be classified as fixed. For decades, Japanese companies provided their workers a lifetime guarantee of employment. Although such a guarantee entails higher fixed labor costs, a firm can benefit from it because workers are more loyal and dedicated, which can improve productivity. However, during an economic downturn, the company risks losing money if its revenues decrease while its fixed costs remain unchanged. The recent global economic crisis has made companies very reluctant to lock in fixed costs. Concepts in Action: Zipcar Helps Twitter Reduce Fixed Costs describes how a car-sharing service offers companies the opportunity to convert the fixed costs of owning corporate cars into variable costs by renting cars on an as-needed basis.

A particular cost item could be variable for one level of activity and fixed for another. Consider annual registration and license costs for a fleet of planes owned by an airline company. Registration and license costs would be a variable cost that would change with the number of planes the company owned. But the registration and license costs for a particular plane are fixed regardless of the miles flown by that plane during a year.

Decision Point

How do managers decide whether a cost is a variable or a fixed cost?

Some costs have both fixed and variable elements and are called *mixed* or *semivariable* costs. For example, a company's telephone costs may consist of a fixed monthly cost as well as a cost per phone-minute used. We discuss mixed costs and techniques to separate out their fixed and variable components in Chapter 10.

Cost Drivers

A **cost driver** is a variable, such as the level of activity or volume, that causally affects costs over a given time span. An *activity* is an event, task, or unit of work with a specified purpose—for example, designing products, setting up machines, or testing products. The level of activity or volume is a cost driver if there is a cause-and-effect relationship between a change in the level of activity or volume and a change in the level of total costs. For example, if product-design costs change with the number of parts in a product, the

Concepts in Action

Zipcar Helps Twitter Reduce Fixed Costs

In many North American and European cities, Avis subsidiary Zipcar has emerged as a way for corporations to reduce the spending on gas, insurance, and parking of corporate cars. Zipcar—which provides an "on-demand" option for urban individuals and businesses to rent a car by the week, the day, or even the hour—has rates beginning around $8 per hour and $75 per day (including gas, insurance, and about 180 miles per day).

Let's think about what Zipcar means for companies. Many small businesses own a company car or two for getting to meetings, making deliveries, and running errands. Similarly, many large companies own a fleet of cars to shuttle visiting executives and clients back and forth from appointments, business lunches, and the airport. Traditionally, owning these cars has involved very high fixed costs, including buying the asset (car), maintenance costs, and insurance for multiple drivers.

Now, however, companies like Twitter can use Zipcar for on-demand mobility while reducing their transportation and overhead costs. Based in downtown San Francisco, Twitter managers use Zipcar to meet venture capitalists and partners in Silicon Valley and when they travel to places like New York and Boston. "We wanted to avoid the cost of taking taxis everywhere or the time delays of mass transit," said Jack Dorsey, the micro-blogging service's co-founder. "Zipcar's the fastest, easiest way to get around town."

From a business perspective, Zipcar allows Twitter and other companies to convert the fixed costs of owning a company car to variable costs. If business slows or a car isn't required to visit a client, Twitter is not saddled with the fixed costs of car ownership. Of course, when business is good, causing Twitter managers to use Zipcar more often, they can end up paying more overall than they would have paid if they purchased and maintained the car themselves.

Along with cutting corporate spending, car sharing services like Zipcar reduce congestion on the road and promote environmental sustainability. Users report reducing their vehicle miles traveled by 44%, and surveys show CO_2 emissions are being cut by up to 50% per user.

Sources: Based on Paul Keegan, "Zipcar–the best new idea in business." *Fortune* (August 27, 2009); Elizabeth Olsen, "Car sharing reinvents the company wheels." *New York Times* (May 7, 2009); John Kell, Avis to Buy Car-Sharing Service Zipcar," *The Wall Street Journal* (Jnauary 2, 2013); Zipcar, Inc., "Zipcar for business case studies"; Zipcar, Inc., "Zipcar rates and plans."

number of parts is a cost driver of product-design costs. Similarly, miles driven is often a cost driver of distribution costs.

The cost driver of a variable cost is the level of activity or volume whose change causes proportionate changes in the variable cost. For example, the number of vehicles assembled is the cost driver of the total cost of steering wheels. If setup workers are paid an hourly wage, the number of setup hours is the cost driver of total (variable) setup costs.

Costs that are fixed in the short run have no cost driver in the short run but may have a cost driver in the long run. Consider the costs of testing, say, 0.1% of the color printers produced at a Hewlett-Packard plant. These costs consist of equipment and staff costs of the testing department, which are difficult to change. Consequently, they are fixed in the short run regardless of changes in the volume of production. In this case, volume of production is not a cost driver of testing costs in the short run. In the long run, however, Hewlett-Packard will increase or decrease the testing department's equipment and staff to the levels needed to support future production volumes. In the long run, volume of production is indeed a cost driver of testing costs. Costing systems that identify the cost of each activity such as testing, design, or setup are called *activity-based costing systems*.

Relevant Range

Relevant range is the band or range of normal activity level or volume in which there is a specific relationship between the level of activity or volume and the cost in question. For example, a fixed cost is fixed only in relation to a given wide range of total activity or volume (at which the company is expected to operate) and only for a given time span (usually a particular budget period). Suppose BMW contracts with Thomas Transport Company (TTC) to transport X6s to BMW dealerships. TTC rents two trucks, and each truck has an annual fixed rental cost of $40,000. The maximum annual usage of each truck is 120,000 miles. In the current year (2014), the predicted combined total hauling of the two trucks is 170,000 miles.

Exhibit 2-4 shows how annual fixed costs behave at different levels of miles of hauling. Up to 120,000 miles, TTC can operate with one truck; from 120,001 to 240,000 miles, it operates with two trucks; and from 240,001 to 360,000 miles, it operates with three trucks. This pattern will continue as TTC adds trucks to its fleet to provide more miles of hauling. Given the predicted 170,000-mile usage for 2014, the range from 120,001 to 240,000 miles hauled is the range in which TTC expects to operate, resulting in fixed rental costs of $80,000. Within this relevant range, changes in miles hauled will not affect the annual fixed costs.

Fixed costs may change from one year to the next, though. For example, if the total rental fee of the two trucks increases by $2,000 for 2015, the total level of fixed costs will increase to $82,000 (all else remaining the same). If that increase occurs, total rental costs will be fixed at this new level ($82,000) for 2015 for the miles hauled in the 120,001 to 240,000 range.

The relevant range also applies to variable costs. Outside the relevant range, variable costs, such as direct materials costs, may no longer change proportionately with changes in production volumes. For example, above a certain volume, the cost of direct materials may increase at a lower rate because a firm may be able to negotiate price discounts for purchasing greater amounts of materials from its suppliers.

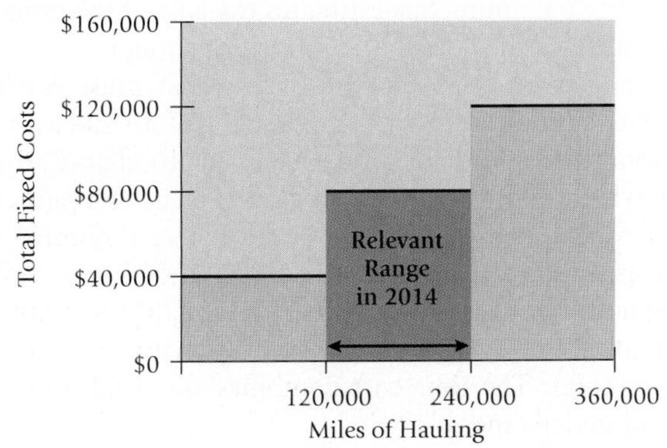

Exhibit 2-4

Fixed-Cost Behavior at Thomas Transport Company

Exhibit 2-5

Examples of Costs in Combinations of the Direct/Indirect and Variable/Fixed Cost Classifications for a Car Manufacturer

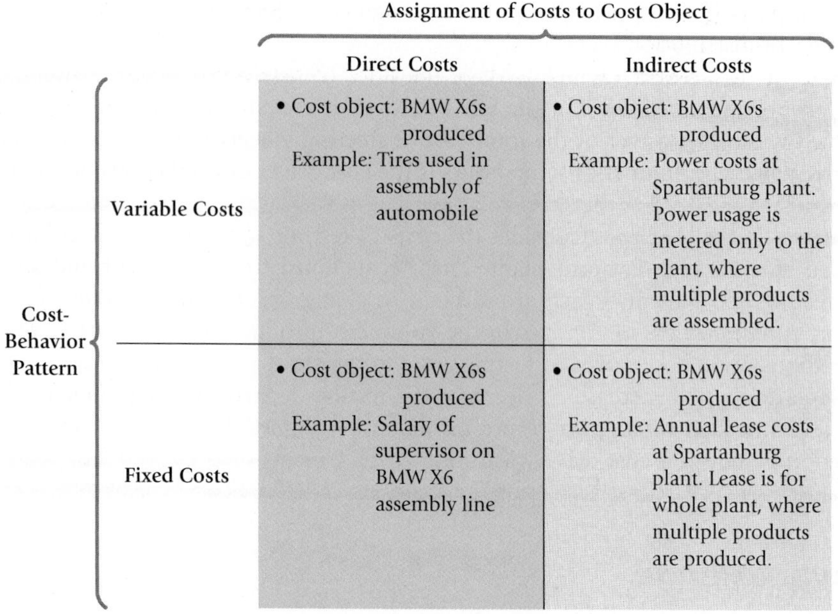

Assignment of Costs to Cost Object
Direct Costs
Indirect Costs
Cost-Behavior Pattern
Variable Costs
• Cost object: BMW X6s produced
Example: Tires used in assembly of automobile
• Cost object: BMW X6s produced
Example: Power costs at Spartanburg plant. Power usage is metered only to the plant, where multiple products are assembled.
Fixed Costs
• Cost object: BMW X6s produced
Example: Salary of supervisor on BMW X6 assembly line
• Cost object: BMW X6s produced
Example: Annual lease costs at Spartanburg plant. Lease is for whole plant, where multiple products are produced.

Relationships Between Types of Costs

We have introduced two major classifications of costs: direct/indirect and variable/fixed. Costs may simultaneously be as follows:

- Direct and variable
- Direct and fixed
- Indirect and variable
- Indirect and fixed

Exhibit 2-5 shows examples of costs in each of these four cost classifications for the BMW X6.

Learning Objective 4

Interpret unit costs cautiously

...for many decisions, managers should use total costs, not unit costs

Total Costs and Unit Costs

The preceding section concentrated on the behavior patterns of total costs in relation to activity or volume levels. We now consider unit costs.

Unit Costs

A **unit cost,** also called an **average cost,** is calculated by dividing the total cost by the related number of units produced. In many decision contexts, calculating a unit cost is essential. Consider the booking agent who has to make the decision to book Paul McCartney to play at Shea Stadium. She estimates the cost of the event to be $4,000,000. This knowledge is helpful for the decision, but it is not enough.

Before reaching a decision, the booking agent also must predict the number of people who will attend. Without knowing the number of attendees, she cannot make an informed decision about the admission price she needs to charge to recover the cost of the event or even on whether to have the event at all. So she computes the unit cost of the event by dividing the total cost ($4,000,000) by the expected number of people who will attend. If 50,000 people attend, the unit cost is $80 ($4,000,000 ÷ 50,000) per person; if 20,000 attend, the unit cost increases to $200 ($4,000,000 ÷ 20,000). Unless the total cost is "unitized" (that is, averaged by the level of activity or volume), the $4,000,000 cost is difficult to interpret. The unit cost combines the total cost and the number of people in a simple and understandable way.

Accounting systems typically report both total-cost amounts and average-cost-per-unit amounts. The units might be expressed in various ways. Examples are automobiles assembled, packages delivered, or hours worked. Consider Tennessee Products, a manufacturer of speaker systems with a plant in Memphis. Suppose that, in 2014, its first year of operations, the company incurs $40,000,000 of manufacturing costs to produce 500,000 speaker systems. Then the unit cost is $80:

$$\frac{\text{Total manufacturing costs}}{\text{Number of units manufactured}} = \frac{\$40{,}000{,}000}{500{,}000 \text{ units}} = \$80 \text{ per unit}$$

If 480,000 units are sold and 20,000 units remain in ending inventory, the unit-cost concept helps managers determine total costs in the income statement and balance sheet and, therefore, the financial results Tennessee Products reports to shareholders, banks, and the government.

Cost of goods sold in the income statement, 480,000 units × $80 per unit	$38,400,000
Ending inventory in the balance sheet, 20,000 units × $80 per unit	1,600,000
Total manufacturing costs of 500,000 units	$40,000,000

Unit costs are found in all areas of the value chain—for example, the unit cost of a product design, a sales visit, and a customer-service call. By summing unit costs throughout the value chain, managers calculate the unit cost of the different products or services they deliver and determine the profitability of each product or service. Managers use this information, for example, to decide the products in which they should invest more resources, such as R&D and marketing, and the prices they should charge.

Use Unit Costs Cautiously

Although unit costs are regularly used in financial reports and for making product mix and pricing decisions, *managers should think in terms of total costs rather than unit costs for many decisions*. Consider the manager of the Memphis plant of Tennessee Products. Assume the $40,000,000 in costs in 2014 consist of $10,000,000 of fixed costs and $30,000,000 of variable costs (at $60 variable cost per speaker system produced). Suppose the total fixed costs and the variable cost per speaker system in 2015 are expected to be unchanged from 2014. The budgeted costs for 2015 at different production levels, calculated on the basis of total variable costs, total fixed costs, and total costs, are:

Units Produced (1)	Variable Cost per Unit (2)	Total Variable Costs (3) = (1) × (2)	Total Fixed Costs (4)	Total Costs (5) = (3) + (4)	Unit Cost (6) = (5) ÷ (1)
100,000	$60	$ 6,000,000	$10,000,000	$16,000,000	$160.00
200,000	$60	$12,000,000	$10,000,000	$22,000,000	$110.00
500,000	$60	$30,000,000	$10,000,000	$40,000,000	$ 80.00
800,000	$60	$48,000,000	$10,000,000	$58,000,000	$ 72.50
1,000,000	$60	$60,000,000	$10,000,000	$70,000,000	$ 70.00

A plant manager who uses the 2014 unit cost of $80 per unit will underestimate actual total costs if the plant's 2015 output is below the 2014 level of 500,000 units. If the volume produced falls to 200,000 units due to, say, the presence of a new competitor and less demand, actual costs would be $22,000,000. The unit cost of $80 times 200,000 units equals $16,000,000, which underestimates the actual total costs by $6,000,000 ($22,000,000 − $16,000,000). In other words, *the unit cost of $80 applies only when the company produces 500,000 units*.

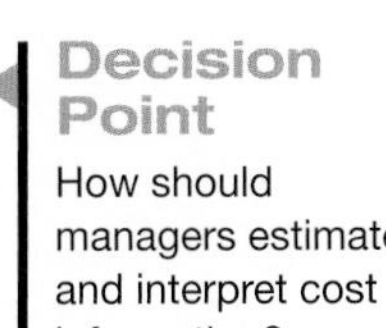

Decision Point
How should managers estimate and interpret cost information?

An overreliance on the unit cost in this situation could lead to insufficient cash being available to pay the company's costs if volume declines to 200,000 units. As the table indicates, for making this decision, managers should think in terms of total variable costs, total fixed costs, and total costs rather than unit cost. As a general rule, first calculate total costs, then compute the unit cost, if it is needed for a particular decision.

Learning Objective 5

Distinguish inventoriable costs

...assets when incurred, then cost of goods sold

from period costs

...expenses of the period when incurred

Business Sectors, Types of Inventory, Inventoriable Costs, and Period Costs

In this section, we describe the different sectors of the economy, the different types of inventory that companies hold, and some commonly used classifications of manufacturing costs.

Manufacturing-, Merchandising-, and Service-Sector Companies

We define three sectors of the economy and provide examples of companies in each sector.

1. **Manufacturing-sector companies** purchase materials and components and convert them into various finished goods. Examples are automotive companies such as Jaguar, cellular-phone producers such as Nokia, food-processing companies such as Heinz, and computer companies such as Toshiba.
2. **Merchandising-sector companies** purchase and then sell tangible products without changing their basic form. This sector includes companies engaged in retailing (for example, bookstores such as Barnes & Noble and department stores such as Target); distribution (for example, a supplier of hospital products, such as Owens and Minor); or wholesaling (for example, a supplier of electronic components such as Arrow Electronics).
3. **Service-sector companies** provide services (intangible products)—for example, legal advice or audits—to their customers. Examples are law firms such as Wachtell, Lipton, Rosen & Katz; accounting firms such as Ernst & Young; banks such as Barclays; mutual fund companies such as Fidelity; insurance companies such as Aetna; transportation companies such as Singapore Airlines; advertising agencies such as Saatchi & Saatchi; television stations such as Turner Broadcasting; Internet service providers such as Comcast; travel agencies such as American Express; and brokerage firms such as Merrill Lynch.

Types of Inventory

Manufacturing-sector companies purchase materials and components and convert them into finished goods. These companies typically have one or more of the following three types of inventory:

1. **Direct materials inventory.** Direct materials in stock that will be used in the manufacturing process (for example, computer chips and components needed to manufacture cellular phones).
2. **Work-in-process inventory.** Goods partially worked on but not yet completed (for example, cellular phones at various stages of completion in the manufacturing process). This is also called **work in progress.**
3. **Finished goods inventory.** Goods (for example, cellular phones) completed but not yet sold.

Merchandising-sector companies purchase tangible products and then sell them without changing their basic form. These companies hold only one type of inventory, which is products in their original purchased form, called *merchandise inventory*. Service-sector companies provide only services or intangible products and do not hold inventories of tangible products.

Commonly Used Classifications of Manufacturing Costs

Three terms commonly used when describing manufacturing costs are *direct materials costs, direct manufacturing labor costs,* and *indirect manufacturing costs*. These terms build on the direct versus indirect cost distinction we described earlier in the context of manufacturing costs.

1. **Direct materials costs** are the acquisition costs of all materials that eventually become part of the cost object (work in process and then finished goods) and can be traced to the cost object in an economically feasible way. The steel and tires used to make the BMW X6 and the computer chips used to make cellular phones are examples of direct material costs. Note that the costs of direct materials include not only the cost of the materials themselves but the freight-in (inward delivery) charges, sales taxes, and customs duties that must be paid to acquire them.
2. **Direct manufacturing labor costs** include the compensation of all manufacturing labor that can be traced to the cost object (work in process and then finished goods) in an economically feasible way. Examples include wages and fringe benefits paid to machine operators and assembly-line workers who convert direct materials to finished goods.
3. **Indirect manufacturing costs** are all manufacturing costs that are related to the cost object (work in process and then finished goods) but cannot be traced to that cost object in an economically feasible way. Examples include supplies, indirect materials such as lubricants, indirect manufacturing labor such as plant maintenance and cleaning labor, plant rent, plant insurance, property taxes on the plant, plant depreciation, and the compensation of plant managers. This cost category is also referred to as **manufacturing overhead costs** or **factory overhead costs**. We use *indirect manufacturing costs* and *manufacturing overhead costs* interchangeably in this book.

We now describe the distinction between inventoriable costs and period costs.

Inventoriable Costs

Inventoriable costs are all costs of a product that are considered assets in a company's balance sheet when the costs are incurred and that are expensed as cost of goods sold only when the product is sold. For manufacturing-sector companies, all manufacturing costs are inventoriable costs. The costs first accumulate as work-in-process inventory assets (in other words, they are "inventoried") and then as finished goods inventory assets. Consider Cellular Products, a manufacturer of cellular phones. The cost of the company's direct materials, such as computer chips, direct manufacturing labor costs, and manufacturing overhead costs create new assets. They start out as work in process inventory and become finished goods inventory (the cellular phones). When the cellular phones are sold, the costs move from being assets to cost of goods sold expense. This cost is matched against **revenues,** which are inflows of assets (usually cash or accounts receivable) received for products or services customers purchase.

Note that the cost of goods sold includes all manufacturing costs (direct materials, direct manufacturing labor, and manufacturing overhead costs) incurred to produce them. The cellular phones may be sold during a different accounting period than the period in which they were manufactured. Thus, inventorying manufacturing costs in the balance sheet during the accounting period when the phones are manufactured and expensing the manufacturing costs in a later income statement when the phones are sold matches revenues and expenses.

For merchandising-sector companies such as Walmart, inventoriable costs are the costs of purchasing goods that are resold in their same form. These costs are made up of the costs of the goods themselves plus any incoming freight, insurance, and handling costs for those goods. Service-sector companies provide only services or intangible products. The absence of inventories of tangible products for sale means service-sector companies have no inventoriable costs.

Period Costs

Period costs are all costs in the income statement other than cost of goods sold. Period costs, such as marketing, distribution, and customer service costs, are treated as expenses of the accounting period in which they are incurred because managers expect these costs

Exhibit 2-6

Examples of Period Costs in Combinations of the Direct/Indirect and Variable/Fixed Cost Classifications at a Bank

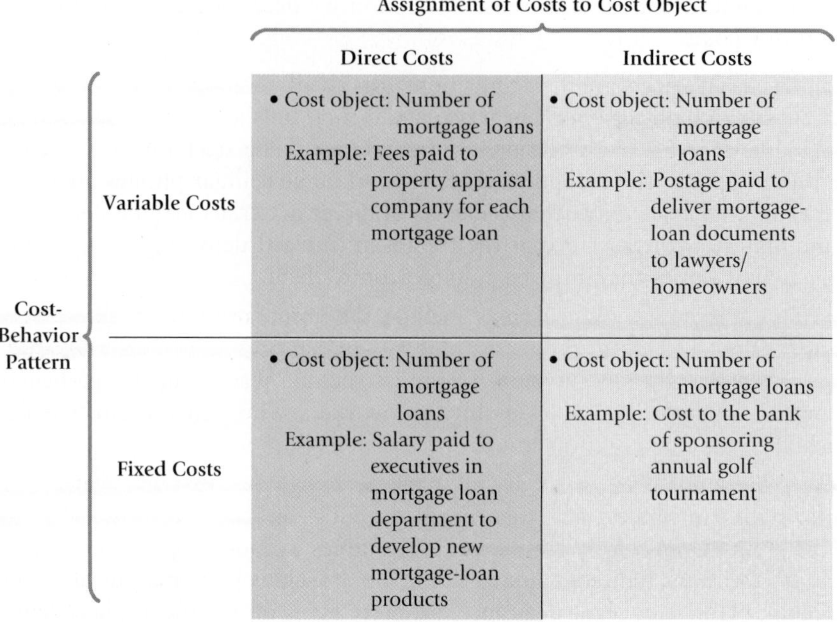

to increase revenues in only that period and not in future periods. Some costs such as R&D costs are treated as period costs because, although these costs may increase revenues in a future period if the R&D efforts are successful, it is highly uncertain if and when these increased revenues will occur. Expensing period costs as they are incurred best matches expenses to revenues.

Decision Point

What are the differences in the accounting for inventoriable versus period costs?

For manufacturing-sector companies, all nonmanufacturing costs (for example, design costs and costs of shipping products to customers) in the income statement are period costs. For merchandising-sector companies, all costs in the income statement not related to the cost of goods purchased for resale are period costs. Examples of these period costs are labor costs of sales-floor personnel and advertising costs. Because there are no inventoriable costs for service-sector companies, all costs in the income statement are period costs.

Exhibit 2-5 showed examples of inventoriable costs in direct/indirect and variable/fixed cost classifications for a car manufacturer. Exhibit 2-6 shows examples of period costs in direct/indirect and variable/fixed cost classifications at a bank.

Learning Objective 6

Illustrate the flow of inventoriable and period costs

...in manufacturing settings, inventoriable costs flow through work-in-process and finished goods accounts and are expensed when goods are sold; period costs are always expensed as incurred

Illustrating the Flow of Inventoriable Costs and Period Costs

We illustrate the flow of inventoriable costs and period costs through the income statement of a manufacturing company, where the distinction between inventoriable costs and period costs is most detailed.

Manufacturing-Sector Example

Follow the flow of costs for Cellular Products in Exhibits 2-7 and 2-8. Exhibit 2-7 visually highlights the differences in the flow of inventoriable and period costs for a manufacturing-sector company. Note how, as described in the previous section, inventoriable costs go through the balance sheet accounts of work-in-process inventory and finished goods inventory before entering the cost of goods sold in the income statement. Period costs are expensed directly in the income statement. Exhibit 2-8 takes the visual presentation in Exhibit 2-7 and shows how inventoriable costs and period expenses would appear in the income statement and schedule of cost of goods manufactured of a manufacturing company.

We start by tracking the flow of direct materials shown on the left in Exhibit 2-7 and in Panel B in Exhibit 2-8. To keep things simple, all numbers are expressed in thousands, except for the per unit amounts.

Step 1: **Cost of direct materials used in 2014.** Note how the arrows in Exhibit 2-7 for beginning inventory, $11,000, and direct material purchases, $73,000, "fill up" the direct materials inventory box and how direct materials used, $76,000, "empties out" direct material inventory, leaving an ending inventory of direct materials of $8,000 that becomes the beginning inventory for the next year.

The cost of direct materials used is calculated in Exhibit 2-8, Panel B (light blue–shaded area), as follows:

Beginning inventory of direct materials, January 1, 2014	$11,000
+ Purchases of direct materials in 2014	73,000
– Ending inventory of direct materials, December 31, 2014	8,000
= Direct materials used in 2014	$76,000

Step 2: **Total manufacturing costs incurred in 2014.** Total manufacturing costs refers to all direct manufacturing costs and manufacturing overhead costs incurred during 2014 for all goods worked on during the year. Cellular Products classifies its manufacturing costs into the three categories described earlier.

(i) Direct materials used in 2014 (shaded light blue in Exhibit 2-8, Panel B)	$ 76,000
(ii) Direct manufacturing labor in 2014 (shaded blue in Exhibit 2-8, Panel B)	9,000
(iii) Manufacturing overhead costs in 2014 (shaded dark blue in Exhibit 2-8, Panel B)	20,000
Total manufacturing costs incurred in 2014	$105,000

Note how in Exhibit 2-7 these costs increase work-in-process inventory.

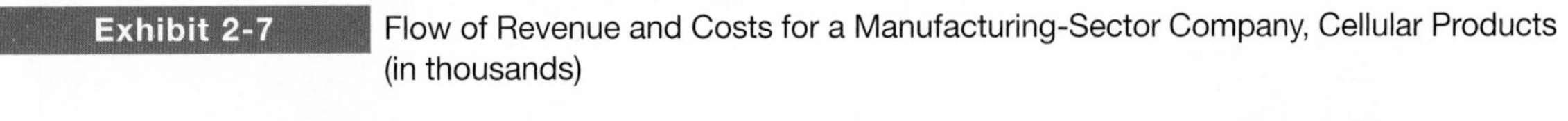

Exhibit 2-7 Flow of Revenue and Costs for a Manufacturing-Sector Company, Cellular Products (in thousands)

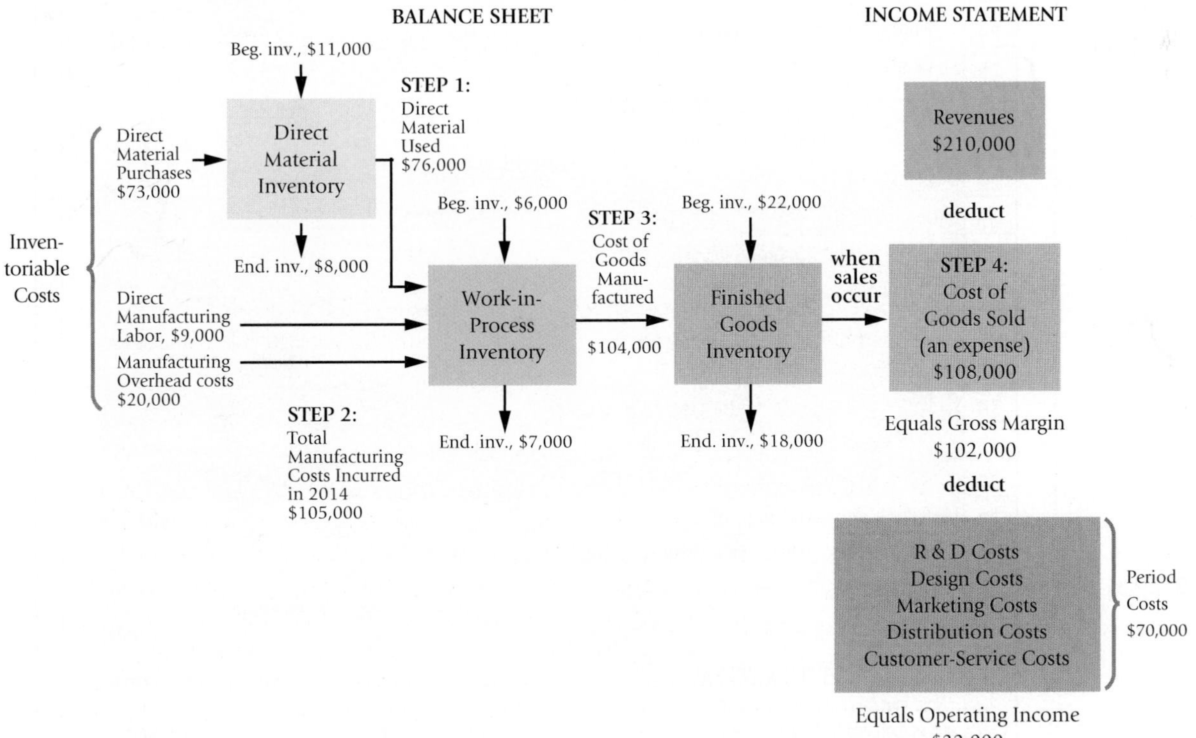

Exhibit 2-8 Income Statement and Schedule of Cost of Goods Manufactured of a Manufacturing-Sector Company, Cellular Products

Home | Insert | Page Layout | Formulas | Data | Review | View

Step		A	B	C	D
	1	**PANEL A: INCOME STATEMENT**			
	2	**Cellular Products**			
	3	**Income Statement**			
	4	**For the Year Ended December 31, 2014 (in thousands)**			
	5	Revenues		$210,000	
STEP 4	6	Cost of goods sold:			
STEP 4	7	Beginning finished goods inventory, January 1, 2014	$ 22,000		
STEP 4	8	Cost of goods manufactured (see Panel B)	104,000		
STEP 4	9	Cost of goods available for sale	126,000		
STEP 4	10	Ending finished goods inventory, December 31, 2014	18,000		
STEP 4	11	Cost of goods sold		108,000	
	12	Gross margin (or gross profit)		102,000	
	13	Operating costs:			
	14	R&D, design, mktg., dist., and cust.-service cost	70,000		
	15	Total operating costs		70,000	
	16	Operating income		$ 32,000	
	17				
	18	**PANEL B: COST OF GOODS MANUFACTURED**			
	19	**Cellular Products**			
	20	**Schedule of Cost of Goods Manufactured**[a]			
	21	**For the Year Ended December 31, 2014 (in thousands)**			
STEP 1	22	Direct materials:			
STEP 1	23	Beginning inventory, January 1, 2014	$11,000		
STEP 1	24	Purchases of direct materials	73,000		
STEP 1	25	Cost of direct materials available for use	84,000		
STEP 1	26	Ending inventory, December 31, 2014	8,000		
STEP 1 / STEP 2	27	Direct materials used		$ 76,000	
STEP 2	28	Direct manufacturing labor		9,000	
STEP 2	29	Manufacturing overhead costs:			
STEP 2	30	Indirect manufacturing labor	$ 7,000		
STEP 2	31	Supplies	2,000		
STEP 2	32	Heat, light, and power	5,000		
STEP 2	33	Depreciation—plant building	2,000		
STEP 2	34	Depreciation—plant equipment	3,000		
STEP 2	35	Miscellaneous	1,000		
STEP 2	36	Total manufacturing overhead costs		20,000	
STEP 2 / STEP 3	37	Manufacturing costs incurred during 2014		105,000	
STEP 3	38	Beginning work-in-process inventory, January 1, 2014		6,000	
STEP 3	39	Total manufacturing costs to account for		111,000	
STEP 3	40	Ending work-in-process inventory, December 31, 2014		7,000	
STEP 3	41	Cost of goods manufactured (to income statement)		$104,000	
	42	[a] Note that this schedule can become a schedule of cost of goods manufactured and sold simply by including the beginning and ending finished goods inventory figures in the supporting schedule rather than in the body of the income statement.			

Step 3: Cost of goods manufactured in 2014. **Cost of goods manufactured** refers to the cost of goods brought to completion, whether they were started before or during the current accounting period.

Note how the work-in-process inventory box in Exhibit 2-7 has a very similar structure to the direct materials inventory box described in Step 1. Beginning work-in-process inventory of $6,000 and total manufacturing costs incurred in 2014 of $105,000 "fill up" the work-in-process inventory box. Some of the manufacturing costs incurred during 2014 are held back as the cost of the ending work-in-process inventory. The ending work-in-process inventory of $7,000 becomes the beginning inventory for the next year, and the $104,000 cost of goods manufactured during 2014 "empties out" the work-in-process inventory while "filling up" the finished goods inventory box.

The cost of goods manufactured in 2014 (shaded green) is calculated in Exhibit 2-8, Panel B, as follows:

Beginning work-in-process inventory, January 1, 2014	$ 6,000
+ Total manufacturing costs incurred in 2014	105,000
= Total manufacturing costs to account for	111,000
− Ending work-in-process inventory, December 31, 2014	7,000
= Cost of goods manufactured in 2014	$104,000

Step 4: Cost of goods sold in 2014. The cost of goods sold is the cost of finished goods inventory sold to customers during the current accounting period. Looking at the finished goods inventory box in Exhibit 2-7, we see that the beginning inventory of finished goods of $22,000 and cost of goods manufactured in 2014 of $104,000 "fill up" the finished goods inventory box. The ending inventory of finished goods of $18,000 becomes the beginning inventory for the next year, and the $108,000 cost of goods sold during 2014 "empties out" the finished goods inventory.

This cost of goods sold is an expense that is matched against revenues. The cost of goods sold for Cellular Products (shaded olive green) is computed in Exhibit 2-8, Panel A, as follows:

Beginning inventory of finished goods, January 1, 2014	$ 22,000
+ Cost of goods manufactured in 2014	104,000
− Ending inventory of finished goods, December 31, 2014	18,000
= Cost of goods sold in 2014	$108,000

Exhibit 2-9 shows related general ledger T-accounts for Cellular Products' manufacturing cost flow. Note how the cost of goods manufactured ($104,000) is the cost of all goods completed during the accounting period. These costs are all inventoriable costs. Goods completed during the period are transferred to finished goods inventory. These costs become cost of goods sold in the accounting period when the goods are sold. Also note that the direct materials, direct manufacturing labor, and manufacturing overhead costs of the units in work-in-process inventory ($7,000) and finished goods inventory ($18,000) as of December 31, 2014, will appear as an asset in the balance sheet. These costs will become expenses next year when the work-in-process inventory is converted to finished goods and the finished goods are sold.

Exhibit 2-9 General Ledger T-Accounts for Cellular Products' Manufacturing Cost Flow (in thousands)

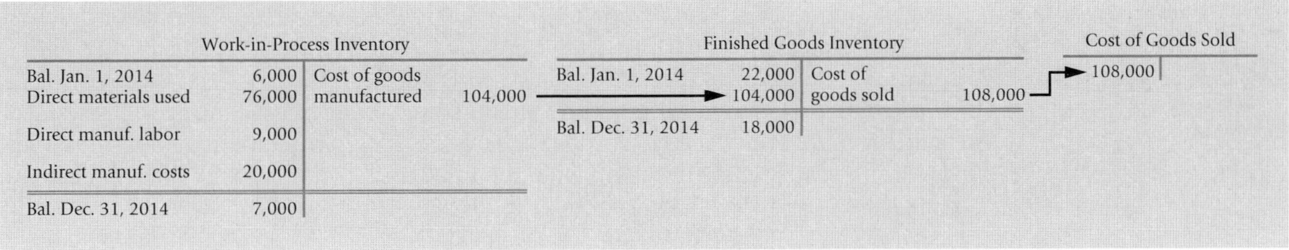

We can now prepare Cellular Products' income statement for 2014. The income statement of Cellular Products is shown on the right side in Exhibit 2-7 and in Exhibit 2-8, Panel A. Revenues of Cellular Products are (in thousands) $210,000. Inventoriable costs expensed during 2014 equal cost of goods sold of $108,000.

Gross margin = Revenues − Cost of goods sold = $210,000 − $108,000 = $102,000.

The $70,000 of operating costs composed of R&D, design, marketing, distribution, and customer-service costs are period costs of Cellular Products. These period costs include, for example, salaries of salespersons, depreciation on computers and other equipment used in marketing, and the cost of leasing warehouse space for distribution. **Operating income** equals total revenues from operations minus cost of goods sold and operating (period) costs (excluding interest expense and income taxes) or, equivalently, gross margin minus period costs. The operating income of Cellular Products is $32,000 (gross margin, $102,000 – period costs, $70,000). If you are familiar with financial accounting, recall that period costs are typically called selling, general, and administrative expenses in the income statement.

Newcomers to cost accounting frequently assume that indirect costs such as rent, telephone, and depreciation are always costs of the period in which they are incurred and are not associated with inventories. When these costs are incurred in marketing or in corporate headquarters, they are period costs. However, when these costs are incurred in manufacturing, they are manufacturing overhead costs and are inventoriable.

Because costs that are inventoried are not expensed until the units associated with them are sold, a manager can produce more units than are expected to be sold in a period without reducing a firm's net income. In fact, building up inventory in this way defers the expensing of the current period's fixed manufacturing costs as manufacturing costs are inventoried and not expensed until the units are sold in a subsequent period. This in turn actually *increases* the firm's gross margin and operating income even though there is no increase in sales, causing outsiders to believe that the company is more profitable than it actually is. We will discuss this risky accounting practice in greater detail in Chapter 9.

Recap of Inventoriable Costs and Period Costs

Exhibit 2-7 highlights the differences between inventoriable costs and period costs for a manufacturing company. The manufacturing costs of finished goods include direct materials, direct manufacturing labor, and manufacturing overhead costs such as supervision, production control, and machine maintenance. All these costs are inventoriable: They are assigned to work-in-process inventory until the goods are completed and then to finished goods inventory until the goods are sold. All nonmanufacturing costs, such as R&D, design, and distribution costs, are period costs.

Decision Point

What is the flow of inventoriable and period costs in manufacturing and merchandising settings?

Inventoriable costs and period costs flow through the income statement at a merchandising company similar to the way costs flow at a manufacturing company. At a merchandising company, however, the flow of costs is much simpler to understand and track. Exhibit 2-10 shows the inventoriable costs and period costs for a retailer or wholesaler, which buys goods for resale. The only inventoriable cost is the cost of merchandise. (This corresponds to the cost of finished goods manufactured for a manufacturing company.) Purchased goods are held as merchandise inventory, the cost of which is shown as an asset in the balance sheet. As the goods are sold, their costs are shown in the income statement as cost of goods sold. A retailer or wholesaler also has a variety of marketing, distribution, and customer-service costs, which are period costs. In the income statement, period costs are deducted from revenues without ever having been included as part of inventory. Concepts in Action: Cost Structure at Nordstrom Spurs Growth shows the importance of having the right cost structure for period expenses for a retailer.

Exhibit 2-10 Flow of Revenues and Costs for a Merchandising Company (Retailer or Wholesaler)

		BALANCE SHEET		INCOME STATEMENT	
				Revenues	
		Beginning Inventory ↓		deduct	
Inventoriable Costs	Merchandise Purchases →	Merchandise Inventory	when sales occur →	Cost of Goods Sold (an expense)	
		↓ Ending Inventory		Equals Gross Margin	
				deduct	
				Design Costs Purchasing Dept. Costs Marketing Costs Distribution Costs Customer-Service Costs	Period Costs
				Equals Operating Income	

Prime Costs and Conversion Costs

Two terms used to describe cost classifications in manufacturing costing systems are *prime costs* and *conversion costs*. **Prime costs** are all direct manufacturing costs. For Cellular Products,

Prime costs = Direct material costs + Direct manufacturing labor costs = $76,000 + $9,000 = $85,000

Concepts in Action

Cost Structure at Nordstrom Spurs Growth

During the recent global recession, the retail industry was hit hard due to declining economic conditions and changing consumer shopping habits. Since 2009, many long-standing retailers including Circuit City, Blockbuster, and Borders went out of business as their revenues failed to keep pace with the high fixed costs of the retail business, which include high rents and payroll. While some retailers closed their doors, however, other retailers became stronger and were prepared to grow as consumer spending recovered.

While many failed retailers had high fixed costs, Nordstrom, an upscale department store chain, has a more variable cost structure. At Nordstrom, the company's operations are mainly based on a variable cost business model with about 40–45% of its selling, general, and administrative (SGA) costs being variable. These costs include compensation (most salespeople earn a commission), benefits, advertising, and shipping and handling. As consumer spending dropped during the recession, the company reduced costs to mitigate the impact of sluggish sales trends on margins. Similarly, its cost structure enabled Nordstrom to quickly capitalize on the emerging opportunities when market conditions improved.

For example, in 2009 Nordstrom's SGA expenses were 25.5% of its $8.2 billion in revenue. In 2011, its SGA expenses increased to 26.7%, but revenues were $10.5 billion. The company's variable cost flexibility allowed the company to first cut costs and then to aggressively pursue growth while incurring slightly higher SGA costs.

Sources: Based on Nordstrom, Inc., 2012. 2011 Annual Report. Seattle, WA: Nordstrom, Inc.; Zacks Equity Research, "Nordstrom Pinned to Neutral," May 22, 2012.

As we have already discussed, the greater the proportion of prime costs (or direct costs) to total costs, the more confident managers can be about the accuracy of the costs of products. As information-gathering technology improves, companies can add more and more direct-cost categories. For example, power costs might be metered in specific areas of a plant and identified as a direct cost of specific products. Furthermore, if a production line were dedicated to manufacturing a specific product, the depreciation on the production equipment would be a direct manufacturing cost and would be included in prime costs. Computer software companies often have a "purchased technology" direct manufacturing cost item. This item, which represents payments to suppliers who develop software algorithms for a product, is also included in prime costs. **Conversion costs** are all manufacturing costs other than direct material costs. Conversion costs represent all manufacturing costs incurred to convert direct materials into finished goods. For Cellular Products,

$$\text{Conversion costs} = \frac{\text{Direct manufacturing}}{\text{labor costs}} + \frac{\text{Manufacturing}}{\text{overhead costs}} = \$9{,}000 + \$20{,}000 = \$29{,}000$$

Note that direct manufacturing labor costs are a part of both prime costs and conversion costs.

Some manufacturing operations, such as computer-integrated manufacturing (CIM) plants, have very few workers. The workers' roles are to monitor the manufacturing process and to maintain the equipment that produces multiple products. The costing systems in CIM plants do not have a direct manufacturing labor cost category because direct manufacturing labor cost is relatively small and because it is difficult to trace this cost to products. In a CIM plant, the only prime cost is the cost of direct materials. The conversion costs for such a plant are largely manufacturing overhead costs.

Learning Objective 7

Explain why product costs are computed in different ways for different purposes

...examples are pricing and product-mix decisions, government contracts, and financial statements

Measuring Costs Requires Judgment

Measuring costs requires judgment. That's because there are alternative ways for managers to define and classify costs. Different companies or sometimes even different subunits within the same company may define and classify costs differently. Be careful to define and understand the ways costs are measured in a company or situation. We first illustrate this point for labor costs.

Measuring Labor Costs

Consider labor costs for software programming at companies such as Apple, where programmers work on different software applications for products like the iMac, the iPad, and the iPhone. Although labor cost classifications vary among companies, many companies use multiple labor cost categories:

- Direct programming labor costs that can be traced to individual products
- Overhead costs (labor related)
  - Indirect labor compensation for
    - Office staff
    - Office security
    - Rework labor (time spent by direct laborers correcting software errors)
    - Overtime premium paid to software programmers (explained next)
    - Idle time (explained next)
  - Salaries for managers, department heads, and supervisors
  - Payroll fringe costs, for example, health care premiums and pension costs (explained later)

To retain information on different categories, *indirect labor costs* are commonly divided into many subclassifications, for example, office staff and idle time costs. Note that managers' salaries usually are not classified as indirect labor costs. Instead, the compensation of supervisors, department heads, and all others who are regarded as management is placed in a separate classification of labor-related overhead.

Overtime Premium and Idle Time

Managers need to pay special attention to two classes of indirect labor—overtime premium and idle time. **Overtime premium** is the wage rate paid to workers (for both direct labor and indirect labor) in *excess* of their straight-time wage rates. Overtime premium is usually considered to be a part of indirect costs or overhead. Consider the example of George Flexner, a junior software programmer who writes software for multiple products. He is paid $40 per hour for straight-time and $60 per hour (time and a half) for overtime. His overtime premium is $20 per overtime hour. If he works 44 hours, including 4 overtime hours, in one week, his gross compensation would be classified as follows:

Direct programming labor: 44 hours × $40 per hour	$1,760
Overtime premium: 4 hours × $20 per hour	80
Total compensation for 44 hours	$1,840

In this example, why is the overtime premium of direct programming labor usually considered an overhead cost rather than a direct cost? After all, the premium can be traced to specific products that George worked on while working overtime. Overtime premium is generally not considered a direct cost because the particular job that George worked on during the overtime hours is a matter of chance. For example, assume that George worked on two products for 5 hours each on a specific workday that lasted 10 hours, including 2 overtime hours. Should the product George worked on during hours 9 and 10 be assigned the overtime premium? Or should the premium be prorated over both products? Prorating the overtime premium does not "penalize"—add to the cost of—a particular product solely because it happened to be worked on during the overtime hours. *Instead, the overtime premium is considered to be attributable to the heavy overall volume of work. Its cost is regarded as part of overhead, which is borne by both products.*

Sometimes, though, overtime can definitely be attributed to a single product. For example, the overtime needed to meet the launch deadline for a new product may clearly be the sole source of overtime. In such instances, the overtime premium is regarded as a direct cost of that product.

Another subclassification of indirect labor is the idle time of both direct and indirect labor. **Idle time** refers to the wages paid for unproductive time caused by lack of orders, machine or computer breakdowns, work delays, poor scheduling, and the like. For example, if George had no work for 3 hours during that week while waiting to receive code from another colleague, George's earnings would be classified as follows:

Direct programming labor: 41 hours × $40/hour	$1,640
Idle time (overhead): 3 hours × $40/hour	120
Overtime premium (overhead): 4 hours × $20/hour	80
Total earnings for 44 hours	$1,840

Clearly, in this case, the idle time is not related to a particular product, nor, as we have already discussed, is the overtime premium. Both the overtime premium and the costs of idle time are considered overhead costs.

Benefits of Defining Accounting Terms

Managers, accountants, suppliers, and others will avoid many problems if they thoroughly understand and agree on the classifications and meanings of the cost terms introduced in this chapter and later in this book. Consider the classification of programming labor *payroll fringe costs,* which include employer payments for employee benefits such as Social Security, life insurance, health insurance, and pensions. Consider, for example, a software programmer who is paid a wage of $40 an hour with fringe benefits totaling, say, $10 per hour. Some companies classify the $40 as a direct programming labor cost of the product for which the software is being written and the $10 as overhead cost. Other companies classify the entire $50 as direct programming labor cost. The latter approach is preferable because the stated wage and the fringe benefit costs together are a fundamental part of acquiring direct software programming labor services.

Caution: In every situation, it is important for managers and management accountants to pinpoint clearly what direct labor includes and what direct labor excludes. This clarity will help prevent disputes regarding cost-reimbursement contracts, income tax payments, and labor union matters, which often can take a substantial amount of time for managers to resolve. Consider that some countries, such as Costa Rica and Mauritius, offer substantial income tax savings to foreign companies that generate employment within their borders. In some cases, to qualify for the tax benefits, the direct labor costs must at least equal a specified percentage of a company's total costs.

When managers do not precisely define direct labor costs, disputes can arise about whether payroll fringe costs should be included as part of direct labor costs when calculating the direct labor percentage for qualifying for such tax benefits. Companies have sought to classify payroll fringe costs as part of direct labor costs to make direct labor costs a higher percentage of total costs. Tax authorities have argued that payroll fringe costs are part of overhead. In addition to payroll fringe costs, other debated items are compensation for training time, idle time, vacations, sick leave, and overtime premium. To prevent disputes, contracts and laws should be as specific as possible about accounting definitions and measurements.

Different Meanings of Product Costs

Many cost terms used by organizations have ambiguous meanings. Consider the term *product cost*. A **product cost** is the sum of the costs assigned to a product for a specific purpose. Different purposes can result in different measures of product cost, as the brackets on the value chain in Exhibit 2-11 illustrate:

- **Pricing and product-mix decisions.** For the purposes of making decisions about pricing and which products provide the most profits, managers are interested in the overall (total) profitability of different products and, consequently, assign costs incurred in all business functions of the value chain to the different products.
- **Reimbursement under government contracts.** Government contracts often reimburse contractors on the basis of the "cost of a product" plus a prespecified margin of profit. A contract such as this is referred to as a "cost-plus" agreement. Cost-plus agreements are typically used for services and development contracts when it is not easy to predict the amount of money required to design, fabricate, and test items. Because these contracts transfer the risk of cost overruns to the government, agencies such as the Department of Defense and the Department of Energy provide detailed guidelines on the cost items they will allow (and disallow) when calculating the cost of a product. For example, many government agencies explicitly exclude marketing, distribution, and customer-service costs from product costs that qualify for reimbursement, and they may only partially reimburse R&D costs. These agencies want to reimburse contractors for only those costs most closely related to delivering products under the contract. The second bracket in Exhibit 2-11 shows how the

Exhibit 2-11

Different Product Costs for Different Purposes

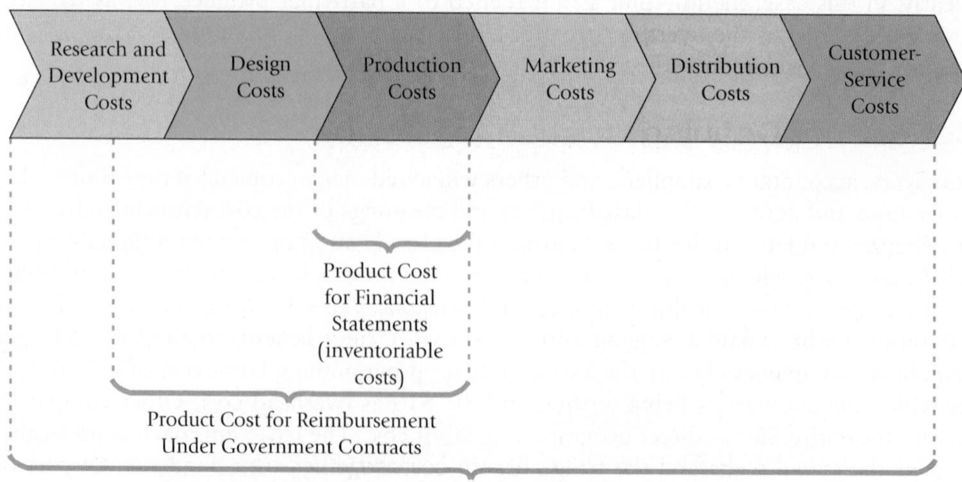

Exhibit 2-12

Alternative Classifications of Costs

1. Business function
   a. Research and development
   b. Design of products and processes
   c. Production
   d. Marketing
   e. Distribution
   f. Customer service
2. Assignment to a cost object
   a. Direct cost
   b. Indirect cost
3. Behavior pattern in relation to the level of activity or volume
   a. Variable cost
   b. Fixed cost
4. Aggregate or average
   a. Total cost
   b. Unit cost
5. Assets or expenses
   a. Inventoriable cost
   b Period cost

product-cost calculations for a specific contract may allow for all design and production costs but only part of R&D costs.

- **Preparing financial statements for external reporting under Generally Accepted Accounting Principles (GAAP).** Under GAAP, only manufacturing costs can be assigned to inventories in the financial statements. For the purposes of calculating inventory costs, product costs include only inventoriable (production) costs.

As Exhibit 2-11 illustrates, product-cost measures range from a narrow set of costs for financial statements—a set that includes only production costs—to a broader set of costs for reimbursement under government contracts to a still broader set of costs for pricing and product-mix decisions.

Decision Point

Why do managers assign different costs to the same cost object?

This section focused on how different purposes result in the inclusion of different cost items of the value chain of business functions when product costs are calculated. The same caution about the need to be clear and precise about cost concepts and their measurement applies to each cost classification introduced in this chapter. Exhibit 2-12 summarizes the key cost classifications. Using the five-step process described in Chapter 1, think about how these different classifications of costs help managers make decisions and evaluate performance.

1. **Identify the problem and uncertainties.** Consider a decision about how much to price a product. This decision often depends on how much it costs to make the product.
2. **Obtain information.** Managers identify the direct and indirect costs of a product in each business function. Managers also gather other information about customers, competitors, and the prices of competing products.
3. **Make predictions about the future.** Managers estimate what it will cost to make the product in the future. This requires managers to predict the quantity of the product they expect the company to sell as well as have an understanding of fixed and variable costs.
4. **Make decisions by choosing among alternatives.** Managers choose a price to charge based on a thorough understanding of costs and other information.
5. **Implement the decision, evaluate performance, and learn.** Managers control costs and learn by comparing the actual total and unit costs against budgeted amounts.

The next section describes how the basic concepts introduced in this chapter lead to a framework for understanding cost accounting and cost management that can then be applied to the study of many topics, such as strategy evaluation, quality, and investment decisions.

A Framework for Cost Accounting and Cost Management

Learning Objective 8

Describe a framework for cost accounting and cost management

...three features that help managers make decisions

The following three features of cost accounting and cost management can be used for a wide range of applications:

1. Calculating the cost of products, services, and other cost objects
2. Obtaining information for planning and control and performance evaluation
3. Analyzing the relevant information for making decisions

We develop these ideas in Chapters 3 through 11. The ideas also form the foundation for the study of various topics later in the book.

Calculating the Cost of Products, Services, and Other Cost Objects

You have already learned that costing systems trace direct costs and allocate indirect costs to products. Chapters 4 and 5 describe systems such as job costing and activity-based costing, which are used to calculate total costs and unit costs of products and services. The chapters also discuss how managers use this information to formulate strategies and make pricing, product-mix, and cost-management decisions.

Obtaining Information for Planning and Control and Performance Evaluation

Budgeting is the most commonly used tool for planning and control. A budget forces managers to look ahead, to translate a company's strategy into plans, to coordinate and communicate within the organization, and to provide a benchmark for evaluating the company's performance. Managers strive to meet their budget targets, so budgeting often affects the behavior of a company's personnel and the decisions they make. Chapter 6 describes budgeting systems.

At the end of a reporting period, managers compare the company's actual results to its planned performance. The manager's tasks are to understand why differences (called variances) between actual and planned performance arise and to use the information provided by these variances as feedback to promote learning and future improvement. Managers also use variances as well as nonfinancial measures, such as defect rates and customer satisfaction ratings, to control and evaluate the performance of various departments, divisions, and managers. Chapters 7 and 8 discuss variance analysis. Chapter 9 describes planning, control, and inventory-costing issues relating to capacity. Chapters 6, 7, 8, and 9 focus on the management accountant's role in implementing strategy.

Analyzing the Relevant Information for Making Decisions

When designing strategies and implementing them, managers must understand which revenues and costs to consider and which ones to ignore. Management accountants help managers identify what information is relevant and what information is irrelevant. Consider a decision about whether to buy a product from an outside vendor or make it in-house. The costing system indicates that it costs \$25 per unit to make the product in-house. A vendor offers to sell the product for \$22 per unit. At first glance, it seems it will cost less for the company to buy the product rather than make it. Suppose, however, that of the \$25 to make the product in-house, \$5 consists of plant lease costs that the company has already paid under a lease contract. Furthermore, if the product is bought, the plant will remain idle because it is too costly to retool the plant to make another product. That is, there is no opportunity to use the plant in some other profitable way. Under these conditions, it will cost less to make the product than to buy it. That's because making the product costs only an *additional* \$20 per unit (\$25 – \$5), compared with an *additional* \$22 per unit if it is bought. The \$5 per unit of lease cost is irrelevant to the decision because it is a *past* (or *sunk*) cost that has already been incurred regardless of whether the product is made or bought. Analyzing relevant information is a key aspect of making decisions.

When making strategic decisions about which products and how much to produce, managers must know how revenues and costs vary with changes in output levels. For this purpose, managers need to distinguish fixed costs from variable costs. Chapter 3 analyzes how operating income changes with changes in units sold and how managers use this information to make decisions such as how much to spend on advertising. Chapter 10 describes methods to estimate the fixed and variable components of costs. Chapter 11 applies the concept of relevance to decision making in many different situations and describes methods managers use to maximize income given the resource constraints they face.

Later chapters in the book discuss topics such as strategy evaluation, customer profitability, quality, just-in-time systems, investment decisions, transfer pricing, and performance evaluation. Each of these topics invariably has product costing, planning and control, and decision-making perspectives. A command of the first 11 chapters will help you master these topics. For example, Chapter 12 on strategy describes the balanced scorecard, a set of financial and nonfinancial measures used to implement strategy that builds on the planning and control functions. The section on strategic analysis of operating income builds on ideas of product costing and variance analysis. The section on downsizing and managing capacity builds on ideas of relevant revenues and relevant costs.

Decision Point

What are the three key features of cost accounting and cost management?

Problem for Self-Study

TEST EXAMPLE

Foxwood Company is a metal- and woodcutting manufacturer, selling products to the home-construction market. Consider the following data for 2014:

Sandpaper	$ 2,000
Materials-handling costs	70,000
Lubricants and coolants	5,000
Miscellaneous indirect manufacturing labor	40,000
Direct manufacturing labor	300,000
Direct materials inventory, Jan. 1, 2014	40,000
Direct materials inventory, Dec. 31, 2014	50,000
Finished goods inventory, Jan. 1, 2014	100,000
Finished goods inventory, Dec. 31, 2014	150,000
Work-in-process inventory, Jan. 1, 2014	10,000
Work-in-process inventory, Dec. 31, 2014	14,000
Plant-leasing costs	54,000
Depreciation—plant equipment	36,000
Property taxes on plant equipment	4,000
Fire insurance on plant equipment	3,000
Direct materials purchased	460,000
Revenues	1,360,000
Marketing promotions	60,000
Marketing salaries	100,000
Distribution costs	70,000
Customer-service costs	100,000

Required

1. Prepare an income statement with a separate supporting schedule of cost of goods manufactured. For all manufacturing items, classify costs as direct costs or indirect costs and indicate by V or F whether each is basically a variable cost or a fixed cost (when the cost object is a product unit). If in doubt, decide on the basis of whether the total cost will change substantially over a wide range of units produced.
2. Suppose that both the direct material costs and the plant-leasing costs are for the production of 900,000 units. What is the direct material cost of each unit produced? What is the plant-leasing cost per unit? Assume that the plant-leasing cost is a fixed cost.
3. Suppose Foxwood Company manufactures 1,000,000 units next year. Repeat the computation in requirement 2 for direct materials and plant-leasing costs. Assume the implied cost-behavior patterns persist.
4. As a management consultant, explain concisely to the company president why the unit cost for direct materials did not change in requirements 2 and 3 but the unit cost for plant-leasing costs did change.

Solution

1.

Foxwood Company
Income Statement
For the Year Ended December 31, 2014

Revenues		$1,360,000
Cost of goods sold		
Beginning finished goods inventory, January 1, 2014	$ 100,000	
Cost of goods manufactured (see the following schedule)	960,000	
Cost of goods available for sale	1,060,000	
Deduct ending finished goods inventory, December 31, 2014	150,000	910,000
Gross margin (or gross profit)		450,000
Operating costs		
Marketing promotions	60,000	
Marketing salaries	100,000	
Distribution costs	70,000	
Customer-service costs	100,000	330,000
Operating income		$ 120,000

Foxwood Company
Schedule of Cost of Goods Manufactured
For the Year Ended December 31, 2014

Direct materials		
Beginning inventory, January 1, 2014		$ 40,000
Purchases of direct materials		460,000
Cost of direct materials available for use		500,000
Ending inventory, December 31, 2014		50,000
Direct materials used		450,000 (V)
Direct manufacturing labor		300,000 (V)
Indirect manufacturing costs		
Sandpaper	$ 2,000 (V)	
Materials-handling costs	70,000 (V)	
Lubricants and coolants	5,000 (V)	
Miscellaneous indirect manufacturing labor	40,000 (V)	
Plant-leasing costs	54,000 (F)	
Depreciation—plant equipment	36,000 (F)	
Property taxes on plant equipment	4,000 (F)	
Fire insurance on plant equipment	3,000 (F)	214,000
Manufacturing costs incurred during 2014		964,000
Beginning work-in-process inventory, January 1, 2014		10,000
Total manufacturing costs to account for		974,000
Ending work-in-process inventory, December 31, 2014		14,000
Cost of goods manufactured (to income statement)		$ 960,000

2. Direct material unit cost = Direct materials used ÷ Units produced
= \$450,000 ÷ 900,000 units = \$0.50 per unit
Plant-leasing unit cost = Plant-leasing costs ÷ Units produced
= \$54,000 ÷ 900,000 units = \$0.06 per unit
3. The direct material costs are variable, so they would increase in total from \$450,000 to \$500,000 (1,000,000 units × \$0.50 per unit). However, their unit cost would be unaffected: \$500,000 ÷ 1,000,000 units = \$0.50 per unit.
In contrast, the plant-leasing costs of \$54,000 are fixed, so they would not increase in total. However, the plant-leasing cost per unit would decline from \$0.060 to \$0.054: \$54,000 ÷ 1,000,000 units = \$0.054 per unit.
4. The explanation would begin with the answer to requirement 3. As a consultant, you should stress that the unitizing (averaging) of costs that have different behavior patterns can be misleading. A common error is to assume that a total unit cost, which is often a sum of variable unit cost and fixed unit cost, is an indicator that total costs change in proportion to changes in production levels. The next chapter demonstrates the necessity for distinguishing between cost-behavior patterns. You must be wary, especially about average fixed cost per unit. Too often, unit fixed cost is erroneously regarded as being indistinguishable from unit variable cost.

▶ Decision Points

The following question-and-answer format summarizes the chapter's learning objectives. Each decision presents a key question related to a learning objective. The guidelines are the answer to that question.

Decision	Guidelines
1. What is a cost object?	A cost object is anything for which a manager needs a separate measurement of cost. Examples include a product, a service, a project, a customer, a brand category, an activity, and a department.
2. How do managers decide whether a cost is a direct or an indirect cost?	A direct cost is any cost that is related to a particular cost object and can be traced to that cost object in an economically feasible way. Indirect costs are related to a particular cost object but cannot be traced to it in an economically feasible way. The same cost can be direct for one cost object and indirect for another cost object. This book uses *cost tracing* to describe the assignment of direct costs to a cost object and *cost allocation* to describe the assignment of indirect costs to a cost object.
3. How do managers decide whether a cost is a variable or a fixed cost?	A variable cost changes *in total* in proportion to changes in the related level of total activity or volume of output produced. A fixed cost remains unchanged *in total* for a given time period despite wide changes in the related level of total activity or volume of output produced.
4. How should managers estimate and interpret cost information?	In general, focus on total costs, not unit costs. When making total cost estimates, think of variable costs as an amount per unit and fixed costs as a total amount. Interpret the unit cost of a cost object cautiously when it includes a fixed-cost component.
5. What are the differences in the accounting for inventoriable versus period costs?	Inventoriable costs are all costs of a product that a company regards as an asset in the accounting period in which they are incurred and which become cost of goods sold in the accounting period in which the product is sold. Period costs are expensed in the accounting period in which they are incurred and are all of the costs in an income statement other than cost of goods sold.

Decision	Guidelines
6. What is the flow of inventoriable and period costs in manufacturing and merchandising settings?	In manufacturing settings, inventoriable costs flow through work-in-process and finished goods accounts, and are expensed as cost of goods sold. Period costs are expensed as they are incurred. In merchandising settings, only the cost of merchandise is treated as inventoriable.
7. Why do managers assign different costs to the same cost objects?	Managers can assign different costs to the same cost object depending on the purpose. For example, for the external reporting purpose in a manufacturing company, the inventoriable cost of a product includes only manufacturing costs. In contrast, costs from all business functions of the value chain often are assigned to a product for pricing and product-mix decisions.
8. What are the three key features of cost accounting and cost management?	Three features of cost accounting and cost management are (1) calculating the cost of products, services, and other cost objects; (2) obtaining information for planning and control and performance evaluation; and (3) analyzing relevant information for making decisions.

Terms to Learn

This chapter contains more basic terms than any other in this book. Do not proceed before you check your understanding of the following terms. The chapter and the Glossary at the end of the book contain definitions of the following important terms:

actual cost **(p. 29)**
average cost **(p. 36)**
budgeted cost **(p. 29)**
conversion costs **(p. 46)**
cost **(p. 29)**
cost accumulation **(p. 29)**
cost allocation **(p. 30)**
cost assignment **(p. 30)**
cost driver **(p. 34)**
cost object **(p. 29)**
cost of goods manufactured **(p. 43)**
cost tracing **(p. 30)**
direct costs of a cost object **(p. 30)**
direct manufacturing labor costs **(p. 39)**
direct material costs **(p. 39)**
direct materials inventory **(p. 38)**
factory overhead costs **(p. 39)**
finished goods inventory **(p. 38)**
fixed cost **(p. 32)**
idle time **(p. 47)**
indirect costs of a cost object **(p. 30)**
indirect manufacturing costs **(p. 39)**
inventoriable costs **(p. 39)**
manufacturing overhead costs **(p. 39)**
manufacturing-sector companies **(p. 38)**
merchandising-sector companies **(p. 38)**
operating income **(p. 44)**
overtime premium **(p. 47)**
period costs **(p. 39)**
prime costs **(p. 45)**
product cost **(p. 48)**
relevant range **(p. 35)**
revenues **(p. 39)**
service-sector companies **(p. 38)**
unit cost **(p. 36)**
variable cost **(p. 32)**
work-in-process inventory **(p. 38)**
work in progress **(p. 38)**

Assignment Material

MyAccountingLab

Questions

2-1 Define cost object and give three examples.
2-2 Define direct costs and indirect costs.
2-3 Why do managers consider direct costs to be more accurate than indirect costs?
2-4 Name three factors that will affect the classification of a cost as direct or indirect.
2-5 Define variable cost and fixed cost. Give an example of each.
2-6 What is a cost driver? Give one example.
2-7 What is the relevant range? What role does the relevant-range concept play in explaining how costs behave?
2-8 Explain why unit costs must often be interpreted with caution.
2-9 Describe how manufacturing-, merchandising-, and service-sector companies differ from one another.
2-10 What are three different types of inventory that manufacturing companies hold?
2-11 Distinguish between inventoriable costs and period costs.

2-12 Define the following: direct material costs, direct manufacturing-labor costs, manufacturing overhead costs, prime costs, and conversion costs.

2-13 Describe the overtime-premium and idle-time categories of indirect labor.

2-14 Define product cost. Describe three different purposes for computing product costs.

2-15 What are three common features of cost accounting and cost management?

Exercises

MyAccountingLab

2-16 Computing and interpreting manufacturing unit costs. Minnesota Office Products (MOP) produces three different paper products at its Vaasa lumber plant: Supreme, Deluxe, and Regular. Each product has its own dedicated production line at the plant. It currently uses the following three-part classification for its manufacturing costs: direct materials, direct manufacturing labor, and manufacturing overhead costs. Total manufacturing overhead costs of the plant in July 2014 are $150 million ($15 million of which are fixed). This total amount is allocated to each product line on the basis of the direct manufacturing labor costs of each line. Summary data (in millions) for July 2014 are as follows:

	Supreme	Deluxe	Regular
Direct material costs	$ 89	$ 57	$ 60
Direct manufacturing labor costs	$ 16	$ 26	$ 8
Manufacturing overhead costs	$ 48	$ 78	$ 24
Units produced	125	150	140

Required

1. Compute the manufacturing cost per unit for each product produced in July 2014.
2. Suppose that, in August 2014, production was 150 million units of Supreme, 190 million units of Deluxe, and 220 million units of Regular. Why might the July 2014 information on manufacturing cost per unit be misleading when predicting total manufacturing costs in August 2014?

2-17 Direct, indirect, fixed, and variable costs. Wonder Bakery manufactures two types of bread, which it sells as wholesale products to various specialty retail bakeries. Each loaf of bread requires a three-step process. The first step is mixing. The mixing department combines all of the necessary ingredients to create the dough and processes it through high-speed mixers. The dough is then left to rise before baking. The second step is baking, which is an entirely automated process. The baking department molds the dough into its final shape and bakes each loaf of bread in a high-temperature oven. The final step is finishing, which is an entirely manual process. The finishing department coats each loaf of bread with a special glaze, allows the bread to cool, and then carefully packages each loaf in a specialty carton for sale in retail bakeries.

Required

1. Costs involved in the process are listed next. For each cost, indicate whether it is a direct variable, direct fixed, indirect variable, or indirect fixed cost, assuming "units of production of each kind of bread" is the cost object.

Costs:

Yeast
Flour
Packaging materials
Depreciation on ovens
Depreciation on mixing machines
Rent on factory building
Fire insurance on factory building
Factory utilities
Finishing department hourly laborers
Mixing department manager
Materials handlers in each department
Custodian in factory
Night guard in factory
Machinist (running the mixing machine)
Machine maintenance personnel in each department
Maintenance supplies for factory
Cleaning supplies for factory

2. If the cost object were the "mixing department" rather than units of production of each kind of bread, which preceding costs would now be direct instead of indirect costs?

2-18 Classification of costs, service sector. Market Focus is a marketing research firm that organizes focus groups for consumer-product companies. Each focus group has eight individuals who are paid $60 per session to provide comments on new products. These focus groups meet in hotels and are led by a trained, independent marketing specialist hired by Market Focus. Each specialist is paid a fixed retainer to conduct a minimum number of sessions and a per session fee of $2,200. A Market Focus staff member attends each session to ensure that all the logistical aspects run smoothly.

Required

Classify each cost item **(A–H)** as follows:

a. Direct or indirect (D or I) costs of each individual focus group.
b. Variable or fixed (V or F) costs of how the total costs of Market Focus change as the number of focus groups conducted changes. (If in doubt, select on the basis of whether the total costs will change substantially if there is a large change in the number of groups conducted.)

You will have two answers (D or I; V or F) for each of the following items:

Cost Item	D or I	V or F
A. Payment to individuals in each focus group to provide comments on new products		
B. Annual subscription of Market Focus to *Consumer Reports* magazine		
C. Phone calls made by Market Focus staff member to confirm individuals will attend a focus group session (Records of individual calls are not kept.)		
D. Retainer paid to focus group leader to conduct 18 focus groups per year on new medical products		
E. Recruiting cost to hire marketing specialists		
F. Lease payment by Market Focus for corporate office		
G. Cost of tapes used to record comments made by individuals in a focus group session (These tapes are sent to the company whose products are being tested.)		
H. Gasoline costs of Market Focus staff for company-owned vehicles (Staff members submit monthly bills with no mileage breakdowns.)		
I. Costs incurred to improve the design of focus groups to make them more effective		

2-19 Classification of costs, merchandising sector. Band Box Entertainment (BBE) operates a large store in Atlanta, Georgia. The store has both a movie (DVD) section and a music (CD) section. BBE reports revenues for the movie section separately from the music section.

Required

Classify each cost item **(A–H)** as follows:

a. Direct or indirect (D or I) costs of the total number of DVDs sold.
b. Variable or fixed (V or F) costs of how the total costs of the movie section change as the total number of DVDs sold changes. (If in doubt, select on the basis of whether the total costs will change substantially if there is a large change in the total number of DVDs sold.)

You will have two answers (D or I; V or F) for each of the following items:

Cost Item	D or I	V or F
A. Annual retainer paid to a video distributor		
B. Cost of store manager's salary		
C. Costs of DVDs purchased for sale to customers		
D. Subscription to *DVD Trends* magazine		
E. Leasing of computer software used for financial budgeting at the BBE store		
F. Cost of popcorn provided free to all customers of the BBE store		
G. Cost of cleaning the store every night after closing		
H. Freight-in costs of DVDs purchased by BBE		

2-20 Classification of costs, manufacturing sector. The Kitakyushu, Japan, plant of Nissan Motor Corporation assembles two types of cars (Teanas and Muranos). Separate assembly lines are used for each type of car.

Required

Classify each cost item **(A–H)** as follows:

a. Direct or indirect (D or I) costs for the total number of Teanas assembled.
b. Variable or fixed (V or F) costs depending on how total costs change as the total number of Teanas assembled changes. (If in doubt, select on the basis of whether the total costs will change substantially if there is a large change in the total number of Teanas assembled.)

You will have two answers (D or I; V or F) for each of the following items:

Cost Item	D or I	V or F
A. Cost of tires used on Teanas		
B. Salary of public relations manager for Kitakyushu plant		
C. Annual awards dinner for Teana suppliers		
D. Cost of lubricant used on the Teana assembly line		

E. Freight costs of Teana engines shipped from Yokohama to Kitakyushu
F. Electricity costs for Teana assembly line (single bill covers entire plant)
G. Wages paid to temporary assembly-line workers hired in periods of high Teana production (paid on hourly basis)
H. Annual fire-insurance policy cost for Kitakyushu plant

2-21 Variable costs, fixed costs, total costs. Bridget Ashton is getting ready to open a small restaurant. She is on a tight budget and must choose between the following long-distance phone plans:

Plan A: Pay 10 cents per minute of long-distance calling.

Plan B: Pay a fixed monthly fee of $15 for up to 240 long-distance minutes and 8 cents per minute thereafter (if she uses fewer than 240 minutes in any month, she still pays $15 for the month).

Plan C: Pay a fixed monthly fee of $22 for up to 510 long-distance minutes and 5 cents per minute thereafter (if she uses fewer than 510 minutes, she still pays $22 for the month).

Required

1. Draw a graph of the total monthly costs of the three plans for different levels of monthly long-distance calling.
2. Which plan should Ashton choose if she expects to make 100 minutes of long-distance calls? 240 minutes? 540 minutes?

2-22 Variable and Fixed Costs. Beacher Motors specializes in producing one specialty vehicle. It is called Surfer and is styled to easily fit multiple surfboards in its back area and top-mounted storage racks. Beacher has the following manufacturing costs:

Plant management costs, $1,200,000 per year

Cost of leasing equipment, $1,800,000 per year

Workers' wages, $700 per Surfer vehicle produced

Direct materials costs: Steel, $1,500 per Surfer; Tires, $125 per tire, each Surfer takes 5 tires (one spare).

City license, which is charged monthly based on the number of tires used in production:

0–500 tires	$ 50,000
501–1,000 tires	$ 74,500
more than 1,000 tires	$200,000

Beacher currently produces 110 vehicles per month.

Required

1. What is the variable manufacturing cost per vehicle? What is the fixed manufacturing cost per month?
2. Plot a graph for the variable manufacturing costs and a second for the fixed manufacturing costs per month. How does the concept of relevant range relate to your graphs? Explain.
3. What is the total manufacturing cost of each vehicle if 100 vehicles are produced each month? 225 vehicles? How do you explain the difference in the manufacturing cost per unit?

2-23 Variable costs, fixed costs, relevant range. Dotball Candies manufactures jaw-breaker candies in a fully automated process. The machine that produces candies was purchased recently and can make 4,400 per month. The machine costs $9,500 and is depreciated using straight-line depreciation over 10 years assuming zero residual value. Rent for the factory space and warehouse and other fixed manufacturing overhead costs total $1,300 per month.

Dotball currently makes and sells 3,100 jaw-breakers per month. Dotball buys just enough materials each month to make the jaw-breakers it needs to sell. Materials cost 10 cents per jawbreaker.

Next year Dotball expects demand to increase by 100%. At this volume of materials purchased, it will get a 10% discount on price. Rent and other fixed manufacturing overhead costs will remain the same.

Required

1. What is Dotball's current annual relevant range of output?
2. What is Dotball's current annual fixed manufacturing cost within the relevant range? What is the annual variable manufacturing cost?
3. What will Dotball's relevant range of output be next year? How, if at all, will total annual fixed and variable manufacturing costs change next year? Assume that if it needs to Dotball could buy an identical machine at the same cost as the one it already has.

2-24 Cost drivers and value chain. Roxbury Mobile Company (RMC) is developing a new touch-screen smartphone to compete in the cellular phone industry. The company will sell the phones at wholesale prices to cell phone companies, which will in turn sell them in retail stores to the final customer. RMC has undertaken the following activities in its value chain to bring its product to market:

Identify customer needs (What do smartphone users want?)

Perform market research on competing brands

Design a prototype of the RMC smartphone
Market the new design to cell phone companies
Manufacture the RMC smartphone
Process orders from cell phone companies
Package the RMC smartphones
Deliver the RMC smartphones to the cell phone companies
Provide online assistance to cell phone users for use of the RMC smartphone
Make design changes to the smartphone based on customer feedback

During the process of product development, production, marketing, distribution, and customer service, RMC has kept track of the following cost drivers:

Number of smartphones shipped by RMC
Number of design changes
Number of deliveries made to cell phone companies
Engineering hours spent on initial product design
Hours spent researching competing market brands
Customer-service hours
Number of smartphone orders processed
Number of cell phone companies purchasing the RMC smartphone
Machine hours required to run the production equipment
Number of surveys returned and processed from competing smartphone users

Required

1. Identify each value chain activity listed at the beginning of the exercise with one of the following value-chain categories:
   a. Design of products and processes
   b. Production
   c. Marketing
   d. Distribution
   e. Customer service
2. Use the list of preceding cost drivers to find one or more reasonable cost drivers for each of the activities in RMC's value chain.

2-25 Cost drivers and functions. The representative cost drivers in the right column of this table are randomized so they do not match the list of functions in the left column.

Function	Representative Cost Driver
1. Accounts payable	**A.** Number of invoices sent
2. Recruiting	**B.** Number of purchase orders
3. Data processing	**C.** Number of research scientists
4. Research and development	**D.** Hours of computer processing unit (CPU)
5. Purchasing	**E.** Number of employees hired
6. Warehousing	**F.** Number of payments processed
7. Billing	**G.** Number of pallets moved

Required

1. Match each function with its representative cost driver.
2. Give a second example of a cost driver for each function.

2-26 Total costs and unit costs, service setting. The Big Event (TBE) recently started a business organizing food and music at weddings and other large events. In order to better understand the profitability of the business, the owner has asked you for an analysis of costs—what costs are fixed, what costs are variable, and so on, for each event. You have the following cost information:

Music costs: $10,000 per event
Catering costs:
  Food: $65 per guest
  Setup/cleanup: $15 per guest
  Fixed fee: $4,000 per event

The Big Event has allowed the caterer, who is also new in business, to place business cards on each table as a form of advertising. This has proved quite effective, and the caterer gives TBE a discount of $5 per guest in exchange for allowing the caterer to advertise.

Required

1. Draw a graph depicting fixed costs, variable costs, and total costs for each event versus the number of guests.
2. Suppose 150 persons attend the next event. What is TBE's total net cost and the cost per attendee?
3. Suppose instead that 200 persons attend. What is TBE's total net cost and the cost per attendee.
4. How should TBE charge customers for its services? Explain briefly.

2-27 Total and unit cost, decision making. Gayle's Glassworks makes glass flanges for scientific use. Materials cost $1 per flange, and the glass blowers are paid a wage rate of $28 per hour. A glass blower blows 10 flanges per hour. Fixed manufacturing costs for flanges are $28,000 per period. Period (nonmanufacturing) costs associated with flanges are $10,000 per period and are fixed.

Required

1. Graph the fixed, variable, and total manufacturing cost for flanges, using units (number of flanges) on the *x*-axis.
2. Assume Gayle's Glassworks manufactures and sells 5,000 flanges this period. Its competitor, Flora's Flasks, sells flanges for $10 each. Can Gayle sell below Flora's price and still make a profit on the flanges?
3. How would your answer to requirement 2 differ if Gayle's Glassworks made and sold 10,000 flanges this period? Why? What does this indicate about the use of unit cost in decision making?

2-28 Inventoriable costs versus period costs. Each of the following cost items pertains to one of these companies: Star Market (a merchandising-sector company), Maytag (a manufacturing-sector company), and Yahoo! (a service-sector company):

a. Cost of lettuce and tomatoes on sale in Star Market's produce department
b. Electricity used to provide lighting for assembly-line workers at a Maytag refrigerator-assembly plant
c. Depreciation on Yahoo!'s computer equipment used to update its Web site
d. Electricity used to provide lighting for Star Market's store aisles
e. Depreciation on Maytag's computer equipment used for quality testing of refrigerator components during the assembly process
f. Salaries of Star Market's marketing personnel planning local-newspaper advertising campaigns
g. Perrier mineral water purchased by Yahoo! for consumption by its software engineers
h. Salaries of Yahoo!'s marketing personnel selling advertising
i. Depreciation on vehicles used to transport Maytag refrigerators to retail stores

Required

1. Distinguish between manufacturing-, merchandising-, and service-sector companies.
2. Distinguish between inventoriable costs and period costs.
3. Classify each of the cost items (**a–h**) as an inventoriable cost or a period cost. Explain your answers.

Problems

MyAccountingLab

2-29 Computing cost of goods purchased and cost of goods sold. The following data are for Marvin Department Store. The account balances (in thousands) are for 2014.

Marketing, distribution, and customer-service costs	$ 37,000
Merchandise inventory, January 1, 2014	27,000
Utilities	17,000
General and administrative costs	43,000
Merchandise inventory, December 31, 2014	34,000
Purchases	155,000
Miscellaneous costs	4,000
Transportation-in	7,000
Purchase returns and allowances	4,000
Purchase discounts	6,000
Revenues	280,000

Required

1. Compute **(a)** the cost of goods purchased and **(b)** the cost of goods sold.
2. Prepare the income statement for 2014.

2-30 Cost of goods purchased, cost of goods sold, and income statement. The following data are for Montgomery Retail Outlet Stores. The account balances (in thousands) are for 2014.

Marketing and advertising costs	$ 48,000
Merchandise inventory, January 1, 2014	90,000
Shipping of merchandise to customers	4,000
Building depreciation	8,400
Purchases	520,000
General and administrative costs	64,000
Merchandise inventory, December 31, 2014	104,000
Merchandise freight-in	20,000
Purchase returns and allowances	22,000
Purchase discounts	18,000
Revenues	640,000

Required

1. Compute **(a)** the cost of goods purchased and **(b)** the cost of goods sold.
2. Prepare the income statement for 2014.

2-31 Flow of Inventoriable Costs. Renka's Heaters selected data for October 2014 are presented here (in millions):

Direct materials inventory 10/1/2014	$ 105
Direct materials purchased	365
Direct materials used	385
Total manufacturing overhead costs	450
Variable manufacturing overhead costs	265
Total manufacturing costs incurred during October 2014	1,610
Work-in-process inventory 10/1/2014	230
Cost of goods manufactured	1,660
Finished goods inventory 10/1/2014	130
Cost of goods sold	1,770

Required

Calculate the following costs:

1. Direct materials inventory 10/31/2014
2. Fixed manufacturing overhead costs for October 2014
3. Direct manufacturing labor costs for October 2014
4. Work-in-process inventory 10/31/2014
5. Cost of finished goods available for sale in October 2014
6. Finished goods inventory 10/31/2014

2-32 Cost of goods manufactured, income statement, manufacturing company. Consider the following account balances (in thousands) for the Peterson Company:

Peterson Company	Beginning of 2014	End of 2014
Direct materials inventory	21,000	23,000
Work-in-process inventory	26,000	25,000
Finished goods inventory	13,000	20,000
Purchases of direct materials		74,000
Direct manufacturing labor		22,000
Indirect manufacturing labor		17,000
Plant insurance		7,000
Depreciation—plant, building, and equipment		11,000
Repairs and maintenance—plant		3,000
Marketing, distribution, and customer-service costs		91,000
General and administrative costs		24,000

Required

1. Prepare a schedule for the cost of goods manufactured for 2014.
2. Revenues for 2014 were $310 million. Prepare the income statement for 2014.

2-33 Cost of goods manufactured, income statement, manufacturing company. Consider the following account balances (in thousands) for the Shaler Corporation:

Shaler Corporation	Beginning of 2014	End of 2014
Direct materials inventory	130,000	68,000
Work-in-process inventory	166,000	144,000
Finished goods inventory	246,000	204,000
Purchases of direct materials		256,000
Direct manufacturing labor		212,000
Indirect manufacturing labor		96,000
Indirect materials		28,000
Plant insurance		4,000
Depreciation—plant, building, and equipment		42,000
Plant utilities		24,000
Repairs and maintenance—plant		16,000
Equipment leasing costs		64,000
Marketing, distribution, and customer-service costs		124,000
General and administrative costs		68,000

Required

1. Prepare a schedule for the cost of goods manufactured for 2014.
2. Revenues (in thousands) for 2014 were $1,200,000. Prepare the income statement for 2014.

2-34 Income statement and schedule of cost of goods manufactured. The Howell Corporation has the following account balances (in millions):

For Specific Date		For Year 2014	
Direct materials inventory, Jan. 1, 2014	$15	Purchases of direct materials	$325
Work-in-process inventory, Jan. 1, 2014	10	Direct manufacturing labor	100
Finished goods inventory, Jan. 1, 2014	70	Depreciation—plant and equipment	80
Direct materials inventory, Dec. 31, 2014	20	Plant supervisory salaries	5
Work-in-process inventory, Dec. 31, 2014	5	Miscellaneous plant overhead	35
Finished goods inventory, Dec. 31, 2014	55	Revenues	950
		Marketing, distribution, and customer-service costs	240
		Plant supplies used	10
		Plant utilities	30
		Indirect manufacturing labor	60

Required

Prepare an income statement and a supporting schedule of cost of goods manufactured for the year ended December 31, 2014. (For additional questions regarding these facts, see the next problem.)

2-35 Interpretation of statements (continuation of 2-34).

Required

1. How would the answer to Problem 2-34 be modified if you were asked for a schedule of cost of goods manufactured and sold instead of a schedule of cost of goods manufactured? Be specific.
2. Would the sales manager's salary (included in marketing, distribution, and customer-service costs) be accounted for any differently if the Howell Corporation were a merchandising-sector company instead of a manufacturing-sector company? Using the flow of manufacturing costs outlined in Exhibit 2-9 (page 43), describe how the wages of an assembler in the plant would be accounted for in this manufacturing company.
3. Plant supervisory salaries are usually regarded as manufacturing overhead costs. When might some of these costs be regarded as direct manufacturing costs? Give an example.

4. Suppose that both the direct materials used and the plant and equipment depreciation are related to the manufacture of 1 million units of product. What is the unit cost for the direct materials assigned to those units? What is the unit cost for plant and equipment depreciation? Assume that yearly plant and equipment depreciation is computed on a straight-line basis.
5. Assume that the implied cost-behavior patterns in requirement 4 persist. That is, direct material costs behave as a variable cost and plant and equipment depreciation behaves as a fixed cost. Repeat the computations in requirement 4, assuming that the costs are being predicted for the manufacture of 1.2 million units of product. How would the total costs be affected?
6. As a management accountant, explain concisely to the president why the unit costs differed in requirements 4 and 5.

2-36 Income statement and schedule of cost of goods manufactured. The following items (in millions) pertain to Chester Corporation:

Chester's manufacturing costing system uses a three-part classification of direct materials, direct manufacturing labor, and manufacturing overhead costs.

For Specific Date		For Year 2014	
Work-in-process inventory, Jan. 1, 2014	$15	Plant utilities	$ 6
Direct materials inventory, Dec. 31, 2014	9	Indirect manufacturing labor	25
Finished goods inventory, Dec. 31, 2014	19	Depreciation—plant and equipment	8
Accounts payable, Dec. 31, 2014	28	Revenues	354
Accounts receivable, Jan. 1, 2014	57	Miscellaneous manufacturing overhead	17
Work-in-process inventory, Dec. 31, 2014	7	Marketing, distribution, and customer-service costs	91
Finished goods inventory, Jan 1, 2014	43	Direct materials purchased	82
Accounts receivable, Dec. 31, 2014	30	Direct manufacturing labor	41
Accounts payable, Jan. 1, 2014	40	Plant supplies used	5
Direct materials inventory, Jan. 1, 2014	39	Property taxes on plant	3

Required

Prepare an income statement and a supporting schedule of cost of goods manufactured. (For additional questions regarding these facts, see the next problem.)

2-37 Terminology, interpretation of statements (continuation of 2-36).

Required

1. Calculate total prime costs and total conversion costs.
2. Calculate total inventoriable costs and period costs.
3. Design costs and R&D costs are not considered product costs for financial statement purposes. When might some of these costs be regarded as product costs? Give an example.
4. Suppose that both the direct materials used and the depreciation on plant and equipment are related to the manufacture of 1 million units of product. Determine the unit cost for the direct materials assigned to those units and the unit cost for depreciation on plant and equipment. Assume that yearly depreciation is computed on a straight-line basis.
5. Assume that the implied cost-behavior patterns in requirement 4 persist. That is, direct material costs behave as a variable cost and depreciation on plant and equipment behaves as a fixed cost. Repeat the computations in requirement 4, assuming that the costs are being predicted for the manufacture of 2 million units of product. Determine the effect on total costs.
6. Assume that depreciation on the equipment (but not the plant) is computed based on the number of units produced because the equipment deteriorates with units produced. The depreciation rate on equipment is $1 per unit. Calculate the depreciation on equipment assuming (a) 1 million units of product are produced and (b) 2 million units of product are produced.

2-38 Labor cost, overtime, and idle time. Louie Anderson works in the production department of Southwest Plasticworks as a machine operator. Louie, a long-time employee of Southwest, is paid on an hourly basis at a rate of $20 per hour. Louie works five 8-hour shifts per week Monday–Friday (40 hours). Any time Louie works over and above these 40 hours is considered overtime for which he is paid at a rate of time and a half ($30 per hour). If the overtime falls on weekends, Louie is paid at a rate of double time ($40 per hour). Louie is also paid an additional $20 per hour for any holidays worked, even if it is part of his regular 40 hours. Louie is paid his regular wages even if the machines are down (not operating) due to regular machine maintenance, slow order periods, or unexpected mechanical problems. These hours are considered "idle time."

During December Louie worked the following hours:

	Hours worked including machine downtime	Machine downtime
Week 1	48	6.4
Week 2	44	2.0
Week 3	43	5.8
Week 4	46	3.5

Included in the total hours worked are two company holidays (Christmas Eve and Christmas Day) during Week 4. All overtime worked by Louie was Monday–Friday, except for the hours worked in Week 3; all of the Week 3 overtime hours were worked on a Saturday.

Required

1. Calculate (a) direct manufacturing labor, (b) idle time, (c) overtime and holiday premium, and (d) total earnings for Louie in December.
2. Is idle time and overtime premium a direct or indirect cost of the products that Louie worked on in December? Explain.

2-39 Missing records, computing inventory costs. Ron Howard recently took over as the controller of Johnson Brothers Manufacturing. Last month, the previous controller left the company with little notice and left the accounting records in disarray. Ron needs the ending inventory balances to report first-quarter numbers.

For the previous month (March 2014) Ron was able to piece together the following information:

Direct materials purchased	$120,000
Work-in-process inventory, 3/1/2014	$ 35,000
Direct materials inventory, 3/1/2014	$ 12, 500
Finished goods inventory, 3/1/2014	$160,000
Conversion costs	$330,000
Total manufacturing costs added during the period	$420,000
Cost of goods manufactured	4 times direct materials used
Gross margin as a percentage of revenues	20%
Revenues	$518,750

Required

Calculate the cost of:

1. Finished goods inventory, 3/31/2014
2. Work-in-process inventory, 3/31/2014
3. Direct materials inventory, 3/31/2014

2-40 Comprehensive problem on unit costs, product costs. Atlanta Office Equipment manufactures and sells metal shelving. It began operations on January 1, 2014. Costs incurred for 2014 are as follows (V stands for variable; F stands for fixed):

Direct materials used	$149,500 V
Direct manufacturing labor costs	34,500 V
Plant energy costs	6,000 V
Indirect manufacturing labor costs	12,000 V
Indirect manufacturing labor costs	17,000 F
Other indirect manufacturing costs	7,000 V
Other indirect manufacturing costs	27,000 F
Marketing, distribution, and customer-service costs	126,000 V
Marketing, distribution, and customer-service costs	47,000 F
Administrative costs	58,000 F

Variable manufacturing costs are variable with respect to units produced. Variable marketing, distribution, and customer-service costs are variable with respect to units sold.

Inventory data are as follows:

	Beginning: January 1, 2014	Ending: December 31, 2014
Direct materials	0 lb	2,300 lbs
Work in process	0 units	0 units
Finished goods	0 units	? units

Production in 2014 was 115,000 units. Two pounds of direct materials are used to make one unit of finished product.

Revenues in 2014 were $540,000. The selling price per unit and the purchase price per pound of direct materials were stable throughout the year. The company's ending inventory of finished goods is carried at the average unit manufacturing cost for 2014. Finished-goods inventory at December 31, 2014, was $15,400.

Required

1. Calculate direct materials inventory, total cost, December 31, 2014.
2. Calculate finished-goods inventory, total units, December 31, 2014.
3. Calculate selling price in 2014.
4. Calculate operating income for 2014.

2-41 Cost classification; ethics. Jason Hand, the new plant manager of Old Tree Manufacturing Plant Number 7, has just reviewed a draft of his year-end financial statements. Hand receives a year-end bonus of 8% of the plant's operating income before tax. The year-end income statement provided by the plant's controller was disappointing to say the least. After reviewing the numbers, Hand demanded that his controller go back and "work the numbers" again. Hand insisted that if he didn't see a better operating income number the next time around he would be forced to look for a new controller.

Old Tree Manufacturing classifies all costs directly related to the manufacturing of its product as product costs. These costs are inventoried and later expensed as costs of goods sold when the product is sold. All other expenses, including finished goods warehousing costs of $3,570,000, are classified as period expenses. Hand had suggested that warehousing costs be included as product costs because they are "definitely related to our product." The company produced 210,000 units during the period and sold 190,000 units.

As the controller reworked the numbers, he discovered that if he included warehousing costs as product costs, he could improve operating income by $340,000. He was also sure these new numbers would make Hand happy.

Required

1. Show numerically how operating income would improve by $340,000 just by classifying the preceding costs as product costs instead of period expenses.
2. Is Hand correct in his justification that these costs are "definitely related to our product"?
3. By how much will Hand profit personally if the controller makes the adjustments in requirement 1?
4. What should the plant controller do?

2-42 Finding unknown amounts. An auditor for the Internal Revenue Service is trying to reconstruct some partially destroyed records of two taxpayers. For each of the cases in the accompanying list, find the unknowns designated by the letters A through D.

	Case 1	Case 2
	(in thousands)	
Accounts receivable, 12/31	$ 9,000	$ 3,150
Cost of goods sold	A	30,000
Accounts payable, 1/1	4, 500	2,550
Accounts payable, 12/31	2,700	2,250
Finished goods inventory, 12/31	B	7,950
Gross margin	16,950	C
Work-in-process inventory, 1/1	0	1,200
Work-in-process inventory, 12/31	0	4,500
Finished goods inventory, 1/1	6,000	6,000
Direct materials used	12,000	18,000
Direct manufacturing labor	4,500	7,500
Manufacturing overhead costs	10,500	D
Purchases of direct materials	13,500	10,500
Revenues	48,000	47,700
Accounts receivable, 1/1	3,000	2,100

3

Cost–Volume–Profit Analysis

Learning Objectives

1. Explain the features of cost–volume–profit (CVP) analysis
2. Determine the breakeven point and output level needed to achieve a target operating income
3. Understand how income taxes affect CVP analysis
4. Explain how managers use CVP analysis to make decisions
5. Explain how sensitivity analysis helps managers cope with uncertainty
6. Use CVP analysis to plan variable and fixed costs
7. Apply CVP analysis to a company producing multiple products
8. Apply CVP analysis in service and not-for-profit organizations
9. Distinguish contribution margin from gross margin

All managers want to know how profits will change as the units sold of a product or service change.

Home Depot managers, for example, might wonder how many units of a new power drill must be sold to break even or make a certain amount of profit. Procter & Gamble managers might ask themselves how expanding their business in Nigeria would affect costs, revenues, and profits. These questions have a common "what-if" theme: What if we sold more power drills? What if we started selling in Nigeria? Examining the results of these what-if possibilities and alternatives helps managers make better decisions.

Managers must also decide how to price their products and understand the effect of their pricing decisions on revenues and profits. The following article explains how the Irish rock band U2 decided whether it should decrease the prices of some of its tickets during a recent world tour. Does lowering ticket prices sound like a wise strategy to you?

How "The Biggest Rock Show Ever" Turned a Big Profit[1]

On its recent world tour across North America, Europe, and Asia, the rock bank U2 performed on an imposing 164-foot-high stage that resembled a spaceship, complete with a massive video screen and footbridges leading to ringed catwalks. U2 used three separate stages—each one costing nearly $40 million dollars. Additional expenses for the tour were $750,000 daily. As a result, the tour's success depended not only on the quality of each night's concert but also on recouping its tremendous fixed costs—costs that did not change with the number of fans in the audience.

To cover its high fixed costs and make a profit, U2 needed to sell a lot of tickets. To maximize the tour's revenue, tickets were sold for as little as $30, and a unique in-the-round stage configuration boosted stadium capacities by roughly 20%. The plan worked. U2 shattered attendance records in most of the venues it played. By the end of the tour, the band played to more than 7 million fans, racking up almost $736 million in ticket and merchandise sales… and went in to the history books as the biggest tour ever. As you read this chapter, you will begin to understand how and why U2 made the decision to lower prices.

Businesses that have high fixed costs have to pay particular attention to the "what-ifs" behind decisions because making the wrong choices can be disastrous. Examples of well-known companies that have high fixed costs are American Airlines

[1] *Sources:* Gundersen, Edna. 2009. U2 turns 360 stadium tour into attendance-shattering sellouts. *USA Today*, October 4; and Waddell, Ray. 2011. U2's "360" Tour Gross: $736,137,344! *Billboard*, July 29.

and General Motors. When companies have high fixed costs, they need significant revenues just to break even. In the airline industry, for example, companies' fixed costs are so high the profits most airlines make come from the last two to five passengers who board each flight! Consequently, when revenues at American Airlines dropped, it was forced to declare bankruptcy. In this chapter, you will see how cost–volume–profit (CVP) analysis helps managers minimize such risks.

Essentials of CVP Analysis

Learning Objective 1

Explain the features of cost–volume–profit (CVP) analysis

...how operating income changes with changes in output level, selling prices, variable costs, or fixed costs

In Chapter 2, we discussed total revenues, total costs, and income. Managers use **cost–volume–profit (CVP) analysis** to study the behavior of and relationship among these elements as changes occur in the number of units sold, the selling price, the variable cost per unit, or the fixed costs of a product. Consider this example:

> Example: Emma Jones is a young entrepreneur who recently used *GMAT Success*, a test-prep book and software package for the business school admission test. Emma loved the book and program so much that after graduating she signed a contract with *GMAT Success*'s publisher to sell the learning materials. She recently sold them at a college fair in Boston and is now thinking of selling them at a college fair in Chicago. Emma knows she can purchase each package (book and software) from the publisher for $120 per package, with the privilege of returning all unsold packages and receiving a full $120 refund per package. She also knows that she must pay $2,000 to rent a booth at the fair. She will incur no other costs. Should she rent the booth or not?

Emma, like most managers who face such a situation, will need to work through the series of steps introduced in Chapter 1 to make the most profitable decisions.

1. **Identify the problem and uncertainties.** Every managerial decision involves selecting a course of action. The decision to rent the booth hinges on how Emma resolves two important uncertainties: the price she can charge and the number of packages she can sell at that price. Emma must decide knowing that the outcome of the action she chooses is uncertain. The more confident she is about selling a large number of packages at a high price, the more willing she will be to rent the booth.
2. **Obtain information.** When faced with uncertainty, managers obtain information that might help them understand the uncertainties more clearly. For example, Emma gathers information about the type of individuals likely to attend the fair and other test-prep packages that might be sold at the fair. She also gathers data from her experience selling the packages at the Boston fair.
3. **Make predictions about the future.** Managers make predictions using all the information available to them. Emma predicts she can charge $200 for the *GMAT Success* package. At that price, she is reasonably confident that she will be able to sell at least 30 packages and possibly as many as 60. Emma must be realistic and exercise judgment when making these predictions. If they are too optimistic, she will rent the booth when she should not. If they are too pessimistic, she will not rent the booth when she should.

Emma's predictions rest on the belief that her experience at the Chicago fair will be similar to her experience at the Boston fair 4 months earlier. Yet Emma is uncertain about several aspects of her prediction. Are the fairs truly comparable? For example, will attendance at the two fairs be the same? Have market conditions changed over the past 4 months? Are there any biases creeping into her thinking? She is keen on selling at the Chicago fair because sales in the last couple of months have been lower than expected. Is this experience making her predictions overly optimistic? Has she ignored some of the competitive risks? Will the other test-prep vendors at the fair reduce their prices? If they do, should she? How many packages can she expect to sell if she does?

Emma rethinks her plan and retests her assumptions. She obtains data about student attendance and total sales in past years from the organizers of the fair. In the end, she feels quite confident that her predictions are reasonable, accurate, and carefully thought through.

4. **Make decisions by choosing among alternatives.** Emma uses the CVP analysis that follows and decides to rent the booth at the Chicago fair.
5. **Implement the decision, evaluate performance, and learn.** Thoughtful managers never stop learning. They compare their actual performance to predicted performance to understand why things worked out the way they did and what they might learn. At the end of the Chicago fair, for example, Emma would want to evaluate whether her predictions about price and the number of packages she could sell were correct. This will help her make better decisions about renting booths at future fairs.

How does Emma use CVP analysis in Step 4 to make her decision? She begins by identifying which costs are fixed and which costs are variable and then calculates *contribution margin.*

Contribution Margin

The booth-rental cost of $2,000 is a fixed cost because it will not change no matter how many packages Emma sells. The total cost of the packages is a variable cost because it increases in proportion to the number of packages sold and she can return whatever she doesn't sell for a full refund.

To understand how her operating income will change by selling different quantities of packages, Emma calculates operating income if sales are 5 packages and if sales are 40 packages.

	5 packages sold	40 packages sold
Revenues	$ 1,000 ($200 per package × 5 packages)	$8,000 ($200 per package × 40 packages)
Variable purchase costs	600 ($120 per package × 5 packages)	4,800 ($120 per package × 40 packages)
Fixed costs	2,000	2,000
Operating income	$(1,600)	$1,200

The only numbers that change from selling different quantities of packages are *total revenues* and *total variable costs*. The difference between total revenues and total variable costs is called **contribution margin**. That is,

Contribution margin = Total revenues − Total variable costs

Contribution margin indicates why operating income changes as the number of units sold changes. The contribution margin when Emma sells 5 packages is $400 ($1,000 in total revenues minus $600 in total variable costs); the contribution margin when Emma sells 40 packages is $3,200 ($8,000 in total revenues minus $4,800 in total variable costs). When calculating the contribution margin, be sure to subtract all variable costs. For example, if Emma incurred some variable selling costs because she paid a commission to salespeople for each package they sold at the fair, variable costs would include the cost of each package plus the sales commission paid on it.

Contribution margin per unit is a useful tool for calculating contribution margin and operating income. It is defined as:

$$\text{Contribution margin per unit} = \text{Selling price} - \text{Variable cost per unit}$$

In the *GMAT Success* example, the contribution margin per package, or per unit, is \$200 − \$120 = \$80. Contribution margin per unit recognizes the tight coupling of selling price and variable cost per unit. Unlike fixed costs, Emma will only incur the variable cost per unit of \$120 when she sells a unit of *GMAT Success*.

Contribution margin per unit provides a second way to calculate contribution margin:

$$\text{Contribution margin} = \text{Contribution margin per unit} \times \text{Number of units sold}$$

For example, when Emma sells 40 packages, contribution margin = \$80 per unit × 40 units = \$3,200.

Even before she gets to the fair, Emma incurs \$2,000 in fixed costs. Because the contribution margin per unit is \$80, Emma will recover \$80 for each package that she sells at the fair. Emma hopes to sell enough packages to fully recover the \$2,000 she spent renting the booth and to then make a profit.

Exhibit 3-1 shows contribution margins for different quantities of packages sold. The income statement in Exhibit 3-1 is called a **contribution income statement** because it groups costs into variable costs and fixed costs to highlight contribution margin.

$$\text{Operating income} = \text{Contribution margin} - \text{Fixed costs}$$

Each additional package sold from 0 to 1 to 5 increases contribution margin by \$80 per package and helps Emma recover more and more of her fixed costs and reduce her operating loss. If Emma sells 25 packages, contribution margin equals \$2,000 (\$80 per package × 25 packages). This quantity exactly recovers her fixed costs and results in \$0 operating income. If Emma sells 40 packages, contribution margin increases by another \$1,200 (\$3,200 − \$2,000), all of which becomes operating income. As you look across Exhibit 3-1 from left to right, you see that the increase in contribution margin exactly equals the increase in operating income (or the decrease in operating loss).

When companies, such as Samsung and Prada, sell multiple products, calculating contribution margin per unit is cumbersome. Instead of expressing contribution margin in dollars per unit, these companies express it as a percentage called **contribution margin percentage** (or **contribution margin ratio**):

$$\text{Contribution margin percentage (or contribution margin ratio)} = \frac{\text{Contribution margin}}{\text{Revenues}}$$

Consider a sales level such as the 40 units sold in Exhibit 3-1:

$$\text{Contribution margin percentage} = \frac{\$3{,}200}{\$8{,}000} = 0.40, \text{ or } 40\%$$

Exhibit 3-1

Contribution Income Statement for Different Quantities of *GMAT Success* Packages Sold

Home | Insert | Page Layout | Formulas | Data | Review | View

	A	B	C	D	E	F	G	H
1				Number of Packages Sold				
2				0	1	5	25	40
3	Revenues	\$ 200	per package	\$ 0	\$ 200	\$ 1,000	\$5,000	\$8,000
4	Variable costs	\$ 120	per package	0	120	600	3,000	4,800
5	Contribution margin	\$ 80	per package	0	80	400	2,000	3,200
6	Fixed costs	\$2,000		2,000	2,000	2,000	2,000	2,000
7	Operating income			\$(2,000)	\$(1,920)	\$(1,600)	\$ 0	\$1,200

Contribution margin percentage is the contribution margin per dollar of revenue. Emma earns 40% for each dollar of revenue (40 cents) she takes in. Contribution margin percentage is a handy way to calculate contribution margin for different dollar amounts of revenue. Rearranging terms in the equation defining contribution margin percentage, we get:

$$\text{Contribution margin} = \text{Contribution margin percentage} \times \text{Revenues (in dollars)}$$

To derive the relationship between operating income and contribution margin percentage, recall that:

$$\text{Operating income} = \text{Contribution margin} - \text{Fixed costs}$$

Substituting for contribution margin in the above equation:

$$\text{Operating income} = \text{Contribution margin percentage} \times \text{Revenues} - \text{Fixed costs}$$

For example, in Exhibit 3-1, if Emma sells 40 packages:

Revenues	$8,000
Contribution margin percentage	40%
Contribution margin, 40% × $8,000	$3,200
Fixed costs	2,000
Operating income	$1,200

When there is only one product, as in our example, we can divide both the numerator and denominator of the contribution margin percentage equation by the quantity of units sold and calculate contribution margin percentage as follows:

$$\text{Contribution margin percentage} = \frac{\text{Contribution margin/Quantity of units sold}}{\text{Revenues/Quantity of units sold}}$$
$$= \frac{\text{Contribution margin per unit}}{\text{Selling price}}$$

In our example,

$$\text{Contribution margin percentage} = \frac{\$80}{\$200} = 0.40, \text{ or } 40\%$$

Contribution margin percentage is a useful tool for calculating how a change in revenues changes contribution margin. As Emma's revenues increase by $3,000 from $5,000 to $8,000, her contribution margin increases from $2,000 to $3,200 (by $1,200):

Contribution margin at revenue of $8,000, 0.40 × $8,000	$3,200
Contribution margin at revenue of $5,000, 0.40 × $5,000	2,000
Change in contribution margin when revenue increases by $3,000, 0.40 × $3,000	$1,200

$$\text{Change in contribution margin} = \text{Contribution margin percentage} \times \text{Change in revenues}$$

Contribution margin analysis is a widely used technique. For example, managers at Home Depot use contribution margin analysis to evaluate how sales fluctuations during a recession will affect the company's profitability.

Expressing CVP Relationships

How was the Excel spreadsheet in Exhibit 3-1 constructed? Underlying the exhibit are some equations that express the CVP relationships. To make good decisions using CVP analysis, we must understand these relationships and the structure of the contribution income statement in Exhibit 3-1. There are three related ways (we will call them "methods") to think more deeply about and model CVP relationships:

1. The equation method
2. The contribution margin method
3. The graph method

As you will learn later in the chapter, different methods are useful for different decisions.

The equation method and the contribution margin method are most useful when managers want to determine operating income at a few specific sales levels (for example, 5, 15, 25, and 40 units sold). The graph method helps managers visualize the relationship between units sold and operating income over a wide range of quantities.

Equation Method

Each column in Exhibit 3-1 is expressed as an equation.

$$\text{Revenues} - \text{Variable costs} - \text{Fixed costs} = \text{Operating income}$$

How are revenues in each column calculated?

$$\text{Revenues} = \text{Selling price } (SP) \times \text{Quantity of units sold } (Q)$$

How are variable costs in each column calculated?

$$\text{Variable costs} = \text{Variable cost per unit } (VCU) \times \text{Quantity of units sold } (Q)$$

So,

$$\left[\begin{pmatrix}\text{Selling}\\ \text{price}\end{pmatrix} \times \begin{pmatrix}\text{Quantity of}\\ \text{units sold}\end{pmatrix} - \begin{pmatrix}\text{Variable cost}\\ \text{per unit}\end{pmatrix} \times \begin{pmatrix}\text{Quantity of}\\ \text{units sold}\end{pmatrix}\right] - \begin{matrix}\text{Fixed}\\ \text{costs}\end{matrix} = \begin{matrix}\text{Operating}\\ \text{income}\end{matrix} \quad \text{(Equation 1)}$$

Equation 1 becomes the basis for calculating operating income for different quantities of units sold. For example, if you go to cell F7 in Exhibit 3-1, the calculation of operating income when Emma sells 5 packages is

$$(\$200 \times 5) - (\$120 \times 5) - \$2{,}000 = \$1{,}000 - \$600 - \$2{,}000 = -\$1{,}600$$

Contribution Margin Method

Rearranging equation 1,

$$\left[\begin{pmatrix}\text{Selling} & - & \text{Variable cost}\\ \text{price} & & \text{per unit}\end{pmatrix} \times \begin{pmatrix}\text{Quantity of}\\ \text{units sold}\end{pmatrix}\right] - \begin{matrix}\text{Fixed}\\ \text{costs}\end{matrix} = \begin{matrix}\text{Operating}\\ \text{income}\end{matrix}$$

$$\begin{pmatrix}\text{Contribution margin} & \times & \text{Quantity of}\\ \text{per unit} & & \text{units sold}\end{pmatrix} - \begin{matrix}\text{Fixed}\\ \text{costs}\end{matrix} = \begin{matrix}\text{Operating}\\ \text{income}\end{matrix} \quad \text{(Equation 2)}$$

In our *GMAT Success* example, contribution margin per unit is \$80 (\$200 − \$120), so when Emma sells 5 packages,

$$\text{Operating income} = (\$80 \times 5) - \$2{,}000 = -\$1{,}600$$

Equation 2 expresses the basic idea we described earlier—each unit sold helps Emma recover \$80 (in contribution margin) of the \$2,000 in fixed costs.

Graph Method

The graph method helps managers visualize the relationships between total revenues and total costs. The graph shows each relationship as a line. Exhibit 3-2 illustrates the graph method for selling *GMAT Success*. Because we have assumed that total costs and total revenues behave in a linear way, we need only two points to plot the line representing each of them.

1. **Total costs line.** The total costs line is the sum of fixed costs and variable costs. Fixed costs are \$2,000 for all quantities of units sold within the relevant range. To plot the

Exhibit 3-2

Cost–Volume Graph for *GMAT Success*

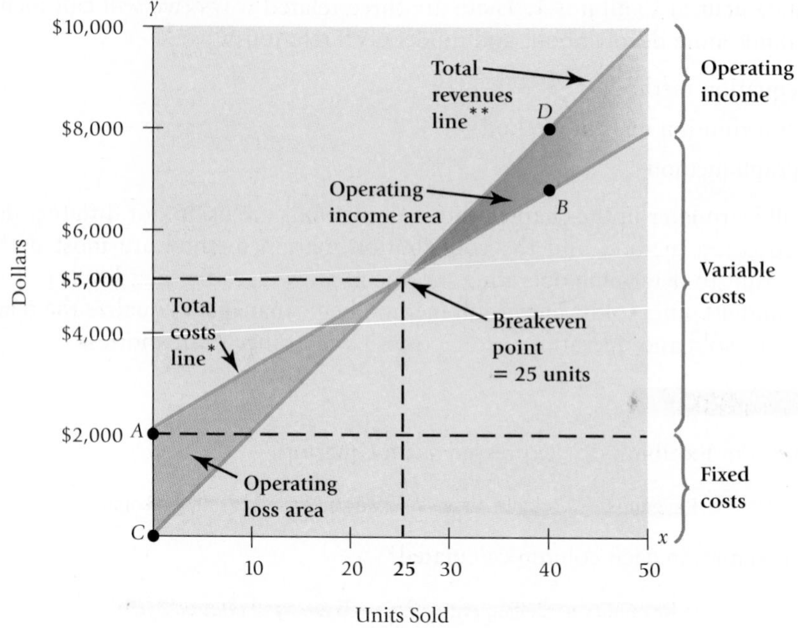

*Slope of the total costs line is the variable cost per unit = $120
**Slope of the total revenues line is the selling price = $200

total costs line, use as one point the $2,000 fixed costs at zero units sold (point A) because variable costs are $0 when no units are sold. Select a second point by choosing any other output level (say, 40 units sold) and determine the corresponding total costs. Total variable costs at this output level are $4,800 (40 units × $120 per unit). Remember, fixed costs are $2,000 at all quantities of units sold within the relevant range, so total costs at 40 units sold equal $6,800 ($2,000 + $4,800), which is point B in Exhibit 3-2. The total costs line is the straight line from point A through point B.

2. **Total revenues line.** One convenient starting point is $0 revenues at 0 units sold, which is point C in Exhibit 3-2. Select a second point by choosing any other convenient output level and determining the corresponding total revenues. At 40 units sold, total revenues are $8,000 ($200 per unit × 40 units), which is point D in Exhibit 3-2. The total revenues line is the straight line from point C through point D.

Decision Point
How can CVP analysis help managers?

The profit or loss at any sales level can be determined by the vertical distance between the two lines at that level in Exhibit 3-2. For quantities fewer than 25 units sold, total costs exceed total revenues, and the purple area indicates operating losses. For quantities greater than 25 units sold, total revenues exceed total costs, and the blue-green area indicates operating incomes. At 25 units sold, total revenues equal total costs. Emma will break even by selling 25 packages.

Like Emma, many companies, particularly small- and medium-sized companies, use the graph method to see how their revenues and costs will change as the quantity of units sold changes. The graph helps them understand their regions of profitability and unprofitability.

Cost–Volume–Profit Assumptions

Now that you know how CVP analysis works, think about the following assumptions we made during the analysis:

1. Changes in revenues and costs arise only because of changes in the number of product (or service) units sold. The number of units sold is the only revenue driver and the only cost driver. Just as a cost driver is any factor that affects costs, a **revenue driver** is a variable, such as volume, that causally affects revenues.
2. Total costs can be separated into two components: a fixed component that does not vary with units sold (such as Emma's $2,000 booth fee) and a variable component that changes based on units sold (such as the $120 cost per *GMAT Success* package).

3. When represented graphically, the behaviors of total revenues and total costs are linear (meaning they can be represented as a straight line) in relation to units sold within a relevant range (and time period).
4. Selling price, variable cost per unit, and total fixed costs (within a relevant range and time period) are known and constant.

As you can tell from these assumptions, to conduct a CVP analysis, you need to correctly distinguish fixed from variable costs. Always keep in mind, however, that whether a cost is variable or fixed depends on the time period for a decision.

The shorter the time horizon, the higher the percentage of total costs considered fixed. For example, suppose an American Airlines plane will depart from its gate in the next hour and currently has 20 seats unsold. A potential passenger arrives with a transferable ticket from a competing airline. American's variable costs of placing one more passenger in an otherwise empty seat (such as the cost of providing the passenger with a free beverage) is negligible. With only an hour to go before the flight departs, virtually all costs (such as crew costs and baggage-handling costs) are fixed.

Alternatively, suppose American Airlines must decide whether to continue to offer this particular flight next year. If American Airlines decides to cancel this flight because very few passengers during the last year have taken it, many more of its costs, including crew costs, baggage-handling costs, and airport fees for the flight, would be considered variable: Over this longer 1-year time period, American Airlines would not have to incur these costs if the flight were no longer operating. Always consider the relevant range, the length of the time horizon, and the specific decision situation when classifying costs as variable or fixed.

Breakeven Point and Target Operating Income

Learning Objective 2

Determine the breakeven point and output level needed to achieve a target operating income

...compare contribution margin and fixed costs

Managers and entrepreneurs like Emma always want to know how much they must sell to earn a given amount of income. Equally important, they want to know how much they must sell to avoid a loss.

Breakeven Point

The **breakeven point (BEP)** is that quantity of output sold at which total revenues equal total costs—that is, the quantity of output sold that results in \$0 of operating income. You have already learned how to use the graph method to calculate the breakeven point. Recall from Exhibit 3-1 that operating income was \$0 when Emma sold 25 units; this is the breakeven point. But by understanding the equations underlying the calculations in Exhibit 3-1, we can calculate the breakeven point directly for selling *GMAT Success* rather than trying out different quantities and checking when operating income equals \$0.

Recall the equation method (equation 1):

$$\left[\left(\begin{array}{c}\text{Selling}\\ \text{price}\end{array} \times \begin{array}{c}\text{Quantity of}\\ \text{units sold}\end{array}\right) - \left(\begin{array}{c}\text{Variable cost}\\ \text{per unit}\end{array} \times \begin{array}{c}\text{Quantity of}\\ \text{units sold}\end{array}\right)\right] - \begin{array}{c}\text{Fixed}\\ \text{costs}\end{array} = \begin{array}{c}\text{Operating}\\ \text{income}\end{array}$$

Setting operating income equal to \$0 and denoting quantity of output units that must be sold by Q,

$$(\$200 \times Q) - (\$120 \times Q) - \$2{,}000 = \$0$$
$$\$80 \times Q = \$2{,}000$$
$$Q = \$2{,}000 \div \$80 \text{ per unit} = 25 \text{ units}$$

If Emma sells fewer than 25 units, she will incur a loss; if she sells 25 units, she will break even; and if she sells more than 25 units, she will make a profit. Although this breakeven point is expressed in units, it can also be expressed in revenues: 25 units × \$200 selling price = \$5,000.

Recall the contribution margin method (equation 2):

$$\left(\text{Contribution margin per unit} \times \text{Quantity of units sold}\right) - \text{Fixed costs} = \text{Operating income}$$

At the breakeven point, operating income is by definition \$0, and so,

$$\text{Contribution margin per unit} \times \text{Breakeven quantity of units} = \text{Fixed costs} \qquad \text{(Equation 3)}$$

Rearranging equation 3 and entering the data,

$$\text{Breakeven number of units} = \frac{\text{Fixed costs}}{\text{Contribution margin per unit}} = \frac{\$2{,}000}{\$80 \text{ per unit}} = 25 \text{ units}$$

$$\begin{aligned}\text{Breakeven revenues} &= \text{Breakeven number of units} \times \text{Selling price}\\ &= 25 \text{ units} \times \$200 \text{ per unit} = \$5{,}000\end{aligned}$$

In practice (because companies have multiple products), management accountants usually calculate the breakeven point directly in terms of revenues using contribution margin percentages. Recall that in the *GMAT Success* example, at revenues of \$8,000, contribution margin is \$3,200:

$$\text{Contribution margin percentage} = \frac{\text{Contribution margin}}{\text{Revenues}} = \frac{\$3{,}200}{\$8{,}000} = 0.40, \text{ or } 40\%$$

That is, 40% of each dollar of revenue, or 40 cents, is the contribution margin. To break even, contribution margin must equal Emma's fixed costs, which are \$2,000. To earn \$2,000 of contribution margin, when \$1 of revenue results in a \$0.40 contribution margin, revenues must equal \$2,000 ÷ 0.40 = \$5,000.

$$\text{Breakeven revenues} = \frac{\text{Fixed costs}}{\text{Contribution margin \%}} = \frac{\$2{,}000}{0.40} = \$5{,}000$$

While the breakeven point tells managers how much they must sell to avoid a loss, managers are equally interested in how they will achieve the operating income targets underlying their strategies and plans. In our example, selling 25 units at a price of \$200 (equal to revenue of \$5,000) assures Emma that she will not lose money if she rents the booth. While this news is comforting, how does Emma determine how much she needs to sell to achieve a targeted amount of operating income?

Target Operating Income

Suppose Emma wants to earn an operating income of \$1,200? How many units must she sell? One approach is to keep plugging in different quantities into Exhibit 3-1 and check when operating income equals \$1,200. Exhibit 3-1 shows that operating income is \$1,200 when 40 packages are sold. A more convenient approach is to use equation 1 from page 71.

$$\left[\left(\text{Selling price} \times \text{Quantity of units sold}\right) - \left(\text{Variable cost per unit} \times \text{Quantity of units sold}\right)\right] - \text{Fixed costs} = \text{Operating income} \qquad \text{(Equation 1)}$$

We denote by Q the unknown quantity of units Emma must sell to earn an operating income of \$1,200. Selling price is \$200, variable cost per package is \$120, fixed costs are \$2,000, and target operating income is \$1,200. Substituting these values into equation 1, we have

$$\begin{aligned}(\$200 \times Q) - (\$120 \times Q) - \$2{,}000 &= \$1{,}200\\ \$80 \times Q &= \$2{,}000 + \$1{,}200 = \$3{,}200\\ Q &= \$3{,}200 \div \$80 \text{ per unit} = 40 \text{ units}\end{aligned}$$

Alternatively, we could use equation 2,

$$\left(\text{Contribution margin per unit} \times \text{Quantity of units sold}\right) - \text{Fixed costs} = \text{Operating income} \qquad \text{(Equation 2)}$$

Given a target operating income ($1,200 in this case), we can rearrange terms to get equation 4.

$$\text{Quantity of units required to be sold} = \frac{\text{Fixed costs} + \text{Target operating income}}{\text{Contribution margin per unit}} \qquad \text{(Equation 4)}$$

$$\text{Quantity of units required to be sold} = \frac{\$2{,}000 + \$1{,}200}{\$80 \text{ per unit}} = 40 \text{ units}$$

Proof:		
	Revenues, $200 per unit × 40 units	$8,000
	Variable costs, $120 per unit × 40 units	4,800
	Contribution margin, $80 per unit × 40 units	3,200
	Fixed costs	2,000
	Operating income	$1,200

The revenues needed to earn an operating income of $1,200 can also be calculated directly by recognizing (1) that $3,200 of contribution margin must be earned (to cover the fixed costs of $2,000 plus earn an operating income of $1,200) and (2) that $1 of revenue earns $0.40 (40 cents) of contribution margin (the contribution margin percentage is 40%). To earn a contribution margin of $3,200, revenues must equal $3,200 ÷ 0.40 = $8,000. That is,

$$\text{Revenues needed to earn target operating income} = \frac{\text{Fixed costs} + \text{Target operating income}}{\text{Contribution margin percentage}}$$

$$\text{Revenues needed to earn operating income of \$1,200} = \frac{\$2{,}000 + \$1{,}200}{0.40} = \frac{\$3{,}200}{0.40} = \$8{,}000$$

Could we use the graph method and the graph in Exhibit 3-2 to figure out how many units Emma must sell to earn an operating income of $1,200? Yes, but it is not as easy to determine the precise point at which the difference between the total revenues line and the total costs line equals $1,200. Recasting Exhibit 3-2 in the form of a profit–volume (PV) graph, however, makes it easier to answer this question.

A **PV graph** shows how changes in the quantity of units sold affect operating income. Exhibit 3-3 is the PV graph for *GMAT Success* (fixed costs, $2,000; selling price, $200; and variable cost per unit, $120). The PV line can be drawn using two points. One convenient

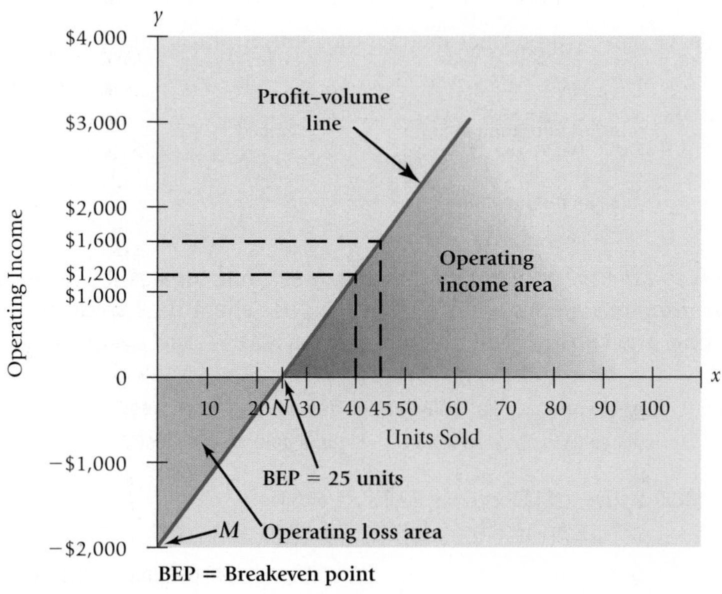

Exhibit 3-3

Profit–Volume Graph for *GMAT Success*

Decision Point

How can managers determine the breakeven point or the output needed to achieve a target operating income?

point (M) is the operating loss at 0 units sold, which is equal to the fixed costs of $2,000 and is shown at −$2,000 on the vertical axis. A second convenient point (N) is the breakeven point, which is 25 units in our example (see page 73). The PV line is the straight line from point M through point N. To find the number of units Emma must sell to earn an operating income of $1,200, draw a horizontal line parallel to the x-axis corresponding to $1,200 on the vertical axis (the y-axis). At the point where this line intersects the PV line, draw a vertical line down to the horizontal axis (the x-axis). The vertical line intersects the x-axis at 40 units, indicating that by selling 40 units Emma will earn an operating income of $1,200.

Just like Emma, managers at larger companies such as California Pizza Kitchen use profit–volume analyses to understand how profits change with sales volumes. They use this understanding to target the sales levels they need to achieve to meet their profit plans.

Learning Objective 3

Understand how income taxes affect CVP analysis

...focus on net income

Target Net Income and Income Taxes

Net income is operating income plus nonoperating revenues (such as interest revenue) minus nonoperating costs (such as interest cost) minus income taxes. For simplicity, throughout this chapter we assume nonoperating revenues and nonoperating costs are zero. So, our net income equation will simply be:

$$\text{Net income} = \text{Operating income} - \text{Income taxes}$$

Until now, we have ignored the effect of income taxes in our CVP analysis. In many companies, managers' income targets are expressed in terms of net income because the company's top executives want them to consider the effect their decisions have on the firm's operating income *after* income taxes. Some decisions might not result in a large operating income, but their tax consequences make them attractive because they have a positive effect on net income—the measure that drives shareholders' dividends and returns.

To make net income evaluations, CVP calculations for target income must be stated in terms of target net income instead of target operating income. For example, Emma may be interested in knowing the quantity of units of *GMAT Success* she must sell to earn a net income of $960, assuming an income tax rate of 40%.

$$\text{Target net income} = \begin{pmatrix}\text{Target}\\ \text{operating income}\end{pmatrix} - \begin{pmatrix}\text{Target}\\ \text{operating income} \times \text{Tax rate}\end{pmatrix}$$

$$\text{Target net income} = (\text{Target operating income}) \times (1 - \text{Tax rate})$$

$$\text{Target operating income} = \frac{\text{Target net income}}{1 - \text{Tax rate}} = \frac{\$960}{1 - 0.40} = \$1{,}600$$

In other words, to earn a target net income of $960, Emma's target operating income is $1,600.

Proof:

Target operating income	$1,600
Tax at 40% (0.40 × $1,600)	640
Target net income	$ 960

The key step is to take the target net income number and convert it into the corresponding target operating income number. We can then use equation 1 to determine the target operating income and substitute numbers from our *GMAT Success* example.

$$\left[\begin{pmatrix}\text{Selling}\\ \text{price}\end{pmatrix} \times \begin{pmatrix}\text{Quantity of}\\ \text{units sold}\end{pmatrix} - \begin{pmatrix}\text{Variable cost}\\ \text{per unit}\end{pmatrix} \times \begin{pmatrix}\text{Quantity of}\\ \text{unit sold}\end{pmatrix}\right] - \begin{matrix}\text{Fixed}\\ \text{costs}\end{matrix} = \begin{matrix}\text{Operating}\\ \text{income}\end{matrix} \qquad \text{(Equation 1)}$$

$$(\$200 \times Q) - (\$120 \times Q) - \$2{,}000 = \$1{,}600$$

$$\$80 \times Q = \$3{,}600$$

$$Q = \$3{,}600 \div \$80 \text{ per unit} = 45 \text{ units}$$

Alternatively, we can calculate the number of units Emma must sell by using the contribution margin method and equation 4:

$$\text{Quantity of units required to be sold} = \frac{\text{Fixed costs} + \text{Target operating income}}{\text{Contribution margin per unit}} \quad \text{(Equation 4)}$$

$$= \frac{\$2{,}000 + \$1{,}600}{\$80 \text{ per unit}} = 45 \text{ units}$$

Proof:

Revenues, \$200 per unit × 45 units	\$9,000
Variable costs, \$120 per unit × 45 units	5,400
Contribution margin	3,600
Fixed costs	2,000
Operating income	1,600
Income taxes, \$1,600 × 0.40	640
Net income	\$ 960

Emma can also use the PV graph in Exhibit 3-3. To earn the target operating income of \$1,600, Emma needs to sell 45 units.

Focusing the analysis on target net income instead of target operating income will not change the breakeven point because, by definition, operating income at the breakeven point is \$0 and no income taxes are paid when there is no operating income.

Decision Point

How can managers incorporate income taxes into CVP analysis?

Using CVP Analysis for Decision Making

Learning Objective 4

Explain how managers use CVP analysis to make decisions

...choose the alternative that maximizes operating income

You have learned how CVP analysis is useful for calculating the units that need to be sold to break even or to achieve a target operating income or target net income. A manager can also use CVP analysis to make other strategic decisions. Consider a decision about choosing the features for a product, such as the engine size, transmission system, or steering system for a new car model. Different choices will affect the vehicle's selling price, variable cost per unit, fixed costs, units sold, and operating income. CVP analysis helps managers make product decisions by estimating the expected profitability of these choices. We return to our *GMAT Success* example to show how Emma can use a CVP analysis to make decisions about advertising and selling price.

Decision to Advertise

Suppose Emma anticipates selling 40 units of the *GMAT Success* package at the fair. Exhibit 3-3 indicates that Emma's operating income will be \$1,200. Emma is considering advertising the product and its features in the fair brochure. The advertisement will be a fixed cost of \$500. Emma thinks that advertising will increase sales by 10% to 44 packages. Should Emma advertise? The following table presents the CVP analysis.

	40 Packages Sold with No Advertising (1)	44 Packages Sold with Advertising (2)	Difference (3) = (2) − (1)
Revenues (\$200 × 40; \$200 × 44)	\$8,000	\$8,800	\$ 800
Variable costs (\$120 × 40; \$120 × 44)	4,800	5,280	480
Contribution margin (\$80 × 40; \$80 × 44)	3,200	3,520	320
Fixed costs	2,000	2,500	500
Operating income	\$1,200	\$1,020	\$ (180)

Operating income will decrease from \$1,200 to \$1,020, so Emma should not advertise. Note that Emma could focus only on the difference column and come to the same conclusion: If Emma advertises, contribution margin will increase by \$320 (revenues,

$800 − variable costs, $480) and fixed costs will increase by $500, resulting in a $180 decrease in operating income.

When using CVP analysis, try evaluating your decisions based on differences rather than mechanically working through the contribution income statement. What if advertising costs were $400 or $600 instead of $500? Analyzing differences allows managers to get to the heart of CVP analysis and sharpens their intuition by focusing only on the revenues and costs that will change as a result of a decision.

Decision to Reduce the Selling Price

Having decided not to advertise, Emma is contemplating whether to reduce the selling price to $175. At this price, she thinks she will sell 50 units. At this quantity, the test-prep package company that supplies *GMAT Success* will sell the packages to Emma for $115 per unit instead of $120. Should Emma reduce the selling price?

Contribution margin from lowering price to $175: ($175 − $115) per unit × 50 units	$3,000
Contribution margin from maintaining price at $200: ($200 − $120) per unit × 40 units	3,200
Change in contribution margin from lowering price	$ (200)

Decreasing the price will reduce contribution margin by $200 and, because the fixed costs of $2,000 will not change, will also reduce Emma's operating income by $200. Emma should not reduce the selling price.

Determining Target Prices

Emma could also ask, "At what price can I sell 50 units (purchased at $115 per unit) and continue to earn an operating income of $1,200?" The answer is $179, as the following calculations show.

	Target operating income	$1,200
	Add fixed costs	2,000
	Target contribution margin	$3,200
	Divided by number of units sold	÷ 50 units
	Target contribution margin per unit	$ 64
	Add variable cost per unit	115
	Target selling price	$ 179
Proof:	Revenues, $179 per unit × 50 units	$8,950
	Variable costs, $115 per unit × 50 units	5,750
	Contribution margin	3,200
	Fixed costs	2,000
	Operating income	$1,200

Decision Point

How do managers use CVP analysis to make decisions?

Emma should also examine the effects of other decisions, such as simultaneously increasing her advertising costs and raising or lowering the price of *GMAT Success* packages. In each case, Emma will estimate the effects these actions are likely to have on the demand for *GMAT Success*. She will then compare the changes in contribution margin (through the effects on selling prices, variable costs, and quantities of units sold) to the changes in fixed costs and choose the alternative that provides the highest operating income.

Strategic decisions invariably entail risk. Managers can use CVP analysis to evaluate how the operating income of their companies will be affected if the outcomes they predict are not achieved—say, if sales are 10% lower than they estimated. Evaluating this risk affects other strategic decisions a manager might make. For example, if the probability of a decline in sales seems high, a manager may take actions to change the cost structure to have more variable costs and fewer fixed costs.

Sensitivity Analysis and Margin of Safety 

Learning Objective 5

Explain how sensitivity analysis helps managers cope with uncertainty

...determine the effect on operating income of different assumptions

Sensitivity analysis is a "what-if" technique managers use to examine how an outcome will change if the original predicted data are not achieved or if an underlying assumption changes. The analysis answers questions such as "What will operating income be if the quantity of units sold decreases by 5% from the original prediction?" and "What will operating income be if variable cost per unit increases by 10%?" This helps visualize the possible outcomes that might occur *before* the company commits to funding a project. For example, companies such as Boeing and Airbus use CVP analysis to evaluate how many airplanes they need to sell in order to recover the multibillion-dollar costs of designing and developing new ones. The managers then do a sensitivity analysis to test how sensitive their conclusions are to different assumptions, such as the size of the market for the airplane, its selling price, and the market share they think it can capture.

Electronic spreadsheets, such as Excel, enable managers to systematically and efficiently conduct CVP-based sensitivity analyses and to examine the effect and interaction of changes in selling price, variable cost per unit, and fixed costs on target operating income. Exhibit 3-4 displays a spreadsheet for the *GMAT Success* example.

Using the spreadsheet, Emma can immediately see how many units she needs to sell to achieve particular operating-income levels, given alternative levels of fixed costs and variable cost per unit that she may face. For example, she must sell 32 units to earn an operating income of $1,200 if fixed costs are $2,000 and variable cost per unit is $100. Emma can also use Exhibit 3-4 to determine that she needs to sell 56 units to break even if the fixed cost of the booth rental at the Chicago fair is raised to $2,800 and if the variable cost per unit charged by the test-prep package supplier increases to $150. Emma can use this information along with sensitivity analysis and her predictions about how much she can sell to decide if she should rent the booth.

Another aspect of sensitivity analysis is **margin of safety**:

$$\text{Margin of safety} = \text{Budgeted (or actual) revenues} - \text{Breakeven revenues}$$
$$\text{Margin of safety (in units)} = \text{Budgeted (or actual) sales quantity} - \text{Breakeven quantity}$$

The margin of safety answers the "what-if" question: If budgeted revenues are above the breakeven point and drop, how far can they fall below budget before the breakeven point is reached? Sales might decrease as a result of factors such as a poorly executed

Exhibit 3-4

Spreadsheet Analysis of CVP Relationships for *GMAT Success*

Home | Insert | Page Layout | Formulas | Data | Review | View

D5 ▼ *fx* =($A5+D$3)/(F1-$B5)

	A	B	C	D	E	F
1			Number of units required to be sold at $200			
2			Selling Price to Earn Target Operating Income of			
3		Variable Costs	$0	$1,200	$1,600	$2,000
4	Fixed Costs	per Unit	(Breakeven point)			
5	$2,000	$100	20	32[a]	36	40
6	$2,000	$120	25	40	45	50
7	$2,000	$150	40	64	72	80
8	$2,400	$100	24	36	40	44
9	$2,400	$120	30	45	50	55
10	$2,400	$150	48	72	80	88
11	$2,800	$100	28	40	44	48
12	$2,800	$120	35	50	55	60
13	$2,800	$150	56	80	88	96
14						
15	[a]Number of units	=	Fixed costs + Target operating income	=	$2,000 + $1,200	= 32
16	required to be sold		Contribution margin per unit		$200 – $100	

$$^{a}\text{Number of units required to be sold} = \frac{\text{Fixed costs} + \text{Target operating income}}{\text{Contribution margin per unit}} = \frac{\$2{,}000 + \$1{,}200}{\$200 - \$100} = 32$$

marketing program or a competitor introducing a better product. Assume that Emma has fixed costs of $2,000, a selling price of $200, and variable cost per unit of $120. From Exhibit 3-1, if Emma sells 40 units, budgeted revenues are $8,000 and budgeted operating income is $1,200. The breakeven point is 25 units or $5,000 in total revenues.

$$\text{Margin of safety} = \frac{\text{Budgeted}}{\text{revenues}} - \frac{\text{Breakeven}}{\text{revenues}} = \$8{,}000 - \$5{,}000 = \$3{,}000$$

$$\frac{\text{Margin of}}{\text{safety (in units)}} = \frac{\text{Budgeted}}{\text{sales (units)}} - \frac{\text{Breakeven}}{\text{sales (units)}} = 40 - 25 = 15 \text{ units}$$

Sometimes margin of safety is expressed as a percentage:

$$\text{Margin of safety percentage} = \frac{\text{Margin of safety in dollars}}{\text{Budgeted (or actual) revenues}}$$

In our example, margin of safety percentage $= \dfrac{\$3{,}000}{\$8{,}000} = 37.5\%$

This result means that revenues would have to decrease substantially, by 37.5%, to reach the breakeven revenues. The high margin of safety gives Emma confidence that she is unlikely to suffer a loss.

MC Question Test

If, however, Emma expects to sell only 30 units, budgeted revenues would be $6,000 ($200 per unit × 30 units) and the margin of safety would equal:

$$\text{Budgeted revenues} - \text{Breakeven revenues} = \$6{,}000 - \$5{,}000 = \$1{,}000$$

$$\frac{\text{Margin of}}{\text{safety percentage}} = \frac{\text{Margin of safety in dollars}}{\text{Budgeted (or actual) revenues}} = \frac{\$1{,}000}{\$6{,}000} = 16.67\%$$

The analysis implies that if revenues fall by more than 16.67%, Emma would suffer a loss. A low margin of safety increases the risk of a loss, which means Emma would need to look for ways to lower the breakeven point by reducing fixed costs or increasing contribution margin. For example, she would need to evaluate if her product is attractive enough to customers to allow her to charge a higher price without reducing the demand for it or if she could purchase the software at a lower cost. If Emma can neither reduce her fixed costs nor increase contribution margin and if she does not have the tolerance for this level of risk, she will prefer not to rent a booth at the fair.

Decision Point

What can managers do to cope with uncertainty or changes in underlying assumptions?

Sensitivity analysis gives managers a good feel for a decision's risks. It is a simple approach to recognizing **uncertainty**, which is the possibility that an actual amount will deviate from an expected amount. A more comprehensive approach to recognizing uncertainty is to compute expected values using probability distributions. This approach is illustrated in the appendix to this chapter.

Learning Objective 6

Use CVP analysis to plan variable and fixed costs

...compare risk of losses versus higher returns

Cost Planning and CVP

Managers have the ability to choose the levels of fixed and variable costs in their cost structures. This is a strategic decision. In this section, we describe various factors that managers and management accountants consider as they make this decision.

Alternative Fixed-Cost/Variable-Cost Structures

CVP-based sensitivity analysis highlights the risks and returns as fixed costs are substituted for variable costs in a company's cost structure. In Exhibit 3-4, compare line 6 and line 11.

			Number of units required to be sold at $200 selling price to earn target operating income of	
	Fixed Cost	Variable Cost	$0 (Breakeven point)	$2,000
Line 6	$2,000	$120	25	50
Line 11	$2,800	$100	28	48

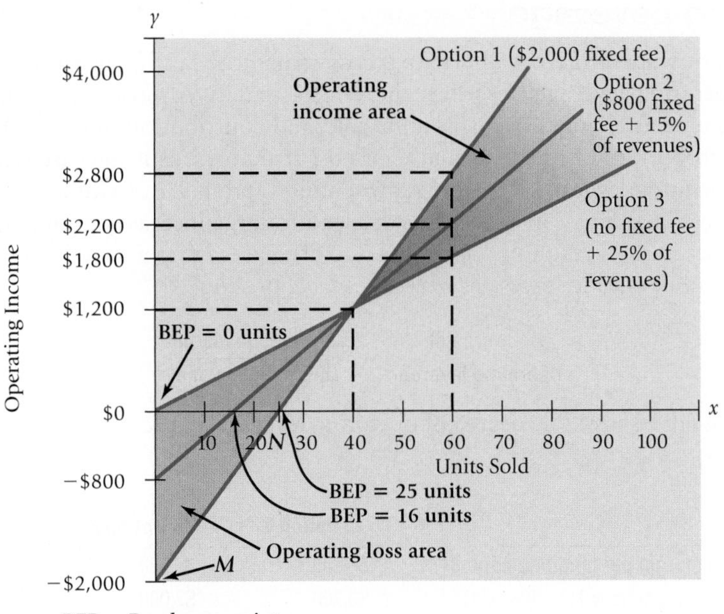

Exhibit 3-5

Profit–Volume Graph for Alternative Rental Options for *GMAT Success*

Line 11, which has higher fixed costs and lower variable costs than line 6, has a higher breakeven point but requires fewer units to be sold (48 vs. 50) to earn an operating income of $2,000. CVP analysis can help managers evaluate various fixed-cost/variable-cost structures. We next consider the effects of these choices in more detail. Suppose the Chicago fair organizers offer Emma three rental alternatives:

Option 1: $2,000 fixed fee

Option 2: $800 fixed fee plus 15% of *GMAT Success* revenues

Option 3: 25% of *GMAT Success* revenues with no fixed fee

Emma is interested in how her choice of a rental agreement will affect the income she earns and the risks she faces. Exhibit 3-5 graphically depicts the profit–volume relationship for each option.

- The line representing the relationship between units sold and operating income for Option 1 is the same as the line in the PV graph shown in Exhibit 3-3 (fixed costs of $2,000 and contribution margin per unit of $80).
- The line representing Option 2 shows fixed costs of $800 and a contribution margin per unit of $50 [selling price, $200, minus variable cost per unit, $120, minus variable rental fees per unit, $30 (0.15 × $200)].
- The line representing Option 3 shows fixed costs of $0 and a contribution margin per unit of $30[$200 − $120 − $50(0.25 × $200)].

Option 3 has the lowest breakeven point (0 units), and Option 1 has the highest breakeven point (25 units). Option 1 is associated with the highest risk of loss if sales are low, but it also has the highest contribution margin per unit ($80) and therefore the highest operating income when sales are high (greater than 40 units).

The choice among Options 1, 2, and 3 is a strategic decision. As with most strategic decisions, what Emma decides will significantly affect her operating income (or loss), depending on the demand for the product. Faced with this uncertainty, Emma's choice will be influenced by her confidence in the level of demand for *GMAT Success* packages and her willingness to risk losses if demand is low. For example, if Emma's tolerance for risk is high, she will choose Option 1 with its high potential rewards. If, however, Emma is risk averse, she will prefer Option 3, where the rewards are smaller if sales are high but where she never suffers a loss if sales are low.

Operating Leverage

The risk-return tradeoff across alternative cost structures can be measured as *operating leverage*. **Operating leverage** describes the effects that fixed costs have on changes in operating income as changes occur in units sold and contribution margin. Organizations with a high proportion of fixed costs in their cost structures, as is the case with Option 1, have high operating leverage. The line representing Option 1 in Exhibit 3-5 is the steepest of the three lines. Small increases in sales lead to large increases in operating income. Small decreases in sales result in relatively large decreases in operating income, leading to a greater risk of operating losses. *At any given level of sales*,

$$\text{Degree of operating leverage} = \frac{\text{Contribution margin}}{\text{Operating income}}$$

The following table shows the **degree of operating leverage** at sales of 40 units for the three rental options.

	Option 1	Option 2	Option 3
1. Contribution margin per unit (see page 81)	$ 80	$ 50	$ 30
2. Contribution margin (row 1 × 40 units)	$3,200	$2,000	$1,200
3. Operating income (from Exhibit 3-5)	$1,200	$1,200	$1,200
4. Degree of operating leverage (row 2 ÷ row 3)	$\frac{\$3,200}{\$1,200} = 2.67$	$\frac{\$2,000}{\$1,200} = 1.67$	$\frac{\$1,200}{\$1,200} = 1.00$

These results indicate that, when sales are 40 units, a 1% change in sales and contribution margin will result in 2.67% change in operating income for Option 1. For Option 3, a 1% change in sales and contribution margin will result in only a 1% change in operating income. Consider, for example, a sales increase of 50% from 40 to 60 units. Contribution margin will increase by 50% under each option. Operating income, however, will increase by 2.67 × 50% = 133% from $1,200 to $2,800 in Option 1, but it will increase by only 1.00 × 50% = 50% from $1,200 to $1,800 in Option 3 (see Exhibit 3-5). The degree of operating leverage at a given level of sales helps managers calculate the effect of sales fluctuations on operating income.

Keep in mind that, in the presence of fixed costs, the degree of operating leverage is different at different levels of sales. For example, at sales of 60 units, the degree of operating leverage under each of the three options is as follows:

	Option 1	Option 2	Option 3
1. Contribution margin per unit (page 81)	$ 80	$ 50	$ 30
2. Contribution margin (row 1 × 60 units)	$4,800	$3,000	$1,800
3. Operating income (from Exhibit 3-5)	$2,800	$2,200	$1,800
4. Degree of operating leverage (row 2 ÷ row 3)	$\frac{\$4,800}{\$2,800} = 1.71$	$\frac{\$3,000}{\$2,200} = 1.36$	$\frac{\$1,800}{\$1,800} = 1.00$

The degree of operating leverage decreases from 2.67 (at sales of 40 units) to 1.71 (at sales of 60 units) under Option 1 and from 1.67 to 1.36 under Option 2. In general, whenever there are fixed costs, the degree of operating leverage decreases as the level of sales increases beyond the breakeven point. If fixed costs are $0 as they are in Option 3, contribution margin equals operating income and the degree of operating leverage equals 1.00 at all sales levels.

It is important for managers to monitor operating leverage carefully. Consider companies such as General Motors and American Airlines. Their high operating leverage was a major reason for their financial problems. Anticipating high demand for their services, these companies borrowed money to acquire assets, resulting in high fixed costs. As their sales declined, these companies suffered losses and could not generate enough cash to service their interest and debt, causing them to seek bankruptcy protection.

Managers and management accountants should distinguish fixed from variable costs and then evaluate how the level of fixed costs and variable costs they choose will affect the risk-return tradeoffs of their firms. As we have explained, distinguishing fixed from variable costs is fairly straightforward in some cases. In others it's more challenging because costs do not vary only with the number of units sold but with the number of different types of products or services offered, the number of batches in which products are produced, or the complexity of operations. Chapter 10 describes techniques managers can use to separate fixed costs from variable costs. Regardless, differentiating fixed from variable costs requires careful judgment.

What actions can managers take to reduce fixed costs? Nike, the shoe and apparel company, does no manufacturing and incurs no fixed costs of operating and maintaining manufacturing plants. Instead, it buys its products from various suppliers. As a result, all of Nike's costs of producing products are variable costs. Nike reduces its risk of loss by increasing variable costs and reducing fixed costs. Concepts in Action: Cost–Volume–Profit Analysis Makes Megabus a Mega-Success describes how Megabus, an intercity bus operator, developed an innovative business model to reduce its fixed costs.

To reduce both fixed costs and variable costs, many companies are moving their manufacturing facilities from the United States to lower-cost countries, such as Mexico and China. Other companies, such as General Electric and Hewlett-Packard, have shifted service functions, such as after-sales customer service, to their customer call centers in countries such as India. These decisions by companies are often controversial. Some economists argue that outsourcing helps keep costs, and therefore prices, low and enables U.S. companies to remain globally competitive. Others argue that outsourcing reduces job opportunities in the United States and hurts working-class families.

Decision Point

How should managers choose among different variable-cost/fixed-cost structures?

Concepts in Action

Cost–Volume–Profit Analysis Makes Megabus a Mega-Success

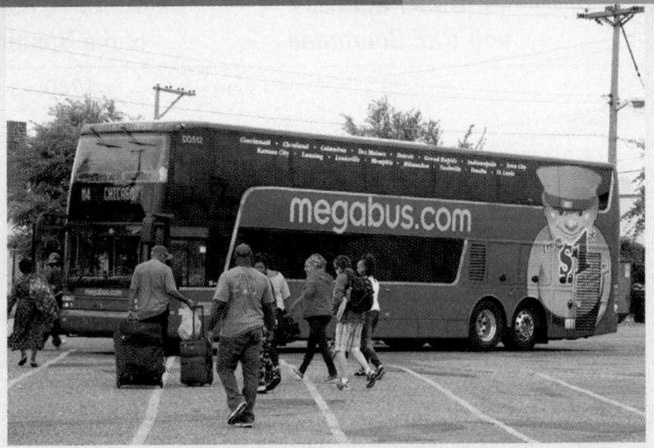

Many travelers are shunning airlines and leaving their cars at home to take the low-fare Megabus between major U.S. cities. Megabus, one of a growing number of express bus services, has a simple business model. Most tickets are sold online and are paperless. The first passengers to reserve seats on each bus get the cheapest prices, often starting at $1, and fares vary based on demand. Buses outfitted with free Wi-Fi connections and other perks link city centers such as Boston, New York, and Washington, D.C. The buses make few if any stops, so travel times are often the same as driving and only slightly longer than taking the train, at a fraction of the price.

To offer rock-bottom prices and good service, Megabus is fanatical about keeping costs down. Aside from buses and a barebones back-office staff, Megabus has virtually no fixed costs. The company has drastically reduced rent and labor expenses, eschewing bus terminals for city-center curbside pickup, and customers pay extra to order tickets from an agent. The bus fleet is also in constant use. As chief executive Dale Moser stated, "You cut all that overhead out of your business, you find you can pass that savings on to customers, thus driving volume." Without high fixed costs, Megabus can also easily add and subtract departures profitably. During the Thanksgiving and Christmas holiday seasons, Megabus sells as many tickets as are requested on its Web site, adding buses as needed.

Since hitting the road in 2006, Megabus has changed the way many Americans—especially those in their 20s and 30s—travel. In 2012, Megabus did $152.8 million in business with profits of $21 million, and the company served its 25 millionth customer.

Sources: Ben Austen, "The Megabus Effect," *Bloomberg Businessweek* (April 7, 2011); Ken Belson, "Thinking Outside Rails and Runways, and Taking the Bus," *The New York Times* (May 5, 2010); Josh Sanburn, "Reinventing The Wheels," *Time* (November 15, 2012); No author, "Stagecoach gets on the buses for improved profits," *Yorkshire Post* (June 27, 2013); Stagecoach Group plc, Preliminary results for the year ended 30 April 2013 (Perth, Scotland: Stagecoach Group plc, 2013).

Learning Objective 7

Apply CVP analysis to a company producing multiple products

...assume sales mix of products remains constant as total units sold changes

Effects of Sales Mix on Income

Sales mix is the quantities (or proportion) of various products (or services) that constitute a company's total unit sales. Suppose Emma is now budgeting for a subsequent college fair in New York. She plans to sell two different test-prep packages—*GMAT Success* and *GRE Guarantee*—and budgets the following:

	GMAT Success	*GRE Guarantee*	Total
Expected sales	60	40	100
Revenues, \$200 and \$100 per unit	\$12,000	\$4,000	\$16,000
Variable costs, \$120 and \$70 per unit	7,200	2,800	10,000
Contribution margin, \$80 and \$30 per unit	\$ 4,800	\$1,200	6,000
Fixed costs			4,500
Operating income			\$ 1,500

What is the breakeven point for Emma's business now? The total number of units that must be sold to break even in a multiproduct company depends on the sales mix. For Emma, this is the combination of the number of units of *GMAT Success* sold and the number of units of *GRE Guarantee* sold. We assume that the budgeted sales mix (60 units of *GMAT Success* sold for every 40 units of *GRE Guarantee* sold, that is, a ratio of 3:2) will not change at different levels of total unit sales. That is, we think of Emma selling a bundle of 3 units of *GMAT Success* and 2 units of *GRE Guarantee*. (Note that this does not mean that Emma physically bundles the two products together into one big package.)

Each bundle yields a contribution margin of \$300, calculated as follows:

	Number of Units of *GMAT Success* and *GRE Guarantee* in Each Bundle	Contribution Margin per Unit for *GMAT Success* and *GRE Guarantee*	Contribution Margin of the Bundle
GMAT *Success*	3	\$80	\$240
GRE *Guarantee*	2	30	60
Total			\$300

To compute the breakeven point, we calculate the number of bundles Emma needs to sell.

$$\text{Breakeven point in bundles} = \frac{\text{Fixed costs}}{\text{Contribution margin per bundle}} = \frac{\$4{,}500}{\$300 \text{ per bundle}} = 15 \text{ bundles}$$

The breakeven point in units of *GMAT Success* and *GRE Guarantee* is as follows:

GMAT Success: 15 bundles × 3 units per bundle	45 units
GRE Guarantee: 15 bundles × 2 units per bundle	30 units
Total number of units to break even	75 units

The breakeven point in dollars for *GMAT Success* and *GRE Guarantee* is as follows:

GMAT Success: 45 units × \$200 per unit	\$ 9,000
GRE Guarantee: 30 units × \$100 per unit	3,000
Breakeven revenues	\$12,000

When there are multiple products, it is often convenient to use the contribution margin percentage. Under this approach, Emma also calculates the revenues from selling a bundle of 3 units of *GMAT Success* and 2 units of *GRE Guarantee*:

	Number of Units of *GMAT Success* and *GRE Guarantee* in Each Bundle	Selling Price for *GMAT Success* and *GRE Guarantee*	Revenue of the Bundle
GMAT *Success*	3	$200	$600
GRE *Guarantee*	2	100	200
Total			$800

$$\text{Contribution margin percentage for the bundle} = \frac{\text{Contribution margin of the bundle}}{\text{Revenue of the bundle}} = \frac{\$300}{\$800} = 0.375, \text{ or } 37.5\%$$

$$\text{Breakeven revenues} = \frac{\text{Fixed costs}}{\text{Contribution margin \% for the bundle}} = \frac{\$4{,}500}{0.375} = \$12{,}000$$

$$\text{Number of bundles required to be sold to break even} = \frac{\text{Breakeven revenues}}{\text{Revenue per bundle}} = \frac{\$12{,}000}{\$800 \text{ per bundle}} = 15 \text{ bundles}$$

The breakeven point in units and dollars for *GMAT Success* and *GRE Guarantee* are as follows:

GMAT Success: 15 bundles × 3 units per bundle = 45 units × $200 per unit = $9,000

GRE Guarantee: 15 bundles × 2 units per bundle = 30 units × $100 per unit = $3,000

Recall that in all our calculations we have assumed that the budgeted sales mix (3 units of *GMAT Success* for every 2 units of *GRE Guarantee*) will not change at different levels of total unit sales.

Of course, there are many different sales mixes (in units) that can result in a contribution margin of $4,500 and cause Emma to break even, as the following table shows:

Sales Mix (Units)		Contribution Margin from		
GMAT Success **(1)**	***GRE Guarantee*** **(2)**	***GMAT Success*** **(3) = $80 × (1)**	***GRE Guarantee*** **(4) = $30 × (2)**	**Total Contribution Margin (5) = (3) + (4)**
48	22	$3,840	$ 660	$4,500
36	54	2,880	1,620	4,500
30	70	2,400	2,100	4,500

If, for example, the sales mix changes to 3 units of *GMAT Success* for every 7 units of *GRE Guarantee*, the breakeven point increases from 75 units to 100 units, composed of 30 units of *GMAT Success* and 70 units of *GRE Guarantee*. The breakeven quantity increases because the sales mix has shifted toward the lower-contribution-margin product, *GRE Guarantee* (which is $30 per unit compared to *GMAT Success*'s $80 per unit). In general, for any given total quantity of units sold, as the sales mix shifts toward units with lower contribution margins (more units of *GRE Guarantee* compared to *GMAT Success*), the lower operating income will be.

How do companies choose their sales mix? They adjust their mix to respond to demand changes. For example, as gasoline prices increase and customers want smaller cars, auto companies, such as Ford, Volkswagen, and Toyota, shift their production mix to produce smaller cars. This shift to smaller cars might result in an increase in the breakeven point because the sales mix has shifted toward lower-contribution-margin products. Despite this increase in the breakeven point, shifting the sales mix to smaller cars is the correct decision because the demand for larger cars has fallen. At no point should a manager focus on changing the sales mix to lower the breakeven point without taking into account customer preferences and demand. Of course, the shift in sales mix to smaller cars prompts managers at Ford, Volkswagen, and Toyota to take other actions such as reducing fixed costs and increasing contribution margins on smaller cars by charging higher prices for features that customers are willing to pay for or lowering variable costs.

Decision Point

How can managers apply CVP analysis to a company producing multiple products?

The multiproduct case has two cost drivers, *GMAT Success* and *GRE Guarantee*, It shows how CVP and breakeven analyses can be adapted when there are multiple cost drivers. The key point is that many different combinations of cost drivers can result in a given contribution margin.

Learning Objective 8

Apply CVP analysis in service and not-for-profit organizations

...define appropriate output measures

CVP Analysis in Service and Not-for-Profit Organizations

So far, our CVP analysis has focused on Emma's merchandising company. Of course, managers at manufacturing companies such as BMW, service companies such as Bank of America, and not-for-profit organizations such as the United Way also use CVP analysis to make decisions. To apply CVP analysis in service and not-for-profit organizations, we need to focus on measuring their output, which is different from the tangible units sold by manufacturing and merchandising companies. Examples of output measures in various service industries (for example, airlines, hotels/motels, and hospitals) and not-for-profit organizations (for example, universities) are as follows:

Industry	Measure of Output
Airlines	Passenger miles
Hotels/motels	Room-nights occupied
Hospitals	Patient days
Universities	Student credit-hours

Consider the Oregon Department of Social Services, a not-for-profit agency that helps disabled people seeking employment. The agency has a \$900,000 budget appropriation from the State of Oregon (its revenue) for 2014. On average, the agency supplements each person's income by \$5,000 annually. The agency's only other costs are fixed costs of rent and administrative salaries equal to \$270,000. The agency manager wants to know how many people could be assisted in 2014. We can use CVP analysis here by setting the agency's operating income to \$0. Let Q be the number of disabled people to be assisted:

$$\text{Revenues} - \text{Variable costs} - \text{Fixed costs} = 0$$
$$\$900{,}000 - \$5{,}000\,Q - \$270{,}000 = 0$$
$$\$5{,}000\,Q = \$900{,}000 - \$270{,}000 = \$630{,}000$$
$$Q = \$630{,}000 \div \$5{,}000 \text{ per person} = 126 \text{ people}$$

Suppose the nonprofit's budget appropriation for 2015 will be reduced by 15% to \$900,000 × (1 − 0.15) = \$765,000. The manager wants to know how many people with disabilities could be assisted with this reduced budget. Assume the monetary assistance per person and the agency's fixed costs don't change:

$$\$765{,}000 - \$5{,}000\,Q - \$270{,}000 = 0$$
$$\$5{,}000\,Q = \$765{,}000 - \$270{,}000 = \$495{,}000$$
$$Q = \$495{,}000 \div \$5{,}000 \text{ per person} = 99 \text{ people}$$

So, in 2015, instead of assisting 126 people, the agency can assist only 99. Note the following two characteristics of the CVP relationships in this nonprofit situation:

1. The percentage drop in the number of people assisted, (126 − 99) ÷ 126, or 21.4%, is greater than the 15% reduction in the budget appropriation. It is greater because

the $270,000 in fixed costs still must be paid, leaving a proportionately lower budget to assist people. In other words, the percentage drop in people assisted exceeds the percentage drop in budget appropriation.

2. Given the reduced budget appropriation (revenues) of $765,000 in 2015, the manager can adjust the agency's operations to stay within this appropriation in one or more of three ways: (a) by reducing the number of people assisted from the current 126, (b) by reducing the variable cost per person (the extent of assistance given a person) from the current $5,000 per person, or (c) by reducing the agency's total fixed costs from the current $270,000.

Decision Point

How do managers apply CVP analysis in service and not-for-profit organizations?

Contribution Margin Versus Gross Margin

Learning Objective 9

Distinguish contribution margin

...revenues minus all variable costs

from gross margin

...revenues minus cost of goods sold

So far, we have developed two important concepts relating to profit margin—contribution margin, which was introduced in this chapter, and gross margin, which was discussed in Chapter 2. Is there a relationship between these two concepts? In the following equations, we clearly distinguish contribution margin, which provides information for CVP analysis, from gross margin, a measure of competitiveness, described in Chapter 2.

$$\text{Gross margin} = \text{Revenues} - \text{Cost of goods sold}$$
$$\text{Contribution margin} = \text{Revenues} - \text{All variable costs}$$

The gross margin measures how much a company can charge for its products over and above the cost of acquiring or producing them. Companies, such as brand-name pharmaceuticals producers, have high gross margins because their products are often patented and provide unique and distinctive benefits to consumers. In contrast, manufacturers of generic medicines and basic chemicals have low gross margins because the market for these products is highly competitive. Contribution margin indicates how much of a company's revenues are available to cover fixed costs. It helps in assessing the risk of losses. For example, the risk of loss is low if the contribution margin exceeds a company's fixed costs even when sales are low. Gross margin and contribution margin are related but give different insights. For example, a company operating in a competitive market with a low gross margin will have a low risk of loss if its fixed costs are small.

Consider the distinction between gross margin and contribution margin in the manufacturing sector. The concepts differ in two ways: fixed manufacturing costs and variable nonmanufacturing costs. The following example (figures assumed) illustrates this difference:

Contribution Income Statement Emphasizing Contribution Margin (in thousands)			Financial Accounting Income Statement Emphasizing Gross Margin (in thousands)	
Revenues		$1,000	Revenues	$1,000
Variable manufacturing costs	$250		Cost of goods sold (variable manufacturing costs, $250 + fixed manufacturing costs, $160)	410
Variable nonmanufacturing costs	270	520		
Contribution margin		480	Gross margin	590
Fixed manufacturing costs	160			
Fixed nonmanufacturing costs	138	298	Nonmanufacturing costs (variable, $270 + fixed $138)	408
Operating income		$ 182	Operating income	$ 182

Fixed manufacturing costs of $160,000 are not deducted from revenues when computing the contribution margin but are deducted when computing the gross margin. The cost of goods sold in a manufacturing company includes all variable manufacturing costs and all fixed manufacturing costs ($250,000 + $160,000). The company's variable nonmanufacturing costs (such as commissions paid to salespersons) of $270,000 are deducted from revenues when computing the contribution margin but are not deducted when computing gross margin.

Decision Point
What is the difference between contribution margin and gross margin?

Like contribution margin, gross margin can be expressed as a total, as an amount per unit, or as a percentage. For example, the **gross margin percentage** is the gross margin divided by revenues—59% ($590 ÷ $1,000) in our manufacturing-sector example.

One reason why managers sometimes confuse gross margin and contribution margin with each other is that the two are often identical in the case of merchandising companies because the cost of goods sold equals the variable cost of goods purchased (and subsequently sold).

Problem for Self-Study

Wembley Travel Agency specializes in flights between Los Angeles and London. It books passengers on United Airlines at $900 per round-trip ticket. Until last month, United paid Wembley a commission of 10% of the ticket price paid by each passenger. This commission was Wembley's only source of revenues. Wembley's fixed costs are $14,000 per month (for salaries, rent, and so on), and its variable costs, such as sales commissions and bonuses, are $20 per ticket purchased for a passenger.

United Airlines has just announced a revised payment schedule for all travel agents. It will now pay travel agents a 10% commission per ticket up to a maximum of $50. Any ticket costing more than $500 generates only a $50 commission, regardless of the ticket price. Wembley's managers are concerned about how United's new payment schedule will affect its breakeven point and profitability.

1. Under the old 10% commission structure, how many round-trip tickets must Wembley sell each month (a) to break even and (b) to earn an operating income of $7,000?
2. How does United's revised payment schedule affect your answers to (a) and (b) in requirement 1?

Solution

1. Wembley receives a 10% commission on each ticket: 10% × $900 = $90. Thus,

$$\text{Selling price} = \$90 \text{ per ticket}$$
$$\text{Variable cost per unit} = \$20 \text{ per ticket}$$
$$\text{Contribution margin per unit} = \$90 - \$20 = \$70 \text{ per ticket}$$
$$\text{Fixed costs} = \$14{,}000 \text{ per month}$$

a. $$\frac{\text{Breakeven number}}{\text{of tickets}} = \frac{\text{Fixed costs}}{\text{Contribution margin per unit}} = \frac{\$14{,}000}{\$70 \text{ per ticket}} = 200 \text{ tickets}$$

b. When target operating income = $7,000 per month,

$$\frac{\text{Quantity of tickets}}{\text{required to be sold}} = \frac{\text{Fixed costs} + \text{Target operating income}}{\text{Contribution margin per unit}}$$
$$= \frac{\$14{,}000 + \$7{,}000}{\$70 \text{ per ticket}} = \frac{\$21{,}000}{\$70 \text{ per ticket}} = 300 \text{ tickets}$$

2. Under the new system, Wembley would receive only $50 on the $900 ticket. Thus,

$$\text{Selling price} = \$50 \text{ per ticket}$$
$$\text{Variable cost per unit} = \$20 \text{ per ticket}$$
$$\text{Contribution margin per unit} = \$50 - \$20 = \$30 \text{ per ticket}$$
$$\text{Fixed costs} = \$14{,}000 \text{ per month}$$

a. $$\frac{\text{Breakeven number}}{\text{of tickets}} = \frac{\$14{,}000}{\$30 \text{ per ticket}} = 467 \text{ tickets (rounded up)}$$

b. $$\frac{\text{Quantity of tickets}}{\text{required to be sold}} = \frac{\$21{,}000}{\$30 \text{ per ticket}} = 700 \text{ tickets}$$

The $50 cap on the commission paid per ticket causes the breakeven point to more than double (from 200 to 467 tickets) and the tickets required to be sold to earn $7,000 per month to also more than double (from 300 to 700 tickets). As would be expected, managers at Wembley reacted very negatively to the United Airlines announcement to change commission payments. Unfortunately for Wembley, other airlines also changed their commission structure in similar ways.

▸ Decision Points

The following question-and-answer format summarizes the chapter's learning objectives. Each decision presents a key question related to a learning objective. The guidelines are the answer to that question.

Decision	Guidelines
1. How can CVP analysis help managers?	CVP analysis assists managers in understanding the behavior of a product's or service's total costs, total revenues, and operating income as changes occur in the output level, selling price, variable costs, or fixed costs.
2. How can managers determine the breakeven point or the output needed to achieve a target operating income?	The breakeven point is the quantity of output at which total revenues equal total costs. The three methods for computing the breakeven point and the quantity of output to achieve target operating income are the equation method, the contribution margin method, and the graph method. Each method is merely a restatement of the others. Managers often select the method they find easiest to use in a specific decision situation.
3. How can managers incorporate income taxes into CVP analysis?	Income taxes can be incorporated into CVP analysis by using the target net income to calculate the target operating income. The breakeven point is unaffected by income taxes because no income taxes are paid when operating income equals zero.
4. How do managers use CVP analysis to make decisions?	Managers compare how revenues, costs, and contribution margins change across various alternatives. They then choose the alternative that maximizes operating income.
5. What can managers do to cope with uncertainty or changes in underlying assumptions?	Sensitivity analysis is a "what-if" technique that examines how an outcome will change if the original predicted data are not achieved or if an underlying assumption changes. When making decisions, managers use CVP analysis to compare contribution margins and fixed costs under different assumptions. Managers also calculate the margin of safety equal to budgeted revenues minus breakeven revenues.
6. How should managers choose among different variable-cost/fixed-cost structures?	Choosing the variable-cost/fixed-cost structure is a strategic decision for companies. CVP analysis helps managers compare the risk of losses when revenues are low and the upside profits when revenues are high for different proportions of variable and fixed costs in a company's cost structure.
7. How can managers apply CVP analysis to a company producing multiple products?	Managers apply CVP analysis in a company producing multiple products by assuming the sales mix of products sold remains constant as the total quantity of units sold changes.
8. How do managers apply CVP analysis in service and not-for-profit organizations?	Managers define output measures such as passenger-miles in the case of airlines or patient-days in the context of hospitals and identify costs that are fixed and those that vary with these measures of output.
9. What is the difference between contribution margin and gross margin?	Contribution margin is revenues minus all variable costs whereas gross margin is revenues minus cost of goods sold. Contribution margin measures the risk of a loss, whereas gross margin measures the competitiveness of a product.

Appendix

Decision Models and Uncertainty[2]

This appendix explores the characteristics of uncertainty, describes an approach managers can use to make decisions in a world of uncertainty, and illustrates the insights gained when uncertainty is recognized in CVP analysis. In the face of uncertainty, managers rely on decision models to help them make the right choices.

Role of a Decision Model

Uncertainty is the possibility that an actual amount will deviate from an expected amount. In the *GMAT Success* example, Emma might forecast sales at 42 units, but actual sales might turn out to be 30 units or 60 units. A decision model helps managers deal with such uncertainty. It is a formal method for making a choice, commonly involving both quantitative and qualitative analyses. The quantitative analysis usually includes the following steps:

Step 1: Identify a choice criterion. A **choice criterion** is an objective that can be quantified, such as maximize income or minimize costs. Managers use the choice criterion to choose the best alternative action. Emma's choice criterion is to maximize expected operating income at the Chicago college fair.

Step 2: Identify the set of alternative actions that can be taken. We use the letter *a* with subscripts $_{1, 2,}$ and $_3$ to distinguish each of Emma's three possible actions:

a_1 = Pay \$2,000 fixed fee

a_2 = Pay \$800 fixed fee plus15% of *GMAT Success* revenues

a_3 = Pay 25% of *GMAT Success* revenues with no fixed fee

Step 3: Identify the set of events that can occur. An **event** is a possible relevant occurrence, such as the actual number of *GMAT Success* packages Emma might sell at the fair. The set of events should be mutually exclusive and collectively exhaustive. Events are mutually exclusive if they cannot occur at the same time. Events are collectively exhaustive if, taken together, they make up the entire set of possible relevant occurrences (no other event can occur). Examples of mutually exclusive and collectively exhaustive events are growth, decline, or no change in industry demand and increase, decrease, or no change in interest rates. Only one event out of the entire set of mutually exclusive and collectively exhaustive events will actually occur.

Suppose Emma's only uncertainty is the number of units of *GMAT Success* that she can sell. For simplicity, suppose Emma estimates that sales will be either 30 or 60 units. This set of events is mutually exclusive because clearly sales of 30 units and 60 units cannot both occur at the same time. It is collectively exhaustive because under our assumptions sales cannot be anything other than 30 or 60 units. We use the letter *x* with subscripts $_1$ and $_2$ to distinguish the set of mutually exclusive and collectively exhaustive events:

x_1 = 30 units

x_2 = 60 units

Step 4: Assign a probability to each event that can occur. A **probability** is the likelihood or chance that an event will occur. The decision model approach to coping with uncertainty assigns probabilities to events. A **probability distribution** describes the likelihood, or the probability, that each of the mutually exclusive and collectively exhaustive set of events will occur. In some cases, there will be much evidence to guide the assignment of probabilities. For example, the probability of obtaining heads in the toss of a coin is 1/2 and that of drawing a particular playing card from a standard, well-shuffled deck is 1/52. In business, the probability of having a specified percentage of defective units may be

[2] *Source:* Based on teaching notes prepared by R. Williamson.

assigned with great confidence on the basis of production experience with thousands of units. In other cases, there will be little evidence supporting estimated probabilities—for example, expected sales of a new pharmaceutical product next year. Suppose that Emma, on the basis of past experience, assesses a 60% chance, or a 6/10 probability, that she will sell 30 units and a 40% chance, or a 4/10 probability, that she will sell 60 units. Using $P(x)$ as the notation for the probability of an event, the probabilities are as follows:

$$P(x_1) = 6/10 = 0.60$$
$$P(x_2) = 4/10 = 0.40$$

The sum of these probabilities must equal 1.00 because these events are mutually exclusive and collectively exhaustive.

Step 5: Identify the set of possible outcomes. **Outcomes** specify, in terms of the choice criterion, the predicted economic results of the various possible combinations of actions and events. In the *GMAT Success* example, the outcomes are the six possible operating incomes displayed in the decision table in Exhibit 3-6. A **decision table** is a summary of the alternative actions, events, outcomes, and probabilities of events.

Distinguish among actions, events, and outcomes. Actions are decision choices available to managers—for example, the particular rental alternatives that Emma can choose. Events are the set of all relevant occurrences that can happen—for example, the different quantities of *GMAT Success* packages that may be sold at the fair. The outcome is operating income, which depends both on the action the manager selects (rental alternative chosen) and the event that occurs (the quantity of packages sold).

Exhibit 3-7 presents an overview of relationships among a decision model, the implementation of a chosen action, its outcome, and subsequent performance evaluation. Thoughtful managers step back and evaluate what happened and learn from their experiences. This learning serves as feedback for adapting the decision model for future actions.

Expected Value

An **expected value** is the weighted average of the outcomes, with the probability of each outcome serving as the weight. When the outcomes are measured in monetary terms, expected value is often called **expected monetary value.** Using information in Exhibit 3-6,

Exhibit 3-6 Decision Table for *GMAT Success*

Home | Insert | Page Layout | Formulas | Data | Review | View

	A	B	C	D	E–F	G	H–I
1	Selling price =	$200		Operating Income			
2	Package cost =	$120		Under Each Possible Event			
3			Percentage				
4		Fixed	of Fair	Event x_1: Units Sold =	30	Event x_2: Units Sold =	60
5	Actions	Fee	Revenues	Probability(x_1) =	0.60	Probability(x_2) =	0.40
6	a_1: Pay $2,000 fixed fee	$2,000	0%	$400[l]		$2,800[m]	
7	a_2: Pay $800 fixed fee plus 15% of revenues	$ 800	15%	$700[n]		$2,200[p]	
8	a_3: Pay 25% of revenues with no fixed fee	$ 0	25%	$900[q]		$1,800[r]	
9							
10	[l]Operating income = ($200 – $120)(30) – $2,000	=	$ 400				
11	[m]Operating income = ($200 – $120)(60) – $2,000	=	$2,800				
12	[n]Operating income = ($200 – $120 – 15% × $200)(30) – $800	=	$ 700				
13	[p]Operating income = ($200 – $120 – 15% × $200)(60) – $800	=	$2,200				
14	[q]Operating income = ($200 – $120 – 25% × $200)(30)	=	$ 900				
15	[r]Operating income = ($200 – $120 – 25% × $200)(60)	=	$1,800				

Exhibit 3-7 A Decision Model and Its Link to Performance Evaluation

Decision Model 1. Choice criterion 2. Set of alternative actions 3. Set of relevant events 4. Set of probabilities 5. Set of possible outcomes	→	Implementation of Chosen Action	Uncertainty Resolved*	→	Outcome of Chosen Action	→	Performance Evaluation

Feedback (from Performance Evaluation back to Decision Model)

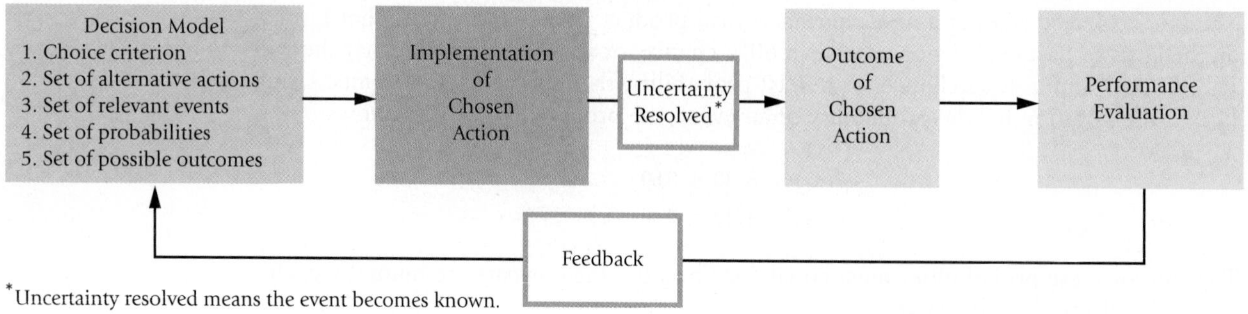

*Uncertainty resolved means the event becomes known.

the expected monetary value of each booth-rental alternative denoted by $E(a_1)$, $E(a_2)$, and $E(a_3)$ is as follows:

Pay \$2,000 fixed fee:	$E(a_1) = (0.60 \times \$400) + (0.40 \times \$2{,}800) = \$1{,}360$
Pay \$800 fixed fee plus 15% of revenues:	$E(a_2) = (0.60 \times \$700) + (0.40 \times \$2{,}200) = \$1{,}300$
Pay 25% of revenues with no fixed fee:	$E(a_3) = (0.60 \times \$900) + (0.40 \times \$1{,}800) = \$1{,}260$

To maximize expected operating income, Emma should select action a_1—*pay* the fair organizers a \$2,000 fixed fee.

To interpret the expected value of selecting action a_1, imagine that Emma attends many fairs, each with the probability distribution of operating incomes given in Exhibit 3-6. For a specific fair, Emma will earn operating income of either \$400, if she sells 30 units, or \$2,800, if she sells 60 units. But if Emma attends 100 fairs, she will expect to earn \$400 operating income 60% of the time (at 60 fairs) and \$2,800 operating income 40% of the time (at 40 fairs), for a total operating income of \$136,000 (\$400 × 60 + \$2,800 × 40). The expected value of \$1,360 is the operating income per fair that Emma will earn when averaged across all fairs (\$136,000 ÷ 100). Of course, in many real-world situations, managers must make one-time decisions under uncertainty. Even in these cases, expected value is a useful tool for choosing among alternatives.

Consider the effect of uncertainty on the preferred action choice. If Emma were certain she would sell only 30 units (that is, $P(x_1) = 1$), she would prefer alternative a_3 —pay 25% of revenues with no fixed fee. To follow this reasoning, examine Exhibit 3-6. When 30 units are sold, alternative a_3 yields the maximum operating income of \$900. Because fixed costs are \$0, booth-rental costs are lower, equal to \$1,500 (25% of revenues = 0.25 × \$200 per unit × 30 units), when sales are low.

However, if Emma were certain she would sell 60 packages (that is, $P(x_2) = 1$), she would prefer alternative a_1—pay a \$2,000 fixed fee. Exhibit 3-6 indicates that when 60 units are sold, alternative a_1 yields the maximum operating income of \$2,800. That's because, when 60 units are sold, rental payments under a_2 (\$800 + 0.15 × \$200 per unit × 60 units = \$2,600) and a_3 (0.25 × \$200 per unit × 60 units = \$3,000) are more than the fixed \$2,000 fee under a_1.

Despite the high probability of selling only 30 units, Emma still prefers to take action a_1, which is to pay a fixed fee of \$2,000. That's because the high risk of low operating income (the 60% probability of selling only 30 units) is more than offset by the high return from selling 60 units, which has a 40% probability. If Emma were more averse to risk (measured in our example by the difference between operating incomes when 30 vs. 60 units are sold), she might have preferred action a_2 or a_3. For example, action a_2 ensures an operating income of at least \$700, greater than the operating income of \$400 that she would earn under action a_1 if only 30 units were sold. Of course, choosing a_2 limits the upside potential to \$2,200 relative to \$2,800 under a_1, if 60 units are sold. If Emma is very concerned about downside risk, however, she may be willing to forgo some upside benefits to protect against a \$400 outcome by choosing a_2.[3]

[3] For more formal approaches, refer to Moore, J., and L. Weatherford, *Decision modeling with Microsoft Excel*, 6th ed. (Upper Saddle River, NJ: Prentice Hall, 2001).

Good Decisions and Good Outcomes

Always distinguish between a good decision and a good outcome. One can exist without the other. Suppose you are offered a one-time-only gamble tossing a coin. You will win $20 if the outcome is heads, but you will lose $1 if the outcome is tails. As a decision maker, you proceed through the logical phases: gathering information, assessing outcomes, and making a choice. You accept the bet. Why? Because the expected value is $9.50 [0.5($20) + 0.5(− $1)]. The coin is tossed and the outcome is tails. You lose. From your viewpoint, this was a good decision but a bad outcome.

A decision can be made only on the basis of information that is available at the time of evaluating and making the decision. By definition, uncertainty rules out guaranteeing that the best outcome will always be obtained. As in our example, it is possible that bad luck will produce bad outcomes even when good decisions have been made. A bad outcome does not mean a bad decision was made. The best protection against a bad outcome is a good decision.

Terms to Learn

This chapter and the Glossary at the end of the book contain definitions of the following important terms:

breakeven point (BEP) **(p. 73)**
choice criterion **(p. 90)**
contribution income statement **(p. 69)**
contribution margin **(p. 68)**
contribution margin per unit **(p. 69)**
contribution margin percentage **(p. 69)**
contribution margin ratio **(p. 69)**
cost–volume–profit (CVP) analysis **(p. 67)**
decision table **(p. 91)**
degree of operating leverage **(p. 82)**
event **(p. 90)**
expected monetary value **(p. 91)**
expected value **(p. 91)**
gross margin percentage **(p. 88)**
margin of safety **(p. 79)**
net income **(p. 76)**
operating leverage **(p. 82)**
outcomes **(p. 91)**
probability **(p. 90)**
probability distribution **(p. 90)**
PV graph **(p. 75)**
revenue driver **(p. 72)**
sales mix **(p. 84)**
sensitivity analysis **(p. 79)**
uncertainty **(p. 80)**

Assignment Material

Note: To underscore the basic CVP relationships, the assignment material ignores income taxes unless stated otherwise.

Questions

MyAccountingLab

3-1 Define cost–volume–profit analysis.
3-2 Describe the assumptions underlying CVP analysis.
3-3 Distinguish between operating income and net income.
3-4 Define contribution margin, contribution margin per unit, and contribution margin percentage.
3-5 Describe three methods that managers can use to express CVP relationships.
3-6 Why is it more accurate to describe the subject matter of this chapter as CVP analysis rather than as breakeven analysis?
3-7 "CVP analysis is both simple and simplistic. If you want realistic analysis to underpin your decisions, look beyond CVP analysis." Do you agree? Explain.
3-8 How does an increase in the income tax rate affect the breakeven point?
3-9 Describe sensitivity analysis. How has the advent of the electronic spreadsheet affected the use of sensitivity analysis?
3-10 Give an example of how a manager can decrease variable costs while increasing fixed costs.
3-11 Give an example of how a manager can increase variable costs while decreasing fixed costs.
3-12 What is operating leverage? How is knowing the degree of operating leverage helpful to managers?
3-13 "There is no such thing as a fixed cost. All costs can be 'unfixed' given sufficient time." Do you agree? What is the implication of your answer for CVP analysis?
3-14 How can a company with multiple products compute its breakeven point?
3-15 "In CVP analysis, gross margin is a less-useful concept than contribution margin." Do you agree? Explain briefly.

MyAccountingLab

Exercises

3-16 CVP computations. Fill in the blanks for each of the following independent cases.

Case	Revenues	Variable Costs	Fixed Costs	Total Costs	Operating Income	Contribution Margin Percentage
a.		$800		$1,200	$1,000	
b.	$2,400		$400		$ 700	
c.	$ 900	$500		$ 900		
d.	$1,800		$400			50%

3-17 CVP computations. Garrett Manufacturing sold 410,000 units of its product for $68 per unit in 2014. Variable cost per unit is $60, and total fixed costs are $1,640,000.

Required

1. Calculate (a) contribution margin and (b) operating income.
2. Garrett's current manufacturing process is labor intensive. Kate Schoenen, Garrett's production manager, has proposed investing in state-of-the-art manufacturing equipment, which will increase the annual fixed costs to $5,330,000. The variable costs are expected to decrease to $54 per unit. Garrett expects to maintain the same sales volume and selling price next year. How would acceptance of Schoenen's proposal affect your answers to (a) and (b) in requirement 1?
3. Should Garrett accept Schoenen's proposal? Explain.

3-18 CVP analysis, changing revenues and costs. Brilliant Travel Agency specializes in flights between Toronto and Jamaica. It books passengers on Ontario Air. Brilliant's fixed costs are $36,000 per month. Ontario Air charges passengers $1,300 per round-trip ticket.

Calculate the number of tickets Brilliant must sell each month to (a) break even and (b) make a target operating income of $12,000 per month in each of the following independent cases.

Required

1. Brilliant's variable costs are $34 per ticket. Ontario Air pays Brilliant 10% commission on ticket price.
2. Brilliant's variable costs are $30 per ticket. Ontario Air pays Brilliant 10% commission on ticket price.
3. Brilliant's variable costs are $30 per ticket. Ontario Air pays $46 fixed commission per ticket to Brilliant. Comment on the results.
4. Brilliant's variable costs are $30 per ticket. It receives $46 commission per ticket from Ontario Air. It charges its customers a delivery fee of $8 per ticket. Comment on the results.

3-19 CVP exercises. The Incredible Donut owns and operates six doughnut outlets in and around Kansas City. You are given the following corporate budget data for next year:

Revenues	$10,400,000
Fixed costs	$ 2,100,000
Variable costs	$ 7,900,000

Variable costs change based on the number of doughnuts sold.

Compute the budgeted operating income for each of the following deviations from the original budget data. (Consider each case independently.)

Required

1. An 11% increase in contribution margin, holding revenues constant
2. An 11% decrease in contribution margin, holding revenues constant
3. A 4% increase in fixed costs
4. A 4% decrease in fixed costs
5. A 7% increase in units sold
6. A 7% decrease in units sold
7. An 11% increase in fixed costs and a 11% increase in units sold
8. A 4% increase in fixed costs and a 4% decrease in variable costs
9. Which of these alternatives yields the highest budgeted operating income? Explain why this is the case.

3-20 CVP exercises. The Doral Company manufactures and sells pens. Currently, 5,000,000 units are sold per year at $0.50 per unit. Fixed costs are $900,000 per year. Variable costs are $0.30 per unit.

Consider each case separately:

Required

1. **a.** What is the current annual operating income?
   b. What is the present breakeven point in revenues?

Compute the new operating income for each of the following changes:

2. A $0.04 per unit increase in variable costs
3. A 10% increase in fixed costs and a 10% increase in units sold
4. A 20% decrease in fixed costs, a 20% decrease in selling price, a 10% decrease in variable cost per unit, and a 40% increase in units sold

Compute the new breakeven point in units for each of the following changes:

5. A 10% increase in fixed costs
6. A 10% increase in selling price and a $20,000 increase in fixed costs

3-21 CVP analysis, income taxes. Brooke Motors is a small car dealership. On average, it sells a car for $27,000, which it purchases from the manufacturer for $23,000. Each month, Brooke Motors pays $48,200 in rent and utilities and $68,000 for salespeople's salaries. In addition to their salaries, salespeople are paid a commission of $600 for each car they sell. Brooke Motors also spends $13,000 each month for local advertisements. Its tax rate is 40%.

Required

1. How many cars must Brooke Motors sell each month to break even?
2. Brooke Motors has a target monthly net income of $51,000. What is its target monthly operating income? How many cars must be sold each month to reach the target monthly net income of $51,000?

3-22 CVP analysis, income taxes. The Swift Meal has two restaurants that are open 24 hours a day. Fixed costs for the two restaurants together total $456,000 per year. Service varies from a cup of coffee to full meals. The average sales check per customer is $9.50. The average cost of food and other variable costs for each customer is $3.80. The income tax rate is 30%. Target net income is $159,600.

Required

1. Compute the revenues needed to earn the target net income.
2. How many customers are needed to break even? To earn net income of $159,600?
3. Compute net income if the number of customers is 145,000.

3-23 CVP analysis, sensitivity analysis. Tuff Kids Jeans Co. sells blue jeans wholesale to major retailers across the country. Each pair of jeans has a selling price of $30 with $21 in variable costs of goods sold. The company has fixed manufacturing costs of $1,200,000 and fixed marketing costs of $300,000. Sales commissions are paid to the wholesale sales reps at 5% of revenues. The company has an income tax rate of 25%.

Required

1. How many jeans must Tuff Kids sell in order to break even?
2. How many jeans must the company sell in order to reach:
   a. a target operating income of $450,000?
   b. a net income of $450,000?
3. How many jeans would TuffKids have to sell to earn the net income in part 2b if (consider each requirement independently).
   a. The contribution margin per unit increases by 10%
   b. The selling price is increased to $32.50
   c. The company outsources manufacturing to an overseas company increasing variable costs per unit by $2.00 and saving 60% of fixed manufacturing costs.

3-24 CVP analysis, margin of safety. Suppose Lattin Corp.'s breakeven point is revenues of $1,500,000. Fixed costs are $720,000.

Required

1. Compute the contribution margin percentage.
2. Compute the selling price if variable costs are $13 per unit.
3. Suppose 90,000 units are sold. Compute the margin of safety in units and dollars.
4. What does this tell you about the risk of Lattin making a loss? What are the most likely reasons for this risk to increase?

3-25 Operating leverage. Carmel Rugs is holding a 2-week carpet sale at Jean's Club, a local warehouse store. Carmel Rugs plans to sell carpets for $1,000 each. The company will purchase the carpets from a local distributor for $400 each, with the privilege of returning any unsold units for a full refund. Jean's Club has offered Carmel Rugs two payment alternatives for the use of space.

- Option 1: A fixed payment of $17,400 for the sale period
- Option 2: 20% of total revenues earned during the sale period

Assume Carmel Rugs will incur no other costs.

Required

1. Calculate the breakeven point in units for (a) option 1 and (b) option 2.
2. At what level of revenues will Carmel Rugs earn the same operating income under either option?
   a. For what range of unit sales will Carmel Rugs prefer option 1?
   b. For what range of unit sales will Carmel Rugs prefer option 2?
3. Calculate the degree of operating leverage at sales of 87 units for the two rental options.
4. Briefly explain and interpret your answer to requirement 3.

3-26 CVP analysis, international cost structure differences. Plush Decor, Inc., is considering three possible countries for the sole manufacturing site of its newest area rug: Italy, Spain, and Singapore. All area rugs are to be sold to retail outlets in the United States for $200 per unit. These retail outlets add their own markup when selling to final customers. Fixed costs and variable cost per unit (area rug) differ in the three countries.

Country	Sales Price to Retail Outlets	Annual Fixed Costs	Variable Manufacturing Cost per Area Rug	Variable Marketing & Distribution Cost per Area Rug
Italy	$200.00	$ 6,386,000	$70.00	$27.00
Spain	200.00	5,043,000	61.00	16.00
Singapore	200.00	12,240,000	84.00	14.00

Required

1. Compute the breakeven point for Plush Decor, Inc., in each country in (a) units sold and (b) revenues.
2. If Plush Decor, Inc., plans to produce and sell 80,000 rugs in 2014, what is the budgeted operating income for each of the three manufacturing locations? Comment on the results.

3-27 Sales mix, new and upgrade customers. Chartz 1-2-3 is a top-selling electronic spreadsheet product. Chartz is about to release version 5.0. It divides its customers into two groups: new customers and upgrade customers (those who previously purchased Chartz 1-2-3 4.0 or earlier versions). Although the same physical product is provided to each customer group, sizable differences exist in selling prices and variable marketing costs:

	New Customers		Upgrade Customers	
Selling price		$195		$115
Variable costs				
Manufacturing	$15		$15	
Marketing	50	65	20	35
Contribution margin		$130		$ 80

The fixed costs of Chartz 1-2-3 5.0 are $16,500,000. The planned sales mix in units is 60% new customers and 40% upgrade customers.

Required

1. What is the Chartz 1-2-3 5.0 breakeven point in units, assuming that the planned 60%/40% sales mix is attained?
2. If the sales mix is attained, what is the operating income when 170,000 total units are sold?
3. Show how the breakeven point in units changes with the following customer mixes:
   a. New 40% and upgrade 60%
   b. New 80% and upgrade 20%
   c. Comment on the results.

3-28 Sales mix, three products. The Janowski Company has three product lines of mugs—A, B, and C—with contribution margins of $5, $4, and $3, respectively. The president foresees sales of 168,000 units in the coming period, consisting of 24,000 units of A, 96,000 units of B, and 48,000 units of C. The company's fixed costs for the period are $405,000.

Required

1. What is the company's breakeven point in units, assuming that the given sales mix is maintained?
2. If the sales mix is maintained, what is the total contribution margin when 168,000 units are sold? What is the operating income?
3. What would operating income be if the company sold 24,000 units of A, 48,000 units of B, and 96,000 units of C? What is the new breakeven point in units if these relationships persist in the next period?
4. Comparing the breakeven points in requirements 1 and 3, is it always better for a company to choose the sales mix that yields the lower breakeven point? Explain.

3-29 CVP, not-for-profit. Genesee Music Society is a not-for-profit organization that brings guest artists to the community's greater metropolitan area. The music society just bought a small concert hall in the center of town to house its performances. The lease payments on the concert hall are expected to be $4,000 per month. The organization pays its guest performers $1,800 per concert and anticipates corresponding ticket sales to be $4,500 per concert. The music society also incurs costs of approximately $1,000 per concert for marketing and advertising. The organization pays its artistic director $33,000 per year and expects to receive $30,000 in donations in addition to its ticket sales.

Required

1. If the Genesee Music Society just breaks even, how many concerts does it hold?
2. In addition to the organization's artistic director, the music society would like to hire a marketing director for $25,500 per year. What is the breakeven point? The music society anticipates that the addition of a marketing director would allow the organization to increase the number of concerts to 41 per year. What is the music society's operating income/(loss) if it hires the new marketing director?
3. The music society expects to receive a grant that would provide the organization with an additional $17,000 toward the payment of the marketing director's salary. What is the breakeven point if the music society hires the marketing director and receives the grant?

3-30 Contribution margin, decision making. McCarthy Men's Clothing's revenues and cost data for 2014 are as follows:

Revenues		$500,000
Cost of goods sold		250,000
Gross margin		250,000
Operating costs:		
Salaries fixed	$160,000	
Sales commissions (11% of sales)	55,000	
Depreciation of equipment and fixtures	15,000	
Store rent ($4,000 per month)	48,000	
Other operating costs	40,000	318,000
Operating income (loss)		$ (68,000)

Mr. McCarthy, the owner of the store, is unhappy with the operating results. An analysis of other operating costs reveals that it includes $35,000 variable costs, which vary with sales volume, and $5,000 (fixed) costs.

Required

1. Compute the contribution margin of McCarthy Men's Clothing.
2. Compute the contribution margin percentage.
3. Mr. McCarthy estimates that he can increase units sold, and hence revenues by 20% by incurring additional advertising costs of $12,000. Calculate the impact of the additional advertising costs on operating income.
4. What other actions can Mr. McCarthy take to improve operating income?

3-31 Contribution margin, gross margin, and margin of safety. Mirabella Cosmetics manufactures and sells a face cream to small ethnic stores in the greater New York area. It presents the monthly operating income statement shown here to George Lopez, a potential investor in the business. Help Mr. Lopez understand Mirabella's cost structure.

	A	B	C	D
1	Mirabella Cosmetics			
2	Operating Income Statement, June 2014			
3	Units sold			10,000
4	Revenues			$100,000
5	Cost of goods sold			
6	Variable manufacturing costs		$55,000	
7	Fixed manufacturing costs		20,000	
8	Total			75,000
9	Gross margin			25,000
10	Operating costs			
11	Variable marketing costs		$ 5,000	
12	Fixed marketing & administration costs		10,000	
13	Total operating costs			15,000
14	Operating income			$ 10,000

Required

1. Recast the income statement to emphasize contribution margin.
2. Calculate the contribution margin percentage and breakeven point in units and revenues for June 2014.
3. What is the margin of safety (in units) for June 2014?
4. If sales in June were only 8,000 units and Mirabella's tax rate is 30%, calculate its net income.

3-32 Uncertainty and expected costs. Hillmart Corp., an international retail giant, is considering implementing a new business-to-business (B2B) information system for processing merchandise orders. The current system costs Hillmart $1,000,000 per month and $45 per order. Hillmart has two options, a partially automated B2B and a fully automated B2B system. The partially automated B2B system will have a fixed cost of $5,000,000 per month and a variable cost of $35 per order. The fully automated B2B system has a fixed cost of $11,000,000 per month and $20 per order.

Based on data from the past two years, Hillmart has determined the following distribution on monthly orders:

Monthly Number of Orders	Probability
300,000	0.15
400,000	0.20
500,000	0.40
600,000	0.15
700,000	0.10

Required

1. Prepare a table showing the cost of each plan for each quantity of monthly orders.
2. What is the expected cost of each plan?
3. In addition to the information systems costs, what other factors should Hillmart consider before deciding to implement a new B2B system?

MyAccountingLab

Problems

3-33 CVP analysis, service firm. Lifetime Escapes generates average revenue of $7,500 per person on its 5-day package tours to wildlife parks in Kenya. The variable costs per person are as follows:

Airfare	$1,600
Hotel accommodations	3,100
Meals	600
Ground transportation	300
Park tickets and other costs	700
Total	$6,300

Annual fixed costs total $570,000.

Required

1. Calculate the number of package tours that must be sold to break even.
2. Calculate the revenue needed to earn a target operating income of $102,000.

3. If fixed costs increase by $19,000, what decrease in variable cost per person must be achieved to maintain the breakeven point calculated in requirement 1?
4. The general manager at Lifetime Escapes proposes to increase the price of the package tour to $8,200 to decrease the breakeven point in units. Using information in the original problem, calculate the new breakeven point in units. What factors should the general manager consider before deciding to increase the price of the package tour?

3-34 CVP, target operating income, service firm. KinderKids provides daycare for children Mondays through Fridays. Its monthly variable costs per child are as follows:

Lunch and snacks	$100
Educational supplies	30
Other supplies (paper products, toiletries, etc.)	20
Total	$150

Monthly fixed costs consist of the following:

Rent	$1,500
Utilities	150
Insurance	200
Salaries	1,700
Miscellaneous	450
Total	$4,000

KinderKids charges each parent $400 per child per month.

Required

1. Calculate the breakeven point.
2. KinderKids' target operating income is $5,000 per month. Compute the number of children who must be enrolled to achieve the target operating income.
3. KinderKids lost its lease and had to move to another building. Monthly rent for the new building is $2,200. At the suggestion of parents, KinderKids plans to take children on field trips. Monthly costs of the field trips are $1,100. By how much should KinderKids increase fees per child to meet the target operating income of $5,000 per month, assuming the same number of children as in requirement 2?

3-35 CVP analysis, margin of safety. (CMA, adapted) Arvin Tax Preparation Services has total budgeted revenues for 2014 of $618,000, based on an average price of $206 per tax return prepared. The company would like to achieve a margin of safety percentage of at least 45%. The company's current fixed costs are $327,600, and variable costs average $24 per customer. (Consider each of the following separately).

Required

1. Calculate Arvin's breakeven point and margin of safety in units.
2. Which of the following changes would help Arvin achieve its desired margin of safety?
   a. Average revenue per customer increases to $224.
   b. Planned number of tax returns prepared increases by 15%
   c. Arvin purchases new tax software that results in a 5% increase to fixed costs but e-files all tax returns, which reduces mailing costs an average $2 per customer.

3-36 CVP analysis, income taxes. (CMA, adapted) J.T.Brooks and Company, a manufacturer of quality handmade walnut bowls, has had a steady growth in sales for the past 5 years. However, increased competition has led Mr. Brooks, the president, to believe that an aggressive marketing campaign will be necessary next year to maintain the company's present growth. To prepare for next year's marketing campaign, the company's controller has prepared and presented Mr. Brooks with the following data for the current year, 2014:

Variable cost (per bowl)	
Direct materials	$ 3.00
Direct manufacturing labor	8.00
Variable overhead (manufacturing, marketing, distribution, and customer service)	7.50
Total variable cost per bowl	$ 18.50
Fixed costs	
Manufacturing	$ 20,000
Marketing, distribution, and customer service	194,500
Total fixed costs	$214,500
Selling price	$ 35.00
Expected sales, 22,000 units	$770,000
Income tax rate	40%

Required

1. What is the projected net income for 2014?
2. What is the breakeven point in units for 2014?
3. Mr. Brooks has set the revenue target for 2015 at a level of $875,000 (or 25,000 bowls). He believes an additional marketing cost of $16,500 for advertising in 2015, with all other costs remaining constant, will be necessary to attain the revenue target. What is the net income for 2015 if the additional $16,500 is spent and the revenue target is met?
4. What is the breakeven point in revenues for 2015 if the additional $16,500 is spent for advertising?
5. If the additional $16,500 is spent, what are the required 2015 revenues for 2015 net income to equal 2014 net income?
6. At a sales level of 25,000 units, what maximum amount can be spent on advertising if a 2015 net income of $108,450 is desired?

3-37 CVP, sensitivity analysis. The Derby Shoe Company produces its famous shoe, the Divine Loafer that sells for $70 per pair. Operating income for 2013 is as follows:

Sales revenue ($70 per pair)	$350,000
Variable cost ($30 per pair)	150,000
Contribution margin	200,000
Fixed cost	100,000
Operating income	$100,000

Derby Shoe Company would like to increase its profitability over the next year by at least 25%. To do so, the company is considering the following options:

Required

1. Replace a portion of its variable labor with an automated machining process. This would result in a 20% decrease in variable cost per unit but a 15% increase in fixed costs. Sales would remain the same.
2. Spend $25,000 on a new advertising campaign, which would increase sales by 10%.
3. Increase both selling price by $10 per unit and variable costs by $8 per unit by using a higher-quality leather material in the production of its shoes. The higher-priced shoe would cause demand to drop by approximately 20%.
4. Add a second manufacturing facility that would double Derby's fixed costs but would increase sales by 60%.

Evaluate each of the alternatives considered by Derby Shoes. Do any of the options meet or exceed Derby's targeted increase in income of 25%? What should Derby do?

3-38 CVP analysis, shoe stores. The HighStep Shoe Company operates a chain of shoe stores that sell 10 different styles of inexpensive men's shoes with identical unit costs and selling prices. A unit is defined as a pair of shoes. Each store has a store manager who is paid a fixed salary. Individual salespeople receive a fixed salary and a sales commission. HighStep is considering opening another store that is expected to have the revenue and cost relationships shown here.

Home Insert Page Layout Formulas Data Review View

	A	B	C	D	E
1	**Unit Variable Data (per pair of shoes)**			**Annual Fixed Costs**	
2	Selling price	$60.00		Rent	$ 30,000
3	Cost of shoes	$37.00		Salaries	100,000
4	Sales commission	3.00		Advertising	40,000
5	Variable cost per unit	$40.00		Other fixed costs	10,000
6				Total fixed costs	$180,000

Consider each question independently:

Required

1. What is the annual breakeven point in (a) units sold and (b) revenues?
2. If 8,000 units are sold, what will be the store's operating income (loss)?

3. If sales commissions are discontinued and fixed salaries are raised by a total of $15,500, what would be the annual breakeven point in (a) units sold and (b) revenues?
4. Refer to the original data. If, in addition to his fixed salary, the store manager is paid a commission of $2.00 per unit sold, what would be the annual breakeven point in (a) units sold and (b) revenues?
5. Refer to the original data. If, in addition to his fixed salary, the store manager is paid a commission of $2.00 *per unit in excess of the breakeven point*, what would be the store's operating income if 12,000 units were sold?

3-39 CVP analysis, shoe stores (continuation of 3-38). Refer to requirement 3 of Problem 3-38. In this problem, assume the role of the owner of HighStep.

Required

1. As owner, which sales compensation plan would you choose if forecasted annual sales of the new store were at least 10,000 units? What do you think of the motivational aspect of your chosen compensation plan?
2. Suppose the target operating income is $69,000. How many units must be sold to reach the target operating income under (a) the original salary-plus-commissions plan and (b) the higher-fixed-salaries-only plan? Which method would you prefer? Explain briefly.
3. You open the new store on January 1, 2014, with the original salary-plus-commission compensation plan in place. Because you expect the cost of the shoes to rise due to inflation, you place a firm bulk order for 11,000 shoes and lock in the $37 price per unit. But toward the end of the year, only 9,500 shoes are sold, and you authorize a markdown of the remaining inventory to $50 per unit. Finally, all units are sold. Salespeople, as usual, get paid a commission of 5% of revenues. What is the annual operating income for the store?

3-40 Alternate cost structures, uncertainty, and sensitivity analysis. Deckle Printing Company currently leases its only copy machine for $1,200 a month. The company is considering replacing this leasing agreement with a new contract that is entirely commission based. Under the new agreement, Deckle would pay a commission for its printing at a rate of $20 for every 500 pages printed. The company currently charges $0.15 per page to its customers. The paper used in printing costs the company $0.04 per page and other variable costs, including hourly labor amounting to $0.05 per page.

Required

1. What is the company's breakeven point under the current leasing agreement? What is it under the new commission-based agreement?
2. For what range of sales levels will Deckle prefer (a) the fixed lease agreement (b) the commission agreement?
3. Do this question only if you have covered the chapter appendix in your class. Deckle estimates that the company is equally likely to sell 20,000, 30,000, 40,000, 50,000, or 60,000 pages of print. Using information from the original problem, prepare a table that shows the expected profit at each sales level under the fixed leasing agreement and under the commission-based agreement. What is the expected value of each agreement? Which agreement should Deckle choose?

3-41 CVP, alternative cost structures. SuperShades operates a kiosk at the local mall, selling sunglasses for $20 each. SuperShades currently pays $800 a month to rent the space and pays two full-time employees to each work 160 hours a month at $10 per hour. The store shares a manager with a neighboring mall and pays 50% of the manager's annual salary of $40,000 and benefits equal to 20% of salary. The wholesale cost of the sunglasses to the company is $5 a pair.

Required

1. How many sunglasses does SuperShades need to sell each month to break even?
2. If SuperShades wants to earn an operating income of $4,500 per month, how many sunglasses does the store need to sell?
3. If the store's hourly employees agreed to a 15% sales-commission-only pay structure, instead of their hourly pay, how many sunglasses would SuperShades need to sell to earn an operating income of $4,500?
4. Assume SuperShades pays its employees hourly under the original pay structure, but is able to pay the mall 8% of its monthly revenue instead of monthly rent. At what sales levels would SuperShades prefer to pay a fixed amount of monthly rent, and at what sales levels would it prefer to pay 8% of its monthly revenue as rent?

3-42 CVP analysis, income taxes, sensitivity. (CMA, adapted) Carlisle Engine Company manufactures and sells diesel engines for use in small farming equipment. For its 2014 budget, Carlisle Engine Company estimates the following:

Selling price	$ 4,000
Variable cost per engine	$ 1,000
Annual fixed costs	$4,800,000
Net income	$1,200,000
Income tax rate	20%

The first-quarter income statement, as of March 31, reported that sales were not meeting expectations. During the first quarter, only 400 units had been sold at the current price of $4,000. The income statement showed that variable and fixed costs were as planned, which meant that the 2014 annual net income projection would not be met unless management took action. A management committee was formed and presented the following mutually exclusive alternatives to the president:

a. Reduce the selling price by 15%. The sales organization forecasts that at this significantly reduced price, 2,100 units can be sold during the remainder of the year. Total fixed costs and variable cost per unit will stay as budgeted.
b. Lower variable cost per unit by $300 through the use of less-expensive direct materials. The selling price will also be reduced by $400, and sales of 1,750 units are expected for the remainder of the year.
c. Reduce fixed costs by 10% and lower the selling price by 30%. Variable cost per unit will be unchanged. Sales of 2,200 units are expected for the remainder of the year.

Required

1. If no changes are made to the selling price or cost structure, determine the number of units that Carlisle Engine Company must sell (a) to break even and (b) to achieve its net income objective.
2. Determine which alternative Carlisle Engine should select to achieve its net income objective. Show your calculations.

3-43 Choosing between compensation plans, operating leverage. (CMA, adapted) BioPharm Corporation manufactures pharmaceutical products that are sold through a network of external sales agents. The agents are paid a commission of 20% of revenues. BioPharm is considering replacing the sales agents with its own salespeople, who would be paid a commission of 13% of revenues and total salaries of $2,240,000. The income statement for the year ending December 31, 2013, under the two scenarios is shown here.

	A	B	C	D	E
1	BioPharm Corporation				
2	Income Statement				
3	For the Year Ended December 31, 2013				
4		Using Sales Agents		Using Own Sales Force	
5	Revenues		$32,000,000		$32,000,000
6	Cost of goods sold				
7	Variable	$12,160,000		$12,160,000	
8	Fixed	3,750,000	15,910,000	3,750,000	15,910,000
9	Gross margin		16,090,000		16,090,000
10	Marketing costs				
11	Commissions	$ 6,400,000		$ 4,160,000	
12	Fixed costs	3,660,000	10,060,000	5,900,000	10,060,000
13	Operating income		$ 6,030,000		$ 6,030,000

Required

1. Calculate BioPharm's 2013 contribution margin percentage, breakeven revenues, and degree of operating leverage under the two scenarios.
2. Describe the advantages and disadvantages of each type of sales alternative.
3. In 2014, BioPharm uses its own salespeople, who demand a 16% commission. If all other cost-behavior patterns are unchanged, how much revenue must the salespeople generate in order to earn the same operating income as in 2013?

3-44 Sales mix, three products. The Ronowski Company has three product lines of belts—A, B, and C—with contribution margins of $3, $2, and $1, respectively. The president foresees sales of 200,000 units in the coming period, consisting of 20,000 units of A, 100,000 units of B, and 80,000 units of C. The company's fixed costs for the period are $255,000.

Required

1. What is the company's breakeven point in units, assuming that the given sales mix is maintained?
2. If the sales mix is maintained, what is the total contribution margin when 200,000 units are sold? What is the operating income?
3. What would operating income be if 20,000 units of A, 80,000 units of B, and 100,000 units of C were sold? What is the new breakeven point in units if these relationships persist in the next period?

3-45 Multiproduct CVP and decision making. Crystal Clear Products produces two types of water filters. One attaches to the faucet and cleans all water that passes through the faucet. The other is a pitcher-cum-filter that only purifies water meant for drinking.

The unit that attaches to the faucet is sold for $100 and has variable costs of $35.
The pitcher-cum-filter sells for $120 and has variable costs of $30.

Crystal Clear sells two faucet models for every three pitchers sold. Fixed costs equal $1,200,000.

Required

1. What is the breakeven point in unit sales and dollars for each type of filter at the current sales mix?
2. Crystal Clear is considering buying new production equipment. The new equipment will increase fixed cost by $208,000 per year and will decrease the variable cost of the faucet and the pitcher units by $5 and $10, respectively. Assuming the same sales mix, how many of each type of filter does Crystal Clear need to sell to break even?
3. Assuming the same sales mix, at what total sales level would Crystal Clear be indifferent between using the old equipment and buying the new production equipment? If total sales are expected to be 24,000 units, should Crystal Clear buy the new production equipment?

3-46 Sales mix, two products. The Stackpole Company retails two products: a standard and a deluxe version of a luggage carrier. The budgeted income statement for next period is as follows:

	Standard Carrier	Deluxe Carrier	Total
Units sold	187,500	62,500	250,000
Revenues at $28 and $50 per unit	$5,250,000	$3,125,000	$8,375,000
Variable costs at $18 and $30 per unit	3,375,000	1,875,000	5,250,000
Contribution margins at $10 and $20 per unit	$1,875,000	$1,250,000	3,125,000
Fixed costs			2,250,000
Operating income			$ 875,000

Required

1. Compute the breakeven point in units, assuming that the company achieves its planned sales mix.
2. Compute the breakeven point in units (a) if only standard carriers are sold and (b) if only deluxe carriers are sold.
3. Suppose 250,000 units are sold but only 50,000 of them are deluxe. Compute the operating income. Compute the breakeven point in units. Compare your answer with the answer to requirement 1. What is the major lesson of this problem?

3-47 Gross margin and contribution margin. The Museum of America is preparing for its annual appreciation dinner for contributing members. Last year, 525 members attended the dinner. Tickets for the dinner were $24 per attendee. The profit report for last year's dinner follows.

Ticket sales	$12,600
Cost of dinner	15,300
Gross margin	(2,700)
Invitations and paperwork	2,500
Profit (loss)	$(5,200)

This year the dinner committee does not want to lose money on the dinner. To help achieve its goal, the committee analyzed last year's costs. Of the $15,300 cost of the dinner, $9,000 were fixed costs and $6,300 were variable costs. Of the $2,500 cost of invitations and paperwork, $1,975 were fixed and $525 were variable.

Required

1. Prepare last year's profit report using the contribution margin format.
2. The committee is considering expanding this year's dinner invitation list to include volunteer members (in addition to contributing members). If the committee expands the dinner invitation list, it expects attendance to double. Calculate the effect this will have on the profitability of the dinner assuming fixed costs will be the same as last year.

3-48 Ethics, CVP analysis. Kirk Corporation produces a molded plastic casing, LX201, for desktop computers. Summary data from its 2013 income statement are as follows:

Revenues	$4,000,000
Variable costs	2,400,000
Fixed costs	1,728,000
Operating income	$ (128,000)

Bridgett Hewitt, Kirk's president, is very concerned about Kirk Corporation's poor profitability. She asks Julian Buckner, production manager, and Seth Madden, controller, to see if there are ways to reduce costs.

After 2 weeks, Julian returns with a proposal to reduce variable costs to 52% of revenues by reducing the costs Kirk currently incurs for safe disposal of wasted plastic. Seth is concerned that this would expose the company to potential environmental liabilities. He tells Julian, "We would need to estimate some of these potential environmental costs and include them in our analysis." "You can't do that," Julian replies. "We are not violating any laws. There is some possibility that we may have to incur environmental costs in the future, but if we bring it up now, this proposal will not go through because our senior management always assumes these costs to be larger than they turn out to be. The market is very tough, and we are in danger of shutting down the company and costing all of us our jobs. The only reason our competitors are making money is because they are doing exactly what I am proposing."

Required

1. Calculate Kirk Corporation's breakeven revenues for 2013.
2. Calculate Kirk Corporation's breakeven revenues if variable costs are 52% of revenues.
3. Calculate Kirk Corporation's operating income for 2013 if variable costs had been 52% of revenues.
4. Given Julian Buckner's comments, what should Seth Madden do?

3-49 Deciding where to produce. (CMA, adapted) Portal Corporation produces the same power generator in two Illinois plants, a new plant in Peoria and an older plant in Moline. The following data are available for the two plants.

Home Insert Page Layout Formulas Data Review View

	A	B	C	D	E
1		Peoria		Moline	
2	Selling price		$150.00		$150.00
3	Variable manufacturing cost per unit	$72.00		$88.00	
4	Fixed manufacturing cost per unit	30.00		15.00	
5	Variable marketing and distribution cost per unit	14.00		14.00	
6	Fixed marketing and distribution cost per unit	19.00		14.50	
7	Total cost per unit		135.00		131.50
8	Operating income per unit		$ 15.00		$ 18.50
9	Production rate per day	400	units	320	units
10	Normal annual capacity usage	240	days	240	days
11	Maximum annual capacity	300	days	300	days

All fixed costs per unit are calculated based on a normal capacity usage consisting of 240 working days. When the number of working days exceeds 240, overtime charges raise the variable manufacturing costs of additional units by $3.00 per unit in Peoria and $8.00 per unit in Moline.

Portal Corporation is expected to produce and sell 192,000 power generators during the coming year. Wanting to take advantage of the higher operating income per unit at Moline, the company's production manager has decided to manufacture 96,000 units at each plant, resulting in a plan in which Moline operates at maximum capacity (320 units per day × 300 days) and Peoria operates at its normal volume (400 units per day × 240 days).

Required

1. Calculate the breakeven point in units for the Peoria plant and for the Moline plant.
2. Calculate the operating income that would result from the production manager's plan to produce 96,000 units at each plant.
3. Determine how the production of 192,000 units should be allocated between the Peoria and Moline plants to maximize operating income for Portal Corporation. Show your calculations.

4 Job Costing

Learning Objectives

1. Describe the building-block concepts of costing systems
2. Distinguish job costing from process costing
3. Describe the approaches to evaluating and implementing job-costing systems
4. Outline the seven-step approach to normal costing
5. Distinguish actual costing from normal costing
6. Track the flow of costs in a job-costing system
7. Dispose of under- or overallocated manufacturing overhead costs at the end of the fiscal year using alternative methods
8. Understand variations from normal costing

No one likes to lose money.

Whether a company is a new startup venture providing marketing consulting services or an established manufacturer of custom-built motorcycles, knowing how to job cost—that is, knowing how much it costs to produce an individual product—is critical if a company is to generate a profit. As the following article shows, KB Home, a leading U.S. homebuilder, knows this all too well.

Job Costing and "Green" Home Construction[1]

Making a profit on a project depends on pricing it correctly. At KB Home, a leading U.S. homebuilder, managers and employees are responsible for the costing and pricing of the company's new "green" ZeroHouse 2.0 homes. These environmentally friendly homes include solar power systems, solar thermal water heaters, LED lights, and even electric-vehicle charging stations to help homeowners enhance their energy efficiency.

For each custom ZeroHouse 2.0 home that KB Home builds, company managers use historical data and marketplace information to carefully estimate all costs associated with the project: direct costs, indirect costs, and general administrative costs. Direct costs include environmentally responsible building materials, solar panels, and direct labor. Indirect costs include the cost of supervisory labor, company-owned equipment, and safety equipment. Finally, general administrative costs allocated to each project include office rent, utilities, and insurance.

Throughout the homebuilding process, on-site managers report on the status of each ZeroHouse 2.0 under construction. These managers are also responsible for identifying any potential problems with a project and determining the alterations necessary to ensure high-quality, on-time delivery within the original project budget.

For KB Home and other "green" homebuilders, job costing is critical ... and will be even more important in the years ahead. In 2011, "green" homes comprised 17% of the home-construction market, and that number is expected to increase 29–38% by 2016, as more homebuyers request environmentally friendly homes that lower their energy use while saving them money.

Just like at KB Home, managers at Nissan want to know how much it costs to manufacture its new Leaf electric car, and managers at Ernst & Young want to know what it costs to audit Whole Foods, the organic grocer. Knowing the costs and profitability of jobs helps managers pursue their business strategies, develop pricing

[1] *Sources*: McGraw-Hill Construction/National Association of Home Builders, *New and Remodeled Green Homes: Transforming the Residential Market*, May 2012; KB Home, *Sustainability Report 2012*, Los Angeles: KB Home, 2013; Robbie Whelan, "Martha Stewart Green Homes—Who Will Buy Them?," Developments blog, *The Wall Street Journal*, January 12, 2011, http://blogs.wsj.com/; and multiple conversations with KB Home managers, 2013 (various dates).

plans, and meet external reporting requirements. Of course, when making decisions, managers combine cost information with noncost information, such as their personal observations about operations, and nonfinancial performance measures, like quality and customer satisfaction.

Building-Block Concepts of Costing Systems

Learning Objective 1

Describe the building-block concepts of costing systems

. . . the building blocks are cost object, direct costs, indirect costs, cost pools, and cost-allocation bases

Before we begin our discussion of costing systems, let's review the cost-related terms from Chapter 2 and introduce the new terms we will need to discuss the topics in this chapter.

1. A *cost object* is anything for which a measurement of costs is desired—for example, a product, such as an iMac computer, or a service, such as the cost of repairing an iMac computer.
2. The *direct costs of a cost object* are costs related to a particular cost object that can be traced to that cost object in an economically feasible (cost-effective) way—for example, the cost of purchasing the main computer board or the cost of parts used to make an iMac computer.
3. The *indirect costs of a cost object* are costs related to a particular cost object that cannot be traced to that cost object in an economically feasible (cost-effective) way—for example, the salaries of supervisors who oversee multiple products, only one of which is the iMac, or the rent paid for the repair facility that repairs many different Apple computer products besides the iMac. Indirect costs are allocated to the cost object using a cost-allocation method. Recall that *cost assignment* is a general term for assigning costs, whether direct or indirect, to a cost object. *Cost tracing* is the process of assigning direct costs. *Cost allocation* is the process of assigning indirect costs. The relationship among these three concepts can be graphically represented as

Cost Assignment

Direct Costs	Cost Tracing →	Cost Object
Indirect Costs	Cost Allocation →	

Throughout this chapter, the costs assigned to a cost object, such as a BMW Mini Cooper car, or a service, such as an audit of the MTV network, include both variable costs and costs that are fixed in the short run. Managers cost products and services to guide their long-run strategic decisions (for example, about the mix of products and services to produce and sell or the prices to charge for various products). In the long run, managers want revenues to exceed total (variable plus fixed) costs.

We also need to introduce and explain two more terms before discussing costing systems:

4. **Cost pool.** A **cost pool** is a grouping of individual indirect cost items. Cost pools can range from broad, such as all manufacturing-plant costs, to narrow, such as the costs of operating metal-cutting machines. Cost pools are often organized in conjunction with cost-allocation bases.
5. **Cost-allocation base.** How should a company allocate the costs of operating metal-cutting machines among different products? One way is based on the number of machine-hours used to produce different products. The **cost-allocation base** (number of machine-hours) is a systematic way to link an indirect cost or group of indirect costs (operating costs of all metal-cutting machines) to cost objects (different products). For example, if the indirect costs of operating metal-cutting machines is \$500,000 based on running these machines for 10,000 hours, the cost-allocation rate is \$500,000 ÷ 10,000 hours = \$50 per machine-hour, where machine-hours is the cost-allocation base. If a product uses 800 machine-hours, it will be allocated \$40,000, \$50 per machine-hour × 800 machine-hours. The ideal cost-allocation base is the cost driver of the indirect costs because there is a cause-and-effect relationship between the cost-allocation base and the indirect costs. A cost-allocation base can be either financial (such as direct labor costs) or nonfinancial (such as the number of machine-hours). When the cost object is a job, product, or customer, the cost-allocation base is also called a **cost-application base.** For example, when the cost object is a department or another cost pool, the cost-allocation base is not called a cost-application base.

   Sometimes a cost may need to be allocated when the cause-and-effect relationship is not clear-cut. Consider a corporatewide advertising program that promotes the general image of a company and its various divisions, rather than the image of an individual product. Many companies, such as PepsiCo, allocate costs like these to their individual divisions on the basis of revenues: The higher a division's revenue, the higher the business's allocated cost of the advertising program. Allocating costs this way is based on the criterion of *benefits received* rather than cause-and-effect. Divisions with higher revenues benefit from the advertising more than divisions with lower revenues and therefore ought to be allocated more of the advertising costs.

   Another criterion for allocating some costs is the cost object's *ability to bear* the costs allocated to it. The city government of Houston, Texas, for example, distributes the costs of the city manager's office to other city departments—including the police department, fire department, library system, and others—based on the size of their budgets. The city's rationale is that larger departments should absorb a larger share of the costs. Organizations generally use the cause-and-effect criterion to allocate costs, followed by benefits received, and finally, and more rarely, by ability to bear.

Decision Point
What are the building block concepts of a costing system?

The concepts represented by these five terms constitute the building blocks we will use to design the costing systems described in this chapter.

Learning Objective 2
Distinguish job costing
...job costing is used to cost a distinct product
from process costing
...process costing is used to cost masses of identical or similar units

Job-Costing and Process-Costing Systems

Management accountants use two basic types of costing systems to assign costs to products or services.

1. **Job-costing system.** In a job-costing system, the cost object is a unit or multiple units of a distinct product or service called a **job.** Each job generally uses different amounts of resources. The product or service is often a single unit, such as a specialized machine made at Hitachi, a construction project managed by Bechtel Corporation, a repair job done at an Audi Service Center, or an advertising campaign produced by Saatchi & Saatchi. Each special machine made by Hitachi is unique and distinct from the other machines made at the plant. An advertising campaign for one client

at Saatchi & Saatchi is unique and distinct from advertising campaigns for other clients. Job costing is also used by companies such as Ethan Allen to cost multiple identical units of distinct furniture products. Because the products and services are distinct, job-costing systems are used to accumulate costs separately for each product or service.

2. **Process-costing system.** In a process-costing system, the cost object is masses of identical or similar units of a product or service. For example, Citibank provides the same service to all its customers when processing customer deposits. Intel provides the same product (say, a Pentium 6 chip) to each of its customers. All Minute Maid consumers receive the same frozen orange juice product. In each period, process-costing systems divide the total costs of producing an identical or similar product or service by the total number of units produced to obtain a per-unit cost. This per-unit cost is the average unit cost that applies to each of the identical or similar units produced in that period.

Exhibit 4-1 presents examples of job costing and process costing in the service, merchandising, and manufacturing sectors. These two types of costing systems lie at opposite ends of a continuum; in between, one type of system can blur into the other to some degree.

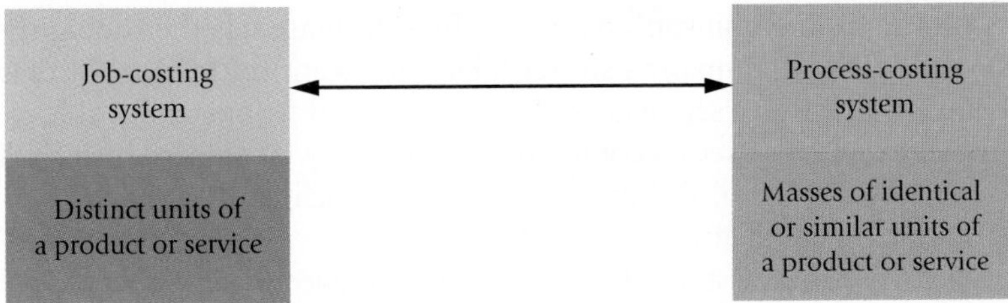

Decision Point

How do you distinguish job costing from process costing?

Many companies have costing systems that are neither pure job-costing systems nor pure process-costing systems but have elements of both, tailored to the underlying operations. For example, Kellogg Corporation uses job costing to calculate the total cost to manufacture each of its different and distinct types of products—such as Corn Flakes,

Exhibit 4-1

Examples of Job Costing and Process Costing in the Service, Merchandising, and Manufacturing Sectors

	Service Sector	Merchandising Sector	Manufacturing Sector
Job Costing Used	• Audit engagements done by PricewaterhouseCoopers • Consulting engagements done by McKinsey & Co. • Advertising-agency campaigns run by Ogilvy & Mather • Individual legal cases argued by Hale & Dorr • Computer-repair jobs done by CompUSA • Movies produced by Universal Studios	• L. L. Bean sending individual items by mail order • Special promotion of new products by Walmart	• Assembly of individual aircrafts at Boeing • Construction of ships at Litton Industries
Process Costing Used	• Bank-check clearing at Bank of America • Postal delivery (standard items) by U.S. Postal Service	• Grain dealing by Arthur Daniel Midlands • Lumber dealing by Weyerhauser	• Oil refining by Shell Oil • Beverage production by PepsiCo

Crispix, and Froot Loops—and process costing to calculate the per-unit cost of producing each identical box of Corn Flakes, each identical box of Crispix, and so on. In this chapter, we focus on job-costing systems. Chapters 17 and 18 discuss process-costing systems.

Learning Objective 3

Describe the approaches to evaluating and implementing job-costing systems

...to determine costs of jobs in a timely manner

Job Costing: Evaluation and Implementation

We illustrate job costing using the example of Robinson Company, which manufactures and installs specialized machinery for the paper-making industry. In early 2013, Robinson receives a request to bid on the manufacturing and installation of a new paper-making machine for the Western Pulp and Paper Company (WPP). Robinson had never made a machine quite like this one, and its managers wonder what to bid for the job. In order to make decisions about the job, Robinson's management team works through the five-step decision-making process.

1. **Identify the problems and uncertainties.** The decision of whether and how much to bid for the WPP job depends on how management resolves two critical uncertainties: (1) what it will cost to complete the job; and (2) the prices Robinson's competitors are likely to bid.
2. **Obtain information.** Robinson's managers first evaluate whether doing the WPP job is consistent with the company's strategy. Do they want to do more of these kinds of jobs? Is this an attractive segment of the market? Will Robinson be able to develop a competitive advantage over its competitors and satisfy customers such as WPP? After completing their research, Robinson's managers conclude that the WPP job fits well with the company's strategy.

   Robinson's managers study the drawings and engineering specifications provided by WPP and decide on the technical details of the machine. They compare the specifications of this machine to similar machines they have made in the past, identify competitors that might bid on the job, and gather information on what these bids might be.
3. **Make predictions about the future.** Robinson's managers estimate the cost of direct materials, direct manufacturing labor, and overhead for the WPP job. They also consider qualitative factors and risk factors and evaluate any biases they might have. For example, do engineers and employees working on the WPP job have the necessary skills and technical competence? Would they find the experience valuable and challenging? How accurate are the cost estimates, and what is the likelihood of cost overruns? What biases do Robinson's managers have to be careful about?
4. **Make decisions by choosing among alternatives.** Robinson's managers consider several alternative bids based on what they believe competing firms will bid, the technical expertise needed for the job, business risks, and other qualitative factors. Ultimately Robinson decides to bid $15,000. The manufacturing cost estimate is $9,705 (as described later in the chapter), which yields a markup of more than 50% on manufacturing cost.
5. **Implement the decision, evaluate performance, and learn.** Robinson wins the bid for the WPP job. As Robinson works on the job, management accountants carefully track all of the costs incurred (which are detailed later in this chapter). Ultimately, Robinson's managers will compare the predicted amounts against actual costs to evaluate how well the company did on the WPP job.

In its job-costing system, Robinson accumulates the costs incurred for a job in different parts of the value chain, such as manufacturing, marketing, and customer service. We focus here on Robinson's manufacturing function (which also includes the product's installation). To make a machine, Robinson purchases some components from outside suppliers and makes other components itself. Each of Robinson's jobs also has a service element: installing a machine at a customer's site, integrating it with the customer's other machines and processes, and ensuring the machine meets the customer's expectations.

One form of a job-costing system Robinson can use is **actual costing**, which is a costing system that traces direct costs to a cost object based on the *actual direct-cost rates* times the actual quantities of the direct-cost inputs used. Indirect costs are allocated based on the *actual indirect-cost rates* times the actual quantities of the cost-allocation bases. An actual indirect-cost rate is calculated by dividing actual annual indirect costs by the actual annual quantity of the cost-allocation base.

$$\text{Actual indirect cost rate} = \frac{\text{Actual annual indirect costs}}{\text{Actual annual quantity of the cost-allocation base}}$$

As its name suggests, actual costing systems calculate the actual costs of jobs. Yet actual costing systems are not commonly found in practice because actual costs cannot be computed in a *timely* manner.[2] The problem is not with computing direct-cost rates for direct materials and direct manufacturing labor. For example, Robinson records the actual prices paid for materials. As it uses these materials, the prices paid serve as actual direct-cost rates for charging material costs to jobs. As we discuss next, calculating actual indirect-cost rates on a timely basis each week or each month is, however, a problem. Robinson can only calculate actual indirect-cost rates at the end of the fiscal year. However, the firm's managers are unwilling to wait that long to learn the costs of various jobs because they need cost information to monitor and manage the cost of jobs while they are in progress. Ongoing cost information about jobs also helps managers bid on new jobs while old jobs are in progress.

Time Period Used to Compute Indirect-Cost Rates

There are two reasons for using longer periods, such as a year, to calculate indirect-cost rates.

1. **The numerator reason (indirect-cost pool).** The shorter the period, the greater is the influence of seasonal patterns on the amount of costs. For example, if indirect-cost rates were calculated each month, the costs of heating (included in the numerator) would be charged to production only during the winter months. An annual period incorporates the effects of all four seasons into a single, annual indirect-cost rate.

   Levels of total indirect costs are also affected by nonseasonal erratic costs. Nonseasonal erratic costs are the costs incurred in a particular month that benefit operations during future months, such as equipment-repair costs and the costs of vacation and holiday pay for employees. If monthly indirect-cost rates were calculated, the jobs done in a month in which there were high, nonseasonal erratic costs would be charged with these higher costs. Pooling all indirect costs together over the course of a full year and calculating a single annual indirect-cost rate helps smooth some of the erratic bumps in costs associated with shorter periods.

2. **The denominator reason (quantity of the cost-allocation base).** Another reason for longer periods is to avoid spreading monthly fixed indirect costs over fluctuating levels of monthly output and fluctuating quantities of the cost-allocation base. Consider the following example.

Reardon and Pane is a firm of tax accountants whose work follows a highly seasonal pattern. Tax season (January–April) is very busy. Other times of the year are less busy. The firm has both variable indirect costs and fixed indirect costs. Variable indirect costs (such as supplies, power, and indirect support labor) vary with the quantity of the cost-allocation base (direct professional labor-hours). Fixed indirect costs (depreciation and general administrative support) do not vary with short-run fluctuations in the quantity of the cost-allocation base:

	Indirect Costs			Direct Professional Labor-Hours	Variable Indirect Cost Rate per Direct Professional Labor-Hour	Fixed Indirect Cost Rate per Direct Professional Labor-Hour	Total Allocation Rate per Direct Professional Labor-Hour
	Variable (1)	Fixed (2)	Total (3)	(4)	(5) = (1) ÷ (4)	(6) = (2) ÷ (4)	(7) = (3) ÷ (4)
High-output month	$40,000	$60,000	$100,000	3,200	$12.50	$18.75	$31.25
Low-output month	10,000	60,000	70,000	800	$12.50	$75.00	87.50

[2] Actual costing is presented in more detail on pages (pages 118–120).

Variable indirect costs change in proportion to changes in the number of direct professional labor-hours worked. Therefore, the variable indirect-cost rate is the same in both the high-output months and the low-output months ($12.50 in both as the table shows). Sometimes overtime payments can cause the variable indirect-cost rate to be higher in high-output months. In such cases, variable indirect costs will be allocated at a higher rate to production in high-output months relative to production in low-output months.

Now consider the fixed costs of $60,000. The fixed costs cause monthly total indirect-cost rates to vary considerably—from $31.25 per hour to $87.50 per hour. Few managers believe that identical jobs done in different months should be allocated such significantly different indirect-cost charges per hour ($87.50 ÷ $31.25 = 2.80, or 280%) because of fixed costs. Furthermore, if fees for preparing tax returns are based on costs, fees would be high in low-output months leading to lost business, when in fact management wants to accept more bids to use the idle capacity during these months (for more details, see Chapter 9).

Reardon and Pane chose a specific level of capacity based on a time horizon far beyond a mere month. An average, annualized rate based on the relationship between total annual indirect costs and the total annual level of output smoothes the effect of monthly variations in output levels. This rate is more representative of the total costs and total output the company's managers considered when choosing the level of capacity and, therefore, fixed costs. Another denominator reason for using annual overhead rates is because the number of Monday-to-Friday workdays in a month affects the calculation of monthly indirect-cost rates. The number of workdays per month varies from 20 to 23 during a year. Because February has the fewest workdays (and consequently labor-hours), if separate rates are computed each month, jobs done in February would bear a greater share of the firm's indirect costs (such as depreciation and property taxes) than identical jobs in other months. An annual period reduces the effect that the number of working days per month has on unit costs.

Decision Point

What is the main challenge of implementing job-costing systems?

Normal Costing

As we indicated, because it's hard to calculate actual indirect-cost rates on a weekly or monthly basis, managers cannot calculate the actual costs of jobs as they are completed. Nonetheless, managers want a close approximation of the costs of various jobs regularly during the year, not just at the end of the fiscal year. They want to know manufacturing costs (and other costs, such as marketing costs) to price jobs, monitor and manage costs, evaluate the success of jobs, learn about what did and did not work, bid on new jobs, and prepare interim financial statements. Because companies need immediate access to job costs, few wait to allocate overhead costs until the end of the accounting year. Instead, a *predetermined* or *budgeted* indirect-cost rate is calculated for each cost pool at the beginning of a fiscal year, and overhead costs are allocated to jobs as work progresses. For the numerator and denominator reasons already described, the **budgeted indirect-cost rate** for each cost pool is computed as follows:

$$\text{Budgeted indirect cost rate} = \frac{\text{Budgeted annual indirect costs}}{\text{Budgeted annual quantity of the cost-allocation base}}$$

Using budgeted indirect-cost rates gives rise to normal costing.

Normal costing is a costing system that (1) traces direct costs to a cost object by using the actual direct-cost rates times the actual quantities of the direct-cost inputs and (2) allocates indirect costs based on the *budgeted* indirect-cost rates times the actual quantities of the cost-allocation bases.

Learning Objective 4

Outline the seven-step approach to normal costing

...the seven-step approach is used to compute direct and indirect costs of a job

General Approach to Job Costing Using Normal Costing

We illustrate normal costing for the Robinson Company example using the following seven steps to assign costs to an individual job. This approach is commonly used by companies in the manufacturing, merchandising, and service sectors.

Step 1: Identify the Job That Is the Chosen Cost Object. The cost object in the Robinson Company example is Job WPP 298, manufacturing a paper-making machine for Western Pulp and Paper (WPP) in 2013. Robinson's managers and management accountants gather information to cost jobs through source documents. A **source document** is an original record (such as a labor time card on which an employee's work hours are recorded) that supports journal entries in an accounting system. The main source document for Job WPP 298 is a job-cost record. A **job-cost record**, also called a **job-cost sheet**, is used to record and accumulate all the costs assigned to a specific job, starting when work begins. Exhibit 4-2 shows the job-cost record for the paper-making machine ordered by WPP. Follow the various steps in costing Job WPP 298 on the job-cost record in Exhibit 4-2.

Exhibit 4-2 Source Documents at Robinson Company: Job-Cost Record

Home Insert Page Layout Formulas Data Review View

	A	B	C	D	E	F
1				**JOB-COST RECORD**		
2	JOB NO:	WPP 298		CUSTOMER:	Western Pulp and Paper	
3	Date Started:	Feb. 4, 2013		Date Completed	Feb. 28, 2013	
4						
5						
6	**DIRECT MATERIALS**					
7	Date	Materials		Quantity	Unit	Total
8	Received	Requisition No.	Part No.	Used	Cost	Costs
9	Feb. 4, 2013	2013: 198	MB 468-A	8	$14	$ 112
10	Feb. 4, 2013	2013: 199	TB 267-F	12	63	756
11						•
12						•
13	Total					$ 4,606
14						
15	**DIRECT MANUFACTURING LABOR**					
16	Period	Labor Time	Employee	Hours	Hourly	Total
17	Covered	Record No.	No.	Used	Rate	Costs
18	Feb. 4-10, 2013	LT 232	551-87-3076	25	$18	$ 450
19	Feb. 4-10, 2013	LT 247	287-31-4671	5	19	95
20	•	•	•	•	•	•
21	•	•	•	•	•	•
22	Total			88		$ 1,579
23						
24	**MANUFACTURING OVERHEAD***					
25		Cost Pool		Allocation Base	Allocation-	Total
26	Date	Category	Allocation Base	Quantity Used	Base Rate	Costs
27	Dec. 31, 2013	Manufacturing	Direct Manufacturing	88 hours	$40	$ 3,520
28			Labor-Hours			
29						
30	Total					$ 3,520
31	**TOTAL MANUFACTURING COST OF JOB**					$ 9,705
32						
33						
34	*The Robinson Company uses a single manufacturing-overhead cost pool. The use of multiple overhead cost pools					
35	would mean multiple entries in the "Manufacturing Overhead" section of the job-cost record.					
36						

Exhibit 4-3 Source Documents at Robinson Company: Materials-Requisition Record and Labor-Time Sheet

PANEL A:

MATERIALS-REQUISITION RECORD

Materials-Requisition Record No. 2013: 198
Job No. WPP 298 Date: FEB. 4, 2013

Part No.	Part Description	Quantity	Unit Cost	Total Cost
MB 468-A	Metal Brackets	8	$14	$112

Issued By: B. Clyde Date: Feb. 4, 2013
Received By: L. Daley Date: Feb. 4, 2013

PANEL B:

LABOR-TIME SHEET

Labor-Time Record No: LT 232
Employee Name: G. L. Cook Employee No: 551-87-3076
Employee Classification Code: Grade 3 Machinist
Hourly Rate: $18
Week Start: Feb. 4, 2013 Week End: Feb. 10, 2013

Job. No.	M	T	W	Th	F	S	Su	Total
WPP 298	4	8	3	6	4	0	0	25
JL 256	3	0	4	2	3	0	0	12
Maintenance	1	0	1	0	1	0	0	3
Total	8	8	8	8	8	0	0	40

Supervisor: R. Stuart Date: Feb. 10, 2013

Step 2: Identify the Direct Costs of the Job. Robinson identifies two direct-manufacturing cost categories: direct materials and direct manufacturing labor.

- **Direct materials:** On the basis of the engineering specifications and drawings provided by WPP, a manufacturing engineer orders materials from the storeroom using a basic source document called a **materials-requisition record**, which contains information about the cost of direct materials used on a specific job and in a specific department. Exhibit 4-3, Panel A, shows a materials-requisition record for the Robinson Company. See how the record specifies the job for which the material is requested (WPP 298) and describes the material (Part Number MB 468-A, metal brackets), the actual quantity (8), the actual unit cost ($14), and the actual total cost ($112). The $112 actual total cost also appears on the job-cost record in Exhibit 4-2. If we add the cost of all materials requisitions, the total actual direct materials cost is $4,606, which is shown in the Direct Materials panel of the job-cost record in Exhibit 4-2.
- **Direct manufacturing labor:** Accounting for direct manufacturing labor is similar to accounting for direct materials. The source document for direct manufacturing labor is a **labor-time sheet**, which contains information about the amount of labor time used for a specific job in a specific department. Exhibit 4-3, Panel B, shows a typical weekly labor-time sheet for a particular employee (G. L. Cook). Each day Cook records the time spent on individual jobs (in this case WPP 298 and JL 256), as well as the time spent on other tasks, such as the maintenance of machines or cleaning, that are not related to a specific job.

  The 25 hours that Cook spent on Job WPP 298 appears on the job-cost record in Exhibit 4-2 at a cost of $450 (25 hours × $18 per hour). Similarly, the job-cost record for Job JL 256 will show a cost of $216 (12 hours × $18 per hour). The three hours of time spent on maintenance and cleaning at $18 per hour equals $54. This cost is part of indirect manufacturing costs because it is not traceable to any particular job. This indirect cost is included as part of the manufacturing-overhead cost pool allocated to jobs. The total direct manufacturing labor costs of $1,579 for the paper-making machine that appears in the Direct Manufacturing Labor panel of the job-cost record in Exhibit 4-2 is the sum of all the direct manufacturing labor costs charged to Job WPP 298 by different employees.

  All costs other than direct materials and direct manufacturing labor are classified as indirect costs.

Step 3: Select the Cost-Allocation Bases to Use for Allocating Indirect Costs to the Job. Recall that indirect manufacturing costs are costs that are necessary to do a job but that cannot be traced to a specific job. It would be impossible to complete a job without incurring indirect costs such as supervision, manufacturing engineering, utilities, and repairs. Moreover, different jobs require different quantities of indirect resources. Because these costs cannot be traced to a specific job, managers must allocate them to jobs in a systematic way.

Companies often use multiple cost-allocation bases to allocate indirect costs because different indirect costs have different cost drivers. For example, some indirect costs such as depreciation and repairs of machines are more closely related to machine-hours. Other indirect costs such as supervision and production support are more closely related to direct manufacturing labor-hours. Robinson, however, chooses direct manufacturing labor-hours as the sole allocation base for linking all indirect manufacturing costs to jobs. The managers do so because, in Robinson's labor-intensive environment, they believe the number of direct manufacturing labor-hours drives the manufacturing overhead resources required by individual jobs. (We will see in Chapter 5 that managers in many manufacturing environments often need to broaden the set of cost drivers.) In 2013, Robinson budgets 28,000 direct manufacturing labor-hours.

Step 4: Identify the Indirect Costs Associated with Each Cost-Allocation Base. Because Robinson believes that a single cost-allocation base—direct manufacturing labor-hours—can be used to allocate indirect manufacturing costs to jobs, Robinson creates a single cost pool called manufacturing overhead costs. This pool represents all indirect costs of the Manufacturing Department that are difficult to trace directly to individual jobs. In 2013, budgeted manufacturing overhead costs total $1,120,000.

As we saw in Steps 3 and 4, managers first identify cost-allocation bases and then identify the costs related to each cost-allocation base, not the other way around. They choose this order because managers must first understand their companies' cost drivers (the reasons why costs are being incurred) before they can determine the costs associated with each cost driver. Otherwise, there is nothing to guide the creation of cost pools. Of course, Steps 3 and 4 are often done almost simultaneously.

Step 5: Compute the Rate per Unit of Each Cost-Allocation Base Used to Allocate Indirect Costs to the Job. For each cost pool, the budgeted indirect-cost rate is calculated by dividing the budgeted total indirect costs in the pool (determined in Step 4) by the budgeted total quantity of the cost-allocation base (determined in Step 3). Robinson calculates the allocation rate for its single manufacturing overhead cost pool as follows:

$$\begin{aligned}\text{Budgeted manufacturing overhead rate} &= \frac{\text{Budgeted manufacturing overhead costs}}{\text{Budgeted total quantity of cost-allocation base}}\\ &= \frac{\$1{,}120{,}000}{\text{28,000 direct manufacturing labor-hours}}\\ &= \$40 \text{ per direct manufacturing labor-hour}\end{aligned}$$

Step 6: Compute the Indirect Costs Allocated to the Job. The indirect costs of a job are calculated by multiplying the *actual* quantity of each different allocation base (one allocation base for each cost pool) associated with the job by the *budgeted* indirect cost rate of each allocation base (computed in Step 5). Recall that Robinson's managers selected direct manufacturing labor-hours as the only cost-allocation base. Robinson uses 88 direct manufacturing labor-hours on the WPP 298 job. Consequently, the manufacturing overhead costs allocated to WPP 298 equal $3,520 ($40 per direct manufacturing labor-hour × 88 hours) and appear in the Manufacturing Overhead panel of the WPP 298 job-cost record in Exhibit 4-2.

Step 7: Compute the Total Cost of the Job by Adding All Direct and Indirect Costs Assigned to the Job. Exhibit 4-2 shows that the total manufacturing costs of the WPP job are $9,705.

Direct manufacturing costs		
Direct materials	$4,606	
Direct manufacturing labor	1,579	$ 6,185
Manufacturing overhead costs		
($40 per direct manufacturing labor-hour × 88 hours)		3,520
Total manufacturing costs of job WPP 298		$9,705

Concepts in Action

The Job Costing "Game Plan" at the New Cowboys Stadium

Although the Dallas Cowboys have won five Super Bowls, many football fans recognize the team for its futuristic home, Cowboys Stadium in Arlington, Texas. The 80,000-seat stadium, built in 3 years, features two arches spanning a quarter-mile in length over the dome, a retractable roof, the largest retractable glass doors in the world (in each end zone), canted glass exterior walls, and a 600-ton video screen. For Manhattan Construction, the company that managed the $1.2 billion Cowboys Stadium project, understanding the costs of these features was critical for making successful pricing decisions and ensuring that the project was profitable.

The Cowboys Stadium project had five stages: (1) conceptualization, (2) design and planning, (3) preconstruction, (4) construction, and (5) finalization and delivery. During this process, Manhattan Construction hired architects and subcontractors, created blueprints, purchased and cleared land, constructed the stadium, built out and finished interiors, and completed last-minute changes before the stadium's 2009 opening. To ensure proper allocation and accounting of resources, project managers used a job-costing system. They then allocated estimated overhead costs (supervisor salaries, rent, materials handling, and so on). Manhattan Construction was able to estimate the project's profitability based on the percentage of work completed and revenue earned, while providing the Dallas Cowboys with clear, concise, and transparent costing data.

Just like quarterback Tony Romo navigating opposing defenses, Manhattan Construction was able to leverage its job-costing system to ensure the successful construction of a stadium as iconic as the blue star on the Cowboys' helmets.

Sources: Based on interview with Mark Penny, Project Manager, Manhattan Construction Co., 2010; David Dillon, "New Cowboys Stadium Has Grand Design, but Discipline Isn't Compromised," *The Dallas Morning News* (June 3, 2009); Brooke Knudson, "Profile: Dallas Cowboys Stadium," *Construction Today* (December 22, 2008); and Dallas Cowboys, "Cowboys Stadium: Architecture Fact Sheet."

Recall that Robinson bid a price of $15,000 for the job. At that revenue, the normal-costing system shows the job's gross margin is $5,295 ($15,000 − $9,705) and its gross-margin percentage is 35.3% ($5,295 ÷ $15,000 = 0.353).

Robinson's manufacturing managers and sales managers can use the gross margin and gross-margin percentage calculations to compare the different jobs to try to understand why some jobs aren't as profitable as others. Were direct materials wasted? Was the direct manufacturing labor cost of the jobs too high? Were the jobs simply underpriced? A job-cost analysis provides the information managers needed to gauge the manufacturing and sales performance of their firms (see Concepts in Action: The Job Costing "Game Plan" at the New Cowboys Stadium).

Decision Point

How do you implement a normal-costing system?

Exhibit 4-4 is an overview of Robinson Company's job-costing system. This exhibit represents the concepts comprising the five building blocks of job-costing systems introduced at the beginning of this chapter: (1) cost objects, (2) the direct costs of a cost object, (3) the indirect (overhead) costs of a cost object, (4) the indirect-cost pool, and (5) the cost-allocation base. (The symbols in the exhibit are used consistently in the costing-system overviews presented in this book. A triangle always identifies a direct cost, a rectangle represents the indirect-cost pool, and an octagon describes the cost-allocation base.) Costing-system overviews such as Exhibit 4-4 are important learning tools. We urge you to sketch one when you need to understand a costing system.

Note the similarities between Exhibit 4-4 and the cost of the WPP 298 job described in Step 7. Exhibit 4-4 shows two direct-cost categories (direct materials and direct

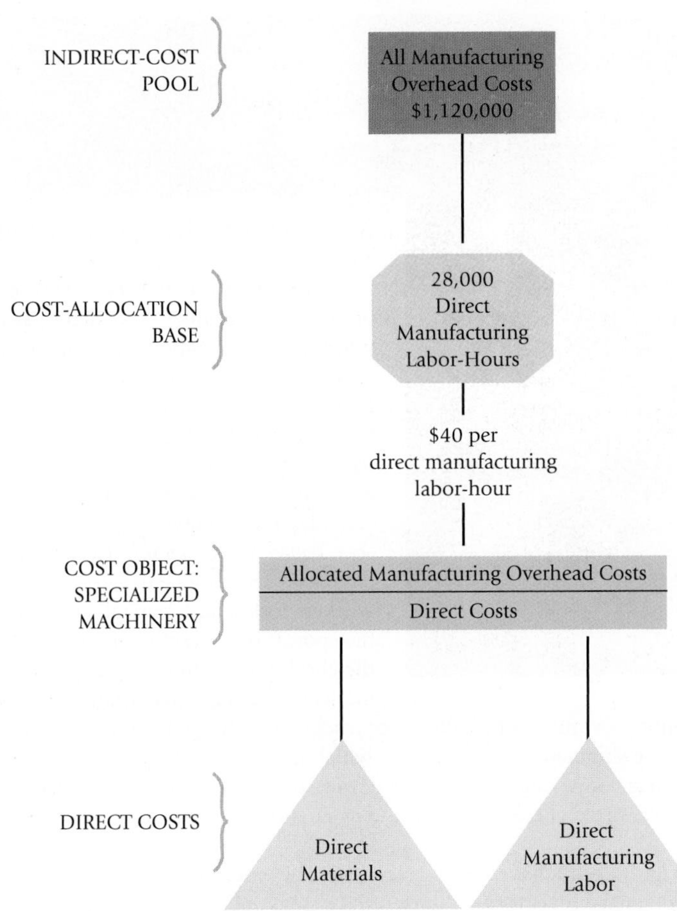

Exhibit 4-4

Job-Costing Overview for Determining Manufacturing Costs of Jobs at Robinson Company.

manufacturing labor) and one indirect-cost category (manufacturing overhead) used to allocate indirect costs. The costs in Step 7 also have three dollar amounts, each corresponding respectively to the two direct-cost and one indirect-cost categories.

The Role of Technology

Information technology gives managers quick and accurate job-costing information, making it easier for them to manage and control jobs. Consider, for example, the direct materials charged to jobs. Managers control these costs as materials are purchased and used. Using Electronic Data Interchange (EDI) technology, companies like Robinson order materials from their suppliers by clicking a few keys on a computer keyboard. EDI, an electronic computer link between a company and its suppliers, ensures that the order is transmitted quickly and accurately with minimal paperwork and costs. A bar code scanner records the receipt of incoming materials, and a computer matches the receipt with the order, prints out a check to the supplier, and records the materials received. When an operator on the production floor transmits a request for materials via a computer terminal, the computer prepares a materials-requisition record, instantly recording the issue of materials in the materials and job-cost records. Each day, the computer sums the materials-requisition records charged to a particular job or manufacturing department. A performance report is then prepared monitoring the actual costs of direct materials. The use of direct materials can be reported hourly if managers believe the benefits exceed the cost of such frequent reporting. The Concepts in Action: Home Depot Undergoes an Inventory Management "Fix-It" describes Home Depot's use of technology to manage its inventory.

Similarly, information about direct manufacturing labor is obtained as employees log into computer terminals and key in job numbers, their employee numbers, and start and end times of their work on different jobs. The computer automatically prints the labor time record and, using hourly rates stored for each employee, calculates the direct manufacturing

Concepts in Action

Home Depot Undergoes an Inventory Management "Fix-It"

At the end of 2012, Home Depot had $10.7 billion worth of inventory. For many years, however, the world's largest home-improvement retailer struggled to know where that entire inventory was at any given time due to dated technology. As a result, Home Depot performed its own renovation to transform its inventory management using state-of-the-art technology across more than 2,200 stores in the United States, Canada, and Mexico.

Today, Home Depot uses advanced databases and mobile devices that help workers locate and manage inventory on the spot. When merchandise is scanned at the checkout, computer systems are automatically alerted when additional inventory is needed on store shelves. While Home Depot previously sent half-empty trucks to individual stores, new "rapid deployment" distribution centers now combine shipments to area stores, which trims costs and cuts truck trips by 50%. The company has deployed 59,000 "First Phone" mobile wireless devices that give store workers instant access to product information, check inventory levels, speed checkout times, and even allow customers to purchase their items through a PayPal account.

Home Depot's inventory management fix-it efforts have yielded significant benefits for the company. The new technology has helped more effectively manage inventory volume, reduce stockouts, reduce the need to sell overstocked items at clearance prices, and churn through inventory at a faster pace. Additionally, Home Depot employees now spend only 45% of their workday on stocking and inventory, down from 60% in 2008. This allows for more time helping customers, which increases sales.

Sources: Based on Miguel Bustillo, "Home Depot Undergoes Renovation," *The Wall Street Journal* (February 24, 2010); Meridith Levinson Sun, "Home Improvement," CIO (August 2004); Rachel Tobin Ramos, "Home Depot Getting Better Handle on Products," *The Atlanta Journal-Constitution* (March 29, 2010); Joel Schectman, "Home Depot Rolls Out New Mobile Devices for Workers," CIO Journal blog, *The Wall Street Journal*, June 21, 2012, http://blogs.wsj.com/; The Home Depot, Inc., 2013 Form 10-K (March 28, 2011).

labor costs of individual jobs. Information technology can also give managers instant feedback to help them control manufacturing overhead costs, jobs in process, jobs completed, and jobs shipped and installed at customer sites.

Learning Objective 5

Distinguish actual costing

...actual costing uses actual indirect-cost rates

from normal costing

...normal costing uses budgeted indirect-cost rates

Actual Costing

How would the cost of Job WPP 298 change if Robinson had used actual costing rather than normal costing? Both actual costing and normal costing trace direct costs to jobs in the same way because source documents identify the actual quantities and actual rates of direct materials and direct manufacturing labor for a job as the work is being done. The only difference between costing a job with normal costing and actual costing is that normal costing uses *budgeted* indirect-cost rates, whereas actual costing uses *actual* indirect-cost rates calculated annually at the end of the year. Exhibit 4-5 distinguishes actual costing from normal costing.

The following actual data for 2013 are for Robinson's manufacturing operations:

	Actual
Total manufacturing overhead costs	$1,215,000
Total direct manufacturing labor-hours	27,000

Exhibit 4-5

Actual Costing and Normal Costing Methods

	Actual Costing	Normal Costing
Direct Costs	*Actual direct-cost rates* × actual quantities of direct-cost inputs	*Actual direct-cost rates* × actual quantities of direct-cost inputs
Indirect Costs	*Actual indirect-cost rates* × actual quantities of cost-allocation bases	*Budgeted indirect-cost rates* × actual quantities of cost-allocation bases

Steps 1 and 2 are the same in both normal and actual costing: Step 1 identifies WPP 298 as the cost object; Step 2 calculates actual direct materials costs of $4,606 and actual direct manufacturing labor costs of $1,579. Recall from Step 3 that Robinson uses a single cost-allocation base, direct manufacturing labor-hours, to allocate all manufacturing overhead costs to jobs. The actual quantity of direct manufacturing labor-hours for 2013 is 27,000 hours. In Step 4, Robinson groups all actual indirect manufacturing costs of $1,215,000 into a single manufacturing overhead cost pool. In Step 5, the **actual indirect-cost rate** is calculated by dividing actual total indirect costs in the pool (determined in Step 4) by the actual total quantity of the cost-allocation base (determined in Step 3). Robinson calculates the actual manufacturing overhead rate in 2013 for its single manufacturing overhead cost pool as follows:

$$\text{Actual manufacturing overhead rate} = \frac{\text{Actual annual manufacturing overhead costs}}{\text{Actual annual quantity of the cost-allocation base}}$$
$$= \frac{\$1{,}215{,}000}{27{,}000 \text{ direct manufacturing labor-hours}}$$
$$= \$45 \text{ per direct manufacturing labor-hour}$$

In Step 6, under an actual-costing system,

$$\text{Manufacturing overhead costs allocated to WPP 298} = \text{Actual manufacturing overhead rate} \times \text{Actual quantity of direct manufacturing labor-hours}$$
$$= \$45 \text{ per direct manuf. labor-hour} \times 88 \text{ direct manufacturing labor-hours}$$
$$= \$3{,}960$$

In Step 7, the cost of the job under actual costing is $10,145, calculated as follows:

Direct manufacturing costs		
Direct materials	$4,606	
Direct manufacturing labor	1,579	$ 6,185
Manufacturing overhead costs		
($45 per direct manufacturing labor-hour × 88 actual direct manufacturing labor-hours)		3,960
Total manufacturing costs of job		$10,145

The manufacturing cost of the WPP 298 job is higher by $440 under actual costing ($10,145) than it is under normal costing ($9,705) because the actual indirect-cost rate is $45 per hour, whereas the budgeted indirect-cost rate is $40 per hour. That is, ($45 – $40) × 88 actual direct manufacturing labor-hours = $440.

As we discussed previously, the manufacturing costs of a job are available much earlier in a normal-costing system. Consequently, Robinson's manufacturing and sales managers can evaluate the profitability of different jobs, the efficiency with which the jobs are done, and the pricing of different jobs as soon as they are completed, while the experience is still fresh in everyone's mind. Another advantage of normal costing is that it provides managers with information earlier—while there is still time to take corrective actions, such as improving the company's labor efficiency or reducing the company's

Decision Point

How do you distinguish actual costing from normal costing?

overhead costs. At the end of the year, though, costs allocated using normal costing will not, in general, equal actual costs incurred. If the differences are significant, adjustments will need to be made so that the cost of jobs and the costs in various inventory accounts are based on actual rather than normal costing. We describe these adjustments later in the chapter.

The next section explains how a normal job-costing system aggregates the costs and revenues for all jobs worked on during a particular month. *Instructors and students who do not wish to explore these details can go directly to page 127 to the section "Budgeted Indirect Costs and End-of-Accounting-Year Adjustments."*

Learning Objective 6

Track the flow of costs in a job-costing system

...from purchase of materials to sale of finished goods

A Normal Job-Costing System in Manufacturing

The following example looks at events that occurred at Robinson Company in February 2013. Before getting into the details of normal costing, study Exhibit 4-6, which provides a broad framework for understanding the flow of costs in job costing.

The upper part of Exhibit 4-6 shows the flow of inventoriable costs from the purchase of materials and other manufacturing inputs to their conversion into work-in-process and finished goods, to the sale of finished goods.

Direct materials used and direct manufacturing labor can be easily traced to jobs. They become part of work-in-process inventory on the balance sheet because direct manufacturing labor transforms direct materials into another asset, work-in-process inventory. Robinson also incurs manufacturing overhead costs (including indirect materials and indirect manufacturing labor) to convert direct materials into work-in-process inventory. The overhead (indirect) costs, however, cannot be easily traced to individual jobs. Manufacturing overhead costs, therefore, are first accumulated in a manufacturing overhead account and then allocated to individual jobs. As manufacturing overhead costs are allocated, they become part of work-in-process inventory.

As individual jobs are completed, work-in-process inventory becomes another balance sheet asset, finished goods inventory. Only when finished goods are sold is the expense of cost of goods sold recognized in the income statement and matched against revenues earned.

The lower part of Exhibit 4-6 shows the period costs—marketing and customer-service costs. These costs do not create any assets on the balance sheet because they are not incurred to transform materials into a finished product. Instead, they are expensed in the income statement as they are incurred to best match revenues.

We next describe the entries made in the general ledger.

Exhibit 4-6 Flow of Costs in Job Costing

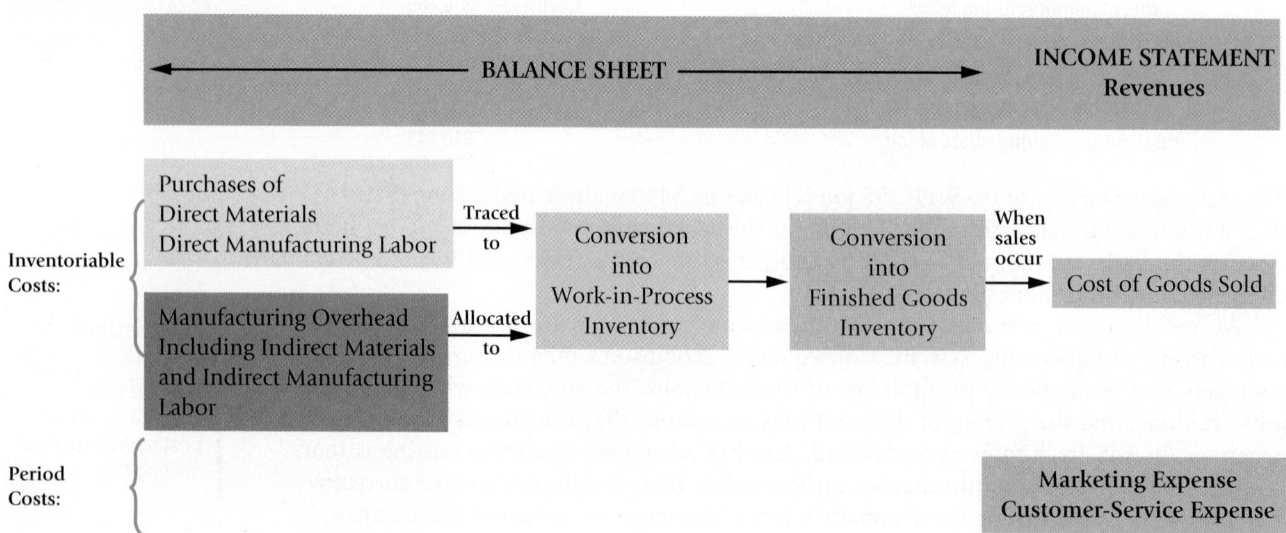

General Ledger

You know by this point that a job-costing system has a separate job-cost record for each job. A summary of the job-cost record is typically found in a subsidiary ledger. The general ledger account Work-in-Process Control presents the total of these separate job-cost records pertaining to all unfinished jobs. The job-cost records and Work-in-Process Control account track job costs from when jobs start until they are complete. When jobs are completed or sold, they are recorded in the finished goods inventory records of jobs in the subsidiary ledger. The general ledger account Finished Goods Control records the total of these separate job-cost records for all jobs completed and subsequently for all jobs sold.

Exhibit 4-7 shows T-account relationships for Robinson Company's general ledger. The general ledger gives a "bird's-eye view" of the costing system. The amounts shown in Exhibit 4-7 are based on the monthly transactions and journal entries that follow. As you go through each journal entry, use Exhibit 4-7 to see how the various entries being made come together. General ledger accounts with "Control" in their titles (for example, Materials Control and Accounts Payable Control) have underlying subsidiary ledgers that contain additional details, such as each type of material in inventory and individual suppliers Robinson must pay.

Some companies simultaneously make entries in the general ledger and subsidiary ledger accounts. Others, such as Robinson, make entries in the subsidiary ledger when transactions occur and entries in the general ledger less frequently, often on a monthly basis.

Exhibit 4-7 Manufacturing Job-Costing System Using Normal Costing: Diagram of General Ledger Relationships for February 2013

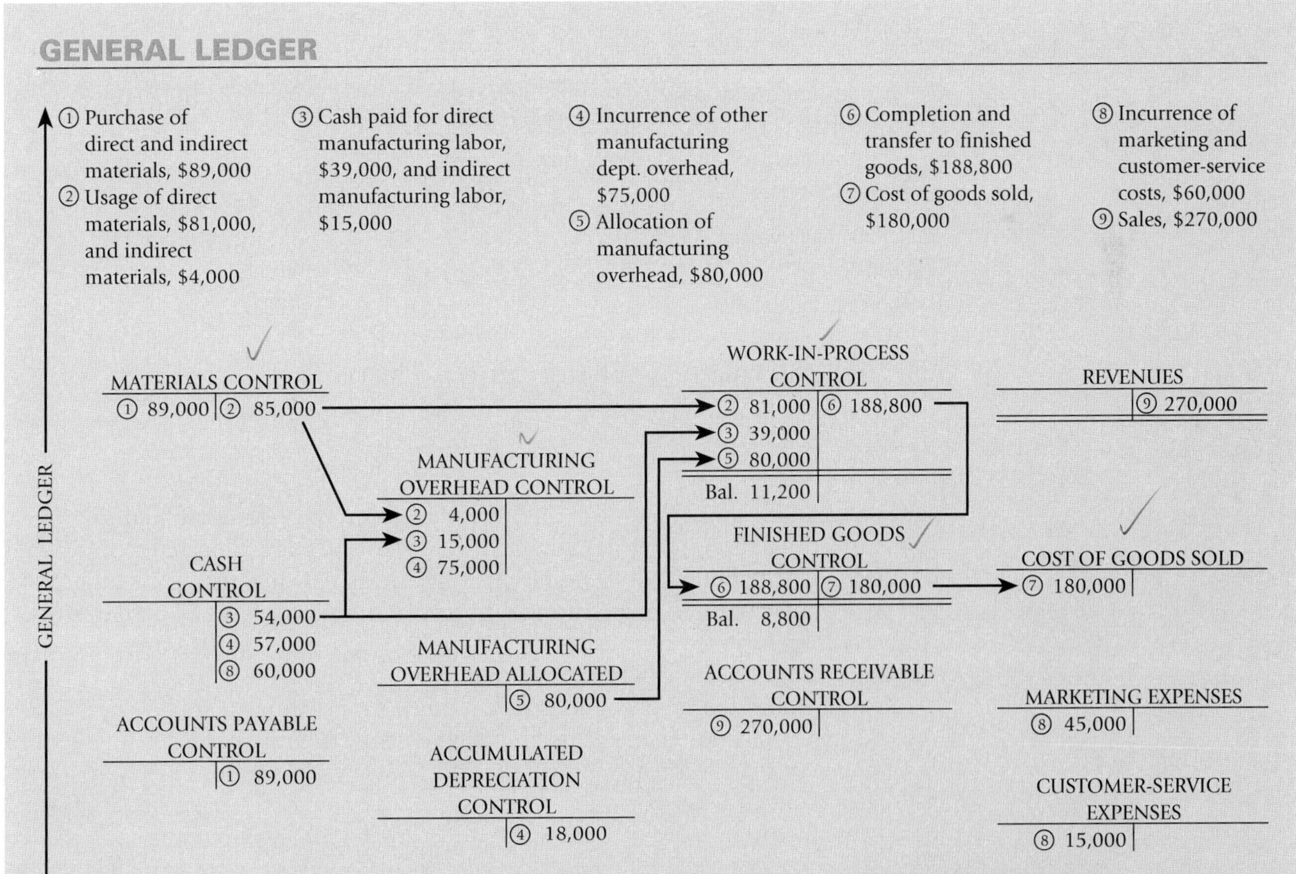

A general ledger should be viewed as only one of many tools managers can use for planning and control. To control operations, managers rely on not only the source documents used to record amounts in the subsidiary ledgers, but also on nonfinancial information such as the percentage of jobs requiring rework.

Explanations of Transactions

We next look at a summary of Robinson Company's transactions for February 2013 and the corresponding journal entries for those transactions.

1. Purchases of materials (direct and indirect) on credit, $89,000

Materials Control	89,000	
Accounts Payable Control		89,000

2. Usage of direct materials, $81,000, and indirect materials, $4,000

Work-in-Process Control	81,000	
Manufacturing Overhead Control	4,000	
Materials Control		85,000

3. Manufacturing payroll for February: direct labor, $39,000, and indirect labor, $15,000, paid in cash

Work-in-Process Control	39,000	
Manufacturing Overhead Control	15,000	
Cash Control		54,000

4. Other manufacturing overhead costs incurred during February, $75,000, consisting of
   - supervision and engineering salaries, $44,000 (paid in cash);
   - plant utilities, repairs, and insurance, $13,000 (paid in cash); and
   - plant depreciation, $18,000

Manufacturing Overhead Control	75,000	
Cash Control		57,000
Accumulated Depreciation Control		18,000

5. Allocation of manufacturing overhead to jobs, $80,000

Work-in-Process Control	80,000	
Manufacturing Overhead Allocated		80,000

Under normal costing, **manufacturing overhead allocated**—or **manufacturing overhead applied**—is the amount of manufacturing overhead costs allocated to individual jobs based on the budgeted rate multiplied by the actual quantity of the allocation base used for each job. Manufacturing overhead allocated contains all manufacturing overhead costs assigned to jobs using a cost-allocation base because overhead costs cannot be traced specifically to jobs in an economically feasible way.

Keep in mind the distinct difference between transactions 4 and 5. In transaction 4, actual overhead costs incurred throughout the month are added (debited) to the Manufacturing Overhead Control account. These costs are not debited to Work-in-Process Control because unlike direct costs, they cannot be traced to individual jobs. Manufacturing overhead costs are added (debited) to individual jobs and to Work-in-Process Control *only when* manufacturing overhead costs are allocated in transaction 5. At the time these costs are allocated, Manufacturing Overhead Control is, *in effect,* decreased (credited) via its contra account, Manufacturing Overhead Allocated. Manufacturing Overhead Allocated is referred to as a *contra account* because the amounts debited to it represent the amounts credited to the Manufacturing

Overhead Control account. Having Manufacturing Overhead Allocated as a contra account allows the job-costing system to separately retain information about the manufacturing overhead costs the company has *incurred* (in the Manufacturing Overhead Control account) as well as the amount of manufacturing overhead costs it has *allocated* (in the Manufacturing Overhead Allocated account). If the allocated manufacturing overhead had been credited to manufacturing overhead control, the company would lose information about the actual manufacturing overhead costs it is incurring.

Under the normal-costing system described in our Robinson Company example, at the beginning of the year, the company calculated the budgeted manufacturing overhead rate of $40 per direct manufacturing labor-hour by predicting the company's annual manufacturing overhead costs and annual quantity of the cost-allocation base. Almost certainly, the actual amounts allocated will differ from the predictions. We discuss what to do with this difference later in the chapter.

6. The sum of all individual jobs completed and transferred to finished goods in February 2013 is $188,800

Finished Goods Control	188,800	
Work-in-Process Control		188,800

7. Cost of goods sold, $180,000

Cost of Goods Sold	180,000	
Finished Goods Control		180,000

8. Marketing costs for February 2013, $45,000, and customer-service costs for February 2013, $15,000, paid in cash

Marketing Expenses	45,000	
Customer-Service Expenses	15,000	
Cash Control		60,000

9. Sales revenues from all jobs sold and delivered in February 2013, all on credit, $270,000

Accounts Receivable Control	270,000	
Revenues		270,000

Subsidiary Ledgers

Exhibits 4-8 and 4-9 present subsidiary ledgers that contain the underlying details—the "worm's-eye view"—that help Robinson's managers keep track of the WPP 298 job, as opposed to the "bird's-eye view" of the general ledger. The sum of all entries in underlying subsidiary ledgers equals the total amount in the corresponding general ledger control accounts.

Materials Records by Type of Material

The subsidiary ledger for materials at Robinson Company—called *Materials Records*—is used to continuously record the quantity of materials received, issued to jobs, and the inventory balances for each type of material. Panel A of Exhibit 4-8 shows the Materials Record for Metal Brackets (Part No. MB 468-A). In many companies, the source documents supporting the receipt and issue of materials (the material requisition record in Exhibit 4-3, Panel A, (page 114)) are scanned into a computer. Software programs then automatically update the Materials Records and make all the necessary accounting entries in the subsidiary and general ledgers. The cost of materials received across all types of direct and indirect material records for February 2013 is $89,000 (Exhibit 4-8, Panel A). The cost of materials issued across all types of direct and indirect material records for February 2013 is $85,000 (Exhibit 4-8, Panel A).

Exhibit 4-8 Subsidiary Ledgers for Materials, Labor, and Manufacturing Department Overhead[1]

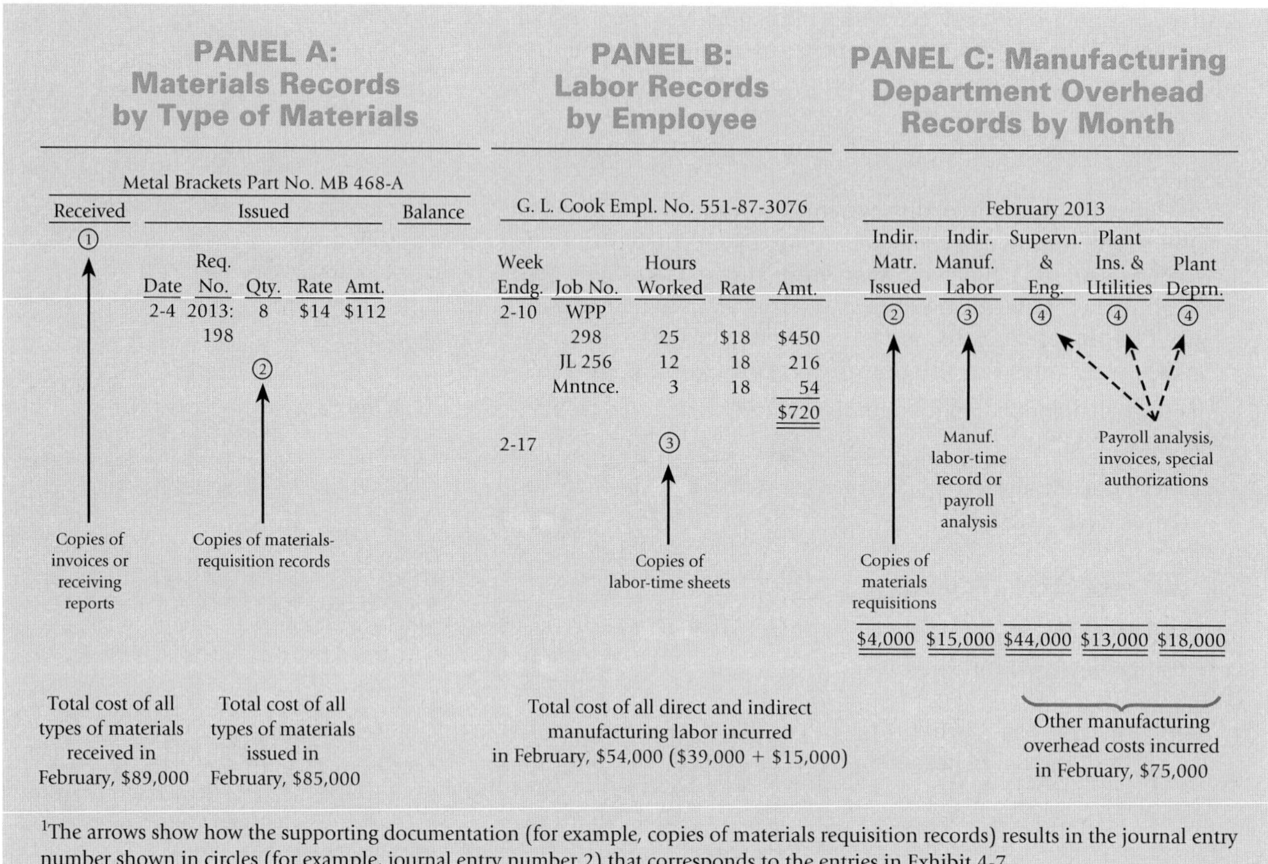

[1]The arrows show how the supporting documentation (for example, copies of materials requisition records) results in the journal entry number shown in circles (for example, journal entry number 2) that corresponds to the entries in Exhibit 4-7.

As direct materials are used, they are recorded as issued in the Materials Records (see Exhibit 4-8, Panel A, for a record of the Metal Brackets issued for the WPP machine job). Direct materials are also charged to Work-in-Process Inventory Records for Jobs, which are the subsidiary ledger accounts for the Work-in-Process Control account in the general ledger. For example, the metal brackets used in the WPP machine job appear as direct material costs of $112 in the subsidiary ledger under the work-in-process inventory record for WPP 298 [Exhibit 4-9, Panel A, which is based on the job-cost record source document in Exhibit 4-2, (page 113)]. The cost of direct materials used across all job-cost records for February 2013 is $81,000 (Exhibit 4-9, Panel A).

As indirect materials (for example, lubricants) are used, they are charged to the Manufacturing Department overhead records (Exhibit 4-8, Panel C), which comprise the subsidiary ledger for the Manufacturing Overhead Control account. The Manufacturing Department overhead records are used to accumulate actual costs in individual overhead categories by each indirect-cost-pool account in the general ledger. Recall that Robinson has only one indirect-cost pool: Manufacturing Overhead. The cost of indirect materials used is not added directly to individual job records. Instead, this cost is allocated to individual job records as a part of manufacturing overhead.

Labor Records by Employee

Labor records by employee (see Exhibit 4-8, Panel B, for G. L. Cook) are used to trace the costs of direct manufacturing labor to individual jobs and to accumulate the costs of indirect manufacturing labor in the Manufacturing Department overhead records (Exhibit 4-8, Panel C). The labor records are based on the labor-time sheet source documents (see Exhibit 4-3, Panel B, (page 114)). The subsidiary ledger for employee

Exhibit 4-9 Subsidiary Ledgers for Individual Jobs[1]

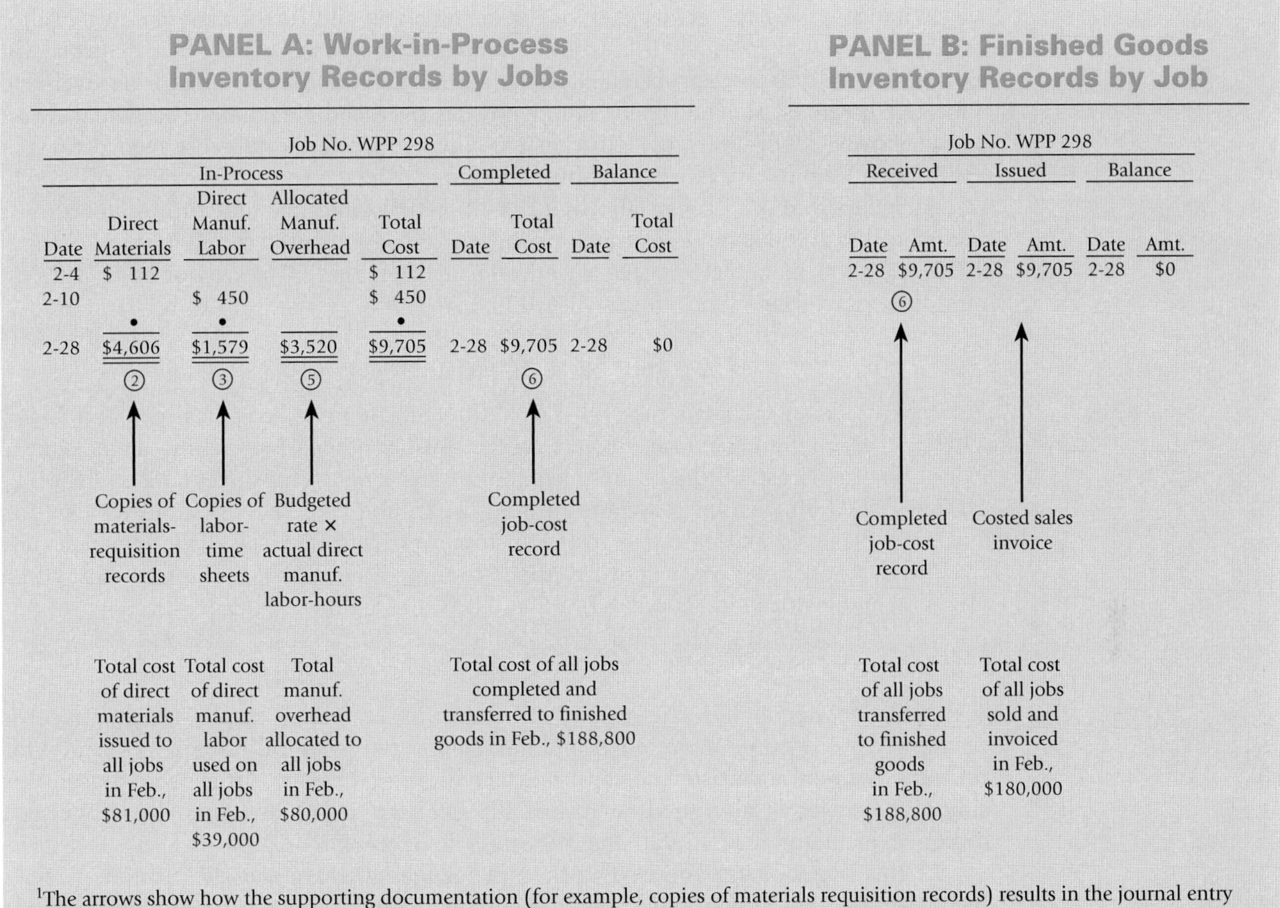

[1]The arrows show how the supporting documentation (for example, copies of materials requisition records) results in the journal entry number shown in circles (for example, journal entry number 2) that corresponds to the entries in Exhibit 4-7.

labor records (Exhibit 4-8, Panel B) shows the different jobs that G. L. Cook, Employee No. 551-87-3076, worked on and the $720 of wages owed to Cook, for the week ending February 10. The sum of total wages owed to all employees for February 2013 is $54,000. The job-cost record for WPP 298 shows direct manufacturing labor costs of $450 for the time Cook spent on the WPP machine job during that week (Exhibit 4-9, Panel A). Total direct manufacturing labor costs recorded in all job-cost records (the subsidiary ledger for Work-in-Process Control) for February 2013 is $39,000.

G. L. Cook's employee record shows $54 for maintenance, which is an indirect manufacturing labor cost. The total indirect manufacturing labor costs of $15,000 for February 2013 appear in the Manufacturing Department overhead records in the subsidiary ledger (Exhibit 4-8, Panel C). These costs, by definition, cannot be traced to an individual job. Instead, they are allocated to individual jobs as a part of manufacturing overhead.

Manufacturing Department Overhead Records by Month

The Manufacturing Department overhead records (see Exhibit 4-8, Panel C) that make up the subsidiary ledger for the Manufacturing Overhead Control account show details of different categories of overhead costs such as indirect materials, indirect manufacturing labor, supervision and engineering, plant insurance and utilities, and plant depreciation. The source documents for these entries include invoices (for example, a utility bill) and special schedules (for example, a depreciation schedule) from the responsible accounting officer. Manufacturing department overhead for February 2013 is indirect materials, $4,000; indirect manufacturing labor, $15,000; and other manufacturing overhead, $75,000 (Exhibit 4-8, Panel C).

Work-in-Process Inventory Records by Jobs

As we have already discussed, the job-cost record for each individual job in the subsidiary ledger is debited by the actual cost of direct materials and direct manufacturing labor used by individual jobs. In Robinson's normal-costing system, the job-cost record for each individual job in the subsidiary ledger is also debited for manufacturing overhead allocated based on the budgeted manufacturing overhead rate times the actual direct manufacturing labor-hours used in that job. For example, the job-cost record for Job WPP 298 (Exhibit 4-9, Panel A) shows Manufacturing Overhead Allocated of $3,520 (the budgeted rate of $40 per labor-hour × 88 actual direct manufacturing labor-hours used). For the 2,000 actual direct manufacturing labor-hours used for all jobs in February 2013, the total manufacturing overhead allocated equals $40 per labor-hour × 2,000 direct manufacturing labor-hours = $80,000.

Finished Goods Inventory Records by Jobs

Exhibit 4-9, Panel A, shows that Job WPP 298 was completed at a cost of $9,705. Job WPP 298 also simultaneously appears in the finished goods records of the subsidiary ledger. The total cost of all jobs completed and transferred to finished goods in February 2013 is $188,800 (Exhibit 4-9, Panels A and B). Exhibit 4-9, Panel B, indicates that Job WPP 298 was sold and delivered to the customer on February 28, 2013, at which time $9,705 was transferred from finished goods to cost of goods sold. The total cost of all jobs sold and invoiced in February 2013 is $180,000 (Exhibit 4-9, Panel B).

Other Subsidiary Records

Just as it does for manufacturing payroll, Robinson maintains employee labor records in subsidiary ledgers for marketing and customer-service payroll as well as records for different types of advertising costs (print, television, and radio). An accounts receivable subsidiary ledger is also used to record the February 2013 amounts due from each customer, including the $15,000 due from the sale of Job WPP 298.

At this point, pause and review the nine entries in this example. Exhibit 4-7 is a handy summary of all nine general-ledger entries presented in the form of T-accounts. Be sure to trace each journal entry, step by step, to T-accounts in the general ledger presented in Exhibit 4-7. Robinson's managers will use this information to evaluate how Robinson has performed on the WPP job.

Exhibit 4-10 provides Robinson's income statement for February 2013 using information from entries 7, 8, and 9. Managers could further subdivide the cost of goods sold calculations and present them in the format of Exhibit 2-8 [(page 42)]. The benefit of using the subdivided format is that it allows managers to discern detailed performance trends that can help them improve the efficiency on future jobs.

Exhibit 4-10

Robinson Company Income Statement for the Month Ending February 2013

Revenues		$270,000
Cost of goods sold ($180,000 + $14,000[1])		194,000
Gross margin		76,000
Operating costs		
Marketing costs	$45,000	
Customer-service costs	15,000	
Total operating costs		60,000
Operating income		$ 16,000

[1]Cost of goods sold has been increased by $14,000, the difference between the Manufacturing overhead control account ($94,000) and the Manufacturing overhead allocated ($80,000). In a later section of this chapter, we discuss this adjustment, which represents the amount by which actual manufacturing overhead cost exceeds the manufacturing overhead allocated to jobs during February 2013.

Nonmanufacturing Costs and Job Costing

In Chapter 2 (pages 48–49), you learned that companies use product costs for different purposes. The product costs reported as inventoriable costs to shareholders may differ from the product costs reported to managers to guide their pricing and product-mix decisions. Managers must keep in mind that even though marketing and customer-service costs are expensed when incurred for financial accounting purposes, companies often trace or allocate these costs to individual jobs for pricing, product-mix, and cost-management decisions.

Robinson can trace direct marketing costs and customer-service costs to jobs the same way in which it traces direct manufacturing costs to jobs. Assume these costs have the same cost-allocation base, revenues, and are included in a single cost pool. Robinson can then calculate a budgeted indirect-cost rate by dividing budgeted indirect marketing costs plus budgeted indirect customer-service costs by budgeted revenues. Robinson can use this rate to allocate these indirect costs to jobs. For example, if this rate were 15% of revenues, Robinson would allocate $2,250 to Job WPP 298 (0.15 × $15,000, the revenue from the job). By assigning both manufacturing costs and nonmanufacturing costs to jobs, Robinson can compare all costs against the revenues that different jobs generate.

Decision Point

How are transactions recorded in a manufacturing job-costing system?

Budgeted Indirect Costs and End-of-Accounting-Year Adjustments

Learning Objective 7

Dispose of under- or overallocated manufacturing overhead costs at the end of the fiscal year using alternative methods

...for example, writing off this amount to the Cost of Goods Sold account

Managers try to closely approximate actual manufacturing overhead costs and actual direct manufacturing labor-hours when calculating the budgeted indirect cost rate. However, for the numerator and denominator reasons explained earlier in the chapter, under normal costing, a company's actual overhead costs incurred each month are not likely to equal its overhead costs allocated each month. Even at the end of the year, allocated costs are unlikely to equal actual costs because they are based on estimates made up to 12 months before actual costs are incurred. We now describe adjustments that management accountants need to make when, at the end of the fiscal year, indirect costs allocated differ from actual indirect costs incurred. These adjustments affect the reported income numbers used to evaluate managerial performance.

Underallocated and Overallocated Indirect Costs

Underallocated indirect costs occur when the allocated amount of indirect costs in an accounting period is less than the actual (incurred) amount. **Overallocated indirect costs** occur when the allocated amount of indirect costs in an accounting period is greater than the actual (incurred) amount.

Underallocated (overallocated) indirect costs = Actual indirect costs incurred − Indirect costs allocated

Underallocated (overallocated) indirect costs are also called **underapplied (overapplied) indirect costs** and **underabsorbed (overabsorbed) indirect costs.**

Consider the manufacturing overhead cost pool at Robinson Company. There are two indirect-cost accounts in the general ledger that have to do with manufacturing overhead:

1. Manufacturing Overhead Control, the record of the actual costs in all the individual overhead categories (such as indirect materials, indirect manufacturing labor, supervision, engineering, utilities, and plant depreciation)
2. Manufacturing Overhead Allocated, the record of the manufacturing overhead allocated to individual jobs on the basis of the budgeted rate multiplied by actual direct manufacturing labor-hours

At the end of the year, the overhead accounts show the following amounts.

Manufacturing Overhead Control			Manufacturing Overhead Allocated	
Bal. Dec. 31, 2013	1,215,000		Bal. Dec. 31, 2013	1,080,000

The $1,080,000 credit balance in Manufacturing Overhead Allocated results from multiplying the 27,000 actual direct manufacturing labor-hours worked on all jobs in 2013 by the budgeted rate of $40 per direct manufacturing labor-hour.

The $135,000 ($1,215,000 – $1,080,000) difference (a net debit) is an underallocated amount because actual manufacturing overhead costs are greater than the allocated amount. This difference arises for two reasons related to the computation of the $40 budgeted hourly rate:

1. **Numerator reason (indirect-cost pool).** Actual manufacturing overhead costs of $1,215,000 are greater than the budgeted amount of $1,120,000.
2. **Denominator reason (quantity of allocation base).** Actual direct manufacturing labor-hours of 27,000 are fewer than the budgeted 28,000 hours.

There are three main approaches to accounting for the $135,000 underallocated manufacturing overhead caused by Robinson underestimating manufacturing overhead costs and overestimating the quantity of the cost-allocation base: (1) adjusted allocation-rate approach, (2) proration approach, and (3) writeoff to cost of goods sold approach.

Adjusted Allocation-Rate Approach

The **adjusted allocation-rate approach** restates all overhead entries in the general ledger and subsidiary ledgers using actual cost rates rather than budgeted cost rates. First, the actual manufacturing overhead rate is computed at the end of the fiscal year. Then the manufacturing overhead costs allocated to every job during the year are recomputed using the actual manufacturing overhead rate (rather than the budgeted manufacturing overhead rate). Finally, end-of-year closing entries are made. The result is that at year-end, every job-cost record and finished goods record—as well as the ending Work-in-Process Control, Finished Goods Control, and Cost of Goods Sold accounts—represent actual manufacturing overhead costs incurred.

The widespread adoption of computerized accounting systems has greatly reduced the cost of using the adjusted allocation-rate approach. In our Robinson example, the actual manufacturing overhead ($1,215,000) exceeds the manufacturing overhead allocated ($1,080,000) by 12.5% [($1,215,000 – $1,080,000) ÷ $1,080,000]. At year-end, Robinson could increase the manufacturing overhead allocated to each job in 2013 by 12.5% using a single software command. The command would adjust both the subsidiary ledgers and the general ledger.

Consider the Western Pulp and Paper machine job, WPP 298. Under normal costing, the manufacturing overhead allocated to the job is $3,520 (the budgeted rate of $40 per direct manufacturing labor-hour × 88 hours). Increasing the manufacturing overhead allocated by 12.5%, or $440 ($3,520 × 0.125), means the adjusted amount of manufacturing overhead allocated to Job WPP 298 equals $3,960 ($3,520 + $440). Note from page (page 119) that using actual costing, manufacturing overhead allocated to this job is $3,960 (the actual rate of $45 per direct manufacturing labor-hour × 88 hours). Making this adjustment under normal costing for each job in the subsidiary ledgers ensures that actual manufacturing overhead costs of $1,215,000 are allocated to jobs.

The adjusted allocation-rate approach yields the benefits of both the *timeliness and convenience of normal costing during the year and the allocation of actual manufacturing overhead costs at year-end.* Each individual job-cost record and the end-of-year account balances for inventories and cost of goods sold are adjusted to actual costs. These adjustments, in turn, will affect the income Robinson reports. Knowing the actual profitability of individual jobs after they are completed provides managers with accurate and useful insights for future decisions about which jobs to undertake, how to price them, and how to manage their costs.

Proration Approach

The **proration** approach spreads underallocated overhead or overallocated overhead among ending work-in-process inventory, finished goods inventory, and cost of goods sold. Materials inventory is not included in this proration because no manufacturing overhead costs have been allocated to it. We illustrate end-of-year proration in the Robinson Company example. Assume the following actual results for Robinson Company in 2013:

	A	B	C
1	Account	Account Balance (Before Proration)	Allocated Manufacturing Overhead Included in Each Account Balance (Before Proration)
2	Work-in-process control	$ 50,000	$ 16,200
3	Finished goods control	75,000	31,320
4	Cost of goods sold	2,375,000	1,032,480
5		$2,500,000	$1,080,000

How should Robinson prorate the underallocated $135,000 of manufacturing overhead at the end of 2013?

Robinson prorates underallocated or overallocated amounts on the basis of the total amount of manufacturing overhead allocated in 2013 (before proration) in the ending balances of Work-in-Process Control, Finished Goods Control, and Cost of Goods Sold accounts. The $135,000 underallocated overhead is prorated over the three accounts in proportion to the total amount of manufacturing overhead allocated (before proration) in column 2 of the following table, resulting in the ending balances (after proration) in column 5 at actual costs.

	A	B	C	D	E	F	G
10		Account Balance (Before Proration)	Allocated Manufacturing Overhead Included in Each Account Balance (Before Proration)	Allocated Manufacturing Overhead Included in Each Account Balance as a Percent of Total	Proration of $135,000 of Underallocated Manufacturing Overhead		Account Balance (After Proration)
11	Account	(1)	(2)	(3) = (2) / $1,080,000	(4) = (3) x $135,000		(5) = (1) + (4)
12	Work-in-process control	$ 50,000	$ 16,200	1.5%	0.015 x $135,000 =	$ 2,025	$ 52,025
13	Finished goods control	75,000	31,320	2.9%	0.029 x 135,000 =	3,915	78,915
14	Cost of goods sold	2,375,000	1,032,480	95.6%	0.956 x 135,000 =	129,060	2,504,060
15	Total	$2,500,000	$1,080,000	100.0%		$135,000	$2,635,000

Prorating on the basis of the manufacturing overhead allocated (before proration) results in Robinson allocating manufacturing overhead based on actual manufacturing overhead costs. Recall that Robinson's actual manufacturing overhead ($1,215,000) in 2013 exceeds its manufacturing overhead allocated ($1,080,000) in 2013 by 12.5%. The proration amounts in column 4 can also be derived by multiplying the balances in column 2 by 0.125. For example, the $3,915 proration to Finished Goods is 0.125 × $31,320. Adding these amounts effectively means allocating manufacturing overhead at 112.5% of what had been allocated before. The journal entry to record this proration is as follows:

Work-in-Process Control	2,025	
Finished Goods Control	3,915	
Cost of Goods Sold	129,060	
Manufacturing Overhead Allocated	1,080,000	
Manufacturing Overhead Control		1,215,000

If manufacturing overhead had been overallocated, the Work-in-Process Control, Finished Goods Control, and Cost of Goods Sold accounts would be decreased (credited) instead of increased (debited).

This journal entry closes (brings to zero) the manufacturing overhead-related accounts and restates the 2013 ending balances for Work-in-Process Control, Finished Goods Control, and Cost of Goods Sold to what they would have been if actual manufacturing overhead rates had been used rather than budgeted manufacturing overhead rates. This method reports the same 2013 ending balances in the general ledger as the adjusted allocation-rate approach does. However, unlike the adjusted allocation-rate approach, the sum of the amounts shown in the subsidiary ledgers will not match the amounts shown in the general ledger after proration because no adjustments from budgeted to actual manufacturing overhead rates are made in the individual job-cost records. The objective of the proration approach is to only adjust the general ledger to actual manufacturing overhead rates for purposes of financial reporting. The increase in cost of goods sold expense by $129,060 as a result of the proration causes Robinson's reported operating income to decrease by the same amount.

Some companies use the proration approach but base it on the ending balances of Work-in-Process Control, Finished Goods Control, and Cost of Goods Sold accounts prior to proration (see column 1 of the preceding table). The following table shows that prorations based on ending account balances are not the same as the more accurate prorations calculated earlier based on the amount of manufacturing overhead allocated to the accounts because the proportions of manufacturing overhead costs to total costs in these accounts are not the same.

	A	B	C	D	E	F
1		Account Balance (Before Proration)	Account Balance as a Percent of Total	Proration of $135,000 of Underallocated Manufacturing Overhead		Account Balance (After Proration)
2	Account	(1)	(2) = (1) / $2,500,000	(3) = (2) x $135,000		(4) = (1) + (3)
3	Work-in-process control	$ 50,000	2.0%	0.02 x $135,000 =	$ 2,700	$ 52,700
4	Finished goods control	75,000	3.0%	0.03 x 135,000 =	4,050	79,050
5	Cost of goods sold	2,375,000	95.0%	0.95 x 135,000 =	128,250	2,503,250
6	Total	$2,500,000	100.0%		$135,000	$2,635,000

However, proration based on ending balances is frequently justified as being an expedient way of approximating the more accurate results from using manufacturing overhead costs allocated.

Writeoff to Cost of Goods Sold Approach

Under the writeoff approach, the total under- or overallocated manufacturing overhead is included in this year's Cost of Goods Sold. For Robinson, the journal entry would be as follows:

Cost of Goods Sold	135,000	
Manufacturing Overhead Allocated	1,080,000	
Manufacturing Overhead Control		1,215,000

Robinson's two Manufacturing Overhead accounts—Manufacturing Overhead Control and Manufacturing Overhead Allocated—are closed with the difference between them included in cost of goods sold. The Cost of Goods Sold account after the writeoff equals $2,510,000, the balance before the writeoff of $2,375,000 *plus the underallocated* manufacturing overhead amount of $135,000. This results in operating income decreasing by $135,000.

Choosing Among Approaches

Which of the three approaches of dealing with underallocated overhead and overallocated overhead is the best one to use? When making this decision, managers should consider the amount of underallocated or overallocated overhead and the purpose of the adjustment, as the following table indicates.

If the purpose of the adjustment is to . . .	and the total amount of underallocation or overallocation is . . .	then managers prefer to use the . . .
state the balance sheet and income statements based on actual rather than budgeted manufacturing overhead rates	big, relative to total operating income, and inventory levels are high	proration method because it is the most accurate method of allocating actual manufacturing overhead costs to the general ledger accounts.
state the balance sheet and income statements based on actual rather than budgeted manufacturing overhead rates	small, relative to total operating income, or inventory levels are low	writeoff to cost of goods sold approach because it is a good approximation of the more accurate proration method.
provide an accurate record of actual individual job costs in order to conduct a profitability analysis, learn how to better manage the costs of jobs, and bid on future jobs	big, relative to total operating income,	adjusted-allocation rate method because it makes adjustments in individual job records in addition to the general ledger accounts.

Many management accountants and managers argue that to the extent that the underallocated overhead cost measures inefficiency during the period, it should be written off to the Cost of Goods Sold account instead of being prorated to the Work-in-Process or Finished Goods inventory accounts. This line of reasoning favors applying a combination of the writeoff and proration methods. For example, the portion of the underallocated overhead cost that is due to inefficiency (say, because of excessive spending or idle capacity) and that could have been avoided should be written off to the Cost of Goods Sold account, whereas the portion that is unavoidable should be prorated. Unlike full proration, this approach avoids making the costs of inefficiency part of inventory assets.

As our discussion suggests, choosing which method to use and determining the amount to be written off is often a matter of judgment. The method managers choose affects the operating income a company reports. In the case of underallocated overhead, the method of writing it off to cost of goods sold results in lower operating income compared to proration. In the case of overallocated overhead, proration results in lower operating income compared to writing the overhead off to cost of goods sold. Reporting lower operating income lowers the company's taxes, saving the company cash and increasing the company's value. Reporting higher operating income, however, can increase the compensation managers earn even though it results in higher taxes for the company. Top managers design compensation plans to encourage managers to take actions that increase a company's value. For example, the compensation plan might reward the managers for after-tax cash flow metrics, in addition to achieving various levels of operating income, to align decision making and performance evaluation. Occasionally, if a company is experiencing financial difficulty, its managers may prefer to report higher operating income to avoid showing losses that could affect the firm's credit rating and result in its loans being called. In general, however, managers should choose the method that increases the company's value and best represents its performance, while consistently applying the same method year after year. At no time should managers make choices that are illegal or unethical. We discuss these issues in more detail in another chapter (Chapter 23).

Decision Point

How should managers dispose of under- or overallocated manufacturing overhead costs at the end of the accounting year?

Robinson's managers believed that a single manufacturing overhead cost pool with direct manufacturing labor-hours as the cost-allocation base was appropriate for allocating all manufacturing overhead costs to jobs. Had Robinson's managers felt that different manufacturing departments (for example, machining and assembly) used overhead resources differently, they would have assigned overhead costs to each department and calculated a separate overhead allocation rate for each department based on the cost driver of the overhead costs in each department. The general ledger would contain Manufacturing Overhead Control and Manufacturing Overhead Allocated accounts for each department, resulting in end-of-year adjustments for underallocated or overallocated overhead costs for each department.

Instructors and students interested in exploring these more detailed allocations can go to Chapter 15, where we continue the Robinson Company example.

Learning Objective 8

Understand variations from normal costing

...some variations from normal costing use budgeted direct-cost rates

Variations from Normal Costing: A Service-Sector Example

Job costing is also very useful in service organizations such as accounting and consulting firms, advertising agencies, auto repair shops, and hospitals. In an accounting firm, each audit is a job. The costs of each audit are accumulated in a job-cost record, much like the document used by Robinson Company, based on the seven-step approach described earlier. On the basis of labor-time sheets, direct labor costs of the professional staff—audit partners, audit managers, and audit staff—are traced to individual jobs. Other direct costs, such as travel, out-of-town meals and lodging, phone, fax, and copying, are also traced to jobs. The costs of secretarial support, office staff, rent, and depreciation of furniture and equipment are indirect costs because these costs cannot be traced to jobs in an economically feasible way. Indirect costs are allocated to jobs, for example, using a cost-allocation base such as number of professional labor-hours.

In some service organizations, a variation from normal costing is helpful because actual direct-labor costs, the largest component of total costs, can be difficult to trace to jobs as they are completed. For example, the actual direct-labor costs of an audit may include bonuses that become known only at the end of the year (a numerator reason). Also, the hours worked each period might vary significantly depending on the number of working days each month and the demand for services (a denominator reason) while the direct-labor costs remain largely fixed. It would be inappropriate to charge a job with higher actual direct labor costs simply because a month had fewer working days or demand for services was low in that month. Using budgeted rates gives a better picture of the direct labor cost per hour that the company had planned when it hired the workers. In situations like these, a company needing timely information during the progress of an audit will use budgeted rates for some direct costs and budgeted rates for other indirect costs. All budgeted rates are calculated at the start of the fiscal year. In contrast, normal costing uses actual cost rates for all direct costs and budgeted cost rates only for indirect costs.

The mechanics of using budgeted rates for direct costs are similar to the methods employed when using budgeted rates for indirect costs in normal costing. We illustrate this for Donahue and Associates, a public accounting firm. For 2013, Donahue budgets total direct-labor costs of \$14,400,000, total indirect costs of \$12,960,000, and total direct (professional) labor-hours of 288,000. In this case,

$$\text{Budgeted direct-labor cost rate} = \frac{\text{Budgeted total direct-labor costs}}{\text{Budgeted total direct-labor hours}}$$

$$= \frac{\$14{,}400{,}000}{288{,}000 \text{ direct labor-hours}} = \$50 \text{ per direct labor-hour}$$

Assuming only one indirect-cost pool and total direct-labor costs as the cost-allocation base,

$$\text{Budgeted indirect cost rate} = \frac{\text{Budgeted total costs in indirect cost pool}}{\text{Budgeted total quantity of cost-allocation base (direct-labor costs)}}$$

$$= \frac{\$12{,}960{,}000}{\$14{,}400{,}000} = 0.90\text{, or 90\% of direct-labor costs}$$

Suppose that in March 2013, an audit of Hanley Transport, a client of Donahue, uses 800 direct labor-hours. Donahue calculates the direct-labor costs of the audit by multiplying the budgeted direct-labor cost rate, $50 per direct labor-hour, by 800, the actual quantity of direct labor-hours. The indirect costs allocated to the Hanley Transport audit are determined by multiplying the budgeted indirect-cost rate (90%) by the direct-labor costs assigned to the job ($40,000). Assuming no other direct costs for travel and the like, the cost of the Hanley Transport audit is as follows:

Direct-labor costs, $50 × 800	$ 40,000
Indirect costs allocated, 90% × $40,000	36,000
Total	$76,000

At the end of the fiscal year, the direct costs traced to jobs using budgeted rates will generally not equal actual direct costs because the actual rate and the budgeted rate are developed at different times using different information. End-of-year adjustments for underallocated or overallocated direct costs would need to be made in the same way that adjustments are made for underallocated or overallocated indirect costs.

The Donahue and Associates example illustrates that all costing systems do not exactly match either the actual-costing system or the normal-costing system described earlier in the chapter. As another example, engineering consulting firms, such as Tata Consulting Engineers in India and Terracon Consulting Engineers in the United States, often use budgeted rates to allocate indirect costs (such as engineering and office-support costs) as well as some direct costs (such as professional labor-hours) and trace some actual direct costs (such as the cost of making blueprints and fees paid to outside experts). Users of costing systems should be aware of the different systems that they may encounter.

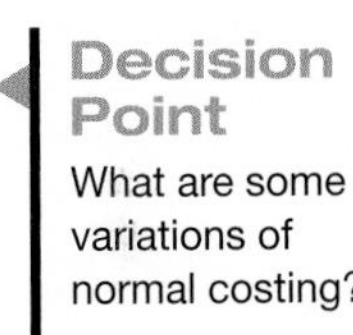

Decision Point
What are some variations of normal costing?

Problem for Self-Study

Your manager asks you to bring the following incomplete accounts of Endeavor Printing, Inc., up to date through January 31, 2014. Consider the data that appear in the T-accounts as well as the following information in items (a) through (j).

Endeavor's normal-costing system has two direct-cost categories (direct material costs and direct manufacturing labor costs) and one indirect-cost pool (manufacturing overhead costs, which are allocated using direct manufacturing labor costs).

Materials Control	
12-31-2013 Bal. 15,000	

Wages Payable Control	
	1-31-2014 Bal. 3,000

Work-in-Process Control	

Manufacturing Overhead Control	
1-31-2014 Bal. 57,000	

Finished Goods Control	
12-31-2013 Bal. 20,000	

Costs of Goods Sold	

Additional information follows:

a. Manufacturing overhead is allocated using a budgeted rate that is set every December. You forecast next year's manufacturing overhead costs and next year's direct manufacturing labor costs. The budget for 2014 is $600,000 for manufacturing overhead costs and $400,000 for direct manufacturing labor costs.
b. The only job unfinished on January 31, 2014, is No. 419, on which direct manufacturing labor costs are $2,000 (125 direct manufacturing labor-hours) and direct material costs are $8,000.
c. Total direct materials issued to production during January 2014 are $90,000.
d. Cost of goods completed during January is $180,000.

e. Materials inventory as of January 31, 2014, is $20,000.
f. Finished goods inventory as of January 31, 2014, is $15,000.
g. All plant workers earn the same wage rate. Direct manufacturing labor-hours used for January total 2,500 hours. Other labor costs total $10,000.
h. The gross plant payroll paid in January equals $52,000. Ignore withholdings.
i. All "actual" manufacturing overhead cost incurred during January has already been posted.
j. All materials are direct materials.

Required

Calculate the following:

1. Materials purchased during January
2. Cost of Goods Sold during January
3. Direct manufacturing labor costs incurred during January
4. Manufacturing Overhead Allocated during January
5. Balance, Wages Payable Control, December 31, 2013
6. Balance, Work-in-Process Control, January 31, 2014
7. Balance, Work-in-Process Control, December 31, 2013
8. Manufacturing Overhead Underallocated or Overallocated for January 2014

Solution

Amounts from the T-accounts are labeled "(T)."

1. From Materials Control T-account, Materials purchased: $90,000 (c) + $20,000 (e) – $15,000 (T) = $95,000
2. From Finished Goods Control T-account, Cost of Goods Sold: $20,000 (T) + $180,000 (d) – $15,000 (f) = $185,000
3. Direct manufacturing wage rate: $2,000 (b) ÷ 125 direct manufacturing labor-hours (b) = $16 per direct manufacturing labor-hour

   Direct manufacturing labor costs: 2,500 direct manufacturing labor-hours (g) × $16 per direct manufacturing labor-hour = $40,000
4. Manufacturing overhead rate: $600,000 (a) ÷ $400,000 (a) = 150%

   Manufacturing Overhead Allocated: 150% of $40,000 (see 3) = 1.50 × $40,000 = $60,000
5. From Wages Payable Control T-account, Wages Payable Control, December 31, 2013: $52,000 (h) + $3,000 (T) – $40,000 (see 3) – $10,000 (g) = $5,000
6. Work-in-Process Control, January 31, 2014: $8,000 (b) + $2,000 (b) + 150% of $2,000 (b) = $13,000 (This answer is used in item 7.)
7. From Work-in-Process Control T-account, Work-in-Process Control, December 31, 2013: $180,000 (d) + $13,000 (see 6) – $90,000 (c) – $40,000 (see 3) – $60,000 (see 4) = $3,000
8. Manufacturing overhead overallocated: $60,000 (see 4) – $57,000 (T) = $3,000.

Letters alongside entries in T-accounts correspond to letters in the preceding additional information. Numbers alongside entries in T-accounts correspond to numbers in the preceding requirements.

Materials Control

December 31, 2013, Bal.	(given)	15,000		
	(1)	95,000*	(c)	90,000
January 31, 2014, Bal.	(e)	20,000		

Work-in-Process Control

December 31, 2013, Bal.	(7)	3,000	(d)	180,000
Direct materials	(c)	90,000		
Direct manufacturing labor	(b) (g) (3)	40,000		
Manufacturing overhead allocated	(3) (a) (4)	60,000		
January 31, 2014, Bal.	(b) (6)	13,000		

*Can be computed only after all other postings in the account have been made.

Finished Goods Control

December 31, 2013, Bal.	(given) 20,000		(2)	185,000
	(d) 180,000			
January 31, 2014, Bal.	(f) 15,000			

Wages Payable Control

	(h) 52,000	December 31, 2013, Bal.	(5)	5,000
			(g) (3)	40,000
			(g)	10,000
		January 31, 2014	(given)	3,000

Manufacturing Overhead Control

Total January charges	(given) 57,000			

Manufacturing Overhead Allocated

			(3) (a) (4)	60,000

Cost of Goods Sold

	(d) (f) (2) 185,000			

▶ Decision Points

The following question-and-answer format summarizes the chapter's learning objectives. Each decision presents a key question related to a learning objective. The guidelines are the answer to that question.

Decision	Guidelines
1. What are the building-block concepts of a costing system?	The building-block concepts of a costing system are a cost object, direct costs of a cost object, indirect costs of a cost object, cost pool, and cost-allocation base. Costing-system overview diagrams represent these concepts in a systematic way. Costing systems aim to report cost numbers that reflect the way cost objects (such as products or services) use the resources of an organization.
2. How do you distinguish job costing from process costing?	Job-costing systems assign costs to distinct units of a product or service. Process-costing systems assign costs to masses of identical or similar units and compute unit costs on an average basis. These two costing systems represent opposite ends of a continuum. The costing systems of many companies combine some elements of both job costing and process costing.
3. What is the main challenge of implementing job-costing systems?	The main challenge of implementing job-costing systems is estimating actual costs of jobs in a timely manner.
4. How do you implement a normal-costing system?	A general seven-step approach to normal costing requires identifying (1) the job, (2) the actual direct costs, (3) the budgeted cost-allocation bases, (4) the budgeted indirect-cost pools, (5) the budgeted cost-allocation rates, (6) the allocated indirect costs (budgeted rates times actual quantities of the cost-allocation bases), and (7) the total direct and indirect costs of a job.
5. How do you distinguish actual costing from normal costing?	Actual costing and normal costing differ in the type of indirect-cost rates used:

	Actual Costing	Normal Costing
Direct-cost rates	Actual rates	Actual rates
Indirect-cost rates	Actual rates	Budgeted rates

Both systems use actual quantities of inputs for tracing direct costs and actual quantities of the cost-allocation bases for allocating indirect costs.

Decision	Guidelines
6. How are transactions recorded in a manufacturing job-costing system?	A job-costing system in manufacturing records the flow of inventoriable costs in the general and subsidiary ledgers for (a) acquisition of materials and other manufacturing inputs, (b) their conversion into work in process, (c) their conversion into finished goods, and (d) the sale of finished goods. The job-costing system expenses period costs, such as marketing costs, as they are incurred.
7. How should managers dispose of under- or overallocated manufacturing overhead costs at the end of the accounting year?	The two standard approaches to disposing of under- or overallocated manufacturing overhead costs at the end of the accounting year for the purposes of stating balance sheet and income statement amounts at actual costs are (1) to adjust the allocation rate and (2) to prorate on the basis of the total amount of the allocated manufacturing overhead cost in the ending balances of Work-in-Process Control, Finished Goods Control, and Cost of Goods Sold accounts. Many companies write off amounts of under- or overallocated manufacturing overhead to Cost of Goods Sold when amounts are immaterial or underallocated overhead costs are the result of inefficiencies.
8. What are some variations of normal costing?	In some variations from normal costing, organizations use budgeted rates to assign direct costs, as well as indirect costs, to jobs.

Terms to Learn

This chapter and the Glossary at the end of the book contain definitions of the following important terms:

actual costing **(p. 110)**
actual indirect-cost rate **(p. 119)**
adjusted allocation-rate approach **(p. 128)**
budgeted indirect-cost rate **(p. 112)**
cost-allocation base **(p. 108)**
cost-application base **(p. 108)**
cost pool **(p. 108)**
job **(p. 108)**
job-cost record **(p. 113)**
job-cost sheet **(p. 113)**
job-costing system **(p. 108)**
labor-time sheet **(p. 114)**
manufacturing overhead allocated **(p. 122)**
manufacturing overhead applied **(p. 122)**
materials-requisition record **(p. 114)**
normal costing **(p. 112)**
overabsorbed indirect costs **(p. 127)**
overallocated indirect costs **(p. 127)**
overapplied indirect costs **(p. 127)**
process-costing system **(p. 109)**
proration **(p. 128)**
source document **(p. 113)**
underabsorbed indirect costs **(p. 127)**
underallocated indirect costs **(p. 127)**
underapplied indirect costs **(p. 127)**

Assignment Material

MyAccountingLab

Questions

4-1 Define cost pool, cost tracing, cost allocation, and cost-allocation base.

4-2 How does a job-costing system differ from a process-costing system?

4-3 Why might an advertising agency use job costing for an advertising campaign by PepsiCo, whereas a bank might use process costing to determine the cost of checking account deposits?

4-4 Describe the seven steps in job costing.

4-5 Give examples of two cost objects in companies using job costing.

4-6 Describe three major source documents used in job-costing systems.

4-7 What is the advantage of using computerized source documents to prepare job-cost records?

4-8 Give two reasons why most organizations use an annual period rather than a weekly or monthly period to compute budgeted indirect-cost rates.

4-9 Distinguish between actual costing and normal costing.

4-10 Describe two ways in which a house-construction company may use job-cost information.

4-11 Comment on the following statement: "In a normal-costing system, the amounts in the Manufacturing Overhead Control account will always equal the amounts in the Manufacturing Overhead Allocated account."

4-12 Describe three different debit entries to the Work-in-Process Control T-account under normal costing.

4-13 Describe three alternative ways to dispose of under- or overallocated overhead costs.

4-14 When might a company use budgeted costs rather than actual costs to compute direct-labor rates?

4-15 Describe briefly why Electronic Data Interchange (EDI) is helpful to managers.

Exercises

MyAccountingLab

4-16 Job costing, process costing. In each of the following situations, determine whether job costing or process costing would be more appropriate.

- **a.** A CPA firm
- **b.** An oil refinery
- **c.** A custom furniture manufacturer
- **d.** A tire manufacturer
- **e.** A textbook publisher
- **f.** A pharmaceutical company
- **g.** An advertising agency
- **h.** An architecture firm
- **i.** A flour mill
- **j.** A paint manufacturer
- **k.** A nursing home
- **l.** A landscaping company
- **m.** A cola-drink-concentrate producer
- **n.** A movie studio
- **o.** A law firm
- **p.** A commercial aircraft manufacturer
- **q.** A management consulting firm
- **r.** A plumbing contractor
- **s.** A catering service
- **t.** A paper mill
- **u.** An auto repair shop

4-17 Actual costing, normal costing, accounting for manufacturing overhead. Destin Products uses a job-costing system with two direct-cost categories (direct materials and direct manufacturing labor) and one manufacturing overhead cost pool. Destin allocates manufacturing overhead costs using direct manufacturing labor costs. Destin provides the following information:

	Budget for 2014	Actual Results for 2014
Direct material costs	$2,000,000	$1,900,000
Direct manufacturing labor costs	1,500,000	1,450,000
Manufacturing overhead costs	2,700,000	2,755,000

Required

1. Compute the actual and budgeted manufacturing overhead rates for 2014.
2. During March, the job-cost record for Job 626 contained the following information:

Direct materials used	$40,000
Direct manufacturing labor costs	$30,000

   Compute the cost of Job 626 using (a) actual costing and (b) normal costing.
3. At the end of 2014, compute the under- or overallocated manufacturing overhead under normal costing. Why is there no under- or overallocated overhead under actual costing?
4. Why might managers at Destin Products prefer to use normal costing?

4-18 Job costing, normal and actual costing. Anderson Construction assembles residential houses. It uses a job-costing system with two direct-cost categories (direct materials and direct labor) and one indirect-cost pool (assembly support). Direct labor-hours is the allocation base for assembly support costs. In December 2013, Anderson budgets 2014 assembly-support costs to be $8,000,000 and 2014 direct labor-hours to be 160,000.

At the end of 2014, Anderson is comparing the costs of several jobs that were started and completed in 2014.

	Laguna Model	Mission Model
Construction period	Feb–June 2014	May–Oct 2014
Direct material costs	$106,650	$127,970
Direct labor costs	$ 36,276	$ 41,750
Direct labor-hours	920	1,040

Direct materials and direct labor are paid for on a contract basis. The costs of each are known when direct materials are used or when direct labor-hours are worked. The 2014 actual assembly-support costs were $7,614,000, and the actual direct labor-hours were 162,000.

Required

1. Compute the (a) budgeted indirect-cost rate and (b) actual indirect-cost rate. Why do they differ?
2. What are the job costs of the Laguna Model and the Mission Model using (a) normal costing and (b) actual costing?
3. Why might Anderson Construction prefer normal costing over actual costing?

4-19 Budgeted manufacturing overhead rate, allocated manufacturing overhead. Gammaro Company uses normal costing. It allocates manufacturing overhead costs using a budgeted rate per machine-hour. The following data are available for 2014:

Budgeted manufacturing overhead costs	$4,200,000
Budgeted machine-hours	175,000
Actual manufacturing overhead costs	$4,050,000
Actual machine-hours	170,000

Required

1. Calculate the budgeted manufacturing overhead rate.
2. Calculate the manufacturing overhead allocated during 2014.
3. Calculate the amount of under- or overallocated manufacturing overhead. Why do Gammaro's managers need to calculate this amount?

4-20 Job costing, accounting for manufacturing overhead, budgeted rates. The Lynn Company uses a normal job-costing system at its Minneapolis plant. The plant has a machining department and an assembly department. Its job-costing system has two direct-cost categories (direct materials and direct manufacturing labor) and two manufacturing overhead cost pools (the machining department overhead, allocated to jobs based on actual machine-hours, and the assembly department overhead, allocated to jobs based on actual direct manufacturing labor costs). The 2014 budget for the plant is as follows:

	Machining Department	Assembly Department
Manufacturing overhead	$1,800,000	$3,600,000
Direct manufacturing labor costs	$1,400,000	$2,000,000
Direct manufacturing labor-hours	100,000	200,000
Machine-hours	50,000	200,000

Required

1. Present an overview diagram of Lynn's job-costing system. Compute the budgeted manufacturing overhead rate for each department.
2. During February, the job-cost record for Job 494 contained the following:

	Machining Department	Assembly Department
Direct materials used	$45,000	$70,000
Direct manufacturing labor costs	$14,000	$15,000
Direct manufacturing labor-hours	1,000	1,500
Machine-hours	2,000	1,000

   Compute the total manufacturing overhead costs allocated to Job 494.
3. At the end of 2014, the actual manufacturing overhead costs were $2,100,000 in machining and $3,700,000 in assembly. Assume that 55,000 actual machine-hours were used in machining and that actual direct manufacturing labor costs in assembly were $2,200,000. Compute the over- or underallocated manufacturing overhead for each department.

4-21 Job costing, consulting firm. Taylor & Associates, a consulting firm, has the following condensed budget for 2014:

Revenues		$20,000,000
Total costs:		
Direct costs		
Professional Labor	$ 5,000,000	
Indirect costs		
Client support	13,000,000	18,000,000
Operating income		$ 2,000,000

Taylor has a single direct-cost category (professional labor) and a single indirect-cost pool (client support). Indirect costs are allocated to jobs on the basis of professional labor costs.

Required

1. Prepare an overview diagram of the job-costing system. Calculate the 2014 budgeted indirect-cost rate for Taylor & Associates.
2. The markup rate for pricing jobs is intended to produce operating income equal to 10% of revenues. Calculate the markup rate as a percentage of professional labor costs.
3. Taylor is bidding on a consulting job for Tasty Chicken, a fast food chain specializing in poultry meats. The budgeted breakdown of professional labor on the job is as follows:

Professional Labor Category	Budgeted Rate per Hour	Budgeted Hours
Director	$200	3
Partner	100	16
Associate	50	40
Assistant	30	160

Calculate the budgeted cost of the Tasty Chicken job. How much will Taylor bid for the job if it is to earn its target operating income of 10% of revenues?

4-22 Time period used to compute indirect cost rates. Plunge Manufacturing produces outdoor wading and slide pools. The company uses a normal-costing system and allocates manufacturing overhead on the basis of direct manufacturing labor-hours. Most of the company's production and sales occur in the first and second quarters of the year. The company is in danger of losing one of its larger customers, Socha Wholesale, due to large fluctuations in price. The owner of Plunge has requested an analysis of the manufacturing cost per unit in the second and third quarters. You have been provided the following budgeted information for the coming year:

	Quarter			
	1	2	3	4
Pools manufactured and sold	565	490	245	100

It takes 1 direct manufacturing labor-hour to make each pool. The actual direct material cost is $14.00 per pool. The actual direct manufacturing labor rate is $20 per hour. The budgeted variable manufacturing overhead rate is $15 per direct manufacturing labor-hour. Budgeted fixed manufacturing overhead costs are $12,250 each quarter.

Required

1. Calculate the total manufacturing cost per unit for the second and third quarter assuming the company allocates manufacturing overhead costs based on the budgeted manufacturing overhead rate determined for each quarter.
2. Calculate the total manufacturing cost per unit for the second and third quarter assuming the company allocates manufacturing overhead costs based on an annual budgeted manufacturing overhead rate.
3. Plunge Manufacturing prices its pools at manufacturing cost plus 30%. Why might Socha Wholesale be seeing large fluctuations in the prices of pools? Which of the methods described in requirements 1 and 2 would you recommend Plunge use? Explain.

4-23 Accounting for manufacturing overhead. Jamison Woodworking uses normal costing and allocates manufacturing overhead to jobs based on a budgeted labor-hour rate and actual direct labor-hours. Under- or overallocated overhead, if immaterial, is written off to Cost of Goods Sold. During 2014, Jamison recorded the following:

Budgeted manufacturing overhead costs	$4,400,000
Budgeted direct labor-hours	200,000
Actual manufacturing overhead costs	$4,650,000
Actual direct labor-hours	212,000

Required

1. Compute the budgeted manufacturing overhead rate.
2. Prepare the summary journal entry to record the allocation of manufacturing overhead.
3. Compute the amount of under- or overallocated manufacturing overhead. Is the amount significant enough to warrant proration of overhead costs, or would it be permissible to write it off to cost of goods sold? Prepare the journal entry to dispose of the under- or overallocated overhead.

4-24 Job costing, journal entries. The University of Chicago Press is wholly owned by the university. It performs the bulk of its work for other university departments, which pay as though the press were an outside business enterprise. The press also publishes and maintains a stock of books for general sale. The press uses normal costing to cost each job. Its job-costing system has two direct-cost categories (direct materials and direct manufacturing labor) and one indirect-cost pool (manufacturing overhead, allocated on the basis of direct manufacturing labor costs).

The following data (in thousands) pertain to 2014:

Direct materials and supplies purchased on credit	$ 800
Direct materials used	710
Indirect materials issued to various production departments	100
Direct manufacturing labor	1,300
Indirect manufacturing labor incurred by various production departments	900
Depreciation on building and manufacturing equipment	400
Miscellaneous manufacturing overhead* incurred by various production departments (ordinarily would be detailed as repairs, photocopying, utilities, etc.)	550
Manufacturing overhead allocated at 160% of direct manufacturing labor costs	?
Cost of goods manufactured	4,120
Revenues	8,000
Cost of goods sold (before adjustment for under- or overallocated manufacturing overhead)	4,020
Inventories, December 31, 2013 (not 2014):	
Materials Control	100
Work-in-Process Control	60
Finished Goods Control	500

Required

1. Prepare an overview diagram of the job-costing system at the University of Chicago Press.
2. Prepare journal entries to summarize the 2014 transactions. As your final entry, dispose of the year-end under- or overallocated manufacturing overhead as a writeoff to Cost of Goods Sold. Number your entries. Explanations for each entry may be omitted.
3. Show posted T-accounts for all inventories, Cost of Goods Sold, Manufacturing Overhead Control, and Manufacturing Overhead Allocated.
4. How did the University of Chicago Press perform in 2014?

4-25 Journal entries, T-accounts, and source documents. Creation Company produces gadgets for the coveted small appliance market. The following data reflect activity for the year 2014:

Costs incurred:	
Purchases of direct materials (net) on credit	$122,000
Direct manufacturing labor cost	83,000
Indirect labor	54,000
Depreciation, factory equipment	32,000
Depreciation, office equipment	7,900
Maintenance, factory equipment	29,000
Miscellaneous factory overhead	9,900
Rent, factory building	78,000
Advertising expense	94,000
Sales commissions	33,000

Inventories:

	January 1, 2014	December 31, 2014
Direct materials	$ 9,800	$13,000
Work in process	6,300	23,000
Finished goods	68,000	27,000

*The term *manufacturing overhead* is not used uniformly. Other terms that are often encountered in printing companies include *job overhead* and *shop overhead*.

Creation Co. uses a normal-costing system and allocates overhead to work in process at a rate of $2.60 per direct manufacturing labor dollar. Indirect materials are insignificant so there is no inventory account for indirect materials.

Required

1. Prepare journal entries to record the transactions for 2014 including an entry to close out over- or underallocated overhead to cost of goods sold. For each journal entry indicate the source document that would be used to authorize each entry. Also note which subsidiary ledger, if any, should be referenced as backup for the entry.
2. Post the journal entries to T-accounts for all of the inventories, Cost of Goods Sold, the Manufacturing Overhead Control Account, and the Manufacturing Overhead Allocated Account.

4-26 Job costing, journal entries. Donald Transport assembles prestige manufactured homes. Its job-costing system has two direct-cost categories (direct materials and direct manufacturing labor) and one indirect-cost pool (manufacturing overhead allocated at a budgeted $31 per machine-hour in 2014). The following data (in millions) show operation costs for 2014:

Materials Control, beginning balance, January 1, 2014	$ 18
Work-in-Process Control, beginning balance, January 1, 2014	9
Finished Goods Control, beginning balance, January 1, 2014	10
Materials and supplies purchased on credit	154
Direct materials used	152
Indirect materials (supplies) issued to various production departments	19
Direct manufacturing labor	96
Indirect manufacturing labor incurred by various production departments	34
Depreciation on plant and manufacturing equipment	28
Miscellaneous manufacturing overhead incurred (ordinarily would be detailed as repairs, utilities, etc., with a corresponding credit to various liability accounts)	13
Manufacturing overhead allocated, 3,000,000 actual machine-hours	?
Cost of goods manufactured	298
Revenues	410
Cost of goods sold	294

Required

1. Prepare an overview diagram of Donald Transport's job-costing system.
2. Prepare journal entries. Number your entries. Explanations for each entry may be omitted. Post to T-accounts. What is the ending balance of Work-in-Process Control?
3. Show the journal entry for disposing of under- or overallocated manufacturing overhead directly as a year-end writeoff to Cost of Goods Sold. Post the entry to T-accounts.
4. How did Donald Transport perform in 2014?

4-27 Job costing, unit cost, ending work in process. Rafael Company produces pipes for concert-quality organs. Each job is unique. In April 2013, it completed all outstanding orders, and then, in May 2013, it worked on only two jobs, M1 and M2:

	A	B	C
1	**Rafael Company, May 2013**	**Job M1**	**Job M2**
2	Direct materials	$ 78,000	$ 51,000
3	Direct manufacturing labor	273,000	208,000

Direct manufacturing labor is paid at the rate of $26 per hour. Manufacturing overhead costs are allocated at a budgeted rate of $20 per direct manufacturing labor-hour. Only Job M1 was completed in May.

Required

1. Calculate the total cost for Job M1.
2. 1,100 pipes were produced for Job M1. Calculate the cost per pipe.
3. Prepare the journal entry transferring Job M1 to finished goods.
4. What is the ending balance in the Work-in-Process Control account?

4-28 Job costing; actual, normal, and variation from normal costing. Cheney & Partners, a Quebec-based public accounting partnership, specializes in audit services. Its job-costing system has a single direct-cost category (professional labor) and a single indirect-cost pool (audit support, which contains all costs of the

Audit Support Department). Audit support costs are allocated to individual jobs using actual professional labor-hours. Cheney & Partners employs 10 professionals to perform audit services.

Budgeted and actual amounts for 2014 are as follows:

	A	B	C
1	**Cheney & Partners**		
2	**Budget for 2014**		
3	Professional labor compensation	$960,000	
4	Audit support department costs	$720,000	
5	Professional labor-hours billed to clients	16,000	hours
6			
7	**Actual results for 2014**		
8	Audit support department costs	$744,000	
9	Professional labor-hours billed to clients	15,500	hours
10	Actual professional labor cost rate	$ 53	per hour

Required

1. Compute the direct-cost rate and the indirect-cost rate per professional labor-hour for 2014 under (a) actual costing, (b) normal costing, and (c) the variation from normal costing that uses budgeted rates for direct costs.
2. Which job-costing system would you recommend Cheney & Partners use? Explain.
3. Cheney's 2014 audit of Pierre & Co. was budgeted to take 170 hours of professional labor time. The actual professional labor time spent on the audit was 185 hours. Compute the cost of the Pierre & Co. audit using (a) actual costing, (b) normal costing, and (c) the variation from normal costing that uses budgeted rates for direct costs. Explain any differences in the job cost.

4-29 Job costing; variation on actual, normal, and variation from normal costing. Creative Solutions designs Web pages for clients in the education sector. The company's job-costing system has a single direct cost category (Web-designing labor) and a single indirect cost pool composed of all overhead costs. Overhead costs are allocated to individual jobs based on direct labor-hours. The company employs six Web designers. Budgeted and actual information regarding Creative Solutions follows:

Budget for 2014:	
Direct labor costs	$273,000
Direct labor-hours	10,500
Overhead costs	$157,500
Actual results for 2014:	
Direct labor costs	$285,000
Direct labor-hours	11,400
Overhead costs	$159,600

Required

1. Compute the direct cost rate and the indirect cost rate per Web-designing labor-hour for 2014 under (a) actual costing, (b) normal costing, and (c) the variation from normal costing that uses budgeted rates for direct costs.
2. Which method would you suggest Creative Solutions use? Explain.
3. Creative Solutions' Web design for Greenville Day School was budgeted to take 86 direct labor-hours. The actual time spent on the project was 79 hours. Compute the cost of the Greenville Day School job using (a) actual costing, (b) normal costing, and (c) the variation from normal costing that uses budgeted rates for direct cost.

4-30 Proration of overhead. The Ride-On-Wave Company (ROW) produces a line of non-motorized boats. ROW uses a normal-costing system and allocates manufacturing overhead using direct manufacturing labor cost. The following data are for 2014:

Budgeted manufacturing overhead cost	$125,000
Budgeted direct manufacturing labor cost	$250,000
Actual manufacturing overhead cost	$117,000
Actual direct manufacturing labor cost	$228,000

Inventory balances on December 31, 2014, were as follows:

Account	Ending balance	2014 direct manufacturing labor cost in ending balance
Work in process	$ 50,700	$ 20,520
Finished goods	245,050	59,280
Cost of goods sold	549,250	148,200

Required

1. Calculate the manufacturing overhead allocation rate.
2. Compute the amount of under- or overallocated manufacturing overhead.
3. Calculate the ending balances in work in process, finished goods, and cost of goods sold if under- or overallocated manufacturing overhead is as follows:
   a. Written off to cost of goods sold
   b. Prorated based on ending balances (before proration) in each of the three accounts
   c. Prorated based on the overhead allocated in 2014 in the ending balances (before proration) in each of the three accounts
4. Which method would you choose? Justify your answer.

Problems

MyAccountingLab

4-31 Job costing, accounting for manufacturing overhead, budgeted rates. The Pisano Company uses a job-costing system at its Dover, Delaware, plant. The plant has a machining department and a finishing department. Pisano uses normal costing with two direct-cost categories (direct materials and direct manufacturing labor) and two manufacturing overhead cost pools (the machining department with machine-hours as the allocation base and the finishing department with direct manufacturing labor costs as the allocation base). The 2014 budget for the plant is as follows:

	Machining Department	Finishing Department
Manufacturing overhead costs	$9,065,000	$8,181,000
Direct manufacturing labor costs	$ 970,000	$4,050,000
Direct manufacturing labor-hours	36,000	155,000
Machine-hours	185,000	37,000

Required

1. Prepare an overview diagram of Pisano's job-costing system.
2. What is the budgeted manufacturing overhead rate in the machining department? In the finishing department?
3. During the month of January, the job-cost record for Job 431 shows the following:

	Machining Department	Finishing Department
Direct materials used	$13,000	$ 5,000
Direct manufacturing labor costs	$ 900	$1,250
Direct manufacturing labor-hours	20	70
Machine-hours	140	20

   Compute the total manufacturing overhead cost allocated to Job 431.
4. Assuming that Job 431 consisted of 300 units of product, what is the cost per unit?
5. Amounts at the end of 2014 are as follows:

	Machining Department	Finishing Department
Manufacturing overhead incurred	$10,000,000	$7,982,000
Direct manufacturing labor costs	$ 1,030,000	$4,100,000
Machine-hours	200,000	34,000

   Compute the under- or overallocated manufacturing overhead for each department and for the Dover plant as a whole.
6. Why might Pisano use two different manufacturing overhead cost pools in its job-costing system?

4-32 Service industry, job costing, law firm. Kidman & Associates is a law firm specializing in labor relations and employee-related work. It employs 30 professionals (5 partners and 25 associates) who work directly with its clients. The average budgeted total compensation per professional for 2014 is $97,500. Each professional is budgeted to have 1,500 billable hours to clients in 2014. All professionals work for clients to their maximum 1,500 billable hours available. All professional labor costs are included in a single direct-cost category and are traced to jobs on a per-hour basis. All costs of Kidman & Associates other than professional labor costs are included in a single indirect-cost pool (legal support) and are allocated to jobs using professional labor-hours as the allocation base. The budgeted level of indirect costs in 2014 is $2,475,000.

Required

1. Prepare an overview diagram of Kidman's job-costing system.
2. Compute the 2014 budgeted direct-cost rate per hour of professional labor.
3. Compute the 2014 budgeted indirect-cost rate per hour of professional labor.
4. Kidman & Associates is considering bidding on two jobs:
   a. Litigation work for Richardson, Inc., which requires 120 budgeted hours of professional labor
   b. Labor contract work for Punch, Inc., which requires 160 budgeted hours of professional labor

   Prepare a cost estimate for each job.

4-33 Service industry, job costing, two direct- and two indirect-cost categories, law firm (continuation of 4-32). Kidman has just completed a review of its job-costing system. This review included a detailed analysis of how past jobs used the firm's resources and interviews with personnel about what factors drive the level of indirect costs. Management concluded that a system with two direct-cost categories (professional partner labor and professional associate labor) and two indirect-cost categories (general support and secretarial support) would yield more accurate job costs. Budgeted information for 2014 related to the two direct-cost categories is as follows:

	Professional Partner Labor	Professional Associate Labor
Number of professionals	5	25
Hours of billable time per professional	1,500 per year	1,500 per year
Total compensation (average per professional)	$210,000	$75,000

Budgeted information for 2014 relating to the two indirect-cost categories is as follows:

	General Support	Secretarial Support
Total costs	$2,025,000	$450,000
Cost-allocation base	Professional labor-hours	Partner labor-hours

Required

1. Compute the 2014 budgeted direct-cost rates for (a) professional partners and (b) professional associates.
2. Compute the 2014 budgeted indirect-cost rates for (a) general support and (b) secretarial support.
3. Compute the budgeted costs for the Richardson and Punch jobs, given the following information:

	Richardson, Inc.	Punch, Inc.
Professional partners	48 hours	32 hours
Professional associates	72 hours	128 hours

4. Comment on the results in requirement 3. Why are the job costs different from those computed in Problem 4-32?
5. Would you recommend Kidman & Associates use the job-costing system in Problem 4-32 or the job-costing system in this problem? Explain.

4-34 Proration of overhead. (Z. Iqbal, adapted) The Zaf Radiator Company uses a normal-costing system with a single manufacturing overhead cost pool and machine-hours as the cost-allocation base. The following data are for 2014:

Budgeted manufacturing overhead costs	$4,800,000
Overhead allocation base	Machine-hours
Budgeted machine-hours	80,000
Manufacturing overhead costs incurred	$4,900,000
Actual machine-hours	75,000

Machine-hours data and the ending balances (before proration of under- or overallocated overhead) are as follows:

	Actual Machine-Hours	2014 End-of-Year Balance
Cost of Goods Sold	60,000	$8,000,000
Finished Goods Control	11,000	1,250,000
Work-in-Process Control	4,000	750,000

Required

1. Compute the budgeted manufacturing overhead rate for 2014.
2. Compute the under- or overallocated manufacturing overhead of Zaf Radiator in 2014. Dispose of this amount using the following:
   a. Writeoff to Cost of Goods Sold
   b. Proration based on ending balances (before proration) in Work-in-Process Control, Finished Goods Control, and Cost of Goods Sold
   c. Proration based on the overhead allocated in 2014 (before proration) in the ending balances of Work-in-Process Control, Finished Goods Control, and Cost of Goods Sold
3. Which method do you prefer in requirement 2? Explain.

4-35 Normal costing, overhead allocation, working backward. Gardi Manufacturing uses normal costing for its job-costing system, which has two direct-cost categories (direct materials and direct manufacturing labor) and one indirect-cost category (manufacturing overhead). The following information is obtained for 2014:

- Total manufacturing costs, $8,300,000
- Manufacturing overhead allocated, $4,100,000 (allocated at a rate of 250% of direct manufacturing labor costs)
- Work-in-process inventory on January 1, 2014, $420,000
- Cost of finished goods manufactured, $8,100,000

Required

1. Use information in the first two bullet points to calculate (a) direct manufacturing labor costs in 2014 and (b) cost of direct materials used in 2014.
2. Calculate the ending work-in-process inventory on December 31, 2014.

4-36 Proration of overhead with two indirect cost pools. Premier Golf Carts makes custom golf carts that it sells to dealers across the Southeast. The carts are produced in two departments, fabrication (a mostly automated department) and custom finishing (a mostly manual department). The company uses a normal-costing system in which overhead in the fabrication department is allocated to jobs on the basis of machine-hours and overhead in the finishing department is allocated to jobs based on direct labor-hours. During May, Premier Golf Carts reported actual overhead of $49,500 in the fabrication department and $22,200 in the finishing department. Additional information follows:

Manufacturing overhead rate (fabrication department)	$20 per machine-hour
Manufacturing overhead rate (finishing department)	$16 per direct labor-hour
Machine-hours (fabrication department) for May	2,000 machine-hours
Direct labor-hours (finishing department) for May	1,200 labor-hours
Work in process inventory, May 31	$50,000
Finished goods inventory, May 31	$150,000
Cost of goods sold, May	$300,000

Premier Golf Carts prorates under- and overallocated overhead monthly to work in process, finished goods, and cost of goods sold based on the ending balance in each account.

Required

1. Calculate the amount of overhead allocated in the fabrication department and the finishing department in May.
2. Calculate the amount of under- or overallocated overhead in each department and in total.
3. How much of the under- or overallocated overhead will be prorated to (a) work in process inventory, (b) finished goods inventory, and (c) cost of goods sold based on the ending balance (before proration) in each of the three accounts? What will be the balance in work in process, finished goods, and cost of goods sold after proration?
4. What would be the effect of writing off under- and overallocated overhead to cost of goods sold? Would it be reasonable for Premier Golf Carts to change to this simpler method?

4-37 General ledger relationships, under- and overallocation. (S. Sridhar, adapted) Southwick Company uses normal costing in its job-costing system. Partially completed T-accounts and additional information for Southwick for 2014 are as follows:

Direct Materials Control

	Debit	Credit
1-1-2014	25,000	234,000
	240,000	

Work-in-Process Control

	Debit	Credit
1-1-2014	44,000	
Dir. manuf. labor	348,000	

Finished Goods Control

	Debit	Credit
1-1-2014	10,000	880,000
	925,000	

Manufacturing Overhead Control

Debit	Credit
514,000	

Manufacturing Overhead Allocated

Debit	Credit

Cost of Goods Sold

Debit	Credit

Additional information follows:

a. Direct manufacturing labor wage rate was $12 per hour.
b. Manufacturing overhead was allocated at $16 per direct manufacturing labor-hour.
c. During the year, sales revenues were $1,050,000, and marketing and distribution costs were $125,000.

Required

1. What was the amount of direct materials issued to production during 2014?
2. What was the amount of manufacturing overhead allocated to jobs during 2014?
3. What was the total cost of jobs completed during 2014?
4. What was the balance of work-in-process inventory on December 31, 2014?
5. What was the cost of goods sold before proration of under- or overallocated overhead?
6. What was the under- or overallocated manufacturing overhead in 2014?
7. Dispose of the under- or overallocated manufacturing overhead using the following:
   a. Writeoff to Cost of Goods Sold
   b. Proration based on ending balances (before proration) in Work-in-Process Control, Finished Goods Control, and Cost of Goods Sold
8. Using each of the approaches in requirement 7, calculate Southwick's operating income for 2014.
9. Which approach in requirement 7 do you recommend Southwick use? Explain your answer briefly.

4-38 Overview of general ledger relationships. Brandon Company uses normal costing in its job-costing system. The company produces custom bikes for toddlers. The beginning balances (December 1) and ending balances (as of December 30) in their inventory accounts are as follows:

	Beginning Balance 12/1	Ending Balance 12/31
Materials Control	$2,100	$ 8,500
Work-in-Process Control	6,700	9,000
Manufacturing Department Overhead Control	—	94,000
Finished Goods Control	4,400	19,400

Additional information follows:

a. Direct materials purchased during December were $66,300.
b. Cost of goods manufactured for December was $234,000.
c. No direct materials were returned to suppliers.
d. No units were started or completed on December 31 and no direct materials were requisitioned on December 31.
e. The manufacturing labor costs for the December 31 working day: direct manufacturing labor, $4,300, and indirect manufacturing labor, $1,400.
f. Manufacturing overhead has been allocated at 110% of direct manufacturing labor costs through December 31.

Required

1. Prepare journal entries for the December 31 payroll.
2. Use T-accounts to compute the following:
   a. The total amount of materials requisitioned into work in process during December
   b. The total amount of direct manufacturing labor recorded in work in process during December (Hint: You have to solve requirements **2b** and **2c** simultaneously)
   c. The total amount of manufacturing overhead recorded in work in process during December
   d. Ending balance in work in process, December 31
   e. Cost of goods sold for December before adjustments for under- or overallocated manufacturing overhead
3. Prepare closing journal entries related to manufacturing overhead. Assume that all under- or overallocated manufacturing overhead is closed directly to Cost of Goods Sold.

4-39 Allocation and proration of overhead. InStep Company prints custom training material for corporations. The business was started January 1, 2014. The company uses a normal-costing system. It has two direct cost pools, materials and labor, and one indirect cost pool, overhead. Overhead is charged to printing jobs on the basis of direct labor cost. The following information is available for 2014.

Budgeted direct labor costs	$225,000
Budgeted overhead costs	$315,000
Costs of actual material used	$148,500
Actual direct labor costs	$213,500
Actual overhead costs	$302,100

There were two jobs in process on December 31, 2014: Job 11 and Job 12. Costs added to each job as of December 31 are as follows:

	Direct materials	Direct labor
Job 11	$4,870	$5,100
Job 12	$5,910	$6,800

InStep Company has no finished goods inventories because all printing jobs are transferred to cost of goods sold when completed.

Required

1. Compute the overhead allocation rate.
2. Calculate the balance in ending work in process and cost of goods sold before any adjustments for under- or overallocated overhead.
3. Calculate under- or overallocated overhead.
4. Calculate the ending balances in work in process and cost of goods sold if the under- or overallocated overhead amount is as follows:
   a. Written off to cost of goods sold
   b. Prorated using the overhead allocated in 2014 (before proration) in the ending balances of cost of goods sold and work-in-process control accounts
5. Which of the methods in requirement 4 would you choose? Explain.

4-40 Job costing, contracting, ethics. Rand Company manufactures modular homes. The company has two main products that it sells commercially: a 1,000-square-foot, one-bedroom model and a 1,500-square-foot, two-bedroom model. The company recently began providing emergency housing (huts) to the Federal Emergency Management Agency (FEMA). The emergency housing is similar to the 1,000-square-foot model.

FEMA has requested Rand to create a bid for 150 emergency huts to be sent for wildfire victims in the West. Your manager has asked that you prepare this bid. In preparing the bid, you find a recent invoice to FEMA for 200 huts provided during the most recent hurricane season in the South. You also have a standard cost sheet for the 1,000-square-foot model sold commercially. Both are provided as follows:

Standard cost sheet: 1,000-sq.-ft., one-bedroom model

Direct materials		$9,500
Direct manufacturing labor	32 hours	704
Manufacturing overhead*	$3.50 per direct labor dollar	2,464
Total cost		$12,668
Retail markup on total cost		25%
Retail price		$15,835

INVOICE

DATE: September 15, 2014

BILL TO: FEMA

FOR: 200 Emergency Huts

SHIP TO: Sarasota, Florida

Direct materials	$2,090,000
Direct manufacturing labor**	164,400
Manufacturing overhead	575,400
Total cost	2,829,800
Government contract markup on total cost	20%
Total due	$3,395,760

Required

1. Calculate the total bid if you base your calculations on the standard cost sheet assuming a cost plus 20% government contract.
2. Calculate the total bid if you base your calculations on the September 15, 2014, invoice assuming a cost plus 20% government contract.
3. What are the main discrepancies between the bids you calculated in requirements 1 and 2?
4. What bid should you present to your manager? What principles from the IMA "Standards of Ethical Conduct for Practitioners of Management Accounting and Financial Management," as described in Chapter 1, should guide your decision? As the manager, what would you do?

4-41 Job costing—service industry. Jordan Brady schedules gigs for local bands and creates CDs and T-shirts to sell at each gig. Brady uses a normal-costing system with two direct-cost pools, labor and materials, and one indirect-cost pool, general overhead. General overhead is allocated to each gig based on 120% of direct labor cost. Actual overhead equaled allocated overhead as of March 2014. Actual overhead in April was $1,980. All costs incurred during the planning stage for a gig and during the gig are gathered in a balance sheet account called "Gigs in Progress (GIP)." When a gig is completed, the costs are transferred to an income statement account called "Cost of Completed Gigs (CCG)." Following is cost information for April 2014:

	From Beginning GIP		Incurred in April	
Band	**Materials**	**Labor**	**Materials**	**Labor**
Irok	$570	$750	$110	$200
Freke Out	700	550	140	100
Bottom Rung	250	475	310	250
Dish Towel	—	—	540	450
Rail Ride	—	—	225	250

*Overhead cost pool includes inspection labor ($15 per hour), setup labor ($12 per hour), and other indirect costs associated with production.

**Direct manufacturing labor includes 30 production hours per unit, 4 inspection hours per unit, and 6 setup hours per unit.

As of April 1, there were three gigs in progress: *Irok, Freke Out,* and *Bottom Rung.* The gigs for *Dish Towel* and *Rail Ride* were started during April. The gigs for *Freke Out* and *Dish Towel* were completed during April.

Required

1. Calculate GIP at the end of April.
2. Calculate CCG for April.
3. Calculate under- or overallocated overhead at the end of April.
4. Calculate the ending balances in GIP and CCG if the under- or overallocated overhead amount is as follows:
   a. Written off to CCG
   b. Prorated based on the ending balances (before proration) in GIP and CCG
   c. Prorated based on the overhead allocated in April in the ending balances of GIP and CCG (before proration)
5. Which method would you choose? Explain. Would your choice depend on whether overhead cost is underallocated or overallocated? Explain.

5 Activity-Based Costing and Activity-Based Management

Learning Objectives

1. Explain how broad averaging undercosts and overcosts products or services
2. Present three guidelines for refining a costing system
3. Distinguish between simple and activity-based costing systems
4. Describe a four-part cost hierarchy
5. Cost products or services using activity-based costing
6. Evaluate the costs and benefits of implementing activity-based costing systems
7. Explain how managers use activity-based costing systems in activity-based management
8. Compare activity-based costing systems and department costing systems

A good mystery never fails to capture the imagination.

Money is stolen or lost, property disappears, or someone meets with foul play. On the surface, many people may view these cases as typical. Someone with a trained eye, however, may uncover hidden facts, details, and patterns. Getting to the bottom of the case, understanding what happened and why, and taking action can make the difference between a solved case and an unsolved one. Business and organizations face similar cases. Their costing systems are often mysteries with unresolved questions: Why are we bleeding red ink? Are we pricing our products accurately? Activity-based costing can help unravel the mystery and result in improved operations, as LG Electronics discovered.

LG Electronics Reduces Costs and Inefficiencies Through Activity-Based Costing[1]

Based in Seoul, South Korea, LG Electronics is one of the world's largest manufacturers of flat-screen televisions and mobile phones. In 2012, the company spent $35.9 billion to purchase the semiconductors, metals, connectors, and other materials to manufacture its many electronic devices.

Until recently, however, LG Electronics did not have a centralized procurement system to leverage its scale and control rising supply costs. When LG Electronics hired its first chief procurement officer in 2009, he turned to activity-based costing (ABC) to identify opportunities for improvement. ABC analysis of the company's procurement system revealed that most company resources were applied to administrative tasks that were done manually and at a very high cost rather than to strategic tasks such as lowering supply costs.

The ABC analysis led LG Electronics to change many of its procurement practices and processes, improve efficiency, and focus on the highest-value tasks such as managing costs of commodity products and negotiating with suppliers. In 2012, LG Electronics saved $4.7 billion in direct material costs. Furthermore, the company

---

[1] *Sources:* Based on J. Carbone, "LG Electronics centralizes purchasing to save," *Purchasing* (April 2009); K. Yoou-chul, "CPO expects to save $1 billion in procurement," *The Korea Times* (April 1, 2009); "Linton's goals" (May 12, 2009); M. Ihlwan, "Innovation Close-up: LG Electronics," *Bloomberg Businessweek* (April 15, 2010); T. Linton and J. Choi, Global Procurement Transformation: New Frontiers for Global Innovation, in Proceedings of 95th Annual International Supply Management Conference, April 2012; and LG Corp., "Business Partners for Win-Win Growth, http://www.lg.com/global/sustainability/business-partner/win-win-growth, accessed May 2013.

developed an innovative global procurement strategy for its televisions, mobile phones, computers, and home-theater systems by implementing competitive bidding among suppliers, standardizing parts across product lines, and developing the capability to purchase more goods in China. As a result, today 44% of LG Electronics' global purchasing is sourced from outside of South Korea.

Most companies, such as Dell, Oracle, JP Morgan Chase, and Honda, offer more than one product (or service). Dell Computer, for example, produces desktops, laptops, and servers. Manufacturing these products entails three basic activities: (1) designing computers, (2) ordering component parts, and (3) assembling the product. Different products require different quantities of the three activities. A server, for example, has a more complex design, many more parts, and a more complex assembly than a desktop computer.

Dell separately tracks activity costs by product in its activity-based costing (ABC) system. In this chapter, we describe these types of systems and how they help companies make better decisions about pricing and product mix. And, just as in the case of LG Electronics, we show how ABC systems help managers make cost management decisions by improving product designs, processes, and efficiency.

Broad Averaging and Its Consequences

Learning Objective 1

Explain how broad averaging undercosts and overcosts products or services

...it does not measure the different resources consumed by different products and services

Historically, companies (such as television and automobile manufacturers) produced a limited variety of products. These companies used few overhead resources to support these simple operations, so indirect (or overhead) costs were a relatively small percentage of total costs. Managers used simple costing systems to allocate overhead costs broadly in an easy, inexpensive, and reasonably accurate way. But as product diversity and indirect costs increased, broad averaging led to inaccurate product costs. That's because simple *peanut-butter costing* (yes, that's what it's called) broadly averages or spreads the cost of resources uniformly to cost objects (such as products or services) when, in fact, the individual products or services use those resources in nonuniform ways.

Undercosting and Overcosting

The following example illustrates how averaging can result in inaccurate and misleading cost data. Consider the cost of a restaurant bill for four colleagues who meet monthly to discuss business developments. Each diner orders separate entrees, desserts, and drinks. The restaurant bill for the most recent meeting is as follows.

	Emma	James	Jessica	Matthew	Total	Average
Entree	$11	$20	$15	$14	$ 60	$15
Dessert	0	8	4	4	16	4
Drinks	4	14	8	6	32	8
Total	$15	$42	$27	$24	$108	$27

If the $108 total restaurant bill is divided evenly, $27 is the average cost per diner. This cost-averaging approach treats each diner the same. When costs are averaged across all four diners, both Emma and Matthew are overcosted, James is undercosted, and Jessica is (by coincidence) accurately costed. Emma, especially, may object to paying the average bill of $27 because her individual bill is only $15.

Broad averaging often leads to undercosting or overcosting of products or services:

- **Product undercosting**—a product consumes a high level of resources per unit but is reported to have a low cost per unit (James's dinner).
- **Product overcosting**—a product consumes a low level of resources per unit but is reported to have a high cost per unit (Emma's dinner).

What are the strategic consequences of product undercosting and overcosting? Suppose a manager uses cost information about products to guide pricing decisions. Undercosted products will be underpriced and may even lead to sales that actually result in losses because the sales may bring in less revenue than the cost of resources they use. Overcosted products will lead to overpricing, causing those products to lose market share to competitors producing similar products. But what if prices are determined by the market based on consumer demand and competition among companies? In this case, product undercosting and overcosting cause managers to focus on the wrong products. Managers give greater attention to overcosted products that show low profits when in fact costs and profits from these products are perfectly reasonable. They give less attention to undercosted products thinking they are highly profitable, when in fact these products consume large amounts of resources and are far less profitable than they appear.

Product-Cost Cross-Subsidization

Product-cost cross-subsidization means that if a company undercosts one of its products, it will overcost at least one of its other products. Similarly, if a company overcosts one of its products, it will undercost at least one of its other products. Product-cost cross-subsidization is very common when a cost is uniformly spread—meaning it is broadly averaged—across multiple products without managers recognizing the amount of resources each product consumes.

In the restaurant-bill example, the amount of cost cross-subsidization of each diner can be readily computed *because all cost items can be traced as direct costs to each diner.* If all diners pay $27, Emma is paying $12 more than her actual cost of $15. She is cross-subsidizing James who is paying $15 less than his actual cost of $42. Calculating the amount of cost cross-subsidization takes more work when there are indirect costs to be considered. Why? Because when two or more diners use the resources represented by indirect costs, we need to find a way to allocate costs to each diner. Consider, for example, a $40 bottle of wine whose cost is shared equally. Each diner would pay $10 ($40 ÷ 4). Suppose Matthew drinks two glasses of wine, while Emma, James, and Jessica drink one glass each for a total of five glasses. Allocating the cost of the bottle of wine on the basis of the glasses of wine that each diner drinks would result in Matthew paying $16 ($40 × 2/5) and each of the others paying $8 ($40 × 1/5). In this case, by sharing the cost equally, Emma, James, and Jessica are each paying $2($10 − $8) more and are cross-subsidizing Matthew who is paying $6($16 − $10) less for his wine for the night.

Decision Point

When does product undercosting or overcosting occur?

To see the effects of broad averaging on direct and indirect costs, we next consider Plastim Corporation's costing system.

Simple Costing System at Plastim Corporation

Plastim Corporation manufactures lenses for the rear taillights of automobiles. A lens, made from black, red, orange, or white plastic, is the part of the taillight visible on the automobile's exterior. Lenses are made by injecting molten plastic into a mold, which gives the lens its desired shape. The mold is cooled to allow the molten plastic to solidify, and the lens is removed.

Plastim has a contract with Giovanni Motors, a major automobile manufacturer, to make two types of lenses: a complex lens called C5 and a simple lens called S3. The complex lens is large and has special features, such as multicolor molding (when more than one color is injected into the mold) and a complex shape that wraps around the corner of the car. Manufacturing C5 lenses is complicated because various parts in the mold must align and fit precisely. The S3 lens is simpler to make because it has a single color and few special features.

Design, Manufacturing, and Distribution Processes

Whether lenses are simple or complex, Plastim follows this sequence of steps to design, produce, and distribute them:

- **Design products and processes.** Each year Giovanni Motors specifies details of the simple and complex lenses it needs for its new models of cars. Plastim's design department designs the new molds and specifies the manufacturing process to make the lenses.
- **Manufacture lenses.** The lenses are molded, finished, cleaned, and inspected.
- **Distribute lenses.** Finished lenses are packed and sent to Giovanni Motors.

Plastim is operating at capacity and incurs very low marketing costs. Because of its high-quality products, Plastim has minimal customer-service costs. Plastim competes with several other companies who also manufacture simple lenses. At a recent meeting, Giovanni's purchasing manager informed Plastim's sales manager that Bandix, which makes only simple lenses, is offering to supply the S3 lens to Giovanni at a price of $53, well below the $63 price that Plastim is currently projecting and budgeting for 2014. Unless Plastim can lower its selling price, it will lose the Giovanni business for the simple lens for the upcoming model year. Fortunately, the same competitive pressures do not exist for the complex lens, which Plastim currently sells to Giovanni at $137 per lens.

Plastim's managers have two primary options:

- Give up the Giovanni business in simple lenses if selling them is unprofitable. Bandix makes only simple lenses and perhaps, therefore, uses simpler technology and processes than Plastim. The simpler operations may give Bandix a cost advantage that Plastim cannot match. If so, it is better for Plastim to not supply the S3 lens to Giovanni.
- Reduce the price of the simple lens and either accept a lower margin or aggressively seek to reduce costs.

To make these long-run strategic decisions, managers first need to understand the costs to design, make, and distribute the S3 and C5 lenses.

Bandix makes only simple lenses and can fairly accurately calculate the cost of a lens by dividing total costs by the number of simple lenses produced. Plastim's costing environment is more challenging because the manufacturing overhead costs support the production of both simple and complex lenses. Plastim's managers and management accountants need to find a way to allocate overhead costs to each type of lens.

In computing costs, Plastim assigns both variable costs and costs that are fixed in the short run to the S3 and C5 lenses. Managers cost products and services to guide long-run strategic decisions, such as what mix of products and services to produce and sell and what prices to charge for them. In the long run, managers have the ability to influence all costs. The firm will only survive in the long run if revenues exceed total costs, regardless of whether these costs are variable or fixed in the short run.

To guide pricing and cost-management decisions, Plastim's managers assign both manufacturing and nonmanufacturing costs to the S3 and C5 lenses. If managers had wanted to calculate the cost of inventory, Plastim's management accountants would have assigned only manufacturing costs to the lenses, as required by Generally Accepted Accounting Principles. Surveys of company practice across the globe indicate that the vast majority of companies use costing systems not just for inventory costing but also for strategic purposes, such as pricing and product-mix decisions and decisions about cost reduction, process improvement, design, and planning and budgeting. Managers of these companies assign all costs to products and services. Even merchandising-sector companies (for whom inventory costing is straightforward) and service-sector companies (who have no inventory) expend considerable resources in designing and operating their costing systems to allocate costs for strategic purposes.

Simple Costing System Using a Single Indirect-Cost Pool

Plastim currently has a simple costing system that allocates indirect costs using a single indirect-cost rate, the type of system described in Chapter 4. The only difference between these two chapters is that Chapter 4 focuses on jobs while here the cost objects are products. Exhibit 5-1 shows an overview of Plastim's simple costing system. Use this exhibit as a guide as you study the following steps, each of which is marked in Exhibit 5-1.

Step 1: Identify the Products That Are the Chosen Cost Objects. The cost objects are the 60,000 simple S3 lenses and the 15,000 complex C5 lenses that Plastim will produce in 2014. Plastim's management accountants first calculate the total costs and then the unit cost of designing, manufacturing, and distributing lenses.

Step 2: Identify the Direct Costs of the Products. The direct costs are direct materials and direct manufacturing labor. Exhibit 5-2 shows the direct and indirect costs for the S3 and the C5 lenses using the simple costing system. The direct cost calculations appear on lines 5, 6, and 7 in Exhibit 5-2. Plastim's simple costing system classifies all costs other than direct materials and direct manufacturing labor as indirect costs.

Step 3: Select the Cost-Allocation Bases to Use for Allocating Indirect (or Overhead) Costs to the Products. A majority of the indirect costs consist of salaries paid to supervisors, engineers, manufacturing support, and maintenance staff that support direct manufacturing labor. Plastim's managers use direct manufacturing labor-hours as the only allocation base to allocate all manufacturing and nonmanufacturing indirect costs to S3 and C5. In 2014, Plastim's managers budget 39,750 direct manufacturing labor-hours.

Exhibit 5-1

Overview of Plastim's Simple Costing System

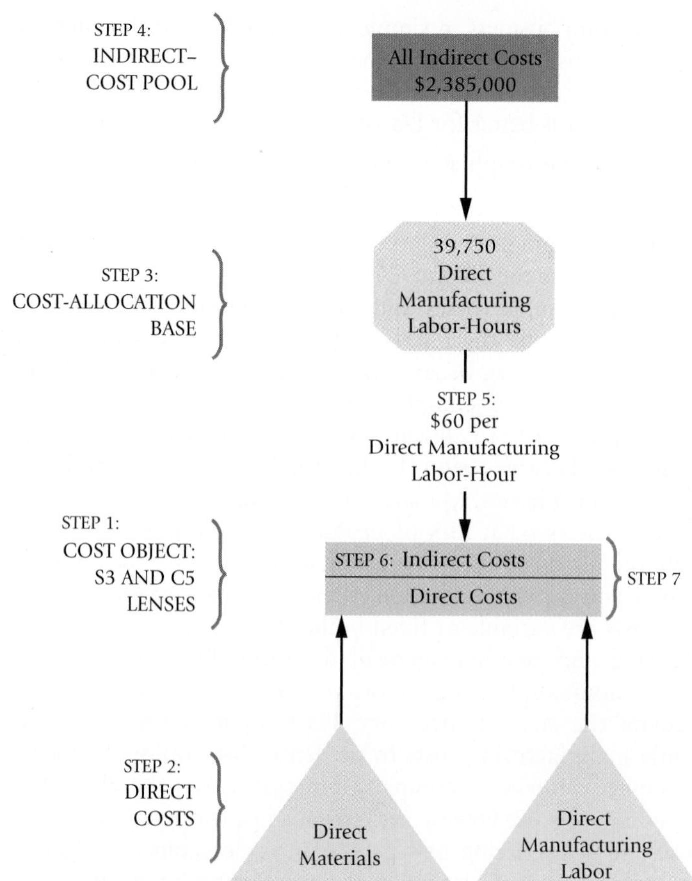

Exhibit 5-2 Plastim's Product Costs Using the Simple Costing System

	A	B	C	D	E	F	G
1		60,000			15,000		
2		Simple Lenses (S3)			Complex Lenses (C5)		
3		Total	per Unit		Total	per Unit	Total
4		(1)	(2) = (1) ÷ 60,000		(3)	(4) = (3) ÷ 15,000	(5) = (1) + (3)
5	Direct materials	$1,125,000	$18.75		$ 675,000	$45.00	$1,800,000
6	Direct manufacturing labor	600,000	10.00		195,000	13.00	795,000
7	Total direct costs (Step 2)	1,725,000	28.75		870,000	58.00	2,595,000
8	Indirect costs allocated (Step 6)	1,800,000	30.00		585,000	39.00	2,385,000
9	Total costs (Step 7)	$3,525,000	$58.75		$1,455,000	$97.00	$4,980,000
10							

Step 4: Identify the Indirect Costs Associated with Each Cost-Allocation Base. Because Plastim uses only a single cost-allocation base, Plastim's management accountants group all budgeted indirect costs of $2,385,000 for 2014 into a single overhead cost pool.

Step 5: Compute the Rate per Unit of Each Cost-Allocation Base.

$$\text{Budgeted indirect-cost rate} = \frac{\text{Budgeted total costs in indirect-cost pool}}{\text{Budgeted total quantity of cost-allocation base}}$$

$$= \frac{\$2{,}385{,}000}{39{,}750 \text{ direct manufacturing labor-hours}}$$

$$= \$60 \text{ per direct manufacturing labor-hour}$$

Step 6: Compute the Indirect Costs Allocated to the Products. Plastim's managers budget 30,000 total direct manufacturing labor-hours to make the 60,000 S3 lenses and 9,750 total direct manufacturing labor-hours to make the 15,000 C5 lenses. Exhibit 5-2 shows indirect costs of $1,800,000 ($60 per direct manufacturing labor-hour × 30,000 direct manufacturing labor-hours) allocated to the simple lens and $585,000 ($60 per direct manufacturing labor-hour × 9,750 direct manufacturing labor-hours) allocated to the complex lens.

Step 7: Compute the Total Cost of the Products by Adding All Direct and Indirect Costs Assigned to the Products. Exhibit 5-2 presents the product costs for the simple and complex lenses. The direct costs are calculated in Step 2 and the indirect costs in Step 6. Be sure you see the parallel between the simple costing system overview diagram (Exhibit 5-1) and the costs calculated in Step 7. Exhibit 5-1 shows two direct-cost categories and one indirect-cost category. Therefore, the budgeted cost of each type of lens in Step 7 (Exhibit 5-2) has three line items: two for direct costs and one for allocated indirect costs. It is very helpful to draw overview diagrams to see the big picture of costing systems before getting into the detailed costing of products and services. The budgeted cost per S3 lens is $58.75, well above the $53 selling price quoted by Bandix. The budgeted cost per C5 lens is $97.

Applying the Five-Step Decision-Making Process at Plastim

To decide how it should respond to the threat that Bandix poses to its S3 lens business, Plastim's managers work through the five-step decision-making process introduced in Chapter 1.

Step 1: Identify the Problem and Uncertainties. The problem is clear: If Plastim wants to retain the Giovanni business for S3 lenses and make a profit, it must find a way to reduce the price and costs of the S3 lens. The two major uncertainties Plastim faces are (1) whether its technology and processes for the S3 lens are competitive with Bandix's and (2) whether Plastim's S3 lens is overcosted by the simple costing system.

Step 2: Obtain Information. Senior management asks a team of design and process engineers to analyze and evaluate the design, manufacturing, and distribution operations for the S3 lens. The team is very confident that the technology and processes for the S3 lens are not inferior to those of Bandix and other competitors because Plastim has many years of experience in manufacturing and distributing the S3 lens with a history and culture of continuous process improvements. The team is less certain about Plastim's capabilities in manufacturing and distributing complex lenses because it only recently started making this type of lens. Given these doubts, senior management is happy that Giovanni Motors considers the price of the C5 lens to be competitive. Plastim's managers are puzzled, though, by how, at the currently budgeted prices, Plastim is expected to earn a very large profit margin percentage (operating income ÷ revenues) on the C5 lenses and a small profit margin on the S3 lenses:

	60,000 Simple Lenses (S3)		15,000 Complex Lenses (C5)		
	Total (1)	per Unit (2) = (1) ÷ 60,000	Total (3)	per Unit (4) = (3) ÷ 15,000	Total (5) = (1) + (3)
Revenues	$3,780,000	$63.00	$2,055,000	$137.00	$5,835,000
Total costs	3,525,000	58.75	1,455,000	97.00	4,980,000
Operating income	$ 255,000	$ 4.25	$ 600,000	$ 40.00	$ 855,000
Profit margin percentage		6.75%		29.20%	

As they continue to gather information, Plastim's managers begin to ponder why the profit margins are under so much pressure for the S3 lens, where the company has strong capabilities, but are high on the newer, less-established C5 lens. Plastim is not deliberately charging a low price for S3, so managers begin to evaluate the costing system. Plastim's simple costing system may be overcosting the simple S3 lens (assigning too much cost to it) and undercosting the complex C5 lens (assigning too little cost to it).

Step 3: Make Predictions About the Future. Plastim's key challenge is to get a better estimate of what it will cost to design, make, and distribute the S3 and C5 lenses. Managers are fairly confident about the direct material and direct manufacturing labor cost of each lens because these costs are easily traced to the lenses. But managers are quite concerned about how accurately the simple costing system measures the indirect resources used by each type of lens. They believe the costing system can be substantially improved.

Even as they come to this conclusion, managers want to avoid biased thinking. In particular, they want to be careful that the desire to be competitive on the S3 lens does not lead to assumptions that bias them in favor of lowering costs of the S3 lens.

Step 4: Make Decisions by Choosing Among Alternatives. On the basis of predicted costs and taking into account how Bandix might respond, Plastim's managers must decide whether they should bid for Giovanni Motors' S3 lens business and, if they do bid, what price they should offer.

Step 5: Implement the Decision, Evaluate Performance, and Learn. If Plastim bids and wins Giovanni's S3 lens business, it must compare actual costs as it makes and ships S3 lenses to predicted costs and learn why actual costs deviate from predicted costs. Such evaluation and learning form the basis for future improvements.

The next few sections focus on Steps 3, 4, and 5: (3) how Plastim improves the allocation of indirect costs to the S3 and C5 lenses, (4) how it uses these predictions to bid for the S3 lens business, and (5) how it evaluates performance, makes product design and process improvements, and learns using the new system.

Refining a Costing System

Learning Objective

Present three guidelines for refining a costing system

...classify more costs as direct costs, expand the number of indirect-cost pools, and identify cost drivers

A **refined costing system** reduces the use of broad averages for assigning the cost of resources to cost objects (such as jobs, products, and services) and provides better measurement of the costs of indirect resources used by different cost objects, no matter how differently various cost objects use indirect resources. Refining a costing system helps managers make better decisions about how to allocate resources and which products to produce.

Reasons for Refining a Costing System

Three principal reasons have accelerated the demand for refinements to the costing system.

1. **Increase in product diversity.** The growing demand for customized products has led managers to increase the variety of products and services their companies offer. Kanthal, a Swedish manufacturer of heating elements, for example, produces more than 10,000 different types of electrical heating wires and thermostats. Banks, such as Barclays Bank in the United Kingdom, offer many different types of accounts and services: special passbook accounts, ATMs, credit cards, and electronic banking products. Producing these products places different demands on resources because of differences in volume, process, technology, and complexity. For example, the computer and network resources needed to support electronic banking products are much greater than the computer and network resources needed to support a passbook savings account. The use of broad averages fails to capture these differences in demand and leads to distorted and inaccurate cost information.
2. **Increase in indirect costs.** The use of product and process technology such as computer-integrated manufacturing (CIM) and flexible manufacturing systems (FMS) has led to an increase in indirect costs and a decrease in direct costs, particularly direct manufacturing labor costs. In CIM and FMS, computers on the manufacturing floor instruct equipment to set up and run quickly and automatically. The computers accurately measure hundreds of production parameters and directly control the manufacturing processes to achieve high-quality output. Managing complex technology and producing diverse products also require additional support function resources for activities such as production scheduling, product and process design, and engineering. Because direct manufacturing labor is not a cost driver of these costs, allocating indirect costs on the basis of direct manufacturing labor (as in Plastim's simple costing system) does not accurately measure how resources are being used by different products.
3. **Competition in product markets.** As markets have become more competitive, managers have felt the need to obtain more accurate cost information to help them make important strategic decisions, such as how to price products and which products to sell. Making correct decisions about pricing and product mix is critical in competitive markets because competitors quickly capitalize on a manager's mistakes. For example, if Plastim overcosts the S3 lens and charges a higher price, a competitor aware of the true costs of making the lens could charge a lower price and gain the S3 business.

The preceding factors explain why managers want to refine cost systems. Refining costing systems requires gathering, validating, analyzing, and storing vast quantities of data. Advances in information technology have drastically reduced the costs of performing these activities.

Guidelines for Refining a Costing System

There are three main guidelines for refining a costing system:

1. **Direct-cost tracing.** Identify as many direct costs as is economically feasible. This guideline aims to reduce the amount of costs classified as indirect, thereby minimizing the extent to which costs have to be allocated rather than traced.
2. **Indirect-cost pools.** Expand the number of indirect-cost pools until each pool is more homogeneous. All costs in a *homogeneous cost pool* have the same or a similar

cause-and-effect (or benefits-received) relationship with a single cost driver that is used as the cost-allocation base. Consider, for example, a single indirect-cost pool containing both indirect machining costs and indirect distribution costs that are allocated to products using machine-hours. This pool is not homogeneous because machine-hours are a cost driver of machining costs but not of distribution costs, which has a different cost driver, number of shipments. If, instead, machining costs and distribution costs are separated into two indirect-cost pools, with machine-hours as the cost-allocation base for the machining cost pool and number of shipments as the cost-allocation base for the distribution cost pool, each indirect-cost pool would become homogeneous.

3. **Cost-allocation bases.** As we describe later in the chapter, whenever possible, managers should use the cost driver (the cause of indirect costs) as the cost-allocation base for each homogeneous indirect-cost pool (the effect).

Decision Point

How do managers refine a costing system?

Learning Objective 3

Distinguish between simple and activity-based costing systems

...unlike simple systems, activity-based costing systems calculate costs of individual activities to cost products

Activity-Based Costing Systems

One of the best tools for refining a costing system is *activity-based costing*. **Activity-based costing (ABC)** refines a costing system by identifying individual activities as the fundamental cost objects. An **activity** is an event, task, or unit of work with a specified purpose—for example, designing products, setting up machines, operating machines, and distributing products. More informally, activities are verbs; they are things that a firm does. To help make strategic decisions, ABC systems identify activities in all functions of the value chain, calculate costs of individual activities, and assign costs to cost objects such as products and services on the basis of the mix of activities needed to produce each product or service.[2]

Fundamental Cost Objects		Assignment to Other Cost Objects
Activities →	Costs of Activities →	Costs of • Products • Services • Customers

Plastim's ABC System

After reviewing its simple costing system and the potential miscosting of product costs, Plastim's managers decide to implement an ABC system. Direct material costs and direct manufacturing labor costs can be traced to products easily, so the ABC system focuses on refining the assignment of indirect costs to departments, processes, products, or other cost objects. To identify activities, Plastim organizes a team of managers from design, manufacturing, distribution, accounting, and administration. Plastim's ABC system then uses these activities to break down its current single indirect cost pool into finer pools of costs related to the various activities.

Defining activities is difficult. The team evaluates hundreds of tasks performed at Plastim. It must decide which tasks should be classified as separate activities and which should be combined. For example, should maintenance of molding machines, operations of molding machines, and process control be regarded as separate activities or combined into a single activity? An activity-based costing system with many activities becomes overly detailed and unwieldy to operate. An activity-based costing system with too few activities may not be refined enough to measure cause-and-effect relationships between cost drivers and various indirect costs. To achieve an effective balance, Plastim's team

[2] For more details on ABC systems, see R. Cooper and R. S. Kaplan, *The Design of Cost Management Systems* (Upper Saddle River, NJ: Prentice Hall, 1999); G. Cokins, *Activity-Based Cost Management: An Executive's Guide* (Hoboken, NJ: John Wiley & Sons, 2001); and R. S. Kaplan and S. Anderson, *Time-Driven Activity-Based Costing: A Simpler and More Powerful Path to Higher Profits* (Boston: Harvard Business School Press, 2007).

focuses on activities that account for a sizable fraction of indirect costs and combines activities that have the same cost driver into a single activity. For example, the team decides to combine maintenance of molding machines, operations of molding machines, and process control into a single activity—molding machine operations—because all these activities have the same cost driver: molding machine-hours.

The team identifies the following seven activities by developing a flowchart of all the steps and processes needed to design, manufacture, and distribute S3 and C5 lenses.

a. Design products and processes
b. Set up molding machines to ensure that the molds are properly held in place and parts are properly aligned before manufacturing starts
c. Operate molding machines to manufacture lenses
d. Clean and maintain the molds after lenses are manufactured
e. Prepare batches of finished lenses for shipment
f. Distribute lenses to customers
g. Administer and manage all processes at Plastim

These activity descriptions (or *activity list* or *activity dictionary*) form the basis of the activity-based costing system. Compiling the list of tasks, however, is only the first step in implementing activity-based costing systems. Plastim must also identify the cost of each activity and the related cost driver by using the three guidelines for refining a costing system described on pages 157–158.

1. **Direct-cost tracing.** Plastim's ABC system subdivides the single indirect cost pool into seven smaller cost pools related to the different activities. The costs in the cleaning and maintenance activity cost pool (item d) consist of salaries and wages paid to workers who clean the mold. These costs are direct costs because they can be economically traced to a specific mold and lens.
2. **Indirect-cost pools.** The remaining six activity cost pools are indirect cost pools. Unlike the single indirect cost pool of Plastim's simple costing system, each of the activity-related cost pools is homogeneous. That is, each activity cost pool includes only those narrow and focused sets of costs that have the same cost driver. For example, the distribution cost pool includes only those costs (such as wages of truck drivers) that, over time, increase as the cost driver of distribution costs, cubic feet of packages delivered, increases. In the simple costing system, Plastim lumped all indirect costs together and the cost-allocation base, direct manufacturing labor-hours, was not a cost driver of the indirect costs. Managers were therefore unable to measure how different cost objects used resources.

   To determine the costs of activity pools, managers assign costs accumulated in various account classifications (such as salaries, wages, maintenance, and electricity) to each of the activity cost pools. This process is commonly called *first-stage allocation*. For example, as we will see later in the chapter, of the $2,385,000 in the total indirect-cost pool, Plastim identifies setup costs of $300,000. Setup costs include depreciation and maintenance costs of setup equipment, wages of setup workers, and allocated salaries of design engineers, process engineers, and supervisors. We discuss *first-stage allocation* in more detail in Chapters 14 and 15. We focus here on the *second-stage allocation*, the allocation of costs of activity cost pools to products.
3. **Cost-allocation bases.** For each activity cost pool, Plastim uses the cost driver (whenever possible) as the cost-allocation base. To identify cost drivers, Plastim's managers consider various alternatives and use their knowledge of operations to choose among them. For example, Plastim's managers choose setup-hours rather than the number of setups as the cost driver of setup costs because Plastim's managers believe that more complex setups take more time and are more costly. Over time, Plastim's managers can use data to test their beliefs. (Chapter 10 discusses several methods to estimate the relationship between a cost driver and costs.)

The logic of ABC systems is twofold. First, when managers structure activity cost pools more finely with cost drivers for each activity cost pool as the cost-allocation base, it leads to more accurate costing of activities. Second, allocating these costs to products by measuring the cost-allocation bases of different activities used by different products leads to more accurate product costs. We illustrate this logic by focusing on the setup activity at Plastim.

Setting up molding machines frequently entails trial runs, fine-tuning, and adjustments. Improper setups cause quality problems such as scratches on the surface of the lens. The resources needed for each setup depend on the complexity of the manufacturing operation. Complex lenses require more setup resources (setup-hours) per setup than simple lenses. Furthermore, complex lenses can be produced only in small batches because the molds for complex lenses need to be cleaned more often than molds for simple lenses. Relative to simple lenses, complex lenses therefore not only use more setup-hours per setup, but they also require more frequent setups.

Setup data for the simple S3 lens and the complex C5 lens are as follows.

		Simple S3 Lens	Complex C5 Lens	Total
1	Quantity of lenses produced	60,000	15,000	
2	Number of lenses produced per batch	240	50	
3 = (1) ÷ (2)	Number of batches	250	300	
4	Setup time per batch	2 hours	5 hours	
5 = (3) × (4)	Total setup-hours	500 hours	1,500 hours	2,000 hours

Recall that in its simple costing system, Plastim uses direct manufacturing labor-hours to allocate all $2,385,000 of indirect costs (which includes $300,000 of indirect setup costs) to products. The following table compares how setup costs allocated to simple and complex lenses will be different if Plastim allocates setup costs to lenses based on setup-hours rather than direct manufacturing labor-hours. Of the $60 total rate per direct manufacturing labor-hour (page 155), the setup cost per direct manufacturing labor-hour amounts to $7.54717 ($300,000 ÷ 39,750 total direct manufacturing labor-hours). The setup cost per setup-hour equals $150 ($300,000 ÷ 2,000 total setup-hours).

	Simple S3 Lens	Complex C5 Lens	Total
Setup cost allocated using direct manufacturing labor-hours:			
$7.54717 × 30,000; $7.54717 × 9,750	$226,415	$ 73,585	$300,000
Setup cost allocated using setup-hours:			
$150 × 500; $150 × 1,500	$ 75,000	$225,000	$300,000

ABC systems that use available time (setup-hours in our example) to calculate the cost of a resource and to allocate costs to cost objects are sometimes called *time-driven activity-based costing (TDABC) systems.* As we have already discussed when presenting guidelines 2 and 3, setup-hours, not direct manufacturing labor-hours, are the cost driver of setup costs. The C5 lens uses substantially more setup-hours than the S3 lens (1,500 hours ÷ 2,000 hours = 75% of the total setup-hours) because the C5 requires a greater number of setups (batches) and each setup is more challenging and requires more setup-hours.

Decision Point

What is the difference between the design of a simple costing system and an activity-based costing (ABC) system?

The ABC system therefore allocates significantly more setup costs to C5 than to S3. When direct manufacturing labor-hours rather than setup-hours are used to allocate setup costs in the simple costing system, the S3 lens is allocated a very large share of the setup costs because the S3 lens uses a larger proportion of direct manufacturing labor-hours (30,000 ÷ 39,750 = 75.47%). As a result, the simple costing system overcosts the S3 lens with regard to setup costs.

As we will see later in the chapter, ABC systems provide valuable information to managers beyond more accurate product costs. For example, identifying setup-hours as the cost driver correctly orients managers' cost reduction efforts on reducing setup-hours and cost per setup-hour. Note that setup-hours are related to batches (or groups) of lenses made, not the number of individual lenses. Activity-based costing attempts to identify the most relevant cause-and-effect relationship for each activity pool without restricting the cost driver to only units of output or variables related to units of output (such as direct manufacturing labor-hours). As our discussion of setups illustrates, limiting cost-allocation bases to only units of output weakens the cause-and-effect relationship between the cost-allocation base and the costs in a cost pool.

Cost Hierarchies

Learning Objective 4

Describe a four-part cost hierarchy

...a four-part cost hierarchy is used to categorize costs based on different types of cost drivers—for example, costs that vary with each unit of a product versus costs that vary with each batch of products

A **cost hierarchy** categorizes various activity cost pools on the basis of the different types of cost drivers, cost-allocation bases, or different degrees of difficulty in determining cause-and-effect (or benefits-received) relationships. ABC systems commonly use a cost hierarchy with four levels to identify cost-allocation bases that are cost drivers of the activity cost pools: (1) output unit–level costs, (2) batch-level costs, (3) product-sustaining costs, and (4) facility-sustaining costs.

Output unit–level costs are the costs of activities performed on each individual unit of a product or service. Machine operations costs (such as the cost of energy, machine depreciation, and repair) related to the activity of running the automated molding machines are output unit–level costs because, over time, the cost of this activity increases with additional units of output produced (or machine-hours used). Plastim's ABC system uses molding machine-hours, an output unit–level cost-allocation base, to allocate machine operations costs to products.

Batch-level costs are the costs of activities related to a group of units of a product or service rather than each individual unit of product or service. In the Plastim example, setup costs are batch-level costs because, over time, the cost of this setup activity increases with setup-hours needed to produce batches (groups) of lenses. As described in the table on page 160, the S3 lens requires 500 setup-hours (2 setup-hours per batch × 250 batches). The C5 lens requires 1,500 setup-hours (5 setup-hours per batch × 300 batches). The total setup costs allocated to S3 and C5 depend on the total setup-hours required by each type of lens, not on the number of units of S3 and C5 produced. (Setup costs being a batch-level cost cannot be avoided by producing one less unit of S3 or C5.) Plastim's ABC system uses setup-hours, a batch-level cost-allocation base, to allocate setup costs to products. Other examples of batch-level costs are material-handling and quality-inspection costs associated with batches (not the quantities) of products produced and costs of placing purchase orders, receiving materials, and paying invoices related to the number of purchase orders placed rather than the quantity or value of materials purchased.

Product-sustaining costs (service-sustaining costs) are the costs of activities undertaken to support individual products or services regardless of the number of units or batches in which the units are produced. In the Plastim example, design costs are product-sustaining costs. Over time, design costs depend largely on the time designers spend on designing and modifying the product, the mold, and the process. These design costs are a function of the complexity of the mold, measured by the number of parts in the mold multiplied by the area (in square feet) over which the molten plastic must flow (12 parts × 2.5 square feet, or 30 parts-square feet for the S3 lens; and 14 parts × 5 square feet, or 70 parts-square feet for the C5 lens). As a result, the total design costs allocated to S3 and C5 depend on the complexity of the mold, regardless of the number of units or batches of production. Plastim can't avoid design costs by producing fewer units or running fewer batches. Plastim's ABC system uses parts-square feet, a product-sustaining cost-allocation base, to allocate design costs to products. Other examples of product-sustaining costs are product research and development costs, costs of making engineering changes, and marketing costs to launch new products.

Facility-sustaining costs are the costs of activities that managers cannot trace to individual products or services but that support the organization as a whole. In the Plastim example and at companies such as Volvo, Samsung, and General Electric, the general administration costs (including top management compensation, rent, and building security) are facility-sustaining costs. It is usually difficult to find a good cause-and-effect

Decision Point

What is a cost hierarchy?

relationship between these costs and the cost-allocation base, so some companies deduct facility-sustaining costs as a separate lump-sum amount from operating income rather than allocate them to products. Managers who follow this approach need to keep in mind that when making decisions based on costs (such as pricing), some lump-sum costs have not been allocated. They must set prices that are much greater than the allocated costs to recover some of the unallocated facility-sustaining costs. Other companies, such as Plastim, allocate facility-sustaining costs to products on some basis—for example, direct manufacturing labor-hours—because management believes all costs should be allocated to products even if it's done in a somewhat arbitrary way. Allocating all costs to products or services ensures that managers have taken into account all costs when making decisions based on costs (such as pricing). So long as managers are aware of the nature of facility-sustaining costs and the pros and cons of allocating them, which method a manager chooses is a matter of personal preference.

Learning Objective 5

Cost products or services using activity-based costing

...use cost rates for different activities to compute indirect costs of a product

Implementing Activity-Based Costing

Now that you understand the basic concepts of ABC, let's see how Plastim's managers refine the simple costing system, evaluate the two systems, and identify the factors to consider when deciding whether to develop the ABC system.

Implementing ABC at Plastim

To implement ABC, Plastim's managers follow the seven-step approach to costing and the three guidelines for refining costing systems (increase direct-cost tracing, create homogeneous indirect-cost pools, and identify cost-allocation bases that have cause-and-effect relationships with costs in the cost pool). Exhibit 5-3 shows an overview of Plastim's ABC system. Use this exhibit as a guide as you study the following steps, each of which is marked in Exhibit 5-3.

Exhibit 5-3 Overview of Plastim's Activity-Based Costing System

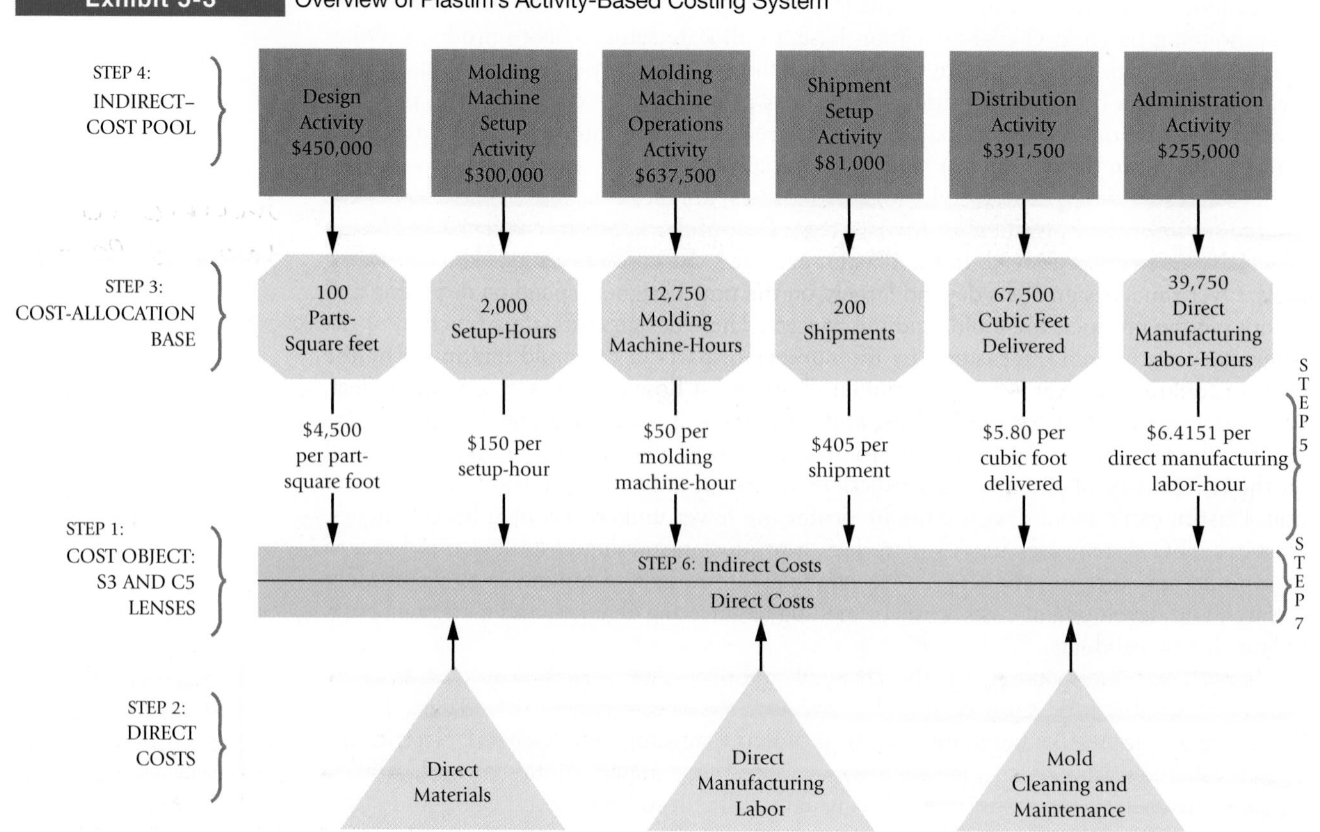

Step 1: Identify the Products That Are the Chosen Cost Objects. The cost objects are the 60,000 S3 and the 15,000 C5 lenses that Plastim will produce in 2014. Plastim's managers want to determine the total costs and then the per-unit cost of designing, manufacturing, and distributing these lenses.

Step 2: Identify the Direct Costs of the Products. The managers identify the following direct costs of the lenses because these costs can be economically traced to a specific mold and lens: direct material costs, direct manufacturing labor costs, and mold cleaning and maintenance costs.

Exhibit 5-5 shows the direct and indirect costs for the S3 and C5 lenses using the ABC system. The direct costs calculations appear on lines 6, 7, 8, and 9 in Exhibit 5-5. Plastim's managers classify all other costs as indirect costs, as we will see in Exhibit 5-4.

Step 3: Select the Activities and Cost-Allocation Bases to Use for Allocating Indirect Costs to the Products. Following guidelines 2 and 3 for refining a costing system (pages 157–158), Plastim's managers identify six activities for allocating indirect costs to products: (a) design, (b) molding machine setups, (c) machine operations, (d) shipment setup, (e) distribution, and (f) administration. Exhibit 5-4, column 2, shows the cost hierarchy category, and column 4 shows the cost-allocation base and the budgeted quantity of the cost-allocation base for each activity described in column 1.

Identifying the cost-allocation bases defines the number of activity pools into which costs must be grouped in an ABC system. For example, rather than define the design activities of product design, process design, and prototyping as separate activities, Plastim's managers define these three activities together as a combined "design" activity and form a homogeneous design cost pool. Why? Because the same cost driver— the complexity of the mold— drives the costs of each design activity. A second consideration for choosing a cost-allocation base is the availability of reliable data and measures. For example, in its ABC system, Plastim's managers measure mold complexity in terms of the number of parts in the mold and the surface area of the mold (parts-square feet). If these data are difficult to obtain or measure, Plastim's managers may be forced to use some other measure of complexity, such as the amount of material flowing through the mold that may only be weakly related to the cost of the design activity.

Exhibit 5-4 Activity-Cost Rates for Indirect-Cost Pools

Home Insert Page Layout Formulas Data Review View

	A	B	C	D	E	F	G	H
1			(Step 4)	(Step 3)		(Step 5)		
2	Activity	Cost Hierarchy Category	Total Budgeted Indirect Costs	Budgeted Quantity of Cost-Allocation Base		Budgeted Indirect Cost Rate		Cause-and-Effect Relationship Between Allocation Base and Activity Cost
3	(1)	(2)	(3)	(4)		(5) = (3) ÷ (4)		(6)
4	Design	Product-sustaining	$450,000	100	parts-square feet	$ 4,500	per part-square foot	Design Department indirect costs increase with more complex molds (more parts, larger surface area).
5	Setup molding machines	Batch-level	$300,000	2,000	setup-hours	$ 150	per setup-hour	Indirect setup costs increase with setup-hours.
6	Machine operations	Output unit-level	$637,500	12,750	molding machine-hours	$ 50	per molding machine-hour	Indirect costs of operating molding machines increases with molding machine-hours.
7	Shipment setup	Batch-level	$ 81,000	200	shipments	$ 405	per shipment	Shipping costs incurred to prepare batches for shipment increase with the number of shipments.
8	Distribution	Output-unit-level	$391,500	67,500	cubic feet delivered	$ 5.80	per cubic foot delivered	Distribution costs increase with the cubic feet of packages delivered.
9	Administration	Facility sustaining	$255,000	39,750	direct manuf. labor-hours	$6.4151	per direct manuf. labor-hour	The demand for administrative resources increases with direct manufacturing labor-hours.

Step 4: Identify the Indirect Costs Associated with Each Cost-Allocation Base. In this step, Plastim's managers try to assign budgeted indirect costs for 2014 to activities (see Exhibit 5-4, column 3) on the basis of a cause-and-effect relationship between the cost-allocation base for an activity and the cost. For example, all costs that have a cause-and-effect relationship to cubic feet of packages moved are assigned to the distribution cost pool. Of course, the strength of the cause-and-effect relationship between the cost-allocation base and the cost of an activity varies across cost pools. For example, the cause-and-effect relationship between direct manufacturing labor-hours and administration activity costs, which as we discussed earlier is somewhat arbitrary, is not as strong as the relationship between setup-hours and setup activity costs, where setup-hours is the cost driver of setup costs.

Some costs can be directly identified with a particular activity. For example, salaries paid to design engineers and depreciation of equipment used in the design department are directly identified with the design activity. Other costs need to be allocated across activities. For example, on the basis of interviews or time records, manufacturing engineers and supervisors estimate the time they will spend on design, molding machine setup, and molding machine operations. If a manufacturing engineer spends 15% of her time on design, 45% of her time managing molding machine setups, and 40% of her time on molding operations, the company will allocate the manufacturing engineer's salary to each of these activities in proportion to the time spent. Still other costs are allocated to activity-cost pools using allocation bases that measure how these costs support different activities. For example, rent costs are allocated to activity cost pools on the basis of square-feet area used by different activities.

As you can see, all costs do not fit neatly into activity categories. Often, costs may first need to be allocated to activities (Stage 1 of the two-stage cost-allocation model) before the costs of the activities can be allocated to products (Stage 2).

The following table shows the assignment of costs to the seven activities identified earlier. Recall that Plastim's management accountants reclassify mold cleaning costs as a direct cost because these costs can be easily traced to a specific mold and lens.

	Design	Molding Machine Setups	Molding Operations	Mold Cleaning	Shipment Setup	Distribution	Administration	Total
Salaries (supervisors, design engineers, process engineers)	$320,000	$105,000	$137,500	$ 0	$21,000	$61,500	$165,000	$ 810,000
Wages of support staff	65,000	115,000	70,000	234,000	34,000	125,000	40,000	683,000
Depreciation	24,000	30,000	290,000	18,000	11,000	140,000	15,000	528,000
Maintenance	13,000	16,000	45,000	12,000	6,000	25,000	5,000	122,000
Power and fuel	18,000	20,000	35,000	6,000	5,000	30,000	10,000	124,000
Rent	10,000	14,000	60,000	0	4,000	10,000	20,000	118,000
Total	$450,000	$300,000	$637,500	$270,000	$81,000	$391,500	$255,000	$2,385,000

Step 5: Compute the Rate per Unit of Each Cost-Allocation Base. Exhibit 5-4, column 5, summarizes the calculation of the budgeted indirect-cost rates using the budgeted quantity of the cost-allocation base from Step 3 and the total budgeted indirect costs of each activity from Step 4.

Step 6: Compute the Indirect Costs Allocated to the Products. Exhibit 5-5 shows total budgeted indirect costs of $1,153,953 allocated to the simple lens and $961,047 allocated to the complex lens. Follow the budgeted indirect cost calculations for each lens in Exhibit 5-5. For each activity, Plastim's operations personnel indicate the total quantity of the cost-allocation base that will be used by each type of lens (recall that Plastim operates at capacity). For example, lines 15 and 16 in Exhibit 5-5 show that of the 2,000 total setup-hours, the S3 lens is budgeted to use 500 hours and the C5 lens 1,500 hours. The budgeted indirect cost rate is $150 per setup-hour (Exhibit 5-4, column 5, line 5). Therefore, the total budgeted cost of the setup activity allocated to the S3 lens is $75,000

Exhibit 5-5 Plastim's Product Costs Using Activity-Based Costing System

	A	B	C	D	E	F	G
1		60,000			15,000		
2		Simple Lenses (S3)			Complex Lenses (C5)		
3		Total	per Unit		Total	per Unit	Total
4	Cost Description	(1)	(2) = (1) ÷ 60,000		(3)	(4) = (3) ÷ 15,000	(5) = (1) + (3)
5	Direct costs						
6	Direct materials	$1,125,000	$18.75		$ 675,000	$ 45.00	$1,800,000
7	Direct manufacturing labor	600,000	10.00		195,000	13.00	795,000
8	Direct mold cleaning and maintenance costs	120,000	2.00		150,000	10.00	270,000
9	Total direct costs (Step 2)	1,845,000	30.75		1,020,000	68.00	2,865,000
10	Indirect Costs of Activities						
11	Design						
12	S3, 30 parts-sq.ft. × $4,500	135,000	2.25				} 450,000
13	C5, 70 parts-sq.ft. × $4,500				315,000	21.00	
14	Setup of molding machines						
15	S3, 500 setup-hours × $150	75,000	1.25				} 300,000
16	C5, 1,500 setup-hours × $150				225,000	15.00	
17	Machine operations						
18	S3, 9,000 molding machine-hours × $50	450,000	7.50				} 637,500
19	C5, 3,750 molding machine-hours × $50				187,500	12.50	
20	Shipment setup						
21	S3, 100 shipments × $405	40,500	0.67				} 81,000
22	C5, 100 shipments × $405				40,500	2.70	
23	Distribution						
24	S3, 45,000 cubic feet delivered × $5.80	261,000	4.35				} 391,500
25	C5, 22,500 cubic feet delivered × $5.80				130,500	8.70	
26	Administration						
27	S3, 30,000 dir. manuf. labor-hours × $6.4151	192,453	3.21				} 255,000
28	C5, 9,750 dir. manuf. labor-hours × $6.4151				62,547	4.17	
29	Total indirect costs allocated (Step 6)	1,153,953	19.23		961,047	64.07	2,115,000
30	Total Costs (Step 7)	$2,998,953	$49.98		$1,981,047	$132.07	$4,980,000
31							

(500 setup-hours × $150 per setup-hour) and to the C5 lens is $225,000 (1,500 setup-hours × $150 per setup-hour). Budgeted setup cost per unit equals $1.25 ($75,000 ÷ 60,000 units) for the S3 lens and $15 ($225,000 ÷ 15,000 units) for the C5 lens.

Step 7: Compute the Total Cost of the Products by Adding All Direct and Indirect Costs Assigned to the Products. Exhibit 5-5 presents the product costs for the simple and complex lenses. The direct costs are calculated in Step 2, and the indirect costs are calculated in Step 6. The ABC system overview in Exhibit 5-3 shows three direct-cost categories and six indirect-cost categories. The budgeted cost of each lens type in Exhibit 5-5 has nine line items, three for direct costs and six for indirect costs. The differences between the ABC product costs of S3 and C5 calculated in Exhibit 5-5 highlight how each of these products uses different amounts of direct and indirect costs in each activity area.

We emphasize two features of ABC systems. First, these systems identify all costs used by products, whether the costs are variable or fixed in the short run. When making long-run strategic decisions using ABC information, managers want revenues to exceed total costs. Otherwise, a company will make losses and will be unable to continue in business. Second, recognizing the hierarchy of costs is critical when allocating costs to products.

Decision Point
How do managers cost products or services using ABC systems?

Management accountants use the cost hierarchy to first calculate the total costs of each product. They then derive per-unit costs by dividing total costs by the number of units produced.

Comparing Alternative Costing Systems

Exhibit 5-6 compares the simple costing system using a single indirect-cost pool (Exhibits 5-1 and 5-2) that Plastim had been using and the ABC system (Exhibits 5-3 and 5-5). Note three points in Exhibit 5-6, consistent with the guidelines for refining a costing system: (1) ABC systems trace more costs as direct costs; (2) ABC systems create homogeneous cost pools linked to different activities; and (3) for each activity-cost pool, ABC systems seek a cost-allocation base that has a cause-and-effect relationship with costs in the cost pool.

The homogeneous cost pools and the choice of cost-allocation bases, tied to the cost hierarchy, give Plastim's managers greater confidence in the activity and product cost numbers from the ABC system. The bottom part of Exhibit 5-6 shows that allocating costs to lenses using only an output unit–level allocation base—direct manufacturing labor-hours, as in the single indirect-cost pool system used prior to ABC—overcosts the simple S3 lens by $8.77 per unit and undercosts the complex C5 lens by $35.07 per unit. The C5 lens uses a disproportionately larger amount of output unit–level, batch-level, and product-sustaining costs than is represented by the direct manufacturing labor-hour cost-allocation base. The S3 lens uses a disproportionately smaller amount of these costs.

Exhibit 5-6 Comparing Alternative Costing Systems

	Simple Costing System Using a Single Indirect-Cost Pool (1)	ABC System (2)	Difference (3) = (2) − (1)
Direct-cost categories	2 Direct materials Direct manufacturing labor	3 Direct materials Direct manufacturing labor Direct mold cleaning and maintenance labor	1
Total direct costs	$2,595,000	$2,865,000	$270,000
Indirect-cost pools	1 Single indirect-cost pool allocated using direct manufacturing labor-hours	6 Design (parts-square feet)[1] Molding machine setup (setup-hours) Machine operations (molding machine-hours) Shipment setup (number of shipments) Distribution (cubic feet delivered) Administration (direct manufacturing labor-hours)	5
Total indirect costs	$2,385,000	$2,115,000	($270,000)
Total costs assigned to simple (S3) lens	$3,525,000	$2,998,953	($526,047)
Cost per unit of simple (S3) lens	$58.75	$49.98	($8.77)
Total costs assigned to complex (C5) lens	$1,455,000	$1,981,047	$526,047
Cost per unit of complex (C5) lens	$97.00	$132.07	$35.07

[1]Cost drivers for the various indirect-cost pools are shown in parentheses.

The benefit of an ABC system is that it provides information to make better decisions. But managers must weigh this benefit against the measurement and implementation costs of an ABC system.

Considerations in Implementing Activity-Based Costing Systems

Learning Objective 6

Evaluate the costs and benefits of implementing activity-based costing systems

. . . measurement difficulties versus more accurate costs that aid in decision making when products make diverse demands on indirect resources

Managers choose the level of detail to use in a costing system by evaluating the expected costs of the system against the expected benefits that result from better decisions.

Benefits and Costs of Activity-Based Costing Systems

Here are some of the telltale signs of when an ABC system is likely to provide the most benefits:

- Significant amounts of indirect costs are allocated using only one or two cost pools.
- All or most indirect costs are identified as output unit–level costs (few indirect costs are described as batch-level costs, product-sustaining costs, or facility-sustaining costs).
- Products make diverse demands on resources because of differences in volume, process steps, batch size, or complexity.
- Products that a company is well-suited to make and sell show small profits; whereas products that a company is less suited to make and sell show large profits.
- Operations staff has substantial disagreement with the reported costs of manufacturing and marketing products and services.

When managers decide to implement ABC, they must make important choices about the level of detail to use. Should managers choose many finely specified activities, cost drivers, and cost pools, or would a few suffice? For example, Plastim's managers could identify a different molding machine-hour rate for each different type of molding machine. In making such choices, managers weigh the benefits against the costs and limitations of implementing a more detailed costing system.

The main costs and limitations of an ABC system are the measurements necessary to implement it. ABC systems require managers to estimate costs of activity pools and to identify and measure cost drivers for these pools to serve as cost-allocation bases. Even basic ABC systems require many calculations to determine costs of products and services. These measurements are costly. Activity-cost rates also need to be updated regularly.

As ABC systems get very detailed and more cost pools are created, more allocations are necessary to calculate activity costs for each cost pool, which increases the chances of misidentifying the costs of different activity cost pools. For example, supervisors are more prone to incorrectly identify the time they spend on different activities if they have to allocate their time over five activities rather than only two activities.

Occasionally, managers are also forced to use allocation bases for which data are readily available rather than allocation bases they would have liked to use. For example, a manager might be forced to use the number of loads moved, instead of the degree of difficulty and distance of different loads moved, as the allocation base for material-handling costs because data on degree of difficulty and distance of moves are difficult to obtain. When incorrect cost-allocation bases are used, activity-cost information can be misleading. For example, if the cost per load moved decreases, a company may conclude that it has become more efficient in its materials-handling operations. In fact, the lower cost per load moved may have resulted solely from moving many lighter loads over shorter distances.

Many companies, such as Kanthal, a Swedish heating elements manufacturer, have found the strategic and operational benefits of a less-detailed ABC system to be good enough to not warrant incurring the costs and challenges of operating a more detailed system. Other organizations, such as Hewlett-Packard, have implemented ABC in only certain divisions (such as the Roseville Networks Division, which manufactures printed circuit boards) or functions (such as procurement and production). As improvements in information technology and accompanying declines in measurement costs continue, more detailed ABC systems have become a practical alternative in many companies. As these advancements become more widespread, more detailed ABC systems will be better able to pass the cost–benefit test.

Global surveys of company practice suggest that ABC implementation varies among companies. Nevertheless, its framework and ideas provide a standard for judging whether any simple costing system is good enough for a particular management's purposes. ABC thinking can help managers improve any simple costing system.

Behavioral Issues in Implementing Activity-Based Costing Systems

Successfully implementing ABC systems requires more than an understanding of the technical details. ABC implementation often represents a significant change in the costing system and, as the chapter indicates, requires a manager to choose how to define activities and the level of detail. What then are some of the behavioral issues that managers and management accountants must be sensitive to?

1. **Gaining support of top management and creating a sense of urgency for the ABC effort.** This requires managers and management accountants to clearly communicate the strategic benefits of ABC, such as improvements in product and process design. For example, at USAA Federal Savings Bank, managers calculated the cost of individual activities such as opening and closing accounts and demonstrated how the information gained from ABC provided insights into the efficiency of bank operations, which were previously unavailable.
2. **Creating a guiding coalition of managers throughout the value chain for the ABC effort.** ABC systems measure how the resources of an organization are used. Managers responsible for these resources have the best knowledge about activities and cost drivers. Getting managers to cooperate and take the initiative for implementing ABC is essential for gaining the required expertise, the proper credibility, greater commitment, valuable coordination, and the necessary leadership.
3. **Educating and training employees in ABC as a basis for employee empowerment.** Management accountants must disseminate information about ABC throughout the organization to enable employees in all areas of a business to use their knowledge of ABC to make improvements. For example, WS Industries, an Indian manufacturer of insulators, not only shared ABC information with its workers but also established an incentive plan that gave them a percentage of the cost savings. The results were dramatic because employees were empowered and motivated to implement numerous cost-saving projects.
4. **Seeking small short-run successes as proof that the ABC implementation is yielding results.** Too often, managers and management accountants seek big results and major changes far too quickly. In many situations, achieving a significant change overnight is difficult. However, showing how ABC information has helped improve a process and save costs, even if only in small ways, motivates the team to stay on course and build momentum. The credibility gained from small victories leads to additional and bigger improvements involving larger numbers of people and different parts of the organization. Eventually ABC becomes rooted in the culture of the organization. Sharing short-term successes also helps motivate employees to be innovative. At USAA Federal Savings Bank, managers created a "process improvement" mailbox in Microsoft Outlook to facilitate the sharing of process improvement ideas.
5. **Recognizing that ABC information is not perfect because it balances the need for better information against the costs of creating a complex system that few managers**

and employees can understand. The management accountant must help managers recognize both the value and the limitations of ABC and not oversell it. Open and honest communication about ABC ensures that managers use ABC thoughtfully to make good decisions. Managers can then make critical judgments without being adversarial and can ask tough questions to help drive better decisions about the system.

Decision Point
What should managers consider when deciding to implement ABC systems?

Activity-Based Management

Learning Objective 7
Explain how managers use activity-based costing systems in activity-based management
...such as pricing decisions, product-mix decisions, and cost reduction

The emphasis of this chapter so far has been on the role of ABC systems in obtaining better product costs. However, Plastim's managers must now use this information to make decisions (Step 4 of the five-step decision process, page 156) and to implement the decision, evaluate performance, and learn (Step 5, page 156). **Activity-based management (ABM)** is a method of management decision making that uses activity-based costing information to improve customer satisfaction and profitability. We define ABM broadly to include decisions about pricing and product mix, cost reduction, process improvement, and product and process design.

Pricing and Product-Mix Decisions

An ABC system gives managers information about the costs of making and selling diverse products. With this information, managers can make pricing and product-mix decisions. For example, the ABC system indicates that Plastim can match its competitor's price of $53 for the S3 lens and still make a profit because the ABC cost of S3 is $49.98 (see Exhibit 5-5).

Plastim's managers offer Giovanni Motors a price of $52 for the S3 lens. Plastim's managers are confident that they can use the deeper understanding of costs that the ABC system provides to improve efficiency and further reduce the cost of the S3 lens. Without information from the ABC system, Plastim managers might have erroneously concluded that they would incur an operating loss on the S3 lens at a price of $53. This incorrect conclusion would have probably caused Plastim to reduce or exit its business in simple lenses and focus instead on complex lenses, where its single indirect-cost-pool system indicated it is very profitable.

Focusing on complex lenses would have been a mistake. The ABC system indicates that the cost of making the complex lens is much higher—$132.07 versus $97 indicated by the direct manufacturing labor-hour-based costing system Plastim had been using. As Plastim's operations staff had thought all along, Plastim has no competitive advantage in making C5 lenses. At a price of $137 per lens for C5, the profit margin is very small ($137.00 − $132.07 = $4.93). As Plastim reduces its prices on simple lenses, it would need to negotiate a higher price for complex lenses with Giovanni Motors.

Cost Reduction and Process Improvement Decisions

Managers use ABC systems to focus on how and where to reduce costs. They set cost reduction targets for the cost per unit of the cost-allocation base in different activity areas. For example, the supervisor of the distribution activity area at Plastim could have a performance target of decreasing distribution cost per cubic foot of products delivered from $5.80 to $5.40 by reducing distribution labor and warehouse rental costs. The goal is to reduce these costs by improving the way work is done without compromising customer service or the actual or perceived value (usefulness) customers obtain from the product or service. That is, the supervisor will attempt to take out only those costs that are *nonvalue added.* Controlling physical cost drivers, such as setup-hours or cubic feet delivered, is another fundamental way that operating personnel manage costs. For example, the distribution department can decrease distribution costs by packing the lenses in a way that reduces the bulkiness of the packages delivered.

The following table shows the reduction in distribution costs of the S3 and C5 lenses as a result of actions that lower cost per cubic foot delivered (from $5.80 to $5.40) and total cubic feet of deliveries (from 45,000 to 40,000 for S3 and 22,500 to 20,000 for C5).

	60,000 (S3) Lenses		15,000 (C5) Lenses	
	Total (1)	per Unit (2) = (1) ÷ 60,000	Total (3)	per Unit (4) = (3) ÷ 15,000
Distribution costs (from Exhibit 5-5)				
S3: 45,000 cubic × $5.80/cubic foot	$261,000	$4.35		
C5: 22,500 cubic × $5.80/cubic foot			$130,500	$8.70
Distribution costs as a result of process improvements				
S3: 40,000 cubic × $5.40/cubic foot	216,000	3.60		
C5: 20,000 cubic × $5.40/cubic foot			108,000	7.20
Savings in distribution costs from process improvements	$ 45,000	$0.75	$ 22,500	$1.50

In the long run, total distribution costs will decrease from $391,500 ($261,000 + $130,500) to $324,000 ($216,000 + $108,000). In the short run, however, distribution costs may be fixed and may not decrease. Suppose all $391,500 of distribution costs are fixed costs in the short run. The efficiency improvements (using less distribution labor and space) mean that the same $391,500 of distribution costs can now be used to distribute $72{,}500\left(= \dfrac{\$391{,}500}{\$5.40 \text{ per cubic feet}}\right)$ cubic feet of lenses. In this case, how should costs be allocated to the S3 and C5 lenses?

ABC systems distinguish costs incurred from resources used to design, manufacture, and deliver products and services. For the distribution activity, after process improvements,

$$\text{Costs incurred} = \$391{,}500$$
$$\text{Resources used} = \$216{,}000 \text{ (for S3 lens)} + \$108{,}000 \text{ (for CL5 lens)} = \$324{,}000$$

On the basis of the resources used by each product, Plastim's ABC system allocates $216,000 to S3 and $108,000 to C5 for a total of $324,000. The difference of $67,500 ($391,500 − $324,000) is shown as costs of unused but available distribution capacity. Plastim's ABC system does not allocate the costs of unused capacity to products so as not to burden the product costs of S3 and C5 with the cost of resources not used by these products. Instead, the system highlights the amount of unused capacity as a separate line item to alert managers to reduce these costs, such as by redeploying labor to other uses or laying off workers. Chapter 9 discusses issues related to unused capacity in more detail.

Design Decisions

ABC systems help managers to evaluate the effect of current product and process designs on activities and costs and to identify new designs to reduce costs. For example, design decisions that decrease the complexity of the mold reduce costs of design, but also materials, labor, machine setups, machine operations, and mold cleaning and maintenance because a less-complex design reduces scrap and the time for setups and operations of the molding machine. Plastim's customers may be willing to give up some features of the lens in exchange for a lower price. Note that Plastim's previous costing system, which used direct manufacturing labor-hours as the cost-allocation base for all indirect costs, would have mistakenly signaled that Plastim choose those designs that most reduce direct manufacturing labor-hours when, in fact, there is a weak cause-and-effect relationship between direct manufacturing labor-hours and indirect costs.

Planning and Managing Activities

Most managers implementing ABC systems for the first time start by analyzing actual costs to identify activity-cost pools and activity-cost rates. Managers then calculate a budgeted rate (as in the Plastim example) that they use for planning, making decisions, and managing activities. At year-end, managers compare budgeted costs and actual costs to evaluate how well activities were managed. Management accountants make adjustments for underallocated or overallocated indirect costs for each activity using methods described in Chapter 4. As activities and processes change, managers calculate new activity-cost rates.

We return to activity-based management in later chapters. Management decisions that use activity-based costing information are described in Chapter 6, where we discuss activity-based budgeting; in Chapter 11, where we discuss outsourcing and adding or dropping business segments; in Chapter 12, where we present reengineering and downsizing; in Chapter 13, where we evaluate alternative design choices to improve efficiency and reduce nonvalue-added costs; in Chapter 14, where we explore managing customer profitability; in Chapter 19, where we explain quality improvements; and in Chapter 20, where we describe how to evaluate suppliers.

Decision Point

How can ABC systems be used to manage better?

Activity-Based Costing and Department Costing Systems

Learning Objective 8

Compare activity-based costing systems and department costing systems

...activity-based costing systems are a refinement of department costing systems into more-focused and homogenous cost pools

Companies often use costing systems that have features of ABC systems—such as multiple cost pools and multiple cost-allocation bases—but that do not emphasize individual activities. Many companies have evolved their costing systems from using a single indirect cost rate system to using separate indirect cost rates for each department (such as design, manufacturing, and distribution) or each subdepartment (such as machining and assembly departments within manufacturing) that can represent broad tasks. ABC systems, with its focus on specific activities, are a further refinement of department costing systems. In this section, we compare ABC systems and department costing systems.

Plastim uses the design department indirect cost rate to cost its design activity. Plastim calculates the design activity rate by dividing total design department costs by total parts-square feet, a measure of the complexity of the mold and the driver of design department costs. Plastim does not find it worthwhile to calculate separate activity rates within the design department for the different design activities, such as designing products, making temporary molds, and designing processes. The complexity of a mold is an appropriate cost-allocation base for costs incurred in each design activity because design department costs are homogeneous with respect to this cost-allocation base.

In contrast, the manufacturing department identifies two activity cost pools—a setup cost pool and a machine operations cost pool—instead of a single manufacturing department overhead cost pool. It identifies these activity cost pools for two reasons. First, each of these activities within manufacturing incurs significant costs and has a different cost driver, setup-hours for the setup cost pool and machine-hours for the machine operations cost pool. Second, the S3 and C5 lenses do not use resources from these two activity areas in the same proportion. For example, C5 uses 75% (1,500 ÷ 2,000) of the setup-hours but only 29.4% (3,750 ÷ 12,750) of the machine-hours. Using only machine-hours, say, to allocate all manufacturing department costs at Plastim would result in C5 being undercosted because it would not be charged for the significant amounts of setup resources it actually uses.

For the reasons we just explained, using department indirect cost rates to allocate costs to products results in similar information as activity cost rates if (1) a single activity accounts for a sizable proportion of the department's costs; or (2) significant costs are incurred on different activities within a department, but each activity has the same cost driver and therefore cost-allocation base (as was the case in Plastim's design department). From a purely product costing standpoint, department and activity indirect cost rates will also result in the same product costs if (1) significant costs are incurred for different activities with different cost-allocation bases within a department but (2) different products use resources from the different activity areas in the same proportions (for example, if C5 had used 65%, say, of the setup-hours and 65% of the machine-hours). In this case, though, not identifying activities and cost drivers within departments conceals activity cost information that would help managers manage costs and improve design and processes.

Decision Point
When can department costing systems be used instead of ABC systems?

We close this section with a note of caution: Do not assume that because department costing systems require the creation of multiple indirect cost pools that they properly recognize the drivers of costs within departments as well as how resources are used by products. As we have indicated, in many situations, department costing systems can be refined using ABC. Emphasizing activities leads to more-focused and homogeneous cost pools, aids in identifying cost-allocation bases for activities that have a better cause-and-effect relationship with the costs in activity cost pools, and leads to better design and process decisions. But these benefits of an ABC system would need to be balanced against its costs and limitations.

ABC in Service and Merchandising Companies

Although many early examples of ABC originated in manufacturing, managers also use ABC in service and merchandising companies. For instance, the Plastim example includes the application of ABC to a service activity—design—and to a merchandising activity—distribution. Companies such as the USAA Federal Savings Bank, Braintree Hospital, BCTel in the telecommunications industry, and Union Pacific in the railroad industry have implemented some form of ABC systems to identify profitable product mixes, improve efficiency, and satisfy customers. Similarly, many retail and wholesale companies—for example, Supervalu, a retailer and distributor of grocery store products, and Owens and Minor, a medical supplies distributor—have used ABC systems. As we describe in Chapter 14, a large number of financial services companies (as well as other companies) employ variations of ABC systems to analyze and improve the profitability of their customer interactions.

The widespread use of ABC systems in service and merchandising companies reinforces the idea that ABC systems are used by managers for strategic decisions rather than for inventory valuation. (Inventory valuation is fairly straightforward in merchandising companies and not needed in service companies.) Service companies, in particular, find great value from ABC because a vast majority of their cost structure is composed of indirect costs. After all, there are few direct costs when a bank makes a loan or when a representative answers a phone call at a call center. As we have seen, a major benefit of ABC is its ability to assign indirect costs to cost objects by identifying activities and cost drivers. As a result, ABC systems provide greater insight than traditional systems into the management of these indirect costs. The general approach to ABC in service and merchandising companies is similar to the ABC approach in manufacturing.

The USAA Federal Savings Bank followed the approach described in this chapter when it implemented ABC in its banking operations. Managers calculated the cost rates of various activities, such as performing ATM transactions, opening and closing accounts, administering mortgages, and processing Visa transactions by dividing the cost of these activities by the time available to do them. Managers used these time-based rates to cost individual products, such as checking accounts, mortgages, and Visa cards, and to calculate the costs of supporting different types of customers. Information from this time-driven activity-based costing system helped the USAA Federal Savings Bank to improve its processes and to identify profitable products and customer segments. Concepts in Action: Hospitals Use Time-Driven Activity-Based Costing to Reduce Costs and Improve Care describes how hospitals, such as the M.D. Anderson Cancer Research Center in Houston and Children's Hospital in Boston, have similarly benefited from using ABC analysis.

Activity-based costing raises some interesting issues when it is applied to a public service institution, such as the U.S. Postal Service. The costs of delivering mail to remote locations are far greater than the costs of delivering mail within urban areas. However, for fairness and community-building reasons, the Postal Service cannot charge higher prices to customers in remote areas. In this case, activity-based costing is valuable for understanding, managing, and reducing costs but not for pricing decisions.

Concepts in Action

Hospitals Use Time-Driven Activity-Based Costing to Reduce Costs and Improve Care

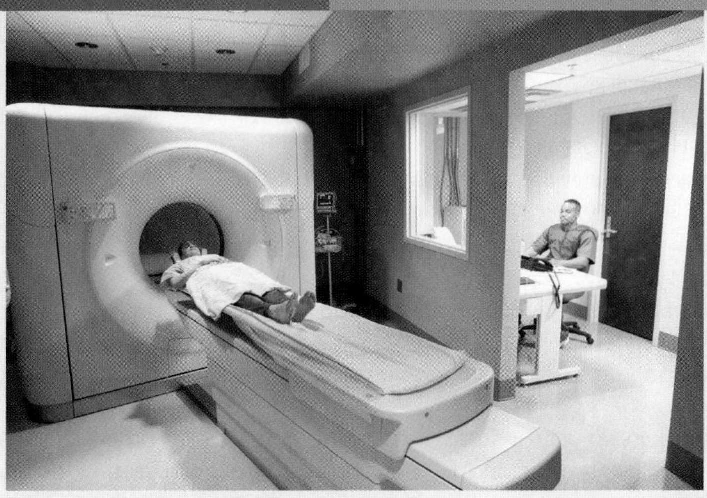

In the United States, health care costs in 2012 exceeded 17% of gross domestic product and are expected to rise to 19.6% by 2021. Several medical centers, such as the M.D. Anderson Cancer Center in Houston and Children's Hospital in Boston, are using time-driven activity-based costing (TDABC) to help bring accurate cost and value measurement practices into the health care delivery system.

TDABC assigns all of the organization's resource costs to cost objects using a framework that requires two sets of estimates. TDABC first calculates the cost of supplying resource capacity, such as a doctor's time. The total cost of resources—including personnel, supervision, insurance, space occupancy, technology, and supplies—is divided by the available capacity—the time available for doctors to do their work—to obtain the capacity cost rate. Next, TDABC uses the capacity cost rate to drive resource costs to cost objects, such as the number of patients seen, by estimating the demand for resource capacity (time) that the cost object requires.

Medical centers implementing TDABC have succeeded in reducing costs. For head and neck procedures at the M.D. Anderson Cancer Center, the TDABC-modified process resulted in a 16% reduction in process time, a 12% decrease in costs for technical staff, and a 36% reduction in total cost per patient. Prior to implementing TDABC, managers did not have the necessary information to make decisions to reduce costs.

More broadly, health care providers implementing TDABC have found that better outcomes for patients often go hand in hand with lower total costs. For example, spending more on early detection and better diagnosis of disease reduces patient suffering and often leads to less-complex and less-expensive care. With the insights from TDABC, health care providers can utilize medical staff, equipment, facilities, and administrative resources far more efficiently; streamline the path of patients through the system; and select treatment approaches that improve outcomes while eliminating services that do not.

Sources: Based on R. S. Kaplan and S. R. Anderson, "The Innovation of Time-Driven Activity-Based Costing," *Cost Management* (March-April 2007); R. S. Kaplan and S. R. Anderson, "Time-Drive Activity-Based Costing" (Boston, MA: Harvard Business School Press, 2007); and R. S. Kaplan and M. E. Porter, "How to Solve the Cost Crisis in Health Care," *Harvard Business Review* (September 2011); and Louise Radnofsky, "Steep Rise in Health Costs Projected," *The Wall Street Journal* (June 12, 2012).

Problem for Self-Study

Family Supermarkets (FS) has decided to increase the size of its Memphis store. It wants information about the profitability of individual product lines: soft drinks, fresh produce, and packaged food. FS provides the following data for 2014 for each product line:

	Soft Drinks	Fresh Produce	Packaged Food
Revenues	$317,400	$840,240	$483,960
Cost of goods sold	$240,000	$600,000	$360,000
Cost of bottles returned	$ 4,800	$ 0	$ 0
Number of purchase orders placed	144	336	144
Number of deliveries received	120	876	264
Hours of shelf-stocking time	216	2,160	1,080
Items sold	50,400	441,600	122,400

FS also provides the following information for 2014:

Activity (1)	Description of Activity (2)	Total Support Costs (3)	Cost-Allocation Base (4)
1. Bottle returns	Returning of empty bottles to store	$ 4,800	Direct tracing to soft-drink line
2. Ordering	Placing of orders for purchases	$ 62,400	624 purchase orders
3. Delivery	Physical delivery and receipt of merchandise	$100,800	1,260 deliveries
4. Shelf-stocking	Stocking of merchandise on store shelves and ongoing restocking	$ 69,120	3,456 hours of shelf-stocking time
5. Customer support	Assistance provided to customers, including checkout and bagging	$122,880	614,400 items sold
Total		$360,000	

Required

1. Family Supermarkets currently allocates store support costs (all costs other than cost of goods sold) to product lines on the basis of cost of goods sold of each product line. Calculate the operating income and operating income as a percentage of revenues for each product line.
2. If Family Supermarkets allocates store support costs (all costs other than cost of goods sold) to product lines using an ABC system, calculate the operating income and operating income as a percentage of revenues for each product line.
3. Comment on your answers in requirements 1 and 2.

Solution

1. The following table shows the operating income and operating income as a percentage of revenues for each product line. All store support costs (all costs other than cost of goods sold) are allocated to product lines using cost of goods sold of each product line as the cost-allocation base. Total store support costs equal $360,000 (cost of bottles returned, $4,800 + cost of purchase orders, $62,400 + cost of deliveries, $100,800 + cost of shelf-stocking, $69,120 + cost of customer support, $122,880). The allocation rate for store support costs = $360,000 ÷ $1,200,000 (soft drinks $240,000 + fresh produce $600,000 + packaged food, $360,000) = 30% of cost of goods sold. To allocate support costs to each product line, FS multiplies the cost of goods sold of each product line by 0.30.

	Soft Drinks	Fresh Produce	Packaged Food	Total
Revenues	$317,400	$840,240	$483,960	$1,641,600
Cost of goods sold	240,000	600,000	360,000	1,200,000
Store support cost				
($240,000; $600,000; $360,000) × 0.30	72,000	180,000	108,000	360,000
Total costs	312,000	780,000	468,000	1,560,000
Operating income	$ 5,400	$ 60,240	$ 15,960	$ 81,600
Operating income ÷ Revenues	1.70%	7.17%	3.30%	4.97%

2. The ABC system identifies bottle-return costs as a direct cost because these costs can be traced to the soft-drink product line. FS then calculates cost-allocation rates for each activity area (as in Step 5 of the seven-step costing system, described earlier on page 164). The activity rates are as follows.

Activity (1)	Cost Hierarchy (2)	Total Costs (3)	Quantity of Cost-Allocation Base (4)	Overhead Allocation Rate (5) = (3) ÷ (4)
Ordering	Batch-level	$ 62,400	624 purchase orders	$100 per purchase order
Delivery	Batch-level	$100,800	1,260 deliveries	$80 per delivery
Shelf-stocking	Output unit–level	$ 69,120	3,456 shelf-stocking hours	$20 per stocking-hour
Customer support	Output unit–level	$122,880	614,400 items sold	$0.20 per item sold

Store support costs for each product line by activity are obtained by multiplying the total quantity of the cost-allocation base for each product line by the activity cost rate. Operating income and operating income as a percentage of revenues for each product line are as follows.

	Soft Drinks	Fresh Produce	Packaged Food	Total
Revenues	$317,400	$840,240	$483,960	$1,641,600
Cost of goods sold	240,000	600,000	360,000	1,200,000
Bottle-return costs	4,800	0	0	4,800
Ordering costs				
(144; 336; 144) purchase orders × $100	14,400	33,600	14,400	62,400
Delivery costs				
(120; 876; 264) deliveries × $80	9,600	70,080	21,120	100,800
Shelf-stocking costs				
(216; 2,160; 1,080) stocking-hours × $20	4,320	43,200	21,600	69,120
Customer-support costs				
(50,400; 441,600; 122,400) items sold × $0.20	10,080	88,320	24,480	122,880
Total costs	283,200	835,200	441,600	1,560,000
Operating income	$ 34,200	$ 5,040	$ 42,360	$ 81,600
Operating income ÷ Revenues	10.78%	0.60%	8.75%	4.97%

3. Managers believe the ABC system is more credible than the simple costing system. The ABC system distinguishes the different types of activities at FS more precisely. It also tracks more accurately how individual product lines use resources. Rankings of relative profitability—operating income as a percentage of revenues—of the three product lines under the simple costing system and under the ABC system are as follows.

Simple Costing System		ABC Systemm	
1. Fresh produce	7.17%	1. Soft drinks	10.78%
2. Packaged food	3.30%	2. Packaged food	8.75%
3. Soft drinks	1.70%	3. Fresh produce	0.60%

The percentage of revenues, cost of goods sold, and activity costs for each product line are as follows.

	Soft Drinks	Fresh Produce	Packaged Food
Revenues	19.34%	51.18%	29.48%
Cost of goods sold	20.00	50.00	30.00
Bottle returns	100.00	0	0
Activity areas:			
Ordering	23.08	53.84	23.08
Delivery	9.53	69.52	20.95
Shelf-stocking	6.25	62.50	31.25
Customer support	8.20	71.88	19.92

Soft drinks have fewer deliveries and require less shelf-stocking time and customer support than either fresh produce or packaged food. Most major soft-drink suppliers deliver merchandise to the store shelves and stock the shelves themselves. In contrast, the fresh produce area has the most deliveries and consumes a large percentage of shelf-stocking time. It also has the highest number of individual sales items and so requires the most customer support. The simple costing system assumed that each product line used the resources in each activity area in the same ratio as their respective individual cost of goods sold to total cost of goods sold. Clearly, this assumption is incorrect. Relative to cost of goods sold, soft drinks and packaged food use fewer resources while fresh produce uses more resources. As a result, the ABC system reduces the costs assigned to soft drinks and packaged food and increases the costs assigned to fresh produce. The simple costing system is an example of averaging that is too broad.

FS managers can use the ABC information to guide decisions such as how to allocate a planned increase in floor space. An increase in the percentage of space allocated to soft drinks is warranted. Note, however, that ABC information is only one input into decisions about shelf-space allocation. In many situations, companies cannot make product decisions in isolation but must consider the effect that dropping or deemphasizing a product might have on customer demand for other products. For example, FS will have a minimum limit on the shelf space allocated to fresh produce because reducing the choice of fresh produce will lead to customers not shopping at FS, resulting in loss of sales of other, more profitable products.

Pricing decisions can also be made in a more informed way with ABC information. For example, suppose a competitor announces a 5% reduction in soft-drink prices. Given the 10.78% margin FS currently earns on its soft-drink product line, it has flexibility to reduce prices and still make a profit on this product line. In contrast, the simple costing system erroneously implied that soft drinks only had a 1.70% margin, leaving little room to counter a competitor's pricing initiatives.

Decision Points

The following question-and-answer format summarizes the chapter's learning objectives. Each decision presents a key question related to a learning objective. The guidelines are the answer to that question.

Decision	Guidelines
1. When does product undercosting or overcosting occur?	Product undercosting (overcosting) occurs when a product or service consumes a high (low) level of resources but is reported to have a low (high) cost. Broad averaging, or peanut-butter costing, a common cause of undercosting or overcosting, is the result of using broad averages that uniformly assign, or spread, the cost of resources to products when the individual products use those resources in a nonuniform way. Product-cost cross-subsidization exists when one undercosted (overcosted) product results in at least one other product being overcosted (undercosted).
2. How do managers refine a costing system?	Refining a costing system means making changes that result in cost numbers that better measure the way different cost objects, such as products, use different amounts of resources of the company. These changes can require additional direct-cost tracing, the choice of more-homogeneous indirect cost pools, or the use of cost drivers as cost-allocation bases.
3. What is the difference between the design of a simple costing system and an activity-based costing (ABC) system?	The ABC system differs from the simple system by its fundamental focus on activities. The ABC system typically has more-homogeneous indirect-cost pools than the simple system, and more cost drivers are used as cost-allocation bases.
4. What is a cost hierarchy?	A cost hierarchy categorizes costs into different cost pools on the basis of the different types of cost-allocation bases or different degrees of difficulty in determining cause-and-effect (or benefits-received) relationships. A four-part hierarchy to cost products consists of output unit–level costs, batch-level costs, product-sustaining or service-sustaining costs, and facility-sustaining costs.
5. How do managers cost products or services using ABC systems?	In ABC, costs of activities are used to assign costs to other cost objects such as products or services based on the activities the products or services consume.
6. What should managers consider when deciding to implement ABC systems?	ABC systems are likely to yield the most decision-making benefits when indirect costs are a high percentage of total costs or when products and services make diverse demands on indirect resources. The main costs of ABC systems are the difficulties of the measurements necessary to implement and update the systems.

7. How can ABC systems be used to manage better?

Activity-based management (ABM) is a management method of decision making that uses ABC information to satisfy customers and improve profits. ABC systems are used for such management decisions as pricing, product-mix, cost reduction, process improvement, product and process redesign, and planning and managing activities.

8. When can department costing systems be used instead of ABC systems?

Activity-based costing systems are a refinement of department costing systems into more-focused and homogeneous cost pools. Cost information in department costing systems approximates cost information in ABC systems only when each department has a single activity (or a single activity accounts for a significant proportion of department costs) or a single cost driver for different activities or when different products use the different activities of the department in the same proportions.

Terms to Learn

This chapter and the Glossary at the end of this book contain definitions of the following important terms:

activity **(p. 158)**
activity-based costing (ABC) **(p. 158)**
activity-based management (ABM) **(p. 169)**
batch-level costs **(p. 161)**
cost hierarchy **(p. 161)**
facility-sustaining costs **(p. 161)**
output unit–level costs **(p. 161)**
product-cost cross-subsidization **(p. 152)**
product overcosting **(p. 152)**
product-sustaining costs **(p. 161)**
product undercosting **(p. 152)**
refined costing system **(p. 157)**
service-sustaining costs **(p. 161)**

Assignment Material

Questions

MyAccountingLab

5-1 What is broad averaging, and what consequences can it have on costs?

5-2 Why should managers worry about product overcosting or undercosting?

5-3 What is costing system refinement? Describe three guidelines for refinement.

5-4 What is an activity-based approach to designing a costing system?

5-5 Describe four levels of a cost hierarchy.

5-6 Why is it important to classify costs into a cost hierarchy?

5-7 What are the key reasons for product cost differences between simple costing systems and ABC systems?

5-8 Describe four decisions for which ABC information is useful.

5-9 "Department indirect-cost rates are never activity-cost rates." Do you agree? Explain.

5-10 Describe four signs that help indicate when ABC systems are likely to provide the most benefits.

5-11 What are the main costs and limitations of implementing ABC systems?

5-12 "ABC systems only apply to manufacturing companies." Do you agree? Explain.

5-13 "Activity-based costing is the wave of the present and the future. All companies should adopt it." Do you agree? Explain.

5-14 "Increasing the number of indirect-cost pools is guaranteed to sizably increase the accuracy of product or service costs." Do you agree? Why?

5-15 The controller of a retail company has just had a $50,000 request to implement an ABC system quickly turned down. A senior vice president, in rejecting the request, noted, "Given a choice, I will always prefer a $50,000 investment in improving things a customer sees or experiences, such as our shelves or our store layout. How does a customer benefit by our spending $50,000 on a supposedly better accounting system?" How should the controller respond?

MyAccountingLab

Exercises

5-16 Cost hierarchy. Forrester, Inc., manufactures karaoke machines for several well-known companies. The machines differ significantly in their complexity and their manufacturing batch sizes. The following costs were incurred in 2014:

a. Indirect manufacturing labor costs such as supervision that supports direct manufacturing labor, $825,000
b. Procurement costs of placing purchase orders, receiving materials, and paying suppliers related to the number of purchase orders placed, $525,000
c. Cost of indirect materials, $160,000
d. Costs incurred to set up machines each time a different product needs to be manufactured, $365,000
e. Designing processes, drawing process charts, and making engineering process changes for products, $287,500
f. Machine-related overhead costs such as depreciation, maintenance, and production engineering, $950,000 (These resources relate to the activity of running the machines.)
g. Plant management, plant rent, and plant insurance, $512,000

Required

1. Classify each of the preceding costs as output unit–level, batch-level, product-sustaining, or facility-sustaining. Explain each answer.
2. Consider two types of karaoke machines made by Forrester, Inc. One machine, designed for professional use, is complex to make and is produced in many batches. The other machine, designed for home use, is simple to make and is produced in few batches. Suppose that Forrester needs the same number of machine-hours to make each type of karaoke machine and that Forrester allocates all overhead costs using machine-hours as the only allocation base. How, if at all, would the machines be miscosted? Briefly explain why.
3. How is the cost hierarchy helpful to Forrester in managing its business?

5-17 ABC, cost hierarchy, service. (CMA, adapted) Vineyard Test Laboratories does heat testing (HT) and stress testing (ST) on materials and operates at capacity. Under its current simple costing system, Vineyard aggregates all operating costs of $1,190,000 into a single overhead cost pool. Vineyard calculates a rate per test-hour of $17 ($1,190,000 ÷ 70,000 total test-hours). HT uses 40,000 test-hours, and ST uses 30,000 test-hours. Gary Celeste, Vineyard's controller, believes that there is enough variation in test procedures and cost structures to establish separate costing and billing rates for HT and ST. The market for test services is becoming competitive. Without this information, any miscosting and mispricing of its services could cause Vineyard to lose business. Celeste divides Vineyard's costs into four activity-cost categories.

a. Direct-labor costs, $146,000. These costs can be directly traced to HT, $100,000, and ST, $46,000.
b. Equipment-related costs (rent, maintenance, energy, and so on), $350,000. These costs are allocated to HT and ST on the basis of test-hours.
c. Setup costs, $430,000. These costs are allocated to HT and ST on the basis of the number of setup-hours required. HT requires 13,600 setup-hours, and ST requires 3,600 setup-hours.
d. Costs of designing tests, $264,000. These costs are allocated to HT and ST on the basis of the time required for designing the tests. HT requires 3,000 hours, and ST requires 1,400 hours.

Required

1. Classify each activity cost as output unit–level, batch-level, product- or service-sustaining, or facility-sustaining. Explain each answer.
2. Calculate the cost per test-hour for HT and ST. Explain briefly the reasons why these numbers differ from the $17 per test-hour that Vineyard calculated using its simple costing system.
3. Explain the accuracy of the product costs calculated using the simple costing system and the ABC system. How might Vineyard's management use the cost hierarchy and ABC information to better manage its business?

5-18 Alternative allocation bases for a professional services firm. The Walliston Group (WG) provides tax advice to multinational firms. WG charges clients for (a) direct professional time (at an hourly rate) and (b) support services (at 30% of the direct professional costs billed). The three professionals in WG and their rates per professional hour are as follows:

Professional	Billing Rate per Hour
Max Walliston	$640
Alexa Boutin	220
Jacob Abbington	100

WG has just prepared the May 2014 bills for two clients. The hours of professional time spent on each client are as follows:

	Hours per Client	
Professional	**San Antonio Dominion**	**Amsterdam Enterprises**
Walliston	26	4
Boutin	5	14
Abbington	39	52
Total	70	70

Required

1. What amounts did WG bill to San Antonio Dominion and Amsterdam Enterprises for May 2014?
2. Suppose support services were billed at $75 per professional labor-hour (instead of 30% of professional labor costs). How would this change affect the amounts WG billed to the two clients for May 2014? Comment on the differences between the amounts billed in requirements 1 and 2.
3. How would you determine whether professional labor costs or professional labor-hours is the more appropriate allocation base for WG's support services?

5-19 Plant-wide, department, and ABC indirect cost rates. Automotive Products (AP) designs and produces automotive parts. In 2014, actual variable manufacturing overhead is $308,600. AP's simple costing system allocates variable manufacturing overhead to its three customers based on machine-hours and prices its contracts based on full costs. One of its customers has regularly complained of being charged noncompetitive prices, so AP's controller Devon Smith realizes that it is time to examine the consumption of overhead resources more closely. He knows that there are three main departments that consume overhead resources: design, production, and engineering. Interviews with the department personnel and examination of time records yield the following detailed information.

	A	B	C	D	E	F
1				Usage of Cost Drivers by Customer Contract		
2	**Department**	**Cost Driver**	**Manufacturing Overhead in 2014**	**United Motors**	**Holden Motors**	**Leland Auto**
3	Design	CAD-design-hours	$ 39,000	110	200	80
4	Production	Engineering-hours	29,600	70	60	240
5	Engineering	Machine-hours	240,000	120	2,800	1,080
6	Total		$308,600			

Required

1. Compute the manufacturing overhead allocated to each customer in 2014 using the simple costing system that uses machine-hours as the allocation base.
2. Compute the manufacturing overhead allocated to each customer in 2014 using department-based manufacturing overhead rates.
3. Comment on your answers in requirements 1 and 2. Which customer do you think was complaining about being overcharged in the simple system? If the new department-based rates are used to price contracts, which customer(s) will be unhappy? How would you respond to these concerns?
4. How else might AP use the information available from its department-by-department analysis of manufacturing overhead costs?
5. AP's managers are wondering if they should further refine the department-by-department costing system into an ABC system by identifying different activities within each department. Under what conditions would it not be worthwhile to further refine the department costing system into an ABC system?

5-20 Plant-wide, department, and activity-cost rates. Triumph Trophies makes trophies and plaques and operates at capacity. Triumph does large custom orders, such as the participant trophies for the Minnetonka Little League. The controller has asked you to compare plant-wide, department, and activity-based cost allocation.

Triumph Trophies Budgeted Information for the Year Ended November 30, 2014

Forming Department	Trophies	Plaques	Total
Direct materials	$26,000	$22,500	$48,500
Direct manufacturing labor	31,200	18,000	49,200
Overhead costs			
Set up			24,000
Supervision			20,772

Assembly Department	Trophies	Plaques	Total
Direct materials	$ 5,200	$18,750	$23,950
Direct manufacturing labor	15,600	21,000	36,600
Overhead costs			
Setup			46,000
Supervision			21,920

Other information follows:

Setup costs in each department vary with the number of batches processed in each department. The budgeted number of batches for each product line in each department is as follows:

	Trophies	Plaques
Forming department	40	116
Assembly department	43	103

Supervision costs in each department vary with direct manufacturing labor costs in each department.

Required

1. Calculate the budgeted cost of trophies and plaques based on a single plant-wide overhead rate, if total overhead is allocated based on total direct costs.
2. Calculate the budgeted cost of trophies and plaques based on departmental overhead rates, where forming department overhead costs are allocated based on direct manufacturing labor costs of the forming department and assembly department overhead costs are allocated based on total direct costs of the assembly department.
3. Calculate the budgeted cost of trophies and plaques if Triumph allocates overhead costs in each department using activity-based costing.
4. Explain how the disaggregation of information could improve or reduce decision quality.

5-21 ABC, process costing. Parker Company produces mathematical and financial calculators and operates at capacity. Data related to the two products are presented here:

	Mathematical	Financial
Annual production in units	50,000	100,000
Direct material costs	$150,000	$300,000
Direct manufacturing labor costs	$ 50,000	$100,000
Direct manufacturing labor-hours	2,500	5,000
Machine-hours	25,000	50,000
Number of production runs	50	50
Inspection hours	1,000	500

Total manufacturing overhead costs are as follows:

	Total
Machining costs	$375,000
Setup costs	120,000
Inspection costs	105,000

Required

1. Choose a cost driver for each overhead cost pool and calculate the manufacturing overhead cost per unit for each product.
2. Compute the manufacturing cost per unit for each product.
3. How might Parker's managers use the new cost information from its activity-based costing system to better manage its business?

5-22 Department costing, service company. CKM is an architectural firm that designs and builds buildings. It prices each job on a cost plus 20% basis. Overhead costs in 2014 are $4,011,780. CKM's simple costing system allocates overhead costs to its jobs based on number of jobs. There were three jobs in 2014. One customer, Sanders, has complained that the cost of its building in Chicago was not competitive. As a result, the controller has initiated a detailed review of the overhead allocation to determine if overhead costs are charged to jobs in proportion to consumption of overhead resources by jobs. She gathers the following information.

			Quantity of Cost Drivers Used by Each Project		
Department	**Cost Driver**	**Overhead Costs in 2014**	**Sanders**	**Hanley**	**Stanley**
Design	Design department hours	$ 1,500,000	1,000	5,000	4,000
Engineering	Number of engineers	$ 500,030	2,000	2,000	2,200
Construction	Labor-hours	$ 2,011,750	20,800	21,500	19,600
		$ 4,011,780			

Required

1. Compute the overhead allocated to each project in 2014 using the simple costing system.
2. Compute the overhead allocated to each project in 2014 using department overhead cost rates.
3. Do you think Sanders had a valid reason for dissatisfaction with the cost? How does the allocation based on department rates change costs for each project?
4. What value, if any, would CKM get by allocating costs of each department based on the activities done in that department?

5-23 Activity-based costing, service company. Speediprint Corporation owns a small printing press that prints leaflets, brochures, and advertising materials. Speediprint classifies its various printing jobs as standard jobs or special jobs. Speediprint's simple job-costing system has two direct-cost categories (direct materials and direct labor) and a single indirect-cost pool. Speediprint operates at capacity and allocates all indirect costs using printing machine-hours as the allocation base.

Speediprint is concerned about the accuracy of the costs assigned to standard and special jobs and therefore is planning to implement an activity-based costing system. Speediprint's ABC system would have the same direct-cost categories as its simple costing system. However, instead of a single indirect-cost pool there would now be six categories for assigning indirect costs: design, purchasing, setup, printing machine operations, marketing, and administration. To see how activity-based costing would affect the costs of standard and special jobs, Speediprint collects the following information for the fiscal year 2014 that just ended.

Home Insert Page Layout Formulas Data Review View

	A	B	C	D	E–H
1		**Standard Job**	**Special Job**	**Total**	**Cause-and-Effect Relationship Between Allocation Base and Activity Cost**
2	Number of printing jobs	400	200		
3	Price per job	$ 600	$ 750		
4	Cost of supplies per job	$ 100	$ 125		
5	Direct labor costs per job	$ 90	$ 100		
6	Printing machine-hours per job	10	10		
7	Cost of printing machine operations			$ 75,000	Indirect costs of operating printing machines
8					increase with printing machine-hours
9	Setup-hours per job	4	7		
10	Setup costs			$ 45,000	Indirect setup costs increase with setup-hours
11	Total number of purchase orders	400	500		
12	Purchase order costs			$ 18,000	Indirect purchase order costs increase with
13					number of purchase orders
14	Design costs	$4,000	$16,000	$ 20,000	Design costs are allocated to standard and special
15					jobs based on a special study of the design department
16	Marketing costs as a percentage of revenues	5%	5%	$ 19,500	
17	Administration costs			$ 24,000	Demand for administrative resources increases with direct labor costs

Required

1. Calculate the cost of a standard job and a special job under the simple costing system.
2. Calculate the cost of a standard job and a special job under the activity-based costing system.
3. Compare the costs of a standard job and a special job in requirements 1 and 2. Why do the simple and activity-based costing systems differ in the cost of a standard job and a special job?
4. How might Speediprint use the new cost information from its activity-based costing system to better manage its business?

5-24 Activity-based costing, manufacturing. Fancy Doors, Inc., produces two types of doors, interior and exterior. The company's simple costing system has two direct cost categories (materials and labor) and one indirect cost pool. The simple costing system allocates indirect costs on the basis of machine-hours. Recently, the owners of Fancy Doors have been concerned about a decline in the market share for their interior doors, usually their biggest seller. Information related to Fancy Doors production for the most recent year follows:

	Interior	Exterior
Units sold	3,200	1,800
Selling price	$ 250	$ 400
Direct material cost per unit	$ 60	$ 90
Direct manufacturing labor cost per hour	$ 32	$ 32
Direct manufacturing labor-hours per unit	1.50	2.25
Production runs	40	85
Material moves	72	168
Machine setups	45	155
Machine-hours	5,500	4,500
Number of inspections	250	150

The owners have heard of other companies in the industry that are now using an activity-based costing system and are curious how an ABC system would affect their product costing decisions. After analyzing the indirect cost pool for Fancy Doors, the owners identify six activities as generating indirect costs: production scheduling, material handling, machine setup, assembly, inspection, and marketing. Fancy Doors collected the following data related to the indirect cost activities:

Activity	Activity Cost	Activity Cost Driver
Production scheduling	$190,000	Production runs
Material handling	$ 90,000	Material moves
Machine setup	$ 50,000	Machine setups
Assembly	$120,000	Machine-hours
Inspection	$ 16,000	Number of inspections

Marketing costs were determined to be 3% of the sales revenue for each type of door.

Required

1. Calculate the cost of an interior door and an exterior door under the existing simple costing system.
2. Calculate the cost of an interior door and an exterior door under an activity-based costing system.
3. Compare the costs of the doors in requirements 1 and 2. Why do the simple and activity-based costing systems differ in the cost of an interior and exterior door?
4. How might Fancy Door, Inc., use the new cost information from its activity-based costing system to address the declining market share for interior doors?

5-25 ABC, retail product-line profitability. Henderson Supermarkets (HS) operates at capacity and decides to apply ABC analysis to three product lines: baked goods, milk and fruit juice, and frozen foods. It identifies four activities and their activity cost rates as follows:

Ordering	$102 per purchase order
Delivery and receipt of merchandise	$ 78 per delivery
Shelf-stocking	$ 21 per hour
Customer support and assistance	$ 0.22 per item sold

The revenues, cost of goods sold, store support costs, activities that account for the store support costs, and activity-area usage of the three product lines are as follows:

	Baked Goods	Milk and Fruit Juice	Frozen Products
Financial data			
Revenues	$59,500	$66,000	$51,000
Cost of goods sold	$36,000	$48,000	$34,000
Store support	$10,800	$14,400	$10,200
Activity-area usage (cost-allocation base)			
Ordering (purchase orders)	25	20	15
Delivery (deliveries)	90	35	30
Shelf-stocking (hours)	190	180	40
Customer support (items sold)	13,500	17,500	8,000

Under its simple costing system, HS allocated support costs to products at the rate of 30% of cost of goods sold.

Required

1. Use the simple costing system to prepare a product-line profitability report for HS.
2. Use the ABC system to prepare a product-line profitability report for HS.
3. What new insights does the ABC system in requirement 2 provide to HS managers?

5-26 ABC, wholesale, customer profitability. Ramirez Wholesalers operates at capacity and sells furniture items to four department-store chains (customers). Mr. Ramirez commented, "We apply ABC to determine product-line profitability. The same ideas apply to customer profitability, and we should find out our customer profitability as well." Ramirez Wholesalers sends catalogs to corporate purchasing departments on a monthly basis. The customers are entitled to return unsold merchandise within a six-month period from the purchase date and receive a full purchase price refund. The following data were collected from last year's operations:

	Chain			
	1	2	3	4
Gross sales	$50,000	$30,000	$100,000	$70,000
Sales returns:				
Number of items	100	26	60	40
Amount	$10,000	$ 5,000	$ 7,000	$ 6,000
Number of orders:				
Regular	40	150	50	70
Rush	10	50	10	30

Ramirez has calculated the following activity rates:

Activity	Cost-Driver Rate
Regular order processing	$20 per regular order
Rush order processing	$100 per rush order
Returned items processing	$10 per item
Catalogs and customer support	$1,000 per customer

Customers pay the transportation costs. The cost of goods sold averages 80% of sales.

Required

Determine the contribution to profit from each chain last year. Comment on your solution.

5-27 ABC, activity area cost-driver rates, product cross-subsidization. Intex Potatoes (IP) operates at capacity and processes potatoes into potato cuts at its highly automated Pocatello plant. It sells potatoes to the retail consumer market and to the institutional market, which includes hospitals, cafeterias, and university dormitories.

IP's simple costing system, which does not distinguish between potato cuts processed for retail and institutional markets, has a single direct-cost category (direct materials; that is, raw potatoes) and a single indirect-cost pool (production support). Support costs, which include packaging materials, are allocated on the basis of pounds of potato cuts processed. The company uses 1,800,000 pounds of raw potatoes to process 1,600,000 pounds of potato cuts. At the end of 2014, IP unsuccessfully bid for a large institutional contract. Its bid was reported to be 30% above the winning bid. This feedback came as a shock because IP included only a minimum profit margin on its bid, and the Pocatello plant was acknowledged as the most efficient in the industry.

As a result of its review process of the lost contract bid, IP decided to explore ways to refine its costing system. The company determined that 90% of the direct materials (raw potatoes) related to the retail market and 10% to the institutional market. In addition, the company identified that packaging materials could be directly traced to individual jobs ($190,000 for retail and $9,000 for institutional). Also, the company used ABC to identify three main activity areas that generated support costs: cleaning, cutting, and packaging.

- **Cleaning Activity Area**—The cost-allocation base is pounds of raw potatoes cleaned.
- **Cutting Activity Area**—The production line produces (a) 150 pounds of retail potato cuts per cutting-hour and (b) 200 pounds of institutional potato cuts per cutting-hour. The cost-allocation base is cutting-hours on the production line.
- **Packaging Activity Area**—The packaging line packages (a) 25 pounds of retail potato cuts per packaging-hour and (b) 80 pounds of institutional potato cuts per packaging-hour. The cost-allocation base is packaging-hours on the production line.

The following table summarizes the actual costs for 2014 before and after the preceding cost analysis.

		After the Cost Analysis			
	Before the Cost Analysis	**Production Support**	**Retail**	**Institutional**	**Total**
Direct materials used					
Potatoes	$ 231,000		$207,900	$23,100	$ 231,000
Packaging			190,000	9,000	199,000
Production support	1,689,000				
Cleaning		$ 270,000			270,000
Cutting		624,000			624,000
Packaging		596,000			596,000
Total	$1,920,000	$1,490,000	$397,900	$32,100	$1,920,000

Required

1. Using the simple costing system, what is the cost per pound of potato cuts produced by IP?
2. Calculate the cost rate per unit of the cost driver in the (a) cleaning, (b) cutting, and (c) packaging activity areas.
3. Suppose IP uses information from its activity cost rates to calculate costs incurred on retail potato cuts and institutional potato cuts. Using the ABC system, what is the cost per pound of (a) retail potato cuts and (b) institutional potato cuts?
4. Comment on the cost differences between the two costing systems in requirements 1 and 3. How might IP use the information in requirement 3 to make better decisions?

5-28 Activity-based costing. The job costing system at Sheri's Custom Framing has five indirect cost pools (purchasing, material handling, machine maintenance, product inspection, and packaging). The company is in the process of bidding on two jobs: Job 215, an order of 15 intricate personalized frames, and Job 325, an order of 6 standard personalized frames. The controller wants you to compare overhead allocated under the current simple job-costing system and a newly designed activity-based job-costing system. Total budgeted costs in each indirect cost pool and the budgeted quantity of activity driver are as follows.

	Budgeted Overhead	Activity Driver	Budgeted Quantity of Activity Driver
Purchasing	$ 35,000	Purchase orders processed	2,000
Material handling	43,750	Material moves	5,000
Machine maintenance	118,650	Machine-hours	10,500
Product inspection	9,450	Inspections	1,200
Packaging	19,950	Units produced	3,800
	$226,800		

Information related to Job 215 and Job 325 follows. Job 215 incurs more batch-level costs because it uses more types of materials that need to be purchased, moved, and inspected relative to Job 325.

	Job 215	Job 325
Number of purchase orders	25	8
Number of material moves	10	4
Machine-hours	40	60
Number of inspections	9	3
Units produced	15	6

Required

1. Compute the total overhead allocated to each job under a simple costing system, where overhead is allocated based on machine-hours.
2. Compute the total overhead allocated to each job under an activity-based costing system using the appropriate activity drivers.
3. Explain why Sheri's Custom Framing might favor the ABC job-costing system over the simple job-costing system, especially in its bidding process.

5-29 ABC, product costing at banks, cross-subsidization. United Savings Bank (USB) is examining the profitability of its Premier Account, a combined savings and checking account. Depositors receive a 7% annual interest rate on their average deposit. USB earns an interest rate spread of 3% (the difference between the rate at which it lends money and the rate it pays depositors) by lending money for home-loan purposes at 10%. Thus, USB would gain $60 on the interest spread if a depositor had an average Premier Account balance of $2,000 in 2014 ($2,000 × 3% = $60).

The Premier Account allows depositors unlimited use of services such as deposits, withdrawals, checking accounts, and foreign currency drafts. Depositors with Premier Account balances of $1,000 or more receive unlimited free use of services. Depositors with minimum balances of less than $1,000 pay a $22-a-month service fee for their Premier Account.

USB recently conducted an activity-based costing study of its services. It assessed the following costs for six individual services. The use of these services in 2014 by three customers is as follows:

	Activity-Based Cost per "Transaction"	Account Usage		
		Lindell	Welker	Colston
Deposit/withdrawal with teller	$ 2.50	44	49	4
Deposit/withdrawal with automatic teller machine (ATM)	0.80	12	24	13
Deposit/withdrawal on prearranged monthly basis	0.50	0	14	58
Bank checks written	8.20	8	2	3
Foreign currency drafts	12.10	6	1	5
Inquiries about account balance	1.70	7	16	6
Average Premier Account balance for 2013		$1,200	$700	$24,900

Assume Lindell and Colston always maintain a balance above $1,000, whereas Welker always has a balance below $1,000.

Required

1. Compute the 2014 profitability of the Lindell, Welker, and Colston Premier Accounts at USB.
2. Why might USB worry about the profitability of individual customers if the Premier Account product offering is profitable as a whole?
3. What changes would you recommend for USB's Premier Account?

MyAccountingLab

Problems

5-30 Job costing with single direct-cost category, single indirect-cost pool, law firm. Bradley Associates is a recently formed law partnership. Emmit Harrington, the managing partner of Bradley Associates, has just finished a tense phone call with Martin Omar, president of Campa Coal. Omar strongly complained about the price Bradley charged for some legal work done for Campa Coal.

Harrington also received a phone call from its only other client (St. Edith's Glass), which was very pleased with both the quality of the work and the price charged on its most recent job.

Bradley Associates operates at capacity and uses a cost-based approach to pricing (billing) each job. Currently it uses a simple costing system with a single direct-cost category (professional labor-hours) and a single indirect-cost pool (general support). Indirect costs are allocated to cases on the basis of professional labor-hours per case. The job files show the following:

	Campa Coal	St. Edith's Glass
Professional labor	150 hours	100 hours

Professional labor costs at Bradley Associates are $80 an hour. Indirect costs are allocated to cases at $100 an hour. Total indirect costs in the most recent period were $25,000.

1. Why is it important for Bradley Associates to understand the costs associated with individual jobs?
2. Compute the costs of the Campa Coal and St. Edith's Glass jobs using Bradley's simple costing system.

5-31 Job costing with multiple direct-cost categories, single indirect-cost pool, law firm (continuation of 5-30). Harrington asks his assistant to collect details on those costs included in the $25,000 indirect-cost pool that can be traced to each individual job. After analysis, Bradley is able to reclassify $15,000 of the $25,000 as direct costs:

Other Direct Costs	Campa Coal	St. Edith's Glass
Research support labor	$1,800	$ 3,850
Computer time	400	1,600
Travel and allowances	700	4,200
Telephones/faxes	250	1,200
Photocopying	300	700
Total	$3,450	$11,550

Harrington decides to calculate the costs of each job as if Bradley had used six direct cost-pools and a single indirect-cost pool. The single indirect-cost pool would have $10,000 of costs and would be allocated to each case using the professional labor-hours base.

Required

1. Calculate the revised indirect-cost allocation rate per professional labor-hour for Bradley Associates when total indirect costs are $10,000.
2. Compute the costs of the Campa and St. Edith's jobs if Bradley Associates had used its refined costing system with multiple direct-cost categories and one indirect-cost pool.
3. Compare the costs of Campa and St. Edith's jobs in requirement 2 with those in requirement 2 of Problem 5-30. Comment on the results.

5-32 Job costing with multiple direct-cost categories, multiple indirect-cost pools, law firm (continuation of 5-30 and 5-31). Bradley has two classifications of professional staff: partners and associates. Harrington asks his assistant to examine the relative use of partners and associates on the recent Campa Coal and St. Edith's jobs. The Campa job used 50 partner-hours and 100 associate-hours. The St. Edith's job used 75 partner-hours and 25 associate-hours. Therefore, totals of the two jobs together were 125 partner-hours and 125 associate-hours. Harrington decides to examine how using separate direct-cost rates for partners and associates and using separate indirect-cost pools for partners and associates would have affected the costs of the Campa and St. Edith's jobs. Indirect costs in each indirect-cost pool would be allocated on the basis of total hours of that category of professional labor. From the total indirect cost-pool of $10,000, $6,000 is attributable to the activities of partners and $4,000 is attributable to the activities of associates.

The rates per category of professional labor are as follows:

Category of Professional Labor	Direct Cost per Hour	Indirect Cost per Hour
Partner	$100	$6,000 ÷ 125 hours = $48
Associate	$ 60	$4,000 ÷ 125 hours = $32

Required

1. Compute the costs of the Campa and St. Edith's cases using Bradley's further refined system, with multiple direct-cost categories and multiple indirect-cost pools.
2. For what decisions might Bradley Associates find it more useful to use this job-costing approach rather than the approaches in Problem 5-30 or 5-31?

5-33 First-stage allocation, activity-based costing, manufacturing sector. Thurgood Devices uses activity-based costing to allocate overhead costs to customer orders for pricing purposes. Many customer orders are won through competitive bidding. Direct material and direct manufacturing labor costs are traced directly to each order. Thurgood's direct manufacturing labor rate is $20 per hour. The company reports the following yearly overhead costs:

Wages and salaries	$480,000
Depreciation	60,000
Rent	120,000
Other overhead	240,000
Total overhead costs	$900,000

Thurgood has established four activity cost pools:

Activity Cost Pool	Activity Measure	Total Activity for the Year
Direct manufacturing labor support	Number of direct manufacturing labor-hours	30,000 direct manufacturing labor-hours
Order processing	Number of customer orders	500 orders
Design support	Number of custom designs	100 custom designs
Other	Facility-sustaining costs allocated to orders based on direct manufacturing labor-hours	30,000 direct manufacturing labor-hours

Only about 20% of Thurgood's yearly orders require custom designs.

Paul Moeller, Thurgood's controller, has prepared the following estimates for distribution of the overhead costs across the four activity cost pools:

	Direct Manufacturing Labor Support	Order Processing	Design Support	Other	Total
Wages and salaries	40%	25%	30%	5%	100%
Depreciation	25%	10%	15%	50%	100%
Rent	30%	25%	10%	35%	100%
Other overhead	20%	30%	35%	15%	100%

Order 448200 required $4,550 of direct materials, 80 direct manufacturing labor-hours, and one custom design.

Required

1. Allocate the overhead costs to each activity cost pool. Calculate the activity rate for each pool.
2. Determine the cost of Order 448200.
3. How does activity-based costing enhance Thurgood's ability to price its orders? Suppose Thurgood used a traditional costing system to allocate all overhead costs to orders on the basis of direct manufacturing labor-hours. How might this have affected Thurgood's pricing decisions?

5-34 First-stage allocation, activity-based costing, service sector. LawnCare USA provides lawn care and landscaping services to commercial clients. LawnCare USA uses activity-based costing to bid on jobs and to evaluate their profitability. LawnCare USA reports the following annual costs:

Wages and salaries	$360,000
Depreciation	72,000
Supplies	120,000
Other overhead	288,000
Total overhead costs	$840,000

John Gilroy, controller of LawnCare USA, has established four activity cost pools:

Activity Cost Pool	Activity Measure	Total Activity for the Year
Estimating jobs	Number of job estimates	250 estimates
Lawn care	Number of direct labor-hours	10,000 direct labor-hours
Landscape design	Number of design hours	500 design hours
Other	Facility-sustaining costs that are not allocated to jobs	Not applicable

Gilroy estimates that LawnCare USA's costs are distributed to the activity-cost pools as follows:

	Estimating Jobs	Lawn Care	Landscape Design	Other	Total
Wages and salaries	5%	70%	15%	10%	100%
Depreciation	10%	65%	10%	15%	100%
Supplies	0%	100%	0%	0%	100%
Other overhead	15%	50%	20%	15%	100%

Sunset Office Park, a new development in a nearby community, has contacted LawnCare USA to provide an estimate on landscape design and annual lawn maintenance. The job is estimated to require a single landscape design requiring 40 design hours in total and 250 direct labor-hours annually. LawnCare USA has a policy of pricing estimates at 150% of cost.

Required

1. Allocate LawnCare USA's costs to the activity-cost pools and determine the activity rate for each pool.
2. Estimate total cost for the Sunset Office Park job.
3. How much should LawnCare USA bid to perform the job?
4. Sunset Office Park asks LawnCare USA to give an estimate for providing its services for a 2-year period. What are the advantages and disadvantages for LawnCare USA to provide a 2-year estimate?

5-35 Department and activity-cost rates, service sector. Raynham's Radiology Center (RRC) performs X-rays, ultrasounds, computer tomography (CT) scans, and magnetic resonance imaging (MRI). RRC has developed a reputation as a top radiology center in the state. RRC has achieved this status because it constantly reexamines its processes and procedures. RRC has been using a single, facility-wide overhead allocation rate. The vice president of finance believes that RRC can make better process improvements if it uses more disaggregated cost information. She says, "We have state-of-the-art medical imaging technology. Can't we have state-of-the-art accounting technology?"

Raynham's Radiology Center Budgeted Information for the Year Ended May 31, 2014

	X-rays	Ultrasound	CT Scan	MRI	Total
Technician labor	$ 62,000	$101,000	$155,000	$ 103,000	$ 421,000
Depreciation	42,240	256,000	424,960	876,800	1,600,000
Materials	22,600	16,400	23,600	31,500	94,100
Administration					20,000
Maintenance					250,000
Sanitation					252,500
Utilities					151,100
	$126,840	$373,400	$603,560	$1,011,300	$2,788,700
Number of procedures	3,842	4,352	2,924	2,482	
Minutes to clean after each procedure	5	5	15	35	
Minutes for each procedure	5	15	25	40	

RRC operates at capacity. The proposed allocation bases for overhead are:

Administration	Number of procedures
Maintenance (including parts)	Capital cost of the equipment (use Depreciation)
Sanitation	Total cleaning minutes
Utilities	Total procedure minutes

Required

1. Calculate the budgeted cost per service for X-rays, ultrasounds, CT scans, and MRI using direct technician labor costs as the allocation basis.
2. Calculate the budgeted cost per service of X-rays, ultrasounds, CT scans, and MRI if RRC allocated overhead costs using activity-based costing.
3. Explain how the disaggregation of information could be helpful to RRC's intention to continuously improve its services.

5-36 Activity-based costing, merchandising. Pharmahelp, Inc., a distributor of special pharmaceutical products, operates at capacity and has three main market segments:

a. General supermarket chains
b. Drugstore chains
c. Mom-and-pop single-store pharmacies

Rick Flair, the new controller of Pharmahelp, reported the following data for 2014

	A	B	C	D	E
1					
2	**Pharmahelp, 2014**	**General**			
3		**Supermarket**	**Drugstore**	**Mom-and-Pop**	
4		**Chains**	**Chains**	**Single Stores**	**Pharmahelp**
5	Revenues	$3,708,000	$3,150,000	$1,980,000	$8,838,000
6	Cost of goods sold	3,600,000	3,000,000	1,800,000	8,400,000
7	Gross margin	$ 108,000	$ 150,000	$ 180,000	438,000
8	Other operating costs				301,080
9	Operating income				$ 136,920

For many years, Pharmahelp has used gross margin percentage [(Revenue – Cost of goods sold) ÷ Revenue] to evaluate the relative profitability of its market segments. But Flair recently attended a seminar on activity-based costing and is considering using it at Pharmahelp to analyze and allocate "other operating costs." He meets with all the key managers and several of his operations and sales staff, and they agree that there are five key activities that drive other operating costs at Pharmahelp:

Activity Area	Cost Driver
Order processing	Number of customer purchase orders
Line-item processing	Number of line items ordered by customers
Delivering to stores	Number of store deliveries
Cartons shipped to store	Number of cartons shipped
Stocking of customer store shelves	Hours of shelf-stocking

Each customer order consists of one or more line items. A line item represents a single product (such as Extra-Strength Tylenol Tablets). Each product line item is delivered in one or more separate cartons. Each store delivery entails the delivery of one or more cartons of products to a customer. Pharmahelp's staff stacks cartons directly onto display shelves in customers' stores. Currently, there is no additional charge to the customer for shelf-stocking and not all customers use Pharmahelp for this activity. The level of each activity in the three market segments and the total cost incurred for each activity in 2014 is as follows:

Home Insert Page Layout Formulas Data Review View

	A	B	C	D	E
13					
14	**Activity-based Cost Data**		**Activity Level**		
15	**Pharmahelp 2014**	**General**			**Total Cost**
16		**Supermarket**	**Drugstore**	**Mom-and-Pop**	**of Activity**
17	**Activity**	**Chains**	**Chains**	**Single Stores**	**in 2014**
18	Orders processed (number)	140	360	1,500	$ 80,000
19	Line-items ordered (number)	1,960	4,320	15,000	63,840
20	Store deliveries made (number)	120	360	1,000	71,000
21	Cartons shipped to stores (number)	36,000	24,000	16,000	76,000
22	Shelf stocking (hours)	360	180	100	10,240
23					$301,080

Required

1. Compute the 2014 gross-margin percentage for each of Pharmahelp's three market segments.
2. Compute the cost driver rates for each of the five activity areas.
3. Use the activity-based costing information to allocate the $301,080 of "other operating costs" to each of the market segments. Compute the operating income for each market segment.
4. Comment on the results. What new insights are available with the activity-based costing information?

5-37 Choosing cost drivers, activity-based costing, activity-based management. Pastel Bags (PB) is a designer of high-quality backpacks and purses. Each design is made in small batches. Each spring, PB comes out with new designs for the backpack and for the purse. The company uses these designs for a year and then moves on to the next trend. The bags are all made on the same fabrication equipment that is expected to operate at capacity. The equipment must be switched over to a new design and set up to prepare for the production of each new batch of products. When completed, each batch of products is immediately shipped to a wholesaler. Shipping costs vary with the number of shipments. Budgeted information for the year is as follows:

Pastel Bags
Budget for Costs and Activities
For the Year Ended February 28, 2014

Direct materials—purses	$ 319,155
Direct materials—backpacks	454,995
Direct manufacturing labor—purses	99,000
Direct manufacturing labor—backpacks	113,000
Setup	64,000
Shipping	73,000
Design	169,000
Plant utilities and administration	221,000
Total	$1,513,150

Other budget information follows:

	Backpacks	Purses	Total
Number of bags	6,175	3, 075	9, 250
Hours of production	1,665	2,585	4,250
Number of batches	120	80	200
Number of designs	2	2	4

Required

1. Identify the cost hierarchy level for each cost category.
2. Identify the most appropriate cost driver for each cost category. Explain briefly your choice of cost driver.
3. Calculate the budgeted cost per unit of cost driver for each cost category.
4. Calculate the budgeted total costs and cost per unit for each product line.
5. Explain how you could use the information in requirement 4 to reduce costs.

5-38 ABC, health care. Crosstown Health Center runs two programs: drug addict rehabilitation and aftercare (counseling and support of patients after release from a mental hospital). The center's budget for 2014 follows.

Professional salaries:		
4 physicians × $150,000	$600,000	
12 psychologists × $75,000	900,000	
16 nurses × $30,000	480,000	$1,980,000
Medical supplies		242,000
Rent and clinic maintenance		138,600
Administrative costs to manage patient charts, food, laundry		484,000
Laboratory services		92,400
Total		$2,937,000

Kim Yu, the director of the center, is keen on determining the cost of each program. Yu compiled the following data describing employee allocations to individual programs:

	Drug	Aftercare	Total Employees
Physicians	4		4
Psychologists	4	8	12
Nurses	6	10	16

Yu has recently become aware of activity-based costing as a method to refine costing systems. She asks her accountant, Gus Gates, how she should apply this technique. Gates obtains the following budgeted information for 2014:

	Drug	Aftercare	Total
Square feet of space occupied by each program	9,000	12,000	21,000
Patient-years of service	50	60	110
Number of laboratory tests	1,400	700	2,100

Required

1. a. Selecting cost-allocation bases that you believe are the most appropriate for allocating indirect costs to programs, calculate the budgeted indirect cost rates for medical supplies; rent and clinic maintenance; administrative costs for patient charts, food, and laundry; and laboratory services.
   b. Using an activity-based costing approach to cost analysis, calculate the budgeted cost of each program and the budgeted cost per patient-year of the drug program.
   c. What benefits can Crosstown Health Center obtain by implementing the ABC system?
2. What factors, other than cost, do you think Crosstown Health Center should consider in allocating resources to its programs?

5-39 Unused capacity, activity-based costing, activity-based management. Zarson's Netballs is a manufacturer of high-quality basketballs and volleyballs. Setup costs are driven by the number of batches. Equipment and maintenance costs increase with the number of machine-hours, and lease rent is paid per square foot. Capacity of the facility is 14,000 square feet, and Zarson is using only 80% of this capacity. Zarson records the cost of unused capacity as a separate line item and not as a product cost. The following is the budgeted information for Zarson:

Zarson's Netballs
Budgeted Costs and Activities
For the Year Ended December 31, 2014

Direct materials—basketballs	$ 168, 100
Direct materials—volleyballs	303,280
Direct manufacturing labor—basketballs	111,800
Direct manufacturing labor—volleyballs	100,820
Setup	157,500
Equipment and maintenance costs	115,200
Lease rent	210,000
Total	$1,166,700

Other budget information follows:

	Basketballs	Volleyballs
Number of balls	58,000	85,000
Machine-hours	13,500	10,500
Number of batches	450	300
Square footage of production space used	3,200	8,000

Required

1. Calculate the budgeted cost per unit of cost driver for each indirect cost pool.
2. What is the budgeted cost of unused capacity?
3. What is the budgeted total cost and the cost per unit of resources used to produce (a) basketballs and (b) volleyballs?
4. Why might excess capacity be beneficial for Zarson? What are some of the issues Zarson should consider before increasing production to use the space?

5-40 Unused capacity, activity-based costing, activity-based management. Whitewater Adventures manufactures two models of kayaks, Basic and Deluxe, using a combination of machining and hand finishing. Machine setup costs are driven by the number of setups. Indirect manufacturing labor costs increase with direct manufacturing labor costs. Equipment and maintenance costs increase with the number of machine-hours, and facility rent is paid per square foot. Capacity of the facility is 6,250 square feet, and Whitewater is using only 80% of this capacity. Whitewater records the cost of unused capacity as a separate line item and not as a product cost. For the current year, Whitewater has budgeted the following:

Whitewater Adventures
Budgeted Costs and Activities
for the Year Ended December 31, 2014

Direct materials—Basic kayaks	$325,000
Direct materials—Deluxe kayaks	240,000
Direct manufacturing labor—Basic kayaks	110,000
Direct manufacturing labor—Deluxe kayaks	130,000
Indirect manufacturing labor costs	72,000
Machine setup costs	40,500
Equipment and maintenance costs	235,000
Facility rent	200,000
Total	$1,352,500

Other budget information follows:

	Basic	Deluxe
Number of kayaks	5,000	3,000
Machine-hours	11,000	12,500
Number of setups	300	200
Square footage of production space used	2,860	2,140

Required

1. Calculate the cost per unit of each cost-allocation base.
2. What is the budgeted cost of unused capacity?
3. Calculate the budgeted total cost and the cost per unit for each model.
4. Why might excess capacity be beneficial for Whitewater? What are some of the issues Whitewater should consider before increasing production to use the space?

5-41 ABC, implementation, ethics. (CMA, adapted) Plum Electronics, a division of Berry Corporation, manufactures two large-screen television models: the Mammoth, which has been produced since 2010 and sells for $990, and the Maximum, a newer model introduced in early 2012 that sells for $1,254. Based on the following income statement for the year ended November 30, 2014, senior management at Berry have decided to concentrate Plum's marketing resources on the Maximum model and to begin to phase out the Mammoth model because Maximum generates a much bigger operating income per unit.

Plum Electronics
Income Statement for the
Fiscal Year Ended November 30, 2014

	Mammoth	Maximum	Total
Revenues	$21,780,000	$5,016,000	$26,796,000
Cost of goods sold	13,794,000	3,511,200	17,305,200
Gross margin	7,986,000	1,504,800	9,490,800
Selling and administrative expense	6,413,000	1,075,800	7,488,800
Operating income	$ 1,573,000	$ 429,000	$ 2,002,000
Units produced and sold	22,000	4,000	
Operating income per unit sold	$ 71.50	$ 107.25	

Details for cost of goods sold for Mammoth and Maximum are as follows:

	Mammoth		Maximum	
	Total	**Per Unit**	**Total**	**Per Unit**
Direct materials	$ 5,033,600	$ 228.80	$2,569,600	$642.40
Direct manufacturing labor[a]	435,600	19.80	184,800	46.20
Machine costs[b]	3,484,800	158.40	316,800	79.20
Total direct costs	$ 8,954,000	$ 407.00	$3,071,200	$767.80
Manufacturing overhead costs[c]	$ 4,840,000	$ 220.00	$ 440,000	$110.00
Total cost of goods sold	$13,794,000	$ 627.00	$3,511,200	$877.80

[a] Mammoth requires 1.5 hours per unit and Maximum requires 3.5 hours per unit. The direct manufacturing labor cost is $13.20 per hour.

[b] Machine costs include lease costs of the machine, repairs, and maintenance. Mammoth requires 8 machine-hours per unit and Maximum requires 4 machine-hours per unit. The machine-hour rate is $19.80 per hour.

[c] Manufacturing overhead costs are allocated to products based on machine-hours at the rate of $27.50 per hour.

Plum's controller, Steve Jacobs, is advocating the use of activity-based costing and activity-based management and has gathered the following information about the company's manufacturing overhead costs for the year ended November 30, 2014.

		Units of the Cost-Allocation Base		
Activity Center (Cost-Allocation Base)	**Total Activity Costs**	**Mammoth**	**Maximum**	**Total**
Soldering (number of solder points)	$1,036,200	1,185,000	385,000	1,570,000
Shipments (number of shipments)	946,000	16,200	3,800	20,000
Quality control (number of inspections)	1,364,000	56,200	21,300	77,500
Purchase orders (number of orders)	1,045,440	80,100	109,980	190,080
Machine power (machine-hours)	63,360	176,000	16,000	192,000
Machine setups (number of setups)	825,000	16,000	14,000	30,000
Total manufacturing overhead	$5,280,000			

After completing his analysis, Jacobs shows the results to Charles Clark, the Plum division president. Clark does not like what he sees. "If you show headquarters this analysis, they are going to ask us to phase out the Maximum line, which we have just introduced. This whole costing stuff has been a major problem for us. First Mammoth was not profitable and now Maximum.

"Looking at the ABC analysis, I see two problems. First, we do many more activities than the ones you have listed. If you had included all activities, maybe your conclusions would be different. Second, you used number of setups and number of inspections as allocation bases. The numbers would be different had you used setup-hours and inspection-hours instead. I know that measurement problems precluded you from using these other cost-allocation bases, but I believe you ought to make some adjustments to our current numbers to compensate for these issues. I know you can do better. We can't afford to phase out either product."

Jacobs knows that his numbers are fairly accurate. As a quick check, he calculates the profitability of Maximum and Mammoth using more and different allocation bases. The set of activities and activity rates he had used results in numbers that closely approximate those based on more detailed analyses. He is confident that headquarters, knowing that Maximum was introduced only recently, will not ask Plum to phase it out. He is also aware that a sizable portion of Clark's bonus is based on division revenues.

Phasing out either product would adversely affect his bonus. Still, he feels some pressure from Clark to do something.

Required

1. Using activity-based costing, calculate the gross margin per unit of the Maximum and Mammoth models.
2. Explain briefly why these numbers differ from the gross margin per unit of the Maximum and Mammoth models calculated using Plum's existing simple costing system.
3. Comment on Clark's concerns about the accuracy and limitations of ABC.
4. How might Plum find the ABC information helpful in managing its business?
5. What should Steve Jacobs do in response to Clark's comments?

5-42 Activity-based costing, activity-based management, merchandising. Main Street Books and Café (MSBC) is a large city bookstore that sells books and music CDs and has a café. MSBC operates at capacity and allocates selling, general, and administration (S, G & A) costs to each product line using the cost of merchandise of each product line. MSBC wants to optimize the pricing and cost management of each product line. MSBC is wondering if its accounting system is providing it with the best information for making such decisions.

Main Street Books and Café
Product Line Information
For the Year Ended December 31, 2014

	Books	CDs	Café
Revenues	$3,720,480	$2,315,360	$736,216
Cost of merchandise	$2,656,727	$1,722,311	$556,685
Cost of café cleaning	—	—	$ 18,250
Number of purchase orders placed	2,800	2,500	2,000
Number of deliveries received	1,400	1,700	1,600
Hours of shelf stocking time	15,000	14,000	10,000
Items sold	124,016	115,768	368,108

Main Street Books and Café incurs the following selling, general, and administration costs:

Main Street Books and Café
Selling, General, and Administration (S, G & A) Costs
For the Year Ended December 31, 2014

Purchasing department expense	$ 474,500
Receiving department expense	432,400
Shelf stocking labor expense	487,500
Customer support expense (cashiers and floor employees)	91,184
	$1,485,584

Required

1. Suppose MSBC uses cost of merchandise to allocate all S, G & A costs. Prepare product line and total company income statements.
2. Identify an improved method for allocating costs to the three product lines. Explain. Use the method for allocating S, G & A costs that you propose to prepare new product line and total company income statements. Compare your results to the results in requirement 1.
3. Write a memo to MSBC management describing how the improved system might be useful for managing the store.

6 Master Budget and Responsibility Accounting

Learning Objectives

1. Describe the master budget and explain its benefits
2. Describe the advantages of budgets
3. Prepare the operating budget and its supporting schedules
4. Use computer-based financial planning models for sensitivity analysis
5. Describe responsibility centers and responsibility accounting
6. Recognize the human aspects of budgeting
7. Appreciate the special challenges of budgeting in multinational companies

No one likes to run out of cash.

During the global recession of 2007–2009, both households and businesses faced economic hardships. Among the hottest innovations to emerge during the recession were Web sites that enabled users to get a snapshot of their financial data, including checking accounts, investment statements, and loans, and to create budgets to manage their spending and saving. Mint.com was one of these Web sites. In 2009, Intuit, the developer of the Quicken and TurboTax products, recognized the growing popularity of these financial Web sites and acquired Mint.com for $170 million.

Businesses, like individuals, need budgets. Without budgets, it's difficult for managers and their employees to know whether they're on target for their growth and spending goals. Adhering to budgets is important for all types of companies: large financial institutions, such as Citigroup, which suffered big financial losses after the bursting of the housing bubble in the mid-2000s; large retailers, such as Walmart, whose profit margins are slim; profitable computer companies, such as Apple, which sell high dollar-value goods; and luxury hotels, such as the Ritz-Carlton, which sell high dollar-value services.

"Scrimping" at the Ritz: Master Budgets

"Ladies and gentlemen serving ladies and gentlemen." That's the motto of the Ritz-Carlton. With locations ranging from Denver to Dubai, the grand hotel chain is known for its indulgent luxury and sumptuous surroundings. However, the aura of the chain's old-world elegance stands in contrast to its emphasis—behind the scenes, of course—on cost control and budgets.

A Ritz hotel's performance is the responsibility of its general manager and controller at each location. Local forecasts and budgets are prepared annually and are the basis of subsequent performance evaluations for the hotel and people who work there.

The hotel's sales director forecasts all revenue including hotel rooms, conventions, weddings, meeting facilities, merchandise, and food and beverage sales. The controller then seeks input about costs. Standard costs, based on cost per occupied room, are used to build the budget for guest room stays. Other standard costs are used to calculate costs for meeting rooms and food and beverages. The completed budgets are sent to corporate headquarters and the hotel's actual performance each month is monitored against the approved budget.

The managers of each hotel meet daily to review the hotel's performance relative to the plan. They have the ability to adjust prices in the reservation system if they so choose. Adjusting prices can be particularly important if a hotel experiences unanticipated changes in occupancy rates. Each month, the controller of each hotel receives a report from headquarters that shows how the hotel performed against budget as well as against the performance of other Ritz hotels. Any ideas for boosting revenues and reducing costs are regularly shared among hotels.

Why do successful companies feel the need to use budgeting to watch their spending so closely? Because, as the Ritz-Carlton example illustrates, budgeting is a critical function in an organization's decision-making process. Southwest Airlines, for example, uses budgets to monitor and manage fluctuating fuel costs. Walmart depends on its budget to maintain razor-thin margins as it competes with Target. Gillette uses budgets to plan marketing campaigns for its razors and blades.

Even though budgeting is essential for businesses, many managers are often frustrated by the budgeting process. They find it difficult to predict the future and dislike superiors challenging them to improve the performance of their departments. They also dislike being personally evaluated on targets that are challenging. It is not uncommon for a manager to view budgeting as a game: "If I lower my performance *expectations,* my *actual* performance will look good," the manager might conclude. We discuss these issues and the ways thoughtful managers deal with them later in this chapter. For now, we highlight some of the benefits managers get from budgeting.

Budgets help managers:

1. Communicate directions and goals to different departments of a company to help them coordinate the actions they must pursue to satisfy customers and succeed in the marketplace.
2. Judge performance by measuring financial results against planned objectives, activities, and timelines and learn about potential problems.
3. Motivate employees to achieve their goals.

Interestingly, even when it comes to entrepreneurial activities, research shows that business planning increases a new venture's probability of survival, as well as its product development and venture-organizing activities.[1] As the old adage goes: "If you fail to plan, you plan to fail."

In this chapter, you will see that a budget is based on an organization's strategy and expresses its operating and financial plans. Most importantly, you will see that budgeting is a human activity that requires judgment and wise interpretation.

[1] For more details, see Frederic Delmar and Scott Shane, "Does Business Planning Facilitate the Development of New Ventures?" *Strategic Management Journal* (December 2003).

Learning Objective 1

Describe the master budget

...the master budget is the initial budget prepared before the start of a period

and explain its benefits

...benefits include planning, coordination, and control

Budgets and the Budgeting Cycle

A *budget* is (a) the quantitative expression of a proposed plan of action by management for a specified period and (b) an aid to coordinate what needs to be done to implement that plan. The budget generally includes both the plan's financial and nonfinancial aspects and serves as a blueprint for the company to follow in an upcoming period. A financial budget quantifies managers' expectations regarding a company's income, cash flows, and financial position. Just as financial statements are prepared for past periods, financial statements can be prepared for future periods—for example, a budgeted income statement, a budgeted statement of cash flows, or a budgeted balance sheet. Managers develop financial budgets using supporting information from nonfinancial budgets for, say, units manufactured or sold, number of employees, and number of new products being introduced to the marketplace.

Strategic Plans and Operating Plans

Budgeting is most useful when it is integrated with a company's strategy. *Strategy* specifies how an organization matches its capabilities with the opportunities in the marketplace to accomplish its objectives. To develop successful strategies, managers must consider questions such as the following:

- What are our objectives?
- How do we create value for our customers while distinguishing ourselves from our competitors?
- Are the markets for our products local, regional, national, or global? What trends affect our markets? How do the economy, our industry, and our competitors affect us?
- What organizational and financial structures serve us best?
- What are the risks and opportunities of alternative strategies, and what are our contingency plans if our preferred plan fails?

A company, such as Home Depot, can have a strategy of providing quality products or services at a low price. Another company, such as Porsche or the Ritz-Carlton, can have a strategy of providing a unique product or service that is priced higher than the products or services of competitors. Exhibit 6-1 shows that strategic plans are expressed through long-run budgets and operating plans are expressed via short-run budgets. But there is more to the story! The exhibit shows arrows pointing backward as well as forward. The backward arrows show that budgets can lead to changes in plans and strategies. Budgets help managers assess strategic risks and opportunities by providing them with feedback about the likely effects of their strategies and plans. Sometimes the feedback prompts managers to revise their plans and possibly their strategies.

Boeing's experience with the 747-8 program illustrates how budgets can help managers rework their operating plans. Boeing believed that utilizing some of the design concepts it was implementing in its 787 Dreamliner program would be a relatively inexpensive way to reconfigure its 747-8 jet. However, continued cost overruns and delays undermined that strategy: In early 2012, the 747-8 program was already $2 billion over budget and a year behind schedule. As a result, the company expected to earn no profit on any of the more than 100 orders for 747-8 planes it had on its books. And with the budget revealing higher-than-expected costs in design, rework, and production, Boeing postponed production plans for the 747-8 program.

Exhibit 6-1

Strategy, Planning, and Budgets

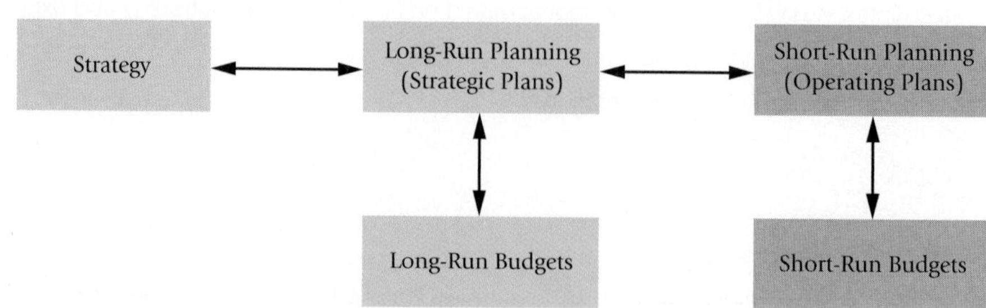

Budgeting Cycle and Master Budget

Well-managed companies usually cycle through the following steps during the course of the fiscal year:

1. Before the start of the fiscal year, managers at all levels take into account the company's past performance, market feedback, and anticipated future changes to initiate plans for the next period. For example, an anticipated economic recovery from a recession may cause managers to plan for sales increases, higher production, and greater promotion expenses. Managers and management accountants work together to develop plans for the company as a whole and the performance of its subunits, such as departments or divisions.
2. At the beginning of the fiscal year, senior managers give subordinate managers a frame of reference, a set of specific financial or nonfinancial expectations against which they will compare actual results.
3. During the course of the year, management accountants help managers investigate any deviations from the plans, such as an unexpected decline in sales. If necessary, corrective action follows, such as changes in a product's features, a reduction in prices to boost sales, or cutting of costs to maintain profitability.

The preceding three steps describe the ongoing budget-related processes. The working document at the core of this process is called the *master budget.* The **master budget** expresses management's operating and financial plans for a specified period, usually a fiscal year, and it includes a set of budgeted financial statements. The master budget is the initial plan of what the company intends to accomplish in the period and evolves from both the operating and financing decisions managers make along the way.

- Operating decisions deal with how to best use the limited resources of an organization.
- Financing decisions deal with how to obtain the funds to acquire those resources.

The terminology used to describe budgets varies among companies. For example, budgeted financial statements are sometimes called **pro forma statements.** Some companies, such as Hewlett-Packard, refer to budgeting as *targeting*. And many companies, such as Nissan Motor Company and Owens Corning, refer to the budget as a *profit plan*. Microsoft refers to goals as *commitments* and distributes firm-level goals across the company, connecting them to organizational, team, and ultimately individual commitments.

This book focuses on how management accounting helps managers make operating decisions, which is why operating budgets are emphasized here. Managers spend a significant part of their time preparing and analyzing budgets because budgeting yields many advantages.

Decision Point

What is the master budget and why is it useful?

Advantages and Challenges of Implementing Budgets

Learning Objective 2

Describe the advantages of budgets

...advantages include coordination, communication, performance evaluation, and managerial motivation

Budgets are an integral part of management control systems. As we have discussed at the start of this chapter, when administered thoughtfully by managers, budgets do the following:

- Promote coordination and communication among subunits within the company
- Provide a framework for judging performance and facilitating learning
- Motivate managers and other employees

Promoting Coordination and Communication

Coordination is meshing and balancing all aspects of production or service and all departments in a company in the best way for the company to meet its goals. *Communication* is making sure all employees understand those goals. Coordination forces executives to think about the relationships among individual departments within the company, as well as between the company and its supply chain partners.

Consider budgeting at Pace, a United Kingdom–based manufacturer of electronic products. A key product is Pace's digital set-top box for decoding satellite broadcasts. The production manager can achieve more timely production by coordinating and communicating with the company's marketing team to understand when set-top boxes need to be shipped to customers. In turn, the marketing team can make better predictions of future demand for set-top boxes by coordinating and communicating with Pace's customers.

Suppose BSkyB, one of Pace's largest customers, is planning to launch a new high-definition personal video recorder service. If Pace's marketing group is able to obtain information about the launch date for the service, it can share this information with Pace's manufacturing group. The manufacturing group must then coordinate and communicate with Pace's materials-procurement group, and so on. The point to understand is that Pace is more likely to have personal video recorders in the quantities customers demand if Pace coordinates and communicates both within its business functions and with its customers and suppliers during the budgeting process as well as during the production process.

Providing a Framework for Judging Performance and Facilitating Learning

Budgets enable a company's managers to measure actual performance against predicted performance. Budgets can overcome two limitations of using past performance as a basis for judging actual results. One limitation is that past results often incorporate past miscues and substandard performance. Suppose the cellular telephone company Mobile Communications is examining the current-year (2014) performance of its sales force. The sales force's 2013 performance incorporated the efforts of an unusually high number of salespeople who have since left the company because they did not have a good understanding of the marketplace. The president of Mobile said of those salespeople, "They could not sell ice cream in a heat wave." Using the sales record of those departed employees would set the performance bar for 2014 much too low.

The other limitation of using past performance is that future conditions can be expected to differ from the past. Consider again Mobile Communications. Suppose, in 2014, Mobile had a 20% revenue increase, compared with a 10% revenue increase in 2013. Does this increase indicate outstanding sales performance? Not if the forecasted and actual 2014 industry growth rate was 40%. In this case, Mobile's 20% actual revenue gain in 2014 doesn't look so good, even though it exceeded the 2013 actual growth rate of 10%. Using the 40% budgeted growth rate for the industry provides Mobile Communications with a better benchmark against which to evaluate its 2014 sales performance than using the 2013 actual growth rate of 10%. This is why many companies also evaluate their performance relative to their peers. Using only the budget to evaluate performance creates an incentive for subordinates to set targets that are relatively easy to achieve.[2] Of course, managers at all levels recognize this incentive and therefore work to make the budget more challenging to achieve for the individuals who report to them. Still, the budget is the end product of negotiations among senior and subordinate managers. At the end of the year, senior managers gain information about the performance of competitors and external market conditions. This is valuable information senior managers can use to judge the performance of subordinate managers.

One of the most valuable benefits of budgeting is that it helps managers gather information for improving future performance. When actual outcomes fall short of budgeted or planned results, it prompts thoughtful senior managers to ask questions about what happened and why and how this knowledge can be used to ensure that such shortfalls do not occur again. This probing and learning is one of the most important reasons why budgeting helps improve performance.

---

[2] For several examples, see Jeremy Hope and Robin Fraser, *Beyond Budgeting* (Boston: Harvard Business School Press, 2003). The authors also criticize the tendency for managers to administer budgets rigidly even when changing market conditions have rendered the budgets obsolete.

Motivating Managers and Other Employees

Research shows that the performance of employees improves when they receive a challenging budget. Why? Because they view not meeting it as a failure. Most employees are motivated to work more intensely to avoid failure than to achieve success. As employees get closer to a goal, they work harder to achieve it. Creating a little anxiety improves performance. However, overly ambitious and unachievable budgets can actually de-motivate employees because they see little chance of avoiding failure. As a result, many executives like to set demanding but achievable goals for their subordinate managers and employees.[3] General Electric's former CEO Jack Welch describes challenging yet achievable budgets as energizing, motivating, and satisfying for managers and other employees and capable of unleashing out-of-the-box and creative thinking. We will return to the topic of setting difficult-to-achieve targets and how it affects employees later in the chapter.

Challenges in Administering Budgets

The budgeting process involves all levels of management. Top managers want lower-level managers to participate in the budgeting process because they have more specialized knowledge and firsthand experience with the day-to-day aspects of running the business. Participation also creates greater commitment and accountability toward the budget among lower-level managers. This is the bottom-up aspect of the budgeting process.

The budgeting process, however, is time-consuming. Estimates suggest that senior managers spend about 10–20% of their time on budgeting, and finance planning departments spend as much as 50% of their time on it.[4] For most organizations, the annual budget process is a months-long exercise that consumes a tremendous amount of resources.

The widespread use of budgets in companies ranging from major multinational corporations to small local businesses indicates that the advantages of budgeting systems outweigh the costs. To gain the benefits of budgeting, management at all levels of a company should understand and support the budget and all aspects of the management control system. This is critical for obtaining lower-level management's participation in the formulation of budgets and for successful administration of budgets. Lower-level managers who feel that top managers do not "believe" in budgets are unlikely to be active participants in a budget process.

Budgets should not be administered rigidly. Attaining the budget is not an end in itself, especially when conditions change dramatically. A manager may commit to a budget, but if a situation arises in which some unplanned repairs or an unplanned advertising program would serve the long-run interests of the company, the manager should undertake the additional spending. On the flip side, the dramatic decline in consumer demand during the 2007–2009 recession led designers such as Gucci to slash their ad budgets and put on hold planned new boutiques. Macy's and other retailers, stuck with shelves of merchandise ordered before the financial crisis, had no recourse but to slash prices and cut their workforces. J. C. Penney eventually missed its sales projections for 2009 by $2 billion. However, its aggressive actions during the year enabled it to survive the recession. Unfortunately, in 2012, J. C. Penney suffered steep declines in sales as a result of changing its strategy away from offering discounts and deals to everyday low pricing.

Decision Point

When should a company prepare budgets? What are the advantages of preparing budgets?

Learning Objective 3

Prepare the operating budget

...the budgeted income statement

and its supporting schedules

...such as cost of goods sold and nonmanufacturing costs

Developing an Operating Budget

Budgets are typically developed for a set period, such as a month, quarter, or year, which can be then broken into subperiods. For example, a 12-month cash budget may be broken into 12 monthly periods so that cash inflows and outflows can be better coordinated.

[3] For a detailed discussion and several examples of the merits of setting specific hard goals, see Gary P. Latham, "The Motivational Benefits of Goal-Setting," *Academy of Management Executive* 18, no. 4 (2004).

[4] See Peter Horvath and Ralf Sauter, "Why Budgeting Fails: One Management System Is Not Enough," *Balanced Scorecard Report* (September 2004).

Time Coverage of Budgets

The motive for creating a budget should guide a manager in choosing the period for the budget. For example, consider budgeting for a new Harley-Davidson 500-cc motorcycle. If the purpose is to budget for the total profitability of this new model, a 5-year period (or more) may be suitable and long enough to cover the product from design to manufacturing, sales, and after-sales support. In contrast, consider budgeting for a seasonal theater production, which is expected to run for a few months. If the purpose is to estimate all cash outlays, a 6-month period from the planning stage to the final performance should suffice.

The most frequently used budget period is 1 year, which is often subdivided into quarters and months. The budgeted data for a year are frequently revised as the year goes on. At the end of the second quarter, management may change the budget for the next two quarters in light of new information obtained during the first 6 months. For example, Amerigroup, a health insurance firm, had to make substantial revisions to its third-quarter and annual cost projections for 2009 because of higher-than-expected costs related to a flu epidemic caused by the H1N1 virus.

Businesses are increasingly using *rolling budgets*. A **rolling budget**, also called a **continuous budget** or **rolling forecast**, is a budget that is always available for a specified future period. It is created by continually adding a month, quarter, or year to the period that just ended. Consider Electrolux, a global appliance company, which has a 3- to 5-year strategic plan and a 4-quarter rolling budget. A 4-quarter rolling budget for the April 2013 to March 2014 period is superseded in the next quarter—that is in June 2013—by a 4-quarter rolling budget for July 2013 to June 2014, and so on. There is always a 12-month budget (for the next year) in place. Rolling budgets constantly force Electrolux's management to think about the forthcoming 12 months, regardless of the quarter at hand. Some companies, such as Borealis, Europe's leading polyolefin plastics manufacturer; Millipore, a life sciences research and manufacturing firm headquartered in Massachusetts; and Nordea, the largest financial services group in the Nordic and Baltic Sea region, prepare rolling financial forecasts that look ahead five quarters. Other companies, such as EMC Corporation, the information infrastructure giant, employ a 6-quarter rolling-forecast process so that budget allocations can be constantly adjusted to meet changing market conditions.

Steps in Preparing an Operating Budget

The best way to learn how to prepare an operating budget is by walking through the steps a company would take to do so. Consider Stylistic Furniture, a company that makes two types of granite-top coffee tables: Casual and Deluxe. It is late 2013 and Stylistic's CEO, Rex Jordan, is very concerned about how to respond to the board of directors' mandate to increase profits by 10% in the coming year. Jordan goes through the five-step decision-making process introduced in Chapter 1.

1. **Identify the Problem and Uncertainties.** The problem is to identify a strategy and to build a budget to achieve a 10% profit growth. There are several uncertainties. Can Stylistic dramatically increase the sales of its more profitable Deluxe tables? What price pressures is Stylistic likely to face? Will the cost of materials increase? Can Stylistic reduce costs through efficiency improvements?
2. **Obtain Information.** Stylistic's managers gather information about sales of tables in the current year. They are delighted to learn that sales of Deluxe tables have been stronger than expected. Moreover, one of the key competitors in Stylistic's Casual tables line has had quality problems that are unlikely to be resolved until 2014. Unfortunately, Stylistic's managers also discover that the prices of direct materials have increased slightly during 2013.
3. **Make Predictions About the Future.** Stylistic's managers feel confident that with a little more marketing, they will be able to grow the Deluxe tables business and even increase prices slightly relative to 2013. They also do not expect significant price pressures on Casual tables during the year because of the quality problems faced by a key competitor.

The purchasing manager anticipates that prices of direct materials will be about the same as in 2013. The manufacturing manager believes that efficiency improvements would allow the costs of manufacturing tables to be maintained at 2013 costs despite an increase in the prices of other inputs. Achieving these efficiency improvements is important if Stylistic is to maintain its 12% operating margin (that is, operating income ÷ sales = 12%) and to grow sales and operating income.

4. **Make Decisions by Choosing Among Alternatives.** Jordan and his managers feel confident about their strategy to increase the sales of Deluxe tables. This decision has some risks but is the best option available for Stylistic to increase its profits by 10%.
5. **Implement the Decision, Evaluate Performance, and Learn.** As we will discuss in Chapters 7 and 8, managers compare a company's actual performance to its predicted performance to learn why things turned out the way they did and how to do better. Stylistic's managers would want to know whether their predictions about the prices of Casual and Deluxe tables were correct. Did the prices of direct materials increase more or less than anticipated? Did efficiency improvements occur? Such learning would be very helpful as Stylistic plans its budgets in subsequent years.

Stylistic's managers begin their work on the 2014 budget. Exhibit 6-2 shows the various parts of the master budget, which is composed of the financial projections for Stylistic's operating and financial budgets for 2014. The light, medium, and dark green boxes in Exhibit 6-2 show the budgeted income statement and its supporting budget schedules, which together are called the **operating budget**.

We show the revenues budget box in light green to indicate that it is often the starting point of the operating budget. The supporting schedules—shown in medium green—quantify the budgets for various business functions of the value chain, from research and development to distribution costs. These schedules build up to the budgeted income statement—the key summary statement in the operating budget—shown in dark green.

The orange and purple boxes in the exhibit are the **financial budget**, which is that part of the master budget made up of the capital expenditures budget, the cash budget, the budgeted balance sheet, and the budgeted statement of cash flows. A financial budget focuses on how operations and planned capital outlays affect cash—shown in orange. Management accountants use the cash budget and the budgeted income statement to prepare two other summary financial statements—the budgeted balance sheet and the budgeted statement of cash flows, which are shown in purple.

Top managers and line managers responsible for various business functions in the value chain finalize the master budget after several rounds of discussions among them. We next present the steps in preparing an operating budget for Stylistic Furniture for 2014. Use Exhibit 6-2 as a guide for the steps that follow. The appendix to this chapter presents Stylistic's cash budget, which is another key component of the master budget. The following details are needed to prepare the budget:

- Stylistic sells two models of granite-top coffee tables: Casual and Deluxe. Revenue unrelated to sales, such as interest income, is zero.
- Work-in-process inventory is negligible and is ignored.
- Direct materials inventory and finished goods inventory are costed using the first-in, first-out (FIFO) method. The unit costs of direct materials purchased and unit costs of finished goods sold remain unchanged throughout each budget year but can change from year to year.
- There are two types of direct materials: red oak (RO) and granite slabs (GS). The direct material costs are variable with respect to units of output—coffee tables.
- Direct manufacturing labor workers are hired on an hourly basis; no overtime is worked.
- There are two cost drivers for manufacturing overhead costs—direct manufacturing labor-hours and setup labor-hours, and two manufacturing overhead cost pools—manufacturing operations overhead and machine setup overhead.
- Direct manufacturing labor-hours is the cost driver for the variable portion of manufacturing operations overhead. The fixed component of manufacturing operations

Exhibit 6-2

Overview of the Master Budget for Stylistic Furniture

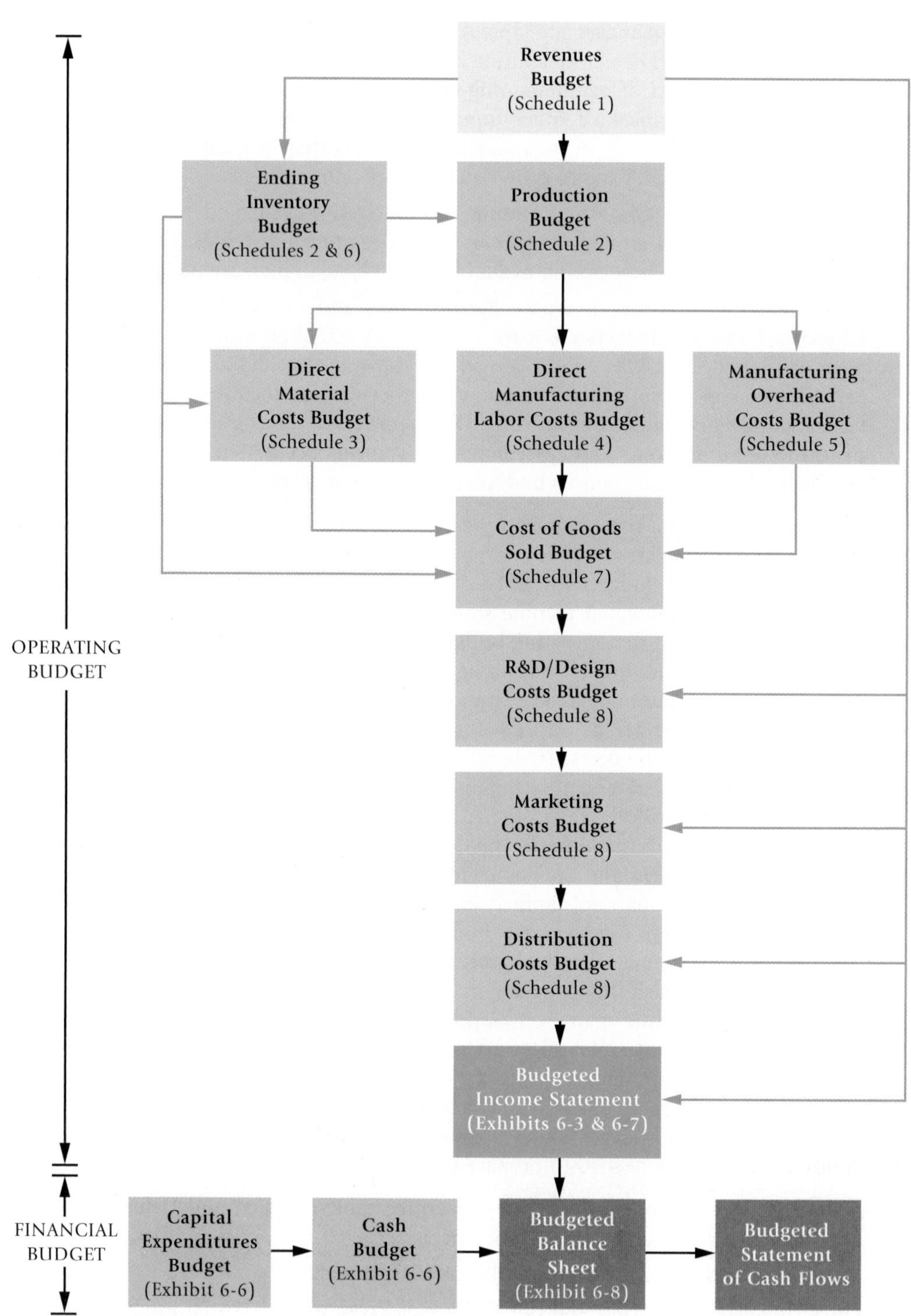

overhead is tied to the manufacturing capacity of 300,000 direct manufacturing labor-hours Stylistic has planned for 2014.

- Setup labor-hours are the cost driver for the variable portion of machine setup overhead. The fixed component of machine setup overhead is tied to the setup capacity of 15,000 setup labor-hours Stylistic has planned for 2014.
- For computing inventoriable costs, Stylistic allocates all (variable and fixed) manufacturing operations overhead costs using direct manufacturing labor-hours and machine setup overhead costs using setup labor-hours.

- Nonmanufacturing costs consist of product design, marketing, and distribution costs. All product design costs are fixed costs for 2014. The variable component of marketing costs equals the 6.5% sales commission on revenues paid to salespeople. The variable portion of distribution costs varies with cubic feet of tables sold and shipped.

The following data are available for the 2014 budget:

Direct materials	
Red oak	$ 7 per board foot (b.f.) (same as in 2013)
Granite	$10 per square foot (sq. ft.) (same as in 2013)
Direct manufacturing labor	$20 per hour

Content of Each Product Unit

	Product	
	Casual Granite Table	**Deluxe Granite Table**
Red oak	12 board feet	12 board feet
Granite	6 square feet	8 square feet
Direct manufacturing labor	4 hours	6 hours

	Product	
	Casual Granite Table	**Deluxe Granite Table**
Expected sales in units	50,000	10,000
Selling price	$ 600	$ 800
Target ending inventory in units	11,000	500
Beginning inventory in units	1,000	500
Beginning inventory in dollars	$384,000	$262,000

	Direct Materials	
	Red oak	**Granite**
Beginning inventory	70,000 b.f.	60,000 sq. ft.
Target ending inventory	80,000 b.f.	20,000 sq. ft.

Stylistic bases its budgeted cost information on the costs it predicts it will incur to support its revenues budget, taking into account the efficiency improvements it expects to make in 2014. Recall from Step 3 of the decision-making process (page 202) that efficiency improvements are critical to offset the anticipated increases in the cost of inputs and to maintain Stylistic's 12% operating margin. Some companies rely heavily on past results when developing budgeted amounts; others rely on detailed engineering studies. Companies differ in how they compute their budgeted amounts.

Most companies have a budget manual that contains a company's particular instructions and information for preparing its budgets. Although the details differ among companies, the following basic steps are common for developing the operating budget for a manufacturing company. Beginning with the revenues budget, each of the other budgets follows step by step in logical fashion. As you go through the details for preparing a budget, think about two things: (1) the information needed to prepare each budget and (2) the actions managers can plan to take to improve the company's performance.

Step 1: Prepare the Revenues Budget. Stylistic currently sells two models of granite-top coffee tables: Casual and Deluxe. During 2013, Stylistic's managers had considered introducing a third coffee-table model but decided against it. They must now budget for the quantities and prices of Casual and Deluxe tables in 2014.

A revenues budget is the usual starting point for the operating budget. Why? Because the forecasted level of unit sales or revenues has a major impact on the production capacity and the inventory levels planned for 2014—and therefore manufacturing and nonmanufacturing costs. Many factors affect the sales forecast, including the sales volume in recent periods, general economic and industry conditions, market research studies, pricing policies, advertising and sales promotions, competition, and regulatory policies. The key to Stylistic achieving its goal of growing its profits by 10% is to grow its sales of Deluxe tables from 8,000 tables in 2013 to 10,000 tables in 2014.

Sales managers and sales representatives build the revenues budget by gathering detailed information about customer needs, market potential, and competitors' products. They debate how best to position, price, and promote Casual and Deluxe tables relative to competitors' products. Together with top management, they consider various actions, such as adding product features, digital advertising, and changing sales incentives, to increase revenues. The cost of these actions are included in the various cost budgets.

Managers often gather information through a customer response management (CRM) or sales management system. Statistical approaches such as regression and trend analysis also help with sales forecasting. These techniques use indicators of economic activity and past sales data to forecast future sales. Managers use statistical analysis only as one input to forecast sales. In the final analysis, the sales forecast represents the collective experience and judgment of managers.

After much discussion, top managers decide on the budgeted sales quantities and prices shown in the revenues budget in Schedule 1. These are difficult targets designed to motivate the organization to achieve higher levels of performance.

Schedule 1: Revenues Budget
for the Year Ending December 31, 2014

	Units	Selling Price	Total Revenues
Casual	50,000	$600	$30,000,000
Deluxe	10,000	800	8,000,000
Total			$38,000,000

The $38,000,000 is the amount of revenues in the budgeted income statement.

Revenues budgets are usually based on expected demand because demand for a company's products is invariably the limiting factor for achieving profit goals. Occasionally, other factors, such as available production capacity (being less than demand) or a manufacturing input in short supply, limit budgeted revenues. In these cases, managers base the revenues budget on the maximum units that can be produced because sales will be limited by that amount.

Step 2: Prepare the Production Budget (in Units). After budgeting revenues, the logical next step is to plan the production of Casual and Deluxe tables so that the product is available when customers need it. The only new information managers need to prepare the production budget is the level of finished goods inventory Stylistic wants to maintain. High inventory levels increase the cost of carrying inventory, the costs of quality, and shrinkage costs. On the flip side, keeping inventory levels too low increases setup costs and results in lost sales from holding inadequate inventory. Over the course of the year, Stylistic's management decides to increase the inventory of Casual tables to avoid some of the supply shortages the company had encountered in the current year but to maintain the inventory level of Deluxe tables.

The manufacturing manager then prepares the production budget, shown in Schedule 2. The total finished goods units to be produced depend on budgeted unit sales (calculated in Step 1), the target ending finished goods inventory, and the beginning finished goods inventory:

$$\begin{array}{c} \text{Budget} \\ \text{production} \\ \text{(units)} \end{array} = \begin{array}{c} \text{Budget} \\ \text{sales} \\ \text{(units)} \end{array} + \begin{array}{c} \text{Target ending} \\ \text{finished goods} \\ \text{inventory} \\ \text{(units)} \end{array} - \begin{array}{c} \text{Beginning} \\ \text{finished goods} \\ \text{inventory} \\ \text{(units)} \end{array}$$

Schedule 2: Production Budget (in Units)
for the Year Ending December 31, 2014

	Product	
	Casual	**Deluxe**
Budgeted unit sales (Schedule 1)	50,000	10,000
Add target ending finished goods inventory	11,000	500
Total required units	61,000	10,500
Deduct beginning finished goods inventory	1,000	500
Units of finished goods to be produced	60,000	10,000

The production budget drives the various budgeted costs (for example, direct materials, direct manufacturing labor, and manufacturing overhead) Stylistic plans to incur in 2014 to support its revenues budget, taking into account the efficiency improvements it plans to make.

Managers are always looking for opportunities to reduce costs, for example, by redesigning products, improving processes, streamlining manufacturing, and reducing the time it takes to complete various activities such as setting up machines or transporting materials. Making these changes improves a company's competitiveness, but it also requires investment. The budgeting exercise is an ideal time for managers to evaluate their plans and request any financial resources that they might need. We start with the budget for direct materials.

Step 3: Prepare the Direct Material Usage Budget and Direct Material Purchases Budget. The number of units to be produced, calculated in Schedule 2, is the key to computing the usage of direct materials in quantities and in dollars. The direct material quantities used depend on the efficiency with which Stylistic's workers use materials to produce a table. In determining budgets, managers are constantly anticipating ways to make process improvements that increase quality and reduce waste, thereby reducing direct material usage and costs. Senior managers set budgets that motivate production managers to reduce direct material costs and keep negligible work-in-process inventory. We ignore work-in-process inventory when preparing Stylistic's budgets for 2014.

Like many companies, Stylistic has a *bill of materials* stored in its computer systems that it constantly updates for efficiency improvements. This document identifies how each product is manufactured, specifying all materials (and components), the sequence in which the materials are used, the quantity of materials in each finished unit, and the work centers where the operations are performed. For example, the bill of materials would indicate that 12 board feet of red oak and 6 square feet of granite are needed to produce each Casual coffee table and 12 board feet of red oak and 8 square feet of granite are needed to produce each Deluxe coffee table. Direct materials inventories are costed using the first-in, first-out (FIFO) method. The management accountant uses this information to calculate the direct materials usage budget in Schedule 3A.

Schedule 3A: Direct Material Usage Budget in Quantity and Dollars
for the Year Ending December 31, 2014

	Material		
	Red oak	**Granite**	**Total**
Physical Units Budget			
Direct materials required for Casual tables (60,000 units × 12 b.f. and 6 sq. ft.)	720,000 b.f.	360,000 sq. ft.	
Direct materials required for Deluxe tables (10,000 units × 12 b.f. and 8 sq. ft.)	120,000 b.f.	80,000 sq. ft.	
Total quantity of direct materials to be used	840,000 b.f.	440,000 sq. ft.	

	Material		
	Red oak	Granite	Total
Cost Budget			
Available from beginning direct materials inventory (under a FIFO cost-flow assumption) (Given)			
Red oak: 70,000 b.f. × $7 per b.f.	$ 490,000		
Granite: 60,000 sq.ft. × $10 per sq. ft.		$ 600,000	
To be purchased and used this period			
Red oak: (840,000 − 70,000) b.f. × $7 per b.f.	5,390,000		
Granite: (440,000 − 60,000) sq. ft. × $10 per sq. ft.		3,800,000	
Direct materials to be used this period	$5,880,000	$4,400,000	$10,280,000

The only new information needed to prepare the direct materials purchases budget is the level of direct materials inventory Stylistic wants to maintain. Over the course of the year, Stylistic's managers decide to increase the inventory of red oak but reduce the inventory of granite to the planned levels of ending inventory described on page 205. The purchasing manager then prepares the budget for direct material purchases, shown in Schedule 3B:

Schedule 3B: Direct Material Purchases Budget for the Year Ending December 31, 2014

	Material		
	Red oak	Granite	Total
Physical Units Budget			
To be used in production (from Schedule 3A)	840,000 b.f.	440,000 sq. ft.	
Add target ending inventory	80,000 b.f.	20,000 sq. ft.	
Total requirements	920,000 b.f.	460,000 sq. ft.	
Deduct beginning inventory	70,000 b.f.	60,000 sq. ft.	
Purchases to be made	850,000 b.f.	400,000 sq. ft.	
Cost Budget			
Red oak: 850,000 b.f. × $7 per b.f.	$5,950,000		
Granite: 400,000 sq. ft. × $10 per sq. ft.		$4,000,000	
Direct materials to be purchased this period	$5,950,000	$4,000,000	$9,950,000

Step 4: Prepare the Direct Manufacturing Labor Costs Budget. To create the budget for direct manufacturing labor costs, Stylistic's managers estimate wage rates, production methods, process and efficiency improvements, and hiring plans. The company hires direct manufacturing labor workers on an hourly basis. These workers do not work overtime. Manufacturing managers use *labor standards*, the time allowed per unit of output, to calculate the direct manufacturing labor costs budget in Schedule 4 based on the information on pages 205 and 207.

Schedule 4: Direct Manufacturing Labor Costs Budget for the Year Ending December 31, 2014

	Output Units Produced (Schedule 2)	Direct Manufacturing Labor-Hours per Unit	Total Hours	Hourly Wage Rate	Total
Casual	60,000	4	240,000	$20	$4,800,000
Deluxe	10,000	6	60,000	20	1,200,000
Total			300,000		$6,000,000

Step 5: Prepare the Manufacturing Overhead Costs Budget. Stylistic's managers next budget for manufacturing overhead costs such as supervision, depreciation, maintenance, supplies, and power. Managing overhead costs is important but also challenging because it requires managers to understand the various activities needed to manufacture products and the cost drivers of those activities. As we described earlier (page 203), Stylistic's managers identify two activities for manufacturing overhead costs in its activity-based costing system: manufacturing operations and machine setups. The following table presents the activities and their cost drivers.

Manufacturing Overhead Costs	Cost Driver of Variable Component of Overhead Costs	Cost Driver of Fixed Component of Overhead Costs	Manufacturing and Setup Capacity in 2014
Manufacturing Operations Overhead Costs	Direct manufacturing labor-hours	Manufacturing capacity	300,000 direct manufacturing labor-hours
Machine Setup Overhead Costs	Setup labor-hours	Setup capacity	15,000 setup labor-hours

The use of activity-based cost drivers gives rise to **activity-based budgeting (ABB)**, a budgeting method that focuses on the budgeted cost of the activities necessary to produce and sell products and services.

In its activity-based costing system, Stylistic's manufacturing managers estimate various line items of overhead costs that comprise manufacturing operations overhead (that is, all costs for which direct manufacturing labor-hours is the cost driver). Managers identify opportunities for process and efficiency improvements, such as reducing defect rates and the time to manufacture a table, and then calculate budgeted manufacturing operations overhead costs in the operating department. They also determine the resources that they will need from the two support departments—kilowatt-hours of energy from the power department and hours of maintenance service from the maintenance department. The support department managers, in turn, plan the costs of personnel and supplies that they will need in order to provide the operating department with the support services it requires. The costs of the support departments are then allocated (first-stage cost allocation) as part of manufacturing operations overhead. Chapter 15 describes the allocation of support department costs to operating departments when support departments provide services to each other and to operating departments. The first half of Schedule 5 (page 210) shows the various line items of costs that constitute manufacturing operations overhead costs—that is, all variable and fixed overhead costs (in the operating and support departments) that are caused by the 300,000 direct manufacturing labor-hours (the cost driver).

Stylistic budgets costs differently for variable and fixed overhead costs. Consider variable overhead costs of supplies: Stylistic's managers use past historical data and their knowledge of operations to estimate the cost of supplies per direct manufacturing labor-hour, which is \$5. The total budgeted cost of supplies for 2014 is therefore \$5 multiplied by the 300,000 budgeted direct manufacturing labor-hours, for a total of \$1,500,000. The total variable manufacturing operations overhead cost equals \$21.60 per direct manufacturing labor-hour multiplied by the 300,000 budgeted direct manufacturing labor-hours, for a total of \$6,480,000.

For fixed overhead costs, Stylistic's managers start the budgeting process by determining the total fixed manufacturing operations overhead costs of \$2,520,000 needed to support the 300,000 direct manufacturing labor-hours of capacity Stylistic's managers have planned. (Stylistic may not operate at full capacity each year, but its fixed manufacturing operations costs will still be \$2,520,000.) Its fixed manufacturing overhead cost is \$2,520,000 ÷ 300,000 = \$8.40 per direct manufacturing labor-hour (regardless of the budgeted direct manufacturing labor-hours, which may be less than 300,000 in a particular year). That is, each direct manufacturing labor-hour will absorb \$21.60 of variable manufacturing operations overhead plus $8.40 of fixed manufacturing operations overhead for a total of $30 of manufacturing operations overhead cost per direct manufacturing labor-hour.

Next, Stylistic's managers determine how setups will be done for the Casual and Deluxe line of tables, taking into account past experiences and potential improvements in setup efficiency.

For example, managers consider the following:

- Increasing the number of tables produced per batch so fewer batches (and therefore fewer setups) are needed for the budgeted production of tables
- Decreasing the setup time per batch
- Reducing the supervisory time needed, for instance by increasing the skill base of workers

Stylistic's managers forecast the following setup information for the Casual and Deluxe tables:

	Casual Tables	Deluxe Tables	Total
1. Quantity of tables to be produced	60,000 tables	10,000 tables	
2. Number of tables to be produced per batch	50 tables/batch	40 tables/batch	
3. Number of batches (1) ÷ (2)	1,200 batches	250 batches	
4. Setup time per batch	10 hours/batch	12 hours/batch	
5. Total setup-hours (3) × (4)	12,000 hours	3,000 hours	15,000 hours
6. Setup-hours per table (5) ÷ (1)	0.2 hour	0.3 hour	

Using an approach similar to the one described for manufacturing operations overhead costs, Stylistic's managers estimate various line items of costs that comprise machine setup overhead costs (supplies, indirect manufacturing labor, power, depreciation, and supervision)—that is, all costs caused by the 15,000 setup labor-hours (the cost driver): The second half of Schedule 5 summarizes (1) total variable machine setup overhead costs per setup labor-hour = $88($26 + $56 + $6) × the budgeted 15,000 setup labor-hours = $1,320,000 and (2) fixed machine setup overhead costs of $1,680,000 needed to support the 15,000 setup labor-hours of capacity that Stylistic's managers have planned. (Again, Stylistic may not operate at full capacity each year. However, the fixed machine setup costs will still be $1,680,000.) The fixed machine setup cost is $1,680,000 ÷ 15,000 = $112 per setup labor-hour (regardless of the budgeted setup labor-hours, which may be less than 15,000 in a particular year). That is, each setup labor-hour will absorb $88 of variable machine setup overhead cost plus $112 of fixed machine setup overhead cost for a total of $200 of machine setup overhead cost per setup labor-hour.

Schedule 5: Manufacturing Overhead Costs Budget
for the Year Ending December 31, 2014

Manufacturing Operations Overhead Costs		
Variable costs (for 300,000 direct manufacturing labor-hours)		
Supplies ($5 per direct manufacturing labor-hour)	$1,500,000	
Indirect manufacturing labor ($5.60 per direct manufacturing labor-hour)	1,680,000	
Power (support department costs) ($7 per direct manufacturing labor-hour)	2,100,000	
Maintenance (support department costs) ($4 per direct manufacturing labor-hour)	1,200,000	$6,480,000
Fixed costs (to support capacity of 300,000 direct manufacturing labor-hours)		
Depreciation	1,020,000	
Supervision	390,000	
Power (support department costs)	630,000	
Maintenance (support department costs)	480,000	2,520,000
Total manufacturing operations overhead costs		$9,000,000

Machine Setup Overhead Costs

Variable costs (for 15,000 setup labor-hours)		
Supplies ($26 per setup labor-hour)	$ 390,000	
Indirect manufacturing labor ($56 per setup labor-hour)	840,000	
Power (support department costs) ($6 per setup labor-hour)	90,000	$ 1,320,000
Fixed costs (to support capacity of 15,000 setup labor-hours)		
Depreciation	603,000	
Supervision	1,050,000	
Power (support department costs)	27,000	1,680,000
Total machine setup overhead costs		$ 3,000,000
Total manufacturing overhead costs		$12,000,000

Note how using activity-based cost drivers provide additional and detailed information that improves decision making compared with budgeting based solely on output-based cost drivers. Of course, managers must always evaluate whether the expected benefit of adding more cost drivers exceeds the expected cost.[5]

Note that Stylistic is scheduled to operate at capacity. Therefore, the budgeted quantity of the cost allocation base/cost driver is the same for variable overhead costs and fixed overhead costs—300,000 direct manufacturing labor-hours for manufacturing operations overhead costs and 15,000 setup labor-hours for machine setup overhead costs. In this case, the budgeted rate for the manufacturing operations overhead cost does not have to be calculated separately for variable costs and for fixed costs. It can be calculated directly by estimating total budgeted manufacturing operations overhead: $9,000,000 ÷ 300,000 direct manufacturing labor-hours = $30 per direct manufacturing labor-hour. Similarly, the budgeted rate for machine setup overhead cost can be calculated as total budgeted machine setup overhead: $3,000,000 ÷ 15,000 budgeted setup hours = $200 per setup-hour.

Step 6: Prepare the Ending Inventories Budget. Schedule 6A shows the computation of the unit cost of coffee tables started and completed in 2014. These calculations are needed to calculate the ending inventories budget and the budgeted cost of goods sold. In accordance with Generally Accepted Accounting Principles, Stylistic treats both variable and fixed manufacturing overhead as inventoriable (product) costs. Manufacturing operations overhead costs are allocated to finished goods inventory at the budgeted rate of $30 per direct manufacturing labor-hour. Machine setup overhead costs are allocated to finished goods inventory at the budgeted rate of $200 per setup-hour.

Schedule 6A: Unit Costs of Ending Finished Goods Inventory December 31, 2014

		Product			
		Casual Tables		Deluxe Tables	
	Cost per Unit of Input	Input per Unit of Output	Total	Input per Unit of Output	Total
Red oak	$ 7	12 b.f.	$ 84	12 b.f.	$ 84
Granite	10	6 sq. ft.	60	8 sq. ft.	80
Direct manufacturing labor	20	4 hrs.	80	6 hrs.	120
Manufacturing operations overhead	30	4 hrs.	120	6 hrs.	180
Machine setup overhead	200	0.2 hrs.	40	0.3 hrs.	60
Total			$384		$524

Under the FIFO method, managers use this unit cost to calculate the cost of target ending inventories of finished goods in Schedule 6B.

[5] The Stylistic example illustrates ABB using manufacturing operations and setup costs included in Stylistic's manufacturing overhead costs budget. ABB implementations in practice include costs in many parts of the value chain. For an example, see Sofia Borjesson, "A Case Study on Activity-Based Budgeting," *Journal of Cost Management* 10, no. 4 (Winter 1997): 7–18.

Schedule 6B: Ending Inventories Budget December 31, 2014

	Quantity	Cost per Unit		Total
Direct materials				
Red oak	80,000*	$7	$ 560,000	
Granite	20,000*	10	200,000	$ 760,000
Finished goods				
Casual	11,000**	$384***	$4,224,000	
Deluxe	500**	524***	262,000	4,486,000
Total ending inventory				$5,246,000

*Data are from page 205. **Data are from page 205. ***From Schedule 6A, this is based on 2014 costs of manufacturing finished goods because under the FIFO costing method, the units in finished goods ending inventory consists of units that are produced during 2014.

Step 7: Prepare the Cost of Goods Sold Budget. The manufacturing and purchase managers, together with the management accountant, use information from Schedules 3–6 to prepare Schedule 7—the cost of goods sold expense that will be matched against revenues to calculate Stylistic's budgeted gross margin for 2014.

Schedule 7: Cost of Goods Sold Budget for the Year Ending December 31, 2014

	From Schedule		Total
Beginning finished goods inventory, January 1, 2014	Given*		$ 646,000
Direct materials used	3A	$10,280,000	
Direct manufacturing labor	4	6,000,000	
Manufacturing overhead	5	12,000,000	
Cost of goods manufactured			28,280,000
Cost of goods available for sale			28,926,000
Deduct ending finished goods inventory, December 31, 2014	6B		4,486,000
Cost of goods sold			$24,440,000

*Based on beginning inventory values in 2014 for Casual tables, $384,000, and Deluxe tables, $262,000 (page 205).

Step 8: Prepare the Nonmanufacturing Costs Budget. Schedules 2–7 represent budgets for Stylistic's manufacturing costs. Stylistic also incurs nonmanufacturing costs in other parts of the value chain—product design, marketing, and distribution. Just as in the case of manufacturing costs, the key to managing nonmanufacturing overhead costs is to understand the various activities that will be needed to support the design, marketing, and distribution of Deluxe and Casual tables in 2014 and the cost drivers of those activities. Managers in these functions of the value chain build in process and efficiency improvements and prepare nonmanufacturing cost budgets on the basis of the quantities of cost drivers planned for 2014.

The number of design changes is the cost driver for product design costs. Product design costs of $1,024,000 are fixed costs for 2014 and adjusted at the start of the year based on the number of design changes planned for 2014.

Total revenue is the cost driver for the variable portion of marketing (and sales) costs. The commission paid to salespeople equals 6.5 cents per dollar (or 6.5%) of revenues. Managers budget the fixed component of marketing costs, $1,330,000, at the start of the year based on budgeted revenues for 2014.

Cubic feet of tables sold and shipped (Casual: 18 cubic feet × 50,000 tables + Deluxe: 24 cubic feet × 10,000 tables = 1,140,000 cubic feet) is the cost driver of the variable component of budgeted distribution costs. Variable distribution costs equal $2 per cubic foot. The fixed component of budgeted distribution costs equal to $1,596,000 varies with the company's distribution capacity, which in 2014 is 1,140,000 cubic feet (to support the distribution of 50,000 Casual tables and 10,000 Deluxe tables). For brevity, Schedule 8 shows the product design, marketing, and distribution costs budget for 2014 in a single schedule.

Exhibit 6-3

Budgeted Income Statement for Stylistic Furniture

	A	B	C	D
1	**Budgeted Income Statement for Stylistic Furniture**			
2	**For the Year Ending December 31, 2014**			
3	Revenues	Schedule 1		$38,000,000
4	Cost of goods sold	Schedule 7		24,440,000
5	Gross margin			13,560,000
6	Operating costs			
7	Product design costs	Schedule 8	$1,024,000	
8	Marketing costs	Schedule 8	3,800,000	
9	Distribution costs	Schedule 8	3,876,000	8,700,000
10	Operating income			$ 4,860,000

Schedule 8: Nonmanufacturing Costs Budget
for the Year Ending December 31, 2014

Business Function	Variable Costs	Fixed Costs	Total Costs
Product design	—	$1,024,000	$1,024,000
Marketing (Variable cost: $38,000,000 × 0.065)	$2,470,000	1,330,000	3,800,000
Distribution (Variable cost: $2 × 1,140,000 cu. ft.)	2,280,000	1,596,000	3,876,000
	$4,750,000	$3,950,000	$8,700,000

Step 9: Prepare the Budgeted Income Statement. The CEO and managers of various business functions, with help from the management accountant, use information in Schedules 1, 7, and 8 to finalize the budgeted income statement, shown in Exhibit 6-3. The style used in Exhibit 6-3 is typical, but managers and accountants could include more details in the income statement. As more details are put in the income statement, fewer supporting schedules are needed.

Budgeting is a cross-functional activity. The strategies developed by top managers for achieving a company's revenue and operating income goals affect the costs planned for the different business functions of the value chain. For example, the budgeted increase in sales at Stylistic based on spending more for marketing must be matched with higher production costs to ensure there is an adequate supply of tables and with higher distribution costs to ensure the timely delivery of tables to customers. Rex Jordan, the CEO of Stylistic Furniture, is very pleased with the 2014 budget. It calls for a 10% increase in operating income compared with 2013. The keys to achieving a higher operating income are a significant increase in sales of Deluxe tables and process improvements and efficiency gains throughout the value chain. As Rex studies the budget more carefully, however, he is struck by two comments appended to the budget: First, to achieve the budgeted number of tables sold, Stylistic may need to reduce its selling prices by 3% to $582 for Casual tables and to $776 for Deluxe tables. Second, a supply shortage in direct materials may result in a 5% increase in the prices of direct materials (red oak and granite) above the material prices anticipated in the 2014 budget. Even if direct materials prices increase, selling prices are anticipated to remain the same. He asks Tina Larsen, a management accountant, to use Stylistic's financial planning model to evaluate how these outcomes will affect budgeted operating income.

Decision Point

What is the operating budget and what are its components?

Learning Objective 4

Use computer-based financial planning models for sensitivity analysis

...for example, understand the effects of changes in selling prices and direct material prices on budgeted income

Financial Planning Models and Sensitivity Analysis

Financial planning models are mathematical representations of the relationships among operating activities, financing activities, and other factors that affect the master budget. Managers can use computer-based systems, such as enterprise resource planning (ERP)

systems, to perform calculations for these planning models. Managers use budgeting tools within ERP systems to simplify budgeting, reduce the need to re-input data, and reduce the time required to prepare budgets. Concepts in Action: Web-Enabled Budgeting and Hendrick Motorsports provides an example of one such company. ERP systems store vast quantities of information about the materials, machines and equipment, labor, power, maintenance, and setups needed to manufacture different products. Once managers identify sales quantities for different products, the software can quickly compute the budgeted costs for manufacturing these products. ERP systems also help managers budget for nonmanufacturing costs.

As they prepare operating budgets, managers do not focus only on what they can achieve. They also identify the risks they face such as a potential decline in demand for the company's products, the entry of a new competitor, or an increase in the prices of different inputs. Sensitivity analysis is a useful tool that helps managers evaluate these risks. *Sensitivity analysis* is a "what-if" technique that examines how a result will change if the original predicted data are not achieved or if an underlying assumption changes. Software packages typically have a sensitivity analysis module managers can use in their planning and budgeting activities.

To see how sensitivity analysis works, we consider two scenarios identified as possibly affecting Stylistic Furniture's budget model for 2014. Either of the two scenarios could happen but not both together.

Scenario 1: A 3% decrease in the selling price of the Casual table and a 3% decrease in the selling price of the Deluxe table.

Scenario 2: A 5% increase in the price per board foot of red oak and a 5% increase in the price per square foot of granite.

Exhibit 6-4 presents the budgeted operating income for the two scenarios.

Note that under Scenario 1, a change in the selling price per table affects revenues (Schedule 1) as well as variable marketing costs (sales commissions, Schedule 8). The Problem for Self-Study at the end of the chapter shows the revised schedules for Scenario 1. Similarly, a change in the price of direct materials affects the direct material usage budget (Schedule 3A), the unit cost of ending finished goods inventory (Schedule 6A), the ending finished goods inventories budget (in Schedule 6B), and the cost of goods sold budget (Schedule 7). Sensitivity analysis is especially useful to managers incorporating these interrelationships into their budgeting decisions.

Decision Point

How can managers plan for changes in the assumptions underlying the budget and manage risk?

Exhibit 6-4 shows that operating income decreases substantially if selling prices decrease but declines much less if direct materials prices increase by 5%. The sensitivity analysis prompts Stylistic's managers to put in place contingency plans. For example, should selling prices decline in 2014, Stylistic may choose to postpone some product development programs that it had included in its 2014 budget but that could be deferred to a later year. More generally, when the success or viability of a venture is highly dependent

Exhibit 6-4 Effect of Changes in Budget Assumptions on Budgeted Operating Income for Stylistic Furniture

Home Insert Page Layout Formulas Data Review View

	A	B	C	D	E	F	G	H	I
1	Key Assumptions								
2		Units Sold		Selling Price		Direct Material Cost		Budgeted Operating Income	
3	What-If Scenario	Casual	Deluxe	Casual	Deluxe	Red Oak	Granite	Dollars	Change from Master Budget
4	Master budget	50,000	10,000	$600	$800	$7.00	$10.00	$4,860,000	
5	Scenario 1	50,000	10,000	582	776	$7.00	$10.00	3,794,100	22% decrease
6	Scenario 2	50,000	10,000	600	800	$7.35	$10.50	4,418,000	9% decrease

Concepts in Action

Web-Enabled Budgeting and Hendrick Motorsports

Many companies use Web-based software packages to manage budgeting and forecasting functions across the organization. One unique company implementing Web-enabled budgeting is Hendrick Motorsports. Featuring drivers Jimmie Johnson and Dale Earnhardt, Jr., Hendrick is the premier NASCAR Sprint Cup stock car racing organization, with four full-time racing teams that bring in more than $125 million in sponsorship money annually.

The tasks at Hendrick include accounting and marketing to engine building and racecar driving. Hendrick has multiple functional areas and units, varied worksites, and an environment that is ever changing. Hendrick uses Microsoft Forecaster software, a Web-based software package, to allow its financial managers to seamlessly manage the planning and budgeting process.

Authorized users from each functional area or team sign on to the application through the corporate intranet and prepare their budgets online. Managers complete the annual budgeting process in only six weeks, a 50% reduction in the time spent budgeting and planning, which is critical given NASCAR's short off-season. Hendrick's system frees the finance department to work on strategy, analysis, and decision making.

Security on the system is tight: Access is limited to only the accounts that a manager is authorized to budget. (For example, Dale Earnhardt, Jr.'s crew chief is not able to see what Jimmie Johnson's team members are doing.) The software allows users at the racetrack to access the application remotely, enabling managers to receive or update real-time "actuals" from the system. In this way, team managers know their allotted expenses for each race.

Sources: Badenhausen, Kurt. 2013. Hendrick "Motorsports Tops List Of Nascar's Most Valuable Teams." Forbes.com, March 13. http://www.forbes.com/sites/kurtbadenhausen/2013/03/13/hendrick-motorsports-tops-list-of-nascars-most-valuable-teams/; Goff, John. 2004. "In the Fast Lane." *CFO Magazine*, December 1; Hendrick Motorsports. 2013. "About Hendrick Motorsports." Hendrick Motorsports Web site, September 26. www.hendrickmotorsports.com; Lampe, Scott. 2003. "NASCAR Racing Team Stays on Track with FRx Software's Comprehensive Budget Planning Solution." *DM Review*, July 1; Microsoft Corporation. 2009. "Microsoft Forecaster: Hendrick Motorsports Customer Video." October 8. http://www.microsoft.com/BusinessSolutions/frx_hendrick_video.mspx

on attaining one or more targets, managers should frequently update their budgets as uncertainty is resolved. These updated budgets can help managers adjust expenditure levels as circumstances change.

Earlier in this chapter we described a rolling budget as a budget that is always available for a specified future period. Rolling budgets are constantly updated to reflect the latest cost and revenue information and make managers responsive to changing conditions and market needs.

Instructors and students who, at this point, want to explore the cash budget and the budgeted balance sheet for the Stylistic Furniture example can skip ahead to the appendix on page 224.

Learning Objective 5

Describe responsibility centers

...a part of an organization that a manager is accountable for

and responsibility accounting

...measurement of plans and actual results that a manager is accountable for

Budgeting and Responsibility Accounting

To attain the goals described in the master budget, top managers must coordinate the efforts of all of the firm's employees—from senior executives through middle levels of management to every supervised worker. To coordinate the company's efforts, top managers assign a certain amount of responsibility to lower-level managers and then hold them accountable for how they perform. Consequently, how each company structures its organization significantly shapes how it coordinates its actions.

Organization Structure and Responsibility

Organization structure is an arrangement of lines of responsibility within an organization. A company such as Exxon Mobil is organized by business function, refining, marketing, and so on—with the president of each business function having decision-making authority over his or her function. Other companies, such as Procter & Gamble, the household-products giant, are organized primarily by product line or brand. The managers of the individual divisions (toothpaste, soap, and so on) have decision-making authority concerning all the business functions (manufacturing, marketing, and so on) within that division.

Each manager, regardless of level, is in charge of a responsibility center. A **responsibility center** is a part, segment, or subunit of an organization whose manager is accountable for a specified set of activities. Higher-level managers supervise centers with broader responsibility and larger numbers of subordinates. **Responsibility accounting** is a system that measures the plans, budgets, actions, and actual results of each responsibility center. There are four types of responsibility centers:

1. **Cost center**—the manager is accountable for costs only.
2. **Revenue center**—the manager is accountable for revenues only.
3. **Profit center**—the manager is accountable for revenues and costs.
4. **Investment center**—the manager is accountable for investments, revenues, and costs.

The maintenance department of a Marriott hotel is a cost center because the maintenance manager is responsible only for costs, and the budget is based only on costs. The sales department is a revenue center because the sales manager is responsible primarily for revenues, and the department's budget is primarily based on revenues. The hotel manager is in charge of a profit center because the manager is accountable for both revenues and costs, and the hotel's budget is based on revenues and costs. The regional manager responsible for determining the amount to be invested in new hotel projects and for revenues and costs generated from these investments is in charge of an investment center. So, this center's budget is based on revenues, costs, and the investment base.

A responsibility center can be structured to promote better alignment of individual and company goals. For example, until recently, OPD, an office products distributor, operated its sales department solely as a revenue center. Each salesperson received a commission of 3% of the revenues per order, regardless of its size, the cost of processing it, or the cost of delivering the office products. Upon analyzing customer profitability, OPD found that many customers were unprofitable. The main reason was the high ordering and delivery costs of small orders. OPD's managers decided to make the sales department a profit center, accountable for revenues and costs, and to change the incentive system for salespeople to 15% of the monthly profits of their customers. The costs for each customer included the ordering and delivery costs. The effect of this change was immediate. The sales department began charging customers for ordering and delivery, and salespeople at OPD actively encouraged customers to consolidate their purchases into fewer orders. As a result, each order began producing larger revenues. The profitability of customers increased because of a 40% reduction in ordering and delivery costs in 1 year.

Feedback

Budgets coupled with responsibility accounting provide feedback to top managers about the performance relative to the budget of different responsibility center managers.

Differences between actual results and budgeted amounts—called *variances*—can help managers implement strategies and evaluate them in three ways:

1. **Early warning.** Variances alert managers early to events not easily or immediately evident. Managers can then take corrective actions or exploit the available opportunities. For example, after observing a small decline in sales during a period, managers may want to investigate if this is an indication of an even steeper decline to come later in the year.

2. **Performance evaluation.** Variances prompt managers to probe how well the company has implemented its strategies. Were materials and labor used efficiently? Was R&D spending increased as planned? Did product warranty costs decrease as planned?
3. **Evaluating strategy.** Variances sometimes signal to managers that their strategies are ineffective. For example, a company seeking to compete by reducing costs and improving quality may find that it is achieving these goals but that it is having little effect on sales and profits. Top management may then want to reevaluate the strategy.

Responsibility and Controllability

Controllability is the degree of influence a specific manager has over costs, revenues, or related items for which he or she is responsible. A **controllable cost** is any cost primarily subject to the influence of a given *responsibility center manager* for a given *period.* A responsibility accounting system could either exclude all uncontrollable costs from a manager's performance report or segregate such costs from the controllable costs. For example, a machining supervisor's performance report might be confined to direct materials, direct manufacturing labor, power, and machine maintenance costs and might exclude costs such as rent and taxes paid on the plant.

In practice, controllability is difficult to pinpoint for two main reasons:

1. Few costs are clearly under the sole influence of one manager. For example, purchasing managers are able to affect the prices their firms pay for direct materials, but these prices also depend on market conditions beyond the managers' control. Similarly, the decisions production managers make can affect the quantities of direct materials used but also depend on the quality of materials purchased. Moreover, managers often work in teams. Think about how difficult it is to evaluate individual responsibility in a team situation.
2. With a long enough time span, all costs will come under somebody's control. However, most performance reports focus on periods of a year or less. A current manager may benefit from a predecessor's accomplishments or may inherit a predecessor's problems and inefficiencies. For example, managers may have to work with undesirable contracts with suppliers or labor unions negotiated by their predecessors. How can we separate what the current manager actually controls from the results of decisions other managers made? Exactly what is the current manager accountable for? The answers may not be clear-cut.

Executives differ in how they embrace the controllability notion when evaluating people reporting to them. Some CEOs regard the budget as a firm commitment subordinates must meet and that "numbers always tell the story." Failing to meet the budget is viewed unfavorably. An executive once noted, "You can miss your plan once, but you wouldn't want to miss it twice." Such an approach forces managers to learn to perform under adverse circumstances and to deliver consistent results year after year. It removes the need to discuss which costs are controllable and which are noncontrollable because it does not matter whether the performance was due to controllable or uncontrollable factors. The disadvantage of this approach is that it subjects a manager's compensation to greater risk. It also de-motivates managers when uncontrollable factors adversely affect their performance evaluations even though they have performed well in terms of factors they can control.

Other CEOs believe that focusing on making the numbers in a budget puts excessive pressure on managers. These CEOs adjust for noncontrollable factors and evaluate managers only on what they can control, such as their performance relative to competitors. Using relative performance measures takes out the effects of favorable or unfavorable business conditions that are outside the manager's control and affect all competing managers in the same way. The challenge is in finding the correct benchmarks. Relative performance measures, however, reduce the pressure on managers to perform when circumstances are difficult.

Managers should avoid thinking about controllability only in the context of performance evaluation. Responsibility accounting is more far-reaching. It focuses on gaining *information and knowledge,* not only on control. *Responsibility accounting helps managers to first focus on whom they should ask to obtain information and not on whom they should blame.* Comparing the shortfall of actual revenues to budgeted revenues is certainly relevant when evaluating the performance of the sales managers of Ritz-Carlton hotels. But the more fundamental purpose of responsibility accounting is to gather information from the sales managers to enable future improvement. Holding them accountable for sales motivates them to learn about market conditions and dynamics outside of their personal control but relevant when deciding the actions the hotels might take to increase their future sales. Similarly, purchasing managers may be held accountable for total purchase costs, not because of their ability to control market prices, but because of their ability to predict and respond to uncontrollable prices and understand their causes.

Decision Point

How do companies use responsibility centers? Should performance reports of responsibility center managers include only costs the manager can control?

Performance reports for responsibility centers are sometimes designed to change managers' behavior in the direction top managers desire even if the reports decrease controllability. Consider a manufacturing department. If the department is designated as a cost center, the manufacturing manager may emphasize efficiency and deemphasize the pleas of sales personnel for faster service and rush orders that reduce efficiency and increase costs. Evaluating the department as a profit center decreases the manufacturing manager's controllability (because the manufacturing manager has limited influence on sales) but it motivates the manager to look more favorably at rush orders that benefit sales. She will weigh the impact of decisions on costs and revenues rather than on costs alone.

Call centers provide another example. If designated as a cost center, the call-center manager will focus on controlling operating costs, for example, by decreasing the time customer representatives spend on each call. If designed as a profit center, the call-center manager will encourage customer-service representatives to balance efficiency with better customer service and efforts to upsell and cross-sell other products. Hewlett-Packard, Microsoft, Oracle, and others offer software platforms designed to prompt and help call center personnel turn their cost centers into profit centers. The new adage is, "Every service call is a sales call."

Learning Objective 6

Recognize the human aspects of budgeting

...to engage subordinate managers in the budgeting process

Human Aspects of Budgeting

Why did we discuss the master budget and responsibility accounting in the same chapter? Primarily to emphasize that human factors are crucial in budgeting. Too often, budgeting is thought of as a mechanical tool because the budgeting techniques themselves are free of emotion. However, the administration of budgeting requires education, persuasion, and intelligent interpretation.

Budgetary Slack

As we discussed earlier in this chapter, budgeting is most effective when lower-level managers actively participate and meaningfully engage in the budgeting process. Participation adds credibility to the budgeting process and makes employees more committed and accountable for meeting the budget. But participation requires "honest" communication about the business from subordinates and lower-level managers to their bosses.

At times, subordinates may try to "play games" and build in *budgetary slack*. **Budgetary slack** is the practice of underestimating budgeted revenues or overestimating budgeted costs to make budgeted targets easier to achieve. This practice frequently occurs when budget variances (the differences between actual results and budgeted amounts) are used to evaluate the performance of line managers and their subordinates. Line managers are also unlikely to be fully honest in their budget communications if top managers mechanically institute across-the-board cost reductions (say, a 10% reduction in all areas) in the face of projected revenue reductions.

Budgetary slack provides managers with a hedge against unexpected adverse circumstances. But budgetary slack also misleads top managers about the true profit potential of the company, which leads to inefficient resource planning and allocation and poor coordination of activities across different parts of the company.

To avoid the problems of budgetary slack, some companies use budgets primarily for planning and to a lesser extent for performance evaluation. They evaluate the performance of managers using multiple indicators that take into account various factors that become known during the course of the year, such as the prevailing business environment and the performance of their industry or their competitors. Evaluating performance in this way takes time and requires careful judgment.

One approach to dealing with budgetary slack is to obtain good benchmark data when setting the budget. Consider the plant manager of a beverage bottler. Suppose top managers could purchase a consulting firm's study of productivity levels—such as the number of bottles filled per hour—at a number of comparable plants owned by other bottling companies. The managers could then share this independent information with the plant manager and use it to set the operations budget. Using external benchmark performance measures reduces a manager's ability to set budget levels that are easy to achieve.

Rolling budgets are another approach to reducing budgetary slack. As we discussed earlier in the chapter, companies that use rolling budgets always have a budget for a defined period, say 12 months, by adding, at the end of each quarter, a budget for one more quarter to replace the quarter just ended. The continuous updating of budget information and the richer information it provides reduce the opportunity to create budgetary slack relative to when budgeting is done only annually.

Some companies, such as IBM, have designed innovative performance evaluation measures that reward managers based on the subsequent accuracy of the forecasts used in preparing budgets. For example, the *higher and more accurate* the budgeted profit forecasts of division managers, the higher their incentive bonuses.[6] Another approach to reducing budgetary slack is for managers to involve themselves regularly in understanding what their subordinates are doing. Such involvement should not result in managers dictating the decisions and actions of subordinates. Rather, a manager's involvement should take the form of providing support, challenging in a motivational way the assumptions subordinates make, and enhancing mutual learning about the operations. Regular interaction with their subordinates allows managers to become knowledgeable about the operations and diminishes the ability of subordinates to create slack in their budgets. Instead, the subordinates and their superiors have in-depth dialogues about the budgets and performance goals. Managers then evaluate the performance of subordinates using both subjective (and objective) measures. Of course, using subjective measures requires subordinates to trust their managers to evaluate them fairly.

In addition to developing their organization's strategies, top managers are responsible for defining a company's core values and norms and building employee commitment toward adhering to them. These values and norms describe what constitutes acceptable and unacceptable behavior. For example, Johnson & Johnson (J & J) has a credo that describes its responsibilities to doctors, patients, employees, communities, and shareholders. Employees are trained in the credo to help them understand the behavior that is expected of them. J & J managers are often promoted from within and are therefore very familiar with the work of the employees reporting to them. J & J also has a strong culture of mentoring subordinates. J & J's values and employee practices create an environment where managers know their subordinates well, which helps to reduce budgetary slack.

Stretch Targets

Many of the best performing companies, such as General Electric, Microsoft, and Novartis, set "stretch" targets. Stretch targets are challenging but achievable levels of expected performance, intended to create a little discomfort. Creating some performance anxiety motivates employees to exert extra effort and attain better performance, but setting targets that are very difficult or impossible to achieve hurts performance because employees give up on trying to achieve them. Organizations such as Goldman Sachs also use "horizontal" stretch goal initiatives. The aim is to enhance professional development of employees by asking them to take on significantly different responsibilities or roles outside their comfort zone.

---

[6] For an excellent discussion of these issues, see Chapter 14 ("Formal Models in Budgeting and Incentive Contracts") in Robert S. Kaplan and Anthony A. Atkinson, *Advanced Management Accounting*, 3rd ed. (Upper Saddle River, NJ: Prentice Hall, 1998).

A major rationale for stretch targets is their psychological motivation. Consider the following two compensation arrangements offered to a salesperson:

- In the first arrangement, the salesperson is paid $80,000 for achieving a sales target of $1,000,000 and 8 cents for every dollar of sales above $1,000,000 up to $1,100,000.
- In the second arrangement, the salesperson is paid $88,000 for achieving a sales target of $1,100,000 (a stretch target) with a reduction in compensation of 8 cents for every dollar of sales less than $1,100,000 up to $1,000,000.

For simplicity we assume that sales will be between $1,000,000 and $1,100,000.

The salesperson receives the same level of compensation under the two arrangements for all levels of sales between $1,000,000 and $1,100,000. The question is whether the psychological motivation is the same in the two compensation arrangements. Many executives who favor stretch targets point to the asymmetric way in which salespeople psychologically perceive the two compensation arrangements. In the first arrangement, achieving the sales target of $1,000,000 is seen as good, and everything above it as a bonus. In the second arrangement, not reaching the stretch sales target of $1,100,000 is seen as a failure. If salespeople are loss averse, that is, they feel the pain of loss more than the joy of success, they will work harder under the second arrangement to achieve sales of $1,100,000 and not fail.

Ethics

At no point should the pressure for performance embedded in stretch targets push employees to engage in illegal or unethical practices. The more a company tries to push performance, the greater the emphasis it must place on training employees to follow its code of conduct to prohibit behavior that is out of bounds (for example, no bribery, side payments, or dishonest dealings) and its norms and values (for example, putting customers first and not compromising on quality).

Ethical questions are sometimes subtle and not clear-cut. Consider, for example, a division manager, faced with the choice of doing maintenance on a machine at the end of 2013 or early in 2014. It is preferable to do the maintenance in 2013 because delaying maintenance increases the probability of the machine breaking down. But doing so would mean that the manager will not reach his 2013 stretch target for operating income and lose some of his bonus. If the risks of a breakdown and loss are substantial, many observers would view delaying maintenance as unethical. If the risk is minimal, there may be more debate as to whether delaying maintenance is unethical.

Many managers regard budgets negatively. To them, the word *budget* is about as popular as, say, *downsizing, layoff,* or *strike.* Top managers must convince their subordinates that the budget is a tool designed to help them set and reach goals. As with all tools of management, it has its benefits and challenges. Budgets must be used thoughtfully and wisely, but whatever the manager's perspective on budgets—pro or con—they are not remedies for weak management talent, faulty organization, or a poor accounting system.

Kaizen Budgeting

Chapter 1 noted the importance of continuous improvement, or *kaizen* in Japanese. **Kaizen budgeting** explicitly incorporates continuous improvement anticipated during the budget period into the budget numbers. A number of companies that focus on cost reduction, including General Electric in the United States and Toyota in Japan, use Kaizen budgeting to continuously reduce costs. Much of the cost reduction associated with Kaizen budgeting arises from many small improvements rather than "quantum leaps." The improvements tend to come from employee suggestions as a result of managers creating a culture that values, recognizes, and rewards these suggestions. Employees who actually do the job, whether in manufacturing, sales, or distribution, have the best information and knowledge of how the job can be done better.

As an example, throughout our nine budgeting steps for Stylistic Furniture, we assumed 4 hours of direct labor time were required to manufacture each Casual coffee table. A Kaizen budgeting approach would incorporate continuous improvement by prescribing 4.00 direct manufacturing labor-hours per table for the first quarter of 2014, 3.95 hours for the second quarter, 3.90 hours for the third quarter, and so on. The implications of these reductions would be lower direct manufacturing labor costs as well as lower variable manufacturing operations overhead costs because direct manufacturing labor is the driver of these costs. If Stylistic Furniture doesn't meet continuous improvement goals, its managers will explore the reasons behind the failure to meet the goals and either adjust the targets or seek input from employees to implement process improvements. Of course, top managers should encourage managers and employees at all levels to try to find a way to achieve bigger (if periodic) cost reductions as well by changing operating processes and supply-chain relationships.

Managers can also apply Kaizen budgeting to activities such as setups with the goal of reducing setup time and setup costs or distribution with the goal of reducing the cost per cubic foot of shipping tables. Kaizen budgeting for specific activities is a key building block of the master budget for companies that use the Kaizen approach.

A growing number of cash-strapped states and agencies in the United States are using Kaizen techniques to bring together government workers, regulators, and end users of government processes to identify ways to reduce inefficiencies and eliminate bureaucratic procedures. Several state environmental agencies, for example, have conducted a Kaizen session or are planning one.[7] The U.S. Postal Service has identified many different programs to reduce its costs. The success of these efforts will depend heavily on human factors such as the commitment and engagement of managers and other employees to make these changes.

Decision Point

Why are human factors crucial in budgeting?

Budgeting in Multinational Companies

Learning Objective 7

Appreciate the special challenges of budgeting in multinational companies

...exposure to currency fluctuations and to different legal, political, and economic environments

Multinational companies, such as FedEx, Kraft, and Pfizer, have operations in many countries. An international presence has benefits—access to new markets and resources—and drawbacks—operating in less-familiar business environments and exposure to currency fluctuations. Multinational companies earn revenues and incur expenses in many different currencies and must translate their operating performance into a single currency (say, U.S. dollars) for reporting results to their shareholders each quarter. This translation is based on the average exchange rates that prevail during the quarter. As a result, managers of multinational companies budget in different currencies and also budget for foreign exchange rates. This requires managers and management accountants to anticipate potential changes in exchange rates that might occur during the year. To reduce the possible negative impact a company could experience as a result of unfavorable exchange rate movements, finance managers frequently use sophisticated techniques such as forward, future, and option contracts to minimize exposure to foreign currency fluctuations (see Chapter 11). Besides currency issues, managers at multinational companies need to understand the political, legal, and, in particular, economic environments of the different countries in which they operate when preparing budgets. For example, in countries such as Turkey, Zimbabwe, and Guinea, annual inflation rates are very high, resulting in sharp declines in the value of the local currency. Managers also need to consider differences in tax regimes, especially when the company transfers goods or services across the many countries in which it operates (see Chapter 22).

When there is considerable business and exchange rate uncertainty related to global operations, a natural question to ask is: "Do the managers of multinational companies find budgeting to be a helpful tool?" The answer is yes. However, in these circumstances the budgeting is not done so much to evaluate the firm's performance relative to its budgets—which can be meaningless when conditions are so volatile—as it is to help managers adapt their plans and coordinate the actions a company needs to take. Senior managers evaluate performance more subjectively, based on how well subordinate managers have managed in these constantly changing and volatile environments.

Decision Point

What are the special challenges involved in budgeting at multinational companies?

[7] For details, see "State Governments, Including Ohio's, Embrace Kaizen to Seek Efficiency via Japanese Methods," http://www.cleveland.com (December 12, 2008).

Problem for Self-Study

Consider the Stylistic Furniture example described earlier. Suppose that to maintain its sales quantities, Stylistic needs to decrease selling prices to $582 per Casual table and $776 per Deluxe table, a 3% decrease in the selling prices used in the chapter illustration. All other data are unchanged.

Required

Prepare a budgeted income statement, including all necessary detailed supporting budget schedules that are different from the schedules presented in the chapter. Indicate those schedules that will remain unchanged.

Solution

Schedules 1 and 8 will change. Schedule 1 changes because a change in selling price affects revenues. Schedule 8 changes because revenues are a cost driver of marketing costs (sales commissions). The remaining Schedules 2–7 will not change because a change in selling price has no effect on manufacturing costs. The revised schedules and the new budgeted income statement follow.

Schedule 1: Revenues Budget
for the Year Ending December 31, 2014

	Selling Price	Units	Total Revenues
Casual tables	$582	50,000	$29,100,000
Deluxe tables	776	10,000	7,760,000
Total			$36,860,000

Schedule 8: Nonmanufacturing Costs Budget
for the Year Ending December 31, 2014

Business Function	Variable Costs	Fixed Costs (as in Schedule 8, page 213)	Total Costs
Product design		$1,024,000	$1,024,000
Marketing (Variable cost: $36,860,000 × 0.065)	$2,395,900	1,330,000	3,725,900
Distribution (Variable cost: $2 × 1,140,000 cu. ft.)	2,280,000	1,596,000	3,876,000
	$4,675,900	$3,950,000	$8,625,900

Stylistic Furniture Budgeted Income Statement
for the Year Ending December 31, 2014

Revenues	Schedule 1		$36,860,000
Cost of goods sold	Schedule 7		24,440,000
Gross margin			12,420,000
Operating costs			
Product design	Schedule 8	$1,024,000	
Marketing costs	Schedule 8	3,725,900	
Distribution costs	Schedule 8	3,876,000	8,625,900
Operating income			$ 3,794,100

Decision Points

The following question-and-answer format summarizes the chapter's learning objectives. Each decision presents a key question related to a learning objective. The guidelines are the answer to that question.

Decision	Guidelines
1. What is the master budget, and why is it useful?	The master budget summarizes the financial projections of all the company's budgets. It expresses management's operating and financing plans—the formalized outline of the company's financial objectives and how they will be attained. Budgets are tools that, by themselves, are neither good nor bad. Budgets are useful when administered skillfully.
2. When should a company prepare budgets? What are the advantages of preparing budgets?	Budgets should be prepared when their expected benefits exceed their expected costs. There are four key advantages of budgets: (a) they compel strategic analysis and planning, (b) they promote coordination and communication among subunits of the company, (c) they provide a framework for judging performance and facilitating learning, and (d) they motivate managers and other employees.
3. What is the operating budget and what are its components?	The operating budget is the budgeted income statement and its supporting budget schedules. The starting point for the operating budget is generally the revenues budget. The following supporting schedules are derived from the revenues budget and the activities needed to support the revenues budget: production budget, direct material usage budget, direct material purchases budget, direct manufacturing labor cost budget, manufacturing overhead costs budget, ending inventories budget, cost of goods sold budget, R&D/product design cost budget, marketing cost budget, distribution cost budget, and customer-service cost budget.
4. How can managers plan for changes in the assumptions underlying the budget and manage risk?	Managers can use financial planning models—mathematical statements of the relationships among operating activities, financing activities, and other factors that affect the budget. These models make it possible for managers to conduct a what-if (sensitivity) analysis of the risks that changes in the original predicted data or changes in underlying assumptions would have on the master budget and to develop plans to respond to changed conditions.
5. How do companies use responsibility centers? Should performance reports of responsibility center managers include only costs the manager can control?	A responsibility center is a part, segment, or subunit of an organization whose manager is accountable for a specified set of activities. Four types of responsibility centers are cost centers, revenue centers, profit centers, and investment centers. Responsibility accounting systems are useful because they measure the plans, budgets, actions, and actual results of each responsibility center. Controllable costs are costs primarily subject to the influence of a given responsibility center manager for a given time period. Performance reports of responsibility center managers often include costs, revenues, and investments that the managers cannot control. Responsibility accounting associates financial items with managers on the basis of which manager has the most knowledge and information about the specific items, regardless of the manager's ability to exercise full control.
6. Why are human factors crucial in budgeting?	The administration of budgets requires education, participation, persuasion, and intelligent interpretation. When wisely administered, budgets create commitment, accountability, and honest communication among employees and can be used as the basis for continuous improvement efforts. When badly managed, budgeting can lead to game-playing and budgetary slack—the practice of making budget targets more easily achievable.

Decision	Guidelines
7. What are the special challenges involved in budgeting at multinational companies?	Budgeting is a valuable tool for multinational companies but is challenging because of the uncertainties posed by operating in multiple countries. In addition to budgeting in different currencies, managers in multinational companies also need to budget for foreign exchange rates and consider the political, legal, and economic environments of the different countries in which they operate. In times of high uncertainty, managers use budgets more to help the organization learn and adapt to its circumstances than to evaluate performance.

Appendix

The Cash Budget

The chapter illustrated the operating budget, which is one part of the master budget. The other part is the financial budget, which is composed of the capital expenditures budget, the cash budget, the budgeted balance sheet, and the budgeted statement of cash flows. This appendix focuses on the cash budget and the budgeted balance sheet. We discuss capital budgeting in Chapter 21. The budgeted statement of cash flows is beyond the scope of this book and generally is covered in financial accounting and corporate finance courses.

Why should Stylistic's managers want a cash budget in addition to the operating income budget presented in the chapter? Recall that Stylistic's management accountants prepared the operating budget on an accrual accounting basis consistent with how the company reports its actual operating income. But Stylistic's managers also need to plan cash flows to ensure that the company has adequate cash to pay vendors, meet payroll, and pay operating expenses as these payments come due. Stylistic could be very profitable, but the pattern of cash receipts from revenues might be delayed and result in insufficient cash being available to make scheduled payments. Stylistic's managers may then need to initiate a plan to borrow money to finance any shortfall. Building a profitable operating plan does not guarantee that adequate cash will be available, so Stylistic's managers need to prepare a cash budget in addition to an operating income budget.

Exhibit 6-5 shows Stylistic Furniture's balance sheet for the year ended December 31, 2013. The budgeted cash flows for 2014 are:

	Quarters			
	1	2	3	4
Collections from customers	$9,136,600	$10,122,000	$10,263,200	$8,561,200
Disbursements				
Direct materials	3,031,400	2,636,967	2,167,900	2,242,033
Direct manufacturing labor payroll	1,888,000	1,432,000	1,272,000	1,408,000
Manufacturing overhead costs	3,265,296	2,476,644	2,199,924	2,435,136
Nonmanufacturing costs	2,147,750	2,279,000	2,268,250	2,005,000
Machinery purchase	—	—	758,000	—
Income taxes	725,000	400,000	400,000	400,000

The quarterly data are based on the budgeted cash effects of the operations formulated in Schedules 1–8 in the chapter, but the details of that formulation are not shown here to keep this illustration as brief and as focused as possible.

Stylistic wants to maintain a $320,000 minimum cash balance at the end of each quarter. The company can borrow or repay money at an interest rate of 12% per year. Management does not want to borrow any more short-term cash than is necessary. By special arrangement with the bank, Stylistic pays interest when repaying the principal. Assume, for simplicity, that borrowing takes place at the beginning and repayment at the end of the quarter under consideration (in multiples of $1,000). Interest is computed to the nearest dollar.

Exhibit 6-5

Balance Sheet for Stylistic Furniture, December 31, 2013

Home Insert Page Layout Formulas Data Review View

	A	B	C	D
1	**Stylistic Furniture Balance Sheet**			
2	**December 31, 2013**			
3	**Assets**			
4	Current assets			
5	Cash		$ 300,000	
6	Accounts receivable		1,711,000	
7	Direct materials inventory		1,090,000	
8	Finished goods inventory		646,000	$ 3,747,000
9	Property, Plant, and equipment			
10	Land		2,000,000	
11	Building and equipment	$ 22,000,000		
12	Accumulated depreciation	(6,900,000)	15,100,000	17,100,000
13	Total			$20,847,000
14	**Liabilities and Stockholders' Equity**			
15	Current liabilities			
16	Accounts payable		$ 904,000	
17	Income taxes payable		325,000	$ 1,229,000
18	Stockholders' equity			
19	Common stock, no-par 25,000 shares outstanding		3,500,000	
20	Retained earnings		16,118,000	19,618,000
21	Total			$20,847,000

Suppose a management accountant at Stylistic receives the preceding data and the other data contained in the budgets in the chapter (pages 203–213). Her manager asks her to:

1. Prepare a cash budget for 2014 by quarter. That is, prepare a statement of cash receipts and disbursements by quarter, including details of borrowing, repayment, and interest.
2. Prepare a budgeted income statement for the year ending December 31, 2014. This statement should include interest expense and income taxes (at a rate of 40% of operating income).
3. Prepare a budgeted balance sheet on December 31, 2014.

Preparation of Budgets

1. The **cash budget** is a schedule of expected cash receipts and disbursements. It predicts the effects on the cash position at the given level of operations. Exhibit 6-6 presents the cash budget by quarters to show the impact of cash flow timing on bank loans and their repayment. In practice, monthly—and sometimes weekly or even daily—cash budgets are critical for cash planning and control. Cash budgets help avoid unnecessary idle cash and unexpected cash deficiencies. They thus keep cash balances in line with needs. Ordinarily, the cash budget has these main sections:
   a. **Cash available for needs (before any financing).** The beginning cash balance plus cash receipts equals the total cash available for needs before any financing. Cash receipts depend on collections of accounts receivable, cash sales, and miscellaneous recurring sources, such as rental or royalty receipts. Information on the expected collectibility of accounts receivable is needed for accurate predictions. Key factors include bad-debt (uncollectible accounts) experience (not an issue in the Stylistic case because Stylistic sells to only a few large wholesalers) and average time lag between sales and collections.

Exhibit 6-6 Cash Budget for Stylistic Furniture for the Year Ending December 31, 2014

	A	B	C	D	E	F
1	**Stylistic Furniture**					
2	**Cash Budget**					
3	**For Year Ending December 31, 2014**					
4		**Quarter 1**	**Quarter 2**	**Quarter 3**	**Quarter 4**	**Year as a Whole**
5	Cash balance, beginning	$ 300,000	$ 320,154	$ 320,783	$ 324,359	$ 300,000
6	Add receipts					
7	Collections from customers	9,136,600	10,122,000	10,263,200	8,561,200	38,083,000
8	Total cash available for needs (x)	9,436,600	10,442,154	10,583,983	8,885,559	38,383,000
9	Deduct disbursements					
10	Direct materials	3,031,400	2,636,967	2,167,900	2,242,033	10,078,300
11	Direct maufacturing labor payroll	1,888,000	1,432,000	1,272,000	1,408,000	6,000,000
12	Manufacturing overhead costs	3,265,296	2,476,644	2,199,924	2,435,136	10,377,000
13	Nonmanufacturing costs	2,147,750	2,279,000	2,268,250	2,005,000	8,700,000
14	Machinery purchase			758,000		
15	Income taxes	725,000	400,000	400,000	400,000	1,925,000
16	Total disbursements (y)	11,057,446	9,224,611	9,066,074	8,490,169	37,080,300
17	Minimum cash balance desired	320,000	320,000	320,000	320,000	320,000
18	Total cash needed	11,377,446	9,544,611	9,386,074	8,810,169	37,400,300
19	Cash excess (deficiency)*	$ (1,940,846)	$ 897,543	$ 1,197,909	$ 75,390	$ 0
20	Financing					
21	Borrowing (at beginning)	$ 1,941,000	$ 0	$ 0	$ 0	$ 1,941,000
22	Repayment (at end)	0	(846,000)	(1,095,000)	0	(1,941,000)
23	Interest (at 12% per year)**	0	(50,760)	(98,550)	0	(149,310)
24	Total effects of financing (z)	1,941,000	(896,760)	(1,193,550)	0	(149,310)
25	Cash balance, ending***	$ 320,154	$ 320,783	$ 324,359	$ 395,390	$ 395,390
26	*Excess of total cash available − Total cash needed before financing					
27	**Note that the short-term interest payments pertain only to the amount of principal being repaid at the end of a quarter. The specific computations regarding interest are $846,000 × 0.12 × 0.5 = $50,760; $1,095,000 × 0.12 × 0.75 = $98,550. Also note that *depreciation does not require a cash outlay.*					
28	***Ending cash balance = Total cash available for needs (x) − Total disbursements (y) + Total effects of financing (z)					

b. **Cash disbursements.** Cash disbursements by Stylistic Furniture include:
   i. *Direct material purchases.* Suppliers are paid in full in the month after the goods are delivered.
   ii. *Direct manufacturing labor and other wage and salary outlays.* All payroll-related costs are paid in the month in which the labor effort occurs.
   iii. *Other costs.* These depend on timing and credit terms. (In the Stylistic case, all other costs are paid in the month in which the cost is incurred.) *Note that depreciation does not require a cash outlay.*
   iv. *Other disbursements.* These include outlays for property, plant, equipment, and other long-term investments.
   v. Income tax payments as shown each quarter.

c. **Financing effects.** Short-term financing requirements depend on how the total cash available for needs [keyed as (x) in Exhibit 6-6] compares with the total cash disbursements [keyed as (y)], plus the minimum ending cash balance desired. The financing plans will depend on the relationship between total cash available for needs and total cash needed. If there is a deficiency of cash, Stylistic obtains loans. If there is excess cash, Stylistic repays any outstanding loans.

d. **Ending cash balance.** The cash budget in Exhibit 6-6 shows the pattern of short-term "self-liquidating" cash loans. In quarter 1, Stylistic budgets a $1,940,846 cash deficiency. The company therefore undertakes short-term borrowing of $1,941,000 that it pays off over the course of the year. Seasonal peaks of production or sales often result in heavy cash disbursements for purchases, payroll, and other operating outlays as the company produces and sells products. Cash receipts from customers typically lag behind sales. The loan is *self-liquidating* in the sense that the company uses the borrowed money to acquire resources that it uses to produce and sell finished goods and uses the proceeds from sales to repay the loan. This self-liquidating cycle is the movement from cash to inventories to receivables and back to cash.

2. The budgeted income statement is presented in Exhibit 6-7. It is merely the budgeted operating income statement in Exhibit 6-3 (page 213) expanded to include interest expense and income taxes.
3. The budgeted balance sheet is presented in Exhibit 6-8. Each item is projected in light of the details of the business plan as expressed in all the previous budget schedules. For example, the ending balance of accounts receivable of $1,628,000 is computed by adding the budgeted revenues of $38,000,000 (from Schedule 1 on page 206) to the beginning balance of accounts receivable of $1,711,000 (from Exhibit 6-5) and subtracting cash receipts of $38,083,000 (from Exhibit 6-6).

For simplicity, this example explicitly gave the cash receipts and disbursements. Usually, the receipts and disbursements are calculated based on the lags between the items reported on the accrual basis of accounting in an income statement and balance sheet and their related cash receipts and disbursements. Consider accounts receivable.

The budgeted sales for the year are broken down into sales budgets for each month and quarter. For example, Stylistic Furniture budgets sales by quarter of $9,282,000, $10,332,000, $10,246,000, and $8,140,000, which equal 2014 budgeted sales of $38,000,000.

Exhibit 6-7

Budgeted Income Statement for Stylistic Furniture for the Year Ending December 31, 2014

	A	B	C	D
1	Stylistic Furniture			
2	Budgeted Income Statement			
3	For the Year Ending December 31, 2014			
4	Revenues	Schedule 1		$38,000,000
5	COGS	Schedule 7		24,440,000
6	Gross margin			13,560,000
7	Operating costs			
8	Product design costs	Schedule 8	$1,024,000	
9	Marketing costs	Schedule 8	3,800,000	
10	Distribution costs	Schedule 8	3,876,000	8,700,000
11	Operating income			4,860,000
12	Interest expense	Exhibit 6-6		149,310
13	Income before income taxes			4,710,690
14	Income taxes (at 40%)			1,884,276
15	Net income			$ 2,826,414

	Quarter 1		Quarter 2		Quarter 3		Quarter 4	
	Casual	Deluxe	Casual	Deluxe	Casual	Deluxe	Casual	Deluxe
Budgeted sales in units	12,270	2,400	13,620	2,700	13,610	2,600	10,500	2,300
Selling price	$ 600	$ 800	$ 600	$ 800	$ 600	$ 800	$ 600	$ 800
Budgeted revenues	$7,362,000	$1,920,000	$ 8,172,000	$2,160,000	$ 8,166,000	$2,080,000	$6,300,000	$1,840,000
	$9,282,000		$10,332,000		$10,246,000		$8,140,000	

Notice that sales are expected to be higher in the second and third quarters relative to the first and fourth quarters when weather conditions limit the number of customers shopping for furniture.

Once Stylistic's managers determine the sales budget, a management accountant prepares a schedule of cash collections that serves as an input for the preparation of the cash budget. Stylistic estimates that 80% of all sales made in a quarter are collected in the same quarter and 20% are collected in the following quarter. Estimated collections from customers each quarter are calculated in the following table.

Schedule of Cash Collections

	Quarters			
	1	2	3	4
Accounts receivable balance on 1-1-2014 (Fourth-quarter sales from prior year collected in first quarter of 2014)	$1,711,000			
From first-quarter 2014 sales ($9,282,000 × 0.80; $9,282,000 × 0.20)	7,425,600	$ 1,856,400		
From second-quarter 2014 sales ($10,332,000 × 0.80; $10,332,000 × 0.20)		8,265,600	$ 2,066,400	
From third-quarter 2014 sales ($10,246,000 × 0.80; $10,246,000 × 0.20)			8,196,800	$2,049,200
From fourth-quarter 2014 sales ($8,140,000 × 0.80)				6,512,000
Total collections	$9,136,600	$10,122,000	$10,263,200	$8,561,200

Uncollected fourth-quarter 2014 sales of $1,628,000 ($8,140,000 × 0.20) appear as accounts receivable on the budgeted balance sheet of December 31, 2014 (see Exhibit 6-8). Note that the quarterly cash collections from customers calculated in this schedule equal the cash collections by quarter shown on page 224.

Sensitivity Analysis and Cash Flows

Exhibit 6-4 (page 214) shows how differing assumptions about selling prices of coffee tables and direct material prices led to differing amounts for budgeted operating income for Stylistic Furniture. A key use of sensitivity analysis is to budget cash flow. Exhibit 6-9 outlines the short-term borrowing implications of the two combinations examined in Exhibit 6-4. Scenario 1, with the lower selling prices per table ($582 for the Casual table and $776 for the Deluxe table), requires $2,146,000 of short-term borrowing in quarter 1 that cannot be fully repaid as of December 31, 2014. Scenario 2, with the 5% higher direct material costs, requires $2,048,000 borrowing by Stylistic Furniture that also cannot be repaid by December 31, 2014. Sensitivity analysis helps managers anticipate such outcomes and take steps to minimize the effects of expected reductions in cash flows from operations.

Exhibit 6-8 Budgeted Balance Sheet for Stylistic Furniture, December 31, 2014

	A	B	C	D
1	**Stylistic Furniture**			
2	**Budgeted Balance Sheet**			
3	**December 31, 2014**			
4	**Assets**			
5	Current assets			
6	Cash (from Exhibit 6-6)		$ 395,390	
7	Accounts receivable (1)		1,628,000	
8	Direct materials inventory (2)		760,000	
9	Finished goods inventory (2)		4,486,000	$ 7,269,390
10	Property, Plant, and equipment			
11	Land (3)		2,000,000	
12	Building and equipment (4)	$22,758,000		
13	Accumulated depreciation (5)	(8,523,000)	14,235,000	16,235,000
14	Total			$23,504,390
15	**Liabilities and Stockholders' Equity**			
16	Current liabilities			
17	Accounts payable (6)		$ 775,700	
18	Income taxes payable (7)		284,276	$ 1,059,976
19	Stockholders' equity			
20	Common stock, no-par, 25,000 shares outstanding (8)		3,500,000	
21	Retained earnings (9)		18,944,414	22,444,414
22	Total			$23,504,390
23				
24	Notes:			
25	Beginning balances are used as the starting point for most of the following computations			
26	(1) $1,711,000 + $38,000,000 revenues − $38,083,000 receipts (Exhibit 6-6) = $1,628,000			
27	(2) From Schedule 6B, p. 212			
28	(3) From opening balance sheet (Exhibit 6-5)			
29	(4) $22,000,000 (Exhibit 6-5) + $758,000 purchases (Exhibit 6-6) = $22,758,000			
30	(5) $6,900,000 (Exhibit 6-5) + $1,020,000 + $603,000 depreciation from Schedule 5, p. 210			
31	(6) $904,000 + $9,950,000 (Schedule 3B) − $10,078,300 (Exhibit 6-6) = $775,300			
32	There are no other current liabilities. From Exhibit 6-6: Cash flows for direct manufacturing labor = $6,000,000 from Schedule 4 Cash flows for manufacturing overhead costs = $10,377,000 ($12,000,000 − depreciation $1,623,000) from Schedule 5 Cash flows for nonmanufacturing costs = $8,700,000 from Schedule 8.			
33	(7) $325,000 + $1,884,276 (from Exhibit 6-7) − $1,925,000 payment (Exhibit 6-6) = $284,276			
34	(8) From opening balance sheet (Exhibit 6-5)			
35	(9) $16,118,000 (Exhibit 6-5) + net income $2,826,414 (Exhibit 6-7) = $18,944,414			

Exhibit 6-9 Sensitivity Analysis: Effects of Key Budget Assumptions in Exhibit 6-4 on 2014 Short-Term Borrowing for Stylistic Furniture

Home Insert Page Layout Formulas Data Review View

	A	B	C	D	E	F	G	H	I	J
1				Direct Material			Short-Term Borrowing and Repayment by Quarter			
2		Selling Price		Purchase Costs		Budgeted		Quarters		
3	Scenario	Casual	Deluxe	Red Oak	Granite	Operating Income	1	2	3	4
4	1	$582	$776	$7.00	$10.00	$3,794,100	$2,146,000	$(579,000)	$(834,000)	$170,000
5	2	$600	$800	7.35	10.50	4,483,800	2,048,000	$(722,000)	$(999,000)	$41,000

Terms to Learn

This chapter and the Glossary at the end of the book contain definitions of the following important terms:

Assignment Material

MyAccountingLab

Questions

6-1 What are the four elements of the budgeting cycle?

6-2 Define master budget.

6-3 "Strategy, plans, and budgets are unrelated to one another." Do you agree? Explain.

6-4 "Budgeted performance is a better criterion than past performance for judging managers." Do you agree? Explain.

6-5 "Production managers and marketing managers are like oil and water. They just don't mix." How can a budget assist in reducing battles between these two areas?

6-6 "Budgets meet the cost–benefit test. They force managers to act differently." Do you agree? Explain.

6-7 Define rolling budget. Give an example.

6-8 Outline the steps in preparing an operating budget.

6-9 "The sales forecast is the cornerstone for budgeting." Why?

6-10 How can sensitivity analysis be used to increase the benefits of budgeting?

6-11 Define Kaizen budgeting.

6-12 Describe how nonoutput-based cost drivers can be incorporated into budgeting.

6-13 Explain how the choice of the type of responsibility center (cost, revenue, profit, or investment) affects behavior.

6-14 What are some additional considerations that arise when budgeting in multinational companies?

6-15 "Cash budgets must be prepared before the operating income budget." Do you agree? Explain.

MyAccountingLab

Exercises

6-16 Sales budget, service setting. In 2014, Rouse & Sons, a small environmental-testing firm, performed 12,200 radon tests for $290 each and 16,400 lead tests for $240 each. Because newer homes are being built with lead-free pipes, lead-testing volume is expected to decrease by 10% next year. However, awareness of radon-related health hazards is expected to result in a 6% increase in radon-test volume each year in the near future. Jim Rouse feels that if he lowers his price for lead testing to $230 per test, he will have to face only a 7% decline in lead-test sales in 2015.

Required

1. Prepare a 2015 sales budget for Rouse & Sons assuming that Rouse holds prices at 2014 levels.
2. Prepare a 2015 sales budget for Rouse & Sons assuming that Rouse lowers the price of a lead test to $230. Should Rouse lower the price of a lead test in 2015 if the company's goal is to maximize sales revenue?

6-17 Sales and production budget. The McKnight Company expects sales in 2015 of 208,000 units of serving trays. McKnight's beginning inventory for 2015 is 18,000 trays, and its target ending inventory is 27,000 trays. Compute the number of trays budgeted for production in 2015.

6-18 Direct material budget. Inglenook Co. produces wine. The company expects to produce 2,500,000 two-liter bottles of Chablis in 2015. Inglenook purchases empty glass bottles from an outside vendor. Its target ending inventory of such bottles is 80,000; its beginning inventory is 50,000. For simplicity, ignore breakage. Compute the number of bottles to be purchased in 2015.

6-19 Budgeting material purchases budget. The Howell Company has prepared a sales budget of 43,000 finished units for a 3-month period. The company has an inventory of 11,000 units of finished goods on hand at December 31 and has a target finished goods inventory of 19,000 units at the end of the succeeding quarter.

It takes 4 gallons of direct materials to make one unit of finished product. The company has an inventory of 66,000 gallons of direct materials at December 31 and has a target ending inventory of 56,000 gallons at the end of the succeeding quarter. How many gallons of direct materials should Howell Company purchase during the 3 months ending March 31?

6-20 Revenues, production, and purchases budgets. The Mochizuki Co. in Japan has a division that manufactures two-wheel motorcycles. Its budgeted sales for Model G in 2015 is 915,000 units. Mochizuki's target ending inventory is 70,000 units, and its beginning inventory is 115,000 units. The company's budgeted selling price to its distributors and dealers is 405,000 yen (¥) per motorcycle.

Mochizuki buys all its wheels from an outside supplier. No defective wheels are accepted. (Mochizuki's needs for extra wheels for replacement parts are ordered by a separate division of the company.) The company's target ending inventory is 72,000 wheels, and its beginning inventory is 55,000 wheels. The budgeted purchase price is 18,000 yen (¥) per wheel.

Required

1. Compute the budgeted revenues in yen.
2. Compute the number of motorcycles that Mochizuki should produce.
3. Compute the budgeted purchases of wheels in units and in yen.
4. What actions can Mochizuki's managers take to reduce budgeted purchasing costs of wheels assuming the same budgeted sales for Model G?

6-21 Revenues and production budget. Price, Inc., bottles and distributes mineral water from the company's natural springs in northern Oregon. Price markets two products: 12-ounce disposable plastic bottles and 1-gallon reusable plastic containers.

Required

1. For 2015, Price marketing managers project monthly sales of 420,000 12-ounce bottles and 170,000 1-gallon containers. Average selling prices are estimated at $0.20 per 12-ounce bottle and $1.50 per 1-gallon container. Prepare a revenues budget for Price, Inc., for the year ending December 31, 2015.
2. Price begins 2015 with 890,000 12-ounce bottles in inventory. The vice president of operations requests that 12-ounce bottles ending inventory on December 31, 2015, be no less than 680,000 bottles. Based on sales projections as budgeted previously, what is the minimum number of 12-ounce bottles Price must produce during 2015?
3. The VP of operations requests that ending inventory of 1-gallon containers on December 31, 2015, be 240,000 units. If the production budget calls for Price to produce 1,900,000 1-gallon containers during 2015, what is the beginning inventory of 1-gallon containers on January 1, 2015?

6-22 Budgeting; direct material usage, manufacturing cost, and gross margin. Xander Manufacturing Company manufactures blue rugs, using wool and dye as direct materials. One rug is budgeted to use 36 skeins of wool at a cost of $2 per skein and 0.8 gallons of dye at a cost of $6 per gallon. All other materials are indirect. At the beginning of the year Xander has an inventory of 458,000 skeins of wool at a cost of $961,800 and 4,000 gallons of dye at a cost of $23,680. Target ending inventory of wool and dye is zero. Xander uses the FIFO inventory cost flow method.

Xander blue rugs are very popular and demand is high, but because of capacity constraints the firm will produce only 200,000 blue rugs per year. The budgeted selling price is $2,000 each. There are no rugs in beginning inventory. Target ending inventory of rugs is also zero.

Xander makes rugs by hand, but uses a machine to dye the wool. Thus, overhead costs are accumulated in two cost pools—one for weaving and the other for dyeing. Weaving overhead is allocated to products based on direct manufacturing labor-hours (DMLH). Dyeing overhead is allocated to products based on machine-hours (MH).

There is no direct manufacturing labor cost for dyeing. Xander budgets 62 direct manufacturing labor-hours to weave a rug at a budgeted rate of $13 per hour. It budgets 0.2 machine-hours to dye each skein in the dyeing process.

The following table presents the budgeted overhead costs for the dyeing and weaving cost pools:

	Dyeing (based on 1,440,000 MH)	Weaving (based on 12,400,000 DMLH)
Variable costs		
Indirect materials	$ 0	$15,400,000
Maintenance	6,560,000	5,540,000
Utilities	7,550,000	2,890,000
Fixed costs		
Indirect labor	347,000	1,700,000
Depreciation	2,100,000	274,000
Other	723,000	5,816,000
Total budgeted costs	$17,280,000	$31,620,000

Required

1. Prepare a direct material usage budget in both units and dollars.
2. Calculate the budgeted overhead allocation rates for weaving and dyeing.
3. Calculate the budgeted unit cost of a blue rug for the year.
4. Prepare a revenues budget for blue rugs for the year, assuming Xander sells (a) 200,000 or (b) 185,000 blue rugs (that is, at two different sales levels).
5. Calculate the budgeted cost of goods sold for blue rugs under each sales assumption.
6. Find the budgeted gross margin for blue rugs under each sales assumption.
7. What actions might you take as a manager to improve profitability if sales drop to 185,000 blue rugs?
8. How might top management at Xander use the budget developed in requirements 1–6 to better manage the company?

6-23 Budgeting, service company. Sunshine Window Washers (SWW) provides window-washing services to commercial clients. The company has enjoyed considerable growth in recent years due to a successful marketing campaign and favorable reviews on service-rating Web sites. Sunshine owner Sam Davis makes sales calls himself and quotes on jobs based on square footage of window surface. Sunshine hires college students to drive the company vans to jobs and wash the windows. A part-time bookkeeper takes care of billing customers and other office tasks. Overhead is accumulated in two cost pools, one for travel to jobs, allocated based on miles driven, and one for window washing, allocated based on direct labor-hours (DLH).

Sam Davis estimates that his window washers will work a total of 2,000 jobs during the year Each job averages 2,000 square feet of window surface and requires 5 direct labor-hours and 12.5 miles of travel. Davis pays his window washers $12 per hour. Taxes and benefits equal 20% of wages. Wages, taxes, and benefits are considered direct labor costs. The following table presents the budgeted overhead costs for the Travel and Window Washing cost pools:

	Travel (based on 25,000 miles driven)	Window Washing (based on 10,000 DLH)
Variable costs		
Supplies ($4.40 per DLH)	$ 0	$ 44,000
Fuel ($0.60 per mile)	15,000	0
Fixed costs (to support capacity of 30,000 miles driven and 12,000 direct labor-hours)		
Indirect labor	0	20,000
Depreciation	40,000	35,000
Other	5,000	23,000
Total budgeted costs	$60,000	$122,000

Required

1. Prepare a direct labor budget in both hours and dollars. Calculate the direct labor rate.
2. Calculate the budgeted overhead allocation rates for travel and window washing based on the budgeted quantity of the cost drivers.
3. Calculate the budgeted total cost of all jobs for the year and the budgeted cost of an average 2,000-square-foot window-washing job.

4. Prepare a revenues budget for the year, assuming that Sunshine charges customers $0.10 per square foot.
5. Calculate the budgeted operating income.
6. Davis believes that spending $15,000 in additional advertising will lead to a 20% increase in the number of jobs. Recalculate the budgeted revenue and operating income assuming this change is made. Calculate expenses by multiplying the existing budgeted cost per job calculated in requirement 3 by the number of jobs and adding the $15,000 advertising cost. Based on the change in budgeted operating income, would you recommend the investment?
7. Do you see any flaw in this analysis? How could the analysis be improved? Should SWW spend $15,000 in additional advertising?
8. What is SWW's profitability if sales should decline to 1,800 jobs annually? What actions can Davis take to improve profitability?

6-24 Budgets for production and direct manufacturing labor. (CMA, adapted) Roletter Company makes and sells artistic frames for pictures of weddings, graduations, and other special events. Bob Anderson, the controller, is responsible for preparing Roletter's master budget and has accumulated the following information for 2015:

	2015				
	January	**February**	**March**	**April**	**May**
Estimated sales in units	10,000	14,000	7,000	8,000	8,000
Selling price	$54.00	$50.50	$50.50	$50.50	$50.50
Direct manufacturing labor-hours per unit	2.0	2.0	1.5	1.5	1.5
Wage per direct manufacturing labor-hour	$12.00	$12.00	$12.00	$13.00	$13.00

In addition to wages, direct manufacturing labor-related costs include pension contributions of $0.50 per hour, worker's compensation insurance of $0.20 per hour, employee medical insurance of $0.30 per hour, and Social Security taxes. Assume that as of January 1, 2015, the Social Security tax rates are 7.5% for employers and 7.5% for employees. The cost of employee benefits paid by Roletter on its employees is treated as a direct manufacturing labor cost.

Roletter has a labor contract that calls for a wage increase to $13 per hour on April 1, 2015. New labor-saving machinery has been installed and will be fully operational by March 1, 2015. Roletter expects to have 17,500 frames on hand at December 31, 2014, and it has a policy of carrying an end-of-month inventory of 100% of the following month's sales plus 50% of the second following month's sales.

Required

1. Prepare a production budget and a direct manufacturing labor budget for Roletter Company by month and for the first quarter of 2015. You may combine both budgets in one schedule. The direct manufacturing labor budget should include labor-hours and show the details for each labor cost category.
2. What actions has the budget process prompted Roletter's management to take?
3. How might Roletter's managers use the budget developed in requirement 1 to better manage the company?

6-25 Activity-based budgeting. The Jerico store of Jiffy Mart, a chain of small neighborhood convenience stores, is preparing its activity-based budget for January 2015. Jiffy Mart has three product categories: soft drinks (35% of cost of goods sold [COGS]), fresh produce (25% of COGS), and packaged food (40% of COGS). The following table shows the four activities that consume indirect resources at the Jerico store, the cost drivers and their rates, and the cost-driver amount budgeted to be consumed by each activity in January 2015.

			January 2015 Budgeted Amount of Cost Driver Used		
Activity	**Cost Driver**	**January 2015 Budgeted Cost-Driver Rate**	**Soft Drinks**	**Fresh Snacks**	**Packaged Food**
Ordering	Number of purchase orders	$ 45	14	24	14
Delivery	Number of deliveries	$ 41	12	62	19
Shelf stocking	Hours of stocking time	$10.50	16	172	94
Customer support	Number of items sold	$ 0.09	4,600	34,200	10,750

Required

1. What is the total budgeted indirect cost at the Jerico store in January 2015? What is the total budgeted cost of each activity at the Jerico store for January 2015? What is the budgeted indirect cost of each product category for January 2015?
2. Which product category has the largest fraction of total budgeted indirect costs?
3. Given your answer in requirement 2, what advantage does Jiffy Mart gain by using an activity-based approach to budgeting over, say, allocating indirect costs to products based on cost of goods sold?

6-26 Kaizen approach to activity-based budgeting (continuation of 6-25). Jiffy Mart has a Kaizen (continuous improvement) approach to budgeting monthly activity costs for each month of 2015. Each successive month, the budgeted cost-driver rate decreases by 0.4% relative to the preceding month. So, for example, February's budgeted cost-driver rate is 0.996 times January's budgeted cost-driver rate, and March's budgeted cost-driver rate is 0.996 times the budgeted February rate. Jiffy Mart assumes that the budgeted amount of cost-driver usage remains the same each month.

Required

1. What are the total budgeted cost for each activity and the total budgeted indirect cost for March 2015?
2. What are the benefits of using a Kaizen approach to budgeting? What are the limitations of this approach, and how might Jiffy Mart management overcome them?

6-27 Responsibility and controllability. Consider each of the following independent situations for Tropical Hot Tubs. Tropical manufactures and sells hot tubs. The company also contracts to service both its own and other brands of hot tubs. Tropical has a manufacturing plant, a supply warehouse that supplies both the manufacturing plant and the service technicians (who often need parts to repair hot tubs), and 10 service vans. The service technicians drive to customer sites to service the hot tubs. Tropical owns the vans, pays for the gas, and supplies hot tub parts, but the technicians own their own tools.

1. In the manufacturing plant, the production manager is not happy with the motors that the purchasing manager has been purchasing. In May, the production manager stops requesting motors from the supply warehouse and starts purchasing them directly from a different motor manufacturer. Actual materials costs in May are higher than budgeted.
2. Overhead costs in the manufacturing plant for June are much higher than budgeted. Investigation reveals a utility rate hike in effect that was not figured into the budget.
3. Gasoline costs for each van are budgeted based on the service area of the van and the amount of driving expected for the month. The driver of van 3 routinely has monthly gasoline costs exceeding the budget for van 3. After investigating, the service manager finds that the driver has been driving the van for personal use.
4. Cascades Resort and Spa, one of Tropical's hot tub service customers, calls the service people only for emergencies and not for routine maintenance. Thus, the materials and labor costs for these service calls exceeds the monthly budgeted costs for a contract customer.
5. Tropical's service technicians are paid an hourly wage, with overtime pay if they exceed 40 hours per week, excluding driving time. Fred Friendly, one of the technicians, frequently exceeds 40 hours per week. Service customers are happy with Fred's work, but the service manager talks to him constantly about working more quickly. Fred's overtime causes the actual costs of service to exceed the budget almost every month.
6. The cost of gasoline has increased by 50% this year, which caused the actual gasoline costs to greatly exceed the budgeted costs for the service vans.

Required

For each situation described, determine where (that is, with whom) (a) responsibility and (b) controllability lie. Suggest ways to solve the problem or to improve the situation.

6-28 Responsibility, controllability, and stretch targets. Consider each of the following independent situations for Happy Tours, a company owned by Jason Haslett that sells motor coach tours to schools and other groups. Happy Tours owns a fleet of 10 motor coaches and employs 12 drivers, 1 maintenance technician, 3 sales representatives, and an office manager. Happy Tours pays for all fuel and maintenance on the coaches. Drivers are paid $0.50 per mile while in transit, plus $15 per hour while idle (time spent waiting while tour groups are visiting their destinations). The maintenance technician and office manager are both full-time salaried employees. The sales representatives work on straight commission.

1. When the office manager receives calls from potential customers, she is instructed to handle the contracts herself. Recently, however, the number of contracts written up by the office manager has declined. At the same time, one of the sales representatives has experienced a significant increase in contracts. The other two representatives believe that the office manager has been colluding with the third representative to send him the prospective customers.
2. One of the motor coach drivers seems to be reaching his destinations more quickly than any of the other drivers and is reporting longer idle time.
3. Fuel costs have increased significantly in recent months. Driving the motor coaches at 60 miles per hour on the highway consumes significantly less fuel than driving them at 65 miles per hour.

4. Regular preventive maintenance of the motor coaches has been proven to improve fuel efficiency and reduce overall operating costs by averting costly repairs. During busy months, however, it is difficult for the maintenance technician to complete all of the maintenance tasks within his 40-hour workweek.
5. Jason Haslett has read about stretch targets, and he believes that a change in the compensation structure of the sales representatives may improve sales. Rather than a straight commission of 10% of sales, he is considering a system where each representative is given a monthly goal of 50 contracts. If the goal is met, the representative is paid a 12% commission. If the goal is not met, the commission falls to 8%. Currently, each sales representative averages 45 contracts per month.

Required

For situations 1–4, discuss which employee has responsibility for the related costs and the extent to which costs are controllable and by whom. What are the risks or costs to the company? What can be done to solve the problem or improve the situation? For situation 5, describe the potential benefits and costs of establishing stretch targets.

6-29 Cash flow analysis, sensitivity analysis. Game Depot is a retail store selling video games. Sales are uniform for most of the year but pick up in June and December both because new releases come out and because consumers purchase games in anticipation of summer or winter holidays. Game Depot also sells and repairs game systems. The forecast of sales and service revenue for the March–June 2014 is as follows:

Sales and Service Revenues Budget March–June 2014

Month	Expected Sales Revenue	Expected Service Revenue	Total Revenue
March	$ 9,000	$1,500	$ 10,500
April	11,000	2,000	13,000
May	12,400	2,800	15,200
June	19,400	5,200	24,600

Almost all the service revenue is paid for by bank credit card, so Game Depot budgets this as 100% bank card revenue. The bank cards charge an average fee of 3% of the total. Half of the sales revenue is also paid for by bank credit card, for which the fee is also 3% on average. About 10% of the sales are paid in cash, and the rest (the remaining 40%) are carried on a store account. Although the store tries to give store credit only to the best customers, it still averages about 2% for uncollectible accounts; 90% of store accounts are paid in the month following the purchase, and 8% are paid 2 months after purchase.

Required

1. Calculate the cash that Game Depot expects to collect in May and in June 2014. Show calculations for each month.
2. Game Depot has budgeted expenditures for May of $8,700 for the purchase of games and game systems, $2,800 for rent and utilities and other costs, and $2,000 in wages for the two part-time employees.
   a. Given your answer to requirement 1, will Game Depot be able to cover its payments for May?
   b. The projections for May are a budget. Assume (independently for each situation) that May revenues might also be 5% less and 10% less and that costs might be 8% higher. Under each of those three scenarios, show the total net cash for May and the amount Game Depot would have to borrow if cash receipts are less than cash payments. Assume the beginning cash balance for May is $200.
3. Why do Game Depot's managers prepare a cash budget in addition to the revenue, expenses, and operating income budget? Has preparing the cash budget been helpful? Explain briefly.
4. Suppose the costs for May are as described in requirement 2, but the expected cash receipts for May are $12,400 and beginning cash balance is $200. Game Depot has the opportunity to purchase the games and game systems on account in May, but the supplier offers the company credit terms of 2/10 net 30, which means if Game Depot pays within 10 days (in May) it will get a 2% discount on the price of the merchandise. Game Depot can borrow money at a rate of 24%. Should Game Depot take the purchase discount?

Problems

MyAccountingLab

6-30 Budget schedules for a manufacturer. Lame Specialties manufactures, among other things, woolen blankets for the athletic teams of the two local high schools. The company sews the blankets from fabric and sews on a logo patch purchased from the licensed logo store site. The teams are as follows:

- Knights, with red blankets and the Knights logo
- Raiders, with black blankets and the Raider logo

Also, the black blankets are slightly larger than the red blankets.

The budgeted direct-cost inputs for each product in 2014 are as follows:

	Knights Blanket	Raiders Blanket
Red wool fabric	4 yards	0 yards
Black wool fabric	0	5
Knight logo patches	1	0
Raider logo patches	0	1
Direct manufacturing labor	3 hours	4 hours

Unit data pertaining to the direct materials for March 2014 are as follows:

Actual Beginning Direct Materials Inventory (3/1/2014)

	Knights Blanket	Raiders Blanket
Red wool fabric	35 yards	0 yards
Black wool fabric	0	15
Knight logo patches	45	0
Raider logo patches	0	60

Target Ending Direct Materials Inventory (3/31/2014)

	Knights Blanket	Raiders Blanket
Red wool fabric	25 yards	0 yards
Black wool fabric	0	25
Knight logo patches	25	0
Raider logo patches	0	25

Unit cost data for direct-cost inputs pertaining to February 2014 and March 2014 are as follows:

	February 2014 (actual)	March 2014 (budgeted)
Red wool fabric (per yard)	$ 9	$10
Black wool fabric (per yard)	12	11
Knight logo patches (per patch)	7	7
Raider logo patches (per patch)	6	8
Manufacturing labor cost per hour	26	27

Manufacturing overhead (both variable and fixed) is allocated to each blanket on the basis of budgeted direct manufacturing labor-hours per blanket. The budgeted variable manufacturing overhead rate for March 2014 is $16 per direct manufacturing labor-hour. The budgeted fixed manufacturing overhead for March 2014 is $14,640. Both variable and fixed manufacturing overhead costs are allocated to each unit of finished goods.

Data relating to finished goods inventory for March 2014 are as follows:

	Knights Blankets	Raiders Blankets
Beginning inventory in units	12	17
Beginning inventory in dollars (cost)	$1,440	$2,550
Target ending inventory in units	22	27

Budgeted sales for March 2014 are 130 units of the Knights blankets and 190 units of the Raiders blankets. The budgeted selling prices per unit in March 2014 are $229 for the Knights blankets and $296 for the Raiders blankets. Assume the following in your answer:

- Work-in-process inventories are negligible and ignored.
- Direct materials inventory and finished goods inventory are costed using the FIFO method.
- Unit costs of direct materials purchased and finished goods are constant in March 2014.

Required

1. Prepare the following budgets for March 2014:
   a. Revenues budget
   b. Production budget in units
   c. Direct material usage budget and direct material purchases budget
   d. Direct manufacturing labor budget
   e. Manufacturing overhead budget
   f. Ending inventories budget (direct materials and finished goods)
   g. Cost of goods sold budget
2. Suppose Lame Specialties decides to incorporate continuous improvement into its budgeting process. Describe two areas where it could incorporate continuous improvement into the budget schedules in requirement 1.

6-31 Budgeted costs, Kaizen improvements. Trendy T-Shirt Factory manufactures plain white and solid-colored T-shirts. Inputs include the following:

	Price	Quantity	Cost per unit of output
Fabric	$ 7 per yard	1 yard per unit	$7 per unit
Labor	$14 per DMLH	0.25 DMLH per unit	$3.50 per unit

Additionally, the colored T-shirts require 3 ounces of dye per shirt at a cost of $0.40 per ounce. The shirts sell for $14 each for white and $18 each for colors. The company expects to sell 12,000 white T-shirts and 60,000 colored T-shirts uniformly over the year.

Trendy has the opportunity to switch from using the dye it currently uses to using an environmentally friendly dye that costs $1.25 per ounce. The company would still need 3 ounces of dye per shirt. Trendy is reluctant to change because of the increase in costs (and decrease in profit), but the Environmental Protection Agency has threatened to fine the company $120,000 if it continues to use the harmful but less expensive dye.

Required

1. Given the preceding information, would Trendy be better off financially by switching to the environmentally friendly dye? (Assume all other costs would remain the same.)
2. Assume Trendy chooses to be environmentally responsible regardless of cost, and it switches to the new dye. The production manager suggests trying Kaizen costing. If Trendy can reduce fabric and labor costs each by 1% per month, how close will it be at the end of 12 months to the profit it would have earned before switching to the more expensive dye? (Round to the nearest dollar for calculating cost reductions.)
3. Refer to requirement 2. How could the reduction in material and labor costs be accomplished? Are there any problems with this plan?

6-32 Revenue and production budgets. (CPA, adapted) The Sabat Corporation manufactures and sells two products: Thingone and Thingtwo. In July 2013, Sabat's budget department gathered the following data to prepare budgets for 2014:

2014 Projected Sales

Product	Units	Price
Thingone	62,000	$172
Thingtwo	46,000	$264

2014 Inventories in Units

	Expected Target	
Product	January 1, 2014	December 31, 2014
Thingone	21,000	26,000
Thingtwo	13,000	14,000

The following direct materials are used in the two products:

		Amount Used per Unit	
Direct Material	Unit	Thingone	Thingtwo
A	pound	5	6
B	pound	3	4
C	each	0	2

Projected data for 2014 for direct materials are:

Direct Material	Anticipated Purchase Price	Expected Inventories January 1, 2014	Target Inventories December 31, 2014
A	$11	37,000 lb.	40,000 lb.
B	6	32,000 lb.	35,000 lb.
C	5	10,000 units	12,000 units

Projected direct manufacturing labor requirements and rates for 2014 are:

Product	Hours per Unit	Rate per Hour
Thingone	3	$11
Thingtwo	4	14

Manufacturing overhead is allocated at the rate of $19 per direct manufacturing labor-hour.

Based on the preceding projections and budget requirements for Thingone and Thingtwo, prepare the following budgets for 2014:

Required

1. Revenues budget (in dollars)
2. What questions might the CEO ask the marketing manager when reviewing the revenues budget? Explain briefly.
3. Production budget (in units)
4. Direct material purchases budget (in quantities)
5. Direct material purchases budget (in dollars)
6. Direct manufacturing labor budget (in dollars)
7. Budgeted finished goods inventory at December 31, 2014 (in dollars)
8. What questions might the CEO ask the production manager when reviewing the production, direct materials, and direct manufacturing labor budgets?
9. How does preparing a budget help Sabat Corporation's top management better manage the company?

6-33 Budgeted income statement. (CMA, adapted) Smart Video Company is a manufacturer of videoconferencing products. Maintaining the videoconferencing equipment is an important area of customer satisfaction. A recent downturn in the computer industry has caused the videoconferencing equipment segment to suffer, leading to a decline in Smart Video's financial performance. The following income statement shows results for 2014:

Smart Video Company Income Statement for the Year Ended December 31, 2014 (in thousands)

Revenues		
Equipment	$8,000	
Maintenance contracts	1,900	
Total revenues		$9,900
Cost of goods sold		4,000
Gross margin		5,900
Operating costs		
Marketing	630	
Distribution	100	
Customer maintenance	1,100	
Administration	920	
Total operating costs		2,750
Operating income		$3,150

Smart Video's management team is preparing the 2015 budget and is studying the following information:

1. Selling prices of equipment are expected to increase by 10% as the economic recovery begins. The selling price of each maintenance contract is expected to remain unchanged from 2014.
2. Equipment sales in units are expected to increase by 6%, with a corresponding 6% growth in units of maintenance contracts.
3. Cost of each unit sold is expected to increase by 5% to pay for the necessary technology and quality improvements.
4. Marketing costs are expected to increase by $290,000, but administration costs are expected to remain at 2014 levels.

5. Distribution costs vary in proportion to the number of units of equipment sold.
6. Two maintenance technicians are to be hired at a total cost of $160,000, which covers wages and related travel costs. The objective is to improve customer service and shorten response time.
7. There is no beginning or ending inventory of equipment.

Required

1. Prepare a budgeted income statement for the year ending December 31, 2015.
2. How well does the budget align with Smart Video's strategy?
3. How does preparing the budget help Smart Video's management team better manage the company?

6-34 Responsibility in a restaurant. Paula Beane owns a restaurant franchise that is part of a chain of "southern homestyle" restaurants. One of the chain's popular breakfast items is biscuits and gravy. Central Warehouse makes and freezes the biscuit dough, which it then sells to the franchise stores where it is thawed and baked in the individual stores by the cook. Each franchise also has a purchasing agent who orders the biscuits (and other items) based on expected demand. In March 2015, one of the freezers in Central Warehouse breaks down and biscuit production is reduced by 25% for 3 days. During those 3 days, Paula's franchise runs out of biscuits but demand does not slow down. Paula's franchise cook, Betty Baker, sends one of the kitchen helpers to the local grocery store to buy refrigerated ready-to-bake biscuits. Although the customers are kept happy, the refrigerated biscuits cost Paula's franchise three times the cost of the Central Warehouse frozen biscuits, and the franchise loses money on this item for those 3 days. Paula is angry with the purchasing agent for not ordering enough biscuits to avoid running out of stock and with Betty for spending too much money on the replacement biscuits.

Required

Who is responsible for the cost of the biscuits? At what level is the cost controllable? Do you agree that Paula should be angry with the purchasing agent? With Betty? Why or why not?

6-35 Comprehensive problem with ABC costing. Animal Gear Company makes two pet carriers, the Cat-allac and the Dog-eriffic. They are both made of plastic with metal doors, but the Cat-allac is smaller. Information for the two products for the month of April is given in the following tables:

Input Prices

Direct materials	
Plastic	$ 5 per pound
Metal	$ 4 per pound
Direct manufacturing labor	$10 per direct manufacturing labor-hour

Input Quantities per Unit of Output

	Cat-allac	Dog-eriffic
Direct materials		
Plastic	4 pounds	6 pounds
Metal	0.5 pounds	1 pound
Direct manufacturing labor-hours	3 hours	5 hours
Machine-hours (MH)	11 MH	19 MH

Inventory Information, Direct Materials

	Plastic	Metal
Beginning inventory	290 pounds	70 pounds
Target ending inventory	410 pounds	65 pounds
Cost of beginning inventory	$1,102	$217

Animal Gear accounts for direct materials using a FIFO cost flow assumption.

Sales and Inventory Information, Finished Goods

	Cat-allac	Dog-eriffic
Expected sales in units	530	225
Selling price	$ 205	$ 310
Target ending inventory in units	30	10
Beginning inventory in units	10	25
Beginning inventory in dollars	$1,000	$4,650

Animal Gear uses a FIFO cost flow assumption for finished goods inventory.

Animal Gear uses an activity-based costing system and classifies overhead into three activity pools: Setup, Processing, and Inspection. Activity rates for these activities are $105 per setup-hour, $10 per machine-hour, and $15 per inspection-hour, respectively. Other information follows:

Cost-Driver Information

	Cat-allac	Dog-eriffic
Number of units per batch	25	9
Setup time per batch	1.50 hours	1.75 hours
Inspection time per batch	0.5 hour	0.7 hour

Nonmanufacturing fixed costs for March equal $32,000, half of which are salaries. Salaries are expected to increase 5% in April. The only variable nonmanufacturing cost is sales commission, equal to 1% of sales revenue.

Prepare the following for April:

Required

1. Revenues budget
2. Production budget in units
3. Direct material usage budget and direct material purchases budget
4. Direct manufacturing labor cost budget
5. Manufacturing overhead cost budgets for each of the three activities
6. Budgeted unit cost of ending finished goods inventory and ending inventories budget
7. Cost of goods sold budget
8. Nonmanufacturing costs budget
9. Budgeted income statement (ignore income taxes)
10. How does preparing the budget help Animal Gear's management team better manage the company?

6-36 Cash budget (continuation of 6-35). Refer to the information in Problem 6-35.

Assume the following: Animal Gear (AG) does not make any sales on credit. AG sells only to the public and accepts cash and credit cards; 90% of its sales are to customers using credit cards, for which AG gets the cash right away, less a 2% transaction fee.

Purchases of materials are on account. AG pays for half the purchases in the period of the purchase and the other half in the following period. At the end of March, AG owes suppliers $8,000.

AG plans to replace a machine in April at a net cash cost of $13,000.

Labor, other manufacturing costs, and nonmanufacturing costs are paid in cash in the month incurred except of course depreciation, which is not a cash flow. Depreciation is $25,000 of the manufacturing cost and $10,000 of the nonmanufacturing cost for April.

AG currently has a $2,000 loan at an annual interest rate of 24%. The interest is paid at the end of each month. If AG has more than $10,000 cash at the end of April it will pay back the loan. AG owes $5,000 in income taxes that need to be remitted in April. AG has cash of $5,900 on hand at the end of March.

Required

1. Prepare a cash budget for April for Animal Gear.
2. Why do Animal Gear's managers prepare a cash budget in addition to the revenue, expenses, and operating income budget?

6-37 Comprehensive operating budget, budgeted balance sheet. Skulas, Inc., manufactures and sells snowboards. Skulas manufactures a single model, the Pipex. In the summer of 2014, Skulas' management accountant gathered the following data to prepare budgets for 2015:

Materials and Labor Requirements

Direct materials	
Wood	9 board feet (b.f.) per snowboard
Fiberglass	10 yards per snowboard
Direct manufacturing labor	5 hours per snowboard

Skulas' CEO expects to sell 2,900 snowboards during 2015 at an estimated retail price of $650 per board. Further, the CEO expects 2015 beginning inventory of 500 snowboards and would like to end 2015 with 200 snowboards in stock.

	Direct Materials Inventories	
	Beginning Inventory 1/1/2015	Ending Inventory 12/31/2015
Wood	2,040 b.f.	1,540 b.f.
Fiberglass	1,040 yards	2,040 yards

Variable manufacturing overhead is $7 per direct manufacturing labor-hour. There are also $81,000 in fixed manufacturing overhead costs budgeted for 2015. Skulas combines both variable and fixed manufacturing overhead into a single rate based on direct manufacturing labor-hours. Variable marketing costs are allocated at the rate of $250 per sales visit. The marketing plan calls for 38 sales visits during 2015. Finally, there are $35,000 in fixed nonmanufacturing costs budgeted for 2015.

Other data include:

	2014 Unit Price	2015 Unit Price
Wood	$32.00 per b.f.	$34.00 per b.f.
Fiberglass	$ 8.00 per yard	$ 9.00 per yard
Direct manufacturing labor	$28.00 per hour	$29.00 per hour

The inventoriable unit cost for ending finished goods inventory on December 31, 2014, is $374.80. Assume Skulas uses a FIFO inventory method for both direct materials and finished goods. Ignore work in process in your calculations.

Budgeted balances at December 31, 2014, in the selected accounts are as follows:

Cash	$ 14,000
Property, plant, and equipment (net)	854,000
Current liabilities	21,000
Long-term liabilities	182,000
Stockholders' equity	857,120

Required

1. Prepare the 2015 revenues budget (in dollars).
2. Prepare the 2015 production budget (in units).
3. Prepare the direct material usage and purchases budgets for 2015.
4. Prepare a direct manufacturing labor budget for 2015.
5. Prepare a manufacturing overhead budget for 2015.
6. What is the budgeted manufacturing overhead rate for 2015?
7. What is the budgeted manufacturing overhead cost per output unit in 2015?
8. Calculate the cost of a snowboard manufactured in 2015.
9. Prepare an ending inventory budget for both direct materials and finished goods for 2015.
10. Prepare a cost of goods sold budget for 2015.
11. Prepare the budgeted income statement for Skulas, Inc., for the year ending December 31, 2015.
12. Prepare the budgeted balance sheet for Skulas, Inc., as of December 31, 2015.
13. What questions might the CEO ask the management team when reviewing the budget? Should the CEO set stretch targets? Explain briefly.
14. How does preparing the budget help Skulas' management team better manage the company?

6-38 Cash budgeting. Retail outlets purchase snowboards from Skulas, Inc., throughout the year. However, in anticipation of late summer and early fall purchases, outlets ramp up inventories from May through August. Outlets are billed when boards are ordered. Invoices are payable within 60 days. From past experience, Skulas' accountant projects 40% of invoices will be paid in the month invoiced, 45% will be paid in the following month, and 15% of invoices will be paid two months after the month of invoice. The average selling price per snowboard is $650.

To meet demand, Skulas increases production from April through July because the snowboards are produced a month prior to their projected sale. Direct materials are purchased in the month of production and are paid for during the following month (terms are payment in full within 30 days of the invoice date). During this period there is no production for inventory and no materials are purchased for inventory.

Direct manufacturing labor and manufacturing overhead are paid monthly. Variable manufacturing overhead is incurred at the rate of $7 per direct manufacturing labor-hour. Variable marketing costs are driven by the number of sales visits. However, there are no sales visits during the months studied. Skulas,

Inc., also incurs fixed manufacturing overhead costs of $7,500 per month and fixed nonmanufacturing overhead costs of $4,500 per month.

Projected Sales

May 480 units	August 500 units
June 520 units	September 460 units
July 750 units	October 440 units

Direct Materials and Direct Manufacturing Labor Utilization and Cost

	Units per Board	Price per Unit	Unit
Wood	9	$34	board feet
Fiberglass	10	9	yard
Direct manufacturing labor	5	29	Hour

The beginning cash balance for July 1, 2015, is $14,000. On October 1, 2014, Skulas had a cash crunch and borrowed $60,000 on a 12% one-year note with interest payable monthly. The note is due October 1, 2015.

Required

1. Prepare a cash budget for the months of July through September 2015. Show supporting schedules for the calculation of receivables and payables.
2. Will Skulas be in a position to pay off the $60,000 one-year note that is due on October 1, 2015? If not, what actions would you recommend to Skulas' management?
3. Suppose Skulas is interested in maintaining a minimum cash balance of $14,000. Will the company be able to maintain such a balance during all three months analyzed? If not, suggest a suitable cash management strategy.
4. Why do Skulas' managers prepare a cash budget in addition to the revenue, expenses, and operating income budget?

6-39 Cash budgeting. On December 1, 2014, the Iaia Wholesale Co. is attempting to project cash receipts and disbursements through January 31, 2015. On this latter date, a note will be payable in the amount of $107,000. This amount was borrowed in September to carry the company through the seasonal peak in November and December.

Selected general ledger balances on December 1 are:

Cash	$ 30,000	
Inventory	111,800	
Accounts payable		$139,000

Sales terms call for a 3% discount if payment is made within the first 10 days of the month after sale, with the balance due by the end of the month after sale. Experience has shown that 50% of the billings will be collected within the discount period, 30% by the end of the month after purchase, and 15% in the following month. The remaining 5% will be uncollectible. There are no cash sales.

The average selling price of the company's products is $170 per unit. Actual and projected sales are:

October actual	$ 287,000
November actual	629,000
December estimated	561,000
January estimated	612,000
February estimated	510,000
Total estimated for year ending June 30, 2015	$3,218,750

All purchases are payable within 15 days. Approximately 60% of the purchases in a month are paid that month and the rest the following month. The average unit purchase cost is $130. Target ending inventories are 570 units plus 20% of the next month's unit sales.

Total budgeted marketing, distribution, and customer-service costs for the year are $670,000. Of this amount, $155,000 are considered fixed (and include depreciation of $43,400). The remainder varies with sales. Both fixed and variable marketing, distribution, and customer-service costs are paid as incurred.

Required

1. Prepare a cash budget for December 2014 and January 2015. Supply supporting schedules for collections of receivables; payments for merchandise; and marketing, distribution, and customer-service costs.
2. Why do Iaia's managers prepare a cash budget in addition to the operating income budget?

6-40 Comprehensive problem; ABC manufacturing, two products. Hazlett, Inc., operates at capacity and makes plastic combs and hairbrushes. Although the combs and brushes are a matching set, they are sold individually and so the sales mix is not 1:1. Hazlett's management is planning its annual budget for fiscal year 2015. Here is information for 2015:

Input Prices

Direct materials	
Plastic	$ 0.30 per ounce
Bristles	$ 0.75 per bunch
Direct manufacturing labor	$ 18 per direct manufacturing labor-hour

Input Quantities per Unit of Output

	Combs	Brushes
Direct materials		
Plastic	5 ounces	8 ounces
Bristles	—	16 bunches
Direct manufacturing labor	0.05 hours	0.2 hours
Machine-hours (MH)	0.025 MH	0.1 MH

Inventory Information, Direct Materials

	Plastic	Bristles
Beginning inventory	1,600 ounces	1,820 bunches
Target ending inventory	1,766 ounces	2,272 bunches
Cost of beginning inventory	$456	$1,419

Hazlett accounts for direct materials using a FIFO cost flow.

Sales and Inventory Information, Finished Goods

	Combs	Brushes
Expected sales in units	12,000	14,000
Selling price	$ 9	$ 30
Target ending inventory in units	1,200	1,400
Beginning inventory in units	600	1,200
Beginning inventory in dollars	$ 2,700	$27,180

Hazlett uses a FIFO cost flow assumption for finished goods inventory.

Combs are manufactured in batches of 200, and brushes are manufactured in batches of 100. It takes 20 minutes to set up for a batch of combs and 1 hour to set up for a batch of brushes.

Hazlett uses activity-based costing and has classified all overhead costs as shown in the following table. Budgeted fixed overhead costs vary with capacity. Hazlett operates at capacity so budgeted fixed overhead cost per unit equals the budgeted fixed overhead costs divided by the budgeted quantities of the cost allocation base.

Cost Type	Budgeted Variable	Budgeted Fixed	Cost Driver/Allocation Base
Manufacturing			
Materials handling	$17,235	$22,500	Number of ounces of plastic used
Setup	10,245	16,650	Setup-hours
Processing	11,640	30,000	Machine-hours
Inspection	10,500	1,560	Number of units produced
Nonmanufacturing			
Marketing	$21,150	$90,000	Sales revenue
Distribution	0	1,170	Number of deliveries

Delivery trucks transport units sold in delivery sizes of 1,000 combs or 1,000 brushes.

Required

Do the following for the year 2015:

1. Prepare the revenues budget.
2. Use the revenues budget to:
   a. Find the budgeted allocation rate for marketing costs.
   b. Find the budgeted number of deliveries and allocation rate for distribution costs.
3. Prepare the production budget in units.
4. Use the production budget to:
   a. Find the budgeted number of setups and setup-hours and the allocation rate for setup costs.
   b. Find the budgeted total machine-hours and the allocation rate for processing costs.
   c. Find the budgeted total units produced and the allocation rate for inspection costs.
5. Prepare the direct material usage budget and the direct material purchases budgets in both units and dollars; round to whole dollars.
6. Use the direct material usage budget to find the budgeted allocation rate for materials-handling costs.
7. Prepare the direct manufacturing labor cost budget.
8. Prepare the manufacturing overhead cost budget for materials handling, setup, processing, and inspection costs.
9. Prepare the budgeted unit cost of ending finished goods inventory and ending inventories budget.
10. Prepare the cost of goods sold budget.
11. Prepare the nonmanufacturing overhead costs budget for marketing and distribution.
12. Prepare a budgeted income statement (ignore income taxes).
13. How does preparing the budget help Hazlett's management team better manage the company?

6-41 Budgeting and ethics. Jayzee Company manufactures a variety of products in a variety of departments and evaluates departments and departmental managers by comparing actual cost and output relative to the budget. Departmental managers help create the budgets and usually provide information about input quantities for materials, labor, and overhead costs.

Kurt Jackson is the manager of the department that produces product Z. Kurt has estimated these inputs for product Z:

Input	**Budget Quantity per Unit of Output**
Direct material	8 pounds
Direct manufacturing labor	30 minutes
Machine time	24 minutes

The department produces about 100 units of product Z each day. Kurt's department always gets excellent evaluations, sometimes exceeding budgeted production quantities. For each 100 units of product Z produced, the company uses, on average, about 48 hours of direct manufacturing labor (eight people working 6 hours each), 790 pounds of material, and 39.5 machine-hours.

Top management of Jayzee Company has decided to implement budget standards that will challenge the workers in each department, and it has asked Kurt to design more challenging input standards for product Z. Kurt provides top management with the following input quantities:

Input	**Budget Quantity per Unit of Output**
Direct material	7.9 pounds
Direct manufacturing labor	29 minutes
Machine time	23.6 minutes

Discuss the following:

1. Are these budget standards challenging for the department that produces product Z?
2. Why do you suppose Kurt picked these particular standards?
3. What steps can Jayzee Company's top management take to make sure Kurt's standards really meet the goals of the firm?

6-42 Human aspects of budgeting in a service firm. Vidal Sanson owns three upscale hair salons: Bristles I, II, and III. Each of the salons has a manager and 10 stylists who rent space in the salons as independent contractors and who pay a fee of 10% of each week's revenue to the salon as rent. In exchange they get to use the facility and utilities, but must bring their own equipment.

The manager of each salon schedules each customer appointment to last an hour and then allows the stylist 10 minutes between appointments to clean up, rest, and prepare for the next appointment. The salons are open from 10:00 a.m. to 6:00 p.m., so each stylist can serve seven customers per day. Stylists each work 5 days a week on a staggered schedule, so the salon is open 7 days a week. Everyone works on Saturdays, but some stylists have Sunday and Monday off, some have Tuesday and Wednesday off, and some have Thursday and Friday off.

Vidal Sanson knows that utility costs are rising. Vidal wants to increase revenues to cover at least some part of rising utility costs, so Vidal tells each of the managers to find a way to increase productivity in the salons so that the stylists will pay more to the salons. Vidal does not want to increase the rental fee above 10% of revenue for fear the stylists will leave. And each salon has only 10 stations, so Vidal feels each salon cannot hire more than 10 full-time stylists.

The manager of Bristles I attacks the problem by simply telling the stylists that, from now on, customers will be scheduled for 40-minute appointments and breaks will be 5 minutes. This will allow each stylist to add one more customer per day.

The manager of Bristles II asks the stylists on a voluntary basis to work one extra hour per day, from 10:00 a.m. to 7:00 p.m., to add an additional customer per stylist per day.

The manager of Bristles III sits down with the stylists and discusses the issue. After considering shortening the appointment and break times or lengthening the hours of operation, one of the stylists says, "I know we rent stations in your store, but I am willing to share my station. You could hire another stylist who will simply work at whatever station is vacant during our days off. Since we use our own equipment, this will not be a problem for me as long as there is a secure place I can leave my equipment on my days off." Most of the other stylists agree that this is a good solution.

Required

1. Which manager's style do you think is most effective? Why?
2. How do you think the stylists will react to the managers of salons I and II? If the stylists are displeased, how can they indicate their displeasure?
3. In Bristles III, if the stylists did not want to share their stations with another party, how else could they find a way to increase revenues?

6-43 Comprehensive budgeting problem; activity-based costing, operating and financial budgets. Tyva makes a very popular undyed cloth sandal in one style, but in Regular and Deluxe. The Regular sandals have cloth soles and the Deluxe sandals have cloth-covered wooden soles. Tyva is preparing its budget for June 2015 and has estimated sales based on past experience.

Other information for the month of June follows:

Input Prices

Direct materials	
Cloth	$5.25 per yard
Wood	$7.50 per board foot
Direct manufacturing labor	$15 per direct manufacturing labor-hour

Input Quantities per Unit of Output (per pair of sandals)

	Regular	Deluxe
Direct materials		
Cloth	1.3 yards	1.5 yards
Wood	0	2 b.f.
Direct manufacturing labor-hours (DMLH)	5 hours	7 hours
Setup-hours per batch	2 hours	3 hours

Inventory Information, Direct Materials

	Cloth	Wood
Beginning inventory	610 yards	800 b.f.
Target ending inventory	386 yards	295 b.f.
Cost of beginning inventory	$3,219	$6,060

Tyva accounts for direct materials using a FIFO cost flow assumption.

Sales and Inventory Information, Finished Goods

	Regular	Deluxe
Expected sales in units (pairs of sandals)	2,000	3,000
Selling price	$ 120	$ 195
Target ending inventory in units	400	600
Beginning inventory in units	250	650
Beginning inventory in dollars	$23,250	$92,625

Tyva uses a FIFO cost flow assumption for finished goods inventory.

All the sandals are made in batches of 50 pairs of sandals. Tyva incurs manufacturing overhead costs, marketing and general administration, and shipping costs. Besides materials and labor, manufacturing costs include setup, processing, and inspection costs. Tyva ships 40 pairs of sandals per shipment. Tyva uses activity-based costing and has classified all overhead costs for the month of June as shown in the following chart:

Cost type	Denominator Activity	Rate
Manufacturing		
Setup	Setup-hours	$18 per setup-hour
Processing	Direct manufacturing labor-hours	$1.80 per DMLH
Inspection	Number of pairs of sandals	$1.35 per pair
Nonmanufacturing		
Marketing and general administration	Sales revenue	8%
Shipping	Number of shipments	$15 per shipment

Required

1. Prepare each of the following for June:
   a. Revenues budget
   b. Production budget in units
   c. Direct material usage budget and direct material purchases budget in both units and dollars; round to dollars
   d. Direct manufacturing labor cost budget
   e. Manufacturing overhead cost budgets for setup, processing, and inspection activities
   f. Budgeted unit cost of ending finished goods inventory and ending inventories budget
   g. Cost of goods sold budget
   h. Marketing and general administration and shipping costs budget
2. Tyva's balance sheet for May 31 follows.

Tyva Balance Sheet as of May 31

Assets		
Cash		$ 9,435
Accounts receivable	$324,000	
Less: Allowance for bad debts	16,200	307,800
Inventories		
Direct materials		9,279
Finished goods		115,875
Fixed assets	$870,000	
Less: Accumulated depreciation	136,335	733,665
Total assets		$1,176,054

Liabilities and Equity	
Accounts payable	$ 15,600
Taxes payable	10,800
Interest payable	750
Long-term debt	150,000
Common stock	300,000
Retained earnings	698,904
Total liabilities and equity	$1,176,054

Use the balance sheet and the following information to prepare a cash budget for Tyva for June. Round to dollars.

- All sales are on account; 60% are collected in the month of the sale, 38% are collected the following month, and 2% are never collected and written off as bad debts.
- All purchases of materials are on account. Tyva pays for 80% of purchases in the month of purchase and 20% in the following month.
- All other costs are paid in the month incurred, including the declaration and payment of a $15,000 cash dividend in June.
- Tyva is making monthly interest payments of 0.5% (6% per year) on a $150,000 long-term loan.
- Tyva plans to pay the $10,800 of taxes owed as of May 31 in the month of June. Income tax expense for June is zero.
- 30% of processing, setup, and inspection costs and 10% of marketing and general administration and shipping costs are depreciation.

3. Prepare a budgeted income statement for June and a budgeted balance sheet for Tyva as of June 30, 2015.

7 Flexible Budgets, Direct-Cost Variances, and Management Control

Learning Objectives

1. Understand static budgets and static-budget variances
2. Examine the concept of a flexible budget and learn how to develop it
3. Calculate flexible-budget variances and sales-volume variances
4. Explain why standard costs are often used in variance analysis
5. Compute price variances and efficiency variances for direct-cost categories
6. Understand how managers use variances
7. Describe benchmarking and explain its role in cost management

Every organization, regardless of its profitability or growth, has to step back and take a hard look at its spending decisions.

And when customers are affected by a recession, the need for managers to use budgeting and variance analysis tools for cost control becomes especially critical. By studying variances, managers can focus on where specific performances have fallen short and use the information they learn to make corrective adjustments and achieve significant savings for their companies. The drive to achieve cost reductions might seem at odds with the growing push for organizations to pursue environmentally sound business practices. To the contrary, managers looking to be more efficient with their plants and operations have found that cornerstones of the sustainability movement, such as reducing waste and power usage, offer fresh ways to help them manage risk and control costs, as the following article shows.

Going for the (Other) Green: Reducing Standard Costs[1]

While Whole Foods and IKEA have long been associated with eco-friendliness, sustainable practices have been spreading far beyond these early adopters to a broad swath of businesses. In recent years, managers in some unlikely industries have discovered that the financial benefits of sustainability can manifest themselves in numerous ways. One surprising way involves companies going green to reduce their standard costs.

At APC Construction, a small road-builder in Colorado, the company increased the amount of recycled asphalt it uses in its production process—purely out of necessity. When the cost of standard asphalt cement skyrocketed from $180 per ton in 2003 to $600 per ton in 2008, the company needed to rein in its standard costs for cement. As a result, the company began increasing the amount of recycled ingredients in its product. "With a 30% recycled product, you're looking at a savings of almost $8 per ton," says Bob Stewart, the company's finance chief. "You're reducing the amount of energy you use to crush the rock and you're preserving natural resources."

Urschel Laboratories, a maker of capital equipment for the food processing and chemical industries, simultaneously reduced its freight costs and carbon footprint. With

[1] *Source:* Kate O'Sullivan, "Going for the Green" Sept. 01, 2011, CFO Magazine.

oil prices rising, some of Urschel's carriers began adding fuel surcharges to ship the company's machinery. Since much of what the company sells is heavy equipment, Urschel found that its customers often had enough lead time to wait 4 to 6 weeks for their orders to arrive by sea, a practice that costs the company half of what air freight—its former standard—costs. This lowered the company's standard costs for shipping while reducing the amount of fuel oil required to ship its equipment to customers around the world.

Understanding the behavior of costs, planning for them, performing variance analysis, and acting appropriately on the results are critical functions for managers. For retailers such as McDonald's and Dunkin' Donuts, an intricate understanding of direct costs is essential in order to make each high-quality food item and beverage at the lowest possible cost. Similarly, organizations ranging from General Electric and Bank of America to sports teams such as the Sacramento Kings have to manage costs and analyze variances for long-term sustainability.

In Chapter 6, you saw how budgets help managers with their planning function. We now explain how budgets, specifically flexible budgets, are used to compute variances, which assist managers in their control function. Flexible budgets and variances enable managers to compare a firm's actual results with its planned performance, understand why the two differ, and learn what improvements can be made. Variance analysis supports the critical final function in the five-step decision-making process by enabling managers to *evaluate performance and learn* after decisions are implemented. In this chapter and the next, we explain how.

Static Budgets and Variances

Learning Objective 1

Understand static budgets

...the master budget based on output planned at start of period

and static-budget variances

...the difference between the actual result and the corresponding budgeted amount in the static budget

A **variance** is the difference between actual results and expected performance. The expected performance is also called **budgeted performance**, which is a point of reference for making comparisons.

The Use of Variances

Variances bring together the planning and control functions of management and facilitate management by exception. **Management by exception** is a practice whereby managers focus more closely on areas that are not operating as expected and less closely on areas that are. Consider the scrap and rework costs at a Maytag appliances plant. If the plant's actual costs are much higher than originally budgeted, the variances will prompt managers to find out why and correct the problem so future operations result in less scrap and rework. Sometimes a large positive variance may occur, such as a significant decrease in the manufacturing costs of a product. Managers will try to understand the reasons for the decrease (better operator training or changes in manufacturing methods, for example) so these practices can be continued and implemented by other divisions within the organization.

Variances are also used for evaluating performance and to motivate managers. Production-line managers at Maytag may have quarterly efficiency incentives linked to achieving a budgeted amount of operating costs.

Sometimes variances suggest that the company should consider a change in strategy. For example, large negative variances caused by excessive defect rates for a new product may suggest a flawed product design. Managers may then want to investigate the product design and potentially change the mix of products being offered. Variances also help managers make more informed predictions about the future and thereby improve the quality of the five-step decision-making process.

The benefits of variance analysis are not restricted to companies. In today's difficult economic environment, public officials have realized that the ability to make timely tactical changes based on variance information can result in their having to make fewer draconian adjustments later. For example, the city of Scottsdale, Arizona, monitors its tax and fee performance against expenditures monthly. Why? One of the city's goals is to keep its water usage rates stable. By monitoring the extent to which the city's water revenues are matching its current expenses, Scottsdale can avoid sudden spikes in the rate it charges residents for water as well as finance water-related infrastructure projects.[2]

How important of a decision-making tool is variance analysis? Very. A recent survey by the United Kingdom's Chartered Institute of Management Accountants found that it was easily the most popular costing tool used by organizations of all sizes.

Static Budgets and Static-Budget Variances

We will take a closer look at variances by examining one company's accounting system. As you study the exhibits in this chapter, note that "level" followed by a number denotes the amount of detail shown by a variance analysis. Level 1 reports the least detail; level 2 offers more information; and so on.

Consider Webb Company, a firm that manufactures and sells jackets. The jackets require tailoring and many other hand operations. Webb sells exclusively to distributors, who in turn sell to independent clothing stores and retail chains. For simplicity, we assume the following:

1. Webb's only costs are in the manufacturing function; Webb incurs no costs in other value-chain functions, such as marketing and distribution.
2. All units manufactured in April 2014 are sold in April 2014.
3. There is no direct materials inventory at either the beginning or the end of the period. No work-in-process or finished goods inventories exist at either the beginning or the end of the period.

Webb has three variable-cost categories. The budgeted variable cost per jacket for each category is as follows:

Cost Category	Variable Cost per Jacket
Direct materials costs	$60
Direct manufacturing labor costs	16
Variable manufacturing overhead costs	12
Total variable costs	$88

The *number of units manufactured* is the cost driver for direct materials, direct manufacturing labor, and variable manufacturing overhead. The relevant range for the cost driver is from 0 to 12,000 jackets. Budgeted and actual data for April 2014 are:

Budgeted fixed costs for production between 0 and 12,000 jackets	$276,000
Budgeted selling price	$ 120 per jacket
Budgeted production and sales	12,000 jackets
Actual production and sales	10,000 jackets

[2] For an excellent discussion and other related examples from governmental settings, see Kavanagh S., and C. Swanson. 2009. Tactical financial management: Cash flow and budgetary variance analysis. *Government Finance Review*, October 1.

Exhibit 7-1

Static-Budget-Based Variance Analysis for Webb Company for April 2014[a]

Level 1 Analysis

	Actual Results (1)	Static-Budget Variances (2) = (1) − (3)	Static Budget (3)
Units sold	10,000	2,000 U	12,000
Revenues	$ 1,250,000	$190,000 U	$1,440,000
Variable costs			
Direct materials	621,600	98,400 F	720,000
Direct manufacturing labor	198,000	6,000 U	192,000
Variable manufacturing overhead	130,500	13,500 F	144,000
Total variable costs	950,100	105,900 F	1,056,000
Contribution margin	299,900	84,100 U	384,000
Fixed costs	285,000	9,000 U	276,000
Operating income	$ 14,900	$ 93,100 U	$ 108,000

$ 93,100 U

Static-budget variance

[a]F = favorable effect on operating income; U = unfavorable effect on operating income.

The **static budget**, or master budget, is based on the level of output planned at the start of the budget period. The master budget is called a static budget because the budget for the period is developed around a single (static) planned output level. Exhibit 7-1, column 3, presents the static budget for Webb Company for April 2014 that was prepared at the end of 2013. For each line item in the income statement, Exhibit 7-1, column 1, displays data for the actual April results. For example, actual revenues are $1,250,000, and the actual selling price is $1,250,000 ÷ 10,000 jackets = $125 per jacket—compared with the budgeted selling price of $120 per jacket. Similarly, actual direct materials costs are $621,600, and the direct material cost per jacket is $621,600 ÷ 10,000 = $62.16 per jacket—compared with the budgeted direct material cost per jacket of $60. We describe potential reasons and explanations for these differences as we discuss different variances throughout the chapter.

The **static-budget variance** (see Exhibit 7-1, column 2) is the difference between the actual result and the corresponding budgeted amount in the static budget.

A **favorable variance**—denoted F in this book —has the effect, when considered in isolation, of increasing operating income relative to the budgeted amount. For revenue items, F means actual revenues exceed budgeted revenues. For cost items, F means actual costs are less than budgeted costs. An **unfavorable variance**—denoted U in this book — has the effect, when viewed in isolation, of decreasing operating income relative to the budgeted amount. Unfavorable variances are also called *adverse variances* in some countries, such as the United Kingdom.

The unfavorable static-budget variance for operating income of $93,100 in Exhibit 7-1 is calculated by subtracting static-budget operating income of $108,000 from actual operating income of $14,900:

$$\begin{aligned}\text{Static-budget variance for operating income} &= \text{Actual result} - \text{Static-budget amount}\\ &= \$14{,}900 - \$108{,}000\\ &= \$93{,}100\ \text{U}.\end{aligned}$$

The analysis in Exhibit 7-1 provides managers with additional information on the static-budget variance for operating income of $93,100 U. The more detailed breakdown indicates how the line items that comprise operating income—revenues, individual variable costs, and fixed costs—add up to the static-budget variance of $93,100.

Decision Point

What are static budgets and static-budget variances?

Recall that Webb produced and sold only 10,000 jackets, although managers anticipated an output of 12,000 jackets in the static budget. *Managers want to know how much of the static-budget variance is due to Webb inaccurately forecasting what it expected to produce and sell and how much is due to how it actually performed manufacturing and selling 10,000 jackets.* Managers, therefore, create a flexible budget, which enables a more in-depth understanding of deviations from the static budget.

Learning Objective 2

Examine the concept of a flexible budget

...the budget that is adjusted (flexed) to recognize the actual output level

and learn how to develop it

...proportionately increase variable costs; keep fixed costs the same

Flexible Budgets

A **flexible budget** calculates budgeted revenues and budgeted costs based on *the actual output in the budget period.* The flexible budget is prepared at the end of the period (April 2014 for Webb), after managers know the actual output of 10,000 jackets. The flexible budget is the *hypothetical* budget that Webb would have prepared at the start of the budget period if it had correctly forecast the actual output of 10,000 jackets. In other words, the flexible budget is not the plan Webb initially had in mind for April 2014 (remember Webb planned for an output of 12,000 jackets). Rather, it is the budget Webb *would have* put together for April if it knew in advance that the output for the month would be 10,000 jackets. In preparing the flexible budget, note that:

- The budgeted selling price is the same $120 per jacket used in the static budget.
- The budgeted unit variable cost is the same $88 per jacket used in the static budget.
- The budgeted *total* fixed costs are the same static-budget amount of $276,000. Why? Because the 10,000 jackets produced falls within the relevant range of 0 to 12,000 jackets. Therefore, Webb would have budgeted the same amount of fixed costs, $276,000, whether it anticipated making 10,000 or 12,000 jackets.

The *only* difference between the static budget and the flexible budget is that the static budget is prepared for the planned output of 12,000 jackets, whereas the flexible budget is prepared retroactively based on the actual output of 10,000 jackets. In other words, the static budget is being "flexed," or adjusted, from 12,000 jackets to 10,000 jackets.[3] The flexible budget for 10,000 jackets assumes all costs are either completely variable or completely fixed with respect to the number of jackets produced.

Webb develops its flexible budget in three steps.

Step 1: Identify the Actual Quantity of Output. In April 2014, Webb produced and sold 10,000 jackets.

Step 2: Calculate the Flexible Budget for Revenues Based on the Budgeted Selling Price and Actual Quantity of Output.

$$\text{Flexible-budget revenues} = \$120 \text{ per jacket} \times 10{,}000 \text{ jackets} = \$1{,}200{,}000$$

Step 3: Calculate the Flexible Budget for Costs Based on the Budgeted Variable Cost per Output Unit, Actual Quantity of Output, and Budgeted Fixed Costs.

Flexible-budget variable costs	
Direct materials, $60 per jacket × 10,000 jackets	$ 600,000
Direct manufacturing labor, $16 per jacket × 10,000 jackets	160,000
Variable manufacturing overhead, $12 per jacket × 10,000 jackets	120,000
Total flexible-budget variable costs	880,000
Flexible-budget fixed costs	276,000
Flexible-budget total costs	$1,156,000

[3] Suppose Webb, when preparing its annual budget for 2014 at the end of 2013, had perfectly anticipated that its output in April 2014 would equal 10,000 jackets. Then the flexible budget for April 2014 would be identical to the static budget.

Exhibit 7-2 Level 2 Flexible-Budget-Based Variance Analysis for Webb Company for April 2014[a]

Level 2 Analysis

	Actual Results (1)	Flexible-Budget Variances (2) = (1) – (3)	Flexible Budget (3)	Sales-Volume Variances (4) = (3) – (5)	Static Budget (5)
Units sold	10,000	0	10,000	2,000 U	12,000
Revenues	$1,250,000	$50,000 F	$1,200,000	$240,000 U	$1,440,000
Variable costs					
Direct materials	621,600	21,600 U	600,000	120,000 F	720,000
Direct manufacturing labor	198,000	38,000 U	160,000	32,000 F	192,000
Variable manufacturing overhead	130,500	10,500 U	120,000	24,000 F	144,000
Total variable costs	950,100	70,100 U	880,000	176,000 F	1,056,000
Contribution margin	299,900	20,100 U	320,000	64,000 U	384,000
Fixed manufacturing costs	285,000	9,000 U	276,000	0	276,000
Operating income	$ 14,900	$29,100 U	$ 44,000	$ 64,000 U	$ 108,000

Level 2 — $29,100 U Flexible-budget variance; $ 64,000 U Sales-volume variance

Level 1 — $93,100 U Static-budget variance

[a]F = favorable effect on operating income; U = unfavorable effect on operating income.

These three steps enable Webb to prepare a flexible budget, as shown in Exhibit 7-2, column 3. The flexible budget allows for a more detailed analysis of the $93,100 unfavorable static-budget variance for operating income.

Decision Point

How can managers develop a flexible budget and why is it useful to do so?

Flexible-Budget Variances and Sales-Volume Variances

Learning Objective 3

Calculate flexible-budget variances

. . . each flexible-budget variance is the difference between an actual result and a flexible-budget amount

and sales-volume variances

. . . each sales-volume variance is the difference between a flexible-budget amount and a static-budget amount

Exhibit 7-2 shows the flexible-budget-based variance analysis for Webb, which subdivides the $93,100 unfavorable static-budget variance for operating income into two parts: a flexible-budget variance of $29,100 U and a sales-volume variance of $64,000 U. The **sales-volume variance** is the difference between a flexible-budget amount and the corresponding static-budget amount. The **flexible-budget variance** is the difference between an actual result and the corresponding flexible-budget amount.

Sales-Volume Variances

Keep in mind that the flexible-budget amounts in column 3 of Exhibit 7-2 and the static-budget amounts in column 5 are both computed using budgeted selling prices, budgeted variable cost per jacket, and budgeted fixed costs. The difference between the static-budget and the flexible-budget amounts is called the sales-volume variance because it arises *solely* from the difference between the 10,000 actual quantity (or volume) of jackets sold and the 12,000 quantity of jackets expected to be sold in the static budget.

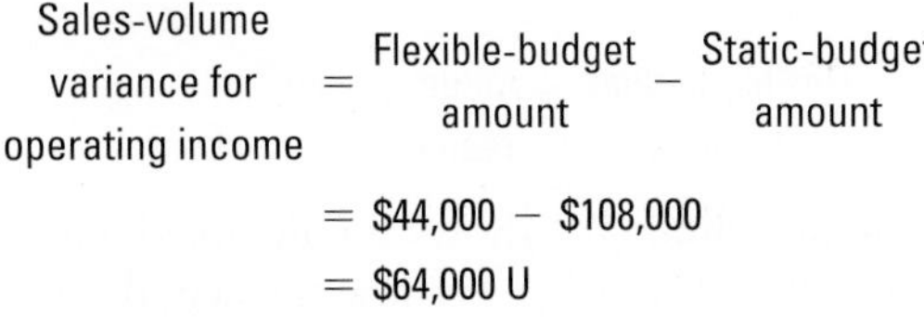

$$\text{Sales-volume variance for operating income} = \text{Flexible-budget amount} - \text{Static-budget amount}$$

$$= \$44{,}000 - \$108{,}000$$

$$= \$64{,}000\ \text{U}$$

The sales-volume variance in operating income for Webb measures the change in the budgeted contribution margin because Webb sold only 10,000 jackets rather than the budgeted 12,000.

$$\begin{aligned}\text{Sales-volume variance for operating income} &= \begin{pmatrix}\text{Budgeted contribution}\\ \text{margin per unit}\end{pmatrix} \times \begin{pmatrix}\text{Actual units} & - & \text{Static-budget}\\ \text{sold} & & \text{units sold}\end{pmatrix}\\ &= \begin{pmatrix}\text{Budgeted selling} & - & \text{Budgeted variable}\\ \text{price} & & \text{cost per unit}\end{pmatrix} \times \begin{pmatrix}\text{Actual units} & - & \text{Static-budget}\\ \text{sold} & & \text{units sold}\end{pmatrix}\\ &= (\$120 \text{ per jacket} - \$88 \text{ per jacket}) \times (10{,}000 \text{ jackets} - 12{,}000 \text{ jackets})\\ &= \$32 \text{ per jacket} \times (-2{,}000 \text{ jackets})\\ &= \$64{,}000\ \text{U}\end{aligned}$$

Exhibit 7-2, column 4, shows the components of this overall variance by identifying the sales-volume variance for each of the line items in the income statement. The unfavorable sales-volume variance in operating income arises because of one or more of the following reasons:

1. Failure of Webb's managers to execute the sales plans
2. Weaker than anticipated overall demand for jackets
3. Competitors taking away market share from Webb
4. Unexpected changes in customer tastes and preferences away from Webb's designs
5. Quality problems leading to customer dissatisfaction with Webb's jackets

How Webb responds to the unfavorable sales-volume variance will depend on what its managers believe caused the variance. For example, if Webb's managers believe the unfavorable sales-volume variance was caused by market-related reasons (reasons 1, 2, 3, or 4), the sales manager would be in the best position to explain what happened and suggest corrective actions that may be needed, such as sales promotions, market studies, or changes to advertising plans. If, however, managers believe the unfavorable sales-volume variance was caused by unanticipated quality problems (reason 5), the production manager would be in the best position to analyze the causes and suggest strategies for improvement, such as changes in the manufacturing process or investments in new machines.

The static-budget variances compared actual revenues and costs for 10,000 jackets against budgeted revenues and costs for 12,000 jackets. A portion of this difference, the sales-volume variance, reflects the effects of selling fewer units or inaccurate forecasting of sales. By removing this component from the static-budget variance, managers can compare their firm's revenues earned and costs incurred for April 2014 against the flexible budget—the revenues and costs Webb would have budgeted for the 10,000 jackets actually produced and sold. *Flexible-budget variances are a better measure of sales price and cost performance than static-budget variances because they compare actual revenues to budgeted revenues and actual costs to budgeted costs for the same 10,000 jackets of output.* Concepts in Action: Flexible Budgets at Corning shows the importance of flexible budgets for conducting variance analysis and in enabling a company to manage its business in an uncertain environment.

Flexible-Budget Variances

The first three columns of Exhibit 7-2 compare Webb's actual results with its flexible-budget amounts. The flexible-budget variances for each line item in the income statement are shown in column 2:

$$\begin{matrix}\text{Flexible-budget} & = & \text{Actual} & - & \text{Flexible-budget}\\ \text{variance} & & \text{result} & & \text{amount}\end{matrix}$$

The operating income line in Exhibit 7-2 shows the flexible-budget variance is \$29,100 U (\$14,900 – \$44,000). The \$29,100 U arises because the actual selling price, actual variable

Concepts in Action

Flexible Budgets at Corning

Historically, the rule of business budgeting was simple: Make a budget and stick to it. In today's fast-changing environment, however, many companies are pairing their annual "static" budget with a flexible budget that adjusts for changes in the volume of activity. Corning, the 160-year-old maker of specialty glass and ceramics, uses a flexible budget to quickly accommodate the impact of significant changes that affect its business.

Each year, Corning pulls together its annual budget. While managers still work to make sure that budget is achieved, it cannot predict the actions of Corning's customers and competitors with 100% accuracy. For instance, Apple uses the company's scratch-resistant Gorilla Glass on its iPhone screens. If Apple decides to expedite the production of its newest iPhone model, Corning may have to unexpectedly ramp up its Gorilla Glass manufacturing, which has both unexpected costs and revenues. At Corning, management accountants and finance executives produce rolling forecasts each month to address what the company thinks will happen for the rest of the quarter. According to Tony Tripeny, Corning's senior vice president and corporate controller, "Based on this analysis, we will go to the business units and say, 'What are you going to do differently? What actions are you going to take, and how is that different from what we had assumed with the budget?'"

By using a flexible budget, Corning managers can analyze uncertainty, improve performance evaluation, and conduct useful variance analysis that helps the company stay on track. So, why does Corning develop a detailed budget at all? It has specific benefits, explains Tripeny. As an example, he cites the relationship of a budget to Corning's resolve to be the lowest-cost producer in its markets. "During the budget process, we set up specific objectives, like targets for manufacturing costs," he says. "Even though the business might change during the year, it normally doesn't change enough to alter the manufacturing-performance targets. From a control standpoint, a budget still has value, but it shouldn't guide how you manage the business, which is about perceiving what's ahead and acting on it quicker than the competition."

Sources: Pogue, David. 2010. Gorilla Glass, the smartphone's unsung hero. Pogue's Posts (blog), *New York Times*, December 9. http://pogue.blogs.nytimes.com; Banham, Russ. 2011. Let it roll. *CFO Magazine*, May.

cost per unit, and actual fixed costs differ from their budgeted amounts. The actual results and budgeted amounts for the selling price and variable cost per unit are as follows:

	Actual Result	Budgeted Amount
Selling price	\$125.00 (\$1,250,000 ÷ 10,000 jackets)	\$120.00 (\$1,200,000 ÷ 10,000 jackets)
Variable cost per jacket	\$ 95.01 (\$ 950,100 ÷ 10,000 jackets)	\$ 88.00 (\$ 880,000 ÷ 10,000 jackets)

The flexible-budget variance for revenues is called the **selling-price variance** because it arises solely from the difference between the actual selling price and the budgeted selling price:

$$\begin{aligned}\text{Selling-price variance} &= \left(\text{Actual selling price} - \text{Budgeted selling price}\right) \times \text{Actual units sold}\\ &= (\$125 \text{ per jacket} - \$120 \text{ per jacket}) \times 10{,}000 \text{ jackets}\\ &= \$50{,}000 \text{ F}\end{aligned}$$

Webb has a favorable selling-price variance because the \$125 actual selling price exceeds the \$120 budgeted amount, which increases operating income. Marketing managers are generally in the best position to understand and explain the reason for a selling price difference. For example, was the difference due to better quality? Or was it due to an overall increase in market prices? Webb's managers concluded it was due to a general increase in prices.

The flexible-budget variance for total variable costs is unfavorable ($70,100 U) for the actual output of 10,000 jackets. It's unfavorable because of one or both of the following:

- Webb used greater quantities of inputs (such as direct manufacturing labor-hours) compared to the budgeted quantities of inputs.
- Webb incurred higher prices per unit for the inputs (such as the wage rate per direct manufacturing labor-hour) compared to the budgeted prices per unit of the inputs.

Higher input quantities and/or higher input prices relative to the budgeted amounts could be the result of Webb deciding to produce a better product than what was planned or the result of inefficiencies related to Webb's manufacturing and purchasing operations or both. *You should always think of variance analysis as providing suggestions for further investigation rather than as establishing conclusive evidence of good or bad performance.*

Decision Point

How are flexible-budget and sales-volume variances calculated?

The actual fixed costs of $285,000 are $9,000 more than the budgeted amount of $276,000. This unfavorable flexible-budget variance reflects unexpected increases in the cost of fixed indirect resources, such as the factory's rent or supervisors' salaries.

In the rest of this chapter, we will focus on variable direct-cost input variances. Chapter 8 emphasizes indirect (overhead) cost variances.

Learning Objective 4

Explain why standard costs are often used in variance analysis

...standard costs exclude past inefficiencies and take into account expected future changes

Standard Costs for Variance Analysis

To gain further insight, a company will subdivide the flexible-budget variance for its direct-cost inputs into two more-detailed variances:

1. A price variance that reflects the difference between an actual input price and a budgeted input price
2. An efficiency variance that reflects the difference between an actual input quantity and a budgeted input quantity

We will call these level 3 variances. Managers generally have more control over efficiency variances than price variances because the quantity of inputs used is primarily affected by factors inside the company (such as the efficiency with which operations are performed), whereas changes in the price of materials or in wage rates may be largely dictated by market forces outside the company.

Obtaining Budgeted Input Prices and Budgeted Input Quantities

To calculate price and efficiency variances, Webb needs to obtain budgeted input prices and budgeted input quantities. Webb's three main sources for this information are: (1) past data, (2) data from similar companies, and (3) standards. Each source has its advantages and disadvantages.

1. **Actual input data from past periods.** Most companies have past data on actual input prices and actual input quantities. These historical data could be analyzed for trends or patterns using some of the techniques we will discuss in another chapter (Chapter 10) to obtain estimates of budgeted prices and quantities.

   Advantages: Past data represent quantities and prices that are real rather than hypothetical, so they can be very useful benchmarks for measuring improvements in performance. Moreover, past data are typically easy to collect at a low cost.

   Disadvantages: A firm's inefficiencies, such as the wastage of direct materials, are incorporated in past data. Consequently, the data do not represent the performance the firm could have ideally attained, only the performance it achieved in the past. Past data also do not incorporate any changes expected for the budget period, such as improvements resulting from new investments in technology.

2. **Data from other companies that have similar processes.** Another source of information is data from peer companies or companies that have similar processes, which can serve as a benchmark. For example, Baptist Healthcare System in Louisville, Kentucky, benchmarks its labor performance data against those of similar top-ranked hospitals.

   Advantages: Data from other companies can provide a firm useful information about how it's performing relative to its competitors.

   Disadvantages: Input-price and input-quantity data from other companies are often not available or may not be comparable to a particular company's situation. Consider American Apparel, which makes more than 1 million articles of clothing a week. At its sole factory, in Los Angeles, workers receive hourly wages, piece rates, and medical benefits well in excess of those paid by its competitors, virtually all of whom are offshore and have significantly lower production costs. (We will discuss benchmarking in more detail later in the chapter.)

3. **Standards developed by the firm itself.** A **standard** is a carefully determined price, cost, or quantity that is used as a benchmark for judging performance. Standards are usually expressed on a per-unit basis. Consider how Webb determines its direct manufacturing labor standards. Webb conducts engineering studies to obtain a detailed breakdown of the steps required to make a jacket. Each step is assigned a standard time based on work performed by a *skilled* worker using equipment operating in an *efficient* manner. Similarly, Webb determines the standard quantity of square yards of cloth based on what is required by a skilled operator to make a jacket.

   Advantages: Standard times (1) aim to exclude past inefficiencies and (2) take into account changes expected to occur in the budget period. An example of the latter would be a decision by Webb's managers to lease new, faster, and more accurate sewing machines. Webb would incorporate the resulting higher level of efficiency into the new standards it sets.

   Disdvantages: Because they are not based on realized benchmarks, the standards might not be achievable, and workers could get discouraged trying to meet them.

The term *standard* refers to many different things:

- A **standard input** is a carefully determined quantity of input, such as square yards of cloth or direct manufacturing labor-hours, required for one unit of output, such as a jacket.
- A **standard price** is a carefully determined price a company expects to pay for a unit of input. In the Webb example, the standard wage rate the firm expects to pay its operators is an example of a standard price of a direct manufacturing labor-hour.
- A **standard cost** is a carefully determined cost of a unit of output, such as the standard direct manufacturing labor cost of a jacket at Webb.

$$\frac{\text{Standard cost per output unit for}}{\text{each variable direct-cost input}} = \frac{\text{Standard input allowed}}{\text{for one output unit}} \times \frac{\text{Standard price}}{\text{per input unit}}$$

Standard direct material cost per jacket: 2 square yards of cloth input allowed per output unit (jacket) manufactured, at $30 standard price per square yard

$$\text{Standard direct material cost per jacket} = 2 \text{ square yards} \times \$30 \text{ per square yard} = \$60$$

Standard direct manufacturing labor cost per jacket: 0.8 manufacturing labor-hour of input allowed per output unit manufactured, at $20 standard price per hour

$$\text{Standard direct manufacturing labor cost per jacket} = 0.8 \text{ labor-hour} \times \$20 \text{ per labor-hour} = \$16$$

How are the words *budget* and *standard* related? Budget is the broader term. To clarify, budgeted input prices, input quantities, and costs need *not* be based on standards. As we saw previously, they could be based on past data or competitive benchmarks. However, when standards *are* used to obtain budgeted input quantities and prices, the terms *standard* and *budget* are used interchangeably. The standard cost of each input required for one unit of output is determined by the standard quantity of the input required for one unit of output and the standard price per input unit. Notice how the standard-cost computations shown previously for direct materials and direct manufacturing labor result in the budgeted direct material cost per jacket of $60 and the budgeted direct manufacturing labor cost of $16 referred to earlier.

In its standard costing system, Webb uses standards that are attainable by operating efficiently but that allow for normal disruptions. A normal disruption could include, for example, a short delay in the receipt of materials needed to produce the jackets or a production delay because a piece of equipment needed a minor repair. An alternative is to set more-challenging standards that are more difficult to attain. As we discussed in Chapter 6, setting challenging standards can increase the motivation of employees and a firm's performance. However, as we have indicated, if workers believe the standards are unachievable, they can become frustrated and the firm's performance could suffer.

Decision Point

What is a standard cost and what are its purposes?

Learning Objective 5

Compute price variances

...each price variance is the difference between an actual input price and a budgeted input price

and efficiency variances

...each efficiency variance is the difference between an actual input quantity and a budgeted input quantity for actual output

for direct-cost categories

Price Variances and Efficiency Variances for Direct-Cost Inputs

Consider Webb's two direct-cost categories. The actual cost for each of these categories for the 10,000 jackets manufactured and sold in April 2014 is as follows:

Direct Materials Purchased and Used[4]	
1. Square yards of cloth input purchased and used	22,200
2. Actual price incurred per square yard	$ 28
3. Direct material costs (22,200 × $28) [shown in Exhibit 7-2, column 1]	$621,600

Direct manufacturing Labor used	
1. Direct manufacturing labor-hours used	9,000
2. Actual price incurred per direct manufacturing labor-hour	$ 22
3. Direct manufacturing labor costs (9,000 × $22) [shown in Exhibit 7-2, column 1]	$198,000

Let's use the Webb Company data to illustrate the price variance and the efficiency variance for direct-cost inputs.

A **price variance** is the difference between actual price and budgeted price, multiplied by the actual input quantity, such as direct materials purchased. A price variance is sometimes called a **rate variance**, especially when it's used to describe the price variance for direct manufacturing labor. An **efficiency variance** is the difference between the actual input quantity used (such as square yards of cloth) and the budgeted input quantity allowed for actual output, multiplied by budgeted price. An efficiency variance is sometimes called a **usage variance**. Let's explore price and efficiency variances in greater detail so we can see how managers use them.

Price Variances

The formula for computing the price variance is as follows:

$$\text{Price variance} = \left(\text{Actual price of input} - \text{Budgeted price of input}\right) \times \text{Actual quantity of input}$$

The price variances for Webb's two direct-cost categories are as follows:

Direct-Cost Category	(**Actual price of input**	− **Budgeted price of input**)	× **Actual quantity of input**	= **Price Variance**
Direct materials	($28 per sq. yard)	− $30 per sq. yard)	× 22,200 square yards	= $44,400 F
Direct manufacturing labor	($22 per hour	− $20 per hour)	× 9,000 hours	= $18,000 U

[4] The Problem for Self-Study (pages 268–269) relaxes the assumption that the quantity of direct materials used equals the quantity of direct materials purchased.

The direct materials price variance is favorable because the actual price of cloth is less than the budgeted price, resulting in an increase in operating income. The direct manufacturing labor price variance is unfavorable because the actual wage rate paid to labor is more than the budgeted rate, resulting in a decrease in operating income.

Managers should always consider a broad range of possible causes for a price variance. For example, Webb's favorable direct materials price variance could be due to one or more of the following:

- Webb's purchasing manager negotiated the direct materials prices more skillfully than was planned for in the budget.
- The purchasing manager switched to a lower-price supplier.
- The purchasing manager ordered larger quantities than the quantities budgeted, thereby obtaining quantity discounts.
- Direct materials prices decreased unexpectedly due to an oversupply of materials in the industry.
- The budgeted purchase prices of direct materials were set too high because managers did not carefully analyze market conditions.
- The purchasing manager negotiated favorable prices because he was willing to accept unfavorable terms on factors other than prices (such as agree to lower-quality material).

How Webb's managers respond to the direct materials price variance depends on what they believe caused it. For example, if they believe the purchasing manager received quantity discounts by ordering a larger amount of materials than budgeted, Webb could investigate whether the larger quantities resulted in higher storage costs for the firm. If the increase in storage and inventory holding costs exceeds the quantity discounts, purchasing in larger quantities is not beneficial. Some companies have reduced their materials storage areas to prevent their purchasing managers from ordering in larger quantities.

Efficiency Variance

For any actual level of output, the efficiency variance is the difference between the actual quantity of input used and the budgeted quantity of input allowed for that output level, multiplied by the budgeted input price:

$$\text{Efficiency variance} = \left(\begin{array}{c}\text{Actual}\\ \text{quantity of}\\ \text{input used}\end{array} - \begin{array}{c}\text{Budgeted quantity}\\ \text{of input allowed}\\ \text{for actual output}\end{array}\right) \times \begin{array}{c}\text{Budgeted price}\\ \text{of input}\end{array}$$

The idea here is that, given a certain output level, a company is inefficient if it uses a larger quantity of input than budgeted. Conversely, a company is efficient if it uses a smaller input quantity than was budgeted for that output level.

The efficiency variances for each of Webb's direct-cost categories are as follows:

Direct-Cost Category	(Actual quantity of input used − Budgeted quantity of input allowed for actual output)	× Budgeted price of input	= Efficiency variance
Direct materials	[22,200 sq. yds. − (10,000 units × 2 sq. yds./unit)]	× \$30 per sq. yard	
	= (22,200 sq. yds. − 20,000 sq. yds.)	× \$30 per sq. yard	= \$66,000 U
Direct manufacturing labor	[9,000 hours − (10,000 units × 0.8 hour/unit)]	× \$20 per hour	
	= (9,000 hours − 8,000 hours)	× \$20 per hour	= 20,000 U

The two manufacturing efficiency variances—the direct materials efficiency variance and the direct manufacturing labor efficiency variance—are each unfavorable. Why? Because given the firm's actual output, more of these inputs were used than were budgeted for. This lowered Webb's operating income.

As with price variances, there is a broad range of possible causes for these efficiency variances. For example, Webb's unfavorable efficiency variance for direct manufacturing labor could be because of one or more of the following:

- Webb's workers took longer to make each jacket because they worked more slowly or made poor-quality jackets that required reworking.
- Webb's personnel manager hired underskilled workers.
- Webb's production scheduler inefficiently scheduled work, resulting in more manufacturing labor time than budgeted being used per jacket.
- Webb's maintenance department did not properly maintain machines, resulting in more manufacturing labor time than budgeted being used per jacket.
- Webb's budgeted time standards were too tight because the skill levels of employees and the environment in which they operated weren't accurately evaluated.

Suppose Webb's managers determine that the unfavorable variance is due to poor machine maintenance. Webb could then establish a team consisting of plant engineers and machine operators to develop a maintenance schedule to reduce future breakdowns and prevent adverse effects on labor time and product quality.[5]

Exhibit 7-3 provides an alternative way to calculate price and efficiency variances. It shows how the price variance and the efficiency variance subdivide the flexible-budget variance. Consider direct materials. The direct materials flexible-budget variance of $21,600 U is the difference between the actual costs incurred (actual input quantity × actual price) of $621,600 shown in column 1 and the flexible budget (budgeted input quantity allowed

Exhibit 7-3 Columnar Presentation of Variance Analysis: Direct Costs for Webb Company for April 2014[a]

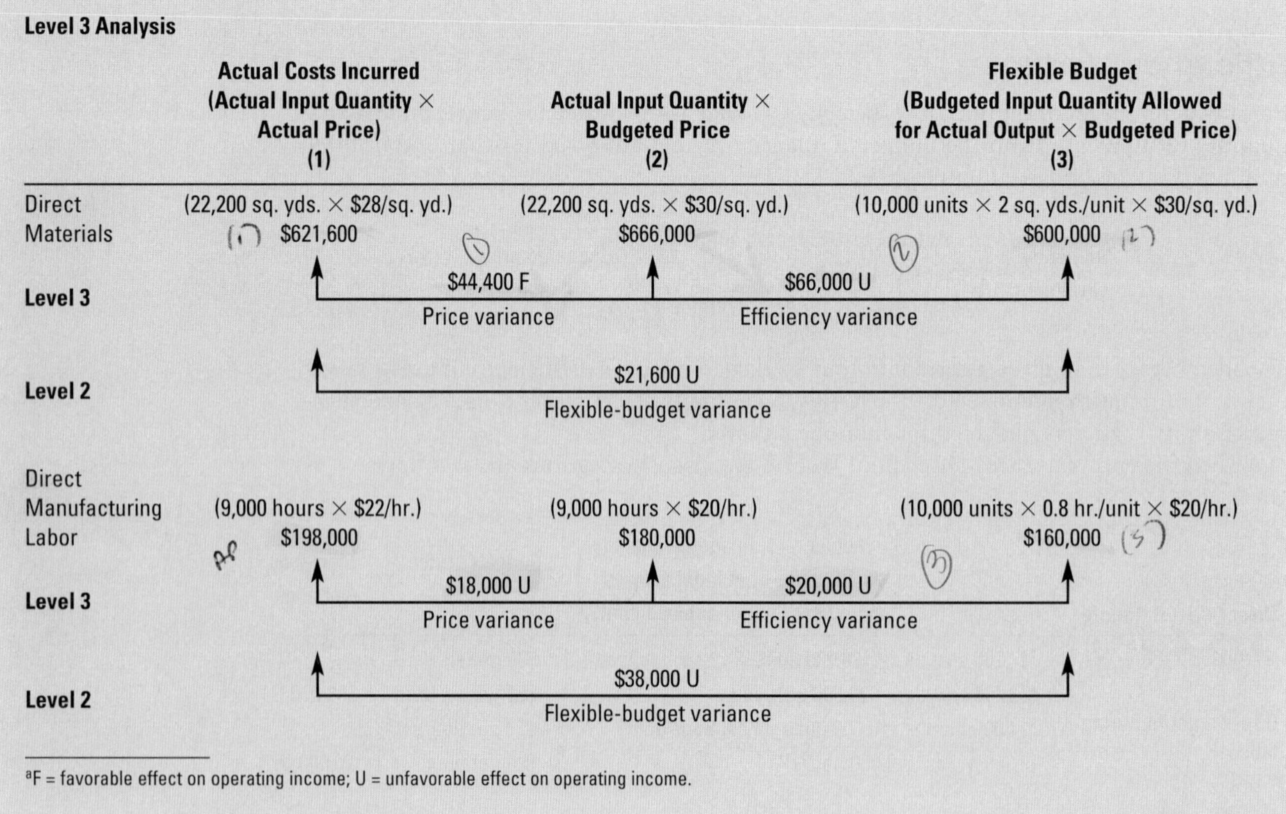

Level 3 Analysis

	Actual Costs Incurred (Actual Input Quantity × Actual Price) (1)		Actual Input Quantity × Budgeted Price (2)		Flexible Budget (Budgeted Input Quantity Allowed for Actual Output × Budgeted Price) (3)
Direct Materials	(22,200 sq. yds. × $28/sq. yd.) $621,600		(22,200 sq. yds. × $30/sq. yd.) $666,000		(10,000 units × 2 sq. yds./unit × $30/sq. yd.) $600,000
Level 3		$44,400 F Price variance		$66,000 U Efficiency variance	
Level 2			$21,600 U Flexible-budget variance		
Direct Manufacturing Labor	(9,000 hours × $22/hr.) $198,000		(9,000 hours × $20/hr.) $180,000		(10,000 units × 0.8 hr./unit × $20/hr.) $160,000
Level 3		$18,000 U Price variance		$20,000 U Efficiency variance	
Level 2			$38,000 U Flexible-budget variance		

[a]F = favorable effect on operating income; U = unfavorable effect on operating income.

[5] When there are multiple inputs, such as different types of materials, that can be substituted for one another, the efficiency variance can be further decomposed into mix and yield variances. The appendix to this chapter describes how these variances are calculated.

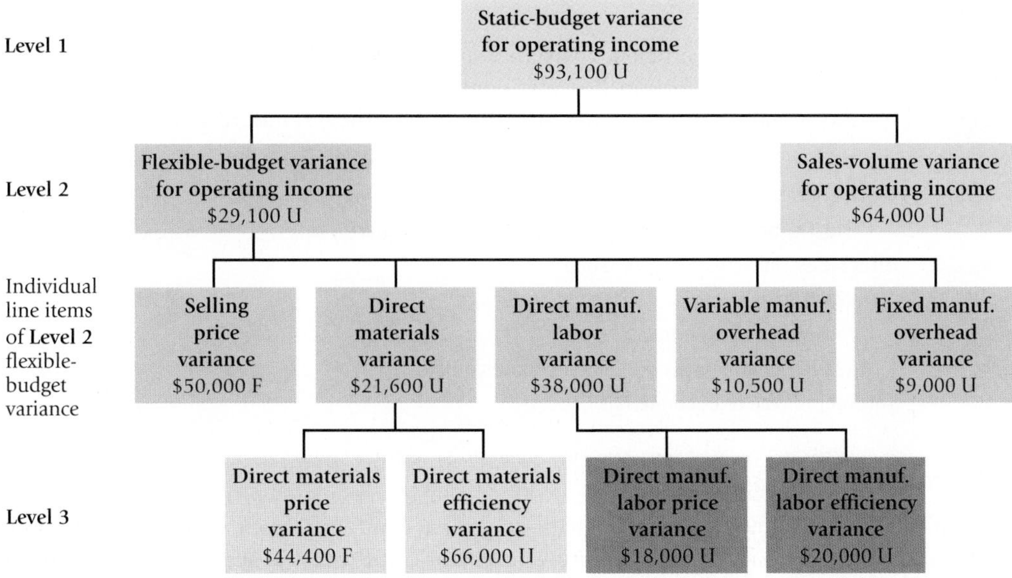

Exhibit 7-4

Summary of Level 1, 2, and 3 Variance Analyses

for actual output × budgeted price) of $600,000 shown in column 3. Column 2 (actual input quantity × budgeted price) is inserted between column 1 and column 3. The difference between columns 1 and 2 is the price variance of $44,400 F. This price variance occurs because the same actual input quantity (22,200 sq. yds.) is multiplied by the *actual price* ($28) in column 1 and the *budgeted price* ($30) in column 2. The difference between columns 2 and 3 is the efficiency variance of $66,000 U because the same budgeted price ($30) is multiplied by the *actual input quantity* (22,200 sq. yds) in column 2 and the *budgeted input quantity allowed for actual output* (20,000 sq. yds.) in column 3. The sum of the direct materials price variance, $44,400 F, and the direct materials efficiency variance, $66,000 U, equals the direct materials flexible budget variance, $21,600 U.

Exhibit 7-4 provides a summary of the different variances. Note how the variances at each higher level provide disaggregated and more detailed information for evaluating performance.

We now present Webb's journal entries under its standard costing system.

Journal Entries Using Standard Costs

Chapter 4 illustrated journal entries when normal costing is used. We will now illustrate journal entries for Webb Company using standard costing. Our focus is on direct materials and direct manufacturing labor. All the numbers included in the following journal entries are found in Exhibit 7-3.

Note: In each of the following entries, unfavorable variances are always debits (they decrease operating income), and favorable variances are always credits (they increase operating income).

Journal Entry 1A

Isolate the direct materials price variance at the time the materials were purchased. This is done by increasing (debiting) the Direct Materials Control account by the standard price Webb established for purchasing the materials. This is the earliest time possible to isolate this variance.

1a.	Direct Materials Control		
	(22,200 square yards × $30 per square yard)	666,000	
	Direct Materials Price Variance		
	(22,200 square yards × $2 per square yard)		44,400
	Accounts Payable Control		
	(22,200 square yards × $28 per square yard)		621,600
	This records the direct materials purchased.		

Journal Entry 1B

Isolate the direct materials efficiency variance at the time the direct materials are used by increasing (debiting) the Work-in-Process Control account. Use the standard quantities allowed for the actual output units manufactured times their standard purchase prices.

1b.	Work-in-Process Control		
	(10,000 jackets × 2 yards per jacket × $30 per square yard)	600,000	
	Direct Materials Efficiency Variance		
	(2,200 square yards × $30 per square yard)	66,000	
	Direct Materials Control		
	(22,200 square yards × $30 per square yard)		666,000
	This records the direct materials used.		

Journal Entry 2

Isolate the direct manufacturing labor price variance and efficiency variance at the time the labor is used by increasing (debiting) the Work-in-Process Control by the standard hours and standard wage rates allowed for the actual units manufactured. Note that the Wages Payable Control account measures the actual amounts payable to workers based on the actual hours they worked and their actual wage rate.

2.	Work-in-Process Control		
	(10,000 jackets × 0.80 hour per jacket × $20 per hour)	160,000	
	Direct Manufacturing Labor Price Variance		
	(9,000 hours × $2 per hour)	18,000	
	Direct Manufacturing Labor Efficiency Variance		
	(1,000 hours × $20 per hour)	20,000	
	Wages Payable Control		
	(9,000 hours × $22 per hour)		198,000
	This records the liability for Webb's direct manufacturing labor costs.		

You have learned how standard costing and variance analysis help managers focus on areas not operating as expected. The journal entries here point to another advantage of standard costing systems: standard costs simplify product costing. As each unit is manufactured, costs are assigned to it using the standard cost of direct materials, the standard cost of direct manufacturing labor, and, as you will see in a later chapter (Chapter 8), the standard manufacturing overhead cost.

From the perspective of control, all variances should be isolated at the earliest possible time. For example, by isolating the direct materials price variance at the time materials are purchased, managers can take corrective actions—such as trying to obtain cost reductions from the firm's current suppliers or obtaining price quotes from other potential suppliers—immediately when a large unfavorable variance is known rather than waiting until after the materials are used in production.

If the variance accounts are immaterial in amount at the end of the fiscal year, they are written off to the cost of goods sold. For simplicity, we assume that the balances in the different direct cost variance accounts as of April 2014 are also the balances at the end of 2014 and are immaterial in total. Webb would record the following journal entry to write off the direct cost variance accounts to the Cost of Goods Sold account.

Cost of Goods Sold	59,600	
Direct Materials Price Variance	44,400	
Direct Materials Efficiency Variance		66,000
Direct Manufacturing Labor Price Variance		18,000
Direct Manufacturing Labor Efficiency Variance		20,000

Alternatively, assuming Webb has inventories at the end of the fiscal year and the variances are material in their amounts, the variance accounts will be prorated among the cost of goods sold and various inventory accounts using the methods described in Chapter 4 (pages 128–129). For example, the Direct Materials Price Variance will be prorated among Materials Control, Work-in-Process Control, Finished Goods Control, and Cost of Goods Sold on the basis of the standard costs of direct materials in each account's ending balance. Direct Materials Efficiency Variance is prorated among Work-in-Process Control, Finished Goods Control, and Cost of Goods Sold on the basis of the direct material costs in each account's ending balance (after proration of the direct materials price variance).

As discussed in Chapter 4, many accountants, industrial engineers, and managers argue that to the extent variances measure inefficiency during the year, they should be written off against income for that period instead of being prorated among inventories and the cost of goods sold. These people believe it's better to apply a combination of the write-off and proration methods for each individual variance. That way, unlike full proration, the firm doesn't end up carrying the costs of inefficiency as part of its inventoriable costs. Consider the efficiency variance: The portion of the variance due to avoidable inefficiencies should be written off to cost of goods sold. In contrast, the portion that is unavoidable should be prorated. Likewise, if a portion of the direct materials price variance is unavoidable because it is entirely caused by general market conditions, it too should be prorated.

Implementing Standard Costing

Standard costing provides valuable information that is used for the management and control of materials, labor, and other activities related to production.

Standard Costing and Information Technology

Both large and small firms are increasingly using computerized standard costing systems. For example, companies such as Sandoz, a maker of generic drugs, and Dell store standard prices and standard quantities in their computer systems. A bar code scanner records the receipt of materials, immediately costing each material using its stored standard price. The receipt of materials is then matched with the firm's purchase orders and recorded in accounts payable, and the direct material price variance is isolated.

The direct materials efficiency variance is calculated as output is completed by comparing the standard quantity of direct materials that should have been used with the computerized request for direct materials submitted by an operator on the production floor. Labor variances are calculated as employees log into production-floor terminals and punch in their employee numbers, start and end times, and the quantity of product they helped produce. Managers use this instantaneous feedback from variances to immediately detect and correct any cost-related problem.

Wide Applicability of Standard Costing

Manufacturing firms as well as firms in the service sector find standard costing to be a useful tool. Companies implementing total quality management programs use standard costing to control materials costs. Service-sector companies such as McDonald's are labor intensive and use standard costs to control labor costs. Companies that have implemented computer-integrated manufacturing (CIM), such as Toyota, use flexible budgeting and standard costing to manage activities such as materials handling and setups. The growing use of Enterprise Resource Planning (ERP) systems, as described in Chapter 6, has made it easy for firms to keep track of the standard, average, and actual costs of items in inventory and to make real-time assessments of variances. Managers use variance information to identify areas of the firm's manufacturing or purchasing process that most need attention.

Decision Point

Why should a company calculate price and efficiency variances?

Concepts in Action

Starbucks Reduces Direct-Cost Variances to Brew a Turnaround

Along with coffee, Starbucks brewed profitable growth for many years. But when consumers tightened their purse strings amid the recent recession, the company was in serious trouble. With customers cutting back and lower-priced competition—from Dunkin' Donuts and McDonald's among others—increasing, Starbucks' profit margins were under attack.

For Starbucks, profitability depends on making each beverage at the lowest possible cost. In each Starbucks store, the two key direct costs are materials and labor. Materials costs at Starbucks include coffee beans, milk, flavoring syrups, pastries, paper cups, and lids. To reduce budgeted costs for materials, Starbucks sought to avoid waste and spoilage by no longer brewing decaffeinated and darker coffee blends in the afternoon and evening, when store traffic is slower. With milk prices rising, the company switched to 2% milk, which is healthier and costs less, and redoubled efforts to reduce milk-related spoilage. To reduce labor costs, stores employed fewer baristas. In other stores, Starbucks adopted many "lean" production techniques to make its drink-making processes more efficient. While some changes seem small—keeping bins of coffee beans on top of the counter so baristas don't have to bend over and moving bottles of flavored syrups closer to where drinks are made—some stores experienced a 10% increase in transactions using the same number of workers or fewer.

Starbucks' focus on reducing direct-cost variances paid off. The company has reduced its store operating expenses from 36.1% of total net revenue in 2008 to 29.5% in 2012. Continued focus on direct-cost variances will remain critical to the company's future success in any economic climate.

Sources: Adamy, Janet. 2009. Starbucks brews up new cost cuts by putting lid on afternoon decaf. *Wall Street Journal,* January 28; Harris, Craig. 2007. Starbucks slips; lattes rise. *Seattle Post Intelligencer,* July 23; Jargon, Julie. 2010. Starbucks growth revives, perked by Via. *Wall Street Journal,* January 21; Jargon, Julie. 2009. Latest Starbucks buzzword: 'Lean' Japanese techniques. *Wall Street Journal,* August 4; Kesmodel, David. 2009. Starbucks sees demand stirring again. *Wall Street Journal,* November 6; Starbucks Corporation, 2012 Annual Report (Seattle: Starbucks Corporation, 2013); and Starbucks Corporation, 2008 Annual Report (Seattle: Starbucks Corporation, 2009).

Learning Objective 6

Understand how managers use variances

. . . managers use variances to improve future performance

Management's Use of Variances

Managers and management accountants use variances to evaluate performance after decisions are implemented, to trigger organization learning, and to make continuous improvements. Variances serve as an early warning system to alert managers to existing problems or to prospective opportunities. When done well, variance analysis enables managers to evaluate the effectiveness of the actions and performance of personnel in the current period, as well as to fine-tune strategies for achieving improved performance in the future. Concepts in Action: Starbucks Reduces Direct-Cost Variances to Brew a Turnaround shows the huge payoff the coffee retailing giant has reaped from paying careful attention to variance analysis wth respect to its direct costs.

Multiple Causes of Variances

To interpret variances correctly and make appropriate decisions based on them, managers need to recognize that variances can have multiple causes. Managers must not interpret variances in isolation of each other. The causes of variances in one part of the value chain can be the result of decisions made in another part of the value chain. Consider an unfavorable direct materials efficiency variance on Webb's production line. Possible operational causes of this variance across the value chain of the company are:

1. Poor design of products or processes
2. Poor work on the production line because of underskilled workers or faulty machines
3. Inappropriate assignment of labor or machines to specific jobs
4. Congestion due to scheduling a large number of rush orders placed by Webb's sales representatives
5. Webb's cloth suppliers not manufacturing materials of uniformly high quality

Item 5 offers an even broader reason for the cause of the unfavorable direct materials efficiency variance by considering inefficiencies in the supply chain of companies—in this case, by the cloth suppliers for Webb's jackets. Whenever possible, managers must attempt to understand the root causes of the variances.

When to Investigate Variances

Because a standard is not a single measure but rather a range of acceptable input quantities, costs, output quantities, or prices, managers should expect small variances to arise. A variance within an acceptable range is considered to be an "in-control occurrence" and calls for no investigation or action by managers. So when do managers need to investigate variances?

Frequently, managers investigate variances based on subjective judgments or rules of thumb. For critical items, such as product defects, even a small variance can prompt an investigation. For other items, such as direct material costs, labor costs, and repair costs, companies generally have rules such as "investigate all variances exceeding $5,000 or 20% of the budgeted cost, whichever is lower." The idea is that a 4% variance in direct material costs of $1 million—a $40,000 variance—deserves more attention than a 15% variance in repair costs of $10,000—a $1,500 variance. In other words, variance analysis is subject to the same cost–benefit test as all other phases of a management control system.

Using Variances for Performance Measurement

Managers often use variance analysis when evaluating the performance of their employees or business units. Two attributes of performance are commonly evaluated:

1. **Effectiveness:** the degree to which a predetermined objective or target is met, such as the sales, market share, and customer satisfaction ratings of Starbucks' VIA® Ready Brew line of instant coffees.
2. **Efficiency:** the relative amount of inputs used to achieve a given output level. For example, the smaller the quantity of Arabica beans used to make a given number of VIA packets or the greater the number of VIA packets made from a given quantity of beans, the greater the efficiency.

As we discussed earlier, it is important to understand the causes of a variance before using it for performance evaluation. Suppose a purchasing manager for Starbucks has just negotiated a deal that results in a favorable price variance for direct materials. The deal could have achieved a favorable variance for any or all of the following reasons:

1. The purchasing manager bargained effectively with suppliers.
2. The purchasing manager secured a discount for buying in bulk with fewer purchase orders. (However, buying larger quantities than necessary for the short run resulted in excessive inventory.)
3. The purchasing manager accepted a bid from the lowest-priced supplier without fully checking the supplier's quality-monitoring procedures.

If the purchasing manager's performance is evaluated solely on price variances, then the evaluation will be positive. Reason 1 would support this conclusion: The purchasing manager bargained effectively. Reasons 2 and 3, buying in bulk or buying without checking the supplier's quality-monitoring procedures, will lead to short-run gains. But should these lead to a positive evaluation for the purchasing manager? Not necessarily. These short-run gains could be offset by higher inventory storage costs or higher inspection costs and defect rates. Starbucks may ultimately lose more money because of reasons 2 and 3 than it gains from the favorable price variance.

Bottom line: Managers should not automatically interpret a favorable variance as "good news" or assume it means their subordinates performed well.

Firms benefit from variance analysis because it highlights individual aspects of performance. However, if any single performance measure (for example, achieving a certain labor efficiency variance or a certain consumer rating) is overemphasized, managers will tend to make decisions that will cause the particular performance measure to look good. These actions may conflict with the company's overall goals, inhibiting the goals from being achieved. This faulty perspective on performance usually arises when top management designs a performance evaluation and reward system that does not emphasize total company objectives.

Organization Learning

The goal of variance analysis is for managers to understand why variances arise, to learn, and to improve their firm's future performance. For instance, to reduce the unfavorable direct materials efficiency variance, Webb's managers may attempt to improve the design of its jackets, the commitment of its workers to do the job right the first time, and the quality of the materials. Sometimes an unfavorable direct materials efficiency variance may signal a need to change the strategy related to a product, perhaps because it cannot be made at a low enough cost. Variance analysis should not be used to "play the blame game" (find someone to blame for every unfavorable variance) but to help managers learn about what happened and how to perform better in the future.

Companies need to strike a delicate balance between using variances to evaluate the performance of managers and employees and improve learning within the organization. If the performance evaluation aspect is overemphasized, managers will focus on setting and meeting targets that are easy to attain rather than targets that are challenging, require creativity and resourcefulness, and result in continuous improvement. For example, Webb's manufacturing manager will prefer an easy standard that allows workers ample time to manufacture a jacket. But that will provide the manufacturing department little incentive to improve processes and identify methods to reduce production times and costs. Alternatively, the manufacturing manager might urge workers to produce jackets within the time allowed, even if this leads to poorer quality jackets being produced, which would later hurt revenues. If variance analysis is seen as a way to promote learning within the organization, negative effects such as these can be minimized.

Continuous Improvement

Managers can also use variance analysis to create a virtuous cycle of continuous improvement. How? By repeatedly identifying the causes of variances, taking corrective actions, and evaluating the results. Improvement opportunities are often easier to identify when the company first produces a product. Once managers identify easy improvements, much more ingenuity may be required to identify successive ones. Some companies use kaizen budgeting (Chapter 6, p. 220) to specifically target reductions in budgeted costs over successive periods. The advantage of kaizen budgeting is that it makes continuous improvement goals explicit.

Financial and Nonfinancial Performance Measures

Almost all companies use a combination of financial and nonfinancial performance measures for planning and control rather than relying exclusively on either type of measure. To control a production process, supervisors cannot wait for an accounting report with variances reported in dollars. Instead, timely nonfinancial performance measures are frequently used for control purposes. For example, Nissan and many other manufacturers display real-time defect rates and production levels on large LED screens throughout their plants for workers and managers to see.

In Webb's cutting room, cloth is laid out and cut into pieces, which are then matched and assembled. Managers exercise control in the cutting room by observing workers and by focusing on *nonfinancial measures*, such as number of square yards of cloth used to produce 1,000 jackets or the percentage of jackets started and completed without requiring any rework. Webb's production workers find these nonfinancial measures easy to understand. Webb's managers also use *financial measures* to evaluate the overall cost efficiency with which operations are being run and to help guide decisions about, say, changing the mix of inputs used in manufacturing jackets. Financial measures are critical in a company because they indicate the economic impact of diverse physical activities. This knowledge allows managers to make trade-offs, such as increasing the costs of one physical activity (say, cutting) to reduce the costs of another physical measure (say, defects).

Decision Point

How do managers use variances?

Benchmarking and Variance Analysis

Learning Objective 7

Describe benchmarking and explain its role in cost management

...benchmarking compares actual performance against the best levels of performance

Webb Company based its budgeted amounts on analysis of its own operations. We now turn to the situation in which companies develop standards based on the operations of other companies. **Benchmarking** is the continuous process of comparing your firm's performance levels against the best levels of performance in competing companies or in companies having similar processes. When benchmarks are used as standards, managers and management accountants know that the company will be competitive in the marketplace if it can meet or beat those standards.

Companies develop benchmarks and calculate variances on items that are the most important to their businesses. A common unit of measurement used to compare the efficiency of airlines is cost per available seat mile. Available seat mile (ASM) is a measure of airline size and equals the total seats in a plane multiplied by the distance the plane traveled. Consider the cost per available seat mile for United. Assume United uses data from each of six competing U.S. airlines in its benchmark cost comparisons. Summary data are in Exhibit 7-5. The benchmark companies are in alphabetical order in column A. Also reported in Exhibit 7-5 are operating cost per ASM, operating revenue per ASM, operating income per ASM, fuel cost per ASM, labor cost per ASM, and total available seat miles for each airline. The slow recovery of the travel industry from the recession induced by the financial crisis is evident in the fact that only five of the seven airlines have positive levels of operating income.

How well did United manage its costs? The answer depends on which specific benchmark is being used for comparison. United's actual operating cost of 14.19 cents per ASM is above the average operating cost of 12.91 cents per ASM of the six other airlines. Moreover, United's operating cost per ASM is 24.2% higher than JetBlue Airways, the lowest-cost competitor at 11.42 cents per ASM [(14.19 − 11.42) ÷ 11.42 = 0.242]. So why is United's operating cost per ASM so high? Columns E and F suggest that both fuel cost and labor cost are possible reasons. These benchmarking data alert management at United that it needs to become more efficient in its use of both material and labor inputs to become more cost competitive.

It can be difficult for firms to find appropriate benchmarks such as those in Exhibit 7-5. Many companies purchase benchmark data from consulting firms. Another problem is ensuring the benchmark numbers are comparable. In other words, there needs to be an "apples to apples" comparison. Differences can exist across companies in their strategies, inventory costing methods, depreciation methods, and so on. For example, JetBlue serves fewer cities and flies mostly long-haul routes compared with United, which serves almost all major U.S. cities and several international cities and flies both long-haul and short-haul routes. Southwest Airlines differs from United because it specializes in short-haul direct flights and offers fewer services on board its planes. Because United's strategy is different from the strategies of JetBlue and Southwest, one might expect its cost per ASM to be different, too. United's strategy is more comparable to the strategies of American, Delta, and U.S. Airways. Note that its costs per ASM are relatively more competitive with these airlines. But United

Exhibit 7-5 Available Seat Mile (ASM) Benchmark Comparison of United Airlines with Six Other Airlines

Airline	Operating Cost (Cents per ASM) (1)	Operating Revenue (Cents per ASM) (2)	Operating Income (Cents per ASM) (3) = (2) – (1)	Fuel Cost (Cents per ASM) (4)	Labor Cost (Cents per ASM) (5)	Total ASMs (Millions) (6)
United Airlines	14.19	13.10	- 1.09	4.90	4.24	216,299
Airlines used as benchmarks:						
Alaska Airlines	11.90	13.09	1.19	4.10	3.53	28,185
American Airlines	14.26	13.47	-0.79	4.90	4.28	152,627
Delta Airlines	13.80	14.48	0.68	5.00	3.86	200,880
JetBlue Airways	11.42	11.96	0.54	4.40	2.76	40,095
Southwest Airlines	12.83	13.29	0.46	4.60	3.90	128,272
U.S. Airways	13.25	13.49	0.24	4.60	3.54	74,204
Average of airlines used as benchmarks	12.91	13.30	0.39	4.60	3.65	104,044

Source: 2012 data from the MIT Global Airline Industry Program

competes head to head with JetBlue and Southwest in several cities and markets, so it still needs to benchmark against these carriers as well.

Decision Point
What is benchmarking and why is it useful?

United's management accountants can use benchmarking data to address several questions. How do factors such as plane size and type or the duration of flights affect the cost per ASM? Do airlines differ in their fixed cost/variable cost structures? To what extent can United's performance be improved by rerouting flights, using different types of aircraft on different routes, or changing the frequency or timing of specific flights? What explains revenue differences per ASM across airlines? Is it differences in the service quality passengers perceive or differences in an airline's competitive power at specific airports? Management accountants are more valuable to managers when they use benchmarking data to provide insight into *why* costs or revenues differ across companies or within plants of the same company, as distinguished from simply reporting the magnitude of the differences.

Problem for Self-Study

O'Shea Company manufactures ceramic vases. It uses its standard costing system when developing its flexible-budget amounts. In September 2014, 2,000 finished units were produced. The following information relates to its two direct manufacturing cost categories: direct materials and direct manufacturing labor.

Direct materials used were 4,400 kilograms (kg). The standard direct materials input allowed for one output unit is 2 kilograms at \$15 per kilogram. O'Shea purchased 5,000 kilograms of materials at \$16.50 per kilogram, a total of \$82,500. (This Problem for Self-Study illustrates how to calculate direct materials variances when the quantity of materials *purchased* in a period differs from the quantity of materials *used* in that period.)

Actual direct manufacturing labor-hours were 3,250, at a total cost of \$66,300. Standard manufacturing labor time allowed is 1.5 hours per output unit, and the standard direct manufacturing labor cost is \$20 per hour.

Required

1. Calculate the direct materials price variance and efficiency variance and the direct manufacturing labor price variance and efficiency variance. Base the direct materials price variance on a flexible budget for *actual quantity purchased*, but base the direct materials efficiency variance on a flexible budget for *actual quantity used*.
2. Prepare journal entries for a standard costing system that isolates variances at the earliest possible time.

Solution

1. Exhibit 7-6 shows how the columnar presentation of variances introduced in Exhibit 7-3 can be adjusted for the difference in timing between purchase and use of materials. Note, in particular, the two sets of computations in column 2 for direct materials—the $75,000 for direct materials purchased and the $66,000 for direct materials used. The direct materials price variance is calculated on purchases so that managers responsible for the purchase can immediately identify and isolate reasons for the variance and initiate any desired corrective action. The efficiency variance is the responsibility of the production manager, so this variance is identified only at the time materials are used.

2.

Materials Control (5,000 kg × $15 per kg)	75,000	
Direct Materials Price Variance (5,000 kg × $1.50 per kg)	7,500	
Accounts Payable Control (5,000 kg × $16.50 per kg)		82,500
Work-in-Process Control (2,000 units × 2 kg per unit × $15 per kg)	60,000	
Direct Materials Efficiency Variance (400 kg × $15 per kg)	6,000	
Materials Control (4,400 kg × $15 per kg)		66,000
Work-in-Process Control (2,000 units × 1.5 hours per unit × $20 per hour)	60,000	
Direct Manufacturing Labor Price Variance (3,250 hours × $0.40 per hour)	1,300	
Direct Manufacturing Labor Efficiency Variance (250 hours × $20 per hour)	5,000	
Wages Payable Control (3,250 hours × $20.40 per hour)		66,300

Note: All the variances are debits because they are unfavorable and therefore reduce operating income.

Exhibit 7-6 Columnar Presentation of Variance Analysis for O'Shea Company: Direct Materials and Direct Manufacturing Labor for September 2014

Level 3 Analysis

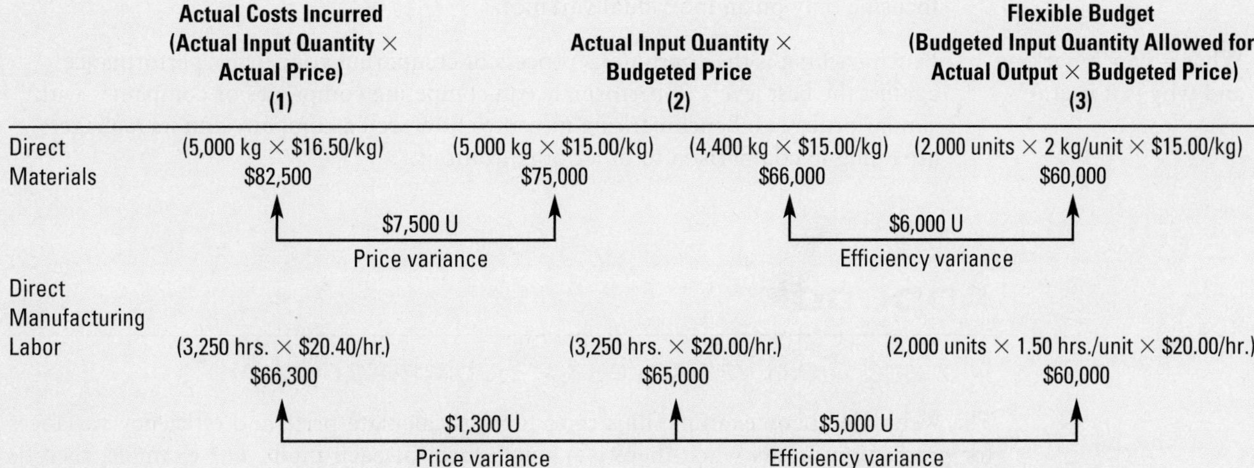

[a]F = favorable effect on operating income; U = unfavorable effect on operating income.

▶ Decision Points

The following question-and-answer format summarizes the chapter's learning objectives. Each decision presents a key question related to a learning objective. The guidelines are the answer to that question.

Decision	Guidelines
1. What are static budgets and static-budget variances?	A static budget is based on the level of output planned at the start of the budget period. The static-budget variance is the difference between the actual result and the corresponding budgeted amount in the static budget.
2. How can managers develop a flexible budget, and why is it useful to do so?	A flexible budget is adjusted (flexed) to recognize the actual output level of the budget period. Managers use a three-step procedure to develop a flexible budget. When all costs are either variable or fixed with respect to output, these three steps require only information about the budgeted selling price, budgeted variable cost per output unit, budgeted fixed costs, and actual quantity of output units. Flexible budgets help managers gain more insight into the causes of variances than is available from static budgets.
3. How are flexible-budget and sales-volume variances calculated?	The static-budget variance can be subdivided into a flexible-budget variance (the difference between the actual result and the corresponding flexible-budget amount) and a sales-volume variance (the difference between the flexible-budget amount and the corresponding static-budget amount).
4. What is a standard cost and what are its purposes?	A standard cost is a carefully determined cost used as a benchmark for judging performance. The purposes of a standard cost are to exclude past inefficiencies and to take into account changes expected to occur in the budget period.
5. Why should a company calculate price and efficiency variables?	The computation of price and efficiency variances helps managers gain insight into two different—but not independent—aspects of performance. The price variance focuses on the difference between the actual input price and the budgeted input price. The efficiency variance focuses on the difference between the actual quantity of input and the budgeted quantity of input allowed for actual output.
6. How do managers use variances?	Managers use variances for control, decision-making, performance evaluation, organization learning, and continuous improvement. When using variances for these purposes, managers should consider several variances together rather than focusing only on an individual variance.
7. What is benchmarking and why is it useful?	Benchmarking is the continuous process of comparing your firm's performance against the best levels of performance in competing companies or companies with similar processes. Benchmarking measures how well a company and its managers are doing in comparison to other organizations.

Appendix

Mix and Yield Variances for Substitutable Inputs

The Webb Company example illustrates how to calculate price and efficiency variances for production inputs when there is a single form of each input. For example, there is a single material (cloth) that is needed for production and a single type of direct labor employed by Webb. But what if managers have leeway in combining and substituting inputs? For example, Del Monte can combine material inputs (such as pineapples, cherries, and grapes) in varying proportions for its cans of fruit cocktail. Within limits, these individual fruits are *substitutable inputs* in making the fruit cocktail.

We illustrate how the efficiency variance discussed in this chapter (pages 259–260) can be subdivided into variances that highlight the financial impact of input mix and input yield when inputs are substitutable. Consider Delpino Corporation, which makes tomato ketchup. Our example focuses on direct material inputs and substitution among three of these inputs. The same approach can also be used to examine substitutable direct manufacturing labor inputs.

To produce ketchup of a specified consistency, color, and taste, Delpino mixes three types of tomatoes grown in different regions: Latin American tomatoes (Latoms), California tomatoes (Caltoms), and Florida tomatoes (Flotoms). Delpino's production standards require 1.60 tons of tomatoes to produce 1 ton of ketchup; 50% of the tomatoes are budgeted to be Latoms, 30% Caltoms, and 20% Flotoms. The direct material inputs budgeted to produce 1 ton of ketchup are as follows:

0.80 (50% of 1.6) ton of Latoms at $70 per ton	$ 56.00
0.48 (30% of 1.6) ton of Caltoms at $80 per ton	38.40
0.32 (20% of 1.6) ton of Flotoms at $90 per ton	28.80
Total budgeted cost of 1.6 tons of tomatoes	$123.20

Budgeted average cost per ton of tomatoes is $123.20 ÷ 1.60 tons = $77 per ton.

Because Delpino uses fresh tomatoes to make ketchup, no inventories of tomatoes are kept. Purchases are made as needed, so all price variances relate to tomatoes purchased and used. Actual results for June 2014 show that a total of 6,500 tons of tomatoes were used to produce 4,000 tons of ketchup:

3,250	tons of Latoms at actual cost of $70 per ton	$227,500
2,275	tons of Caltoms at actual cost of $82 per ton	186,550
975	tons of Flotoms at actual cost of $96 per ton	93,600
6,500	tons of tomatoes	507,650
Budgeted cost of 4,000 tons of ketchup at $123.20 per ton		492,800
Flexible-budget variance for direct materials		$ 14,850 U

Given the standard ratio of 1.60 tons of tomatoes to 1 ton of ketchup, 6,400 tons of tomatoes should be used to produce 4,000 tons of ketchup. At standard mix, quantities of each type of tomato required are as follows:

Latoms:	0.50 × 6,400 = 3,200 tons
Caltoms:	0.30 × 6,400 = 1,920 tons
Flotoms:	0.20 × 6,400 = 1,280 tons

Direct Materials Price and Efficiency Variances

Exhibit 7-7 presents in columnar format the analysis of the flexible-budget variance for direct materials discussed in the body of the chapter. The materials price and efficiency variances are calculated separately for each input material and then added together. The variance analysis prompts Delpino to investigate the unfavorable price and efficiency variances. Why did it pay more for tomatoes and use greater quantities than it had budgeted? Were actual market prices of tomatoes higher, in general, or could the purchasing department have negotiated lower prices? Did the inefficiencies result from inferior tomatoes or from problems in processing?

Direct Materials Mix and Direct Materials Yield Variances

Managers sometimes have discretion to substitute one material for another. The manager of Delpino's ketchup plant has some leeway in combining Latoms, Caltoms, and Flotoms without affecting the ketchup's quality. We will assume that to maintain quality, mix percentages of each type of tomato can only vary up to 5% from standard mix. For example, the percentage of Caltoms in the mix can vary between 25% and 35% (30% ± 5%).

Exhibit 7-7 Direct Materials Price and Efficiency Variances for the Delpino Corporation for June 2014

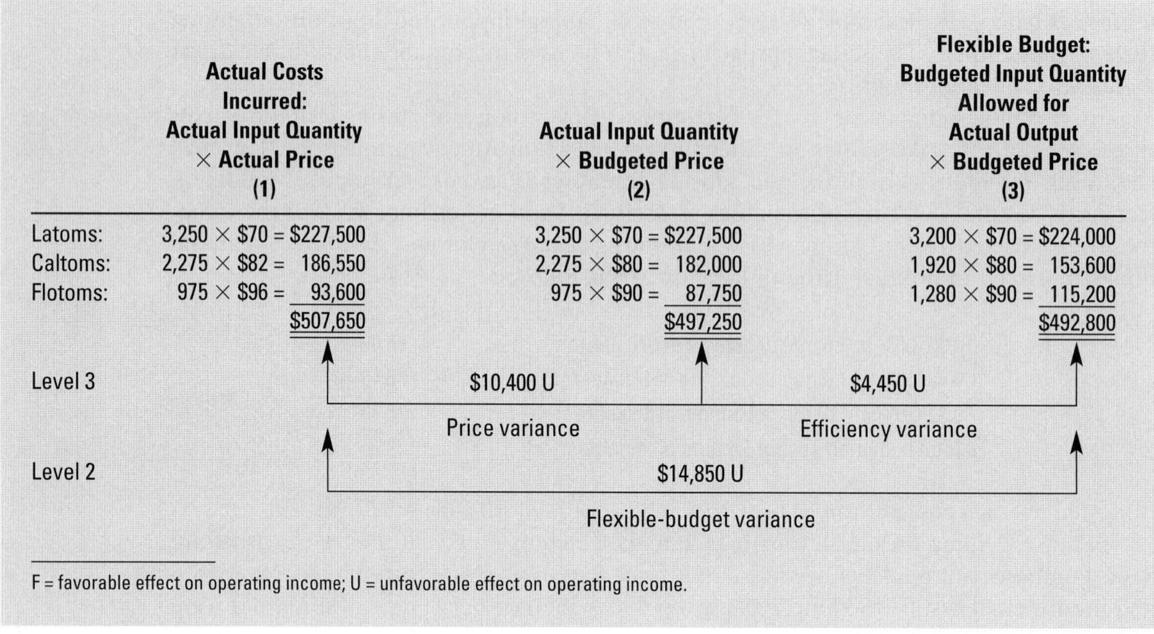

	Actual Costs Incurred: Actual Input Quantity × Actual Price (1)	Actual Input Quantity × Budgeted Price (2)	Flexible Budget: Budgeted Input Quantity Allowed for Actual Output × Budgeted Price (3)
Latoms:	3,250 × \$70 = \$227,500	3,250 × \$70 = \$227,500	3,200 × \$70 = \$224,000
Caltoms:	2,275 × \$82 = 186,550	2,275 × \$80 = 182,000	1,920 × \$80 = 153,600
Flotoms:	975 × \$96 = 93,600	975 × \$90 = 87,750	1,280 × \$90 = 115,200
	\$507,650	\$497,250	\$492,800

Level 3: \$10,400 U Price variance; \$4,450 U Efficiency variance

Level 2: \$14,850 U Flexible-budget variance

F = favorable effect on operating income; U = unfavorable effect on operating income.

When inputs are substitutable, direct materials efficiency improvement relative to budgeted costs can come from two sources: (1) using a cheaper mix to produce a given quantity of output, measured by the direct materials mix variance, and (2) using less input to achieve a given quantity of output, measured by the direct materials yield variance.

Holding actual total quantity of all direct materials inputs used constant, the total **direct materials mix variance** is the difference between (1) budgeted cost for actual mix of actual total quantity of direct materials used and (2) budgeted cost of budgeted mix of actual total quantity of direct materials used. Holding budgeted input mix constant, the **direct materials yield variance** is the difference between (1) budgeted cost of direct materials based on actual total quantity of direct materials used and (2) flexible-budget cost of direct materials based on budgeted total quantity of direct materials allowed for actual output produced. Exhibit 7-8 presents the direct materials mix and yield variances for the Delpino Corporation.

Direct Materials Mix Variance

The total direct materials mix variance is the sum of the direct materials mix variances for each input:

$$\begin{matrix}\text{Direct} \\ \text{materials} \\ \text{mix variance} \\ \text{for each input}\end{matrix} = \begin{matrix}\text{Actual total} \\ \text{quantity of all} \\ \text{direct materials} \\ \text{inputs used}\end{matrix} \times \left(\begin{matrix}\text{Actual} \\ \text{direct materials} \\ \text{input mix} \\ \text{percentage}\end{matrix} - \begin{matrix}\text{Budgeted} \\ \text{direct materials} \\ \text{input mix} \\ \text{percentage}\end{matrix}\right) \times \begin{matrix}\text{Budegeted} \\ \text{price of} \\ \text{direct materials} \\ \text{input}\end{matrix}$$

The direct materials mix variances are as follows:

Latoms:	6,500 tons × (0.50 − 0.50) × \$70 per ton = 6,500 × 0.00 × \$70	= \$ 0
Caltoms:	6,500 tons × (0.35 − 0.30) × \$80 per ton = 6,500 × 0.05 × \$80	= 26,000 U
Flotoms:	6,500 tons × (0.15 − 0.20) × \$90 per ton = 6,500 × −0.05 × \$90	= 29,250 F
Total direct materials mix variance		\$ 3,250 F

Exhibit 7-8 Total Direct Materials Yield and Mix Variances for the Delpino Corporation for June 2014

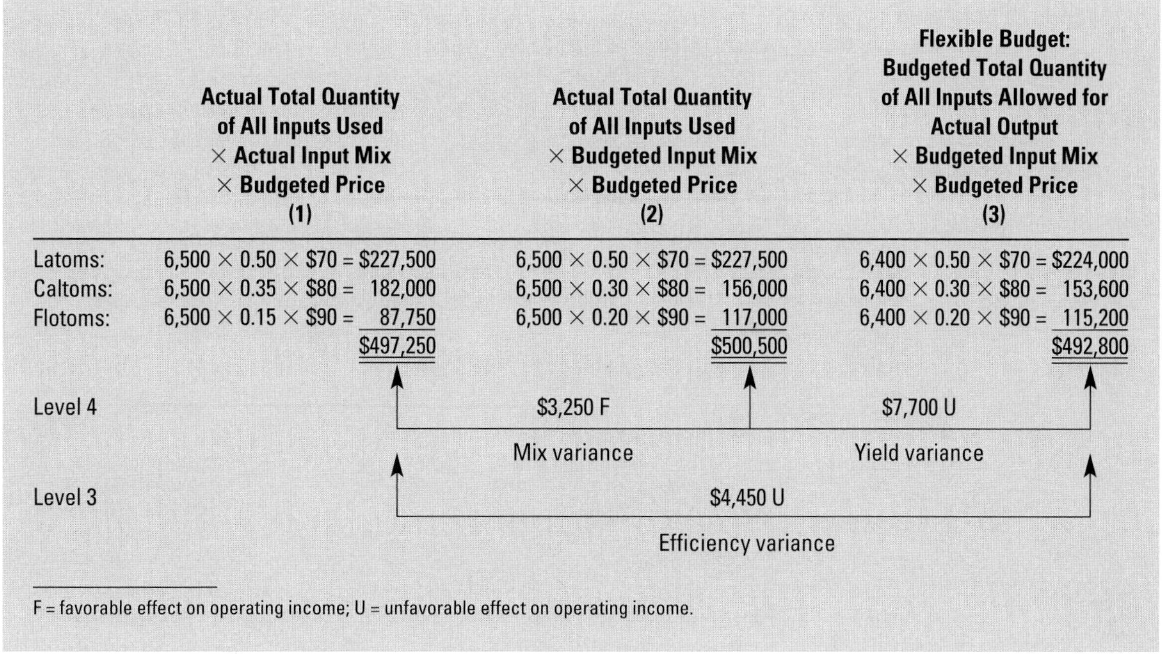

	Actual Total Quantity of All Inputs Used × Actual Input Mix × Budgeted Price (1)	Actual Total Quantity of All Inputs Used × Budgeted Input Mix × Budgeted Price (2)	Flexible Budget: Budgeted Total Quantity of All Inputs Allowed for Actual Output × Budgeted Input Mix × Budgeted Price (3)
Latoms:	6,500 × 0.50 × $70 = $227,500	6,500 × 0.50 × $70 = $227,500	6,400 × 0.50 × $70 = $224,000
Caltoms:	6,500 × 0.35 × $80 = 182,000	6,500 × 0.30 × $80 = 156,000	6,400 × 0.30 × $80 = 153,600
Flotoms:	6,500 × 0.15 × $90 = 87,750	6,500 × 0.20 × $90 = 117,000	6,400 × 0.20 × $90 = 115,200
	$497,250	$500,500	$492,800

Level 4: $3,250 F Mix variance; $7,700 U Yield variance

Level 3: $4,450 U Efficiency variance

F = favorable effect on operating income; U = unfavorable effect on operating income.

The total direct materials mix variance is favorable because relative to the budgeted mix, Delpino substitutes 5% of the cheaper Caltoms for 5% of the more-expensive Flotoms.

Direct Materials Yield Variance

The direct materials yield variance is the sum of the direct materials yield variances for each input:

$$\begin{matrix}\text{Direct}\\\text{materials}\\\text{yield variance}\\\text{for each input}\end{matrix} = \left(\begin{matrix}\text{Actual total}\\\text{quantity of}\\\text{all direct}\\\text{materials}\\\text{inputs used}\end{matrix} - \begin{matrix}\text{Budgeted total}\\\text{quantity of all}\\\text{direct materials}\\\text{input allowed}\\\text{for actual output}\end{matrix}\right) \times \begin{matrix}\text{Budgeted}\\\text{direct materials}\\\text{input mix}\\\text{percentage}\end{matrix} \times \begin{matrix}\text{Budegeted}\\\text{price of}\\\text{direct materials}\\\text{input}\end{matrix}$$

The direct materials yield variances are as follows:

Latoms:	(6,500 − 6,400) tons × 0.50 × $70 per ton = 100 × 0.50 × $70 =	$3,500 U
Caltoms:	(6,500 − 6,400) tons × 0.30 × $80 per ton = 100 × 0.30 × $80 =	2,400 U
Flotoms:	(6,500 − 6,400) tons × 0.20 × $90 per ton = 100 × 0.20 × $90 =	1,800 U
Total direct materials yield variance		$7,700 U

The total direct materials yield variance is unfavorable because Delpino used 6,500 tons of tomatoes rather than the 6,400 tons that it should have used to produce 4,000 tons of ketchup. Holding the budgeted mix and budgeted prices of tomatoes constant, the budgeted cost per ton of tomatoes in the budgeted mix is $77 per ton. The unfavorable yield variance represents the budgeted cost of using 100 more tons of tomatoes, (6,500 – 6,400) tons × $77 per ton = $7,700 U. Delpino would want to investigate reasons for this unfavorable yield variance. For example, did the substitution of the cheaper Caltoms for Flotoms that resulted in the favorable mix variance also cause the unfavorable yield variance?

The direct materials variances computed in Exhibits 7-7 and 7-8 can be summarized as follows:

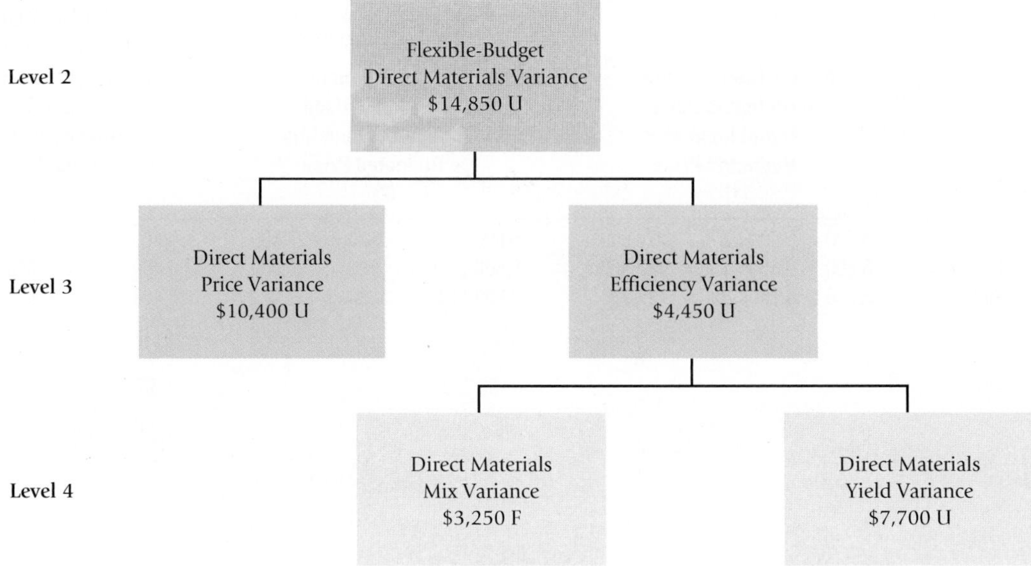

Terms to Learn

This chapter and the Glossary at the end of the book contain definitions of the following important terms:

benchmarking **(p. 267)**
budgeted performance **(p. 249)**
direct materials mix variance **(p. 272)**
direct materials yield variance **(p. 272)**
effectiveness **(p. 265)**
efficiency **(p. 265)**
efficiency variance **(p. 258)**
favorable variance **(p. 251)**
flexible budget **(p. 252)**
flexible-budget variance **(p. 253)**
management by exception **(p. 249)**
price variance **(p. 258)**
rate variance **(p. 258)**
sales-volume variance **(p. 253)**
selling-price variance **(p. 255)**
standard **(p. 257)**
standard cost **(p. 257)**
standard input **(p. 257)**
standard price **(p. 257)**
static budget **(p. 251)**
static-budget variance **(p. 251)**
unfavorable variance **(p. 251)**
usage variance **(p. 258)**
variance **(p. 249)**

Assignment Material

MyAccountingLab

Questions

7-1 What is the relationship between management by exception and variance analysis?

7-2 What are two possible sources of information a company might use to compute the budgeted amount in variance analysis?

7-3 Distinguish between a favorable variance and an unfavorable variance.

7-4 What is the key difference between a static budget and a flexible budget?

7-5 Why might managers find a flexible-budget analysis more informative than a static-budget analysis?

7-6 Describe the steps in developing a flexible budget.

7-7 List four reasons for using standard costs.

7-8 How might a manager gain insight into the causes of a flexible-budget variance for direct materials?

7-9 List three causes of a favorable direct materials price variance.

7-10 Describe three reasons for an unfavorable direct manufacturing labor efficiency variance.

7-11 How does variance analysis help in continuous improvement?

7-12 Why might an analyst examining variances in the production area look beyond that business function for explanations of those variances?

7-13 Comment on the following statement made by a plant manager: "Meetings with my plant accountant are frustrating. All he wants to do is pin the blame on someone for the many variances he reports."

7-14 How can the sales-volume variance be decomposed further to obtain useful information?

7-15 "Benchmarking against other companies enables a company to identify the lowest-cost producer. This amount should become the performance measure for next year." Do you agree?

Exercises

MyAccountingLab

7-16 Flexible budget. Brabham Enterprises manufactures tires for the Formula I motor racing circuit. For August 2014, it budgeted to manufacture and sell 3,000 tires at a variable cost of $74 per tire and total fixed costs of $54,000. The budgeted selling price was $110 per tire. Actual results in August 2014 were 2,800 tires manufactured and sold at a selling price of $112 per tire. The actual total variable costs were $229,600, and the actual total fixed costs were $50,000.

Required

1. Prepare a performance report (akin to Exhibit 7-2, page 253) that uses a flexible budget and a static budget.
2. Comment on the results in requirement 1.

7-17 Flexible budget. Connor Company's budgeted prices for direct materials, direct manufacturing labor, and direct marketing (distribution) labor per attaché case are $40, $8, and $12, respectively. The president is pleased with the following performance report:

	Actual Costs	Static Budget	Variance
Direct materials	$364,000	$400,000	$36,000 F
Direct manufacturing labor	78,000	80,000	2,000 F
Direct marketing (distribution) labor	110,000	120,000	10,000 F

Actual output was 8,800 attaché cases. Assume all three direct-cost items shown are variable costs.

Required

Is the president's pleasure justified? Prepare a revised performance report that uses a flexible budget and a static budget.

7-18 Flexible-budget preparation and analysis. Bank Management Printers, Inc., produces luxury checkbooks with three checks and stubs per page. Each checkbook is designed for an individual customer and is ordered through the customer's bank. The company's operating budget for September 2014 included these data:

Number of checkbooks	15,000
Selling price per book	$ 20
Variable cost per book	$ 8
Fixed costs for the month	$145,000

The actual results for September 2014 were as follows:

Number of checkbooks produced and sold	12,000
Average selling price per book	$ 21
Variable cost per book	$ 7
Fixed costs for the month	$150,000

The executive vice president of the company observed that the operating income for September was much lower than anticipated, despite a higher-than-budgeted selling price and a lower-than-budgeted variable cost per unit. As the company's management accountant, you have been asked to provide explanations for the disappointing September results.

Bank Management develops its flexible budget on the basis of budgeted per-output-unit revenue and per-output-unit variable costs without detailed analysis of budgeted inputs.

Required

1. Prepare a static-budget-based variance analysis of the September performance.
2. Prepare a flexible-budget-based variance analysis of the September performance.
3. Why might Bank Management find the flexible-budget-based variance analysis more informative than the static-budget-based variance analysis? Explain your answer.

7-19 Flexible budget, working backward. The Clarkson Company produces engine parts for car manufacturers. A new accountant intern at Clarkson has accidentally deleted the calculations on the company's variance analysis calculations for the year ended December 31, 2014. The following table is what remains of the data.

	A	B	C	D	E	F
1	**Performance Report, Year Ended December 31, 2014**					
2						
3		**Actual Results**	**Flexible-Budget Variances**	**Flexible Budget**	**Sales-Volume Variances**	**Static Budget**
4	Units sold	130,000				120,000
5	Revenues (sales)	$715,000				$420,000
6	Variable costs	515,000				240,000
7	Contribution margin	200,000				180,000
8	Fixed costs	140,000				120,000
9	Operating income	$ 60,000				$ 60,000

Required

1. Calculate all the required variances. (If your work is accurate, you will find that the total static-budget variance is $0.)
2. What are the actual and budgeted selling prices? What are the actual and budgeted variable costs per unit?
3. Review the variances you have calculated and discuss possible causes and potential problems. What is the important lesson learned here?

7-20 Flexible-budget and sales volume variances. Luster, Inc., produces the basic fillings used in many popular frozen desserts and treats—vanilla and chocolate ice creams, puddings, meringues, and fudge. Luster uses standard costing and carries over no inventory from one month to the next. The ice-cream product group's results for June 2014 were as follows:

	A	B	C
1	**Performance Report, June 2014**		
2		**Actual Results**	**Static Budget**
3	Units (pounds)	350,000	335,000
4	Revenues	$2,012,500	$1,976,500
5	Variable manufacturing costs	1,137,500	1,038,500
6	Contribution margin	$875,000	$938,000

Sam Adler, the business manager for ice-cream products, is pleased that more pounds of ice cream were sold than budgeted and that revenues were up. Unfortunately, variable manufacturing costs went up, too. The bottom line is that contribution margin declined by $63,000, which is less than 3% of the budgeted revenues of $1,976,500. Overall, Adler feels that the business is running fine.

Required

1. Calculate the static-budget variance in units, revenues, variable manufacturing costs, and contribution margin. What percentage is each static-budget variance relative to its static-budget amount?
2. Break down each static-budget variance into a flexible-budget variance and a sales-volume variance.
3. Calculate the selling-price variance.
4. Assume the role of management accountant at Luster. How would you present the results to Sam Adler? Should he be more concerned? If so, why?

7-21 Price and efficiency variances. Peterson Foods manufactures pumpkin scones. For January 2014, it budgeted to purchase and use 15,000 pounds of pumpkin at $0.89 a pound. Actual purchases and usage for January 2014 were 16,000 pounds at $0.82 a pound. Peterson budgeted for 60,000 pumpkin scones. Actual output was 60,800 pumpkin scones.

Required

1. Compute the flexible-budget variance.
2. Compute the price and efficiency variances.
3. Comment on the results for requirements 1 and 2 and provide a possible explanation for them.

7-22 Materials and manufacturing labor variances. Consider the following data collected for Great Homes, Inc.:

	Direct Materials	Direct Manufacturing Labor
Cost incurred: Actual inputs × actual prices	$200,000	$90,000
Actual inputs × standard prices	214,000	86,000
Standard inputs allowed for actual output × standard prices	225,000	80,000

Required

Compute the price, efficiency, and flexible-budget variances for direct materials and direct manufacturing labor.

7-23 Direct materials and direct manufacturing labor variances. SallyMay, Inc., designs and manufactures T-shirts. It sells its T-shirts to brand-name clothes retailers in lots of one dozen. SallyMay's May 2013 static budget and actual results for direct inputs are as follows:

Static Budget	
Number of T-shirt lots (1 lot = 1 dozen)	400
Per Lot of T-shirts:	
Direct materials	14 meters at $1.70 per meter = $23.80
Direct manufacturing labor	1.6 hours at $8.10 per hour = $12.96
Actual Results	
Number of T-shirt lots sold	450
Total Direct Inputs:	
Direct materials	6,840 meters at $1.95 per meter = $13,338
Direct manufacturing labor	675 hours at $8.20 per hour = $5,535

SallyMay has a policy of analyzing all input variances when they add up to more than 10% of the total cost of materials and labor in the flexible budget, and this is true in May 2013. The production manager discusses the sources of the variances: "A new type of material was purchased in May. This led to faster cutting and sewing, but the workers used more material than usual as they learned to work with it. For now, the standards are fine."

Required

1. Calculate the direct materials and direct manufacturing labor price and efficiency variances in May 2013. What is the total flexible-budget variance for both inputs (direct materials and direct manufacturing labor) combined? What percentage is this variance of the total cost of direct materials and direct manufacturing labor in the flexible budget?
2. Sally King, the CEO, is concerned about the input variances. But she likes the quality and feel of the new material and agrees to use it for one more year. In May 2014, SallyMay again produces 450 lots of T-shirts. Relative to May 2013, 2% less direct material is used, direct material price is down 5%, and 2% less direct manufacturing labor is used. Labor price has remained the same as in May 2013. Calculate the direct materials and direct manufacturing labor price and efficiency variances in May 2014. What is the total flexible-budget variance for both inputs (direct materials and direct manufacturing labor) combined? What percentage is this variance of the total cost of direct materials and direct manufacturing labor in the flexible budget?
3. Comment on the May 2014 results. Would you continue the "experiment" of using the new material?

7-24 Price and efficiency variances, journal entries. The Schuyler Corporation manufactures lamps. It has set up the following standards per finished unit for direct materials and direct manufacturing labor:

Direct materials: 10 lb. at $4.50 per lb.	$45.00
Direct manufacturing labor: 0.5 hour at $30 per hour	15.00

The number of finished units budgeted for January 2014 was 10,000; 9,850 units were actually produced.

Actual results in January 2014 were as follows:

Direct materials: 98,055 lb. used	
Direct manufacturing labor: 4,900 hours	$154,350

Assume that there was no beginning inventory of either direct materials or finished units.

During the month, materials purchased amounted to 100,000 lb., at a total cost of $465,000. Input price variances are isolated upon purchase. Input-efficiency variances are isolated at the time of usage.

Required

1. Compute the January 2014 price and efficiency variances of direct materials and direct manufacturing labor.
2. Prepare journal entries to record the variances in requirement 1.
3. Comment on the January 2014 price and efficiency variances of Schuyler Corporation.
4. Why might Schuyler calculate direct materials price variances and direct materials efficiency variances with reference to different points in time?

7-25 Materials and manufacturing labor variances, standard costs. Dunn, Inc., is a privately held furniture manufacturer. For August 2014, Dunn had the following standards for one of its products, a wicker chair:

	Standards per Chair
Direct materials	2 square yards of input at $5 per square yard
Direct manufacturing labor	0.5 hour of input at $10 per hour

The following data were compiled regarding *actual performance*: actual output units (chairs) produced, 2,000; square yards of input purchased and used, 3,700; price per square yard, $5.10; direct manufacturing labor costs, $8,820; actual hours of input, 900; labor price per hour, $9.80.

1. Show computations of price and efficiency variances for direct materials and direct manufacturing labor. Give a plausible explanation of why each variance occurred.
2. Suppose 6,000 square yards of materials were purchased (at $5.10 per square yard), even though only 3,700 square yards were used. Suppose further that variances are identified at their most timely control point; accordingly, direct materials price variances are isolated and traced at the time of purchase to the purchasing department rather than to the production department. Compute the price and efficiency variances under this approach.

7-26 Journal entries and T-accounts (continuation of 7-25). Prepare journal entries and post them to T-accounts for all transactions in Exercise 7-25, including requirement 2. Summarize how these journal entries differ from the normal-costing entries described in Chapter 4, pages 121–123.

7-27 Price and efficiency variances, benchmarking. Topiary Co. produces molded plastic garden pots and other plastic containers. In June 2014, Topiary produces 1,000 lots (each lot is 12 dozen pots) of its most popular line of pots, the 14-inch "Grecian urns," at each of its two plants, which are located in Mineola and Bayside. The production manager, Janice Roberts, asks her assistant, Alastair Ramy, to find out the precise per-unit budgeted variable costs at the two plants and the variable costs of a competitor, Land Art, who offers similar-quality pots at cheaper prices. Ramy pulls together the following information for each lot:

Per lot	Mineola Plant	Bayside Plant	Land Art
Direct materials	13.50 lbs. @ $9.20 per lb.	14.00 lbs. @ $9.00 per lb.	13.00 lbs. @ $8.80 per lb.
Direct labor	3 hrs. @ $10.15 per hr.	2.7 hrs. @ $10.20 per hr.	2.5 hrs. @ $10.00 per hr.
Variable overhead	$12 per lot	$11 per lot	$11 per lot

Required

1. What is the budgeted variable cost per lot at the Mineola Plant, the Bayside Plant, and at Land Art?
2. Using the Land Art data as the standard, calculate the direct materials and direct labor price and efficiency variances for the Mineola and Bayside plants.
3. What advantage does Topiary get by using Land Art's benchmark data as standards in calculating its variances? Identify two issues that Roberts should keep in mind in using the Land Art data as the standards.

7-28 Static and flexible budgets, service sector. Student Finance (StuFi) is a startup that aims to use the power of social communities to transform the student loan market. It connects participants through a dedicated lending pool, enabling current students to borrow from a school's alumni community. StuFi's revenue model is to take an upfront fee of 40 basis points (0.40%) *each* from the alumni investor and the student borrower for every loan originated on its platform.

StuFi hopes to go public in the near future and is keen to ensure that its financial results are in line with that ambition. StuFi's budgeted and actual results for the third quarter of 2014 are presented below.

	A	B	C	D	E
1		Static Budget		Actual Results	
2	New loans originated	8,200		10,250	
3	Average amount of loan	$145,000		$162,000	
4	Variable costs per loan:				
5	Professional labor	$360	(8 hrs at $45 per hour)	$475	(9.5 hrs at $50 per hour)
6	Credit verification	$100		$100	
7	Federal documentation fees	$120		$125	
8	Courier services	$50		$54	
9	Administrative costs (fixed)	$800,000		$945,000	
10	Technology costs (fixed)	$1,300,000		$1,415,000	

Required

1. Prepare StuFi's static budget of operating income for the third quarter of 2014.
2. Prepare an analysis of variances for the third quarter of 2014 along the lines of Exhibit 7-2; identify the sales volume and flexible budget variances for operating income.
3. Compute the professional labor price and efficiency variances for the third quarter of 2014.
4. What factors would you consider in evaluating the effectiveness of professional labor in the third quarter of 2014.

Problems

MyAccountingLab

7-29 Flexible budget, direct materials, and direct manufacturing labor variances. Milan Statuary manufactures bust statues of famous historical figures. All statues are the same size. Each unit requires the same amount of resources. The following information is from the static budget for 2014:

Expected production and sales	6,100 units
Expected selling price per unit	$ 700
Total fixed costs	$1,350,000

Standard quantities, standard prices, and standard unit costs follow for direct materials and direct manufacturing labor:

	Standard Quantity	Standard Price	Standard Unit Cost
Direct materials	16 pounds	$14 per pound	$224
Direct manufacturing labor	3.8 hours	$ 30 per hour	$114

During 2014, actual number of units produced and sold was 5,100, at an average selling price of $730. Actual cost of direct materials used was $1,149,400, based on 70,000 pounds purchased at $16.42 per pound. Direct manufacturing labor-hours actually used were 17,000, at the rate of $33.70 per hour. As a result, actual direct manufacturing labor costs were $572,900. Actual fixed costs were $1,200,000. There were no beginning or ending inventories.

1. Calculate the sales-volume variance and flexible-budget variance for operating income.
2. Compute price and efficiency variances for direct materials and direct manufacturing labor.

Required

7-30 Variance analysis, nonmanufacturing setting. Marcus McQueen has run In-A-Flash Car Detailing for the past 10 years. His static budget and actual results for June 2014 are provided next. Marcus has one employee who has been with him for all 10 years that he has been in business. In addition, at any given time he also employs two other less experienced workers. It usually takes each employee 2 hours to detail a vehicle, regardless of his or her experience. Marcus pays his experienced employee $30 per vehicle and the other two employees $15 per vehicle. There were no wage increases in June.

In-A-Flash Car Detailing
Actual and Budgeted Income Statements
For the Month Ended June 30, 2014

	Budget	Actual
Cars detailed	280	320
Revenue	$53,200	$72,000
Variable costs		
Costs of supplies	1,260	1,360
Labor	6,720	8,400
Total variable costs	7,980	9,760
Contribution margin	45,220	62,240
Fixed costs	9,800	9,800
Operating income	$35,420	$52,440

Required

1. How many cars, on average, did Marcus budget for each employee? How many cars did each employee actually detail?
2. Prepare a flexible budget for June 2014.
3. Compute the sales price variance and the labor efficiency variance for each labor type.
4. What information, in addition to that provided in the income statements, would you want Marcus to gather, if you wanted to improve operational efficiency?

7-31 Comprehensive variance analysis, responsibility issues. (CMA, adapted) Ultra, Inc., manufactures a full line of well-known sunglasses frames and lenses. Ultra uses a standard costing system to set attainable standards for direct materials, labor, and overhead costs. Ultra reviews and revises standards annually as necessary. Department managers, whose evaluations and bonuses are affected by their department's performance, are held responsible to explain variances in their department performance reports.

Recently, the manufacturing variances in the Delta prestige line of sunglasses have caused some concern. For no apparent reason, unfavorable materials and labor variances have occurred. At the monthly staff meeting, John Puckett, manager of the Image line, will be expected to explain his variances and suggest ways of improving performance. Barton will be asked to explain the following performance report for 2014:

	Actual Results	Static-Budget Amounts
Units sold	7,300	7,800
Revenues	$576,700	$608,400
Variable manufacturing costs	346,604	273,000
Fixed manufacturing costs	111,000	114,000
Gross margin	119,096	221,400

Barton collected the following information:

Three items comprised the standard variable manufacturing costs in 2014:

- Direct materials: Frames. Static budget cost of $35,880. The standard input for 2014 is 2.00 ounces per unit.
- Direct materials: Lenses. Static budget costs of $96,720. The standard input for 2014 is 4.00 ounces per unit.
- Direct manufacturing labor: Static budget costs of $140,400. The standard input for 2014 is 1 hour per unit.

Assume there are no variable manufacturing overhead costs.

The actual variable manufacturing costs in 2014 were as follows:

- Direct materials: Frames. Actual costs of $70,080. Actual ounces used were 4.00 ounces per unit.
- Direct materials: Lenses. Actual costs of $131,400. Actual ounces used were 6.00 ounces per unit.
- Direct manufacturing labor: Actual costs of $145,124. The actual labor rate was $14.20 per hour.

Required

1. Prepare a report that includes the following:
   a. Selling-price variance
   b. Sales-volume variance and flexible-budget variance for operating income in the format of the analysis in Exhibit 7-2

c. Price and efficiency variances for the following:
   - Direct materials: frames
   - Direct materials: lenses
   - Direct manufacturing labor
2. Give three possible explanations for each of the three price and efficiency variances at Ultra in requirement 1c.

7-32 Possible causes for price and efficiency variances. You are a student preparing for a job interview with a *Fortune* 100 consumer products manufacturer. You are applying for a job in the finance department. This company is known for its rigorous case-based interview process. One of the students who successfully obtained a job with them upon graduation last year advised you to "know your variances cold!" When you inquired further, she told you that she had been asked to pretend that she was investigating wage and materials variances. Per her advice, you have been studying the causes and consequences of variances. You are excited when you walk in and find that the first case deals with variance analysis. You are given the following data for May for a detergent bottling plant located in Mexico:

Actual	
Bottles filled	360,000
Direct materials used in production	6,300,000 oz.
Actual direct material cost	2,205,000 pesos
Actual direct manufacturing labor-hours	24,500 hours
Actual direct labor cost	739,165 pesos

Standards	
Purchase price of direct materials	0.34 pesos/oz
Bottle size	15 oz.
Wage rate	29.30 pesos/hour
Bottles per minute	0.50

30/HR

Please respond to the following questions as if you were in an interview situation:

Required

1. Calculate the materials efficiency and price variance and the wage and labor efficiency variances for the month of May.
2. You are given the following context: "Union organizers are targeting our detergent bottling plant in Puebla, Mexico, for a union." Can you provide a better explanation for the variances that you have calculated on the basis of this information?

7-33 Material cost variances, use of variances for performance evaluation. Katharine Johnson is the owner of Best Bikes, a company that produces high-quality cross-country bicycles. Best Bikes participates in a supply chain that consists of suppliers, manufacturers, distributors, and elite bicycle shops. For several years Best Bikes has purchased titanium from suppliers in the supply chain. Best Bikes uses titanium for the bicycle frames because it is stronger and lighter than other metals and therefore increases the quality of the bicycle. Earlier this year, Best Bikes hired Michael Bentfield, a recent graduate from State University, as purchasing manager. Michael believed that he could reduce costs if he purchased titanium from an online marketplace at a lower price.

Best Bikes established the following standards based upon the company's experience with previous suppliers. The standards are as follows:

Cost of titanium	$18 per pound
Titanium used per bicycle	8 lbs.

Actual results for the first month using the online supplier of titanium are as follows:

Bicycles produced	400
Titanium purchased	5,200 lb. for $88,400
Titanium used in production	4,700 lb.

Required

1. Compute the direct materials price and efficiency variances.
2. What factors can explain the variances identified in requirement 1? Could any other variances be affected?
3. Was switching suppliers a good idea for Best Bikes? Explain why or why not.

4. Should Michael Bentfield's performance evaluation be based solely on price variances? Should the production manager's evaluation be based solely on efficiency variances? Why is it important for Katharine Johnson to understand the causes of a variance before she evaluates performance?
5. Other than performance evaluation, what reasons are there for calculating variances?
6. What future problems could result from Best Bikes' decision to buy a lower quality of titanium from the online marketplace?

7-34 Direct manufacturing labor and direct materials variances, missing data. (CMA, heavily adapted) Young Bay Surfboards manufactures fiberglass surfboards. The standard cost of direct materials and direct manufacturing labor is $223 per board. This includes 40 pounds of direct materials, at the budgeted price of $2 per pound, and 10 hours of direct manufacturing labor, at the budgeted rate of $14.30 per hour. Following are additional data for the month of July:

Units completed	5,500 units
Direct material purchases	160,000 pounds
Cost of direct material purchases	$432,000
Actual direct manufacturing labor-hours	41,000 hours
Actual direct labor cost	$594,500
Direct materials efficiency variance	$ 1,700 F

There were no beginning inventories.

Required

1. Compute direct manufacturing labor variances for July.
2. Compute the actual pounds of direct materials used in production in July.
3. Calculate the actual price per pound of direct materials purchased.
4. Calculate the direct materials price variance.

7-35 Direct materials efficiency, mix, and yield variances. Nature's Best Nuts produces specialty nut products for the gourmet and natural foods market. Its most popular product is Zesty Zingers, a mixture of roasted nuts that are seasoned with a secret spice mixture and sold in 1-pound tins. The direct materials used in Zesty Zingers are almonds, cashews, pistachios, and seasoning. For each batch of 100 tins, the budgeted quantities and budgeted prices of direct materials are as follows:

	Quantity for One Batch	Price of Input
Almonds	180 cups	$1 per cup
Cashews	300 cups	$2 per cup
Pistachios	90 cups	$3 per cup
Seasoning	30 cups	$6 per cup

Changing the standard mix of direct material quantities slightly does not significantly affect the overall end product, particularly for the nuts. In addition, not all nuts added to production end up in the finished product, as some are rejected during inspection.

In the current period, Nature's Best made 2,500 tins of Zesty Zingers in 25 batches with the following actual quantity, cost, and mix of inputs:

	Actual Quantity	Actual Cost	Actual Mix
Almonds	5,280 cups	$ 5,280	33%
Cashews	7,520 cups	15,040	47%
Pistachios	2,720 cups	8,160	17%
Seasoning	480 cups	2,880	3%
Total actual	16,000 cups	$31,360	100%

Required

1. What is the budgeted cost of direct materials for the 2,500 tins?
2. Calculate the total direct materials efficiency variance.
3. Why is the total direct materials price variance zero?
4. Calculate the total direct materials mix and yield variances. What are these variances telling you about the 2,500 tins produced this period? Are the variances large enough to investigate?

7-36 Direct materials and manufacturing labor variances, solving unknowns. (CPA, adapted) On May 1, 2014, Lowell Company began the manufacture of a new paging machine known as Dandy. The company installed a standard costing system to account for manufacturing costs. The standard costs for a unit of Dandy follow:

Direct materials (2 lb. at $3 per lb.)	$6.00
Direct manufacturing labor (1/2 hour at $16 per hour)	8.00
Manufacturing overhead (80% of direct manufacturing labor costs)	6.40
	$20.40

The following data were obtained from Lowell's records for the month of May:

	Debit	Credit
Revenues		$150,000
Accounts payable control (for May's purchases of direct materials)		36,300
Direct materials price variance	$4,500	
Direct materials efficiency variance	2,900	
Direct manufacturing labor price variance	1,700	
Direct manufacturing labor efficiency variance		2,000

Actual production in May was 4,700 units of Dandy, and actual sales in May were 3,000 units.

The amount shown for direct materials price variance applies to materials purchased during May. There was no beginning inventory of materials on May 1, 2014.

Compute each of the following items for Lowell for the month of May. Show your computations.

Required

1. Standard direct manufacturing labor-hours allowed for actual output produced
2. Actual direct manufacturing labor-hours worked
3. Actual direct manufacturing labor wage rate
4. Standard quantity of direct materials allowed (in pounds)
5. Actual quantity of direct materials used (in pounds)
6. Actual quantity of direct materials purchased (in pounds)
7. Actual direct materials price per pound

7-37 Direct materials and manufacturing labor variances, journal entries. Zanella's Smart Shawls, Inc., is a small business that Zanella developed while in college. She began hand-knitting shawls for her dorm friends to wear while studying. As demand grew, she hired some workers and began to manage the operation. Zanella's shawls require wool and labor. She experiments with the type of wool that she uses, and she has great variety in the shawls she produces. Zanella has bimodal turnover in her labor. She has some employees who have been with her for a very long time and others who are new and inexperienced.

Zanella uses standard costing for her shawls. She expects that a typical shawl should take 3 hours to produce, and the standard wage rate is $9.00 per hour. An average shawl uses 13 skeins of wool. Zanella shops around for good deals and expects to pay $3.40 per skein.

Zanella uses a just-in-time inventory system, as she has clients tell her what type and color of wool they would like her to use.

For the month of April, Zanella's workers produced 200 shawls using 580 hours and 3,500 skeins of wool. Zanella bought wool for $9,000 (and used the entire quantity) and incurred labor costs of $5,520.

Required

1. Calculate the price and efficiency variances for the wool and the price and efficiency variances for direct manufacturing labor.
2. Record the journal entries for the variances incurred.
3. Discuss logical explanations for the combination of variances that Zanella experienced.

7-38 Use of materials and manufacturing labor variances for benchmarking. You are a new junior accountant at In Focus Corporation, maker of lenses for eyeglasses. Your company sells generic-quality lenses for a moderate price. Your boss, the controller, has given you the latest month's report for the lens trade association. This report includes information related to operations for your firm and three of your competitors within the trade association. The report also includes information related to the industry benchmark for each line item in the report. You do not know which firm is which, except that you know you are Firm A.

Unit Variable Costs
Member Firms
For the Month Ended September 30, 2014

	Firm A	Firm B	Firm C	Firm D	Industry Benchmark	
Materials input	2.15	2.00	2.20	2.60	2.15	oz. of glass
Materials price	$ 5.00	$ 5.25	$ 5.10	$ 4.50	$ 5.10	per oz.
Labor-hours used	0.75	1.00	0.65	0.70	0.70	hours
Wage rate	$14.50	$14.00	$14.25	$15.25	$12.50	per DLH
Variable overhead rate	$ 9.25	$14.00	$ 7.75	$11.75	$12.25	per DLH

Required

1. Calculate the total variable cost per unit for each firm in the trade association. Compute the percent of total for the material, labor, and variable overhead components.
2. Using the trade association's industry benchmark, calculate direct materials and direct manufacturing labor price and efficiency variances for the four firms. Calculate the percent over standard for each firm and each variance.
3. Write a brief memo to your boss outlining the advantages and disadvantages of belonging to this trade association for benchmarking purposes. Include a few ideas to improve productivity that you want your boss to take to the department heads' meeting.

7-39 Direct labor variances: price, efficiency, mix, and yield. Trevor Joseph employs two workers in his guitar-making business. The first worker, George, has been making guitars for 20 years and is paid $30 per hour. The second worker, Earl, is less experienced and is paid $20 per hour. One guitar requires, on average, 10 hours of labor. The budgeted direct labor quantities and prices for one guitar are as follows:

	Quantity	Price per Hour of Labor	Cost for One Guitar
George	6 hours	$30 per hour	$180
Earl	4 hours	$20 per hour	80

That is, each guitar is budgeted to require 10 hours of direct labor, composed of 60% of George's labor and 40% of Earl's, although sometimes Earl works more hours on a particular guitar and George less, or vice versa, with no obvious change in the quality or function of the guitar.

During the month of August, Joseph manufactures 25 guitars. Actual direct labor costs are as follows:

George (145 hours)	$4,350
Earl (108 hours)	2,160
Total actual direct labor cost	$6,510

Required

1. What is the budgeted cost of direct labor for 25 guitars?
2. Calculate the total direct labor price and efficiency variances.
3. For the 25 guitars, what is the total actual amount of direct labor used? What is the actual direct labor input mix percentage? What is the budgeted amount of George's and Earl's labor that should have been used for the 25 guitars?
4. Calculate the total direct labor mix and yield variances. How do these numbers relate to the total direct labor efficiency variance? What do these variances tell you?

7-40 Direct-cost and selling price variances. MicroDisk is the market leader in the Secure Digital (SD) card industry and sells memory cards for use in portable devices such as mobile phones, tablets, and digital cameras. Its most popular card is the Mini SD, which it sells to OEMs as well as through outlets such as Target and Walmart for an average selling price of $8. MicroDisk has a standard monthly production level of

420,000 Mini SDs in its Taiwan facility. The standard input quantities and prices for direct-cost inputs are as follows:

	A	B	C	D	E
1		Quantity per		Standard	
2	Cost Item	Mini SD card		Unit Costs	
3	Direct materials				
4	Specialty polymer	17	mm	$0.05	/mm
5	Connector pins	10	units	0.10	/unit
6	Wi-Fi transreceiver	1	unit	0.50	/unit
7					
8	Direct manufacturing labor				
9	Setup	1	min.	24.00	/hr.
10	Fabrication	2	min.	30.00	/hr.

Phoebe King, the CEO, is disappointed with the results for June 2014, especially in comparison to her expectations based on the standard cost data.

	Performance Report, June 2014						
14		Actual		Budget		Variance	
15	Output units	462,000		420,000		42,000	F
16	Revenues	$3,626,700		$3,360,000		$266,700	F
17	Direct materials	1,200,000		987,000		213,000	U
18	Direct manufacturing labor	628,400		588,000		40,400	U

King observes that despite the significant increase in the output of Mini SDs in June, the product's contribution to the company's profitability has been lower than expected. She gathers the following information to help analyze the situation:

21	Input Usage Report, June 2014			
22	Cost Item	Quantity		Actual Cost
23	Direct materials			
24	Specialty polymer	8,300,000	mm	$415,000
25	Connector pins	5,000,000	units	550,000
26	Wi-Fi transreceiver	470,000	units	235,000
27				
28	Direct manufacturing labor			
29	Setup	455,000	min.	182,000
30	Fabrication	864,000	min.	446,400

Calculate the following variances. Comment on the variances and provide potential reasons why they might have arisen, with particular attention to the variances that may be related to one another:

Required

1. Selling-price variance
2. Direct materials price variance, for each category of materials
3. Direct materials efficiency variance, for each category of materials

4. Direct manufacturing labor price variance, for setup and fabrication
5. Direct manufacturing labor efficiency variance, for setup and fabrication.

7-41 Comprehensive variance analysis review. Vivus Bioscience produces a generic statin pill that is used to treat patients with high cholesterol. The pills are sold in blister packs of 10. Vivus employs a team of sales representatives who are paid varying amounts of commission.

Given the narrow margins in the generic drugs industry, Vivus relies on tight standards and cost controls to manage its operations. Vivus has the following budgeted standards for the month of April 2014:

Average selling price per pack	$ 7.20
Total direct materials cost per pack	$ 1.80
Direct manufacturing labor cost per hour	$ 14.40
Average labor productivity rate (packs per hour)	280
Sales commission cost per unit	$ 0.36
Fixed administrative and manufacturing overhead	$960,000

Vivus budgeted sales of 1,400,000 packs for April. At the end of the month, the controller revealed that actual results for April had deviated from the budget in several ways:

- Unit sales and production were 90% of plan.
- Actual average selling price increased to $7.30.
- Productivity dropped to 250 packs per hour.
- Actual direct manufacturing labor cost was $14.60 per hour.
- Actual total direct material cost per unit increased to $1.90.
- Actual sales commissions were $0.30 per unit.
- Fixed overhead costs were $12,000 above budget.

Calculate the following amounts for Vivus for April 2014:

Required

1. Static-budget and actual operating income
2. Static-budget variance for operating income
3. Flexible-budget operating income
4. Flexible-budget variance for operating income
5. Sales-volume variance for operating income
6. Price and efficiency variances for direct manufacturing labor
7. Flexible-budget variance for direct manufacturing labor

7-42 Price and efficiency variances, benchmarking and ethics. Sunto Scientific manufactures GPS devices for a chain of retail stores. Its most popular model, the Magellan XS, is assembled in a dedicated facility in Savannah, Georgia. Sunto is keenly aware of the competitive threat from smartphones that use Google Maps and has put in a standard cost system to manage production of the Magellan XS. It has also implemented a just-in-time system so the Savannah facility operates with no inventory of any kind.

Producing the Magellan XS involves combining a navigation system (imported from Sunto's plant in Dresden at a fixed price), an LCD screen made of polarized glass, and a casing developed from specialty plastic. The budgeted and actual amounts for Magellan XS for July 2014 were as follows:

	Budgeted Amounts	Actual Amounts
Magellan XS units produced	4,000	4,400
Navigation system cost	$81,600	$89,000
Navigation systems	4,080	4,450
Polarized glass cost	$40,000	$40,300
Sheets of polarized glass used	800	816
Plastic casing cost	$12,000	$12,500
Ounces of specialty plastic used	4,000	4,250
Direct manufacturing labor costs	$36,000	$37,200
Direct manufacturing labor-hours	2,000	2,040

The controller of the Savannah plant, Jim Williams, is disappointed with the standard costing system in place. The standards were developed on the basis of a study done by an outside consultant at the start of the year. Williams points out that he has rarely seen a significant unfavorable variance under this system. He observes that even at the present level of output, workers seem to have a substantial amount of idle time. Moreover, he is concerned that the production supervisor, John Kelso, is aware of the issue but is unwilling to tighten the standards because the current lenient benchmarks make his performance look good.

Required

1. Compute the price and efficiency variances for the three categories of direct materials and for direct manufacturing labor in July 2014.
2. Describe the types of actions the employees at the Savannah plant may have taken to reduce the accuracy of the standards set by the outside consultant. Why would employees take those actions? Is this behavior ethical?
3. If Williams does nothing about the standard costs, will his behavior violate any of the standards of ethical conduct for practitioners described in the IMA Statement of Ethical Professional Practice (see Exhibit 1-7 on page 18)?
4. What actions should Williams take?
5. Williams can obtain benchmarking information about the estimated costs of Sunto's competitors such as Garmin and TomTom from the Competitive Intelligence Institute (CII). Discuss the pros and cons of using the CII information to compute the variances in requirement 1.

8 Flexible Budgets, Overhead Cost Variances, and Management Control

Learning Objectives

1. Explain the similarities and differences in planning variable overhead costs and fixed overhead costs
2. Develop budgeted variable overhead cost rates and budgeted fixed overhead cost rates
3. Compute the variable overhead flexible-budget variance, the variable overhead efficiency variance, and the variable overhead spending variance
4. Compute the fixed overhead flexible-budget variance, the fixed overhead spending variance, and the fixed overhead production-volume variance
5. Show how the 4-variance analysis approach reconciles the actual overhead incurred with the overhead amounts allocated during the period
6. Explain the relationship between the sales-volume variance and the production-volume variance
7. Calculate variances in activity-based costing
8. Examine the use of overhead variances in nonmanufacturing settings

What do this week's weather forecast and an organization's performance have in common?

Much of the time, reality doesn't match what people expect. Rain that results in a little league game being canceled may suddenly give way to sunshine. Business owners expecting to "whistle their way to the bank" may change their tune after tallying their monthly bills and discovering that skyrocketing operational costs have significantly reduced their profits. Differences, or variances, are all around us.

Analyzing variances is a valuable activity for firms because the process highlights the areas where performance most lags expectations. By using this information to make corrective adjustments, companies can achieve significant savings. Furthermore, the process of setting up standards requires firms to have a thorough understanding of their fixed and variable overhead costs, which brings its own benefits, as the following article shows.

Planning Fixed and Variable Overhead Costs at Tesla Motors[1]

Managers frequently review the differences, or variances, in overhead costs and make changes in the operations of a business. Sometimes staffing levels are increased or decreased, while at other times managers identify ways to use fewer resources like, say, office supplies and travel for business meetings that don't add value to the products and services that customers buy.

Tesla Motors is a Silicon Valley–based electric car manufacturer. To develop its renowned Model S all-electric plug-in sedan—*Consumer Reports* recently called it the best car it ever tested—Tesla Motors required an in-depth understanding of its fixed and variable overhead costs for planning and control purposes.

Automobile manufacturing is an industry with significant fixed overhead costs. As a new company, Tesla Motors made the strategic decision to make up-front fixed

[1] *Sources:* Ohnsman, Alan. 2012. Tesla Motors cuts factory cost to try to generate profit. *Bloomberg*, http://www.bloomberg.com/news/2012-04-12/tesla-motors-cuts-factory-cost-to-try-to-generate-profit.html, April 12; Tesla Motors, Inc. 2013. March 31, 2013 Form 10-Q (filed May 10); Valdes-Dapena, Peter. 2013. Tesla: Consumer Reports' best car ever tested. *CNNMoney.com*, http://money.cnn.com/2013/05/09/autos/tesla-models-consumer-reports/index.html, May 9; White, Joseph. 2013. Tesla has a fresh $1 billion—and lots of ways to spend it. *Corporate Intelligence (blog), The Wall Street Journal*, http://blogs.wsj.com/corporate-intelligence/, May 17.

investments designed to benefit the company for many years. These resulted in various fixed overhead costs including depreciation and taxes on its new state-of-the-art factory, assembly line supervisors, insurance, and salaries for the engineers that design the battery packs and electric motors that power its specially designed vehicles. Variable costs for Tesla Motors include utilities, office supplies, advertising, and promotion costs among many others.

Understanding its fixed and variable overhead costs allows Tesla Motors' management accountants to develop the company's budgeted fixed and variable overhead cost rates for each Model S produced. Also, using flexible budgeting, the company can make strategic changes based on activity. For instance, when Tesla Motors began expanding sales beyond North America in early 2013, the company added new sales and marketing staff to support the growth of the business, which then resulted in a new variable overhead cost rate.

Companies such as DuPont, International Paper, and U.S. Steel, which invest heavily in capital equipment, and Amazon.com and Yahoo!, which invest large amounts in software, have high overhead costs. As the Tesla example suggests, understanding the behavior of overhead costs, planning for them, analyzing the variances related to them, and acting appropriately on the results are critical for a company.

In Chapter 7, you learned how managers use flexible budgets and variance analysis to help plan and control the direct-cost categories of direct materials and direct manufacturing labor. In this chapter, you will learn how managers plan for and control the indirect-cost categories of variable manufacturing overhead and fixed manufacturing overhead. This chapter also explains why managers should be careful when interpreting variances based on overhead-cost concepts developed primarily for financial reporting purposes.

Planning of Variable and Fixed Overhead Costs

Learning Objective 1

Explain the similarities and differences in planning variable overhead costs and fixed overhead costs

...for both, plan only essential activities and be efficient; fixed overhead costs are usually determined well before the budget period begins

We'll use the Webb Company example again to illustrate the planning and control of variable and fixed overhead costs. Recall that Webb manufactures jackets it sells to distributors, who in turn sell them to independent clothing stores and retail chains. Because we assume Webb's only costs are manufacturing costs, for simplicity we use the term "overhead costs" instead of "manufacturing overhead costs" in this chapter. Webb's variable overhead costs include energy, machine maintenance, engineering support, and indirect materials. Webb's fixed overhead costs include plant leasing costs, depreciation on plant equipment, and the salaries of the plant managers.

Planning Variable Overhead Costs

To effectively plan variable overhead costs for a product or service, managers must focus on the activities that create a superior product or service for their customers and eliminate activities that do not add value. For example, customers expect Webb's jackets to last, so

Webb's managers consider sewing to be an essential activity. Therefore, maintenance activities for sewing machines, which are included in Webb's variable overhead costs, are also essential activities for which management must plan. Such maintenance should be done in a cost-effective way, such as by scheduling periodic equipment maintenance rather than waiting for sewing machines to break down. For many companies today, it is critical to plan for ways to reduce the consumption of energy, a rapidly growing component of variable overhead costs. Webb installs smart meters in order to monitor energy use in real time and steer production operations away from peak consumption periods.

Planning Fixed Overhead Costs

Planning fixed overhead costs is similar to planning variable overhead costs—undertake only essential activities and then plan to be efficient in that undertaking. But there is an additional strategic issue when it comes to planning fixed overhead costs: choosing the appropriate level of capacity or investment that will benefit the company in the long run. Consider Webb's leasing of sewing machines, each of which has a fixed cost per year. Leasing too many machines will result in overcapacity and unnecessary fixed leasing costs. Leasing too few machines will result in an inability to meet demand, lost sales of jackets, and unhappy customers. Consider AT&T, which did not initially foresee the iPhone's appeal or the proliferation of "apps" and consequently did not upgrade its network sufficiently to handle the resulting data traffic. AT&T subsequently had to impose limits on how customers could use the iPhone (such as by curtailing tethering and the streaming of Webcasts). This explains why following the iPhone's release, at one point AT&T had the lowest customer satisfaction ratings among all major carriers.

Decision Point

How do managers plan variable overhead costs and fixed overhead costs?

The planning of fixed overhead costs differs from the planning of variable overhead costs in another regard as well: timing. At the start of a budget period, management will have made most of the decisions determining the level of fixed overhead costs to be incurred. But it's the day-to-day, ongoing operating decisions that mainly determine the level of variable overhead costs incurred in that period. For example, the variable overhead costs of hospitals, which include the costs of disposable supplies, doses of medication, suture packets, and medical waste disposal, are a function of the number and nature of procedures carried out, as well as the practice patterns of the physicians. However, most of the costs of providing hospital service are fixed overhead costs—those related to buildings, equipment, and salaried labor. These costs are unrelated to a hospital's volume of activity.[2]

Learning Objective 2

Develop budgeted variable overhead cost rates

...budgeted variable costs divided by quantity of cost-allocation base

and budgeted fixed overhead cost rates

...budgeted fixed costs divided by quantity of cost-allocation base

Standard Costing at Webb Company

Webb uses standard costing. Chapter 7 explained how the standards for Webb's direct manufacturing costs were developed. This chapter explains how the standards for Webb's manufacturing overhead costs are developed. **Standard costing** is a costing system that (1) traces direct costs to output produced by multiplying the standard prices or rates by the standard quantities of inputs allowed for actual outputs produced and (2) allocates overhead costs on the basis of the standard overhead-cost rates times the standard quantities of the allocation bases allowed for the actual outputs produced.

The standard cost of Webb's jackets can be computed at the start of the budget period. This feature of standard costing simplifies record keeping because no record is needed of the actual overhead costs or of the actual quantities of the cost-allocation bases used for making the jackets. What managers *do* need are the standard overhead cost rates for Webb's variable and fixed overhead. Management accountants calculate these cost rates based on the planned amounts of variable and fixed overhead and the standard

[2] Free-standing surgery centers have thrived because they have lower fixed overhead costs compared to traditional hospitals. For an enlightening summary of costing issues in health care, see A. Macario. 2010. "What does one minute of operating room time cost?" *Journal of Clinical Anesthesia*, June.

quantities of the allocation bases. We describe these computations next. Note that once managers set these standards, the costs of using standard costing are low relative to the costs of using actual costing or normal costing.

Developing Budgeted Variable Overhead Rates

Budgeted variable overhead cost-allocation rates can be developed in four steps. Throughout the chapter, we use the broader term *budgeted rate* rather than *standard rate* to be consistent with the term used to describe normal costing in earlier chapters. When standard costing is used, the budgeted rates are standard rates.

Step 1: Choose the Period to Be Used for the Budget. Webb uses a 12-month budget period. Chapter 4 (page 111) provided two reasons for using annual overhead rates rather than, say, monthly rates. The first relates to the numerator, such as reducing the influence of seasonality on the firm's cost structure. The second relates to the denominator, such as reducing the effect of varying output and number of days in a month. In addition, setting overhead rates once a year rather than 12 times a year saves managers time.

Step 2: Select the Cost-Allocation Bases to Use in Allocating the Variable Overhead Costs to the Output Produced. Webb's operating managers select machine-hours as the cost-allocation base because they believe that machine-hours is the only cost driver of variable overhead. Based on an engineering study, Webb estimates it will take 0.40 of a machine-hour per actual output unit. For its budgeted output of 144,000 jackets in 2014, Webb budgets 57,600 (0.40 × 144,000) machine-hours.

Step 3: Identify the Variable Overhead Costs Associated with Each Cost-Allocation Base. Webb groups all of its variable overhead costs, including the costs of energy, machine maintenance, engineering support, indirect materials, and indirect manufacturing labor, in a single cost pool. Webb's total budgeted variable overhead costs for 2014 are $1,728,000.

Step 4: Compute the Rate per Unit of Each Cost-Allocation Base Used to Allocate the Variable Overhead Costs to the Output Produced. Dividing the amount in Step 3 ($1,728,000) by the amount in Step 2 (57,600 machine-hours), Webb estimates a rate of $30 per standard machine-hour for allocating its variable overhead costs.

When standard costing is used, the variable overhead rate per unit of the cost-allocation base ($30 per machine-hour for Webb) is generally expressed as a standard rate per output unit. Webb calculates the budgeted variable overhead cost rate per output unit as follows:

$$\begin{array}{c}\text{Budgeted variable}\\\text{overhead cost rate}\\\text{per output unit}\end{array} = \begin{array}{c}\text{Budgeted input}\\\text{allowed per}\\\text{output unit}\end{array} \times \begin{array}{c}\text{Budgeted variable}\\\text{overhead cost rate}\\\text{per input unit}\end{array}$$

$$= \text{0.40 hour per jacket} \times \$30 \text{ per hour}$$

$$= \$12 \text{ per jacket}$$

The $12-per-jacket rate is the budgeted variable overhead cost rate in Webb's static budget for 2014 as well as in the monthly performance reports the firm prepares during 2014.

The $12-per-jacket rate represents the amount by which managers expect Webb's variable overhead costs to change when the amount of output changes. As the number of jackets manufactured increases, the variable overhead costs allocated to output (for inventory costing) increase at the rate of $12 per jacket. The $12 per jacket represents the firm's total variable overhead costs per unit of output, including the costs of energy, repairs, indirect labor, and so on. Managers help control variable overhead costs by setting a budget for each of these line items and then investigating the possible causes of any significant variances.

Developing Budgeted Fixed Overhead Rates

Fixed overhead costs are, by definition, a lump sum of costs that remains unchanged for a given period, despite wide changes in a firm's level of activity or output. Fixed costs are included in flexible budgets, but they remain the same within the relevant range of activity regardless of the output level chosen to "flex" the variable costs and revenues. Recall from Exhibit 7-2 and the steps in developing a flexible budget that Webb's monthly fixed overhead costs of $276,000 are the same in the static budget as they are in the flexible budget. Do not assume, however, that these costs can never be changed. Managers can reduce them by selling equipment or laying off employees, for example. But the costs are fixed in the sense that, unlike variable costs such as direct material costs, fixed costs do not *automatically* increase or decrease with the level of activity within the relevant range.

The process of developing the budgeted fixed overhead rate is the same as the one for calculating the budgeted variable overhead rate. The steps are as follows:

Step 1: Choose the Period to Use for the Budget. As with variable overhead costs, the budget period for fixed overhead costs is typically one year, to help smooth out seasonal effects.

Step 2: Select the Cost-Allocation Bases to Use in Allocating the Fixed Overhead Costs to the Output Produced. Webb uses machine-hours as the only cost-allocation base for the firm's fixed overhead costs. Why? Because Webb's managers believe that, in the long run, the company's fixed overhead costs will increase or decrease to the levels needed to support the amount of machine-hours. Therefore, in the long run, the amount of machine-hours used is the only cost driver of fixed overhead costs. The number of machine-hours is the denominator in the budgeted fixed overhead rate computation and is called the **denominator level**. For simplicity, we assume Webb expects to operate at capacity in fiscal year 2014, with a budgeted usage of 57,600 machine-hours for a budgeted output of 144,000 jackets.[3]

Step 3: Identify the Fixed Overhead Costs Associated with Each Cost-Allocation Base. Because Webb identifies a single cost-allocation base—machine-hours—to allocate fixed overhead costs, it groups all such costs into a single cost pool. Costs in this pool include depreciation on plant and equipment, plant and equipment leasing costs, and the plant manager's salary. Webb's fixed overhead budget for 2014 is $3,312,000.

Step 4: Compute the Rate per Unit of Each Cost-Allocation Base Used to Allocate Fixed Overhead Costs to the Output Produced. By dividing the $3,312,000 from Step 3 by the 57,600 machine-hours from Step 2, Webb estimates a fixed overhead cost rate of $57.50 per machine-hour:

$$\begin{array}{c}\text{Budgeted fixed}\\\text{overhead cost per}\\\text{unit of cost-allocation}\\\text{base}\end{array} = \frac{\text{Budgeted total costs in fixed overhead cost pool}}{\text{Budgeted total quantity of cost-allocation base}} = \frac{\$3{,}312{,}000}{57{,}600} = \$57.50 \text{ per machine-hour}$$

Under standard costing, the $57.50 fixed overhead cost per machine-hour is usually expressed as a standard cost per output unit. Recall that Webb's engineering study estimates that it will take 0.40 machine-hour per output unit. Webb can now calculate the budgeted fixed overhead cost per output unit as follows:

$$\begin{array}{c}\text{Budgeted fixed}\\\text{overhead cost per}\\\text{output unit}\end{array} = \begin{array}{c}\text{Budgeted quantity}\\\text{of cost-allocation}\\\text{base allowed per}\\\text{output unit}\end{array} \times \begin{array}{c}\text{Budgeted fixed}\\\text{overhead cost}\\\text{per unit of}\\\text{cost-allocation base}\end{array}$$

$$= 0.40 \text{ of a machine-hour per jacket} \times \$57.50 \text{ per machine-hour}$$

$$= \$23.00 \text{ per jacket}$$

Decision Point

How are budgeted variable overhead and fixed overhead cost rates calculated?

When preparing monthly budgets for 2014, Webb divides the $3,312,000 annual total fixed costs into 12 equal monthly amounts of $276,000.

[3] Because Webb plans its capacity over multiple periods, anticipated demand in 2014 could be such that budgeted output for 2014 is less than Webb's capacity. Companies vary in the denominator levels they choose. Some choose budgeted output and others choose capacity. In either case, the approach and analysis presented in this chapter is unchanged. Chapter 9 discusses in more detail the implications of choosing a denominator level.

Variable Overhead Cost Variances

Learning Objective 3

Compute the variable overhead flexible-budget variance,

...difference between actual variable overhead costs and flexible-budget variable overhead amounts

the variable overhead efficiency variance,

...difference between actual quantity of cost-allocation base and budgeted quantity of cost-allocation base

and the variable overhead spending variance

...difference between actual variable overhead cost rate and budgeted variable overhead cost rate

We now illustrate how the budgeted variable overhead rate is used to compute Webb's variable overhead cost variances. The following data are for April 2014, when Webb produced and sold 10,000 jackets:

	Actual Result	Flexible-Budget Amount
1. Output units (jackets)	10,000	10,000
2. Machine-hours per output unit	0.45	0.40
3. Machine-hours (1 × 2)	4,500	4,000
4. Variable overhead costs	$130,500	$120,000
5. Variable overhead costs per machine-hour (4 ÷ 3)	$ 29.00	$ 30.00
6. Variable overhead costs per output unit (4 ÷ 1)	$ 13.05	$ 12.00

As we saw in Chapter 7, the flexible budget enables Webb to highlight the differences between actual costs and actual quantities versus budgeted costs and budgeted quantities for the actual output level of 10,000 jackets.

Flexible-Budget Analysis

The **variable overhead flexible-budget variance** measures the difference between actual variable overhead costs incurred and flexible-budget variable overhead amounts.

$$\begin{aligned}\text{Variable overhead flexible-budget variance} &= \text{Actual costs incurred} - \text{Flexible-budget amount}\\ &= \$130{,}500 - \$120{,}000\\ &= \$10{,}500\text{ U}\end{aligned}$$

This $10,500 unfavorable flexible-budget variance means Webb's actual variable overhead exceeded the flexible-budget amount by $10,500 for the 10,000 jackets actually produced and sold. Webb's managers would want to know why. Did Webb use more machine-hours than planned to produce the 10,000 jackets? If so, was it because workers were less skilled than expected in using machines? Or did Webb spend more on variable overhead costs, such as maintenance?

Just as we illustrated in Chapter 7 with the flexible-budget variance for direct-cost items, Webb's managers can get further insight into the reason for the $10,500 unfavorable variance by subdividing it into the efficiency variance and spending variance.

Variable Overhead Efficiency Variance

The **variable overhead efficiency variance** is the difference between actual quantity of the cost-allocation base used and budgeted quantity of the cost-allocation base that should have been used to produce the actual output, multiplied by the budgeted variable overhead cost per unit of the cost-allocation base.

$$\begin{aligned}\text{Variable overhead efficiency variance} &= \left(\text{Actual quantity of variable overhead cost-allocation base used for actual output} - \text{Budgeted quantity of variable overhead cost-allocation base allowed for actual output}\right) \times \text{Budgeted variable overhead cost per unit of cost-allocation base}\\ &= (4{,}500\text{ hours} - 0.40\text{ hr./unit} \times 10{,}000\text{ units}) \times \$30\text{ per hour}\\ &= (4{,}500\text{ hours} - 4{,}000\text{ hours}) \times \$30\text{ per hour}\\ &= \$15{,}000\text{ U}\end{aligned}$$

Columns 2 and 3 of Exhibit 8-1 depict the variable overhead efficiency variance. Note the variance arises solely because of the difference between the actual quantity (4,500 hours)

Exhibit 8-1 Columnar Presentation of Variable Overhead Variance Analysis: Webb Company for April 2014[a]

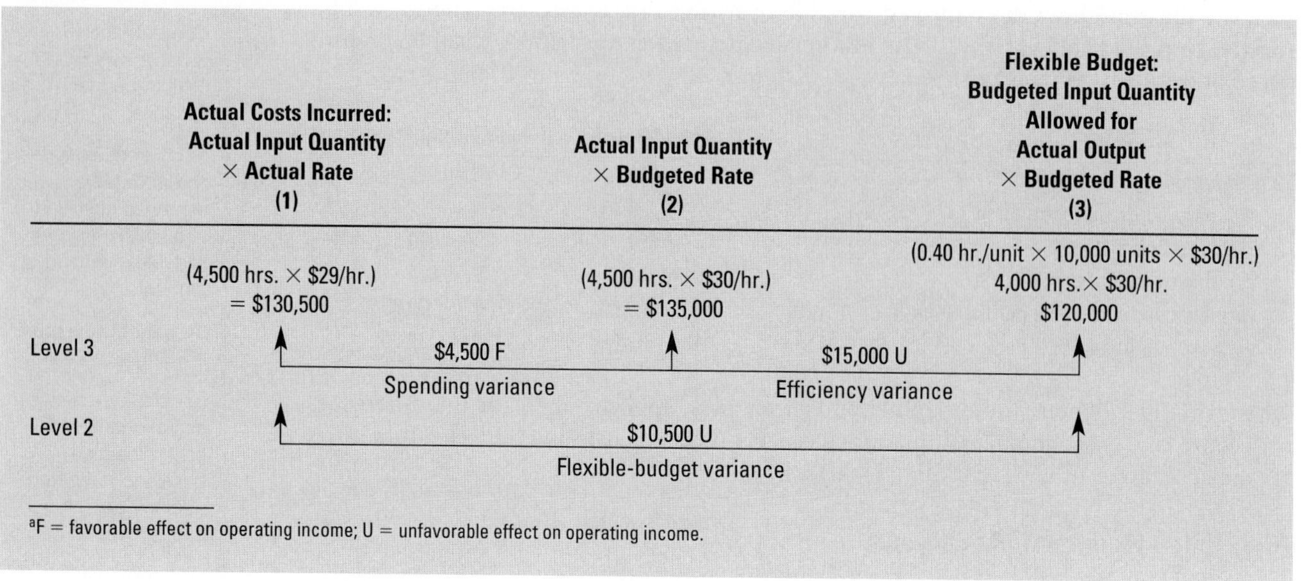

and budgeted quantity (4,000 hours) of the cost-allocation base. The variable overhead efficiency variance is computed the same way the efficiency variance for direct-cost items is (Chapter 7, pages 259–261). However, the interpretation of the variance is somewhat different. The efficiency variances for direct-cost items are based on the differences between the actual inputs used and the budgeted inputs allowed for the actual output produced. For example, a forensic laboratory (the kind popularized by television shows such as *CSI* and *Dexter*) would calculate a direct labor efficiency variance based on whether the lab used more or fewer hours than the standard hours allowed for the actual number of DNA tests. In contrast, the efficiency variance for variable overhead is based on the efficiency with which *the cost-allocation base* is used. Webb's unfavorable variable overhead efficiency variance of $15,000 means that the actual machine-hours (the cost-allocation base) of 4,500 hours was higher than the budgeted machine-hours of 4,000 hours allowed to manufacture 10,000 jackets and this, to the extent machine-hours are a cost driver for variable overhead, pushed up the potential spending on variable overhead.

The following table shows possible causes for Webb's actual machine-hours exceeding the budgeted machine-hours and Webb's potential responses to each of these causes.

Possible Causes for Exceeding Budget	Potential Management Responses
1. Workers were less efficient than expected in using machines.	1. Encourage the human resources department to implement better employee-hiring practices and training procedures.
2. The production scheduler inefficiently scheduled jobs, resulting in more machine-hours used than budgeted.	2. Improve plant operations by installing production-scheduling software.
3. Machines were not maintained in good operating condition.	3. Ensure preventive maintenance is done on all machines.
4. Webb's sales staff promised a distributor a rush delivery, which resulted in more machine-hours used than budgeted.	4. Coordinate production schedules with sales staff and distributors and share information with them.
5. Budgeted machine time standards were set too tight.	5. Commit more resources to develop appropriate standards.

Note how, depending on the cause(s) of the $15,000 U variance, corrective actions may need to be taken not just in manufacturing but also in other business functions of the value chain, such as sales and distribution.

Webb's managers discovered that one reason for the unfavorable variance was that workers were underskilled. As a result, Webb is improving its hiring and training practices. Insufficient maintenance performed in the 2 months prior to April 2014 was another reason. A former plant manager had delayed the maintenance in an attempt to meet Webb's monthly cost targets. As we discussed in Chapter 6, managers should not focus on meeting short-run cost targets if they are likely to result in harmful long-run consequences. For example, if Webb's employees were to hurt themselves while operating poorly maintained machinery, the consequences would not only be harmful, they could be deadly. Webb is now strengthening its internal maintenance procedures so that failure to do monthly maintenance as needed will raise a "red flag" that must be immediately explained to management. Webb is also taking a hard look at its evaluation practices to determine if they inadvertently pressure managers to fixate on short-term targets to the long-run detriment of the firm.

Variable Overhead Spending Variance

The **variable overhead spending variance** is the difference between the actual variable overhead cost per unit of the cost-allocation base and the budgeted variable overhead cost per unit of the cost-allocation base, multiplied by the actual quantity of variable overhead cost-allocation base used.

$$\begin{aligned}\begin{matrix}\text{Variable}\\ \text{overhead}\\ \text{spending}\\ \text{variance}\end{matrix} &= \left(\begin{matrix}\text{Actual variable}\\ \text{overhead cost per unit}\\ \text{of cost-allocation base}\end{matrix} - \begin{matrix}\text{Budgeted variable}\\ \text{overhead cost per unit}\\ \text{of cost-allocation base}\end{matrix}\right) \times \begin{matrix}\text{Actual quantity of}\\ \text{variable overhead}\\ \text{cost-allocation base}\\ \text{used}\end{matrix}\\ &= (\$29 \text{ per machine-hour} - \$30 \text{ per machine-hour}) \times 4{,}500 \text{ machine-hours}\\ &= (-\$1 \text{ per machine-hour}) \times 4{,}500 \text{ machine-hours}\\ &= \$4{,}500 \text{ F}\end{aligned}$$

Webb operated in April 2014 with a lower-than-budgeted variable overhead cost per machine-hour, so there is a favorable variable overhead spending variance. Columns 1 and 2 in Exhibit 8-1 depict this variance.

To understand why the favorable variable overhead spending variance occurred, Webb's managers need to recognize why *actual* variable overhead cost per unit of the cost-allocation base ($29 per machine-hour) is *lower* than the *budgeted* variable overhead cost per unit of the cost-allocation base ($30 per machine-hour).

Overall, Webb used 4,500 machine-hours, which is 12.5% greater than the flexible-budget amount of 4,000 machine-hours. However, actual variable overhead costs of $130,500 are only 8.75% greater than the flexible-budget amount of $120,000. Thus, relative to the flexible budget, the percentage increase in actual variable overhead costs is *less* than the percentage increase in machine-hours. Consequently, the actual variable overhead cost per machine-hour is lower than the budgeted amount, resulting in a favorable variable overhead spending variance.

Recall that variable overhead costs include costs of energy, machine maintenance, indirect materials, and indirect labor. Two possible reasons why the percentage increase in actual variable overhead costs is less than the percentage increase in machine-hours are as follows:

1. The actual prices of the individual inputs included in variable overhead costs, such as the price of energy, indirect materials, or indirect labor, are lower than budgeted prices of these inputs. For example, the actual price of electricity may only be $0.09 per kilowatt-hour, compared with a price of $0.10 per kilowatt-hour in the flexible budget.
2. Relative to the flexible budget, the percentage increase in the actual use of individual items in the variable overhead-cost pool is less than the percentage increase in machine-hours. Compared with the flexible-budget amount of 30,000 kilowatt-hours, suppose the actual energy use was 32,400 kilowatt-hours, or 8% higher. The fact that this is a smaller percentage increase than the 12.5% increase in machine-hours (4,500 actual

machine-hours versus a flexible budget of 4,000 machine-hours) will lead to a favorable variable overhead spending variance, which can be partially or completely traced to the efficient use of energy and other variable overhead items.

As part of the last stage of the five-step decision-making process, Webb's managers will need to examine the signals provided by the variable overhead variances to *evaluate the firm's performance and learn*. By understanding the reasons for these variances, Webb can take appropriate actions and make more precise predictions in order to achieve improved results in future periods.

For example, Webb's managers must examine why the actual prices of variable overhead cost items are different from the budgeted prices. The differences could be the result of skillful negotiation on the part of the purchasing manager, oversupply in the market, or lower quality of inputs such as indirect materials. Webb's response depends on what is believed to be the cause of the variance. If the concerns are about quality, for instance, Webb may want to put in place new quality management systems.

Similarly, Webb's managers should understand the possible causes for the efficiency with which variable overhead resources are used. These causes include the skill levels of workers, maintenance of machines, and the efficiency of the manufacturing process. Webb's managers discovered that Webb used fewer indirect labor resources per machine-hour because of manufacturing process improvements. As a result, the firm began organizing cross-functional teams to see if more process improvements could be achieved.

We emphasize that a manager should not always view a favorable variable overhead spending variance as desirable. For example, the variable overhead spending variance would be favorable if Webb's managers purchased lower-priced, poor-quality indirect materials, hired less-talented supervisors, or performed less machine maintenance. These decisions, however, are likely to hurt product quality and harm the long-run prospects of the business.

To clarify the concepts of variable overhead efficiency variance and variable overhead spending variance, consider the following example. Suppose that (a) energy is the only item of variable overhead cost and machine-hours is the cost-allocation base; (b) actual machine-hours used equals the number of machine-hours under the flexible budget; and (c) the actual price of energy equals the budgeted price. From (a) and (b), it follows that there is no efficiency variance—the company has been efficient with respect to the number of machine-hours (the cost-allocation base) used to produce the actual output. However, and despite (c), there could still be a spending variance. Why? Because even though the company used the correct number of machine-hours, the energy consumed *per machine-hour* could be higher than budgeted (for example, because the machines have not been maintained correctly). The cost of this higher energy usage would be reflected in an unfavorable spending variance.

Journal Entries for Variable Overhead Costs and Variances

We now prepare journal entries for the Variable Overhead Control account and the contra account Variable Overhead Allocated.

Entries for variable overhead for April 2014 (data from Exhibit 8-1) are as follows:

	Debit	Credit
1. Variable Overhead Control	130,500	
Accounts Payable and various other accounts		130,500
To record actual variable overhead costs incurred.		
2. Work-in-Process Control	120,000	
Variable Overhead Allocated		120,000
To record variable overhead cost allocated (0.40 machine-hour/unit × 10,000 units × $30/machine-hour). (The costs accumulated in Work-in-Process Control are transferred to Finished Goods Control when production is completed and to Cost of Goods Sold when the products are sold.)		

3. Variable Overhead Allocated	120,000	
Variable Overhead Efficiency Variance	15,000	
Variable Overhead Control		130,500
Variable Overhead Spending Variance		4,500
This records the variances for the accounting period.		

These variances are the underallocated or overallocated variable overhead costs. At the end of the fiscal year, the variance accounts are written off to cost of goods sold if immaterial in amount. If the variances are material in amount, they are prorated among the Work-in-Process Control, Finished Goods Control, and Cost of Goods Sold accounts on the basis of the variable overhead allocated to these accounts, as described in Chapter 4, pages 127–132. As we discussed in Chapter 7, only unavoidable costs are prorated. Any part of the variances attributable to avoidable inefficiency is written off in the period. Assume that the balances in the variable overhead variance accounts as of April 2014 are also the balances at the end of the 2014 fiscal year and are immaterial in amount. The following journal entry records the write-off of the variance accounts to the cost of goods sold:

Cost of Goods Sold	10,500	
Variable Overhead Spending Variance	4,500	
Variable Overhead Efficiency Variance		15,000

Next we demonstrate how to calculate fixed overhead cost variances.

Decision Point

What variances can be calculated for variable overhead costs?

Fixed Overhead Cost Variances

Learning Objective 4

Compute the fixed overhead flexible-budget variance,

...difference between actual fixed overhead costs and flexible-budget fixed overhead amounts

the fixed overhead spending variance,

...same as the preceding explanation

and the fixed overhead production-volume variance

...difference between budgeted fixed overhead and fixed overhead allocated on the basis of actual output produced

The flexible-budget amount for a fixed-cost item is also the amount included in the static budget prepared at the start of the period. No adjustment is required for differences between actual output and budgeted output for fixed costs because fixed costs are unaffected by changes in the output level within the relevant range. At the start of 2014, Webb budgeted its fixed overhead costs to be $276,000 per month. The actual amount for April 2014 turned out to be $285,000. The **fixed overhead flexible-budget variance** is the difference between actual fixed overhead costs and fixed overhead costs in the flexible budget:

$$\text{Fixed overhead flexible-budget variance} = \text{Actual costs incurred} - \text{Flexible-budget amount}$$
$$= \$285{,}000 - \$276{,}000$$
$$= \$9{,}000 \text{ U}$$

The variance is unfavorable because the $285,000 actual fixed overhead costs exceed the $276,000 budgeted for April 2014, which decreases that month's operating income by $9,000.

The variable overhead flexible-budget variance described earlier in this chapter was subdivided into a spending variance and an efficiency variance. There is no efficiency variance for fixed overhead costs. That's because a given lump sum of fixed overhead costs will be unaffected by how efficiently machine-hours are used to produce output in a given budget period. As we will see later on, this does not mean that a company cannot be efficient or inefficient in its use of fixed-overhead-cost resources. As Exhibit 8-2 shows, because there is no efficiency variance, the **fixed overhead spending variance** is the same amount as the fixed overhead flexible-budget variance:

$$\text{Fixed overhead spending variance} = \text{Actual costs incurred} - \text{Flexible-budget amount}$$
$$= \$285{,}000 - \$276{,}000$$
$$= \$9{,}000 \text{ U}$$

Reasons for the unfavorable spending variance could be higher plant-leasing costs, higher depreciation on plant and equipment, or higher administrative costs, such as a higher-than-budgeted

Exhibit 8-2 Columnar Presentation of Fixed Overhead Variance Analysis: Webb Company for April 2014[a]

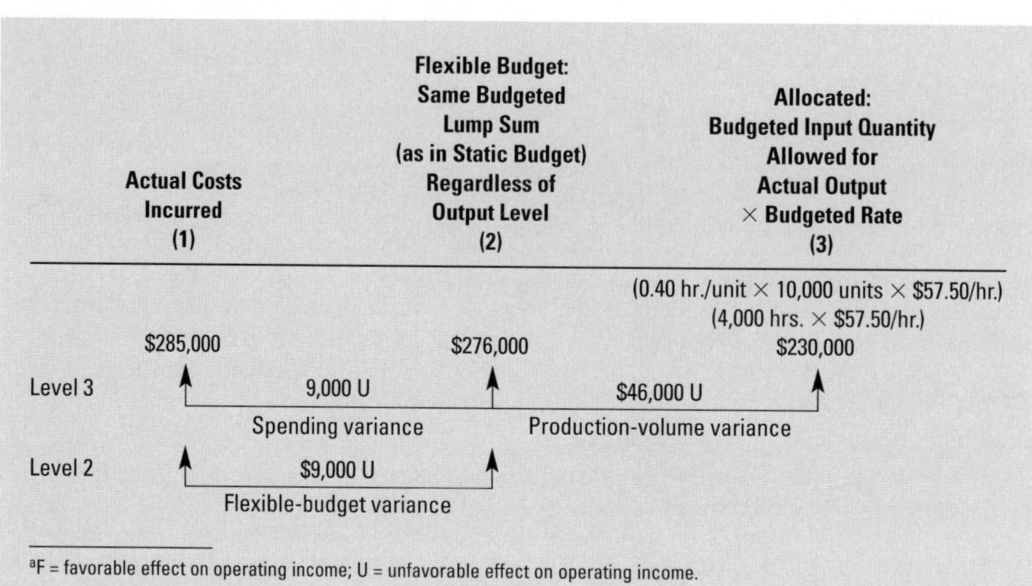

salary paid to the plant manager. Webb investigated this variance and found that there was a $9,000 per month unexpected increase in its equipment-leasing costs. However, managers concluded that the new lease rates were competitive with lease rates available elsewhere. If this were not the case, Webb would look to lease equipment from other suppliers.

Production-Volume Variance

The **production-volume variance** arises only for fixed costs. It is the difference between the budgeted fixed overhead and the fixed overhead allocated on the basis of actual output produced. Recall that at the start of the year, Webb calculated a budgeted fixed overhead rate of $57.50 per machine-hour based on monthly budgeted fixed overhead costs of $276,000. Under standard costing, Webb's fixed overhead costs are allocated to the actual output produced during each period at the rate of $57.50 per standard machine-hour, which is equivalent to a rate of $23 per jacket (0.40 machine-hour per jacket × $57.50 per machine-hour). If Webb produces 1,000 jackets, $23,000 ($23 per jacket × 1,000 jackets) out of April's budgeted fixed overhead costs of $276,000 will be allocated to the jackets. If Webb produces 10,000 jackets, $230,000 ($23 per jacket × 10,000 jackets) will be allocated. Only if Webb produces 12,000 jackets (that is, operates, as budgeted, at capacity) will all $276,000 ($23 per jacket × 12,000 jackets) of the budgeted fixed overhead costs be allocated to the jacket output. The key point here is that even though Webb budgeted its fixed overhead costs to be $276,000, it does not necessarily allocate all these costs to output. The reason is that Webb budgets $276,000 of fixed costs to support its planned production of 12,000 jackets. If Webb produces fewer than 12,000 jackets, it only allocates the budgeted cost of capacity actually needed and used to produce the jackets.

The production-volume variance, also referred to as the **denominator-level variance,** is the difference between the budgeted and allocated fixed overhead amounts. Note that the allocated overhead can be expressed in terms of allocation-base units (machine-hours for Webb) or in terms of the budgeted fixed cost per unit:

$$\text{Production volume variance} = \text{Budgeted fixed overhead} - \text{Fixed overhead allocated for actual output units produced}$$

$$= \$276{,}000 - (0.40 \text{ hour per jacket} \times \$57.50 \text{ per hour} \times 10{,}000 \text{ jackets})$$

$$= \$276{,}000 - (\$23 \text{ per jacket} \times 10{,}000 \text{ jackets})$$

$$= \$276{,}000 - \$230{,}000$$

$$= \$46{,}000 \text{ U}$$

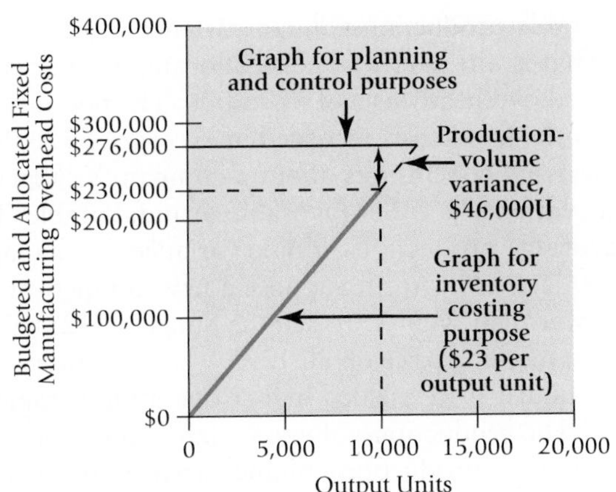

Exhibit 8-3

Behavior of Fixed Manufacturing Overhead Costs: Budgeted for Planning and Control Purposes and Allocated for Inventory Costing Purposes for Webb Company for April 2014

As shown in Exhibit 8-2, the budgeted fixed overhead ($276,000) will be the lump sum shown in the static budget and also in any flexible budget within the relevant range. The fixed overhead allocated ($230,000) is the amount of fixed overhead costs allocated; it is calculated by multiplying the number of output units produced during the budget period (10,000 units) by the budgeted cost per output unit ($23). The $46,000 U production-volume variance can also be thought of as $23 per jacket × 2,000 jackets that were *not* produced. We will explore possible causes for the unfavorable production-volume variance and its management implications in the following section.

Exhibit 8-3 shows Webb's production-volume variance. For planning and control purposes, Webb's fixed (manufacturing) overhead costs do not change in the 0- to 12,000-unit relevant range. Contrast this behavior of fixed costs with how these costs are depicted for the purpose of inventory costing in Exhibit 8-3. Under Generally Accepted Accounting Principles (GAAP), fixed (manufacturing) overhead costs are allocated as an inventoriable cost to the output units produced. Every output unit that Webb manufactures will increase the fixed overhead allocated to products by $23. That is, for purposes of allocating fixed overhead costs to jackets, these costs are viewed *as if* they had a variable-cost behavior pattern. As the graph in Exhibit 8-3 shows, the difference between the $276,000 in fixed overhead costs budgeted and the $230,000 of costs allocated is the $46,000 unfavorable production-volume variance.

Managers should always be careful to distinguish the true behavior of fixed costs from the manner in which fixed costs are assigned to products. In particular, although fixed costs are unitized and allocated for inventory costing purposes, managers should be wary of using the same unitized fixed overhead costs for planning and control purposes. When forecasting fixed costs, managers should concentrate on total lump-sum costs instead of unitized costs. Similarly, when managers are looking to assign costs for control purposes or identify the best way to use capacity resources fixed in the short run, we will see in Chapters 9 and 11 that the use of unitized fixed costs often leads to incorrect decisions.

Interpreting the Production-Volume Variance

Lump-sum fixed costs represent the costs of acquiring capacity. These costs do not decrease automatically if the capacity needed turns out to be less than the capacity acquired. Sometimes costs are fixed for a specific time period for contractual reasons, such as an annual lease contract for a plant. At other times, costs are fixed because capacity has to be acquired or disposed of in fixed increments, or lumps. For example, suppose that acquiring a sewing machine gives Webb the ability to produce 1,000 jackets. If it is not possible to buy or lease a fraction of a machine, Webb can add capacity only in increments of 1,000 jackets. That is, Webb may choose capacity levels of 10,000, 11,000, or 12,000 jackets, but nothing in between.

Webb's management would want to analyze the $46,000 unfavorable production-volume variance. Why did this overcapacity occur? Why were 10,000 jackets produced instead of 12,000? Is demand weak? Should Webb reevaluate its product and marketing strategies? Is there a quality problem? Or did Webb make a strategic mistake by acquiring too much capacity? The causes of the $46,000 unfavorable production-volume variance will determine the actions Webb's managers take in response to the variance.

In contrast, a favorable production-volume variance indicates an overallocation of fixed overhead costs. That is, the overhead costs allocated to the actual output produced exceed the budgeted fixed overhead costs of $276,000. The favorable production-volume variance is composed of the fixed costs recorded in excess of $276,000.

Be careful when drawing conclusions about a company's capacity planning whether the production-volume variance is either favorable or unfavorable. To correctly interpret Webb's $46,000 unfavorable production-volume variance, its managers should consider why it sold only 10,000 jackets in April. Suppose a new competitor gained market share by pricing its jackets lower than Webb's. To sell the budgeted 12,000 jackets, Webb might have had to reduce its own selling price on all 12,000 jackets. Suppose it decided that selling 10,000 jackets at a higher price yielded higher operating income than selling 12,000 jackets at a lower price. The production-volume variance does not take into account such information. The failure of the production-volume variance to consider such information is why Webb should not interpret the $46,000 U amount as the total economic cost of selling 2,000 jackets fewer than the 12,000 jackets budgeted. If, however, Webb's managers anticipate they will not need capacity beyond 10,000 jackets, they may reduce the excess capacity, say, by canceling the lease on some of the machines.

Companies plan their plant capacity strategically on the basis of market information about how much capacity will be needed over some future time horizon. For 2014, Webb's budgeted quantity of output is equal to the maximum capacity of the plant for that budget period. Actual demand (and quantity produced) turned out to be below the budgeted quantity of output, so Webb reports an unfavorable production-volume variance for April 2014. However, it would be incorrect to conclude that Webb's management made a poor planning decision regarding its plant capacity. The demand for Webb's jackets might be highly uncertain. Given this uncertainty and the cost of not having sufficient capacity to meet sudden demand surges (including lost contribution margins as well as reduced repeat business), Webb's management may have made a wise capacity choice for 2014.

So what should Webb's managers ultimately do about the unfavorable variance in April? Should they try to reduce capacity, increase sales, or do nothing? Based on their analysis of the situation, Webb's managers decided to reduce some capacity but continued to maintain some excess capacity to accommodate unexpected surges in demand. Chapters 9 and 12 examine these issues in more detail. Concepts in Action: Variance Analysis and Standard Costing Help Sandoz Manage Its Overhead Costs highlights another example of managers using variances to help guide their decisions.

Next we describe the journal entries Webb would make to record fixed overhead costs using standard costing.

Journal Entries for Fixed Overhead Costs and Variances

We illustrate journal entries for fixed overhead costs for April 2014 using the Fixed Overhead Control account and the contra account Fixed Overhead Allocated (data from Exhibit 8-2).

1. Fixed Overhead Control	285,000	
Salaries Payable, Accumulated Depreciation, and various other accounts		285,000
To record actual fixed overhead costs incurred.		
2. Work-in-Process Control	230,000	
Fixed Overhead Allocated		230,000
To record fixed overhead costs allocated.		
(0.40 machine-hour/unit × 10,000 units × $57.50/machine-hour). (The costs accumulated in Work-in-Process Control are transferred to Finished Goods Control when production is completed and to the Cost of Goods Sold when the products are sold.)		
3. Fixed Overhead Allocated	230,000	
Fixed Overhead Spending Variance	9,000	
Fixed Overhead Production-Volume Variance	46,000	
Fixed Overhead Control		285,000
To record variances for the accounting period.		

Concepts in Action

Variance Analysis and Standard Costing Help Sandoz Manage Its Overhead Costs

Sandoz US, the $8.7 billion subsidiary of Swiss-based Novartis AG, is one of the world's largest generic drug manufacturers. Market pricing pressure means that Sandoz operates on razor-thin margins. As a result, Sandoz must tackle the challenge of accounting for overhead costs. Sandoz uses standard costing and variance analysis to manage its overhead costs.

Each year, Sandoz prepares an overhead budget based on a detailed production plan, planned overhead spending, and other factors. Sandoz then uses activity-based costing to assign budgeted overhead costs to different work centers (for example, mixing, blending, tableting, testing, and packaging). Finally, overhead costs are assigned to products based on the activity levels required by each product at each work center. The resulting standard product cost is used in product profitability analysis and as a basis for making pricing decisions. The two main focal points in Sandoz's performance analyses are overhead absorption analysis and manufacturing overhead variance analysis.

Each month, Sandoz uses absorption analysis to compare its actual production and actual costs to the standard costs of its processed inventory. The monthly analysis evaluates two key trends:

1. Are costs in line with the budget? If not, the reasons are examined and the accountable managers are notified.
2. Are production volume and product mix conforming to plan? If not, Sandoz reviews and adjusts the capacities of its machines, and the absorption trend is deemed to be permanent.

Manufacturing overhead variances are examined at the work center level. These variances help determine when equipment is not running as expected so it can be repaired or replaced. Variances also help in identifying inefficiencies in processing and setup and cleaning times, which leads to more efficient ways to use equipment. Sometimes, the manufacturing overhead variance analysis leads to the review and improvement of the standards themselves—a critical element in planning the level of plant capacity. Managers also review the company's current and future capacity on a monthly basis to identify constraints and future capital needs.

Sources: Novartis AG. 2013. December 31, 2012 Form 20-F (filed January 23, 2013), accessed May 2013; and conversations with and documents prepared by Eric Evans and Erich Erchr (of Sandoz US), 2004.

Overall, $285,000 of fixed overhead costs were incurred during April, but only $230,000 were allocated to jackets. The difference of $55,000 is precisely the underallocated fixed overhead costs we introduced when studying normal costing in Chapter 4. The third entry illustrates how the fixed overhead spending variance of $9,000 and the fixed overhead production-volume variance of $46,000 together record this amount in a standard costing system.

At the end of the fiscal year, the fixed overhead spending variance is written off to the cost of goods sold if it is immaterial in amount or prorated among Work-in-Process Control, Finished Goods Control, and Cost of Goods Sold on the basis of the fixed overhead allocated to these accounts as described in Chapter 4, pages 127–132. Some companies combine the write-off and proration methods—that is, they write off the portion of the variance that is due to inefficiency and could have been avoided and prorate the portion of the variance that is unavoidable. Assume that the balance in the Fixed

Overhead Spending Variance account as of April 2014 is also the balance at the end of 2014 and is immaterial in amount. The following journal entry records the write-off to Cost of Goods Sold.

Cost of Goods Sold	9,000	
Fixed Overhead Spending Variance		9,000

We now consider the production-volume variance. Assume that the balance in the Fixed Overhead Production-Volume Variance account as of April 2014 is also the balance at the end of 2014. Also assume that some of the jackets manufactured during 2014 are in work-in-process and finished goods inventory at the end of the year. Many management accountants make a strong argument for writing off to Cost of Goods Sold and not prorating an unfavorable production-volume variance. Proponents of this argument contend that the unfavorable production-volume variance of \$46,000 measures the cost of resources expended for 2,000 jackets that were not produced (\$23 per jacket × 2,000 jackets = \$46,000). Prorating these costs would inappropriately allocate the fixed overhead costs incurred for the 2,000 jackets not produced to the jackets that were produced. The jackets produced already bear their representative share of fixed overhead costs of \$23 per jacket. Therefore, this argument favors charging the unfavorable production-volume variance against the year's revenues so that fixed costs of unused capacity are not carried in work-in-process inventory and finished goods inventory.

There is, however, an alternative view. This view regards the denominator level as a "soft" rather than a "hard" measure of the fixed resources required and needed to produce each jacket. Suppose that either because of the design of the jacket or the functioning of the machines, it took more machine-hours than previously thought to manufacture each jacket. Consequently, Webb could make only 10,000 jackets rather than the planned 12,000 in April. In this case, the \$276,000 of budgeted fixed overhead costs support the production of the 10,000 jackets manufactured. Under this reasoning, prorating the fixed overhead production-volume variance would appropriately spread the fixed overhead costs among the Work-in-Process Control, Finished Goods Control, and Cost of Goods Sold accounts.

What about a favorable production-volume variance? Suppose Webb manufactured 13,800 jackets in April 2014.

$$
\begin{aligned}
\text{Production-volume variance} &= \begin{array}{c}\text{Budgeted}\\ \text{fixed}\\ \text{overhead}\end{array} - \begin{array}{c}\text{Fixed overhead allocated using}\\ \text{budgeted cost per output unit overhead}\\ \text{allowed for actual output produced}\end{array}\\
&= \$276{,}000 - (\$23 \text{ per jacket} \times 13{,}800 \text{ jackets})\\
&= \$276{,}000 - \$317{,}400 = \$41{,}400\text{ F}
\end{aligned}
$$

Because actual production exceeded the planned capacity level, clearly the fixed overhead costs of \$276,000 supported the production of all 13,800 jackets and should therefore be allocated to them. Prorating the favorable production-volume variance achieves this outcome and reduces the amounts in the Work-in-Process Control, Finished Goods Control, and Cost of Goods Sold accounts. Proration is also the more conservative approach in the sense that it results in a lower operating income than if the entire favorable production-volume variance were credited to Cost of Goods Sold.

Another point relevant to this discussion is that if variances are always written off to Cost of Goods Sold, a company could set its standards to either increase (for financial reporting purposes) or decrease (for tax purposes) its operating income. In other words, always writing off variances invites gaming behavior. For example, Webb could generate a favorable production-volume variance by setting the denominator level used to allocate the firm's fixed overhead costs low and thereby increase its operating income. Or the firm could do just the opposite if it wanted to decrease its operating income to lower its taxes. The proration method has the effect of approximating the allocation of fixed costs based on actual costs and actual output, so it is not susceptible to this type of manipulation.

There is no clear-cut or preferred approach for closing out the production-volume variance. The appropriate accounting procedure is a matter of judgment and depends on the circumstances of each case. Variations of the proration method may be desirable. For example, a company may choose to write off a portion of the production-volume variance and prorate the rest. The goal is to write off that part of the production-volume variance that represents the cost of capacity not used to support the production of output during the period. The rest of the production-volume variance is prorated to Work-in-Process Control, Finished Goods Control, and Cost of Goods Sold.

If Webb were to write off the production-volume variance to Cost of Goods Sold, it would make the following journal entry.

Cost of Goods Sold	46,000	
Fixed Overhead Production-Volume Variance		46,000

Decision Point

What variances can be calculated for fixed overhead costs?

Integrated Analysis of Overhead Cost Variances

Learning Objective 5

Show how the 4-variance analysis approach reconciles the actual overhead incurred with the overhead amounts allocated during the period

...the 4-variance analysis approach identifies spending and efficiency variances for variable overhead costs and spending and production-volume variances for fixed overhead costs

As our discussion indicates, the variance calculations for variable overhead and fixed overhead differ:

- Variable overhead has no production-volume variance.
- Fixed overhead has no efficiency variance.

Exhibit 8-4 presents an integrated summary of the variable overhead variances and the fixed overhead variances computed using standard costs for April 2014. Panel A shows the variances for variable overhead, whereas Panel B contains the fixed overhead variances. As you study Exhibit 8-4, note how the columns in Panels A and B are aligned to measure the different variances. In both Panels A and B,

- the difference between columns 1 and 2 measures the spending variance.
- the difference between columns 2 and 3 measures the efficiency variance (if applicable).
- the difference between columns 3 and 4 measures the production-volume variance (if applicable).

Panel A contains an efficiency variance; Panel B has no efficiency variance for fixed overhead. As we discussed, a lump-sum amount of fixed costs will be unaffected by the degree of operating efficiency in a given budget period.

Panel A does not have a production-volume variance because the amount of variable overhead allocated is always the same as the flexible-budget amount. Variable costs never have any unused capacity. When production and sales decline from 12,000 jackets to 10,000 jackets, budgeted variable overhead costs proportionately decline. Fixed costs are different. Panel B has a production-volume variance (see Exhibit 8-3) because Webb did not use some of the fixed overhead capacity it had acquired when it planned to produce 12,000 jackets.

4-Variance Analysis

When all of the overhead variances are presented together as in Exhibit 8-4, we refer to it as a 4-variance analysis:

	4-Variance Analysis		
	Spending Variance	**Efficiency Variance**	**Production-Volume Variance**
Variable overhead	\$4,500 F	\$15,000 U	Never a variance
Fixed overhead	\$9,000 U	Never a variance	\$46,000 U

Note that the 4-variance analysis provides the same level of information as the variance analysis carried out earlier for variable overhead and fixed overhead separately

Exhibit 8-4 Columnar Presentation of Integrated Variance Analysis: Webb Company for April 2014[a] 

PANEL A: Variable (Manufacturing) Overhead

Actual Costs Incurred: Actual Input Quantity × Actual Rate (1)	Actual Input Quantity × Budgeted Rate (2)	Flexible Budget: Budgeted Input Quantity Allowed for Actual Output × Budgeted Rate (3)	Allocated: Budgeted Input Quantity Allowed for Actual Output × Budgeted Rate (4)
		(0.40 hrs./unit × 10,000 units × $30/hr.)	(0.40 hrs./unit × 10,000 units × $30/hr.)
(4,500 hrs. × $29/hr.)	(4,500 hrs. × $30/hr.)	(4,000 hrs. × $30/hr.)	(4,000 hrs. × $30/hr.)
$130,500	$135,000	$120,000	$120,000

(1)–(2): $4,500 F Spending variance; (2)–(3): $15,000 U Efficiency variance; (3)–(4): Never a variance

(1)–(3): $10,500 U Flexible-budget variance; (3)–(4): Never a variance

(1)–(4): $10,500 U Underallocated variable overhead (Total variable overhead variance)

PANEL B: Fixed (Manufacturing) Overhead

Actual Costs Incurred (1)	Same Budgeted Lump Sum (as in Static Budget) Regardless of Output Level (2)	Flexible Budget: Same Budgeted Lump Sum (as in Static Budget) Regardless of Output Level (3)	Allocated: Budgeted Input Quantity Allowed for Actual Output × Budgeted Rate (4)
			(0.40 hrs./unit × 10,000 units × $57.50/hr.)
			(4,000 hrs. × $57.50/hr.)
$285,000	$276,000	$276,000	$230,000

(1)–(2): $9,000 U Spending variance; (2)–(3): Never a variance; (3)–(4): $46,000 U Production-volume variance

(1)–(3): $9,000 U Flexible-budget variance; (3)–(4): $46,000 U Production-volume variance

(1)–(4): $55,000 U Underallocated fixed overhead (Total fixed overhead variance)

[a]F = favorable effect on operating income; U = unfavorable effect on operating income.

(in Exhibits 8-1 and 8-2, respectively), but it does so in a unified presentation that also indicates those variances that are never present.

As with other variances, the variances in Webb's 4-variance analysis are not necessarily independent of each other. For example, Webb may purchase lower-quality machine fluids (leading to a favorable variable overhead spending variance), which results in the machines taking longer to operate than budgeted (causing an unfavorable variable overhead efficiency variance), and producing less than budgeted output (causing an unfavorable production-volume variance).

Combined Variance Analysis

To keep track of all that is happening within their areas of responsibility, managers in large, complex businesses, such as General Electric and Disney, use detailed 4-variance analysis. Doing so helps them identify and focus attention on the areas not operating as expected. Managers of small businesses understand their operations better based on personal observations and nonfinancial measures. They find less value in doing the additional measurements required for 4-variance analyses. For example, to simplify their costing systems, small companies may not distinguish variable overhead incurred from fixed overhead incurred because making this distinction is often not clear-cut. As we saw in Chapter 2 and will see in Chapter 10, many costs such as supervision, quality control, and materials handling have both variable- and fixed-cost components that may not be easy to separate. Managers may therefore use a less detailed analysis that *combines* the variable overhead and fixed overhead into a single total overhead cost.

When a single total overhead cost category is used, it can still be analyzed in depth. The variances are now the sums of the variable overhead and fixed overhead variances for that level, as computed in Exhibit 8-4. The combined variance analysis looks as follows:

	Combined 3-Variance Analysis		
	Spending Variance	**Efficiency Variance**	**Production-Volume Variance**
Total overhead	$4,500 U	$15,000 U	$46,000 U

The accounting for 3-variance analysis is simpler than for 4-variance analysis, but some information is lost because the variable and fixed overhead spending variances are combined into a single total overhead spending variance.

Finally, the overall **total-overhead variance** is given by the sum of the preceding variances. In the Webb example, this equals $65,500 U. Note that this amount, which aggregates the flexible-budget and production-volume variances, equals the total amount of underallocated (or underapplied) overhead costs. (Recall our discussion of underallocated overhead costs in normal costing from Chapter 4, pages 127–128.) Using figures from Exhibit 8-4, the $65,500 U total-overhead variance is the difference between (a) the total actual overhead incurred ($130,500 + $285,000 = $415,500) and (b) the overhead allocated ($120,000 + $230,000 = $350,000) to the actual output produced. If the total-overhead variance were favorable, it would have corresponded instead to the amount of overapplied overhead costs.

Decision Point

What is the most detailed way for a company to reconcile actual overhead incurred with the amount allocated during a period?

Production-Volume Variance and Sales-Volume Variance

Learning Objective 6

Explain the relationship between the sales-volume variance and the production-volume variance

...the production-volume and operating-income volume variances together comprise the sales-volume variance

As we complete our study of variance analysis for Webb Company, it is helpful to step back to see the "big picture" and to link the accounting and performance evaluation functions of standard costing. Exhibit 7-1, page 251, first identified a static-budget variance of $93,100 U as the difference between the static budget operating income of $108,000 and the actual operating income of $14,900. Exhibit 7-2, page 253, then subdivided the static-budget variance of $93,100 U into a flexible-budget variance of $29,100 U and a sales-volume variance of $64,000 U. In both Chapter 7 and this chapter, we presented more detailed variances that subdivided, whenever possible, individual flexible-budget variances for the selling price, direct materials, direct manufacturing labor, and variable overhead. For the fixed overhead, we noted that the flexible-budget variance is the same as the spending variance. Where does the production-volume variance belong then? As you shall see, the production-volume variance is a component of the sales-volume variance. Under our assumption of actual production and sales of 10,000 jackets, Webb's costing system debits to Work-in-Process Control the standard costs of the 10,000 jackets produced. These amounts are then transferred to Finished Goods and finally to Cost of Goods Sold:

Direct materials (Chapter 7, page 262, entry 1b)	
($60 per jacket × 10,000 jackets)	$ 600,000
Direct manufacturing labor (Chapter 7, page 262, entry 2)	
($16 per jacket × 10,000 jackets)	160,000
Variable overhead (Chapter 8, page 300, entry 2)	
($12 per jacket × 10,000 jackets)	120,000
Fixed overhead (Chapter 8, page 300, entry 2)	
($23 per jacket × 10,000 jackets)	230,000
Cost of goods sold at standard cost	
($111 per jacket × 10,000 jackets)	$1,110,000

Webb's costing system also records the revenues from the 10,000 jackets sold at the budgeted selling price of $120 per jacket. The net effect of these entries on Webb's budgeted operating income is as follows:

Revenues at budgeted selling price	
($120 per jacket × 10,000 jackets)	$1,200,000
Cost of goods sold at standard cost	
($111 per jacket × 10,000 jackets)	1,110,000
Operating income based on budgeted profit per jacket	
($9 per jacket × 10,000 jackets)	$ 90,000

A crucial point to keep in mind is that under standard costing, fixed overhead costs are treated as if they are a variable cost. That is, in determining the budgeted operating income of $90,000, only $230,000 ($23 per jacket × 10,000 jackets) of the fixed overhead costs are considered, whereas the budgeted fixed overhead costs are $276,000. Webb's accountants then record the $46,000 unfavorable production-volume variance (the difference between the budgeted fixed overhead costs, $276,000, and allocated fixed overhead costs, $230,000, page 300, entry 2), as well as the various flexible-budget variances (including the fixed overhead spending variance) that total $29,100 unfavorable (see Exhibit 7-2, page 253). This results in actual operating income of $14,900 as follows:

Operating income based on budgeted profit per jacket	
($9 per jacket × 10,000 jackets)	$ 90,000
Unfavorable production-volume variance	(46,000)
Flexible-budget operating income (Exhibit 7-2)	44,000
Unfavorable flexible-budget variance for operating income (Exhibit 7-2)	(29,100)
Actual operating income (Exhibit 7-2)	$ 14,900

In contrast, the static-budget operating income of $108,000 (page 253) is not entered in Webb's costing system because standard costing records budgeted revenues, standard costs, and variances only for the 10,000 jackets actually produced and sold, not for the 12,000 jackets that were *planned* to be produced and sold. As a result, the sales-volume variance of $64,000 U, which is the difference between the static-budget operating income of $108,000 and the flexible-budget operating income of $44,000 (Exhibit 7-2, page 253), is never actually recorded under standard costing. Nevertheless, the sales-volume variance is useful because it helps managers understand the lost contribution margin from selling 2,000 fewer jackets (the sales-volume variance assumes fixed costs remain at the budgeted level of $276,000).

The sales-volume variance has two components. They are as follows:

1. A difference between the static-budget operating income of $108,000 for 12,000 jackets and the budgeted operating income of $90,000 for 10,000 jackets. This is the

operating-income volume variance of $18,000 U ($108,000 − $90,000). It reflects the fact that Webb produced and sold 2,000 fewer units than budgeted.

2. A difference between the budgeted operating income of $90,000 and the flexible budget operating income of $44,000 (Exhibit 7-2, page 253) for the 10,000 actual units. This difference arises because Webb's costing system treats fixed costs as if they behave in a variable manner and assumes fixed costs equal the allocated amount of $230,000, rather than the budgeted fixed costs of $276,000. Of course, this difference is precisely the production-volume variance of $46,000 U.

In summary, we have the following:

	Operating-income volume variance	$18,000 U
(+)	Production-volume variance	46,000 U
Equals	Sales-volume variance	$64,000 U

We can now provide a summary (see Exhibit 8-5) that formally disaggregates the static-budget variance of $93,100 U into its components. Note how the comprehensive chart incorporates all of the variances you have studied in Chapters 7 and 8.

We next describe the use of variance analysis in activity-based costing systems.

Decision Point

What is the relationship between the sales-volume variance and the production-volume variance?

Variance Analysis and Activity-Based Costing

Learning Objective 7

Calculate variances in activity-based costing

...compare budgeted and actual overhead costs of activities

Activity-based costing (ABC) systems focus on individual activities as the fundamental cost objects. ABC systems classify the costs of various activities into a cost hierarchy—output unit-level costs, batch-level costs, product-sustaining costs, and facility-sustaining costs (see page 161). In this section, we show how a company that has an ABC system and batch-level costs can benefit from variance analysis. Batch-level costs are the costs of activities related to a group of units of products or services rather than to each individual

Exhibit 8-5 Summary of Levels 1, 2, and 3 Variance Analysis: Webb Company for April 2014

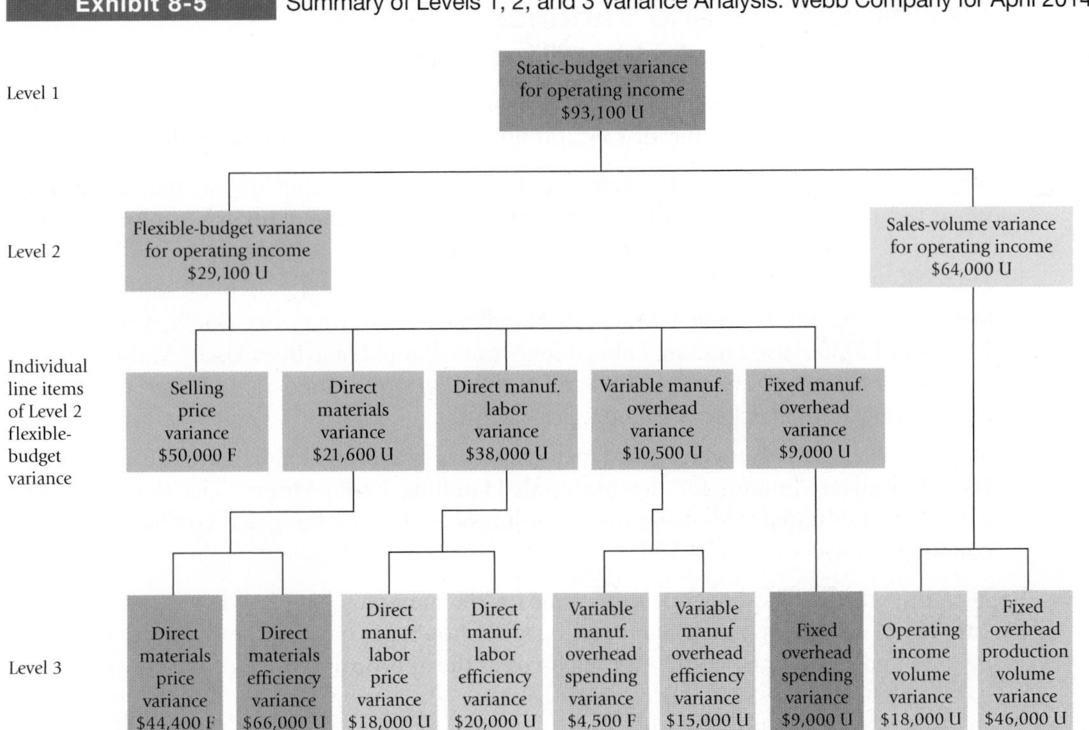

unit of product or service. We illustrate variance analysis for variable batch-level direct costs and fixed batch-level setup overhead costs.[4]

Consider Lyco Brass Works, which manufactures many different types of faucets and brass fittings. Because of the wide range of products it produces, Lyco uses an activity-based costing system. In contrast, Webb uses a simple costing system because it makes only one type of jacket. One of Lyco's products is Elegance, a decorative brass faucet for home spas. Lyco produces Elegance in batches.

For each product Lyco makes, it uses dedicated materials-handling labor to bring materials to the production floor, transport items in process from one work center to the next, and take the finished goods to the shipping area. Therefore, materials-handling labor costs for Elegance are direct costs of Elegance. Because the materials for a batch are moved together, materials-handling labor costs vary with number of batches rather than with number of units in a batch. Materials-handling labor costs are variable direct batch-level costs.

To manufacture a batch of Elegance, Lyco must set up the machines and molds. Employees must be highly skilled to set up the machines and molds. Hence, a separate setup department is responsible for setting up the machines and molds for different batches of products. Setup costs are overhead costs. For simplicity, assume that setup costs are fixed with respect to the number of setup-hours. The costs consist of salaries paid to engineers and supervisors and the costs of leasing setup equipment.

Information regarding Elegance for 2014 follows:

	Actual Result	Static-Budget Amount
1. Units of Elegance produced and sold	151,200	180,000
2. Batch size (units per batch)	140	150
3. Number of batches (Line 1 ÷ Line 2)	1,080	1,200
4. Materials-handling labor-hours per batch	5.25	5
5. Total materials-handling labor-hours (Line 3 × Line 4)	5,670	6,000
6. Cost per materials-handling labor-hour	\$ 14.50	\$ 14
7. Total materials-handling labor costs (Line 5 × Line 6)	\$ 82,215	\$ 84,000
8. Setup-hours per batch	6.25	6
9. Total setup-hours (Line 3 × Line 8)	6,750	7,200
10. Total fixed setup overhead costs	\$220,000	\$216,000

Flexible Budget and Variance Analysis for Direct Materials-Handling Labor Costs

To prepare the flexible budget for the materials-handling labor costs, Lyco starts with the actual units of output produced, 151,200 units, and proceeds with the following steps.

Step 1: Using the Budgeted Batch Size, Calculate the Number of Batches that Should Have Been Used to Produce the Actual Output. At the budgeted batch size of 150 units per batch, Lyco should have produced the 151,200 units of output in 1,008 batches (151,200 units ÷ 150 units per batch).

Step 2: Using the Budgeted Materials-Handling Labor-Hours per Batch, Calculate the Number of Materials-Handling Labor-Hours that Should Have Been Used. At the budgeted quantity of 5 hours per batch, 1,008 batches should have required 5,040 materials-handling labor-hours (1,008 batches × 5 hours per batch).

Step 3: Using the Budgeted Cost per Materials-Handling Labor-Hour, Calculate the Flexible-Budget Amount for the Materials-Handling Labor-Hours. The flexible-budget amount is 5,040 materials-handling labor-hours × the \$14 budgeted cost per materials-handling labor-hour = \$70,560.

Note how the flexible-budget calculations for the materials-handling labor costs focus on batch-level quantities (materials-handling labor-hours per batch rather than per unit). The flexible-budget quantity computations focus at the appropriate level of the cost hierarchy.

[4] The techniques we demonstrate can be applied to analyze variable batch-level overhead costs as well.

For example, because materials handling is a batch-level cost, the flexible-budget quantity calculations are made at the batch level—the quantity of materials-handling labor-hours that Lyco should have used based on the number of batches it should have used to produce the actual quantity of 151,200 units. If a cost had been a product-sustaining cost—such as product design cost—the flexible-budget quantity computations would focus at the product-sustaining level, for example, by evaluating the actual complexity of the product's design relative to the budget.

The flexible-budget variance for the materials-handling labor costs can now be calculated as follows:

$$\begin{aligned}\text{Flexible-budget variance} &= \text{Actual costs} - \text{Flexible-budget costs}\\ &= (5{,}670 \text{ hours} \times \$14.50 \text{ per hour}) - (5{,}040 \text{ hours} \times \$14 \text{ per hour})\\ &= \$82{,}215 - \$70{,}560\\ &= \$11{,}655 \text{ U}\end{aligned}$$

The unfavorable variance indicates that materials-handling labor costs were $11,655 higher than the flexible-budget target. We can get some insight into the possible reasons for this unfavorable outcome by examining the price and efficiency components of the flexible-budget variance. Exhibit 8-6 presents the variances in columnar form.

$$\begin{aligned}\text{Price variance} &= \left(\text{Actual price of input} - \text{Budgeted price of input}\right) \times \text{Actual quantity of input}\\ &= (\$14.50 \text{ per hour} - \$14 \text{ per hour}) \times 5{,}670 \text{ hours}\\ &= \$0.50 \text{ per hour} \times 5{,}670 \text{ hours}\\ &= \$2{,}835 \text{ U}\end{aligned}$$

The unfavorable price variance for materials-handling labor indicates that the $14.50 actual cost per materials-handling labor-hour exceeds the $14.00 budgeted cost per materials-handling labor-hour. This variance could be the result of Lyco's human resources manager negotiating wage rates less skillfully or of wage rates increasing unexpectedly due to a scarcity of labor.

$$\begin{aligned}\text{Efficiency variance} &= \left(\text{Actual quantity of input used} - \text{Budgeted quantity of input allowed for actual output}\right) \times \text{Budgeted price of input}\\ &= (5{,}670 \text{ hours} - 5{,}040 \text{ hours}) \times \$14 \text{ per hour}\\ &= 630 \text{ hours} \times \$14 \text{ per hour}\\ &= \$8{,}820 \text{ U}\end{aligned}$$

Exhibit 8-6 Columnar Presentation of Variance Analysis for Direct Materials-Handling Labor Costs: Lyco Brass Works for 2014[a]

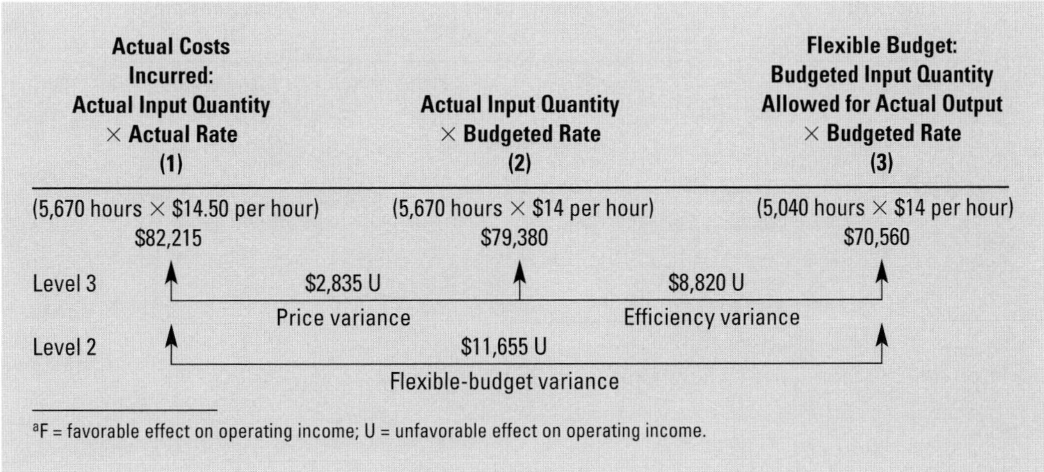

The unfavorable efficiency variance indicates that the 5,670 actual materials-handling labor-hours exceeded the 5,040 budgeted materials-handling labor-hours for the actual output. Possible reasons for the unfavorable efficiency variance are as follows:

- Smaller actual batch sizes of 140 units, instead of the budgeted batch sizes of 150 units, resulted in Lyco producing the 151,200 units in 1,080 batches instead of 1,008 (151,200 ÷ 150) batches
- The actual materials-handling labor-hours per batch (5.25 hours) were higher than the budgeted materials-handling labor-hours per batch (5 hours)

Reasons for smaller-than-budgeted batch sizes could include quality problems when batch sizes exceed 140 faucets and high costs of carrying inventory.

Possible reasons for the larger actual materials-handling labor-hours per batch are as follows:

- Inefficient layout of the Elegance production line
- Materials-handling labor having to wait at work centers before picking up or delivering materials
- Unmotivated, inexperienced, and underskilled employees
- Very tight standards for materials-handling time

Identifying the reasons for the efficiency variance helps Lyco's managers develop a plan for improving its materials-handling labor efficiency and take corrective action that will be incorporated into future budgets.

We now consider fixed setup overhead costs.

Flexible Budget and Variance Analysis for Fixed Setup Overhead Costs

Exhibit 8-7 presents the variances for fixed setup overhead costs in columnar form.

Exhibit 8-7 Columnar Presentation of Fixed Setup Overhead Variance Analysis: Lyco Brass Works for 2014[a]

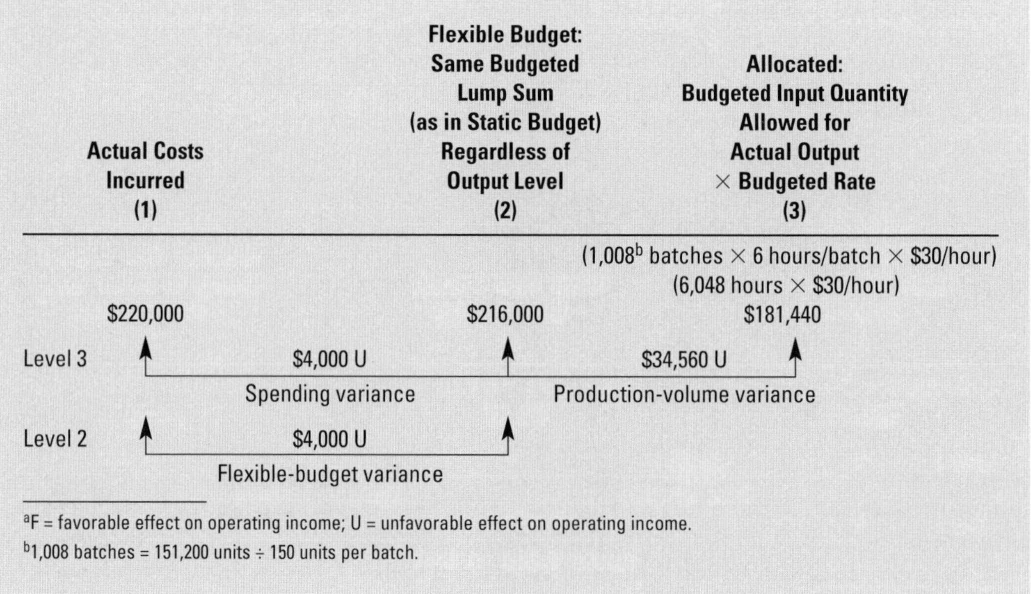

Lyco's fixed setup overhead flexible-budget variance is calculated as follows:

$$\begin{aligned}\text{Fixed-setup overhead flexible-budget variance} &= \text{Actual costs incurred} - \text{Flexible-budget costs}\\ &= \$220{,}000 - \$216{,}000\\ &= \$4{,}000\text{ U}\end{aligned}$$

Note that the flexible-budget amount for the fixed setup overhead costs equals the static-budget amount of $216,000. That's because there is no "flexing" of fixed costs. Moreover, because the fixed overhead costs have no efficiency variance, the fixed setup overhead spending variance is the same as the fixed overhead flexible-budget variance. The spending variance could be unfavorable because of higher leasing costs of new setup equipment or higher salaries paid to engineers and supervisors. Lyco may have incurred these costs to alleviate some of the difficulties it was having in setting up machines.

To calculate the production-volume variance, Lyco first computes the budgeted cost-allocation rate for the fixed setup overhead costs using the same four-step approach described on page 292.

Step 1: Choose the Period to Use for the Budget. Lyco uses a period of 12 months (the year 2014).

Step 2: Select the Cost-Allocation Base to Use in Allocating the Fixed Overhead Costs to the Output Produced. Lyco uses budgeted setup-hours as the cost-allocation base for fixed setup overhead costs. Budgeted setup-hours in the static budget for 2014 are 7,200 hours.

Step 3: Identify the Fixed Overhead Costs Associated with the Cost-Allocation Base. Lyco's fixed setup overhead cost budget for 2014 is $216,000.

Step 4: Compute the Rate per Unit of the Cost-Allocation Base Used to Allocate the Fixed Overhead Costs to the Output Produced. Dividing the $216,000 from Step 3 by the 7,200 setup-hours from Step 2, Lyco estimates a fixed setup overhead cost rate of $30 per setup-hour:

$$\begin{aligned}\text{Budgeted fixed setup overhead cost per unit of cost-allocation base} &= \frac{\text{Budgeted total costs in fixed overhead cost pool}}{\text{Budgeted total quantity of cost-allocation base}} = \frac{\$216{,}000}{7{,}200\text{ setup hours}}\\ &= \$30\text{ per setup-hour}\end{aligned}$$

$$\begin{aligned}\text{Production-volume variance for fixed setup overhead costs} &= \text{Budgeted fixed setup overhead costs} - \text{Fixed setup overhead allocation using budgeted input allowed for actual output units produced}\\ &= \$216{,}000 - (1{,}008\text{ batches} \times 6\text{ hours/batch}) \times \$30\text{/hour}\\ &= \$216{,}000 - (6{,}048\text{ hours} \times \$30\text{/hour})\\ &= \$216{,}000 - \$181{,}440\\ &= \$34{,}560\text{ U}\end{aligned}$$

During 2014, Lyco planned to produce 180,000 units of Elegance but actually produced 151,200 units. The unfavorable production-volume variance measures the amount of extra fixed setup costs Lyco incurred for setup capacity it did not use. One interpretation is that the unfavorable $34,560 production-volume variance represents an inefficient use of the company's setup capacity. However, Lyco may have earned higher operating income by selling 151,200 units at a higher price than 180,000 units at a lower price. As a result, Lyco's managers should interpret the production-volume variance cautiously because it does not consider the effect of output on selling prices and operating income.

Decision Point

How can variance analysis be used in an activity-based costing system?

Learning Objective 8

Examine the use of overhead variances in nonmanufacturing settings

...analyze nonmanufacturing variable overhead costs for decision making and cost management; fixed overhead variances are especially important in service settings

Overhead Variances in Nonmanufacturing Settings

Our Webb Company example examined variable and fixed manufacturing overhead costs. Managers can also use variance analysis to examine the overhead costs of the nonmanufacturing areas of the company and to make decisions about (1) pricing, (2) managing costs, and (3) the mix of products to make. For example, when product distribution costs are high, as they are in the automobile, consumer durables, cement, and steel industries, standard costing can provide managers with reliable and timely information on variable distribution overhead spending variances and efficiency variances.

What about service-sector companies such as airlines, hospitals, hotels, and railroads? How can they benefit from variance analyses? The output measures these companies commonly use are passenger-miles flown, patient days provided, room-days occupied, and ton-miles of freight hauled, respectively. Few costs can be traced to these outputs in a cost-effective way. Most of the costs are fixed overhead costs, such as the costs of equipment, buildings, and staff. Using capacity effectively is the key to profitability, and fixed overhead variances can help managers in this task. Retail businesses, such as Kmart, also have high capacity-related fixed costs (lease and occupancy costs). In the case of Kmart, sales declines resulted in unused capacity and unfavorable fixed-cost variances. Kmart reduced its fixed costs by closing some of its stores, but it also had to file for Chapter 11 bankruptcy.

Consider the following data for United Airlines for selected years from the past decade. Available seat miles (ASMs) are the actual seats in an airplane multiplied by the distance the plane traveled.

Year	Total ASMs (Millions) (1)	Operating Revenue per ASM (2)	Operating Cost per ASM (3)	Operating Income per ASM (4) = (2) − (3)
2000	175,493	10.2 cents	10.0 cents	0.2 cents
2003	136,566	8.6 cents	9.8 cents	−1.2 cents
2006	143,085	10.6 cents	10.8 cents	−0.2 cents
2008	135,859	11.9 cents	13.6 cents	−1.4 cents
2011	118,973	13.1 cents	13.5 cents	−0.4 cents

When air travel declined after terrorists hijacked a number of commercial jets on September 11, 2001, United's revenues fell. However most of the company's fixed costs—for its airport facilities, equipment, personnel, and so on—did not. United had a large unfavorable production-volume variance because its capacity was underutilized. As column 1 of the table indicates, United responded by reducing its capacity substantially over the next few years. Available seat miles (ASMs) declined from 175,493 million in 2000 to 136,566 million in 2003. Yet United was unable to fill even the planes it had retained, so its revenue per ASM declined (column 2) and its cost per ASM stayed roughly the same (column 3). United filed for Chapter 11 bankruptcy in December 2002 and began seeking government guarantees to obtain the loans it needed. Subsequently, strong demand for airline travel, as well as productivity improvements resulting from the more efficient use of resources and networks, led to increased traffic and higher average ticket prices. By maintaining a disciplined approach to capacity and tight control over growth, United saw over a 20% increase in its revenue per ASM between 2003 and 2006. The improvement in performance allowed United to come out of bankruptcy on February 1, 2006. In the past few years, however, the global recession and soaring jet fuel prices have had a significant negative impact on United's performance, as reflected in the continued negative operating incomes and the further decline in capacity. In May 2010, a merger agreement was reached between United and Continental Airlines, and Continental was dissolved in 2012.

Financial and Nonfinancial Performance Measures

The overhead variances discussed in this chapter are examples of financial performance measures. As the preceding examples illustrate, nonfinancial measures such as those related to capacity utilization and physical measures of input usage also provide useful information. The nonfinancial measures that managers of Webb would likely find helpful in planning and controlling its overhead costs include the following:

1. Quantity of actual indirect materials used per machine-hour, relative to the quantity of budgeted indirect materials used per machine-hour
2. Actual energy used per machine-hour, relative to the budgeted energy used per machine-hour
3. Actual machine-hours per jacket, relative to the budgeted machine-hours per jacket

These performance measures, like the financial variances discussed in this chapter and Chapter 7, alert managers to problems and probably would be reported daily or hourly on the production floor. The overhead variances we discussed in this chapter capture the financial effects of items such as the three factors listed, which in many cases first appear as nonfinancial performance measures. An especially interesting example along these lines comes from Japan: Some Japanese companies have begun reining in their CO_2 emissions in part by doing a budgeted-to-actual variance analysis of the emissions. The goal is to make employees aware of the emissions and reduce them in advance of greenhouse-gas reduction plans being drawn up by the Japanese government.

Finally, both financial and nonfinancial performance measures are used to evaluate the performance of managers. Exclusive reliance on either is always too simplistic because each gives a different perspective on performance. Nonfinancial measures (such as those described previously) provide feedback on individual aspects of a manager's performance, whereas financial measures evaluate the overall effect of and the tradeoffs among different nonfinancial performance measures. We provide further discussion of these issues in Chapters 12, 19, and 23.

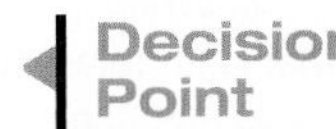

Decision Point

How are overhead variances useful in nonmanufacturing settings?

Problem for Self-Study

Nina Garcia is the newly appointed president of Laser Products. She is examining the May 2014 results for the Aerospace Products Division. This division manufactures wing parts for satellites. Garcia's current concern is with manufacturing overhead costs at the Aerospace Products Division. Both variable and fixed overhead costs are allocated to the wing parts on the basis of laser-cutting-hours. The following budget information is available:

Budgeted variable overhead rate	$200 per hour
Budgeted fixed overhead rate	$240 per hour
Budgeted laser-cutting time per wing part	1.5 hours
Budgeted production and sales for May 2014	5,000 wing parts
Budgeted fixed overhead costs for May 2014	$1,800,000

Actual results for May 2014 are as follows:

Wing parts produced and sold	4,800 units
Laser-cutting-hours used	8,400 hours
Variable overhead costs	$1,478,400
Fixed overhead costs	$1,832,200

Required

1. Compute the spending variance and the efficiency variance for variable overhead.
2. Compute the spending variance and the production-volume variance for fixed overhead.
3. Give two explanations for each of the variances calculated in requirements 1 and 2.

Solution

1 and 2. See Exhibit 8-8.

3. a. Variable overhead spending variance, $201,600 F. One possible reason for this variance is that the actual prices of individual items included in variable overhead (such as cutting fluids) are lower than budgeted prices. A second possible reason is that the percentage increase in the actual quantity usage of individual items in the variable overhead cost pool is less than the percentage increase in laser-cutting-hours compared to the flexible budget.

   b. Variable overhead efficiency variance, $240,000 U. One possible reason for this variance is inadequate maintenance of laser machines, causing them to take more

Exhibit 8-8 Columnar Presentation of Integrated Variance Analysis: Laser Products for May 2014[a]

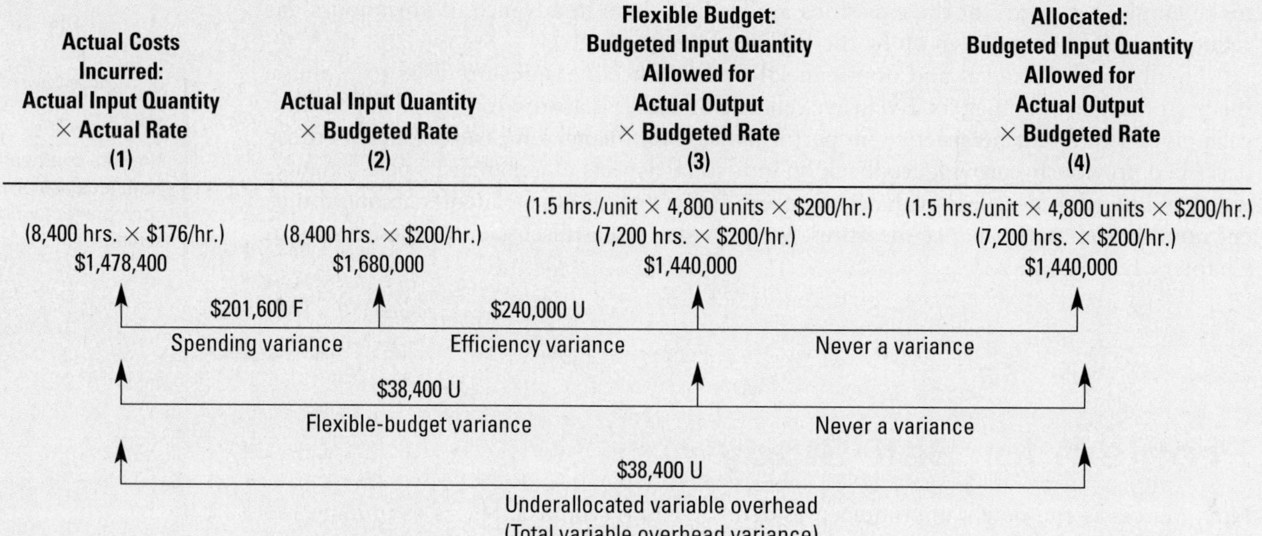

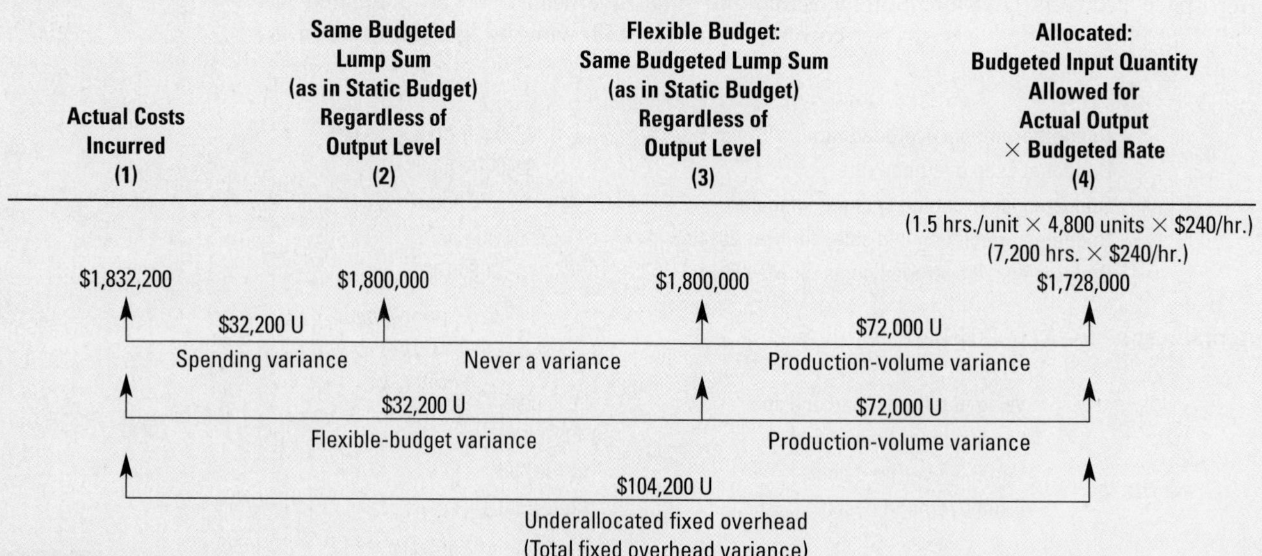

[a]F = favorable effect on operating income; U = unfavorable effect on operating income.

Source: Republished with permission of Strategic Finance by Paul Sherman. Copyright 2003 by Institute of Management Accountants. Permission conveyed through Copyright Clearance Center, Inc.

laser-cutting time per wing part. A second possible reason is use of undermotivated, inexperienced, or underskilled workers operating the laser-cutting machines, resulting in more laser-cutting time per wing part.

c. Fixed overhead spending variance, $32,200 U. One possible reason for this variance is that the actual prices of individual items in the fixed-cost pool unexpectedly increased from the prices budgeted (such as an unexpected increase in the cost of leasing each machine). A second possible reason is that the Aerospace Products Division had to lease more machines or hire more supervisors than had been budgeted.

d. Production-volume variance, $72,000 U. Actual production of wing parts is 4,800 units, compared with 5,000 units budgeted. One possible reason for this variance is demand factors, such as a decline in an aerospace program that led to a decline in demand for aircraft parts. A second possible reason is supply factors, such as a production stoppage due to labor problems or machine breakdowns.

Decision Points

The following question-and-answer format summarizes the chapter's learning objectives. Each decision presents a key question related to a learning objective. The guidelines are the answer to that question.

Decision	Guidelines
1. How do managers plan variable overhead costs and fixed overhead costs?	Planning of both variable and fixed overhead costs involves undertaking only activities that add value and then being efficient in that undertaking. The key difference is that for variable-cost planning, ongoing decisions during the budget period play a much larger role; for fixed-cost planning, most key decisions are made before the start of the period.
2. How are budgeted variable overhead and fixed overhead cost rates calculated?	The budgeted variable (fixed) overhead cost rate is calculated by dividing the budgeted variable (fixed) overhead costs by the denominator level of the cost-allocation base.
3. What variances can be calculated for variable overhead costs?	When the flexible budget for variable overhead is developed, an overhead efficiency variance and an overhead spending variance can be computed. The variable overhead efficiency variance focuses on the difference between the actual quantity of the cost-allocation base used relative to the budgeted quantity of the cost-allocation base. The variable overhead spending variance focuses on the difference between the actual variable overhead cost per unit of the cost-allocation base relative to the budgeted variable overhead cost per unit of the cost-allocation base.
4. What variances can be calculated for fixed overhead costs?	For fixed overhead, the static and flexible budgets coincide. The difference between the budgeted and actual amount of fixed overhead is the flexible-budget variance, also referred to as the spending variance. The production-volume variance measures the difference between the budgeted fixed overhead and the fixed overhead allocated on the basis of actual output produced.
5. What is the most detailed way for a company to reconcile actual overhead incurred with the amount allocated during a period?	A 4-variance analysis presents spending and efficiency variances for variable overhead costs and spending and production-volume variances for fixed overhead costs. By analyzing these four variances together, managers can reconcile the actual overhead costs with the amount of overhead allocated to the output produced during a period.
6. What is the relationship between the sales-volume variance and the production-volume variance?	The production-volume variance is a component of the sales-volume variance. The production-volume and operating-income volume variances together comprise the sales-volume variance.

Decision	Guidelines
7. How can variance analysis be used in an activity-based costing system?	Flexible budgets in ABC systems give insight into why actual activity costs differ from budgeted activity costs. Using output and input measures for an activity, a comprehensive variance analysis can be conducted.
8. How are overhead variances useful in nonmanufacturing settings?	Managers can analyze variances for all variable overhead costs, including those outside the manufacturing function. The analysis can be used to make pricing and product mix decisions and to manage costs. Fixed overhead variances are especially important in service settings, where using capacity effectively is the key to profitability. In all cases, the information provided by variances can be supplemented by the use of suitable nonfinancial metrics.

Terms to Learn

The chapter and the Glossary at the end of the book contain definitions of the following important terms:

denominator level **(p. 292)**
denominator-level variance **(p. 298)**
fixed overhead flexible-budget variance **(p. 297)**
fixed overhead spending variance **(p. 297)**
operating-income volume variance **(p. 307)**
production-volume variance **(p. 298)**
standard costing **(p. 290)**
total-overhead variance **(p. 305)**
variable overhead efficiency variance **(p. 293)**
variable overhead flexible-budget variance **(p. 293)**
variable overhead spending variance **(p. 295)**

Assignment Material

MyAccountingLab

Questions

8-1 How do managers plan for variable overhead costs?

8-2 How does the planning of fixed overhead costs differ from the planning of variable overhead costs?

8-3 How does standard costing differ from actual costing?

8-4 What are the steps in developing a budgeted variable overhead cost-allocation rate?

8-5 What are the factors that affect the spending variance for variable manufacturing overhead?

8-6 Assume variable manufacturing overhead is allocated using machine-hours. Give three possible reasons for a favorable variable overhead efficiency variance.

8-7 Describe the difference between a direct materials efficiency variance and a variable manufacturing overhead efficiency variance.

8-8 What are the steps in developing a budgeted fixed overhead rate?

8-9 Why is the flexible-budget variance the same amount as the spending variance for fixed manufacturing overhead?

8-10 Explain how the analysis of fixed manufacturing overhead costs differs for (a) planning and control and (b) inventory costing for financial reporting.

8-11 Provide one caveat that will affect whether a production-volume variance is a good measure of the economic cost of unused capacity.

8-12 "The production-volume variance should always be written off to Cost of Goods Sold." Do you agree? Explain.

8-13 What are the variances in a 4-variance analysis?

8-14 "Overhead variances should be viewed as interdependent rather than independent." Give an example.

8-15 Describe how flexible-budget variance analysis can be used in the control of costs of activity areas.

MyAccountingLab

Exercises

8-16 Variable manufacturing overhead, variance analysis. Esquire Clothing is a manufacturer of designer suits. The cost of each suit is the sum of three variable costs (direct material costs, direct manufacturing labor costs, and manufacturing overhead costs) and one fixed-cost category (manufacturing overhead costs). Variable manufacturing overhead cost is allocated to each suit on the basis of budgeted direct manufacturing labor-hours per suit. For June 2014, each suit is budgeted to take 4 labor-hours. Budgeted variable manufacturing overhead cost per labor-hour is $12. The budgeted number of suits to be manufactured in June 2014 is 1,040.

Actual variable manufacturing costs in June 2014 were $52,164 for 1,080 suits started and completed. There were no beginning or ending inventories of suits. Actual direct manufacturing labor-hours for June were 4,536.

Required

1. Compute the flexible-budget variance, the spending variance, and the efficiency variance for variable manufacturing overhead.
2. Comment on the results.

8-17 Fixed manufacturing overhead, variance analysis (continuation of 8-16). Esquire Clothing allocates fixed manufacturing overhead to each suit using budgeted direct manufacturing labor-hours per suit. Data pertaining to fixed manufacturing overhead costs for June 2014 are budgeted, $62,400, and actual, $63,916.

Required

1. Compute the spending variance for fixed manufacturing overhead. Comment on the results.
2. Compute the production-volume variance for June 2014. What inferences can Esquire Clothing draw from this variance?

8-18 Variable manufacturing overhead variance analysis. The French Bread Company bakes baguettes for distribution to upscale grocery stores. The company has two direct-cost categories: direct materials and direct manufacturing labor. Variable manufacturing overhead is allocated to products on the basis of standard direct manufacturing labor-hours. Following is some budget data for the French Bread Company:

Direct manufacturing labor use	0.02 hours per baguette
Variable manufacturing overhead	$10.00 per direct manufacturing labor-hour

The French Bread Company provides the following additional data for the year ended December 31, 2014:

Planned (budgeted) output	3,200,000	baguettes
Actual production	2,800,000	baguettes
Direct manufacturing labor	50,400	hours
Actual variable manufacturing overhead	$680,400	

Required

1. What is the denominator level used for allocating variable manufacturing overhead? (That is, for how many direct manufacturing labor-hours is French Bread budgeting?)
2. Prepare a variance analysis of variable manufacturing overhead. Use Exhibit 8-4 (page 304) for reference.
3. Discuss the variances you have calculated and give possible explanations for them.

8-19 Fixed manufacturing overhead variance analysis (continuation of 8-18). The French Bread Company also allocates fixed manufacturing overhead to products on the basis of standard direct manufacturing labor-hours. For 2014, fixed manufacturing overhead was budgeted at $4.00 per direct manufacturing labor-hour. Actual fixed manufacturing overhead incurred during the year was $272,000.

Required

1. Prepare a variance analysis of fixed manufacturing overhead cost. Use Exhibit 8-4 (page 304) as a guide.
2. Is fixed overhead underallocated or overallocated? By what amount?
3. Comment on your results. Discuss the variances and explain what may be driving them.

8-20 Manufacturing overhead, variance analysis. The Principles Corporation is a manufacturer of centrifuges. Fixed and variable manufacturing overheads are allocated to each centrifuge using budgeted assembly-hours. Budgeted assembly time is 2 hours per unit. The following table shows the budgeted amounts and actual results related to overhead for June 2014.

Home Insert Page Layout Formulas Data Review View

	A–E	F	G
1	**The Principles Corporation (June 2014)**	**Actual Results**	**Static Budget**
2	Number of centrifuges assembled and sold	225	110
3	Hours of assembly time	360	
4	Variable manufacturing overhead cost per hour of assembly time		$32.00
5	Variable manufacturing overhead costs	$11,933	
6	Fixed manufacturing overhead costs	$12,180	$10,780

Required

1. Prepare an analysis of all variable manufacturing overhead and fixed manufacturing overhead variances using the columnar approach in Exhibit 8-4 (page 304).
2. Prepare journal entries for Principles' June 2014 variable and fixed manufacturing overhead costs and variances; write off these variances to cost of goods sold for the quarter ending June 30, 2014.
3. How does the planning and control of variable manufacturing overhead costs differ from the planning and control of fixed manufacturing overhead costs?

8-21 4-variance analysis, fill in the blanks. Rozema, Inc., produces chemicals for large biotech companies. It has the following data for manufacturing overhead costs during August 2015:

	Variable	Fixed
Actual costs incurred	$31,000	$18,000
Costs allocated to products	33,000	14,600
Flexible budget	———	13,400
Actual input × budgeted rate	30,800	———

Use F for favorable and U for unfavorable:

	Variable	Fixed
(1) Spending variance	$____	$____
(2) Efficiency variance	____	____
(3) Production-volume variance	____	____
(4) Flexible-budget variance	____	____
(5) Underallocated (overallocated) manufacturing overhead	____	____

8-22 Straightforward 4-variance overhead analysis. The Lopez Company uses standard costing in its manufacturing plant for auto parts. The standard cost of a particular auto part, based on a denominator level of 4,000 output units per year, included 6 machine-hours of variable manufacturing overhead at $8 per hour and 6 machine-hours of fixed manufacturing overhead at $15 per hour. Actual output produced was 4,400 units. Variable manufacturing overhead incurred was $245,000. Fixed manufacturing overhead incurred was $373,000. Actual machine-hours were 28,400.

Required

1. Prepare an analysis of all variable manufacturing overhead and fixed manufacturing overhead variances, using the 4-variance analysis in Exhibit 8-4 (page 304).
2. Prepare journal entries using the 4-variance analysis.
3. Describe how individual fixed manufacturing overhead items are controlled from day to day.
4. Discuss possible causes of the fixed manufacturing overhead variances.

8-23 Straightforward coverage of manufacturing overhead, standard-costing system. The Singapore division of a Canadian telecommunications company uses standard costing for its machine-paced production of telephone equipment. Data regarding production during June are as follows:

Variable manufacturing overhead costs incurred	$618,840
Variable manufacturing overhead cost rate	$8 per standard machine-hour
Fixed manufacturing overhead costs incurred	$145,790
Fixed manufacturing overhead costs budgeted	$144,000
Denominator level in machine-hours	72,000
Standard machine-hour allowed per unit of output	1.2
Units of output	65,500
Actual machine-hours used	76,400
Ending work-in-process inventory	0

Required

1. Prepare an analysis of all manufacturing overhead variances. Use the 4-variance analysis framework illustrated in Exhibit 8-4 (page 304).
2. Prepare journal entries for manufacturing overhead costs and their variances.
3. Describe how individual variable manufacturing overhead items are controlled from day to day.
4. Discuss possible causes of the variable manufacturing overhead variances.

8-24 Overhead variances, service sector. Easy Meals Now (EMN) operates a meal home-delivery service. It has agreements with 20 restaurants to pick up and deliver meals to customers who phone or fax orders to EMN. EMN allocates variable and fixed overhead costs on the basis of delivery time. EMN's owner, Steve Roberts, obtains the following information for May 2014 overhead costs:

	A	B	C
1	Easy Meals Now (May 2014)	Actual Results	Static Budget
2	Output units (number of deliveries)	8,600	12,000
3	Hours per delivery		0.70
4	Hours of delivery time	5,660	
5	Variable overhead cost per hour of delivery time		$1.75
6	Variable overhead costs	$11,320	
7	Fixed overhead costs	$39,600	$33,600

Required

1. Compute spending and efficiency variances for EMN's variable overhead in May 2014.
2. Compute the spending variance and production-volume variance for EMN's fixed overhead in May 2014.
3. Comment on EMN's overhead variances and suggest how Steve Roberts might manage EMN's variable overhead differently from its fixed overhead costs.

8-25 Total overhead, 3-variance analysis. Ames Air Force Base has a bay that specializes in maintenance for aircraft engines. It uses standard costing and flexible budgets to account for this activity. For 2014, budgeted variable overhead at a level of 8,000 standard monthly direct labor-hours was $64,000; budgeted total overhead at 10,000 standard monthly direct labor-hours was $197,600. The standard cost allocated to repair output included a total overhead rate of 120% of standard direct labor costs.

For February, Ames incurred total overhead of $249,000 and direct labor costs of $202,440. The direct labor price variance was $9,640 unfavorable. The direct labor flexible-budget variance was $14,440 unfavorable. The standard labor price was $16 per hour. The production-volume variance was $14,000 favorable.

Required

1. Compute the direct labor efficiency variance.
2. Compute the denominator level and the spending and efficiency variances for total overhead.
3. Describe how individual variable overhead items are controlled from day to day. Also, describe how individual fixed overhead items are controlled.

8-26 Production-volume variance analysis and sales volume variance. Marissa Designs, Inc., makes jewelry in the shape of geometric patterns. Each piece is handmade and takes an average of 1.5 hours to produce because of the intricate design and scrollwork. Marissa uses direct labor-hours to allocate the overhead cost to production. Fixed overhead costs, including rent, depreciation, supervisory salaries, and other production expenses, are budgeted at $10,800 per month. These costs are incurred for a facility large enough to produce 1,200 pieces of jewelry a month.

During the month of February, Marissa produced 720 pieces of jewelry and actual fixed costs were $11,400.

Required

1. Calculate the fixed overhead spending variance and indicate whether it is favorable (F) or unfavorable (U).
2. If Marissa uses direct labor-hours available at capacity to calculate the budgeted fixed overhead rate, what is the production-volume variance? Indicate whether it is favorable (F) or unfavorable (U).
3. An unfavorable production-volume variance could be interpreted as the economic cost of unused capacity. Why would Marissa be willing to incur this cost?
4. Marissa's budgeted variable cost per unit is $25, and it expects to sell its jewelry for $55 apiece. Compute the sales-volume variance and reconcile it with the production-volume variance calculated in requirement 2. What does each concept measure?

8-27 Overhead variances, service setting. Munich Partners provides a diverse array of back office services to its clients in the financial services industry, ranging from record keeping and compliance to order processing and trade settlement. Munich has grown increasingly reliant on technology to acquire, retain, and serve its clients. Worried that its spending on information technology is getting out of control, Munich has recently embraced variance analysis as a tool for cost management.

After some study, Munich determines that its variable and fixed technology overhead costs are both driven by the processing time involved in meeting client requests. This is typically measured in CPU units of usage of a high-performance computing cluster. Munich's primary measure of output is the number of client interactions its partners have in a given period.

The following information pertains to the first quarter of 2014 (dollars in thousands):

Budgeted Output Units	14,000 client interactions
Budgeted Fixed Technology Overhead	$ 11,200
Budgeted Variable Technology Overhead	$ 1.50 per CPU unit
Budgeted CPU units	0.2 units per client interaction
Fixed Technology Overhead incurred	$ 12,200
CPU Units used	4,000
Variable Technology Overhead incurred	$ 5,500
Actual Output Units	15,000 client interactions

Required

1. Calculate the variable overhead spending and efficiency variances, and indicate whether each is favorable (F) or unfavorable (U).
2. Calculate the fixed overhead spending and production volume variances, and indicate whether each is favorable (F) or unfavorable (U).
3. Comment on Munich Partners' overhead variances. In your view, is the firm right to be worried about its control over technology spending?

8-28 Identifying favorable and unfavorable variances. Purdue, Inc., manufactures tires for large auto companies. It uses standard costing and allocates variable and fixed manufacturing overhead based on machine-hours. For each independent scenario given, indicate whether each of the manufacturing variances will be favorable or unfavorable or, in case of insufficient information, indicate "CBD" (cannot be determined).

Scenario	Variable Overhead Spending Variance	Variable Overhead Efficiency Variance	Fixed Overhead Spending Variance	Fixed Overhead Production-Volume Variance
Production output is 6% less than budgeted, and actual fixed manufacturing overhead costs are 5% more than budgeted				
Production output is 13% less than budgeted; actual machine-hours are 7% more than budgeted				
Production output is 10% more than budgeted				
Actual machine-hours are 20% less than flexible-budget machine-hours				
Relative to the flexible budget, actual machine-hours are 15% less, and actual variable manufacturing overhead costs are 20% greater				

8-29 Flexible-budget variances, review of Chapters 7 and 8. Michael Roberts is a cost accountant and business analyst for Darby Design Company (DDC), which manufactures expensive brass doorknobs. DDC uses two direct cost categories: direct materials and direct manufacturing labor. Roberts feels that manufacturing overhead is most closely related to material usage. Therefore, DDC allocates manufacturing overhead to production based upon pounds of materials used.

At the beginning of 2014, DDC budgeted annual production of 410,000 doorknobs and adopted the following standards for each doorknob:

	Input	Cost/Doorknob
Direct materials (brass)	0.3 lb. @ $9/lb.	$ 2.70
Direct manufacturing labor	1.2 hours @ $16/hour	19.20
Manufacturing overhead:		
Variable	$4/lb. × 0.3 lb.	1.20
Fixed	$14/lb. × 0.3 lb.	4.20
Standard cost per doorknob		$27.30

Actual results for April 2014 were as follows:

Production	32,000 doorknobs
Direct materials purchased	12,900 lb. at $10/lb.
Direct materials used	9,000 lbs.
Direct manufacturing labor	29,600 hours for $621,600
Variable manufacturing overhead	$ 64,900
Fixed manufacturing overhead	$160,000

Required

1. For the month of April, compute the following variances, indicating whether each is favorable (F) or unfavorable (U):
   a. Direct materials price variance (based on purchases)
   b. Direct materials efficiency variance
   c. Direct manufacturing labor price variance
   d. Direct manufacturing labor efficiency variance
   e. Variable manufacturing overhead spending variance
   f. Variable manufacturing overhead efficiency variance
   g. Production-volume variance
   h. Fixed manufacturing overhead spending variance
2. Can Roberts use any of the variances to help explain any of the other variances? Give examples.

Problems

MyAccountingLab

8-30 Comprehensive variance analysis. Chef Whiz manufactures premium food processors. The following are some manufacturing overhead data for Chef Whiz for the year ended December 31, 2014:

Manufacturing Overhead	Actual Results	Flexible Budget	Allocated Amount
Variable	$51,480	$79,950	$79,950
Fixed	350,210	343,980	380,250

Budgeted number of output units: 588
Planned allocation rate: 3 machine-hours per unit
Actual number of machine-hours used: 1,170
Static-budget variable manufacturing overhead costs: $72,324

Required

Compute the following quantities (you should be able to do so in the prescribed order):

1. Budgeted number of machine-hours planned
2. Budgeted fixed manufacturing overhead costs per machine-hour
3. Budgeted variable manufacturing overhead costs per machine-hour
4. Budgeted number of machine-hours allowed for actual output produced
5. Actual number of output units
6. Actual number of machine-hours used per output unit

8-31 Journal entries (continuation of 8-30).

Required

1. Prepare journal entries for variable and fixed manufacturing overhead (you will need to calculate the various variances to accomplish this).
2. Overhead variances are written off to the Cost of Goods Sold (COGS) account at the end of the fiscal year. Show how COGS is adjusted through journal entries.

8-32 Graphs and overhead variances. Best Around, Inc., is a manufacturer of vacuums and uses standard costing. Manufacturing overhead (both variable and fixed) is allocated to products on the basis of budgeted machine-hours. In 2014, budgeted fixed manufacturing overhead cost was $17,000,000. Budgeted variable manufacturing overhead was $10 per machine-hour. The denominator level was 1,000,000 machine-hours.

Required

1. Prepare a graph for fixed manufacturing overhead. The graph should display how Best Around, Inc.'s fixed manufacturing overhead costs will be depicted for the purposes of (a) planning and control and (b) inventory costing.

2. Suppose that 1,125,000 machine-hours were allowed for actual output produced in 2014, but 1,200,000 actual machine-hours were used. Actual manufacturing overhead was $12,075,000, variable, and $17,100,000, fixed. Compute (a) the variable manufacturing overhead spending and efficiency variances and (b) the fixed manufacturing overhead spending and production-volume variances. Use the columnar presentation illustrated in Exhibit 8-4 (page 304).
3. What is the amount of the under- or overallocated variable manufacturing overhead and the under- or overallocated fixed manufacturing overhead? Why are the flexible-budget variance and the under- or overallocated overhead amount always the same for variable manufacturing overhead but rarely the same for fixed manufacturing overhead?
4. Suppose the denominator level was 1,700,000 rather than 1,000,000 machine-hours. What variances in requirement 2 would be affected? Recompute them.

8-33 Overhead variance, missing information. Consider the following two situations—cases A and B—independently. Data refer to operations for April 2014. For each situation, assume standard costing. Also assume the use of a flexible budget for control of variable and fixed manufacturing overhead based oı machine-hours.

	Cases	
	A	B
(1) Fixed manufacturing overhead incurred	$ 84,920	$23,180
(2) Variable manufacturing overhead incurred	$120,400	—
(3) Denominator level in machine-hours	—	1,000
(4) Standard machine-hours allowed for actual output achieved	6,200	—
(5) Fixed manufacturing overhead (per standard machine-hour)	—	—
Flexible-Budget Data:		
(6) Variable manufacturing overhead (per standard machine-hour)	—	$ 42.00
(7) Budgeted fixed manufacturing overhead	$ 88,200	$20,000
(8) Budgeted variable manufacturing overhead[a]	—	—
(9) Total budgeted manufacturing overhead[a]	—	—
Additional Data:		
(10) Standard variable manufacturing overhead allocated	$124,000	—
(11) Standard fixed manufacturing overhead allocated	$ 86,800	—
(12) Production-volume variance	—	$ 4,000 F
(13) Variable manufacturing overhead spending variance	$ 5,000 F	$ 2,282 F
(14) Variable manufacturing overhead efficiency variance	—	$ 2,478 F
(15) Fixed manufacturing overhead spending variance	—	—
(16) Actual machine-hours used	—	—

[a]For standard machine-hours allowed for actual output produced.

Required

Fill in the blanks under each case. [*Hint:* Prepare a worksheet similar to that in Exhibit 8-4 (page 304). Fill in the knowns and then solve for the unknowns.]

8-34 Flexible budgets, 4-variance analysis. (CMA, adapted) Wilson Products uses standard costing. It allocates manufacturing overhead (both variable and fixed) to products on the basis of standard direct manufacturing labor-hours (DLH). Wilson Products develops its manufacturing overhead rate from the current annual budget. The manufacturing overhead budget for 2014 is based on budgeted output of 672,000 units, requiring 3,360,000 DLH. The company is able to schedule production uniformly throughout the year.

A total of 72,000 output units requiring 321,000 DLH was produced during May 2014. Manufacturing overhead (MOH) costs incurred for May amounted to $355,800. The actual costs, compared with the annual budget and 1/12 of the annual budget, are as follows:

Annual Manufacturing Overhead Budget 2014

	Total Amount	Per Output Unit	Per DLH Input Unit	Monthly MOH Budget May 2014	Actual MOH Costs for May 2014
Variable MOH					
Indirect manufacturing labor	$1,008,000	$1.50	$0.30	$ 84,000	$ 84,000
Supplies	672,000	1.00	0.20	56,000	117,000
Fixed MOH					
Supervision	571,200	0.85	0.17	47,600	41,000
Utilities	369,600	0.55	0.11	30,800	55,000
Depreciation	705,600	1.05	0.21	58,800	88,800
Total	$3,326,400	$4.95	$0.99	$277,200	$355,800

Calculate the following amounts for Wilson Products for May 2014:

Required

1. Total manufacturing overhead costs allocated
2. Variable manufacturing overhead spending variance
3. Fixed manufacturing overhead spending variance
4. Variable manufacturing overhead efficiency variance
5. Production-volume variance

Be sure to identify each variance as favorable (F) or unfavorable (U).

8-35 Activity-based costing, batch-level variance analysis. Audrina's Fleet Feet, Inc., produces dance shoes for stores all over the world. While the pairs of shoes are boxed individually, they are crated and shipped in batches. The shipping department records both variable direct batch-level costs and fixed batch-level overhead costs. The following information pertains to shipping department costs for 2014.

	Static-Budget Amounts	Actual Results
Pairs of shoes shipped	225,000	180,000
Average number of pairs of shoes per crate	15	10
Packing hours per crate	0.9 hours	1.1 hour
Variable direct cost per hour	$18	$16
Fixed overhead cost	$54,000	$56,500

Required

1. What is the static budget number of crates for 2014?
2. What is the flexible budget number of crates for 2014?
3. What is the actual number of crates shipped in 2014?
4. Assuming fixed overhead is allocated using crate-packing hours, what is the predetermined fixed overhead allocation rate?
5. For variable direct batch-level costs, compute the price and efficiency variances.
6. For fixed overhead costs, compute the spending and the production-volume variances.

8-36 Overhead variances and sales volume variance. Birken Company manufactures shopping bags made of recycled plastic that it plans to sell for $5 each. Birken budgets production and sales of 800,000 bags for 2014, with a standard of 400,000 machine-hours for the whole year. Budgeted fixed overhead costs are $500,000, and variable overhead cost is $1.60 per machine-hour.

Because of increased demand, Birken actually produced and sold 900,000 bags in 2014, using a total of 440,000 machine-hours. Actual variable overhead costs are $699,600 and actual fixed overhead is $501,900. Actual selling price is $6 per bag.

Direct materials and direct labor actual costs were the same as standard costs, which were $1.20 per unit and $1.80 per unit, respectively.

Required

1. Calculate the variable overhead and fixed overhead variances (spending, efficiency, spending, and volume).
2. Create a chart like that in Exhibit 7-2 showing Flexible Budget Variances and Sales Volume Variances for revenues, costs, contribution margin, and operating income.
3. Calculate the operating income based on budgeted profit per shopping bag.

4. Reconcile the budgeted operating income from requirement 3 to the actual operating income from your chart in requirement 2.
5. Calculate the operating income volume variance and show how the sales volume variance is composed of the production volume variance and the operating income volume variance.

8-37 Activity-based costing, batch-level variance analysis. Rae Steven Publishing Company specializes in printing specialty textbooks for a small but profitable college market. Due to the high setup costs for each batch printed, Rae Steven holds the book requests until demand for a book is approximately 520. At that point Rae Steven will schedule the setup and production of the book. For rush orders, Rae Steven will produce smaller batches for an additional charge of $987 per setup.

Budgeted and actual costs for the printing process for 2014 were as follows:

	Static-Budget Amounts	Actual Results
Number of books produced	197,600	225,680
Average number of books per setup	520	496
Hours to set up printers	7 hours	7.5 hours
Direct variable cost per setup-hour	$130	$70
Total fixed setup overhead costs	$53,200	$68,000

Required

1. What is the static budget number of setups for 2014?
2. What is the flexible budget number of setups for 2014?
3. What is the actual number of setups in 2014?
4. Assuming fixed setup overhead costs are allocated using setup-hours, what is the predetermined fixed setup overhead allocation rate?
5. Does Rae Steven's charge of $987 cover the budgeted direct variable cost of an order? The budgeted total cost?
6. For direct variable setup costs, compute the price and efficiency variances.
7. For fixed setup overhead costs, compute the spending and the production-volume variances.
8. What qualitative factors should Rae Steven consider before accepting or rejecting a special order?

8-38 Comprehensive review of Chapters 7 and 8, working backward from given variances. The Gallo Company uses a flexible budget and standard costs to aid planning and control of its machining manufacturing operations. Its costing system for manufacturing has two direct-cost categories (direct materials and direct manufacturing labor—both variable) and two overhead-cost categories (variable manufacturing overhead and fixed manufacturing overhead, both allocated using direct manufacturing labor-hours).

At the 50,000 budgeted direct manufacturing labor-hour level for August, budgeted direct manufacturing labor is $1,250,000, budgeted variable manufacturing overhead is $500,000, and budgeted fixed manufacturing overhead is $1,000,000.

The following actual results are for August:

Direct materials price variance (based on purchases)	$179,300 F
Direct materials efficiency variance	75,900 U
Direct manufacturing labor costs incurred	535,500
Variable manufacturing overhead flexible-budget variance	10,400 U
Variable manufacturing overhead efficiency variance	18,100 U
Fixed manufacturing overhead incurred	957,550

The standard cost per pound of direct materials is $11.50. The standard allowance is 6 pounds of direct materials for each unit of product. During August, 20,000 units of product were produced. There was no beginning inventory of direct materials. There was no beginning or ending work in process. In August, the direct materials price variance was $1.10 per pound.

In July, labor unrest caused a major slowdown in the pace of production, resulting in an unfavorable direct manufacturing labor efficiency variance of $40,000. There was no direct manufacturing labor price variance. Labor unrest persisted into August. Some workers quit. Their replacements had to be hired at higher wage rates, which had to be extended to all workers. The actual average wage rate in August exceeded the standard average wage rate by $0.50 per hour.

Required

1. Compute the following for August:
   a. Total pounds of direct materials purchased
   b. Total number of pounds of excess direct materials used
   c. Variable manufacturing overhead spending variance
   d. Total number of actual direct manufacturing labor-hours used
   e. Total number of standard direct manufacturing labor-hours allowed for the units produced
   f. Production-volume variance
2. Describe how Gallo's control of variable manufacturing overhead items differs from its control of fixed manufacturing overhead items.

8-39 Review of Chapters 7 and 8, 3-variance analysis. (CPA, adapted) The Brown Manufacturing Company's costing system has two direct-cost categories: direct materials and direct manufacturing labor. Manufacturing overhead (both variable and fixed) is allocated to products on the basis of standard direct manufacturing labor-hours (DLH). At the beginning of 2014, Beal adopted the following standards for its manufacturing costs:

	Input	Cost per Output Unit
Direct materials	5 lb. at $4 per lb.	$ 20.00
Direct manufacturing labor	4 hrs. at $16 per hr.	64.00
Manufacturing overhead:		
Variable	$8 per DLH	32.00
Fixed	$9 per DLH	36.00
Standard manufacturing cost per output unit		$152.00

The denominator level for total manufacturing overhead per month in 2014 is 37,000 direct manufacturing labor-hours. Beal's flexible budget for January 2014 was based on this denominator level. The records for January indicated the following:

Direct materials purchased	40,300 lb. at $3.80 per lb.
Direct materials used	37,300 lb.
Direct manufacturing labor	31,400 hrs. at $16.25 per hr.
Total actual manufacturing overhead (variable and fixed)	$650,000
Actual production	7,600 output units

Required

1. Prepare a schedule of total standard manufacturing costs for the 7,600 output units in January 2014.
2. For the month of January 2014, compute the following variances, indicating whether each is favorable (F) or unfavorable (U):
   a. Direct materials price variance, based on purchases
   b. Direct materials efficiency variance
   c. Direct manufacturing labor price variance
   d. Direct manufacturing labor efficiency variance
   e. Total manufacturing overhead spending variance
   f. Variable manufacturing overhead efficiency variance
   g. Production-volume variance

8-40 Non-financial variances. Max Canine Products produces high-quality dog food distributed only through veterinary offices. To ensure that the food is of the highest quality and has taste appeal, Max Canine has a rigorous inspection process. For quality control purposes, Max Canine has a standard based on the pounds of food inspected per hour and the number of pounds that pass or fail the inspection.

Max Canine expects that for every 13,000 pounds of food produced, 1,300 pounds of food will be inspected. Inspection of 1,300 pounds of dog food should take 1 hour. Max Canine also expects that 5% of the food inspected will fail the inspection. During the month of May, Supreme produced 2,990,000 pounds of food and inspected 292,500 pounds of food in 200 hours. Of the 292,500 pounds of food inspected, 15,625 pounds of food failed to pass the inspection.

Required

1. Compute two variances that help determine whether the time spent on inspections was more or less than expected. (Follow a format similar to the one used for the variable overhead spending and efficiency variances, but without prices.)
2. Compute two variances that can be used to evaluate the percentage of the food that fails the inspection.

8-41 Overhead variances, service sector. Cavio is a cloud service provider that offers computing resources to handle enterprise-wide applications. For March 2014, Cavio estimates that it will provide 18,000 RAM hours of services to clients. The budgeted variable overhead rate is $6 per RAM hour.

At the end of March, there is a $500 favorable spending variance for variable overhead and a $1,575 unfavorable spending variance for fixed overhead. For the services actually provided during the month, 14,850 RAM hours are budgeted and 15,000 RAM hours are actually used. Total actual overhead costs are $119,875.

Required

1. Compute efficiency and flexible-budget variances for Cavio's variable overhead in March 2014. Will variable overhead be over- or underallocated? By how much?
2. Compute production-volume and flexible-budget variances for Cavio's fixed overhead in March 2014. Will fixed overhead be over- or underallocated? By how much?

8-42 Direct-cost and overhead variances, income statement. The Kordell Company started business on January 1, 2013, in Raleigh. The company adopted a standard absorption costing system for its one product—a football for use in collegiate intramural sports. Because of the extensive handcrafting needed to do quality assurance on the final product, Kordell chose direct labor as the application base for overhead and decided to use the proration method to account for variances at year-end.

Kordell expected to make and sell 80,000 footballs the first year; each football was budgeted to use 1 pound of leather and require 15 minutes of direct labor work. The company expected to pay $1 for each pound of leather and compensate workers at an hourly wage of $16. Kordell has no variable overhead costs, but expected to spend $200,000 on fixed manufacturing overhead in 2013.

In 2013, Kordell actually made 100,000 footballs and sold 80,000 of them for a total revenue of $1 million. The expenses incurred were as follows:

Fixed manufacturing costs	$300,000
Leather costs (110,000 pounds bought and used)	$121,000
Direct labor costs (30,000 hours)	$465,000

Required

1. Compute the following variances for 2013, and indicate whether each is favorable (F) or unfavorable (U):
   a. Direct materials efficiency variance
   b. Direct materials price variance
   c. Direct labor efficiency variance
   d. Direct labor price variance
   e. Total manufacturing overhead spending variance
   f. Fixed overhead flexible budget variance
   g. Fixed overhead production-volume variance
2. Compute Kordell Company's gross margin for its first year of operation.

8-43 Overhead variances, ethics. Hartmann Company uses standard costing. The company has two manufacturing plants, one in Georgia and the other in Alabama. For the Georgia plant, Hartmann has budgeted annual output of 2,000,000 units. Standard labor-hours per unit are 0.50, and the variable overhead rate for the Georgia plant is $3.30 per direct labor-hour. Fixed overhead for the Georgia plant is budgeted at $2,400,000 for the year.

For the Alabama plant, Hartmann has budgeted annual output of 2,100,000 units with standard labor-hours also 0.50 per unit. However, the variable overhead rate for the Alabama plant is $3.10 per hour, and the budgeted fixed overhead for the year is only $2,205,000.

Firm management has always used variance analysis as a performance measure for the two plants and has compared the results of the two plants.

Tom Saban has just been hired as a new controller for Hartmann. Tom is good friends with the Alabama plant manager and wants him to get a favorable review. Tom suggests allocating the firm's budgeted common fixed costs of $3,150,000 to the two plants, but on the basis of one-third to the Alabama plant and two-thirds to the Georgia plant. His explanation for this allocation base is that Georgia is a more expensive state than Alabama.

At the end of the year, the Georgia plant reported the following actual results: output of 1,950,000 using 1,020,000 labor-hours in total, at a cost of $3,264,000 in variable overhead and $2,440,000 in fixed overhead.

Actual results for the Alabama plant are an output of 2,175,000 units using 1,225,000 labor-hours with a variable cost of $3,920,000 and fixed overhead cost of $2,300,000. The actual common fixed costs for the year were $3,075,000.

Required

1. Compute the budgeted fixed cost per labor-hour for the fixed overhead separately for each plant:
   a. Excluding allocated common fixed costs
   b. Including allocated common fixed costs
2. Compute the variable overhead spending variance and the variable overhead efficiency variance separately for each plant.
3. Compute the fixed overhead spending and volume variances for each plant:
   a. Excluding allocated common fixed costs
   b. Including allocated common fixed costs
4. Did Tom Saban's attempt to make the Alabama plant look better than the Georgia plant by allocating common fixed costs work? Why or why not?
5. Should common fixed costs be allocated in general when variances are used as performance measures? Why or why not?
6. What do you think of Tom Saban's behavior overall?

9 Inventory Costing and Capacity Analysis

Learning Objectives

1. Identify what distinguishes variable costing from absorption costing.
2. Compute income under variable costing and absorption costing, and explain the difference in income.
3. Understand how absorption costing can provide undesirable incentives for managers to build up inventory.
4. Differentiate throughput costing from variable costing and absorption costing.
5. Describe the various capacity concepts that firms can use in absorption costing.
6. Examine the key factors managers use to choose a capacity level to compute the budgeted fixed manufacturing cost rate.
7. Understand other issues that play an important role in capacity planning and control.

Few numbers capture the attention of managers and shareholders more than operating profits.

In industries that require significant upfront investments in capacity, two key decisions have a substantial impact on corporate profits: (1) How much money a firm spends on fixed investments and (2) the extent to which the firm eventually utilizes capacity to meet customer demand. Unfortunately, the compensation and reward systems of a firm, as well as the choice of inventory-costing methods, may induce managers to make decisions that benefit short-term earnings at the expense of a firm's long-term health. It may take a substantial external shock, like a sharp economic slowdown, to motivate managers to make the right capacity and inventory choices, as the following article illustrates.

Lean Manufacturing Helps Companies Reduce Inventory and Survive the Recession[1]

Can changing the way a mattress is pieced together help a company stay in business and remain profitable during a recession? For Sealy, the world's largest mattress manufacturer, the answer was a resounding "yes!"

Sealy used to manufacture as many mattresses as its resources allowed, regardless of customer orders. While factories operated at peak capacity, inventory often piled up, which cost the company millions of dollars each year. During the recent recession, Sealy was among thousands of manufacturers that remained profitable by changing its production plans to become more cost-efficient. Sealy adopted a policy of lean manufacturing, that is, producing only completed units and initiating production only in response to actual customer orders.

While Sealy launched its lean strategy in 2004, it intensified that strategy during the recession. The firm reconfigured old manufacturing processes to be more efficient. As a result:

- Each bed is now completed in 4 hours, down from 21.
- Median delivery times from Sealy to its retailers were cut to 60 hours, down from 72.

[1] *Sources:* Davidson, Paul. 2009. Lean manufacturing helps companies survive recession. *USA Today*, November 2; Sealy Corporation. 2011 Annual Report. Trinity, NC: Sealy Corporation, 2012; Sealy Corporation. 2009 Annual Report. Trinity, NC: Sealy Corporation, 2010; Hsu, Tiffany. 2012. Mattress mates: Tempur-Pedic buys Sealy for $1.3 billion. *The Los Angeles Times*, September 27.

- Raw-material inventories were cut by 50%.
- The company now adheres to a precise production schedule based on orders from retailers. While factories no longer run at full capacity, no mattress is made now until a customer orders it.

Sealy's manufacturing and inventory strategy was key to its survival during the recession and beyond. From 2008 to 2011, Sealy's lean manufacturing successfully reduced its inventory costs by 12%, or $7.6 million. This reduction enhanced the company's operations and made it an attractive acquisition target. In 2012, rival Tempur-Pedic purchased Sealy for $1.3 billion to create one of the largest companies in the competitive bedding industry.

Managers in industries with high fixed costs, like manufacturing, must manage capacity levels and make decisions about how to use available capacity. Managers must also decide on a production and inventory policy (as Sealy did). These decisions and the accounting choices managers make affect the operating incomes of manufacturing companies. This chapter focuses on two types of cost accounting choices:

1. *The inventory-costing choice* determines which manufacturing costs are treated as inventoriable costs. Recall from Chapter 2 (page 39) that *inventoriable costs* are all costs of a product that are regarded as assets when they are incurred and expensed as cost of goods sold when the product is sold. There are three types of inventory costing methods: absorption costing, variable costing, and throughput costing.
2. *The denominator-level capacity choice* focuses on the cost allocation base used to set budgeted fixed manufacturing cost rates. There are four possible choices of capacity levels: theoretical capacity, practical capacity, normal capacity utilization, and master-budget capacity utilization.

Variable and Absorption Costing

Learning Objective 1

Identify what distinguishes variable costing

...fixed manufacturing costs excluded from inventoriable costs

from absorption costing

...fixed manufacturing costs included in inventoriable costs

The two most common methods of costing inventories in manufacturing companies are *variable costing* and *absorption costing*. We describe each in this section and then discuss them in detail, using a hypothetical telescope-manufacturing company as an example.

Variable Costing

Variable costing is a method of inventory costing in which all variable manufacturing costs (direct and indirect) are included as inventoriable costs. All fixed manufacturing costs are excluded from inventoriable costs and are instead treated as costs of the period in which they are incurred. Note that *variable costing* is an imprecise term to describe this inventory-costing method because only variable manufacturing costs are inventoried; variable nonmanufacturing costs are still treated as period costs and are expensed. Another common term used to describe this method is **direct costing**. This term is also imprecise because variable costing considers variable manufacturing overhead (an indirect cost) as inventoriable, while excluding direct marketing costs, for example.

Absorption Costing

Absorption costing is a method of inventory costing in which all variable manufacturing costs and all fixed manufacturing costs are included as inventoriable costs. That is, inventory "absorbs" all manufacturing costs. The job costing system you studied in Chapter 4 is an example of absorption costing.

Under both variable costing and absorption costing, all variable manufacturing costs are inventoriable costs and all nonmanufacturing costs in the value chain (such as research and development and marketing), whether variable or fixed, are period costs and are recorded as expenses when incurred.

Comparing Variable and Absorption Costing

The easiest way to understand the difference between variable costing and absorption costing is with an example. In this chapter, we will study Stassen Company, an optical consumer-products manufacturer, and focus on its product line of high-end telescopes for aspiring astronomers.

Stassen uses standard costing:

- Direct costs are traced to products using standard prices and standard inputs allowed for actual outputs produced.
- Indirect (overhead) manufacturing costs are allocated using standard indirect rates times standard inputs allowed for actual outputs produced.

Stassen's management wants to prepare an income statement for 2014 (the fiscal year just ended) to evaluate the performance of the telescope product line. The operating information for the year is as follows:

	A	B
1		**Units**
2	Beginning inventory	0
3	Production	8,000
4	Sales	6,000
5	Ending inventory	2,000

Actual price and cost data for 2014 are as follows:

	A	B
10	Selling price	$ 1,000
11	Variable manufacturing cost per unit	
12	Direct material cost per unit	$ 110
13	Direct manufacturing labor cost per unit	40
14	Manufacturing overhead cost per unit	50
15	Total variable manufacturing cost per unit	$ 200
16	Variable marketing cost per unit sold	$ 185
17	Fixed manufacturing costs (all indirect)	$1,080,000
18	Fixed marketing costs (all indirect)	$1,380,000

For simplicity and to focus on the main ideas, we assume the following about Stassen:

- Stassen incurs manufacturing and marketing costs only. The cost driver for all variable manufacturing costs is units produced; the cost driver for variable marketing costs is units sold. There are no batch-level costs and no product-sustaining costs.

- There are no price variances, efficiency variances, or spending variances. Therefore, the *budgeted* (standard) price and cost data for 2014 are the same as the *actual* price and cost data.
- Work-in-process inventory is zero.
- Stassen budgeted production of 8,000 units for 2014. This was used to calculate the budgeted fixed manufacturing cost per unit of $135 ($1,080,000/8,000 units).[2]
- Stassen budgeted sales of 6,000 units for 2014, which is the same as the actual sales for 2014.
- The actual production for 2014 is 8,000 units. As a result, there is no production-volume variance for manufacturing costs in 2014. A later example, based on data for 2015, does include production-volume variances. However, even in that case, the income statement contains no variances other than the production-volume variance.
- Variances are written off to cost of goods sold in the period (year) in which they occur.

Based on the preceding information, Stassen's inventoriable costs per unit produced in 2014 under the two inventory costing methods are as follows:

	Variable Costing		Absorption Costing	
Variable manufacturing cost per unit produced:				
Direct materials	$110		$110	
Direct manufacturing labor	40		40	
Manufacturing overhead	50	$200	50	$200
Fixed manufacturing cost per unit produced		—		135
Total inventoriable cost per unit produced		$200		$335

To summarize, the main difference between variable costing and absorption costing is the accounting for fixed manufacturing costs:

- Under variable costing, fixed manufacturing costs are not inventoried; they are treated as an expense of the period.
- Under absorption costing, fixed manufacturing costs are inventoriable costs. In our example, the standard fixed manufacturing cost is $135 per unit ($1,080,000 ÷ 8,000 units) produced.

Decision Point

How does variable costing differ from absorption costing?

Variable vs. Absorption Costing: Operating Income and Income Statements

Learning Objective 2

Compute income under absorption costing

...using the gross-margin format

and variable costing,

...using the contribution-margin format

and explain the difference in income

...affected by the unit level of production and sales under absorption costing, but only the unit level of sales under variable costing

When comparing variable and absorption costing, we must also take into account whether we are looking at short- or long-term numbers. How does the data for a one-year period differ from that of a two-year period under variable and absorption costing?

Comparing Income Statements for One Year

What will Stassen's operating income be if it uses variable costing or absorption costing? The differences between these methods are apparent in Exhibit 9-1. Panel A shows the variable costing income statement and Panel B the absorption-costing income statement for Stassen's telescope product line for 2014. The variable-costing income statement uses the contribution-margin format (introduced in Chapter 3). The absorption-costing income statement uses the gross-margin format (introduced in Chapter 2). Why these different formats? The distinction between variable costs and fixed costs is central to

[2] Throughout this section, we use budgeted output as the basis for calculating the fixed manufacturing cost per unit for ease of exposition. In the latter half of this chapter, we consider the relative merits of alternative denominator-level choices for calculating this unit cost.

Exhibit 9-1 Comparison of Variable Costing and Absorption Costing for Stassen Company: Telescope Product-Line Income Statements for 2014

	A	B	C	D	E	F	G
1	**Panel A: VARIABLE COSTING**				**Panel B: ABSORPTION COSTING**		
2	Revenues: $1,000 × 6,000 units		$6,000,000		Revenues: $1,000 × 6,000 units		$6,000,000
3	Variable cost of goods sold:				Cost of goods sold:		
4	Beginning inventory	$ 0			Beginning inventory	$ 0	
5	Variable manufacturing costs: $200 × 8,000 units	1,600,000			Variable manufacturing costs: $200 × 8,000 units	1,600,000	
6					Allocated fixed manufacturing costs: $135 × 8,000 units	1,080,000	
7	Cost of goods available for sale	1,600,000			Cost of goods available for sale	2,680,000	
8	Deduct ending inventory: $200 × 2,000 units	(400,000)			Deduct ending inventory: $335 × 2,000 units	(670,000)	
9	Variable cost of goods sold		1,200,000		Cost of goods sold		2,010,000
10	Variable marketing costs: $185 × 6,000 units sold		1,110,000				
11	Contribution margin		3,690,000		Gross Margin		3,990,000
12	Fixed manufacturing costs		1,080,000		Variable marketing costs: $185 × 6,000 units sold		1,110,000
13	Fixed marketing costs		1,380,000		Fixed marketing costs		1,380,000
14	Operating income		$1,230,000		Operating Income		$1,500,000
15							
16	Manufacturing costs expensed in Panel A:				Manufacturing costs expensed in Panel B:		
17	Variable cost of goods sold		$1,200,000				
18	Fixed manufacturing costs		1,080,000				
19	Total		$2,280,000		Cost of goods sold		$2,010,000

variable costing, and it is highlighted by the contribution-margin format. Similarly, the distinction between manufacturing and nonmanufacturing costs is central to absorption costing, and it is highlighted by the gross-margin format.

Absorption-costing income statements do not need to differentiate between variable and fixed costs. However, we will make this distinction between variable and fixed costs in the Stassen example to show how individual line items are classified differently under variable costing and absorption costing. In Exhibit 9-1, Panel B, note that inventoriable cost is $335 per unit under absorption costing: allocated fixed manufacturing costs of $135 per unit plus variable manufacturing costs of $200 per unit.

Notice how the fixed manufacturing costs of $1,080,000 are accounted for under variable costing and absorption costing in Exhibit 9-1. The income statement under variable costing deducts the $1,080,000 lump sum as an expense for 2014. In contrast, under absorption costing, the $1,080,000 ($135 per unit × 8,000 units) is initially treated as an inventoriable cost in 2014. Of this $1,080,000, $810,000 ($135 per unit × 6,000 units sold) subsequently becomes a part of cost of goods sold in 2014, and $270,000 ($135 per unit × 2,000 units) remains an asset—part of ending finished goods inventory on December 31, 2014.

Operating income is $270,000 higher under absorption costing compared with variable costing because only $810,000 of fixed manufacturing costs are expensed under absorption costing, whereas all $1,080,000 of fixed manufacturing costs are expensed under variable costing. Note that the variable manufacturing cost of $200 per unit is accounted for the same way in both income statements in Exhibit 9-1.

These points can be summarized as follows:

	Variable Costing	**Absorption Costing**
Variable manufacturing costs: $200 per telescope produced	Inventoriable	Inventoriable
Fixed manufacturing costs: $1,080,000 per year	Deducted as an expense of the period	Inventoriable at $135 per telescope produced using budgeted denominator level of 8,000 units produced per year ($1,080,000 ÷ 8,000 units = $135 per unit)

The basis of the difference between variable costing and absorption costing is how fixed manufacturing costs are accounted for. If inventory levels change, operating income will differ between the two methods because of the difference in accounting for fixed manufacturing costs. To see this difference, let's compare telescope sales of 6,000, 7,000, and 8,000 units by Stassen in 2014, when 8,000 units were produced. Of the $1,080,000 total fixed manufacturing costs, the amount expensed in the 2014 income statement under each of these scenarios would be as follows:

	A	B	C	D	E	G	H
1			Variable Costing			Absorption Costing	
2						Fixed Manufacturing Costs	
3	Units	Ending	Fixed Manufacturing Costs			Included in Inventory	Amount Expensed
4	Sold	Inventory	Included in Inventory	Amount Expensed		=$135 × Ending Inv.	=$135 × Units Sold
5	6,000	2,000	$0	$1,080,000		$270,000	$ 810,000
6	7,000	1,000	$0	$1,080,000		$135,000	$ 945,000
7	8,000	0	$0	$1,080,000		$ 0	$1,080,000

In the last scenario, where 8,000 units are produced and sold, both variable and absorption costing report the same net income because inventory levels are unchanged. This chapter's appendix describes how the choice of variable costing or absorption costing affects the breakeven quantity of sales when inventory levels are allowed to vary.

Comparing Income Statements for Multiple Years

To get a more comprehensive view of the effects of variable costing and absorption costing, Stassen's management accountants prepare income statements for two years of operations, starting with 2014. The data are given in units in the following table:

	E	F	G
1		2014	2015
2	Budgeted production	8,000	8,000
3	Beginning inventory	0	2,000
4	Actual production	8,000	5,000
5	Sales	6,000	6,500
6	Ending inventory	2,000	500

All other 2014 data given earlier for Stassen also apply for 2015.

In 2015, Stassen has a production-volume variance because actual telescope production differs from the budgeted level of production of 8,000 units per year used to calculate the budgeted fixed manufacturing cost per unit. The actual quantity sold for 2015 is 6,500 units, which is the same as the sales quantity budgeted for that year.

Exhibit 9-2 presents the income statement under variable costing in Panel A and the income statement under absorption costing in Panel B for 2014 and 2015. As you study Exhibit 9-2, note that the 2014 columns in both Panels A and B show the same figures as Exhibit 9-1. The 2015 column is similar to 2014 *except for the production-volume variance line item under absorption costing in Panel B*. Keep in mind the following points about absorption costing as you study Panel B of Exhibit 9-2:

1. The $135 fixed manufacturing cost rate is based on the budgeted denominator capacity level of 8,000 units in 2014 and 2015 ($1,080,000 ÷ 8,000 units = $135 per unit). Whenever production (the quantity produced, not the quantity sold) deviates from the denominator level, there will be a production-volume variance. The amount of Stassen's production-volume variance is determined by multiplying $135 per unit by the difference between the actual level of production and the denominator level.

Exhibit 9-2 Comparison of Variable Costing and Absorption Costing for Stassen Company: Telescope Product-Line Income Statements for 2014 and 2015

	A	B	C	D	E
1	**Panel A: VARIABLE COSTING**				
2			**2014**		**2015**
3	Revenues: $1,000 × 6,000; 6,500 units		$6,000,000		$6,500,000
4	Variable cost of goods sold:				
5	Beginning inventory: $200 × 0; 2,000 units	$ 0		$ 400,000	
6	Variable manufacturing costs: $200 × 8,000; 5,000 units	1,600,000		1,000,000	
7	Cost of goods available for sale	1,600,000		1,400,000	
8	Deduct ending inventory: $200 × 2,000; 500 units	(400,000)		(100,000)	
9	Variable cost of goods sold		1,200,000		1,300,000
10	Variable marketing costs: $185 × 6,000; 6,500 units		1,110,000		1,202,500
11	Contribution margin		3,690,000		3,997,500
12	Fixed manufacturing costs		1,080,000		1,080,000
13	Fixed marketing costs		1,380,000		1,380,000
14	Operating income		$1,230,000		$1,537,500
15					
16	**Panel B: ABSORPTION COSTING**				
17			**2014**		**2015**
18	Revenues: $1,000 × 6,000; 6,500 units		$6,000,000		$6,500,000
19	Cost of goods sold:				
20	Beginning inventory: $335 × 0; 2,000 units	0		670,000	
21	Variable manufacturing costs: $200 × 8,000; 5,000 units	1,600,000		1,000,000	
22	Allocated fixed manufacturing costs: $135 × 8,000; 5,000 units	1,080,000		675,000	
23	Cost of goods available for sale	2,680,000		2,345,000	
24	Deduct ending inventory: $335 × 2,000; 500 units	(670,000)		(167,500)	
25	Adjustment for production-volume variance[a]	$ 0		$ 405,000	U
26	Cost of goods sold		2,010,000		2,582,500
27	Gross Margin		3,990,000		3,917,500
28	Variable marketing costs: $185 × 6,000; 6,500 units		1,110,000		1,202,500
29	Fixed marketing costs		1,380,000		1,380,000
30	Operating Income		$1,500,000		$1,335,000
31					
32	[a]Production-volume variance = Budgeted fixed manufacturing costs – Fixed manufacturing overhead allocated using budgeted cost per output unit allowed for actual output produced (Panel B, line 22)				
33	2014: $1,080,000 – ($135 × 8,000) = $1,080,000 – $1,080,000 = $0				
34	2015: $1,080,000 – ($135 × 5,000) = $1,080,000 – $675,000 = $405,000 U				
35					
36	Production-volume variance can also be calculated as follows:				
37	Fixed manufacturing cost per unit × (Denominator level – Actual output units produced)				
38	2014: $135 × (8,000 – 8,000) units = $135 × 0 = $0				
39	2015: $135 × (8,000 – 5,000) units = $135 × 3,000 = $405,000 U				

Recall how standard costing works under absorption costing. Each time a unit is manufactured, $135 of fixed manufacturing costs is included in the cost of goods manufactured and available for sale. In 2015, when 5,000 units are manufactured, $675,000 ($135 per unit × 5,000 units) of fixed manufacturing costs is included in the cost of goods available for sale (see Exhibit 9-2, Panel B, line 22). Total fixed manufacturing costs for 2015 are $1,080,000. The production-volume variance of $405,000 U equals the difference between $1,080,000 and $675,000. In Panel B, note how, for each year, the fixed manufacturing costs included in the cost of goods available for sale plus the production-volume variance always equals $1,080,000.

2. As a result of the production-volume variance, note that the absorption costing income is lower in 2015 than in 2014 even though Stassen sold 500 more units. We explore the impact of production levels on income under absorption costing in greater detail later in this chapter.

3. The production-volume variance, which relates only to fixed manufacturing overhead, exists under absorption costing but not under variable costing. Under variable costing, fixed manufacturing costs of $1,080,000 are always treated as an expense of the period, regardless of the level of production (and sales).

Here's a summary (using information from Exhibit 9-2) of the operating-income differences for Stassen Company during 2014 and 2015:

	2014	2015
1. Absorption-costing operating income	$1,500,000	$1,335,000
2. Variable-costing operating income	$1,230,000	$1,537,500
3. Difference: (1) – (2)	$ 270,000	$ (202,500)

The sizeable differences in the preceding table illustrate why managers whose performance is measured by reported income are concerned about the choice between variable costing and absorption costing.

Why do variable costing and absorption costing report different operating income numbers? In general, if inventory increases during an accounting period, less operating income will be reported under variable costing than absorption costing. Conversely, if inventory decreases, more operating income will be reported under variable costing than absorption costing. The difference in reported operating income is due solely to (a) moving fixed manufacturing costs into inventories as inventories increase and (b) moving fixed manufacturing costs out of inventories as inventories decrease under absorption costing.

The difference between operating income under absorption costing and variable costing can be computed by formula 1, which focuses on fixed manufacturing costs in beginning inventory and ending inventory:

	A	B	C	D	E	F	G	H
1	Formula 1							
2						Fixed manufacturing		Fixed manufacturing
3		Absorption-costing	–	Variable-costing	=	costs in ending inventory	–	costs in beginning inventory
4		operating income		operation income		under absorption costing		under absorption costing
5	2014	$1,500,000	–	$1,230,000	=	($135 × 2,000 units)	–	($135 × 0 units)
6			$270,000		=		$270,000	
7								
8	2015	$1,335,000	–	$1,537,500	=	($135 × 500 units)	–	($135 × 2,000 units)
9			($202,500)		=		($202,500)	

Fixed manufacturing costs in ending inventory are deferred to a future period under absorption costing. For example, $270,000 of fixed manufacturing overhead is deferred to 2015 at December 31, 2014. Under variable costing, all $1,080,000 of fixed manufacturing costs are treated as an expense of 2014.

Recall that

$$\text{Beginning inventory} + \text{Cost of goods manufactured} = \text{Cost of goods sold} + \text{Ending Inventory}$$

Therefore, instead of focusing on fixed manufacturing costs in ending and beginning inventory (as in formula 1), we could alternatively look at fixed manufacturing costs in units produced and units sold. The latter approach (see formula 2) highlights how fixed manufacturing costs move between units produced and units sold during the fiscal year.

	A	B	C	D	E	F	G	H
12	Formula 2							
13						Fixed manufacturing costs		Fixed manufacturing costs
14		Absorption-costing	–	Variable-costing	=	inventoried in units produced	–	in cost of goods sold
15		operating income		operation income		under absorption costing		under absorption costing
16	2014	$1,500,000	–	$1,230,000	=	($135 × 8,000 units)	–	($135 × 6,000 units)
17		$270,000			=	$270,000		
18								
19	2015	$1,335,000	–	$1,537,500	=	($135 × 5,000 units)	–	($135 × 6,500 units)
20		($202,500)			=	($202,500)		

Managers face increasing pressure to reduce inventory levels. Some companies are achieving steep reductions in inventory levels using policies such as just-in-time production—a production system under which products are manufactured only when needed. Formula 1 illustrates that, as Stassen reduces its inventory levels, operating income differences between absorption costing and variable costing become immaterial. Consider, for example, the formula for 2014. If instead of 2,000 units in ending inventory, Stassen had only 2 units in ending inventory, the difference between absorption-costing operating income and variable-costing operating income would drop from $270,000 to just $270.

Variable Costing and the Effect of Sales and Production on Operating Income

Given a constant contribution margin per unit and constant fixed costs, the period-to-period change in operating income under variable costing is *driven solely by changes in the quantity of units actually sold*. Consider the variable-costing operating income of Stassen in 2015 versus 2014. Recall the following:

$$\text{Contribution margin per unit} = \text{Selling price} - \text{Variable manufacturing cost per unit} - \text{Variable marketing cost per unit}$$

$$= \$1{,}000 \text{ per unit} - \$200 \text{ per unit} - \$185 \text{ per unit}$$

$$= \$615 \text{ per unit}$$

$$\text{Change in variable-costing operating income} = \text{Contribution margin per unit} \times \text{Change in quantity of units sold}$$

$$\text{2015 vs. 2014: } \$1{,}537{,}500 - \$1{,}230{,}000 = \$615 \text{ per unit} \times (6{,}500 \text{ unit} - 6{,}000 \text{ units})$$

$$\$307{,}500 = \$307{,}500$$

Decision Point
How does income differ under variable and absorption costing?

Under variable costing, Stassen managers cannot increase operating income by "producing for inventory." Why not? Because, as you can see from the preceding computations, when using variable costing, only the quantity of units sold drives operating income. We'll explain later in this chapter that absorption costing enables managers to increase operating income by increasing the unit level of sales, as well as by producing more units. Before you proceed to the next section, make sure that you examine Exhibit 9-3 for a detailed comparison of the differences between variable costing and absorption costing.

Exhibit 9-3 Comparative Income Effects of Variable Costing and Absorption Costing

Question	Variable Costing	Absorption Costing	Comment
Are fixed manufacturing costs inventoried?	No	Yes	Basic theoretical question of when these costs should be expensed
Is there a production-volume variance?	No	Yes	Choice of denominator level affects measurement of operating income under absorption costing only
Are classifications between variable and fixed costs routinely made?	Yes	Infrequently	Absorption costing can be easily modified to obtain subclassifications for variable and fixed costs, if desired (for example, see Exhibit 9-1, Panel B)
How do changes in unit inventory levels affect operating income?[a]			Differences are attributable to the timing of when fixed manufacturing costs are expensed
Production = sales	Equal	Equal	
Production > sales	Lower[b]	Higher[c]	
Production < sales	Higher	Lower	
What are the effects on cost-volume-profit relationship (for a given level of fixed costs and a given contribution margin per unit)?	Driven by unit level of sales	Driven by (a) unit level of sales, (b) unit level of production, and (c) chosen denominator level	Management control benefit: Effects of changes in production level on operating income are easier to understand under variable costing

[a]Assuming that all manufacturing variances are written off as period costs, that no change occurs in work-in-process inventory, and no change occurs in the budgeted fixed manufacturing cost rate between accounting periods.
[b]That is, lower operating income than under absorption costing.
[c]That is, higher operating income than under variable costing.

Absorption Costing and Performance Measurement

Learning Objective 3

Understand how absorption costing can provide undesirable incentives for managers to build up inventory

. . . producing more units for inventory absorbs fixed manufacturing costs and increases operating income

Absorption costing is the required inventory method for external financial reporting in most countries (we provide potential reasons for this rule later in the chapter). Many companies use absorption costing for internal accounting as well because:

- It is cost-effective and less confusing for managers to use one common method of inventory costing for both external and internal reporting and performance evaluation.
- It can help prevent managers from taking actions that make their performance measure look good but that hurt the income they report to shareholders.
- It measures the cost of all manufacturing resources, whether variable or fixed, necessary to produce inventory. Many companies use inventory costing information for long-run decisions, such as pricing and choosing a product mix. For these long-run decisions, inventory costs should include both variable *and* fixed costs.

An important attribute of absorption costing is that it enables a manager to increase margins and operating income by producing more ending inventory. Producing for inventory is justified when a firm's managers anticipate rapid growth in demand and want to produce and store additional units to deal with possible production shortages in the next year. For example, with the recent improvement in the national economy, manufacturers of energy-efficient doors and windows are stepping up production in order to take advantage of an anticipated rebound in the housing market. But, under absorption costing, Stassen's managers may be tempted to produce inventory even when they *do not* anticipate customer demand to grow. The reason is that this production leads to higher operating income, which can benefit managers in two ways: directly, because higher incomes typically result in a higher bonus for the manager, and indirectly, because greater income levels have a positive effect on stock price, which increases managers' stock-based compensation. But higher income results in the company paying higher taxes. Shareholders and supporters of good corporate governance would also argue that it is unethical for managers to take actions that are intended solely to increase their compensation rather than to improve the company. Producing for inventory is a risky strategy, especially in industries with volatile demand or high risk of product obsolescence because of the pace at which innovation is occuring. For example, the new BlackBerry Z10 smartphone has seen declining sell-through rates and higher levels of inventory and is being sold at deeply discounted prices in the United Kingdom. Concepts in Action: Absorption Costing and the Bankruptcy of U.S. Automakers illustrates the dramatic negative impact of producing for inventory in the auto industry.

To reduce the undesirable incentives to build up inventories that absorption costing can create, a number of companies use variable costing for internal reporting. Variable costing focuses attention on distinguishing variable manufacturing costs from fixed manufacturing costs. This distinction is important for short-run decision making (as in cost-volume-profit analysis in Chapter 3 and in planning and control in Chapters 6, 7, and 8).

Companies that use both methods for internal reporting—variable costing for short-run decisions and performance evaluation and absorption costing for long-run decisions—benefit from the different advantages of both. Surveys sponsored by Chartered Institute of Management Accountants (United Kingdom), the world's largest professional body of management accountants, have shown that while most organizations employ absorption costing systems, more than 75% indicate the use of variable costing information as either the most important or second most important measure for decision-making purposes.

In the next section, we explore in more detail the challenges that arise from absorption costing.

Concepts in Action: Absorption Costing and the Bankruptcy of U.S. Automakers

In the years leading up to the 2008 recession, General Motors, Ford, and Chrysler were producing new vehicles in excess of market demand. This led to large inventories on car dealers' lots across the United States. At the same time, profits were rising and executives at these three companies were achieving their short-term incentive targets. How is this possible? Absorption costing may hold the answer.

In 2009, General Motors and Chrysler filed for bankruptcy and appealed for government aid. Yet these automakers had abundant excess capacity. They also had enormous fixed costs, from factories and machinery to workers whose contracts protected them from layoffs when demand was low. To "absorb" these costs, the automakers produced more cars while using absorption costing. The more vehicles they made, the lower the cost per vehicle, and the higher the profits on their income statements. In effect, the automakers shifted costs from their income statements to their balance sheets.

Ultimately, this practice hurt the automakers by driving up advertising and inventory costs. "When the dealers couldn't sell the cars, they would sit on the lots," says Dr. Karen Sedatole, a Michigan State professor who recently co-authored a study on the topic. "They'd have to go in and replace the tires, and there were costs associated with that." The companies also had to pay to advertise their cars, often at discounted prices using rebates, employee pricing, and 0% financing promotions. General Motors and Chrysler ran out of cash for operations and making loans available for car buyers. In January 2009, the U.S. government used $24.9 billion in bailout funds to rescue General Motors and Chrysler.

Sources: Based on Marielle Segarra, "Lots of Trouble," *CFO Magazine* (March 2012); and Bruggen, A., R. Krishnan, and K. L. Sedatole. 2011. Drivers and Consequences of Short-Term Production Decisions: Evidence from the Auto Industry. *Contemporary Accounting Research* 28 (1):83–123.

Undesirable Buildup of Inventories

If a manager's bonus is based on reported absorption-costing operating income, that manager may be motivated to build up an undesirable level of inventories. Assume that Stassen's managers have such a bonus plan. Exhibit 9-4 shows how Stassen's absorption costing operating income for 2015 changes as the production level changes. This exhibit assumes that the production-volume variance is written off to cost of goods sold at the end of each year. Beginning inventory of 2,000 units and sales of 6,500 units for 2015 are unchanged from the case shown in Exhibit 9-2. *As you review* Exhibit 9-4, *keep in mind that the computations are basically the same as those in* Exhibit 9-2.

Exhibit 9-4 shows that production of 4,500 units meets the 2015 sales budget of 6,500 units (2,000 units from beginning inventory +4,500 units produced). Operating income at this production level is $1,267,500. By producing more than 4,500 units, commonly referred to as *producing for inventory*, Stassen increases absorption-costing operating income. Each additional unit in 2015 ending inventory will increase operating income by $135. For example, if 9,000 units are produced (column H in Exhibit 9-4), ending inventory will be 4,500 units and operating income increases to $1,875,000. This amount is $607,500 more than the operating income with zero ending inventory ($1,875,000 – $1,267,500, or 4,500 units × $135 per unit = $607,500). By producing 4,500 units for inventory, the company using absorption costing includes $607,500 of fixed manufacturing costs in finished goods inventory, so those costs are not expensed in 2015.

The scenarios outlined in Exhibit 9-4 raise three other important points. First, column D is the base-case setting and just restates the 2015 absorption costing results from Panel B of Exhibit 9-2. Second, column F highlights that when inventory levels are unchanged, that is, production equals sales, the absorption costing income equals the income under variable costing (see Panel A of Exhibit 9-2 for comparison). Third, the example in Exhibit 9-4 focuses on one year, 2015. A Stassen manager who built up an inventory of 4,500 telescopes at the end of 2015 would have to further increase ending inventories in 2016 to increase that year's operating income by producing for inventory. There are limits to how much inventory levels can be increased over time because of physical constraints

Exhibit 9-4 Effect on Absorption-Costing Operating Income of Different Production Levels for Stassen Company: Telescope Product-Line Income Statement for 2015 at Sales of 6,500 Units

Home Insert Page Layout Formulas Data Review View

	A	B	C	D	E	F	G	H	I
1	**Unit Data**								
2	Beginning inventory	2,000		2,000		2,000		2,000	
3	Production	4,500		5,000		6,500		9,000	
4	Goods available for sale	6,500		7,000		8,500		11,000	
5	Sales	6,500		6,500		6,500		6,500	
6	Ending inventory	0		500		2,000		4,500	
7									
8	**Income Statement**								
9	Revenues	$6,500,000		$6,500,000		$6,500,000		$6,500,000	
10	Cost of goods sold:								
11	Beginning inventory: $335 × 2,000	670,000		670,000		670,000		670,000	
12	Variable manufacturing costs: $200 × production	900,000		1,000,000		1,300,000		1,800,000	
13	Allocated fixed manufacturing costs: $135 × production	607,500		675,000		877,500		1,215,000	
14	Cost of goods available for sale	2,177,500		2,345,000		2,847,500		3,685,000	
15	Deduct ending inventory: $335 × ending inventory	0		(167,500)		(670,000)		(1,507,500)	
16	Adjustment for production-volume variance[a]	472,500	U	405,000	U	202,500	U	(135,000)	F
17	Cost of goods sold	2,650,000		2,582,500		2,380,000		2,042,500	
18	Gross Margin	3,850,000		3,917,500		4,120,000		4,457,500	
19	Marketing costs: $1,380,000 + ($185 per unit × 6,500 units sold)	2,582,500		2,582,500		2,582,500		2,582,500	
20	Operating Income	$1,267,500		$1,335,000		$1,537,500		$1,875,000	
21									
22	[a]Production-volume variance = Budgeted fixed manufacturing costs – Allocated fixed manufacturing costs (Income Statement, line 13)								
23	At production of 4,500 units: $1,080,000 – $607,500 = $472,500 U								
24	At production of 5,000 units: $1,080,000 – $675,000 = $405,000 U								
25	At production of 6,500 units: $1,080,000 – $877,500 = $202,500 U								
26	At production of 9,000 units: $1,080,000 – $1,215,000 = ($135,000) F								

on storage space and management controls. Such limits reduce the likelihood of incurring some of absorption costing's undesirable effects. Nevertheless, managers do have the ability and incentive to move costs in and out of inventory in order to manage operating income under absorption costing.

Top management can implement checks and balances that limit managers from producing for inventory under absorption costing. However, the practice cannot be completely prevented. There are many subtle ways a manager can produce for inventory that may not be easy to detect. For example, consider the following scenarios:

- A plant manager may switch to manufacturing products that absorb the highest amount of fixed manufacturing costs, regardless of the customer demand for these products (called "cherry picking" the production line). Delaying the production of items that absorb the least or lower fixed manufacturing costs could lead to failure to meet promised customer delivery dates (which, over time, can result in unhappy customers).
- A plant manager may accept a particular order to increase production, even though another plant in the same company is better suited to handle that order.
- To increase production, a manager may defer maintenance of equipment beyond the current period. Although operating income in this period may increase as a result, future operating income could decrease by a larger amount if repair costs increase and equipment becomes less efficient.

Proposals for Revising Performance Evaluation

Top management, with help from the controller and management accountants, can take several steps to reduce the undesirable effects of absorption costing.

- Focus on careful budgeting and inventory planning to reduce management's freedom to build up excess inventory. For example, the budgeted monthly balance sheets have estimates of the dollar amount of inventories. If actual inventories exceed these dollar amounts, top management can investigate the inventory buildups.
- Incorporate a carrying charge for inventory in the internal accounting system. For example, the company could assess an inventory carrying charge of 1% per month on the investment tied up in inventory and for spoilage and obsolescence when it evaluates a manager's performance. An increasing number of companies are beginning to adopt this inventory carrying charge.
- Change the period used to evaluate performance. Critics of absorption costing give examples in which managers take actions that maximize quarterly or annual income at the potential expense of long-run income. When their performance is evaluated over a three- to five-year period, managers will be less tempted to produce for inventory.
- Include nonfinancial as well as financial variables in the measures used to evaluate performance. Examples of nonfinancial measures that can be used to monitor the performance of Stassen's managers in 2015 (see column H of Exhibit 9-4) are as follows:

$$\text{(a)}\ \frac{\text{Ending inventory in units in 2015}}{\text{Beginning inventory in units in 2015}} = \frac{4{,}500}{2{,}000} = 2.25$$

$$\text{(b)}\ \frac{\text{Units produced in 2015}}{\text{Units sold in 2015}} = \frac{9{,}000}{6{,}500} = 1.38$$

Decision Point

Why might managers build up finished goods inventory if they use absorption costing?

Top management would want to see production equal to sales and relatively stable levels of inventory. Companies that manufacture or sell several products could report these two measures for each of the products they manufacture and sell.

Besides the formal performance measurement systems, companies develop codes of conduct to discourage behavior that benefits managers but not the company and build values and cultures that focus on behaving ethically. We discuss these topics in Chapter 23.

Comparing Inventory Costing Methods

Learning Objective 4

Differentiate throughput costing

...direct material costs inventoried

from variable costing

...variable manufacturing costs inventoried

and absorption costing

...variable and fixed manufacturing costs inventoried

Before we begin our discussion of capacity, we will look at *throughput costing*, a variation of variable costing, and compare the various costing methods.

Throughput Costing

Some managers believe that even variable costing promotes an excessive amount of costs being inventoried. They argue that only direct materials, such as the lenses, casing, scope, and mount in the case of Stassen's telescopes, are "truly variable" in output. **Throughput costing,** which is also called **super-variable costing,** is an extreme form of variable costing in which only direct material costs are included as inventoriable costs. All other costs are costs of the period in which they are incurred. In particular, variable direct manufacturing labor costs and variable manufacturing overhead costs are regarded as period costs and are deducted as expenses of the period.

Exhibit 9-5 is the throughput-costing income statement for Stassen Company for 2014 and 2015. *Throughput margin* equals revenues minus all direct material cost of the goods sold. Compare the operating income amounts reported in Exhibit 9-5 with those for absorption costing and variable costing:

	2014	2015
Absorption-costing operating income	$1,500,000	$1,335,000
Variable-costing operating income	$1,230,000	$1,537,500
Throughput-costing operating income	$1,050,000	$1,672,500

Only the $110 direct material cost per unit is inventoriable under throughput costing, compared with $335 per unit for absorption costing and $200 per unit for variable costing. When the production quantity exceeds sales, as in 2014, throughput costing results in the largest amount of expenses in the current period's income statement. Advocates of throughput costing say it provides managers less incentive to produce for inventory than either variable costing or, especially, absorption costing. Throughput costing is a more

Exhibit 9-5

Throughput Costing for Stassen Company: Telescope Product-Line Income Statements for 2014 and 2015

Home Insert Page Layout Formulas Data Review View

	A	B	C
1		2014	2015
2	Revenues: $1,000 × 6,000; 6,500 units	$6,000,000	$6,500,000
3	Direct material cost of goods sold		
4	Beginning inventory: $110 × 0; 2,000 units	0	220,000
5	Direct materials: $110 × 8,000; 5,000 units	880,000	550,000
6	Cost of goods available for sale	880,000	770,000
7	Deduct ending inventory: $110 × 2,000; 500 units	(220,000)	(55,000)
8	Direct material cost of goods sold	660,000	715,000
9	Throughput margin[a]	5,340,000	5,785,000
10	Manufacturing costs (other than direct materials)[b]	1,800,000	1,530,000
11	Marketing costs[c]	2,490,000	2,582,500
12	Operating income	$1,050,000	$1,672,500
13			
14	[a]Throughput margin equals revenues minus all direct material cost of goods sold		
15	[b]Fixed manuf. costs + [(variable manuf. labor cost per unit + variable manuf. overhead cost per unit) × units produced]; $1,080,000 + [($40 + $50) × 8,000; 5,000 units]		
16	[c]Fixed marketing costs + (variable marketing cost per unit × units sold);		
17	$1,380,000 + ($185 × 6,000; 6,500 units)		

recent phenomenon in comparison with variable costing and absorption costing and has avid supporters, but so far it has not been widely adopted.[3]

A Comparison of Alternative Inventory-Costing Methods

Variable costing and absorption costing may be combined with actual, normal, or standard costing. Exhibit 9-6 compares product costing under these six alternative inventory-costing systems.

Variable costing has been controversial among accountants because of how it affects *external reporting*, not because of disagreement about the need to delineate between variable and fixed costs for internal planning and control. Accountants who favor variable costing for external reporting maintain that the fixed portion of manufacturing costs is more closely related to the capacity to produce than to the actual production of specific units. Fixed costs should therefore be expensed, not inventoried.

Accountants who support absorption costing for *external reporting* maintain that inventories should carry a fixed-manufacturing-cost component because both variable manufacturing costs and fixed manufacturing costs are necessary to produce goods. Therefore, both types of costs should be inventoried in order to match all manufacturing costs to revenues, regardless of their different behavior patterns. For external reporting to shareholders, companies around the globe tend to follow the generally accepted accounting principle that all manufacturing costs are inventoriable. This also eases the burden on firms and auditors to attempt to disentangle fixed and variable costs of production, a distinction that is not always clear-cut in practice.

Similarly, for tax reporting in the United States, managers must take direct production costs, as well as fixed and variable indirect production costs, into account in the computation of inventoriable costs in accordance with the "full absorption" method of inventory costing. Indirect production costs include items such as rent, utilities, maintenance, repair

Exhibit 9-6 Comparison of Alternative Inventory-Costing Systems

			Actual Costing	Normal Costing	Standard Costing
Absorption Costing	Variable Costing	**Variable Direct Manufacturing Cost**	Actual prices × Actual quantity of inputs used	Actual prices × Actual quantity of inputs used	Standard prices × Standard quantity of inputs allowed for actual output achieved
Absorption Costing	Variable Costing	**Variable Manufacturing Overhead Costs**	Actual variable overhead rates × Actual quantity of cost-allocation bases used	Budgeted variable overhead rates × Actual quantity of cost-allocation bases used	Standard variable overhead rates × Standard quantity of cost-allocation bases allowed for actual output achieved
Absorption Costing		**Fixed Direct Manufacturing Costs**	Actual prices × Actual quantity of inputs used	Actual prices × Actual quantity of inputs used	Standard prices × Standard quantity of inputs allowed for actual output achieved
Absorption Costing		**Fixed Manufacturing Overhead Costs**	Actual fixed overhead rates × Actual quantity of cost-allocation bases used	Budgeted fixed overhead rates × Actual quantity of cost-allocation bases used	Standard fixed overhead rates × Standard quantity of cost-allocation bases allowed for actual output achieved

[3] See E. Goldratt, *The Theory of Constraints* (New York: North River Press, 1990); E. Noreen, D. Smith, and J. Mackey, *The Theory of Constraints and Its Implications for Management Accounting* (New York: North River Press, 1995).

expenses, indirect materials, and indirect labor. For other indirect cost categories (including depreciation, insurance, taxes, officers' salaries, factory administrative expenses, and strike-related costs), the portion of the cost that is "incident to and necessary for production or manufacturing operations or processes" is inventoriable for tax purposes *only* if it is treated as inventoriable for the purposes of financial reporting. Accordingly, managers must often allocate costs between those portions related to manufacturing activities and those not related to manufacturing.[4]

Decision Point

How does throughput costing differ from variable costing and absorption costing?

Denominator-Level Capacity Concepts and Fixed-Cost Capacity Analysis

Learning Objective 5

Describe the various capacity concepts that can be used in absorption costing

...supply-side: theoretical and practical capacity; demand-side: normal and master-budget capacity utilization

We have seen that the difference between variable and absorption costing methods arises solely from the treatment of fixed manufacturing costs. Spending on fixed manufacturing costs enables firms to obtain the scale or capacity needed to satisfy the expected market demand from customers. Determining the "right" amount of spending, or the appropriate level of capacity, is one of the most strategic and most difficult decisions managers face. Having too much capacity to produce relative to that needed to meet market demand means firms will incur some costs of unused capacity. Having too little capacity to produce means that demand from some customers may be unfilled. These customers may go to other sources of supply and never return. Both managers and accountants must understand these issues that arise with capacity costs.

We start this section by analyzing a key question in absorption costing: Given a firm's level of spending on fixed manufacturing costs, what capacity level should managers and accountants use to compute the fixed manufacturing cost per unit produced? We then study the broader question of how a firm should decide on its level of capacity investment.

Absorption Costing and Alternative Denominator-Level Capacity Concepts

Earlier chapters, especially Chapters 4, 5, and 8, highlighted how normal costing and standard costing report costs in an ongoing timely manner throughout a fiscal year. The choice of the capacity level used to allocate budgeted fixed manufacturing costs to products can greatly affect the operating income reported under normal costing or standard costing and the product-cost information available to managers.

Consider the Stassen Company example again. Recall that the annual fixed manufacturing costs of the production facility are $1,080,000. Stassen currently uses absorption costing with standard costs for external reporting purposes, and it calculates its budgeted fixed manufacturing rate on a per unit basis. We will now examine four different capacity levels used as the denominator to compute the budgeted fixed manufacturing cost rate: theoretical capacity, practical capacity, normal capacity utilization, and master-budget capacity utilization.

Theoretical Capacity and Practical Capacity

- SUPPLY DRIVEN

In business and accounting, capacity ordinarily means a "constraint," an "upper limit." **Theoretical capacity** is the level of capacity based on producing at full efficiency all the time. Stassen can produce 25 units per shift when the production lines are operating at maximum speed. If we assume 360 days per year, the theoretical annual capacity for 2 shifts per day is as follows:

$$25 \text{ units per shift} \times 2 \text{ shifts per day} \times 360 \text{ days} = 18{,}000 \text{ units}$$

[4] Details regarding tax rules can be found in Section 1.471-11 of the U.S. Internal Revenue Code: Inventories of Manufacturers (see http://ecfr.gpoaccess.gov). Recall from Chapter 2 that costs not related to production, such as marketing, distribution, or research expenses, are treated as period expenses for financial reporting. Under U.S. tax rules, a firm can still consider these costs as inventoriable for tax purposes provided that it does so consistently.

Theoretical capacity is theoretical in the sense that it does not allow for any slowdowns due to plant maintenance, shutdown periods, or interruptions because of downtime on the assembly lines. Theoretical capacity levels are unattainable in the real world, but they represent the ideal goal of capacity utilization a company can aspire to.

Practical capacity is the level of capacity that reduces theoretical capacity by considering unavoidable operating interruptions, such as scheduled maintenance time and shutdowns for holidays. Assume that practical capacity is the practical production rate of 20 units per shift (as opposed to 25 units per shift under theoretical capacity) for 2 shifts per day for 300 days a year (as opposed to 360 days a year under theoretical capacity). The practical annual capacity is as follows:

20 units per shift × 2 shifts per day × 300 days = 12,000 units

Engineering and human resource factors are both important when estimating theoretical or practical capacity. Engineers at the Stassen facility can provide input on the technical capabilities of machines for cutting and polishing lenses. Human resources can evaluate employee safety factors, such as increased injury risk when the line operates at faster speeds.

Normal Capacity Utilization and Master-Budget Capacity Utilization

Both theoretical capacity and practical capacity measure capacity levels in terms of what a plant can *supply*—available capacity. In contrast, normal capacity utilization and master-budget capacity utilization measure capacity levels in terms of *demand* for the output of the plant, that is, the amount of available capacity the plant expects to use based on the demand for its products. In many cases, budgeted demand is well below production capacity available.

Normal capacity utilization is the level of capacity utilization that satisfies average customer demand over a period (say, two to three years) that includes seasonal, cyclical, and trend factors. **Master-budget capacity utilization** is the level of capacity utilization that managers expect for the current budget period, which is typically one year. These two capacity-utilization levels can differ quite significantly in industries that face cyclical demand patterns. For example:

- The automobile industry may have a period of high demand due to low interest rates or a period of low demand due to a recession.
- The semiconductor industry may have a period of high demand if companies update employee computers or a period of low demand if companies downsize.

Consider Stassen's master budget for 2014, based on production of 8,000 telescopes per year. Despite using this master-budget capacity-utilization level of 8,000 telescopes for 2014, top management believes that over the next three years the normal (average) annual production level will be 10,000 telescopes. It views 2014's budgeted production level of 8,000 telescopes to be "abnormally" low because a major competitor has been sharply reducing its selling price and spending a lot of money on advertising. Stassen expects that the competitor's lower price and advertising blitz will not be a long-run phenomenon and that, by 2015 and beyond, Stassen's production and sales will be higher.

Effect on Budgeted Fixed Manufacturing Cost Rate

We now illustrate how each of these four denominator levels affects the budgeted fixed manufacturing cost rate. Stassen has budgeted (standard) fixed manufacturing overhead costs of $1,080,000 for 2014. This lump-sum is incurred to provide the capacity to produce telescopes. The amount includes, among other costs, leasing costs for the facility and the compensation of the facility managers. The budgeted fixed manufacturing cost rates for 2014 for each of the four capacity-level concepts are as follows:

Denominator-Level Capacity Concept (1)	Budgeted Fixed Manufacturing Costs per Year (2)	Budget Capacity Level (in units) (3)	Budgeted Fixed Manufacturing Cost per Unit (4) = (2)/(3)
Theoretical capacity	$1,080,000	18,000	$ 60
Practical capacity	$1,080,000	12,000	$ 90
Normal capacity utilization	$1,080,000	10,000	$108
Master-budget capacity utilization	$1,080,000	8,000	$135

The significant difference in cost rates (from $60 to $135) arises because of large differences in budgeted capacity levels under the different capacity concepts.

Budgeted (standard) variable manufacturing cost is $200 per unit. The total budgeted (standard) manufacturing cost per unit for alternative capacity-level concepts is as follows:

Denominator-Level Capacity Concept (1)	Budgeted Variable Manufacturing Cost per Unit (2)	Budgeted Fixed Manufacturing Cost per Unit (3)	Budgeted Total Manufacturing Cost per Unit (4) = (2) + (3)
Theoretical capacity	$200	$ 60	$260
Practical capacity	$200	$ 90	$290
Normal capacity utilization	$200	$108	$308
Master-budget capacity utilization	$200	$135	$335

Because different denominator-level capacity concepts yield different budgeted fixed manufacturing costs per unit, Stassen must decide which capacity level to use. Stassen is not required to use the same capacity-level concept, say, for management planning and control, external reporting to shareholders, and income tax purposes.

Decision Point

What are the various capacity levels a company can use to compute the budgeted fixed manufacturing cost rate?

Choosing a Capacity Level

Learning Objective 6

Examine the key factors in choosing a capacity level to compute the budgeted fixed manufacturing cost rate

...managers must consider the effect a capacity level has on product costing, pricing decisions, performance evaluation, and financial and tax statements

As we just saw, at the start of each fiscal year, managers determine different denominator levels for the different capacity concepts and calculate different budgeted fixed manufacturing costs per unit. We now discuss different denominator-level choices for different purposes, including (a) product costing and capacity management, (b) pricing, (c) performance evaluation, (d) external reporting, and (e) tax requirements.

Product Costing and Capacity Management

Data from normal costing or standard costing are often used in pricing or product-mix decisions. As the Stassen example illustrates, use of theoretical capacity results in an unrealistically small fixed manufacturing cost per unit because it is based on an idealistic and unattainable level of capacity. Theoretical capacity is rarely used to calculate budgeted fixed manufacturing cost per unit because it departs significantly from the real capacity available to a company.

Many companies favor practical capacity as the denominator to calculate budgeted fixed manufacturing cost per unit. Practical capacity in the Stassen example represents the maximum number of units (12,000) that Stassen can reasonably expect to produce per year for the $1,080,000 it will spend annually on capacity. If Stassen had consistently planned to produce fewer units, say 6,000 telescopes each year, it would have built a smaller plant and incurred lower costs.

Stassen budgets $90 in fixed manufacturing cost per unit based on the $1,080,000 it costs to acquire the capacity to produce 12,000 units. This level of plant capacity is an important strategic decision that managers make well before Stassen uses the capacity and even before Stassen knows how much of the capacity it will actually use. That is, budgeted fixed manufacturing cost of $90 per unit measures the *cost per unit of supplying the capacity*.

Demand for Stassen's telescopes in 2014 is expected to be 8,000 units, which is 4,000 units lower than the practical capacity of 12,000 units. However, it costs Stassen $1,080,000 per year to acquire the capacity to make 12,000 units, so the cost of *supplying* the capacity needed to make 12,000 units is still $90 per unit. The capacity and its cost are fixed *in the short run*; unlike variable costs, the capacity supplied does not automatically reduce to match the capacity needed in 2014. As a result, not all of the capacity supplied at $90 per unit will be needed or used in 2014. Using practical capacity as the denominator level, managers can subdivide the cost of resources supplied into used and unused components. At the supply cost of $90 per unit, the manufacturing resources that Stassen will use equal $720,000 ($90 per unit × 8,000 units). Manufacturing resources that Stassen will not use are $360,000 [$90 per unit × (12,000 − 8,000) units].

Using practical capacity as the denominator level sets the cost of capacity at the cost of supplying the capacity, regardless of the demand for the capacity. Highlighting the cost of capacity acquired but not used directs managers' attention toward managing unused capacity, perhaps by designing new products to fill unused capacity, by leasing unused capacity to others, or by eliminating unused capacity. In contrast, using either of the capacity levels based on the demand for Stassen's telescopes—master-budget capacity utilization or normal capacity utilization—hides the amount of unused capacity. If Stassen had used master-budget capacity utilization as the capacity level, it would have calculated budgeted fixed manufacturing cost per unit as $135 ($1,080,000 ÷ 8,000 units). This calculation does not use data about practical capacity, so it does not separately identify the cost of unused capacity. Note, however, that the cost of $135 per unit includes a charge for unused capacity: It is composed of the $90 fixed manufacturing resource that would be used to produce each unit at practical capacity plus the cost of unused capacity allocated to each unit, $45 per unit ($360,000 ÷ 8,000 units).

From the perspective of long-run product costing, which cost of capacity should Stassen use for pricing purposes or for benchmarking its product cost structure against competitors: $90 per unit based on practical capacity or $135 per unit based on master-budget capacity utilization? Probably the $90 per unit based on practical capacity. Why? Because $90 per unit represents the budgeted cost per unit of only the capacity used to produce the product, and it explicitly excludes the cost of any unused capacity. Stassen's customers will be willing to pay a price that covers the cost of the capacity actually used but will not want to pay for unused capacity that provides no other benefits to them. Customers expect Stassen to manage its unused capacity or to bear the cost of unused capacity, not pass it along to them. Moreover, if Stassen's competitors manage unused capacity more effectively, the cost of capacity in the competitors' cost structures (which guides competitors' pricing decisions) is likely to approach $90. In the next section, we show how using normal capacity utilization or master-budget capacity utilization can result in managers setting selling prices that are not competitive.

Pricing Decisions and the Downward Demand Spiral

The **downward demand spiral** for a company is the continuing reduction in the demand for its products that occurs when competitor prices are not met; as demand drops further, higher and higher unit costs result in greater reluctance to meet competitors' prices.

The easiest way to understand the downward demand spiral is with an example. Assume Stassen uses master-budget capacity utilization of 8,000 units for product costing in 2014. The resulting manufacturing cost is $335 per unit ($200 variable manufacturing cost per unit + $135 fixed manufacturing cost per unit). Assume that in December 2013, a competitor offers to supply a major customer of Stassen (a customer who was expected to purchase 2,000 units in 2014) telescopes at $300 per unit. The Stassen manager doesn't want to show a loss on the account and wants to recoup all costs in the long run, so the manager declines to match the competitor's price. The account is lost. The loss means budgeted fixed manufacturing costs of $1,080,000 will be spread over the remaining master-budget volume of 6,000 units at a rate of $180 per unit ($1,080,000 ÷ 6,000 units).

Suppose yet another Stassen customer, who also accounts for 2,000 units of budgeted volume, receives a bid from a competitor at a price of $350 per unit. The Stassen manager compares this bid with his revised unit cost of $380 ($200 + $180) and declines to match the competition, and the account is lost. Planned output would shrink further to 4,000 units. Budgeted fixed manufacturing cost per unit for the remaining 4,000 telescopes would now be $270 ($1,080,000 ÷ 4,000 units). The following table shows the effect of spreading fixed manufacturing costs over a shrinking amount of master-budget capacity utilization:

Home | Insert | Page Layout | Formulas | Data | Review | View

	A	B	C	D
1	Master-Budget		Budgeted Fixed	
2	Capacity Utilization	Budgeted Variable	Manufacturing	Budgeted Total
3	Denominator Level	Manufacturing Cost	Cost per Unit	Manufacturing
4	(Units)	per Unit	[$1,080,000 ÷ (1)]	Cost per Unit
5	(1)	(2)	(3)	(4) = (2) + (3)
6	8,000	$200	$135	$335
7	6,000	$200	$180	$380
8	4,000	$200	$270	$470
9	3,000	$200	$360	$560

Practical capacity, by contrast, is a stable measure. The use of practical capacity as the denominator to calculate budgeted fixed manufacturing cost per unit avoids the recalculation of unit costs when expected demand levels change because the fixed cost rate is calculated based on *capacity available* rather than *capacity used to meet demand*. Managers who use reported unit costs in a mechanical way to set prices are less likely to promote a downward demand spiral when they use practical capacity than when they use normal capacity utilization or master-budget capacity utilization.

Using practical capacity as the denominator level also gives the manager a more accurate idea of the resources needed and used to produce a unit by excluding the cost of unused capacity. As discussed earlier, the cost of manufacturing resources supplied to produce a telescope is $290 ($200 variable manufacturing cost per unit plus $90 fixed manufacturing cost per unit). This cost is lower than the prices Stassen's competitors offer and would have correctly led the manager to match the prices and retain the accounts (assuming for purposes of this discussion that Stassen has no other costs). If, however, the prices competitors offered were lower than $290 per unit, the Stassen manager would not recover the cost of resources used to supply telescopes. This would signal to the manager that Stassen was noncompetitive even if it had no unused capacity. The only way for Stassen to be profitable and retain customers in the long run would be to reduce its manufacturing cost per unit.[5]

Performance Evaluation

Consider how the choice among normal capacity utilization, master-budget capacity utilization, and practical capacity affects how a company evaluates its marketing manager. Normal capacity utilization is often used as a basis for long-run plans. Normal

[5] The downward demand spiral is currently at work in the traditional landline phone industry. As more telephone customers shift services to wireless or Internet-based options, Verizon and AT&T, the two largest telephone service providers in the United States, are reducing their focus on providing copper-wire telephone service to homes and business. As AT&T told the U.S. Federal Communications Commission, "The business model for legacy phone services is in a death spiral."

capacity utilization depends on the time span selected and the forecasts made for each year. *However, normal capacity utilization is an average that provides no meaningful feedback to the marketing manager for a particular year.* Using normal capacity utilization to judge current performance of a marketing manager is an example of a company misusing a long-run measure for a short-run purpose. The company should use master-budget capacity utilization, rather than normal capacity utilization or practical capacity, to evaluate a marketing manager's performance in the current year because the master budget is the principal short-run planning and control tool. Managers feel more obligated to reach the levels specified in the master budget, which the company should have carefully set in relation to the maximum opportunities for sales in the current year.

When large differences exist between practical capacity and master-budget capacity utilization, several companies (such as Texas Instruments, Polysar, and Sandoz) classify the difference as *planned unused capacity*. One reason for this approach is performance evaluation. Consider our Stassen telescope example. The managers in charge of capacity planning usually do not make pricing decisions. Top management decided to build a production facility with 12,000 units of practical capacity, focusing on demand over the next five years. But Stassen's marketing managers, who are mid-level managers, make the pricing decisions. These marketing managers believe they should be held accountable only for the manufacturing overhead costs related to their potential customer base in 2014. The master-budget capacity utilization suggests a customer base in 2014 of 8,000 units (2/3 of the 12,000 practical capacity). Using responsibility accounting principles (see Chapter 6, pages 215–218), only 2/3 of the budgeted total fixed manufacturing costs ($1,080,000 × 2/3 = $720,000) would be attributed to the fixed capacity costs of meeting 2014 demand. The remaining 1/3 of the numerator ($1,080,000 × 1/3 = $360,000) would be separately shown as the capacity cost of meeting increases in long-run demand expected to occur beyond 2014.[6]

External Reporting

The magnitude of the favorable/unfavorable production-volume variance under absorption costing is affected by the choice of the denominator level used to calculate the budgeted fixed manufacturing cost per unit. Assume the following actual operating information for Stassen in 2014:

	A	B	C
1	Beginning inventory	0	
2	Production	8,000	units
3	Sales	6,000	units
4	Ending inventory	2,000	units
5	Selling price	$ 1,000	per unit
6	Variable manufacturing cost	$ 200	per unit
7	Fixed manufacturing costs	$ 1,080,000	
8	Variable marketing cost	$ 185	per unit sold
9	Fixed marketing costs	$ 1,380,000	

Note that this is the same data used to calculate the income under variable and absorption costing for Stassen in Exhibit 9-1. As before, we assume that there are no price, spending, or efficiency variances in manufacturing costs.

[6] For further discussion, see T. Klammer, *Capacity Measurement and Improvement* (Chicago: Irwin, 1996). This research was facilitated by CAM-I, an organization promoting innovative cost management practices. CAM-I's research on capacity costs explores how companies can identify types of capacity costs that can be reduced (or eliminated) without affecting the required output to meet customer demand. An example is improving processes to successfully eliminate the costs of capacity held in anticipation of handling difficulties due to imperfect coordination with suppliers and customers.

Recall from Chapter 8 the equation used to calculate the production-volume variance:

$$\text{Production-volume variance} = \left(\text{Budgeted fixed manufacturing overhead}\right) - \left(\begin{array}{c}\text{Fixed manufacturing overhead allocated using} \\ \text{budgeted cost per output unit} \\ \text{allowed for actual output produced}\end{array}\right)$$

The four different capacity-level concepts result in four different budgeted fixed manufacturing overhead cost rates per unit. The different rates will result in different amounts of fixed manufacturing overhead costs allocated to the 8,000 units actually produced and different amounts of production-volume variance. Using the budgeted fixed manufacturing costs of $1,080,000 (equal to actual fixed manufacturing costs) and the rates calculated on page 345 for different denominator levels, the production-volume variance computations are as follows:

Production-volume variance (theoretical capacity)	= $1,080,000 − (8,000 units × $60 per unit)
	= $1,080,000 − 480,000
	= $600,000 U
Production-volume variance (practical capacity)	= $1,080,000 − (8,000 units × $90 per unit)
	= $1,080,000 − 720,000
	= $360,000 U
Production-volume variance (normal capacity utilization)	= $1,080,00 − (8,000 units × $108 per unit)
	= $1,080,000 − 864,000
	= $216,000 U
Production-volume variance (master-budget capacity utilization)	= $1,080,000 − (8,000 units × $135 per unit)
	= $1,080,000 − 1,080,000
	= $0

How Stassen disposes of its production-volume variance at the end of the fiscal year will determine the effect this variance has on the company's operating income. We now discuss the three alternative approaches Stassen can use to dispose of the production-volume variance. These approaches were first discussed in Chapter 4 (pages 127–132).

1. **Adjusted allocation-rate approach.** This approach restates all amounts in the general and subsidiary ledgers by using actual rather than budgeted cost rates. Given that actual fixed manufacturing costs are $1,080,000 and actual production is 8,000 units, the recalculated fixed manufacturing cost is $135 per unit ($1,080,000 ÷ 8,000 actual units). Under the adjusted allocation-rate approach, the choice of the capacity level used to calculate the budgeted fixed manufacturing cost per unit has no impact on year-end financial statements. In effect, actual costing is adopted at the end of the fiscal year.
2. **Proration approach.** The underallocated or overallocated overhead is spread among ending balances in Work-in-Process Control, Finished Goods Control, and Cost of Goods Sold. The proration restates the ending balances in these accounts to what they would have been if actual cost rates had been used rather than budgeted cost rates. The proration approach also results in the choice of the capacity level used to calculate the budgeted fixed manufacturing cost per unit having no effect on year-end financial statements.
3. **Write-off variances to cost of goods sold approach.** Exhibit 9-7 shows how use of this approach affects Stassen's operating income for 2014. Recall that the ending inventory on December 31, 2014, is 2,000 units. Using master-budget capacity utilization as the denominator level results in assigning the highest amount of fixed manufacturing cost per unit to the 2,000 units in ending inventory (see the line item "deduct ending inventory" in Exhibit 9-7). Accordingly, operating income is highest using master-budget capacity utilization. The differences in operating income for the four denominator-level

concepts in Exhibit 9-7 are due to these different amounts of fixed manufacturing overhead being inventoried at the end of 2014:

Fixed Manufacturing Overhead in December 31, 2014, Inventory	
Theoretical capacity	2,000 units × \$60 per unit = \$120,000
Practical capacity	2,000 units × \$90 per unit = \$180,000
Normal capacity utilization	2,000 units × \$108 per unit = \$216,000
Master-budget capacity utilization	2,000 units × \$135 per unit = \$270,000

In Exhibit 9-7, for example, the \$54,000 difference (\$1,500,000 – \$1,446,000) in operating income between master-budget capacity utilization and normal capacity utilization is due to the difference in fixed manufacturing overhead inventoried (\$270,000 – \$216,000).

To summarize, the common factor behind the increasing operating-income numbers in Exhibit 9-4 (page 339) and Exhibit 9-7 is the increasing amount of fixed manufacturing costs incurred that is included in ending inventory. The amount of fixed manufacturing costs inventoried depends on two factors: the number of units in ending inventory and the rate at which fixed manufacturing costs are allocated to each unit. Exhibit 9-4 shows the effect on operating income of increasing the number of units in ending inventory (by increasing production). Exhibit 9-7 shows the effect on operating income of increasing the

Exhibit 9-7 Income-Statement Effects of Using Alternative Capacity-Level Concepts: Stassen Company for 2014

Home Insert Page Layout Formulas Data Review View

	A	B	C	D	E	F	G	H
1		Theoretical Capacity		Practical Capacity		Normal Capacity Utilization		Master-Budget Capacity Utilization
2	Denominator level in units	18,000		12,000		10,000		8,000
3	Revenues[a]	\$6,000,000		\$6,000,000		\$6,000,000		\$6,000,000
4	Cost of goods sold							
5	Beginning inventory	0		0		0		0
6	Variable manufacturing costs[b]	1,600,000		1,600,000		1,600,000		1,600,000
7	Fixed manufacturing costs[c]	480,000		720,000		864,000		1,080,000
8	Cost of goods available for sale	2,080,000		2,320,000		2,464,000		2,680,000
9	Deduct ending inventory[d]	(520,000)		(580,000)		(616,000)		(670,000)
10	Cost of goods sold (at standard cost)	1,560,000		1,740,000		1,848,000		2,010,000
11	Adjustment for production-volume variance	600,000	U	360,000	U	216,000	U	0
12	Cost of goods sold	2,160,000		2,100,000		2,064,000		2,010,000
13	Gross margin	3,840,000		3,900,000		3,936,000		3,990,000
14	Marketing costs[e]	2,490,000		2,490,000		2,490,000		2,490,000
15	Operating income	\$1,350,000		\$1,410,000		\$1,446,000		\$1,500,000
16								
17	[a]\$1,000 × 6,000 units = \$6,000,000			[d]Ending inventory costs:				
18	[b]\$200 × 8,000 units = \$1,600,000			(\$200 + \$60) × 2,000 units = \$520,000				
19	[c]Fixed manufacturing overhead costs:			(\$200 + \$90) × 2,000 units = \$580,000				
20	\$60 × 8,000 units = \$ 480,000			(\$200 + \$108) × 2,000 units = \$616,000				
21	\$90 × 8,000 units = \$ 720,000			(\$200 + \$135) × 2,000 units = \$670,000				
22	\$108 × 8,000 units = \$ 864,000			[e]Marketing costs:				
23	\$135 × 8,000 units = \$1,080,000			\$1,380,000 + (\$185 × 6,000 units) = \$2,490,000				

fixed manufacturing cost allocated per unit (by decreasing the denominator level used to calculate the rate).

Chapter 8 (pages 301–303) discusses the various issues managers and management accountants must consider when deciding whether to prorate the production-volume variance among inventories and cost of goods sold or to simply write off the variance to cost of goods sold. The objective is to write off the portion of the production-volume variance that represents the cost of capacity not used to support the production of output during the period. Determining this amount is almost always a matter of judgment.

Tax Requirements

For tax reporting purposes in the United States, the Internal Revenue Service (IRS) requires companies to assign inventoriable indirect production costs by a "method of allocation which fairly apportions such costs among the various items produced." The IRS accepts approaches that involve the use of either overhead rates (which the IRS terms the "manufacturing burden rate method") or standard costs. Under either approach, U.S. tax reporting requires end-of-period reconciliation between actual and applied indirect costs using the adjusted allocation-rate method or the proration method.[7] More interestingly, under either approach, the IRS permits the use of practical capacity to calculate budgeted fixed manufacturing cost per unit. Further, the production-volume variance generated this way can be deducted for tax purposes in the year in which the cost is incurred. The tax benefits from this policy are evident from Exhibit 9-7. Note that the operating income when the denominator is set to practical capacity (column D, where the production volume variance of $360,000 is written off to cost of goods sold) is lower than those under normal capacity utilization (column F) or master-budget capacity utilization (column H).

Decision Point

What are the major factors managers consider in choosing the capacity level to compute the budgeted fixed manufacturing cost rate?

Planning and Control of Capacity Costs

Learning Objective 7

Understand other issues that play an important role in capacity planning and control

...uncertainty regarding the expected spending on capacity costs and the demand for installed capacity, the role of capacity-related issues in nonmanufacturing areas, and the possible use of activity-based costing techniques in allocating capacity costs

In addition to the issues previously discussed, managers must take a variety of other factors into account when planning capacity levels and in deciding how best to control and assign capacity costs. These other factors include the level of uncertainty about both the expected costs and the expected demand for the installed capacity; the presence of capacity-related issues in nonmanufacturing settings; and the potential use of activity-based costing techniques in allocating capacity costs.

Difficulties in Forecasting Chosen Denominator-Level Concept

Practical capacity measures the available supply of capacity. Managers can usually use engineering studies and human resource considerations (such as worker safety) to obtain a reliable estimate of this denominator level for the budget period. It is more difficult to obtain reliable estimates of demand-side denominator-level concepts, especially longer-term normal capacity utilization figures. For example, many U.S. steel companies in the 1980s believed they were in the downturn of a demand cycle that would have an upturn within two or three years. After all, steel had been a cyclical business in which upturns followed downturns, making the notion of normal capacity utilization appear reasonable. Unfortunately, the steel cycle in the 1980s did not turn up, resulting in some companies and numerous plants closing. The recent global economic slowdown demonstrated the extent to which demand projections could be inaccurate. Consider that in 2006 auto analysts forecast that annual demand in India for cars and passenger vehicles would hit 1.92 million in the year 2009–2010. In early 2009, the forecast for the same period was revised downward to 1.37 million vehicles. Inaccurate forecasts are not exclusive to the auto industry. In April

[7] For example, Section 1.471-11 of the U.S. Internal Revenue Code states, "The proper use of the standard cost method... requires that a taxpayer must reallocate to the goods in ending inventory a pro rata portion of any net negative or net positive overhead variances." Of course, if the variances are not material in amount, they can be expensed (i.e., written off to cost of goods sold), provided the same treatment is carried out in the firm's financial reports.

2013, the world's largest miner, BHP Billiton, scrapped plans for projects worth $40 billion in Australia to reflect dropping prices for major metals in response to slowing demand from China, the largest commodities consumer. In addition to dealing with economic cycles and inaccurate forecasts, companies also face the problem of marketing managers who may overestimate their ability to regain lost sales and market share. Their estimate of "normal" demand for their product may consequently be based on an overly optimistic outlook. Master-budget capacity utilization focuses only on the expected demand for the next year. Therefore, companies can more reliably estimate master-budget capacity utilization than normal capacity utilization. However, master-budget capacity utilization is still just a forecast, and the true demand realization can be either higher or lower than this estimate.

It is important to understand that costing systems, such as normal costing or standard costing, do not recognize uncertainty the way managers recognize it. A single amount, rather than a range of possible amounts, is used as the denominator level when calculating the budgeted fixed manufacturing cost per unit in absorption costing. Consider Stassen's facility, which has an estimated practical capacity of 12,000 units. The estimated master-budget capacity utilization for 2014 is 8,000 units. However, there is still substantial doubt about the actual number of units Stassen will have to manufacture in 2014 and in future years. Managers recognize uncertainty in their capacity-planning decisions. Stassen built its current plant with a 12,000-unit practical capacity in part to provide the capability to meet possible demand surges. Even if such surges do not occur in a given period, do not conclude that capacity unused in a given period is wasted resources. The gains from meeting sudden demand surges may well require having unused capacity in some periods.

Difficulties in Forecasting Fixed Manufacturing Costs

The fixed manufacturing cost rate is based on a numerator (budgeted fixed manufacturing costs) and a denominator (some measure of capacity or capacity utilization). Our discussion so far has emphasized issues concerning the choice of the denominator. Challenging issues also arise in measuring the numerator. For example, deregulation of the U.S. electric utility industry has resulted in many electric utilities becoming unprofitable. This situation has led to write-downs in the values of the utilities' plants and equipment. The write-downs reduce the numerator because there is less depreciation expense included in the calculation of fixed capacity cost per kilowatt-hour of electricity produced. The difficulty that managers face in this situation is that the amount of write-downs is not clear-cut but, rather, a matter of judgment. In several industries, the increased emphasis on sustainability and attention to the environment has led to unexpected increases in the fixed costs of operations. On the other hand, infrastructure costs for information technology have continued to plummet and have moved from fixed to variable costs in many cases because of the capabilities offered by providers such as Amazon Web Services.

Nonmanufacturing Costs

Capacity costs also arise in nonmanufacturing parts of the value chain. Stassen may acquire a fleet of vehicles capable of distributing the practical capacity of its production facility. When actual production is below practical capacity, there will be unused-capacity cost issues with the distribution function, as well as with the manufacturing function.

As you saw in Chapter 8, capacity cost issues are prominent in many service-sector companies, such as airlines, hospitals, and railroads—even though these companies carry no inventory and so have no inventory costing problems. For example, in calculating the fixed overhead cost per patient-day in its obstetrics and gynecology department, a hospital must decide which denominator level to use: practical capacity, normal capacity utilization, or master-budget capacity utilization. The hospital's decision may have implications for capacity management, as well as pricing and performance evaluation.

Activity-Based Costing

To maintain simplicity, the Stassen example in this chapter assumed that all costs were either variable or fixed. In particular, there were no batch-level costs and no product-sustaining costs. It is easy to see that the distinction between variable and absorption costing carries over directly into activity-based costing systems, with batch-level costs acting as variable costs and product-sustaining ones as fixed costs, as a function of the number of units produced.

In order to focus on the choice of denominator to calculate the budgeted fixed manufacturing cost rate, our Stassen example assumed that all fixed manufacturing costs had a single cost driver: telescope units produced. As you saw in Chapter 5, activity-based costing systems have multiple overhead cost pools at the output-unit, batch, product-sustaining, and facility-sustaining levels—each with its own cost driver. In calculating activity cost rates (for fixed costs of setups and material handling, say), management must choose a capacity level for the quantity of the cost driver (setup-hours or loads moved). Should management use practical capacity, normal capacity utilization, or master-budget capacity utilization? For all the reasons described in this chapter (such as pricing and capacity management), most proponents of activity-based costing argue that managers should use practical capacity as the denominator level to calculate activity cost rates.

Decision Point

What issues must managers take into account when planning capacity levels and for assigning capacity costs?

Problem for Self-Study

Assume Stassen Company on January 1, 2014, decides to contract with another company to preassemble a large percentage of the components of its telescopes. The revised manufacturing cost structure during the 2014–2015 period is as follows:

Variable manufacturing cost per unit produced	
Direct materials	$ 250
Direct manufacturing labor	20
Manufacturing overhead	5
Total variable manufacturing cost per unit produced	$ 275
Fixed manufacturing costs	$480,000

Under the revised cost structure, a larger percentage of Stassen's manufacturing costs are variable for units produced. The denominator level of production used to calculate budgeted fixed manufacturing cost per unit in 2014 and 2015 is 8,000 units. Assume no other change from the data underlying Exhibits 9-1 and 9-2. Summary information pertaining to absorption-costing operating income and variable-costing operating income with this revised cost structure are as follows:

	2014	2015
Absorption-costing operating income	$1,500,000	$1,560,000
Variable-costing operating income	1,380,000	1,650,000
Difference	$ 120,000	$ (90,000)

Required

1. Compute the budgeted fixed manufacturing cost per unit in 2014 and 2015.
2. Explain the difference between absorption-costing operating income and variable-costing operating income in 2014 and 2015, focusing on fixed manufacturing costs in beginning and ending inventory.
3. Why are these differences smaller than the differences in Exhibit 9-2?
4. Assume the same preceding information, except that for 2014, the master-budget capacity utilization is 10,000 units instead of 8,000. How would Stassen's absorption-costing income for 2014 differ from the $1,500,000 shown previously? Show your computations.

Solution

1. $$\text{Budgeted fixed manufacturing cost per unit} = \frac{\text{Budgeted fixed manufacturing costs}}{\text{Budgeted production units}}$$

$$= \frac{\$480{,}000}{8{,}000 \text{ units}}$$

$$= \$60 \text{ per unit}$$

2. $$\text{Absorption-costing operating income} - \text{Variable-costing operating income} = \text{Fixed manufacturing costs in ending inventory under absorption costing} - \text{Fixed manufacturing costs in beginning inventory under absorption costing}$$

2014: $\$1{,}500{,}000 - \$1{,}380{,}000 = (\$60 \text{ per unit} \times 2{,}000 \text{ units}) - (\$60 \text{ per unit} \times 0 \text{ units})$

$\$120{,}000 = \$120{,}000$

2015: $\$1{,}560{,}000 - \$1{,}650{,}000 = (\$60 \text{ per unit} \times 500 \text{ units}) - (\$60 \text{ per unit} \times 2{,}000 \text{ units})$

$-\$90{,}000 = -\$90{,}000$

3. Subcontracting a large part of manufacturing has greatly reduced the magnitude of fixed manufacturing costs. This reduction, in turn, means differences between absorption costing and variable costing are much smaller than in Exhibit 9-2.
4. Given the higher master-budget capacity utilization level of 10,000 units, the budgeted fixed manufacturing cost rate for 2014 is now as follows:

$$\frac{\$480{,}000}{10{,}000 \text{ units}} = \$48 \text{ per unit}$$

The manufacturing cost per unit is \$323 (\$275 + \$48). So, the production-volume variance for 2014 is

$$(10{,}000 \text{ units} - 8{,}000 \text{ units}) \times \$48 \text{ per unit} = \$96{,}000 \text{ U}$$

The absorption-costing income statement for 2014 is as follows:

Revenues: \$1,000 per unit × 6,000 units	\$6,000,000
Cost of goods sold:	
Beginning inventory	0
Variable manufacturing costs: \$275 per unit × 8,000 units	2,200,000
Fixed manufacturing costs: \$48 per unit × 8,000 units	384,000
Cost of goods available for sale	2,584,000
Deduct ending inventory: \$323 per unit × 2,000 units	(646,000)
Cost of goods sold (at standard costs)	1,938,000
Adjustment for production-volume variance	96,000 U
Cost of goods sold	2,034,000
Gross margin	3,966,000
Marketing costs: \$1,380,000 fixed + (\$185 per unit × 6,000 units sold)	2,490,000
Operating income	\$1,476,000

The higher denominator level used to calculate the budgeted fixed manufacturing cost per unit means that fewer fixed manufacturing costs are inventoried (\$48 per unit × 2,000 units = \$96,000) than when the master-budget capacity utilization was 8,000 units (\$60 per unit × 2,000 units = \$120,000). This difference of \$24,000 (\$120,000 − \$96,000) results in operating income being lower by \$24,000 relative to the prior calculated income level of \$1,500,000.

Decision Points

The following question-and-answer format summarizes the chapter's learning objectives. Each decision presents a key question related to a learning objective. The guidelines are the answer to that question.

Decision	Guidelines
1. How does variable costing differ from absorption costing?	Variable costing and absorption costing differ in only one respect: how to account for fixed manufacturing costs. Under variable costing, fixed manufacturing costs are excluded from inventoriable costs and are a cost of the period in which they are incurred. Under absorption costing, fixed manufacturing costs are inventoriable and become a part of cost of goods sold in the period when sales occur.
2. How does income differ under variable and absorption costing?	The variable-costing income statement is based on the contribution-margin format. Under it, operating income is driven by the unit level of sales. Under absorption costing, the income statement follows the gross-margin format. Operating income is driven by the unit level of production, the unit level of sales, and the denominator level used for assigning fixed costs.
3. Why might managers build up finished goods inventory if they use absorption costing?	When absorption costing is used, managers can increase current operating income by producing more units for inventory. Producing for inventory absorbs more fixed manufacturing costs into inventory and reduces costs expensed in the period. Critics of absorption costing label this manipulation of income as the major negative consequence of treating fixed manufacturing costs as inventoriable costs.
4. How does throughput costing differ from variable costing and absorption costing?	Throughput costing treats all costs except direct materials as costs of the period in which they are incurred. Throughput costing results in a lower amount of manufacturing costs being inventoried than either variable or absorption costing.
5. What are the various capacity levels a company can use to compute the budgeted fixed manufacturing cost rate?	Capacity levels can be measured in terms of capacity supplied—theoretical capacity or practical capacity. Capacity can also be measured in terms of output demanded—normal capacity utilization or master-budget capacity utilization.
6. What are the major factors managers consider in choosing the capacity level to compute the budgeted fixed manufacturing cost rate?	The major factors managers consider in choosing the capacity level to compute the budgeted fixed manufacturing cost rate are (a) effect on product costing and capacity management, (b) effect on pricing decisions, (c) effect on performance evaluation, (d) effect on financial statements, and (e) regulatory requirements.
7. What issues must managers take into account when planning capacity levels and for assigning capacity costs?	Critical factors when planning capacity levels and for assigning capacity costs include the uncertainty about the expected spending on capacity costs and the demand for the installed capacity; the role of capacity-related issues in nonmanufacturing areas; and the possible use of activity-based costing techniques in allocating capacity costs.

Appendix

Breakeven Points in Variable Costing and Absorption Costing

Chapter 3 introduced cost-volume-profit analysis. If variable costing is used, the breakeven point (that's where operating income is $0) is computed in the usual manner. There is only one breakeven point in this case, and it depends on (1) fixed (manufacturing and operating) costs and (2) contribution margin per unit.

The formula for computing the breakeven point under variable costing is a special case of the more general target operating income formula from Chapter 3 (page 73):

$$\text{Let } Q = \text{Number of units sold to earn the target operating income}$$

$$\text{Then } Q = \frac{\text{Total fixed costs} + \text{Target operating income}}{\text{Contribution margin per unit}}$$

Breakeven occurs when the target operating income is $0. In our Stassen illustration for 2014 (see Exhibit 9-1, page 332):

$$Q = \frac{(\$1{,}080{,}000 + \$1{,}380{,}000) + \$0}{(\$1{,}000 - (\$200 + \$185))} = \frac{\$2{,}460{,}000}{\$615}$$

$$= 4{,}000 \text{ units}$$

We now verify that Stassen will achieve breakeven under variable costing by selling 4,000 units:

Revenues, $1,000 × 4,000 units	$4,000,000
Variable costs, $385 × 4,000 units	1,540,000
Contribution margin, $615 × 4,000 units	2,460,000
Fixed costs	2,460,000
Operating income	$ 0

If absorption costing is used, the required number of units to be sold to earn a specific target operating income is not unique because of the number of variables involved. The following formula shows the factors that will affect the target operating income under absorption costing:

$$Q = \frac{\begin{matrix}\text{Total} \\ \text{fixed} \\ \text{costs}\end{matrix} + \begin{matrix}\text{Target} \\ \text{operating} \\ \text{income}\end{matrix} + \left[\begin{matrix}\text{Fixed} \\ \text{manufacturing} \\ \text{cost rate}\end{matrix} \times \left(\begin{matrix}\text{Breakeven} \\ \text{sales} \\ \text{in units}\end{matrix} - \begin{matrix}\text{Units} \\ \text{produced}\end{matrix}\right)\right]}{\text{Contribution margin per unit}}$$

In this formula, the numerator is the sum of three terms (from the perspective of the two "+" signs), compared with two terms in the numerator of the variable-costing formula stated earlier. The additional term in the numerator under absorption costing is as follows:

$$\left[\begin{matrix}\text{Fixed manufacturing} \\ \text{cost rate}\end{matrix} \times \left(\begin{matrix}\text{Breakeven sales} \\ \text{in units}\end{matrix} - \begin{matrix}\text{Units} \\ \text{produced}\end{matrix}\right)\right]$$

This term reduces the fixed costs that need to be recovered when units produced exceed the breakeven sales quantity. When production exceeds the breakeven sales quantity, some of the fixed manufacturing costs that are expensed under variable costing are not expensed under absorption costing; they are instead included in finished goods inventory. The breakeven sales quantity under absorption costing is correspondingly lower than under variable costing.[8]

[8] The reverse situation, where production is lower than the breakeven sales quantity, is not possible unless the firm has opening inventory. In that case, provided the variable manufacturing cost per unit and the fixed manufacturing cost rate are constant over time, the breakeven formula given is still valid. The breakeven sales quantity under absorption costing would then exceed that under variable costing.

For Stassen Company in 2014, suppose that actual production is 5,280 units. Then one breakeven point, Q, under absorption costing is as follows:

$$Q = \frac{(\$1{,}080{,}000 + \$1{,}380{,}000) + \$0 + [\$135 \times (Q - 5{,}280)]}{(\$1{,}000 - (\$200 + \$185))}$$

$$= \frac{(\$2{,}460{,}000 + \$135Q - \$712{,}800)}{\$615}$$

$$\$615Q = \$1{,}747{,}200 + \$135Q$$

$$\$480Q = \$1{,}747{,}200$$

$$Q = 3{,}640$$

We next verify that production of 5,280 units and sales of 3,640 units will lead Stassen to break even under absorption costing:

Revenues, $1,000 × 3,640 units		$3,640,000
Cost of goods sold:		
Cost of goods sold at standard cost, $335 × 3,640 units	$1,219,400	
Production-volume variance, $135 × (8,000 − 5,280) units	367,200 U	1,586,600
Gross margin		2,053,400
Marketing costs:		
Variable marketing costs, $185 × 3,640 units	673,400	
Fixed marketing costs	1,380,000	2,053,400
Operating income		$ 0

The breakeven point under absorption costing depends on (1) fixed manufacturing costs, (2) fixed operating (marketing) costs, (3) contribution margin per unit, (4) unit level of production, and (5) the capacity level chosen as the denominator to set the fixed manufacturing cost rate. For Stassen in 2014, a combination of 3,640 units sold, fixed manufacturing costs of $1,080,000, fixed marketing costs of $1,380,000, contribution margin per unit of $615, an 8,000-unit denominator level, and production of 5,280 units would result in an operating income of $0. *Note, however, that there are many combinations of these five factors that would give an operating income of $0.* For example, holding all other factors constant, a combination of 6,240 units produced and 3,370 units sold also results in an operating income of $0 under absorption costing. We provide verification of this alternative breakeven point next:

Revenues, $1,000 × 3,370 units		$3,370,000
Cost of goods sold:		
Cost of goods sold at standard cost, $335 × 3,370 units	$1,128,950	
Production-volume variance, $135 × (8,000 − 6,240) units	237,600 U	1,366,550
Gross margin		2,003,450
Marketing costs:		
Variable marketing costs, $185 × 3,370 units	623,450	
Fixed marketing costs	1,380,000	2,003,450
Operating income		$ 0

Suppose actual production in 2014 was equal to the denominator level, 8,000 units, and there were no units sold and no fixed marketing costs. All the units produced would be placed in inventory, so all the fixed manufacturing costs would be included in inventory. There would be no production-volume variance. Under these conditions, the company could break even under absorption costing with no sales whatsoever! In contrast, under variable costing, the operating loss would be equal to the fixed manufacturing costs of $1,080,000.

Terms to Learn

This chapter and the Glossary at the end of the book contain definitions of the following important terms:

absorption costing **(p. 330)**
direct costing **(p. 329)**
downward demand spiral **(p. 346)**
master-budget capacity utilization **(p. 344)**
normal capacity utilization **(p. 344)**
practical capacity **(p. 344)**
super-variable costing **(p. 341)**
theoretical capacity **(p. 343)**
throughput costing **(p. 341)**
variable costing **(p. 329)**

Assignment Material

MyAccountingLab

Questions

9-1 Differences in operating income between variable costing and absorption costing are due solely to accounting for fixed costs. Do you agree? Explain.

9-2 Why is the term *direct costing* a misnomer?

9-3 Do companies in either the service sector or the merchandising sector make choices about absorption costing versus variable costing?

9-4 Explain the main conceptual issue under variable costing and absorption costing regarding the timing for the release of fixed manufacturing overhead as expense.

9-5 "Companies that make no variable-cost/fixed-cost distinctions must use absorption costing, and those that do make variable-cost/fixed-cost distinctions must use variable costing." Do you agree? Explain.

9-6 The main trouble with variable costing is that it ignores the increasing importance of fixed costs in manufacturing companies. Do you agree? Why?

9-7 Give an example of how, under absorption costing, operating income could fall even though the unit sales level rises.

9-8 What are the factors that affect the breakeven point under (a) variable costing and (b) absorption costing?

9-9 Critics of absorption costing have increasingly emphasized its potential for leading to undesirable incentives for managers. Give an example.

9-10 What are two ways of reducing the negative aspects associated with using absorption costing to evaluate the performance of a plant manager?

9-11 What denominator-level capacity concepts emphasize the output a plant can supply? What denominator-level capacity concepts emphasize the output customers demand for products produced by a plant?

9-12 Describe the downward demand spiral and its implications for pricing decisions.

9-13 Will the financial statements of a company always differ when different choices at the start of the accounting period are made regarding the denominator-level capacity concept?

9-14 What is the IRS's requirement for tax reporting regarding the choice of a denominator-level capacity concept?

9-15 "The difference between practical capacity and master-budget capacity utilization is the best measure of management's ability to balance the costs of having too much capacity and having too little capacity." Do you agree? Explain.

MyAccountingLab

Exercises

9-16 Variable and absorption costing, explaining operating-income differences. Nascar Motors assembles and sells motor vehicles and uses standard costing. Actual data relating to April and May 2014 are as follows:

	A	B	C	D
1		**April**		**May**
2	Unit data			
3	Beginning inventory	0		150
4	Production	500		400
5	Sales	350		520
6	Variable costs			
7	Manufacturing cost per unit produced	$ 10,000		$ 10,000
8	Operating (marketing) cost per unit sold	3,000		3,000
9	Fixed costs			
10	Manufacturing costs	$2,000,000		$2,000,000
11	Operating (marketing) costs	600,000		600,000

The selling price per vehicle is $24,000. The budgeted level of production used to calculate the budgeted fixed manufacturing cost per unit is 500 units. There are no price, efficiency, or spending variances. Any production-volume variance is written off to cost of goods sold in the month in which it occurs.

Required

1. Prepare April and May 2014 income statements for Nascar Motors under (a) variable costing and (b) absorption costing.
2. Prepare a numerical reconciliation and explanation of the difference between operating income for each month under variable costing and absorption costing.

9-17 Throughput costing (continuation of 9-16). The variable manufacturing costs per unit of Nascar Motors are as follows:

	A	B	C
1		**April**	**May**
7	Direct material cost per unit	$6,700	$6,700
8	Direct manufacturing labor cost per unit	1,500	1,500
9	Manufacturing overhead cost per unit	1,800	1,800

Required

1. Prepare income statements for Nascar Motors in April and May 2014 under throughput costing.
2. Contrast the results in requirement 1 with those in requirement 1 of Exercise 9-16.
3. Give one motivation for Nascar Motors to adopt throughput costing.

9-18 Variable and absorption costing, explaining operating-income differences. Crystal Clear Corporation manufactures and sells 50-inch television sets and uses standard costing. Actual data relating to January, February, and March 2014 are as follows:

	January	February	March
Unit data			
Beginning inventory	0	100	100
Production	1,400	1,375	1,430
Sales	1,300	1,375	1,455
Variable costs			
Manufacturing cost per unit produced	$ 950	$ 950	$ 950
Operating (marketing) cost per unit sold	$ 725	$ 725	$ 725
Fixed costs			
Manufacturing costs	$490,000	$490,000	$490,000
Operating (marketing) costs	$120,000	$120,000	$120,000

The selling price per unit is $3,500. The budgeted level of production used to calculate the budgeted fixed manufacturing cost per unit is 1,400 units. There are no price, efficiency, or spending variances. Any production-volume variance is written off to cost of goods sold in the month in which it occurs.

1. Prepare income statements for Crystal Clear in January, February, and March 2014 under (a) variable costing and (b) absorption costing.
2. Explain the difference in operating income for January, February, and March under variable costing and absorption costing.

9-19 Throughput costing (continuation of 9-18). The variable manufacturing costs per unit of Crystal Clear Corporation are as follows:

	January	February	March
Direct material cost per unit	$550	$550	$550
Direct manufacturing labor cost per unit	175	175	175
Manufacturing overhead cost per unit	225	225	225
	$950	$950	$950

Required

1. Prepare income statements for Crystal Clear in January, February, and March 2014 under throughput costing.
2. Contrast the results in requirement 1 with those in requirement 1 of Exercise 9-18.
3. Give one motivation for Crystal Clear to adopt throughput costing.

9-20 Variable versus absorption costing. The Zwatch Company manufactures trendy, high-quality, moderately priced watches. As Zwatch's senior financial analyst, you are asked to recommend a method of inventory costing. The CFO will use your recommendation to prepare Zwatch's 2014 income statement. The following data are for the year ended December 31, 2014:

Beginning inventory, January 1, 2014	85,000 units
Ending inventory, December 31, 2014	34,500 units
2014 sales	345,400 units
Selling price (to distributor)	$22.00 per unit
Variable manufacturing cost per unit, including direct materials	$5.10 per unit
Variable operating (marketing) cost per unit sold	$1.10 per unit sold
Fixed manufacturing costs	$1,440,000
Denominator-level machine-hours	6,000
Standard production rate	50 units per machine-hour
Fixed operating (marketing) costs	$1,080,000

Required

Assume standard costs per unit are the same for units in beginning inventory and units produced during the year. Also, assume no price, spending, or efficiency variances. Any production-volume variance is written off to cost of goods sold in the month in which it occurs.

1. Prepare income statements under variable and absorption costing for the year ended December 31, 2014.
2. What is Zwatch's operating income as percentage of revenues under each costing method?
3. Explain the difference in operating income between the two methods.
4. Which costing method would you recommend to the CFO? Why?

9-21 Absorption and variable costing. (CMA) Osawa, Inc., planned and actually manufactured 200,000 units of its single product in 2014, its first year of operation. Variable manufacturing cost was $20 per unit produced. Variable operating (nonmanufacturing) cost was $10 per unit sold. Planned and actual fixed manufacturing costs were $600,000. Planned and actual fixed operating (nonmanufacturing) costs totaled $400,000. Osawa sold 120,000 units of product at $40 per unit.

Required

1. Osawa's 2014 operating income using absorption costing is (a) $440,000, (b) $200,000, (c) $600,000, (d) $840,000, or (e) none of these. Show supporting calculations.
2. Osawa's 2014 operating income using variable costing is (a) $800,000, (b) $440,000, (c) $200,000, (d) $600,000, or (e) none of these. Show supporting calculations.

9-22 Absorption versus variable costing. Regina Company manufacturers a professional-grade vacuum cleaner and began operations in 2014. For 2014, Regina budgeted to produce and sell 20,000 units. The company had no price, spending, or efficiency variances and writes off production-volume variance to cost of goods sold. Actual data for 2014 are given as follows:

Home | Insert | Page Layout | Formulas | Data

	A	B
1	Units produced	18,000
2	Units sold	17,500
3	Selling price	$ 450
4	Variable costs:	
5	Manufacturing cost per unit produced	
6	Direct materials	$ 30
7	Direct manufacturing labor	25
8	Manufacturing overhead	60
9	Marketing cost per unit sold	45
10	Fixed costs:	
11	Manufacturing costs	$1,200,000
12	Administrative costs	965,450
13	Marketing	1,366,400

1. Prepare a 2014 income statement for Regina Company using variable costing.
2. Prepare a 2014 income statement for Regina Company using absorption costing.
3. Explain the differences in operating incomes obtained in requirements 1 and 2.
4. Regina's management is considering implementing a bonus for the supervisors based on gross margin under absorption costing. What incentives will this bonus plan create for the supervisors? What modifications could Regina management make to improve such a plan? Explain briefly.

Required

9-23 Variable and absorption costing, sales, and operating-income changes. Smart Safety, a three-year-old company, has been producing and selling a single type of bicycle helmet. Smart Safety uses standard costing. After reviewing the income statements for the first three years, Stuart Weil, president of Smart Safety, commented, "I was told by our accountants—and in fact, I have memorized—that our breakeven volume is 52,000 units. I was happy that we reached that sales goal in each of our first two years. But here's the strange thing: In our first year, we sold 52,000 units and indeed we broke even. Then in our second year we sold the same volume and had a positive operating income. I didn't complain, of course... but here's the bad part. In our third year, we *sold 20% more* helmets, but our *operating income fell by more than 80%* relative to the second year! We didn't change our selling price or cost structure over the past three years and have no price, efficiency, or spending variances... so what's going on?!"

	A	B	C	D
1	**Absorption Costing**			
2		**2013**	**2014**	**2015**
3	Sales (units)	52,000	52,000	62,400
4	Revenues	$2,236,000	$2,236,000	$2,683,200
5	Cost of goods sold			
6	Beginning inventory	0	0	405,600
7	Production	2,028,000	2,433,600	2,028,000
8	Available for sale	2,028,000	2,433,600	2,433,600
9	Deduct ending inventory	0	(405,600)	0
10	Adjustment for production-volume variance	0	(260,600)	0
11	Cost of goods sold	2,028,000	1,768,000	2,433,600
12	Gross margin	208,000	468,600	249,600
13	Selling and administrative expenses (all fixed)	208,000	208,000	208,000
14	Operating income	$ 0	$ 260,000	$ 41,600
15				
16	Beginning inventory	0	0	10,400
17	Production (units)	52,000	62,400	52,000
18	Sales (units)	52,000	52,000	62,400
19	Ending inventory	0	10,400	0
20	Variable manufacturing cost per unit	$ 14	$ 14	$ 14
21	Fixed manufacturing overhead costs	$1,300,000	$1,300,000	$1,300,000
22	Fixed manuf. costs allocated per unit produced	$ 25	$ 25	$ 25

Required

1. What denominator level is Smart Safety using to allocate fixed manufacturing costs to the bicycle helmets? How is Smart Safety disposing of any favorable or unfavorable production-volume variance at the end of the year? Explain your answer briefly.
2. How did Smart Safety's accountants arrive at the breakeven volume of 52,000 units?
3. Prepare a variable costing-based income statement for each year. Explain the variation in variable costing operating income for each year based on contribution margin per unit and sales volume.
4. Reconcile the operating incomes under variable costing and absorption costing for each year, and use this information to explain to Stuart Weil the positive operating income in 2014 and the drop in operating income in 2015.

9-24 Capacity management, denominator-level capacity concepts. Match each of the following numbered descriptions with one or more of the denominator-level capacity concepts by putting the appropriate letter(s) by each item:

a. Theoretical capacity
b. Practical capacity
c. Normal capacity utilization
d. Master-budget capacity utilization

1. Measures the denominator level in terms of what a plant can supply
2. Is based on producing at full efficiency all the time
3. Represents the expected level of capacity utilization for the next budget period
4. Measures the denominator level in terms of demand for the output of the plant
5. Takes into account seasonal, cyclical, and trend factors
6. Should be used for performance evaluation in the current year
7. Represents an ideal benchmark
8. Highlights the cost of capacity acquired but not used
9. Should be used for long-term pricing purposes
10. Hides the cost of capacity acquired but not used
11. If used as the denominator-level concept, would avoid the restatement of unit costs when expected demand levels change

9-25 Denominator-level problem. Thunder Bolt, Inc., is a manufacturer of the very popular G36 motorcycles. The management at Thunder Bolt has recently adopted absorption costing and is debating which denominator-level concept to use. The G36 motorcycles sell for an average price of \$8,200. Budgeted fixed manufacturing overhead costs for 2014 are estimated at \$6,480,000. Thunder Bolt, Inc., uses subassembly operators that provide component parts. The following are the denominator-level options that management has been considering:

a. Theoretical capacity—based on three shifts, completion of five motorcycles per shift, and a 360-day year—$3 \times 5 \times 360 = 5{,}400$.
b. Practical capacity—theoretical capacity adjusted for unavoidable interruptions, breakdowns, and so forth—$3 \times 4 \times 320 = 3{,}840$.
c. Normal capacity utilization—estimated at 3,240 units.
d. Master-budget capacity utilization—the strengthening stock market and the growing popularity of motorcycles have prompted the marketing department to issue an estimate for 2014 of 3,600 units.

Required

1. Calculate the budgeted fixed manufacturing overhead cost rates under the four denominator-level concepts.
2. What are the benefits to Thunder Bolt, Inc., of using either theoretical capacity or practical capacity?
3. Under a cost-based pricing system, what are the negative aspects of a master-budget denominator level? What are the positive aspects?

9-26 Variable and absorption costing and breakeven points. Artesa, a leading firm in the semiconductor industry, produces digital integrated circuits (ICs) for the communications and defense markets.

For the year ended December 31, 2013, Artesa sold 242,400 ICs at an average selling price of \$47 per unit. The following information also relates to 2013 (assume constant unit costs and no variances of any kind):

Inventory, January 1, 2013:	32,600 ICs
Inventory, December 31, 2013:	24,800 ICs
Fixed manufacturing costs:	\$1,876,800
Fixed administrative costs:	\$3,284,400
Direct materials costs:	\$13 per IC
Direct labor costs:	\$11 per IC

Required

1. How many integrated circuits did Artesa produce in 2013?
2. Calculate the breakeven point (number of ICs sold) in 2013 under:
   a. Variable costing
   b. Absorption costing
3. Due to difficulties in obtaining high-quality silicon, Artesa expects that direct materials costs will increase to \$15 per IC in 2014. Assuming all other data are the same, calculate the minimum number of ICs Artesa must sell in 2014 to break even under:
   a. Variable costing
   b. Absorption costing

9-27 Variable costing versus absorption costing. The Mavis Company uses an absorption-costing system based on standard costs. Total variable manufacturing cost, including direct material cost, is \$3 per unit; the standard production rate is 10 units per machine-hour. Total budgeted and actual fixed manufacturing overhead costs are \$420,000. Fixed manufacturing overhead is allocated at \$7 per machine-hour (\$420,000 ÷ 60,000 machine-hours of denominator level). Selling price is \$5 per unit. Variable operating (nonmanufacturing) cost, which is driven by units sold, is \$1 per unit. Fixed operating (nonmanufacturing) costs are \$120,000. Beginning inventory in 2014 is 30,000 units; ending inventory is 40,000 units. Sales in 2014 are 540,000 units. The same standard unit costs persisted throughout 2013 and 2014. For simplicity, assume that there are no price, spending, or efficiency variances.

Required

1. Prepare an income statement for 2014 assuming that the production-volume variance is written off at year-end as an adjustment to cost of goods sold.
2. The president has heard about variable costing. She asks you to recast the 2014 statement as it would appear under variable costing.
3. Explain the difference in operating income as calculated in requirements 1 and 2.
4. Graph how fixed manufacturing overhead is accounted for under absorption costing. That is, there will be two lines: one for the budgeted fixed manufacturing overhead (which is equal to the actual fixed manufacturing overhead in this case) and one for the fixed manufacturing overhead allocated. Show the production-volume variance in the graph.

5. Critics have claimed that a widely used accounting system has led to undesirable buildups of inventory levels. (a) Is variable costing or absorption costing more likely to lead to such buildups? Why? (b) What can managers do to counteract undesirable inventory buildups?

Problems

9-28 Variable costing and absorption costing, the All-Fixed Company. (R. Marple, adapted) It is the end of 2013. The All-Fixed Company began operations in January 2012. The company is so named because it has no variable costs. All its costs are fixed; they do not vary with output.

The All-Fixed Company is located on the bank of a river and has its own hydroelectric plant to supply power, light, and heat. The company manufactures a synthetic fertilizer from air and river water and sells its product at a price that is not expected to change. It has a small staff of employees, all paid fixed annual salaries. The output of the plant can be increased or decreased by adjusting a few dials on a control panel.

The following budgeted and actual data are for the operations of the All-Fixed Company. All-Fixed uses budgeted production as the denominator level and writes off any production-volume variance to cost of goods sold.

	2012	2013[a]
Sales	10,000 tons	10,000 tons
Production	20,000 tons	0 tons
Selling price	$ 30 per ton	$ 30 per ton
Costs (all fixed):		
Manufacturing	$280,000	$280,000
Operating (nonmanufacturing)	$ 40,000	$ 40,000

[a] Management adopted the policy, effective January 1, 2013, of producing only as much product as needed to fill sales orders. During 2013, sales were the same as for 2012 and were filled entirely from inventory at the start of 2013.

Required

1. Prepare income statements with one column for 2012, one column for 2013, and one column for the two years together using (a) variable costing and (b) absorption costing.
2. What is the breakeven point under (a) variable costing and (b) absorption costing?
3. What inventory costs would be carried in the balance sheet on December 31, 2012 and 2013, under each method?
4. Assume that the performance of the top manager of the company is evaluated and rewarded largely on the basis of reported operating income. Which costing method would the manager prefer? Why?

9-29 Comparison of variable costing and absorption costing. Gammaro Company uses standard costing. Tim Sweeney, the new president of Gammaro Company, is presented with the following data for 2014:

	A	B	C
1	Gammaro Company		
2	Income Statements for the Year Ended December 31, 2014		
3		Variable	Absorption
4		Costing	Costing
5	Revenues	$9,350,000	$9,350,000
6	Cost of goods sold (at standard costs)	4,695,000	5,855,000
7	Fixed manufacturing overhead (budgeted)	1,350,000	-
8	Fixed manufacturing overhead variances (all unfavorable):		
9	Spending	125,000	125,000
10	Production volume	-	405,000
11	Total marketing and administrative costs (all fixed)	1,570,000	1,570,000
12	Total costs	7,740,000	7,955,000
13	Operating income	$1,610,000	$1,395,000
14			
15	Inventories (at standard costs)		
16	December 31, 2013	$1,345,000	$1,730,000
17	December 31, 2014	45,000	215,000

Required

1. At what percentage of denominator level was the plant operating during 2014?
2. How much fixed manufacturing overhead was included in the 2013 and the 2014 ending inventory under absorption costing?
3. Reconcile and explain the difference in 2014 operating incomes under variable and absorption costing.
4. Tim Sweeney is concerned: He notes that despite an increase in sales over 2013, 2014 operating income has actually declined under absorption costing. Explain how this occurred.

9-30 Effects of differing production levels on absorption costing income: Metrics to minimize inventory buildups. Horizon Press produces textbooks for college courses. The company recently hired a new editor, Billie White, to handle production and sales of books for an introduction to accounting course. Billie's compensation depends on the gross margin associated with sales of this book. Billie needs to decide how many copies of the book to produce. The following information is available for the fall semester 2013:

Estimated sales	26,000 books
Beginning inventory	0 books
Average selling price	$ 81 per book
Variable production costs	$ 45 per book
Fixed production costs	$416,000 per semester

The fixed cost allocation rate is based on expected sales and is therefore equal to $416,000/26,000 books = $16 per book.

Billie has decided to produce either 26,000, 32,500, or 33,800 books.

Required

1. Calculate expected gross margin if Billie produces 26,000, 32,500, or 33,800 books. (Make sure you include the production-volume variance as part of cost of goods sold.)
2. Calculate ending inventory in units and in dollars for each production level.
3. Managers who are paid a bonus that is a function of gross margin may be inspired to produce a product in excess of demand to maximize their own bonus. The chapter suggested metrics to discourage managers from producing products in excess of demand. Do you think the following metrics will accomplish this objective? Show your work.
   a. Incorporate a charge of 5% of the cost of the ending inventory as an expense for evaluating the manager.
   b. Include nonfinancial measures (such as the ones recommended on page 340) when evaluating management and rewarding performance.

9-31 Alternative denominator-level capacity concepts, effect on operating income. Castle Lager has just purchased the Jacksonville Brewery. The brewery is two years old and uses absorption costing. It will "sell" its product to Castle Lager at $47 per barrel. Peter Bryant, Castle Lager's controller, obtains the following information about Jacksonville Brewery's capacity and budgeted fixed manufacturing costs for 2014:

Home Insert Page Layout Formulas Data Review View

	A	B	C	D	E
1		Budgeted Fixed	Days of	Hours of	
2	Denominator-Level	Manufacturing	Production	Production	Barrels
3	Capacity Concept	Overhead per Period	per Period	per Day	per Hour
4	Theoretical capacity	$27,900,000	358	22	545
5	Practical capacity	$27,900,000	348	20	510
6	Normal capacity utilization	$27,900,000	348	20	410
7	Master-budget capacity for each half year				
8	(a) January–June 2014	$13,950,000	174	20	315
9	(b) July–December 2014	$13,950,000	174	20	505

Required

1. Compute the budgeted fixed manufacturing overhead rate per barrel for each of the denominator-level capacity concepts. Explain why they are different.

2. In 2014, the Jacksonville Brewery reported these production results:

	A	B
12	Beginning inventory in barrels, 1-1-2014	0
13	Production in barrels	2,670,000
14	Ending inventory in barrels, 12-31-2014	210,000
15	Actual variable manufacturing costs	$80,634,000
16	Actual fixed manufacturing overhead costs	$26,700,000

There are no variable cost variances. Fixed manufacturing overhead cost variances are written off to cost of goods sold in the period in which they occur. Compute the Jacksonville Brewery's operating income when the denominator-level capacity is (a) theoretical capacity, (b) practical capacity, and (c) normal capacity utilization.

9-32 Motivational considerations in denominator-level capacity selection (continuation of 9-31).

Required

1. If the plant manager of the Jacksonville Brewery gets a bonus based on operating income, which denominator-level capacity concept would he prefer to use? Explain.
2. What denominator-level capacity concept would Castle Lager prefer to use for U.S. income-tax reporting? Explain.
3. How might the IRS limit the flexibility of an absorption-costing company like Castle Lager attempting to minimize its taxable income?

9-33 Denominator-level choices, changes in inventory levels, effect on operating income. Donaldson Corporation is a manufacturer of computer accessories. It uses absorption costing based on standard costs and reports the following data for 2014:

	A	B	C
1	Theoretical capacity	275,000	units
2	Practical capacity	265,000	units
3	Normal capacity utilization	233,200	units
4	Selling price	$ 39	per unit
5	Beginning inventory	35,000	units
6	Production	235,000	units
7	Sales volume	250,000	units
8	Variable budgeted manufacturing cost	$ 8	per unit
9	Total budgeted fixed manufacturing costs	$2,915,000	
10	Total budgeted operating (nonmanuf.) costs (all fixed)	$ 200,000	

There are no price, spending, or efficiency variances. Actual operating costs equal budgeted operating costs. The production-volume variance is written off to cost of goods sold. For each choice of denominator level, the budgeted production cost per unit is also the cost per unit of beginning inventory.

Required

1. What is the production-volume variance in 2014 when the denominator level is (a) theoretical capacity, (b) practical capacity, and (c) normal capacity utilization?
2. Prepare absorption costing–based income statements for Donaldson Corporation using theoretical capacity, practical capacity, and normal capacity utilization as the denominator levels.
3. Why is the operating income under normal capacity utilization lower than the other two scenarios?
4. Reconcile the difference in operating income based on theoretical capacity and practical capacity with the difference in fixed manufacturing overhead included in inventory.

9-34 Variable and absorption costing and breakeven points. Whistler, Inc., manufactures a specialized snowboard made for the advanced snowboarder. Whistler began 2014 with an inventory of 240 snowboards. During the year, it produced 900 boards and sold 995 for $750 each. Fixed production costs were $280,000, and variable production costs were $325 per unit. Fixed advertising, marketing, and other general and administrative expenses were $112,000, and variable shipping costs were $15 per board. Assume that the cost of each unit in beginning inventory is equal to 2014 inventory cost.

Required

1. Prepare an income statement assuming Whistler uses variable costing.
2. Prepare an income statement assuming Whistler uses absorption costing. Whistler uses a denominator level of 1,000 units. Production-volume variances are written off to cost of goods sold.
3. Compute the breakeven point in units sold assuming Whistler uses the following:
   a. Variable costing   b. Absorption costing (Production = 900 boards)

4. Provide proof of your preceding breakeven calculations.
5. Assume that $20,000 of fixed administrative costs were reclassified as fixed production costs. Would this reclassification affect breakeven point using variable costing? What if absorption costing were used? Explain.
6. The company that supplies Whistler with its specialized impact-resistant material has announced a price increase of $30 for each board. What effect would this have on the breakeven points previously calculated?

9-35 Downward demand spiral. Gostkowski Company is about to enter the highly competitive personal electronics market with a new optical reader. In anticipation of future growth, the company has leased a large manufacturing facility and has purchased several expensive pieces of equipment. In 2013, the company's first year, Gostkowski budgets for production and sales of 24,000 units, compared with its practical capacity of 48,000. The company's cost data are as follows:

	A	B
1	Variable manufacturing costs per unit:	
2	Direct materials	$ 20
3	Direct manufacturing labor	35
4	Manufacturing overhead	9
5	Fixed manufacturing overhead	$576,000

Required

1. Assume that Gostkowski uses absorption costing and uses budgeted units produced as the denominator for calculating its fixed manufacturing overhead rate. Selling price is set at 130% of manufacturing cost. Compute Gostkowski's selling price.
2. Gostkowski enters the market with the selling price computed previously. However, despite growth in the overall market, sales are not as robust as the company had expected, and a competitor has priced its product $16 lower than Gostkowski's. Enrico Gostkowski, the company's president, insists that the competitor must be pricing its product at a loss and that the competitor will be unable to sustain that. In response, Gostkowski makes no price adjustments but budgets production and sales for 2014 at 18,000 units. Variable and fixed costs are not expected to change. Compute Gostkowski's new selling price. Comment on how Gostkowski's choice of budgeted production affected its selling price and competitive position.
3. Recompute the selling price using practical capacity as the denominator level of activity. How would this choice have affected Gostkowski's position in the marketplace? Generally, how would this choice affect the production-volume variance?

9-36 Absorption costing and production-volume variance—alternative capacity bases. Planet Light First (PLF), a producer of energy-efficient light bulbs, expects that demand will increase markedly over the next decade. Due to the high fixed costs involved in the business, PLF has decided to evaluate its financial performance using absorption costing income. The production-volume variance is written off to cost of goods sold. The variable cost of production is $2.40 per bulb. Fixed manufacturing costs are $1,170,000 per year. Variable and fixed selling and administrative expenses are $0.20 per bulb sold and $220,000, respectively. Because its light bulbs are currently popular with environmentally conscious customers, PLF can sell the bulbs for $9.80 each.

PLF is deciding among various concepts of capacity for calculating the cost of each unit produced. Its choices are as follows:

Theoretical capacity	900,000 bulbs
Practical capacity	520,000 bulbs
Normal capacity	260,000 bulbs (average expected output for the next three years)
Master budget capacity	225,000 bulbs expected production this year

Required

1. Calculate the inventoriable cost per unit using each level of capacity to compute fixed manufacturing cost per unit.
2. Suppose PLF actually produces 300,000 bulbs. Calculate the production-volume variance using each level of capacity to compute the fixed manufacturing overhead allocation rate.
3. Assume PLF has no beginning inventory. If this year's actual sales are 225,000 bulbs, calculate operating income for PLF using each type of capacity to compute fixed manufacturing cost per unit.

9-37 Operating income effects of denominator-level choice and disposal of production-volume variance (continuation of 9-36).

Required

1. If PLF sells all 300,000 bulbs produced, what would be the effect on operating income of using each type of capacity as a basis for calculating manufacturing cost per unit?

2. Compare the results of operating income at different capacity levels when 225,000 bulbs are sold and when 300,000 bulbs are sold. What conclusion can you draw from the comparison?
3. Using the original data (that is, 300,000 units produced and 225,000 units sold) if PLF had used the proration approach to allocate the production-volume variance, what would operating income have been under each level of capacity? (Assume that there is no ending work in process.)

9-38 Variable and absorption costing, actual costing. The Iron City Company started business on January 1, 2014. Iron City manufactures a specialty honey beer, which it sells directly to state-owned distributors in Pennsylvania. Honey beer is produced and sold in six-packs, and in 2014, Iron City produced more six-packs than it was able to sell. In addition to variable and fixed manufacturing overhead, Iron City incurred direct materials costs of $880,000, direct manufacturing labor costs of $400,000, and fixed marketing and administrative costs of $295,000. For the year, Iron City sold a total of 180,000 six-packs for a sales revenue of $2,250,000.

Iron City's CFO is convinced that the firm should use an actual costing system but is debating whether to follow variable or absorption costing. The controller notes that Iron City's operating income for the year would be $438,000 under variable costing and $461,000 under absorption costing. Moreover, the ending finished goods inventory would be valued at $7.15 under variable costing and $8.30 under absorption costing.

Iron City incurs no variable nonmanufacturing expenses.

Required

1. What is Iron City's total contribution margin for 2014?
2. Iron City incurs fixed manufacturing costs in addition to its fixed marketing and administrative costs. How much did Iron City incur in fixed manufacturing costs in 2014?
3. How many six-packs did Iron City produce in 2014?
4. How much in variable manufacturing overhead did Iron City incur in 2014?
5. For 2014, how much in total manufacturing overhead is expensed under variable costing, either through Cost of Goods Sold or as a period expense?

9-39 Cost allocation, downward demand spiral. Top Catering operates a chain of 10 hospitals in the Los Angeles area. Its central food-catering facility, Topman, prepares and delivers meals to the hospitals. It has the capacity to deliver up to 1,025,000 meals a year. In 2014, based on estimates from each hospital controller, Topman budgeted for 925,000 meals a year. Budgeted fixed costs in 2014 were $1,517,000. Each hospital was charged $6.24 per meal—$4.60 variable costs plus $1.64 allocated budgeted fixed cost.

Recently, the hospitals have been complaining about the quality of Topman's meals and their rising costs. In mid-2014, Top Catering's president announces that all Top Catering hospitals and support facilities will be run as profit centers. Hospitals will be free to purchase quality-certified services from outside the system. Ron Smith, Topman's controller, is preparing the 2015 budget. He hears that three hospitals have decided to use outside suppliers for their meals, which will reduce the 2015 estimated demand to 820,000 meals. No change in variable cost per meal or total fixed costs is expected in 2015.

Required

1. How did Smith calculate the budgeted fixed cost per meal of $1.64 in 2014?
2. Using the same approach to calculating budgeted fixed cost per meal and pricing as in 2014, how much would hospitals be charged for each Topman meal in 2015? What would the reaction of the hospital controllers be to the price?
3. Suggest an alternative cost-based price per meal that Smith might propose and that might be more acceptable to the hospitals. What can Topman and Smith do to make this price profitable in the long run?

9-40 Cost allocation, responsibility accounting, ethics (continuation of 9-39). In 2015, only 740,000 Topman meals were produced and sold to the hospitals. Smith suspects that hospital controllers had systematically inflated their 2015 meal estimates.

Required

1. Recall that Topman uses the master-budget capacity utilization to allocate fixed costs and to price meals. What was the effect of production-volume variance on Topman's operating income in 2015?
2. Why might hospital controllers deliberately overestimate their future meal counts?
3. What other evidence should Top Catering's president seek to investigate Smith's concerns?
4. Suggest two specific steps that Smith might take to reduce hospital controllers' incentives to inflate their estimated meal counts.

9-41 Absorption, variable, and throughput costing. Tesla Motors assembles the fully electric Model S-85 automobile at its Fremont, California, plant. The standard variable manufacturing cost per vehicle in 2014 is $58,800, which consists of:

Direct materials	$36,000
Direct manufacturing labor	$10,800
Variable manufacturing overhead	$12,000

Variable manufacturing overhead is allocated to vehicles on the basis of assembly time. The standard assembly time per vehicle is 20 hours.

The Fremont plant is highly automated and has a practical capacity of 4,000 vehicles per month. The budgeted monthly fixed manufacturing overhead is $45 million. Fixed manufacturing overhead is allocated on the basis of the standard assembly time for the budgeted normal capacity utilization of the plant. For 2014, the budgeted normal capacity utilization is 3,000 vehicles per month.

Tesla started production of the Model S-85 in 2014. The actual production and sales figures for the first three months of the year are:

	January	February	March
Production	3,200	2,400	3,800
Sales	2,000	2,900	3,200

Franz Holzhausen is SVP of Tesla and director of the Fremont plant. His compensation includes a bonus that is 0.25% of quarterly operating income, calculated using absorption costing. Tesla prepares absorption-costing income statements monthly, which include an adjustment for the production-volume variance occurring in that month. There are no variable cost variances or fixed overhead spending variances in the first three months of 2014.

The Fremont plant is credited with revenue (net of marketing costs) of $96,000 for the sale of each Tesla S-85 vehicle.

Required

1. Compute (a) the fixed manufacturing cost per unit and (b) the total manufacturing cost per unit.
2. Compute the monthly operating income for January, February, and March under absorption costing. What amount of bonus is paid each month to Franz Holzhausen?
3. How much would the use of variable costing change Holzhausen's bonus each month if the same 0.25% figure were applied to variable-costing operating income?
4. Explain the differences in Holzhausen's bonuses in requirements 2 and 3.
5. How much would the use of throughput costing change Holzhausen's bonus each month if the same 0.25% figure were applied to throughput-costing operating income?
6. What are the different approaches Tesla Motors could take to reduce possible undesirable behavior associated with the use of absorption costing at its Fremont plant?

9-42 Costing methods and variances, comprehensive. Rob Kapito, the controller of Blackstar Paint Supply Company, has been exploring a variety of internal accounting systems. Rob hopes to get the input of Blackstar's board of directors in choosing one. To prepare for his presentation to the board, Rob applies four different cost accounting methods to the firm's operating data for 2013. The four methods are actual absorption costing, normal absorption costing, standard absorption costing, and standard variable costing.

With the help of a junior accountant, Rob prepares the following alternative income statements:

	A	B	C	D
Sales Revenue	$ 900,000	$ 900,000	$ 900,000	$ 900,000
Cost of Goods Sold	$ 375,000	$ 250,000	$ 420,000	$ 395,000
(+) Variances:				
Direct Materials	15,000	15,000	—	—
Direct Labor	5,000	5,000	—	—
Manufacturing Overhead	25,000	—	—	25,000
(+) Other Costs (All Fixed)	350,000	475,000	350,000	350,000
Total Costs	$ 770,000	$ 745,000	$ 770,000	$ 770,000
Net Income	$ 130,000	$ 155,000	$ 130,000	$ 130,000

Where applicable, Rob allocates both fixed and variable manufacturing overhead using direct labor hours as the driver. Blackstar carries no work-in-process inventory. Standard costs have been stable over time, and Rob writes off all variances to cost of goods sold. For 2013, there was no flexible budget variance for fixed overhead. In addition, the direct labor variance represents a price variance.

Required

1. Match each method below with the appropriate income statement (A, B, C, or D):

   Actual Absorption costing _____
   Normal Absorption costing _____
   Standard Absorption costing _____
   Standard Variable costing _____

2. During 2013, how did Blackstar's level of finished goods inventory change? In other words, is it possible to know whether Blackstar's finished goods inventory increased, decreased, or stayed constant during the year?
3. From the four income statements, can you determine how the actual volume of production during the year compared to the denominator (expected) volume level?
4. Did Blackstar have a favorable or unfavorable variable overhead spending variance during 2013?

10 Determining How Costs Behave

Learning Objectives

1. Describe linear cost functions and three common ways in which they behave
2. Explain the importance of causality in estimating cost functions
3. Understand various methods of cost estimation
4. Outline six steps in estimating a cost function using quantitative analysis
5. Describe three criteria used to evaluate and choose cost drivers
6. Explain nonlinear cost functions, in particular those arising from learning curve effects
7. Be aware of data problems encountered in estimating cost functions

What is the value of looking at the past?

Perhaps it is to recall fond memories of family and friends or help you understand historical events. Maybe recalling the past helps you better understand and predict the future. An organization looks at the past to analyze its performance and make the best decisions for improving its future performance. This activity requires managers to gather information about costs and how they behave so that managers can predict what they will be "down the road." Understanding how costs behave is a valuable technical skill, and the knowledge gained in this process can motivate an organization to reorganize its operations in innovative ways and tackle important challenges. Managers look to management accountants to help them identify cost drivers, estimate cost relationships, and determine the fixed and variable components of costs. To be effective, management accountants must have a clear understanding of the business's strategy in order to identify new opportunities to reduce costs and increase profitability. As the following article shows, management accountants' in-depth understanding of a company's operations can lead to lower costs, while also supporting environmental sustainability.

Cisco Understands Its Costs While Helping the Environment[1]

Can understanding how costs behave contribute to environmental sustainability? At Cisco Systems, an in-depth understanding of the company's costs and operations led to reduced costs, while also helping the environment. Cisco, makers of computer networking equipment including routers and wireless switches, traditionally regarded the used equipment it received back from its business customers as scrap and recycled it at a cost of about $8 million a year. In 2005, Cisco began trying to find uses for the equipment, mainly because 80% of the returns were in working condition.

A value recovery team at Cisco identified groups within the company that could use the returned equipment. These included its customer service group, which supports warranty claims and service contracts, and the labs that provide technical support, training, and product demonstrations. Based on the initial success of the value recovery team, Cisco designated its recycling group as a company business unit, set clear objectives for it, and assigned the group its own income statement. As a result, the reuse of equipment rose from 5% in 2004 to 45% in 2008, and Cisco's recycling costs fell by 40%. By 2010, the company reused or recycled all returned

[1] *Sources:* Cisco Systems, Inc. 2013. *2012 corporate social responsibility report.* San Jose, CA: Cisco Systems, Inc.; Nidumolu, R., C. Prahalad, and M. Rangaswami. 2009. Why sustainability is now the key driver of innovation. *Harvard Business Review,* September.

electronic equipment. The unit has become a profit center that contributed $286 million to Cisco's bottom line in 2012. Beyond recycling, Cisco now reduces costs by cutting energy consumption in its labs—saving $9 million annually—and installing solar panels on its data centers.

As the Cisco example illustrates, managers must understand how costs behave to make strategic and operating decisions that have a positive environmental impact. Consider several other examples. Managers at FedEx decided to replace old planes with new Boeing 757s that reduced fuel consumption by 36%, while increasing capacity by 20%. At Clorox, managers decided to create a new line of non-synthetic cleaning products that were better for the environment and helped create a new category of "green" cleaning products worth about $200 million annually.

In each situation, knowing how costs behave was essential to answer key managerial questions. This chapter will focus on how managers determine cost-behavior patterns—that is, how costs change in relation to changes in activity levels, in the quantity of products produced, and so on.

Basic Assumptions and Examples of Cost Functions

Learning Objective 1

Describe linear cost functions

...graph of cost function is a straight line

and three common ways in which they behave

...variable, fixed, and mixed

Managers are able to understand cost behavior through cost functions, which are the basic building blocks for estimating costs. A **cost function** is a mathematical description of how a cost changes with changes in the level of an activity relating to that cost. Cost functions can be plotted on a graph by measuring the level of an activity, such as number of batches produced or number of machine-hours used, on the horizontal axis (called the x-axis). The amount of total costs corresponding to—or dependent on—the levels of that activity are measured on the vertical axis (called the y-axis).

Basic Assumptions

Managers often estimate cost functions based on two assumptions:

1. Variations in the level of a single activity (the cost driver) explain the variations in the related total costs.
2. Cost behavior is approximated by a linear cost function within the relevant range. Recall from Chapter 2 that a *relevant range* is the range of the activity in which there is a relationship between total cost and the level of activity. For a **linear cost function**, total cost versus the level of a single activity related to that cost is a straight line within the relevant range.

We use these assumptions throughout most, but not all, of this chapter. Not all cost functions are linear and can be explained by a single activity. Later sections will discuss cost functions that do not rely on these assumptions.

Linear Cost Functions

To understand three basic types of linear cost functions and to see the role of cost functions in business decisions, consider the negotiations between StoreBox, a technology startup, and Forest Web Services (FWS) for enterprise-class cloud computing services.

- **Alternative 1:** \$0.50 per CPU hour used. Total cost to StoreBox changes in proportion to the number of CPU hours used. The number of CPU hours used is the only factor whose change causes a change in total cost.

  Panel A in Exhibit 10-1 presents this *variable cost* for StoreBox. Under alternative 1, there is no fixed cost for cloud services. We write the cost function in Panel A of Exhibit 10-1 as

  $$y = \$0.50X$$

  where X measures the number of CPU hours used (on the x-axis) and y measures the total cost of the CPU hours used (on the y-axis), calculated using the cost function. Panel A illustrates the \$0.50 **slope coefficient**, the amount by which total cost changes when a one-unit change occurs in the level of activity (one hour of CPU usage in the StoreBox example). *Throughout the chapter, uppercase letters, such as X, refer to the actual observations, and lowercase letters, such as y, represent estimates or calculations made using a cost function.*

- **Alternative 2:** The total cost will be fixed at \$1,000 per month, regardless of the number of CPU hours used. (We use the same activity measure, number of CPU hours used, to compare cost-behavior patterns under the three alternatives.)

  Panel B in Exhibit 10-1 shows the fixed cost alternative for StoreBox. We write the cost function in Panel B as

  $$y = \$1{,}000$$

  The fixed cost of \$1,000 is called a **constant**; it is the component of the total cost that does not vary with changes in the level of the activity. The constant accounts for all the cost because there is no variable cost. Graphically, the slope coefficient of this cost function is zero; this cost function intersects the y-axis at a constant value. Therefore, the *constant* is also called the **intercept**.

- **Alternative 3:** \$300 per month plus \$0.20 per CPU hour used. This is an example of a mixed cost. A **mixed cost**—also called a **semivariable cost**—is a cost that has both fixed and variable elements.

  Panel C in Exhibit 10-1 shows the mixed cost alternative for StoreBox. We write the cost function in Panel C of Exhibit 10-1 as

  $$y = \$300 + \$0.20X$$

Exhibit 10-1 Examples of Linear Cost Functions

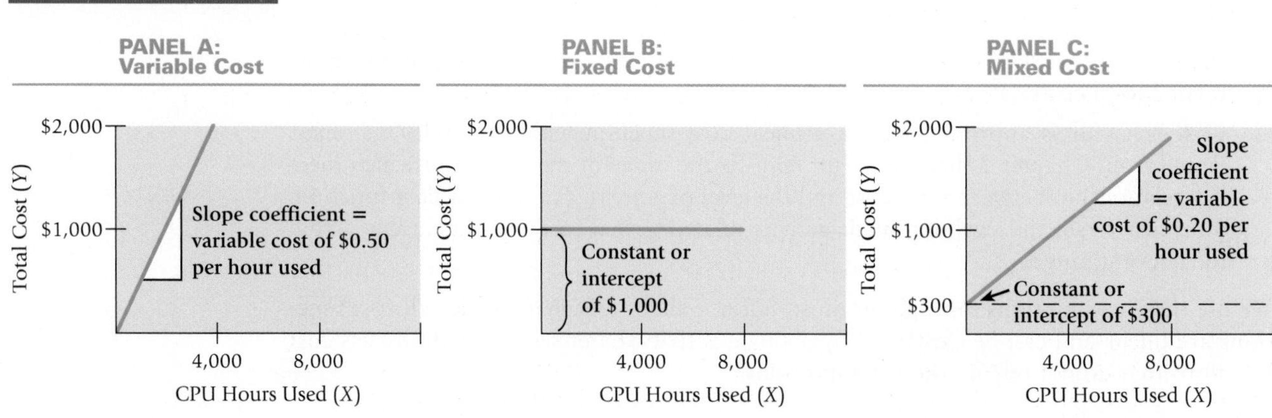

Unlike the graphs for alternatives 1 and 2, Panel C has both a constant, or intercept, value of \$300 and a slope coefficient of \$0.20. In the case of a mixed cost, the total cost in the relevant range increases as the number of CPU hours used increases. Note that the total cost does not vary strictly in proportion to the number of CPU hours used within the relevant range. For example, when 4,000 hours are used, the total cost equals \$1,100 [\$300 + (0.20 per hour × 4,000 hours)], but when 8,000 hours are used, the total cost equals \$1,900 [\$300 + (\$0.20 per hour × 8,000 hours)]. Although the usage in terms of hours has doubled, the total cost has increased by only about 73% [(\$1,900 − \$1,100) ÷ \$1,100].

StoreBox's managers must understand the cost-behavior patterns in the three alternatives to choose the best deal with FWS. Suppose StoreBox expects to use at least 4,000 hours of CPU time each month. Its cost for 4,000 hours under the three alternatives would be as follows:

- **Alternative 1:** \$2,000 (\$0.50 per hour × 4,000 hours)
- **Alternative 2:** \$1,000
- **Alternative 3:** \$1,100 [\$300 + (\$0.20 per hour × 4,000 hours)]

Alternative 2 is the least costly. Moreover, if StoreBox were to use more than 4,000 hours, as is likely to be the case, alternatives 1 and 3 would be even more costly. StoreBox's managers, therefore, should choose alternative 2.

Note that the graphs in Exhibit 10-1 are linear. That is, they appear as straight lines. We simply need to know the constant, or intercept, amount (commonly designated a) and the slope coefficient (commonly designated b). For any linear cost function based on a single activity (recall our two assumptions discussed at the start of this section), knowing a and b is sufficient to describe and graphically plot all the values within the relevant range of number of hours used. The general form of this linear cost function is

$$y = a + bX$$

Under alternative 1, $a = \$0$ and $b = \$0.50$ per CPU hour used; under alternative 2, $a = \$1,000$ and $b = \$0$ per hour used; and under alternative 3, $a = \$300$ and $b = \$0.20$ per hour used. To plot the mixed-cost function in Panel C, we draw a line starting from the point marked \$300 on the y-axis. This is the fixed part of the rate. If StoreBox uses 1,000 CPU hours, total costs increase by \$200 (\$0.20 per hour × 1,000 hours) to \$500 (\$300 + \$200). Similarly, at 2,000 hours, total costs increase by \$400 (\$0.20 per hour × 2,000 hours) to \$700 (\$300 + \$400), and so on.

Review of Cost Classification

Before we discuss the issues related to estimating cost functions, we briefly review the three criteria laid out in Chapter 2 for classifying a cost into its variable and fixed components.

Choice of Cost Object

A particular cost item could be variable for one cost object and fixed for another cost object. Consider Super Shuttle, an airport transportation company. If the fleet of vans it owns is the cost object, then the annual van registration and license costs would be variable costs for the number of vans owned. But if a particular van is the cost object, then the registration and license costs for that van are fixed costs for the miles driven during a year.

Time Horizon

Whether a cost is variable or fixed for a particular activity depends on the time horizon managers are considering when making decisions. The longer the time horizon, all other things being equal, the more likely the cost will be variable. For example, inspection costs at Boeing Company are typically fixed in the short run because inspectors earn a fixed salary in a given year regardless of the number of inspection-hours of work done. But, in the long run, Boeing's total inspection costs will vary with the inspection-hours required.

Exhibit 10-2

Linearity Within Relevant Range for Winter Sports Authority, Inc.

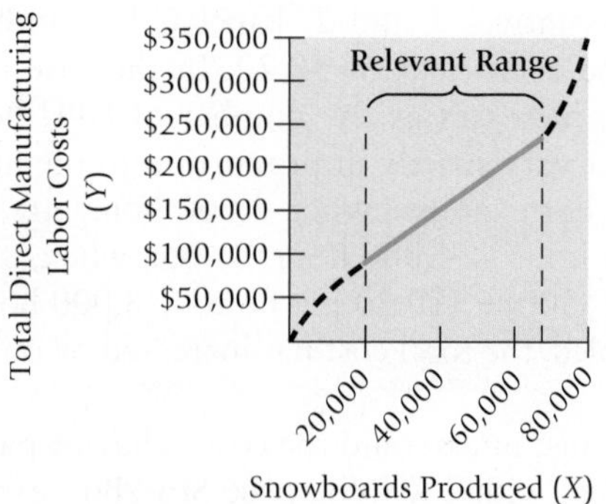

More inspectors will be hired if more inspection-hours are needed, and some inspectors will be reassigned to other tasks or laid off if fewer inspection-hours are needed.

Relevant Range

Decision Point

What is a linear cost function and what types of cost behavior can it represent?

Variable and fixed cost-behavior patterns are valid for linear cost functions only within a given relevant range. Outside the relevant range, variable and fixed cost-behavior patterns change, causing costs to become nonlinear (nonlinear means the plot of the relationship on a graph is not a straight line). For example, Exhibit 10-2 plots the relationship (over several years) between total direct manufacturing labor costs and the number of snowboards produced each year by Winter Sports Authority at its Vermont plant. In this case, the nonlinearities outside the relevant range occur because of labor and other inefficiencies (first because workers are learning to produce snowboards and later because capacity limits are being stretched). Knowing the relevant range is essential to properly classify costs.

Learning Objective 2

Explain the importance of causality in estimating cost functions

...only a cause-and-effect relationship establishes an economically plausible relationship between an activity and its costs

Identifying Cost Drivers

In the StoreBox/FWS example, we discussed variable-, fixed-, and mixed-cost functions using information about *future* cost structures StoreBox was considering. Often, however, cost functions are estimated from *past* cost data. Managers use **cost estimation** to measure a relationship based on data from past costs and the related level of an activity. Managers are interested in estimating past cost functions primarily because they can help them make more accurate **cost predictions**, or forecasts, of future costs. For example, to choose the design features for its new TV models, Sony's managers use past cost functions to evaluate the costs of alternative designs and combine this information with insights about what customers are willing to pay. Similarly, marketing managers at Volkswagen use cost estimation to understand what causes their customer-service costs to change from year to year (for example, the number of new car models introduced or the total number of cars sold) and the fixed and variable components of these costs. Better cost predictions help Volkswagen's managers make more informed planning and control decisions, such as preparing next year's customer-service budget. But better management decisions, cost predictions, and estimation of cost functions can be achieved only if managers correctly identify the factors that affect costs.

The Cause-and-Effect Criterion

The most important issue in estimating a cost function is determining whether a cause-and-effect relationship exists between the level of an activity and the costs related to it. Without a cause-and-effect relationship, managers will be less confident about their ability to estimate or predict costs. Recall from Chapter 2 that when a cause-and-effect relationship exists between a change in the level of an activity and a change in the level of total costs, we refer to the activity measure as a *cost driver*. We use the terms *level of activity* and *level of cost driver* interchangeably when estimating cost functions.

Understanding the drivers of costs is critical for managing costs. The cause-and-effect relationship might arise as a result of the following:

- **A physical relationship between the level of activity and the costs.** Direct materials costs and production are an example. Producing more snowboards requires more plastic, which results in higher total direct materials costs.
- **A contractual arrangement.** Consider the contract between StoreBox and FWS. The contract specifies the number of CPU hours used as the level of activity that affects the cloud services costs. Consequently, there is a direct cause and effect between the two.
- **Knowledge of operations.** An example of knowledge of operations is when the number of parts is used as the activity measure of ordering costs. A Lenovo computer with many parts will incur higher ordering costs than will a newer model that has fewer parts.

Managers must be careful not to interpret a high correlation, or connection, between two variables to mean that either variable causes the other. Consider the total direct materials costs and labor costs for Winston Furniture, which makes two types of (otherwise identical) tables, one with a granite surface and the other with a wooden surface. Granite tables have higher direct material costs than wooden tables because granite is a more expensive input. However, granite is available in precut blocks, so the granite tables require less direct manufacturing labor costs than the wooden tables. Winston currently sells 10,000 granite tables and 30,000 wooden ones.

If Winston sells 20% more of each type of table, then the total direct materials costs and total direct manufacturing labor costs for each type will increase by 20%. The two cost categories are highly correlated in this case. However, it is important to note that neither causes the other, so using one cost to predict the other is problematic.

To see why, suppose Winston sells 20% more tables (or a total of 48,000 again), but now 4,000 of them are granite tables and 44,000 are wooden tables. The direct manufacturing labor costs are higher for wooden tables compared with granite ones, so Winston's total direct manufacturing labor costs will increase by more than 20%. In contrast, because granite is so much more expensive than wood, Winston's total direct materials costs will actually decrease. Consequently, using Winston's total direct manufacturing labor costs to predict its total direct materials costs would be a mistake. Other factors, such as the number of each type of table produced, would have more accurately predicted the changes in the company's total direct materials costs.

Only a cause-and-effect relationship—not merely correlation—establishes an economically plausible relationship between the level of an activity and its costs. Economic plausibility is critical because it gives analysts and managers confidence that the estimated relationship will appear again and again in other sets of data. Identifying cost drivers also gives managers insights into ways to reduce costs and the confidence that reducing the quantity of the cost drivers will lead to a decrease in costs.

Cost Drivers and the Decision-Making Process

To correctly identify cost drivers in order to make decisions, managers should always use a long time horizon. Why? Because costs may be fixed in the short run (during which time they have no cost driver), but they are usually variable and have a cost driver in the long run. Focusing on the short run may inadvertently cause a manager to believe that a cost has no cost driver.

Consider Elegant Rugs, which uses state-of-the-art automated weaving machines to produce carpets for homes and offices. Management has altered manufacturing processes and wants to introduce new styles of carpets. Elegant Rugs' managers follow the five-step decision-making process outlined in Chapter 1 to evaluate how these changes have affected costs and what styles of carpets they should introduce.

Step 1: Identify the problem and its uncertainties. The manufacturing process was changed to reduce Elegant Rugs' indirect manufacturing labor costs. Now managers want to know whether the firm's supervision, maintenance, and quality control costs did, in fact, decrease. One option is to simply compare the firm's indirect manufacturing labor costs before and after the process change. The problem with this approach, however, is that the volume of activity and the style of carpets produced before and after the process change are very different, so the costs need to be compared after taking into account these changes.

Elegant Rugs' managers are fairly confident about the direct materials and direct manufacturing labor costs of the new styles of carpets. They are less certain about the impact that the choice of different styles would have on indirect manufacturing costs.

Step 2: Obtain information. Managers gather information about potential cost drivers—such as machine-hours or direct manufacturing labor-hours—that cause indirect manufacturing labor costs to be incurred. They also begin to consider different techniques (discussed in the next section) for estimating the magnitude of the effect a cost driver has on the firm's indirect manufacturing labor costs. Their goal is to identify the best possible single cost driver.

Step 3: Make predictions about the future. Managers use past data to estimate the relationship between the cost drivers and costs and use this relationship to predict future costs.

Step 4: Make decisions by choosing among alternatives. As we will describe later (pages 385–387), the managers chose machine-hours as the cost driver. Using a regression analysis, they estimated the indirect manufacturing labor costs per machine-hour of alternative styles of carpets and chose to produce the most profitable styles.

Decision Point

What is the most important issue in estimating a cost function?

Step 5: Implement the decision, evaluate performance, and learn. A year later the managers evaluated the results of their decision. Comparing predicted to actual costs helped them determine how accurate the estimates were, set targets for continuous improvement, and seek ways to improve Elegant Rugs' efficiency and effectiveness.

Learning Objective 3

Understand various methods of cost estimation

...for example, the regression analysis method determines the line that best fits past data

Cost Estimation Methods

Four methods of cost estimation are (1) the industrial engineering method, (2) the conference method, (3) the account analysis method, and (4) the quantitative analysis method (which takes different forms). These methods differ in terms of how expensive they are to implement, the assumptions they make, and the information they provide about the accuracy of the estimated cost function. The methods are not mutually exclusive, so many organizations use a combination of methods.

Industrial Engineering Method

Description of method

The **industrial engineering method**, also called the **work-measurement method**, estimates cost functions by analyzing the relationship between inputs and outputs in physical terms. Elegant Rugs uses inputs of cotton, wool, dyes, direct manufacturing labor, machine time, and power. Production output is square yards of carpet. Time-and-motion studies analyze the time required to perform the various operations to produce the carpet. For example, a time-and-motion study may conclude that to produce 10 square yards of carpet requires one hour of direct manufacturing labor. Standards and budgets transform these physical input measures into costs. The result is an estimated cost function relating direct manufacturing labor costs to the cost driver, square yards of carpet produced.

Advantages and challenges

The industrial engineering method is a very thorough and detailed way to estimate a cost function when there is a physical relationship between inputs and outputs. Although it can be time consuming, some government contracts mandate its use. Many organizations, such as Bose and Nokia, use it to estimate direct manufacturing costs but find it too costly or impractical for analyzing their entire cost structure. For example, the physical relationships between inputs and outputs are difficult to specify for some items, such as indirect manufacturing costs, R&D costs, and advertising costs.

Conference Method

Description of method

The **conference method** estimates cost functions on the basis of analysis and opinions about costs and their drivers gathered from various departments of a company (purchasing, process engineering, manufacturing, employee relations, and so on). Some banks, for example, develop cost functions for their retail banking products (such as checking accounts, VISA cards, and mortgages) based on the consensus estimates from personnel from various departments. Relying on the collective judgment of experts is the most popular strategy for estimating the cost of software development projects. Elegant Rugs gathers opinions from supervisors and production engineers about how indirect manufacturing labor costs vary with machine-hours and direct manufacturing labor-hours.

Advantages and challenges

The conference method encourages interdepartmental cooperation. The pooling of expert knowledge from different business functions of the value chain gives the conference method credibility. Because the conference method does not require a detailed analysis of data, cost functions and cost estimates can be developed quickly. However, because opinions are being used, the accuracy of the cost estimates depends largely on the care and skill of the people providing the inputs.

Account Analysis Method

Description of method

The **account analysis method** estimates cost functions by classifying various cost accounts as variable, fixed, or mixed in regard to the identified level of activity. Typically, managers use qualitative rather than quantitative analysis when making these cost-classification decisions.

Consider the indirect manufacturing labor costs for a small production area (or cell) at Elegant Rugs. These include the wages paid for supervision, maintenance, quality control, and setups. During the most recent 12-week period, Elegant Rugs ran the machines in the cell for a total of 862 hours and incurred total indirect manufacturing labor costs of $12,501. Using qualitative analysis, the manager and the management accountant determine that over this 12-week period the indirect manufacturing labor costs are mixed costs with only one cost driver—machine-hours. As the machine-hours vary, one component of the cost (such as the supervision cost) is fixed, whereas another component (such as the maintenance cost) is variable. The manager and management accountant want to estimate a linear cost function for the cell's indirect manufacturing labor costs using the number of machine-hours as the cost driver. To do so, they must distinguish between the variable and fixed cost components. Using their experience and judgment they separate the cell's total indirect manufacturing labor costs ($12,501) into costs that are fixed ($2,157, based on 950 hours of machine capacity for the cell over a 12-week period) and costs that are variable ($10,344) based on the number of machine-hours used. The variable cost per machine-hour is $10,344 ÷ 862 machine-hours = $12 per machine-hour. Therefore, the linear cost equation, $y = a + bX$, is:

Indirect manufacturing labor costs = $2,157 +
($12 per machine-hour × Number of machine-hours)

Elegant Rugs' managers can use the cost function to estimate the indirect manufacturing labor costs of using, say, 950 machine-hours to produce carpet in the next 12-week period. The estimated costs equal $2,157 + (950 machine-hours × $12 per machine-hour) = $13,557. The indirect manufacturing labor cost per machine-hour is currently $12,501 ÷ 862 machine-hours = $14.50 per machine-hour. It decreases to $13,557 ÷ 950 machine-hours = $14.27 per machine-hour, as fixed costs of $2,157 are spread over a greater number of machine-hours.

Advantages and challenges

The account analysis method is widely used because it is reasonably accurate, cost effective, and easy to use. To obtain reliable estimates of the fixed and variable components of cost, organizations must take care to ensure that individuals with thorough knowledge of the operations make the cost-classification decisions. Supplementing the account analysis method with the conference method improves credibility. The accuracy of the account analysis method depends on the accuracy of the qualitative judgments that managers and management accountants make about which costs are fixed and which are variable.

Concepts in Action: What Does It Cost AT&T Wireless to Send a Text Message illustrates external experts' analysis of the fixed and variable cost components of a critical modern communication medium—text messages.

Quantitative Analysis Method

Description of method

Quantitative analysis uses a formal mathematical method to fit cost functions to past data observations. Excel is a useful tool for performing quantitative analysis. Columns B

Concepts in Action

What Does It Cost AT&T Wireless to Send a Text Message?

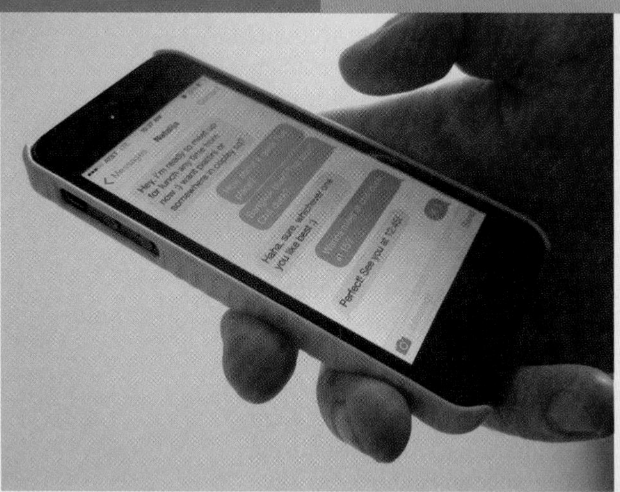

In 2011, customers sent an estimated 5 *trillion* text messages from mobile phones worldwide. Despite the volume, text messaging is a very lucrative business. How, you ask? After understanding how text messaging costs behave, you learn that it is very inexpensive for AT&T Wireless and other wireless carriers to provide this wildly popular service.

Text messaging does not require AT&T Wireless to add any additional infrastructure, equipment, or wireless spectrum. A text message travels wirelessly from a phone to the closest base tower station and is then transferred through wired links to the digital pipes of the telephone network. Then, near its destination, it is converted back into a wireless signal to traverse the final leg, from tower to the recipient's phone. Text messages do not require extra spectrum. Generally limited to 160 characters, small text messaging files are "free riders" tucked into what's called a control channel, or the space reserved for operation of the wireless network.

Other text messaging costs are semi-variable and minimal. For billing, each text message triggers a control message back to the AT&T Wireless billing system with the identity of the sender and the receiver so their monthly bills can be updated. If a text message cannot be delivered, it must be stored until the recipient is available. AT&T Wireless pays for its message storage system based on capacity: the higher the capacity, the greater the cost, though data storage is fairly inexpensive. Finally, AT&T Wireless maintains a database that stores billing information. Its database costs are small and do not vary with increased text message volume.

So what does it cost AT&T Wireless to send a text message? The company will not disclose the information, but University of Waterloo professor Srinivasan Keshav has calculated the cost: 0.3 cent. That's right, three-tenths of one cent! Dr. Keshav found that wireless channels contribute about a tenth of a cent to the carrier's cost, that accounting charges are twice that, and that, due to volume, the other costs basically round to zero because texting requires so little of AT&T Wireless's infrastructure. As you can see, the text messaging business is incredibly profitable for AT&T Wireless.

Sources: Radcliffe, Vaughan, Mitchell Stein, and Michael Lickver. 2012. AT&T Wireless: Text Messaging. Richard Ivey School of Business No. W11049, London, ON: University of Western Ontario; Stross, Randall. 2008. What Carriers Aren't Eager to Tell You About Texting. *The New York Times*, December 28; and Bender, Eric. 2009. Guess What Texting Costs Your Wireless Provider? *Time*, September 10.

	A	B	C
1	Week	Cost Driver: Machine-Hours	Indirect Manufacturing Labor Costs
2		(X)	(Y)
3	1	68	$ 1,190
4	2	88	1,211
5	3	62	1,004
6	4	72	917
7	5	60	770
8	6	96	1,456
9	7	78	1,180
10	8	46	710
11	9	82	1,316
12	10	94	1,032
13	11	68	752
14	12	48	963
15	Total	862	$12,501
16			

Exhibit 10-3

Weekly Indirect Manufacturing Labor Costs and Machine-Hours for Elegant Rugs

and C of Exhibit 10-3 show the breakdown of Elegant Rugs' total machine-hours (862) and total indirect manufacturing labor costs ($12,501) into weekly data for the most recent 12-week period. Note that the data are paired; for each week, there is data for the number of machine-hours and corresponding indirect manufacturing labor costs. For example, week 12 shows 48 machine-hours and indirect manufacturing labor costs of $963. The next section uses the data in Exhibit 10-3 to illustrate how to estimate a cost function using quantitative analysis. We examine two techniques: the relatively simple high-low method as well as the more common quantitative tool used to examine and understand data, regression analysis.

Decision Point

What are the different methods that can be used to estimate a cost function?

Advantages and challenges

Quantitative analysis is the most rigorous approach to estimate costs. Computer programs have made performing quantitative analysis and, in particular, regression analysis much easier. However, regression analysis requires more detailed information about costs, cost drivers, and cost functions and is therefore more time consuming to implement.

Estimating a Cost Function Using Quantitative Analysis

Learning Objective 4

Outline six steps in estimating a cost function using quantitative analysis

...the end result (Step 6) is to evaluate the cost driver of the estimated cost function

There are six steps in estimating a cost function using quantitative analysis of past data. We illustrate the steps using the Elegant Rugs example.

Step 1: Choose the dependent variable. Which **dependent variable** (the cost to be predicted and managed) managers choose will depend on the specific cost function being estimated. In the Elegant Rugs example, the dependent variable is indirect manufacturing labor costs.

Step 2: Identify the independent variable, or cost driver. The **independent variable** (level of activity or cost driver) is the factor used to predict the dependent variable (costs). When the cost is an indirect cost, as it is with Elegant Rugs, the independent variable is also called a cost-allocation base. Although these terms are sometimes used interchangeably, we use the term *cost driver* to describe the independent variable. Frequently, the management accountant, working with the management team, will cycle through the six steps several times, trying alternative economically plausible cost drivers to identify the one that best fits the data.

Recall that a cost driver should be measurable and have an *economically plausible* relationship with the dependent variable. Economic plausibility means that the relationship (describing how changes in the cost driver lead to changes in the costs being considered) is based on a physical relationship, a contract, or knowledge of operations and makes economic sense to the operating manager and the management accountant. As you learned in Chapter 5, all the individual items of costs included in the dependent variable should have the same cost driver, that is, the cost pool should be homogenous. When all items of costs in the dependent variable do not have the same cost driver, the management accountant should investigate the possibility of creating homogenous cost pools and estimating more than one cost function, one for each cost item/cost driver pair.

As an example, consider several types of fringe benefits paid to employees and the cost drivers of the benefits:

Fringe Benefit	Cost Driver
Health benefits	Number of employees
Cafeteria meals	Number of employees
Pension benefits	Salaries of employees
Life insurance	Salaries of employees

The costs of health benefits and cafeteria meals can be combined into one homogenous cost pool because they have the same cost driver—the number of employees. Pension benefits and life insurance costs have a different cost driver—the salaries of employees—and, therefore, should not be combined with health benefits and cafeteria meals. Instead, pension benefits and life insurance costs should be combined into a separate homogenous cost pool. The cost pool composed of pension benefits and life insurance costs can be estimated using the salaries of employees receiving these benefits as the cost driver.

Step 3: Collect data on the dependent variable and the cost driver. This is usually the most difficult step in cost analysis. Management accountants obtain data from company documents, from interviews with managers, and through special studies. These data may be time-series data or cross-sectional data.

Time-series data pertain to the same entity (such as an organization, plant, or activity) over successive past periods. Weekly observations of Elegant Rugs' indirect manufacturing labor costs and number of machine-hours are examples of time-series data. The ideal time-series database would contain numerous observations for a company whose operations have not been affected by economic or technological change. A stable economy and stable technology ensure that data collected during the estimation period represent the same underlying relationship between the cost driver and the dependent variable. Moreover, the periods used to measure the dependent variable and the cost driver should be consistent throughout the observations.

Cross-sectional data pertain to different entities during the same period. For example, studies of loans processed and the related personnel costs at 50 individual, yet similar, branches of a bank during March 2014 would produce cross-sectional data for that month. The cross-sectional data should be drawn from entities that, within each entity, have a similar relationship between the cost driver and costs. Later in this chapter, we describe the problems that arise in data collection.

Step 4: Plot the data. The general relationship between the cost driver and costs can be readily seen in a plot of the data once it's graphed. The plot provides insight into the relevant range of the cost function and reveals whether the relationship between the driver and costs is approximately linear. Moreover, the plot highlights extreme observations (observations outside the general pattern) that analysts should check. Was there an error in recording the data or an unusual event, such as a work stoppage, that makes these observations unrepresentative of the normal relationship between the cost driver and the costs?

Exhibit 10-4 is a plot of the weekly data from columns B and C of the Excel spreadsheet in Exhibit 10-3. This graph provides strong visual evidence of a positive linear

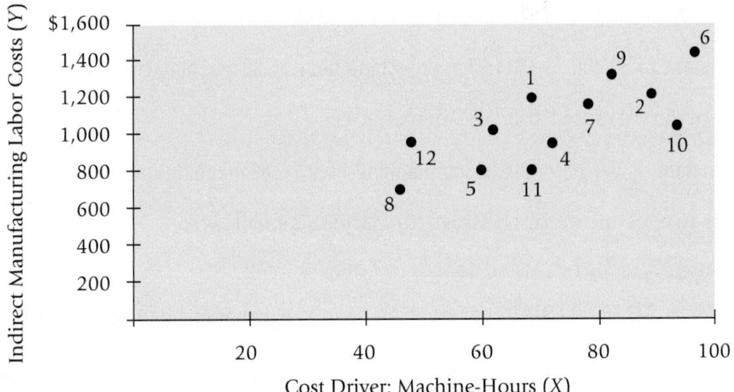

Exhibit 10-4

Plot of Weekly Indirect Manufacturing Labor Costs and Machine-Hours for Elegant Rugs

relationship between Elegant Rugs' number of machine-hours and indirect manufacturing labor costs (when machine-hours go up, so do indirect manufacturing labor costs). There do not appear to be any extreme observations in Exhibit 10-4. The relevant range is from 46 to 96 machine-hours per week (weeks 8 and 6, respectively).

Step 5: Estimate the cost function. The two most common forms of quantitative analysis managers and accountants use to estimate a cost function are the high-low method and regression analysis. Even though computer programs such as Excel make regression analysis much easier, we will describe the high-low method to provide some basic intuition for the idea of drawing a line to "fit" a number of data points. We present these methods after Step 6.

Step 6: Evaluate the cost driver of the estimated cost function. In this step, we describe the criteria for evaluating the cost driver of the estimated cost function. But to do so you first need to understand both the high-low method and regression analysis. Identifying cost drivers is a critical aspect of managing costs and improving profitability and therefore a vital component in a manager's toolkit.

High-Low Method

The simplest form of quantitative analysis to "fit" a line to data points is the **high-low method.** It uses only the highest and lowest observed values of the cost driver within the relevant range and their respective costs to estimate the slope coefficient and the constant of the cost function. It provides a quick first look at the relationship between a cost driver and costs. We illustrate the high-low method using data from Exhibit 10-3.

	Cost Driver: Machine-Hours (X)	Indirect Manufacturing Labor Costs (Y)
Highest observation of cost driver (week 6)	96	$1,456
Lowest observation of cost driver (week 8)	46	710
Difference	50	$ 746

The slope coefficient, b, is calculated as follows:

$$\text{Slope coefficient} = \frac{\text{Difference between costs associated with highest and lowest observations of the cost driver}}{\text{Difference between highest and lowest observations of the cost driver}}$$

$$= \$746 \div 50 \text{ machine-hours} = \$14.92 \text{ per machine-hour}$$

To compute the constant, we can use either the highest or the lowest observation of the cost driver. Both calculations yield the same answer because the method solves two linear equations with two unknowns, the slope coefficient and the constant. Because

$$y = a + bX$$
$$a = y - bX$$

At the highest observation of the cost driver, the constant, a, is:

$$\text{Constant} = \$1{,}456 - (\$14.92 \text{ per machine-hour} \times 96 \text{ machine-hours}) = \$23.68$$

At the lowest observation of the cost driver, a is:

$$\text{Constant} = \$710 - (\$14.92 \text{ per machine-hour} \times 46 \text{ machine-hours}) = \$23.68$$

Thus, the high-low estimate of the cost function is as follows:

$$y = a + bX$$
$$y = \$23.68 + (\$14.92 \text{ per machine-hour} \times \text{Number of machine-hours})$$

The blue line in Exhibit 10-5 shows the estimated cost function using the high-low method (based on the data in Exhibit 10-3). The estimated cost function is a straight line joining the observations with the highest and lowest values of the cost driver (number of machine-hours). Note how this simple high-low line falls "in between" the data points with three observations on the line, four above it and five below it. The intercept (a = \$23.68), the point where the dashed extension of the blue line meets the y-axis, is the constant component of the equation that provides the best linear approximation of how a cost behaves *within the relevant range* of 46–96 machine-hours. Managers should *not* interpret the intercept as an estimate of the fixed costs if no machines were run. The reason is that running no machines and shutting down the plant—that is, using zero machine-hours—is *outside the relevant range.*

Suppose Elegant Rugs' indirect manufacturing labor costs in week 6 were \$1,280, instead of \$1,456, and that 96 machine-hours were used. In this case, the highest observation of the cost driver (96 machine-hours in week 6) will not coincide with the newer highest observation of the costs (\$1,316 in week 9). How would this change affect our high-low calculation? Given that the cause-and-effect relationship runs *from* the cost driver *to* the costs in a cost function, we choose the highest and lowest observations of the cost driver (the factor that causes the costs to change). The high-low method would still estimate the new cost function using data from weeks 6 (high) and 8 (low).

The high-low method is simple to compute and easy to understand. It gives the managers of Elegant Rugs quick initial insight into how the cost driver—the number of machine-hours—affects the firm's indirect manufacturing labor costs. However, it is dangerous for managers to rely on only two observations to estimate a cost function. Suppose that because a labor contract guarantees certain minimum payments in week 8, indirect manufacturing labor costs in week 8 were \$1,000, instead of \$710, when only 46 machine-hours were used. The green line in Exhibit 10-5 shows the cost function that would be estimated by the high-low method using this revised cost. Other than the two points used to draw the line, all other data lie on or below the line! In this case, choosing the highest and lowest observations for machine-hours would result in an estimated cost function that poorly describes the underlying linear cost relationship between number

Exhibit 10-5

High-Low Method for Weekly Indirect Manufacturing Labor Costs and Machine-Hours for Elegant Rugs

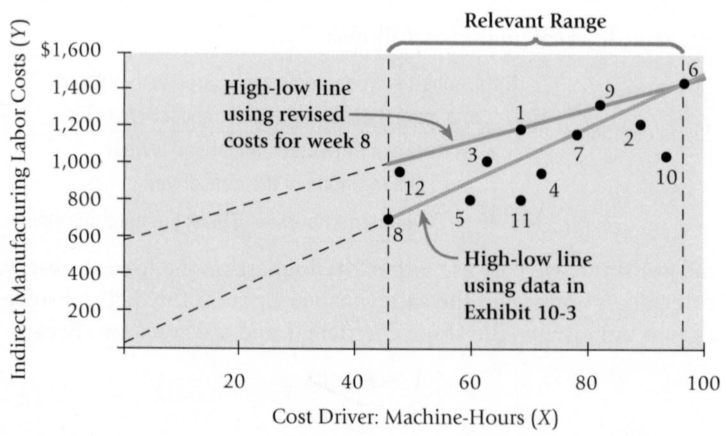

of machine-hours and indirect manufacturing labor costs. In such a situation, managers can modify the high-low method so that the two observations chosen to estimate the cost function are a *representative high* and a *representative low*. By making this adjustment, managers can avoid having extreme observations, which arise from abnormal events, influence the estimate of the cost function. The modification allows managers to estimate a cost function that is representative of the relationship between the cost driver and costs and, therefore, is more useful for making decisions (such as pricing and performance evaluation). Next we describe the regression analysis method. Rather than just high and low values, it uses all available data to estimate the cost function.

Regression Analysis Method

Regression analysis is a statistical method that measures the average amount of change in the dependent variable associated with a unit change in one or more independent variables. The method is widely used because it helps managers "get behind the numbers" so they understand why costs behave the way they do and what managers can do to influence them. For example, at Analog Devices, a maker of digital and analog integrated circuits, managers use regression analysis to evaluate how and why defect rates and product quality change over time. Managers who understand these relationships gain greater insight into their businesses, make more judicious decisions, and manage more effectively.

Simple regression analysis estimates the relationship between the dependent variable and *one* independent variable. In the Elegant Rugs example, the dependent variable is total indirect manufacturing labor costs; the single independent variable, or cost driver, is the number of machine-hours. **Multiple regression** analysis estimates the relationship between the dependent variable and *two or more* independent variables. Multiple regression analysis for Elegant Rugs might use as the independent variables the number of machine-hours and number of batches. The appendix to this chapter explores simple regression and multiple regression in more detail.

In later sections, we will explain how to use Excel to do regression analysis. Here we will discuss how managers interpret and use the output from programs such as Excel to make critical strategic decisions. Exhibit 10-6 shows the line developed using regression analysis that best fits the data in columns B and C of Exhibit 10-3. Excel estimates the cost function to be

$$y = \$300.98 + \$10.31X$$

The regression line in Exhibit 10-6 is derived using the least-squares technique. The least-squares technique determines the regression line by minimizing the sum of the squared vertical differences from the data points (the various points in the graph) to the regression line. The vertical difference, called the **residual term**, measures the distance between actual cost and estimated cost for each observation of the cost driver. Exhibit 10-6 shows the residual term for the week 1 data. The line from the observation to the regression line is drawn perpendicular to the horizontal axis, or x-axis. The smaller the residual

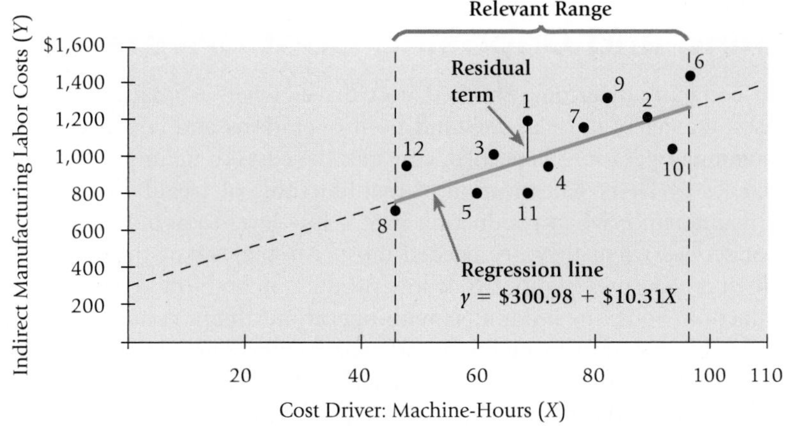

Exhibit 10-6

Regression Model for Weekly Indirect Manufacturing Labor Costs and Machine-Hours for Elegant Rugs

terms, the better is the fit between the actual cost observations and estimated costs. *Goodness of fit* indicates the strength of the relationship between the cost driver and costs. The regression line in Exhibit 10-6 rises from left to right. The positive slope of this line and small residual terms indicate that, on average, indirect manufacturing labor costs increase as the number of machine-hours increases. The vertical dashed lines in Exhibit 10-6 indicate the relevant range, the range within which the cost function applies.

Instructors and students who want to explore the technical details of estimating the least-squares regression line can go to the appendix, pages 398–403, and return to this point without any loss of continuity.

The estimate of the slope coefficient, *b*, indicates that indirect manufacturing labor costs vary at the average amount of $10.31 for every machine-hour used within the relevant range. Managers can use the regression equation when setting budgets for future indirect manufacturing labor costs. For instance, if 90 machine-hours are budgeted for the upcoming week, the predicted indirect manufacturing labor costs would be

$$y = \$300.98 + (\$10.31 \text{ per machine-hour} \times 90 \text{ machine-hours}) = \$1{,}228.88$$

As we have already mentioned, the regression method is more accurate than the high-low method because the regression equation estimates costs using information from all observations, whereas the high-low equation uses information from only two observations. The inaccuracies of the high-low method can mislead managers. Consider the high-low method equation in the preceding section, y = $23.68 + ($14.92 per machine-hour × Number of machine-hours). For 90 machine-hours, the predicted weekly costs using the high-low method equation are $23.68 + ($14.92 per machine-hour × 90 machine-hours) = $1,366.48. Suppose that for 7 weeks over the next 12-week period, Elegant Rugs runs its machines for 90 hours each week. Assume the average indirect manufacturing labor costs for those 7 weeks are $1,300. Based on the high-low method prediction of $1,366.48, Elegant Rugs would conclude it has performed well because actual costs are less than predicted costs. But comparing the $1,300 performance with the more-accurate $1,228.88 prediction of the regression model tells a different story and would probably prompt Elegant Rugs to search for ways to improve its cost performance.

Suppose the manager at Elegant Rugs is interested in evaluating whether recent strategic decisions that led to changes in the production process and resulted in the data in Exhibit 10-3 have reduced the firm's indirect manufacturing labor costs, such as the costs of supervision, maintenance, and quality control. Using data on number of machine-hours used and indirect manufacturing labor costs of the previous process (not shown here), the manager estimates the regression equation to be

Decision Point

What are the steps to estimate a cost function using quantitative analysis?

$$y = \$546.26 + (\$15.86 \text{ per machine-hour} \times \text{Number of machine-hours})$$

The constant ($300.98 versus $545.26) and the slope coefficient ($10.31 versus $15.86) are both smaller for the new process relative to the old process. It appears that the new process has decreased the company's indirect manufacturing labor costs.

Learning Objective 5

Describe three criteria used to evaluate and choose cost drivers

...economically plausible relationships, goodness of fit, and significant effect of the cost driver on costs

Evaluating and Choosing Cost Drivers

How does a company determine the best cost driver when estimating a cost function? In many cases, managers must understand both operations and cost accounting. To see why understanding operations is needed, consider the costs to maintain and repair metal-cutting machines at Helix Corporation, a manufacturer of treadmills. Helix schedules repairs and maintenance when production is at a low level to avoid having to take machines out of service when they are needed most. An analysis of the monthly data will then show high repair costs in months of low production and low repair costs in months of high production. Someone unfamiliar with operations might conclude that there is an inverse relationship between production and repair costs. The engineering link between units produced and repair costs, however, is usually clear-cut. Over time, there is a cause-and-effect relationship: the higher the level of production, the higher the repair costs.

	A	B	C	D
1	Week	Original Cost Driver: Machine-Hours	Alternate Cost Driver: Direct Manufacturing Labor-Hours (*X*)	Indirect Manufacturing Labor Costs (*Y*)
2	1	68	30	$ 1,190
3	2	88	35	1,211
4	3	62	36	1,004
5	4	72	20	917
6	5	60	47	770
7	6	96	45	1,456
8	7	78	44	1,180
9	8	46	38	710
10	9	82	70	1,316
11	10	94	30	1,032
12	11	68	29	752
13	12	48	38	963
14	Total	862	462	$12,501
15				

Exhibit 10-7

Weekly Indirect Manufacturing Labor Costs, Machine-Hours, and Direct Manufacturing Labor-Hours for Elegant Rugs

To estimate the relationship correctly, operating managers and analysts will recognize that repair costs will tend to lag behind periods of high production, and hence, they will use production of prior periods as the cost driver.

In other cases, choosing a cost driver is more subtle and difficult. Consider again the indirect manufacturing labor costs at Elegant Rugs. Although both the number of machine-hours and the number of direct manufacturing labor-hours are plausible cost drivers of the firm's indirect manufacturing labor costs, managers are not sure which is the better driver. Exhibit 10-7 presents weekly data (in Excel) on the indirect manufacturing labor costs and number of machine-hours for the most recent 12-week period from Exhibit 10-3, together with data on the number of direct manufacturing labor-hours for the same period.

What guidance do the different cost-estimation methods provide for choosing among cost drivers? The industrial engineering method relies on analyzing physical relationships between cost drivers and costs, relationships that are difficult to specify in this case. The conference method and the account analysis method use subjective assessments to choose a cost driver and to estimate the fixed and variable components of the cost function. In these cases, managers must rely on their best judgment. Managers cannot use these methods to test and try alternative cost drivers. The major advantages of quantitative methods are that they are objective, so managers can use them to evaluate different cost drivers. We use the regression analysis approach to illustrate how to evaluate different cost drivers.

First, the cost analyst at Elegant Rugs enters data in columns C and D of Exhibit 10-7 in Excel and estimates the following regression equation for the firm's indirect manufacturing labor costs based on the number of direct manufacturing labor-hours:

$$y = \$744.67 + \$7.72X$$

Exhibit 10-8 shows the plot of the data points for number of direct manufacturing labor-hours and indirect manufacturing labor costs and the regression line that best fits the data. Recall that Exhibit 10-6 shows the corresponding graph when number of machine-hours is the cost driver. To decide which of the two cost drivers Elegant Rugs should choose,

Exhibit 10-8

Regression Model for Weekly Indirect Manufacturing Labor Costs and Direct Manufacturing Labor-Hours for Elegant Rugs

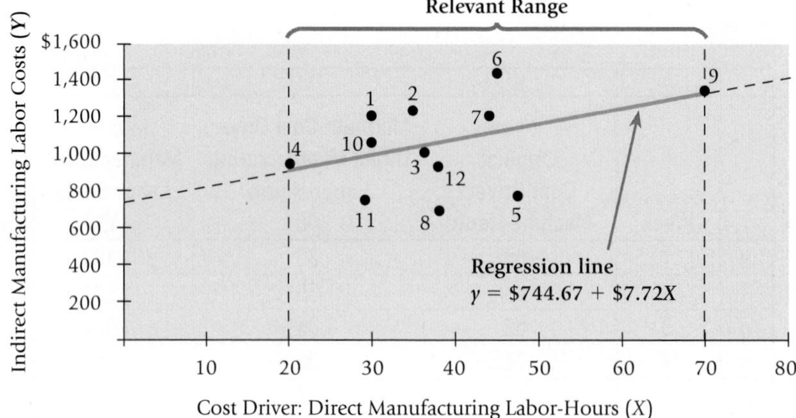

the analyst compares the machine-hour regression equation and the direct manufacturing labor-hour regression equation. There are three criteria used to make this evaluation.

1. **Economic plausibility.** Both cost drivers are economically plausible. However, in the state-of-the-art, highly automated production environment at Elegant Rugs, managers familiar with the operations believe that indirect manufacturing labor costs such as machine maintenance costs are likely to be more closely related to the number of machine-hours used than the number of direct manufacturing labor-hours used.
2. **Goodness of fit.** Compare Exhibits 10-6 and 10-8. The vertical differences between the actual costs and predicted costs are much smaller for the machine-hours regression than for the direct manufacturing labor-hours regression. The number of machine-hours used, therefore, has a stronger relationship—or goodness of fit—with the indirect manufacturing labor costs.
3. **Significance of the independent variable.** Again compare Exhibits 10-6 and 10-8 (both of which have been drawn to roughly the same scale). The machine-hours regression line has a steep slope relative to the slope of the direct manufacturing labor-hours regression line. *For the same (or more) scatter of observations about the line (goodness of fit)*, a flat or slightly sloped regression line indicates a weak relationship between the cost driver and costs. In our example, changes in the direct manufacturing labor-hours appear to have a small effect on the indirect manufacturing labor costs.

Based on this evaluation, managers at Elegant Rugs select the number of machine-hours as the cost driver and use the cost function y = $300.98 + ($10.31 per machine-hour × Number of machine-hours) to predict future indirect manufacturing labor costs.

Instructors and students who want to explore how regression analysis techniques can be used to choose among different cost drivers can go to the appendix, pages 403–407, and return to this point without any loss of continuity.

Why is choosing the correct cost driver to estimate the indirect manufacturing labor costs important? Because identifying the wrong drivers or misestimating cost functions can lead management to incorrect (and costly) decisions along a variety of dimensions. Consider the following strategic decision Elegant Rugs' managers must make. The company is thinking of introducing a new style of carpet that, from a manufacturing standpoint, is similar to the carpets it has manufactured in the past. The company expects to sell 650 square yards of this carpet each week. Managers estimate 72 machine-hours and 21 direct manufacturing labor-hours are required per week to produce this amount of output. Using the machine-hour regression equation, Elegant Rugs would predict indirect manufacturing labor costs of y = $300.98 + ($10.31 per machine-hour × 72 machine-hours) = $1,043.30. If the company used direct manufacturing labor-hours as the cost driver, it would incorrectly predict costs of $744.67 + ($7.72 per labor-hour × 21 labor-hours) = $906.79. If Elegant Rugs chose similarly incorrect cost drivers for other indirect costs as well and systematically underestimated costs, it would conclude that the costs of manufacturing the new style of carpet would be low and basically fixed (fixed because the regression line is nearly flat). But the actual costs driven by the number of machine-hours used and other correct cost drivers would be higher. By failing to identify the proper cost drivers, managers would believe the new style of carpet to be more profitable than it actually is. If the managers had used the correct cost driver, they would have realized the new carpet was not as profitable and may have decided not to introduce it.

Incorrectly estimating the cost function would also affect Elegant Rugs' cost management and cost control activities. Suppose the number of direct manufacturing labor-hours were used as the cost driver, and actual indirect manufacturing labor costs for the new carpet were $970. The actual costs would then be higher than the predicted costs of $906.79. The firm's managers would then feel compelled to cut costs. In fact, on the basis of the preferred machine-hour cost driver, the plant would have actual costs lower than the $1,043.30 predicted costs—a performance that management should seek to replicate, not change!

Cost Drivers and Activity-Based Costing

Activity-based costing (ABC) systems focus on individual activities, such as product design, machine setup, materials handling, distribution, and customer service, as the fundamental cost objects. To implement ABC systems, managers must identify a cost driver for each activity. Consider, for example, a manager at Westronics, a manufacturer of electronic products. Using methods described in this chapter, the manager must decide whether the number of loads moved or the weight of loads moved is the cost driver of the firm's materials-handling costs.

To choose the cost driver, the manager collects data on materials-handling costs and the quantities of the two competing cost drivers over a reasonably long period. Why a

Concepts in Action: Activity-Based Costing: Identifying Cost Drivers

Many cost estimation methods presented in this chapter are essential when implementing activity-based costing across the globe. In the United Kingdom, the City of London police force uses input–output relationships (the industrial engineering method) to identify cost drivers and the cost of an activity. Using a surveying methodology, officials can determine the total costs associated with responding to house robberies, dealing with burglaries, and filling out police reports. The industrial engineering method is also used by U.S. government agencies such as the U.S. Postal Service, to determine the cost of each post office transaction, and the U.S. Patent and Trademark Office, to identify the costs of each patent examination.

Managers are increasingly using quantitative analysis to determine the cost drivers of activities. At DHL Express, the international shipping company recently switched from the conference method to performing in-depth quantitative analysis on its "big data" system. Now managers have a single, worldwide activity-based costing system that shows the cost and profitability for every shipment in its network. By rigorously analyzing its database, DHL Express can link the profit of what's being shipped on a particular flight with the cost of shipping it and then determine which of its 250 airplanes would be best for the job.

Sources: Carter, T., A. Sedaghat, and T. Williams. 1998. How ABC changed the post office. *Management Accounting,* February; Leapman, B. 2006. Police spend £500 m filling in forms. *The Daily Telegraph,* January 22; Peckenpaugh, J. 2002. Teaching the ABCs. *Government Executive,* April 1; The United Kingdom Home Office. 2007. *The police service national ABC model: Manual of guidance.* London: Her Majesty's Stationary Office; Provost, T. 2013. How DHL's big data boosts performance. *CFO.com,* January 30.

long period? Because in the short run, materials-handling costs may be fixed and, therefore, will not vary with changes in the level of the cost driver. In the long run, however, there is a clear cause-and-effect relationship between materials-handling costs and the cost driver. Suppose the number of loads moved is the cost driver. Increases in the number of loads moved will require more materials-handling labor and equipment; decreases in the number of loads moved will result in equipment being sold and labor being reassigned to other tasks.

ABC systems have a great number and variety of cost drivers and cost pools. This means the systems require managers to estimate many cost relationships. When estimating the cost function for each cost pool, the manager must pay careful attention to the cost hierarchy. For example, if a cost is a batch-level cost such as setup cost, the manager must only consider batch-level cost drivers like number of setup-hours. In some cases, the costs in a cost pool may have more than one cost driver from different levels of the cost hierarchy. The cost drivers for Elegant Rugs' indirect manufacturing labor costs could be machine-hours and the number of production batches of carpet manufactured. Furthermore, it may be difficult to subdivide the indirect manufacturing labor costs into two cost pools and to measure the costs associated with each cost driver. In cases like these, companies use multiple regression to estimate costs based on more than one independent variable. The appendix to this chapter discusses multiple regression in more detail.

Decision Point

How should a company evaluate and choose cost drivers?

Concepts in Action: Activity-Based Costing: Identifying Cost Drivers illustrates the variety of methods—industrial engineering, conference, and regression analysis—that managers implementing ABC systems use to estimate slope coefficients. In making these choices, managers trade off level of detail, accuracy, feasibility, and costs of estimating cost functions. For example, to estimate the cost of an activity such as opening a bank account or making a transfer payment, Bankinter in Spain uses work measurement methods, while Royal Bank of Canada uses advanced analytical techniques, including regression.

Learning Objective 6

Explain nonlinear cost functions

...graph of cost function is not a straight line, for example, because of quantity discounts or costs changing in steps

in particular those arising from learning curve effects

...either cumulative average-time learning, where cumulative average time per unit declines by a constant percentage, as units produced double

...or incremental unit-time learning, in which incremental time to produce last unit declines by constant percentage, as units produced double

Nonlinear Cost Functions

As we explained, cost functions are not always linear. A **nonlinear cost function** is a cost function for which the graph of total costs (based on the level of a single activity) is not a straight line within the relevant range. To see what a nonlinear cost function looks like, return to Exhibit 10-2 (page 374). The relevant range is currently set at 20,000 to 65,000 snowboards. But if we extend the relevant range to cover the region from 0 to 80,000 snowboards produced, it is evident that the cost function over this expanded range is graphically represented by a line that is not straight.

Consider another example. Economies of scale may enable an advertising agency to produce double the number of advertisements for less than double the costs. Even direct materials costs are not always linear. As Panel A of Exhibit 10-9 shows, total direct materials costs rise as the units of direct materials purchased increase. But, because of quantity discounts, these costs rise more slowly (as indicated by the slope coefficient) as the units of direct materials purchased increase. This cost function has $b = \$25$ per unit for 1–1,000 units purchased, $b = \$15$ per unit for 1,001–2,000 units purchased, and $b = \$10$ per unit for 2,001–3,000 units purchased. The direct materials cost per unit falls with each price cut. The cost function is nonlinear over the relevant range from 1 to 3,000 units. Over a more narrow relevant range (for example, from 1 to 1,000 units), the cost function is linear.

Step cost functions are also nonlinear cost functions. A **step cost function** is a cost function in which the cost remains the same over various ranges of the level of activity, but the cost increases by discrete amounts—that is, increases in steps—as the level of activity increases from one range to the next. Panel B in Exhibit 10-9 shows a *step variable-cost function*, a step cost function in which cost remains the same over *narrow* ranges of the level of activity in each relevant range. Panel B shows the relationship between units of production and setup costs. The pattern is a step cost function because, as we described in Chapter 5 on activity-based costing, setup costs are related to each production batch started. If the relevant range is considered to be from 0 to 6,000 production units, the

Exhibit 10-9 Examples of Nonlinear Cost Functions

PANEL A: Effects of Quantity Discounts on Slope Coefficient of Direct Material Cost Function

PANEL C: Step Fixed-Cost Function

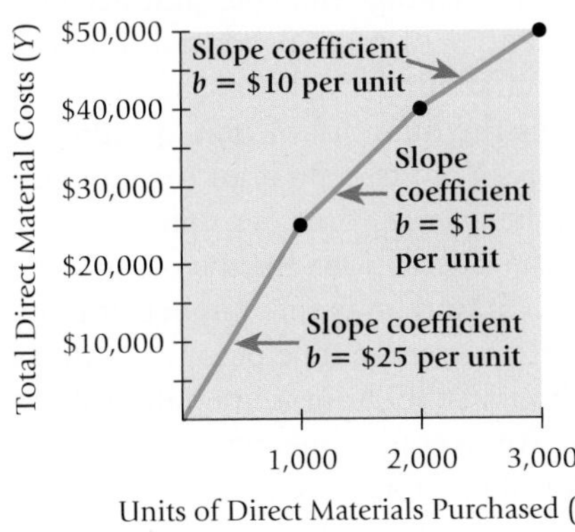

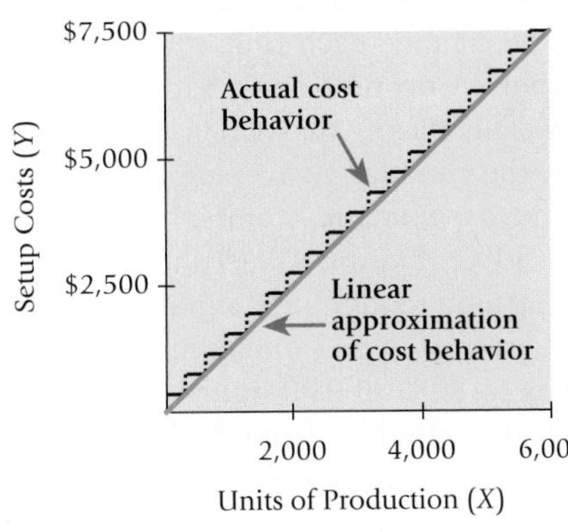

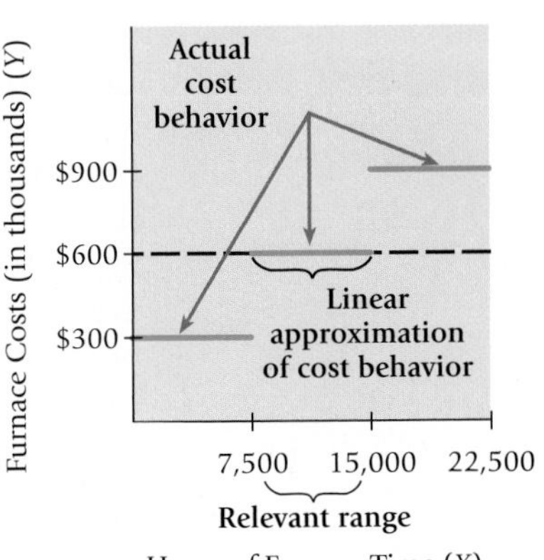

cost function is nonlinear. However, as shown by the green line in Panel B, managers often approximate step variable costs with a continuously variable cost function. This type of step cost pattern also occurs when production inputs such as materials-handling labor, supervision, and process engineering labor are acquired in discrete quantities but used in fractional quantities.

Panel C in Exhibit 10-9 shows a *step fixed-cost function* for Crofton Steel, a company that operates large heat-treatment furnaces to harden steel parts. Looking at Panel C and Panel B, you can see that the main difference between a step variable-cost function and a step fixed-cost function is that with a step fixed-cost function the cost remains the same over *wide* ranges of the activity in each relevant range. The ranges indicate the number of furnaces being used (operating costs of each furnace are $300,000). The cost increases from one range to the next higher range when another furnace is used. The relevant range of 7,500–15,000 hours of furnace time indicates that the company expects to operate with two furnaces at a cost of $600,000. Managers consider the cost of operating furnaces a fixed cost within this relevant range of operation. However, if the relevant range is from 0 to 22,500 hours, the cost function is nonlinear: The graph in Panel C is not a single straight line; it is three broken lines.

Learning Curves

Nonlinear cost functions also result from learning curves. A **learning curve** is a function that measures how labor-hours per unit decline as units of production increase because workers are learning and becoming better at their jobs. Managers use learning curves to predict how labor-hours, or labor costs, will increase as more units are produced.

The aircraft-assembly industry first documented the effect learning has on efficiency. In general, as workers become more familiar with their tasks, their efficiency improves. Managers learn how to more efficiently schedule work and operate the plant. As a result, unit costs decrease as productivity increases, and the unit-cost function behaves nonlinearly. These nonlinearities must be considered when estimating and predicting unit costs.

The term *experience curve* describes a broader application of the learning curve—one that extends to other business functions in the value chain, such as marketing, distribution, and customer service. An **experience curve** measures the decline in the cost per unit of these various business functions as the amount of these activities increases. For companies such as Dell Computer, Walmart, and McDonald's, learning curves and experience curves are key elements of their profit-maximization strategies. These companies use learning curves and experience curves to reduce costs and increase customer satisfaction, market share, and profitability.

We now describe two learning-curve models: the cumulative average-time learning model and the incremental unit-time learning model.

Cumulative Average-Time Learning Model

In the **cumulative average-time learning model**, cumulative average time per unit declines by a constant percentage each time the cumulative quantity of units produced doubles. Consider Rayburn Corporation, a radar systems manufacturer. Rayburn has an 80% learning curve. This means that when Rayburn doubles the quantity of units produced, from X to 2X, the cumulative average time *per unit* for 2X units is 80% of the cumulative average time *per unit* for X units. In other words, the average time per unit drops by 20% (100% – 80%). Exhibit 10-10 shows (in Excel) the calculations for the cumulative average-time learning model for Rayburn Corporation. Note that as the number of units produced doubles from 1 to 2 in column A, the cumulative average time per unit declines from 100 hours to 80% of 100 hours (0.80 × 100 hours = 80 hours) in column B. As the number of units doubles from 2 to 4, the cumulative average time per unit declines to 80% of 80 hours = 64 hours, and so on. To obtain the cumulative total time in column D, multiply the cumulative average time per unit by the cumulative number of units produced. For example, to produce 4 cumulative units would require 256 labor-hours (4 units × 64 cumulative average labor-hours per unit).

Exhibit 10-10 Cumulative Average-Time Learning Model for Rayburn Corporation

Home Insert Page Layout Formulas Data Review View

	A	B	C	D	E
1	**Cumulative Average-Time Learning Model for Rayburn Corporation**				
2					
3		**80% Learning Curve**			
4					
5	**Cumulative**	**Cumulative**		**Cumulative**	**Individual Unit**
6	**Number**	**Average Time**		**Total Time:**	**Time for *X*th**
7	**of Units (*X*)**	**per Unit (*y*)*: Labor-Hours**		**Labor-Hours**	**Unit: Labor-Hours**
8					
9				**D = Col A × Col B**	
10					
11	1	100.00		100.00	100.00
12	2	80.00	= (100 × 0.8)	160.00	60.00
13	3	70.21		210.63	50.63
14	4	64.00	= (80 × 0.8)	256.00	45.37
15	5	59.56		297.82	41.82
16	6	56.17		337.01	39.19
17	7	53.45		374.14	37.13
18	8	51.20	= (64 × 0.8)	409.60	35.46
19	9	49.29		443.65	34.05
20	10	47.65		476.51	32.86
21	11	46.21		508.32	31.81
22	12	44.93		539.22	30.89
23	13	43.79		569.29	30.07
24	14	42.76		598.63	29.34
25	15	41.82		627.30	28.67
26	16	40.96	= (51.2 × 0.8)	655.36	28.06
27					

E13 = D13 – D12
= 210.63 – 160.00

*The mathematical relationship underlying the cumulative average-time learning model is as follows:

$$y = aX^b$$

where y = Cumulative average time (labor-hours) per unit
X = Cumulative number of units produced
a = Time (labor-hours) required to produce the first unit
b = Factor used to calculate cumulative average time to produce units

The value of b is calculated as

$$\frac{\ln(\text{learning-curve \% in decimal form})}{\ln 2}$$

For an 80% learning curve, $b = \ln 0.8/\ln 2 = -0.2231/0.6931 = -0.3219$
For example, when $X = 3$, $a = 100$, $b = -0.3219$,

$$y = 100 \times 3^{-0.3219} = 70.21 \text{ labor-hours}$$

The cumulative total time when $X = 3$ is $70.21 \times 3 = 210.63$ labor-hours.
Numbers in table may not be exact because of rounding.

Incremental Unit-Time Learning Model

In the **incremental unit-time learning model**, the incremental time needed to produce the last unit declines by a constant percentage each time the cumulative quantity of units produced doubles. Again, consider Rayburn Corporation and an 80% learning curve. With this model, the 80% means that when the quantity of units produced is doubled from X to $2X$, the time needed to produce the unit corresponding to $2X$ is 80% of the time needed to produce the Xth unit. Exhibit 10-11 shows the Excel calculations for the incremental unit-time learning model for Rayburn Corporation based on an 80% learning curve. Note how when the units produced double from 2 to 4 in column A, the time to produce unit 4 (the last unit when 4 units are produced) is 64 hours in column B, which is 80% of the 80 hours needed to produce unit 2 (the last unit when 2 units are produced). We obtain the cumulative total time in column D by summing the individual unit times in column B. For example, to produce 4 cumulative units would require 314.21 labor-hours (100.00 + 80.00 + 70.21 + 64.00).

Exhibit 10-12 shows the cumulative average-time learning model (using data from Exhibit 10-10) and the incremental unit-time learning model (using data from Exhibit 10-11). Panel A illustrates the cumulative average time per unit as a function of cumulative units produced for each model (column A in Exhibit 10-10 or 10-11). The curve for the cumulative average-time learning model is plotted using the data from Exhibit 10-10, column B, whereas the curve for the incremental unit-time learning model is plotted using the data from Exhibit 10-11, column E. Panel B graphically illustrates the cumulative total labor-hours, again as a function of cumulative units produced for each model. The curve for the cumulative average-time learning model is plotted using the data from Exhibit 10-10, column D, while that for the incremental unit-time learning model is plotted using the data from Exhibit 10-11, column D.

Exhibit 10-11 Incremental Unit-Time Learning Model for Rayburn Corporation

Home Insert Page Layout Formulas Data Review View

	A	B	C	D	E
1	Incremental Unit-Time Learning Model for Rayburn Corporation				
2					
3		80% Learning Curve			
4					
5	Cumulative	Individual Unit Time		Cumulative	Cumulative
6	Number	for Xth Unit (*y*)*:		Total Time:	Average Time
7	of Units (*X*)	Labor-Hours		Labor-Hours	per Unit:
8					Labor-Hours
9					
10					E = Col D ÷ Col A
11					
12	1	100.00		100.00	100.00
13	2	80.00	= (100 × 0.8)	180.00	90.00
14	3	70.21		250.21	83.40
15	4	64.00	= (80 × 0.8)	314.21	78.55
16	5	59.56		373.77	74.75
17	6	56.17		429.94	71.66
18	7	53.45		483.39	69.06
19	8	51.20	= (64 × 0.8)	534.59	66.82
20	9	49.29		583.89	64.88
21	10	47.65		631.54	63.15
22	11	46.21		677.75	61.61
23	12	44.93		722.68	60.22
24	13	43.79		766.47	58.96
25	14	42.76		809.23	57.80
26	15	41.82		851.05	56.74
27	16	40.96	= (51.2 × 0.8)	892.01	55.75
28					

D14 = D13 + B14
= 180.00 + 70.21

*The mathematical relationship underlying the incremental unit-time learning model is as follows:

$$y = aX^b$$

where y = Time (labor-hours) taken to produce the last single unit
X = Cumulative number of units produced
a = Time (labor-hours) required to produce the first unit
b = Factor used to calculate incremental unit time to produce units

$$= \frac{\ln(\text{learning-curve \% in decimal form})}{\ln 2}$$

For an 80% learning curve, $b = \ln 0.8 \div \ln 2 = -0.2231 \div 0.6931 = -0.3219$

For example, when $X = 3$, $a = 100$, $b = -0.3219$,

$$y = 100 \times 3^{-0.3219} = 70.21 \text{ labor-hours}$$

The cumulative total time when $X = 3$ is 100 + 80 + 70.21 = 250.21 labor-hours.
Numbers in the table may not be exact because of rounding.

Exhibit 10-12 Plots for Cumulative Average-Time Learning Model and Incremental Unit-Time Learning Model for Rayburn Corporation

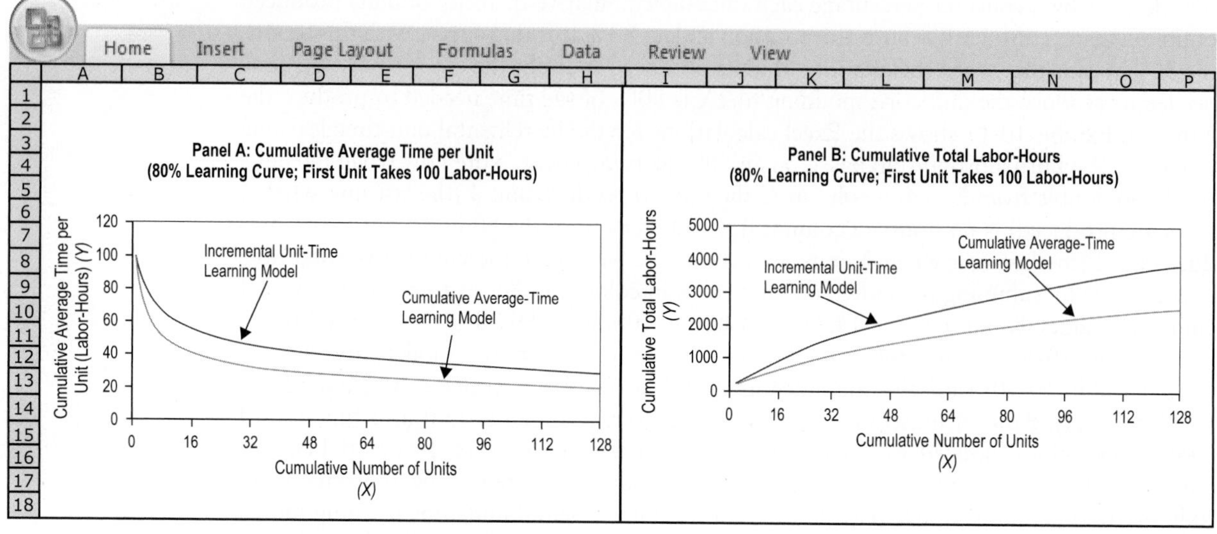

Assuming the learning rate is the same for both models, the cumulative average-time learning model represents a faster pace of learning. This is evidenced by the fact that in Exhibit 10-12, Panel B, the cumulative total labor-hours graph for the 80% incremental unit-time learning model lies above the graph for the 80% cumulative average-time learning model. If we compare the results in Exhibit 10-10 (column D) with the results in Exhibit 10-11 (column D), to produce 4 cumulative units, the 80% incremental unit-time learning model predicts 314.21 labor-hours, whereas the 80% cumulative average-time learning model predicts 256.00 labor-hours. That's because under the cumulative average-time learning model the *average labor-hours needed to produce all 4 units* is 64 hours; the labor-hour amount needed to produce unit 4 is much less than 64 hours—it is 45.37 hours (see Exhibit 10-10). Under the incremental unit-time learning model, the labor-hour amount needed to produce unit 4 is 64 hours, and the labor-hours needed to produce the first 3 units is more than 64 hours, so the average time needed to produce all 4 units is more than 64 hours.

How do managers choose which model and what percent learning curve to use? They do so on a case-by-case basis. For example, if the behavior of manufacturing labor-hour usage as production levels increase follows a pattern like the one predicted by the 80% learning curve cumulative average-time learning model, then the 80% learning curve cumulative average-time learning model should be used. Engineers, plant managers, and workers are good sources of information on the amount and type of learning actually occurring as production increases. Plotting this information and estimating the model that best fits the data are helpful when selecting the appropriate model.[2]

Incorporating Learning-Curve Effects into Prices and Standards

How do companies use learning curves? Consider the data in Exhibit 10-10 for the cumulative average-time learning model at Rayburn Corporation. Suppose the variable costs subject to learning effects are direct manufacturing labor, at $20 per hour, and related overhead, at $30 per direct manufacturing labor-hour. Managers should predict the costs shown in Exhibit 10-13.

[2] For details, see Bailey, C. 2000. Learning curve estimation of production costs and labor-hours using a free Excel add-in. *Management Accounting Quarterly,* Summer: 25–31. Free software for estimating learning curves is available at Dr. Bailey's Web site, www.profbailey.com.

Exhibit 10-13

Predicting Costs Using Learning Curves at Rayburn Corporation

	A	B	C	D	E	F
1		Cumulative				
2	Cumulative	Average Time	Cumulative	Cumulative Costs		Additions to
3	Number of	per Unit:	Total Time:	at $50 per		Cumulative
4	Units	Labor-Hours[a]	Labor-Hours[a]	Labor-Hour		Costs
5	1	100.00	100.00	$ 5,000	(100.00 × $50)	$ 5,000
6	2	80.00	160.00	8,000	(160.00 × $50)	3,000
7	4	64.00	256.00	12,800	(256.00 × $50)	4,800
8	8	51.20	409.60	20,480	(409.60 × $50)	7,680
9	16	40.96	655.36	32,768	(655.36 × $50)	12,288
10						
11	[a]Based on the cumulative average-time learning model. See Exhibit 10-10 for the computations					
12	of these amounts.					

These data show that the effects of the learning curve could have a major impact on the decisions Rayburn Corporation's managers make. For example, the managers might price the firm's radar systems extremely low to generate high demand. As production of the systems increases to meet the growing demand, the cost per unit drops, and Rayburn "rides the product down the learning curve" as it gains market share. Although it may have earned little operating income on its first unit sold—it may actually have lost money on that unit—Rayburn earns more operating income per unit as output increases.

Alternatively, depending on legal and other factors, Rayburn's managers might set a low price on just the final 8 units. After all, the total labor and related overhead costs per unit for these units are predicted to be only $12,288 ($32,768 − $20,480). On these final 8 units, the $1,536 cost per unit ($12,288 ÷ 8 units) is much lower than the $5,000 cost per unit of the first unit produced.

Many companies, such as Pizza Hut and Home Depot, also use learning curves to evaluate performance levels. The Nissan Motor Company sets assembly-labor efficiency standards for new models of cars after taking into account the learning that will occur as more units are produced. Employees are expected to learn on the job, and their performance is evaluated accordingly.

Decision Point

What is a nonlinear cost function and in what ways do learning curves give rise to nonlinear costs?

The learning-curve models examined in Exhibits 10-10 to 10-13 assume that learning is driven by a single variable (production output). Other models of learning have been developed (by companies such as Analog Devices and Hewlett-Packard) that focus on how quality—rather than manufacturing labor-hours—will change over time, regardless of whether more units are produced. Studies indicate that factors other than production output, such as job rotation and organizing workers into teams, contribute to learning that improves quality.

Data Collection and Adjustment Issues

Learning Objective 7

Be aware of data problems encountered in estimating cost functions

...for example, unreliable data and poor record keeping, extreme observations, treating fixed costs as if they are variable, and a changing relationship between a cost driver and cost

The ideal database for estimating cost functions quantitatively has two characteristics:

1. **The database should contain numerous reliably measured observations of the cost driver (the independent variable) and the related costs (the dependent variable).** Errors in measuring the costs and the cost driver are serious. They result in inaccurate estimates of the effect of the cost driver on costs.
2. **The database should consider many values spanning a wide range for the cost driver.** Using only a few values of the cost driver that are grouped closely together causes managers to consider too small a segment of the relevant range and reduces the accuracy of the estimates obtained.

Unfortunately, management accountants typically do not have the advantage of working with a database having both characteristics. This section outlines some frequently encountered data problems and steps you can take to overcome these problems. Managers should ask about these problems and assess how they have been resolved before they rely on cost estimates generated from the data.

- **The time period for measuring the dependent variable does not properly match the period for measuring the cost driver.** This problem often arises when a company does not keep accounting records on the accrual basis. Consider a cost function for a transportation company with engine-lubricant costs as the dependent variable and the number of truck-hours as the cost driver. Assume that the lubricant is purchased sporadically and stored for later use. Records maintained on the basis of lubricants purchased will indicate small lubricant costs in many months and large lubricant costs in other months. These records present an obviously inaccurate picture of what is actually taking place. The analyst should use accrual accounting to measure the cost of lubricants consumed to better match these costs with the truck-hours cost driver in this example.
- **Fixed costs are allocated as if they are variable.** For example, costs such as depreciation, insurance, or rent may be allocated to products to calculate the cost per unit of output. *The danger for managers is to regard these costs as variable rather than as fixed.* The costs appear to be variable, but that is related to the allocation methods used, not the actual behavior of the costs. To avoid this problem, the analyst should carefully distinguish fixed costs from variable costs and not treat allocated fixed cost per unit as a variable cost.
- **Data are either not available for all observations or are not uniformly reliable.** Missing cost observations often arise because they haven't been recorded or haven't been classified correctly. For example, a firm's marketing costs may be understated because the costs of sales visits to customers may be incorrectly recorded as customer-service costs. Recording the data manually rather than electronically tends to result in a higher percentage of missing observations and erroneously entered observations. Errors also arise when data on cost drivers originate outside the internal accounting system. For example, the accounting department may obtain data on testing-hours for medical instruments from the company's manufacturing department and data on number of items shipped to customers from the distribution department. One or both of these departments might not keep accurate records. To minimize these problems, the cost analyst should design data collection reports that regularly and routinely obtain the required data and should follow up immediately whenever data are missing.
- **Extreme values of observations occur.** These values arise from (a) errors in recording costs (for example, a misplaced decimal point), (b) nonrepresentative periods (for example, from a period in which a major machine breakdown occurred or a delay in delivery of materials from an international supplier curtailed production), or (c) observations outside the relevant range. Analysts should adjust or eliminate unusual observations before estimating a cost relationship.
- **There is no homogeneous relationship between the cost driver and the individual cost items in the dependent variable-cost pool.** A homogeneous relationship exists when each activity whose costs are included in the dependent variable has the same cost driver. In this case, a single cost function can be estimated. As discussed in Step 2 for estimating a cost function using quantitative analysis (pages 379–380), when the cost driver for each activity is different, separate cost functions (each with its own cost driver) should be estimated for each activity. Alternatively, as discussed on pages 404–407, the analyst should estimate the cost function with more than one independent variable using multiple regression.
- **The relationship between the cost driver and the cost is not stationary.** This occurs when the underlying process that generated the observations has not remained stable over time. For example, the relationship between number of machine-hours and manufacturing overhead costs is unlikely to be stationary when the data cover a period in

which new technology was introduced. One way to see if the relationship is stationary is to split the sample into two parts and estimate separate cost relationships—one for the period before the technology was introduced and one for the period after the technology was introduced. Then, if the estimated coefficients for the two periods are similar, the analyst can pool the data to estimate a single cost relationship. When feasible, pooling data provides a larger data set for the estimation, which increases confidence in the cost predictions being made.

- **Inflation has affected costs, the cost driver, or both.** For example, inflation may cause costs to change even when there is no change in the level of the cost driver. To study the underlying cause-and-effect relationship between the level of the cost driver and costs, the analyst should remove purely inflationary price effects from the data by dividing each cost by the price index on the date the cost was incurred.

Decision Point

What are the common data problems a company must watch for when estimating costs?

In many cases, a cost analyst must expend considerable effort to reduce the effect of these problems before estimating a cost function on the basis of past data. Before making any decisions, a manager should carefully review any data that seem suspect and work closely with the company's analysts and accountants to obtain and process the correct and relevant information.

Problem for Self-Study

The Helicopter Division of GLD, Inc., is examining helicopter assembly costs at its Indiana plant. It has received an initial order for eight of its new land-surveying helicopters. GLD can adopt one of two methods of assembling the helicopters:

Home Insert Page Layout Formulas Data Review View

	A	B	C	D	E
1		Labor-Intensive Assembly Method		Machine-Intensive Assembly Method	
2	Direct material cost per helicopter	$ 40,000		$36,000	
3	Direct-assembly labor time for first helicopter	2,000	labor-hours	800	labor-hours
4	Learning curve for assembly labor time per helicopter	85%	cumulative average time*	90%	incremental unit time**
5	Direct-assembly labor cost	$ 30	per hour	$ 30	per hour
6	Equipment-related indirect manufacturing cost	$ 12	per direct-assembly labor-hour	$ 45	per direct-assembly labor-hour
7	Material-handling-related indirect manufacturing cost	50%	of direct material cost	50%	of direct material cost
8					
9					
10	*Using the formula (page 390), for an 85% learning curve, b =	$\frac{\ln 0.85}{\ln 2}$ =	$\frac{-0.162519}{0.693147}$ = −0.234465		
11					
12					
13					
14					
15	**Using the formula (page 390), for a 90% learning curve, b =	$\frac{\ln 0.90}{\ln 2}$ =	$\frac{-0.105361}{0.693147}$ = −0.152004		
16					
17					

Required

1. How many direct-assembly labor-hours are required to assemble the first eight helicopters under (a) the labor-intensive method and (b) the machine-intensive method?
2. What is the total cost of assembling the first eight helicopters under (a) the labor-intensive method and (b) the machine-intensive method?

Solution

1. a. The following calculations show the labor-intensive assembly method based on an 85% cumulative average-time learning model (using Excel):

	G	H	I	J	K
1	Cumulative	Cumulative		Cumulative	Individual
2	Number	Average Time		Total Time:	time for
3	of Units	per Unit (*y*):		Labor-Hours	*X*th unit:
4		Labor-Hours			Labor-Hours
5				Col J = Col G × Col H	
6	1	2,000		2,000	2,000
7	2	1,700	(2,000 × 0.85)	3,400	1,400
8	3	1,546		4,637	1,237
9	4	1,445	(1,700 × 0.85)	5,780	1,143
10	5	1,371		6,857	1,077
11	6	1,314		7,884	1,027
12	7	1,267		8,871	987
13	8	1,228.25	(1,445 × 0.85)	9,826	955
14					

Cumulative average-time per unit for the *X*th unit in column H is calculated as $y = aX^b$; see Exhibit 10-10 (page 390). For example, when $X = 3$, $y = 2{,}000 \times 3^{-0.234465} = 1{,}546$ labor-hours.

b. The following calculations show the machine-intensive assembly method based on a 90% incremental unit-time learning model:

	G	H	I	J	K
1	Cumulative	Individual		Cumulative	Cumulative
2	Number	Unit Time		Total Time:	Average Time
3	of Units	for *X*th Unit (*y*):		Labor-Hours	Per Unit:
4		Labor-Hours			Labor-Hours
5					Col K = Col J ÷ Col G
6	1	800		800	800
7	2	720	(800 × 0.9)	1,520	760
8	3	677		2,197	732
9	4	648	(720 × 0.9)	2,845	711
10	5	626		3,471	694
11	6	609		4,081	680
12	7	595		4,676	668
13	8	583	(648 × 0.9)	5,258	657

Individual unit time for the *X*th unit in column H is calculated as $y = aX^b$; see Exhibit 10-11 (page 391). For example, when $X = 3$, $y = 800 \times 3^{-0.152004} = 677$ labor-hours.

2. Total costs of assembling the first eight helicopters are as follows:

	O	P	Q
1		Labor-Intensive	Machine-Intensive
2		Assembly Method	Assembly Method
3		(using data from part 1a)	(using data from part 1b)
4	Direct materials:		
5	8 helicopters × $40,000; $36,000 per helicopter	$320,000	$288,000
6	Direct-assembly labor:		
7	9,826 hrs.; 5,258 hrs. × $30/hr.	294,780	157,740
8	Indirect manufacturing costs		
9	Equipment related		
10	9,826 hrs. × $12/hr.; 5,258 hrs. × $45/hr.	117,912	236,610
11	Materials-handling related		
12	0.50 × $320,000; $288,000	160,000	144,000
13	Total assembly costs	$892,692	$826,350

The machine-intensive method's assembly costs are $66,342 lower than the labor-intensive method ($892,692 – $826,350).

Decision Points

The following question-and-answer format summarizes the chapter's learning objectives. Each decision presents a key question related to a learning objective. The guidelines are the answer to that question.

Decision	Guidelines
1. What is a linear cost function, and what types of cost behavior can it represent?	A linear cost function is a cost function in which, within the relevant range, the graph of total costs based on the level of a single activity is a straight line. Linear cost functions can be described by a constant, *a*, which represents the estimate of the total cost component that, within the relevant range, does not vary with changes in the level of the activity; and a slope coefficient, *b*, which represents the estimate of the amount by which total costs change for each unit change in the level of the activity within the relevant range. Three types of linear cost functions are variable, fixed, and mixed (or semivariable).
2. What is the most important issue in estimating a cost function?	The most important issue in estimating a cost function is determining whether a cause-and-effect relationship exists between the level of an activity and the costs related to it. Only a cause-and-effect relationship—not merely correlation—establishes an economically plausible relationship between the level of an activity and its costs.
3. What are the different methods that can be used to estimate a cost function?	Four methods for estimating cost functions are the industrial engineering method, the conference method, the account analysis method, and the quantitative analysis method (which includes the high-low method and the regression analysis method). If possible, the cost analyst should use more than one method. Each method is a check on the others.
4. What are the steps to estimate a cost function using quantitative analysis?	Six steps need to be taken to estimate a cost function using quantitative analysis: (a) Choose the dependent variable; (b) identify the cost driver; (c) collect data on the dependent variable and the cost driver; (d) plot the data; (e) estimate the cost function; and (f) evaluate the cost driver of the estimated cost function. In most situations, working closely with operations managers, the cost analyst will cycle through these steps several times before identifying an acceptable cost function.

Decision	Guidelines
5. How should a company evaluate and choose cost drivers?	Three criteria for evaluating and choosing cost drivers are (a) economic plausibility, (b) goodness of fit, and (c) the significance of the independent variable.
6. What is a nonlinear cost function, and in what ways do learning curves give rise to nonlinear costs?	A nonlinear cost function is one in which the graph of total costs based on the level of a single activity is not a straight line within the relevant range. Nonlinear costs can arise because of quantity discounts, step cost functions, and learning-curve effects. Due to learning curves, labor-hours per unit decline as units of production increase. With the cumulative average-time learning model, the cumulative average-time per unit declines by a constant percentage each time the cumulative quantity of units produced doubles. With the incremental unit-time learning model, the time needed to produce the last unit declines by a constant percentage each time the cumulative quantity of units produced doubles.
7. What are the common data problems a company must watch for when estimating costs?	The most difficult task in cost estimation is collecting high-quality, reliably measured data on the costs and the cost driver. Common problems include missing data, extreme values of observations, changes in technology, and distortions resulting from inflation.

Appendix

Regression Analysis

This appendix describes estimation of the regression equation, several commonly used regression statistics, and how to choose among cost functions that have been estimated by regression analysis. We use the data for Elegant Rugs presented in Exhibit 10-3 (page 379) and displayed here again for easy reference.

Week	Cost Driver: Machine-Hours (*X*)	Indirect Manufacturing Labor Costs (*Y*)
1	68	$ 1,190
2	88	1,211
3	62	1,004
4	72	917
5	60	770
6	96	1,456
7	78	1,180
8	46	710
9	82	1,316
10	94	1,032
11	68	752
12	48	963
Total	862	$12,501

Estimating the Regression Line

The least-squares technique for estimating the regression line minimizes the sum of the squares of the vertical deviations from the data points to the estimated regression line (also called *residual term* in Exhibit 10-6, page 383). The objective is to find the values of a and b in the linear cost function $y = a + bX$, where y is the *predicted* cost value as distinguished from the *observed* cost value, which we denote by Y. We wish to find the numerical values of a and b that minimize $\Sigma(Y - y)^2$, the sum of the squares of the vertical deviations between Y and y. Generally, these computations are done using software packages such as Excel. For the data in our example,[3] a = \$300.98 and b = \$10.31, so that the equation of the regression line is y = \$300.98 + \$10.31X.

Goodness of Fit

Goodness of fit measures how well the predicted values, y, based on the cost driver, X, match actual cost observations, Y. The regression analysis method computes a measure of goodness of fit, called the **coefficient of determination.** The coefficient of determination (r^2) measures the percentage of variation in Y explained by X (the independent variable). It is more convenient to express the coefficient of determination as 1 minus the proportion of total variance that is *not* explained by the independent variable—that is, 1 minus the ratio of unexplained variation to total variation. The unexplained variance arises because of differences between the actual values, Y, and the predicted values, y, which in the Elegant Rugs example is given by[4]

$$r^2 = 1 - \frac{\text{Unexplained variation}}{\text{Total variation}} = 1 - \frac{\Sigma(Y - y)^2}{\Sigma(Y - \bar{Y})^2} = 1 - \frac{290{,}824}{607{,}699} = 0.52$$

The calculations indicate that r^2 increases as the predicted values, y, more closely approximate the actual observations, Y. The range of r^2 is from 0 (implying no explanatory power) to 1 (implying perfect explanatory power). Generally, an r^2 of 0.30 or higher passes the goodness-of-fit test. However, do not rely exclusively on goodness of fit. It can lead to the indiscriminate inclusion of independent variables that increase r^2 but have no economic plausibility as cost drivers. *Goodness of fit has meaning only if the relationship between the cost drivers and costs is economically plausible.*

An alternative and related way to evaluate goodness of fit is to calculate the *standard error of the regression*. The **standard error of the regression** is the standard deviation of the residuals. It is equal to

$$S = \sqrt{\frac{\Sigma(Y - y)^2}{\text{Degrees of freedom}}} = \sqrt{\frac{\Sigma(Y - y)^2}{n - 2}} = \sqrt{\frac{290{,}824}{12 - 2}} = \$170.54$$

Degrees of freedom equal the number of observations, 12, *minus* the number of coefficients estimated in the regression (in this case two, a and b). On average, actual Y and

[3] The formulae for a and b are as follows:

$$a = \frac{(\Sigma Y)(\Sigma X^2) - (\Sigma X)(\Sigma XY)}{n(\Sigma X^2) - (\Sigma X)(\Sigma X)} \text{ and } b = \frac{n(\Sigma XY) - (\Sigma X)(\Sigma Y)}{n(\Sigma X^2) - (\Sigma X)(\Sigma X)}$$

where for the Elegant Rugs data in Exhibit 10-3,

n = number of data points = 12

ΣX = sum of the given X values = 68 + 88 + ⋯ + 48 = 862

ΣX^2 = sum of squares of the X values = $(68)^2 + (88)^2 + \cdots + (48)^2$ + 4,624 + 7,744 + ⋯ + 2,304 = 64,900

ΣY = sum of given Y values = 1,190 + 1,211 + ⋯ + 963 = 12,501

ΣXY = sum of the amounts obtained by multiplying each of the given X values by the associated observed Y value = (68) (1,190) + (88) (1,211) + ⋯ + (48) (963) = 80,920 + 106,568 + ⋯ + 46,224 = 928,716

$$a = \frac{(12{,}501)(64{,}900) - (862)(928{,}716)}{12(64{,}900) - (862)(862)} = \$300.98$$

$$b = \frac{12(928{,}716) - (862)(12{,}501)}{12(64{,}900) - (862)(862)} = \$10.31$$

[4] From footnote 3, ΣY = 12,501 and $\bar{Y}$ = 12,501 ÷ 12 = 1,041.75

$$\Sigma(Y - \bar{Y})^2 = (1{,}190 - 1{,}041.75)^2 + (1{,}211 - 1{,}041.75)^2 + \cdots + (963 - 1{,}041.75)^2 = 607{,}699$$

Each value of X generates a predicted value of y. For example, in week 1, y = \$300.98 + (10.31 × 68) = \$1002.06; in week 2, y = \$300.98 + (\$10.31 × 88) = \$1,208.26; and in week 12, y = \$300.98 + (\$10.31 × 48) = \$795.86. Comparing the predicted and actual values,

$$\Sigma(Y - y)^2 = (1{,}190 - 1{,}002.06)^2 + (1{,}211 - 1208.26)^2 + \cdots + (963 - 795.86)^2 = 290{,}824.$$

the predicted value, y, differ by \$170.54. For comparison, $\overline{Y}$, the average value of Y, is \$1,041.75. The smaller the standard error of the regression, the better the fit and the better the predictions for different values of X.

Significance of Independent Variables

Exhibit 10-14 shows a convenient format (in Excel) for summarizing the regression results for number of machine-hours and indirect manufacturing labor costs. Do changes in the economically plausible independent variable result in significant changes in the dependent variable? Or alternatively stated, is the slope coefficient, b = \$10.31, of the regression line statistically significant (that is, different from \$0)? Recall, for example, that in the regression of number of machine-hours and indirect manufacturing labor costs in the Elegant Rugs illustration, b is estimated from a sample of 12 weekly observations. The estimate, b, is subject to random factors, as are all sample statistics. That is, a different sample of 12 data points would undoubtedly give a different estimate of b. The **standard error of the estimated coefficient** indicates how much the estimated value, b, is likely to be affected by random factors.

The t-value of a coefficient measures how large the value of the estimated coefficient is relative to its standard error. The t-value (called t Stat in the Excel output) for the slope coefficient b is the value of the estimated coefficient, \$10.31 ÷ the standard error of the estimated coefficient, \$3.12 = 3.30. This is compared to a critical or cutoff value to ensure that a relationship exists between the independent variable and the dependent variable that cannot be attributed to random chance alone. The cutoff t-value for making inferences is a function of the number of degrees of freedom and the significance level. It is typical to look for a 5% level of significance, which indicates that there is less than a 5% probability that random factors could have affected the coefficient b. The cutoff t-value at the 5% significance level and 10 degrees of freedom is 2.228. Because the t-value for the slope coefficient b is 3.30, which exceeds 2.228, we can conclude that there is a statistically significant relationship between machine-hours and indirect manufacturing labor costs.[5]

An alternative way to test that the coefficient b is significantly different from zero is in terms of a *confidence interval*: There is less than a 5% chance that the true value of the machine-hours coefficient lies outside the range \$10.31 ± (\$2.228 × \$3.12), or \$10.31 ± \$6.95, or from \$3.36 to \$17.26. Because 0 does not appear in the confidence interval, we can conclude that changes in the number of machine-hours do affect indirect

Exhibit 10-14 Simple Regression Results with Indirect Manufacturing Labor Costs as Dependent Variable and Machine-Hours as Independent Variable (Cost Driver) for Elegant Rugs

Home | Insert | Page Layout | Formulas | Data | Review | View

	A	B	C	D	E	F
1		**Coefficients**	**Standard Error**	***t* Stat**		= Coefficient/Standard Error
2		**(1)**	**(2)**	**(3) = (1) ÷ (2)**		= B3/C3
3	Intercept	\$300.98	\$229.75	1.31 →		= \$300.98/\$229.75
4	Independent Variable: Machine-Hours (X)	\$ 10.31	\$ 3.12	3.30		
5						
6	**Regression Statistics**					
7	R Square	0.52				
8	Durbin-Watson Statistic	2.05				

[5] If the estimated coefficient is negative, then a t-value lower than −2.228 would denote a statistically significant relationship. As one would expect, the absolute value of the cutoff is lower if the estimated relationship is based on a greater number of observations. For example, with 60 degrees of freedom, the cutoff t-value at the 5% significance level is 2.00.

manufacturing labor costs. Similarly, using data from Exhibit 10-14, the *t*-value for the constant term *a* is \$300.98 ÷ \$229.75 = 1.31, which is less than 2.228. This *t*-value indicates that, within the relevant range, the constant term is *not* significantly different from zero. The Durbin-Watson statistic in Exhibit 10-14 will be discussed in the following section.

Specification Analysis of Estimation Assumptions

Specification analysis is the testing of the assumptions of regression analysis. If the assumptions of (1) linearity within the relevant range, (2) constant variance of residuals, (3) independence of residuals, and (4) normality of residuals all hold, then the simple regression procedures give reliable estimates of coefficient values. This section provides a brief overview of specification analysis. When these assumptions are not satisfied, more-complex regression procedures are necessary to obtain the best estimates.[6]

1. **Linearity within the relevant range.** A common assumption—and one that appears to be reasonable in many business applications—is that a linear relationship exists between the independent variable *X* and the dependent variable *Y* within the relevant range. If a linear regression model is used to estimate a nonlinear relationship, however, the coefficient estimates obtained will be inaccurate.

   When there is only one independent variable, the easiest way to check for linearity is to study the data plotted in a scatter diagram, a step that often is unwisely skipped. Exhibit 10-6 (page 383) presents a scatter diagram for the indirect manufacturing labor costs and machine-hours variables of Elegant Rugs shown in Exhibit 10-3 (page 379). The scatter diagram reveals that linearity appears to be a reasonable assumption for these data.

   The learning-curve models discussed in this chapter (pages 389–392) are examples of nonlinear cost functions. Costs increase when the level of production increases, but by lesser amounts than would occur with a linear cost function. In this case, the analyst should estimate a nonlinear cost function that incorporates learning effects.

2. **Constant variance of residuals.** The vertical deviation of the observed value *Y* from the regression line estimate *y* is called the *residual term, disturbance term*, or *error term*, $u = Y - y$. The assumption of constant variance implies that the residual terms are unaffected by the level of the cost driver. The assumption also implies that there is a uniform scatter, or dispersion, of the data points about the regression line as in Exhibit 10-15, Panel A. This assumption is likely to be violated, for example, in cross-sectional estimation of costs in operations of different sizes. For example, suppose Elegant Rugs has production areas of varying sizes. The company collects data from these different production areas to estimate the relationship between machine-hours and indirect manufacturing labor costs. It is possible that the residual terms in this regression will be larger for the larger production areas that have higher machine-hours and higher indirect manufacturing labor costs. There would not be a uniform scatter of data points about the regression line (see Exhibit 10-15, Panel B). Constant variance is also known as *homoscedasticity.* Violation of this assumption is called *heteroscedasticity*.

   Heteroscedasticity does not affect the accuracy of the regression estimates *a* and *b*. It does, however, reduce the reliability of the estimates of the standard errors and thus affects the precision with which inferences about the population parameters can be drawn from the regression estimates.

3. **Independence of residuals.** The assumption of independence of residuals is that the residual term for any one observation is not related to the residual term for any other observation. The problem of *serial correlation* (also called *autocorrelation*) in the residuals arises when there is a systematic pattern in the sequence of residuals such that the residual in observation *n* conveys information about the residuals in

[6] For details see, for example, Greene, W. H. *Econometric Analysis*, 7th ed. (Upper Saddle River, NJ: Prentice Hall, 2011).

Exhibit 10-15 Constant Variance of Residuals Assumption

PANEL A:
Constant Variance
(Uniform Scatter of Data Points Around Regression Line)

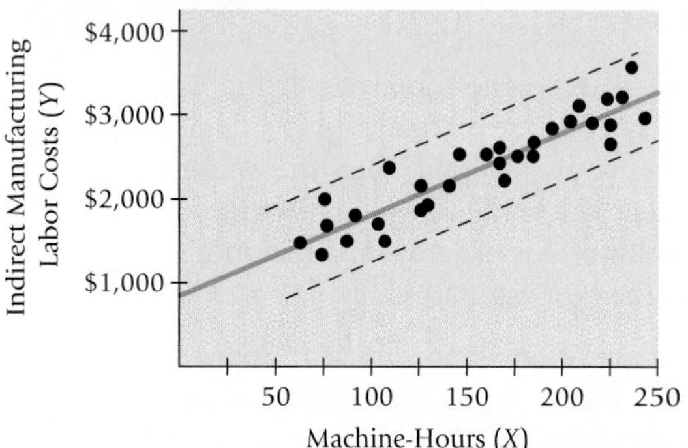

PANEL B:
Nonconstant Variance
(Higher Outputs Have Larger Residuals)

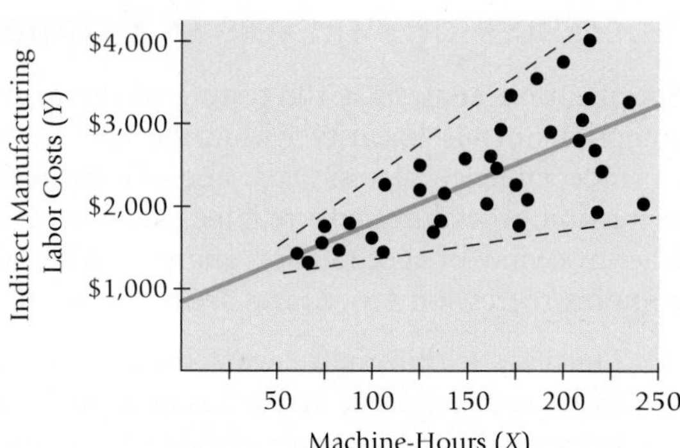

observations $n + 1$, $n + 2$, and so on. Consider another production cell at Elegant Rugs that has, over a 20-week period, seen an increase in production and hence machine-hours. Exhibit 10-16, Panel B, is a scatter diagram of machine-hours and indirect manufacturing labor costs. Observe the systematic pattern of the residuals in Panel B—positive residuals for extreme (high and low) quantities of machine-hours and negative residuals for moderate quantities of machine-hours. One reason for this observed pattern at low values of the cost driver is the "stickiness" of costs. When machine-hours are below 50 hours, indirect manufacturing labor costs do not decline. When machine-hours increase over time as production is ramped up, indirect manufacturing labor costs increase more as managers at Elegant Rugs struggle to manage the higher volume. How would the plot of residuals look if there were no auto-correlation? Like the plot in Exhibit 10-16, Panel A, that shows no pattern in the residuals.

Like nonconstant variance of residuals, serial correlation does not affect the accuracy of the regression estimates *a* and *b*. It does, however, affect the standard errors of the coefficients, which in turn affect the precision with which inferences about the population parameters can be drawn from the regression estimates.

Exhibit 10-16 Independence of Residuals Assumption

PANEL A:
Independence of Residuals
(No Pattern in Residuals)

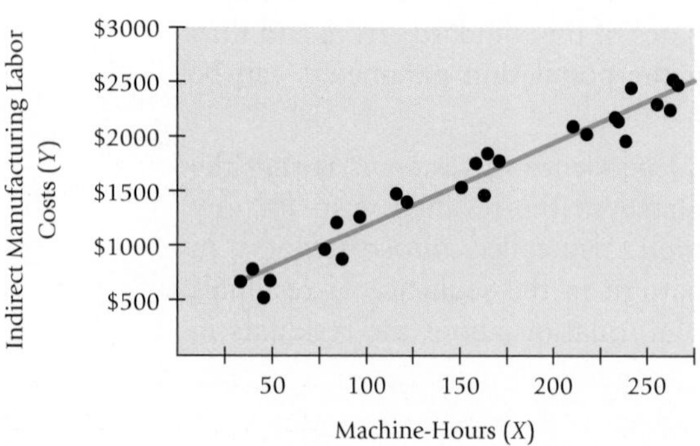

PANEL B:
Serial Correlation in Residuals
(A Pattern of Positive Residuals for Extreme Machine-Hours Used; Negative Residuals for Moderate Machine-Hours Used)

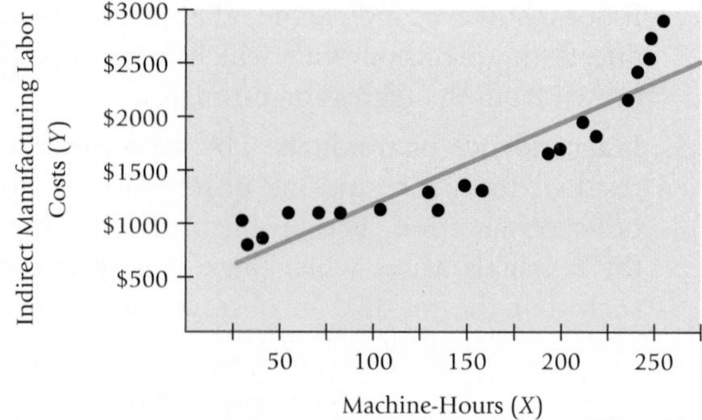

The Durbin-Watson statistic is one measure of serial correlation in the estimated residuals. For samples of 10 to 20 observations, a Durbin-Watson statistic in the 1.10–2.90 range indicates that the residuals are independent. The Durbin-Watson statistic for the regression results of Elegant Rugs in Exhibit 10-14 is 2.05. Therefore, an assumption of independence in the estimated residuals is reasonable for this regression model.

4. **Normality of residuals.** The normality of residuals assumption means that the residuals are distributed normally around the regression line. The normality of residuals assumption is frequently satisfied when using regression analysis on real cost data. Even when the assumption does not hold, accountants can still generate accurate estimates based on the regression equation, but the resulting confidence interval around these estimates is likely to be inaccurate.

Using Regression Output to Choose Cost Drivers of Cost Functions

Consider the two choices of cost drivers we described earlier in this chapter for indirect manufacturing labor costs (y):

$$y = a + (b \times \text{Number of machine-hours})$$

$$y = a + (b \times \text{Number of direct manufacturing labor-hours})$$

Exhibits 10-6 and 10-8 show plots of the data for the two regressions. Exhibit 10-14 reports regression results for the cost function using number of machine-hours as the independent variable. Exhibit 10-17 presents comparable regression results (in Excel) for the cost function using number of direct manufacturing labor-hours as the independent variable.

On the basis of the material presented in this appendix, which regression is better? Exhibit 10-18 compares these two cost functions in a systematic way. For several criteria, the cost function based on machine-hours is preferable to the cost function based on direct manufacturing labor-hours. The economic plausibility criterion is especially important.

Do not always assume that any one cost function will perfectly satisfy all the criteria in Exhibit 10-18. A cost analyst must often make a choice among "imperfect" cost functions, in the sense that the data of any particular cost function will not perfectly meet one or more of the assumptions underlying regression analysis. For example, both of the cost functions in Exhibit 10-18 are imperfect because, as stated in the section on specification analysis of estimation assumptions, inferences drawn from only 12 observations are not reliable.

Exhibit 10-17 Simple Regression Results with Indirect Manufacturing Labor Costs as Dependent Variable and Direct Manufacturing Labor-Hours as Independent Variable (Cost Driver) for Elegant Rugs

Home | Insert | Page Layout | Formulas | Data | Review | View

	A	B	C	D	E	F	G	H
1		**Coefficients**	**Standard Error**	***t* Stat**				
2		**(1)**	**(2)**	**(3) = (1) ÷ (2)**				
3	Intercept	$744.67	$217.61	3.42				
4	Independent Variable: Direct Manufacturing Labor-Hours (X)	$ 7.72	$ 5.40	1.43 →		= Coefficient/Standard Error = B4/C4 = $7.72/$5.40		
5								
6	**Regression Statistics**							
7	R Square	0.17						
8	Durbin-Watson Statistic	2.26						

Exhibit 10-18 Comparison of Alternative Cost Functions for Indirect Manufacturing Labor Costs Estimated with Simple Regression for Elegant Rugs

Criterion	Cost Function 1: Machine-Hours as Independent Variable	Cost Function 2: Direct Manufacturing Labor-Hours as Independent Variable
Economic plausibility	A positive relationship between indirect manufacturing labor costs (technical support labor) and machine-hours is economically plausible in Elegant Rugs' highly automated plant	A positive relationship between indirect manufacturing labor costs and direct manufacturing labor-hours is economically plausible, but less so than machine-hours in Elegant Rugs' highly automated plant on a week-to-week basis.
Goodness of fit[a]	$r^2 = 0.52$; standard error of regression = \$170.50. Excellent goodness of fit.	$r^2 = 0.17$; standard error of regression = \$224.60. Poor goodness of fit.
Significance of independent variable(s)	The *t*-value of 3.30 is significant at the 0.05 level.	The *t*-value of 1.43 is not significant at the 0.05 level.
Specification analysis of estimation assumptions	Plot of the data indicates that assumptions of linearity, constant variance, independence of residuals (Durbin-Watson statistic = 2.05), and normality of residuals hold, but inferences drawn from only 12 observations are not reliable.	Plot of the data indicates that assumptions of linearity, constant variance, independence of residuals (Durbin-Watson statistic = 2.26), and normality of residuals hold, but inferences drawn from only 12 observations are not reliable.

[a]If the number of observations available to estimate the machine-hours regression differs from the number of observations available to estimate the direct manufacturing labor-hours regression, an *adjusted* r^2 can be calculated to take this difference (in degrees of freedom) into account. Programs such as Excel calculate and present *adjusted* r^2.

Multiple Regression and Cost Hierarchies

In some cases, a satisfactory estimation of a cost function may be based on only one independent variable, such as number of machine-hours. In many cases, however, basing the estimation on more than one independent variable (that is, *multiple regression*) is more economically plausible and improves accuracy. The most widely used equations to express relationships between two or more independent variables and a dependent variable are linear in the form

$$y = a + b_1X_1 + b_2X_2 + \cdots + u$$

where,

y = Cost to be predicted
$X_1, X_2, \ldots$ = Independent variables on which the prediction is to be based
$a, b_1, b_2, \ldots$ = Estimated coefficients of the regression model
u = Residual term that includes the net effect of other factors not in the model as well as measurement errors in the dependent and independent variables

Example: Consider the Elegant Rugs data in Exhibit 10-19. The company's ABC analysis indicates that indirect manufacturing labor costs include large amounts incurred for setup and changeover costs when a new batch of carpets is started. Management believes that in addition to number of machine-hours (an output unit-level cost driver), indirect

Exhibit 10-19

Weekly Indirect Manufacturing Labor Costs, Machine-Hours, Direct Manufacturing Labor-Hours, and Number of Production Batches for Elegant Rugs

	A	B	C	D	E
1	Week	Machine-Hours (X_1)	Number of Production Batches (X_2)	Direct Manufacturing Labor-Hours	Indirect Manufacturing Labor Costs (Y)
2	1	68	12	30	$ 1,190
3	2	88	15	35	1,211
4	3	62	13	36	1,004
5	4	72	11	20	917
6	5	60	10	47	770
7	6	96	12	45	1,456
8	7	78	17	44	1,180
9	8	46	7	38	710
10	9	82	14	70	1,316
11	10	94	12	30	1,032
12	11	68	7	29	752
13	12	48	14	38	963
14	Total	862	144	462	$12,501
15					

manufacturing labor costs are also affected by the number of batches of carpet produced during each week (a batch-level driver). Elegant Rugs estimates the relationship between two independent variables, number of machine-hours and number of production batches of carpet manufactured during the week, and indirect manufacturing labor costs.

Exhibit 10-20 presents results (in Excel) for the following multiple regression model, using data in columns B, C, and E of Exhibit 10-19:

$$y = \$42.58 + \$7.60X_1 + \$37.77X_2$$

where X_1 is the number of machine-hours and X_2 is the number of production batches. It is economically plausible that both number of machine-hours and number of production batches would help explain variations in indirect manufacturing labor costs at Elegant Rugs.

Exhibit 10-20 Multiple Regression Results with Indirect Manufacturing Labor Costs and Two Independent Variables of Cost Drivers (Machine-Hours and Production Batches) for Elegant Rugs

	A	B	C	D	E	F
1		Coefficients	Standard Error	*t* Stat		
2		(1)	(2)	(3) = (1) ÷ (2)		
3	Intercept	$42.58	$213.91	0.20		
4	Independent Variable 1: Machine-Hours (*X1*)	$ 7.60	$ 2.77	2.74	→	= Coefficient/Standard Error = B4/C4 = $7.60/$2.77
5	Independent Variable 2: Number of Production Batches (*X2*)	$37.77	$ 15.25	2.48		
6						
7	Regression Statistics					
8	R Square	0.72				
9	Durbin-Watson Statistic	2.49				

The r^2 of 0.52 for the simple regression using number of machine-hours (Exhibit 10-14) increases to 0.72 with the multiple regression in Exhibit 10-20. The t-values suggest that the independent variable coefficients of both number of machine-hours ($7.60) and number of production batches ($37.77) are significantly different from zero ($t = 2.74$ is the t-value for number of machine-hours, and $t = 2.48$ is the t-value for number of production batches, compared to the cut-off t-value of 2.26). The multiple regression model in Exhibit 10-20 satisfies both economic plausibility and statistical criteria, and it explains much greater variation (that is, r^2 of 0.72 versus r^2 of 0.52) in indirect manufacturing labor costs than the simple regression model using only number of machine-hours as the independent variable.[7] The standard error of the regression equation that includes number of batches as an independent variable is

$$\sqrt{\frac{\Sigma(Y - y)^2}{n - 3}} = \sqrt{\frac{170{,}156}{9}} = \$137.50$$

which is lower than the standard error of the regression with only machine-hours as the independent variable, $170.50. That is, even though adding a variable reduces the degrees of freedom in the denominator, it substantially improves fit so that the numerator, $\Sigma(Y - y)^2$, decreases even more. Number of machine-hours and number of production batches are both important cost drivers of indirect manufacturing labor costs at Elegant Rugs.

In Exhibit 10-20, the slope coefficients—$7.60 for number of machine-hours and $37.77 for number of production batches—measure the change in indirect manufacturing labor costs associated with a unit change in an independent variable (assuming that the other independent variable is held constant). For example, indirect manufacturing labor costs increase by $37.77 when one more production batch is added, assuming that the number of machine-hours is held constant.

An alternative approach would create two separate cost pools for indirect manufacturing labor costs: one for costs related to number of machine-hours and another for costs related to number of production batches. Elegant Rugs would then estimate the relationship between the cost driver and the costs in each cost pool. The difficult task under this approach is to properly subdivide the indirect manufacturing labor costs into the two cost pools.

Multicollinearity

A major concern that arises with multiple regression is multicollinearity. **Multicollinearity** exists when two or more independent variables are highly correlated with each other. Generally, users of regression analysis believe that a *coefficient of correlation* between independent variables greater than 0.70 indicates multicollinearity. Multicollinearity increases the standard errors of the coefficients of the individual variables. That is, variables that are economically and statistically significant will appear not to be significantly different from zero.

[7] Adding another variable always increases r^2. The question is whether adding another variable increases r^2 sufficiently. One way to get insight into this question is to calculate an adjusted r^2 as follows:

Adjusted $r^2 = 1 - (1 - r^2)\frac{n - 1}{n - p - 1}$, where n is the number of observations and p is the number of coefficients estimated. In the model with only machine-hours as the independent variable, adjusted $r^2 = 1 - (1 - 0.52)\frac{12 - 1}{12 - 2 - 1} = 0.41$. In the model with both machine-hours and number of batches as independent variables, adjusted $r^2 = 1 - (1 - 0.72)\frac{12 - 1}{12 - 3 - 1} = 0.62$. Adjusted r^2 does not have the same interpretation as r^2, but the increase in adjusted r^2 when number of batches is added as an independent variable suggests that adding this variable significantly improves the fit of the model in a way that more than compensates for the degree of freedom lost by estimating another coefficient.

The matrix of correlation coefficients of the different variables described in Exhibit 10-19 are as follows:

	Indirect Manufacturing Labor Costs	Machine-Hours	Number of Production Batches	Direct Manufacturing Labor-Hours
Indirect manufacturing labor costs	1			
Machine-hours	0.72	1		
Number of production batches	0.69	0.4	1	
Direct manufacturing labor-hours	0.41	0.12	0.31	1

These results indicate that multiple regressions using any pair of the independent variables in Exhibit 10-19 are not likely to encounter multicollinearity problems.

When multicollinearity exists, try to obtain new data that do not suffer from multicollinearity problems. Do not drop an independent variable (cost driver) that should be included in a model because it is correlated with another independent variable. Omitting such a variable will cause the estimated coefficient of the independent variable included in the model to be biased away from its true value.

Terms to Learn

This chapter and the Glossary at the end of this book contain definitions of the following important terms:

account analysis method **(p. 377)**
coefficient of determination (r^2) **(p. 399)**
conference method **(p. 377)**
constant **(p. 372)**
cost estimation **(p. 374)**
cost function **(p. 371)**
cost predictions **(p. 374)**
cumulative average-time learning model **(p. 390)**
dependent variable **(p. 379)**
experience curve **(p. 389)**
high-low method **(p. 381)**
incremental unit-time learning model **(p. 391)**
independent variable **(p. 379)**
industrial engineering method **(p. 376)**
intercept **(p. 372)**
learning curve **(p. 389)**
linear cost function **(p. 371)**
mixed cost **(p. 372)**
multicollinearity **(p. 406)**
multiple regression **(p. 383)**
nonlinear cost function **(p. 388)**
regression analysis **(p. 383)**
residual term **(p. 383)**
semivariable cost **(p. 372)**
simple regression **(p. 383)**
slope coefficient **(p. 372)**
specification analysis **(p. 401)**
standard error of the estimated coefficient **(p. 400)**
standard error of the regression **(p. 399)**
step cost function **(p. 388)**
work-measurement method **(p. 376)**

Assignment Material

Questions

MyAccountingLab

10-1 What two assumptions are frequently made when estimating a cost function?

10-2 Describe three alternative linear cost functions.

10-3 What is the difference between a linear and a nonlinear cost function? Give an example of each type of cost function.

10-4 "High correlation between two variables means that one is the cause and the other is the effect." Do you agree? Explain.

10-5 Name four approaches to estimating a cost function.

10-6 Describe the conference method for estimating a cost function. What are two advantages of this method?

10-7 Describe the account analysis method for estimating a cost function.

10-8 List the six steps in estimating a cost function on the basis of an analysis of a past cost relationship. Which step is typically the most difficult for the cost analyst?

10-9 When using the high-low method, should you base the high and low observations on the dependent variable or on the cost driver?

10-10 Describe three criteria for evaluating cost functions and choosing cost drivers.

10-11 Define learning curve. Outline two models that can be used when incorporating learning into the estimation of cost functions.

10-12 Discuss four frequently encountered problems when collecting cost data on variables included in a cost function.

10-13 What are the four key assumptions examined in specification analysis in the case of simple regression?

10-14 "All the independent variables in a cost function estimated with regression analysis are cost drivers." Do you agree? Explain.

10-15 "Multicollinearity exists when the dependent variable and the independent variable are highly correlated." Do you agree? Explain.

MyAccountingLab

Exercises

10-16 Estimating a cost function. The controller of the Ijiri Company wants you to estimate a cost function from the following two observations in a general ledger account called Maintenance:

Month	Machine-Hours	Maintenance Costs Incurred
January	6,000	$4,000
February	10,000	5,400

Required

1. Estimate the cost function for maintenance.
2. Can the constant in the cost function be used as an estimate of fixed maintenance cost per month? Explain.

10-17 Identifying variable-, fixed-, and mixed-cost functions. The Pacific Corporation operates car rental agencies at more than 20 airports. Customers can choose from one of three contracts for car rentals of one day or less:

- Contract 1: $50 for the day
- Contract 2: $30 for the day plus $0.20 per mile traveled
- Contract 3: $1 per mile traveled

Required

1. Plot separate graphs for each of the three contracts, with costs on the vertical axis and miles traveled on the horizontal axis.
2. Express each contract as a linear cost function of the form $y = a + bX$.
3. Identify each contract as a variable-, fixed-, or mixed-cost function.

10-18 Various cost-behavior patterns. (CPA, adapted).

The vertical axes of the graphs below represent total cost, and the horizontal axes represent units produced during a calendar year. In each case, the zero point of dollars and production is at the intersection of the two axes.

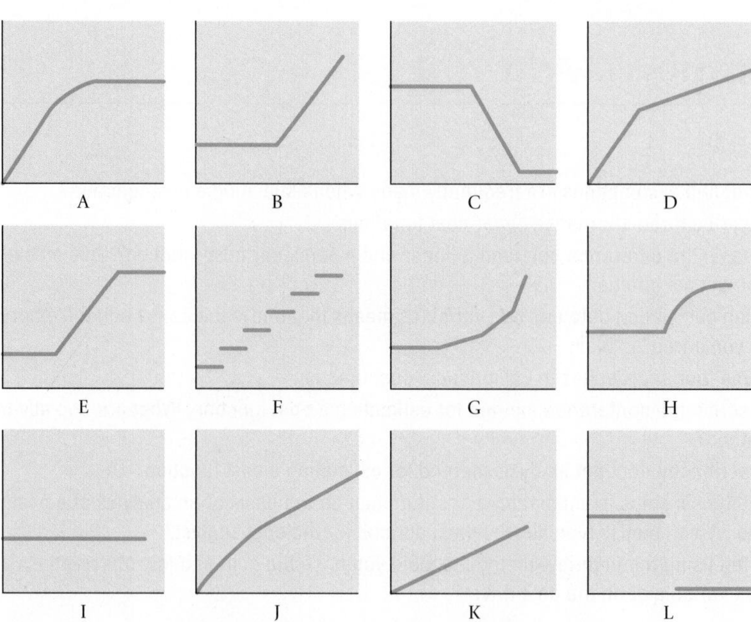

Required

Select the graph that matches the numbered manufacturing cost data (requirements 1-9). Indicate by letter which graph best fits the situation or item described. The graphs may be used more than once.

1. Annual depreciation of equipment, where the amount of depreciation charged is computed by the machine-hours method.
2. Electricity bill—a flat fixed charge, plus a variable cost after a certain number of kilowatt-hours are used, in which the quantity of kilowatt-hours used varies proportionately with quantity of units produced.
3. City water bill, which is computed as follows:

First 1,000,000 gallons or less	$1,000 flat fee
Next 10,000 gallons	$0.003 per gallon used
Next 10,000 gallons	$0.006 per gallon used
Next 10,000 gallons	$0.009 per gallon used
and so on	and so on

   The gallons of water used vary proportionately with the quantity of production output.
4. Cost of direct materials, where direct material cost per unit produced decreases with each pound of material used (for example, if 1 pound is used, the cost is $10; if 2 pounds are used, the cost is $19.98; if 3 pounds are used, the cost is $29.94), with a minimum cost per unit of $9.20.
5. Annual depreciation of equipment, where the amount is computed by the straight-line method. When the depreciation schedule was prepared, it was anticipated that the obsolescence factor would be greater than the wear-and-tear factor.
6. Rent on a manufacturing plant donated by the city, where the agreement calls for a fixed-fee payment unless 200,000 labor-hours are worked, in which case no rent is paid.
7. Salaries of repair personnel, where one person is needed for every 1,000 machine-hours or less (that is, 0 to 1,000 hours requires one person, 1,001 to 2,000 hours requires two people, and so on).
8. Cost of direct materials used (assume no quantity discounts).
9. Rent on a manufacturing plant donated by the county, where the agreement calls for rent of $100,000 to be reduced by $1 for each direct manufacturing labor-hour worked in excess of 200,000 hours, but a minimum rental fee of $20,000 must be paid.

10-19 Matching graphs with descriptions of cost and revenue behavior. (D. Green, adapted) Given here are a number of graphs.

The horizontal axis of each graph represents the units produced over the year, and the vertical axis represents total cost or revenues.

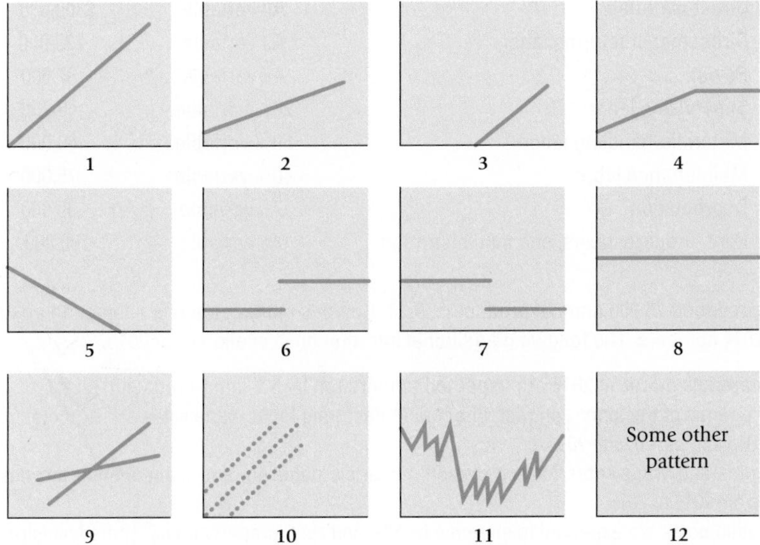

Required

Indicate by number which graph best fits the situation or item described (a–h). Some graphs may be used more than once; some may not apply to any of the situations.

a. Direct material costs
b. Supervisors' salaries for one shift and two shifts
c. A cost-volume-profit graph
d. Mixed costs—for example, car rental fixed charge plus a rate per mile driven

e. Depreciation of plant, computed on a straight-line basis
f. Data supporting the use of a variable-cost rate, such as manufacturing labor cost of $14 per unit produced
g. Incentive bonus plan that pays managers $0.10 for every unit produced above some level of production
h. Interest expense on $2 million borrowed at a fixed rate of interest

10-20 Account analysis, high-low. Luwak Coffees wants to find an equation to estimate monthly utility costs. Luwak has been in business for one year and has collected the following cost data for utilities:

Month	Electricity Bill	Kilowatt Hours Used	Telephone Bill	Telephone Minutes Used	Water Bill	Gallons of Water Used
January	$ 720	2,400	$184.00	2,200	$120	61,120
February	$ 840	2,800	$182.40	2,120	$120	53,400
March	$1,098	3,660	$189.60	2,480	$120	62,900
April	$ 810	2,700	$179.20	1,960	$120	59,930
May	$1,176	3,920	$196.00	2,800	$120	61,136
June	$1,248	4,160	$197.60	2,880	$120	51,080
July	$1,044	3,480	$186.80	2,340	$120	65,380
August	$1,194	3,980	$192.40	2,620	$120	62,444
September	$1,260	4,200	$191.20	2,560	$120	67,080
October	$1,230	4,100	$187.60	2,380	$120	63,940
November	$1,188	3,960	$182.00	2,100	$120	57,200
December	$1,266	4,220	$ 97.00	2,700	$120	68,200

Required

1. Which of the preceding costs is variable? Fixed? Mixed? Explain.
2. Using the high-low method, determine the cost function for each cost.
3. Combine the preceding information to get a monthly utility cost function for Java Joe's.
4. Next month, Luwak expects to use 4,400 kilowatt hours of electricity, make 3,000 minutes of telephone calls, and use 64,000 gallons of water. Estimate total cost of utilities for the month.

10-21 Account analysis method. Gower, Inc., a manufacturer of plastic products, reports the following manufacturing costs and account analysis classification for the year ended December 31, 2014.

Account	Classification	Amount
Direct materials	All variable	$300,000
Direct manufacturing labor	All variable	225,000
Power	All variable	37,500
Supervision labor	20% variable	56,250
Materials-handling labor	50% variable	60,000
Maintenance labor	40% variable	75,000
Depreciation	0% variable	95,000
Rent, property taxes, and administration	0% variable	100,000

Gower, Inc., produced 75,000 units of product in 2014. Gower's management is estimating costs for 2015 on the basis of 2014 numbers. The following additional information is available for 2015.

a. Direct materials prices in 2015 are expected to increase by 5% compared with 2014.
b. Under the terms of the labor contract, direct manufacturing labor wage rates are expected to increase by 10% in 2015 compared with 2014.
c. Power rates and wage rates for supervision, materials handling, and maintenance are not expected to change from 2014 to 2015.
d. Depreciation costs are expected to increase by 5%, and rent, property taxes, and administration costs are expected to increase by 7%.
e. Gower expects to manufacture and sell 80,000 units in 2015.

Required

1. Prepare a schedule of variable, fixed, and total manufacturing costs for each account category in 2015. Estimate total manufacturing costs for 2015.
2. Calculate Gower's total manufacturing cost per unit in 2014, and estimate total manufacturing cost per unit in 2015.
3. How can you obtain better estimates of fixed and variable costs? Why would these better estimates be useful to Gower?

10-22 Estimating a cost function, high-low method. Reisen Travel offers helicopter service from suburban towns to John F. Kennedy International Airport in New York City. Each of its 10 helicopters makes between 1,000 and 2,000 round-trips per year. The records indicate that a helicopter that has made 1,000 round-trips in the year incurs an average operating cost of $350 per round-trip, and one that has made 2,000 round-trips in the year incurs an average operating cost of $300 per round-trip.

Required

1. Using the high-low method, estimate the linear relationship $y = a + bX$, where y is the total annual operating cost of a helicopter and X is the number of round-trips it makes to JFK airport during the year.
2. Give examples of costs that would be included in a and in b.
3. If Reisen Travel expects each helicopter to make, on average, 1,200 round-trips in the coming year, what should its estimated operating budget for the helicopter fleet be?

10-23 Estimating a cost function, high-low method. Laurie Daley is examining customer-service costs in the southern region of Capitol Products. Capitol Products has more than 200 separate electrical products that are sold with a 6-month guarantee of full repair or replacement with a new product. When a product is returned by a customer, a service report is prepared. This service report includes details of the problem and the time and cost of resolving the problem. Weekly data for the most recent 8-week period are as follows:

Week	Customer-Service Department Costs	Number of Service Reports
1	$13,700	190
2	20,900	275
3	13,000	115
4	18,800	395
5	14,000	265
6	21,500	455
7	16,900	340
8	21,000	305

Required

1. Plot the relationship between customer-service costs and number of service reports. Is the relationship economically plausible?
2. Use the high-low method to compute the cost function, relating customer-service costs to the number of service reports.
3. What variables, in addition to number of service reports, might be cost drivers of weekly customer-service costs of Capitol Products?

10-24 Linear cost approximation. Terry Lawler, managing director of the Little Rock Reviewers Company, is examining how overhead costs behave with changes in monthly professional labor-hours billed to clients. Assume the following historical data:

Total Overhead Costs	Professional Labor-Hours Billed to Clients
$330,000	3,000
395,000	4,000
425,000	5,000
467,000	6,000
521,000	7,500
577,000	8,500

Required

1. Compute the linear cost function, relating total overhead costs to professional labor-hours, using the representative observations of 4,000 and 7,500 hours. Plot the linear cost function. Does the constant component of the cost function represent the fixed overhead costs of the Little Rock Reviewers Company? Why?
2. What would be the predicted total overhead costs for (a) 5,000 hours and (b) 8,500 hours using the cost function estimated in requirement 1? Plot the predicted costs and actual costs for 5,000 and 8,500 hours.
3. Lawler had a chance to accept a special job that would have boosted professional labor-hours from 4,000 to 5,000 hours. Suppose Lawler, guided by the linear cost function, rejected this job because it would have brought a total increase in contribution margin of $31,000, before deducting the predicted increase in total overhead cost, $36,000. What is the total contribution margin actually forgone?

10-25 Cost-volume-profit and regression analysis. Goldstein Corporation manufactures a children's bicycle, model CT8. Goldstein currently manufactures the bicycle frame. During 2014, Goldstein made 32,000 frames at a total cost of $1,056,000. Ryan Corporation has offered to supply as many frames as Goldstein wants at a cost of $32.50 per frame. Goldstein anticipates needing 35,000 frames each year for the next few years.

Required

1. **a.** What is the average cost of manufacturing a bicycle frame in 2014? How does it compare to Ryan's offer?
   b. Can Goldstein use the answer in requirement 1a to determine the cost of manufacturing 35,000 bicycle frames? Explain.
2. Goldstein's cost analyst uses annual data from past years to estimate the following regression equation with total manufacturing costs of the bicycle frame as the dependent variable and bicycle frames produced as the independent variable:

$$y = \$435{,}000 + \$19X$$

   During the years used to estimate the regression equation, the production of bicycle frames varied from 31,000 to 35,000. Using this equation, estimate how much it would cost Goldstein to manufacture 35,000 bicycle frames. How much more or less costly is it to manufacture the frames rather than to acquire them from Ryan?
3. What other information would you need to be confident that the equation in requirement 2 accurately predicts the cost of manufacturing bicycle frames?

10-26 Regression analysis, service company. (CMA, adapted) Stan Baiman owns a catering company that prepares food and beverages for banquets and parties. For a standard party the cost on a per-person basis is as follows:

Food and beverages	$30
Labor (0.5 hour × $20 per hour)	10
Overhead (0.5 hour × $14 per hour)	7
Total cost per person	$47

Baiman is quite certain about his estimates of the food, beverages, and labor costs but is not as comfortable with the overhead estimate. The overhead estimate was based on the actual data for the past 12 months, which are presented here. These data indicate that overhead costs vary with the direct labor-hours used. The $14 estimate was determined by dividing total overhead costs for the 12 months by total labor-hours.

Month	Labor-Hours	Overhead Costs
January	5,000	$ 110,000
February	5,400	118,000
March	6,000	120,000
April	8,400	128,000
May	15,000	154,000
June	11,000	142,000
July	13,000	148,000
August	9,000	134,000
September	14,000	150,000
October	9,000	136,000
November	6,200	124,000
December	13,000	146,000
Total	115,000	$1,610,000

Baiman has recently become aware of regression analysis. He estimated the following regression equation with overhead costs as the dependent variable and labor-hours as the independent variable:

$$y = \$96{,}541 + \$3.93X$$

Required

1. Plot the relationship between overhead costs and labor-hours. Draw the regression line and evaluate it using the criteria of economic plausibility, goodness of fit, and slope of the regression line.
2. Using data from the regression analysis, what is the variable cost per person for a standard party?
3. Stan Baiman has been asked to prepare a bid for a 200-person standard party to be given next month. Determine the minimum bid price that Baiman would be willing to submit to recoup variable costs.

10-27 High-low, regression. Mandy Knox is the new manager of the materials storeroom for Timken Manufacturing. Mandy has been asked to estimate future monthly purchase costs for part #696, used in two of Timken's products. Mandy has purchase cost and quantity data for the past 9 months as follows:

Month	Cost of Purchase	Quantity Purchased
January	$12,468	2,700 parts
February	12,660	2,820
March	17,280	4,068
April	15,816	3,744
May	13,164	2,988
June	13,896	3,216
July	15,228	3,636
August	10,272	2,316
September	14,940	3,552

Estimated monthly purchases for this part based on expected demand of the two products for the rest of the year are as follows:

Month	Purchase Quantity Expected
October	3,360 parts
November	3,720
December	3,000

Required

1. The computer in Mandy's office is down, and Mandy has been asked to immediately provide an equation to estimate the future purchase cost for part #696. Mandy grabs a calculator and uses the high-low method to estimate a cost equation. What equation does she get?
2. Using the equation from requirement 1, calculate the future expected purchase costs for each of the last 3 months of the year.
3. After a few hours Mandy's computer is fixed. Mandy uses the first 9 months of data and regression analysis to estimate the relationship between the quantity purchased and purchase costs of part #696. The regression line Mandy obtains is as follows:

$$y = \$2,135.5 + 3.67X$$

   Evaluate the regression line using the criteria of economic plausibility, goodness of fit, and significance of the independent variable. Compare the regression equation to the equation based on the high-low method. Which is a better fit? Why?
4. Use the regression results to calculate the expected purchase costs for October, November, and December. Compare the expected purchase costs to the expected purchase costs calculated using the high-low method in requirement 2. Comment on your results.

10-28 Learning curve, cumulative average-time learning model. Northern Defense manufactures radar systems. It has just completed the manufacture of its first newly designed system, RS-32. Manufacturing data for the RS-32 follow:

	A	B	C
1	Direct material cost	$ 84,000	per unit of RS-32
2	Direct manufacturing labor time for first unit	4,400	direct manufacturing labor hours
3	Learning curve for manufacturing labor time per radar system	85%	cumulative average time[a]
4	Direct manufacturing labor cost	$ 27	per direct manufacturing labor-hour
5	Variable manufacturing overhead cost	$ 13	per direct manufacturing labor-hour
6			
7	[a]Using the formula (p 390), for an 85% learning curve, $b = \frac{\ln 0.85}{\ln 2} = \frac{-0.162519}{0.693147} = -0.234465$		

Required

Calculate the total variable costs of producing 2, 4, and 8 units.

10-29 Learning curve, incremental unit-time learning model. Assume the same information for Northern Defense as in Exercise 10-28, except that Northern Defense uses an 85% incremental unit-time learning model as a basis for predicting direct manufacturing labor-hours. (An 85% learning curve means $b = -0.234465$.)

Required

1. Calculate the total variable costs of producing 2, 3, and 4 units.
2. If you solved Exercise 10-28, compare your cost predictions in the two exercises for 2 and 4 units. Why are the predictions different? How should Northern Defense decide which model it should use?

10-30 High-low method. Ken Howard, financial analyst at KMW Corporation, is examining the behavior of quarterly maintenance costs for budgeting purposes. Howard collects the following data on machine-hours worked and maintenance costs for the past 12 quarters:

Quarter	Machine-Hours	Maintenance Costs
1	100,000	$205,000
2	120,000	240,000
3	110,000	220,000
4	130,000	260,000
5	95,000	190,000
6	115,000	235,000
7	105,000	215,000
8	125,000	255,000
9	105,000	210,000
10	125,000	245,000
11	115,000	200,000
12	140,000	280,000

Required

1. Estimate the cost function for the quarterly data using the high-low method.
2. Plot and comment on the estimated cost function.
3. Howard anticipates that KMW will operate machines for 100,000 hours in quarter 13. Calculate the predicted maintenance costs in quarter 13 using the cost function estimated in requirement 1.

MyAccountingLab

Problems

10-31 High-low method and regression analysis. Fresh Choice, a cooperative of organic family-owned farms outside of Madison, Wisconsin, has recently started a fresh produce club to provide support to the group's member farms and to promote the benefits of eating organic, locally produced food to the nearby suburban community. Families pay a seasonal membership fee of $75 and place their orders a week in advance for a price of $35 per order. In turn, Fresh Choice delivers fresh-picked seasonal local produce to several neighborhood distribution points. Seven hundred families joined the club for the first season, but the number of orders varied from week to week.

Daniel Craig has run the produce club for the first 10-week season. Before becoming a farmer, Daniel had been a business major in college, and he remembers a few things about cost analysis. In planning for next year, he wants to know how many orders will be needed each week for the club to break even, but first he must estimate the club's fixed and variable costs. He has collected the following data over the club's first 10 weeks of operation:

Week	Number of Orders per Week	Weekly Total Costs
1	353	$19,005
2	390	22,605
3	414	22,850
4	450	22,500
5	422	21,950
6	491	24,750
7	449	23,650
8	472	23,005
9	529	25,275
10	508	24,350

Required

1. Plot the relationship between number of orders per week and weekly total costs.
2. Estimate the cost equation using the high-low method, and draw this line on your graph.
3. Harvey uses his computer to calculate the following regression formula:

$$\text{Total weekly costs} = \$10{,}048 + (\$28.91 \times \text{Number of weekly orders})$$

   Draw the regression line on your graph. Use your graph to evaluate the regression line using the criteria of economic plausibility, goodness of fit, and significance of the independent variable. Is the cost function estimated using the high-low method a close approximation of the cost function estimated using the regression method? Explain briefly.
4. Did Fresh Choice break even this season? Remember that each of the families paid a seasonal membership fee of $75.
5. Assume that 850 families join the club next year and that prices and costs do not change. How many orders, on average, must Fresh Choice receive each week to break even?

10-32 High-low method; regression analysis. (CIMA, adapted) Anna Schaub, the financial manager at the Mangiamo restaurant, is checking to see if there is any relationship between newspaper advertising and sales revenues at the restaurant. She obtains the following data for the past 10 months:

Month	Revenues	Advertising Costs
March	$51,000	$1,500
April	72,000	3,500
May	56,000	1,000
June	64,000	4,000
July	56,000	500
August	64,000	1,500
September	43,000	1,000
October	83,000	4,500
November	56,000	2,000
December	61,000	2,000

She estimates the following regression equation:

$$\text{Monthly revenues} = \$46{,}443 + (\$6.584 \times \text{Advertising costs})$$

Required

1. Plot the relationship between advertising costs and revenues. Also draw the regression line and evaluate it using the criteria of economic plausibility, goodness of fit, and slope of the regression line.
2. Use the high-low method to compute the function relating advertising costs and revenues.
3. Using (a) the regression equation and (b) the high-low equation, what is the increase in revenues for each $1,000 spent on advertising within the relevant range? Which method should Schaub use to predict the effect of advertising costs on revenues? Explain briefly.

10-33 Regression, activity-based costing, choosing cost drivers. Parker Manufacturing has been using activity-based costing to determine the cost of product X-678. One of the activities, "Inspection," occurs just before the product is finished. Fitzgerald inspects every 10th unit and has been using "number of units inspected" as the cost driver for inspection costs. A significant component of inspection costs is the cost of the test kit used in each inspection.

Sharon MacPhen, the line manager, is wondering if inspection labor-hours might be a better cost driver for inspection costs. Sharon gathers information for weekly inspection costs, units inspected, and inspection labor-hours as follows:

Week	Units Inspected	Inspection Labor-Hours	Inspection Costs
1	1,800	210	$3,600
2	800	90	1,700
3	2,100	250	4,400
4	2,800	260	5,700
5	2,500	230	5,200
6	1,100	110	2,300
7	1,300	130	2,800

Sharon runs regressions on each of the possible cost drivers and estimates these cost functions:

Inspection Costs = \$98.79 + (\$2.02 × Number of units inspected)

Inspection Costs = \$3.89 + (\$20.06 × Inspection labor-hours)

Required

1. Explain why number of units inspected and inspection labor-hours are plausible cost drivers of inspection costs.
2. Plot the data and regression line for units inspected and inspection costs. Plot the data and regression line for inspection labor-hours and inspection costs. Which cost driver of inspection costs would you choose? Explain.
3. Sharon expects inspectors to work 160 hours next period and to inspect 1,500 units. Using the cost driver you chose in requirement 2, what amount of inspection costs should Sharon budget? Explain any implications of Sharon choosing the cost driver you did not choose in requirement 2 to budget inspection costs.

10-34 Interpreting regression results. Spirit Freightways is a leader in transporting agricultural products in the western provinces of Canada. Reese Brown, a financial analyst at Spirit Freightways, is studying the behavior of transportation costs for budgeting purposes. Transportation costs at Spirit are of two types: (a) operating costs (such as labor and fuel) and (b) maintenance costs (primarily overhaul of vehicles).

Brown gathers monthly data on each type of cost, as well as the total freight miles traveled by Spirit vehicles in each month. The data collected are shown below (all in thousands):

Month	Operating Costs	Maintenance Costs	Freight Miles
January	\$ 942	\$ 974	1,710
February	1,008	776	2,655
March	1,218	686	2,705
April	1,380	694	4,220
May	1,484	588	4,660
June	1,548	422	4,455
July	1,568	352	4,435
August	1,972	420	4,990
September	1,190	564	2,490
October	1,302	788	2,610
November	962	762	2,240
December	772	1,028	1,490

Required

1. Conduct a regression using the monthly data of operating costs on freight miles. You should obtain the following result:

Regression: Operating costs = a + (b × Number of freight miles)

Variable	Coefficient	Standard Error	t-Value
Constant	\$445.76	\$112.97	3.95
Independent variable: No. of freight miles	\$ 0.26	\$ 0.03	7.83
r^2 = 0.86; Durbin-Watson statistic = 2.18			

2. Plot the data and regression line for the above estimation. Evaluate the regression using the criteria of economic plausibility, goodness of fit, and slope of the regression line.
3. Brown expects Spirit to generate, on average, 3,600 freight miles each month next year. How much in operating costs should Brown budget for next year?
4. Name three variables, other than freight miles, that Brown might expect to be important cost drivers for Spirit's operating costs.
5. Brown next conducts a regression using the monthly data of maintenance costs on freight miles. Verify that she obtained the following result:

Regression: Maintenance costs = a + (b × Number of freight miles)

Variable	Coefficient	Standard Error	t-Value
Constant	\$1,170.57	\$91.07	12.85
Independent variable: No. of freight miles	\$ −0.15	\$ 0.03	−5.83
r^2 = 0.77; Durbin-Watson statistic = 1.94			

6. Provide a reasoned explanation for the observed sign on the cost driver variable in the maintenance cost regression. What alternative data or alternative regression specifications would you like to use to better capture the above relationship?

10-35 Cost estimation, cumulative average-time learning curve. The Blue Seas Company, which is under contract to the U.S. Navy, assembles troop deployment boats. As part of its research program, it completes the assembly of the first of a new model (PT109) of deployment boats. The Navy is impressed with the PT109. It requests that Blue Seas submit a proposal on the cost of producing another six PT109s.

Blue Seas reports the following cost information for the first PT109 assembled and uses a 90% cumulative average-time learning model as a basis for forecasting direct manufacturing labor-hours for the next six PT109s. (A 90% learning curve means b = −0.152004.)

	A	B	C
1	Direct material	$201,000	
2	Direct manufacturing labor time for first boat	15,700	labor-hours
3	Direct manufacturing labor rate	$ 43	per direct manufacturing labor-hour
4	Variable manufacturing overhead cost	$ 24	per direct manufacturing labor-hour
5	Other manufacturing overhead	15%	of direct manufacturing labor costs
6	Tooling costs[a]	$281,000	
7	Learning curve for manufacturing labor time per boat	90%	cumulative average time[b]
8			
9	[a]Tooling can be reused at no extra cost because all of its cost has been assigned to the first deployment boat.		
10			
11	[b]Using the formula (page 390), for a 90% learning curve, $b = \frac{\ln 0.9}{\ln 2} = \frac{-0.105361}{0.693147} = -0.152004$		

Required

1. Calculate predicted total costs of producing the six PT109s for the Navy. (Blue Seas will keep the first deployment boat assembled, costed at $1,533,900, as a demonstration model for potential customers.)
2. What is the dollar amount of the difference between (a) the predicted total costs for producing the six PT109s in requirement 1 and (b) the predicted total costs for producing the six PT109s, assuming that there is no learning curve for direct manufacturing labor? That is, for (b) assume a linear function for units produced and direct manufacturing labor-hours.

10-36 Cost estimation, incremental unit-time learning model. Assume the same information for the Blue Seas Company as in Problem 10-35 with one exception. This exception is that Blue Seas uses a 90% incremental unit-time learning model as a basis for predicting direct manufacturing labor-hours in its assembling operations. (A 90% learning curve means $b = -0.152004$.)

Required

1. Prepare a prediction of the total costs for producing the six PT109s for the Navy.
2. If you solved requirement 1 of Problem 10-35, compare your cost prediction there with the one you made here. Why are the predictions different? How should Blue Seas decide which model it should use?

10-37 Regression; choosing among models. Apollo Hospital specializes in outpatient surgeries for relatively minor procedures. Apollo is a nonprofit institution and places great emphasis on controlling costs in order to provide services to the community in an efficient manner.

Apollo's CFO, Julie Chen, has been concerned of late about the hospital's consumption of medical supplies. To better understand the behavior of this cost, Julie consults with Rhett Bratt, the person responsible for Apollo's cost system. After some discussion, Julie and Rhett conclude that there are two potential cost drivers for the hospital's medical supplies costs. The first driver is the total number of procedures performed. The second is the number of patient-hours generated by Apollo. Julie and Rhett view the latter as a potentially better cost driver because the hospital does perform a variety of procedures, some more complex than others.

Rhett provides the following data relating to the past year to Julie.

	A	B	C	D
1	Month	Medical Supplies costs	Number of procedures	Number of patient-hours
2	1	$106,000	320	2,000
3	2	230,000	500	3,900
4	3	84,000	240	1,900
5	4	238,000	520	4,100
6	5	193,000	240	3,400
7	6	180,000	340	3,700
8	7	210,000	420	3,100
9	8	92,000	360	1,200
10	9	222,000	320	3,000
11	10	78,000	180	1,300
12	11	127,000	440	2,800
13	12	225,000	380	3,800

Required

1. Estimate the regression equation for (a) medical supplies costs and number of procedures and (b) medical supplies costs and number of patient-hours. You should obtain the following results:

Regression 1: Medical supplies costs $= a + (b \times$ Number of procedures)

Variable	Coefficient	Standard Error	*t*-Value
Constant	$36,939.77	$56,504.86	0.65
Independent variable: No. of procedures	$ 361.91	$ 152.93	2.37

$r^2 = 0.36$; Durbin-Watson statistic $= 2.48$

Regression 2: Medical supplies costs $= a + (b \times$ Number of patient-hours)

Variable	Coefficient	Standard Error	*t*-Value
Constant	$3,654.86	$23,569.51	0.16
Independent variable: No. of patient-hours	$ 56.76	$ 7.82	7.25

$r^2 = 0.84$; Durbin-Watson statistic $= 1.91$

2. On different graphs plot the data and the regression lines for each of the following cost functions:
   a. Medical supplies costs $= a + (b \times$ Number of procedures)
   b. Medical supplies costs $= a + (b \times$ Number of patient-hours)
3. Evaluate the regression models for "Number of procedures" and "Number of patient-hours" as the cost driver according to the format of Exhibit 10-18 (page 404).
4. Based on your analysis, which cost driver should Julie Chen adopt for Apollo Hospital? Explain your answer.

10-38 Multiple regression (continuation of 10-37). After further discussion, Julie and Rhett wonder if they should view both the number of procedures and number of patient-hours as cost drivers in a multiple regression estimation in order to best understand Apollo's medical supplies costs.

Required

1. Conduct a multiple regression to estimate the regression equation for medical supplies costs using both number of procedures and number of patient-hours as independent variables. You should obtain the following result:

Regression 3: Medical supplies costs $= a + (b_1 \times$ No. of procedures) $+ (b_2 \times$ No. of patient-hours)

Variable	Coefficient	Standard Error	*t*-Value
Constant	–$3,103.76	$30,406.54	–0.10
Independent variable 1: No. of procedures	$ 38.24	$ 100.76	0.38
Independent variable 2: No. of patient-hours	$ 54.37	$ 10.33	5.26

$r^2 = 0.84$; Durbin-Watson statistic $= 1.96$

2. Evaluate the multiple regression output using the criteria of economic plausibility goodness of fit, significance of independent variables, and specification of estimation assumptions.
3. What potential issues could arise in multiple regression analysis that are not present in simple regression models? Is there evidence of such difficulties in the multiple regression presented in this problem? Explain.
4. Which of the regression models from Problems 10-37 and 10-38 would you recommend Julie Chen use? Explain.

10-39 Cost estimation. Hankuk Electronics started production on a sophisticated new smartphone running the Android operating system in January 2013. Given the razor-thin margins in the consumer electronics industry, Hankuk's success depends heavily on being able to produce the phone as economically as possible.

At the end of the first year of production, Hankuk's controller, Inbee Kim, gathered data on its monthly levels of output, as well as monthly consumption of direct labor-hours (DLH). Inbee views labor-hours as the key driver of Hankuk's direct and overhead costs. The information collected by Inbee is provided below:

	A	B	C
1	**Month**	**Output (Units)**	**Direct Labor-Hours**
2	January	684	1,400
3	February	492	820
4	March	660	875
5	April	504	670
6	May	612	760
7	June	636	765
8	July	648	735
9	August	600	660
10	September	648	695
11	October	696	710
12	November	672	690
13	December	675	700

Required

1. Inbee is keen to examine the relationship between direct labor consumption and output levels. She decides to estimate this relationship using a simple linear regression based on the monthly data. Verify that the following is the result obtained by Inbee:

Regression 1: Direct labor-hours $= a + (b \times \text{Output units})$

Variable	Coefficient	Standard Error	t-Value
Constant	345.24	589.07	0.59
Independent variable: Output units	0.71	0.93	0.76

$r^2 = 0.054$; Durbin-Watson statistic $= 0.50$

2. Plot the data and regression line for the above estimation. Evaluate the regression using the criteria of economic plausibility, goodness of fit, and slope of the regression line.
3. Inbee estimates that Hankuk has a variable cost of $17.50 per direct labor-hour. She expects that Hankuk will produce 650 units in the next month, January 2014. What should she budget as the expected variable cost? How confident is she of her estimate?

10-40 Cost estimation, learning curves (continuation of 10-39). Inbee is concerned that she still does not understand the relationship between output and labor consumption. She consults with Jim Park, the head of engineering, and shares the results of her regression estimation. Jim indicates that the production of new smartphone models exhibits significant learning effects—as Hankuk gains experience with production, it can produce additional units using less time. He suggests that it is more appropriate to specify the following relationship:

$$y = ax^b$$

where x is *cumulative production* in units, y is the *cumulative average* direct labor-hours per unit (i.e., cumulative DLH divided by cumulative production), and a and b are parameters of the learning effect.

To estimate this, Inbee and Jim use the original data to calculate the cumulative output and cumulative average labor-hours per unit for each month. They then take natural logarithms of these variables in order to be able to estimate a regression equation. Here is the transformed data:

	A	B	C	D	E	F
21	Month	Cumulative Output (x)	Cumulative DLH	Cumulative Avg DLH (y)	LN (y)	LN (x)
22	January	684	1,400	2.047	0.716	6.528
23	February	1,176	2,220	1.888	0.635	7.070
24	March	1,836	3,095	1.686	0.522	7.515
25	April	2,340	3,765	1.609	0.476	7.758
26	May	2,952	4,525	1.533	0.427	7.990
27	June	3,588	5,290	1.474	0.388	8.185
28	July	4,236	6,025	1.422	0.352	8.351
29	August	4,836	6,685	1.382	0.324	8.484
30	September	5,484	7,380	1.346	0.297	8.610
31	October	6,180	8,090	1.309	0.269	8.729
32	November	6,852	8,780	1.281	0.248	8.832
33	December	7,527	9,480	1.259	0.231	8.926

Required

1. Estimate the relationship between the cumulative average direct labor-hours per unit and cumulative output (both in logarithms). Verify that the following is the result obtained by Inbee and Jim:

   Regression 1: Ln (Cumulative avg DLH per unit) $= a + [b \times$ Ln(Cumulative Output)]

Variable	Coefficient	Standard Error	*t*-Value
Constant	2.087	0.024	85.44
Independent variable: Ln (Cum Output)	−0.208	0.003	−69.046
$r^2 = 0.054$; Durbin-Watson statistic $= 2.66$			

2. Plot the data and regression line for the above estimation. Evaluate the regression using the criteria of economic plausibility, goodness of fit, and slope of the regression line.
3. Verify that the estimated slope coefficient corresponds to an 86.6% cumulative average-time learning curve.
4. Based on this new estimation, how will Inbee revise her budget for Hankuk's variable cost for the expected output of 650 units in January 2014? How confident is she of this new cost estimate?

10-41 Interpreting regression results, matching time periods. Nandita Summers works at Modus, a store that caters to fashion for young adults. Nandita is responsible for the store's online advertising and promotion budget. For the past year, she has studied search engine optimization and has been purchasing keywords and display advertising on Google, Facebook, and Twitter. In order to analyze the effectiveness of her efforts and to decide whether to continue online advertising or move her advertising dollars back to traditional print media, Nandita collects the following data:

	A	B	C
1	**Month**	**Online Ad Expense**	**Sales Revenue**
2	September	$5,125	$44,875
3	October	5,472	42,480
4	November	3,942	53,106
5	December	1,440	64,560
6	January	4,919	34,517
7	February	4,142	59,438
8	March	1,290	51,840
9	April	5,722	36,720
10	May	5,730	62,564
11	June	2,214	59,568
12	July	1,716	35,450
13	August	1,875	36,211

Required

1. Nandita performs a regression analysis, comparing each month's online advertising expense with that month's revenue. Verify that she obtains the following result:

$$\text{Revenue} = \$51{,}999.64 - (0.98 \times \text{Online advertising expense})$$

Variable	**Coefficient**	**Standard Error**	***t*-Value**
Constant	$51,999.64	7,988.68	6.51
Independent variable: Online advertising expense	–0.98	1.99	–0.49
$r^2 = 0.02$; Standard error = 11,837.30			

2. Plot the preceding data on a graph and draw the regression line. What does the cost formula indicate about the relationship between monthly online advertising expense and monthly revenues? Is the relationship economically plausible?
3. After further thought, Nandita realizes there may have been a flaw in her approach. In particular, there may be a lag between the time customers click through to the Modus website and peruse its social media content (which is when the online ad expense is incurred) and the time they actually shop in the physical store. Nandita modifies her analysis by comparing each month's sales revenue to the advertising expense in the *prior* month. After discarding September revenue and August advertising expense, show that the modified regression yields the following:

$$\text{Revenue} = \$28{,}361.37 + (5.38 \times \text{Online advertising expense})$$

Variable	**Coefficient**	**Standard Error**	***t*-Value**
Constant	$28,361.37	5,428.69	5.22
Independent variable: Previous month's online advertising expense	5.38	1.31	4.12
$r^2 = 0.65$; Standard error = 7,393.92			

4. What does the revised formula indicate? Plot the revised data on a graph. Is this relationship economically plausible?
5. Can Nandita conclude that there is a cause-and-effect relationship between online advertising expense and sales revenue? Why or why not?

10-42 Purchasing department cost drivers, activity-based costing, simple regression analysis. Designer Wear operates a chain of 10 retail department stores. Each department store makes its own purchasing decisions. Barry Lee, assistant to the president of Designer Wear, is interested in better understanding the drivers of purchasing department costs. For many years, Designer Wear has allocated purchasing department costs to products on the basis of the dollar value of merchandise purchased. A $100 item is allocated 10 times as many overhead costs associated with the purchasing department as a $10 item.

Lee recently attended a seminar titled "Cost Drivers in the Retail Industry." In a presentation at the seminar, Couture Fabrics, a leading competitor that has implemented activity-based costing, reported number of purchase orders and number of suppliers to be the two most important cost drivers of purchasing department costs. The dollar value of merchandise purchased in each purchase order was not found to be a significant cost driver. Lee interviewed several members of the purchasing department at the Designer Wear store in Miami. They believed that Couture Fabrics' conclusions also applied to their purchasing department.

Lee collects the following data for the most recent year for Designer Wear's 10 retail department stores:

	A	B	C	D	E
1	**Department Store**	**Purchasing Department Costs (PDC)**	**Dollar Value of Merchandise Purchased (MP$)**	**Number of Purchase Orders (No. of POs)**	**Number of Suppliers (No. of Ss)**
2	Baltimore	$1,525,000	$ 68,325,000	4,350	130
3	Chicago	1,120,000	33,450,000	2,555	225
4	Los Angeles	535,000	121,100,000	1,438	12
5	Miami	2,042,000	119,550,000	5,940	193
6	New York	1,050,000	33,520,000	2,795	20
7	Phoenix	522,000	29,847,000	1,315	39
8	Seattle	1,533,000	102,886,000	7,592	112
9	St. Louis	1,748,000	38,665,000	3,610	124
10	Toronto	1,618,000	139,315,000	1,710	215
11	Vancouver	1,251,000	130,940,000	4,725	208

Lee decides to use simple regression analysis to examine whether one or more of three variables (the last three columns in the table) are cost drivers of purchasing department costs. Summary results for these regressions are as follows:

Regression 1: PDC $= a + (b \times$ MP$)

Variable	Coefficient	Standard Error	*t*-Value
Constant	$1,040,594	$344,830	3.02
Independent variable 1: MP$	0.0031	0.0037	0.83
$r^2 = 0.08$; Durbin-Watson statistic $= 2.42$			

Regression 2: PDC $= a(b \times$ No. of POs)

Variable	Coefficient	Standard Error	*t*-Value
Constant	$731,687	$267,395	2.74
Independent variable 1: No. of POs	$ 156.18	$ 65.19	2.40
$r^2 = 0.42$; Durbin-Watson statistic $= 1.99$			

Regression 3: PDC $= a + (b \times$ No. of Ss)

Variable	Coefficient	Standard Error	*t*-Value
Constant	$802,629	$248,566	3.23
Independent variable 1: No. of Ss	$ 3,848	$ 1,660	2.32
$r^2 = 0.40$; Durbin-Watson statistic $= 2.00$			

1. Compare and evaluate the three simple regression models estimated by Lee. Graph each one. Also, use the format employed in Exhibit 10-18 (page 404) to evaluate the information.
2. Do the regression results support the Couture Fabrics' presentation about the purchasing department's cost drivers? Which of these cost drivers would you recommend in designing an ABC system?
3. How might Lee gain additional evidence on drivers of purchasing department costs at each of Designer Wear's stores?

10-43 Purchasing department cost drivers, multiple regression analysis (continuation of 10-42). Barry Lee decides that the simple regression analysis used in Problem 10-42 could be extended to a multiple regression analysis. He finds the following results for two multiple regression analyses:

Regression 4: PDC $= a + (b_1 \times$ No. of POs$) + (b_2 \times$ No. of Ss$)$

Variable	Coefficient	Standard Error	*t*-Value
Constant	\$481,186	\$259,020	1.86
Independent variable 1: No. of POs	\$ 121.37	\$ 58.04	2.09
Independent variable 2: No. of Ss	\$ 2,941	\$ 1,458	2.02
$r^2 = 0.63$; Durbin-Watson statistic $= 1.91$			

Regression 5: PDC $= a + (b_1 \times$ No. of POs$) + (b_2 \times$ No. of Ss$) + (b_3 \times$ MP\$$)$

Variable	Coefficient	Standard Error	*t*-Value
Constant	\$496,544	\$311,137	1.60
Independent variable 1: No. of POs	\$ 122.73	\$ 63.79	1.92
Independent variable 2: No. of Ss	\$ 2,996	\$ 1,646	1.82
Independent variable 3: MP\$	−0.00002	−0.0030	−0.11
$r^2 = 0.63$; Durbin-Watson statistic $= 1.92$			

The coefficients of correlation between combinations of pairs of the variables are as follows:

	PDC	MP\$	No. of POs
MP\$	0.28		
No. of POs	0.65	0.27	
No. of Ss	0.63	0.35	0.30

Required

1. Evaluate regression 4 using the criteria of economic plausibility, goodness of fit, significance of independent variables, and specification analysis. Compare regression 4 with regressions 2 and 3 in Problem 10-42. Which one of these models would you recommend that Lee use? Why?
2. Compare regression 5 with regression 4. Which one of these models would you recommend that Lee use? Why?
3. Lee estimates the following data for the Baltimore store for next year: dollar value of merchandise purchased, \$77,000,000; number of purchase orders, 4,200; number of suppliers, 120. How much should Lee budget for purchasing department costs for the Baltimore store for next year?
4. What difficulties do not arise in simple regression analysis that may arise in multiple regression analysis? Is there evidence of such difficulties in either of the multiple regressions presented in this problem? Explain.
5. Give two examples of decisions in which the regression results reported here (and in Problem 10-42) could be informative.

11

Decision Making and Relevant Information

Learning Objectives

1. Use the five-step decision-making process
2. Distinguish relevant from irrelevant information in decision situations
3. Explain the concept of opportunity cost and why managers should consider it when making insourcing-versus-outsourcing decisions
4. Know how to choose which products to produce when there are capacity constraints
5. Explain how to manage bottlenecks
6. Discuss the factors managers must consider when adding or dropping customers or business units
7. Explain why book value of equipment is irrelevant to managers making equipment-replacement decisions
8. Explain how conflicts can arise between the decision model a manager uses and the performance-evaluation model top management uses to evaluate managers

How many decisions have you made today?

Maybe you made a big decision today, such as accepting a job offer. Or maybe your decision was as simple as making plans for the weekend or choosing a restaurant for dinner. Regardless of whether decisions are significant or routine, most people follow a simple, logical process when making them. This process involves gathering information, making predictions, making a choice, acting on the choice, and evaluating results. The process also includes evaluating the costs and benefits of each choice. For decisions that involve costs, some costs are irrelevant. For example, once you purchase a coffee maker, its cost is irrelevant when calculating how much money you save each time you brew coffee at home versus buy it at Starbucks. You incurred the cost of the coffee maker in the past, and you can't recoup that cost. This chapter will explain which costs and benefits are relevant and which are not—and how you should think of them when choosing among alternatives.

Relevant Costs, JetBlue, and Twitter[1]

What does it cost JetBlue to fly a customer on a round-trip flight from New York City to Nantucket? The incremental cost is very small, around $5 for beverages, because the other costs (the plane, pilots, ticket agents, fuel, airport landing fees, and baggage handlers) are fixed. Because most costs are fixed, would it be worthwhile for JetBlue to fill a seat provided it earns at least $5 for that seat? The answer depends on whether the flight is full.

Suppose JetBlue normally charges $344 for this round-trip ticket. If the flight is full, JetBlue would not sell the ticket for anything less than $344 because there are still customers willing to pay this fare for the flight. But what if there are empty seats? Selling a ticket for something more than $5 is better than leaving the seat empty and earning nothing.

If a customer uses the Internet to purchase the ticket a month in advance, JetBlue will likely quote $344 because it expects the flight to be full. If, on the Monday before the scheduled Friday departure, JetBlue finds that the plane will not be full, the airline may be willing to lower its prices dramatically in hopes of attracting more customers and earning a profit on the unfilled seats.

[1] *Source*: Jones, Charisse. 2009. JetBlue and United give twitter a try to sell airline seats fast. *USA Today*, August 2. www.usatoday.com/travel/flights/2009-08-02-jetblue-united-twitter-airfares_N.htm

Enter Twitter. The widespread microblogging service allows JetBlue to quickly connect with customers and fill seats on flights that might otherwise take off less than full. When Twitter followers learned that $344 round-trip tickets from New York City to Nantucket were available for just $18, the flights filled up quickly. To use such a pricing strategy managers must have a deep understanding of costs in different decision situations.

Just like at JetBlue, managers in corporations around the world use a decision process. Managers at JPMorgan Chase gather information about financial markets, consumer preferences, and economic trends before determining whether to offer new services to customers. Managers at Macy's examine all the relevant information related to domestic and international clothing manufacturing before selecting vendors. Managers at Porsche gather cost information to decide whether to manufacture a component part or purchase it from a supplier. The decision process may not always be easy, but as Peter Drucker said, "Wherever you see a successful business, someone once made a courageous decision."

Information and the Decision Process

Learning Objective 1

Use the five-step decision-making process

...the five steps are identify the problem and uncertainties; obtain information; make predictions about the future; make decisions by choosing among alternatives; and implement the decision, evaluate performance, and learn

Managers usually follow a *decision model* for choosing among different courses of action. A **decision model** is a formal method of making a choice that often involves both quantitative and qualitative analyses. Management accountants analyze and present relevant data to guide managers' decisions.

Consider a strategic decision facing managers at Precision Sporting Goods, a manufacturer of golf clubs: Should the company reorganize its manufacturing operations to reduce manufacturing labor costs? Precision Sporting Goods has only two alternatives: do not reorganize or reorganize.

Reorganization will eliminate all manual handling of materials. Current manufacturing labor consists of 20 workers: 15 workers operate machines and 5 workers handle materials. The 5 materials-handling workers have been hired on contracts that permit layoffs without additional payments. Each worker works 2,000 hours annually. Reorganization is predicted to cost $90,000 each year (mostly for new equipment leases). The reorganization will not affect the production output of 25,000 units, the selling price of $250, the direct material cost per unit of $50, manufacturing overhead of $750,000, or marketing costs of $2,000,000.

Managers use the five-step decision-making process presented in Exhibit 11-1 and first introduced in Chapter 1 to make this decision. Study the sequence of steps in this exhibit and note how Step 5 evaluates performance to provide feedback about actions taken in the previous steps. This feedback might affect future predictions, the prediction methods used, the way choices are made, or the implementation of the decision.

Decision Point

What is the five-step process that managers can use to make decisions?

Exhibit 11-1

Five-Step Decision-Making Process for Precision Sporting Goods

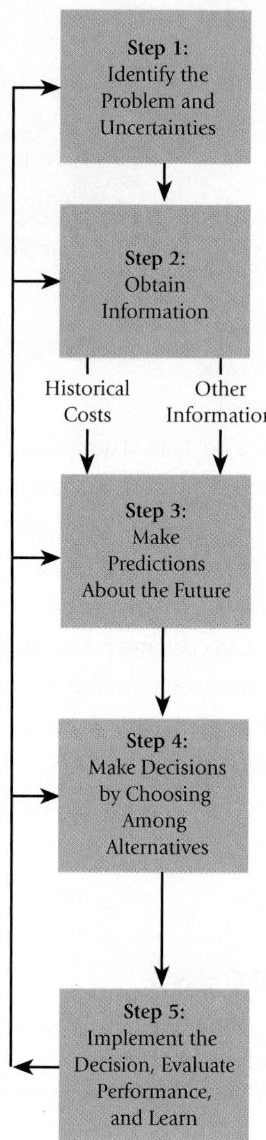

Should Precision Sporting Goods reorganize its manufacturing operations to reduce manufacturing labor costs? An important uncertainty is how the reorganization will affect employee morale.

Historical hourly wage rates are $14 per hour. However, a recently negotiated increase in employee benefits of $2 per hour will increase wages to $16 per hour. The reorganization of manufacturing operations is expected to reduce the number of workers from 20 to 15 by eliminating all 5 workers who handle materials. The reorganization is likely to have negative effects on employee morale.

Managers use information from Step 2 as a basis for predicting future manufacturing labor costs. Under the existing do-not-reorganize alternative, costs are predicted to be $640,000 (20 workers × 2,000 hours per worker per year × $16 per hour), and under the reorganize alternative, costs are predicted to be $480,000 (15 workers × 2,000 hours per worker per year ×$16 per hour). Recall, the reorganization is predicted to cost $90,000 per year.

Managers compare the predicted benefits calculated in Step 3 ($640,000 − $480,000 = $160,000—that is, savings from eliminating materials-handling labor costs, 5 workers × 2,000 hours per worker per year × $16 per hour = $160,000) against the cost of the reorganization ($90,000) along with other considerations (such as likely negative effects on employee morale). Management chooses the reorganize alternative because the financial benefits are significant and the effects on employee morale are expected to be temporary and relatively small.

Evaluating performance after the decision is implemented provides critical feedback for managers, and the five-step sequence is then repeated in whole or in part. Managers learn from actual results that the new manufacturing labor costs are $540,000, rather than the predicted $480,000, because of lower-than-expected manufacturing labor productivity. This (now) historical information can help managers make better subsequent predictions. Managers will also try to improve implementation via employee training and better supervision.

Learning Objective 2

Distinguish relevant from irrelevant information in decision situations

...only costs and revenues that are expected to occur in the future and differ among alternative courses of action are relevant

The Concept of Relevance

Much of this chapter focuses on Step 4 in Exhibit 11-1 and on the concepts of relevant costs and relevant revenues when choosing among alternatives.

Relevant Costs and Relevant Revenues

Relevant costs are *expected future costs* and **relevant revenues** are *expected future revenues* that differ among the alternative courses of action being considered. Costs and revenues that are *not relevant* are called *irrelevant*. It is important to recognize that relevant costs and relevant revenues *must:*

- **Occur in the future**—every decision deals with a manager selecting a course of action based on its expected future results.
- **Differ among the alternative courses of action**—costs and revenues that do not differ will not matter and, therefore, will have no bearing on the decision being made.

The question is always, "What difference will a particular action make?"

Exhibit 11-2 presents the financial data underlying the choice between the do-not-reorganize and reorganize alternatives for Precision Sporting Goods. Managers can analyze the data in two ways: by considering "all costs and revenues" or considering only "relevant costs and revenues."

The first two columns describe the first way and present *all data*. The last two columns describe the second way and present *only relevant costs:* the $640,000 and $480,000 expected future manufacturing labor costs and the $90,000 expected future reorganization costs that differ between the two alternatives. Managers can ignore the revenues, direct materials, manufacturing overhead, and marketing items because these costs will remain the same whether or not Precision Sporting Goods reorganizes. These costs do not differ between the alternatives and, therefore, are irrelevant.

Notice that the past (historical) manufacturing hourly wage rate of $14 and total past (historical) manufacturing labor costs of $560,000 (20 workers × 2,000 hours per worker per year × $14 per hour) do not appear in Exhibit 11-2. *Although they may be a useful basis for making informed predictions of the expected future manufacturing labor costs of $640,000 and $480,000, historical costs themselves are past costs that, therefore, are irrelevant to decision making.* Past costs are also called **sunk costs** because they are unavoidable and cannot be changed no matter what action is taken.

The analysis in Exhibit 11-2 indicates that reorganizing the manufacturing operations will increase predicted operating income by $70,000 each year. Note that the managers at Precision Sporting Goods reach the same conclusion whether they use all data or include only relevant data in the analysis. By confining the analysis to only relevant data, managers can clear away the clutter of potentially confusing irrelevant data. Focusing on relevant data is especially helpful when all the information needed to prepare a detailed income statement is unavailable. Understanding which costs are relevant and which are irrelevant helps the decision maker concentrate on obtaining only the pertinent data.

Qualitative and Quantitative Relevant Information

Managers divide the outcomes of decisions into two broad categories: *quantitative* and *qualitative*. **Quantitative factors** are outcomes that are measured in numerical terms. Some quantitative factors are financial; they can be expressed in monetary terms. Examples include the cost of direct materials, direct manufacturing labor, and marketing. Other quantitative factors are nonfinancial; they can be measured numerically, but they are not

Exhibit 11-2 Determining Relevant Revenues and Relevant Costs for Precision Sporting Goods

	All Revenues and Costs		Relevant Revenues and Costs	
	Alternative 1: Do Not Reorganize	Alternative 2: Reorganize	Alternative 1: Do Not Reorganize	Alternative 2: Reorganize
Revenues[a]	$6,250,000	$6,250,000	—	—
Costs:				
Direct materials[b]	1,250,000	1,250,000	—	—
Manufacturing labor	640,000[c]	480,000[d]	$ 640,000[c]	$ 480,000[d]
Manufacturing overhead	750,000	750,000	—	—
Marketing	2,000,000	2,000,000	—	—
Reorganization costs	—	90,000	—	90,000
Total costs	4,640,000	4,570,000	640,000	570,000
Operating income	$1,610,000	$1,680,000	$(640,000)	$(570,000)
	$70,000 Difference		$70,000 Difference	

[a]25,000 units × $250 per unit = $6,250,000

[b]25,000 units × $50 per unit = $1,250,000

[c]20 workers × 2,000 hours per worker × $16 per hour = $640,000

[d]15 workers × 2,000 hours per worker × $16 per hour = $480,000

Exhibit 11-3 Key Features of Relevant Information

- Past (historical) costs may be helpful as a basis for making *predictions*. However, past costs themselves are always irrelevant when making *decisions*.
- Different alternatives can be compared by examining differences in expected total future revenues and expected total future costs.
- Not all expected future revenues and expected future costs are relevant. Expected future revenues and expected future costs that do not differ among alternatives are irrelevant and, therefore, can be eliminated from the analysis. The key question is always, "What difference will an action make?"
- Appropriate weight must be given to qualitative factors and quantitative nonfinancial factors.

expressed in monetary terms. Examples include reduction in new product-development time for companies such as Microsoft and the percentage of on-time flight arrivals for companies such as Jet Blue. **Qualitative factors** are outcomes that are difficult to measure accurately in numerical terms. Employee morale is an example.

Relevant-cost analysis generally emphasizes quantitative factors that can be expressed in financial terms. *Although qualitative factors and quantitative nonfinancial factors are difficult to measure in financial terms, they are important for managers to consider.* In the Precision Sporting Goods example, managers carefully considered the negative effect on employee morale of laying off materials-handling workers, a qualitative factor, before choosing the reorganize alternative. It is often challenging for managers to compare and trade off nonfinancial and financial considerations.

Exhibit 11-3 summarizes the key features of relevant information. The concept of relevance applies to all decision situations. We present some of these decision situations in this chapter. Later chapters describe other decision situations that require managers to apply the relevance concept, such as joint costs (Chapter 16); quality and timeliness (Chapter 19); inventory management and supplier evaluation (Chapter 20); capital investment (Chapter 21); and transfer pricing (Chapter 22). We start our discussion on relevance by considering managerial decisions that affect output levels, such as whether to introduce a new product or to try to sell more units of an existing product.

One-Time-Only Special Orders

One type of decision that affects output levels involves accepting or rejecting special orders when there is idle production capacity and the special orders have no long-run implications. We use the term **one-time-only special order** to describe these conditions.

Example 1: Surf Gear manufactures quality beach towels at its highly automated Burlington, North Carolina, plant. The plant has a production capacity of 45,000 towels each month. Current monthly production is 30,000 towels. Retail department stores account for all existing sales. Exhibit 11-4 shows the expected results for the coming month (August). (These amounts are predictions based on past costs.) We assume that in the short run all costs can be classified as either fixed or variable for a single cost driver (units of output).

Azelia is a luxury hotel chain that purchases towels from Mugar Corporation. The workers at Mugar are on strike, so Azelia must find a new supplier. In August, Azelia contacts Surf Gear and offers to buy 5,000 towels from them at $11 per towel. Based on the following facts, should Surf Gear's managers accept Azelia's offer?

The management accountant gathers the following additional information.

- No subsequent sales to Azelia are anticipated.
- Fixed manufacturing costs are based on the 45,000-towel production capacity. That is, fixed manufacturing costs relate to the production capacity available and not the

Exhibit 11-4

Budgeted Income Statement for August, Absorption-Costing Format for Surf Gear

	A	B	C	D
1		Total	Per Unit	
2	Units sold	30,000		
3				
4	Revenues	$600,000	$20.00	
5	Cost of goods sold (manufacturing costs)			
6	Variable manufacturing costs	225,000	7.50[b]	
7	Fixed manufacturing costs	135,000	4.50[c]	
8	Total cost of goods sold	360,000	12.00	
9	Marketing costs			
10	Variable marketing costs	150,000	5.00	
11	Fixed marketing costs	60,000	2.00	
12	Total marketing costs	210,000	7.00	
13	Full costs of the product	570,000	19.00	
14	Operating income	$ 30,000	$ 1.00	
15				
16	[a]Surf Gear incurs no R&D, product-design, distribution, or customer-service costs			
17	[b]Variable manufacturing = Direct material + Variable direct manufacturing + Variable manufacturing			
18	cost per unit — cost per unit — labor cost per unit — overhead cost per unit			
19	= $6.00 + $0.50 + $1.00 = $7.50			
20	[c]Fixed manufacturing = Fixed direct manufacturing + Fixed manufacturing			
21	cost per unit — labor cost per unit — overhead cost per unit			
22	= $1.50 + $3.00 = $4.50			

actual capacity used. If Surf Gear accepts the special order, it will use existing idle capacity to produce the 5,000 towels and fixed manufacturing costs will not change.

- No marketing costs will be necessary for the 5,000-unit one-time-only special order.
- Accepting this special order is not expected to affect the selling price or the quantity of towels sold to regular customers.

The management accountant prepares the data shown in Exhibit 11-4 on an absorption-costing basis (both variable and fixed manufacturing costs are included in inventoriable costs and cost of goods sold). In this exhibit, the manufacturing cost of $12 per unit and the marketing cost of $7 per unit include both variable and fixed costs. The sum of all costs (variable and fixed) in a particular business function of the value chain, such as manufacturing costs or marketing costs, are called **business function costs. Full costs of the product,** in this case $19 per unit, are the sum of all variable and fixed costs in all business functions of the value chain (R&D, design, production, marketing, distribution, and customer service). For Surf Gear, full costs of the product consist of costs in manufacturing and marketing because these are the only business functions. Because no marketing costs are necessary for the special order, the manager of Surf Gear will focus only on manufacturing costs. Based on the manufacturing cost per unit of $12, which is greater than the $11-per-unit price Azelia offered, the manager might decide to reject the offer.

In Exhibit 11-5, the management accountant separates manufacturing and marketing costs into their variable- and fixed-cost components and presents data in the format of a contribution income statement. The relevant revenues and costs are the expected future revenues and costs that differ as a result of Surf Gear accepting the special offer: revenues of $55,000 ($11 per unit × 5,000 units) and variable manufacturing costs of $37,500 ($7.50 per unit × 5,000 units). The fixed manufacturing costs and all marketing costs (*including variable marketing costs*) are irrelevant in this case because these costs will not change in total whether the special order is accepted or rejected. Surf Gear would gain an additional $17,500 (relevant revenues, $55,000 − relevant costs, $37,500) in operating income by accepting the special order. In this example, by comparing total amounts for 30,000 units versus 35,000 units or focusing only on the relevant amounts in the difference

Exhibit 11-5

One-Time-Only Special-Order Decision for Surf Gear: Comparative Contribution Income Statements

	A	B	C	D	E	F	G	H
1		Without the Special Order				With the Special Order		Difference: Relevant Amounts
2		30,000				35,000		for the
3		Units to Be Sold				Units to Be Sold		5,000
4		Per Unit		Total		Total		Units Special Order
5		(1)		(2) = (1) × 30,000		(3)		(4) = (3) – (2)
6	Revenues	$20.00		$600,000		$655,000		$55,000[a]
7	Variable costs:							
8	Manufacturing	7.50		225,000		262,500		37,500[b]
9	Marketing	5.00		150,000		150,000		0[c]
10	Total variable costs	12.50		375,000		412,500		37,500
11	Contribution margin	7.50		225,000		242,500		17,500
12	Fixed costs:							
13	Manufacturing	4.50		135,000		135,000		0[d]
14	Marketing	2.00		60,000		60,000		0[d]
15	Total fixed costs	6.50		195,000		195,000		0
16	Operating income	$ 1.00		$ 30,000		$ 47,500		$17,500
17								
18	[a]5,000 units × $11.00 per unit = $55,000.							
19	[b]5,000 units × $7.50 per unit = $37,500.							
20	[c]No variable marketing costs would be incurred for the 5,000-unit one-time-only special order.							
21	[d]Fixed manufacturing costs and fixed marketing costs would be unaffected by the special order.							

column in Exhibit 11-5, the manager avoids a misleading implication: to reject the special order because the $11-per-unit selling price is lower than the manufacturing cost per unit of $12 (Exhibit 11-4), which includes both variable and fixed manufacturing costs.

The assumption of no long-run or strategic implications is crucial to a manager's analysis of the one-time-only special-order decision. Suppose the manager concludes that the retail department stores (Surf Gear's regular customers) will demand a lower price if Surf Gear sells towels at $11 apiece to Azelia. In this case, revenues from regular customers will be relevant. Why? Because the future revenues from regular customers will differ depending on whether Surf Gear accepts the special order. The Surf Gear manager would need to modify the relevant-revenue and relevant-cost analysis of the Azelia order to consider both the short-run benefits from accepting the order and the long-run consequences on profitability if Surf Gear lowered prices to all regular customers.

Potential Problems in Relevant-Cost Analysis

Managers should avoid two potential problems in relevant-cost analysis. First, they must watch for incorrect general assumptions, such as all variable costs are relevant and all fixed costs are irrelevant. In the Surf Gear example, the variable marketing cost of $5 per unit is irrelevant because Surf Gear will incur no extra marketing costs by accepting the special order. But fixed manufacturing costs could be relevant. The extra production of 5,000 towels per month from 30,000 towels to 35,000 towels does not affect fixed manufacturing costs because we assumed that the existing level of fixed manufacturing cost can support any level of production in the relevant range from 30,000 to 45,000 towels per month. In some cases, however, producing the extra 5,000 towels might increase fixed manufacturing costs (and also increase variable manufacturing cost per unit). Suppose Surf Gear would need to run three shifts of 15,000 towels per shift to achieve full capacity of 45,000 towels per month. Increasing monthly production from 30,000 to 35,000 would require a partial third shift (or overtime payments) because two shifts could produce only 30,000 towels. The partial shift would increase fixed manufacturing costs, thereby making these additional fixed manufacturing costs relevant for this decision.

Second, unit-fixed-cost data can potentially mislead managers in two ways:

1. **When irrelevant costs are included.** Consider the $4.50 of fixed manufacturing cost per unit (direct manufacturing labor, $1.50 per unit, plus manufacturing overhead, $3.00 per unit) included in the $12-per-unit manufacturing cost in the one-time-only special-order decision (see Exhibits 11-4 and 11-5). This $4.50-per-unit cost is irrelevant because this cost will not change if the one-time-only special order is accepted, and so managers should not consider it.
2. **When the same unit fixed costs are used at different output levels.** Generally, managers use total fixed costs rather than unit fixed costs because total fixed costs are easier to work with and reduce the chance for erroneous conclusions. Then, if desired, the total fixed costs can be unitized. In the Surf Gear example, total fixed manufacturing costs remain at $135,000 even if the company accepts the special order and produces 35,000 towels. Including the fixed manufacturing cost per unit of $4.50 as a cost of the special order would lead managers to the erroneous conclusion that total fixed manufacturing costs would increase to $157,500 ($4.50 per towel × 35,000 towels).

The best way for managers to avoid these two potential problems is to keep focusing on (1) total fixed costs (rather than unit fixed cost) and (2) the relevance concept. Managers should always require all items included in an analysis to be expected total future revenues and expected total future costs that differ among the alternatives.

Short-Run Pricing Decisions

In the one-time-only special-order decision in the previous section, Surf Gear's managers had to decide whether to accept or reject Azelia's offer to supply towels at $11 each. Sometimes managers must decide how much to bid on a one-time-only special order. This is an example of a short-run pricing decision—decisions that have a time horizon of only a few months.

Consider a short-run pricing decision facing managers at Surf Gear. Cranston Corporation has asked Surf Gear to bid on supplying 5,000 towels in September after Surf Gear has fulfilled its obligation to Azelia in August. Cranston is unlikely to place any future orders with Surf Gear. Cranston will sell Surf Gear's towels under its own brand name in regions and markets where Surf Gear does not sell its towels. Whether Surf Gear accepts or rejects this order will not affect Surf Gear's revenues—neither the units sold nor the selling price—from existing sales channels.

Relevant Costs for Short-Run Pricing Decisions

As before, Surf Gear's managers estimate how much it will cost to supply the 5,000 towels. There are no incremental marketing costs, so the relevant costs are the variable manufacturing costs of $7.50 calculated in the previous section. As before, the extra production of 5,000 towels in September from 30,000 to 35,000 towels does not affect fixed manufacturing costs because the relevant range is from 30,000 to 45,000 towels per month. Any selling price above $7.50 will improve Surf Gear's profitability in the short run. What price should Surf Gear's managers bid for the order of 5,000 towels?

Strategic and Other Factors in Short-Run Pricing

Based on market intelligence, Surf Gear's managers believe that competing bids will be between $10 and $11 per towel, so they decide to bid $10 per towel. If Surf Gear wins this bid, operating income will increase by $12,500 (relevant revenues, $10 × 5,000 = $50,000 − relevant costs, $7.50 × 5,000 = $37,500). In light of the extra capacity and strong competition, management's strategy is to bid as high above $7.50 as possible while remaining lower than competitors' bids. Note how Surf Gear chooses the price after looking at the problem through the eyes of its competitors, not based on just its own costs.

What if Surf Gear was the only supplier and Cranston could undercut Surf Gear's selling price in Surf Gear's current markets? The relevant cost of the bidding decision would then include the contribution margin lost on sales to existing customers. What if there were many parties eager to bid and win the Cranston contract? In this case, the contribution margin lost on sales to Surf Gear's existing customers would be irrelevant to the decision because Cranston would undercut the existing business regardless of whether Surf Gear wins the contract.

Decision Point

When is a revenue or cost item relevant for a particular decision and what potential problems should managers avoid in relevant-cost analysis?

In contrast to the Surf Gear case, in some short-run situations, a company may experience strong demand for its products or have limited capacity. In these circumstances, managers will strategically increase prices in the short run to as much as the market will bear. We observe high short-run prices in the case of new products or new models of older products, such as microprocessors, computer chips, cellular telephones, and software.

Learning Objective 3

Explain the concept of opportunity-cost and why managers should consider it when making insourcing-versus-outsourcing decisions

...in all decisions, it is important to consider the contribution to income forgone by choosing a particular alternative and rejecting others

Insourcing-Versus-Outsourcing and Make-or-Buy Decisions

We now apply the concept of relevance to another strategic decision: whether a company should make a component part or buy it from a supplier. We again assume idle capacity.

Outsourcing and Idle Facilities

Outsourcing is purchasing goods and services from outside vendors rather than **insourcing,** producing the same goods or providing the same services within an organization. For example, Kodak prefers to manufacture its own motion-picture film (insourcing) but has IBM do its data processing (outsourcing). Honda relies on outside vendors to supply some component parts (outsourcing) but chooses to manufacture other parts internally (insourcing).

Decisions about whether a producer of goods or services will insource or outsource are called **make-or-buy decisions.** Surveys of companies indicate that managers consider quality, dependability of suppliers, and costs as the most important factors in the make-or-buy decision. Sometimes, however, qualitative factors dominate management's make-or-buy decision. For example, Dell Computer buys the Pentium chip for its personal computers from Intel because Dell does not have the know-how and technology to make the chip itself. In contrast, to maintain the secrecy of its formula, Coca-Cola does not outsource the manufacture of its concentrate.

Example 2: The Soho Company manufactures a two-in-one video system consisting of a DVD player and a digital media receiver (that downloads movies and video from Internet sites such as Netflix). Columns 1 and 2 of the following table show the expected total and per-unit costs for manufacturing the DVD player. Soho plans to manufacture the 250,000 units in 2,000 batches of 125 units each. Variable batch-level costs of $625 per batch vary with the number of batches, not the total number of units produced.

Broadfield, Inc., a manufacturer of DVD players, offers to sell Soho 250,000 DVD players next year for $64 per unit on Soho's preferred delivery schedule. Assume that financial factors will be the basis of this make-or-buy decision. Should Soho's managers make or buy the DVD player?

	Expected Total Costs of Producing 250,000 Units in 2,000 Batches Next Year (1)	Expected Cost per Unit (2) = (1) ÷ 250,000
Direct materials ($36 per unit × 250,000 units)	$ 9,000,000	$36.00
Direct manufacturing labor ($10 per unit × 250,000 units)	2,500,000	10.00
Variable manufacturing overhead costs of power and utilities ($6 per unit × 250,000 units)	1,500,000	6.00
Mixed (variable and fixed) batch-level manufacturing overhead costs of materials handling and setup [$750,000 + ($625 per batch × 2,000 batches)]	2,000,000	8.00
Fixed manufacturing overhead costs of plant lease, insurance, and administration	3,000,000	12.00
Total manufacturing cost	$18,000,000	$72.00

Columns 1 and 2 of the preceding table indicate the expected total costs and expected cost per unit of producing 250,000 DVD players next year. The expected manufacturing cost per unit for next year is $72. At first glance, it appears that Soho's managers should buy DVD players because the expected $72-per-unit cost of making the DVD player is more than the $64 per unit to buy it. But a make-or-buy decision is rarely obvious. To make a decision, managers need to answer the question, "What is the difference in relevant costs between the alternatives?"

For the moment, suppose (1) the capacity now used to make the DVD players will become idle next year if the DVD players are purchased; (2) the $3,000,000 of fixed manufacturing overhead will continue to be incurred next year regardless of the decision made; and (3) the $750,000 in fixed salaries to support materials handling and setup will not be incurred if the manufacture of DVD players is completely shut down.

Exhibit 11-6 presents the relevant-cost computations, which show that Soho will *save* $1,000,000 by making the DVD players rather than buying them from Broadfield. Based on this analysis, Soho's managers decide to make the DVD players.

Note how the key concepts of relevance presented in Exhibit 11-3 apply here:

- Exhibit 11-6 compares differences in expected total future revenues and expected total future costs. Past costs are always irrelevant when making decisions.
- Exhibit 11-6 shows $2,000,000 of future materials-handling and setup costs under the make alternative but not under the buy alternative. Why? Because buying DVD players and not manufacturing them will save $2,000,000 in future variable costs per batch and avoidable fixed costs. The $2,000,000 represents future costs that differ between the alternatives and so is relevant to the make-or-buy decision.
- Exhibit 11-6 excludes the $3,000,000 of plant-lease, plant-insurance, and plant-administration costs under both alternatives. Why? Because these future costs will not differ between the alternatives, so they are irrelevant.

A common term in decision making is *incremental cost*. An **incremental cost** is the additional total cost incurred for an activity. In Exhibit 11-6, the incremental cost of making DVD players is the additional total cost of $15,000,000 that Soho will incur if it decides to make DVD players. The $3,000,000 of fixed manufacturing overhead is not an incremental cost because Soho will incur these costs whether or not it makes DVD players. Similarly, the incremental cost of buying DVD players from Broadfield is the additional total cost of $16,000,000 that Soho will incur if it decides to buy DVD players. A **differential cost** is the difference in total (relevant) cost between two alternatives. In Exhibit 11-6, the differential cost between the make-DVD-players and buy-DVD-players alternatives is $1,000,000 ($16,000,000 − $15,000,000). Note that *incremental cost* and *differential cost* are sometimes used interchangeably in practice. When faced with these terms, always be sure to clarify what they mean.

Exhibit 11-6

Relevant (Incremental) Items for Make-or-Buy Decision for DVD Players at Soho Company

	Total Relevant Costs		Relevant Cost Per Unit	
Relevant Items	**Make**	**Buy**	**Make**	**Buy**
Outside purchase of parts ($64 × 250,000 units)		$16,000,000		$64
Direct materials	$ 9,000,000		$36	
Direct manufacturing labor	2,500,000		10	
Variable manufacturing overhead	1,500,000		6	
Mixed (variable and fixed) materials-handling and setup overhead	2,000,000		8	
Total relevant costs[a]	$15,000,000	$16,000,000	$60	$64
Difference in favor of making DVD players	$1,000,000		$4	

[a]The $3,000,000 of plant-lease, plant-insurance, and plant-administration costs could be included under both alternatives. Conceptually, they do not belong in a listing of relevant costs because these costs are irrelevant to the decision. Practically, some managers may want to include them in order to list all costs that will be incurred under each alternative.

We define *incremental revenue* and *differential revenue* similarly to incremental cost and differential cost. **Incremental revenue** is the additional total revenue from an activity. **Differential revenue** is the difference in total revenue between two alternatives.

Strategic and Qualitative Factors

Strategic and qualitative factors affect outsourcing decisions. For example, Soho's managers may prefer to manufacture DVD players in-house to retain control over design, quality, reliability, and delivery schedules. Conversely, despite the cost advantages documented in Exhibit 11-6, Soho's managers may prefer to outsource, become a leaner organization, and focus on areas of its core competencies, the manufacture and sale of video systems. For example, advertising companies, such as J. Walter Thompson, only focus on the creative and planning aspects of advertising (their core competencies) and outsource production activities, such as film, photographs, and illustrations.

Outsourcing is risky. As a company's dependence on its suppliers increases, suppliers could increase prices and let quality and delivery performance slip. To minimize these risks, managers generally enter into long-run contracts specifying costs, quality, and delivery schedules with their suppliers. Wise managers go so far as to build close partnerships or alliances with a few key suppliers. For example, Toyota sends its own engineers to improve the processes of its suppliers. Suppliers of companies such as Ford, Hyundai, Panasonic, and Sony have researched and developed innovative products, met demands for increased quantities, maintained quality and on-time delivery, and lowered costs—actions that the companies themselves would not have had the competencies to achieve.

Outsourcing decisions invariably have a long-run horizon in which the financial costs and benefits of outsourcing become more uncertain. Almost always, strategic and qualitative factors become important determinants of the outsourcing decision. Weighing all these factors requires managers to exercise considerable judgment and care.

International Outsourcing

What additional factors would Soho's managers have to consider if the DVD-player supplier was based in Mexico? One important factor would be exchange-rate risk. Suppose the Mexican supplier offers to sell Soho 250,000 DVD players for 192,000,000 pesos. Should Soho make or buy? The answer depends on the exchange rate that Soho's managers expect next year. If they forecast an exchange rate of 12 pesos per $1, Soho's expected purchase cost equals $16,000,000 (192,000,000 pesos ÷ 12 pesos per $), greater than the \$15,000,000 relevant costs for making the DVD players in Exhibit 11-6, so Soho's managers would prefer to make DVD players rather than buy them. If, however, Soho's managers anticipate an exchange rate of 13.50 pesos per \$1, Soho's expected purchase cost equals \$14,222,222 (192,000,000 pesos ÷ 13.50 pesos per \$), which is less than the \$15,000,000 relevant costs for making the DVD players, so Soho's managers would prefer to buy rather than make the DVD players.

Soho's managers have yet another option. Soho could enter into a forward contract to purchase 192,000,000 pesos. A forward contract allows Soho to contract today to purchase pesos next year at a predetermined, fixed cost, thereby protecting itself against exchange-rate risk. If Soho's managers choose this route, they would make (buy) DVD players if the cost of the contract is greater (less) than \$15,000,000.

International outsourcing requires managers to evaluate manufacturing and transportation costs, exchange-rate risks, and the other strategic and qualitative factors discussed earlier such as quality, reliability, and efficiency of the supply chain. *Concepts in Action:* "The LEGO Group" describes how LEGO struggled with outsourcing production to lower-cost countries and eventually brought back all production to Denmark.

The Total Alternatives Approach

In the simple make-or-buy decision in Exhibit 11-6, we assumed that the capacity currently used to make DVD players will remain idle if Soho purchases DVDs from Broadfield. Often, however, the released capacity can be used for other, profitable purposes. In this case, Soho's managers must choose whether to make or buy based on how best to use available production capacity.

Concepts in Action: The LEGO Group

For decades, Denmark-based LEGO Group has delighted children of all ages with its sets of construction toys. The fifth-largest toymaker in the world produces billions of its small building bricks annually, but a decision to outsource a major chunk of its production nearly jeopardized the company's global supply chain and operations.

In response to near bankruptcy in 2004, the company outsourced 80% of its internal Western European production to three lower-cost countries: the Czech Republic, Hungary, and Mexico. While LEGO Group sought to reduce costs and gain economies of scale, it failed to account for managing the complexity of an outsourced global production network. LEGO Group's challenges included controlling its multi-continent production facilities, transferring production knowledge to its outsourcing partners, and allowing for seasonal fluctuations in demand (60% of LEGO production occurs in the second half of the year to accommodate Christmas holiday demand).

These problems led to unanticipated production delays and costs. As a result, the company canceled its outsourcing contracts and brought all production back in-house by 2009.

LEGO Group's experience demonstrates the costs of outsourcing and offshoring, the outsourcing of business processes and jobs to other countries. While offshoring often yields significant cost savings, there are significant costs associated with international taxation, global supply chain coordination, and shuttering existing facilities.

Sources: Based on LEGO Group, Annual Report 2011 (Billund, Denmark: LEGO Group, 2012); LEGO Group, Annual Report 2012 (Billund, Denmark: LEGO Group, 2013); Marcus Møller Larsen, Torben Pedersen, and Dmitrij Slepniov, *Lego Group: An Offshore Outsourcing Journey Towards a New Future*, No. 910M94 (London, Ontario: Richard Ivey School of Business, 2010).

Example 3: If Soho decides to buy DVD players for its video systems from Broadfield, then Soho's best use of the capacity that becomes available is to produce 100,000 Digiteks, a portable, stand-alone DVD player. From a manufacturing standpoint, Digiteks are similar to DVD players made for the video system. With help from operating managers, Soho's management accountant estimates the following future revenues and costs if Soho decides to manufacture and sell Digiteks:

Incremental future revenues		$8,000,000
Incremental future costs		
Direct materials	$3,400,000	
Direct manufacturing labor	1,000,000	
Variable overhead (such as power, utilities)	600,000	
Materials-handling and setup overheads	500,000	
Total incremental future costs		5,500,000
Incremental future operating income		$2,500,000

Because of capacity constraints, Soho can make either DVD players for its video-system unit or Digiteks, but not both. Which of the two alternatives should Soho's managers choose: (1) make video-system DVD players and do not make Digiteks or (2) buy video-system DVD players and make Digiteks?

Exhibit 11-7, Panel A, summarizes the "total-alternatives" approach, the future costs and revenues for *all* products. Soho's managers will choose Alternative 2, buy video-system DVD players, and use the available capacity to make and sell Digiteks. The future incremental costs of buying video-system DVD players from an outside supplier ($16,000,000) exceed the future incremental costs of making video-system DVD players in-house ($15,000,000). But Soho can use the capacity freed up by buying video-system DVD players to gain $2,500,000 in operating income (incremental future revenues of $8,000,000 minus total incremental future costs of $5,500,000) by making and selling Digiteks. The *net relevant* costs of buying video-system DVD players and making and selling Digiteks are $16,000,000 − $2,500,000 = $13,500,000.

The Opportunity-Cost Approach

Deciding to use a resource one way means a manager must forgo the opportunity to use the resource in any other way. This lost opportunity is a cost that the manager must consider when making a decision. **Opportunity cost** is the contribution to operating income that is forgone by not using a limited resource in its next-best alternative use. For example, the (relevant) cost of going to school for a BS in accounting degree is not only the cost of tuition, books, lodging, and food, but also the income sacrificed (opportunity cost) by not working. Presumably, however, the estimated future benefits of obtaining a BS in accounting (such as a higher-paying career) will exceed these out-of-pocket and opportunity costs.

Exhibit 11-7, Panel B, displays the opportunity-cost approach for analyzing the alternatives Soho faces. *Note that the alternatives are defined differently under the two approaches:*

In the total alternatives approach:	In the opportunity cost approach:
1. Make video-system DVD players and do not make Digitek	1. Make video-system DVD players
2. Buy video-system DVD players and make Digitek	2. Buy video-system DVD players

The opportunity cost approach does not reference Digiteks. Under the opportunity-cost approach, the cost of each alternative includes (1) the incremental costs and (2) the opportunity cost, the profit forgone from not making Digiteks. This opportunity cost arises because Digitek is excluded from formal consideration in the alternatives.

Exhibit 11-7 Total-Alternatives Approach and Opportunity-Cost Approach to Make-or-Buy Decisions for Soho Company

	Alternatives for Soho	
Relevant Items	**1. Make Video-System DVD Players and Do Not Make Digitek**	**2. Buy Video-System DVD Players and Make Digitek**
PANEL A Total-Alternatives Approach to Make-or-Buy Decisions		
Total incremental future costs of making/buying video-system DVD players (from Exhibit 11-6)	$15,000,000	$16,000,000
Deduct excess of future revenues over future costs from Digitek	0	(2,500,000)
Total relevant costs under total-alternatives approach	$15,000,000	$13,500,000
	1. Make Video-System DVD Players	**2. Buy Video-System DVD Players**
PANEL B Opportunity-Cost Approach to Make-or-Buy Decisions		
Total incremental future costs of making/buying video-system DVD players (from Exhibit 11-6)	$15,000,000	$16,000,000
Opportunity cost: Profit contribution forgone because capacity will not be used to make Digitek, the next-best alternative	2,500,000	0
Total relevant costs under opportunity-cost approach	$17,500,000	$16,000,000

Note that the differences in costs across the columns in Panels A and B are the same: The cost of alternative 2 is $1,500,000 less than the cost of alternative 1.

Consider alternative 1, making video-system DVD players. What are all the costs of making video-system DVD players? Certainly Soho will incur $15,000,000 of incremental costs to make video-system DVD players, but is this the entire cost? No, because by deciding to use limited manufacturing resources to make video-system DVD players, Soho will give up the opportunity to earn $2,500,000 by not using these resources to make Digiteks. Therefore, the relevant costs of making video-system DVD players are the incremental costs of $15,000,000 plus the opportunity cost of $2,500,000.

Next, consider alternative 2, buy video-system DVD players. The incremental cost of buying video-system DVD players is $16,000,000. The opportunity cost is zero. Why? Because by choosing this alternative, Soho will not forgo the profit it can earn from making and selling Digiteks.

Panel B leads managers to the same conclusion as Panel A: buying video-system DVD players and making Digiteks is the preferred alternative.

Panels A and B in Exhibit 11-7 describe two consistent approaches to decision making with capacity constraints. The total-alternatives approach in Panel A includes all future incremental costs and revenues. For example, under alternative 2, the additional future operating income from *using capacity to make and sell Digiteks* ($2,500,000) is subtracted from the future incremental cost of buying video-system DVD players ($16,000,000). The opportunity-cost analysis in Panel B takes the opposite approach. It focuses only on video-system DVD players. Whenever capacity is not going to be used to make and sell Digiteks, the future forgone operating income is added as an opportunity cost of making video-system DVD players, as in alternative 1. (Note that when Digiteks are made, as in alternative 2, there is no "opportunity cost of not making Digiteks.") Therefore, whereas Panel A *subtracts* $2,500,000 under alternative 2, Panel B *adds* $2,500,000 under alternative 1. *Panel B highlights the idea that when capacity is constrained, the relevant revenues and costs of any alternative equal (1) the incremental future revenues and costs plus (2) the opportunity cost.* However, when managers are considering more than two alternatives simultaneously, it is generally easier for them to use the total-alternatives approach.

Opportunity costs are not recorded in financial accounting systems. Why? Because historical record keeping is limited to transactions involving alternatives that managers *actually selected* rather than alternatives that they rejected. Rejected alternatives do not produce transactions and are not recorded. If Soho makes video-system DVD players, it will not make Digiteks, and it will not record any accounting entries for Digiteks. Yet the opportunity cost of making video-system DVD players, which equals the operating income that Soho forgoes by not making Digiteks, is a crucial input into the make-or-buy decision. Consider again Exhibit 11-7, Panel B. On the basis of only the incremental costs that are systematically recorded in accounting systems, it is less costly for Soho to make rather than buy video-system DVD players. Recognizing the opportunity cost of $2,500,000 leads to a different conclusion: buying video-system DVD players is preferable to making them.

Suppose Soho has sufficient capacity to make Digiteks even if it makes video-system DVD players. In this case, the opportunity cost of making video-system DVD players is $0 because Soho does not give up the $2,500,000 operating income from making and selling Digiteks even if it chooses to make video-system DVD players. The relevant costs are $15,000,000 (incremental costs of $15,000,000 plus opportunity cost of $0). Under these conditions, Soho's managers would prefer to make video-system DVD players, rather than buy them, and also make Digiteks.

Besides quantitative considerations, managers also consider strategic and qualitative factors in make-or-buy decisions. In deciding to buy video-system DVD players from an outside supplier, Soho's managers consider factors such as the supplier's reputation for quality and timely delivery. They also consider the strategic consequences of selling Digiteks. For example, will selling Digiteks take Soho's focus away from its video-system business?

Carrying Costs of Inventory

To see another example of an opportunity cost, consider the following data for Soho's DVD player purchasing decision:

Annual estimated video-system DVD player requirements for next year	250,000 units
Cost per unit when each purchase is equal to 2,500 units	$64.00
Cost per unit when each purchase is equal to or greater than 30,000 units ($64 − 0.5% discount)	$63.68
Cost of a purchase order	$150
Soho's managers are evaluating the following alternatives:	
A. Make 100 purchases (twice a week) of 2,500 units each during next year	
B. Make 8 purchases (twice a quarter) of 31,250 units during the year	
Average investment in inventory:	
A. (2,500 units × $64.00 per unit) ÷ 2[a]	$80,000
B. (31,250 units × $ 63.68 per unit) ÷ 2[a]	$995,000
Annual rate of return if cash is invested elsewhere (for example, bonds or stocks) at the same level of risk as investment in inventory	12%

[a] The example assumes that video-system-DVD-player purchases will be used uniformly throughout the year. The average investment in inventory during the year is the cost of the inventory when a purchase is received plus the cost of inventory just before the next purchase is delivered (in our example, zero) divided by 2.

Soho will pay cash for the video-system DVD players it buys. Which purchasing alternative is more economical for Soho?

The management accountant presents the following analysis to the company's managers using the total alternatives approach, recognizing that Soho has, on average, $995,000 of cash available to invest. If Soho invests only $80,000 in inventory as in alternative A, it will have $915,000 ($995,000 − $80,000) of cash available to invest elsewhere, which at a 12% rate of return will yield a total return of $109,800. This income is subtracted from the ordering and purchasing costs incurred under alternative A. If Soho invests all $995,000 in inventory as in alternative B, it will have $0 ($995,000 − $995,000) available to invest elsewhere and will earn no return on the cash.

	Alternative A: Make 100 Purchases of 2,500 Units Each During the Year and Invest Any Excess Cash (1)	Alternative B: Make 8 Purchases of 31,250 Units Each During the Year and Invest Any Excess Cash (2)	Difference (3) = (1) − (2)
Annual purchase-order costs (100 purch. orders × $150/purch. order; 8 purch. orders × $150/purch. order)	$ 15,000	$ 1,200	$ 13,800
Annual purchase costs (250,000 units × $64.00/unit; 250,000 units × $63.68/unit)	16,000,000	15,920,000	80,000
Deduct annual rate of return earned by investing cash not tied up in inventory elsewhere at the same level of risk [0.12 × ($995,000 − $80,000); 0.12 × ($995,000 − $995,000)]	(109,800)	0	(109,800)
Relevant costs	$15,905,200	$15,921,200	$ (16,000)

Consistent with the trends toward holding smaller inventories, it is more economical for Soho's managers to purchase smaller quantities of 2,500 units 100 times a year than to purchase 31,250 units 8 times a year by $16,000.

The following table presents the management accountant's analysis of the two alternatives using the opportunity cost approach. Each alternative is defined only in terms of the two purchasing choices with no explicit reference to investing the excess cash.

	Alternative A: Make 100 Purchases of 2,500 Units Each During the Year (1)	Alternative B: Make 8 Purchases of 31,250 Units Each During the Year (2)	Difference (3) = (1) − (2)
Annual purchase-order costs (100 purch. orders × $150/purch. order; 8 purch. orders × $150/purch. order)	$ 15,000	$ 1,200	$ 13,800
Annual purchase costs (250,000 units × $64.00/unit; 250,000 units × $63.68/unit)	16,000,000	15,920,000	80,000
Opportunity cost: Annual rate of return that could be earned if investment in inventory were invested elsewhere at the same level of risk (0.12 × $80,000; 0.12 × $995,000)	9,600	119,400	(109,800)
Relevant costs	$16,024,600	$16,040,600	$ (16,000)

Recall that under the opportunity-cost approach, the relevant cost of any alternative is (1) the incremental cost of the alternative plus (2) the opportunity cost of the profit forgone from choosing that alternative. The opportunity cost of holding inventory is the income forgone by tying up money in inventory and not investing it elsewhere. The opportunity cost would not be recorded in the accounting system because, once the money is invested in inventory, there is no money available to invest elsewhere and so no return related to this investment to record. On the basis of the costs recorded in the accounting system (purchase-order costs and purchase costs), Soho's managers would erroneously conclude that making eight purchases of 31,250 units each is the less costly alternative. Column 3, however, indicates that, as in the total-alternatives approach, purchasing smaller quantities of 2,500 units 100 times a year is more economical than purchasing 31,250 units eight times during the year by $16,000. Why? Because the lower

Decision Point

What is an opportunity cost and why should managers consider it when making insourcing-versus-outsourcing decisions?

opportunity cost of holding smaller inventory exceeds the higher purchase and ordering costs. If the opportunity cost of money tied up in inventory were greater than 12% per year, or if other incremental benefits of holding lower inventory were considered, such as lower insurance, materials-handling, storage, obsolescence, and breakage cost, making 100 purchases would be even more economical.

Learning Objective 4

Know how to choose which products to produce when there are capacity constraints

...select the product with the highest contribution margin per unit of the limiting resource

Product-Mix Decisions with Capacity Constraints

We now examine how the concept of relevance applies to **product-mix decisions,** the decisions managers make about which products to sell and in what quantities. These decisions usually have only a short-run focus because they typically arise in the context of capacity constraints that can be relaxed in the long run. In the short run, for example, BMW, the German car manufacturer, continually adapts the mix of its different models of cars (for example, 325i, 525i, and 740i) to fluctuations in selling prices and demand.

To determine product mix, managers maximize operating income, subject to constraints such as capacity and demand. Throughout this section, we assume that as short-run changes in product mix occur, the only costs that change are costs that are variable with the number of units produced (and sold). Under this assumption, the analysis of individual product contribution margins provides insight into the product mix that maximizes operating income.

Example 4: Power Recreation assembles two engines, a snowmobile engine and a boat engine, at its Lexington, Kentucky, plant. The following table shows the selling prices, costs, and contribution margins of these two engines:

	Snowmobile Engine	Boat Engine
Selling price	$800	$1,000
Variable cost per unit	560	625
Contribution margin per unit	$240	$ 375
Contribution margin percentage ($240 ÷ $800; $375 ÷ $1,000)	30%	37.5%

Only 600 machine-hours are available daily for assembling engines. Additional capacity cannot be obtained in the short run. Power Recreation can sell as many engines as it produces. The constraining resource, then, is machine-hours. It takes two machine-hours to produce one snowmobile engine and five machine-hours to produce one boat engine. What product mix should Power Recreation's managers choose to maximize operating income?

In terms of contribution margin per unit and contribution margin percentage, the data in Example 4 shows that boat engines are more profitable than snowmobile engines. The product that Power Recreation should produce and sell, however, is not necessarily the product with the higher individual contribution margin per unit or contribution margin percentage. As the following table shows, managers should choose the product with *the highest contribution margin per unit of the constraining resource (factor).* That's the resource that restricts or limits the production or sale of products.

	Snowmobile Engine	Boat Engine
Contribution margin per unit	$240	$375
Machine-hours required to produce one unit	2 machine-hours	5 machine-hours
Contribution margin per machine-hour		
$240 per unit ÷ 2 machine-hours/unit	$120/machine-hour	
$375 per unit ÷ 5 machine-hours/unit		$75/machine-hour
Total contribution margin for 600 machine-hours		
$120/machine-hour × 600 machine-hours	$72,000	
$75/machine-hour × 600 machine-hours		$45,000

The number of machine-hours is the constraining resource in this example, and snowmobile engines earn more contribution margin per machine-hour ($120/machine-hour) compared with boat engines ($75/machine-hour). Therefore, choosing to produce and sell snowmobile engines maximizes *total* contribution margin ($72,000 vs. $45,000 from producing and selling boat engines) and operating income. Other constraints in manufacturing settings can be the availability of direct materials, components, or skilled labor, as well as financial and sales factors. In a retail department store, the constraining resource may be linear feet of display space. Regardless of the specific constraining resource, managers should always focus on maximizing *total* contribution margin by choosing products that give the highest contribution margin per unit of the constraining resource.

In many cases, a manufacturer or retailer has the challenge of trying to maximize total operating income for a variety of products, each with more than one constraining resource. Some constraints may require a manufacturer or retailer to stock minimum quantities of products even if these products are not very profitable. For example, supermarkets must stock less-profitable products, such as paper towels and toilet paper, because customers will be willing to shop at a supermarket only if it carries a wide range of products. To determine the most profitable production schedule and the most profitable product mix, the manufacturer or retailer needs to determine the maximum total contribution margin in the face of many constraints. Optimization techniques, such as linear programming discussed in the appendix to this chapter, help solve these more complex problems.

Finally, there is the question of managing the bottleneck constraint to increase output and, therefore, contribution margin. Can the available machine-hours for assembling engines be increased beyond 600, for example, by reducing idle time? Can the time needed to assemble each snowmobile engine (two machine-hours) or each boat engine (five machine-hours) be reduced, for example, by reducing setup time and processing time of assembly? Can some of the assembly operations be outsourced to allow more engines to be built?

In the following section, we examine how managers can deal with the bottleneck constraint to increase output and, therefore, the contribution margin when some operations are bottlenecks and others are not.

Decision Point

When a resource is constrained, how should managers choose which of multiple products to produce and sell?

Bottlenecks, Theory of Constraints, and Throughput-Margin Analysis

Learning Objective 5

Explain how to manage bottlenecks

...keep bottlenecks busy and increase their efficiency and capacity by increasing throughput (contribution) margin

Suppose Power Recreation's snowmobile engine must go through a forging operation before it goes to the assembly operation. The company has 1,200 hours of daily forging capacity dedicated to the manufacture of snowmobile engines. The company takes 3 hours to forge each snowmobile engine, so Power Recreation can forge 400 snowmobile engines per day (1,200 hours ÷ 3 hours per snowmobile engine). Recall that it can assemble only 300 snowmobile engines per day (600 machine-hours ÷ 2 machine-hours per snowmobile engine). The production of snowmobile engines is constrained by the assembly operation, not the forging operation.

The **theory of constraints (TOC)** describes methods to maximize operating income when faced with some bottleneck and some nonbottleneck operations.[2] The TOC defines these three measures:

1. **Throughput margin** equals revenues minus the direct material costs of the goods sold.
2. *Investments* equal the sum of (a) material costs in direct materials, work-in-process, and finished goods inventories; (b) R&D costs; and (c) capital costs of equipment and buildings.
3. *Operating costs* equal all costs of operations (other than direct materials) incurred to earn throughput margin. Operating costs include costs such as salaries and wages, rent, utilities, and depreciation.

---

[2] See Eliyahu M. Goldratt and Jeff Cox, *The Goal* (New York: North River Press, 1986); Eliyahu M. Goldratt, *The Theory of Constraints* (New York: North River Press, 1990); Eric W. Noreen, Debra A. Smith, and James T. Mackey, *The Theory of Constraints and Its Implications for Management Accounting* (New York: North River Press, 1995); and Mark J. Woeppel, *Manufacturers' Guide to Implementing the Theory of Constraints* (Boca Raton, FL: Lewis Publishing, 2000).

The objective of the TOC is to increase throughput margin while decreasing investments and operating costs. *The TOC considers a short-run time horizon of a few months and assumes operating costs are fixed and direct material costs are the only variable costs. In a situation where some of the operating costs are also variable in the short run, throughput margin is replaced by contribution margin.* In the Power Recreation example, each snowmobile engine sells for $800. We assume that the variable costs of $560 consist only of direct material costs (incurred in the forging department), so throughput margin equals contribution margin. For ease of exposition and consistency with the previous section, we use the term *contribution margin* instead of *throughput margin* throughout this section.

TOC focuses on managing bottleneck operations, as explained in the following steps:

Step 1: Recognize that the bottleneck operation determines the contribution margin of the entire system. In the Power Recreation example, output in the assembly operation determines the output of snowmobile engines.

Step 2: Identify the bottleneck operation by identifying operations with large quantities of inventory waiting to be worked on. As snowmobile engines are produced at the forging operation, inventories will build up at the assembly operation because daily assembly capacity of 300 snowmobile engines is less than the daily forging capacity of 400 snowmobile engines.

Step 3: Keep the bottleneck operation busy and subordinate all nonbottleneck operations to the bottleneck operation. That is, the needs of the bottleneck operation determine the production schedule of the nonbottleneck operations. To maximize operating income, the manager must maximize contribution margin of the constrained or bottleneck resource. The bottleneck assembly operation must always be kept running; the workers should not be waiting to assemble engines. To achieve this objective, Power Recreation's managers maintain a small buffer inventory of snowmobile engines that have gone through the forging operation and are waiting to be assembled. The bottleneck assembly operation sets the pace for the nonbottleneck forging operations. Operating managers maximize contribution margin by ensuring the assembly operation is operating at capacity by developing a detailed production schedule at the forging operation to ensure that the assembly operation is not waiting for work. At the same time, forging more snowmobile engines that cannot be assembled does not increase output or contribution margin; it only creates excess inventory of unassembled snowmobile engines.

Step 4: Take actions to increase the efficiency and capacity of the bottleneck operation as long as the incremental contribution margin exceeds the incremental costs of increasing efficiency and capacity.

We illustrate Step 4 using data from the forging and assembly operations of Power Recreation.

	Forging	Assembly
Capacity per day	400 units	300 units
Daily production and sales	300 units	300 units
Other fixed operating costs per day (excluding direct materials)	$24,000	$18,000
Other fixed operating costs per unit produced ($24,000 ÷ 300 units; $ 18,000 ÷ 300 units)	$80 per unit	$60 per unit

Power Recreation's output is constrained by the capacity of 300 units in the assembly operation. What can Power Recreation's managers do to relieve the bottleneck constraint of the assembly operation?

Desirable actions include the following:

1. **Eliminate idle time at the bottleneck operation (time when the assembly machine is neither being set up to assemble nor actually assembling snowmobile engines).** Power Recreation's manager is evaluating permanently positioning two workers at the assembly operation to unload snowmobile engines as soon as they are assembled

and to set up the machine to begin assembling the next batch of snowmobile engines. This action will cost $320 per day and bottleneck output will increase by 3 snowmobile engines per day. Should Power Recreation's managers incur the additional costs? Yes, because Power Recreation's contribution margin will increase by $720 per day ($240 per snowmobile engine × 3 snowmobile engines), which is greater than the incremental cost of $320 per day. All other costs are irrelevant.

2. **Shift products that do not have to be made on the bottleneck machine to nonbottleneck machines or to outside processing facilities.** Suppose Spartan Corporation, an outside contractor, offers to assemble 5 snowmobile engines each day at $75 per snowmobile engine from engines that have gone through the forging operation at Power Recreation. Spartan's quoted price is greater than Power Recreation's own operating costs in the assembly department of $60 per snowmobile engine. Should Power Recreation's managers accept the offer? Yes, because assembly is the bottleneck operation. Getting Spartan to assemble additional snowmobile engines will increase contribution margin by $1,200 per day ($240 per snowmobile engine × 5 snowmobile engines), while the relevant cost of increasing capacity will be $375 per day ($75 per snowmobile engine × 5 snowmobile engines). The fact that Power Recreation's unit cost is less than Spartan's quoted price is irrelevant.

   Suppose Gemini Industries, another outside contractor, offers to do the forging operation for 8 snowmobile engines per day for $65 per snowmobile engine from direct materials supplied by Power Recreation. Gemini's price is lower than Power Recreation's operating cost of $80 per snowmobile engine in the forging department. Should Power Recreation's managers accept Gemini's offer? No, because other operating costs are fixed costs. Power Recreation will not save any costs by subcontracting the forging operations. Instead, its costs will increase by $520 per day ($65 per snowmobile engine × 8 snowmobile engines) with no increase in contribution margin, which is constrained by assembly capacity.

3. **Reduce setup time and processing time at bottleneck operations (for example, by simplifying the design or reducing the number of parts in the product).** Suppose Power Recreation can assemble 10 more snowmobile engines each day at a cost of $1,000 per day by reducing setup time at the assembly operation. Should Power Recreation's managers incur this cost? Yes, because the contribution margin will increase by $2,400 per day ($240 per snowmobile engine × 10 snowmobile engines), which is greater than the incremental costs of $1,000 per day. Will Power Recreation's managers find it worthwhile to incur costs to reduce machining time at the nonbottleneck forging operation? No. Other operating costs will increase, while the contribution margin will remain unchanged because bottleneck capacity of the assembly operation will not increase.

4. **Improve the quality of parts or products manufactured at the bottleneck operation.** Poor quality is more costly at a bottleneck operation than at a nonbottleneck operation. The cost of poor quality at a nonbottleneck operation is the cost of materials wasted. If Power Recreation produces 5 defective snowmobile engines at the forging operation, the cost of poor quality is $2,800 (direct material cost per snowmobile engine, $560 × 5 snowmobile engines). No contribution margin is forgone because forging has unused capacity. Despite the defective production, forging can produce and transfer 300 good-quality snowmobile engines to the assembly operation. At a bottleneck operation, the cost of poor quality is the cost of materials wasted *plus* the opportunity cost of lost contribution margin. Bottleneck capacity not wasted in producing defective snowmobile engines could be used to generate additional contribution margin. If Power Recreation produces 5 defective units at the assembly operation, the cost of poor quality is the lost revenue of $4,000 ($800 per snowmobile engine × 5 snowmobile engines) or, alternatively stated, direct material costs of $2,800 (direct material cost per snowmobile engine, $560 × 5 snowmobile engines) plus the forgone contribution margin of $1,200($240 per snowmobile engine × 5 snowmobile engines).

   The high cost of poor quality at the bottleneck operation means that bottleneck time should not be wasted processing units that are defective. That is, engines should be inspected before the bottleneck operation to ensure that only good-quality parts are processed at the bottleneck operation. Furthermore, quality-improvement programs should place special emphasis on minimizing defects at bottleneck machines.

If successful, the actions in Step 4 will increase the capacity of the assembly operation until it eventually exceeds the capacity of the forging operation. The bottleneck will then shift to the forging operation. Power Recreation would then focus continuous-improvement actions on increasing forging operation efficiency and capacity. For example, the contract with Gemini Industries to forge 8 snowmobile engines per day at $65 per snowmobile engine from direct material supplied by Power Recreation will become attractive because the contribution margin will increase by $1,920 per day ($240 per snowmobile engine × 8 snowmobile engines), which is greater than the incremental costs of $520 ($65 per snowmobile engine × 8 snowmobile engines).

Decision Point

What steps can managers take to manage bottlenecks?

The theory of constraints emphasizes management of bottleneck operations as the key to improving performance of production operations as a whole. It focuses on short-run maximization of contribution margin. Because TOC regards operating costs as difficult to change in the short run, it does not identify individual activities and drivers of costs. Therefore, TOC is less useful for the long-run management of costs. In contrast, activity-based costing (ABC) systems take a long-run perspective and focus on improving processes by eliminating non-value-added activities and reducing the costs of performing value-added activities. ABC systems are therefore more useful than TOC for long-run pricing, cost control, and capacity management. The short-run TOC emphasis on maximizing contribution margin by managing bottlenecks complements the long-run strategic-cost-management focus of ABC.[3]

Learning Objective 6

Discuss the factors managers must consider when adding or dropping customers or business units

...managers should focus on how total revenues and costs differ among alternatives and ignore allocated overhead costs

Customer Profitability and Relevant Costs

We have seen how managers make choices about which products and how much of each product to produce. In addition, managers must often make decisions about adding or dropping a product line or a business segment. Similarly, if the cost object is a customer, managers must decide about adding or dropping customers (analogous to a product line) or a branch office (analogous to a business segment or division). We illustrate relevant-revenue and relevant-cost analysis for these kinds of decisions using customers rather than products as the cost object.

Example 5: Allied West, the West Coast sales office of Allied Furniture, a wholesaler of specialized furniture, supplies furniture to three local retailers: Vogel, Brenner, and Wisk. Exhibit 11-8 presents expected revenues and costs of Allied West by customer for the upcoming year using its activity-based costing system. Allied West's management accountant assigns costs to customers based on the activities needed to support each customer. Information on Allied West's costs for different activities at various levels of the cost hierarchy are:

- Furniture-handling labor costs vary with the number of units of furniture shipped to customers.
- Allied West reserves different areas of the warehouse to stock furniture for different customers. For simplicity, we assume that furniture-handling equipment in an area and depreciation costs on the equipment that Allied West has already acquired are identified with individual customers (customer-level costs). Any unused equipment remains idle. The equipment has a one-year useful life and zero disposal value.

[3] For an excellent evaluation of TOC, operations management, cost accounting, and the relationship between TOC and activity-based costing, see Anthony Atkinson, *Cost Accounting, the Theory of Constraints, and Costing* (Issue Paper, CMA Canada, December 2000).

Exhibit 11-8

Customer Profitability Analysis for Allied West

	Customer			
	Vogel	Brenner	Wisk	Total
Revenues	$500,000	$300,000	$400,000	$1,200,000
Cost of goods sold	370,000	220,000	330,000	920,000
Furniture-handling labor	41,000	18,000	33,000	92,000
Furniture-handling equipment cost written off as depreciation	12,000	4,000	9,000	25,000
Rent	14,000	8,000	14,000	36,000
Marketing support	11,000	9,000	10,000	30,000
Sales-order and delivery processing	13,000	7,000	12,000	32,000
General administration	20,000	12,000	16,000	48,000
Allocated corporate-office costs	10,000	6,000	8,000	24,000
Total costs	491,000	284,000	432,000	1,207,000
Operating income	$ 9,000	$ 16,000	$ (32,000)	$ (7,000)

- Allied West allocates its fixed rent costs to each customer on the basis of the amount of warehouse space reserved for that customer.
- Marketing costs vary with the number of sales visits made to customers.
- Sales-order costs are batch-level costs that vary with the number of sales orders received from customers. Delivery-processing costs are batch-level costs that vary with the number of shipments made.
- Allied West allocates fixed general-administration costs (facility-level costs) to customers on the basis of customer revenues.
- Allied Furniture allocates its fixed corporate-office costs to sales offices on the basis of the budgeted costs of each sales office. Allied West then allocates these costs to customers on the basis of customer revenues.

In the following sections, we consider several decisions that Allied West's managers face: Should Allied West drop the Wisk account? Should it add a fourth customer, Loral? Should Allied Furniture close down Allied West? Should it open another sales office, Allied South, whose revenues and costs are identical to those of Allied West?

Relevant-Revenue and Relevant-Cost Analysis of Dropping a Customer

Exhibit 11-8 indicates a loss of $32,000 on the Wisk account. Allied West's managers believe the reason for the loss is that Wisk places low-margin orders with Allied and has relatively high sales-order, delivery-processing, furniture-handling, and marketing costs. Allied West's managers are considering several possible actions for the Wisk account: reducing the costs of supporting Wisk by becoming more efficient; cutting back on some of the services Allied West offers Wisk; asking Wisk to place larger, less frequent orders; charging Wisk higher prices; or dropping the Wisk account. The following analysis focuses on the operating-income effect of dropping the Wisk account for the year.

Allied West's managers and management accountants first identify the relevant revenues and relevant costs. Dropping the Wisk account will:

- Save cost of goods sold, furniture-handling labor, marketing support, sales-order and delivery-processing costs incurred on the account.
- Leave idle the warehouse space and furniture-handling equipment currently used to supply products to Wisk.
- Not affect the fixed rent costs, general-administration costs, or corporate-office costs.

Exhibit 11-9

Relevant-Revenue and Relevant-Cost Analysis for Dropping the Wisk Account and Adding the Loral Account

	(Incremental Loss in Revenues) and Incremental Savings in Costs from Dropping Wisk Account (1)	Incremental Revenues and (Incremental Costs) from Adding Loral Account (2)
Revenues	$(400,000)	$400,000
Cost of goods sold	330,000	(330,000)
Furniture-handling labor	33,000	(33,000)
Furniture-handling equipment cost written off as depreciation	0	(9,000)
Rent	0	0
Marketing support	10,000	(10,000)
Sales-order and delivery processing	12,000	(12,000)
General administration	0	0
Corporate-office costs	0	0
Total costs	385,000	(394,000)
Effect on operating income (loss)	$ (15,000)	$ 6,000

Exhibit 11-9, column 1, presents the relevant-revenue and relevant-cost analysis using data from the Wisk column in Exhibit 11-8. The $385,000 cost savings from dropping the Wisk account will not be enough to offset the $400,000 loss in revenues. Because Allied West's operating income will be $15,000 lower if it drops the Wisk account, Allied West's managers decide to keep the Wisk account. They will, of course, continue to find ways to become more efficient, change Wisk's ordering patterns, or charge higher prices.

Depreciation on equipment that Allied West has already acquired is a past cost and therefore irrelevant. Rent, general-administration, and corporate-office costs are future costs that will not change if Allied West drops the Wisk account and are also irrelevant.

Overhead costs allocated to the sales office and individual customers are always irrelevant. The only question is, will expected total corporate office costs decrease as a result of dropping the Wisk account? In our example, they will not, so these costs are irrelevant. *If expected total corporate-office costs* were to decrease by dropping the Wisk account, those savings would be relevant even if *the amount allocated to Wisk did not change.*

Note that there is no opportunity cost of using warehouse space and equipment for Wisk because there is no alternative use for them. That is, the space and equipment will remain idle if managers drop the Wisk account. But suppose Allied West could lease the available extra space and equipment to Sanchez Corporation for $20,000 per year. Then $20,000 would be Allied West's opportunity cost of continuing to use the warehouse to service Wisk. Allied West would gain $5,000 by dropping the Wisk account ($20,000 from lease revenue minus lost operating income of $15,000). Under the total alternatives approach, the revenue loss from dropping the Wisk account would be $380,000 ($400,000 − $20,000) versus the savings in costs of $385,000 (Exhibit 11-9, column 1). Before reaching a decision, Allied West's managers must examine whether Wisk can be made more profitable so that supplying products to Wisk earns more than the $20,000 from leasing to Sanchez. The managers must also consider strategic factors such as the effect of dropping the Wisk account on Allied West's reputation for developing stable, long-run business relationships with its customers.

Relevant-Revenue and Relevant-Cost Analysis of Adding a Customer

Suppose that Allied West's managers are evaluating the profitability of adding another customer, Loral, to its existing customer base of Vogel, Brenner, and Wisk. There is no other alternative use of the Allied West facility. Loral has a customer profile much like Wisk's. Suppose Allied West's managers predict revenues and costs of doing business with Loral to be the same as the revenues and costs described under the Wisk column in Exhibit 11-8. In particular, Allied West would have to acquire furniture-handling equipment for the Loral account costing $9,000, with a one-year useful life and zero disposal value. If Loral is added as a customer, warehouse rent costs ($36,000), general-administration costs ($48,000), and *actual total* corporate-office costs will not change. Should Allied West's managers add Loral as a customer?

Exhibit 11-9, column 2, shows relevant revenues exceed relevant costs by $6,000. The opportunity cost of adding Loral is $0 because there is no alternative use of the Allied West facility. On the basis of this analysis, Allied West's managers would recommend adding Loral as a customer. Rent, general-administration, and corporate-office costs are irrelevant because these costs will not change if Loral is added as a customer. However, the cost of new equipment to support the Loral order (written off as depreciation of $9,000 in Exhibit 11-9, column 2) is relevant. That's because this cost can be avoided if Allied West decides not to add Loral as a customer. Note the critical distinction here: *Depreciation cost is irrelevant in deciding whether to drop Wisk as a customer because depreciation on equipment that has already been purchased is a past cost, but the cost of purchasing new equipment in the future that will then be written off as depreciation is relevant in deciding whether to add Loral as a customer.*

Relevant-Revenue and Relevant-Cost Analysis of Closing or Adding Branch Offices or Business Divisions

Companies periodically confront decisions about closing or adding branch offices or business divisions. For example, given Allied West's expected loss of $7,000 (see Exhibit 11-8), should Allied Furniture's managers close Allied West for the year? Closing Allied West will save all costs currently incurred at Allied West. Recall that there is no disposal value for the equipment that Allied West has already acquired. Closing Allied West will have no effect on total corporate-office costs and there is no alternative use for the Allied West space.

Exhibit 11-10, column 1, presents the relevant-revenue and relevant-cost analysis using data from the "Total" column in Exhibit 11-8. The revenue losses of $1,200,000 will exceed the cost savings of $1,158,000, leading to a decrease in operating income of $42,000. Allied

Exhibit 11-10 Relevant-Revenue and Relevant-Cost Analysis for Closing Allied West and Opening Allied South

	(Incremental Loss in Revenues) and Incremental Savings in Costs from Closing Allied West (1)	Incremental Revenues and (Incremental Costs) from Opening Allied South (2)
Revenues	$(1,200,000)	$1,200,000
Cost of goods sold	920,000	(920,000)
Furniture-handling labor	92,000	(92,000)
Furniture-handling equipment cost written off as depreciation	0	(25,000)
Rent	36,000	(36,000)
Marketing support	30,000	(30,000)
Sales-order and delivery processing	32,000	(32,000)
General administration	48,000	(48,000)
Corporate-office costs	0	0
Total costs	1,158,000	(1,183,000)
Effect on operating income (loss)	$ (42,000)	$ 17,000

Decision Point

In deciding to add or drop customers or to add or discontinue branch offices or business divisions, what should managers focus on and how should they take into account allocated overhead costs?

West should not be closed. The key reasons are that closing Allied West will not save depreciation cost or actual total corporate-office costs. Depreciation cost is past or sunk because it represents the cost of equipment that Allied West has already purchased. Corporate-office costs allocated to various sales offices will change, *but the total amount of these costs will not decline*. The $24,000 no longer allocated to Allied West will be allocated to other sales offices. Therefore, the $24,000 of allocated corporate-office costs is irrelevant because it does not represent expected cost savings from closing Allied West.

Finally suppose Allied Furniture has the opportunity to open another sales office, Allied South, whose revenues and costs are identical to Allied West's costs, including a cost of $25,000 to acquire furniture-handling equipment with a one-year useful life and zero disposal value. Opening this office will have no effect on total corporate-office costs. Should Allied Furniture's managers open Allied South? Exhibit 11-10, column 2, indicates that they should because opening Allied South will increase operating income by $17,000. As before, the cost of new equipment to be purchased in the future (and written off as depreciation) is relevant and *allocated* corporate-office costs are irrelevant because total corporate-office costs will not change if Allied South is opened.

Learning Objective 7

Explain why book value of equipment is irrelevant to managers making equipment-replacement decisions

. . .it is a past cost

Irrelevance of Past Costs and Equipment-Replacement Decisions

At several points in this chapter, we reasoned that past (historical or sunk) costs are irrelevant to decision making. That's because a decision cannot change something that has already happened. We now apply this concept to decisions about replacing equipment. We stress the idea that **book value**—original cost minus accumulated depreciation—of existing equipment is a past cost that is irrelevant.

Example 6: Toledo Company, a manufacturer of aircraft components, is considering replacing a metal-cutting machine with a newer model. The new machine is more efficient than the old machine, but it has a shorter life. Revenues from aircraft parts ($1.1 million per year) will be unaffected by the replacement decision. Here are the data the management accountant prepares for the existing (old) machine and the replacement (new) machine:

	Old Machine	New Machine
Original cost	$1,000,000	$600,000
Useful life	5 years	2 years
Current age	3 years	0 years
Remaining useful life	2 years	2 years
Accumulated depreciation	$ 600,000	Not acquired yet
Book value	$ 400,000	Not acquired yet
Current disposal value (in cash)	$ 40,000	Not acquired yet
Terminal disposal value (in cash 2 years from now)	$ 0	$ 0
Annual operating costs (maintenance, energy, repairs, coolants, and so on)	$ 800,000	$460,000

Toledo Corporation uses straight-line depreciation. To focus on relevance, we ignore the time value of money and income taxes.[4] Should Toledo's managers replace its old machine?

[4] See Chapter 21 for a discussion of time-value-of-money and income-tax considerations in capital investment decisions.

Exhibit 11-11 Operating Income Comparison: Replacement of Machine, Relevant, and Irrelevant Items for Toledo Company

	Two Years Together		
	Keep (1)	**Replace (2)**	**Difference (3) = (1) – (2)**
Revenues	$2,200,000	$2,200,000	—
Operating costs			
Cash operating costs ($800,000/yr. × 2 years; $460,000/yr. × 2 years)	1,600,000	920,000	$ 680,000
Book value of old machine			
Periodic write-off as depreciation or	400,000	—	—
Lump-sum write-off	—	400,000[a]	
Current disposal value of old machine	—	(40,000)[a]	40,000
New machine cost, written off periodically as depreciation	—	600,000	(600,000)
Total operating costs	2,000,000	1,880,000	120,000
Operating income	$ 200,000	$ 320,000	$(120,000)

[a]In a formal income statement, these two items would be combined as "loss on disposal of machine" of $360,000.

Exhibit 11-11 presents a cost comparison of the two machines. Consider why each of the following four items in Toledo's equipment-replacement decision are relevant or irrelevant:

1. **Book value of old machine, $400,000.** Irrelevant, because it is a past or sunk cost. All past costs are "down the drain." Nothing can change what the company has already spent or what has already happened.
2. **Current disposal value of old machine, $40,000.** Relevant, because it is an expected future benefit that will only occur if the company replaces the machine.
3. **Loss on disposal, $360,000.** This is the difference between amounts in items 1 and 2. This amount is a meaningless combination blurring the distinction between the irrelevant book value and the relevant disposal value. Managers should consider each value separately, as was done in items 1 and 2.
4. **Cost of new machine, $600,000.** Relevant, because it is an expected future cost that will only occur if the company purchases the machine.

Exhibit 11-11 should clarify these four assertions. Column 3 in Exhibit 11-11 shows that the book value of the old machine does not differ between the alternatives and could be ignored for decision-making purposes. No matter what the timing of the write-off—whether a lump-sum charge in the current year or depreciation charges over the next 2 years—the total amount is still $400,000 because it is a past (historical) cost. In contrast, the $600,000 cost of the new machine and the current disposal value of $40,000 for the old machine are relevant because they would not arise if Toledo's managers decided not to replace the machine. Considering the cost of replacing the machine and savings in cash operating costs, Toledo's managers should replace the machine because the operating income from replacing it is $120,000 higher for the 2 years together.

Decision Point

Is book value of existing equipment relevant in equipment replacement decisions?

Exhibit 11-12 concentrates only on relevant items and leads to the same answer—replacing the machine leads to lower costs and higher operating income of $120,000—even though book value is omitted from the calculations. The only relevant items are the cash operating costs, the disposal value of the old machine, and the cost of the new machine, which is represented as depreciation in Exhibit 11-12.

Exhibit 11-12 Cost Comparison: Replacement of Machine, Relevant Items Only, for Toledo Company

	Two Years Together		
	Keep (1)	Replace (2)	Difference (3) = (1) – (2)
Cash operating costs	$1,600,000	$ 920,000	$680,000
Current disposal value of old machine	—	(40,000)	40,000
New machine, written off periodically as depreciation	—	600,000	(600,000)
Total relevant costs	$1,600,000	$1,480,000	$120,000

Decisions and Performance Evaluation

Consider our equipment-replacement example in light of the five-step sequence in Exhibit 11-1 (page 426):

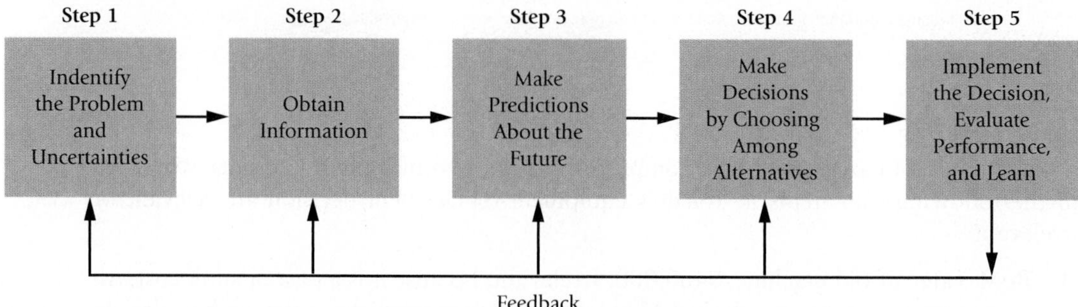

Learning Objective 8

Explain how conflicts can arise between the decision model a manager uses and the performance-evaluation model top management uses to evaluate managers

...tell managers to take a multiple-year view in decision making but judge their performance only on the basis of the current year's operating income

The decision model analysis (Step 4), which is presented in Exhibits 11-11 and 11-12, dictates replacing the machine rather than keeping it. In the real world, however, would the manager replace it? An important factor in replacement decisions is the manager's perception of whether the decision model is consistent with how the company will judge his or her performance after the decision is implemented (the performance-evaluation model in Step 5).

From the perspective of their own careers, it is no surprise that managers tend to favor the alternative that makes their performance look better. In our examples throughout this chapter, the decision model and the performance-evaluation model were consistent. If, however, the performance-evaluation model conflicts with the decision model, the performance-evaluation model often prevails in influencing managers' decisions. The following table compares Toledo's accrual accounting income for the first year and the second year when the manager decides to keep the machine versus when the manager decides to replace the machine.

	Accrual Accounting First-Year Results		Accrual Accounting Second-Year Results	
	Keep	Replace	Keep	Replace
Revenues	$1,100,000	$1,100,000	$1,100,000	$1,100,000
Operating costs				
Cash-operating costs	800,000	460,000	800,000	460,000
Depreciation	200,000	300,000	200,000	300,000
Loss on disposal	—	360,000	—	—
Total operating costs	1,000,000	1,120,000	1,000,000	760,000
Operating income (loss)	$ 100,000	$ (20,000)	$ 100,000	$ 340,000

Total accrual accounting income for the 2 years together is $120,000 higher if the machine is replaced, as in Exhibit 11-11. But if the promotion or bonus of the manager at Toledo hinges on his or her first year's operating income performance under accrual accounting, the manager would be very tempted to keep the old machine. Why? Because the accrual accounting model for measuring performance will show a first-year operating income of $100,000 if the old machine is kept versus an operating loss of $20,000 if the machine is replaced. Even though top management's goals encompass the 2-year period (consistent with the decision model), the manager will focus on first-year results if top management evaluates his or her performance on the basis of short-run measures such as the first-year's operating income.

Managers frequently find it difficult to resolve the conflict between the decision model and the performance-evaluation model. In theory, resolving the difficulty seems obvious: Managers should design models that are consistent. Consider our replacement example. Year-by-year effects on operating income of replacement can be budgeted for the 2-year planning horizon. The manager then would be evaluated on the expectation that the first year would be poor and the next year would be much better. Doing this for every decision, however, makes the performance-evaluation model very cumbersome. As a result of these practical difficulties, accounting systems rarely track each decision separately. Performance evaluation focuses on responsibility centers for a specific period, not on projects or individual items of equipment over their useful lives. Thus, the effects of many different decisions are combined in a single performance report and evaluation measure, say operating income. Lower-level managers make decisions to maximize operating income, and top management—through the reporting system—is rarely aware of particular desirable alternatives that lower-level managers did *not* choose because of conflicts between the decision and performance-evaluation models.

Consider another conflict between the decision model and the performance-evaluation model. Suppose a manager buys a particular machine only to discover shortly afterward that he or she could have purchased a better machine instead. The decision model may suggest replacing the machine that was just bought with the better machine, but will the manager do so? Probably not. Why? Because replacing the machine so soon after its purchase will reflect badly on the manager's capabilities and performance. If the manager's bosses have no knowledge of the better machine, the manager may prefer to keep the recently purchased machine rather than alert them to the better machine.

Many managers consider it unethical to take actions that make their own performance look good when these actions are not in the best interests of the firm. Critics believe that it was precisely these kinds of behaviors that contributed to the recent global financial crisis. To discourage such behaviors, managers develop codes of conduct, emphasize values, and build cultures that focus on doing the right things. Chapter 23 discusses performance-evaluation models, ethics, and ways to reduce conflict between the decision model and the performance-evaluation model in more detail.

Decision Point

How can conflicts arise between the decision model a manager uses and the performance evaluation model top-management uses to evaluate that manager?

Problem for Self-Study

Wally Lewis is manager of the engineering development division of Goldcoast Products. Lewis has just received a proposal signed by all 15 of his engineers to replace the workstations with networked personal computers (networked PCs). Lewis is not enthusiastic about the proposal.

Data on workstations and networked PCs are:

	Workstations	Networked PCs
Original cost	$ 300,000	$ 135,000
Useful life	5 years	3 years
Current age	2 years	0 years
Remaining useful life	3 years	3 years

	Workstations	Networked PCs
Accumulated depreciation	$ 120,000	Not acquired yet
Current book value	$ 180,000	Not acquired yet
Current disposal value (in cash)	$ 95,000	Not acquired yet
Terminal disposal value (in cash 3 years from now)	$ 0	$ 0
Annual computer-related cash operating costs	$ 40,000	$ 10,000
Annual revenues	$1,000,000	$1,000,000
Annual non-computer-related cash operating costs	$ 880,000	$ 880,000

Lewis's annual bonus includes a component based on division operating income. He has a promotion possibility next year that would make him a group vice president of Goldcoast Products.

Required

1. Compare the costs of workstations and networked PCs. Consider the cumulative results for the 3 years together, ignoring the time value of money and income taxes.
2. Why might Lewis be reluctant to purchase the networked PCs?

Solution

1. The following table considers all cost items when comparing future costs of workstations and networked PCs:

	Three Years Together		
All Items	Workstations (1)	Networked PCs (2)	Difference (3) = (1) − (2)
Revenues	$3,000,000	$3,000,000	—
Operating costs			
Non-computer-related cash operating costs ($880,000 per year × 3 years)	2,640,000	2,640,000	—
Computer-related cash operating costs ($40,000 per year; $10,000 per year × 3 years)	120,000	30,000	$ 90,000
Workstations' book value			
Periodic write-off as depreciation or	180,000	—	—
Lump-sum write-off	—	180,000	
Current disposal value of workstations	—	(95,000)	95,000
Networked PCs, written off periodically as depreciation	—	135,000	(135,000)
Total operating costs	2,940,000	2,890,000	50,000
Operating income	$ 60,000	$ 110,000	$(50,000)

Alternatively, the analysis could focus on only those items in the preceding table that differ between the alternatives.

	Three Years Together		
Relevant Items	Workstations	Networked PCs	Difference
Computer-related cash operating costs ($40,000 per year × 3 years; $10,000 per year × 3 years)	$120,000	$ 30,000	$ 90,000
Current disposal value of workstations	—	(95,000)	95,000
Networked PCs, written off periodically as depreciation	—	135,000	(135,000)
Total relevant costs	$120,000	$ 70,000	$ 50,000

The analysis suggests that it is cost-effective to replace the workstations with the networked PCs.

2. The accrual-accounting operating incomes *for the first year* under the alternatives of "keep workstations" versus the "buy networked PCs" are:

	Keep Workstations		Buy Networked PCs	
Revenues		$1,000,000		$1,000,000
Operating costs				
Non-computer-related operating costs	$880,000		$880,000	
Computer-related cash operating costs	40,000		10,000	
Depreciation	60,000		45,000	
Loss on disposal of workstations	—		85,000[a]	
Total operating costs		980,000		1,020,000
Operating income (loss)		$ 20,000		$ (20,000)

[a]$85,000 = Book value of workstations, $180,000 − Current disposal value, $95,000.

Lewis would be less happy with the expected operating loss of $20,000 if the networked PCs are purchased than he would be with the expected operating income of $20,000 if the workstations are kept. Buying the networked PCs would eliminate the component of his bonus based on operating income. He might also perceive the $20,000 operating loss as reducing his chances of being promoted to group vice president.

Decision Points

The following question-and-answer format summarizes the chapter's learning objectives. Each decision presents a key question related to a learning objective. The guidelines are the answer to that question.

Decision	Guidelines
1. What is the five-step process that managers can use to make decisions?	The five-step decision-making process is (a) identify the problem and uncertainties, (b) obtain information, (c) make predictions about the future, (d) make decisions by choosing among alternatives, and (e) implement the decision, evaluate performance, and learn.
2. When is a revenue or cost item relevant for a particular decision, and what potential problems should managers avoid in relevant-cost analysis?	To be relevant for a particular decision, a revenue or cost item must meet two criteria: (a) It must be an expected future revenue or expected future cost and (b) it must differ among alternative courses of action. Relevant revenue and relevant cost analysis only consider quantitative outcomes that can be expressed in financial terms. Quantitative outcomes are outcomes that can be measured in numerical terms. The outcomes of alternative actions can also have nonfinancial quantitative and qualitative effects. Qualitative factors, such as employee morale, are difficult to measure accurately in numerical terms. But managers must consider both qualitative factors and nonfinancial quantitative factors when making decisions. Two potential problems to avoid in relevant-cost analysis are (a) making incorrect general assumptions—such as all variable costs are relevant and all fixed costs are irrelevant—and (b) losing sight of total fixed costs and focusing instead on unit fixed costs.
3. What is an opportunity cost, and why should managers consider it when making insourcing-versus-outsourcing decisions?	Opportunity cost is the contribution to income that is forgone by not using a limited resource in its next-best alternative use. Opportunity cost is included in decision making because the relevant cost of any decision is (a) the incremental cost of the decision plus (b) the opportunity cost of the profit forgone from making that decision. When capacity is constrained, managers must consider the opportunity cost of using the capacity when deciding whether to produce the product in-house versus outsourcing it.

Decision	Guidelines
4. When a resource is constrained, how should managers choose which of multiple products to produce and sell?	When a resource is constrained, managers should select the product that yields the highest contribution margin per unit of the constraining or limiting resource (factor). In this way, total contribution margin will be maximized.
5. What steps can managers take to manage bottlenecks?	Managers can take four steps to manage bottlenecks: (a) recognize that the bottleneck operation determines throughput (contribution) margin, (b) identify the bottleneck, (c) keep the bottleneck busy and subordinate all nonbottleneck operations to the bottleneck operation, and (d) increase bottleneck efficiency and capacity.
6. In deciding to add or drop customers or to add or discontinue branch offices or business divisions, what should managers focus on and how should they take into account allocated overhead costs?	When making decisions about adding or dropping customers or adding or discontinuing branch offices and business divisions, managers should focus on only those costs that will change and any opportunity costs. Managers should ignore allocated overhead costs.
7. Is book value of existing equipment relevant in equipment-replacement decisions?	Book value of existing equipment is a past (historical or sunk) cost and, therefore, is irrelevant in equipment-replacement decisions.
8. How can conflicts arise between the decision model a manager uses and the performance-evaluation model top management uses to evaluate that manager?	Top management faces a persistent challenge: making sure that the performance-evaluation model of lower-level managers is consistent with the decision model. A common inconsistency is to tell these managers to take a multiple-year view in their decision making but then to judge their performance only on the basis of the current year's operating income.

Appendix

Linear Programming

In this chapter's Power Recreation example (pages 440–441), suppose both the snowmobile and boat engines must be tested on a very expensive machine before they are shipped to customers. The available machine-hours for testing are limited. Production data are:

		Use of Capacity in Hours per Unit of Product		Daily Maximum Production in Units	
Department	Available Daily Capacity in Hours	Snowmobile Engine	Boat Engine	Snowmobile Engine	Boat Engine
Assembly	600 machine-hours	2.0 machine-hours	5.0 machine-hours	300[a] snow engines	120 boat engines
Testing	120 testing-hours	1.0 machine-hour	0.5 machine-hour	120 snow engines	240 boat engines

[a] For example, 600 machine-hours ÷ 2.0 machine-hours per snowmobile engine = 300, the maximum number of snowmobile engines that the assembly department can make if it works exclusively on snowmobile engines.

Exhibit 11-13 Operating Data for Power Recreation

	Department Capacity (per Day) In Product Units				
	Assembly	Testing	Selling Price	Variable Cost per Unit	Contribution Margin per Unit
Only snowmobile engines	300	120	$ 800	$560	$240
Only boat engines	120	240	$1,000	$625	$375

Exhibit 11-13 summarizes these and other relevant data. In addition, as a result of material shortages for boat engines, Power Recreation cannot produce more than 110 boat engines per day. How many engines of each type should Power Recreation's managers produce and sell daily to maximize operating income?

Because there are multiple constraints, managers can use a technique called *linear programming (LP)* to determine the number of each type of engine to produce. LP models typically assume that all costs are either variable or fixed for a single cost driver (units of output). We will see that LP models also require certain other linear assumptions to hold. When these assumptions fail, managers should consider other decision models.[5]

Steps in Solving an LP Problem

We use the data in Exhibit 11-13 to illustrate the three steps in solving an LP problem. Throughout this discussion, S equals the number of units of snowmobile engines produced and sold, and B equals the number of units of boat engines produced and sold.

Step 1: **Determine the Objective Function.** The **objective function** of a linear program expresses the objective or goal to be maximized (say, operating income) or minimized (say, operating costs). In our example, the objective is to find the combination of snowmobile engines and boat engines that maximizes total contribution margin. Fixed costs remain the same regardless of the product-mix decision and are irrelevant. The linear function expressing the objective for the total contribution margin (TCM) is:

$$TCM = \$240S + \$375B$$

Step 2: **Specify the Constraints.** A **constraint** is a mathematical inequality or equality that must be satisfied by the variables in a mathematical model. The following linear inequalities express the relationships in our example:

Assembly department constraint	$2S + 5B \leq 600$
Testing department constraint	$1S + 0.5B \leq 120$
Materials-shortage constraint for boat engines	$B \leq 110$
Negative production is impossible	$S \geq 0$ and $B \geq 0$

The three solid lines on the graph in Exhibit 11-14 show the existing constraints for assembly and testing and the materials-shortage constraint.[6] The feasible or technically possible alternatives are those combinations of quantities of snowmobile engines and boat engines that satisfy all the constraining resources or factors. The shaded "area of feasible solutions" in Exhibit 11-14 shows the boundaries of those product combinations that are feasible.

[5] Other decision models are described in Barry Render, Ralph M. Stair, and Michael E. Hanna, *Quantitative Analysis for Management*, 11th ed. (Upper Saddle River, NJ: Prentice Hall, 2012); and Steven Nahmias, *Production and Operations Analysis*, 6th ed. (New York: McGraw-Hill/Irwin, 2008).

[6] As an example of how the lines are plotted in Exhibit 11-14, use equal signs instead of inequality signs and assume for the assembly department that $B = 0$; then $S = 300$ (600 machine-hours ÷ 2 machine-hours per snowmobile engine). Assume that $S = 0$; then $B = 120$ (600 machine-hours ÷ 5 machine-hours per boat engine). Connect those two points with a straight line.

Exhibit 11-14

Linear Programming: Graphic Solution for Power Recreation

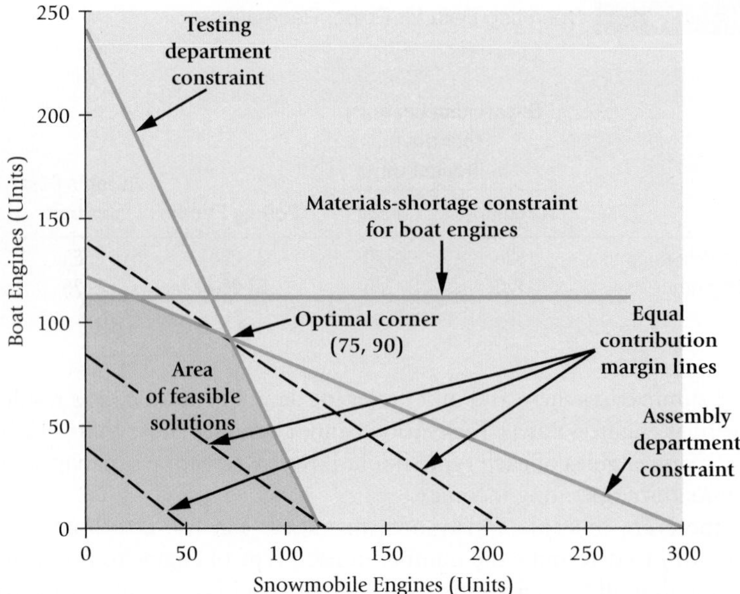

Step 3: **Compute the Optimal Solution. Linear programming (LP)** is an optimization technique used to maximize the *objective function* when there are multiple *constraints*. We present two approaches for finding the optimal solution using LP: trial-and-error approach and graphic approach. These approaches are easy to use in our example because there are only two variables in the objective function and a small number of constraints. Understanding these approaches provides insight into LP. In most real-world LP applications, managers use computer software packages to calculate the optimal solution.[7]

Trial-and-Error Approach

Managers can find the optimal solution by trial and error, by working with coordinates of the corners of the area of feasible solutions.

First, select any set of corner points and compute the total contribution margin. Five corner points appear in Exhibit 11-14. It is helpful to use simultaneous equations to obtain the exact coordinates in the graph. To illustrate, the corner point ($S = 75, B = 90$) can be derived by solving the two pertinent constraint inequalities as simultaneous equations:

	$2S + 5B = 600$	(1)
	$1S + 0.5B = 120$	(2)
Multiplying (2) *by* 2:	$2S + B = 240$	(3)
Subtracting (3) from (1):	$4B = 360$	
Therefore,	$B = 360 \div 4 = 90$	
Substituting for B in (2):	$1S + 0.5(90) = 120$	
	$S = 120 - 45 = 75$	

Given $S = 75$ snowmobile engines and $B = 90$ boat engines, TCM = (\$240 per snowmobile engine × 75 snowmobile engines) + (\$375 per boat engine × 90 boat engines) = \$51,750.

Second, move from corner point to corner point and compute the total contribution margin at each corner point.

[7] Standard computer software packages rely on the *simplex method*, which is an iterative step-by-step procedure for determining the optimal solution to an LP problem. This method starts with a specific feasible solution and then tests it by substitution to see whether the result can be improved. These substitutions continue until no further improvement is possible and the optimal solution is obtained.

Trial	Corner Point (*S, B*)	Snowmobile Engines (*S*)	Boat Engines (*B*)	Total Contribution Margin
1	(0, 0)	0	0	\$240(0) + \$375(0) = \$0
2	(0, 110)	0	110	\$240(0) + \$375(110) = \$41,250
3	(25,110)	25	110	\$240(25) + \$375(110) = \$47,250
4	(75, 90)	75	90	\$240(75) + \$375(90) = \$51,750[a]
5	(120, 0)	120	0	\$240(120) + \$375(0) = \$28,800

[a] The optimal solution.

The optimal product mix is the mix that yields the highest total contribution: 75 snowmobile engines and 90 boat engines. To understand the solution, consider what happens when moving from the point (25, 110) to (75, 90). Power Recreation gives up \$7,500 [\$375 × (110 − 90)] in contribution margin from boat engines while gaining \$12,000 [\$240 × (75 − 25)] in contribution margin from snowmobile engines. This results in a net increase in contribution margin of \$4,500 (\$12,000 − \$7,500), from \$47,250 to \$51,750.

Graphic Approach

Consider all possible combinations that will produce the same total contribution margin of, say, \$12,000. That is,

$$\$240S + \$375B = \$12,000$$

This set of \$12,000 contribution margins is a straight dashed line through [S = 50 (\$12,000 ÷ \$240); B = 0] and [S = 0, B = 32 (\$12,000 ÷ \$375)] in Exhibit 11-14. Other equal total contribution margins can be represented by lines parallel to this one. In Exhibit 11-14, we show three dashed lines. Lines drawn farther from the origin represent more sales of both products and higher amounts of equal contribution margins.

The optimal line is the one farthest from the origin but still passing through a point in the area of feasible solutions. This line represents the highest total contribution margin. The optimal solution—the number of snowmobile engines and boat engines that will maximize the objective function, total contribution margin—is the corner point (S = 75, B = 90). This solution will become apparent if you put a straight-edge ruler on the graph and move it outward from the origin and parallel with the \$12,000 contribution margin line. Move the ruler as far away from the origin as possible—that is, increase the total contribution margin—without leaving the area of feasible solutions. In general, the optimal solution in a maximization problem lies at the corner where the dashed line intersects an extreme point of the area of feasible solutions. Moving the ruler out any farther puts it outside the area of feasible solutions.

Sensitivity Analysis

What are the implications of uncertainty about the accounting or technical coefficients used in the objective function (such as the contribution margin per unit of snowmobile engines or boat engines) or the constraints (such as the number of machine-hours it takes to make a snowmobile engine or a boat engine)? Consider how a change in the contribution margin of snowmobile engines from \$240 to \$300 per unit would affect the optimal solution. Assume the contribution margin for boat engines remains unchanged at \$375 per unit. The revised objective function will be:

$$TCM = \$300S + \$375B$$

Using the trial-and-error approach to calculate the total contribution margin for each of the five corner points described in the previous table, the optimal solution is still (S = 75, B = 90). What if the contribution margin of snowmobile engines falls to \$160 per unit? The optimal solution remains the same (S = 75, B = 90). Thus, big changes in the contribution margin per unit of snowmobile engines have no effect on the optimal solution in this case. That's because, although the slopes of the equal contribution margin lines in Exhibit 11-14 change as the contribution margin of snowmobile engines changes from \$240 to \$300 to \$160 per unit, the farthest point at which the equal contribution margin lines intersect the area of feasible solutions is still ($S = 75, B = 90$).

Terms to Learn

This chapter and the Glossary at the end of the book contain definitions of the following important terms:

book value **(p. 448)**
business function costs **(p. 429)**
constraint **(p. 455)**
decision model **(p. 425)**
differential cost **(p. 433)**
differential revenue **(p. 434)**
full costs of the product **(p. 429)**
incremental cost **(p. 433)**
incremental revenue **(p. 434)**
insourcing **(p. 432)**
linear programming (LP) **(p. 456)**
make-or-buy decisions **(p. 432)**
objective function **(p. 455)**
one-time-only special order **(p. 428)**
opportunity cost **(p. 436)**
outsourcing **(p. 432)**
product-mix decisions **(p. 440)**
qualitative factors **(p. 428)**
quantitative factors **(p. 427)**
relevant costs **(p. 426)**
relevant revenues **(p. 426)**
sunk costs **(p. 427)**
theory of constraints (TOC) **(p. 441)**
throughput margin **(p. 441)**

Assignment Material

MyAccountingLab

Questions

11-1 Outline the five-step sequence in a decision process.

11-2 Define relevant costs. Why are historical costs irrelevant?

11-3 "All future costs are relevant." Do you agree? Why?

11-4 Distinguish between quantitative and qualitative factors in decision making.

11-5 Describe two potential problems that should be avoided in relevant-cost analysis.

11-6 "Variable costs are always relevant, and fixed costs are always irrelevant." Do you agree? Why?

11-7 "A component part should be purchased whenever the purchase price is less than its total manufacturing cost per unit." Do you agree? Why?

11-8 Define opportunity cost.

11-9 "Managers should always buy inventory in quantities that result in the lowest purchase cost per unit." Do you agree? Why?

11-10 "Management should always maximize sales of the product with the highest contribution margin per unit." Do you agree? Why?

11-11 "A branch office or business segment that shows negative operating income should be shut down." Do you agree? Explain briefly.

11-12 "Cost written off as depreciation on equipment already purchased is always irrelevant." Do you agree? Why?

11-13 "Managers will always choose the alternative that maximizes operating income or minimizes costs in the decision model." Do you agree? Why?

11-14 Describe the three steps in solving a linear programming problem.

11-15 How might the optimal solution of a linear programming problem be determined?

MyAccountingLab

Exercises

11-16 Disposal of assets. Answer the following questions.

1. A company has an inventory of 1,250 assorted parts for a line of missiles that has been discontinued. The inventory cost is \$76,000. The parts can be either (a) remachined at total additional costs of \$26,500 and then sold for \$33,500 or (b) sold as scrap for \$2,500. Which action is more profitable? Show your calculations.
2. A truck, costing \$100,500 and uninsured, is wrecked its first day in use. It can be either (a) disposed of for \$18,000 cash and replaced with a similar truck costing \$103,000 or (b) rebuilt for \$88,500 and thus be brand-new as far as operating characteristics and looks are concerned. Which action is less costly? Show your calculations.

11-17 Relevant and irrelevant costs. Answer the following questions.

1. DeCesare Computers makes 5,200 units of a circuit board, CB76, at a cost of $280 each. Variable cost per unit is $190 and fixed cost per unit is $90. Peach Electronics offers to supply 5,200 units of CB76 for $260. If DeCesare buys from Peach it will be able to save $10 per unit in fixed costs but continue to incur the remaining $80 per unit. Should DeCesare accept Peach's offer? Explain.
2. LN Manufacturing is deciding whether to keep or replace an old machine. It obtains the following information:

	Old Machine	New Machine
Original cost	$10,700	$9,000
Useful life	10 years	3 years
Current age	7 years	0 years
Remaining useful life	3 years	3 years
Accumulated depreciation	$7,490	Not acquired yet
Book value	$3,210	Not acquired yet
Current disposal value (in cash)	$2,200	Not acquired yet
Terminal disposal value (3 years from now)	$0	$0
Annual cash operating costs	$17,500	$15,500

LN Manufacturing uses straight-line depreciation. Ignore the time value of money and income taxes. Should LN Manufacturing replace the old machine? Explain.

11-18 Multiple choice. (CPA) Choose the best answer.

1. The Dalton Company manufactures slippers and sells them at $12 a pair. Variable manufacturing cost is $5.00 a pair, and allocated fixed manufacturing cost is $1.25 a pair. It has enough idle capacity available to accept a one-time-only special order of 5,000 pairs of slippers at $6.25 a pair. Dalton will not incur any marketing costs as a result of the special order. What would the effect on operating income be if the special order could be accepted without affecting normal sales: (a) $0, (b) $6,250 increase, (c) $28,750 increase, or (d) $31,250 increase? Show your calculations.
2. The Sacramento Company manufactures Part No. 498 for use in its production line. The manufacturing cost per unit for 30,000 units of Part No. 498 is as follows:

Direct materials	$ 5
Direct manufacturing labor	22
Variable manufacturing overhead	8
Fixed manufacturing overhead allocated	15
Total manufacturing cost per unit	$50

The Counter Company has offered to sell 30,000 units of Part No. 498 to Sacramento for $47 per unit. Sacramento will make the decision to buy the part from Counter if there is an overall savings of at least $30,000 for Sacramento. If Sacramento accepts Counter's offer, $8 per unit of the fixed overhead allocated would be eliminated. Furthermore, Sacramento has determined that the released facilities could be used to save relevant costs in the manufacture of Part No. 575. For Sacramento to achieve an overall savings of $30,000, the amount of relevant costs that would have to be saved by using the released facilities in the manufacture of Part No. 575 would be which of the following: (a) $90,000, (b) $150,000, (c) $180,000, or (d) $210,000? Show your calculations. What other factors might Sacramento consider before outsourcing to Counter?

11-19 Special order, activity-based costing. (CMA, adapted) The Gold Plus Company manufactures medals for winners of athletic events and other contests. Its manufacturing plant has the capacity to produce 11,000 medals each month. Current production and sales are 10,000 medals per month. The company normally charges $150 per medal. Cost information for the current activity level is as follows:

Variable costs that vary with number of units produced	
Direct materials	$ 350,000
Direct manufacturing labor	375,000
Variable costs (for setups, materials handling, quality control, and so on) that vary with number of batches, 200 batches × $500 per batch	100,000
Fixed manufacturing costs	300,000
Fixed marketing costs	275,000
Total costs	$1,400,000

Gold Plus has just received a special one-time-only order for 1,000 medals at $100 per medal. Accepting the special order would not affect the company's regular business. Gold Plus makes medals for its existing customers in batch sizes of 50 medals (200 batches × 50 medals per batch = 10,000 medals). The special order requires Gold Plus to make the medals in 25 batches of 40 medals.

Required

1. Should Gold Plus accept this special order? Show your calculations.
2. Suppose plant capacity were only 10,500 medals instead of 11,000 medals each month. The special order must either be taken in full or be rejected completely. Should Gold Plus accept the special order? Show your calculations.
3. As in requirement 1, assume that monthly capacity is 11,000 medals. Gold Plus is concerned that if it accepts the special order, its existing customers will immediately demand a price discount of $10 in the month in which the special order is being filled. They would argue that Gold Plus's capacity costs are now being spread over more units and that existing customers should get the benefit of these lower costs. Should Gold Plus accept the special order under these conditions? Show your calculations.

11-20 Make versus buy, activity-based costing. The Svenson Corporation manufactures cellular modems. It manufactures its own cellular modem circuit boards (CMCB), an important part of the cellular modem. It reports the following cost information about the costs of making CMCBs in 2014 and the expected costs in 2015:

	Current Costs in 2014	Expected Costs in 2015
Variable manufacturing costs		
Direct material cost per CMCB	$ 180	$ 170
Direct manufacturing labor cost per CMCB	50	45
Variable manufacturing cost per batch for setups, materials handling, and quality control	1,600	1,500
Fixed manufacturing cost		
Fixed manufacturing overhead costs that can be avoided if CMCBs are not made	320,000	320,000
Fixed manufacturing overhead costs of plant depreciation, insurance, and administration that cannot be avoided even if CMCBs are not made	800,000	800,000

Svenson manufactured 8,000 CMCBs in 2014 in 40 batches of 200 each. In 2015, Svenson anticipates needing 10,000 CMCBs. The CMCBs would be produced in 80 batches of 125 each.

The Minton Corporation has approached Svenson about supplying CMCBs to Svenson in 2015 at $300 per CMCB on whatever delivery schedule Svenson wants.

Required

1. Calculate the total expected manufacturing cost per unit of making CMCBs in 2015.
2. Suppose the capacity currently used to make CMCBs will become idle if Svenson purchases CMCBs from Minton. On the basis of financial considerations alone, should Svenson make CMCBs or buy them from Minton? Show your calculations.
3. Now suppose that if Svenson purchases CMCBs from Minton, its best alternative use of the capacity currently used for CMCBs is to make and sell special circuit boards (CB3s) to the Essex Corporation. Svenson estimates the following incremental revenues and costs from CB3s:

Total expected incremental future revenues	$2,000,000
Total expected incremental future costs	$2,150,000

On the basis of financial considerations alone, should Svenson make CMCBs or buy them from Minton? Show your calculations.

11-21 Inventory decision, opportunity costs. Best Trim, a manufacturer of lawn mowers, predicts that it will purchase 204,000 spark plugs next year. Best Trim estimates that 17,000 spark plugs will be required each month. A supplier quotes a price of $9 per spark plug. The supplier also offers a special discount option: If all 204,000 spark plugs are purchased at the start of the year, a discount of 2% off the $9 price will be given. Best Trim can invest its cash at 10% per year. It costs Best Trim $260 to place each purchase order.

Required

1. What is the opportunity cost of interest forgone from purchasing all 204,000 units at the start of the year instead of in 12 monthly purchases of 17,000 units per order?
2. Would this opportunity cost be recorded in the accounting system? Why?

3. Should Best Trim purchase 204,000 units at the start of the year or 17,000 units each month? Show your calculations.
4. What other factors should Best Trim consider when making its decision?

11-22 Relevant costs, contribution margin, product emphasis. The Snack Shack is a take-out food store at a popular beach resort. Susan Sexton, owner of the Snack Shack, is deciding how much refrigerator space to devote to four different drinks. Pertinent data on these four drinks are as follows:

	Cola	Lemonade	Punch	Natural Orange Juice
Selling price per case	$18.80	$20.75	$26.90	$39.30
Variable cost per case	$13.80	$16.25	$20.10	$30.10
Cases sold per foot of shelf space per day	7	12	24	6

Sexton has a maximum front shelf space of 12 feet to devote to the four drinks. She wants a minimum of 1 foot and a maximum of 6 feet of front shelf space for each drink.

Required

1. Calculate the contribution margin per case of each type of drink.
2. A coworker of Sexton's recommends that she maximize the shelf space devoted to those drinks with the highest contribution margin per case. Do you agree with this recommendation? Explain briefly.
3. What shelf-space allocation for the four drinks would you recommend for the Snack Shack? Show your calculations.

11-23 Selection of most profitable product. Fitness Gym, Inc., produces two basic types of weight-lifting equipment, Model 9 and Model 14. Pertinent data are as follows:

	A	B	C
1		Per Unit	
2		Model A	Model B
3	Selling price	$130.00	$105.00
4	Costs		
5	Direct material	26.00	20.00
6	Direct manufacturing labor	20.00	16.00
7	Variable manufacturing overhead	10.00	11.00
8	Fixed manufacturing overhead*	6.00	3.00
9	Marketing (all variable)	10.00	9.00
10	Total cost	72.00	59.00
11	Operating income	$ 58.00	$ 46.00
12			
13	*Allocated on the basis of machine-hours		

The weight-lifting craze suggests that Fitness Gym can sell enough of either Model 9 or Model 14 to keep the plant operating at full capacity. Both products are processed through the same production departments. Which product should the company produce? Briefly explain your answer.

Required

11-24 Theory of constraints, throughput margin, relevant costs. The Pierce Corporation manufactures filing cabinets in two operations: machining and finishing. It provides the following information:

	Machining	Finishing
Annual capacity	110,000 units	90,000 units
Annual production	90,000 units	90,000 units
Fixed operating costs (excluding direct materials)	$540,000	$270,000
Fixed operating costs per unit produced ($540,000 ÷ 90,000; $270,000 ÷ 90,000)	$6 per unit	$3 per unit

Each cabinet sells for $70 and has direct material costs of $30 incurred at the start of the machining operation. Pierce has no other variable costs. Pierce can sell whatever output it produces. The following requirements refer only to the preceding data. There is no connection between the requirements.

Required

1. Pierce is considering using some modern jigs and tools in the finishing operation that would increase annual finishing output by 1,150 units. The annual cost of these jigs and tools is $35,000. Should Pierce acquire these tools? Show your calculations.
2. The production manager of the Machining Department has submitted a proposal to do faster setups that would increase the annual capacity of the Machining Department by 9,000 units and would cost $4,000 per year. Should Pierce implement the change? Show your calculations.
3. An outside contractor offers to do the finishing operation for 9,500 units at $9 per unit, triple the $3 per unit that it costs Pierce to do the finishing in-house. Should Pierce accept the subcontractor's offer? Show your calculations.
4. The Hammond Corporation offers to machine 5,000 units at $3 per unit, half the $6 per unit that it costs Pierce to do the machining in-house. Should Pierce accept Hammond's offer? Show your calculations.
5. Pierce produces 1,700 defective units at the machining operation. What is the cost to Pierce of the defective items produced? Explain your answer briefly.
6. Pierce produces 1,700 defective units at the finishing operation. What is the cost to Pierce of the defective items produced? Explain your answer briefly.

11-25 Closing and opening stores. Sanchez Corporation runs two convenience stores, one in Connecticut and one in Rhode Island. Operating income for each store in 2014 is as follows:

	Connecticut Store	Rhode Island Store
Revenues	$1,070,000	$ 860,000
Operating costs		
Cost of goods sold	750,000	660,000
Lease rent (renewable each year)	90,000	75,000
Labor costs (paid on an hourly basis)	42,000	42,000
Depreciation of equipment	25,000	22,000
Utilities (electricity, heating)	43,000	46,000
Allocated corporate overhead	50,000	40,000
Total operating costs	1,000,000	885,000
Operating income (loss)	$ 70,000	$ (25,000)

The equipment has a zero disposal value. In a senior management meeting, Maria Lopez, the management accountant at Sanchez Corporation, makes the following comment, "Sanchez can increase its profitability by closing down the Rhode Island store or by adding another store like it."

Required

1. By closing down the Rhode Island store, Sanchez can reduce overall corporate overhead costs by $44,000. Calculate Sanchez's operating income if it closes the Rhode Island store. Is Maria Lopez's statement about the effect of closing the Rhode Island store correct? Explain.
2. Calculate Sanchez's operating income if it keeps the Rhode Island store open and opens another store with revenues and costs identical to the Rhode Island store (including a cost of $22,000 to acquire equipment with a one-year useful life and zero disposal value). Opening this store will increase corporate overhead costs by $4,000. Is Maria Lopez's statement about the effect of adding another store like the Rhode Island store correct? Explain.

11-26 Choosing customers. Rodeo Printers operates a printing press with a monthly capacity of 4,000 machine-hours. Rodeo has two main customers: Trent Corporation and Julie Corporation. Data on each customer for January are:

	Trent Corporation	Julie Corporation	Total
Revenues	$210,000	$140,000	$350,000
Variable costs	84,000	85,000	169,000
Contribution margin	126,000	55,000	181,000
Fixed costs (allocated)	102,000	68,000	170,000
Operating income	$ 24,000	$ (13,000)	$ 11,000
Machine-hours required	3,000 hours	1,000 hours	4,000 hours

Julie Corporation indicates that it wants Rodeo to do an *additional* $140,000 worth of printing jobs during February. These jobs are identical to the existing business Rodeo did for Julie in January in terms of variable costs and machine-hours required. Rodeo anticipates that the business from Trent Corporation in February will be the same as that in January. Rodeo can choose to accept as much of the Trent and Julie business for February as its capacity allows. Assume that total machine-hours and fixed costs for February will be the same as in January.

Required

What action should Rodeo take to maximize its operating income? Show your calculations. What other factors should Rodeo consider before making a decision?

11-27 Relevance of equipment costs. Papa's Pizza is considering replacement of its pizza oven with a new, more energy-efficient model. Information related to the old and new pizza ovens follows:

Old oven—original cost	$60,000
Old oven—book value	$50,000
Old oven—current market value	$42,000
Old oven—annual operating cost	$14,000
New oven—purchase price	$75,000
New oven—installation cost	$ 2,000
New oven—annual operating cost	$ 6,000

The old oven had been purchased a year ago. Papa's Pizza estimates that either oven has a remaining useful life of five years. At the end of five years, either oven would have a zero salvage value. Ignore the effect of income taxes and the time value of money.

Required

1. Which of the costs and benefits above are relevant to the decision to replace the oven?
2. What information is irrelevant? Why is it irrelevant?
3. Should Papa's Pizza purchase the new oven? Provide support for your answer.
4. Is there any conflict between the decision model and the incentives of the manager who has purchased the "old" oven and is considering replacing it a year later?
5. At what purchase price would Papa's Pizza be indifferent between purchasing the new oven and continuing to use the old oven?

11-28 Equipment upgrade versus replacement. (A. Spero, adapted) The TechGuide Company produces and sells 7,500 modular computer desks per year at a selling price of $750 each. Its current production equipment, purchased for $1,800,000 and with a five-year useful life, is only two years old. It has a terminal disposal value of $0 and is depreciated on a straight-line basis. The equipment has a current disposal price of $450,000. However, the emergence of a new molding technology has led TechGuide to consider either upgrading or replacing the production equipment. The following table presents data for the two alternatives:

Home Insert Page Layout Formulas Data Review

	A	B	C
1		**Upgrade**	**Replace**
2	One-time equipment costs	$3,000,000	$4,800,000
3	Variable manufacturing cost per desk	$ 150	$ 75
4	Remaining useful life of equipment (years)	3	3
5	Terminal disposal value of equipment	$ 0	$ 0

All equipment costs will continue to be depreciated on a straight-line basis. For simplicity, ignore income taxes and the time value of money.

Required

1. Should TechGuide upgrade its production line or replace it? Show your calculations.
2. Now suppose the one-time equipment cost to replace the production equipment is somewhat negotiable. All other data are as given previously. What is the maximum one-time equipment cost that TechGuide would be willing to pay to replace rather than upgrade the old equipment?
3. Assume that the capital expenditures to replace and upgrade the production equipment are as given in the original exercise, but that the production and sales quantity is not known. For what production and sales quantity would TechGuide (i) upgrade the equipment or (ii) replace the equipment?
4. Assume that all data are as given in the original exercise. Dan Doria is TechGuide's manager, and his bonus is based on operating income. Because he is likely to relocate after about a year, his current bonus is his primary concern. Which alternative would Doria choose? Explain.

MyAccountingLab

Problems

11-29 Special order, short-run pricing. Slugger Corporation produces baseball bats for kids that it sells for $36 each. At capacity, the company can produce 50,000 bats a year. The costs of producing and selling 50,000 bats are as follows:

	Cost per Bat	Total Costs
Direct materials	$13	$ 650,000
Direct manufacturing labor	5	250,000
Variable manufacturing overhead	2	100,000
Fixed manufacturing overhead	6	300,000
Variable selling expenses	3	150,000
Fixed selling expenses	2	100,000
Total costs	$31	$1, 550,000

Required

1. Suppose Slugger is currently producing and selling 40,000 bats. At this level of production and sales, its fixed costs are the same as given in the preceding table. Bench Corporation wants to place a one-time special order for 10,000 bats at $23 each. Slugger will incur no variable selling costs for this special order. Should Slugger accept this one-time special order? Show your calculations.
2. Now suppose Slugger is currently producing and selling 50,000 bats. If Slugger accepts Bench's offer it will have to sell 10,000 fewer bats to its regular customers. (a) On financial considerations alone, should Slugger accept this one-time special order? Show your calculations. (b) On financial considerations alone, at what price would Slugger be indifferent between accepting the special order and continuing to sell to its regular customers at $36 per bat. (c) What other factors should Slugger consider in deciding whether to accept the one-time special order?

11-30 Short-run pricing, capacity constraints. Ohio Acres Dairy, maker of specialty cheeses, produces a soft cheese from the milk of Holstein cows raised on a special corn-based diet. One kilogram of soft cheese, which has a contribution margin of $8, requires 4 liters of milk. A well-known gourmet restaurant has asked Ohio Acres to produce 2,000 kilograms of a hard cheese from the same milk of Holstein cows. Knowing that the dairy has sufficient unused capacity, Elise Princiotti, owner of Ohio Acres, calculates the costs of making one kilogram of the desired hard cheese:

Milk (10 liters × $1.50 per liter)	$15
Variable direct manufacturing labor	4
Variable manufacturing overhead	2
Fixed manufacturing cost allocated	5
Total manufacturing cost	$26

Required

1. Suppose Ohio Acres can acquire all the Holstein milk that it needs. What is the minimum price per kilogram the company should charge for the hard cheese?
2. Now suppose that the Holstein milk is in short supply. Every kilogram of hard cheese Ohio Acres produces will reduce the quantity of soft cheese that it can make and sell. What is the minimum price per kilogram the company should charge to produce the hard cheese?

11-31 International outsourcing. Cuddly Critters, Inc., manufactures plush toys in a facility in Cleveland, Ohio. Recently, the company designed a group of collectible resin figurines to go with the plush toy line. Management is trying to decide whether to manufacture the figurines themselves in existing space in the Cleveland facility or to accept an offer from a manufacturing company in Indonesia. Data concerning the decision are:

Expected annual sales of figurines (in units)	400,000
Average selling price of a figurine	$5
Price quoted by Indonesian company, in Indonesian Rupiah (IDR), for each figurine	27,300 IDR
Current exchange rate	9,100 IDR = $1
Variable manufacturing costs	$2.85 per unit
Incremental annual fixed manufacturing costs associated with the new product line	$200,000
Variable selling and distribution costs[a]	$0.50 per unit
Annual fixed selling and distribution costs[a]	$285,000

[a] Selling and distribution costs are the same regardless of whether the figurines are manufactured in Cleveland or imported.

Required

1. Should Cuddly Critters manufacture the 400,000 figurines in the Cleveland facility or purchase them from the Indonesian supplier? Explain.
2. Cuddly Critters believes that the U.S. dollar may weaken in the coming months against the Indonesian rupiah and does not want to face any currency risk. Assume that Cuddly Critters can enter into a forward contract today to purchase 27,300 IDRs for $3.40. Should Cuddly Critters manufacture the 400,000 figurines in the Cleveland facility or purchase them from the Indonesian supplier? Explain.
3. What are some of the qualitative factors that Cuddly Critters should consider when deciding whether to outsource the figurine manufacturing to Indonesia?

11-32 Relevant costs, opportunity costs. Gavin Martin, the general manager of Oregano Software, must decide when to release the new version of Oregano's spreadsheet package, Easyspread 2.0. Development of Easyspread 2.0 is complete; however, the diskettes, compact discs, and user manuals have not yet been produced. The product can be shipped starting July 1, 2014.

The major problem is that Oregano has overstocked the previous version of its spreadsheet package, Easyspread 1.0. Martin knows that once Easyspread 2.0 is introduced, Oregano will not be able to sell any more units of Easyspread 1.0. Rather than just throwing away the inventory of Easyspread 1.0, Martin is wondering if it might be better to continue to sell Easyspread 1.0 for the next three months and introduce Easyspread 2.0 on October 1, 2014, when the inventory of Easyspread 1.0 will be sold out.

The following information is available:

	Easyspread 1.0	Easyspread 2.0
Selling price	$165	$215
Variable cost per unit of diskettes, compact discs, user manuals	24	38
Development cost per unit	60	95
Marketing and administrative cost per unit	31	41
Total cost per unit	115	174
Operating income per unit	$ 50	$ 41

Development cost per unit for each product equals the total costs of developing the software product divided by the anticipated unit sales over the life of the product. Marketing and administrative costs are fixed costs in 2014, incurred to support all marketing and administrative activities of Oregano Software. Marketing and administrative costs are allocated to products on the basis of the budgeted revenues of each product. The preceding unit costs assume Easyspread 2.0 will be introduced on October 1, 2014.

Required

1. On the basis of financial considerations alone, should Martin introduce Easyspread 2.0 on July 1, 2014, or wait until October 1, 2014? Show your calculations, clearly identifying relevant and irrelevant revenues and costs.
2. What other factors might Gavin Martin consider in making a decision?

11-33 Opportunity costs and relevant costs. Jason Wu operates Exclusive Limousines, a fleet of 10 limousines used for weddings, proms, and business events in Washington, D.C. Wu charges customers a flat fee of $250 per car taken on contract plus an hourly fee of $80. His income statement for May follows:

Revenue (200 contracts × $250) + (1,250 hours × $80)	$150,000
Operating expenses:	
Driver wages and benefits ($35 per hour × 1,250 hours)	43,750
Depreciation on limousines	19,000
Fuel costs ($12.80 per hour × 1,250 hours)	16,000
Maintenance	18,400
Liability and casualty insurance	2,500
Advertising	10,500
Administrative expenses	24,200
Total expenses	134,350
Operating income	$ 15,650

All expenses are fixed, with the exception of driver wages and benefits and fuel costs, which are both variable per hour. During May, the company's limousines were fully booked. In June, Wu expects that Exclusive Limousines will be operating near capacity. Shelly Worthington, a prominent Washington socialite, has asked Wu to bid on a large charity event she is hosting in late June. The limousine company she had hired has canceled at the last minute, and she needs the service of five limousines for four hours each. She will only hire Exclusive Limousines if they take the entire job. Wu checks his schedule and finds that he only has three limousines available that day.

Required

1. If Wu accepts the contract with Worthington, he would either have to (a) cancel two prom contracts each for 1 car for 6 hours or (b) cancel one business event for three cars contracted for two hours each. What are the relevant opportunity costs of accepting the Worthington contract in each case? Which contract should he cancel?
2. Wu would like to win the bid on the Worthington job because of the potential for lucrative future business. Assume that Wu cancels the contract in part 1 with the lowest opportunity cost, and assume that the three currently available cars would go unrented if the company does not win the bid. What is the lowest amount he should bid on the Worthington job?
3. Another limousine company has offered to rent Exclusive Limousines two additional cars for $300 each per day. Wu would still need to pay for fuel and driver wages on these cars for the Worthington job. Should Wu rent the two cars to avoid canceling either of the other two contracts?

11-34 Opportunity costs. (H. Schaefer, adapted) The Wild Orchid Corporation is working at full production capacity producing 13,000 units of a unique product, Everlast. Manufacturing cost per unit for Everlast is:

Direct materials	$10
Direct manufacturing labor	2
Manufacturing overhead	14
Total manufacturing cost	$26

Manufacturing overhead cost per unit is based on variable cost per unit of $8 and fixed costs of $78,000 (at full capacity of 13,000 units). Marketing cost per unit, all variable, is $4, and the selling price is $52.

A customer, the Apex Company, has asked Wild Orchid to produce 3,500 units of Stronglast, a modification of Everlast. Stronglast would require the same manufacturing processes as Everlast. Apex has offered to pay Wild Orchid $40 for a unit of Stronglast and share half of the marketing cost per unit.

Required

1. What is the opportunity cost to Wild Orchid of producing the 3,500 units of Stronglast? (Assume that no overtime is worked.)
2. The Chesapeake Corporation has offered to produce 3,500 units of Everlast for Wild Orchid so that Wild Orchid may accept the Apex offer. That is, if Wild Orchid accepts the Chesapeake offer, Wild Orchid would manufacture 9,500 units of Everlast and 3,500 units of Stronglast and purchase 3,500 units of Everlast from Chesapeake. Chesapeake would charge Wild Orchid $36 per unit to manufacture Everlast. On the basis of financial considerations alone, should Wild Orchid accept the Chesapeake offer? Show your calculations.
3. Suppose Wild Orchid had been working at less than full capacity, producing 9,500 units of Everlast, at the time the Apex offer was made. Calculate the minimum price Wild Orchid should accept for Stronglast under these conditions. (Ignore the previous $40 selling price.)

11-35 Make or buy, unknown level of volume. (A. Atkinson, adapted) Denver Engineering manufactures small engines that it sells to manufacturers who install them in products such as lawn mowers. The company currently manufactures all the parts used in these engines but is considering a proposal from an external supplier who wishes to supply the starter assemblies used in these engines.

The starter assemblies are currently manufactured in Division 3 of Denver Engineering. The costs relating to the starter assemblies for the past 12 months were as follows:

Direct materials	$ 400,000
Direct manufacturing labor	300,000
Manufacturing overhead	800,000
Total	$1,500,000

Over the past year, Division 3 manufactured 150,000 starter assemblies. The average cost for each starter assembly is $10($1,500,000 ÷ 150,000).

Further analysis of manufacturing overhead revealed the following information. Of the total manufacturing overhead, only 25% is considered variable. Of the fixed portion, $300,000 is an allocation of general overhead that will remain unchanged for the company as a whole if production of the starter assemblies is discontinued. A further $200,000 of the fixed overhead is avoidable if production of the starter assemblies is discontinued. The balance of the current fixed overhead, $100,000, is the division manager's salary. If Denver Engineering discontinues production of the starter assemblies, the manager of Division 3 will be transferred to Division 2 at the same salary. This move will allow the company to save the $80,000 salary that would otherwise be paid to attract an outsider to this position.

Required

1. Tutwiler Electronics, a reliable supplier, has offered to supply starter-assembly units at $8 per unit. Because this price is less than the current average cost of $10 per unit, the vice president of manufacturing is eager to accept this offer. On the basis of financial considerations alone, should Denver Engineering accept the outside offer? Show your calculations. (*Hint:* Production output in the coming year may be different from production output in the past year.)
2. How, if at all, would your response to requirement 1 change if the company could use the vacated plant space for storage and, in so doing, avoid $100,000 of outside storage charges currently incurred? Why is this information relevant or irrelevant?

11-36 Make versus buy, activity-based costing, opportunity costs. The Lexington Company produces gas grills. This year's expected production is 20,000 units. Currently, Lexington makes the side burners for its grills. Each grill includes two side burners. Lexington's management accountant reports the following costs for making the 40,000 burners:

	Cost per Unit	Costs for 40,000 Units
Direct materials	$8.00	$320,000
Direct manufacturing labor	4.00	160,000
Variable manufacturing overhead	2.00	80,000
Inspection, setup, materials handling		8,000
Machine rent		12,000
Allocated fixed costs of plant administration, taxes, and insurance		80,000
Total costs		$660,000

Lexington has received an offer from an outside vendor to supply any number of burners Lexington requires at $14.80 per burner. The following additional information is available:

a. Inspection, setup, and materials-handling costs vary with the number of batches in which the burners are produced. Lexington produces burners in batch sizes of 1,000 units. Lexington will produce the 40,000 units in 40 batches.
b. Lexington rents the machine it uses to make the burners. If Lexington buys all of its burners from the outside vendor, it does not need to pay rent on this machine.

Required

1. Assume that if Lexington purchases the burners from the outside vendor, the facility where the burners are currently made will remain idle. On the basis of financial considerations alone, should Lexington accept the outside vendor's offer at the anticipated volume of 40,000 burners? Show your calculations.
2. For this question, assume that if the burners are purchased outside, the facilities where the burners are currently made will be used to upgrade the grills by adding a rotisserie attachment. (*Note:* Each grill contains two burners and one rotisserie attachment.) As a consequence, the selling price of grills will be raised by $48. The variable cost per unit of the upgrade would be $38, and additional tooling costs of $160,000 per year would be incurred. On the basis of financial considerations alone, should Lexington make or buy the burners, assuming that 20,000 grills are produced (and sold)? Show your calculations.
3. The sales manager at Lexington is concerned that the estimate of 20,000 grills may be high and believes that only 16,000 grills will be sold. Production will be cut back, freeing up work space. This space can be used to add the rotisserie attachments whether Lexington buys the burners or makes them in-house. At this lower output, Lexington will produce the burners in 32 batches of 1,000 units each. On the basis of financial considerations alone, should Lexington purchase the burners from the outside vendor? Show your calculations.

11-37 Product mix, constrained resource. Wechsler Company produces three products: A110, B382, and C657. All three products use the same direct material, Voxx. Unit data for the three products are:

	Product		
	A110	B382	C657
Selling price	$168	$112	140
Variable costs			
Direct materials	48	30	18
Labor and other costs	56	54	80
Quantity of Voxx per unit	8 lb.	5 lb.	3 lb.

The demand for the products far exceeds the direct materials available to produce the products. Voxx costs $6 per pound, and a maximum of 5,000 pounds is available each month. Wechsler must produce a minimum of 200 units of each product.

Required

1. How many units of product A110, B382, and C657 should Wechsler produce?
2. What is the maximum amount Wechsler would be willing to pay for another 1,200 pounds of Voxx?

11-38 Product mix, special order. (N. Melumad, adapted) Gormley Precision Tools makes cutting tools for metalworking operations. It makes two types of tools: A6, a regular cutting tool, and EX4, a high-precision cutting tool. A6 is manufactured on a regular machine, but EX4 must be manufactured on both the regular machine and a high-precision machine. The following information is available:

	A6	EX4
Selling price	$ 200	$ 300
Variable manufacturing cost per unit	$ 120	$ 200
Variable marketing cost per unit	$ 30	$ 70
Budgeted total fixed overhead costs	$700,000	$1,100,000
Hours required to produce one unit on the regular machine	1.0	0.5

Additional information includes the following:

a. Gormley faces a capacity constraint on the regular machine of 50,000 hours per year.
b. The capacity of the high-precision machine is not a constraint.
c. Of the $1,100,000 budgeted fixed overhead costs of EX4, $600,000 are lease payments for the high-precision machine. This cost is charged entirely to EX4 because Gormley uses the machine exclusively to produce EX4. The company can cancel the lease agreement for the high-precision machine at any time without penalties.
d. All other overhead costs are fixed and cannot be changed.

Required

1. What product mix—that is, how many units of A6 and EX4—will maximize Gormley's operating income? Show your calculations.
2. Suppose Gormley can increase the annual capacity of its regular machines by 15,000 machine-hours at a cost of $300,000. Should Gormley increase the capacity of the regular machines by 15,000 machine-hours? By how much will Gormley's operating income increase or decrease? Show your calculations.
3. Suppose that the capacity of the regular machines has been increased to 65,000 hours. Gormley has been approached by Clark Corporation to supply 20,000 units of another cutting tool, V2, for $240 per unit. Gormley must either accept the order for all 20,000 units or reject it totally. V2 is exactly like A6 except that its variable manufacturing cost is $140 per unit. (It takes 1 hour to produce one unit of V2 on the regular machine, and variable marketing cost equals $30 per unit.) What product mix should Gormley choose to maximize operating income? Show your calculations.

11-39 Theory of constraints, throughput margin, and relevant costs. Nebraska Industries manufactures electronic testing equipment. Nebraska also installs the equipment at customers' sites and ensures that it functions smoothly. Additional information on the manufacturing and installation departments is as follows (capacities are expressed in terms of the number of units of electronic testing equipment):

	Equipment Manufactured	Equipment Installed
Annual capacity	310 units per year	275 units per year
Equipment manufactured and installed	275 units per year	275 units per year

Nebraska manufactures only 275 units per year because the installation department has only enough capacity to install 275 units. The equipment sells for $45,000 per unit (installed) and has direct material costs of $20,000. All costs other than direct material costs are fixed. The following requirements refer only to the preceding data. There is no connection between the requirements.

Required

1. Nebraska's engineers have found a way to reduce equipment manufacturing time. The new method would cost an additional $50 per unit and would allow Nebraska to manufacture 20 additional units a year. Should Nebraska implement the new method? Show your calculations.
2. Nebraska's designers have proposed a change in direct materials that would increase direct material costs by $2,000 per unit. This change would enable Nebraska to install 310 units of equipment each year. If Nebraska makes the change, it will implement the new design on all equipment sold. Should Nebraska use the new design? Show your calculations.

3. A new installation technique has been developed that will enable Nebraska's engineers to install 7 additional units of equipment a year. The new method will increase installation costs by $55,000 each year. Should Nebraska implement the new technique? Show your calculations.
4. Nebraska is considering how to motivate workers to improve their productivity (output per hour). One proposal is to evaluate and compensate workers in the manufacturing and installation departments on the basis of their productivities. Do you think the new proposal is a good idea? Explain briefly.

11-40 Theory of constraints, contribution margin, sensitivity analysis. Talking Toys (TT) produces dolls in two processes: molding and assembly. TT is currently producing two models: Chatty Chelsey and Talking Tanya. Production in the molding department is limited by the amount of materials available. Production in the assembly department is limited by the amount of trained labor available. The only variable costs are materials in the molding department and labor in the assembly department. Following are the requirements and limitations by doll model and department:

	Molding Materials	Assembly Time	Selling Price
Chatty Chelsey	2 pounds per doll	15 minutes per doll	$39 per doll
Talking Tanya	3 pounds per doll	20 minutes per doll	$50 per doll
Materials/Labor Available	36,000 pounds	8,500 hours	
Cost	$8 per pound	$12 per hour	

The following requirements refer only to the preceding data. There is no connection between the requirements.

Required

1. If there were enough demand for either doll, which doll would TT produce? How many of these dolls would it make and sell?
2. If TT sells three Chatty Chelseys for each Talking Tanya, how many dolls of each type would it produce and sell? What would be the total contribution margin?
3. If TT sells three Chatty Chelseys for each Talking Tanya, how much would production and contribution margin increase if the molding department could buy 900 more pounds of materials for $8 per pound?
4. If TT sells three Chatty Chelseys for each Talking Tanya, how much would production and contribution margin increase if the assembly department could get 65 more labor hours at $12 per hour?

11-41 Closing down divisions. Ainsley Corporation has four operating divisions. The budgeted revenues and expenses for each division for 2014 follows:

	Division			
	A	B	C	D
Sales	$504,000	$ 948,000	$960,000	$1,240,000
Cost of goods sold	440,000	930,000	765,000	925,000
Selling, general, and administrative expenses	96,000	202,500	144,000	210,000
Operating income/loss	$ (32,000)	$(184,500)	$ 51,000	$ 105,000

Further analysis of costs reveals the following percentages of variable costs in each division:

Cost of goods sold	90%	80%	90%	85%
Selling, general, and administrative expenses	50%	50%	60%	60%

Closing down any division would result in savings of 40% of the fixed costs of that division.

Top management is very concerned about the unprofitable divisions (A and B) and is considering closing them for the year.

Required

1. Calculate the increase or decrease in operating income if Ainsley closes division A.
2. Calculate the increase or decrease in operating income if Ainsley closes division B.
3. What other factors should the top management of Ainsley consider before making a decision?

11-42 Dropping a product line, selling more tours. Mechum River Anglers, a division of Old Dominion Travel, offers two types of guided fly fishing tours, Basic and Deluxe. Operating income for each tour type in 2014 is as follows:

	Basic	Deluxe
Revenues (500 × \$900; 400 × \$1,650)	\$450,000	\$ 660,000
Operating costs		
Administrative salaries	120,000	100,000
Guide wages	130,000	380,000
Supplies	50,000	100,000
Depreciation of equipment	25,000	60,000
Vehicle fuel	30,000	24,000
Allocated corporate overhead	45,000	66,000
Total operating costs	400,000	730,000
Operating income (loss)	\$ 40,000	\$ (70,000)

The equipment has a zero disposal value. Guide wages, supplies, and vehicle fuel are variable costs with respect to the number of tours. Administrative salaries are fixed costs with respect to the number of tours. Brad Barrett, Mechum River Anglers' president, is concerned about the losses incurred on the deluxe tours. He is considering dropping the deluxe tour and offering only the basic tour.

Required

1. If the deluxe tours are discontinued, one administrative position could be eliminated, saving the company \$50,000. Assuming no change in the sales of basic tours, what effect would dropping the deluxe tour have on the company's operating income?
2. Refer back to the original data. If Mechum River Anglers drops the deluxe tours, Barrett estimates that sales of basic tours would increase by 50%. He believes that he could still eliminate the \$50,000 administrative position. Equipment currently used for the deluxe tours would be used by the additional basic tours. Should Barrett drop the deluxe tour? Explain.
3. What additional factors should Barrett consider before dropping the deluxe tours?

11-43 Optimal product mix. (CMA adapted) Della Simpson, Inc., sells two popular brands of cookies: Della's Delight and Bonny's Bourbon. Della's Delight goes through the Mixing and Baking departments, and Bonny's Bourbon, a filled cookie, goes through the Mixing, Filling, and Baking departments.

Michael Shirra, vice president for sales, believes that at the current price, Della Simpson can sell all of its daily production of Della's Delight and Bonny's Bourbon. Both cookies are made in batches of 3,000. In each department, the time required per batch and the total time available each day are as follows:

	A	B	C	D
1		Department Minutes		
2		Mixing	Filling	Baking
3	Della's Delight	30	0	10
4	Bonny's Bourbon	15	15	15
5	Total available per day	660	270	300

Revenue and cost data for each type of cookie are as follows:

	A	B	C
7		Della's	Bonny's
8		Delight	Bourbon
9	Revenue per batch	\$ 475	\$ 375
10	Variable cost per batch	175	125
11	Contribution margin per batch	\$ 300	\$ 250
12	Monthly fixed costs		
13	(allocated to each product)	\$18,650	\$22,350

Required

1. Using *D* to represent the batches of Della's Delight and *B* to represent the batches of Bonny's Bourbon made and sold each day, formulate Shirra's decision as an LP model.
2. Compute the optimal number of batches of each type of cookie that Della Simpson, Inc., should make and sell each day to maximize operating income.

11-44 Dropping a customer, activity-based costing, ethics. Jason Ackerman is the management accountant for Carey Restaurant Supply (CRS). Beth Donaldson, the CRS sales manager, and Jason are meeting to discuss the profitability of one of the customers, Martha Leone's Pizza. Jason hands Beth the following analysis of Martha Leone's activity during the last quarter, taken from Central's activity-based costing system:

Sales	$21,840
Cost of goods sold (all variable)	13,090
Order processing (25 orders processed at $280 per order)	7,000
Delivery (2,500 miles driven at $0.70 per mile)	1,750
Rush orders (3 rush orders at $154 per rush order)	462
Sales calls (3 sales calls at $140 per call)	420
Profits	$ (882)

Beth looks at the report and remarks, "I'm glad to see all my hard work is paying off with Martha Leone's. Sales have gone up 10% over the previous quarter!"

Jason replies, "Increased sales are great, but I'm worried about Martha Leone's margin, Beth. We were showing a profit with Martha Leone's at the lower sales level, but now we're showing a loss. Gross margin percentage this quarter was 40%, down five percentage points from the prior quarter. I'm afraid that corporate will push hard to drop them as a customer if things don't turn around."

"That's crazy," Beth responds. "A lot of that overhead for things like order processing, deliveries, and sales calls would just be allocated to other customers if we dropped Martha Leone's. This report makes it look like we're losing money on Martha Leone's when we're not. In any case, I am sure you can do something to make its profitability look closer to what we think it is. No one doubts that Martha Leone's is a very good customer."

Required

1. Assume that Beth is partly correct in her assessment of the report. Upon further investigation, it is determined that 10% of the order processing costs and 20% of the delivery costs would not be avoidable if CRS were to drop Martha Leone's. Would CRS benefit from dropping Martha Leone's? Show your calculations.
2. Beth's bonus is based on meeting sales targets. Based on the preceding information regarding gross margin percentage, what might Beth have done last quarter to meet her target and receive her bonus? How might CRS revise its bonus system to address this?
3. Should Jason rework the numbers? How should he respond to Beth's comments about making Martha Leone's look more profitable?

11-45 Equipment replacement decisions and performance evaluation. Sean Fitzpatrick manages the Peoria plant of Garcia Manufacturing. A representative of Darien Engineering approaches Fitzpatrick about replacing a large piece of manufacturing equipment that Garcia uses in its process with a more efficient model. While the representative made some compelling arguments in favor of replacing the 3-year-old equipment, Fitzpatrick is hesitant. Fitzpatrick is hoping to be promoted next year to manager of the larger Detroit plant, and he knows that the accrual-basis net operating income of the Peoria plant will be evaluated closely as part of the promotion decision. The following information is available concerning the equipment replacement decision:

- The historic cost of the old machine is $600,000. It has a current book value of $240,000, two remaining years of useful life, and a market value of $144,000. Annual depreciation expense is $120,000. It is expected to have a salvage value of $0 at the end of its useful life.
- The new equipment will cost $360,000. It will have a 2-year useful life and a $0 salvage value. Garcia uses straight-line depreciation on all equipment.
- The new equipment will reduce electricity costs by $70,000 per year and will reduce direct manufacturing labor costs by $60,000 per year.

For simplicity, ignore income taxes and the time value of money.

Required

1. Assume that Fitzpatrick's priority is to receive the promotion and he makes the equipment replacement decision based on next year's accrual-based net operating income. Which alternative would he choose? Show your calculations.
2. What are the relevant factors in the decision? Which alternative is in the best interest of the company over the next 2 years? Show your calculations.
3. At what cost would Fitzpatrick be willing to purchase the new equipment? Explain.

12 Strategy, Balanced Scorecard, and Strategic Profitability Analysis

Learning Objectives

1. Recognize which of two generic strategies a company is using
2. Understand what comprises reengineering
3. Understand the four perspectives of the balanced scorecard
4. Analyze changes in operating income to evaluate strategy
5. Identify unused capacity and how to manage it

Olive Garden wants to know.

So do Barnes and Noble, PepsiCo, and L.L. Bean. Even your local car dealer and transit authority are curious. They all want to know if they are meeting their goals. Many companies have successfully used the balanced scorecard approach to measure their progress. Volkswagen do Brasil is one of them.

The Balanced Scorecard at Volkswagen do Brasil

In 2009, Volkswagen do Brasil, the German automaker's Brazilian subsidiary, began to feel the impact of the global financial crisis. Sales were plummeting and newly produced vehicles were parked around Volkswagen's Brazilian plants waiting for consumers to begin spending again. As CEO Thomas Schmall temporarily cut back production and reduced spending, he turned to the company's balanced scorecard to guide his executive team as it managed through the crisis.

Volkswagen do Brasil had introduced the balanced scorecard in 2007 to reverse years of market share declines and financial losses. The initial turnaround was successful. New enthusiasm among the workforce, customers, suppliers, and dealers had led to strong sales increases and a return to profitability. The scorecard focused on satisfying consumer expectations, improving the company's image, growing market share, and achieving sustainable and positive financial results.

As the 2009 crisis unfolded, Schmall was cautious about whether it was time to restore funding or wait until sales recovered before increasing production and resuming spending. Further cutbacks in production schedules and investment would jeopardize plans for market share expansion and new product development. Guided by the balanced scorecard, Schmall continued Volkswagen do Brasil's investments in strategic projects and began to ramp up production. As emerging markets recovered in 2009, the demand for goods shipped from Brazil increased and Volkswagen do Brasil thrived. Following the crisis, Volkswagen do Brasil has become the

Source: Based on Kaplan, Robert S., and Ricardo Reisen de Pinho. 2011. "Volkswagen do Brasil: Driving Strategy with the Balanced Scorecard." HBS No. 9-111-049. Boston: Harvard Business School Publishing, 2011.

second-largest producer of Volkswagens in the world, surpassing Germany and trailing only China.

This chapter focuses on how management accounting information helps companies such as Infosys, Merck, Verizon, and Volkswagen implement and evaluate their strategies. Strategy drives the operations of a company and guides managers' short-run and long-run decisions. We describe the balanced scorecard approach to implementing strategy and methods to analyze operating income to evaluate the success of a strategy. We also show how management accounting information helps strategic initiatives, such as productivity improvement, reengineering, and downsizing.

What Is Strategy?

Learning Objective 1

Recognize which of two generic strategies a company is using

...product differentiation or cost leadership

Strategy specifies how an organization matches its own capabilities with the opportunities in the marketplace to accomplish its objectives. In other words, strategy describes how an organization can create value for its customers while differentiating itself from its competitors. For example, Walmart, the retail giant, creates value for its customers by locating stores in suburban and rural areas and by offering low prices, a wide range of product categories, and few choices within each product category. Consistent with this strategy, Walmart has developed the capability to keep costs down by aggressively negotiating low prices with its suppliers in exchange for high volumes and by maintaining a no-frills, cost-conscious environment with minimal sales staff.

In formulating its strategy, an organization must first thoroughly understand its industry. Industry analysis focuses on five forces: (1) competitors, (2) potential entrants into the market, (3) equivalent products, (4) bargaining power of customers, and (5) bargaining power of input suppliers.[1] The collective effect of these forces shapes an organization's profit potential. In general, profit potential decreases with greater competition, stronger potential entrants, products that are similar, and more demanding customers and suppliers. Below we illustrate these five forces for Chipset, Inc., a maker of linear integrated circuit devices (LICDs) used in modems and communication networks. Chipset produces a single specialized product, CX1, a standard, high-performance microchip that can be used in multiple applications. Chipset designed CX1 after extensive market research and input from its customer base.

1. **Competitors.** The CX1 model faces severe competition based on price, timely delivery, and quality. Companies in the industry have high fixed costs and persistent pressures to reduce selling prices and utilize capacity fully. Price reductions spur growth because it makes LICDs a cost-effective option in applications such as digital subscriber lines (DSLs).
2. **Potential entrants into the market.** The small profit margins and high capital costs discourage new entrants. Moreover, incumbent companies such as Chipset have experience lowering costs and building close relationships with customers and suppliers.

[1] Michael Porter, *Competitive Strategy* (New York: Free Press, 1998); Michael Porter, *Competitive Advantage* (New York: Free Press, 1998); and Michael Porter, "What Is Strategy?" *Harvard Business Review* (November–December 1996): 61–78.

3. **Equivalent products.** Chipset tailors CX1 to customer needs and lowers prices by continuously improving CX1's design and processes to reduce production costs. This reduces the risk of equivalent products or new technologies replacing CX1.
4. **Bargaining power of customers.** Customers, such as EarthLink and Verizon, negotiate aggressively with Chipset and its competitors to keep prices down because they buy large quantities of product.
5. **Bargaining power of input suppliers.** To produce CX1, Chipset requires high-quality materials (such as silicon wafers, pins for connectivity, and plastic or ceramic packaging) and skilled engineers, technicians, and manufacturing labor. The skill sets that suppliers and employees bring give them bargaining power to demand higher prices and wages.

In summary, strong competition and the bargaining powers of customers and suppliers put significant pressure on Chipset's selling prices. To respond to these challenges, Chipset must choose between two basic strategies: *differentiating its product* or *achieving cost leadership*.

Product differentiation is an organization's ability to offer products or services its customers perceive to be superior and unique relative to the products or services of its competitors. Apple Inc. has successfully differentiated its products in the consumer electronics industry, as have Johnson & Johnson in the pharmaceutical industry and Coca-Cola in the soft drink industry. These companies have achieved differentiation through innovative product R&D, careful development and promotion of their brands, and the rapid push of products to market. Managers use differentiation to increase brand loyalty and charge higher prices.

Cost leadership is an organization's ability to achieve lower costs relative to competitors through productivity and efficiency improvements, elimination of waste, and tight cost control. Cost leaders in their respective industries include Walmart (consumer retailing), Home Depot and Lowe's (building products), Texas Instruments (consumer electronics), and Emerson Electric (electric motors). These companies provide products and services that are similar to—not differentiated from—their competitors, but at a lower cost to the customer. Lower selling prices, rather than unique products or services, provide a competitive advantage for these cost leaders.

To evaluate the success of its strategy, a company must trace the sources of its profitability to product differentiation or cost leadership. For example, an analysis of Porsche's profitability shows that the increase in its profitability is due to successful implementation of its product-differentiation strategy. Product differentiation enabled Porsche to increase its profit margins and grow sales. Changes in Home Depot's profitability are due to successful implementation of its cost-leadership strategy through productivity and quality improvements.

What strategy should Chipset follow? In order to make this decision, Chipset managers develop the customer preference map shown in Exhibit 12-1. The *y*-axis describes various attributes of the product desired by customers. The *x*-axis describes how well Chipset and its competitor, Visilog, which follows a product-differentiation strategy, do along various attributes desired by customers from 1 (poor) to 5 (very good). The map highlights the trade-offs in any strategy. It shows the advantages CX1 enjoys in terms of price, scalability,[2] and customer service. Visilog's chips, however, are faster and more powerful and are customized for various applications such as different types of modems and communication networks.

CX1 is somewhat differentiated from competing products. Differentiating CX1 further would be costly, but Chipset may be able to charge a higher price. Conversely, reducing the cost of manufacturing CX1 would allow Chipset to lower prices, spur growth, and increase market share. The scalability of CX1 makes it an effective solution for meeting varying customer needs. Also, consistent with its strategy, Chipset has, over the years, recruited an engineering staff that is more skilled at making product and process

[2] The ability to achieve different performance levels by altering the number of CX1 units in a product.

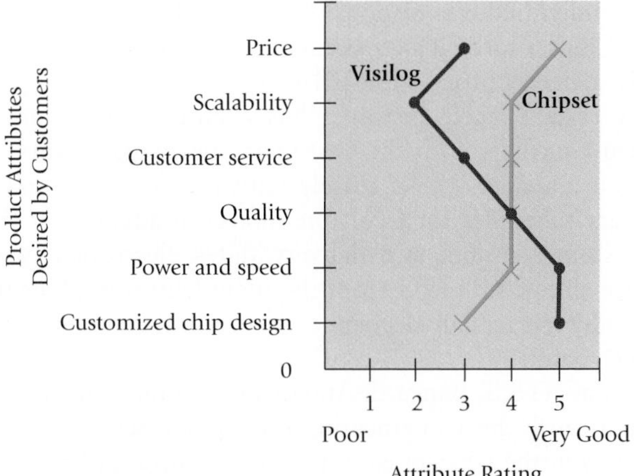

Exhibit 12-1

Customer Preference Map for LICDs

improvements than at creatively designing new products and technologies. The market benefit from lowering prices by improving manufacturing efficiency through process improvements leads Chipset to choose a cost-leadership strategy.

To achieve its cost-leadership strategy, Chipset must further improve its own internal capabilities. It must enhance quality and also reengineer processes to downsize and eliminate excess capacity. At the same time, Chipset's management team does not want to make cuts in personnel that would hurt company morale and hinder future growth. We explore these actions in the next section.

Decision Point

What are two generic strategies a company can use?

Building Internal Capabilities: Quality Improvement and Reengineering at Chipset

Learning Objective 2

Understand what comprises reengineering

...redesigning business processes to improve performance by reducing cost and improving quality

To improve product quality—that is, to reduce defect rates and improve manufacturing yields—Chipset must maintain process parameters within tight ranges based on real-time data about manufacturing-process parameters, such as temperature and pressure. Chipset must also train workers in quality-management techniques to identify the root causes of defects and to take actions to improve quality.

The second component of Chipset's strategy is to reengineer its order-delivery process. Some of Chipset's customers have complained about the lengthening time span between ordering products and receiving them. **Reengineering** is the fundamental rethinking and redesign of business processes to achieve improvements in critical measures of performance, such as cost, quality, service, speed, and customer satisfaction.[3] To illustrate reengineering, consider the order-delivery system at Chipset in 2012. When Chipset received an order from a customer, a copy was sent to manufacturing, where a production scheduler began planning the manufacturing of the ordered products. Frequently, a considerable amount of time elapsed before equipment became available for production to begin. After manufacturing was complete, CX1 chips moved to the shipping department, which matched the quantities of CX1 to be shipped against customer orders. Often, completed CX1 chips stayed in inventory until a truck became available for shipment. If the quantity to be shipped was less than the number of chips the customer requested, the shipping department made a special shipment for the balance of the chips. Shipping documents moved to the billing department for issuing invoices. Special staff in the accounting department followed up with customers for payments.

The many transfers of CX1 chips and information across departments (sales, manufacturing, shipping, billing, and accounting) to satisfy a customer's order created delays.

[3] See Michael Hammer and James Champy, *Reengineering the Corporation: A Manifesto for Business Revolution* (New York: Harper, 1993); Edwin Ruhli, Christoph Treichler, and Sascha L. Schmidt, "From Business Reengineering to Management Reengineering—A European Study," *Management International Review* (1995): 361–371; and Kirsten D. Sandberg, "Reengineering Tries a Comeback—This Time for Growth, Not Just for Cost Savings," *Harvard Management Update* (November 2001).

Moreover, no single individual was responsible for fulfilling a customer order. To respond to these challenges, Chipset formed a cross-functional team in late 2012 and implemented a reengineered order-delivery process for 2013.

Under the new system, each customer has a customer-relationship manager who negotiates long-term contracts with the customer, specifying quantities and prices. The customer-relationship manager works closely with the customer and with manufacturing to specify delivery schedules for CX1 one month in advance of shipment and sends the schedule of customer orders and delivery dates electronically to manufacturing. Completed chips are shipped directly from the manufacturing plant to customers. Each shipment automatically triggers an electronic invoice, and customers electronically transfer funds to Chipset's bank.

Companies such as AT&T, Banca di America e di Italia, Cigna Insurance, and Cisco have benefited significantly by reengineering their processes across design, production, and marketing (just as in the Chipset example). Reengineering has limited benefits when reengineering efforts focus on only a single activity such as shipping or invoicing rather than the entire order-delivery process. To be successful, reengineering efforts must focus on an entire process, change roles and responsibilities, eliminate unnecessary activities and tasks, use information technology, and develop employee skills.

Decision Point

What is reengineering?

Take another look at Exhibit 12-1 and note the interrelatedness and consistency in Chipset's strategy. To help meet customer preferences for price, quality, and customer service, Chipset decides on a cost-leadership strategy. And to achieve cost leadership, Chipset builds internal capabilities by improving quality and by reengineering its processes. Chipset's next challenge is to effectively implement its strategy.

Learning Objective 3

Understand the four perspectives of the balanced scorecard

...financial, customer, internal business process, and learning and growth

Strategy Implementation and the Balanced Scorecard

Many organizations, such as Allstate Insurance, Bank of Montreal, British Petroleum, and Dow Chemical, have introduced a *balanced scorecard* approach to track progress and manage the implementation of their strategies.

The Balanced Scorecard

The **balanced scorecard** translates an organization's mission and strategy into a set of performance measures that provides the framework for implementing its strategy.[4] Not only does the balanced scorecard focus on achieving financial objectives, it also highlights the nonfinancial objectives that an organization must achieve to meet and sustain its financial objectives. The scorecard measures an organization's performance from four perspectives:

1. Financial: the profits and value created for shareholders
2. Customer: the success of the company in its target market
3. Internal business processes: the internal operations that create value for customers
4. Learning and growth: the people and system capabilities that support operations

The measures that a company uses to track performance depend on its strategy. This set of measures is called a "balanced scorecard" because it balances the use of financial and

[4] See Robert S. Kaplan and David P. Norton, *The Balanced Scorecard* (Boston: Harvard Business School Press, 1996); Robert S. Kaplan and David P. Norton, *The Strategy-Focused Organization: How Balanced Scorecard Companies Thrive in the New Business Environment* (Boston: Harvard Business School Press, 2001); Robert S. Kaplan and David P. Norton, *Strategy Maps: Converting Intangible Assets into Tangible Outcomes* (Boston: Harvard Business School Press, 2004); and Robert S. Kaplan and David P. Norton, *Alignment: Using the Balanced Scorecard to Create Corporate Synergies* (Boston: Harvard Business School Press, 2006).

For simplicity, this chapter, and much of the literature, emphasizes long-run financial objectives as the primary goal of for-profit companies. For-profit companies interested in long-run financial, environmental, and social objectives adapt the balanced scorecard to implement all three objectives, as we discuss in a later section.

nonfinancial performance measures to evaluate short-run and long-run performance in a single report. The balanced scorecard reduces managers' emphasis on short-run financial performance, such as quarterly earnings, because the key strategic nonfinancial and operational indicators, such as product quality and customer satisfaction, measure changes that a company is making for the long run. The financial benefits of these long-run changes may not show up immediately in short-run earnings; however, strong improvement in nonfinancial measures usually indicates the creation of future economic value. For example, an increase in customer satisfaction, as measured by customer surveys and repeat purchases, signals a strong likelihood of higher sales and income in the future. By balancing the mix of financial and nonfinancial measures, the balanced scorecard broadens management's attention to short-run *and* long-run performance. In many for-profit companies, the primary goal of the balanced scorecard is to sustain long-run financial performance. Nonfinancial measures simply serve as leading indicators for the hard-to-measure long-run financial performance. Other companies explicitly set long-term financial, social, and environmental goals. As we discuss in a later section, these companies use the balanced scorecard to implement multiple goals.

Strategy Maps and the Balanced Scorecard

In this section, we use the Chipset example to develop strategy maps and the four perspectives of the balanced scorecard. The objectives and measures Chipset's managers choose for each perspective relate to the action plans for furthering Chipset's cost-leadership strategy: *improving quality* and *reengineering processes.*

Strategy Maps

A useful first step in designing a balanced scorecard is a *strategy map*. A **strategy map** is a diagram that describes how an organization creates value by connecting strategic objectives in explicit cause-and-effect relationships with each other in the financial, customer, internal-business-process, and learning-and-growth perspectives. Exhibit 12-2 presents Chipset's strategy map. Follow the arrows to see how a strategic objective affects other strategic objectives. For example, empowering the workforce helps align employee and organization goals and improves processes, which improves manufacturing quality and productivity, reduces customer delivery time, meets specified delivery dates, and improves post-sales service, all of which increase customer satisfaction. Improving manufacturing quality and productivity grows operating income directly and also increases customer satisfaction that, in turn, increases market share, operating income, and shareholder value.

To compete successfully, Chipset invests in its employees, implements new technology and process controls, improves quality, and reengineers processes. The strategy map helps Chipset evaluate whether these activities are generating financial returns.

Chipset could include many other cause-and-effect relationships in the strategy map in Exhibit 12-2. But Chipset, like other companies implementing the balanced scorecard, focuses on only those relationships that it believes to be the most significant so that the scorecard does not become unwieldy and difficult to understand.

Chipset uses the strategy map from Exhibit 12-2 to build the balanced scorecard presented in Exhibit 12-3. The scorecard highlights the four perspectives of performance: financial, customer, internal business process, and learning and growth. The first column presents the strategic objectives from the strategy map in Exhibit 12-2. At the beginning of 2013, the company's managers specify the strategic objectives, measures, initiatives (the actions necessary to achieve the objectives), and target performance (the first four columns of Exhibit 12-3).

Chipset wants to use the balanced scorecard targets to drive the organization to higher levels of performance. Managers therefore set targets at a level of performance that is achievable yet distinctly better than competitors. Chipset's managers complete the fifth column, reporting actual performance at the end of 2013. This column compares Chipset's performance relative to target.

Exhibit 12-2 Strategy Map for Chipset, Inc., for 2013

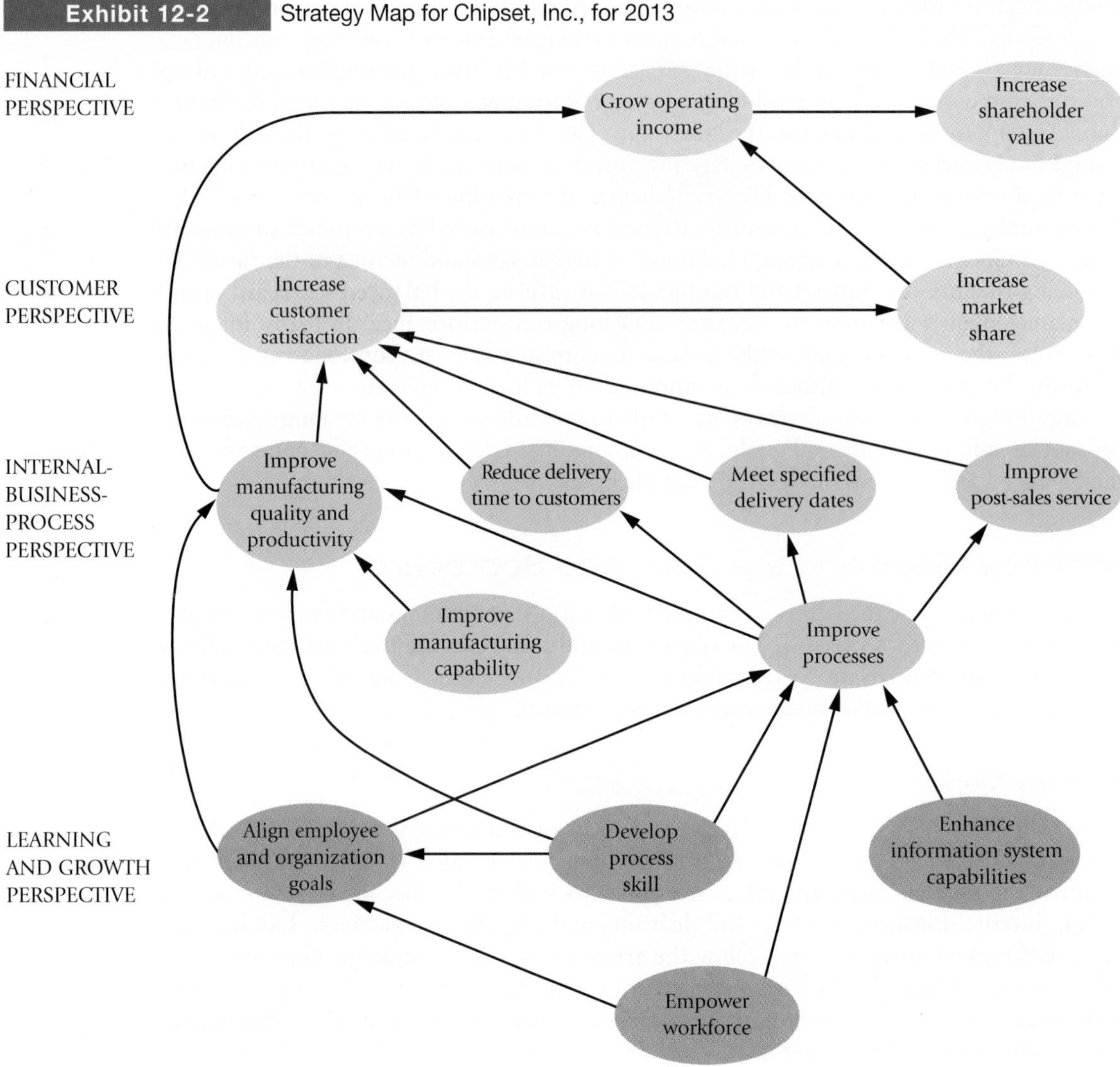

Four Perspectives of the Balanced Scorecard

We next describe the perspectives in general terms and illustrate each using the measures Chipset managers chose in the context of its strategy.

1. **Financial perspective.** This perspective evaluates the profitability of the strategy and the creation of shareholder value. Because Chipset's key strategic initiatives are cost reduction relative to competitors' costs and sales growth, the financial perspective focuses on revenue growth and how much operating income results from reducing costs and selling more units of CX1.
2. **Customer perspective.** This perspective identifies targeted customer and market segments and measures the company's success in these segments. To monitor its customer objectives, Chipset's managers use (a) market research, such as surveys and interviews, to determine market share in the communication-networks segment, and (b) information about the number of new customers and customer-satisfaction ratings from its customer management systems.
3. **Internal-business-process perspective.** This perspective focuses on internal operations that create value for customers that, in turn, help achieve financial performance. Managers at Chipset determine internal-business-process improvement targets after benchmarking against its main competitors. Benchmarking involves getting information about competitors from published financial statements, prevailing prices,

Exhibit 12-3 The Balanced Scorecard for Chipset, Inc., for 2013

Strategic Objectives	Measures	Initiatives	Target Performance	Actual Performance
Financial Perspective				
Grow operating income	Operating income from productivity gain	Manage costs and unused capacity	$1,850,000	$1,912,500
Increase shareholder value	Operating income from growth	Build strong customer relationships	$2,500,000	$2,820,000
	Revenue growth		9%	10%[a]
Customer Perspective				
Increase market share	Market share in communication-networks segment	Identify future needs of customers	6%	7%
Increase customer satisfaction	Number of new customers	Identify new target-customer segments	1	1[b]
	Customer-satisfaction ratings	Increase customer focus of sales organization	90% of customers give top two ratings	87% of customers give top two ratings
Internal-Business-Process Perspective				
Improve postsales service	Service response time	Improve customer-service process	Within 4 hours	Within 3 hours
Improve manufacturing quality and productivity	Yield	Identify root causes of problems and improve quality	78%	79.3%
Reduce delivery time to customers	Order-delivery time	Reengineer order-delivery process	30 days	30 days
Meet specified delivery dates	On-time delivery	Reengineer order-delivery process	92%	90%
Improve processes	Number of major improvements in manufacturing and business processes	Organize teams from manufacturing and sales to modify processes	5	5
Improve manufacturing capability	Percentage of processes with advanced controls	Organize R&D/manufacturing teams to implement advanced controls	75%	75%
Learning-and-Growth Perspective				
Align employee and organization goals	Employee-satisfaction ratings	Employee participation and suggestions program to build teamwork	80% of employees give top two ratings	88% of employees give top two ratings
Empower workforce	Percentage of line workers empowered to manage processes	Have supervisors act as coaches rather than decision makers	85%	90%
Develop process skill	Percentage of employees trained in process and quality management	Employee training programs	90%	92%
Enhance information-system capabilities	Percentage of manufacturing processes with real-time feedback	Improve online and offline data gathering	80%	80%

[a](Revenues in 2013 – Revenues in 2012) ÷ Revenues in 2012 = ($25,300,000 – $23,000,000) ÷ $23,000,000 = 10%.

[b]Number of customers increased from seven to eight in 2013.

customers, suppliers, former employees, industry experts, and financial analysts. The internal-business-process perspective is composed of three subprocesses:

- **Innovation process:** Creating products, services, and processes that will meet the needs of customers. This is a very important process for companies that follow a product-differentiation strategy and must constantly design and develop innovative new products to remain competitive in the marketplace. Chipset's innovation focuses on improving its manufacturing capability and process controls to lower costs and improve quality. Chipset measures innovation by the number of improvements in manufacturing processes and percentage of processes with advanced controls.
- **Operations process:** Producing and delivering existing products and services that will meet the needs of customers. Chipset's strategic initiatives are (a) improving manufacturing quality, (b) reducing delivery time to customers, and (c) meeting specified delivery dates, so it measures yield, order-delivery time, and on-time deliveries.
- **Postsales-service process:** Providing service and support to the customer after the sale of a product or service. Chipset monitors how quickly and accurately it is responding to customer-service requests.

4. **Learning-and-growth perspective.** This perspective identifies the people and information capabilities necessary for an organization to learn, improve, and grow. These capabilities help achieve superior internal processes that in turn create value for customers and shareholders. Chipset's learning-and-growth perspective emphasizes three capabilities:
   - Information-system capabilities, measured by the percentage of manufacturing processes with real-time feedback
   - Employee capabilities, measured by the percentage of employees trained in process and quality management
   - Motivation, measured by employee satisfaction and the percentage of manufacturing and sales employees (also called line employees) empowered to manage processes

The arrows in Exhibit 12-3 indicate the *broad* cause-and-effect linkages: how gains in the learning-and-growth perspective lead to improvements in internal business processes, which lead to higher customer satisfaction and market share, and finally lead to superior financial performance. Note how the scorecard describes elements of Chipset's strategy implementation. Worker training and empowerment improve employee satisfaction and lead to manufacturing and business-process improvements that improve quality and reduce delivery time, which, in turn, results in increased customer satisfaction and higher market share. Exhibit 12-3 indicates that Chipset's actions have been successful from a financial perspective. Chipset has earned significant operating income from executing its cost-leadership strategy, and that strategy has also led to growth.

To sustain long-run financial performance, a company must strengthen all links across its different balanced scorecard perspectives. For example, Southwest Airlines' high employee satisfaction levels and low employee turnover (learning-and-growth perspective) lead to greater efficiency and customer-friendly service (internal-business-process perspective) that enhances customer satisfaction (customer perspective) and boosts profits and return on investment (financial perspective).

A major benefit of the balanced scorecard is that it promotes causal thinking as described in the previous paragraph—where improvement in one activity causes an improvement in another. Think of the balanced scorecard as a *linked scorecard* or a *causal scorecard*. Managers must search for empirical evidence (rather than rely on intuition alone) to test the validity and strength of the various connections. A causal scorecard enables a company to focus on the key drivers that steer the implementation of the strategy. Without convincing links, the scorecard loses much of its value.

Implementing a Balanced Scorecard

To successfully implement a balanced scorecard, subordinate managers and executives require commitment and leadership from top management. At Chipset, the vice president of strategic planning headed the team building the balanced scorecard. The team conducted interviews with senior managers; asked executives about customers, competitors, and technological developments; and sought proposals for balanced scorecard objectives across the four perspectives. The team then met to discuss the responses and build a prioritized list of objectives.

In a meeting with all senior managers, the team sought to achieve consensus on the scorecard objectives. The vice president of strategic management then divided senior management into four groups, with each group responsible for one of the perspectives. In addition, each group broadened the base of inputs by including representatives from the next-lower levels of management and key functional managers. The groups identified measures for each objective and the sources of information for each measure. The groups then met to finalize scorecard objectives, measures, targets, and the initiatives to achieve the targets. Management accountants played an important role in the design and implementation of the balanced scorecard, particularly in determining measures to represent the realities of the business. This required management accountants to understand the economic environment of the industry, Chipset's customers and competitors, and internal business issues such as human resources, operations, and distribution.

Managers at Chipset made sure that employees understood the scorecard and the scorecard process. The final balanced scorecard was communicated to all employees. Sharing the scorecard allowed engineers and operating personnel, for example, to understand the reasons for customer satisfaction and dissatisfaction and to make suggestions for improving internal processes directly aimed at satisfying customers and implementing Chipset's strategy. Too often, only a select group of managers see scorecards. By limiting the scorecard's exposure, Chipset would lose the opportunity for widespread organization engagement and alignment. Companies such as Citibank, Exxon Mobil, and Novartis share their scorecards widely across their divisions and departments.

Chipset also encourages each department to develop its own scorecard that ties into Chipset's main scorecard described in Exhibit 12-3. For example, the quality control department's scorecard has measures that its department managers use to improve yield—number of quality circles, statistical process control charts, Pareto diagrams, and root-cause analyses (see Chapter 19, pages 739–742, for more details). Department scorecards help align the actions of each department to implement Chipset's strategy.

Companies frequently use balanced scorecards to evaluate and reward managerial performance and to influence managerial behavior. Using the balanced scorecard for performance evaluation widens the performance management lens and motivates managers to give greater attention to nonfinancial drivers of performance. Surveys indicate, however, that companies continue to assign more weight to the financial perspective (55%) than to the other perspectives—customer (19%), internal business process (12%), and learning and growth (14%). Companies cite several reasons for the relatively smaller weight on nonfinancial measures, including difficulty evaluating the relative importance of nonfinancial measures; challenges in measuring and quantifying qualitative, nonfinancial data; and difficulty in compensating managers despite poor financial performance (see Chapter 23 for a more detailed discussion of performance evaluation). More and more companies in the manufacturing, merchandising, and service sectors are giving greater weight to nonfinancial measures when promoting employees because they believe that nonfinancial measures—such as customer satisfaction, process improvements, and employee motivation—better assess a manager's potential to succeed at senior levels of management. As this trend continues, operating managers will put more weight on nonfinancial factors when making decisions even though these factors carry smaller weights when determining their annual compensation. For the balanced scorecard to be effective, however, managers must view it as a fair way to assess and reward all important aspects of a manager's performance and promotion prospects.

Different Strategies Lead to Different Scorecards

Recall that while Chipset follows a cost-leadership strategy, its competitor, Visilog, follows a product-differentiation strategy by designing custom chips for modems and communication networks. Visilog designs its balanced scorecard to fit its strategy. For

Exhibit 12-4 Frequently Cited Balanced Scorecard Measures

Financial Perspective
Income measures: Operating income, gross margin percentage
Revenue and cost measures: Revenue growth, revenues from new products, cost reductions in key areas
Income and investment measures: Economic value added[a] (EVA®), return on investment
Customer Perspective
Market share, customer satisfaction, customer-retention percentage, time taken to fulfill customers' requests, number of customer complaints
Internal-Business-Process Perspective
Innovation Process: Operating capabilities, number of new products or services, new-product development times, and number of new patents
Operations Process: Yield, defect rates, time taken to deliver product to customers, percentage of on-time deliveries, average time taken to respond to orders, setup time, manufacturing downtime
Postsales Service Process: Time taken to replace or repair defective products, hours of customer training for using the product
Learning-and-Growth Perspective
Employee measures: Employee education and skill levels, employee-satisfaction ratings, employee turnover rates, percentage of employee suggestions implemented, percentage of compensation based on individual and team incentives
Technology measures: Information system availability, percentage of processes with advanced controls

[a]This measure is described in Chapter 23.

example, in the financial perspective, Visilog evaluates how much of its operating income comes from charging premium prices for its products. In the customer perspective, Visilog measures the percentage of its revenues from new products and new customers. In the internal-business-process perspective, Visilog measures the number of new products introduced and new product development time. In the learning-and-growth perspective, Visilog measures the development of advanced manufacturing capabilities to produce custom chips. Visilog also uses some of the measures described in Chipset's balanced scorecard in Exhibit 12-3. For example, revenue growth, customer satisfaction ratings, order-delivery time, on-time delivery, percentage of frontline workers empowered to manage processes, and employee-satisfaction ratings are also important measures under the product-differentiation strategy. The goal is to align the balanced scorecard with company strategy.[5] Exhibit 12-4 presents some common measures found on company scorecards in the service, retail, and manufacturing sectors.

Environmental and Social Performance and the Balanced Scorecard

Companies are increasingly recognizing that they must continually earn the right to operate in the communities and countries in which they do business. Failure to perform adequately on environmental and social processes puts at risk a company's ability to deliver future value to shareholders. Citizens and governments are becoming much more active in pushing companies to live up to and to report on what they see as their environmental and social obligations. For example in 2010, the Securities and Exchange Commission (SEC) issued a statement intended to remind companies of their obligations under existing federal securities laws and regulations "to consider climate change and its consequences as they prepare disclosure documents to be filed with us and provided to investors."

[5] For simplicity, we have presented the balanced scorecard in the context of companies that have followed either a cost-leadership or a product-differentiation strategy. Of course, a company may have some products for which cost leadership is critical and other products for which product differentiation is important. The company will then develop separate scorecards to implement the different product strategies. In still other contexts, product differentiation may be of primary importance, but some cost leadership must also be achieved. The balanced scorecard measures would then be linked in a cause-and-effect way to this strategy.

As we discussed in Chapter 1, many managers are promoting sustainability—the development and implementation of strategies to achieve:

- Long-term financial performance
- Social performance, such as minimizing employee injuries, improving product safety, and eliminating corruption
- Environmental performance, such as reducing greenhouse gas emissions and non-recycled waste

The Brundtland Commission[6] defined a sustainable society as one where "the current generation meets its needs without jeopardizing the ability of future generations to meet their needs."

There are a wide variety of opinions on this issue. Some believe that managers should only focus on long-run financial performance and not be distracted by pursuing social and environmental goals beyond the minimum levels required by law. Others believe that managers must act to attain environmental and social objectives beyond what is legally required, while achieving good financial performance—often called the *triple bottom line*—as part of a company's social responsibility. Still others believe that there is no conflict between achieving social and environmental goals and long-run financial performance.

Many managers recognize that good environmental and social performance helps to attract and inspire outstanding employees, improves employee safety and health, increases productivity, and lowers operating costs. Environmental and social performance also enhances a company's reputation with socially conscious customers and investors and boosts its image with governments and citizens, all contributing to long-run financial performance. Experienced financial analysts are publishing favorable reports about companies with strong environmental and social performance because of their greater transparency and engagement with multiple stakeholders. A distinguishing organizational characteristic of companies that emphasize environmental and social performance is their long-term orientation. Some recent research suggests that taking the long-term view and engaging with multiple stakeholders results in superior financial performance. Companies, such as Natura, China Light & Power, and Dow Chemical, that focus on the triple bottom line of financial, environmental, and social performance benefit from innovating in technologies, processes, products, and business models to reduce the trade-offs between financial and sustainability goals. These companies also build transformational and transitional leadership and change capabilities needed to implement the strategies to achieve the triple bottom line.

Managers interested in measuring environmental and social performance are incorporating these factors into their balanced scorecards to set priorities for initiatives, guide decisions and actions, and fuel discussions around strategies and business models to improve performance. Suppose Chipset decides to emphasize environmental and social goals in its balanced scorecard. What measures might it add to the balanced scorecard presented in Exhibit 12-3? Chipset, like all companies that emphasize environmental and social goals, integrates its sustainability goals and measures presented in Exhibit 12-5 with the business goals and measures presented in Exhibit 12-3 into a single scorecard. Chipset gains the following benefits from measuring environmental and social performance.

1. **Creating shared value.** A major benefit of measuring environmental and social performance is the opportunity it provides to create shared value[7]—recognizing that the competitiveness of Chipset and its social activities are mutually dependent. In this view, achieving environmental and social objectives is seen as providing strategic

[6] The Brundtland Commission was set up by the United Nations as the World Commission on Environment and Development. It issued its report, *Our Common Future*, in 1987.

[7] Porter, M., and M. Kramer. 2011. Creating shared value: Redefining capitalism and the role of the corporation in society. *Harvard Business Review*, January/February, Volume 89, Issue 1/2, pp. 62–77.

Exhibit 12-5 Environmental and Social Balanced Scorecard Measures for Chipset, Inc., for 2013

Strategic Objectives	Measures	Initiatives	Target Performance	Actual Performance
Financial Perspective				
Reduce waste	Cost savings from reducing energy use and waste	Quality improvement programs	$400,000	$415,000
Reduce cost of time lost from work injuries and illness	Cost savings from fewer work injuries and illness	Train workers in safety methods and hygiene	$50,000	$55,000
Customer Perspective				
Enhance reputation for sustainability with customers	Percentage of customers giving top two ratings for environmental and social performance	Communicate environmental and social goals and performance	90%	92%
Internal-Business-Process Perspective				
Reduce greenhouse gas emissions	Greenhouse gas emissions per million dollars of sales	Increase energy efficiency and reduce carbon footprint by planting trees	27 grams/$1 million of sales	25.6 grams/$1 million of sales
Reduce operational waste not recycled	Hazardous and non-hazardous waste not recycled per million dollars of sales	Increase recycling programs and redesign products	130 grams/$1 million of sales	126 grams/$1 million of sales
Reduce work-related injuries and illnesses	Days of lost time per worker per year due to injury or illness	Redesign processes to improve worker safety and hygiene	0.20 days per worker per year	0.18 days per worker per year
Learning-and-Growth Perspective				
Inspiring employees through environmental and social goals	Percentage of employees giving top two ratings for environmental and social performance	Training employees about environmental and social benefits	87%	90%
Diversity of employees	Percentage of women and minorities in managerial positions	Develop human resource practices to support mentoring and coaching for women and minorities	40%	42%

advantage to the business. For example, reducing greenhouse gas emissions motivates Chipset to redesign its product and processes to reduce energy consumption. Measuring non-recycled hazardous and nonhazardous waste prompts Chipset to work with its suppliers to redesign and reduce packaging and toxic substances in its materials and components. Measuring worker-related injuries and illnesses motivates Chipset to redesign processes to lessen the number of such incidents. In each of these initiatives, Chipset achieves environmental and social goals as well as gains competitive advantage by pushing itself to innovate and building a social and environmental value proposition into its business strategy.

2. **Identifying cause-and-effect relationships to evaluate benefits.** Together with developing the kinds of skills in processes and information systems described in Exhibit 12-3, Chipset's top management creates a culture that encourages hiring employees from a wide variety of backgrounds, particularly women and minorities. This furthers the company's social goals but also gives it access to top talent from a broad cross-section of society. The company trains and mentors employees to create shared value. This training improves internal business processes to decrease greenhouse gases, hazardous and nonhazardous waste, and work-related injuries. These actions, in turn, improve customer measures such as Chipset's reputation for sustainability with customers and customer satisfaction. The financial benefits are the cost savings from shared value such as lower energy consumption and waste. If Chipset can measure growth in revenue or operating income from customers attracted to Chipset's environmental and social actions with reasonable accuracy, the company might add that measure in its financial perspective. The scorecard shows that Chipset has achieved all its environmental and social goals, indicating that its environmental and social actions are translating into financial gains. These results would encourage Chipset to continue its environmental and social efforts.
3. **Reducing risks.** A final benefit of measuring environmental and social performance is to help manage downside risk by acting as a good corporate citizen. This involves being responsive to different stakeholders and reducing any adverse environmental or social effects of business activities. For example, reducing greenhouse gases might ward off fines or more stringent carbon emission caps from the U.S. environmental protection agency. Increase in greenhouse gases or waste might result in fines and lawsuits and lead to negative media attention and stakeholder activism that damages a company's reputation.

Companies use a variety of measures for environmental and social performance in addition to the ones described in the Chipset example:

1. **Financial perspective.** Cost of preventing and remediating environmental damage (training, cleanup, legal costs, and costs of consumer boycotts); cost of recycled materials to total cost of materials
2. **Customer perspective.** Brand image (percentage of survey respondents who rate the company high on trust)
3. **Internal-business perspective.** Energy consumption (joules per $1,000 of sales), water use (millions of cubic meters); waste water discharge (thousands of cubic meters); individual quantities of different greenhouse gases, for example, carbon dioxide, nitrous oxide, sulphur dioxide (grams per $1 million in sales); number of environmental incidents (such as unexpected discharge of air, water, or solid waste); codes of conduct violations (percentage of total employees); contributions to community-based nonprofit organizations; number of joint ventures and partnerships between the company and community organizations
4. **Learning-and-growth perspective.** Implementation of ISO 14000 environmental management standards (subjective score); employees trained and certified in codes of conduct (percentage of total employees); employees trained in United Nations global compact, for example, human rights, fair wage, no child labor, corruption and bribery prevention (percentage of total employees)

Features of a Good Balanced Scorecard

A well-designed balanced scorecard has several features:

1. **It tells the story of a company's strategy, articulating a sequence of cause-and-effect relationships—the links among the various perspectives that align implementation of the strategy.** In for-profit companies, each measure in the scorecard is part of a cause-and-effect chain leading to financial outcomes. Not-for-profit organizations, such as the World Bank and Teach for America, design the cause-and-effect chain to achieve

their strategic service objectives—for example, reducing the number of people in poverty or raising high school graduation rates.

2. **The balanced scorecard helps to communicate the strategy to all members of the organization by translating the strategy into a coherent and linked set of understandable and measurable operational targets.** Guided by the scorecard, managers and employees take actions and make decisions to achieve the company's strategy. Companies that have distinct strategic business units (SBUs)—such as consumer products and pharmaceuticals at Johnson & Johnson—develop their balanced scorecards at the SBU level. Each SBU has its own unique strategy and implementation goals, so building separate scorecards allows managers of each SBU to choose measures that help implement its distinctive strategy.
3. **In for-profit companies, the balanced scorecard must motivate managers to take actions that eventually result in improvements in financial performance.** Managers sometimes tend to focus too much on quality and customer satisfaction as ends in themselves. For example, Xerox discovered that higher customer satisfaction, through service guarantees, did not increase customer loyalty and financial returns because customers also wanted product innovations, such as high-speed color printing, that met their needs. Some companies use statistical methods, such as regression analysis, to test the anticipated cause-and-effect relationships among nonfinancial measures and financial performance. The data for this analysis can come from either time-series data (collected over time) or cross-sectional data (collected, for example, across multiple stores of a retail chain). In the Chipset example, improvements in nonfinancial factors have, in fact, already led to improvements in financial factors.
4. **The balanced scorecard limits the number of measures, identifying only the most critical ones.** Chipset's scorecard, for example, has 16 measures, between three and six measures for each perspective. Limiting the number of measures focuses managers' attention on those that most affect strategy implementation. Using too many measures makes it difficult for managers to process relevant information.
5. **The balanced scorecard highlights less-than-optimal trade-offs that managers may make when they fail to consider operational and financial measures together.** For example, a company with a strategy of innovation and product differentiation spends a lot of money on R&D. That company could achieve superior short-run financial performance by reducing spending on R&D. A good balanced scorecard would signal that the short-run financial performance might have been achieved by taking actions that hurt future financial performance because a leading indicator of that performance, R&D spending and R&D output, has declined.

Pitfalls in Implementing a Balanced Scorecard

Pitfalls to avoid in implementing a balanced scorecard include the following:

1. **Managers should not assume the cause-and-effect linkages are precise.** These linkages are merely hypotheses. Over time, a company must gather evidence of the strength and timing of the linkages among the nonfinancial and financial measures. With experience, organizations should alter their scorecards to include those nonfinancial strategic objectives and measures that are the best leading indicators (the causes) of financial performance (a lagging indicator or the effect). Understanding that the scorecard evolves over time helps managers avoid wasting time and money trying to design the "perfect" scorecard at the outset. Moreover, as the business environment and strategy change over time, the measures in the scorecard also need to change. For example, when Sandoz, a manufacturer of generic pharmaceutical chemicals, shifted its strategy to produce biologic medicines that required significant investment in new technologies and patient trials, its balanced scorecard also changed from only emphasizing productivity and cost efficiency to also measuring innovation.

2. **Managers should not seek improvements across all of the measures all of the time.** For example, strive for quality and on-time performance but not beyond the point at which further improvement in these objectives is so costly that it is inconsistent with long-run profit maximization. Cost–benefit considerations should always be central when designing a balanced scorecard.
3. **Managers should not use only objective measures in the balanced scorecard.** Chipset's balanced scorecard includes both objective measures (such as operating income from cost leadership, market share, and manufacturing yield) and subjective measures (such as customer- and employee-satisfaction ratings). When using subjective measures, however, managers must be careful that the benefits of this potentially rich information are not lost by using measures that are inaccurate or that can be easily manipulated.
4. **Despite challenges of measurement, top management should not ignore nonfinancial measures when evaluating managers and other employees.** Managers tend to focus on the measures used to reward their performance. Excluding nonfinancial measures (such as customer satisfaction or product quality) when evaluating the performance of managers will reduce their significance and importance to managers.

Decision Point

How can an organization translate its strategy into a set of performance measures?

Evaluating the Success of Strategy and Implementation

To evaluate how successful Chipset's strategy and its implementation have been, its management compares the target- and actual-performance columns in the balanced scorecard (Exhibit 12-3). Chipset met most targets set on the basis of competitor benchmarks in 2013 itself because improvements in Chipset's learning-and-growth perspective quickly rippled through to the financial perspective. While Chipset will continue to make improvements to achieve the targets it did not meet, managers were satisfied that the strategic initiatives that Chipset identified and measured for learning and growth resulted in improvements in internal business processes, customer measures, and financial performance.

How would Chipset know if it had problems in strategy implementation? If it did not meet its targets on the two perspectives that are more internally focused: learning and growth and internal business processes.

What if Chipset performed well on learning and growth and internal business processes, but customer measures and financial performance in this year and the next still did not improve? Chipset's managers would then conclude that Chipset did a good job of implementation, as the various internal nonfinancial measures it targeted improved, but that its strategy was faulty because there was no effect on customers or on long-run financial performance and value creation. In this case, management had failed to identify the correct causal links and did a good job implementing the wrong strategy! Management would then reevaluate the strategy and the factors that drive it.

Strategic Analysis of Operating Income

Learning Objective 4

Analyze changes in operating income to evaluate strategy

...growth, price recovery, and productivity

As we have discussed, Chipset performed well on its various nonfinancial measures, and operating income over this year and the next also increased. Chipset's managers might be tempted to declare the cost-leadership strategy a success, but, in fact, they cannot conclude with any confidence that Chipset successfully formulated and implemented its intended strategy. Operating income could have increased simply because prices of inputs decreased or the entire market expanded. Alternatively, a company that has chosen a cost-leadership strategy, like Chipset, may find that its operating-income increase actually resulted from some degree of product differentiation. *To evaluate the success of a strategy, managers and management accountants need to link strategy to the sources of operating-income increases.* These are the kinds of details that top management and boards of directors routinely discuss in their meetings when evaluating performance. Managers who have mastered the strategic analysis of operating income changes gain an understanding of the levers of strategy and strategy implementation that help them deliver sustained operating performance.

For Chipset managers to conclude that they were successful in implementing their strategy, they must demonstrate that improvements in the company's financial performance and operating income over time resulted from achieving targeted cost savings and growth in market share. Fortunately, the top two rows of Chipset's balanced scorecard in Exhibit 12-3 show that operating-income gains from productivity ($1,912,500) and growth ($2,820,000) exceeded targets. (The next section of this chapter describes how these numbers were calculated.) Because its strategy has been successful, Chipset's management can be more confident that the gains will be sustained in subsequent years.

Chipset's management accountants subdivide changes in operating income into components that can be identified with product differentiation, cost leadership, and growth. Managers look to growth because successful product differentiation or cost leadership generally increases market share and helps a company to grow. Subdividing the change in operating income to evaluate the success of a strategy is conceptually similar to the variance analysis discussed in Chapters 7 and 8. One difference, however, is that management accountants compare actual operating performance over *two different periods,* not actual to budgeted numbers in the *same time period* as in variance analysis.[8] A second difference is that the analysis in this section breaks down changes in operating income rather than focusing on differences in individual categories of costs (direct materials, direct manufacturing labor, and overheads) as we did in Chapters 7 and 8.

We next explain how the change in operating income from one period to *any* future period can be subdivided into product differentiation, cost leadership, and growth components.[9] We illustrate the analysis using data from 2012 and 2013 because Chipset implemented key elements of its strategy in late 2012 and early 2013 and expects the financial consequences of these strategies to occur in 2013. Suppose the financial consequences of these strategies had been expected to affect operating income in only 2014. Then we could just as easily have compared 2012 to 2014. If necessary, we could also have compared 2012 to 2013 and 2014 taken together.

Chipset's data for 2012 and 2013 follow:

	2012	2013
1. Units of CX1 produced and sold	1,000,000	1,150,000
2. Selling price	$23	$22
3. Direct materials (square centimeters of silicon wafers)	3,000,000	2,900,000
4. Direct material cost per square centimeter	$1.40	$1.50
5. Manufacturing processing capacity (in square centimeters of silicon wafer)	3,750,000	3,500,000
6. Conversion costs (all manufacturing costs other than direct material costs)	$16,050,000	$15,225,000
7. Conversion cost per unit of capacity (row 6 ÷ row 5)	$4.28	$4.35

Chipset managers obtain the following additional information:

1. Conversion costs (labor and overhead costs) for each year depend on production processing capacity defined in terms of the quantity of square centimeters of silicon wafers that Chipset can process. These costs do not vary with the actual quantity of silicon wafers processed.
2. Chipset incurs no R&D costs. Its marketing, sales, and customer-service costs are small relative to the other costs. Chipset has 8 customers, each purchasing

[8] Other examples of focusing on actual performance over two periods rather than comparisons of actuals with budgets can be found in J. Hope and R. Fraser, *Beyond Budgeting* (Boston, MA: Harvard Business School Press, 2003).

[9] For other details, see Rajiv D. Banker, Srikant M. Datar, and Robert S. Kaplan, "Productivity Measurement and Management Accounting," *Journal of Accounting, Auditing and Finance* (1989): 528–554; and Anthony J. Hayzens, and James M. Reeve, "Examining the Relationships in Productivity Accounting," *Management Accounting Quarterly* (2000): 32–39.

roughly the same quantities of CX1. Because of the highly technical nature of the product, Chipset uses a cross-functional team for its marketing, sales, and customer-service activities. This cross-functional approach ensures that, although marketing, sales, and customer-service costs are small, the entire Chipset organization, including manufacturing engineers, remains focused on increasing customer satisfaction and market share. (The Problem for Self-Study at the end of this chapter describes a situation in which marketing, sales, and customer-service costs are significant.)

3. Chipset's asset structure is very similar in 2012 and 2013.
4. Operating income for each year is as follows:

	2012	2013
Revenues		
($23 per unit × 1,000,000 units; $22 per unit × 1,150,000 units)	$23,000,000	$25,300,000
Costs		
Direct material costs		
($1.40/sq. cm. × 3,000,000 sq. cm.; $1.50/sq. cm. × 2,900,000 sq. cm.)	4,200,000	4,350,000
Conversion costs		
($4.28/sq. cm. × 3,750,000 sq. cm.; $4.35/sq. cm. × 3,500,000 sq. cm.)	16,050,000	15,225,000
Total costs	20,250,000	19,575,000
Operating income	$ 2,750,000	$ 5,725,000
Change in operating income	$2,975,000 F	

The goal of Chipset's managers is to evaluate how much of the $2,975,000 increase in operating income was caused by the successful implementation of the company's cost-leadership strategy. To do this evaluation, management accountants start by analyzing three main factors: (1) growth, (2) price recovery, and (3) productivity.

The **growth component** measures the change in operating income attributable solely to the change in the quantity of output sold between 2012 and 2013.The **price-recovery component** measures the change in operating income attributable solely to changes in Chipset's prices of inputs and outputs between 2012 and 2013. The price-recovery component measures change in output price compared with changes in input prices. A company that has successfully pursued a strategy of product differentiation will be able to increase its output price faster than the increase in its input prices, boosting profit margins and operating income: The company will show a large positive price-recovery component.

The **productivity component** measures the change in costs attributable to a change in the quantity of inputs used in 2013 relative to the quantity of inputs that would have been used in 2012 to produce the 2013 output. The productivity component measures the amount by which operating income increases by using inputs efficiently to lower costs. A company that has successfully pursued a strategy of cost leadership will be able to produce a given quantity of output with a lower cost of inputs and will show a large positive productivity component. Given Chipset's strategy of cost leadership, managers expect the increase in operating income to be attributable to the productivity and growth components, not to price recovery. We now examine these three components in detail.

Growth Component of Change in Operating Income

The growth component of the change in operating income measures the increase in revenues minus the increase in costs from selling more units of CX1 in 2013 (1,150,000 units) than in 2012 (1,000,000 units), *assuming nothing else has changed.*

Revenue Effect of Growth

$$\text{Revenue effect of growth} = \left(\begin{array}{c}\text{Actual units of}\\\text{output sold}\\\text{in 2013}\end{array} - \begin{array}{c}\text{Actual units of}\\\text{output sold}\\\text{in 2012}\end{array}\right) \times \begin{array}{c}\text{Selling}\\\text{price}\\\text{in 2012}\end{array}$$

$$= (1{,}150{,}000 \text{ units} - 1{,}000{,}000 \text{ units}) \times \$23 \text{ per unit}$$

$$= \$3{,}450{,}000\text{ F}$$

This growth component is favorable (F) because the increase in output sold in 2013 increases operating income. Components that decrease operating income are unfavorable (U).

Note that Chipset uses the 2012 price of CX1 and focuses only on the increase in units sold between 2012 and 2013 because the revenue effect of the growth component measures how much revenues would have changed in 2012 if Chipset had sold 1,150,000 units instead of 1,000,000 units.

Cost Effect of Growth

The cost effect of growth measures how much costs would have changed in 2012 if Chipset had produced 1,150,000 units of CX1 instead of 1,000,000 units. To measure the cost effect of growth, Chipset's managers distinguish variable costs such as direct material costs from fixed costs such as conversion costs because as units produced (and sold) increase, variable costs increase proportionately but fixed costs, generally, do not change.

$$\begin{array}{c}\text{Cost effect of}\\\text{growth for}\\\text{variable costs}\end{array} = \left(\begin{array}{c}\text{Units of input}\\\text{required to}\\\text{produce 2013}\\\text{output in 2012}\end{array} - \begin{array}{c}\text{Actual units of}\\\text{input used}\\\text{to produce}\\\text{2012 output}\end{array}\right) \times \begin{array}{c}\text{Input}\\\text{price}\\\text{in 2012}\end{array}$$

$$\begin{array}{c}\text{Cost effect of}\\\text{growth for}\\\text{direct materials}\end{array} = \left(3{,}000{,}000 \text{ sq. cm} \times \frac{1{,}150{,}000 \text{ units}}{1{,}000{,}000 \text{ units}} - 3{,}000{,}000 \text{ sq. cm.}\right) \times \$1.40 \text{ per sq. cm.}$$

$$= (3{,}450{,}000 \text{ sq. cm.} - 3{,}000{,}000 \text{ sq. cm.}) \times \$1.40 \text{ per sq. cm.} = \$630{,}000\text{ U}$$

The units of input required to produce 2013 output in 2012 can also be calculated as follows:

$$\text{Units of input per unit of output in 2012} = \frac{3{,}000{,}000 \text{ sq. cm}}{1{,}000{,}000 \text{ units}} = 3 \text{ sq. cm./unit}$$

Units of input required to produce 2013 output of 1,150,000 units in 2012 = 3 sq. cm. per unit × 1,150,000 units = 3,450,000 sq. cm.

$$\begin{array}{c}\text{Cost effect of}\\\text{growth for}\\\text{fixed costs}\end{array} = \left(\begin{array}{c}\text{Actual units of capacity in}\\\text{2012 because adequate capacity}\\\text{exists to produce 2013 output in 2012}\end{array} - \begin{array}{c}\text{Actual units}\\\text{of capacity}\\\text{in 2012}\end{array}\right) \times \begin{array}{c}\text{Price per}\\\text{unit of}\\\text{capacity}\\\text{in 2012}\end{array}$$

$$\begin{array}{c}\text{Cost effect of}\\\text{growth for}\\\text{conversion costs}\end{array} = (3{,}750{,}000 \text{ sq. cm.} - 3{,}750{,}000 \text{ sq. cm.}) \times \$4.28 \text{ per sq. cm.} = \$0$$

Conversion costs are fixed costs at a given level of capacity. Chipset has manufacturing capacity to process 3,750,000 square centimeters of silicon wafers in 2012 at a cost of $4.28 per square centimeter (rows 5 and 7 of data on page 488). To produce 1,150,000 units of output in 2012, Chipset needs to process 3,450,000 square centimeters of direct materials, which is less than the available capacity of 3,750,000 sq. cm. Throughout this chapter, we assume adequate capacity exists in the current year (2012) to produce next year's (2013) output. Under this assumption, the cost effect of growth for capacity-related fixed costs is, by definition, $0. Had 2012 capacity been inadequate to produce 2013 output in 2012, we would need to calculate the additional capacity required to produce 2013 output in 2012. These calculations are beyond the scope of the book.

In summary, the net increase in operating income attributable to growth equals the following:

Revenue effect of growth		$3,450,000 F
Cost effect of growth		
Direct material costs	$630,000 U	
Conversion costs	0	630,000 U
Change in operating income due to growth		$2,820,000 F

Price-Recovery Component of Change in Operating Income

Assuming that the 2012 relationship between inputs and outputs continued in 2013, the price-recovery component of the change in operating income measures solely the effect of price changes on revenues and costs to produce and sell the 1,150,000 units of CX1 in 2013.

Revenue Effect of Price Recovery

$$\text{Revenue effect of price recovery} = \left(\text{Selling price in 2013} - \text{Selling price in 2012}\right) \times \text{Acutal units of output sold in 2013}$$

$$= (\$22 \text{ per unit} - \$23 \text{ per unit}) \times 1{,}150{,}000 \text{ units}$$

$$= \$1{,}150{,}000 \text{ U}$$

Note that the calculation focuses on revenue changes caused by the decrease in the selling price of CX1 between 2012 ($23) and 2013 ($22).

Cost Effect of Price Recovery

Chipset's management accountants calculate the cost effects of price recovery separately for variable costs and for fixed costs, just as they did when calculating the cost effect of growth.

$$\text{Cost effect of price recovery for variable costs} = \left(\text{Input price in 2013} - \text{Input price in 2012}\right) \times \text{Units of input required to produce 2013 output in 2012}$$

$$\text{Cost effect of price recovery for direct materials} = (\$1.50 \text{ per sq. cm.} - \$1.40 \text{ per sq. cm.}) \times 3{,}450{,}000 \text{ sq. cm.} = \$345{,}000 \text{ U}$$

Recall that the direct materials of 3,450,000 square centimeters required to produce 2013 output in 2012 had already been calculated when computing the cost effect of growth (page 490).

$$\text{Cost effect of price recovery for fixed costs} = \left(\text{Price per unit of capacity in 2013} - \text{Price per unit of capacity in 2012}\right) \times \text{Actual units of capacity in 2012 (because adequate capacity exists to produce 2013 output in 2012)}$$

Cost effect of price recovery for fixed costs is as follows:

Conversion costs: ($4.35 per sq. cm. − $4.28 per sq. cm.) × 3,750,000 sq. cm. = $262,500 U

Recall that the detailed analyses of capacities were presented when computing the cost effect of growth (pages 490–491).

In summary, the net decrease in operating income attributable to price recovery equals the following:

Revenue effect of price recovery		$1,150,000 U
Cost effect of price recovery		
Direct material costs	$345,000 U	
Conversion costs	262,500 U	607,500 U
Change in operating income due to price recovery		$1,757,500 U

The price-recovery analysis indicates that, even as the prices of its inputs increased, the selling prices of CX1 decreased and Chipset could not pass on input-price increases to its customers.

Productivity Component of Change in Operating Income

The productivity component of the change in operating income uses 2013 input prices to measure how costs have decreased as a result of using fewer inputs, a better mix of inputs, and/or less capacity to produce 2013 output, compared with the inputs and capacity that would have been used to produce this output in 2012.

The productivity-component calculations use 2013 prices and output because the productivity component isolates the change in costs between 2012 and 2013 caused solely by the change in the quantities, mix, and/or capacities of inputs.[10]

$$\text{Cost effect of productivity for variable costs} = \left(\begin{array}{c}\text{Actual units of input used}\\ \text{to produce 2013 output}\end{array} - \begin{array}{c}\text{Units of input required to}\\ \text{produce 2013 output in 2012}\end{array}\right) \times \begin{array}{c}\text{Input price}\\ \text{in 2013}\end{array}$$

Using the 2013 data given on page 488 and the calculation of units of input required to produce 2013 output in 2012 when discussing the cost effects of growth (page 490),

$$\begin{aligned}\text{Cost effect of productivity for direct materials} &= (2{,}900{,}000 \text{ sq. cm.} - 3{,}450{,}000 \text{ sq. cm.}) \times \$1.50 \text{ per sq. cm.}\\ &= 550{,}000 \text{ sq. cm.} \times \$1.50 \text{ per sq. cm.} = \$825{,}000 \text{ F}\end{aligned}$$

Chipset's quality and yield improvements reduced the quantity of direct materials needed to produce output in 2013 relative to 2012.

$$\text{Cost effect of productivity for fixed costs} = \left(\begin{array}{c}\text{Actual units of}\\ \text{capacity in 2013}\end{array} - \begin{array}{c}\text{Actual units of capacity in 2012 because adequate}\\ \text{capacity exists to produce 2013 output in 2012}\end{array}\right) \times \begin{array}{c}\text{Price per unit of}\\ \text{capacity in 2013}\end{array}$$

To calculate the cost effect of productivity for fixed costs, we use the 2013 data (page 488) and the analyses of capacity required to produce 2013 output in 2012 when discussing the cost effect of growth (pages 490–491).

[10] Note that the productivity-component calculation uses actual 2013 input prices, whereas its counterpart, the efficiency variance in Chapters 7 and 8, uses budgeted prices. (In effect, the budgeted prices correspond to 2012 prices.) Year 2013 prices are used in the productivity calculation because Chipset wants its managers to choose input quantities to minimize costs in 2013 based on currently prevailing prices. If 2012 prices had been used in the productivity calculation, managers would choose input quantities based on irrelevant input prices that prevailed a year ago! Why does using budgeted prices in Chapters 7 and 8 not pose a similar problem? Because, unlike 2012 prices that describe what happened a year ago, budgeted prices represent prices that are expected to prevail in the current period. Moreover, budgeted prices can be changed, if necessary, to bring them in line with actual current-period prices.

Cost effects of productivity for fixed costs are

Conversion costs: (3,500,000 sq. cm − 3,750,000 sq. cm.) × $4.35 per sq. cm. = $1,087,500 F

Chipset's managers decreased manufacturing capacity in 2013 to 3,500,000 square centimeters by selling off old equipment and reducing the workforce using a combination of retirements and layoffs.

In summary, the net increase in operating income attributable to productivity equals:

Cost effect of productivity	
Direct material costs	$ 825,000 F
Conversion costs	1,087,500 F
Change in operating income due to productivity	$1,912,500 F

The productivity component indicates that Chipset was able to increase operating income by improving quality and productivity and eliminating capacity to reduce costs. The appendix to this chapter examines partial and total factor productivity changes between 2012 and 2013 and describes how the management accountant can obtain a deeper understanding of Chipset's cost-leadership strategy. Note that the productivity component focuses exclusively on costs, so there is no revenue effect for this component.

Exhibit 12-6 summarizes the growth, price-recovery, and productivity components of the changes in operating income. Generally, companies that have been successful at cost leadership will show favorable productivity and growth components. Companies that have successfully differentiated their products will show favorable price-recovery and growth components. In Chipset's case, consistent with its strategy and its implementation, productivity contributed $1,912,500 to the increase in operating income and growth contributed $2,820,000. Price recovery decreased operating income by $1,757,500 because even as input prices increased, the selling price of CX1 decreased. Had Chipset been able to differentiate its product and charge a higher price, the price-recovery effects might have been less unfavorable or perhaps even favorable. As a result, Chipset's managers plan to evaluate some modest changes in product features that might help differentiate CX1 somewhat more from competing products.

Further Analysis of Growth, Price-Recovery, and Productivity Components

As in all variance and profit analysis, Chipset's managers may want to further analyze the change in operating income. For example, Chipset's growth might have been helped by an increase in industry market size. Therefore, at least part of the increase in operating income may be attributable to favorable economic conditions in the industry rather than to any successful implementation of strategy. Some of the growth might relate to the management

Exhibit 12-6 Strategic Analysis of Profitability

	Income Statement Amounts in 2012 (1)	Revenue and Cost Effects of Growth Component in 2013 (2)	Revenue and Cost Effects of Price-Recovery Component in 2013 (3)	Cost Effect of Productivity Component in 2013 (4)	Income Statement Amounts in 2013 (5) = (1) + (2) + (3) + (4)
Revenues	$23,000,000	$3,450,000 F	$1,150,000 U	—	$25,300,000
Costs	20,250,000	630,000 U	607,500 U	$1,912,500 F	19,575,000
Operating income	$ 2,750,000	$2,820,000 F	$1,757,500 U	$1,912,500 F	$ 5,725,000
			$2,975,000 F		
			Change in operating income		

decision to decrease selling price, made possible by the productivity gains. In this case, the increase in operating income from cost leadership must include operating income from productivity-related growth in market share in addition to the productivity gain.

We illustrate these ideas, using the Chipset example and the following additional information. *Instructors who do not wish to cover these detailed calculations can go to the next section on "Applying the Five-Step Decision-Making Framework to Strategy" without any loss of continuity.*

- The market growth rate in the industry is 8% in 2013. Of the 150,000 (1,150,000 − 1,000,000) units of increased sales of CX1 between 2012 and 2013, 80,000 (0.08 × 1,000,000) units are due to an increase in industry market size (which Chipset should have benefited from regardless of its productivity gains), and the remaining 70,000 units are due to an increase in market share.
- During 2013, Chipset could have maintained the price of CX1 at the 2012 price of $23 per unit. But management decided to take advantage of the productivity gains to reduce the price of CX1 by $1 to grow market share leading to the 70,000-unit increase in sales.

The effect of the industry-market-size factor on operating income (not any specific strategic action) is as follows:

Change in operating income due to growth in industry market size

$$\$2{,}820{,}000 \text{ (Exhibit 12-6, column 2)} \times \frac{80{,}000 \text{ units}}{150{,}000 \text{ units}} = \$1{,}504{,}000 \text{ F}$$

Lacking a differentiated product, Chipset could have maintained the price of CX1 at $23 per unit even while the prices of its inputs increased.

The effect of product differentiation on operating income is as follows:

Change in prices of inputs (cost effect of price recovery)	$607,500 U
Change in operating income due to product differentiation	$607,500 U

To exercise cost and price leadership, Chipset made the strategic decision to cut the price of CX1 by $1. This decision resulted in an increase in market share and 70,000 units of additional sales.

The effect of cost leadership on operating income is as follows:

Productivity component	$1,912,500 F
Effect of strategic decision to reduce price ($1/unit × 1,150,000 units)	1,150,000 U
Growth in market share due to productivity improvement and strategic decision to reduce prices	
$\$2{,}820{,}000 \text{ (Exhibit 12-6, column 2)} \times \frac{70{,}000 \text{ units}}{150{,}000 \text{ units}}$	1,316,000 F
Change in operating income due to cost leadership	$2,078,500 F

A summary of the change in operating income between 2012 and 2013 follows.

Change due to industry market size	$1,504,000 F
Change due to product differentiation	607,500 U
Change due to cost leadership	2,078,500 F
Change in operating income	$2,975,000 F

Consistent with its cost-leadership strategy, the productivity gains of $1,912,500 in 2013 were a big part of the increase in operating income from 2012 to 2013. Chipset took advantage of these productivity gains to decrease price by $1 per unit at a cost of $1,150,000 to gain $1,316,000 in operating income by selling 70,000 additional units. The Problem for Self-Study on pages 498–502 describes the analysis of the growth, price-recovery, and productivity components for a company following a product-differentiation

Concepts in Action: Operating Income Analysis Reveals Strategic Challenges at Best Buy

In 2008, Best Buy was the undisputed king of electronics retailing after its largest competitor, Circuit City, went bankrupt. Without another bricks-and-mortar competitor, Best Buy reaffirmed its previously successful strategy of aggressive "big box" store expansion. From 2008 to 2012, Best Buy added 532 stores across the United States, increasing capacity by 49% and growing annual revenue by $10.6 billion.

By 2012, however, an analysis of the company's operating income revealed strategic challenges. Though revenue was growing, operating income fell by 50% from 2008 to 2012. Meanwhile, same-store sales were declining and selling, general, and administrative expenses were rising. These numbers revealed that e-commerce was eroding Best Buy's performance. While the company pursued strategic differentiation through customer experience and add-on services, many consumers were drawn to the low prices of Amazon and other online retailers to buy flat-screen televisions, computers, and digital cameras—three of Best Buy's largest categories. To respond to this challenge, Best Buy ramped up spending on advertising and its e-commerce capabilities, which increased its overall costs.

To turn the company around, Best Buy announced plans to (1) close some existing "big box" stores and open smaller stores focused on selling smartphones, including Samsung mini-shops inside 1,400 locations; (2) further expand its online presence—and introduce a price-match guarantee—to compete better with Amazon; and (3) sell more services through its "Geek Squad" customer-support business.

Sources: Miguel Bustillo, "Best Buy to Shrink 'Big Box' Store Strategy," *The Wall Street Journal* (April 15, 2011); Andria Cheng, "Best Buy to Scale Back Big-Box Strategy," *MarketWatch* (April 14, 2012); Kevin Kelleher, "Best Buy: Not Your Standard Corporate Comeback," *Fortune* (June 12, 2013); Salvador Rogriguez, "Samsung Opening 1,400 Mini-Shops Inside Best Buy Stores Across U.S.," *Los Angeles Times* (May 7, 2013); Best Buy, Inc. Form 10-K. Best Buy, Inc., Richfield, MN: 2010; and Best Buy, Inc. Form 10-K. Best Buy, Inc., Richfield, MN: 2012.

strategy. The Concepts in Action: Operating Income Analysis Reveals Strategic Challenges at Best Buy describes how an analysis of its operating income helped Best Buy change its strategy to compete with Amazon.

Under different assumptions about the change in selling price of CX1, the analysis will attribute different amounts to the different strategies.

Decision Point

How can a company analyze changes in operating income to evaluate the success of its strategy?

Applying the Five-Step Decision-Making Framework to Strategy

We next briefly describe how the five-step decision-making framework, introduced in Chapter 1, is also useful in making decisions about strategy.

1. **Identify the problem and uncertainties.** Chipset's strategy choice depends on resolving two uncertainties: (1) whether Chipset can add value to its customers that its competitors cannot copy and (2) whether Chipset can develop the necessary internal capabilities to add this value.
2. **Obtain information.** Chipset's managers develop customer preference maps to identify various product attributes customers want and the competitive advantage or disadvantage it has on each attribute relative to competitors. The managers also gather data on Chipset's internal capabilities. How good is Chipset in designing and developing innovative new products? How good are its process and marketing capabilities?

3. **Make predictions about the future.** Chipset's managers conclude that they will not be able to develop innovative new products in a cost-effective way. They believe that Chipset's strength lies in improving quality, reengineering processes, reducing costs, and delivering products faster to customers.
4. **Make decisions by choosing among alternatives.** Chipset's managers decide to follow a cost-leadership rather than a product-differentiation strategy. They decide to introduce a balanced scorecard to align and measure Chipset's quality improvement and process reengineering efforts.
5. **Implement the decision, evaluate performance, and learn.** On its balanced scorecard, Chipset's managers compare actual and targeted performance and evaluate possible cause-and-effect relationships. They learn, for example, that increasing the percentage of processes with advanced controls improves yield. As a result, just as they had anticipated, productivity and growth initiatives result in increases in operating income in 2013. The one change Chipset's managers plan for 2014 is to make modest changes in product features that might help differentiate CX1 somewhat from competing products. In this way, feedback and learning help in the development of future strategies and implementation plans.

Learning Objective 5

Identify unused capacity

...capacity available minus capacity used for engineered costs but difficult to determine for discretionary costs

and how to manage it

...downsize to reduce capacity

Downsizing and the Management of Processing Capacity

As we saw in our discussion of the productivity component (page 492), fixed costs are tied to capacity. Unlike variable costs, fixed costs do not change automatically with changes in activity level (for example, fixed conversion costs do not change with changes in the quantity of silicon wafers started into production). How then can managers reduce capacity-based fixed costs? By measuring and managing **unused capacity**, which is the amount of productive capacity available over and above the productive capacity employed to meet customer demand in the current period. To understand unused capacity, it is necessary to distinguish *engineered costs* from *discretionary costs.*

Engineered and Discretionary Costs

Engineered costs result from a cause-and-effect relationship between the cost driver—output—and the (direct or indirect) resources used to produce that output. Engineered costs have a detailed, physically observable, and repetitive relationship with output. In the Chipset example, direct material costs are *direct engineered costs.* Conversion costs are an example of *indirect engineered costs.* Consider 2013. The output of 1,150,000 units of CX1 and the efficiency with which inputs are converted into outputs result in 2,900,000 square centimeters of silicon wafers being started into production. Manufacturing-conversion-cost resources used equal $12,615,000 ($4.35 per sq. cm. × 2,900,000 sq. cm.), but actual conversion costs ($15,225,000) are higher because Chipset has manufacturing capacity to process 3,500,000 square centimeters of silicon wafer ($4.35 per sq. cm. × 3,500,000 sq. cm. = $15,225,000). Although these costs are fixed in the short run, over the long run there is a cause-and-effect relationship between output and manufacturing capacity required (and conversion costs needed). In the long run, Chipset will try to match its capacity to its needs.

In general, cost leadership requires managers to pay special attention to engineered costs and capacity. Companies such as United Airlines have struggled to achieve profitability because of the difficulties they have had in managing capacity-related engineered costs. United's cost structure varies with the number of flights on its schedule. For a given number of flights, most of United's costs such as the cost of airplane leases, fuel, and wages are fixed. United must anticipate future revenues and decide on a level of capacity and the related costs. If revenues fall short, it is difficult for United Airlines to reduce its costs quickly.

Discretionary costs have two important features: (1) They arise from periodic (usually annual) decisions regarding the maximum amount to be incurred and (2) they have no measurable cause-and-effect relationship between output and resources used.

Examples of discretionary costs include advertising, executive training, R&D, and corporate-staff department costs such as legal, human resources, and public relations. Unlike engineered costs, the relationship between discretionary costs and output is weak and unclear because the relationship is nonrepetitive and nonroutine. A noteworthy aspect of discretionary costs is that managers are seldom confident that the "correct" amounts are being spent. The founder of Lever Brothers, an international consumer-products company, once noted, "Half the money I spend on advertising is wasted; the trouble is, I don't know which half!"[11]

Identifying Unused Capacity for Engineered and Discretionary Overhead Costs

Identifying unused capacity is very different for engineered costs compared to discretionary costs. Consider engineered conversion costs.

At the start of 2013, Chipset had capacity to process 3,750,000 square centimeters of silicon wafers. Quality and productivity improvements made during 2013 enabled Chipset to produce 1,150,000 units of CX1 by processing 2,900,000 square centimeters of silicon wafers. Unused manufacturing capacity is 850,000 (3,750,000 − 2,900,000) square centimeters of silicon-wafer processing capacity at the beginning of 2013 when Chipset makes its capacity decisions for the year. At the 2013 conversion cost of $4.35 per square centimeter,

$$\text{Cost of unused capacity} = \text{Cost of capacity at the beginning of the year} - \text{Manufacturing resources used during the year}$$

$$= (3{,}750{,}000 \text{ sq. cm.} \times \$4.35 \text{ per sq. cm.}) - (2{,}900{,}000 \text{ sq. cm.} \times \$4.35 \text{ per sq. cm.})$$

$$= \$16{,}312{,}500 - \$12{,}615{,}000 = \$3{,}697{,}500$$

The absence of a cause-and-effect relationship makes identifying unused capacity for discretionary costs difficult. For example, management cannot determine the R&D resources used for the actual output produced. And without a measure of capacity used, it is not possible to compute unused capacity.

Managing Unused Capacity

What actions can Chipset management take when it identifies unused capacity? In general, it has two alternatives: eliminate unused capacity or grow output to utilize the unused capacity.

In recent years, many companies have *downsized* in an attempt to eliminate unused capacity. **Downsizing** (also called **rightsizing**) is an integrated approach of configuring processes, products, and people to match costs to the activities that need to be performed to operate effectively and efficiently in the present and future. Companies such as AT&T, Delta Airlines, Ford Motor Company, and IBM have downsized to focus on their core businesses and have instituted organization changes to increase efficiency, reduce costs, and improve quality. However, downsizing often means eliminating jobs, which can adversely affect employee morale and the culture of a company.

Consider Chipset's alternatives for dealing with unused manufacturing capacity. Because it needed to process 2,900,000 square centimeters of silicon wafers in 2013, the company could have reduced capacity to 3,000,000 square centimeters (Chipset can add or reduce manufacturing capacity in increments of 250,000 sq. cm.), resulting in cost

[11] Managers also describe some costs as infrastructure costs—costs that arise from having property, plant, and equipment and a functioning organization. Examples are depreciation, long-run lease rental, and the acquisition of long-run technical capabilities. These costs are generally fixed costs because a company purchases property, plant, and equipment before using them. Infrastructure costs can be engineered or discretionary. For instance, manufacturing-overhead cost incurred at Chipset to acquire manufacturing capacity is an infrastructure cost that is an example of an engineered cost. In the long run, there is a cause-and-effect relationship between output and manufacturing-overhead costs needed to produce that output. R&D cost incurred to acquire technical capability is an infrastructure cost that is an example of a discretionary cost. There is no measurable cause-and-effect relationship between output and R&D cost incurred.

savings of $3,262,500 [(3,750,000 sq. cm. − 3,000,000 sq. cm.) × $4.35 per sq. cm.]. Chipset's strategy, however, is not just to reduce costs but also to grow its business. So in early 2013, Chipset reduces its manufacturing capacity by only 250,000 square centimeters—from 3,750,000 square centimeters to 3,500,000 square centimeters—saving $1,087,500 ($4.35 per sq. cm. × 250,000 sq. cm.). It retains some extra capacity for future growth. By avoiding greater reductions in capacity, it also maintains the morale of its skilled and capable workforce. The success of this strategy will depend on Chipset achieving the future growth it has projected.

Decision Point

How can a company identify and manage unused capacity?

Identifying unused capacity for discretionary costs, such as R&D costs, is difficult, so downsizing or otherwise managing this unused capacity is also difficult. Management must exercise considerable judgment in deciding the level of R&D costs that would generate the needed product and process improvements. Unlike engineered costs, there is no clear-cut way to know whether management is spending too much (or too little) on R&D.

Problem for Self-Study

Following a strategy of product differentiation, Westwood Corporation makes a high-end kitchen range hood, KE8. Westwood's data for 2012 and 2013 are:

	2012	2013
1. Units of KE8 produced and sold	40,000	42,000
2. Selling price	$100	$110
3. Direct materials (square feet)	120,000	123,000
4. Direct material cost per square foot	$10	$11
5. Manufacturing capacity for KE8	50,000 units	50,000 units
6. Conversion costs	$1,000,000	$1,100,000
7. Conversion cost per unit of capacity (row 6 ÷ row 5)	$20	$22
8. Selling and customer-service capacity	30 customers	29 customers
9. Selling and customer-service costs	$720,000	$725,000
10. Cost per customer of selling and customer-service capacity (row 9 ÷ row 8)	$24,000	$25,000

In 2013, Westwood produced no defective units and reduced direct material usage per unit of KE8. Conversion costs in each year are tied to manufacturing capacity. Selling and customer service costs are related to the number of customers that the selling and service functions are designed to support. Westwood had 23 customers (wholesalers) in 2012 and 25 customers in 2013.

Required

1. Describe briefly the elements you would include in Westwood's balanced scorecard.
2. Calculate the growth, price-recovery, and productivity components that explain the change in operating income from 2012 to 2013.
3. Suppose during 2013, the market size for high-end kitchen range hoods grew 3% in terms of number of units and all increases in market share (that is, increases in the number of units sold greater than 3%) are due to Westwood's product-differentiation strategy. Calculate how much of the change in operating income from 2012 to 2013 is due to the industry-market-size factor, cost leadership, and product differentiation.
4. How successful has Westwood been in implementing its strategy? Explain.

Solution

1. The balanced scorecard should describe Westwood's product-differentiation strategy. Elements that should be included in its balanced scorecard are as follows:
   - **Financial perspective.** Increase in operating income from higher margins on KE8 and from growth

- **Customer perspective.** Customer satisfaction and market share in the high-end market
- **Internal-business-process perspective.** New product features, development time for new products, improvements in manufacturing processes, manufacturing quality, order-delivery time, and on-time delivery
- **Learning-and-growth perspective.** Number of employees in product development, percentage of employees trained in process and quality management, and employee satisfaction ratings

2. Operating income for each year is:

	2012	2013
Revenues		
($100 per unit × 40,000 units; $110 per unit × 42,000 units)	$4,000,000	$ 4,620,000
Costs		
Direct material costs		
($10 per sq. ft. × 120,000 sq. ft.; $11 per sq. ft. × 123,000 sq. ft.)	1,200,000	1,353,000
Conversion costs		
($20 per unit × 50,000 units; $22 per unit × 50,000 units)	1,000,000	1,100,000
Selling and customer-service cost		
($24,000 per customer × 30 customers;		
$25,000 per customer × 29 customers)	720,000	725,000
Total costs	2,920,000	3,178,000
Operating income	$1,080,000	$1,442,000
Change in operating income	$362,000 F	

Growth Component of Operating Income Change

$$\text{Revenue effect of growth} = \left(\begin{array}{c}\text{Actual units of}\\ \text{output sold}\\ \text{in 2013}\end{array} - \begin{array}{c}\text{Actual units of}\\ \text{output sold}\\ \text{in 2012}\end{array}\right) \times \begin{array}{c}\text{Selling}\\ \text{price}\\ \text{in 2012}\end{array}$$

$$= (42{,}000 \text{ units} - 40{,}000 \text{ units}) \times \$100 \text{ per unit} = \$200{,}000 \text{ F}$$

$$\begin{array}{c}\text{Cost effect}\\ \text{of growth for}\\ \text{variable costs}\end{array} = \left(\begin{array}{c}\text{Units of input}\\ \text{required to produce}\\ \text{2013 output in 2012}\end{array} - \begin{array}{c}\text{Actual units of input}\\ \text{used to produce}\\ \text{2012 output}\end{array}\right) \times \begin{array}{c}\text{Input}\\ \text{price}\\ \text{in 2012}\end{array}$$

$$\begin{array}{c}\text{Cost effect}\\ \text{of growth for}\\ \text{direct materials}\end{array} = \left(120{,}000 \text{ sq. ft.} \times \frac{42{,}000 \text{ units}}{40{,}000 \text{ units}} - 120{,}000 \text{ sq. ft.}\right) \times \$10 \text{ per sq. ft.}$$

$$= (126{,}000 \text{ sq. ft.} - 120{,}000 \text{ sq. ft.}) \times \$10 \text{ per sq. ft.} = \$60{,}000 \text{ U}$$

$$\begin{array}{c}\text{Cost effect}\\ \text{of growth for}\\ \text{fixed costs}\end{array} = \left(\begin{array}{c}\text{Actual units of capacity in}\\ \text{2012 because adequate capacity}\\ \text{exists to produce 2013 output in 2012}\end{array} - \begin{array}{c}\text{Actual units}\\ \text{of capacity}\\ \text{in 2012}\end{array}\right) \times \begin{array}{c}\text{Price per}\\ \text{unit of}\\ \text{capacity}\\ \text{in 2012}\end{array}$$

$$\begin{array}{c}\text{Cost effect of}\\ \text{growth for}\\ \text{fixed conversion costs}\end{array} = (50{,}000 \text{ units} - 50{,}000 \text{ units}) \times \$20 \text{ per unit} = \$0$$

$$\begin{array}{c}\text{Cost effect of growth for}\\ \text{fixed selling and}\\ \text{customer-service costs}\end{array} = (30 \text{ customers} - 30 \text{ customers}) \times \$24{,}000 \text{ per customer} = \$0$$

In summary, the net increase in operating income attributable to growth equals:

Revenue effect of growth		$200,000 F
Cost effect of growth		
Direct material costs	$60,000 U	
Conversion costs	0	
Selling and customer-service costs	0	60,000 U
Change in operating income due to growth		$140,000 F

Price-Recovery Component of Operating-Income Change

$$\text{Revenue effect of price recovery} = \left(\text{Selling price in 2013} - \text{Selling price in 2012}\right) \times \text{Actual units of output sold in 2013}$$

$$= (\$110 \text{ per unit} - \$100 \text{ per unit}) \times 42{,}000 \text{ units} = \$420{,}000 \text{ F}$$

$$\text{Cost effect of price recovery for variable costs} = \left(\text{Input price in 2013} - \text{Input price in 2012}\right) \times \text{Units of input required to produce 2013 output in 2012}$$

$$\text{Direct material costs: } (\$11 \text{ per sq. ft.} - \$10 \text{ per sq. ft.}) \times 126{,}000 \text{ sq. ft.} = \$126{,}000 \text{ U}$$

$$\text{Cost effect of price recovery for direct materials} = \left(\text{Price per unit of capacity in 2013} - \text{Price per unit of capacity in 2012}\right) \times \text{Actual units of capacity in 2012 because adequate capacity exists to produce 2013 output in 2012}$$

Cost effects of price recovery for fixed costs are:

$$\text{Conversion costs: } (\$22 \text{ per unit} - 20 \text{ per unit}) \times 50{,}000 \text{ units} = \$100{,}000 \text{ U}$$

$$\text{Selling and cust.-service costs: } (\$25{,}000 \text{ per cust.} - \$24{,}000 \text{ per cust.}) \times 30 \text{ customers} = \$30{,}000 \text{ U}$$

In summary, the net increase in operating income attributable to price recovery equals:

Revenue effect of price recovery		$420,000 F
Cost effect of price recovery		
Direct material costs	$126,000 U	
Conversion costs	100,000 U	
Selling and customer-service costs	30,000 U	256,000 U
Change in operating income due to price recovery		$164,000 F

Productivity Component of Operating-Income Change

$$\text{Cost effect of productivity for variable costs} = \left(\text{Actual units of input used to produce 2013 output} - \text{Units of input required to produce 2013 output in 2012}\right) \times \text{Input price in 2013}$$

$$\text{Cost effect of productivity for direct materials} = (123{,}000 \text{ sq. ft.} - 126{,}000 \text{ sq. ft.}) \times \$11 \text{ per sq. ft.} = \$33{,}000 \text{ F}$$

$$\text{Cost effect of productivity for fixed costs} = \left(\text{Actual units of capacity in 2013} - \text{Actual units of capacity in 2012 because adequate capacity exists to produce 2013 output in 2012}\right) \times \text{Price per unit of capacity in 2013}$$

Cost effects of productivity for fixed costs are:

Conversion costs: (50,000 units − 50,000 units) × $22 per unit = $0

Selling and customer-service costs: (29 customers − 30 customers) × $25,000/customer = $25,000 F

In summary, the net increase in operating income attributable to productivity equals:

Cost effect of productivity:	
Direct material costs	$33,000 F
Conversion costs	0
Selling and customer-service costs	25,000 F
Change in operating income due to productivity	$58,000 F

A summary of the change in operating income between 2012 and 2013 follows.

	Income Statement Amounts in 2012 (1)	Revenue and Cost Effects of Growth Component in 2013 (2)	Revenue and Cost Effects of Price-Recovery Component in 2013 (3)	Cost Effect of Productivity Component in 2013 (4)	Income Statement Amounts in 2013 (5) = (1) + (2) + (3) + (4)
Revenue	$4,000,000	$200,000 F	$420,000 F	—	$4,620,000
Costs	2,920,000	60,000 U	256,000 U	$58,000 F	3,178,000
Operating income	$1,080,000	$140,000 F	$164,000 F	$58,000 F	$1,442,000
			$362,000 F		

Change in operating income

3. **Effect of the Industry-Market-Size Factor on Operating Income**
Of the increase in sales from 40,000 to 42,000 units, 3%, or 1,200 units (0.03 × 40,000), is due to growth in market size, and 800 units (2,000 − 1,200) are due to an increase in market share. The change in Westwood's operating income from the industry-market-size factor rather than specific strategic actions is as follows:

$$\$140{,}000 \text{ (column 2 of preceding table)} \times \frac{1{,}200 \text{ units}}{2{,}000 \text{ units}} \qquad \$84{,}000 \text{ F}$$

Effect of Product Differentiation on Operating Income

Increase in the selling price of KE8 (revenue effect of the price-recovery component)	$420,000 F
Increase in prices of inputs (cost effect of the price-recovery component)	256,000 U
Growth in market share due to product differentiation	
$\$140{,}000 \text{ (column 2 of preceding table)} \times \frac{800 \text{ units}}{2{,}000 \text{ units}}$	56,000 F
Change in operating income due to product differentiation	$220,000 F

Effect of Cost Leadership on Operating Income

Productivity component	$ 58,000 F

A summary of the net increase in operating income from 2012 to 2013 follows:

Change due to the industry-market-size factor	$ 84,000 F
Change due to product differentiation	220,000 F
Change due to cost leadership	58,000 F
Change in operating income	$362,000 F

4. The analysis of operating income indicates that a significant amount of the increase in operating income resulted from Westwood's successful implementation of its product-differentiation strategy (operating income attributable to product differentiation, $220,000 F). The company was able to continue to charge a premium price for KE8 while increasing market share. Westwood was also able to earn additional operating income from improving its cost leadership through productivity improvement (operating income attributable to cost leadership, $58,000 F).

Decision Points

The following question-and-answer format summarizes the chapter's learning objectives. Each decision presents a key question related to a learning objective. The guidelines are the answer to that question.

Decision	Guidelines
1. What are two generic strategies a company can use?	Two generic strategies are product differentiation and cost leadership. Product differentiation is offering products and services that customers perceive as superior and unique. Cost leadership is achieving low costs relative to competitors. A company chooses its strategy based on an understanding of customer preferences and its own internal capabilities, while differentiating itself from its competitors.
2. What is reengineering?	Reengineering is the rethinking of business processes, such as the order-delivery process, to improve critical performance measures such as cost, quality, and customer satisfaction.
3. How can an organization translate its strategy into a set of performance measures?	An organization can develop a balanced scorecard that provides the framework for a strategic measurement and management system. The balanced scorecard measures performance from four perspectives: (1) financial, (2) customer, (3) internal business processes, and (4) learning and growth. To build their balanced scorecards, organizations often create strategy maps to represent the cause-and-effect relationships across various strategic objectives.
4. How can a company analyze changes in operating income to evaluate the success of its strategy?	To evaluate the success of its strategy, a company can subdivide the change in operating income into growth, price-recovery, and productivity components. The growth component measures the change in revenues and costs from selling more or less units, assuming nothing else has changed. The price-recovery component measures changes in revenues and costs solely as a result of changes in the prices of outputs and inputs. The productivity component measures the decrease in costs from using fewer inputs, using a better mix of inputs, and reducing capacity. If a company is successful in implementing its strategy, changes in components of operating income align closely with strategy.
5. How can a company identify and manage unused capacity?	A company must first distinguish engineered costs from discretionary costs. Engineered costs result from a cause-and-effect relationship between output and the resources needed to produce that output. Discretionary costs arise from periodic (usually annual) management decisions regarding the amount of cost to be incurred. Discretionary costs are not tied to a cause-and-effect relationship between inputs and outputs. Identifying unused capacity is easier for engineered costs and more difficult for discretionary costs. Downsizing is an approach to managing unused capacity that matches costs to the activities that need to be performed to operate effectively.

Appendix

Productivity Measurement

Productivity measures the relationship between actual inputs used (both quantities and costs) and actual outputs produced. The lower the inputs for a given quantity of outputs or the higher the outputs for a given quantity of inputs, the higher the productivity. Measuring productivity improvements over time highlights the specific input–output relationships that contribute to cost leadership.

Partial Productivity Measures

Partial productivity, the most frequently used productivity measure, compares the quantity of output produced with the quantity of an individual input used. In its most common form, partial productivity is expressed as a ratio:

$$\text{Partial productivity} = \frac{\text{Quantity of output produced}}{\text{Quantity of input used}}$$

The higher the ratio, the greater the productivity.

Consider direct materials productivity at Chipset in 2013.

$$\begin{aligned}\text{Direct materials partial productivity} &= \frac{\text{Quantity of CX1 units produced during 2013}}{\text{Quantity of direct materials used to produce CX1 in 2013}}\\ &= \frac{\text{1,150,000 units of CX1}}{\text{2,900,000 sq. cm. of direct materials}}\\ &= \text{0.397 units of CX1 per sq. cm. of direct materials}\end{aligned}$$

Note direct materials partial productivity ignores Chipset's other input, manufacturing conversion capacity. Partial-productivity measures become more meaningful when comparisons are made that examine productivity changes over time, either across different facilities or relative to a benchmark. Exhibit 12-7 presents partial-productivity measures for Chipset's inputs for 2013 and the comparable 2012 inputs that would have been used to produce 2013 output, using information from the productivity-component calculations on pages 492–493. These measures compare actual inputs used in 2013 to produce 1,150,000 units of CX1 with inputs that would have been used in 2013 had the input–output relationship from 2012 continued in 2013.

Evaluating Changes in Partial Productivities

Note how the partial-productivity measures differ for variable-cost and fixed-cost components. For variable-cost elements, such as direct materials, productivity improvements measure the reduction in input resources used to produce output (3,450,000 square centimeters

Exhibit 12-7 Comparing Chipset's Partial Productivities in 2012 and 2013

Input (1)	Partial Productivity in 2013 (2)	Comparable Partial Productivity Based on 2012 Input–Output Relationships (3)	Percentage Change from 2012 to 2013 (4)
Direct materials	$\frac{1{,}150{,}000}{2{,}900{,}000} = 0.397$	$\frac{1{,}150{,}000}{3{,}450{,}000} = 0.333$	$\frac{0.397 - 0.333}{0.333} = 19.2\%$
Manufacturing conversion capacity	$\frac{1{,}150{,}000}{3{,}500{,}000} = 0.329$	$\frac{1{,}150{,}000}{3{,}750{,}000} = 0.307$	$\frac{0.329 - 0.307}{0.307} = 7.2\%$

of silicon wafers to 2,900,000 square centimeters). For fixed-cost elements such as manufacturing conversion capacity, partial productivity measures the reduction in overall capacity from 2012 to 2013 (3,750,000 square centimeters of silicon wafers to 3,500,000 square centimeters) regardless of the amount of capacity actually used in each period.

An advantage of partial-productivity measures is that they focus on a single input. As a result, they are simple to calculate and easy for operations personnel to understand. Managers and operators examine these numbers and try to understand the reasons for the productivity changes—such as better training of workers, lower labor turnover, better incentives, improved methods, or substitution of materials for labor. Isolating the relevant factors helps Chipset implement and sustain these practices in the future.

For all their advantages, partial-productivity measures also have serious drawbacks. Because partial productivity focuses on only one input at a time rather than on all inputs simultaneously, managers cannot evaluate the effect on overall productivity, if (say) manufacturing-conversion-capacity partial productivity increases while direct materials partial productivity decreases. Total factor productivity (TFP), or total productivity, is a measure of productivity that considers all inputs simultaneously.

Total Factor Productivity

Total factor productivity (TFP) is the ratio of the quantity of output produced to the costs of all inputs used based on current-period prices.

$$\text{Total factor productivity} = \frac{\text{Quantity of output produced}}{\text{Costs of all inputs used}}$$

TFP considers all inputs simultaneously and the trade-offs across inputs based on current input prices. Do not think of all productivity measures as physical measures lacking financial content—how many units of output are produced per unit of input. TFP is intricately tied to minimizing total cost—a financial objective.

Calculating and Comparing Total Factor Productivity

We first calculate Chipset's TFP in 2013, using 2013 prices and 1,150,000 units of output produced (based on information from the first part of the productivity-component calculations on pages 492–493).

$$\begin{aligned}\begin{array}{c}\text{Total factor productivity}\\\text{for 2013 using 2013 prices}\end{array} &= \frac{\text{Quantity of output produced in 2013}}{\text{Costs of inputs used in 2013 based on 2013 prices}}\\ &= \frac{1{,}150{,}000}{(2{,}900{,}000 \times \$1.50) + (3{,}500{,}000 \times \$4.35)}\\ &= \frac{1{,}150{,}000}{\$19{,}575{,}000}\\ &= 0.058748 \text{ units of output per dollar of input cost}\end{aligned}$$

By itself, the 2013 TFP of 0.058748 units of CX1 per dollar of input costs is not particularly helpful. We need something to compare the 2013 TFP against. One alternative is to compare TFPs of other similar companies in 2013. However, finding similar companies and obtaining accurate comparable data are often difficult. Companies, therefore, usually compare their own TFPs over time. In the Chipset example, we use as a benchmark TFP calculated using the inputs that Chipset would have used in 2012 to produce 1,150,000 units of CX1 at 2013 prices (that is, we use the costs calculated from the second part of the productivity-component calculations on pages 492–493). Why do we use 2013 prices? Because using the current year's prices in both calculations controls for input-price differences and focuses the analysis on adjustments the manager made in quantities of inputs in response to changes in prices.

$$\text{Benchmark TFP} = \frac{\text{Quantity of output produced in 2013}}{\text{Costs of inputs at 2013 prices that would have been used in 2012 to produce 2013 output}}$$

$$= \frac{1{,}150{,}000}{(3{,}450{,}000 \times \$1.50) + (3{,}750{,}000 \times \$4.35)}$$

$$= \frac{1{,}150{,}000}{\$21{,}487{,}500}$$

$$= 0.053519 \text{ units of output per dollar of input cost}$$

Using 2013 prices, TFP increased 9.8% [(0.058748 − 0.053519) ÷ 0.053519 = 0.098, or 9.8%] from 2012 to 2013. Note that the 9.8% increase in TFP also equals the $1,912,500 gain (Exhibit 12-6, column 4) divided by the $19,575,000 of actual costs incurred in 2013 (Exhibit 12-6, column 5). Total factor productivity increased because Chipset produced more output per dollar of input cost in 2013 relative to 2012, measured in both years using 2013 prices. The gain in TFP occurs because Chipset increases the partial productivities of individual inputs and, consistent with its strategy, combines inputs to lower costs. Note that increases in TFP cannot be due to differences in input prices because we used 2013 prices to evaluate both the inputs that Chipset would have used in 2012 to produce 1,150,000 units of CX1 and the inputs actually used in 2013.

Using Partial and Total Factor Productivity Measures

A major advantage of TFP is that it measures the combined productivity of all inputs used to produce output and explicitly considers gains from using fewer physical inputs as well as substitution among inputs. Managers can analyze these numbers to understand the reasons for changes in TFP—for example, better human resource management practices, higher quality of materials, or improved manufacturing methods.

Although TFP measures are comprehensive, operations personnel find financial TFP measures more difficult to understand and less useful than physical partial-productivity measures. For example, companies that are more labor intensive than Chipset use manufacturing-labor partial-productivity measures. However, if productivity-based bonuses depend on gains in manufacturing-labor partial productivity alone, workers have incentives to substitute materials (and capital) for labor. This substitution improves their own productivity measure, while possibly decreasing the overall productivity of the company as measured by TFP. To overcome these incentive problems, companies—for example, TRW, Eaton, and Whirlpool—explicitly adjust bonuses based on manufacturing-labor partial productivity for the effects of other factors such as investments in new equipment and higher levels of scrap. That is, they combine partial productivity with TFP-like measures.

Many companies such as Behlen Manufacturing, a steel fabricator, and Dell Computers use both partial productivity and total factor productivity to evaluate performance. *Partial productivity and TFP measures work best together because the strengths of one offset the weaknesses of the other.*

Terms to Learn

This chapter and the Glossary at the end of the book contain definitions of the following important terms:

balanced scorecard **(p. 476)**
cost leadership **(p. 474)**
discretionary costs **(p. 496)**
downsizing **(p. 497)**
engineered costs **(p. 496)**
growth component **(p. 489)**
partial productivity **(p. 503)**
price-recovery component **(p. 489)**
product differentiation **(p. 474)**
productivity **(p. 503)**
productivity component **(p. 489)**
reengineering **(p. 475)**
rightsizing **(p. 497)**
strategy map **(p. 477)**
total factor productivity (TFP) **(p. 504)**
unused capacity **(p. 496)**

Assignment Material

MyAccountingLab

Questions

12-1 Define strategy.

12-2 Describe the five key forces to consider when analyzing an industry.

12-3 Describe two generic strategies.

12-4 What is a customer preference map, and why is it useful?

12-5 What is reengineering?

12-6 What are four key perspectives in the balanced scorecard?

12-7 What is a strategy map?

12-8 Describe three features of a good balanced scorecard.

12-9 What are three important pitfalls to avoid when implementing a balanced scorecard?

12-10 Describe three key components in doing a strategic analysis of operating income.

12-11 Why might an analyst incorporate the industry-market-size factor and the interrelationships among the growth, price-recovery, and productivity components into a strategic analysis of operating income?

12-12 How does an engineered cost differ from a discretionary cost?

12-13 What is downsizing?

12-14 What is a partial-productivity measure?

12-15 "We are already measuring total factor productivity. Measuring partial productivities would be of no value." Do you agree? Comment briefly.

MyAccountingLab

Exercises

12-16 Balanced scorecard. Ridgecrest Electric manufactures electric motors. It competes and plans to grow by selling high-quality motors at a low price and by delivering them to customers quickly after receiving customers' orders. There are many other manufacturers who produce similar motors. Ridgecrest believes that continuously improving its manufacturing processes and having satisfied employees are critical to implementing its strategy in 2013.

Required

1. Is Ridgecrest's 2013 strategy one of product differentiation or cost leadership? Explain briefly.
2. Kearney Corporation, a competitor of Ridgecrest, manufactures electric motors with more sizes and features than Ridgecrest at a higher price. Kearney's motors are of high quality but require more time to produce and so have longer delivery times. Draw a simple customer preference map as in Exhibit 12-1 for Ridgecrest and Kearney using the attributes of price, delivery time, quality, and design features.
3. Draw a strategy map as in Exhibit 12-2 with two strategic objectives you would expect to see under each balanced scorecard perspective.
4. For each strategic objective indicate a measure you would expect to see in Ridgecrest's balanced scorecard for 2013.

12-17 Analysis of growth, price-recovery, and productivity components (continuation of 12-16). An analysis of Ridgecrest's operating-income changes between 2012 and 2013 shows the following:

Operating income for 2012	$1, 900,000
Add growth component	95,000
Deduct price-recovery component	(82,000)
Add productivity component	160,000
Operating income for 2013	$2, 073,000

The industry market size for electric motors did not grow in 2013, input prices did not change, and Ridgecrest reduced the prices of its motors.

Required

1. Was Ridgecrest's gain in operating income in 2013 consistent with the strategy you identified in requirement 1 of Exercise 12-16?
2. Explain the productivity component. In general, does it represent savings in only variable costs, only fixed costs, or both variable and fixed costs?

12-18 Strategy, balanced scorecard, merchandising operation. Ramiro & Sons buys T-shirts in bulk, applies its own trendsetting silk-screen designs, and then sells the T-shirts to a number of retailers. Ramiro wants to be known for its trendsetting designs, and it wants every teenager to be seen in a distinctive Ramiro T-shirt. Ramiro presents the following data for its first two years of operations, 2012 and 2013.

	2012	2013
1 Number of T-shirts purchased	225,500	257,000
2 Number of T-shirts discarded	20,500	24,000
3 Number of T-shirts sold (row 1 − (row 2)	205,000	233,000
4 Average selling price	$ 32.00	$ 33.00
5 Average cost per T-shirt	$ 17.00	$ 15.00
6 Administrative capacity (number of customers)	4,700	4,450
7 Administrative costs	$1,739,000	$1,691,000
8 Administrative cost per customer (row 8 ÷ row 7)	$ 370	$ 380

Administrative costs depend on the number of customers Ramiro has created capacity to support, not on the actual number of customers served. Ramiro had 4,300 customers in 2012 and 4,200 customers in 2013.

Required

1. Is Ramiro's strategy one of product differentiation or cost leadership? Explain briefly.
2. Describe briefly the key measures Ramiro should include in its balanced scorecard and the reasons for doing so.

12-19 Strategic analysis of operating income (continuation of 12-18). Refer to Exercise 12-18.

Required

1. Calculate Ramiro's operating income in both 2012 and 2013.
2. Calculate the growth, price-recovery, and productivity components that explain the change in operating income from 2012 to 2013.
3. Comment on your answers in requirement 2. What does each of these components indicate?

12-20 Analysis of growth, price-recovery, and productivity components (continuation of 12-19). Refer to Exercise 12-19. Suppose that the market for silk-screened T-shirts grew by 10% during 2013. All increases in sales greater than 10% are the result of Ramiro's strategic actions.

Calculate the change in operating income from 2012 to 2013 due to growth in market size, product differentiation, and cost leadership. How successful has Ramiro been in implementing its strategy? Explain.

12-21 Identifying and managing unused capacity (continuation of 12-18). Refer to Exercise 12-18.

Required

1. Calculate the amount and cost of unused administrative capacity at the beginning of 2013, based on the actual number of customers Ramiro served in 2013.
2. Suppose Ramiro can only add or reduce administrative capacity in increments of 250 customers. What is the maximum amount of costs that Ramiro can save in 2013 by downsizing administrative capacity?
3. What factors, other than cost, should Ramiro consider before it downsizes administrative capacity?

12-22 Strategy, balanced scorecard. Stanmore Corporation makes a special-purpose machine, D4H, used in the textile industry. Stanmore has designed the D4H machine for 2013 to be distinct from its competitors. It has been generally regarded as a superior machine. Stanmore presents the following data for 2012 and 2013.

	2012	2013
1. Units of D4H produced and sold	200	210
2. Selling price	$40,000	$42,000
3. Direct materials (kilograms)	300,000	310,000
4. Direct material cost per kilogram	$8	$8.50
5. Manufacturing capacity in units of D4H	250	250
6. Total conversion costs	$2,000,000	$2,025,000
7. Conversion cost per unit of capacity (row 6 ÷ row 5)	$8,000	$8,100
8. Selling and customer-service capacity	100 customers	95 customers
9. Total selling and customer-service costs	$1,000,000	$940,500
10. Selling and customer-service capacity cost per customer (row 9 ÷ row 8)	$10,000	$9,900

Stanmore produces no defective machines, but it wants to reduce direct materials usage per D4H machine in 2013. Conversion costs in each year depend on production capacity defined in terms of D4H units that can be produced, not the actual units produced. Selling and customer-service costs depend on the number of customers that Stanmore can support, not the actual number of customers it serves. Stanmore has 75 customers in 2012 and 80 customers in 2013.

Required

1. Is Stanmore's strategy one of product differentiation or cost leadership? Explain briefly.
2. Describe briefly key measures that you would include in Stanmore's balanced scorecard and the reasons for doing so.

12-23 Strategic analysis of operating income (continuation of 12-22). Refer to Exercise 12-22.

Required

1. Calculate the operating income of Stanmore Corporation in 2012 and 2013.
2. Calculate the growth, price-recovery, and productivity components that explain the change in operating income from 2012 to 2013.
3. Comment on your answer in requirement 2. What do these components indicate?

12-24 Analysis of growth, price-recovery, and productivity components (continuation of 12-23). Suppose that during 2013, the market for Stanmore's special-purpose machines grew by 3%. All increases in market share (that is, sales increases greater than 3%) are the result of Stanmore's strategic actions.

Calculate how much of the change in operating income from 2012 to 2013 is due to the industry-market-size factor, product differentiation, and cost leadership. How successful has Stanmore been in implementing its strategy? Explain.

12-25 Identifying and managing unused capacity (continuation of 12-22). Refer to Exercise 12-22.

Required

1. Calculate the amount and cost of (a) unused manufacturing capacity and (b) unused selling and customer-service capacity at the beginning of 2013 based on actual production and actual number of customers served in 2013.
2. Suppose Stanmore can add or reduce its manufacturing capacity in increments of 30 units. What is the maximum amount of costs that Stanmore could save in 2013 by downsizing manufacturing capacity?
3. Stanmore, in fact, does not eliminate any of its unused manufacturing capacity. Why might Stanmore not downsize?

12-26 Strategy, balanced scorecard, service company. Southland Corporation is a small information-systems consulting firm that specializes in helping companies implement standard sales-management software. The market for Southland's services is very competitive. To compete successfully, Southland must deliver quality service at a low cost. Southland presents the following data for 2012 and 2013.

	2012	2013
1. Number of jobs billed	40	55
2. Selling price per job	$45,000	$42,000
3. Software-implementation labor-hours	25,000	28,000
4. Cost per software-implementation labor-hour	$58	$60
5. Software-implementation support capacity (number of jobs it can do)	70	70
6. Total cost of software-implementation support	$224,000	$252,000
7. Software-implementation support-capacity cost per job (row 6 ÷ row 5)	$3,200	$3,600

Software-implementation labor-hour costs are variable costs. Software-implementation support costs for each year depend on the software-implementation support capacity Southland chooses to maintain each year (that is, the number of jobs it can do each year). Software-implementation support costs do not vary with the actual number of jobs done that year.

Required

1. Is Southland Corporation's strategy one of product differentiation or cost leadership? Explain briefly.
2. Describe key measures you would include in Southland's balanced scorecard and your reasons for doing so.

12-27 Strategic analysis of operating income (continuation of 12-26). Refer to Exercise 12-26.

Required

1. Calculate the operating income of Southland Corporation in 2012 and 2013.
2. Calculate the growth, price-recovery, and productivity components that explain the change in operating income from 2012 to 2013.
3. Comment on your answer in requirement 2. What do these components indicate?

12-28 Analysis of growth, price-recovery, and productivity components (continuation of 12-27). Suppose that during 2013, the market for implementing sales-management software increases by 10%. Assume that any increase in market share more than 10% and any decrease in selling price are the result of strategic choices by Southland's management to implement its strategy.

Calculate how much of the change in operating income from 2012 to 2013 is due to the industry-market-size factor, product differentiation, and cost leadership. How successful has Southland been in implementing its strategy? Explain.

12-29 Identifying and managing unused capacity (continuation of 12-26). Refer to Exercise 12-26.

Required

1. Calculate the amount and cost of unused software-implementation support capacity at the beginning of 2013, based on the number of jobs actually done in 2013.
2. Suppose Southland can add or reduce its software-implementation support capacity in increments of 10 units. What is the maximum amount of costs that Southland could save in 2013 by downsizing software-implementation support capacity?
3. Southland, in fact, does not eliminate any of its unused software-implementation support capacity. Why might Southland not downsize?

Problems

MyAccountingLab

12-30 Balanced scorecard and strategy. Scott Company manufactures a DVD player called the Maxus. The company sells the player to discount stores throughout the country. This player is significantly less expensive than similar products sold by Scott's competitors, but the Maxus offers just DVD playback, compared with DVD and Blu-ray playback offered by competitor Nomad Manufacturing. Furthermore, the Maxus has experienced production problems that have resulted in significant rework costs. Nomad's model has an excellent reputation for quality.

Required

1. Draw a simple customer preference map for Scott and Nomad using the attributes of price, quality, and playback features. Use the format of Exhibit 12-1.
2. Is Scott's current strategy that of product differentiation or cost leadership?
3. Scott would like to improve quality and decrease costs by improving processes and training workers to reduce rework. Scott's managers believe the increased quality will increase sales. Draw a strategy map as in Exhibit 12-2 describing the cause-and-effect relationships among the strategic objectives you would expect to see in Scott's balanced scorecard.
4. For each strategic objective, suggest a measure you would recommend in Scott's balanced scorecard.

12-31 Strategic analysis of operating income (continuation of 12-30). Refer to Problem 12-30. As a result of the actions taken, quality has significantly improved in 2013 while rework and unit costs of the Maxus have decreased. Scott has reduced manufacturing capacity because capacity is no longer needed to support rework. Scott has also lowered the Maxus's selling price to gain market share and unit sales have increased. Information about the current period (2013) and last period (2012) follows.

	2012	2013
1. Units of Maxus produced and sold	8,000	11,000
2. Selling price	$95	$80
3. Direct materials used (kits*)	10,000	11,000
4. Direct material cost per kit*	$32	$32
5. Manufacturing capacity in kits processed	14,000	13,000
6. Total conversion costs	$280,000	$260,000
7. Conversion cost per unit of capacity (row 6 ÷ row 5)	$20	$20
8. Selling and customer-service capacity	90 customers	90 customers
9. Total selling and customer-service costs	$13,500	$16,200
10. Selling and customer-service capacity cost per customer (row 9 ÷ row 8)	$150	$180

* A kit is composed of all the major components needed to produce a DVD player.

Conversion costs in each year depend on production capacity defined in terms of kits that can be processed, not the actual kits started. Selling and customer-service costs depend on the number of customers that Scott can support, not the actual number of customers it serves. Scott has 70 customers in 2012 and 80 customers in 2013.

Required

1. Calculate operating income of Scott Company for 2012 and 2013.
2. Calculate the growth, price-recovery, and productivity components that explain the change in operating income from 2012 to 2013.
3. Comment on your answer in requirement 2. What do these components indicate?

12-32 Analysis of growth, price-recovery, and productivity components (continuation of 12-31). Suppose that during 2013, the market for DVD players grew 10%. All increases in market share (that is, sales increases greater than 10%) and decreases in the selling price of the Maxus are the result of Scott's strategic actions.

Required

Calculate how much of the change in operating income from 2012 to 2013 is due to the industry-market-size factor, product differentiation, and cost leadership. How does this relate to Scott's strategy and its success in implementation? Explain.

12-33 Identifying and managing unused capacity (continuation of 12-31). Refer to the information for Scott Company in Problem 12-31.

Required

1. Calculate the amount and cost of (a) unused manufacturing capacity and (b) unused selling and customer-service capacity at the beginning of 2013 based on actual production and actual number of customers served in 2013.
2. Suppose Scott can add or reduce its selling and customer-service capacity in increments of five customers. What is the maximum amount of costs that Scott could save in 2013 by downsizing selling and customer-service capacity?
3. Scott, in fact, does not eliminate any of its unused selling and customer-service capacity. Why might Scott not downsize?

12-34 Balanced scorecard. Following is a random-order listing of perspectives, strategic objectives, and performance measures for the balanced scorecard.

Perspectives	Performance Measures
Internal business process	Percentage of defective-product units
Customer	Return on assets
Learning and growth	Number of patents
Financial	Employee turnover rate
Strategic Objectives	Net income
Acquire new customers	Customer profitability
Increase shareholder value	Percentage of processes with real-time feedback
Retain customers	Return on sales
Improve manufacturing quality	Average job-related training-hours per employee
Develop profitable customers	Return on equity
Increase proprietary products	Percentage of on-time deliveries by suppliers
Increase information-system capabilities	Product cost per unit
Enhance employee skills	Profit per salesperson
On-time delivery by suppliers	Percentage of error-free invoices
Increase profit generated by each salesperson	Customer cost per unit
Introduce new products	Earnings per share
Minimize invoice-error rate	Number of new customers
	Percentage of customers retained

Required

For each perspective, select those strategic objectives from the list that best relate to it. For each strategic objective, select the most appropriate performance measure(s) from the list.

12-35 Balanced scorecard. (R. Kaplan, adapted) Petrocal, Inc., refines gasoline and sells it through its own Petrocal gas stations. On the basis of market research, Petrocal determines that 60% of the overall gasoline market consists of "service-oriented customers," medium- to high-income individuals who are willing to pay a higher price for gas if the gas stations can provide excellent customer service, such as a clean facility, a convenience store, friendly employees, a quick turnaround, the ability to pay by credit card, and high-octane premium gasoline. The remaining 40% of the overall market are "price shoppers" who look to buy the cheapest gasoline available. Petrocal's strategy is to focus on the 60% of service-oriented customers. Petrocal's balanced scorecard for 2013 follows. For brevity, the initiatives taken under each objective are omitted.

Objectives	Measures	Target Performance	Actual Performance
Financial Perspective			
Increase shareholder value	Operating-income changes from price recovery	$80,000,000	$85,000,000
	Operating-income changes from growth	$60,000,000	$62,000,000
Customer Perspective			
Increase market share	Market share of overall gasoline market	4%	3.8%
Internal-Business-Process Perspective			
Improve gasoline quality	Quality index	92 points	93 points
Improve refinery performance	Refinery-reliability index (%)	91%	91%
Ensure gasoline availability	Product-availability index (%)	99%	99.5%
Learning-and-Growth Perspective			
Increase refinery process capability	Percentage of refinery processes with advanced controls	94%	95%

Required

1. Was Petrocal successful in implementing its strategy in 2013? Explain your answer.
2. Would you have included some measure of employee satisfaction and employee training in the learning-and-growth perspective? Are these objectives critical to Petrocal for implementing its strategy? Why or why not? Explain briefly.
3. Explain how Petrocal did not achieve its target market share in the total gasoline market but still exceeded its financial targets. Is "market share of overall gasoline market" the correct measure of market share? Explain briefly.
4. Is there a cause-and-effect linkage between improvements in the measures in the internal-business-process perspective and the measure in the customer perspective? That is, would you add other measures to the internal-business-process perspective or the customer perspective? Why or why not? Explain briefly.
5. Do you agree with Petrocal's decision not to include measures of changes in operating income from productivity improvements under the financial perspective of the balanced scorecard? Explain briefly.

12-36 Balanced scorecard. Vic Corporation manufactures various types of color laser printers in a highly automated facility with high fixed costs. The market for laser printers is competitive. The various color laser printers on the market are comparable in terms of features and price. Vic believes that satisfying customers with products of high quality at low costs is key to achieving its target profitability. For 2013, Vic plans to achieve higher quality and lower costs by improving yields and reducing defects in its manufacturing operations. Vic will train workers and encourage and empower them to take the necessary actions. Currently, a significant amount of Vic's capacity is used to produce products that are defective and cannot be sold. Vic expects that higher yields will reduce the capacity that Vic needs to manufacture products. Vic does not anticipate that improving manufacturing will automatically lead to lower costs because Vic has high fixed costs. To reduce fixed costs per unit, Vic could lay off employees and sell equipment, or it could use the capacity to produce and sell more of its current products or improved models of its current products.

Vic's balanced scorecard (initiatives omitted) for the just-completed fiscal year 2013 follows.

Objectives	Measures	Target Performance	Actual Performance
Financial Perspective			
Increase shareholder value	Operating-income changes from productivity improvements	$2,000,000	$1,200,000
	Operating-income changes from growth	$2,500,000	$1,100,000
Customer Perspective			
Increase market share	Market share in color laser printers	4%	3.6%
Internal-Business-Process Perspective			
Improve manufacturing quality	Yield	88%	90%
Reduce delivery time to customers	Order-delivery time	23 days	20 days

Objectives	Measures	Target Performance	Actual Performance
Learning-and-Growth Perspective			
Develop process skills	Percentage of employees trained in process and quality management	92%	93%
Enhance information-system capabilities	Percentage of manufacturing processes with real-time feedback	90%	92%

Required

1. Was Vic successful in implementing its strategy in 2013? Explain.
2. Is Vic's balanced scorecard useful in helping the company understand why it did not reach its target market share in 2013? If it is, explain why. If it is not, explain what other measures you might want to add under the customer perspective and why.
3. Would you have included some measure of employee satisfaction in the learning-and-growth perspective and new-product development in the internal-business-process perspective? That is, do you think employee satisfaction and development of new products are critical for Vic to implement its strategy? Why or why not? Explain briefly.
4. What problems, if any, do you see in Vic improving quality and significantly downsizing to eliminate unused capacity?

12-37 Balanced scorecard, environmental, and social performance. Cerebral Chocolates makes custom-labeled, high-quality, specialty candy bars for special events and advertising purposes. The company employs several chocolatiers who were trained in Germany. The company offers many varieties of chocolate, including milk, semi-sweet, white, and dark chocolate. It also offers a variety of ingredients, such as coffee, berries, and fresh mint. The real appeal for the company's product, however, is its custom labeling. Customers can order labels for special occasions (for example, wedding invitation labels) or business purposes (for example, business card labels). The company's balanced scorecard for 2013 follows. For brevity, the initiatives taken under each objective are omitted.

Objectives	Measures	Target Performance	Actual Performance
Financial Perspective			
Increase shareholder value	Operating-income changes from price recovery	$500,000	$750,000
	Operating-income changes from growth	$100,000	$125,000
	Cost savings due to reduced packaging size	$20,000	$25,000
Customer Perspective			
Increase market share	Market share of overall candy bar market	8%	7.8%
Increase the number of new product offerings	Number of new product offerings	5	7
Increase customer acquisitions due to sustainability efforts	Percentage of new customers surveyed who required recycled paper options	35%	40%
Internal-Business-Process Perspective			
Reduce time to customer	Average design time	3 days	3 days
Increase quality	Internal quality rating (10-point scale)	7 points	8 points
Increase use of recycled materials	Recycled materials used as a percentage of total materials used	30%	32%
Learning-and-Growth Perspective			
Increase number of professional chocolatiers	Number of chocolatiers	5	6
Increase number of women and minorities in the workforce	Percentage of women and minorities in the workforce	40%	38%

Required

1. Was Cerebral successful in implementing its strategy in 2013? Explain your answer.
2. Would you have included some measure of customer satisfaction in the customer perspective? Are these objectives critical to Cerebral for implementing its strategy? Why or why not? Explain briefly.
3. Explain why Cerebral did not achieve its target market share in the candy bar market but still exceeded its financial targets. Is "market share of overall candy bar market" a good measure of market share for Cerebral? Explain briefly.
4. Do you agree with Cerebral's decision not to include measures of changes in operating income from productivity improvements under the financial perspective of the balanced scorecard? Explain briefly.
5. Why did Cerebral include balanced scorecard standards relating to environmental and social performance? Is the company meeting its performance objectives in these areas?

12-38 Balanced scorecard, social performance. Rocky Plain Company provides cable and Internet services in the greater Denver area. There are many competitors that provide similar services. Rocky Plain believes that the key to financial success is to offer a quality service at the lowest cost. Rocky Plain currently spends a significant amount of hours on installation and post-installation support. This is one area that the company has targeted for cost reduction. Rocky Plain's balanced scorecard for 2013 follows.

Objectives	Measures	Target Performance	Actual Performance
Financial Perspective			
Increase shareholder value	Operating-income changes from productivity	$1,200,000	$400,000
	Operating-income changes from growth	$260,000	$125,000
	Increase in revenue from new customer acquisition	$25,000	$12,000
Customer Perspective			
Increase customer satisfaction	Positive customer survey responses	70%	65%
Increase customer acquisition	New customers acquired through company sponsored community events	475	350
Internal-Business-Process Perspective			
Develop innovative services	Research and development costs as a percentage of revenue	5%	6%
Increase installation efficiency	Installation time per customer	5 hours	4.5 hours
Increase community involvement	Number of new programs with community organizations;	12	15
Decrease workplace injuries	Number of employees injured in the workplace	<3	7
Learning-and-Growth Perspective			
Increase employee competence	Number of annual training-hours per employee	10	11
Increase leadership skills	Number of leadership workshops offered	2	1
Increase employee safety awareness	Percent of employees who have completed safety certification training	100%	95%

Required

1. Was Rocky Plain successful in implementing its strategy in 2013? Explain.
2. Do you agree with Rocky Plain's decision to include measures of developing innovative services (research and development costs) in the internal-business-process perspective of the balanced scorecard? Explain briefly.
3. Is there a cause-and-effect linkage between the measures in the internal-business-process perspective and the customer perspective? That is, would you add other measures to the internal-business-process perspective or the customer perspective? Why or why not? Explain briefly.
4. Why do you think Rocky Plain included balanced scorecard measures relating to employee safety and community engagement? How well is the company doing on these measures?

12-39 Balanced scorecard, environmental, and social performance. SmoothAir is a no-frills airline that services the Midwest. Its mission is to be the only short-haul, low-fare, high-frequency, point-to-point carrier in the Midwest. However, there are several large commercial carriers offering air transportation, and SmoothAir knows that it cannot compete with them based on the services those carriers provide. SmoothAir has chosen to reduce costs by not offering many inflight services, such as food and entertainment options. Instead, the company is dedicated to providing the highest quality transportation at the lowest fare. SmoothAir's balanced scorecard measures (and actual results) for 2013 follow:

Objectives	Measures	Target Performance	Actual Performance
Financial Perspective			
Increase shareholder value	Operating-income changes from productivity	$1,200,000	$1,400,000
	Operating-income changes from price recovery	$450,000	$600,000
	Operating-income changes from growth	$500,000	$660,000
	Cost savings due to reduction in jet fuel consumption	$150,000	$180,000
Customer Perspective			
Increase the number of on-time arrivals	FAA on-time arrival ranking	1st in industry	2nd in industry
Improve brand image	Percentage of customer survey respondents with greater than 90% approval rating on company's sustainability efforts	100%	96%
Internal-Business-Process Perspective			
Reduce turnaround time	On-ground time	<25 minutes	30 minutes
Reduce CO2 emissions	Number of engineering changes that decreased CO2 emissions	10	9
Learning-and-Growth Perspective			
Align ground crews	% of ground crew stockholders	70%	68%
Acquire new energy management tool and technology	Achieve ISO 50001 certification in energy management	Acquire certification by Dec. 31	Acquired certification by Dec. 31

Required

1. What is SmoothAir's strategy? Was SmoothAir successful in implementing its strategy in 2013? Explain your answer.
2. Based on the strategy identified in requirement 1 above, what role does the price-recovery component play in explaining the success of SmoothAir?
3. Would you have included customer-service measures in the customer perspective? Why or why not? Explain briefly.
4. Would you have included some measure of employee satisfaction and employee training in the learning-and-growth perspective? Would you consider this objective critical to SmoothAir for implementing its strategy? Why or why not? Explain briefly.
5. Why do you think Smooth Air has introduced environmental measures in its balanced scorecard? Is the company meeting its performance objectives in this area?

12-40 Partial productivity measurement. Gable Company manufactures wallets from fabric. In 2013, Gable made 2,160,000 wallets using 1,600,000 yards of fabric. In 2013, Gable has capacity to make 2,448,000 wallets and incurs a cost of $8,568,000 for this capacity. In 2014, Gable plans to make 2,203,200 wallets, make fabric use more efficient, and reduce capacity.

Suppose that in 2014 Gable makes 2,203,200 wallets, uses 1,440,000 yards of fabric, and reduces capacity to 2,295,000 wallets at a cost of $7,803,000.

Required

1. Calculate the partial-productivity ratios for materials and conversion (capacity costs) for 2014, and compare them to a benchmark for 2013 calculated based on 2014 output.
2. How can Gable Company use the information from the partial-productivity calculations?

12-41 Total factor productivity (continuation of 12-40). Refer to the data for Problem 12-40. Assume the fabric costs $4.00 per yard in 2014 and $4.10 per yard in 2013.

Required

1. Compute Gable Company's total factor productivity (TFP) for 2014.
2. Compare TFP for 2014 with a benchmark TFP for 2013 inputs based on 2014 prices and output.
3. What additional information does TFP provide that partial productivity measures do not?

13 Pricing Decisions and Cost Management

Learning Objectives

1. Discuss the three major factors that affect pricing decisions
2. Understand how companies make long-run pricing decisions
3. Price products using the target-costing approach
4. Apply the concepts of cost incurrence and locked-in costs
5. Price products using the cost-plus approach
6. Use life-cycle budgeting and costing when making pricing decisions
7. Describe two pricing practices in which noncost factors are important
8. Explain the effects of antitrust laws on pricing

Most companies carefully analyze their input costs and the prices of their products.

They know if the price is too high, customers will go to competitors; if the price is too low, the company won't be able to cover the cost of making the product. A company must also know how its customers will react to particular pricing strategies. When J. C. Penney changed its pricing strategy, its customers were not happy.

Fair and Square: Not What J. C. Penney Customers Wanted

A company's pricing decisions rely on a deep understanding of customers, competitors, and costs. J. C. Penney, once considered America's most venerated department store chain, radically altered its pricing strategy in February 2012. Under pressure from big box retailers and smaller specialty stores, J. C. Penney switched from its existing high-low pricing strategy, in which the retailer ran frequent sales promotions at deep discounts off its higher list prices, to an everyday low pricing model that eschewed sales and clearance discounting.

Dubbed "Fair and Square" pricing by chief executive officer Ron Johnson, the new pricing strategy was meant to simplify J. C. Penney's pricing strategy and make it more straightforward for customers. With consistent prices every day and less frequent price promotions, J. C. Penney touted its new pricing strategy as offering "no games, no gimmicks" and invited customers to "do the math" to see how it offered them cheaper prices on a regular basis. The company viewed its new strategy as a way to escape the high cost and downward spiral of escalating price promotions. In 2011, J. C. Penney spent $1.2 billion to execute 590 sales events and promotions and generated 72% of its $17.3 billion in annual revenue from products sold at steep discounts of more than 50% off the list price.

Launched without any consumer testing, the new pricing strategy failed dramatically. Customers voted with their feet, leaving the retailer in droves when they could not get products at the discounted price they had come to expect. In 2012, J. C. Penney's sales fell by 25%, or $4.3 billion. In response, the company's board fired Ron Johnson

Sources: Based on Elie Ofek and Jill Avery, *J. C. Penney's 'Fair and Square' Pricing Strategy,* HBS No. 9-513-036 (Boston: Harvard Business School Publishing, 2013); and Joann Lublin and Dana Mattioli, "Penney CEO Out, Old Boss Back In," *The Wall Street Journal* (April 8, 2013).

and re-hired his predecessor, Myron Ullman, to undo "Fair and Square" pricing. "I wouldn't recommend that we go back to the way J. C. Penney was when I left. Things change," Ullman said. But, he added, "there's no reason to try and alienate customers who want to try and shop at J. C. Penney."

Managers at many companies, such as IKEA, Unilever, and Walmart, are strategic in their pricing decisions. This chapter describes how managers evaluate demand at different prices and manage customers and costs across the value chain and over a product's life cycle to achieve profitability.

Major Factors that Affect Pricing Decisions

Learning Objective 1

Discuss the three major factors that affect pricing decisions

...customers, competitors, and costs

Consider for a moment how managers at Adidas might price their newest line of sneakers or how decision makers at Comcast would determine how much to charge for a monthly subscription for Internet service. How managers price a product or a service ultimately depends on demand and supply. Three influences on demand and supply are customers, competitors, and costs.

Customers

Customers influence price through their effect on the demand for a product or service. The demand is affected by factors such as the features of a product and its quality. Managers always examine pricing decisions through the eyes of their customers and then manage costs to earn a profit.

Competitors

No business operates in a vacuum. Managers must always be aware of the actions of their competitors. At one extreme, for companies such as Home Depot or Texas Instruments, alternative or substitute products of competitors hurt demand and cause them to lower prices. At the other extreme, companies such as Apple and Porsche have distinctive products and limited competition and are free to set higher prices. When there are competitors, managers try to learn about competitors' technologies, plant capacities, and operating strategies to estimate competitors' costs—valuable information when setting prices.

Because competition spans international borders, fluctuations in exchange rates between different countries' currencies affect costs and pricing decisions. For example, if the yuan weakens against the U.S. dollar, Chinese producers receive more yuan for each dollar of sales. These producers can lower prices and still make a profit; Chinese products become cheaper for American consumers and, consequently, more competitive in U.S. markets.

Costs

Costs influence prices because they affect supply. The lower the cost of producing a product, such as a Toyota Prius or a Nokia cell phone, the greater the quantity of product the company is willing to supply. As companies increase supply, the cost of producing an additional unit initially declines but eventually increases and companies supply products as long as the revenue from selling additional units exceeds the cost of producing them. Managers who understand the cost of producing products set prices that make the products attractive to customers while maximizing operating income.

Weighing Customers, Competitors, and Costs

Surveys indicate that managers weigh customers, competitors, and costs differently when making pricing decisions. At one extreme, companies operating in a perfectly competitive market sell very similar commodity products, such as wheat, rice, steel, and aluminum. The managers at these companies have no control over setting prices and must accept the price determined by a market consisting of many participants. Cost information only helps managers decide the quantity of output to produce to maximize operating income.

In less-competitive markets, such as those for cameras, televisions, and cellular phones, products are differentiated, and all three factors affect prices: The value customers place on a product and the prices charged for competing products affect demand, and the costs of producing and delivering the product affect supply.

As competition lessens even more, such as in microprocessors and operating software, the key factor affecting pricing decisions is the customer's willingness to pay based on the value that customers place on the product or service, not costs or competitors. In the extreme, there are monopolies. A monopolist has no competitors and has much more leeway to set high prices. Nevertheless, there are limits. The higher the price a monopolist sets, the lower the demand for the monopolist's product because customers will either seek substitute products or forgo buying the product.

Decision Point

What are the three major factors affecting pricing decisions?

Learning Objective 2

Understand how companies make long-run pricing decisions

...consider all future variable and fixed costs and earn a target return on investment

Costing and Pricing for the Long Run

Long-run pricing is a strategic decision designed to build long-run relationships with customers based on stable and predictable prices. Managers prefer a stable price because it reduces the need for continuous monitoring of prices, improves planning, and builds long-run buyer–seller relationships. McDonald's maintains a stable price with its Dollar Menu of fast food items, as does Apple, which always prices its new entry-level iPad at $499. But to charge a stable price and earn the target long-run return, managers must know and manage long-run costs of supplying products to customers, which includes *all* future direct and indirect costs. Recall that *indirect costs* of a particular cost object are costs that are related to that cost object but cannot be traced to it in an economically feasible (cost-effective) way. These costs often comprise a large percentage of the overall costs assigned to cost objects such as products, customers, and distribution channels.

Consider cost-allocation issues at Astel Computers. Astel manufactures two products: a server called Deskpoint and a Pentium chip–based personal computer called Provalue. The following figure illustrates six business functions in Astel's value chain.

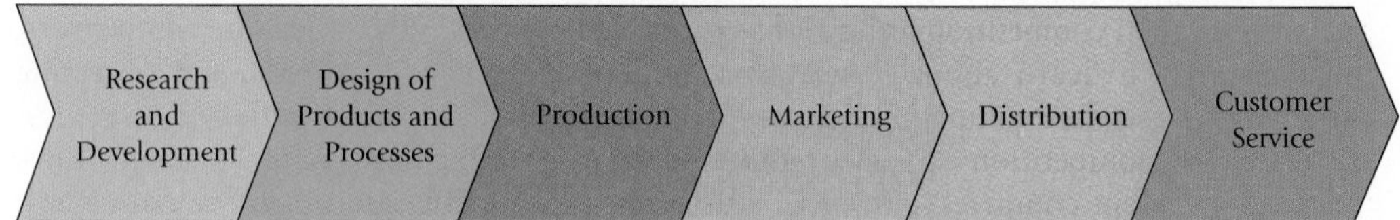

Exhibit 13-1 illustrates four purposes of cost allocation. Different sets of costs are appropriate for different purposes described in the exhibit. When making pricing decisions for Deskpoint and Provalue, Astel's managers allocate indirect costs from all six business functions. Why? Because in the long run, it is only worthwhile to sell a product if the price customers are willing to pay for the product exceeds all costs incurred to produce and sell it while earning a reasonable return on invested capital.

Cost allocations and product profitability analyses affect the products that managers promote. Compensating salespersons on product profitability, calculated based on fully allocated costs, motivates the sales staff to promote higher-margin products. Cost

Exhibit 13-1 Purposes of Cost Allocation

Purpose	Examples
1. To provide information for economic decisions	To decide on the selling price for a product or service To decide whether to add a new product feature
2. To motivate managers and other employees	To encourage the design of products that are simpler to manufacture or less costly to service To encourage sales representatives to emphasize high-margin products or services
3. To justify costs or compute reimbursement amounts	To cost products at a "fair" price, often required by law and government defense contracts To compute reimbursement for a consulting firm based on a percentage of the cost savings resulting from the implementation of its recommendations
4. To measure income and assets	To cost inventories for reporting to external parties To cost inventories for reporting to tax authorities

allocations also influence managers' cost management decisions. For example, to manage purchasing and ordering costs, Astel's managers might ask designers to use fewer components to manufacture Provalue. These design decisions will affect costs in some, but not all, value-chain categories (manufacturing costs but not customer service costs).

Cost allocations are sometimes used to justify cost reimbursements. Astel's contract to supply computers to the U.S. government is based on costs. The cost reimbursement rules for the U.S. government allow fully allocated manufacturing and design costs plus a profit margin but explicitly exclude marketing costs.

Inventory valuation for income and asset measurement requires cost allocation to calculate the cost of manufacturing inventory. For this purpose, Astel allocates only manufacturing costs to products and no costs from other parts of the value chain such as R&D, marketing, or distribution.

Cost allocation is another example of the different costs for different purposes theme of the book. We will discuss cost-allocation in the next several chapters. In this chapter, we focus on the role of cost allocation when making long-run pricing decisions based on costs throughout the value chain.

Calculating Product Costs for Long-Run Pricing Decisions

Astel's market research indicates that the market for Provalue is becoming increasingly competitive. Astel's managers face an important decision about the price to charge for Provalue.

The managers start by reviewing data for the year just ended, 2013. Astel has no beginning or ending inventory of Provalue and manufactures and sells 150,000 units during the year. Astel uses activity-based costing (ABC) to allocate costs and calculate the manufacturing cost of Provalue. Astel's ABC system has:

- Three direct manufacturing costs: direct materials, direct manufacturing labor, and direct machining costs.
- Three manufacturing overhead cost pools: ordering and receiving components, testing and inspection of final products, and rework (correcting and fixing errors and defects).

Astel considers machining costs as a direct cost of Provalue because these machines are dedicated to manufacturing Provalue.[1]

[1] Recall that Astel makes a server, Deskpoint, and a PC, Provalue. If Deskpoint and Provalue had shared the same machines, Astel would have allocated machining costs on the basis of the budgeted machine-hours used to manufacture the two products and would have treated these costs as fixed overhead costs.

Astel uses a long-run time horizon to price Provalue. Over this horizon, Astel's managers observe the following:

- Direct material costs vary with the number of units of Provalue produced.
- Direct manufacturing labor costs vary with the number of direct manufacturing labor-hours used.
- Direct machining costs are fixed costs of leasing 300,000 machine-hours of capacity each year for multiple years. These costs do not vary with the number of machine-hours used each year. Each unit of Provalue requires 2 machine-hours. In 2013, Astel uses the entire machining capacity to manufacture Provalue (2 machine-hours per unit × 150,000 units = 300,000 machine-hours).
- Ordering and receiving, testing and inspection, and rework costs vary with the quantity of their respective cost drivers. For example, ordering and receiving costs vary with the number of orders. In the long run, staff members responsible for placing orders can be reassigned or laid off if fewer orders need to be placed or increased if more orders need to be processed.

The following Excel spreadsheet summarizes manufacturing cost information to produce 150,000 units of Provalue in 2013. Astel's managers derive the indirect cost per unit of the cost driver in column (6) by dividing the total costs in each cost pool by the quantity of cost driver calculated in column (5). (Calculations not shown.)

	A	B	C	D	E	F	G	H
1		Manufacturing Cost Information						
2		to Produce 150,000 Units of Provalue						
3	Cost Category	Cost Driver	Details of Cost Driver Quantities				Total Quantity of Cost Driver	Cost per Unit of Cost Driver
4	(1)	(2)	(3)		(4)		(5) = (3) × (4)	(6)
5	Direct Manufacturing Costs							
6	Direct materials	No. of kits	1	kit per unit	150,000	units	150,000	$460
7	Direct manufacturing labor (DML)	DML-hours	3.2	DML-hours per unit	150,000	units	480,000	$ 20
8	Direct machining (fixed)	Machine-hours					300,000	$ 38
9	Manufacturing Overhead Costs							
10	Ordering and receiving	No. of orders	50	orders per component	450	components	22,500	$ 80
11	Testing and inspection	Testing-hours	30	testing-hours per unit	150,000	units	4,500,000	$ 2
12	Rework				8%	defect rate		
13		Rework-hours	2.5	rework-hours per defective unit	12,000[a]	defective units	30,000	$ 40
14								
15	[a]8% defect rate × 150,000 units = 12,000 defective units							

Exhibit 13-2 shows the total cost of manufacturing Provalue in 2013 of $102 million subdivided into the various categories of direct costs and indirect costs. The

Exhibit 13-2

Manufacturing Costs of Provalue for 2013 Using Activity-Based Costing

	A	B	C
1		Total Manufacturing	
2		Costs for	Manufacturing
3		150,000 Units	Cost per Unit
4		(1)	(2) = (1) ÷ 150,000
5	Direct manufacturing costs		
6	Direct material costs		
7	(150,000 kits × $460 per kit)	$ 69,000,000	$460
8	Direct manufacturing labor costs		
9	(480,000 DML-hours × $20 per hour)	9,600,000	64
10	Direct machining costs		
11	(300,000 machine-hours × $38 per machine-hour)	11,400,000	76
12	Direct manufacturing costs	90,000,000	600
13			
14	Manufacturing overhead costs		
15	Ordering and receiving costs		
16	(22,500 orders × $80 per order)	1,800,000	12
17	Testing and inspection costs		
18	(4,500,000 testing-hours × $2 per hour)	9,000,000	60
19	Rework costs		
20	(30,000 rework-hours × $40 per hour)	1,200,000	8
21	Manufacturing overhead cost	12,000,000	80
22	Total manufacturing costs	$102,000,000	$680

manufacturing cost per unit in Exhibit 13-2 is $680. Manufacturing, however, is just one business function in the value chain. To set long-run prices, Astel's managers must calculate the *full cost* of producing and selling Provalue by allocating costs in all functions of the value chain.

For each nonmanufacturing business function, Astel's managers trace direct costs to products and allocate indirect costs using cost pools and cost drivers that measure cause-and-effect relationships (supporting calculations not shown). Exhibit 13-3 summarizes Provalue's 2013 operating income and shows that Astel earned $15 million from Provalue, or $100 per unit sold in 2013.

Alternative Long-Run Pricing Approaches

How should managers at Astel use product cost information to price Provalue in 2014? Two different approaches for pricing decisions are

1. Market-based
2. Cost-based, which is also called cost-plus

The market-based approach to pricing starts by asking, "Given what our customers want and how our competitors will react to what we do, what price should we charge?" Based on this price, managers control costs to earn a target return on investment. The cost-based approach to pricing starts by asking, "Given what it costs us to make this product, what price should we charge that will recoup our costs and achieve a target return on investment?"

Companies operating in *competitive* markets (for example, commodities such as steel, oil, and natural gas) use the market-based approach. The products produced or services provided by one company are very similar to products produced or services provided by others. Companies in these markets must accept the prices set by the market.

Exhibit 13-3

Profitability of Provalue Division for 2013 Using Value-Chain Activity-Based Costing

	A	B	C
1		Total Amounts	
2		for 150,000 Units	Per Unit
3		(1)	(2) = (1) ÷ 150,000
4	Revenues	$150,000,000	$1,000
5	Costs of goods sold[a] (from Exhibit 13-2)	102,000,000	680
6	Operating costs[b]		
7	R&D costs	2,400,000	16
8	Design costs of product and proces	3,000,000	20
9	Marketing and administration costs	15,000,000	100
10	Distribution costs	9,000,000	60
11	Customer-service costs	3,600,000	24
12	Operating costs	33,000,000	220
13	Full cost of the product	135,000,000	900
14	Operating income	$ 15,000,000	$ 100
15			
16	[a]Cost of goods sold = Total manufacturing costs because there is no beginning or ending inventory		
17	of Provalue in 2013		
18	[b]Numbers for operating cost line-items are assumed without supporting calculations		

Companies operating in *less competitive* markets offer products or services that differ from each other (for example, automobiles, computers, management consulting, and legal services) and can use either the market-based or cost-based approach as the starting point for pricing decisions. Some companies use the cost-based approach: They first look at costs because cost information is more easily available and then consider customers and competitors. Other companies use the market-based approach: They first look at customers and competitors and then look at costs. Both approaches consider customers, competitors, and costs. Only their starting points differ. Managers must always keep in mind market forces, regardless of which pricing approach they use. For example, building contractors often bid on a cost-plus basis but then reduce their prices during negotiations to respond to other lower-cost bids.

Decision Point

How do companies make long-run pricing decisions?

Companies operating in markets that are *not competitive* favor cost-based approaches. That's because these companies do not need to respond or react to competitors' prices. The margin they add to costs to determine price depends on the ability and willingness of customers to pay for the product or service.

We consider first the market-based approach.

Learning Objective 3

Price products using the target-costing approach

...target costing identifies an estimated price customers are willing to pay and then computes a target cost to earn the desired profit

Market-Based Approach: Target Costing for Target Pricing

Market-based pricing starts with a **target price**, which is the estimated price for a product or service that potential customers are willing to pay. Managers base this estimate on an understanding of customers' perceived value for a product or service and how competitors will price competing products or services. In today's business context, managers need to understand customers and competitors for three reasons:

1. Lower-cost competitors continually restrain prices.
2. Products have shorter lives, which leaves companies less time and opportunity to recover from pricing mistakes, loss of market share, and loss of profitability.
3. Customers are more knowledgeable because they have easy access to price and other information online and demand high-quality products at low prices.

Understanding Customers' Perceived Value

A company's sales and marketing organization, through close contact and interaction with customers, identifies customer needs and perceptions of product value. Companies such as Toshiba and Dell also conduct market research on what customers want and the prices they are willing to pay.

Competitor Analysis

To gauge how competitors might react to a prospective price, a manager must understand competitors' technologies, products or services, costs, and financial conditions. In general, the more distinctive a product or service, the higher the price a company can charge. Where do companies obtain information about their competitors? Usually from former customers, suppliers, and employees of competitors. Some companies *reverse-engineer*—disassemble and analyze competitors' products to determine product designs and materials and to understand the technologies competitors use. At no time should a manager resort to illegal or unethical means to obtain information about competitors. For example, a manager should never bribe current employees or pose as a supplier or customer in order to obtain competitor information.

Implementing Target Pricing and Target Costing

We use the Provalue example to illustrate the five steps in developing target prices and target costs.

Step 1: **Develop a Product That Satisfies the Needs of Potential Customers.** Astel's managers use customer feedback and information about competitors' products to finalize product features and design modifications for Provalue in 2014. Their market research indicates that customers do not value Provalue's extra features, such as special audio elements and designs that accommodate upgrades to make the PC run faster. Instead, customers want Astel to redesign Provalue into a no-frills but reliable PC and to sell it at a much lower price.

Step 2: **Choose a Target Price.** Astel's managers expect competitors to lower the prices of PCs to \$850. Astel's managers want to respond aggressively, reducing the price the company charges for Provalue by 20%, from \$1,000 to \$800 per unit. At this lower price, Astel's marketing manager forecasts an increase in annual sales from 150,000 to 200,000 units.

Step 3: **Derive a Target Cost per Unit by Subtracting Target Operating Income per Unit from the Target Price. Target operating income per unit** is the operating income that a company aims to earn per unit of a product or service sold. **Target cost per unit** is the estimated long-run cost per unit of a product or service that enables the company to achieve its target operating income per unit when selling at the target price.[2] *Target cost per unit* is the target price minus *target operating income per unit.* It often needs to be lower than the existing *full cost of the product.* Target cost per unit is really just that—a target—something the company must strive to achieve.

To earn the target return on capital, Astel needs to earn 10% target operating income per unit on the 200,000 units of Provalue it plans to sell.

Total target revenues	= \$800 per unit × 200,000 units = \$160,000,000
Total target operating income	= 10% × \$160,000,000 = \$16,000,000
Target operating income per unit	= \$16,000,000 ÷ 200,000 units = \$80 per unit
Target cost per unit	= Target price − Target operating income per unit
	= \$800 per unit − \$80 per unit = \$720 per unit
Total current full costs of Provalue	= \$135,000,000 (from Exhibit 13-3)
Current full cost per unit of Provalue	= \$135,000,000 ÷ 150,000 units = \$900 per unit

[2] For a more detailed discussion of target costing, see Shahid L. Ansari, Jan E. Bell, and the CAM-I Target Cost Core Group, *Target Costing: The Next Frontier in Strategic Cost Management* (Martinsville, IN: Mountain Valley Publishing, 2009). For implementation information, see Shahid L. Ansari, Dan Swenson, and Jan E. Bell, "A Template for Implementing Target Costing," *Cost Management* (September–October 2006): 20–27.

Provalue's \$720 target cost per unit is \$180 below its existing \$900 unit cost. Astel's managers must reduce costs in all parts of the value chain, from R&D to customer service, for example, by reducing prices of materials and components while maintaining quality.

Target costs include *all* future costs, variable costs, and costs that are fixed in the short run because in the long run a company's prices and revenues must recover all its costs if it is to remain in business. In contrast, for short-run pricing or one-time-only special order decisions, managers consider only those costs that change in the short run, which are mostly, but not exclusively, variable costs.

Step 4: **Perform Cost Analysis.** Astel's managers analyze specific aspects of the product to target for cost reduction:

- The functions performed by different component parts, such as the motherboard, disk drives, and graphics and video cards.
- The importance customers place on different functional features. For example, Provalue's customers value reliability more than video quality.
- The relationship and tradeoffs among functional features and component parts. For example, a simpler motherboard enhances reliability but cannot support a top-of-the-line video card.

Concepts in Action

Extreme Target Pricing and Cost Management at IKEA

IKEA is a global furniture retailing industry phenomenon. Known for products named after Swedish towns, modern design, flat packaging, and do-it-yourself instructions, IKEA has grown into the world's largest furniture retailer with 343 stores worldwide. How did this happen? Through aggressive target pricing, coupled with relentless cost management. IKEA's prices typically run 30% to 50% below its competitors' prices. Moreover, while the prices of other companies' products have increased over time, IKEA's prices have dropped 2% to 3% each year since 2000.

When IKEA decides to create new items, product developers survey competitors to determine how much they charge for similar items, if offered, and then select a target price that is 30% to 50% less than competitors' prices. With a product and price established, IKEA then determines what materials will be used and selects one of its 1,800 suppliers to manufacture the item through a competitive-bidding process. This value-engineering process promotes volume-based cost efficiencies throughout design and production. Aggressive cost management does not stop there. All IKEA products are designed to be shipped unassembled in flat packages, as the company estimates that shipping costs would be at least six times greater if all products were assembled before shipping.

What about products that have already been developed? IKEA applies the same cost management techniques to those products, too. For example, one of IKEA's best-selling products is the Lack bedside table, which has retailed for the same low price since 1981. Since hitting store shelves, more than 100 technical development projects have been performed on the Lack table. Despite the steady increase in the cost of raw materials and wages, IKEA has aggressively sought to reduce product and distribution costs to maintain the Lack table's initial retail price without jeopardizing the company's profit on the product. As founder Ingvar Kamprad once summarized, "Waste of resources is a mortal sin at IKEA. Expensive solutions are a sign of mediocrity, and an idea without a price tag is never acceptable."

Sources: Lisa Margonelli, "How IKEA designs its sexy price tags," *Business 2.0* (October 2002); Enrico Baraldi and Torkel Strömsten, "Managing product development the IKEA way. Using target costing in interorganizational networks," Working Paper, December 2009; Daniel Terdiman, "Anatomy of an IKEA product," CNET News.com, April 19, 2008, http://news.cnet.com/8301-13772_3-9923315-52.html, accessed June 2013; and Anna Ringstrom, "Ikea Founder to Leave Board," *The New York Times* (June 5, 2013).

Step 5: **Perform Value Engineering to Achieve Target Cost. Value engineering** is a systematic evaluation of all aspects of the value chain, with the objective of reducing costs and achieving a quality level that satisfies customers. Value engineering entails improvements in product designs, changes in materials specifications, and modifications in process methods. The Concepts in Action: Extreme Target Pricing and Cost Management at IKEA describes IKEA's approach to target pricing and target costing.

Decision Point

How do companies determine target costs?

Value Engineering, Cost Incurrence, and Locked-In Costs

Learning Objective 4

Apply the concepts of cost incurrence

...when resources are consumed

and locked-in costs

...when resources are committed to be incurred in the future

To implement value engineering, managers distinguish value-added activities and costs from non-value-added activities and costs. A **value-added cost** is a cost that, if eliminated, would reduce the actual or perceived value or utility (usefulness) customers experience from using the product or service. In the Provalue example, value-added costs are specific product features and attributes desired by customers, such as reliability, adequate memory, preloaded software, clear images, and prompt customer service.

A **non-value-added cost** is a cost that, if eliminated, would not reduce the actual or perceived value or utility (usefulness) customers gain from using the product or service. Examples of non-value-added costs are the costs of defective products and machine breakdowns. Companies seek to minimize non-value-added costs because they do not provide benefits to customers.

Activities and costs do not always fall neatly into value-added or non-value-added categories, so managers often have to apply judgment to classify costs. Several costs, such as supervision and production control, have both value-added and non-value-added components. When in doubt, some managers prefer to classify costs as non-value-added to focus organizational attention on cost reduction. The risk with this approach is that an organization may cut some costs that are value-adding, leading to poor customer experiences.

Despite these difficult gray areas, managers find it useful to distinguish value-added from non-value-added costs for value engineering. In the Provalue example, direct materials, direct manufacturing labor, and direct machining costs are value-added costs; ordering, receiving, testing, and inspection costs have both value-added and non-value-added components; and rework costs are non-value-added costs.

Astel's managers next distinguish cost incurrence from locked-in costs. **Cost incurrence** describes when a resource is consumed (or benefit forgone) to meet a specific objective. Costing systems measure cost incurrence. For example, Astel recognizes direct material costs of Provalue only when Provalue is assembled and sold. But Provalue's direct material cost per unit is *locked in,* or *designed in,* much earlier, when product designers choose the specific components in Provalue. **Locked-in costs,** or **designed-in costs,** are costs that have not yet been incurred but will be incurred in the future based on decisions that have already been made.

The best opportunity to manage costs is before costs are locked in, so Astel's managers model the effect of different product design choices on costs such as scrap and rework that will only be incurred later during manufacturing. They then control these costs by making wise design choices. Similarly, managers in the software industry reduce costly and difficult-to-fix errors that appear during coding and testing through better software design and analysis.

Exhibit 13-4 illustrates the locked-in cost curve and the cost-incurrence curve for Provalue. The bottom curve uses information from Exhibit 13-3 to plot the cumulative cost per unit incurred in different business functions of the value chain. The top curve plots cumulative locked-in costs. (The specific numbers underlying this curve are not presented.) Total cumulative cost per unit for both curves is $900, but there is *wide divergence between locked-in costs and costs incurred.* For example, product design decisions lock in more than 86% ($780 ÷ $900) of the unit cost of Provalue (including costs of direct materials, ordering, testing, rework, distribution, and customer service), when Astel incurs only about 4% ($36 ÷ $900) of the unit cost!

Exhibit 13-4

Pattern of Cost Incurrence and Locked-In Costs for Provalue

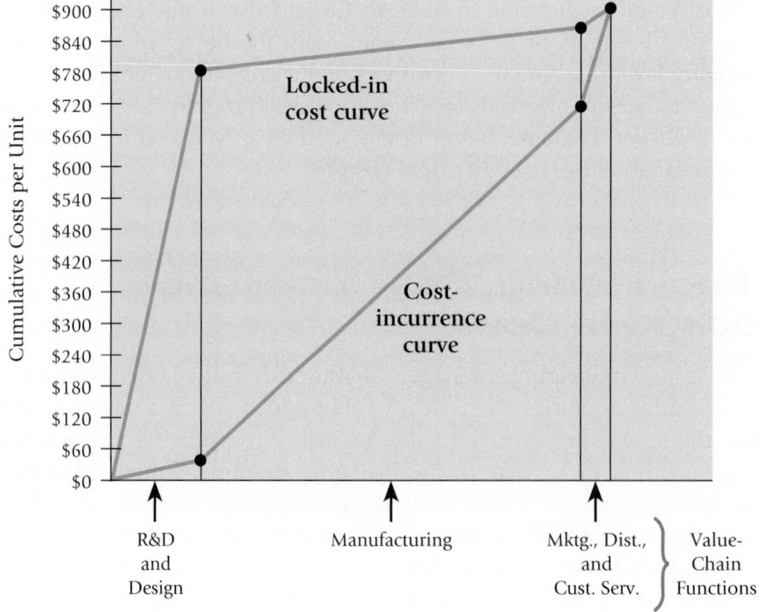

Value-Chain Analysis and Cross-Functional Teams

A cross-functional value-engineering team consisting of marketing managers, product designers, manufacturing engineers, purchasing managers, suppliers, dealers, and management accountants redesign Provalue—called Provalue II—to reduce costs while retaining features that customers value. Some of the team's ideas are:

- Use a simpler, more reliable motherboard without complex features to reduce manufacturing and repair costs.
- Snap-fit rather than solder parts together to decrease direct manufacturing labor-hours and related costs.
- Use fewer components to decrease ordering, receiving, testing, and inspection costs.
- Make Provalue lighter and smaller to reduce distribution and packaging costs.

Management accountants use their understanding of the value chain to estimate cost savings.

The team focuses on design decisions to reduce costs before costs get locked in. However, not all costs are locked in at the design stage. Managers use *kaizen,* or *continuous improvement* techniques, to reduce the time it takes to complete a task, eliminate waste, and improve operating efficiency and productivity. To summarize, the key steps in value-engineering are:

1. Understanding customer requirements and value-added and non-value-added costs.
2. Anticipating how costs are locked in before they are incurred.
3. Using cross-functional teams to redesign products and processes to reduce costs while meeting customer needs.

Achieving the Target Cost per Unit for Provalue

Exhibit 13-5 uses an activity-based approach to compare cost-driver quantities and rates for the 150,000 units of Provalue manufactured and sold in 2013 and the 200,000 units of Provalue II budgeted for 2014. Value engineering decreases both value-added costs (by designing Provalue II to reduce direct materials and component costs, direct manufacturing labor-hours, and testing-hours) and non-value-added costs (by simplifying Provalue II's design to reduce rework). Value engineering also reduces the machine-hours

Exhibit 13-5 Cost-Driver Quantities and Rates for Provalue in 2013 and Provalue II for 2014 Using Activity-Based Costing

	A	B	C	D	E	F	G	H	I	J	K	L	M	N
1–2			**Manufacturing Cost Information for 150,000 Units of Provalue in 2013**						**Manufacturing Cost Information for 200,000 Units of Provalue II for 2014**					
3	**Cost Category**	**Cost Driver**	**Details of Actual Cost Driver Quantities**				**Actual Total Quantity of Cost Driver**	**Actual Cost per Unit of Cost Driver (p.520)**	**Details of Budgeted Cost Driver Quantities**				**Budgeted Total Quantity of Cost Driver**	**Budgeted Cost per Unit of Cost Driver (Given)**
4	**(1)**	**(2)**	**(3)**		**(4)**		**(5)=(3)×(4)**	**(6)**	**(7)**		**(8)**		**(9)=(7)×(8)**	**(10)**
5	**Direct Manufacturing Costs**													
6	Direct materials	No. of kits	1	kit per unit	150,000	units	150,000	$460	1	kit per unit	200,000	units	200,000	$385
7	Direct manuf. labor (DML)	DML hours	3.2	DML hours per unit	150,000	units	480,000	$ 20	2.65	DML hours per unit	200,000	units	530,000	$ 20
8	Direct machining (fixed)	Machine-hours					300,000	$ 38					300,000	$ 38
9	**Manufacturing Overhead Costs**													
10	Ordering and receiving	No. of orders	50	orders per component	450	compo-nents	22,500	$ 80	50	orders per compo-nent	425	compo-nents	21,250	$ 80
11	Testing and inspection	Testing-hours	30	testing-hours per unit	150,000	units	4,500,000	$ 2	15	testing hours per unit	200,000	units	3,000,000	$ 2
12	Rework				8%	defect rate					6.5%	defect rate		
13		Rework-hours	2.5	rework-hours per defective unit	12,000[a]	defective units	30,000	$ 40	2.5	rework-hours per defective unit	13,000[b]	defective units	32,500	$ 40
14														
15	[a]8% defect rate × 150,000 units = 12,000 defective units													
16	[b]6.5% defect rate × 200,000 units = 13,000 defective units													

required to manufacture Provalue II to 1.5 hours per unit. Astel can now use the 300,000 machine-hours of capacity to make 200,000 units of Provalue II (vs. 150,000 units for Provalue), reducing machining cost per unit. For simplicity, we assume that value engineering will not reduce the $20 cost per direct manufacturing labor-hour, the $80 cost per order, the $2 cost per testing-hour, or the $40 cost per rework-hour. (The Problem for Self-Study, pages 536–538, explores how value engineering can also reduce these cost-driver rates.)

Exhibit 13-6 presents the target manufacturing costs of Provalue II, using cost driver and cost-driver rate data from Exhibit 13-5. For comparison, Exhibit 13-6 also shows the actual 2013 manufacturing cost per unit of Provalue from Exhibit 13-2. Astel's managers expect the new design to reduce total manufacturing cost per unit by $140 (from $680

Exhibit 13-6 Target Manufacturing Costs of Provalue II for 2014

	A	B	C	D	E	F
1		PROVALUE II				PROVALUE
2		Budgeted		Budgeted		Actual Manufacturing
3		Manufacturing Costs		Manufacturing		Cost per Unit
4		for 200,000 Units		Cost per Unit		(Exhibit 13-2)
5		(1)		(2) = (1) ÷ 200,000		(3)
6	Direct manufacturing costs					
7	Direct material costs					
8	(200,000 kits × $385 per kit)	$ 77,000,000		$385.00		$460.00
9	Direct manufacturing labor costs					
10	(530,000 DML-hours × $20 per hour)	10,600,000		53.00		64.00
11	Direct machining costs					
12	(300,000 machine-hours × $38 per machine-hour)	11,400,000		57.00		76.00
13	Direct manufacturing costs	99,000,000		495.00		600.00
14	Manufacturing overhead costs					
15	Ordering and receiving costs					
16	(21,250 orders × $80 per order)	1,700,000		8.50		12.00
17	Testing and inspection costs					
18	(3,000,000 testing-hours × $2 per hour)	6,000,000		30.00		60.00
19	Rework costs					
20	(32,500 rework-hours × $40 per hour)	1,300,000		6.50		8.00
21	Manufacturing overhead costs	9,000,000		45.00		80.00
22	Total manufacturing costs	$108,000,000		$540.00		$680.00

to $540) and cost per unit in other business functions from $220 (Exhibit 13-3) to $180 (calculations not shown) at the budgeted sales quantity of 200,000 units. The budgeted full unit cost of Provalue II is 720 ($540 + $180), the target cost per unit. At the end of 2014, Astel's managers will compare actual costs and target costs to understand improvements they can make in subsequent target-costing efforts.

Unless managed properly, value engineering and target costing can have undesirable effects:

- Employees may feel frustrated if they fail to attain target costs.
- The cross-functional team may add too many features just to accommodate the different wishes of team members.
- A product may be in development for a long time as the team repeatedly evaluates alternative designs.
- Organizational conflicts may develop as the burden of cutting costs falls unequally on different business functions in the company's value chain, for example, more on manufacturing than on marketing.

Decision Point

Why is it important for managers to distinguish cost incurrence from locked-in costs?

To avoid these pitfalls, target-costing efforts should always (1) encourage employee participation and celebrate small improvements toward achieving the target cost, (2) focus on the customer, (3) pay attention to schedules, and (4) set cost-cutting targets for all value-chain functions to encourage a culture of teamwork and cooperation.

The target pricing approach is another illustration of the five-step decision-making process introduced in Chapter 1.

1. *Identify the problem and uncertainties.* The problem is the price to charge for Provalue in 2014. The uncertainties are identifying what customers want, how competitors will respond, and how to manage costs.
2. *Obtain information.* Astel's managers do market research to identify customer needs, the prices that competitors are likely to charge, and opportunities to reduce costs.

3. *Make predictions about the future.* Managers make predictions about the effect of different prices on sales volumes and how much they can reduce costs through value engineering and product redesign.
4. *Make decisions by choosing among alternatives.* Managers decide to reduce Provalue's price from $1,000 to $800, anticipating sales to increase from 150,000 units to 200,000 units in 2014.
5. *Implement the decision, evaluate performance, and learn.* Cross-functional value-engineering teams redesign Provalue to achieve a target cost of $720 per unit, considerably lower than the current cost of $900. At the end of 2014, managers will compare actual and target costs to evaluate performance and to identify ways to reduce costs even further.

Cost-Plus Pricing

Learning Objective 5

Price products using the cost-plus approach

...cost-plus pricing is based on some measure of cost plus a markup

Instead of using the market-based approach for long-run pricing decisions, managers sometimes use a cost-based approach. The general formula for setting a cost-based selling price adds a markup component to the cost base. Because a markup is added, cost-based pricing is often called cost-plus pricing, where the plus refers to the markup component. Costco uses cost-plus pricing when deciding how much to charge for products in its warehouse stores. Managers use the cost-plus pricing formula as a starting point. The markup component is usually flexible, depending on the behavior of customers and competitors. In other words, market conditions ultimately determine the markup component.[3] For example, Costco managers will reduce the prices of products if competitors such as Sam's Club offer these products at lower prices.

Cost-Plus Target Rate of Return on Investment

Suppose Astel uses a 12% markup on the full unit cost of Provalue II to compute the selling price. The cost-plus price is:

Cost base (full unit cost of Provalue II)	$720.00
Markup component of 12% (0.12 × $720)	86.40
Prospective selling price	$806.40

How do managers determine the markup percentage of 12%? One way is to choose a markup to earn a **target rate of return on investment,** which is the target annual operating income divided by invested capital. Invested capital can be defined in many ways. In this chapter, we define it as total assets—that is, long-term assets plus current assets. Suppose Astel's (pretax) target rate of return on investment is 18%, and Provalue II's capital investment is $96 million. The target annual operating income for Provalue II is:

Invested capital	$96,000,000
Target rate of return on investment	18%
Target annual operating income (0.18 × $96,000,000)	$17,280,000
Target operating income per unit of Provalue II ($17,280,000 ÷ 200,000 units)	$ 86.40

This calculation indicates that Astel needs to earn a target operating income of $86.40 on each unit of Provalue II. The markup ($86.40) expressed as a percentage of the full unit cost of the product ($720) equals 12% ($86.40 ÷ $720).

[3] Exceptions are pricing of electricity and natural gas in many countries, where prices are set by the government on the basis of costs plus a return on invested capital. In these situations, products are not subject to competitive forces and cost accounting techniques substitute for markets as the basis for setting prices.

Do not confuse the 18% target rate of return on investment with the 12% markup percentage.

- The 18% target rate of return on investment expresses Astel's expected annual operating income as a percentage of investment.
- The 12% markup expresses operating income per unit as a percentage of the full product cost per unit.

Astel uses the target rate of return on investment to calculate the markup percentage.

Alternative Cost-Plus Methods

Computing the specific amount of capital invested in a product is challenging because it requires difficult and arbitrary allocations of investments in equipment and buildings to individual products. The following table uses alternative cost bases (without supporting calculations) and assumed markup percentages to set prospective selling prices for Provalue II without explicitly calculating invested capital to set prices.

Cost Base	Estimated Cost per Unit (1)	Markup Percentage (2)	Markup Component (3) = (1) × (2)	Prospective Selling Price (4) = (1) + (3)
Variable manufacturing cost	$475.00	65%	$308.75	$783.75
Variable cost of the product	547.00	45	246.15	793.15
Manufacturing cost	540.00	50	270.00	810.00
Full cost of the product	720.00	12	86.40	806.40

The different cost bases and markup percentages give four prospective selling prices that are close to each other. In practice, a company chooses a reliable cost base and markup percentage to recover its costs and earn a return on investment. For example, consulting companies often choose the full cost of a client engagement as their cost base because it is difficult to distinguish variable costs from fixed costs.

The markup percentages in the preceding table vary a great deal, from a high of 65% on variable manufacturing cost to a low of 12% on full cost of the product. Why the wide variation? When determining a prospective selling price, a cost base such as variable manufacturing cost that includes fewer costs requires a higher markup percentage because the price needs to be set to earn a profit margin *and* to recover costs (fixed manufacturing costs and all nonmanufacturing costs) that have been excluded from the base.

Surveys indicate that most managers use the full cost of the product for cost-based pricing decisions—that is, they include variable costs and costs that are fixed in the short run when calculating the cost per unit. Managers include fixed cost per unit in the cost base for several reasons:

1. **Full recovery of all costs of the product.** In the long run, the price of a product must exceed the full cost of the product if a company is to remain in business. Using just the variable cost as a base may tempt managers to cut prices as long as prices are above variable cost and generate a positive contribution margin. As the experience in the airline industry has shown, price wars, when airline companies cut prices as long as they exceed variable costs, have caused airlines to lose money because revenues are too low to recover the full cost of the product. Using the full cost of the product as a basis for pricing reduces the temptation to cut prices below full costs.
2. **Price stability.** Limiting the ability and temptation of salespeople to cut prices by using the full cost of a product as the basis for pricing decisions also promotes price stability. Stable prices facilitate more accurate forecasting and planning for both sellers and buyers.
3. **Simplicity.** A full-cost formula for pricing does not require the management accountant to perform a detailed analysis of cost-behavior patterns to separate product costs into variable and fixed components. Variable and fixed cost components are difficult to identify for many costs such as testing, inspection, and setups.

Including fixed cost per unit in the cost base for pricing can be challenging. Allocating fixed costs to products can be arbitrary. Also, calculating fixed cost per unit requires a denominator level that is based on an estimate of capacity or expected units of future sales. Errors in these estimates will cause actual full cost per unit of the product to differ from the estimated amount. Despite these challenges, managers generally include fixed costs when making cost-based pricing decisions.

Cost-Plus Pricing and Target Pricing

The selling prices computed under cost-plus pricing are *prospective* prices. Suppose Astel's initial product design results in a $750 full cost for Provalue II. Assuming a 12% markup, Astel sets a prospective price of $840 [$750 + (0.12 × $750)]. In the competitive personal computer market, customer and competitor reactions to this price may force Astel to reduce the markup percentage and lower the price to, say, $800. Astel may then want to redesign Provalue II to reduce the full cost to $720 per unit, as in our example, and achieve a markup close to 12% while keeping the price at $800. The eventual design and cost-plus price must balance cost, markup, and customer reactions.

The target-pricing approach reduces the need to go back and forth among prospective cost-plus prices, customer reactions, and design modifications. In contrast to cost-plus pricing, target pricing first determines product characteristics and target price on the basis of customer preferences and expected competitor responses and then computes a target cost.

Suppliers who provide unique products and services, such as accountants and management consultants, usually use cost-plus pricing. Professional service firms set prices based on hourly cost-plus billing rates of partners, managers, and associates. These prices are, however, lowered in competitive situations. Professional service firms also take a multiple-year client perspective when deciding prices because clients prefer to work with a firm over multiple periods. Certified public accountants, for example, sometimes charge a client a low price initially to get the account and recover the lower profits or losses in the initial years by charging higher prices in later years.

Service companies such as home repair services, automobile repair services, and architectural firms use a cost-plus pricing method called the *time-and-materials method.* Individual jobs are priced based on materials and labor time. The price charged for materials equals the cost of materials plus a markup. The price charged for labor represents the cost of labor plus a markup. That is, the price charged for each direct cost item includes its own markup. Companies choose the markups to recover overhead costs and to earn a profit.

Decision Point

How do companies price products using the cost-plus approach?

Life-Cycle Product Budgeting and Costing

Learning Objective 6

Use life-cycle budgeting and costing when making pricing decisions

...accumulate all costs of a product from initial R&D to final customer service for each year of the product's life

Managers sometimes need to consider target prices and target costs over a multiple-year product life cycle. The **product life cycle** spans the time from initial R&D on a product to when customer service and support is no longer offered for that product. For automobile companies such as BMW, Ford, and Nissan, the product life cycle is 12 to 15 years to design, introduce, sell, and service different car models. For pharmaceutical products, the life cycle at companies such as Pfizer, Merck, and GlaxoSmithKline may be 15 to 20 years. For banks such as Wells Fargo and Chase, a product such as a newly designed savings account with specific privileges can have a life cycle of 10 to 20 years. Personal computers have a shorter life cycle of 2 to 3 years because rapid innovations in the computing power and speed of microprocessors that run the computers make older models obsolete.

In **life-cycle budgeting,** managers estimate the revenues and business function costs across the entire value chain from a product's initial R&D to its final customer service and support. **Life-cycle costing** tracks and accumulates business function costs across the entire value chain from a product's initial R&D to its final customer service and support. Life-cycle budgeting and life-cycle costing span several years.

Life-Cycle Budgeting and Pricing Decisions

Budgeted life-cycle costs provide useful information for strategically evaluating pricing decisions. Consider Insight, Inc., a computer software company, which is developing a new accounting package, "General Ledger." Assume the following budgeted amounts for General Ledger over a 6-year product life cycle:

Years 1 and 2

	Total Fixed Costs
R&D costs	$240,000
Design costs	160,000

Years 3 to 6

	Total Fixed Costs	Variable Cost per Package
Production costs	$100,000	$25
Marketing costs	70,000	24
Distribution costs	50,000	16
Customer-service costs	80,000	30

Exhibit 13-7 presents the 6-year life-cycle budget for General Ledger for three alternative-selling-price/sales-quantity combinations.

Exhibit 13-7 Budgeting Life-Cycle Revenues and Costs for "General Ledger" Software Package of Insight, Inc.[a]

	Alternative-Selling-Price/ Sales-Quantity Combinations		
	A	B	C
Selling price per package	$400	$480	$600
Sales quantity in units	5,000	4,000	2,500
Life-cycle revenues			
($400 × 5,000; $480 × 4,000; $600 × 2,500)	$2,000,000	$1,920,000	$1,500,000
Life-cycle costs			
R&D costs	240,000	240,000	240,000
Design costs of product/process	160,000	160,000	160,000
Production costs			
$100,000 + ($25 × 5,000); $100,000 + ($25 × 4,000); $100,000 + ($25 × 2,500)	225,000	200,000	162,500
Marketing costs			
$70,000 + ($24 × 5,000); $70,000 + ($24 × 4,000); $70,000 + ($24 × 2,500)	190,000	166,000	130,000
Distribution costs			
$50,000 + ($16 × 5,000); $50,000 + ($16 × 4,000); $50,000 + ($16 × 2,500)	130,000	114,000	90,000
Customer-service costs			
$80,000 + ($30 × 5,000); $80,000 + ($30 × 4,000); $80,000 + ($30 × 2,500)	230,000	200,000	155,000
Total life-cycle costs	1,175,000	1,080,000	937,500
Life-cycle operating income	$ 825,000	$ 840,000	$ 562,500

[a]This exhibit does not take into consideration the time value of money when computing life-cycle revenues or life-cycle costs. Chapter 21 outlines how this important factor can be incorporated into such calculations.

Some features of costs make life-cycle budgeting particularly important:

1. **The development period for R&D and design is long and costly.** When a company incurs a large percentage of total life-cycle costs before any production begins and any revenues are received, as in the General Ledger example, managers need to evaluate revenues and costs over the life cycle of the product in order to decide whether to begin the costly R&D and design activities.
2. **Many costs are locked in at R&D and design stages, even if R&D and design costs themselves are small.** In our General Ledger example, a poorly designed accounting software package, which is difficult to install and use, would result in higher marketing, distribution, and customer-service costs in several subsequent years. These costs would be even higher if the product failed to meet promised quality performance levels. A life-cycle revenue-and-cost budget prevents Insight's managers from overlooking these multiple-year relationships among business-function costs. Life-cycle budgeting highlights costs throughout the product's life cycle and, in doing so, facilitates target pricing, target costing, and value engineering at the design stage before costs are locked in. The amounts presented in Exhibit 13-7 are the outcome of value engineering.

Insight's managers decide to sell the General Ledger package for $480 per package because this price maximizes life-cycle operating income. They then compare actual costs to life-cycle budgets to obtain feedback and to learn about how to estimate costs better for subsequent products. Exhibit 13-7 assumes that the selling price per package is the same over the entire life cycle. For strategic reasons, however, Insight's managers may decide to *skim the market*, which means the company would charge higher prices to eager customers when General Ledger is first introduced and then lower prices later as the product matures. Or managers may decide to add new features in later years to differentiate the product to maintain prices and sales. The life-cycle budget must then incorporate the revenues and costs of these strategies.

Managing Environmental Costs

Managing environmental costs is another example of life-cycle costing and value engineering. Environmental laws like the U.S. Clean Air Act and the U.S. Superfund Amendment and Reauthorization Act have introduced tougher environmental standards, imposed stringent cleanup requirements, and introduced severe penalties for polluting the air and contaminating subsurface soil and groundwater. Environmental costs that are incurred over several years of the product's life cycle are often locked in at the product- and process-design stage. To avoid environmental liabilities, managers in industries such as oil refining, chemical processing, and automobile manufacturing practice value engineering; they design products and processes to prevent and reduce pollution over the product's life cycle. For example, laptop computer manufacturers like Hewlett-Packard and Apple have introduced costly recycling programs to ensure that chemicals from nickel-cadmium batteries do not leak hazardous chemicals into the soil.

Customer Life-Cycle Costing

In the previous section, we considered life-cycle costs from the perspective of a product or service. **Customer life-cycle costs** focus on the total costs incurred by a customer to acquire, use, maintain, and dispose of a product or service. Customer life-cycle costs influence the prices a company can charge for its products. For example, Ford can charge a higher price and/or gain market share if its cars require minimal maintenance for 100,000 miles. Similarly, Maytag charges higher prices for appliances that save electricity and have low maintenance costs. Boeing Corporation justifies a higher price for the Boeing 777 because the plane's design allows mechanics easier access to different areas of the plane to perform routine maintenance, reduces the time and cost of maintenance, and significantly decreases the life-cycle cost of owning the plane.

Decision Point

Describe life-cycle budgeting and lifecycle costing and when companies should use these techniques.

Learning Objective 7

Describe two pricing practices in which noncost factors are important

...price discrimination—charging different customers different prices for the same product—and peak-load pricing—charging higher prices when demand approaches capacity limits

Non-Cost Factors In Pricing Decisions

In some cases, cost is *not* a major factor in setting prices. We explore some of the ways that ability to pay, capacity limits, and purchasing power of customers influence price-setting independent of cost.

Price Discrimination

Consider the prices airlines charge for a round-trip flight from Boston to San Francisco. A coach-class ticket for a flight with a 7-day advance purchase is $450 if the passenger stays in San Francisco over a Saturday night. The ticket is $1,000 if the passenger returns without staying over a Saturday night. Can this price difference be explained by the difference in the cost to the airline of these round-trip flights? No, because it costs the same amount to transport the passenger from Boston to San Francisco and back, regardless of whether the passenger stays in San Francisco over a Saturday night. This difference in price is due to *price discrimination.*

Price discrimination is the practice of charging different customers different prices for the same product or service. How does price discrimination work in the airline example? The demand for airline tickets comes from two main sources: business travelers and pleasure travelers. Business travelers must travel to conduct business for their organizations, so their demand for air travel is relatively insensitive to price. Airlines can earn higher operating incomes by charging business travelers higher prices. Insensitivity of demand to price changes is called *demand inelasticity.* Also, business travelers generally go to their destinations, complete their work, and return home without staying over a Saturday night. Pleasure travelers, in contrast, usually don't need to return home during the week and prefer to spend weekends at their destinations. Because they pay for their tickets themselves, pleasure travelers' demand is price-elastic; lower prices stimulate demand while higher prices restrict demand. Airlines can earn higher operating incomes by charging pleasure travelers lower prices.

How can airlines keep fares high for business travelers while keeping fares low for pleasure travelers? Requiring a Saturday night stay discriminates between the two customer segments. The airlines price-discriminate by taking advantage of different sensitivities to prices exhibited by business travelers and pleasure travelers. Prices differ even though there is no difference in cost in serving the two customer segments.

What if economic conditions weaken such that business travelers become more sensitive to price? The airlines may then need to lower the prices they charge to business travelers. Following the terrorist attacks on the Unites States on September 11, 2001, airlines started offering discounted fares on certain routes without requiring a Saturday night stay to stimulate business travel. Business travel picked up and airlines started filling more seats than they otherwise would have. Unfortunately, travel did not pick up enough, and the airline industry as a whole suffered severe losses over the next few years.

Peak-Load Pricing

In addition to price discrimination, other noncost factors such as capacity constraints affect pricing decisions. **Peak-load pricing** is the practice of charging a higher price for the same product or service when demand approaches the physical limit of the capacity to produce that product or service. When demand is high and production capacity and therefore supply are limited, customers are willing to pay more to get the product or service. In contrast, slack or excess capacity leads companies to lower prices in order to stimulate demand and utilize capacity. Peak-load pricing occurs in the telephone, telecommunications, hotel, car rental, and electric-utility industries. During the 2012 Summer Olympics in London, for example, hotels charged very high rates and required multiple-night stays. Airlines charged high fares for flights into and out of many cities in the region for roughly a month around the time of the Games. Demand far exceeded capacity and the hospitality industry and airlines employed peak-load pricing to increase their profits.

International Pricing

Another example of factors other than costs affecting prices occurs when the same product is sold in different countries. Consider software, books, and medicines produced in one country and sold globally. The prices charged in each country vary much more than the costs of delivering the product to each country. These price differences arise because of differences in the purchasing power of consumers in different countries (a form of price discrimination) and government restrictions that may limit the prices that companies can charge.

Decision Point

Describe price discrimination, peak-load pricing, and price differences across countries.

Antitrust Laws and Pricing Decisions

Learning Objective 8

Explain the effects of antitrust laws on pricing

...antitrust laws attempt to counteract pricing below costs to drive out competitors or fixing prices artificially high to harm consumers

Legal considerations also affect pricing decisions. Companies are not always free to charge whatever price they like. For example, under the U.S. Robinson-Patman Act of 1936, a manufacturer cannot price-discriminate between two customers if the intent is to lessen or prevent competition for customers. Two key features of price-discrimination laws are:

1. Price discrimination is permissible if differences in prices can be justified by differences in costs.
2. Price discrimination is illegal only if the intent is to lessen or prevent competition.

The price discrimination by airline companies described earlier is legal because their practices do not hinder competition.

Predatory Pricing

To comply with U.S. antitrust laws, such as the Sherman Act, the Clayton Act, the Federal Trade Commission Act, and the Robinson-Patman Act, pricing must not be predatory.[4] A company engages in **predatory pricing** when it deliberately prices below its costs in an effort to drive competitors out of the market and restrict supply and then raises prices rather than enlarge demand.[5]

The U.S. Supreme Court established the following conditions to prove that predatory pricing has occurred:

- The predator company charges a price below an appropriate measure of its costs.
- The predator company has a reasonable prospect of recovering in the future, through larger market share or higher prices, the money it lost by pricing below cost.

The Supreme Court has not specified the "appropriate measure of costs."[6]

Most courts in the United States have defined the "appropriate measure of costs" as the short-run marginal or average variable costs.[7] In the case of *Adjustor's Replace-a-Car v. Agency Rent-a-Car,* Adjustor's (the plaintiff) claimed that it was forced to withdraw from the Austin and San Antonio, Texas, markets because Agency had engaged in predatory pricing.[8] To prove predatory pricing, Adjustor pointed to "the net loss from operations" in Agency's income statement, calculated after allocating Agency's headquarters overhead. The judge, however, ruled that Agency had not engaged in predatory pricing because the price it charged for a rental car never dropped below its average variable costs.

---

[4] Discussion of the Sherman Act and the Clayton Act is in Arnold I. Barkman and John D. Jolley, "Cost Defenses for Antitrust Cases," *Management Accounting* 67, No. 10 (1986): 37–40.

[5] For more details, see W. Kip Viscusi, John M. Vernon, and Joseph E. Harrington, *Economics of Regulation and Antitrust,* 4th ed. (Cambridge, MA: MIT Press, 2006); and Jessica L. Goldstein, "Single Firm Predatory Pricing in Antitrust Law: The Rose Acre Recoupment Test and the Search for an Appropriate Judicial Standard," *Columbia Law Review* 91 (1991): 1557–1592.

[6] *Brooke Group v. Brown & Williamson Tobacco,* 113 S. Ct. (1993); Timothy J. Trujillo, "Predatory Pricing Standards Under Recent Supreme Court Decisions and Their Failure to Recognize Strategic Behavior as a Barrier to Entry," *Iowa Journal of Corporation Law* (Summer 1994): 809–831.

[7] An exception is *McGahee v. Northern Propane Gas Co.* [858 F, 2d 1487 (1988)], in which the Eleventh Circuit Court held that prices below average total cost constitute evidence of predatory intent. For more discussion, see Phillip Areeda and Donald F. Turner, "Predatory Pricing and Related Practices under Section 2 of Sherman Act," *Harvard Law Review* 88 (1975): 697–733. For an overview of case law, see W. Kip Viscusi, John M. Vernon, and Joseph E. Harrington, *Economics of Regulation and Antitrust,* 4th ed. (Cambridge, MA: MIT Press, 2006). See also the "Legal Developments" section of the *Journal of Marketing* for summaries of court cases.

[8] *Adjustor's Replace-a-Car, Inc. v. Agency Rent-a-Car,* 735 2d 884 (1984).

The Supreme Court decision in *Brooke Group v. Brown & Williamson Tobacco* (*BWT*) made it more difficult for companies to prove predatory pricing. The Court ruled that pricing below average variable costs is not predatory if the company does not have a reasonable chance of later increasing prices or market share to recover its losses.[9] The defendant, BWT, a cigarette manufacturer, sold brand-name cigarettes and had 12% of the cigarette market. The introduction of generic cigarettes threatened BWT's market share. BWT responded by introducing its own version of generics priced below average variable cost, thereby making it difficult for generic manufacturers to continue in business. The Supreme Court ruled that BWT's action was a competitive response and not predatory pricing. That's because, given BWT's small 12% market share and the existing competition within the industry, it would be unable to later charge a monopoly price to recoup its losses.

Dumping

Closely related to predatory pricing is dumping. Under U.S. laws, **dumping** occurs when a non-U.S. company sells a product in the United States at a price below the market value in the country where it is produced, and this lower price materially injures or threatens to materially injure an industry in the United States. If dumping is proven, an antidumping duty can be imposed under U.S. tariff laws equal to the amount by which the foreign price exceeds the U.S. price. Cases related to dumping have occurred in the cement, computer, lumber, paper, semiconductor, steel, sweater, and tire industries. In November 2012, the U.S. Commerce Department announced it would place import duties of 24% to 36% on imports of imported Chinese-made solar panels. The U.S. International Trade Commission ruled that U.S. solar-panel makers had lost market share in the United States as a result of Chinese companies selling solar panels in the U.S. market below the market price in China. China said the ruling was "unfair" and plans to challenge the decision to the dispute settlement panel of the World Trade Organization (WTO), an international institution created with the goal of promoting and regulating trade practices among countries.[10]

Collusive Pricing

Decision Point
How do antitrust laws affect pricing?

Another violation of antitrust laws is **collusive pricing,** which occurs when companies in an industry conspire in their pricing and production decisions to achieve a price above the competitive price and so restrain trade. In 2013, for example, a federal judge ruled that Apple colluded with five major U.S. book publishers to drive up the prices of e-books.[11]

[9] *Brooke Group v. Brown & Williamson Tobacco,* 113 S. Ct. (1993).
[10] Ryan Tracy, "Washington to Hit Beijing With Solar-Panel Tariffs," *The Wall Street Journal* (November 8, 2012).
[11] Chad Bray, Joe Palazzolo, and Ian Sherr, "U.S. Judge Says Apple Colluded In E-Books," *The Wall Street Journal* (July 11, 2013).

Problem for Self-Study

Reconsider the Astel Computer example (pages 518–522). Astel's marketing manager realizes that a further reduction in price is necessary to sell 200,000 units of Provalue II. To maintain a target profitability of $16 million, or $80 per unit, Astel will need to reduce costs of Provalue II by $6 million, or $30 per unit. Astel targets a reduction of $4 million, or $20 per unit, in manufacturing costs, and $2 million, or $10 per unit, in marketing, distribution, and customer-service costs. The cross-functional team assigned to this task proposes the following changes to manufacture a different version of Provalue, called Provalue III:

1. Reduce direct materials and ordering costs by purchasing subassembled components rather than individual components.
2. Reengineer ordering and receiving to reduce ordering and receiving costs per order.
3. Reduce testing time and the labor and power required per hour of testing.
4. Develop new rework procedures to reduce rework costs per hour.

No changes are proposed in direct manufacturing labor cost per unit and in total machining costs.

The following table summarizes the cost-driver quantities and the cost per unit of each cost driver for Provalue III compared with Provalue II.

Home Insert Page Layout Formulas Data Review View

	A	B	C	D	E	F	G	H	I	J	K	L	M	N
1			Manufacturing Cost Information						Manufacturing Cost Information					
2			for 200,000 Units of Provalue II for 2014						for 200,000 Units of Provalue III for 2014					
3	Cost Category	Cost Driver	Details of Budgeted Cost Driver Quantities				Budgeted Total Quantity of Cost Driver	Budgeted Cost per Unit of Cost Driver	Details of Budgeted Cost Driver Quantities				Budgeted Total Quantity of Cost Driver	Budgeted Cost per Unit of Cost Driver
4	(1)	(2)	(3)		(4)		(5)=(3)×(4)	(6)	(7)		(8)		(9)=(7)×(8)	(10)
5	Direct materials	No. of kits	1	kit per unit	200,000	units	200,000	$385	1	kit per unit	200,000	units	200,000	$ 375
6	Direct manuf. labor (DML)	DML hours	2.65	DML hours per unit	200,000	units	530,000	$ 20	2.65	DML hours per unit	200,000	units	530,000	$ 20
7	Direct machining (fixed)	Machine-hours					300,000	$ 38					300,000	$ 38
8	Ordering and receiving	No. of orders	50	orders per component	425	components	21,250	$ 80	50	orders per component	400	components	20,000	$ 60
9	Test and inspection	Testing-hours	15	testing-hours per unit	200,000	units	3,000,000	$ 2	14	testing-hours per unit	200,000	units	2,800,000	$1.70
10	Rework				6.5%	defect rate					6.5%	defect rate		
11		Rework-hours	2.5	rework-hours per defective unit	13,000[a]	defective units	32,500	$ 40	2.5	rework-hours per defective unit	13,000[a]	defective units	32,500	$ 32
12														
13	[a]6.5% defect rate × 200,000 units = 13,000 defective units													

Required

Will the proposed changes achieve Astel's targeted reduction of $4 million, or $20 per unit, in manufacturing costs for Provalue III? Show your computations.

Solution

Exhibit 13-8 presents the manufacturing costs for Provalue III based on the proposed changes. Manufacturing costs will decline from $108 million, or $540 per unit (Exhibit 13-6), to $104 million, or $520 per unit (Exhibit 13-8), and will achieve the target reduction of $4 million, or $20 per unit.

Exhibit 13-8 Target Manufacturing Costs of Provalue III for 2014 Based on Proposed Changes

	A	B	C	D
1		**Budgeted**		**Budgeted**
2		**Manufacturing Costs**		**Manufacturing**
3		**for 200,000 Units**		**Cost per Unit**
4		**(1)**		**(2) = (1) ÷ 200,000**
5	Direct manufacturing costs			
6	Direct material costs			
7	(200,000 kits × $375 per kit)	$ 75,000,000		$375.00
8	Direct manufacturing labor costs			
9	(530,000 DML-hours × $20 per hour)	10,600,000		53.00
10	Direct machining costs			
11	(300,000 machine-hours × $38 per machine-hour)	11,400,000		57.00
12	Direct manufacturing costs	97,000,000		485.00
13				
14	Manufacturing overhead costs			
15	Ordering and receiving costs			
16	(20,000 orders × $60 per order)	1,200,000		6.00
17	Testing and inspection costs			
18	(2,800,000 testing-hours × $1.70 per hour)	4,760,000		23.80
19	Rework costs			
20	(32,500 rework-hours × $32 per hour)	1,040,000		5.20
21	Manufacturing overhead costs	7,000,000		35.00
22	Total manufacturing costs	$104,000,000		$520.00

Decision Points

The following question-and-answer format summarizes the chapter's learning objectives. Each decision presents a key question related to a learning objective. The guidelines are the answers to that question.

Decision	Guidelines
1. What are the three major factors affecting pricing decisions?	Customers, competitors, and costs influence prices through their effects on demand and supply; customers and competitors affect demand, and costs affect supply.
2. How do companies make long-run pricing decisions?	Companies consider all future costs (whether variable or fixed in the short run) and use a market-based or a cost-based pricing approach to earn a target return on investment.
3. How do companies determine target costs?	One approach to long-run pricing is to use a target price. Target price is the estimated price that potential customers are willing to pay for a product or service. Target cost per unit equals target price minus target operating income per unit. Target cost per unit is the estimated long-run cost of a product or service that when sold enables the company to achieve target operating income per unit. Value-engineering methods help a company make the cost improvements necessary to achieve target cost.

Decision	Guidelines
4. Why is it important for managers to distinguish cost incurrence from locked-in costs?	Cost incurrence describes when a resource is sacrificed. Locked-in costs are costs that have not yet been incurred but, based on decisions that have already been made, will be incurred in the future. To reduce costs, techniques such as value engineering are most effective *before* costs are locked in.
5. How do companies price products using the cost-plus approach?	The cost-plus approach to pricing adds a markup component to a cost base as the starting point for pricing decisions. Many different costs, such as full cost of the product or manufacturing cost, can serve as the cost base in applying the cost-plus formula. Prices are then modified on the basis of customers' reactions and competitors' responses. Therefore, the size of the "plus" is determined by the marketplace.
6. Describe life-cycle budgeting and life-cycle costing and when companies should use these techniques.	Life-cycle budgeting estimates and life-cycle costing tracks and accumulates the costs (and revenues) attributable to a product from its initial R&D to its final customer service and support. These life-cycle techniques are particularly important when (a) a high percentage of total life-cycle costs are incurred before production begins and revenues are earned over several years and (b) a high fraction of the life-cycle costs are locked in at the R&D and design stages.
7. Describe price discrimination, peak-load pricing, and price differences across countries.	Price discrimination is charging some customers a higher price for a given product or service than other customers. Peak-load pricing is charging a higher price for the same product or service when demand approaches physical-capacity limits. Under price discrimination and peak-load pricing, prices differ among different types of customers and across time periods even though the cost of providing the product or service is approximately the same. Prices for the same product differ across countries because of differences in the purchasing power of consumers and government restrictions.
8. How do antitrust laws affect pricing?	To comply with antitrust laws, a company must not engage in predatory pricing, dumping, or collusive pricing, which lessens competition; puts another company at an unfair competitive disadvantage; or harms consumers.

Terms to Learn

The chapter and the Glossary at the end of the book contain definitions of the following important terms:

collusive pricing **(p. 536)**
cost incurrence **(p. 525)**
customer life-cycle costs **(p. 533)**
designed-in costs **(p. 525)**
dumping **(p. 536)**
life-cycle budgeting **(p. 531)**
life-cycle costing **(p. 531)**
locked-in costs **(p. 525)**
non-value-added cost **(p. 525)**
peak-load pricing **(p. 534)**
predatory pricing **(p. 535)**
price discrimination **(p. 534)**
product life cycle **(p. 531)**
target cost per unit **(p. 523)**
target operating income per unit **(p. 523)**
target price **(p. 522)**
target rate of return on investment **(p. 529)**
value-added cost **(p. 525)**
value engineering **(p. 525)**

Assignment Material

Questions

MyAccountingLab

13-1 What are the three major influences on pricing decisions?

13-2 "Relevant costs for pricing decisions are full costs of the product." Do you agree? Explain.

13-3 Describe four purposes of cost allocation.

13-4 How is activity-based costing useful for pricing decisions?

13-5 Describe two alternative approaches to long-run pricing decisions.

13-6 What is a target cost per unit?

13-7 Describe value engineering and its role in target costing.

13-8 Give two examples of a value-added cost and two examples of a non-value-added cost.

13-9 "It is not important for a company to distinguish between cost incurrence and locked-in costs." Do you agree? Explain.

13-10 What is cost-plus pricing?

13-11 Describe three alternative cost-plus pricing methods.

13-12 Give two examples in which the difference in the costs of two products or services is much smaller than the difference in their prices.

13-13 What is life-cycle budgeting?

13-14 What are three benefits of using a product life-cycle reporting format?

13-15 Define predatory pricing, dumping, and collusive pricing.

MyAccountingLab

Exercises

13-16 Value-added, non-value-added costs. The Magill Repair Shop repairs and services machine tools. A summary of its costs (by activity) for 2013 is as follows:

a. Materials and labor for servicing machine tools	$1,100,000
b. Rework costs	90,000
c. Expediting costs caused by work delays	65,000
d. Materials-handling costs	80,000
e. Materials-procurement and inspection costs	45,000
f. Preventive maintenance of equipment	55,000
g. Breakdown maintenance of equipment	75,000

Required

1. Classify each cost as value-added, non-value-added, or in the gray area between.
2. For any cost classified in the gray area, assume 60% is value-added and 40% is non-value-added. How much of the total of all seven costs is value-added and how much is non-value-added?
3. Magill is considering the following changes: (a) introducing quality-improvement programs whose net effect will be to reduce rework and expediting costs by 40% and materials and labor costs for servicing machine tools by 5%; (b) working with suppliers to reduce materials-procurement and inspection costs by 20% and materials-handling costs by 30%; and (c) increasing preventive-maintenance costs by 70% to reduce breakdown-maintenance costs by 50%. Calculate the effect of programs (a), (b), and (c) on value-added costs, non-value-added costs, and total costs. Comment briefly.

13-17 Target operating income, value-added costs, service company. Calvert Associates prepares architectural drawings to conform to local structural-safety codes. Its income statement for 2013 is as follows:

Revenues	$701,250
Salaries of professional staff (7,500 hours × $52 per hour)	390,000
Travel	15,000
Administrative and support costs	171,600
Total costs	576,600
Operating income	$124,650

Following is the percentage of time spent by professional staff on various activities:

Making calculations and preparing drawings for clients	77%
Checking calculations and drawings	3
Correcting errors found in drawings (not billed to clients)	8
Making changes in response to client requests (billed to clients)	5
Correcting own errors regarding building codes (not billed to clients)	7
Total	100%

Assume administrative and support costs vary with professional-labor costs. Consider each requirement independently.

Required

1. How much of the total costs in 2013 are value-added, non-value-added, or in the gray area between? Explain your answers briefly. What actions can Calvert take to reduce its costs?
2. What are the consequences of misclassifying a non-value-added cost as a value-added cost? When in doubt, would you classify a cost as a value-added or non-value-added cost? Explain briefly.
3. Suppose Calvert could eliminate all errors so that it did not need to spend any time making corrections and, as a result, could proportionately reduce professional-labor costs. Calculate Calvert's operating income for 2013.
4. Now suppose Calvert could take on as much business as it could complete, but it could not add more professional staff. Assume Calvert could eliminate all errors so that it does not need to spend any time correcting errors. Assume Calvert could use the time saved to increase revenues proportionately. Assume travel costs will remain at $15,000. Calculate Calvert's operating income for 2013.

13-18 Target prices, target costs, activity-based costing. Snappy Tiles is a small distributor of marble tiles. Snappy identifies its three major activities and cost pools as ordering, receiving and storage, and shipping, and it reports the following details for 2013:

Activity	Cost Driver	Quantity of Cost Driver	Cost per Unit of Cost Driver
1. Placing and paying for orders of marble tiles	Number of orders	500	$50 per order
2. Receiving and storage	Loads moved	4,000	$30 per load
3. Shipping of marble tiles to retailers	Number of shipments	1,500	$40 per shipment

For 2013, Snappy buys 250,000 marble tiles at an average cost of $3 per tile and sells them to retailers at an average price of $4 per tile. Assume Snappy has no fixed costs and no inventories.

Required

1. Calculate Snappy's operating income for 2013.
2. For 2014, retailers are demanding a 5% discount off the 2013 price. Snappy's suppliers are only willing to give a 4% discount. Snappy expects to sell the same quantity of marble tiles in 2014 as in 2013. If all other costs and cost-driver information remain the same, calculate Snappy's operating income for 2014.
3. Suppose further that Snappy decides to make changes in its ordering and receiving-and-storing practices. By placing long-run orders with its key suppliers, Snappy expects to reduce the number of orders to 200 and the cost per order to $25 per order. By redesigning the layout of the warehouse and reconfiguring the crates in which the marble tiles are moved, Snappy expects to reduce the number of loads moved to 3,125 and the cost per load moved to $28. Will Snappy achieve its target operating income of $0.30 per tile in 2014? Show your calculations.

13-19 Target costs, effect of product-design changes on product costs. Neuro Instruments uses a manufacturing costing system with one direct-cost category (direct materials) and three indirect-cost categories:

a. Setup, production order, and materials-handling costs that vary with the number of batches
b. Manufacturing-operations costs that vary with machine-hours
c. Costs of engineering changes that vary with the number of engineering changes made

In response to competitive pressures at the end of 2012, Neuro Instruments used value-engineering techniques to reduce manufacturing costs. Actual information for 2012 and 2013 is as follows:

	2012	2013
Setup, production-order, and materials-handling costs per batch	$ 8,900	$8,000
Total manufacturing-operations cost per machine-hour	$ 64	$ 48
Cost per engineering change	$16,000	$8,000

The management of Neuro Instruments wants to evaluate whether value engineering has succeeded in reducing the target manufacturing cost per unit of one of its products, HJ6, by 5%.

Actual results for 2012 and 2013 for HJ6 are:

	Actual Results for 2012	Actual Results for 2013
Units of HJ6 produced	2,700	4,600
Direct material cost per unit of HJ6	$ 1,400	$ 1,300
Total number of batches required to produce HJ6	60	70
Total machine-hours required to produce HJ6	20,000	30,000
Number of engineering changes made	24	7

Required

1. Calculate the manufacturing cost per unit of HJ6 in 2012.
2. Calculate the manufacturing cost per unit of HJ6 in 2013.
3. Did Neuro Instruments achieve the target manufacturing cost per unit for HJ6 in 2013? Explain.
4. Explain how Neuro Instruments reduced the manufacturing cost per unit of HJ6 in 2013.
5. What challenges might managers at Neuro Instruments encounter in achieving the target cost? How might they overcome these challenges?

13-20 Target costs, effect of process-design changes on service costs. Sun Systems provides energy audits in residential areas of southern Ohio. The energy audits provide information to homeowners on the benefits of solar energy. A consultant from Sun Systems educates the homeowner about federal and state rebates and tax credits available for purchases and installations of solar heating systems. A successful energy audit results in the homeowner purchasing a solar heating system. Sun Systems does not install the solar heating system, but arranges for the installation with a local company. Sun Systems completes all necessary paperwork related to the rebates, tax credits, and financing. The company has identified three major activities that drive the cost of energy audits: identifying new contacts (that varies with the number of new contacts); traveling to and between appointments (that varies with the number of miles driven); and preparing and filing rebates and tax forms (that varies with the number of clerical hours). Actual costs for each of these activities in 2012 and 2013 are:

	2012	2013
Consultant labor cost per hour	$35.00	$35.00
Average cost per new contact	9.00	7.00
Travel cost per mile	0.55	0.65
Preparing and filing cost per clerical hour	9.10	9.50

In 2013, Sun Systems used value engineering to reduce the cost of the energy audits. Managers at Sun Systems want to evaluate whether value engineering has succeeded in reducing the target cost per audit by 5%.

Actual results for 2012 and 2013 for Sun Systems are:

	Actual Results for 2012	Actual Results for 2013
Successful audits performed	150	178
Number of new contacts	215	275
Miles driven	1,756	1,327
Total clerical hours	1,218	1,367
Consultant labor hours per audit	2.2	2

Required

1. Calculate the cost per audit in 2012.
2. Calculate the cost per audit in 2013.
3. Did Sun Systems achieve the target cost per audit in 2013? Explain.
4. What challenges might managers at Sun Systems encounter in achieving the target cost and how might they overcome these challenges?

13-21 Cost-plus target return on investment pricing. John Branch is the managing partner of a business that has just finished building a 60-room motel. Branch anticipates that he will rent these rooms for 16,000 nights next year (or 16,000 room-nights). All rooms are similar and will rent for the same price. Branch estimates the following operating costs for next year:

Variable operating costs	$4 per room-night
Fixed costs	
Salaries and wages	$170,000
Maintenance of building and pool	48,000
Other operating and administration costs	122,000
Total fixed costs	$340,000

The capital invested in the motel is $1,000,000. The partnership's target return on investment is 20%. Branch expects demand for rooms to be uniform throughout the year. He plans to price the rooms at full cost plus a markup on full cost to earn the target return on investment.

Required

1. What price should Branch charge for a room-night? What is the markup as a percentage of the full cost of a room-night?
2. Branch's market research indicates that if the price of a room-night determined in requirement 1 is reduced by 10%, the expected number of room-nights Branch could rent would increase by 10%. Should Branch reduce prices by 10%? Show your calculations.

13-22 Cost-plus, target pricing, working backward. TinRoof, Inc., manufactures and sells a do-it-yourself storage shed kit. In 2013, it reported the following:

Units produced and sold	3,200
Investment	$2,400,000
Markup percentage on full cost	8%
Rate of return on investment	12%
Variable cost per unit	$500

Required

1. What was TinRoof's operating income in 2013? What was the full cost per unit? What was the selling price? What was the percentage markup on variable cost?
2. TinRoof is considering increasing the annual spending on advertising by $175,000. The managers believe that the investment will translate into a 10% increase in unit sales. Should the company make the investment? Show your calculations.
3. Refer back to the original data. In 2014, TinRoof believes that it will only be able to sell 2,900 units at the price calculated in requirement 1. Management has identified $125,000 in fixed cost that can be eliminated. If TinRoof wants to maintain an 8% markup on full cost, what is the target variable cost per unit?

13-23 Life-cycle budgeting and costing, Jurgensen Manufacturing, Inc., plans to develop a new industrial-powered vacuum sweeper for household use that runs exclusively on rechargeable batteries. The product will take 6 months to design and test. The company expects the vacuum sweeper to sell 10,000 units during the first 6 months of sales; 20,000 units per year over the following 2 years; and 5,000 units over the final 6 months of the product's life cycle. The company expects the following costs:

Period	Cost	Total Fixed Cost for the Period	Variable Cost per Unit
Months 0–6	Design costs	$500,000	
Months 7–12	Production	$1,300,000	$90 per unit
	Marketing	$1,000,000	
	Distribution	$200,000	$10 per unit
Months 13–36	Production	$4,900,000	$70 per unit
	Marketing	$2,325,000	
	Distribution	$700,000	$8 per unit
Months 37–42	Production	$800,000	$60 per unit
	Marketing	$475,000	
	Distribution	$100,000	$7 per unit

Ignore time value of money.

Required

1. If Jurgensen prices the sweepers at $375 each, how much operating income will the company make over the product's life cycle? What is the operating income per unit?
2. Excluding the initial product design costs, what is the operating income in each of the three sales phases of the product's life cycle, assuming the price stays at $375?
3. How would you explain the change in budgeted operating income over the product's life cycle? What other factors does the company need to consider before developing the new vacuum sweeper?
4. Jurgensen is concerned about the operating income it will report in the first sales phase. It is considering pricing the vacuum sweeper at $425 for the first 6 months and decreasing the price to $375 thereafter. With this pricing strategy, Jurgensen expects to sell 9,500 units instead of 10,000 units in the first 6 months, 19,000 each year over the next 2 years, and 5,000 over the last 6 months. Assuming the same cost structure given in the problem, which pricing strategy would you recommend? Explain.

13-24 Considerations other than cost in pricing decisions. Fun Stay Express operates a 100-room hotel near a busy amusement park. During June, a 30-day month, Fun Stay Express experienced a 65% occupancy rate from Monday evening through Thursday evening (weeknights). On Friday through Sunday evenings (weekend nights), however, occupancy increases to 90%. (There were 18 weeknights and 12 weekend nights in June.) Fun Stay Express charges $85 per night for a suite. The company recently hired Gina Johnson to manage the hotel to increase the hotel's profitability. The following information relates to Fun Stay Express' costs:

	Fixed Cost	Variable Cost
Depreciation	$25,000 per month	
Administrative costs	$38,000 per month	
Housekeeping and supplies	$16,000 per month	$30 per room-night
Breakfast	$12,000 per month	$6 per breakfast served

Fun Stay Express offers free breakfast to guests. In June, there were an average of two breakfasts served per room-night on weeknights and 4 breakfasts served per room-night on weekend nights.

Required

1. Calculate the average cost per room-night for June. What was Fun Stay Express' operating income or loss for the month?
2. Gina Johnson estimates that if Fun Stay Express decreases the nightly rates to $75, weeknight occupancy will increase to 75%. She also estimates that if the hotel increases the nightly rate on weekend nights to $105, occupancy on those nights will remain at 90%. Would this be a good move for Fun Stay Express? Show your calculations.
3. Why would the guests tolerate a $30 price difference between weeknights and weekend nights?
4. A discount travel clearinghouse has approached Fun Stay Express with a proposal to offer last-minute deals on empty rooms on both weeknights and weekend nights. Assuming that there will be an average of three breakfasts served per night per room, what is the minimum price that Fun Stay Express could accept on the last-minute rooms?

MyAccountingLab

Problems

13-25 Cost-plus, target pricing, working backward. The new CEO of Rusty Manufacturing has asked for a variety of information about the operations of the firm from last year. The CEO is given the following information, but with some data missing:

Total sales revenue	?
Number of units produced and sold	500,000 units
Selling price	?
Operating income	$180,000
Total investment in assets	$2,250,000
Variable cost per unit	$4.00
Fixed costs for the year	$2,500,000

Required

1. Find (a) total sales revenue, (b) selling price, (c) rate of return on investment, and (d) markup percentage on full cost for this product.
2. The new CEO has a plan to reduce fixed costs by $225,000 and variable costs by $0.30 per unit while continuing to produce and sell 500,000 units. Using the same markup percentage as in requirement 1, calculate the new selling price.

3. Assume the CEO institutes the changes in requirement 2 including the new selling price. However, the reduction in variable cost has resulted in lower product quality resulting in 5% fewer units being sold compared with before the change. Calculate operating income (loss).
4. What concerns, if any, other than the quality problem described in requirement 3, do you see in implementing the CEO's plan? Explain briefly.

13-26 Value engineering, target pricing, and target costs. Tiffany Cosmetics manufactures, and sells a variety of makeup and beauty products. The company has come up with its own patented formula for a new anti-aging cream The company president wants to make sure the product is priced competitively because its purchase will also likely increase sales of other products. The company anticipates that it will sell 400,000 units of the product in the first year with the following estimated costs:

Product design and licensing	$ 1,000,000
Direct materials	1,800,000
Direct manufacturing labor	1,200,000
Variable manufacturing overhead	600,000
Fixed manufacturing overhead	2,000,000
Fixed marketing	3,000,000

Required

1. The company believes that it can successfully sell the product for $38 a bottle. The company's target operating income is 40% of revenue. Calculate the target full cost of producing the 400,000 units. Does the cost estimate meet the company's requirements? Is value engineering needed?
2. A component of the direct materials cost requires the nectar of a specific plant in South America. If the company could eliminate this special ingredient, the materials cost would drop by 45%. However, this would require design changes of $300,000 to engineer a chemical equivalent of the ingredient. Will this design change allow the product to meet its target cost?
3. The company president does not believe that the formula should be altered for fear it will tarnish the company's brand. She prefers that the company spend more on marketing and increase the price. The company's accountants believe that if marketing costs are increase by $400,000 then the company can achieve a selling price of $42 per bottle without losing any sales. At this price, will the company achieve its target operating income of 40% of revenue?
4. What are the advantages and disadvantages of pursuing alternative 2 and alternative 3 above?

13-27 Target service costs, value engineering, activity-based costing. Lagoon is an amusement park that offers family-friendly entertainment and attractions. The park boasts more than 25 acres of fun. The admission price to enter the park, which includes access to all attractions, is $35. At this entrance price, Lagoon's target profit is 35% of revenues. Lagoon's managers have identified the major activities that drive the cost of operating the park. The activity cost pools, the cost driver for each activity, and the cost per unit of the cost driver for each pool are:

Activity	Description of Activity	Cost Driver	Cost per Unit of Cost Driver
1. Ticket sales	Selling tickets on-site for entry into the park	Number of tickets sold on-site	$2 per ticket sold
2. Ticket verification	Verifying tickets purchased at park and online ticket purchases	Number of patrons	$1.50 per patron
3. Operating attractions	Loading, monitoring, off-loading patrons on attraction	Number of runs	$90 per run
4. Litter patrol	Roaming the park and cleaning up waste as necessary	Number of litter patrol hours	$20 per hour

The following additional information describes the existing operations:

a. The park operating hours are 10:00 a.m.–8:00 p.m., 7 days a week. The average number of patrons per week is 55,000.
b. Lagoon maintains an online Web site for advance ticket purchases. This site is maintained by an outside company that charges $1 per ticket sold. Only 15% of the tickets are purchased online.
c. Once the ticket is purchased, another park employee checks the ticket and stamps the patron for potential exit and reentry.
d. The park has 27 attractions. A run is the complete cycle of loading, monitoring, and off-loading of patrons. On average, the attractions can make 6 runs an hour. The cost of operating the attractions includes wages of operator, maintenance, and depreciation of equipment.
e. Cleaning crew members are assigned to 1-acre areas. One person can cover approximately 1 acre per hour. Each acre is covered continuously. The cost of litter patrol includes the wages of the employee and cleaning supplies.

In response to competitive pressures and to continue to attract 55,000 patrons per week, Lagoon has decided to lower ticket prices to $33 per patron. To maintain the same level of profits as before, Lagoon is looking to make the following improvements to reduce operating costs:

a. Spend $1,000 per week on advertising to promote awareness of the available online ticket purchase. Lagoon's managers expect that this advertising will increase online purchases to 40% of total ticket sales. At this volume, the cost per online ticket sold will decrease to $0.75.
b. Reduce the operating hours for eight of the attractions that are not very popular from 10 hours per day to 7 hours per day.
c. Increase the number of refuse containers in the park at an additional cost of $250 per week. Litter patrol employees will be able to cover 1.25 acres per hour.

The cost per unit of cost driver for all other activities will remain the same.

Required

1. Does Lagoon currently achieve its target profit of 35% of sales?
2. Will the new changes and improvements allow Lagoon to achieve the same target profit in dollars? Show your calculations.
3. What challenges might managers at Lagoon encounter in achieving the target cost? How might they overcome these challenges?

13-28 Cost-plus, target return on investment pricing. Zoom-o-licious makes candy bars for vending machines and sells them to vendors in cases of 30 bars. Although Zoom-o-licious makes a variety of candy, the cost differences are insignificant, and the cases all sell for the same price.

Zoom-o-licious has a total capital investment of $15,000,000. It expects to produce and sell 300,000 cases of candy next year. Zoom-o-licious requires a 10% target return on investment.

Expected costs for next year are:

Variable production costs	$4.00 per case
Variable marketing and distribution costs	$1.00 per case
Fixed production costs	$300,000
Fixed marketing and distribution costs	$400,000
Other fixed costs	$200,000

Zoom-o-licious prices the cases of candy at full cost plus markup to generate profits equal to the target return on capital.

Required

1. What is the target operating income?
2. What is the selling price Zoom-o-licious needs to charge to earn the target operating income? Calculate the markup percentage on full cost.
3. Zoom-o-licious's closest competitor has just increased its candy case price to $16, although it sells 36 candy bars per case. Zoom-o-licious is considering increasing its selling price to $15 per case. Assuming production and sales decrease by 4%, calculate Zoom-o-licious' return on investment. Is increasing the selling price a good idea?

13-29 Cost-plus, time and materials, ethics. A & L Mechanical sells and services plumbing, heating, and air-conditioning systems. A & L's cost accounting system tracks two cost categories: direct labor and direct materials. A & L uses a time-and-materials pricing system, with direct labor marked up 80% and direct materials marked up 60% to recover indirect costs of support staff, support materials, and shared equipment and tools and to earn a profit.

During a hot summer day, the central air conditioning in Michelle Lowry's home stops working. A & L technician Tony Dickenson arrives at Lowry's home and inspects the air conditioner. He considers two options: replace the compressor or repair it. The cost information available to Dickenson follows:

	Labor	Materials
Repair option	7 hrs.	$120
Replace option	4 hrs.	$230
Labor rate	$45 per hr.	

Required

1. If Dickenson presents Lowry with the replace or repair options, what price would he quote for each?
2. If the two options were equally effective for the 3 years that Lowry intends to live in the home, which option would she choose?
3. If Dickenson's objective is to maximize profits, which option would he recommend to Lowry? What would be the ethical course of action?

13-30 Cost-plus and market-based pricing. Georgia Temps, a large labor contractor, supplies contract labor to building-construction companies. For 2014, Georgia Temps has budgeted to supply 84,000 hours of contract labor. Its variable costs are $13 per hour, and its fixed costs are $168,000. Roger Mason, the general manager, has proposed a cost-plus approach for pricing labor at full cost plus 20%.

Required

1. Calculate the price per hour that Georgia Temps should charge based on Mason's proposal.
2. The marketing manager supplies the following information on demand levels at different prices:

Price per Hour	Demand (Hours)
$16	124,000
17	104,000
18	84,000
19	74,000
20	61,000

Georgia Temps can meet any of these demand levels. Fixed costs will remain unchanged for all the demand levels. On the basis of this additional information, calculate the price per hour that Georgia Temps should charge to maximize operating income.

3. Comment on your answers to requirements 1 and 2. Why are they the same or different?

13-31 Cost-plus and market-based pricing. (CMA, adapted) Quick Test Laboratories evaluates the reaction of materials to extreme increases in temperature. Much of the company's early growth was attributable to government contracts, but recent growth has come from expansion into commercial markets. Two types of testing at Quick Test are Heat Testing (HTT) and Arctic-Condition Testing (ACT). Currently, all of the budgeted operating costs are collected in a single overhead pool. All of the estimated testing-hours are also collected in a single pool. One rate per test-hour is used for both types of testing. This hourly rate is marked up by 30% to recover administrative costs and taxes and to earn a profit.

George Barton, Quick Test's controller, believes that there is enough variation in the test procedures and cost structure to establish separate costing rates and billing rates at a 30% markup. He also believes that the inflexible rate structure the company is currently using is inadequate in today's competitive environment. After analyzing the company data, he has divided operating costs into the following three cost pools:

Labor and supervision	$ 436,800
Setup and facility costs	351,820
Utilities	435,600
Total budgeted costs for the period	$1,224,220

George Barton budgets 112,000 total test-hours for the coming period. Test-hours is also the cost driver for labor and supervision. The budgeted quantity of cost driver for setup and facility costs is 700 setup hours. The budgeted quantity of cost driver for utilities is 12,000 machine-hours.

George has estimated that HTT uses 70% of the test-hours, 20% of the setup-hours, and half the machine-hours.

Required

1. Find the single rate for operating costs based on test-hours and the hourly billing rate for HTT and ACT.
2. Find the three activity-based rates for operating costs.
3. What will the billing rate for HTT and ACT be based on the activity-based costing structure? State the rates in terms of test-hours. Referring to both requirements 1 and 2, which rates make more sense for Quick Test?
4. If Quick Test's competition all charge $23 per hour for arctic testing, what can Quick Test do to stay competitive?

13-32 Life-cycle costing. Maximum Metal Recycling and Salvage receives the opportunity to salvage scrap metal and other materials from an old industrial site. The current owners of the site will sign over the site to Maximum at no cost. Maximum intends to extract scrap metal at the site for 24 months and then will clean up the site, return the land to useable condition, and sell it to a developer. Projected costs associated with the project follow:

		Fixed	Variable
Months 1–24	Metal extraction and processing	$2,000 per month	$80 per ton
Months 1–27	Rent on temporary buildings	$1,000 per month	—
	Administration	$6,000 per month	—
Months 25–27	Clean-up	$20,000 per month	—
	Land restoration	$23,000 total	—
	Cost of selling land	$80,000 total	—

Ignore time value of money.

Required

1. Assuming that Maximum expects to salvage 70,000 tons of metal from the site, what is the total project life cycle cost?
2. Suppose Maximum can sell the metal for $110 per ton and wants to earn a profit (before taxes) of $30 per ton. At what price must Maximum sell the land at the end of the project to achieve its target profit per ton?
3. Now suppose Maximum can only sell the metal for $100 per ton and the land at $110,000 less than what you calculated in requirement 2. If Maximum wanted to maintain the same markup percentage on total project life-cycle cost as in requirement 2, by how much would the company have to reduce its total project life-cycle cost?

13-33 Airline pricing, considerations other than cost in pricing. Northern Airways is about to introduce a daily round-trip flight from New York to Los Angeles and is determining how to price its round-trip tickets.

The market research group at Northern Airways segments the market into business and pleasure travelers. It provides the following information on the effects of two different prices on the number of seats expected to be sold and the variable cost per ticket, including the commission paid to travel agents:

		Number of Seats Expected to Be Sold	
Price Charged	**Variable Cost per Ticket**	**Business**	**Pleasure**
$ 800	$ 85	300	150
1,800	195	285	30

Pleasure travelers start their travel during one week, spend at least one weekend at their destination, and return the following week or thereafter. Business travelers usually start and complete their travel within the same work week. They do not stay over weekends.

Assume that round-trip fuel costs are fixed costs of $24,700 and that fixed costs allocated to the round-trip flight for airplane-lease costs, ground services, and flight-crew salaries total $183,000.

Required

1. If you could charge different prices to business travelers and pleasure travelers, would you? Show your computations.
2. Explain the key factor (or factors) for your answer in requirement 1.
3. How might Northern Airways implement price discrimination? That is, what plan could the airline formulate so that business travelers and pleasure travelers each pay the price the airline desires?

13-34 Anti-trust laws and pricing. USA Airlines is a major airline carrier for both domestic and international travel. The company guarantees the "lowest price" ticket for travel within the United States. In order to get the lowest price airfare, the customer needs to book a flight with USA Airlines and show the booking agent a computer-generated quote from any other airline in the country for the same travel route at a lower rate. USA Airlines will match the rate, plus give the customer an additional 10% discount. USA Airlines has entered into a contract with several regional carriers, which requires them to also price below the competition in order to do business with USA Airlines customers. The "lowest price" ticket guarantee does not apply for travel on Monday mornings and Friday evenings, which are busy travel times for business travelers.

Required

1. Do these pricing practices of USA Airlines violate any anti-trust laws? Why or why not?
2. Why is USA Airlines not offering a price guarantee for flights on Monday mornings and Friday evenings? Do you agree with this policy? Explain briefly.
3. What other factors should USA Airlines consider before implementing these pricing policies?

13-35 Ethics and pricing. Instyle Interior Designs has been requested to prepare a bid to decorate four model homes for a new development. Winning the bid would be a big boost for sales representative Jim Doogan, who works entirely on commission. Sara Groom, the cost accountant for Instyle, prepares the bid based on the following cost information:

Direct costs		
Design costs		$ 20,000
Furniture and artwork		70,000
Direct labor		10,000
Delivery and installation		20,000
Overhead costs		
Design software	5,200	
Furniture handling	4,800	
General and administration	8,000	
Total overhead costs		18,000
Full product costs		$138,000

Based on the company policy of pricing at 120% of full cost, Groom gives Doogan a figure of $165,600 to submit for the job. Doogan is very concerned. He tells Groom that at that price, Instyle has no chance of winning the job. He confides in her that he spent $600 of company funds to take the developer to a basketball playoff game where the developer disclosed that a bid of $156,000 would win the job. He hadn't planned to tell Groom because he was confident that the bid she developed would be below that amount. Doogan reasons that the $600 he spent will be wasted if Instyle doesn't capitalize on this valuable information. In any case, the company will still make money if it wins the bid at $156,000 because it is higher than the full cost of $138,000.

Required

1. Is the $600 spent on the basketball tickets relevant to the bid decision? Why or why not?
2. Groom suggests that if Doogan is willing to use cheaper furniture and artwork, he can achieve a bid of $156,000. The designs have already been reviewed and accepted and cannot be changed without additional cost, so the entire amount of reduction in cost will need to come from furniture and artwork. What is the target cost of furniture and artwork that will allow Doogan to submit a bid of $156,000 assuming a target markup of 20% of full cost?
3. Evaluate whether Groom's suggestion to Doogan to use the developer's tip is unethical. Would it be unethical for Doogan to redo the project's design to arrive at a lower bid? What steps should Doogan and Groom take to resolve this situation?

13-36 Value engineering, target pricing, and locked-in costs. Wood Creations designs, manufactures, and sells modern wood sculptures. Sally Jensen is an artist for the company. Jensen has spent much of the past month working on the design of an intricate abstract piece. Jim Smoot, product development manager, likes the design. However, he wants to make sure that the sculpture can be priced competitively. Alexis Nampa, Wood's cost accountant, presents Smoot with the following cost data for the expected production of 75 sculptures:

Design cost	$ 8,000
Direct materials	32,000
Direct manufacturing labor	38,000
Variable manufacturing overhead	32,000
Fixed manufacturing overhead	26,000
Marketing	14,000

Required

1. Smoot thinks that Wood Creations can successfully market each piece for $2,500. The company's target operating income is 25% of revenue. Calculate the target full cost of producing the 75 sculptures. Does the cost estimate Nampa developed meet Wood's requirements? Is value engineering needed?
2. Smoot discovers that Jensen has designed the sculpture using the highest-grade wood available, rather than the standard grade of wood that Wood Creations normally uses. Replacing the grade of wood will lower the cost of direct materials by 60%. However, the redesign will require an additional $1,100 of design cost, and the sculptures will be sold for $2,400 each. Will this design change allow the sculpture to meet its target cost? Is the cost of wood a locked-in cost?
3. Jensen insists that the higher-grade wood is a necessity in terms of the sculpture's design. She believes that spending an additional $3,000 on better marketing will allow Wood Creations to sell each sculpture for $2,700. If this is the case, will the sculptures' target cost be achieved without any value engineering?
4. Compare the total operating income on the 75 sculptures for requirements 2 and 3. What do you recommend Wood Creations do, based solely on your calculations? Explain briefly.
5. What challenges might managers at Wood Creations encounter in achieving the target cost and how might they overcome these challenges?

14 Cost Allocation, Customer-Profitability Analysis, and Sales-Variance Analysis

Learning Objectives

1. Discuss why a company's revenues and costs differ across customers
2. Identify the importance of customer-profitability profiles
3. Understand the cost-hierarchy-based operating income statement
4. Understand criteria to guide cost-allocation decisions
5. Discuss decisions faced when collecting and allocating indirect costs to customers
6. Subdivide the sales-volume variance into the sales-mix variance and the sales-quantity variance and the sales-quantity variance into the market-share variance and the market-size variance

Companies desperately want to make their customers happy.

But how far should they go to please them, and at what price? Should a company differentiate among its customers and not treat all customers the same? The following article explains why it's so important for managers to be able to figure out the profitability of each of their customers.

Starwood Hotels: Not All Guests Are the Same[1]

In 2013, Starwood Hotels & Resorts Worldwide, Inc.—owner and operator of nine hotel brands including Westin, Sheraton, and W Hotels—announced new benefits for its most frequent customers. Starwood added features including rolling 24-hour check-in and check-out times and personal travel assistants, dubbed "ambassadors." The new perks cost the company $25 million. Why invest so much money in frequent travelers? Customer profitability-analysis shows that high-frequency guests drive a disproportionate share of Starwood's profitability.

Starwood found that just 2% of its guests drove 30% of the company's earnings before interest, taxes, depreciation, and amortization ("EBITDA"). EBITDA is a key profitability measure in the hotel industry. For 2013, Starwood expects $284 million of its projected $980 million EBITDA to come from these guests. The use of the new perks is determined by the frequency of stays in Starwood hotels, with guests who spend 100 nights a year qualifying for the highest level of service. The company estimates that the number of customers who will qualify for this level is "in the low ten thousands."

Starwood's focus on frequent travelers is part of a continuing race by hotel companies to generate more business from recurring guests. As competition grows, expect hotels to continue to match each other and ratchet up benefits for their most profitable customer segments.

To determine which product, customer, program, or department is profitable, organizations need to allocate costs. In this chapter and the next, we build on ideas

[1] *Source:* Based on Alexandra Berzon, "Starwood Perks Up Loyalty Program," *Wall Street Journal* (February 1, 2012).

such as activity-based costing introduced in Chapter 5 and provide insight into cost allocation. The emphasis in this chapter is on macro issues in cost allocation: allocation of costs to divisions and customers. Chapter 15 describes micro issues in cost allocation—allocating support-department costs to operating departments and allocating costs to different users and activities—as well as revenue allocations.

Customer-Profitability Analysis

Learning Objective 1

Discuss why a company's revenues and costs differ across customers

...revenues differ because of differences in quantities purchased and price discounts while costs differ because of different demands placed on a company's resources

Customer-profitability analysis is the reporting and assessment of revenues earned from customers and the costs incurred to earn those revenues. An analysis of customer differences in revenues and costs reveals why differences exist in the operating income earned from different customers. Managers use this information to ensure that customers making large contributions to the operating income of a company receive a high level of attention from the company and that loss-making customers do not use more resources than the revenues they provide. As described at the start of this chapter, at Starwood Hotels, managers use customer-profitability analysis to segment customers into profitable customers who stay frequently at the hotel and are given many perks and other customers who are much less profitable and are given less service.

Consider again Astel Computers from Chapter 13. Recall that Astel has two divisions: the Deskpoint Division manufactures and sells servers, and the Provalue Divison manufactures and sells Pentium chip-based personal computers (PCs). Exhibit 14-1, which is the same as Exhibit 13-3, presents data for the Provalue Division of Astel Computers for the year ended 2013. Astel sells and distributes Provalue through two channels: (1) wholesalers who sell Provalue to retail outlets and (2) direct sales to business customers. Astel sells the same Provalue computer to wholesalers and to business customers, so the full manufacturing cost of Provalue, \$680, is the same regardless of where it is sold. Provalue's listed selling price in 2013 was \$1,100, but price discounts reduced the average selling price to \$1,000. We focus on customer-profitability for the Provalue Division's 10 wholesale distributors.

Customer-Revenue Analysis

Consider revenues from four of Provalue's 10 wholesale customers in 2013:

	A	B	C	D	E
1			CUSTOMER		
2		A	B	G	J
3	Units of Provalue sold	30,000	25,000	5,000	4,000
4	List selling price	$ 1,100	$ 1,100	$ 1,100	$ 1,100
5	Price discount	$ 100	$ 50	$ 150	—
6	Invoice price	$ 1,000	$ 1,050	$ 950	$ 1,100
7	Revenues (Row 3 x Row 6)	$30,000,000	$26,250,000	$4,750,000	$4,400,000

Exhibit 14-1

Profitability of Provalue Division for 2013 Using Value-Chain Activity-Based Costing

	A	B	C
1		Total Amounts	
2		for 150,000 Units	Per Unit
3		(1)	(2) = (1) ÷ 150,000
4	Revenues	$150,000,000	$1,000
5	Costs of goods sold[a] (from Exhibit 13-2)	102,000,000	680
6	Operating costs[b]		
7	R&D costs	2,400,000	16
8	Design costs of product and process	3,000,000	20
9	Marketing and administration costs	15,000,000	100
10	Distribution costs	9,000,000	60
11	Customer-service costs	3,600,000	24
12	Operating costs	33,000,000	220
13	Full cost of the product	135,000,000	900
14	Operating income	$ 15,000,000	$ 100
15			
16	[a]Cost of goods sold = Total manufacturing costs because there is no beginning or ending inventory		
17	of Provalue in 2013		
18	[b]Numbers for operating cost line-items are assumed without supporting calculations		

Two variables explain revenue differences across these four wholesale customers: (1) the number of computers they purchased and (2) the magnitude of price discounting. A **price discount** is the reduction in selling price below list selling price to encourage customers to purchase more quantities. Companies that record only the final invoice price in their information system cannot readily track the magnitude of their price discounting.[2]

Price discounts are a function of multiple factors, including the volume of product purchased (higher-volume customers receive higher discounts) and the desire to sell to a customer who might help promote sales to other customers. In some cases, discounts result from poor negotiating by a salesperson or the unwanted effect of a company's incentive plan based only on revenues. At no time, however, should price discounts stem from illegal activities such as price discrimination, predatory pricing, or collusive pricing (pages 535–536).

Tracking price discounts by customer and by salesperson helps improve customer profitability. For example, the Provalue Division managers may decide to strictly enforce its volume-based price discounting policy. The company may also require its salespeople to obtain approval for giving large discounts to customers who do not normally qualify for them. In addition, the company could track future sales to customers who have received sizable price discounts on the basis of their "high growth potential." For example, managers should track future sales to Customer G to see if the $150-per-computer discount translates into higher future sales.

Customer revenues are one element of customer profitability. The other, equally important element is the cost of acquiring, serving, and retaining customers.

Customer-Cost Analysis

We apply to customers the cost hierarchy discussed in Chapter 5 (page 161). A **customer-cost hierarchy** categorizes costs related to customers into different cost pools on the basis of different types of cost drivers, or cost-allocation bases, or different degrees of difficulty

[2] Further analysis of customer revenues could distinguish gross revenues from net revenues. This approach highlights differences across customers in sales returns. Additional discussion of ways to analyze revenue differences across customers is in Robert S. Kaplan and Robin Cooper, *Cost and Effect: Using Integrated Cost Systems to Drive Profitability and Performance* (Boston: Harvard Business School Press, 1998), Chapter 10; and Gary Cokins, *Activity-Based Cost Management: An Executive's Guide* (New York: Wiley, 2001), Chapter 3.

in determining cause-and-effect or benefits-received relationships. The Provalue Division customer costs are composed of (1) marketing and administration costs, $15,000,000; (2) distribution costs, $9,000,000; and (3) customer-service costs, $3,600,000 (see Exhibit 14-1). Managers identify five categories of indirect costs in its customer-cost hierarchy:

1. **Customer output unit-level costs**—costs of activities to sell each unit (computer) to a customer. An example is product-handling costs of each computer sold.
2. **Customer batch-level costs**—costs of activities related to a group of units (computers) sold to a customer. Examples are costs incurred to process orders or to make deliveries.
3. **Customer-sustaining costs**—costs of activities to support individual customers, regardless of the number of units or batches of product delivered to the customer. Examples are costs of visits to customers or costs of displays at customer sites.
4. **Distribution-channel costs**—costs of activities related to a particular distribution channel rather than to each unit of product, each batch of product, or specific customers. An example is the salary of the manager of the Provalue Division's wholesale distribution channel.
5. **Division-sustaining costs**—costs of division activities that cannot be traced to individual customers or distribution channels. The salary of the Provalue Division manager is an example of a division-sustaining cost.

Note from these descriptions that four of the five levels of Provalue Division's cost hierarchy closely parallel the cost hierarchy described in Chapter 5 except that the Provalue Division focuses on *customers* whereas the cost hierarchy in Chapter 5 focused on *products*. The Provalue Division has one additional cost hierarchy category, distribution-channel costs, for the costs it incurs to support its wholesale and business-sales channels.

Customer-Level Costs

Exhibit 14-2 summarizes details of the costs incurred in marketing and administration, distribution, and customer service by activity. The exhibit also identifies the cost driver (where appropriate), the total costs incurred for the activity, the total quantity of the cost

Exhibit 14-2 Marketing, Distribution, and Customer Service Activities, Costs, and Cost Driver Information for Provalue Division in 2013

Home | Insert | Page Layout | Formulas | Data | Review | View

	A	B	C	D	E	F	G	H
1	Marketing, Distribution, and Customer Service Costs for 150,000 units of Provalue in 2013							
2								
3	Activity Area	Cost Driver	Total Cost of Activity	Total Quantity of Cost Driver		Rate per Unit of Cost Driver		Cost Hierarchy Category
4	(1)	(2)	(3)	(4)		(5) = (3) ÷ (4)		(6)
5	**Marketing and Administration**							
6	Sales order	Number of sales orders	$ 6,750,000	6,000	sales orders	$1,125	per sales order	Customer batch-level costs
7	Customer visits	Number of customer visits	4,200,000	750	customer visits	$5,600	per customer visit	Customer-sustaining costs
8	Wholesale channel marketing		800,000					Distribution-channel costs
9	Business-sales channel marketing		1,350,000					Distribution-channel costs
10	Provalue division administration		1,900,000					Division-sustaining costs
11	Total marketing & administration costs		$15,000,000					
12								
13	**Distribution**							
14	Product handling	Number of cubic feet moved	$ 4,500,000	300,000	cubic feet	$ 15	per cubic foot	Customer output unit-level costs
15	Regular shipments	Number of regular shipments	3,750,000	3,000	regular shipments	$1,250	per regular shipment	Customer batch-level costs
16	Rush shipments	Number of rush shipments	750,000	150	rush shipments	$5,000	per rush shipment	Customer batch-level costs
17	Total distribution costs		$ 9,000,000					
18								
19	**Customer Service**							
20	Customer service	Number of units shipped	$ 3,600,000	150,000	units shipped	$ 24	per unit shipped	Customer output unit-level costs

driver, the cost per unit of the cost driver, and the customer cost-hierarchy category for each activity.

For example, here is a breakdown of Provalue Division's $15,000,000 of marketing and administration costs:

- $6,750,000 on the sales order activity, which includes negotiating, finalizing, issuing, and collecting on 6,000 sales orders at a cost of $1,125($6,750,000 ÷ 6,000) per sales order. Recall that sales-order costs are customer batch-level costs because these costs vary with the number of sales orders issued and not with the number of Provalue computers in a sales order.
- $4,200,000 for customer visits, which are customer-sustaining costs. The amount per customer varies with the number of visits rather than the number of units or batches of Provalue delivered to a customer.
- $800,000 on managing the wholesale channel, which are distribution-channel costs.
- $1,350,000 on managing the business-sales channel, which are distribution-channel costs.
- $1,900,000 on general administration of the Provalue Division, which are division-sustaining costs.

The Provalue Division managers are particularly interested in analyzing *customer-level indirect costs*—costs incurred in the first three categories of the customer-cost hierarchy: customer output unit–level costs, customer batch-level costs, and customer-sustaining costs. Managers want to work with customers to reduce these costs because they believe customer actions will have more impact on customer-level (indirect) costs than on distribution-channel and division-sustaining costs. Information on the quantity of cost drivers used by each of four representative wholesale customers follows:

	A	B	C	D	E	F
1				CUSTOMER		
2	**Activity**	**Quantity of Cost Driver**	**A**	**B**	**G**	**J**
3	**Marketing**					
4	Sales orders	Number of sales orders	1,200	1,000	600	300
5	Customer visits	Number of customer visits	150	100	50	25
6	**Distribution**					
7	Product handling	Number of cubic feet moved	60,000	50,000	10,000	8,000
8	Regular shipments	Number of regular shipments	600	400	300	120
9	Rush shipments	Number of rush shipments	25	5	20	3
10	**Customer Service**					
11	Customer service	Number of units shipped	30,000	25,000	5,000	4,000

Exhibit 14-3 shows customer-level operating income for the four wholesale customers using information on customer revenues previously presented (page 551) and customer-level indirect costs, obtained by multiplying the rate per unit of cost driver (from Exhibit 14-2) by the quantities of the cost driver used by each customer (in the table above). Exhibit 14-3 shows that the Provalue Division is losing money on Customer G (the cost of resources used by Customer G exceeds revenues) while it makes money on Customer J on smaller revenues. The Provalue Division sells fewer computers to Customer B compared to Customer A but has higher operating income from Customer B than Customer A.

The Provalue Division's managers can use the information in Exhibit 14-3 to work with customers to reduce the quantity of activities needed to support them. Consider, for example, a comparison of Customer G and Customer J. Customer G purchases 25% more computers than Customer J purchases (5,000 versus 4,000) but the company offers Customer G significant price discounts to achieve these sales. Compared with Customer J, Customer

Exhibit 14-3 Customer-Profitability Analysis for Provalue Division's Four Wholesale Channel Customers for 2013

	A	B	C	D	E
1		**A**	**B**	**G**	**J**
2	Revenues at list price	$33,000,000	$27,500,000	$5,500,000	$4,400,000
3	Price discount	3,000,000	1,250,000	750,000	-
4	Revenues	30,000,000	26,250,000	4,750,000	4,400,000
5					
6	Cost of goods sold[a]	20,400,000	17,000,000	3,400,000	2,720,000
7					
8	Gross margin	9,600,000	9,250,000	1,350,000	1,680,000
9					
10	Customer-level costs				
11	Marketing costs				
12	Sales orders[b]	1,350,000	1,125,000	675,000	337,500
13	Customer visits[c]	840,000	560,000	280,000	140,000
14	Distribution costs				
15	Product handling[d]	900,000	750,000	150,000	120,000
16	Regular shipments[e]	750,000	500,000	375,000	150,000
17	Rush shipments[f]	125,000	25,000	100,000	15,000
18	Customer service costs				
19	Customer service[g]	720,000	600,000	120,000	96,000
20					
21	Total customer-level costs	4,685,000	3,560,000	1,700,000	858,500
22					
23	Customer-level operating income	$ 4,915,000	$ 5,690,000	$ (350,000)	$ 821,500
24	[a]$680 x 30,000; 25,000; 5,000; 4,000 [b]$1,125 x 1,200; 1,000; 600; 300 [c]$5,600 x 150; 100; 50; 25 [d]$15 x 60,000; 50,000; 10,000;				
25	8,000 [e]$1,250 x 600; 400; 300; 120 [f]$5,000 x 25; 5; 20; 3 [g]$24 x 30,000; 25,000; 5,000; 4,000				

G places twice as many sales orders, requires twice as many customer visits, and generates two-and-a-half times as many regular shipments and almost seven times as many rush shipments. Selling smaller quantities of units is profitable, provided the Provalue Division's salespeople limit the amount of price discounting and customers do not use large amounts of Provalue Division's resources. For example, by implementing an additional charge for customers who use large amounts of marketing and distribution services, managers might be able to prevail upon Customer G to place fewer but larger sales orders and require fewer customer visits, regular shipments, and rush shipments while looking to increase sales in the future. The Provalue Division's managers would perform a similar analysis to understand the reasons for the lower profitability of Customer A relative to Customer B.

Owens and Minor, a distributor of medical supplies to hospitals, follows this approach. Owens and Minor strategically prices each of its services separately. For example, if a hospital wants a rush delivery or special packaging, Owens and Minor charges the hospital an additional price for each particular service. How have its customers reacted? Hospitals that value these services continue to demand and pay for them, while hospitals that do not value these services stop asking for them, saving Owens and Minor some costs. This pricing strategy influences customer behavior in a way that increases Owens and Minor's revenues or decreases its costs.

The ABC system also highlights a second opportunity for cost reduction. The Provalue Division's managers can reduce the costs of each activity by applying the same value-engineering process described in Chapter 13 to nonmanufacturing costs. For example, improving the efficiency of the ordering process (such as by having customers order electronically) reduces sales order costs even if customers place the same number of orders.

Simplifying the design and reducing the weight of the newly designed Provalue II for 2014 reduces the cost per cubic foot of handling Provalue and total product-handling costs. By influencing customer behavior and improving marketing, distribution, and customer service operations, Provalue Division's managers aim to reduce the nonmanufacturing cost of Provalue to $180 per computer and achieve the target cost of $720 for Provalue II.

Decision Point

How can a company's revenues and costs differ across customers?

Learning Objective 2

Identify the importance of customer-profitability profiles

...expand relationships with profitable customers and change behavior patterns of unprofitable customers and highlight that a small percentage of customers contributes a large percentage of operating income

Customer Profitability Profiles

Customer-profitability profiles are a useful tool for managers. Exhibit 14-4 ranks the Provalue Division's 10 wholesale customers based on customer-level operating income. (We analyzed four of these customers in Exhibit 14-3.)

Column 4, computed by adding the individual amounts in column 1, shows the cumulative customer-level operating income. For example, Customer C shows a cumulative income of $13,260,000 in column 4. This $13,260,000 is the sum of $5,690,000 for Customer B, $4,915,000 for Customer A, and $2,655,000 for Customer C.

Column 5 shows what percentage the $13,260,000 *cumulative* total for customers B, A, and C is of the total customer-level operating income of $15,027,500 earned in the wholesale distribution channel from all 10 customers. The three most profitable customers contribute 88% of total customer-level operating income. These customers deserve the highest service and priority. Companies try to keep their best customers happy in a number of ways, including special phone numbers and upgrade privileges for elite-level frequent flyers and free usage of luxury hotel suites and big credit limits for high rollers at casinos. In many companies, it is common for a small number of customers to contribute a high percentage of operating income. Microsoft uses the phrase "not all revenue dollars are endowed equally in profitability" to stress this point.

Exhibit 14-4 Cumulative Customer-Profitability Analysis for Provalue Division's Wholesale Channel Customers: Astel Computers, 2013

Home Insert Page Layout Formulas Data Review View

	A	B	C	D	E	F
1	Retail Customer Code	Customer-Level Operating Income	Customer Revenue	Customer-Level Operating Income Divided by Revenue	Cumulative Customer-Level Operating Income	Cumulative Customer-Level Operating Income as a % of Total Customer-Level Operating Income
2		(1)	(2)	(3) = (1) ÷ (2)	(4)	(5) = (4) ÷ $15,027,500
3	B	$ 5,690,000	$26,250,000	21.7%	$ 5,690,000	38%
4	A	4,915,000	30,000,000	16.4%	10,605,000	71%
5	C	2,655,000	13,000,000	20.4%	13,260,000	88%
6	D	1,445,000	7,250,000	19.9%	14,705,000	98%
7	F	986,000	5,100,000	19.3%	15,691,000	104%
8	J	821,500	4,400,000	18.7%	16,512,500	110%
9	E	100,000	1,800,000	5.6%	16,612,500	111%
10	G	(350,000)	4,750,000	−7.4%	16,262,500	108%
11	H	(535,000)	2,400,000	−22.3%	15,727,500	105%
12	I	(700,000)	2,600,000	−26.9%	15,027,500	100%
13	Total	$15,027,500	$97,550,000			

Column 3 shows the profitability per dollar of revenue by customer. This measure of customer profitability indicates that, although Customer A contributes the second-highest operating income, the profitability per dollar of revenue is lowest among the top six customers because of high price discounts and higher customer-level costs. Provalue Division managers would like to increase profit margins for Customer A by decreasing price discounts or saving customer-level costs while maintaining or increasing sales. Customers D, F, and J have high profit margins but low total sales. The challenge with these customers is to maintain margins while increasing sales. With Customers E, G, H, and I, managers have the dual challenge of boosting profits and sales.

Presenting Profitability Analysis

Exhibit 14-5 illustrates two common ways of displaying the results of customer-profitability analysis. Managers often find the bar chart presentation in Panel A (based on Exhibit 14-4, Column 1) to be an intuitive way to visualize customer profitability because (1) the highly profitable customers clearly stand out and (2) the number of "unprofitable" customers and the magnitude of their losses are apparent. Panel B of Exhibit 14-5 is a popular alternative way to express customer profitability. It plots the contents of column 5

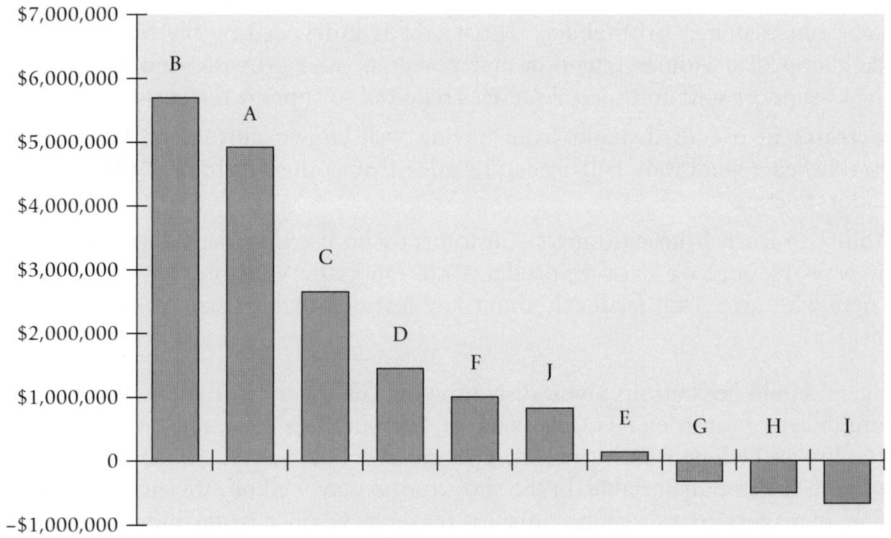

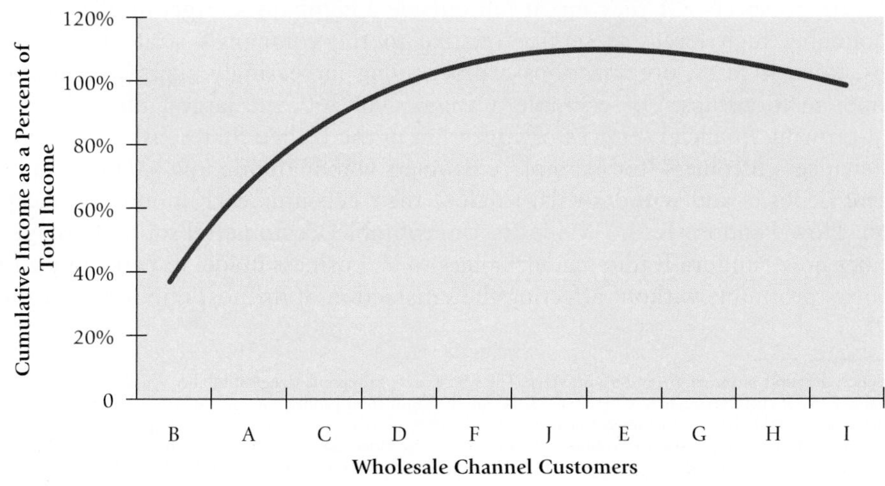

Exhibit 14-5

Panel A: Bar Chart of Customer-Level Operating Income for Provalue Division's Wholesale Channel Customers in 2013

Panel B: The Whale Curve of Cumulative Profitability for Provalue Division's Wholesale Channel Customers in 2013

in Exhibit 14-4. This chart is called the **whale curve** because it is backward-bending at the point where customers start to become unprofitable and thus resembles a humpback whale.[3]

The Provalue Division managers must explore ways to make unprofitable customers profitable. Exhibits 14-2 to 14-5 emphasize annual customer profitability. Managers should also consider other factors when allocating resources among customers, including:

- **Likelihood of customer retention.** The more likely a customer will continue to do business with a company, the more valuable the customer, for example, wholesalers who have sold Provalue each year over the last several years. Customers differ in their loyalty and their willingness to frequently "shop their business."
- **Potential for sales growth.** The higher the likely growth of the customer's sales, the more valuable the customer. Moreover, customers to whom a company can cross-sell other products profitably are more desirable, for example, wholesalers willing to distribute both Astel's Provalue and Deskpoint brands. The analysis has focused on customer profitability as it relates to Provalue. To get the full picture of Astel's relationship with a customer, managers need to do a similar customer profitability analysis for the Deskpoint Division and examine total customer profitability for those customers that sell both Provalue and Deskpoint. To simplify the exposition, we assume that the customers of the Provalue and Deskpoint divisions are distinct.
- **Long-run customer profitability.** This factor is influenced by the first two factors—likelihood of customer retention and potential sales growth—and the cost of customer-support staff and special services required to support the customer.
- **Increases in overall demand from having well-known customers.** Customers with established reputations help generate sales from other customers through product endorsements.
- **Ability to learn from customers.** Customers who provide ideas about new products or ways to improve existing products are especially valuable, for example, wholesalers who give Astel feedback about key features such as size of memory or video displays.

Managers should be cautious about discontinuing customers. In Exhibit 14-4, the current unprofitability of Customer G, for example, may provide misleading signals about G's profitability in the long run. Moreover, as in any ABC-based system, the costs assigned to Customer G are not all variable. In the short run, it may well be efficient for the Provalue Division managers to use spare capacity to serve G on a contribution-margin basis. Discontinuing Customer G will not eliminate all costs assigned to Customer G and may result in losing more revenues relative to costs saved.

Of course, particular customers might be chronically unprofitable and hold limited future prospects. Or they might fall outside a company's target market or require unsustainably high levels of service relative to the company's strategies and capabilities. In such cases, organizations are becoming increasingly aggressive in severing customer relationships. For example, Capital One 360, the largest direct lender and fastest-growing financial services organization in the United States, asks 10,000 "high-maintenance" customers (for example, customers who maintain low balances and make frequent deposits and withdrawals) to close their accounts each month.[4] Concepts in Action: How Pandora Radio Made Its Unprofitable Customers Profitable (page 559) describes how Pandora Radio made changes to its business model to make unprofitable customers profitable without affecting the satisfaction of its most important customers.

[3] In practice, the curve of the chart can be quite steep. The whale curve for cumulative profitability usually reveals that the most profitable 20% of customers generate between 150% and 300% of total profits, the middle 70% of customers break even, and the least profitable 10% of customers lose from 50% to 200% of total profits (see Robert S. Kaplan and V. G. Narayanan, "Measuring and Managing Customer Profitability," *Journal of Cost Management* (September/October 2001): 1–11).

[4] See, for example, "The New Math of Customer Relationships" at http://hbswk.hbs.edu/item/5884.html.

Concepts in Action

How Pandora Radio Made Its Unprofitable Customers Profitable

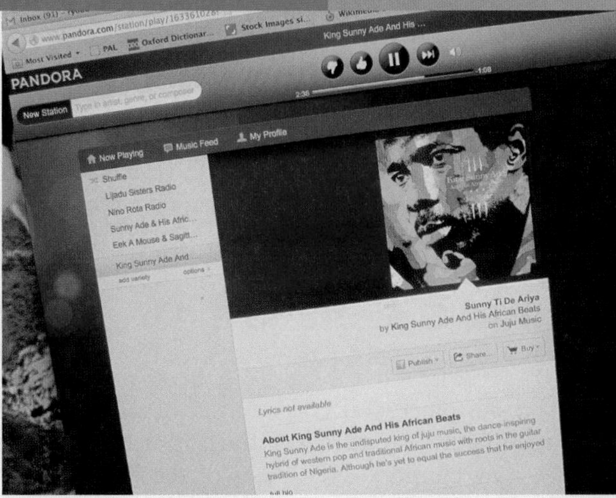

In 2009, Pandora Radio was growing rapidly. While the startup company was still unprofitable, widespread adoption gave founder Tim Westergren hope of turning a profit. Some venture capitalists, however, wanted Pandora to get rid of its heaviest users or at least recover the cost of supporting them. Essentially, they wanted Pandora to fire its unprofitable customers!

The venture capitalists found a troubling trend in Pandora's advertising-supported free service. The company's business model was based on selling advertising at a rate of $6 to $7 for every 1,000 customer impressions. That is, advertisers paid for reach, not duration. While Pandora streamed music at no charge to listeners, the company was contractually bound to pay a royalty on each song played. Thus, heavy users cost Pandora more. In fact, the "sweet spot" for Pandora would have been a lot of users who were in the light- to middle-usage range. Some potential investors wanted Pandora to charge the heavy users for the service or deliver more advertising to them if they listened to the radio for a longer period of time.

Westergren worried about whether such changes were really in the company's best interests, as heavy users were Pandora's greatest evangelists. Pandora ultimately decided not to fire its unprofitable customers. The company announced that free listening would be limited to 40 hours per month, but could be extended to unlimited listening for that month for $0.99. By the end of 2009, Pandora turned consistently profitable. The company grew to 43 million members, achieved $50 million in revenues, and became the second-largest volume streamer of bits on the Internet after YouTube. Today, more than 200 million users—including 140 million mobile users—enjoy music through Pandora's profitable service.

Sources: Based on Willy Shih and Halle Tesco, "Pandora Radio: Fire Unprofitable Customers?" HBS No. 9-610-077 (Boston: Harvard Business School Publishing, 2011); and "Pandora is Now 200 Million Music Fans Strong," Pandora Media, Inc. (Oakland, CA, April 9, 2013).

Using the Five-Step Decision-Making Process to Manage Customer Profitability

In this section, we apply the five-step decision-making process (introduced in Chapter 1) to help understand how managers use different types of customer analyses to allocate resources across customers.

1. *Identify the problem and uncertainties.* The problem is how to manage and allocate resources across customers.
2. *Obtain information.* Managers identify past revenues generated by each customer and customer-level costs incurred in the past to support each customer.
3. *Make predictions about the future.* Managers estimate the revenues they expect from each customer and the customer-level costs they will incur in the future. In making these predictions, managers consider the effects that future price discounts will have on revenues, the effect that pricing for different services (such as rush deliveries) will have on the demand for these services by customers, and ways to reduce the cost of providing services. For example, Deluxe Corporation, a leading check printer, initiated process modifications to rein in its cost to serve customers by opening an electronic channel to shift customers from paper to automated ordering.

4. *Make decisions by choosing among alternatives.* Managers use the customer-profitability profiles to identify the small set of customers who deserve the highest service and priority and also to identify ways to make less-profitable customers (such as Astel's Customer G) more profitable. Banks, for example, often impose minimum balance requirements on customers. Distribution firms may require minimum order quantities or levy a surcharge for smaller or customized orders. In making resource-allocation decisions, managers also consider long-term effects, such as the potential for future sales growth and the opportunity to leverage a particular customer account to make sales to other customers.

Decision Point

How do customer-profitability profiles help managers?

5. *Implement the decision, evaluate performance, and learn.* After the decision is implemented, managers compare actual results to predicted outcomes to evaluate the decision they made, its implementation, and ways in which they might improve profitability.

Learning Objective 3

Understand the cost-hierarchy-based operating income statement

...allocate only those costs that will be affected by actions at a particular hierarchical level

Cost Hierarchy-Based Operating Income Statement

Our analysis so far has focused on customer-level costs—costs of activities that the Provalue Division managers can work with customers to influence such as sales orders, customer visits, and shipments. We now consider other costs of the Provalue Division (such as R&D and design costs, costs to manage different distribution channels, and costs of division administration) and corporate costs incurred by Astel Computers (such as corporate brand advertising and general administration costs). Customer actions do not influence these costs, which raises two important questions: (1) Should these costs be allocated to customers when calculating customer profitability, and (2) if they are allocated, on what basis should they be allocated given the weak cause-and-effect relationship between these costs and customer actions? We start by considering the first question and introduce the cost-hierarchy-based operating income statement, which does not allocate the noncustomer-level costs.

Exhibit 14-6 shows an operating income statement for the Provalue Division for 2013. The customer-level operating income of Customers A and B in Exhibit 14-3 is shown in columns 3 and 4 in Exhibit 14-6. The format of Exhibit 14-6 is based on the

Exhibit 14-6 Income Statement of Provalue Division for 2013 Using the Cost Hierarchy

	A	B	C	D	E	F	G H	I	J	K	L	M	N	O
1				CUSTOMER DISTRIBUTION CHANNELS										
2				Wholesale Customers						Business-Sales Customers				
3		Total	Total	A**		B**	A3			Total	A	B	C	
4		(1) = (2) + (7)	(2)	(3)		(4)	(5)	(6)		(7)	(8)	(9)	(10)	(11)
5	Revenues (at actual prices)	$150,000,000	$97,550,000	$30,000,000		$26,250,000	-	-		$52,450,000	$7,000,000	$6,250,000	-	-
6	Cost of goods sold plus customer-level costs	125,550,000*	82,522,500	25,085,000	a	20,560,000	-	-		43,027,500	5,385,000	4,760,000	-	-
7	Customer-level operating income	24,450,000	15,027,500	$ 4,915,000		$ 5,690,000	-	-		9,422,500	$1,615,000	$1,490,000	-	-
8	Distribution-channel costs	2,150,000	800,000							1,350,000				
9	Distribution-channel-level operating income	22,300,000	$14,227,500							$ 8,072,500				
10	Division-sustaining costs													
11	Administration costs	1,900,000												
12	R&D Costs	2,400,000												
13	Design Costs	3,000,000												
14	Total division-sustaining costs	7,300,000												
15	Division operating income	$ 15,000,000												
16	*Cost of goods sold, $102,000,000 (Exhibit 14-1) + Sales order costs, $6,750,000 + Customer visit costs, $4,200,000 + Product handling costs, $4,500,000 + Regular shipment costs, $3,750,000 + Rush shipment costs, $750,000 + Customer service costs, $3,600,000 (all from Exhibit 14-2)													
17	**Full details are presented in Exhibit 14-3													
18	[a]Cost of goods sold + total customer-level costs from Exhibit 14-3 for Customer A = $20,400,000 + $4,685,000 = $25,085,000.													

Provalue Division's cost hierarchy. As described in Exhibit 14-2, some costs of serving customers, such as the salary of the wholesale distribution-channel manager, are not customer-level costs and are therefore not allocated to customers in Exhibit 14-6. Managers identify these costs as distribution-channel costs because changes in customer behavior will have no effect on these costs. Only decisions pertaining to the channel, such as a decision to discontinue wholesale distribution, will influence these costs. Managers also believe that salespeople responsible for managing individual customer accounts would lose motivation if sales bonuses were adversely affected as a result of allocating to customers distribution-channel costs over which they had minimal influence.

Next, consider division-sustaining costs such as R&D and design costs and administration costs of the Provalue Division. Managers believe there is no direct cause-and-effect relationship between these costs and customer or sales manager's actions. Under this view, allocating division-sustaining costs serves no useful purpose in decision making, performance evaluation, or motivation. Suppose, for example, that the Provalue Division allocates the $7,300,000 of division-sustaining costs to its distribution channels and that in some subsequent period this allocation results in the business-sales channel showing a loss. Should the Provalue Division shut down the business-sales distribution channel? Not if (as we discussed in Chapter 11) division-sustaining costs are unaffected by shutting down the business-sales distribution channel. Allocating division-sustaining costs to distribution channels gives the misleading impression that potential cost savings from discontinuing a distribution channel are greater than the likely amount.

In a cost hierarchy-based income statement, how should we treat the corporate costs for brand advertising, $1,050,000, and administration, $4,400,000, incurred by Astel Computers to support the Provalue and Deskpoint divisions? The Deskpoint Division has revenues of $200,000,000 and operating costs of $170,000,000. Exhibit 14-7 presents the cost hierarchy-based income statement for Astel Computers as a whole. Corporate-sustaining costs are not allocated either to divisions or to customers. That's because, as discussed earlier in the context of division-sustaining costs, there is no direct cause-and-effect relationship between these costs and the profitability of different customers. These costs are unaffected by the actions of division managers or customers, so corporate sustaining costs are subtracted as a lump-sum amount after aggregating operating incomes of the divisions.

Other managers and management accountants advocate fully allocating all costs to distribution channels and to customers because all costs are incurred to support the sales of products to customers. Allocating all corporate costs motivates division managers to examine how corporate costs are planned and controlled. Similarly allocating division costs to distribution channels motivates the managers of the distribution channels to monitor costs incurred in the division. Managers that want to calculate the full costs of serving customers must allocate all corporate, division, and distribution channel costs to customers. These managers and management accountants argue that, in the long run, customers and products must eventually be profitable on a full-cost basis. As we discussed in Chapter 13, for some decisions such as pricing, allocating all costs ensures that long-run prices are set at a level to cover the cost of all resources used to produce and sell products. In this case, the sum of operating incomes of all customers equals companywide operating income.

Exhibit 14-7

Income Statement of Astel Computers for 2013 Using the Cost Hierarchy

Home Insert Page Layout Formulas Data Review View

	A	B	C	D
1	**Income Statement of Astel Computers for 2013 Using the Cost Hierachy**			
2				
3		**Total**	**Provalue Division**	**Deskpoint Division**
4				
5	Revenues	$350,000,000	$150,000,000	$200,000,000
6	Division operating costs	(305,000,000)	(135,000,000)*	(170,000,000)
7	Division operating income before corporate costs	45,000,000	$ 15,000,000	$ 30,000,000
8	Corporate advertising	(1,050,000)		
9	Corporate administration	(4,400,000)		
10	Operating income	$ 39,550,000		
11	*135,000,000 = $125,550,000 + $2,150,000 + $7,300,000 all from Exhibit 14-6, Column 1			

Still other companies allocate only those corporate costs, division costs, or channel costs to customers that are widely perceived as causally related to customer actions or that provide explicit benefits to customer profitability. Corporate advertising is an example of such a cost. These companies exclude other costs such as corporate administration or donations to charitable foundations because the benefits to the customers are less evident or too remote. If a company decides not to allocate some or all corporate, division, or channel costs, it results in total company profitability being less than the sum of individual customer profitabilities.

For some decision purposes, allocating some but not all indirect costs to customers may be the preferred alternative. Consider the performance evaluation of the wholesale channel manager of the Provalue Division. The controllability notion (see page 217) is frequently used to justify excluding corporate costs such as salaries of the top management at corporate headquarters from responsibility accounting reports of the wholesale channel manager. Although the wholesale channel manager tends to benefit from these corporate costs, he or she has no say in ("is not responsible for") how much of these corporate resources to use or how much they cost.

Nevertheless, the value of the hierarchical format in Exhibits 14-6 and 14-7 is to distinguish among various degrees of objectivity when allocating costs so that it dovetails with the different levels at which managers make decisions and evaluate performance. The issue of when and what costs to allocate is another example of the "different costs for different purposes" theme emphasized throughout this book.

Decision Point

Why do managers prepare cost-hierarchy-based operating income statements?

In the next section, we consider what happens if Astel's managers decided to allocate distribution channel costs (such as costs of the wholesale channel), division-sustaining costs (such as costs of R&D and design), and corporate-sustaining costs (such as corporate administration costs of Astel Computers) to individual customers.

Learning Objective 4

Understand criteria to guide cost-allocation decisions

...such as identifying factors that cause resources to be consumed

Criteria to Guide Cost Allocations

Exhibit 14-8 presents four criteria managers use to guide cost-allocation decisions. These decisions affect both the number of indirect-cost pools and the cost-allocation base for each indirect-cost pool. As done throughout this book, we emphasize the superiority of the cause-and-effect and the benefits-received criteria, especially when the purpose of cost allocation is to provide information for economic decisions or to motivate managers and employees.[5] Cause and effect is the primary criterion used in activity-based costing (ABC) applications. ABC systems use the concept of a cost hierarchy to identify the cost drivers that best demonstrate the cause-and-effect relationship between each activity and the costs in the related cost pool. The cost drivers are then chosen as cost-allocation bases. Cause and effect is often difficult to determine in the case of division-sustaining and corporate-sustaining costs. In these situations, managers and management accountants interested in allocating costs use other methods summarized in Exhibit 14-8.

The best way to allocate costs if cause and effect cannot be established is to use the benefits-received criterion by identifying the beneficiaries of the output of the cost object. Consider, for example, the cost of managing the wholesale channel for Provalue, such as the salary of the manager of the wholesale channel. There is no cause-and-effect relationship between these costs and sales made by wholesalers. But it is plausible to assume that the customers with higher revenues benefited more from the wholesale channel support than customers with lower revenues. The benefits-received criterion justifies allocating the costs of managing the wholesale channel of $800,000 to customers based on customer revenues.

Fairness and ability to bear are less frequently used and more problematic criteria than cause and effect or benefits received. It's difficult for two parties to agree on criteria

[5] The Federal Accounting Standards Advisory Board (which sets standards for management accounting for U.S. government departments and agencies) recommends the following: "Cost assignments should be performed by: (a) directly tracing costs whenever feasible and economically practicable, (b) assigning costs on a cause-and-effect basis, and (c) allocating costs on a reasonable and consistent basis" (*FASAB*, 1995, p. 12).

Exhibit 14-8 Criteria for Cost-Allocation Decisions

1. **Cause and Effect.** Using this criterion, managers identify the variables that cause resources to be consumed. For example, managers may use number of sales orders as the variable when allocating the costs of order taking to products and customers. Cost allocations based on the cause-and-effect criterion are likely to be the most credible to operating personnel.
2. **Benefits Received.** Using this criterion, managers identify the beneficiaries of the outputs of the cost object. The costs of the cost object are allocated among the beneficiaries in proportion to the benefits each receives. Consider a corporatewide advertising program that promotes the general image of the corporation rather than any individual product. The costs of this program may be allocated on the basis of division revenues; the higher the revenues, the higher the division's allocated cost of the advertising program. The rationale behind this allocation is that divisions with higher revenues apparently benefited from the advertising more than divisions with lower revenues and, therefore, ought to be allocated more of the advertising costs.
3. **Fairness or Equity.** This criterion is often cited in government contracts when cost allocations are the basis for establishing a price satisfactory to the government and its suppliers. Cost allocation here is viewed as a "reasonable" or "fair" means of establishing a selling price in the minds of the contracting parties. For most allocation decisions, fairness is a matter of judgment rather than an operational criterion.
4. **Ability to Bear.** This criterion advocates allocating costs in proportion to the cost object's ability to bear costs allocated to it. An example is the allocation of corporate administration costs on the basis of division operating income. The presumption is that the more-profitable divisions have a greater ability to absorb corporate administration costs.

for fairness. What one party views as fair another party may view as unfair.[6] For example, a university may view allocating a share of general administrative costs to government contracts for scientific and medical research as fair because general administrative costs are incurred to support all activities of the university. The government may view the allocation of such costs as unfair because the general administrative costs would have been incurred by the university regardless of whether the government contract existed. Perhaps the fairest way to resolve this issue is to understand, as well as possible, the cause-and-effect relationship between the government contract activity and general administrative costs. This is difficult. In other words, fairness is more a matter of judgment than an easily implementable choice criterion.

To get a sense of the issues that arise when using the ability-to-bear criterion, consider Customer G where customer-level costs exceed revenues before any allocation of any division-sustaining or corporate-sustaining costs. This customer has no ability to bear any of the division- or corporate-sustaining costs, so under the ability-to-bear criterion none of these costs will be allocated to Customer G. Costs are not allocated because managers are expected to reduce their dependence on these more remote division- and corporate-sustaining costs (such as administration costs) to support loss-making customers in order to bring the customer relationship back to profitability. However, if the indirect costs are not reduced but simply allocated to other customers, these other customers would be subsidizing the customer that is losing money. The ability-to-bear criterion would then result in a distorted view of lower customer and service profitability for profitable customers and the potential for incorrect actions, such as increasing prices to restore profitability, which could then invite competitors to undercut artificially higher-priced services.

Most importantly, companies must weigh the costs and benefits when designing and implementing their cost allocations. Companies incur costs not only in collecting data but also in taking the time to educate managers about cost allocations. In general, the more complex the cost allocations, the higher these education costs.

[6] Kaplow and Shavell, in a review of the legal literature, note that "notions of fairness are many and varied. They are analyzed and rationalized by different writers in different ways, and they also typically depend upon the circumstances under consideration. Accordingly, it is not possible to identify a consensus view on these notions…" See Louis Kaplow and Steven Shavell, "Fairness Versus Welfare," *Harvard Law Review* (February 2001); and Louis Kaplow and Steven Shavell, *Fairness Versus Welfare* (Boston: Harvard University Press, 2002).

Decision Point

What criteria should managers use to guide cost-allocation decisions?

The costs of designing and implementing complex cost allocations are highly visible. Unfortunately, the benefits from using well-designed cost allocations, such as enabling managers to make better-informed sourcing decisions, pricing decisions, cost-control decisions, and so on, are difficult to measure. Nevertheless, when making cost allocations, managers should consider the benefits as well as the costs. As costs of collecting and processing information decrease, companies are building more detailed cost allocations.

Learning Objective 5

Discuss decisions faced when collecting and allocating indirect costs to customers

...determining the number of cost pools and the costs to be included in each cost pool

Fully Allocated Customer Profitability

In this section, we focus on the first purpose of cost allocation (see Exhibit 13-1): to provide information for economic decisions, such as pricing, by measuring the full costs of delivering products to different customers based on an ABC system.

We continue with the Astel Computers example introduced earlier in this chapter and focus on the fully allocated customer profitability calculations for the 10 wholesale customers in the Provalue Division. The Provalue Division also uses a direct sales channel to sell Provalue computers directly to business customers. Recall that Astel also has another division, the Deskpoint Division, that sells servers. We will use the Astel Computers example to illustrate how costs incurred in different parts of a company can be assigned, and then reassigned, to calculate customer profitability.

We summarize the cost categories as:

- **Corporate costs**—There are two major categories of corporate costs:
  1. **Corporate advertising costs**—advertising and promotion costs to promote the Astel brand, $1,050,000.
  2. **Corporate administration costs**—executive salaries, rent, and general administration costs, $4,400,000.
- **Division costs**—The Provalue Division, which is the focus of our analysis, has three indirect-cost pools—one cost pool each corresponding to the different cost drivers for allocating division costs to distribution channels: (1) cost pool 1 that aggregates all division costs that are allocated to the wholesale and business-sales channels based on revenues of each channel; (2) cost pool 2 that accumulates R&D and design costs that are allocated to the distribution channels on some fair and equitable basis; and (3) cost pool 3 that aggregates all division costs that are allocated to the wholesale and business-sales channels based on the operating incomes of each channel before such allocations (if positive). The cost pools are *homogeneous*, that is, all costs in a cost pool have the same or similar cause-and-effect, benefits-received, or fair-and-equitable relationship with the cost-allocation base. Different cost pools need different cost allocation bases to allocate the costs in the cost pools to distribution channels.
- **Channel costs** —Each distribution channel in the Provalue Division has two indirect cost pools: (1) a cost pool that aggregates all channel costs that are allocated to customers based on customer revenues and (2) a cost pool that aggregates all channel costs that are allocated to customers based on operating incomes of customers before such allocations (if positive).

Exhibit 14-9 presents an overview diagram of the allocation of corporate, division, and distribution-channel indirect costs to wholesale customers of the Provalue Division. Note that the Deskpoint Division has its own indirect-cost pools used to allocate costs to its customers. These cost pools and cost-allocation bases parallel the indirect-cost pools and allocation bases for the Provalue Division.

Implementing Corporate and Division Cost Allocations

Exhibit 14-10 allocates all overhead costs to customers based on the overview diagram in Exhibit 14-9. We describe some of the allocation choices based on the criteria for allocating costs explained in Exhibit 14-8.

Exhibit 14-9 Overview Diagram for Allocating Corporate, Division, and Channel Indirect Costs to Wholesale Customers of Provalue Division

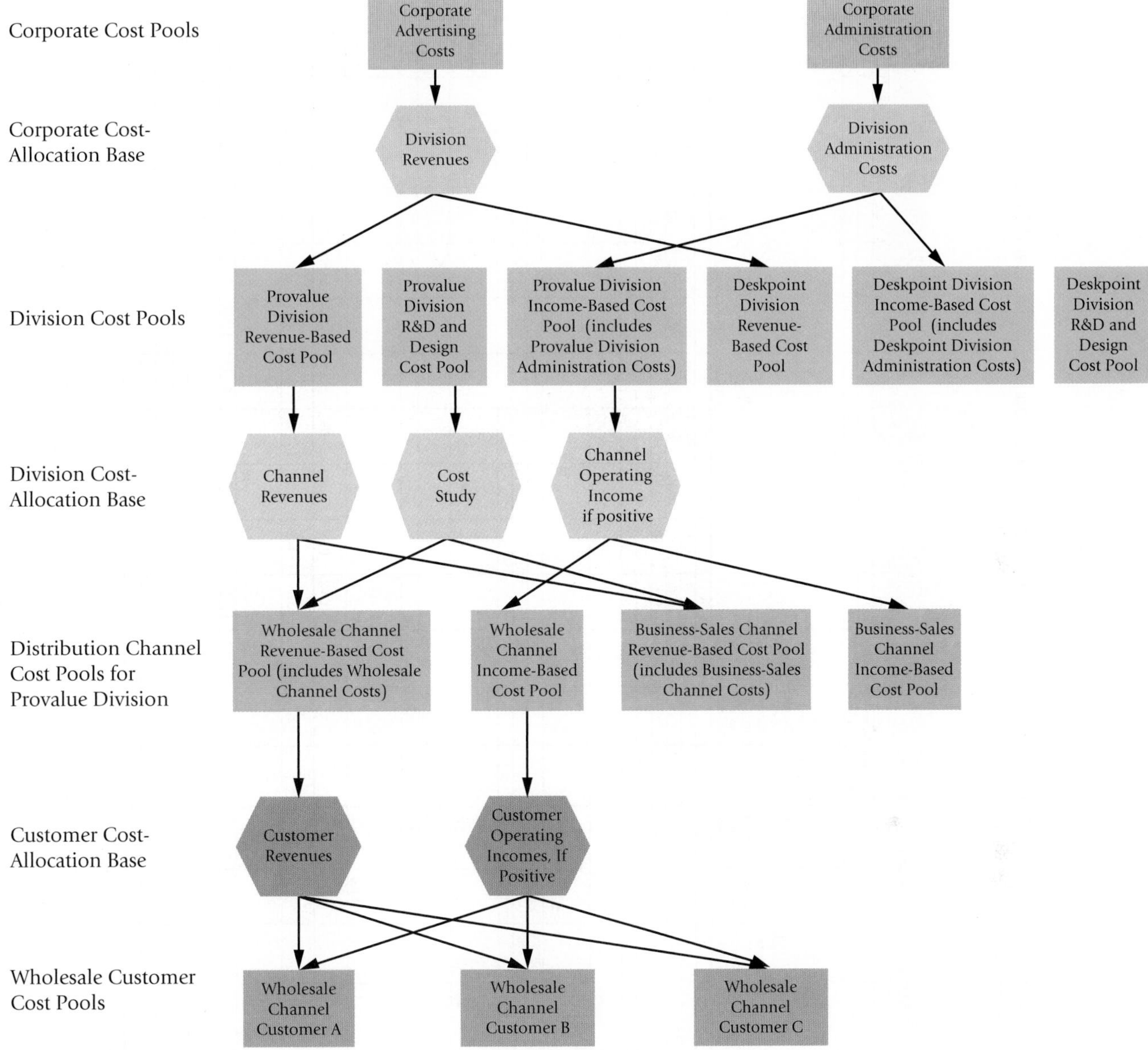

1. Start at the top of Exhibit 14-9 and the allocation of corporate advertising and corporate adminisitration costs based on the demands that the Provalue Division and Deskpoint Division customers place on corporate resources. The first two columns in Exhibit 14-10 present the allocation of corporate advertising and corporate administration costs to the Provalue and Deskpoint divisions.
   a. Astel allocates a total of \$1,050,000 of corporate advertising costs to the two divisions on the basis of the revenues of each division (benefits received). It is plausible to assume that customers with higher revenues benefited more from corporate advertising costs than customers with lower revenues (see Exhibit 14-7 for information on revenues of each division):

$$\text{Provalue Division: } \$1{,}050{,}000 \times \frac{\$150{,}000{,}000}{\$150{,}000{,}000 + \$200{,}000{,}000} = \$450{,}000$$

$$\text{Deskpoint Division: } \$1{,}050{,}000 \times \frac{\$200{,}000{,}000}{\$150{,}000{,}000 + \$200{,}000{,}000} = \$600{,}000$$

Exhibit 14-10 Profitability of Wholesale Customers of Provalue Division After Fully Allocating Corporate, Division, and Channel Indirect Costs (in thousands, rounded)

	A	B	C	D	E	F	G				H	I	J	K	L	M	N	O	P	Q	R
1							Provalue Division														
2		Astel Corporation Cost Pools		Provalue Division Cost Pools			Distribution Channel Cost Pools														
3		Costs Allocated Based on Division Revenues	Costs Allocated Based on Division Administration Costs	Costs Allocated Based on Channel Revenues	R&D and Design Cost Allocation Pool	Costs Allocated Based on Channel Operating Incomes	Wholesale Channel Costs Allocated Based on Customer Revenues	Wholesale Channel Costs Allocated Based on Customer Operating Incomes	Business-Sales Channel Costs Allocated Based on Customer Revenues	Business-Sales Channel Costs Allocated Based on Customer Operating Incomes	Wholesale Channel Customers										
4											A	B	C	D	E	F	G	H	I	J	Total
5	Revenues (Exhibit 14-4)										$30,000	$26,250	$13,000	$7,250	$1,800	$5,100	$4,750	$2,400	$2,600	$4,400	$97,550
6	Customer-level costs (Exh. 14-4, Col. 2-Col.1)										(25,085)	(20,560)	(10,345)	(5,805)	(1,700)	(4,114)	(5,100)	(2,935)	(3,300)	(3,578)	(82,522)
7	Customer-level operating income (Exh. 14-4)										4,915	5,690	2,655	1,445	100	986	(350)	(535)	(700)	822	15,028
8	Astel corporate advertising costs	$(1,050)																			
9	Astel corporate administration costs		$(4,400)																		
10	Allocate corporate advertising costs to divisions based on division revenues[1]	1,050		$(450)																	
11	Allocate corporate administration costs to divisions based on division administration costs[2]		4,400			$(2,090)															
12	R&D costs				$(2,400)																
13	Design costs				(3,000)																
14	Division administration costs					(1,900)															
15	Allocate corporate advertising costs from Provalue Division to wholesale channel based on channel revenues[3]			450			$ (293)		$ (157)												
16	Allocate R&D and Design costs to channels based on fairness[4]				5,400		(2,700)		(2,700)												
17	Distribution channel costs						(800)		(1,350)												
18	Allocate division administration costs from Provalue division to wholesale channel based on channel operating incomes[5]					3,990		$(2,725)		$(1,265)											
19	Allocate wholesale channel costs to customers based on customer revenues						3,793				(1,166)	(1,021)	(505)	(282)	(70)	(198)	(185)	(93)	(101)	(172)	(3,793)
20	Operating income before allocation of division and corporate administration										3,749	4,669	2,150	1,163	30	788	(535)	(628)	(801)	650	11,235
21	Allocate wholesale channel costs to customers based on customer operating income, if positive (ability to bear)							2,725			(774)	(964)	(444)	(240)	(6)	(163)				(134)	(2,725)
22	Fully allocated customer profitability										$ 2,975	$ 3,705	$ 1,706	$ 923	$ 24	$ 625	$ (535)	$ (628)	$ (801)	$ 516	$ 8,510
23																					
24	[1]$1,050 x $150,000 / ($150,000 + $200,000) = $450																				
25	[2]$4,400 x $1,900 / ($1,900 + $2,100) = $2,090																				
26	[3]$450 x $97,550 / $150,000 = $293; $450 x $52,450 / $150,000 = $157																				
27	[4]$5,400 / 2 = $2,700																				
28	[5]$3,990 x $11,235 / $16,450 = $2,725; $3,990 x $5,215 / $16,450 = $1,265																				

b. Using the benefits-received criterion, Astel allocates corporate administration costs of $4,400,000 to each division on the basis of division-administration costs because corporate administration's main role is to support division administration. Exhibit 14-6 shows division-administration costs for Provalue Division of $1,900,000. Division administration costs for Deskpoint Division are $2,100,000. The allocations are:

$$\text{Provalue Division: } \$4{,}400{,}000 \times \frac{\$1{,}900{,}000}{\$1{,}900{,}000 + \$2{,}100{,}000} = \$2{,}090{,}000$$

$$\text{Deskpoint Division: } \$4{,}400{,}000 \times \frac{\$2{,}100{,}000}{\$1{,}900{,}000 + \$2{,}100{,}000} = \$2{,}310{,}000$$

2. Next, drop down one level in Exhibit 14-9 and focus on the allocation of costs from the division cost pools to the distribution-channel cost pools for the Provalue Division. The three columns labeled "Provalue Division Cost Pools" in Exhibit 14-10 show the allocations of the Provalue Division costs to the wholesale channel and the business-sales channel.
   a. Using the benefits-received criterion, the corporate advertising cost of $450,000 that had been allocated to the Provalue Division is now reallocated to the wholesale channel and the business-sales channel on the basis of the revenues of each channel (see Exhibit 14-6).

$$\text{Wholesale Channel: } \$450{,}000 \times \frac{\$97{,}550{,}000}{\$97{,}550{,}000 + \$52{,}450{,}000} = \$292{,}650$$

$$\text{Business-Sales Channel: } \$450{,}000 \times \frac{\$52{,}450{,}000}{\$52{,}450{,}000 + \$97{,}550{,}000} = \$157{,}350$$

   b. The R&D costs and design costs are aggregated into one homogeneous cost pool and allocated to channels on the basis of a study analyzing the demand for R&D and design resources by the wholesale and business-sales channels. A significant amount of the R&D and design costs arise as a result of modifications to the Provalue computer demanded by the more sophisticated business customers. Using the results of the study and the fairness criterion, the Provalue Division allocates half of the R&D and design costs to the business-sales channel (and half to the wholesale channel) even though the business-sales channel accounts for only about one-third of the total sales of the Provalue Division. Exhibit 14-10 shows that the Provalue Division allocates $2,700,000 ($5,400,000 ÷ 2) each to the wholesale and business-sales channels.
   c. Each division adds the allocated corporate-administration costs to the division-administration cost pool. The costs in this cost pool are facility-sustaining costs and do not have a cause-and-effect relationship with any of the activities in the distribution channels. Astel, however, allocates all costs to products so that managers are aware of all costs when making pricing and other decisions. The Provalue Division allocates the total costs of $3,990,000 in the Provalue Division Administration cost pool to the wholesale channel and business-sales channel based on operating incomes of the wholesale and business-sales channels, representing the ability of each channel to bear division-administration costs (including allocated corporate-administration costs). The lower the operating income of a channel, the lower the division costs allocated to it. As described earlier in the chapter, the rationale for the ability-to-bear criterion is that divisions with lower incomes would work hard to reduce these overhead costs if they could manage these costs. From Exhibit 14-10, the operating income of the wholesale channel after subtracting all costs that have been allocated to it thus far is $11,234,850 ($15,027,500 (Cell R7) − $292,650 (Cell G15) − $2,700,000 (Cell G16) − $800,000 (Cell G17)) while the operating income of the business-sales channel is $5,215,150 (calculations not shown).

$$\text{Wholesale Channel: } \$3{,}990{,}000 \times \frac{\$11{,}234{,}850}{\$11{,}234{,}850 + \$5{,}215{,}150} = \$2{,}725{,}049$$

$$\text{Business-Sales Channel: } \$3{,}990{,}000 \times \frac{\$5{,}215{,}150}{\$11{,}234{,}850 + \$5{,}215{,}150} = \$1{,}264{,}951$$

3. Finally, focus on the bottom rows in Exhibit 14-9 and the allocation of costs from the distribution channel cost pools for the Provalue Division to individual wholesale channel customers. The four columns labeled "Provalue Division Distribution Channel Cost Pools" in Exhibit 14-10 show that the costs accumulated in the wholesale channel and the business-sales channel are allocated to customers. Exhibit 14-10 only presents the allocation of wholesale channel costs to wholesale customers.
   a. Some of the wholesale channel costs are allocated to individual wholesale customers on the basis of revenues because revenues are a good measure of how individual customers benefit from these costs. The costs in this cost pool total \$3,792,650 and are composed of three costs: (1) \$292,650 of corporate advertising costs allocated to the wholesale channel in step 2a, (2) \$2,700,000 of R&D and design costs allocated to the wholesale channel in step 2b, and (3) \$800,000 of costs of the wholesale-distribution channel itself (Exhibit 14-6). In Exhibit 14-10, the costs allocated to Customer A and Customer B are:

$$\text{Customer A: } \$3{,}792{,}650 \times \frac{\$30{,}000{,}000}{\$97{,}550{,}000} = \$1{,}166{,}371$$

$$\text{Customer B: } \$3{,}792{,}650 \times \frac{\$26{,}250{,}000}{\$97{,}550{,}000} = \$1{,}020{,}574$$

   b. The second wholesale channel cost pool is composed of \$2,725,049 of the division-administrative costs allocated to the wholesale channel in step 2c. These costs are allocated to individual wholesale customers on the basis of operating incomes (if positive) (see Exhibit 14-10, row 21) because operating incomes represent the ability of customers to bear these costs. In Exhibit 14-10, the sum of all the positive amounts in row 20 equals \$13,195, 922. The costs allocated to Customer A and Customer B are:

$$\text{Customer A: } \$2{,}725{,}049 \times \frac{\$3{,}748{,}629}{\$13{,}195{,}922} = \$774{,}117$$

$$\text{Customer B: } \$2{,}725{,}049 \times \frac{\$4{,}669{,}426}{\$13{,}195{,}922} = \$964{,}269$$

Issues in Allocating Corporate Costs to Divisions and Customers

Astel's management team makes several choices when accumulating and allocating corporate costs to divisions. We present two such issues next.

1. When allocating corporate costs to divisions, should Astel allocate only costs that vary with division activity or assign fixed costs as well? Managers allocate both variable and fixed costs to divisions and then to customers because the resulting costs are useful for making long-run strategic decisions, such as which customers to emphasize and what prices to offer. To make good long-run decisions, managers need to know the cost of all resources (whether variable or fixed in the short run) required to sell products to customers. Why? Because in the long run, firms can manage the levels of virtually all of their costs; very few costs are truly fixed. Moreover, to survive and prosper in the long run, firms must ensure that the revenues received from a customer exceed the total resources consumed to support the customer, regardless of whether these costs are variable or fixed in the short run.

   At the same time, companies that allocate corporate costs to divisions must carefully identify relevant costs for specific decisions. Suppose a division is profitable before any corporate costs are allocated but "unprofitable" after allocation of corporate costs. Should the division be closed down? The relevant corporate costs in this case are not the allocated corporate costs but those corporate costs that will be saved if the division is closed. If division profits exceed the relevant corporate costs, the division should not be closed.

2. When allocating costs to divisions, channels, and customers, how many cost pools should Astel use? One extreme is to aggregate all costs into a single cost pool. The other extreme is to have numerous individual cost pools. As discussed in Chapter 5, a major consideration is to construct **homogeneous cost pools** so that all of the costs in the cost pool have the same or a similar cause-and-effect or benefits-received relationship with the cost-allocation base.

For example, when allocating corporate costs to divisions, Astel can combine corporate advertising costs and corporate administration costs into a single cost pool if both cost categories have the same or similar cause-and-effect relationship with the same cost-allocation base. If, however, as is the case here, each cost category has a cause-and-effect or benefits-received relationship with a different cost-allocation base (for example, revenues of each division affect corporate advertising costs whereas division-administration costs of each division affect corporate administration costs), the company will prefer to maintain separate cost pools for each of these costs. Determining homogeneous cost pools requires judgment and should be revisited on a regular basis.

Managers must balance the benefit of using a multiple cost-pool system against the costs of implementing it. Advances in information-gathering technology make it more likely that multiple cost-pool systems will pass the cost–benefit test.

Decision Point

What are two key decisions managers must make when collecting costs in indirect-cost pools?

Using Fully Allocated Costs for Decision Making

How might Astel's managers use the fully allocated customer-profitability analysis in Exhibit 14-10? As we discussed in Chapter 13 when discussing product pricing, managers frequently favor using the full cost of a product when making pricing decisions. There are similar benefits to calculating fully allocated customer costs.

Consider, for example, Customer E, who shows a profitability of $24,000 in Exhibit 14-10. If this customer demanded a price reduction of $50,000, how should the Provalue Division respond? Based on the analysis in Exhibit 14-4, Customer E shows a profitability of $100,000 and it would appear that even a $50,000 reduction in price would still leave Customer E as a profitable customer. But in the long run, Customer E must generate sufficient profits to recover all the division-support costs of the Provalue Division and the corporate costs of Astel. A $50,000 reduction in price may not be sustainable in the long run. As the Provalue Division begins making plans for Provalue II (see Chapter 13), it simultaneously must consider what it can do to better manage its customers to improve profitability.

Another advantage of allocating costs to customers is that it highlights opportunities to manage costs. For example, the manager of the wholesale channel might want to probe whether the amounts spent on corporate advertising or on R&D and design help in promoting sales to wholesale customers. These discusssions might prompt a reevalaution of the amount and type of advertising, R&D, and design activity.

Sales Variances

The customer-profitability analysis in the previous section focused on the actual profitability of individual customers within a distribution channel (wholesale, for example) and their effect on the Provalue Division's profitability for 2013. At a more strategic level, however, recall that Provalue Division sells Provalues in two different markets: wholesale and directly to businesses. The operating margins in the business-sales market are higher than the operating margins in the wholesale market. In 2013, the Provalue Division had budgeted to sell 60% of its Provalues through wholesalers and 40% directly to businesses. It sold more Provalues in total than it had budgeted, but its actual sales mix (in computers) was 66.67% to wholesalers and 33.33% directly to businesses. Regardless of the profitability of sales to individual customers within each of the wholesale and business-sales channels, the Provalue Division's actual operating income, relative to the master budget, is likely to be positively affected by the higher number of Provalues sold

Learning Objective 6

Subdivide the sales-volume variance into the sales-mix variance

...this variance arises because actual sales mix differs from budgeted sales mix

and the sales-quantity variance

...this variance arises because actual total unit sales differ from budgeted total unit sales

and the sales-quantity variance into the market-share variance

...this variance arises because actual market share differs from budgeted market share

and the market-size variance

...this variance arises because actual market size differs from budgeted market size

and negatively affected by the shift in mix toward the less profitable wholesale customers. Sales-quantity and sales-mix variances can identify the effect of each of these factors on the Provalue Division's profitability. Companies such as Cisco, GE, and Hewlett-Packard perform similar analyses because they sell their products through multiple distribution channels like the Internet, over the telephone, and retail stores.

The Provalue Division classifies all customer-level costs, other than fixed machining costs of $11,400,000, as variable costs and distribution-channel and corporate-sustaining costs as fixed costs. To simplify the sales-variance analysis and calculations, we assume that all of the variable costs are variable with respect to Provalue computers sold. (This means that average batch sizes remain the same as the total number of Provalue computers sold vary.) Without this assumption, the analysis would become more complex and would have to be done using the ABC-variance analysis approach described in Chapter 8, pages 307–311. The basic insights, however, would not change.

Budgeted and actual operating data for 2013 are as follows:

Budget Data for 2013

	Selling Price (1)	Variable Cost per Unit (2)	Contribution Margin per Unit (3) = (1) − (2)	Sales Volume in Units (4)	Sales Mix (Based on Units) (5)	Contribution Margin (6) = (3) × (4)
Wholesale channel	$ 980	$755	$225	93,000	60%[a]	$20,925,000
Business-sales channel	1,050	775	275	62,000	40%	17,050,000
Total				155,000	100%	$37,975,000

[a]Percentage of unit sales to wholesale channel = 93,000 units ÷ 155,000 total unit = 60%.

Actual Results for 2013

	Selling Price (1)	Variable Cost per Unit (2)	Contribution Margin per Unit (3) = (1) − (2)	Sales Volume in Units (4)	Sales Mix (Based on Units) (5)	Contribution Margin (6) = (3) × (4)
Wholesale channel	$ 975.50	$749.225	$226.275	100,000	66.67%[a]	$22,627,500
Business-sales channel	1,049.00	784.55	264.45	50,000	33.33%	13,222,500
Total				150,000	100.00%	$35,850,000

[a]Percentage of unit sales to wholesale channel = 100,000 units ÷ 150,000 total unit = 66.67%.

The budgeted and actual fixed distribution-channel costs, division costs, and corporate-level costs are the same (see Exhibit 14-6, page 560, and Exhibit 14-7, page 561).

Recall that the levels of detail introduced in Chapter 7 (pages 250–256) included the static-budget variance (level 1), the flexible-budget variance (level 2), and the sales-volume variance (level 2). The sales-quantity and sales-mix variances are level 3 variances that subdivide the sales-volume variance.[7]

Static-Budget Variance

The *static-budget variance* is the difference between an actual result and the corresponding budgeted amount in the static budget. Our analysis focuses on the difference between actual and budgeted contribution margins (column 6 in the preceding tables). The total static-budget variance is $2,125,000 U (actual contribution margin of $35,850,000 – budgeted contribution margin of $37,975,000). Exhibit 14-11 (columns 1 and 3) uses the columnar format introduced in Chapter 7 to show detailed calculations of the static-budget variance. Managers can gain more insight about the static-budget variance by subdividing it into the flexible-budget variance and the sales-volume variance.

[7] The presentation of the variances in this chapter and the appendix draws on teaching notes prepared by J. K. Harris.

Exhibit 14-11 Flexible-Budget and Sales-Volume Variance Analysis of Provalue Division for 2013

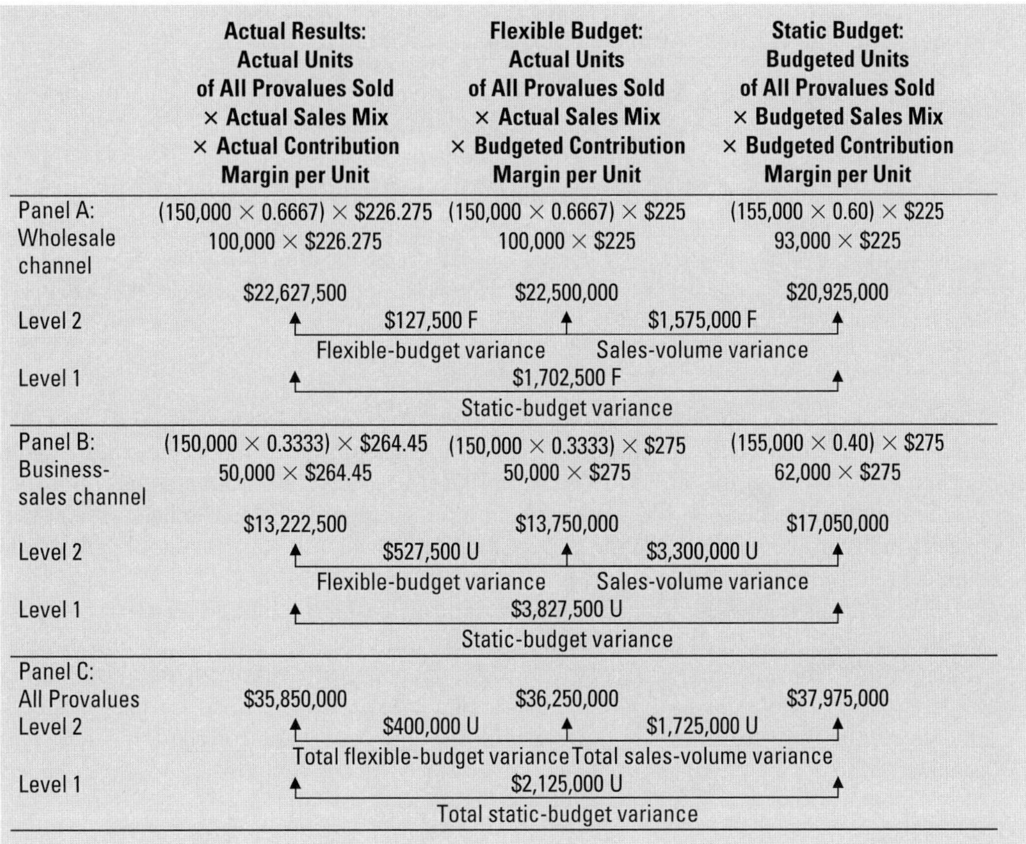

	Actual Results: Actual Units of All Provalues Sold × Actual Sales Mix × Actual Contribution Margin per Unit		Flexible Budget: Actual Units of All Provalues Sold × Actual Sales Mix × Budgeted Contribution Margin per Unit		Static Budget: Budgeted Units of All Provalues Sold × Budgeted Sales Mix × Budgeted Contribution Margin per Unit
Panel A: Wholesale channel	(150,000 × 0.6667) × $226.275 100,000 × $226.275		(150,000 × 0.6667) × $225 100,000 × $225		(155,000 × 0.60) × $225 93,000 × $225
	$22,627,500		$22,500,000		$20,925,000
Level 2		$127,500 F Flexible-budget variance		$1,575,000 F Sales-volume variance	
Level 1			$1,702,500 F Static-budget variance		
Panel B: Business-sales channel	(150,000 × 0.3333) × $264.45 50,000 × $264.45		(150,000 × 0.3333) × $275 50,000 × $275		(155,000 × 0.40) × $275 62,000 × $275
	$13,222,500		$13,750,000		$17,050,000
Level 2		$527,500 U Flexible-budget variance		$3,300,000 U Sales-volume variance	
Level 1			$3,827,500 U Static-budget variance		
Panel C: All Provalues Level 2	$35,850,000		$36,250,000		$37,975,000
		$400,000 U Total flexible-budget variance		$1,725,000 U Total sales-volume variance	
Level 1			$2,125,000 U Total static-budget variance		

Flexible-Budget Variance and Sales-Volume Variance

The *flexible-budget variance* is the difference between an actual result and the corresponding flexible-budget amount based on actual output level in the budget period. The flexible budget contribution margin is equal to budgeted contribution margin per unit times actual units sold of each product. Exhibit 14-11, column 2, shows the flexible-budget calculations. The flexible budget measures the contribution margin that the Provalue Division would have budgeted for the actual quantities of cases sold. The flexible-budget variance is the difference between columns 1 and 2 in Exhibit 14-11. The only difference between columns 1 and 2 is that actual units sold of each product is multiplied by actual contribution margin per unit in column 1 and budgeted contribution margin per unit in column 2. The $400,000 U total flexible-budget variance arises because actual contribution margin on business sales of $264.45 per Provalue is lower than the budgeted amount of $275 per Provalue and offsets the slightly higher actual contribution margin of $226.275 versus the budgeted contribution margin of $225 on wholesale channel sales. The Provalue Division managers are aware that the lower contribution margin of $10.55 ($275 – $264.45) per computer on business sales resulted from higher variable ordering and testing costs and have put in place action plans to reduce these costs in the future.

The *sales-volume variance* is the difference between a flexible-budget amount and the corresponding static-budget amount. In Exhibit 14-11, the sales-volume variance shows the effect on budgeted contribution margin of the difference between actual quantity of units sold and budgeted quantity of units sold. The sales-volume variance of $1,725,000 U is the difference between columns 2 and 3 in Exhibit 14-11. In this case, it is unfavorable overall because while wholesale channel sales of Provalue were higher than budgeted, business sales, which are expected to be more profitable on a per computer basis, were below budget. Provalue Division managers can gain substantial insight into the sales-volume variance by subdividing it into the sales-mix variance and the sales-quantity variance.

Sales-Mix Variance

The **sales-mix variance** is the difference between (1) budgeted contribution margin for the *actual sales mix* and (2) budgeted contribution margin for the *budgeted sales mix*. The formula and computations (using data from page 570) are as follows:

	Actual Units of All Provalues Sold	×	(Actual Sales-Mix Percentage	−	Budgeted Sales-Mix Percentage)	×	Budgeted Contribution Margin per Unit	=	Sales-Mix Variance
Wholesale	150,000 units	×	(0.66667 – 0.60)			×	$225 per unit	=	$2,250,000 F
Business-Sales	150,000 units	×	(0.33333 – 0.40)			×	$275 per unit	=	2,750,000 U
Total sales-mix variance									$ 500,000 U

A favorable sales-mix variance arises for the wholesale channel because the 66.67% actual sales-mix percentage exceeds the 60% budgeted sales-mix percentage. In contrast, the business-sales channel has an unfavorable variance because the 33.33% actual sales-mix percentage is less than the 40% budgeted sales-mix percentage. The total sales-mix variance is unfavorable because actual sales mix shifted toward the less profitable wholesale channel relative to budgeted sales mix.

The concept underlying the sales-mix variance is best explained in terms of composite units. A **composite unit** is a hypothetical unit with weights based on the mix of individual units. Given the budgeted sales for 2013, the composite unit consists of 0.60 units of sales to the wholesale channel and 0.40 units of sales to the business-sales channel. Therefore, the budgeted contribution margin per composite unit for the budgeted sales mix is as follows:

$$0.60 \times \$225 + 0.40 \times \$275 = \$245^{8}$$

Similarly, for the actual sales mix, the composite unit consists of 0.66667 units of sales to the wholesale channel and 0.33333 units of sales to the business-sales channel. The budgeted contribution margin per composite unit for the actual sales mix is therefore:

$$0.66667 \times \$225 + 0.33333 \times \$275 = \$241.6667$$

The impact of the shift in sales mix is now evident. The Provalue Division obtains a lower budgeted contribution margin per composite unit of \$3.3333 (\$245 − \$241.6667). For the 150,000 units actually sold, this decrease translates to a \$500,000 U sales-mix variance (\$3.3333 per unit × 150,000 units).

Managers should probe why the $500,000 U sales-mix variance occurred in 2013. Is the shift in sales mix because profitable business customers proved to be more difficult to find? Is it because of a competitor in the business-sales channel providing better service at a lower price? Or is it because the initial sales-volume estimates were made without adequate analysis of the potential market?

Exhibit 14-12 uses the columnar format to calculate the sales-mix variance and the sales-quantity variances.

Sales-Quantity Variance

The **sales-quantity variance** is the difference between (1) budgeted contribution margin based on *actual units sold of all products* at the budgeted mix and (2) contribution margin in the static budget (which is based on *budgeted units of all products to be sold*

[8] Budgeted contribution margin per composite unit can be computed in another way by dividing total budgeted contribution margin of $37,975,000 by total budgeted units of 155,000 (page 570): $37,975,000 ÷ 155,000 units = $245 per unit.

Exhibit 14-12 Sales-Mix and Sales-Quantity Variance Analysis of Provalue Division for 2013

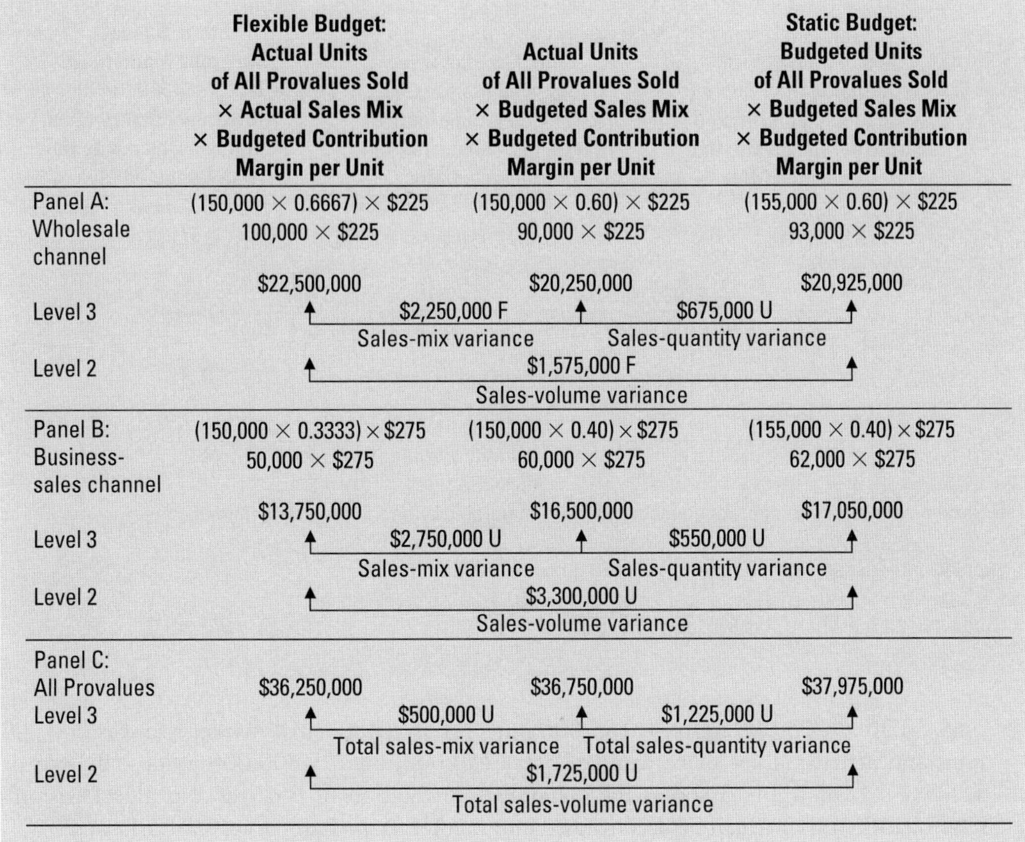

	Flexible Budget: Actual Units of All Provalues Sold × Actual Sales Mix × Budgeted Contribution Margin per Unit		Actual Units of All Provalues Sold × Budgeted Sales Mix × Budgeted Contribution Margin per Unit		Static Budget: Budgeted Units of All Provalues Sold × Budgeted Sales Mix × Budgeted Contribution Margin per Unit
Panel A: Wholesale channel	(150,000 × 0.6667) × $225 100,000 × $225		(150,000 × 0.60) × $225 90,000 × $225		(155,000 × 0.60) × $225 93,000 × $225
	$22,500,000		$20,250,000		$20,925,000
Level 3		$2,250,000 F Sales-mix variance		$675,000 U Sales-quantity variance	
Level 2			$1,575,000 F Sales-volume variance		
Panel B: Business-sales channel	(150,000 × 0.3333) × $275 50,000 × $275		(150,000 × 0.40) × $275 60,000 × $275		(155,000 × 0.40) × $275 62,000 × $275
	$13,750,000		$16,500,000		$17,050,000
Level 3		$2,750,000 U Sales-mix variance		$550,000 U Sales-quantity variance	
Level 2			$3,300,000 U Sales-volume variance		
Panel C: All Provalues	$36,250,000		$36,750,000		$37,975,000
Level 3		$500,000 U Total sales-mix variance		$1,225,000 U Total sales-quantity variance	
Level 2			$1,725,000 U Total sales-volume variance		

at budgeted mix). The formula and computations (using data from page 570) are as follows:

	Actual total Provalues sold − Budgeted total Provalues sold	×	Budgeted Sales-Mix Percentages	×	Budgeted Contribution Margin per Unit	=	Sales-Quantity Variance
Wholesale	(150,000 units − 155,000 units)	×	0.60	×	$225 per unit	=	$ 675,000 U
Business sales	(150,000 units − 155,000 units)	×	0.40	×	$275 per unit	=	550,000 U
Total sales-quantity variance							$1,225,000 U

This variance is unfavorable when actual units of all products sold are less than the budgeted units of all products sold. The Provalue Division sold 5,000 fewer Provalues than were budgeted, resulting in a $1,225,000 sales-quantity variance (also equal to budgeted contribution margin per composite unit for the budgeted sales mix times fewer units sold, $245 × 5,000). Managers would want to probe the reasons for the decrease in sales. Did lower sales come as a result of a competitor's aggressive marketing? Poorer customer service? Or decline in the overall market? Managers can gain additional insight into the causes of the sales-quantity variance by analyzing changes in Provalue Division's share of the total industry market and in the size of that market. The sales-quantity variance can be decomposed into market-share and market-size variances, as we describe in the next section.

Market-Share and Market-Size Variances

The total quantity of Provalues sold depends on overall demand for similar computers in the market, as well as Provalue Division's share of the market. Assume that the Provalue Division derived its total unit sales budget of 155,000 Provalue computers for 2013 from a management estimate of a 20% market share and a budgeted industry market size of 775,000

Exhibit 14-13 Market-Share and Market-Size Variance Analysis of Provalue Division of Astel Computers for 2013[a]

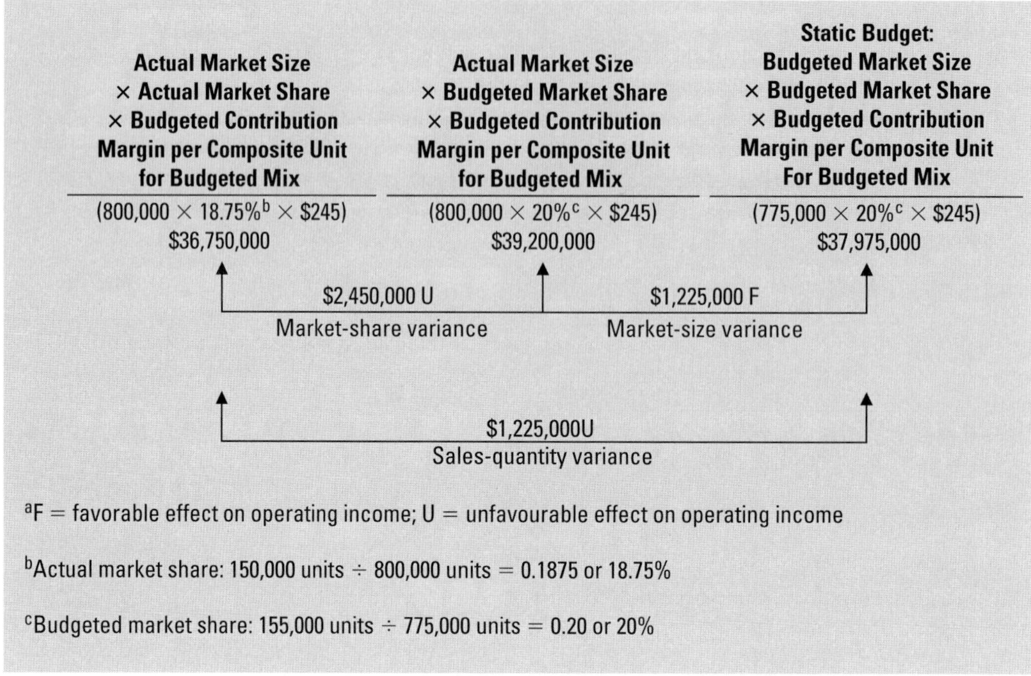

units (0.20 × 775,000 units = 155,000 units). For 2013, actual market size was 800,000 units and actual market share was 18.75% (150,000 units ÷ 800,000 units = 0.1875 or 18.75%). Exhibit 14-13 shows the columnar presentation of how the Provalue Division's sales-quantity variance can be decomposed into market-share and market-size variances.

Market-Share Variance

The **market-share variance** is the difference in budgeted contribution margin for actual market size in units caused solely by *actual market share* being different from *budgeted market share*. The formula for computing the market-share variance is as follows:

$$\text{Market-share variance} = \begin{matrix}\text{Actual}\\ \text{market size}\\ \text{in units}\end{matrix} \times \left(\begin{matrix}\text{Actual}\\ \text{market}\\ \text{share}\end{matrix} - \begin{matrix}\text{Budgeted}\\ \text{market}\\ \text{share}\end{matrix}\right) \times \begin{matrix}\text{Budgeted contribution}\\ \text{margin per composite unit}\\ \text{for budgeted mix}\end{matrix}$$

$$= 800{,}000 \text{ units} \times (0.1875 - 0.20) \times \$245 \text{ per unit}$$

$$= \$2{,}450{,}000 \text{ U}$$

The Provalue Division lost 1.25 market-share percentage points—from the 20% budgeted share to the actual share of 18.75%. The $2,450,000 U market-share variance is the decline in contribution margin as a result of those lost sales.

Market-Size Variance

The **market-size variance** is the difference in budgeted contribution margin at budgeted market share caused solely by *actual market size in units* being different from *budgeted market size in units*. The formula for computing the market-size variance is as follows:

$$\text{Market-size variance} = \left(\begin{matrix}\text{Actual}\\ \text{market}\\ \text{size}\end{matrix} - \begin{matrix}\text{Budgeted}\\ \text{market}\\ \text{size}\end{matrix}\right) \times \begin{matrix}\text{Budgeted}\\ \text{market}\\ \text{share}\end{matrix} \times \begin{matrix}\text{Budgeted contribution}\\ \text{margin per composite unit}\\ \text{for budgeted mix}\end{matrix}$$

$$= (800{,}000 \text{ units} - 775{,}000 \text{ units}) \times 0.20 \times \$245 \text{ per unit}$$

$$= \$1{,}225{,}000 \text{ F}$$

The market-size variance is favorable because actual market size increased 3.23% [(800,000 − 775,000) ÷ 775,000 = 0.0323, or 3.23%] compared to budgeted market size.

Managers should probe the reasons for the market-size and market-share variances for 2013. Is the $1,225,000 F market-size variance because of an increase in market size that can be expected to continue in the future? If yes, the Provalue Division has much to gain by attaining or exceeding its budgeted 20% market share. Was the $2,450,000 unfavorable market-share variance because of competitors providing better offerings or greater value to customers? Did competitors aggressively cut prices to stimulate market demand? Although Provalue Divison managers reduced prices a little relative to the budget, should they have reduced prices even more, particularly for business-sales customers where Provalue sales were considerably below budget and selling prices significantly higher than the prices charged to wholesalers? Was the quality and reliability of Provalue computers as good as the quality and reliability of competitors?

Some companies place more emphasis on the market-share variance than the market-size variance when evaluating their managers. That's because they believe the market-size variance is influenced by economy-wide factors and shifts in consumer preferences that are outside the managers' control, whereas the market-share variance measures how well managers performed relative to their peers.

Be cautious when computing the market-size variance and the market-share variance. Reliable information on market size and market share is not available for all industries. The automobile, computer, and television industries are cases in which market-size and market-share statistics are widely available. In other industries, such as management consulting and personal financial planning, information about market size and market share is far less reliable.

Decision Point

What are the two components of the sales-volume variance and two components of the sales-quantity variance?

Exhibit 14-14 presents an overview of the sales-mix, sales-quantity, market-share, and market-size variances for the Provalue Division. These variances can also be calculated in a multiproduct company, in which each individual product has a different contribution margin per unit. The Problem for Self-Study presents such a setting.

Exhibit 14-14

Overview of Variances for Provalue Division for 2013

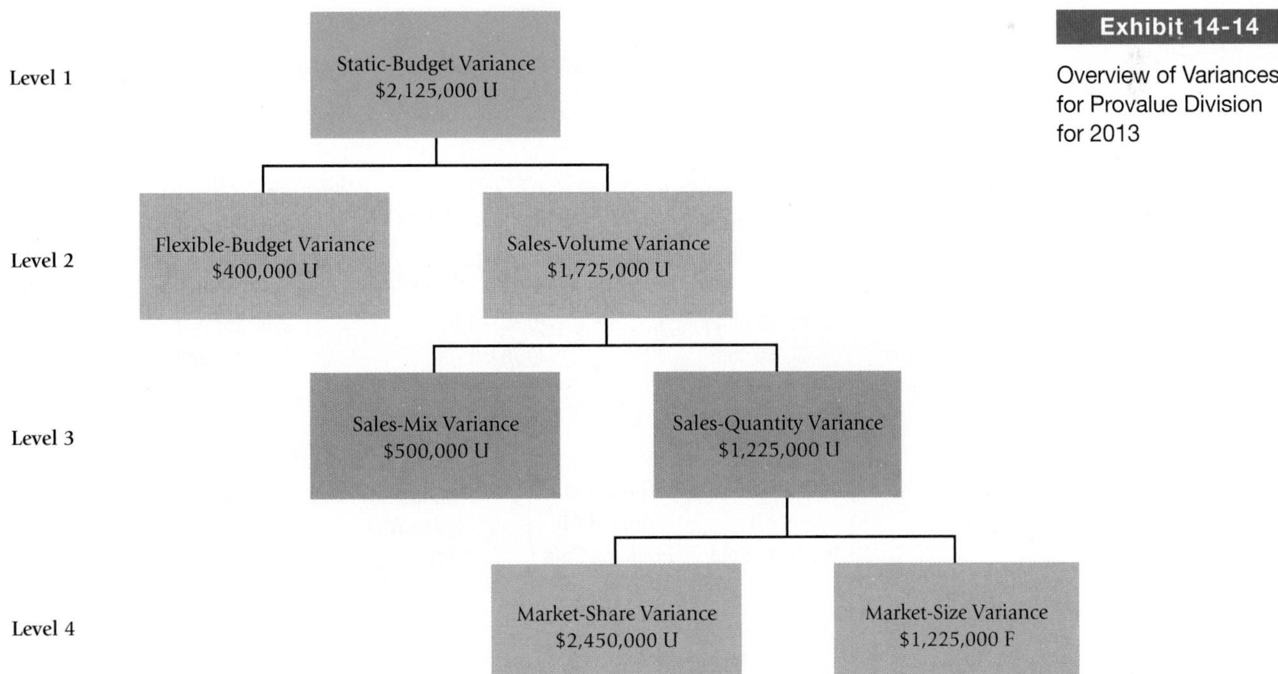

F = favorable effect on operating income; U = unfavorable effect on operating income

Problem for Self Study

The Payne Company manufactures two types of vinyl flooring. Budgeted and actual operating data for 2013 are as follows:

	Static Budget			Actual Results		
	Commercial	Residential	Total	Commercial	Residential	Total
Unit sales in rolls	20,000	60,000	80,000	25,200	58,800	84,000
Contribution margin	$10,000,000	$24,000,000	$34,000,000	$11,970,000	$24,696,000	$36,666,000

In late 2012, a marketing research firm estimated industry volume for commercial and residential vinyl flooring for 2013 at 800,000 rolls. Actual industry volume for 2013 was 700,000 rolls.

Required

1. Compute the sales-mix variance and the sales-quantity variance by type of vinyl flooring and in total. (Compute all variances in terms of contribution margins.)
2. Compute the market-share variance and the market-size variance.
3. What insights do the variances calculated in requirements 1 and 2 provide about Payne Company's performance in 2013?

Solution

1. Actual sales-mix percentage:

Commercial = 25,200 ÷ 84,000 = 0.30, or 30%

Residential = 58,800 ÷ 84,000 = 0.70, or 70%

Budgeted sales-mix percentage:

Commercial = 20,000 ÷ 80,000 = 0.25, or 25%

Residential = 60,000 ÷ 80,000 = 0.75, or 75%

Budgeted contribution margin per unit:

Commercial = $10,000,000 ÷ 20,000 units = $500 per unit

Residential = $24,000,000 ÷ 60,000 units = $400 per unit

	Actual Units of All Products Sold	×	(Actual Sales-Mix Percentage − Budgeted Sales-Mix Percentage)	×	Budgeted Contribution Margin per Unit	=	Sales-Mix Variance
Commercial	84,000 units	×	(0.30 – 0.25)	×	$500 per unit	=	$2,100,000 F
Residential	84,000 units	×	(0.70 – 0.75)	×	$400 per unit	=	1,680,000 U
Total sales-mix variance							$ 420,000 F

	(Actual Units of All Products Sold − Budgeted Units of All Products Sold)	×	Budgeted Sales-Mix Percentage	×	Budgeted Contribution Margin per Unit	=	Sales-Quantity Variance
Commercial	(84,000 units – 80,000 units)	×	0.25	×	$500 per unit	=	$ 500,000 F
Residential	(84,000 units – 80,000 units)	×	0.75	×	$400 per unit	=	1,200,000 F
Total sales-quantity variance							$1,700,000 F

2. Actual market share = 84,000 ÷ 700,000 = 0.12, or 12%
Budgeted market share = 80,000 ÷ 800,000 units = 0.10, or 10%

$$\text{Budgeted contribution margin per composite unit of budgeted mix} = \$34{,}000{,}000 \div 80{,}000 \text{ units} = \$425 \text{ per unit}$$

Budgeted contribution margin per composite unit of budgeted mix can also be calculated as follows:

Commercial: 500 per unit × 0.25	=	$125
Residential: 400 per unit × 0.75	=	300
Budgeted contribution margin per composite unit	=	$425

$$\text{Market-share variance} = \text{Actual market size in units} \times \left(\text{Actual market share} - \text{Budgeted market share}\right) \times \text{Budgeted contribution margin per composite unit for budgeted mix}$$

$$= 700{,}000 \text{ units} \times (0.12 - 0.10) \times \$425 \text{ per unit}$$

$$= \$5{,}950{,}000 \text{ F}$$

$$\text{Market-size variance} = \left(\text{Actual market size in units} - \text{Budgeted market size in units}\right) \times \text{Budgeted market share} \times \text{Budgeted contribution margin per composite unit for budgeted mix}$$

$$= (700{,}000 \text{ units} - 800{,}000 \text{ units}) \times 0.10 \times \$425 \text{ per unit}$$

$$= \$4{,}250{,}000 \text{ U}$$

Note that the algebraic sum of the market-share variance and the market-size variance is equal to the sales-quantity variance: $5,950,000 F + $4,250,000 U = $1,700,000 F.

3. Both the total sales-mix variance and the total sales-quantity variance are favorable. The favorable sales-mix variance occurred because the actual mix was composed of more of the higher-margin commercial vinyl flooring. The favorable total sales-quantity variance occurred because the actual total quantity of rolls sold exceeded the budgeted amount.

   The company's large favorable market-share variance is due to a 12% actual market share compared with a 10% budgeted market share. The market-size variance is unfavorable because the actual market size was 100,000 rolls less than the budgeted market size. Payne's performance in 2013 appears to be very good. Although overall market size declined, the company sold more units than budgeted and gained market share.

▶ Decision Points

The following question-and-answer format summarizes the chapter's learning objectives. Each decision presents a key question related to a learning objective. The guidelines are the answer to that question.

Decision	Guidelines
1. How can a company's revenues and costs differ across customers?	Revenues differ because of differences in the quantity purchased and price discounts. Costs differ because different customers place different demands on a company's resources in terms of processing sales orders, making deliveries, and customer support.
2. How do customer-profitability profiles help managers?	Companies should be aware of and devote sufficient resources to maintaining and expanding relationships with customers who contribute significantly to profitability and design incentives to change behavior patterns of unprofitable customers. Customer-profitability profiles often highlight that a small percentage of customers contributes a large percentage of operating income.

Decision	Guidelines
3. Why do managers prepare cost-hierarchy-based operating incomes statements?	Cost-hierarchy-based operating income statements allocate only those costs that will be affected by actions at a particular hierarchical level. For example, costs such as sales-order costs and shipment costs are allocated to customers because customer actions can affect these costs, but costs of managing the wholesale channel are not allocated to customers because changes in customer behavior will have no effect on these costs.
4. What criteria should managers use to guide cost-allocation decisions?	Managers should use the cause-and-effect and the benefits-received criteria to guide most cost-allocation decisions. Other criteria are fairness or equity and ability to bear.
5. What are two key decisions managers must make when collecting costs in indirect-cost pools?	Two key decisions related to indirect-cost pools are the number of indirect-cost pools to form and the individual cost items to be included in each cost pool to make homogeneous cost pools. Generally, managers allocate both variable costs and costs that are fixed in the short-run.
6. What are the two components of the sales-volume variance and two components of the sales-quantity variance?	The two components of sales-volume variance are (a) the difference between actual sales mix and budgeted sales mix (the sales-mix variance) and (b) the difference between actual unit sales and budgeted unit sales (the sales-quantity variance). The two components of the the sales-quantity variance are (a) the difference between the actual market share and the budgeted market share (the market-share variance) and (b) the difference between the actual market size in units and the budgeted market size in units (the market-size variance).

Terms to Learn

The chapter and the Glossary at the end of the book contain definitions of the following important terms:

composite unit **(p. 572)**
customer-cost hierarchy **(p. 552)**
customer-profitability analysis **(p. 551)**
homogeneous cost pools **(p. 569)**
market-share variance **(p. 574)**
market-size variance **(p. 574)**
price discount **(p. 552)**
sales-mix variance **(p. 572)**
sales-quantity variance **(p. 572)**
whale curve **(p. 558)**

Assignment Material

MyAccountingLab

Questions

14-1 "I'm going to focus on the customers of my business and leave cost-allocation issues to my accountant." Do you agree with this comment by a division president? Explain.

14-2 Why is customer-profitability analysis an important topic to managers?

14-3 How can a company track the extent of price discounting on a customer-by-customer basis?

14-4 "A customer-profitability profile highlights those customers a company should drop to improve profitability." Do you agree? Explain.

14-5 Give examples of three different levels of costs in a customer-cost hierarchy.

14-6 What information does the whale curve provide?

14-7 "A company should not allocate all of its corporate costs to its divisions." Do you agree? Explain.

14-8 What criteria might managers use to guide cost-allocation decisions? Which are the dominant criteria?

14-9 "Once a company allocates corporate costs to divisions, these costs should not be reallocated to the indirect-cost pools of the division." Do you agree? Explain.

14-10 "A company should not allocate costs that are fixed in the short run to customers." Do you agree? Explain briefly.

14-11 How many cost pools should a company use when allocating costs to divisions, channels, and customers?

14-12 Show how managers can gain insight into the causes of a sales-volume variance by subdividing the components of this variance.

14-13 How can the concept of a composite unit be used to explain why an unfavorable total sales-mix variance of contribution margin occurs?

14-14 Explain why a favorable sales-quantity variance occurs.

14-15 How can the sales-quantity variance be decomposed further?

Exercises

MyAccountingLab

14-16 Cost allocation in hospitals, alternative allocation criteria. Dave Meltzer vacationed at Lake Tahoe last winter. Unfortunately, he broke his ankle while skiing and spent two days at the Sierra University Hospital. Meltzer's insurance company received a $4,800 bill for his two-day stay. One item that caught Meltzer's attention was an $11.52 charge for a roll of cotton. Meltzer is a salesman for Johnson & Johnson and knows that the cost to the hospital of the roll of cotton is between $2.20 and $3.00. He asked for a breakdown of the $11.52 charge. The accounting office of the hospital sent him the following information:

a. Invoiced cost of cotton roll	$ 2.40
b. Cost of processing of paperwork for purchase	0.60
c. Supplies-room management fee	0.70
d. Operating-room and patient-room handling costs	1.60
e. Administrative hospital costs	1.10
f. University teaching-related costs	0.60
g. Malpractice insurance costs	1.20
h. Cost of treating uninsured patients	2.72
i. Profit component	0.60
Total	$11.52

Meltzer believes the overhead charge is outrageous . He comments, "There was nothing I could do about it. When they come in and dab your stitches, it's not as if you can say, 'Keep your cotton roll. I brought my own.'"

Required

1. Compute the overhead rate Sierra University Hospital charged on the cotton roll.
2. What criteria might Sierra use to justify allocation of the overhead items **b–i** in the preceding list? Examine each item separately and use the allocation criteria listed in Exhibit 14-8 (page 563) in your answer.
3. What should Meltzer do about the $11.52 charge for the cotton roll?

14-17 Customer profitability, customer-cost hierarchy. Enviro-Tech has only two retail and two wholesale customers. Information relating to each customer for 2013 follows (in thousands):

	Wholesale Customers		**Retail Customers**	
	North America Wholesaler	**South America Wholesaler**	**Green Energy**	**Global Power**
Revenues at list prices	$375,000	$590,000	$175,000	$130,000
Discounts from list prices	25,800	47,200	8,400	590
Cost of goods sold	285,000	510,000	144,000	95,000
Delivery costs	4,550	6,710	2,230	2,145
Order processing costs	3,820	5,980	2,180	1,130
Cost of sales visit	6,300	2,620	2,620	1,575

Enviro-Tech's annual distribution-channel costs are $33 million for wholesale customers and $12 million for retail customers. The company's annual corporate-sustaining costs, such as salary for top management and general-administration costs, are $48 million. There is no cause-and-effect or benefits-received relationship between any cost-allocation base and corporate-sustaining costs. That is, Enviro-Tech could save corporate-sustaining costs only if the company completely shuts down.

Required

1. Calculate customer-level operating income using the format in Exhibit 14-3.
2. Prepare a customer-cost hierarchy report, using the format in Exhibit 14-6.
3. Enviro-Tech's management decides to allocate all corporate-sustaining costs to distribution channels: $38 million to the wholesale channel and $10 million to the retail channel. As a result,

distribution channel costs are now $71million($33 million + $38 million) for the wholesale channel and $22 million($12 million + $10 million) for the retail channel. Calculate the distribution channel–level operating income. On the basis of these calculations, what actions, if any, should Enviro-Tech's managers take? Explain.

4. How might Enviro-Tech use the new cost information from its activity-based costing system to better manage its business?

14-18 Customer profitability, service company. Instant Service (IS) repairs printers and photocopiers for five multisite companies in a tristate area. IS's costs consist of the cost of technicians and equipment that are directly traceable to the customer site and a pool of office overhead. Until recently, IS estimated customer profitability by allocating the office overhead to each customer based on share of revenues. For 2013, IS reported the following results:

	A	B	C	D	E	F	G
1		Avery	Okie	Wizard	Grainger	Duran	Total
2	Revenues	$260,000	$200,000	$322,000	$122,000	$212,000	$1,116,000
3	Technician and equipment cost	182,000	175,000	225,000	107,000	178,000	867,000
4	Office overhead allocated	31,859	24,507	39,457	14,949	25,978	136,750
5	Operating income	$ 46,141	$ 493	$ 57,543	$ 51	$ 8,022	$ 112,250

Tina Sherman, IS's new controller, notes that office overhead is more than 10% of total costs, so she spends a couple of weeks analyzing the consumption of office overhead resources by customers. She collects the following information:

	I	J	K
1	Activity Area	Cost Driver Rate	
2	Service call handling	$75	per service call
3	Parts ordering	$80	per Web-based parts order
4	Billing and collection	$50	per bill (or reminder)
5	Customer database maintenance	$10	per service call

	A	B	C	D	E	F
8		Avery	Okie	Wizard	Grainger	Duran
9	Number of service calls	150	240	40	120	180
10	Number of Web-based parts orders	120	210	60	150	150
11	Number of bills (or reminders)	30	90	90	60	120

Required

1. Compute customer-level operating income using the new information that Sherman has gathered.
2. Prepare exhibits for IS similar to Exhibits 14-4 and 14-5. Comment on the results.
3. What options should IS consider, with regard to individual customers, in light of the new data and analysis of office overhead?

14-19 Customer profitability, distribution. Best Drugs is a distributor of pharmaceutical products. Its ABC system has five activities:

Activity Area	Cost Driver Rate in 2013
1. Order processing	$42 per order
2. Line-item ordering	$5 per line item
3. Store deliveries	$47 per store delivery
4. Carton deliveries	$4 per carton
5. Shelf-stocking	$13 per stocking-hour

Rick Flair, the controller of Best Drugs, wants to use this ABC system to examine individual customer profitability within each distribution market. He focuses first on the Ma and Pa single-store distribution market. Using only two customers helps highlight the insights available with the ABC approach. Data pertaining to these two customers in August 2013 are as follows:

	Ann Arbor Pharmacy	San Diego Pharmacy
Total orders	13	7
Average line items per order	11	19
Total store deliveries	5	7
Average cartons shipped per store delivery	21	18
Average hours of shelf-stocking per store delivery	0.5	0.75
Average revenue per delivery	$2,600	$1,900
Average cost of goods sold per delivery	$2,100	$1,700

Required

1. Use the ABC information to compute the operating income of each customer in August 2013. Comment on the results and what, if anything, Flair should do.
2. Flair ranks the individual customers in the Ma and Pa single-store distribution market on the basis of monthly operating income. The cumulative operating income of the top 20% of customers is $58,120. Best Drugs reports operating losses of $23,670 for the bottom 40% of its customers. Make four recommendations that you think Best Drugs should consider in light of this new customer-profitability information.

14-20 Cost allocation and decision making. Greenbold Manufacturing has four divisions named after its locations: Arizona, Colorado, Delaware, and Florida. Corporate headquarters is in Minnesota. Greenbold corporate headquarters incurs $8,400,000 per period, which is an indirect cost of the divisions. Corporate headquarters currently allocates this cost to the divisions based on the revenues of each division. The CEO has asked each division manager to suggest an allocation base for the indirect headquarters costs from among revenues, segment margin, direct costs, and number of employees. The following is relevant information about each division:

	Arizona	Colorado	Delaware	Florida
Revenues	$11,700,000	$12,750,000	$9,300,000	$8,250,000
Direct costs	7,950,000	6,150,000	6,450,000	6,900,000
Segment margin	$ 3,750,000	$ 6,600,000	$2,850,000	$1,350,000
Number of employees	3,000	6,000	2,250	750

Required

1. Allocate the indirect headquarters costs of Greenbold Manufacturing to each of the four divisions using revenues, direct costs, segment margin, and number of employees as the allocation bases. Calculate operating margins for each division after allocating headquarters costs.
2. Which allocation base do you think the manager of the Florida division would prefer? Explain.
3. What factors would you consider in deciding which allocation base Greenbold should use?
4. Suppose the Greenbold CEO decides to use direct costs as the allocation base. Should the Florida division be closed? Why or why not?

14-21 Cost allocation to divisions. Rembrandt Hotel & Casino is situated on beautiful Lake Tahoe in Nevada. The complex includes a 300-room hotel, a casino, and a restaurant. As Rembrandt's new controller, your manager asks you to recommend the basis the hotel should use for allocating fixed overhead costs to the three divisions in 2014. You are presented with the following income statement information for 2013:

	Hotel	Restaurant	Casino
Revenues	$16,425,000	$5,256,000	$12,340,000
Direct costs	9,819,260	3,749,172	4,248,768
Segment margin	$ 6,605,740	$1,506,828	$ 8,091,232

You are also given the following data on the three divisions:

	Hotel	Restaurant	Casino
Floor space (square feet)	80,000	16,000	64,000
Number of employees	200	50	250

You are told that you may choose to allocate indirect costs based on one of the following: direct costs, floor space, or the number of employees. Total fixed overhead costs for 2013 were $14,550,000.

Required

1. Calculate division margins in percentage terms prior to allocating fixed overhead costs.
2. Allocate indirect costs to the three divisions using each of the three allocation bases suggested. For each allocation base, calculate division operating margins after allocations in dollars and as a percentage of revenues.
3. Discuss the results. How would you decide how to allocate indirect costs to the divisions? Why?
4. Would you recommend closing any of the three divisions (and possibly reallocating resources to other divisions) as a result of your analysis? If so, which division would you close and why?

14-22 Cost allocation to divisions. Holbrook Corporation has three divisions: pulp, paper, and fibers. Holbrook's new controller, Paul Weber, is reviewing the allocation of fixed corporate-overhead costs to the three divisions. He is presented with the following information for each division for 2013:

	Pulp	Paper	Fibers
Revenues	$ 9,800,00	$17,100,000	$25,500,000
Direct manufacturing costs	3,500,000	7,800,000	11,100,000
Division administrative costs	3,300,000	2,000,000	4,700,000
Division margin	$3,000,000	$ 7,300,000	9,700,000
Number of employees	300	150	550
Floor space (square feet)	53,200	35,340	101,460

Until now, Holbrook Corporation has allocated fixed corporate-overhead costs to the divisions on the basis of division margins. Weber asks for a list of costs that comprise fixed corporate overhead and suggests the following new allocation bases:

Fixed Corporate Overhead Costs		Suggested Allocation Bases
Human resource management	$ 2,300,000	Number of employees
Facility	3,200,000	Floor space (square feet)
Corporate administration	4,600,000	Division administrative costs
Total	$10,100,000	

Required

1. Allocate 2013 fixed corporate-overhead costs to the three divisions using division margin as the allocation base. What is each division's operating margin percentage (division margin minus allocated fixed corporate-overhead costs as a percentage of revenues)?
2. Allocate 2013 fixed costs using the allocation bases suggested by Weber. What is each division's operating margin percentage under the new allocation scheme?
3. Compare and discuss the results of requirements 1 and 2. If division performance is linked to operating margin percentage, which division would be most receptive to the new allocation scheme? Which division would be the least receptive? Why?
4. Which allocation scheme should Holbrook Corporation use? Why? How might Weber overcome any objections that may arise from the divisions?

14-23 Variance analysis, multiple products. The Chicago Wolves play in the American Ice Hockey League. The Wolves play in the Downtown Arena, which is owned and managed by the City of Chicago. The arena has a capacity of 17,500 seats (6,500 lower-tier seats and 11,000 upper-tier seats). The arena charges the Wolves a per-ticket charge for use of its facility. All tickets are sold by the Reservation Network, which charges the Wolves a reservation fee per ticket. The Wolves' budgeted contribution margin for each type of ticket in 2013 is computed as follows:

	Lower-Tier Tickets	Upper-Tier Tickets
Selling price	$32	$14
Downtown Arena fee	9	4
Reservation Network fee	6	2
Contribution margin per ticket	$17	$ 8

The budgeted and actual average attendance figures per game in the 2013 season are as follows:

	Budgeted Seats Sold	Actual Seats Sold
Lower tier	5,500	3,600
Upper tier	7,000	6,400
Total	12,500	10,000

There was no difference between the budgeted and actual contribution margin for lower-tier or upper-tier seats.

The manager of the Wolves was unhappy that actual attendance was 20% below budgeted attendance per game, especially given the booming state of the local economy in the past six months.

Required

1. Compute the sales-volume variance for each type of ticket and in total for the Chicago Wolves in 2013. (Calculate all variances in terms of contribution margins.)
2. Compute the sales-quantity and sales-mix variances for each type of ticket and in total in 2013.
3. Present a summary of the variances in requirements 1 and 2. Comment on the results.

14-24 Variance analysis, working backward. The Hiro Corporation sells two brands of wine glasses: Plain and Chic. Hiro provides the following information for sales in the month of June 2014:

Static-budget total contribution margin	$15,525
Budgeted units to be sold of all glasses	2,300 units
Budgeted contribution margin per unit of Plain	$5 per unit
Budgeted contribution margin per unit of Chic	$12 per unit
Total sales-quantity variance	$2,700 U
Actual sales-mix percentage of Plain	60%

All variances are to be computed in contribution-margin terms.

Required

1. Calculate the sales-quantity variances for each product for June 2014.
2. Calculate the individual-product and total sales-mix variances for June 2014. Calculate the individual-product and total sales-volume variances for June 2014.
3. Briefly describe the conclusions you can draw from the variances.

14-25 Variance analysis, multiple products. Soda-King manufactures and sells two soft drinks: Kola and Limor. Budgeted and actual results for 2014 are as follows:

	Budget for 2014			Actual for 2014		
Product	Selling Price	Variable Cost per Carton	Cartons Sold	Selling Price	Variable Cost per Carton	Cartons Sold
Kola	$10.00	$5.50	500,000	$10.10	$5.75	504,300
Limor	$ 7.50	$4.00	750,000	$ 7.75	$3.70	725,700

Required

1. Compute the total sales-volume variance, the total sales-mix variance, and the total sales-quantity variance. (Calculate all variances in terms of contribution margin.) Show results for each product in your computations.
2. What inferences can you draw from the variances computed in requirement 1?

14-26 Market-share and market-size variances (continuation of 14-25). Soda-King prepared the budget for 2014 assuming a 12.5% market share based on total sales in the western region of the United States. The total soft drinks market was estimated to reach sales of 10 million cartons in the region. However, actual total sales volume in the western region was 12.3 million cartons.

Required

Calculate the market-share and market-size variances for Soda-King in 2014. (Calculate all variances in terms of contribution margin.) Comment on the results.

Problems

MyAccountingLab

14-27 Purposes of cost allocation. Sarah Reynolds recently started a job as an administrative assistant in the cost accounting department of Mize Manufacturing. New to the area of cost accounting, Sarah is puzzled by the fact that one of Mize's manufactured products, SR460, has a different cost depending on who asks for it. When the marketing department requested the cost of SR460 in order to determine pricing for the new catalog, Sarah was told to report one amount, but when a request came in the very next day from the financial reporting department for the cost of SR460, she was told to report a very different cost. Sarah runs a report using Mize's cost accounting system, which produces the following cost elements for one unit of SR460:

Direct materials	$57.00
Direct manufacturing labor	32.70
Variable manufacturing overhead	17.52
Allocated fixed manufacturing overhead	65.68
Research and development costs specific to SR460[a]	12.40
Marketing costs[a]	11.90
Sales commissions[a]	22.80
Allocated administrative costs of production department	10.76
Allocated administrative costs of corporate headquarters	37.20
Customer service costs[a]	6.10
Distribution costs[a]	17.60

[a]These costs are specific to SR460, but would not be eliminated if SR460 were purchased from an outside supplier. Allocated costs would be reallocated elsewhere in the company should the company cease production of SR460.

Required

1. Explain to Sarah why the cost given to the marketing and financial reporting departments would be different.
2. Calculate the cost of one unit of SR460 to determine the following:
   a. The selling price of SR460
   b. The cost of inventory for financial reporting
   c. Whether to continue manufacturing SR460 or to purchase it from an outside source (Assume that SR460 is used as a component in one of Mize's other products.)
   d. The ability of Mize's production manager to control costs

14-28 Customer profitability. Bracelet Delights is a new company that manufactures custom jewelry. Bracelet Delights currently has six customers referenced by customer number: 01, 02, 03, 04, 05, and 06. Besides the costs of making the jewelry, the company has the following activities:

Required

1. Customer orders. The salespeople, designers, and jewelry makers spend time with the customer. The cost driver rate is $42 per hour spent with a customer.
2. Customer fittings. Before the jewelry piece is completed, the customer may come in to make sure it looks right and fits properly. Cost driver rate is $30 per hour.
3. Rush orders. Some customers want their jewelry quickly. The cost driver rate is $90 per rush order.
4. Number of customer return visits. Customers may return jewelry up to 30 days after the pickup of the jewelry to have something refitted or repaired at no charge. The cost driver rate is $40 per return visit.

Information about the six customers follows. Some customers purchased multiple items. The cost of the jewelry is 60% of the selling price.

Customer number	**01**	**02**	**03**	**04**	**05**	**06**
Sales revenue	$850	$4,500	$280	$2,200	$5,500	$650
Cost of item(s)	$510	$2,700	$168	$1,320	$3,300	$390
Hours spent on customer order	3	10	1	8	17	5
Hours on fittings	1	6	0	0	4	0
Number of rush orders	0	2	1	2	3	0
Number of return visits	0	0	0	0	0	1

Required

1. Calculate the customer-level operating income for each customer. Rank the customers in order of most to least profitable and prepare a customer-profitability analysis, as in Exhibits 14-3 and 14-4.
2. Are any customers unprofitable? What is causing this? What should Bracelet Delights do about these customers?

14-29 Customer profitability, distribution. Green Paper Delivery has decided to analyze the profitability of five new customers. It buys recycled paper at $20 per case and sells to retail customers at a list price of $26 per case. Data pertaining to the five customers are:

	Customer				
	1	2	3	4	5
Cases sold	1,830	6,780	44,500	31,200	1,950
List selling price	$26	$26	$26	$26	$26
Actual selling price	$26	$25.20	$24.30	$25.80	$23.90
Number of purchase orders	10	18	35	16	35
Number of customer visits	3	5	12	4	12
Number of deliveries	12	28	65	25	35
Miles traveled per delivery	14	4	8	6	45
Number of expedited deliveries	0	0	0	0	3

Green Paper Delivery's five activities and their cost drivers are:

Activity	Cost Driver Rate
Order taking	$90 per purchase order
Customer visits	$75 per customer visit
Deliveries	$3 per delivery mile traveled
Product handling	$1.20 per case sold
Expedited deliveries	$250 per expedited delivery

Required

1. Compute the customer-level operating income of each of the five retail customers now being examined (1, 2, 3, 4, and 5). Comment on the results.
2. What insights do managers gain by reporting both the list selling price and the actual selling price for each customer?
3. What factors should managers consider in deciding whether to drop one or more of the five customers?

14-30 Customer profitability in a manufacturing firm. Antelope Manufacturing makes a component called A1030. This component is manufactured only when ordered by a customer, so Antelope keeps no inventory of A1030. The list price is $115 per unit, but customers who place "large" orders receive a 12% discount on price. The customers are manufacturing firms. Currently, the salespeople decide whether an order is large enough to qualify for the discount. When the product is finished, it is packed in cases of 10. If the component needs to be exchanged or repaired, customers can come back within 10 days for free exchange or repair.

The full cost of manufacturing a unit of A1030 is $95. In addition, Antelope incurs customer-level costs. Customer-level cost-driver rates are:

Order taking	$360 per order
Product handling	$15 per case
Rush order processing	$560 per rush order
Exchange and repair costs	$50 per unit

Information about Antelope's five biggest customers follows:

	A	B	C	D	E
Number of units purchased	5,400	1,800	1,200	4,400	8,100
Discounts given	12%	12%	0	12%	12% on half the units
Number of orders	8	16	52	20	16
Number of cases	540	180	120	440	810
Number of rush orders	1	6	1	0	5
Number of units exchanged/repaired	14	72	16	40	180

All customers except E ordered units in the same order size. Customer E's order quantity varied, so E got a discount part of the time but not all the time.

Required

1. Calculate the customer-level operating income for these five customers. Use the format in Exhibit 14-3. Prepare a customer-profitability analysis by ranking the customers from most to least profitable, as in Exhibit 14-4.
2. Discuss the results of your customer-profitability analysis. Does Antelope have unprofitable customers? Is there anything Antelope should do differently with its five customers?

14-31 Customer-cost hierarchy, customer profitability. Denise Nelson operates Interiors by Denise, an interior design consulting and window treatment fabrication business. Her business is made up of two different distribution channels, a consulting business in which Denise serves two architecture firms (Attractive Abodes and Better Buildings) and a commercial window treatment business in which Denise designs and constructs window treatments for three commercial clients (Cheery Curtains, Delightful Drapes, and Elegant Extras). Denise would like to evaluate the profitability of her two architecture firm clients and three commercial window treatment clients, as well as evaluate the profitability of each of the two channels and the business as a whole. Information about her most recent quarter follow:

Gross revenue from Attractive Abodes (AA)	$117,000
Gross revenue from Better Buildings (BB)	94,400
Gross revenue from Cheery Curtains (CC)	178,690
Gross revenue from Delightful Drapes (DD)	73,920
Gross revenue from Elegant Extras (EE)	36,600
Costs specific to AA	73,500
Costs specific to BB	58,600
Costs specific to CC	109,290
Costs specific to DD	57,860
Costs specific to EE	28,520
Overhead costs[a]	170,200

[a]Denise has determined that 25% of her overhead costs relate directly to her architectural business, 40% relate directly to her window treatment business, and the remainder are general in nature.

On the revenues indicated above, Denise gave a 10% discount to Attractive Abodes in order to lure it away from a competitor and gave a 5% discount to Elegant Extras for advance payment in cash.

Required

1. Prepare a customer-cost hierarchy report for Interiors by Denise, using the format in Exhibit 14-6.
2. Prepare a customer-profitability analysis for the five customers, using the format in Exhibit 14-4.
3. Comment on the results of the preceding reports. What recommendations would you give Denise?

14-32 Allocation of corporate costs to divisions. Dusty Rhodes, controller of Richfield Oil Company, is preparing a presentation to senior executives about the performance of its four divisions. Summary data (dollar amounts in millions) related to the four divisions for the most recent year are as follows:

	A	B	C	D	E	F
1		DIVISIONS				
2		Oil & Gas Upstream	Oil & Gas Downstream	Chemical Products	Copper Mining	Total
3	Revenues	$ 8,000	$16,000	$4,800	$3,200	$32,000
4	Operating Costs	3,000	15,000	3,800	3,500	25,300
5	Operating Income	$ 5,000	$ 1,000	$1,000	$ (300)	$ 6,700
6						
7	Identifiable assets	$14,000	$ 6,000	$3,000	$2,000	$25,000
8	Number of employees	9,000	12,000	6,000	3,000	30,000

Under the existing accounting system, costs incurred at corporate headquarters are collected in a single cost pool ($3,228 million in the most recent year) and allocated to each division on the basis of its actual revenues. The top managers in each division share in a division-income bonus pool. Division income is defined as operating income less allocated corporate costs.

Rhodes has analyzed the components of corporate costs and proposes that corporate costs be collected in four cost pools. The components of corporate costs for the most recent year (dollar amounts in millions) and Rhodes' suggested cost pools and allocation bases are as follows:

	A	B	C	D	E	F
11	**Corporate Cost Category**	**Amount**	**Suggested Cost Pool**	**Suggested Allocation Base**		
12	Interest on debt	$2,000	Cost Pool 1	Identifiable assets		
13	Corporate salaries	150	Cost Pool 2	Division revenues		
14	Accounting and control	110	Cost Pool 2			
15	General marketing	200	Cost Pool 2			
16	Legal	140	Cost Pool 2			
17	Research and development	200	Cost Pool 2			
18	Public affairs	203	Cost Pool 3	Positive operating income*		
19	Personnel and payroll	225	Cost Pool 4	Number of employees		
20	Total	$3,228				
21						
22	*Because public affairs cost includes the cost of public relations staff, lobbyists, and donations to					
23	environmental charities, Rhodes proposes that this cost be allocated using operating income (if positive)					
24	of divisions, with only divisions with positive operating income included in the allocation base.					

Required

1. Discuss two reasons why Richfield Oil should allocate corporate costs to each division.
2. Calculate the operating income of each division when all corporate costs are allocated based on revenues of each division.
3. Calculate the operating income of each division when all corporate costs are allocated using the four cost pools.
4. How do you think the division managers will receive the new proposal? What are the strengths and weaknesses of Rhodes' proposal relative to the existing single-cost-pool method?

14-33 Cost allocation to divisions. Forber Bakery makes baked goods for grocery stores and has three divisions: bread, cake, and doughnuts. Each division is run and evaluated separately, but the main headquarters incurs costs that are indirect costs for the divisions. Costs incurred in the main headquarters are as follows:

Human resources (HR) costs	$1,900,000
Accounting department costs	1,400,000
Rent and depreciation	1,200,000
Other	600,000
Total costs	$5,100,000

The Forber upper management currently allocates this cost to the divisions equally. One of the division managers has done some research on activity-based costing and proposes the use of different allocation bases for the different indirect costs—number of employees for HR costs, total revenues for accounting department costs, square feet of space for rent and depreciation costs, and equal allocation among the divisions of "other" costs. Information about the three divisions follows:

	Bread	**Cake**	**Doughnuts**
Total revenues	$20,900,000	$4,500,000	$13,400,000
Direct costs	14,500,000	3,200,000	7,250,000
Segment margin	$ 6,400,000	$1,300,000	$ 6,150,000
Number of employees	400	100	300
Square feet of space	10,000	4,000	6,000

Required

1. Allocate the indirect costs of Forber to each division equally. Calculate division operating income after allocation of headquarter costs.
2. Allocate headquarter costs to the individual divisions using the proposed allocation bases. Calculate the division operating income after allocation. Comment on the allocation bases used to allocate headquarter costs.
3. Which division manager do you think suggested this new allocation. Explain briefly. Which allocation do you think is "better?"

14-34 Cost-hierarchy income statement and allocation of corporate, division, and channel costs to customers. Rod Manufacturing Company produces metal rods for their customers. Its wholesale division is the focus of our analysis.

Management of the company wishes to analyze the profitability of the three key customers in the division and has gathered the following information.

	Customer A	Customer B	Customer C	Other Customers	Division
Revenue	1,054,826	1,544,680	2,210,162	480,332	5,290,000
Customer-level costs	675,378	951,669	1,517,895	266,058	3,411,000
Customer-level operating income	379,448	593,011	692,267	214,274	1,879,000
Customer-level operating income percentage	35.973%	38.391%	31.322%	44.610%	35.5%

The company allocates wholesale channel costs to customers based on one cost pool and division costs based on two cost pools as follows. Customer actions do not influence these costs.

	Total	Allocation basis
Wholesale-channel cost pool	$740,000	Customer-level operating income
Division costs		
Marketing costs	$560,000	Customer revenue
Administration costs	$240,000	Customer-level costs

Required

1. Calculate customer profitability as a percentage of revenue after assigning customer-level costs, distribution-channel costs, and division costs. Comment on your results.
2. What are the advantages and disadvantages of Rod Manufacturing allocating wholesale-channel and division costs to customers?

14-35 Cost-hierarchy income statement and allocation of corporate, division, and channel costs to customers. Basic Boards makes keyboards that are sold to different customers in two main distribution channels. Recently, the company's profitability has decreased. Management would like to analyze the profitability of each channel based on the following information:

	Distribution Channel A	Distribution Channel B	Total
Revenue	$2,599,506	$2,690,494	$5,290,000
Customer-level costs	1,627,047	1,783,953	3,411,000
Customer-level operating income	$ 972,459	$ 906,541	$1,879,000
Customer-level operating income as a percentage of revenue	37.409%	33.694%	35.5%

The company allocates distribution costs to the two channels as follows:

	Total	Allocation basis
Distribution costs		
Marketing costs	$560,000	Channel revenue
Administration costs	$240,000	Customer-level costs

Based on a special study, the company allocates corporate costs to the two channels based on the corporate resources demanded by the channels as follows: Distribution Channel A, $440,000, and Distribution Channel B, $500,000. If the company were to close a distribution channel, none of the corporate costs would be saved.

Required

1. Calculate the operating income for each distribution channel as a percentage of revenue after assigning customer-level costs, distribution costs, and corporate costs.
2. Should Basic Boards close down any distribution channel? Explain briefly.
3. Would you allocate corporate costs to divisions? Why is allocating these costs helpful? What actions would it help you take?

14-36 Variance analysis, sales-mix and sales-quantity variances. Houston Infonautics, Inc., produces handheld Windows CE™-compatible organizers. Houston Infonautics markets three different handheld models: PalmPro is a souped-up version for the executive on the go, PalmCE is a consumer-oriented version, and PalmKid is a stripped-down version for the young adult market. You are Houston Infonautics' senior vice president of marketing. The CEO has discovered that the total contribution margin came in lower than budgeted, and it is your responsibility to explain to him why actual results are different from the budget. Budgeted and actual operating data for the company's third quarter of 2014 are as follows:

Budgeted Operating Data, Third Quarter 2014

	Selling Price	Variable Cost per Unit	Contribution Margin per Unit	Sales Volume in Units
PalmPro	$380	$185	$195	5,550
PalmCE	274	97	177	44,400
PalmKid	146	65	81	61,050
				111,000

Actual Operating Data, Third Quarter 2014

	Selling Price	Variable Cost per Unit	Contribution Margin per Unit	Sales Volume in Units
PalmPro	$351	$180	$ 171	4,600
PalmCE	284	92	192	49,450
PalmKid	115	73	42	60,950
				115,000

Required

1. Compute the actual and budgeted contribution margins in dollars for each product and in total for the third quarter of 2014.
2. Calculate the actual and budgeted sales mixes for the three products for the third quarter of 2014.
3. Calculate total sales-volume, sales-mix, and sales-quantity variances for the third quarter of 2014. (Calculate all variances in terms of contribution margins.)
4. Given that your CEO is known to have temper tantrums, you want to be well prepared for this meeting. In order to prepare, write a paragraph or two comparing actual results to budgeted amounts.

14-37 Market-share and market-size variances (continuation of 14-36). Houston Infonautics' senior vice president of marketing prepared his budget at the beginning of the third quarter assuming a 25% market share based on total sales. Foolinstead Research estimated that the total handheld-organizer market would reach sales of 444,000 units worldwide in the third quarter. However, actual sales in the third quarter were 500,000 units.

1. Calculate the market-share and market-size variances for Houston Infonautics in the third quarter of 2014 (calculate all variances in terms of contribution margins).
2. Explain what happened based on the market-share and market-size variances.
3. Calculate the actual market size, in units, that would have led to no market-size variance (again using budgeted contribution margin per unit). Use this market-size figure to calculate the actual market share that would have led to a zero market-share variance.

14-38 Variance analysis, multiple products. The Robin's Basket operates a chain of Italian gelato stores. Although the Robin's Basket charges customers the same price for all flavors, production costs vary, depending on the type of ingredients. Budgeted and actual operating data of its Washington, D.C., store for August 2014 are as follows:

Budget for August 2014

	Selling Price per Pint	Variable Cost per Pint	Contribution Margin per Pints	Sales Volume in Pints
Mint chocolate chip	$9.00	$4.80	$4.20	35,000
Vanilla	9.00	3.20	5.80	45,000
Rum raisin	9.00	5.00	4.00	20,000
				100,000

Actual for August 2014

	Selling Price per Pint	Variable Cost per Pound	Contribution Margin per Pound	Sales Volume in Pounds
Mint chocolate chip	$9.00	$4.60	$4.40	33,750
Vanilla	9.00	3.25	5.75	56,250
Rum raisin	9.00	5.15	3.85	22,500
				112,500

The Robin's Basket focuses on contribution margin in its variance analysis.

Required

1. Compute the total sales-volume variance for August 2014.
2. Compute the total sales-mix variance for August 2014.
3. Compute the total sales-quantity variance for August 2014.
4. Comment on your results in requirements 1, 2, and 3.

14-39 Customer profitability and ethics. KC Corporation manufactures an air-freshening device called GoodAir, which it sells to six merchandising firms. The list price of a GoodAir is $30, and the full manufacturing costs are $18. Salespeople receive a commission on sales, but the commission is based on number of orders taken, not on sales revenue generated or number of units sold. Salespeople receive a commission of $10 per order (in addition to regular salary).

KC Corporation makes products based on anticipated demand. KC carries an inventory of GoodAir, so rush orders do not result in any extra manufacturing costs over and above the $18 per unit. KC ships finished product to the customer at no additional charge for either regular or expedited delivery. KC incurs significantly higher costs for expedited deliveries than for regular deliveries. Customers occasionally return shipments to KC, and the company subtracts these returns from gross revenue. The customers are not charged a restocking fee for returns.

Budgeted (expected) customer-level cost driver rates are:

Order taking (excluding sales commission)	$15 per order
Product handling	$1 per unit
Delivery	$1.20 per mile driven
Expedited (rush) delivery	$175 per shipment
Restocking	$50 per returned shipment
Visits to customers	$125 per customer

Because salespeople are paid $10 per order, they often break up large orders into multiple smaller orders. This practice reduces the actual order-taking cost by $7 per smaller order (from $15 per order to $8 per order) because the smaller orders are all written at the same time. This lower cost rate is not included in budgeted rates because salespeople create smaller orders without telling management or the accounting department. All other actual costs are the same as budgeted costs.

Information about KC's clients follows:

	AC	DC	MC	JC	RC	BC
Total number of units purchased	225	520	295	110	390	1,050
Number of actual orders	5	20	4	6	9	18
Number of written orders	10	20*	9	12	24	36
Total number of miles driven to deliver all products	360	580	350	220	790	850
Total number of units returned	15	40	0	0	35	40
Number of returned shipments	3	2	0	0	1	5
Number of expedited deliveries	0	8	0	0	3	4

* Because DC places 20 separate orders, its order costs are $15 per order. All other orders are multiple smaller orders and so have actual order costs of $8 each.

Required

1. Classify each of the customer-level operating costs as a customer output unit–level, customer batch-level, or customer-sustaining cost.
2. Using the preceding information, calculate the expected customer-level operating income for the six customers of KC Corporation. Use the number of written orders at $15 each to calculate expected order costs.
3. Recalculate the customer-level operating income using the number of written orders but at their actual $8 cost per order instead of $15 (except for DC, whose actual cost is $15 per order). How will KC Corporation evaluate customer-level operating cost performance this period?
4. Recalculate the customer-level operating income if salespeople had not broken up actual orders into multiple smaller orders. Don't forget to also adjust sales commissions.
5. How is the behavior of the salespeople affecting the profit of KC Corporation? Is their behavior ethical? What could KC Corporation do to change the behavior of the salespeople?

15 Allocation of Support-Department Costs, Common Costs, and Revenues

Learning Objectives

1. Distinguish the single-rate method from the dual-rate method
2. Understand how the choice between allocation based on budgeted and actual rates and between budged and actual usage can affect the incentives of division managers
3. Allocate multiple support-department costs using the direct method, the step-down method, and the reciprocal method
4. Allocate common costs using the stand-alone method and the incremental method
5. Explain the importance of explicit agreement between contracting parties when the reimbursement amount is based on costs incurred
6. Understand how bundling of products causes revenue allocation issues and the methods managers use to allocate revenues

How a company allocates its overhead and internal support costs—costs related to marketing, advertising, and other internal services—among its various production departments or projects can have a big impact on how profitable those departments or projects are.

While the allocation may not affect the firm's profit as a whole, if the allocation isn't done properly, it can make some departments and projects (and their managers) look better or worse than they should profit-wise. As the following article shows, the method of allocating costs for a project affects not just the firm but also the consumer. Based on the method used, consumers may spend more, or less, for the same service.

Cost Allocation and the Future of "Smart Grid" Energy Infrastructure[1]

Across the globe, countries are adopting alternative methods of generating and distributing energy. The United States is moving toward a "Smart Grid"—that is, making transmission and power lines operate and communicate in a more effective and efficient manner using technology, computers, and software. This proposed system would also integrate with emerging clean-energy sources, such as solar farms and geothermal systems, to help create a more sustainable electricity supply that reduces carbon emissions.

Electric Power Resource Institute is an independent, nonprofit organization headquartered in California. According to this Institute, the cost of developing the "Smart Grid" is between $338 billion and $476 billion over the next two decades. These costs include new infrastructure and technology improvements—mostly to power lines—as well as costs for upgrading the power system. Private utilities and the U.S. government will pay for the costs of "Smart Grid" development, but those costs will be recouped over time by charging energy consumers. A controversy emerged as the U.S. government debated two cost allocation methods for charging consumers. One method was

[1] *Sources*: Josie Garthwaite, "The $160B Question: Who Should Foot the Bill for Transmission Buildout?" *Salon.com* (March 12, 2009); Mark Jaffe, "Cost of Smart-Grid Projects Shocks Consumer Advocates," *The Denver Post* (February 14, 2010).

interconnection-wide cost allocation. Under this system, everybody in the region where a new technology was deployed would have to help pay for it. For example, if new power lines and "smart" energy meters were deployed in Denver, Colorado, everybody in Colorado would help pay for them. Supporters argued that this method would help lessen the costs of actual consumers for the significant investments in new technology.

A competing proposal would allocate costs only to utility ratepayers who actually benefited from the new "Smart Grid" system. In the previous example, only utility customers in Denver would be charged for the new power lines and energy meters. Supporters of this method believed that customers with new "Smart Grid" systems should not be subsidized by those not receiving any of the benefits.

Ultimately, the government decided to only charge the consumers who benefited. These customers would see their average monthly electricity bill increase by $9 to $12, but Smart Grid technology would provide greater grid reliability, integration of solar rooftop generation and plug-in vehicles, reductions in electricity demand, and stronger cybersecurity.

The same allocation dilemmas apply when costs of corporate support departments are allocated across multiple divisions or operating departments at manufacturing companies such as Nestle, service companies such as Comcast, merchandising companies such as Trader Joe's, and academic institutions such as Auburn University. This chapter focuses on several challenges that managers face when making decisions about cost and revenue allocations.

Allocating Support Department Costs Using the Single-Rate and Dual-Rate Methods

Learning Objective 1

Distinguish the single-rate method

...one rate for allocating costs in a cost pool

from the dual-rate method

...two rates for allocating costs in a cost pool—one for variable costs and one for fixed costs

Companies distinguish operating departments (and operating divisions) from support departments. An **operating department**, also called a **production department**, directly adds value to a product or service. Examples are manufacturing departments where products are made. A **support department**, also called a **service department**, provides the services that assist other internal departments (operating departments and other support departments) in the company. Examples of support departments are information systems, production control, materials management, and plant maintenance. Managers face two questions when allocating the costs of a support department to operating departments or divisions: (1) Should fixed costs of support departments, such as the salary of the department manager, be allocated to operating divisions? (2) If fixed costs are allocated, should variable and fixed costs of the support department be allocated in the same way? With regard to the first question, most companies believe that fixed costs of support departments should be allocated because the support department needs to incur these fixed costs to provide operating divisions with the services they require. Depending on the answer to the first question, there are two approaches to allocating support-department costs: the *single-rate cost-allocation method* and the *dual-rate cost-allocation method*.

Single-Rate and Dual-Rate Methods

The **single-rate method** does not distinguish between fixed and variable costs. It allocates costs in each cost pool (support department in this section) to cost objects (operating divisions in this section) using the same rate per unit of a single allocation base. By contrast, the **dual-rate method** partitions the cost of each support department into two pools, a variable-cost pool and a fixed-cost pool, and allocates each pool using a different cost-allocation base. When using either the single-rate method or the dual-rate method, managers can allocate support-department costs to operating divisions based on either a *budgeted* rate or the eventual *actual* cost rate. The latter approach is neither conceptually preferred nor widely used in practice (we explain why in the next section). Accordingly, we illustrate the single-rate and dual-rate methods next based on the use of *budgeted* rates.

We continue the Robinson Company example first presented in Chapter 4. Recall that Robinson manufactures and installs specialized machinery for the paper-making industry. In Chapter 4 we used a single manufacturing overhead cost pool with direct manufacturing labor-hours as the cost-allocation base to allocate all manufacturing overhead costs to jobs. In this chapter, we present a more detailed accounting system to take into account the different operating and service departments within Robinson's manufacturing department.

Robinson has two operating departments—the Machining Department and the Assembly Department—where production occurs and three support departments—Plant Administration, Engineering and Production Control, and Materials Management—that provide essential services to the operating departments for manufacturing the specialized machinery.

- The Plant Adminstration Department is responsible for managing all activities in the plant. That is, its costs are incurred to support, and can be considered part of the supervision costs of, all the other departments.
- The Engineering and Production Control Department supports all the engineering activity in the other departments. In other words, its costs are incurred to support the engineering costs of the other departments and so can be considered part of the engineering costs of those departments.
- The Materials Management Department is responsible for managing and moving materials and components required for different jobs. Each job at Robinson is different and requires small quantities of unique components to be machined and assembled. Materials Management Department costs vary with the number of material-handling labor-hours incurred to support each department. The Materials Management Department invests a substantial number of material-handling labor-hours in support of the Assembly Department.

The specialized machinery that Robinson manufactures does not go through the service departments and so the costs of the service departments must be allocated to the operating departments to determine the full cost of making the specialized machinery. Once costs are accumulated in the operating departments, they can be absorbed into the different specialized machines that Robinson manufactures. Different jobs need different amounts of machining and assembly resources. Each operating department has a different overhead cost driver to absorb overhead costs to machines produced: machine-hours in the Machining Department and assembly labor-hours in the Assembly Department.

We first focus on the allocation of the Materials Management Department costs to the Machining Department and the Assembly Department. The following data relate to the 2013 budget:

Practical capacity	4,000 hours
Fixed costs of the materials management department in the 3,000 labor-hour to 4,000 labor-hour relevant range	$144,000
Budgeted usage (quantity) in labor-hours:	
Machining department	800 hours
Assembly department	2,800 hours
Total	3,600 hours

Budgeted variable cost per material-handling labor-hour in the 3,000 labor-hour to 4,000 labor-hour relevant range	\$30 per hour used
Actual usage in 2013 in labor-hours:	
Machining department	1,200 hours
Assembly department	2,400 hours
Total	3,600 hours

The budgeted rates for materials management department costs can be computed based on either the demand for materials-handling services or the supply of materials-handling services. We consider the allocation of materials management department costs based first on the demand for (or usage of) materials-handling services and then on the supply of materials-handling services.

Allocation Based on the Demand for (or Usage of) Materials-handling Services

We present the single-rate method followed by the dual-rate method.

Single-Rate Method

In this method, a combined budgeted rate is used for fixed and variable costs. The rate is calculated as follows:

Budgeted usage	3,600 hours
Budgeted total cost pool: \$144,000 + (3,600 hours × \$30/hour)	\$252,000
Budgeted total rate per hour: \$252,000 ÷ 3,600 hours	\$70 per hour used
Allocation rate for machining department	\$70 per hour used
Allocation rate for assembly department	\$70 per hour used

Note that the budgeted rate of \$70 per hour is substantially higher than the \$30 budgeted *variable* cost per hour. That's because the \$70 rate includes an allocated amount of \$40 per hour (budgeted fixed costs, \$144,000 ÷ budgeted usage, \$3,600 hours) for the *fixed* costs of operating the facility.

Under the single-rate method, departments are charged the budgeted rate for each hour of *actual* use of the central facility. Applying this to our example, Robinson allocates materials management department costs based on the \$70 per hour budgeted rate and the actual hours the operating departments use. The support costs allocated to the two departments under this method are as follows:

Machining department: \$70 per hour × 1,200 hours	\$ 84,000
Assembly department: \$70 per hour × 2,400 hours	\$168,000

Dual-Rate Method

When a company uses the dual-rate method, managers must choose allocation bases for both the variable and fixed-cost pools of the materials management department. As in the single-rate method, variable costs are assigned based on the *budgeted* variable cost per hour of \$30 for *actual* hours each department uses. However, fixed costs are assigned based on *budgeted* fixed costs per hour and the *budgeted* number of hours for each department. Given the budgeted usage of 800 hours for the machining department and 2,800 hours for the assembly department, the budgeted fixed-cost rate is \$40 per hour (\$144,000 ÷ 3,600 hours), as before. Because this rate is charged on the basis of the *budgeted* usage, however, the fixed costs are effectively allocated in advance as a lump sum based on the relative proportions of the materials management facilities the operating departments expect to use.

The costs allocated to the machining department in 2013 under the dual-rate method would be as follows:

Fixed costs: $40 per hour × 800 (budgeted) hours	$32,000
Variable costs: $30 per hour × 1,200 (actual) hours	36,000
Total costs	$68,000

The costs allocated to the assembly department in 2013 would be as follows:

Fixed costs: $40 per hour × 2,800 (budgeted) hours	$112,000
Variable costs: $30 per hour × 2,400 (actual) hours	72,000
Total costs	$184,000

Note that each operating department is charged the same amount for variable costs under the single-rate and dual-rate methods ($30 per hour multiplied by the actual hours of use). However, the overall assignment of costs differs under the two methods because the single-rate method allocates fixed costs of the support department based on actual usage of materials-handling resources by the operating departments, whereas the dual-rate method allocates fixed costs based on budgeted usage.

We next consider the alternative approach of allocating materials management department costs based on the capacity of materials-handling services supplied.

Allocation Based on the Supply of Capacity

We illustrate this approach using the 4,000 hours of practical capacity of the materials management department. The budgeted rate is then determined as follows:

Budgeted fixed-cost rate per hour, $144,000 ÷ 4,000 hours	$36 per hour
Budgeted variable-cost rate per hour	30 per hour
Budgeted total-cost rate per hour	$66 per hour

Using the same procedures for the single-rate and dual-rate methods as in the previous section, the Materials Management Department costs allocated to the operating departments are as follows:

Single-Rate Method

Machining department: $66 per hour × 1,200 (actual) hours	$ 79,200
Assembly department: $66 per hour × 2,400 (actual) hours	158,400
Fixed costs of unused materials-handling capacity:	
$36 per hour × 400 hours[a]	14,400

[a]400 hours = Practical capacity of 4,000 − (1,200 hours used by machining department + 2,400 hours used by assembly department).

Dual-Rate Method

Machining department	
Fixed costs: $36 per hour × 800 (budgeted) hours	$28,800
Variable costs: $30 per hour × 1,200 (actual) hours	36,000
Total costs	$64,800
Assembly department	
Fixed costs: $36 per hour × 2,800 (budgeted) hours	$100,800
Variable costs: $30 per hour × 2,400 (actual) hours	72,000
Total costs	$172,800
Fixed costs of unused materials-handling capacity:	
$36 per hour × 400 hours[b]	$14,400

[b]400 hours = Practical capacity of 4,000 hours − (800 hours budgeted to be used by machining department + 2,800 hours budgeted to be used by assembly department).

When a company uses practical capacity to allocate costs, the single-rate method allocates only the actual fixed-cost resources used by the machining and assembly departments, while the dual-rate method allocates the budgeted fixed-cost resources to be used by the operating departments. Unused materials management department resources are highlighted but usually not allocated to the departments.[2]

The advantage of using practical capacity to allocate costs is that it focuses management's attention on managing unused capacity (described in Chapter 9, pages 346–347, and Chapter 12, pages 496–498). Using practical capacity also avoids burdening the user departments with the cost of unused capacity of the materials management department. In contrast, when costs are allocated on the basis of the demand for materials-handling services, all $144,000 of budgeted fixed costs, including the cost of unused capacity, are allocated to user departments. If costs are used as a basis for pricing, then charging user departments for unused capacity could result in the downward demand spiral (see page 346).

Recently, the dual-rate method has been receiving more attention. Resource Consumption Accounting (RCA), an emerging management accounting system, employs an allocation procedure similar to a dual-rate system. For each cost/resource pool, cost assignment rates for fixed costs are based on practical capacity supplied, while rates for proportional costs (i.e., costs that vary with regard to the output of the resource pool) are based on planned quantities.[3]

There are advantages and disadvantages of using the single-rate and dual-rate methods. We discuss these next.

Advantages and Disadvantages of Single-Rate Method

Advantages (1) **The single-rate method is less costly to implement** because it avoids the often expensive analysis necessary to classify the individual cost items of a department into fixed and variable categories. (2) **It offers user departments some operational control over the charges they bear** by conditioning the final allocations on the actual usage of support services, rather than basing them solely on uncertain forecasts of expected demand.

Disadvantage The single-rate method may lead operating department managers to make sub-optimal decisions that are in their own best interest but that may be inefficient from the standpoint of the organization as a whole. This occurs because under the single-rate method, the allocated fixed costs of the support department appear as variable costs to the operating departments. Consider the setting where managers make allocations based on the demand for materials-handling services. In this case, each user department is charged $70 per hour under the single-rate method (recall that $40 of this charge relates to the allocated fixed costs of the materials management department). Suppose an external provider offers the machining department material-handling labor services at a rate of $55 per hour, at a time when the materials management department has unused capacity. The machining department's managers would be tempted to use this vendor because it would lower the department's costs ($55 per hour instead of the $70 per hour internal charge for materials-handling services). In the short run, however, the fixed costs of the materials management department remain unchanged in the relevant range (between 3,000 hours of usage and the practical capacity of 4,000 hours). Robinson will therefore incur an additional cost of $25 per hour if the managers were to take this offer—the difference between the $55 external purchase price and the true internal variable cost of $30 of using the materials management department.

[2] In our example, the costs of unused capacity under the single-rate and the dual-rate methods coincide (each equals $14,400). This occurs because the total actual usage of the facility matches the total expected usage of 3,600 hours. The budgeted cost of unused capacity (in the dual-rate method) can be either greater or lower than the actual cost (in the single-rate method), depending on whether the total actual usage is lower or higher than the budgeted usage.

[3] Other important features of Resource Consumption Accounting (RCA) include (1) the selective use of activity-based costing, (2) the nonassignment of fixed costs when causal relationships cannot be established, and (3) the depreciation of assets based on their replacement cost. RCA has its roots in the nearly 50-year-old German cost accounting system called Grenzplankostenrechnung (GPK), which is used by organizations such as Mercedes-Benz, Porsche, and Stihl. For further details, as well as illustrations of the use of RCA and GPK in organizations, see Sally Webber and Douglas B. Clinton, "Resource Consumption Accounting Applied: The Clopay Case," *Management Accounting Quarterly* (Fall 2004); and Brian Mackie, "Merging GPK and ABC on the Road to RCA," *Strategic Finance* (November 2006).

The divergence created under the single-rate method between Robinson's interests and those of its department managers is lessened when allocation is based on practical capacity. The variable cost per hour the operating department managers perceive is now $66 (rather than the $70 rate when allocation is based on budgeted usage). However, any external offer above $30 (Robinson's true variable cost) and below $66 (the single-rate charge per hour) will still result in the user manager preferring to outsource the service at the expense of Robinson's overall profits.

Advantages and Disadvantages of Dual-Rate Method

Advantages (1) **The dual-rate method guides department managers to make decisions that benefit both the organization as a whole and each department** because it signals to department managers how variable costs and fixed costs behave differently. For example, using an external provider of materials-handling services that charges more than $30 per hour would result in Robinson's being worse off than if its own materials management department were used because the latter has a variable cost of $30 per hour. Under the dual-rate method, neither department manager has an incentive to pay more than $30 per hour for an external provider because the internal charge for materials-handling services is precisely that amount. By charging the fixed costs of resources budgeted to be used by the departments as a lump sum, the dual-rate method succeeds in removing fixed costs from the department managers' consideration when making marginal decisions to outsource services. The dual-rate method therefore avoids the potential conflict of interest that can arise under the single-rate method. (2) **Allocating fixed costs based on budgeted usage helps user departments with both short-run and long-run planning because user departments know the costs allocated to them in advance.** Companies commit to infrastructure costs (such as the fixed costs of a support department) on the basis of a long-run planning horizon; budgeted usage measures the long-run demands of the user departments for support-department services.

Decision Point

When should managers use the dual-rate method over the single-rate method?

Disadvantages (1) **The dual-rate method requires managers to distinguish variable costs from fixed costs, which is often a challenging task.** (2) **The dual-rate method does not indicate to operating managers the cost of fixed support department resources used because fixed costs are allocated to operating departments based on budgeted rather than actual usage.** Thus, the Machining Department manager is allocated fixed costs of the Materials Management Department based on the budgeted usage of 800 labor-hours even though the Machining Department actually uses 1,200 labor-hours. (3) **Allocating fixed costs on the basis of budgeted long-run usage may tempt some managers to underestimate their planned usage.** Underestimating will result in their departments bearing a lower percentage of fixed costs (assuming all other managers do not similarly underestimate their usage). If all user department managers underestimate usage, it might also lead to Robinson underestimating its total support department needs. To discourage such underestimates, some companies offer bonuses or other rewards—the "carrot" approach—to managers who make accurate forecasts of long-run usage. Other companies impose cost penalties—the "stick" approach—for underestimating long-run usage. For instance, a higher cost rate is charged after a department exceeds its budgeted usage.

Learning Objective 2

Understand how the choice between allocation based on budgeted and actual rates

...budgeted rates provide certainty to users about charges and motivate the support division to engage in cost control

and between budgeted and actual usage can affect the incentives of division managers

...budgeted usage helps in planning and efficient utilization of fixed resources; actual usage controls consumption of variable resources

Budgeted Versus Actual Costs and the Choice of Allocaton Base

The allocation methods previously outlined follow specific procedures in terms of the support department costs that are considered as well as the manner in which costs are assigned to the operating departments. In this section, we examine these choices in greater detail and consider the impact of alternative approaches. We show that the decision whether to use actual or budgeted costs, as well as the choice between actual and budgeted usage as allocation base, has a significant impact on the cost allocated to each operating department and the incentives of the operating department managers.

Budgeted Versus Actual Rates

In both the single-rate and dual-rate methods, Robinson uses budgeted rates to assign support department costs (fixed as well as variable costs). An alternative approach would involve using the actual rates based on the support costs realized during the period. This method is much less common because of the level of uncertainty it imposes on user departments. When allocations are made using budgeted rates, managers of departments to which costs are allocated know with certainty the rates to be used in that budget period. Users can then determine the amount of the service to request and—if company policy allows—whether to use the internal source or an external vendor. In contrast, when actual rates are used for cost allocation, user departments are not informed of their charges until the end of the budget period.

Budgeted rates also help motivate the manager of the support (or supplier) department (for example, the materials management department) to improve efficiency. During the budget period, the support department, not the user departments, bears the risk of any unfavorable cost variances. That's because user departments do not pay for any costs or inefficiencies of the supplier department that cause actual rates to exceed budgeted rates.

The manager of the supplier department would likely view the budgeted rates negatively if unfavorable cost variances occur due to price increases outside of his or her control. Some organizations try to identify these uncontrollable factors and relieve the support department manager of responsibility for these variances. In other organizations, the supplier department and the user department agree to share the risk (through an explicit formula) of a large, uncontrollable increase in the prices of inputs used by the supplier department. This procedure avoids imposing the risk completely on either the supplier department (as when budgeted rates are used) or the user department (as in the case of actual rates).

For the rest of this chapter, we will continue to consider only allocation methods that are based on budgeted rates.

Budgeted Versus Actual Usage

In both the single-rate and dual-rate methods, the variable costs are assigned on the basis of budgeted rates and actual usage. Because the variable costs are directly and causally linked to usage, charging them as a function of the actual usage is appropriate. Moreover, allocating variable costs on the basis of budgeted usage would provide the user departments with no incentive to control their consumption of support services.

What about the fixed costs? Consider the budget of $144,000 fixed costs at the Materials Management Department of Robinson Company. Recall that budgeted usage is 800 hours for the Machining Department and 2,800 hours for the Assembly Department. Assume that actual usage by the Machining Department is always equal to budgeted usage. We consider three cases:

Case 1: When actual usage by the Assembly Department equals budgeted usage.

Case 2: When actual usage by the Assembly Department is greater than budgeted usage.

Case 3: When actual usage by the Assembly Department is lower than budgeted usage.

Fixed-Cost Allocation Based on Budgeted Rates and Budgeted Usage

This is the dual-rate procedure outlined in the previous section. When budgeted usage is the allocation base, regardless of the actual usage of facilities (i.e., whether Case 1, 2, or 3 occurs), user departments receive a preset lump-sum fixed-cost charge. If rates are based on expected demand of $40 per hour ($144,000 ÷ 3,600 hours), the Machining Department is assigned $32,000 ($40 per hour × 800 hours) and the Assembly Department, $112,000 ($40 per hour × 2,800 hours). If rates are set using practical capacity of $36 per hour ($144,000 ÷ 4,000 hours), the Machining Department is charged $28,800 ($36 per hour × 800 hours), the Assembly Department is allocated $100,800 ($36 per hour × 2,800 hours), and the remaining $14,400 ($36 per hour × 400 hours) is the unallocated cost of excess capacity.

Fixed-Cost Allocation Based on Budgeted Rates and Actual Usage

Column 2 of Exhibit 15-1 shows the allocations when the budgeted rate is based on expected demand ($40 per hour), while column 3 shows the allocations when practical capacity is used to derive the rate ($36 per hour). Note that each operating department's fixed-cost allocation varies based on its actual usage of support facilities. However, variations in actual usage in one department do not affect the costs allocated to the other department. The Machining Department is allocated either $32,000 or $28,800, depending on the budgeted rate chosen, independent of the Assembly Department's actual usage.

Note, however, that this allocation procedure for fixed costs is exactly the same as that under the single-rate method. The procedure therefore shares the advantages of the single-rate method, such as advanced knowledge of budgeted rates, as well as control over the costs charged to them based on actual usage.[4] The procedure also shares the disadvantages of the single-rate method discussed in the previous section, such as charging excessively high costs, including the cost of unused capacity, when rates are based on expected usage. In Case 1, for example, actual usage equals budgeted usage of 3,600 materials-handling labor-hours and is less than the practical capacity of 4,000 labor-hours. However, all $144,000 of fixed costs of the Materials Management Department are allocated to the operating departments even though the Materials Handling Department has idle capacity. On the other hand, when actual usage (4,000 labor-hours) is more than the budgeted amount (3,600 labor-hours) as in Case 2, a total of $160,000 is allocated, which is more than the fixed costs of $144,000. This results in overallocation of fixed costs requiring end-of period adjustments, as discussed in Chapters 4 and 8.

Allocating fixed costs based on practical capacity avoids these problems by explicitly recognizing the costs of unused capacity. However, as we have discussed earlier, allocating fixed-cost rates based on actual usage induces conflicts of interest between the user departments and the firm when evaluating outsourcing possibilities.

Allocating Budgeted Fixed Costs Based on Actual Usage

Finally, consider the impact of having actual usage as the allocation base when the firm assigns total budgeted fixed costs to operating departments (rather than specifying budgeted fixed-cost rates, as we have thus far). If the budgeted fixed costs of $144,000 are

Exhibit 15-1 Effect of Variations in Actual Usage on Fixed-Cost Allocation to Operating Divisions

	(1) Actual Usage		(2) Budgeted Rate Based on Expected Demand[a]		(3) Budgeted Rate Based on Practical Capacity[b]		(4) Allocation of Budgeted Total Fixed Cost	
Case	**Mach. Dept.**	**Assmb. Dept.**	**Mach. Dept.**	**Assmb. Dept.**	**Mach. Dept.**	**Assmb. Dept.**	**Mach. Dept.**	**Assmb. Dept.**
1	800 hours	2,800 hours	$ 32,000	$ 112,000	$ 28,800	$ 100,800	$ 32,000[c]	$ 112,000[d]
2	800 hours	3,200 hours	$ 32,000	$ 128,000	$ 28,800	$ 115,200	$ 28,800[e]	$ 115,200[f]
3	800 hours	2,400 hours	$ 32,000	$ 96,000	$ 28,800	$ 86,400	$ 36,000[g]	$ 108,000[h]

a $\frac{\$144{,}000}{(800 + 2{,}800)\text{ hours}} = \$40\text{ per hour}$ b $\frac{\$144{,}000}{4{,}000\text{ hours}} = \$36\text{ per hour}$ c $\frac{800}{(800 + 2{,}800)} \times \$144{,}000$ d $\frac{2{,}800}{(800 + 2{,}800)} \times \$144{,}000$

e $\frac{800}{(800 + 3{,}200)} \times \$144{,}000$ f $\frac{3{,}200}{(800 + 3{,}200)} \times \$144{,}000$ g $\frac{800}{(800 + 2{,}400)} \times \$144{,}000$ h $\frac{2{,}400}{(800 + 2{,}400)} \times \$144{,}000$

[4] The total amount of fixed costs allocated to divisions will in general not equal the actual realized costs. Adjustments for overallocations and underallocations would then be made using the methods discussed previously in Chapters 4, 7, and 8.

allocated using budgeted usage, we are back in the familiar dual-rate setting. On the other hand, if the actual usage of the facility is the basis for allocation, the charges would equal the amounts in Exhibit 15-1, column 4:

- In Case 1, the fixed-cost allocation equals the amount based on budgeted usage (which is also the same as the charge under the dual-rate method based on demand for material-handling services).
- In Case 2, the fixed-cost allocation is $3,200 less to the Machining Department than the amount based on budgeted usage ($28,800 versus $32,000).
- In Case 3, the fixed-cost allocation is $4,000 more to the Machining Department than the amount based on budgeted usage ($36,000 versus $32,000).

Why does the Machining Department receive $4,000 more in costs in Case 3, even though its actual usage equals its budgeted usage? Because the total fixed costs of $144,000 are now spread over 400 fewer hours of actual total usage. In other words, the lower usage by the Assembly Department leads to an increase in the fixed costs allocated to the Machining Department. When budgeted fixed costs are allocated based on actual usage, user departments will not know their fixed-cost allocations until the end of the budget period. This method therefore shares the same flaw as those methods that rely on the use of actual cost rates rather than budgeted cost rates.

To summarize, there are excellent economic and motivational reasons to justify the precise forms of the single-rate and dual-rate methods considered in the previous section and, in particular, to recommend the dual-rate allocation procedure.

Decision Point

What factors should managers consider when deciding between allocation based on budgeted and actual rates, and budgeted and actual usage?

Allocating Costs of Multiple Support Departments

Learning Objective 3

Allocate multiple support-department costs using the direct method,

...allocates support-department costs directly to operating departments

the step-down method,

...partially allocates support-department costs to other support departments

and the reciprocal method

...fully allocates support-department costs to other support departments

In the previous section, we examined general issues that arise when allocating costs from one support department to operating departments. In this section, we examine the special cost-allocation problems that arise when two or more of the support departments whose costs are being allocated provide reciprocal support to each other as well as to operating departments. An example of reciprocal support is Robinson's Materials Management Department providing material-handling labor services to all other departments, including the Engineering and Production Control Department, while also utilizing the services of the Engineering and Production Control Department for managing material-handling equipment and scheduling materials movement to the production floor. More accurate support-department cost allocations result in more accurate product, service, and customer costs.

Exhibit 15-2, column 6, provides details of Robinson's total budgeted manufacturing overhead costs of $1,120,000 for 2013 (see page 115), for example, supervision salaries, $200,000; depreciation and maintenance, $193,000; indirect labor, $195,000; and rent, utilities and insurance, $160,000. Robinson allocates the $1,120,000 of total budgeted manufacturing overhead costs to the Machining and Assembly Departments in several steps.

Step A: Trace or Allocate Each Cost to Various Support and Operating Departments. Exhibit 15-2, columns (1) through (5), show calculations for this step. For example, supervision salaries are traced to the departments in which the supervisors work. As described on page 30, supervision costs are an indirect cost of individual jobs because supervisory costs cannot be traced to individual jobs. They are a direct cost of the different departments, however, because they can be identified with each department in an economically feasible way. Rent, utilities, and insurance costs cannot be traced to each department because these costs are incurred for all of Robinson's manufacturing facility. These costs are therefore allocated to different departments on the basis of the square feet area—the cost driver for rent, utilities, and insurance costs.

Step B: Allocate Plant Administration Costs to Other Support Departments and Operating Departments. Plant adminstration supports supervisors in each department, so plant administration costs are allocated to departments on the basis of supervision costs.

Exhibit 15-2 Details of Budgeted Manufacturing Overhead at Robinson Company for 2013 and Allocation of Plant Administration Department Costs

	A	B	C	D	E	F	G
1		Support Departments			Operating Departments		
2	Step A	Plant Administration Department (1)	Engineering and Production Control Department (2)	Materials Management Department (3)	Machining Department (4)	Assembly Department (5)	Total (6)
3	Plant manager's salary	$ 92,000					$ 92,000
4	Supervision salaries (traced to each department)		$ 48,000	$ 40,000	$ 52,000	$ 60,000	200,000
5	Engineering salaries (traced to each department)		110,000	36,000	60,000	24,000	230,000
6	Depreciation and maintenance (traced to each department)		39,000	55,000	79,000	20,000	193,000
7	Indirect materials (traced to each department)		20,000	12,000	11,000	7,000	50,000
8	Indirect labor (traced to each department)		43,000	77,000	37,000	38,000	195,000
9	Rent, utilities, and insurance (allocated to each department based on square feet area; $8[1] × 1,000; 2,000; 3,000; 8,000; 6,000 sq. ft.)	8,000	16,000	24,000	64,000	48,000	160,000
10	Total	$ 100,000	$276,000	$244,000	$303,000	$197,000	$1,120,000
11							
12	Step B						
13	Allocation of plant administration costs 0.50[2] × $48,000; $40,000; $52,000; $60,000	(100,000)	24,000	20,000	26,000	30,000	
14		$ 0	$300,000	$264,000	$329,000	$227,000	
15	[1]$160,000 ÷ 20,000 total square feet area = $8 per square foot						
16	[2]Plant administration cost-allocation rate = Total plant administration costs / Total supervision salaries = $100,000 / $200,000 = 0.50						

Some companies prefer not to allocate plant adminstration costs to jobs, products, or customers because these costs are fixed and independent of the level of activity in the plant. However, most companies, like Robinson, allocate plant adminstration costs to departments and jobs, products, or customers because allocating all costs allows companies to calculate the full manufacturing costs of products. Robinson calculates the plant administration cost-allocation rate as follows:

$$\text{Plant administration cost-allocation rate} = \frac{\text{Total plant administration costs}}{\text{Total supervision salaries}} = \frac{\$100{,}000}{\$200{,}000} = 0.50$$

The bottom part of Exhibit 15-2 shows how Robinson uses the 0.50 cost-allocation rate and supervision salaries to allocate plant adminstration costs to the other support and operating departments.

Step C: Allocate Engineering and Production Control and Materials Management Costs to the Machining and Assembly Operating Departments. Note that the two support departments whose costs are being allocated—Engineering and Production Control and Materials Management—provide reciprocal support to each other as well as support to the operating departments. That is, the Engineering and Production Control Department provides services to the Materials Management Department (for example, engineering services for material-handling equipment and scheduling material movement to the production floor), while the Materials Management Department provides services to the Engineering and Production Control Department (for example, delivering materials).

Consider again the Materials Management Department. As we saw in the previous section, this department is budgeted to provide 800 hours of materials-handling labor services to the Machining Department and 2,800 hours of materials-handling labor services to the Assembly Department. In this section, we further assume that the Materials Handling Department provides an additional 400 hours of materials-handling labor services to the Engineering and Production Control Department. Recall from the previous section that the Materials Management Department has budgeted fixed costs (for example, plant administration, depreciation, and rent) of $144,000 and budgeted variable costs (for example, indirect materials, indirect labor, and maintenance) of $30 per labor-hour. Thus, for the analysis in this section the total budgeted costs of the Materials Management Department equal $264,000 [$144,000 + $30 × (800 + 2,800 + 400) labor-hours] as shown in Exhibit 15-2.[5]

Exhibit 15-3 displays the data for budgeted overhead costs from Exhibit 15-2 after allocating Plant Administration Department costs but before any further interdepartment cost allocations and the services provided by each support department to the other departments. To understand the percentages in this exhibit, consider the Engineering and Production Control Department. This department supports the engineering activity in the other departments and so the costs of this department are allocated based on engineering salaries in each of the other departments. From Exhibit 15-2, budgeted engineering salaries are $36,000 in the Materials Management Department, $60,000 in the Machining Department, and $24,000 in the Assembly Department for a total of $120,000 ($36,000 + $60,000 + $24,000). Thus, the Engineering and Production Control Department provides support of 30% ($36,000 ÷ $120,000 = 0.30) to the Materials Management Department, 50% ($60,000 ÷ $120,000 = 0.50) to the Machining Department, and 20% ($24,000 ÷ $120,000 = 0.20) to the Assembly Department. Similarly, the Materials Management Department provides a total of 4,000 material-handling labor-hours of support work: 10% (400 ÷ 4,000 = 0.10) for the Engineering and Production Control Department, 20% (800 ÷ 4,000 = 0.20) for the Machining Department, and 70% (2,800 ÷ 4,000 = 0.70) for the Assembly Department.

We describe three methods of allocating budgeted overhead costs from the support departments to the Machining Department and the Assembly Department: *direct*, *step-down*, and *reciprocal*. Throughout this section, we use budgeted costs and budgeted hours. Why? Because our goal is to determine the budgeted costs of the operating departments (Machining and Assembly) after Robinson allocates the budgeted costs of the support

Exhibit 15-3 Data for Allocating Support Department Costs at Robinson Company for 2013

Home Insert Page Layout Formulas Data Review View

	A	B	C	D	E	F	G
1		**SUPPORT DEPARTMENTS**			**OPERATING DEPARTMENTS**		
2		**Engineering and Production Control**	**Materials Management**		**Machining**	**Assembly**	**Total**
3	Budgeted overhead costs						
4	before any interdepartment cost allocations	$300,000	$264,000		$329,000	$227,000	$1,120,000
5	Support work furnished:						
6	By Engineering and Production Control						
7	Budgeted engineering salaries	—	$36,000		$60,000	$24,000	$120,000
8	Percentage	—	30%		50%	20%	100%
9	By Materials Management						
10	Budgeted material-handling labor-hours	400	—		800	2,800	4,000
11	Percentage	10%	—		20%	70%	100%

[5] The previous section assumed that the Materials Management Department only provided services to the Machining and Assembly Departments and not to the Engineering and Production Control Department, resulting in total budgeted costs of $252,000 [$144,000 + $30 × (800 + 2,800) labor-hours].

departments (Materials Management and Engineering and Production Control) to the operating departments. The budgeted costs of the Machining Department will be divided by the budgeted machine-hours in the Machining Department and the budgeted costs of the Assembly Department will be divided by the budgeted direct manufacturing labor-hours in the Assembly Department to calculate the budgeted overhead allocation rates in each operating department. These overhead rates will be used to allocate overhead costs to each job as it passes through an operating department based on the actual number of machine-hours used in the Machining Department and the actual number of direct manufacturing labor-hours used in the Assembly Department. To simplify the explanation and to focus on concepts, we use the single-rate method to allocate the costs of each support department. (The Problem for Self-Study illustrates the dual-rate method for allocating reciprocal support-department costs.)

Direct Method

The **direct method** allocates each support-department's costs to operating departments only. The direct method does not allocate support department costs to other support departments. Exhibit 15-4 illustrates this method using the data in Exhibit 15-3. The base used to allocate Engineering and Production Control costs to the operating departments is the budgeted engineering salaries in the operating departments: $60,000 + $24,000 = $84,000. This amount excludes the $36,000 of budgeted engineering salaries representing services to be provided by Engineering and Production Control to Materials Management. Similarly, the base used for allocation of Materials Management costs to the operating departments is 800 + 2,800 = 3,600 budgeted material-handling labor-hours, which excludes the 400 hours of budgeted support time provided by Materials Management to Engineering and Production Control.

An equivalent approach to implementing the direct method involves calculating a budgeted rate for each support department's costs. For example, the rate for the Engineering

Exhibit 15-4

Direct Method of Allocating Support-Department Costs at Robinson Company for 2013

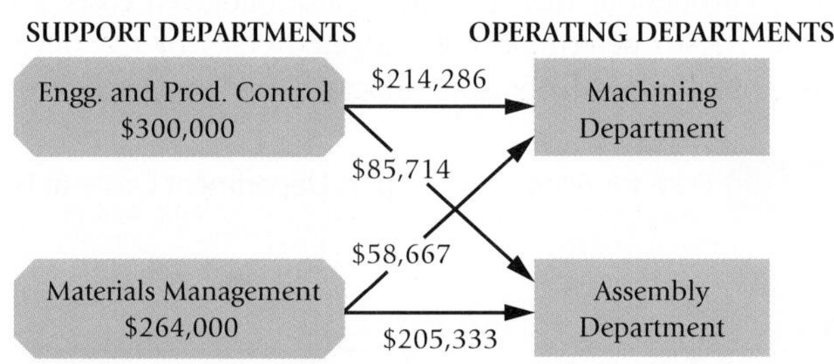

	A	B	C	D	E	F	G
1		SUPPORT DEPARTMENTS			OPERATING DEPARTMENTS		
2		Engineering and Production Control	Materials Management		Machining	Assembly	Total
3	Budgeted overhead costs						
4	before any interdepartment cost allocations	$300,000	$264,000		$329,000	$227,000	$1,120,000
5	Allocation of Engg. And Prod. Control (5/7, 2/7)[a]	(300,000)			214,286	85,714	
6	Allocation of Materials Management (2/9, 7/9)[b]		(264,000)		58,667	205,333	
7							
8	Total budgeted overhead of operating departments	$ 0	$ 0		$601,953	$518,047	$1,120,000
9							
10	[a] Base is ($60,000 + $24,000), or $84,000; $60,000 ÷ $84,000 = 5/7; $24,000 ÷ $84,000 = 2/7.						
11	[b] Base is (800 + 2,800), or 3,600 hours; 800 ÷ 3,600 = 2/9; 2,800 ÷ 3,600 = 7/9.						

and Production Control Department costs is ($300,000 ÷ $84,000), or 357.143%. The Machining Department is then allocated $214,286 (357.143% × $60,000), while the Assembly Department is allocated $85,714 (357.143% × $24,000). For ease of explanation throughout this section, we will use the fraction of the support department services used by other departments, rather than calculate budgeted rates, to allocate support department costs.

Most managers adopt the direct method because it is easy to use. The benefit of the direct method is simplicity. Managers do not need to predict the usage of support department services by other support departments. A disadvantage of the direct method is that it ignores information about reciprocal services provided among support departments and can therefore lead to inaccurate estimates of the cost of operating departments. We now examine a second approach, which partially recognizes the services provided among support departments.

Step-Down Method

Some organizations use the **step-down method**—also called the **sequential allocation method**—which allocates support-department costs to other support departments and to operating departments in a sequential manner that partially recognizes the mutual services provided among all support departments.

Exhibit 15-5 shows the step-down method. The Engineering and Production Control costs of $300,000 are allocated first. Exhibit 15-3 shows that Engineering and Production Control provides 30% of its services to Materials Management, 50% to Machining, and 20% to Assembly. Therefore, $90,000 is allocated to Materials Management (30% of $300,000), $150,000 to Machining (50% of $300,000), and $60,000 to Assembly (20% of $300,000). The Materials Management Department costs now total $354,000: budgeted costs of the Materials Management Department before any interdepartmental cost allocations, $264,000, plus $90,000 from the allocation of Engineering and Production Control

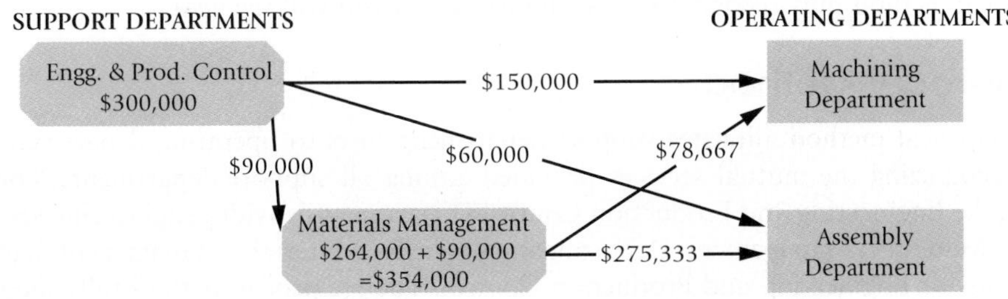

Exhibit 15-5

Step-Down Method of Allocating Support-Department Costs at Robinson Company for 2013

	A	B	C	D	E	F	G
1		SUPPORT DEPARTMENTS			OPERATING DEPARTMENTS		
2		Engineering and Production Control	Materials Management		Machining	Assembly	Total
3	Budgeted overhead costs before any						
4	interdepartment cost allocations	$300,000	$264,000		$329,000	$227,000	$1,120,000
5	Allocation of Engg. and Prod. Control (3/10, 5/10, 2/10)[a]	(300,000)	90,000		150,000	60,000	
6			354,000				
7	Allocation of Materials Management (2/9, 7/9)[b]		(354,000)		78,667	275,333	
8							
9	Total budgeted overhead of operating departments	$ 0	$ 0		$557,667	$562,333	$1,120,000
10							
11	[a] Base is ($36,000 + $60,000 + $24,000), or $120,000 ; $36,000 ÷ $120,000 = 3/10; $60,000 ÷ $120,000 = 5/10; $24,000 ÷ $120,000 = 2/10.						
12	[b] Base is (800 + 2,800), or 3,600 hours; 800 ÷ 3,600 = 2/9; 2,800 ÷ 3,600 = 7/9.						

costs to the Materials Management Department. The $354,000 is then only allocated between the two operating departments based on the proportion of the Materials Management Department services provided to Machining and Assembly. From Exhibit 15-3, the Materials Management Department provides 20% of its services to Machining and 70% to Assembly, so $78,667 (2/9 × $354,000) is allocated to Machining and $275,333 (7/9 × $354,000) is allocated to Assembly.

Note that this method requires managers to rank (sequence) the support departments in the order that the step-down allocation is to proceed. In our example, the costs of the Engineering and Production Control Department were allocated first to all other departments, including the Materials Management Department. The costs of the Materials Management support department were allocated second, but only to the two operating departments. Different sequences will result in different allocations of support-department costs to operating departments—for example, if the Materials Management Department costs had been allocated first and the Engineering and Production Control Department costs second. A popular step-down sequence begins with the support department that renders the highest percentage of its total services to *other support departments*. The sequence continues with the department that renders the next-highest percentage, and so on, ending with the support department that renders the lowest percentage.[6] In our example, costs of the Engineering and Production Control Department were allocated first because it provides 30% of its services to the Materials Management Department, whereas the Materials Management Department provides only 10% of its services to the Engineering and Production Control Department (see Exhibit 15-3).

Under the step-down method, once a support department's costs have been allocated, no subsequent support-department costs are allocated back to it. Once the Engineering and Production Control Department costs are allocated, it receives no further allocation from other (lower-ranked) support departments. The result is that the step-down method does not recognize the total services that support departments provide to each other. The reciprocal method fully recognizes all such services, as you will see next.

Reciprocal Method

The **reciprocal method** allocates support-department costs to operating departments by fully recognizing the mutual services provided among all support departments. For example, the Engineering and Production Control Department provides engineering services to the Materials Management Department. Similarly, Materials Management handles materials for Engineering and Production Control. The reciprocal method fully incorporates interdepartmental relationships into the support-department cost allocations.

Exhibit 15-6 presents one way to understand the reciprocal method as an extension of the step-down method. First, Engineering and Production Control costs are allocated to all other departments, including the Materials Management support department (Materials Management, 30%; Machining, 50%; Assembly, 20%). The costs in the Materials Management Department then total $354,000 ($264,000 + $90,000 from the first-round allocation), as in Exhibit 15-5. The $354,000 is then allocated to all other departments that the Materials Management Department supports, including the Engineering and Production Control support department—Engineering and Production Control, 10%; Machining, 20%; and Assembly, 70% (see Exhibit 15-3). The Engineering and Production Control costs that had been brought down to $0 now have $35,400 from the Materials Management Department allocation. These costs are again reallocated to all other departments, including Materials Management, in the same ratio that the Engineering and Production Control costs were previously assigned. Now the Materials Management Department costs that had been brought down to $0 have $10,620 from the Engineering and Production Control Department allocations. These costs are again allocated in the same ratio that the Materials Management Department costs were previously assigned.

[6] An alternative approach to selecting the sequence of allocations is to begin with the support department that renders the highest dollar amount of services to other support departments. The sequence ends with the allocation of the costs of the department that renders the lowest dollar amount of services to other support departments.

Exhibit 15-6 Reciprocal Method of Allocating Support-Department Costs Using Repeated Iterations at Robinson Company for 2013

	A	B	C	D	E	F	G
1		Engineering and					
2		Production Control	Materials Management		Machining Department	Assembly Department	Total
3	Budgeted overhead costs before any						
4	interdepartment cost allocations	$300,000	$264,000		$329,000	$227,000	$1,120,000
5	1st Allocation of Engg. and Prod. Control (3/10,5/10,2/10)[a]	(300,000)	90,000		150,000	60,000	
6			354,000				
7	1st Allocation of Materials Management (1/10,2/10,7/10)[b]	35,400	(354,000)		70,800	247,800	
8	2nd Allocation of Engg. and Prod. Control (3/10,5/10,2/10)[a]	(35,400)	10,620		17,700	7,080	
9	2nd Allocation of Materials Management (1/10,2/10,7/10)[b]	1,062	(10,620)		2,124	7,434	
10	3rd Allocation of Engg. and Prod. Control (3/10,5/10,2/10)[a]	(1,062)	319		531	212	
11	3rd Allocation of Materials Management (1/10,2/10,7/10)[b]	32	(319)		63	224	
12	4th Allocation of Engg. and Prod. Control (3/10,5/10,2/10)[a]	(32)	10		16	6	
13	4th Allocation of Materials Management (1/10,2/10,7/10)[b]	1	(10)		2	7	
14	5th Allocation of Engg. and Prod. Control (3/10,5/10,2/10)[a]	(1)	0		1	0	
15							
16	Total budgeted overhead of operating departments	$ 0	$ 0		$570,237	$549,763	$1,120,000
17							
18	Total support department amounts allocated and reallocated (the numbers in parentheses in the first two columns):						
19	Engineering and Production Control: $300,000 + $35,400 + $1,062 + $32 + $1 = $336,495						
20	Materials Management: $354,000 + $10,620 + $319 + $10 = $364,949						
21							
22	[a]Base is $36,000 + $60,000 + $24,000 = $120,000; $36,000 ÷ $120,000 = 3/10; $60,000 ÷ $120,000 = 5/10; $24,000 ÷ $120,000 = 2/10						
23	[b]Base is 400 + 800 + 2,800 = 4,000 labor-hours; 400 ÷ 4,000 = 1/10; 800 ÷ 4,000 = 2/10; 2,800 ÷ 4,000 = 7/10						

Successive rounds result in smaller and smaller amounts being allocated to and reallocated from the support departments until eventually all support department costs are allocated to the Machining Department and the Assembly Department.

An alternative way to implement the reciprocal method is to formulate and solve linear equations. This implementation requires three steps.

Step 1: Express Support Department Costs and Reciprocal Relationships in the Form of Linear Equations. Let *EPC* be the *complete reciprocated costs* of Engineering and Production Control and *MM* be the *complete reciprocated costs* of Materials Management. By **complete reciprocated costs,** we mean the support department's own costs plus any interdepartmental cost allocations. We then express the data in Exhibit 15-3 as follows:

$$EPC = \$300{,}000 + 0.1\,MM \qquad (1)$$

$$MM = \$264{,}000 + 0.3\,EPC \qquad (2)$$

The $0.1MM$ term in equation (1) is the percentage of the Materials Management services *used by* Engineering and Production Control. The $0.3EPC$ term in equation (2) is the percentage of Engineering and Production Control services *used by* Materials Management. The complete reciprocated costs in equations (1) and (2) are sometimes called the **artificial costs** of the support departments.

Step 2: Solve the Set of Linear Equations to Obtain the Complete Reciprocated Costs of Each Support Department. Substituting equation (1) into (2):

$$MM = \$264,000 + [0.3\,(\$300,000 + 0.1\,MM)]$$
$$MM = \$264,000 + \$90,000 + 0.03\,MM$$
$$0.97\,MM = \$354,000$$
$$MM = \$364,949$$

Substituting this into equation (1):

$$EPC = \$300,000 + 0.1\,(\$364,949)$$
$$EPC = \$300,000 + \$36,495 = \$336,495$$

The complete reciprocated costs or artificial costs for the Materials Management Department are $364,949 and for the Engineering and Production Control Department are $336,495. The complete-reciprocated-cost figures also appear at the bottom of Exhibit 15-6 as the total amounts allocated and reallocated.When there are more than two support departments with reciprocal relationships, managers can use software such as Excel to calculate the complete reciprocated costs of each support department. Because the calculations involve finding the inverse of a matrix, the reciprocal method is also sometimes referred to as the **matrix method**.[7]

Step 3: Allocate the Complete Reciprocated Costs of Each Support Department to All Other Departments (Both Support Departments and Operating Departments) on the Basis of the Usage Percentages (Based on Total Units of Service Provided to All Departments). Consider the Materials Management Department. The complete reciprocated costs of $364,949 are allocated as follows:

To Engineering and Production Control (1/10) × $364,949	= $ 36,495
To Machining (2/10) × $364,949	= $ 72,990
To Assembly (7/10) × $364,949	= $255,464
Total	$364,949

Similarly, the $336,495 in reciprocated costs of the Engineering and Production Control Department are allocated to the Materials Management Department (3/10), Machining Department (5/10), and Assembly Department (2/10).

Exhibit 15-7 presents summary data based on the reciprocal method.

Robinson's $701,444 complete reciprocated costs of the support departments exceeds the budgeted amount of $564,000.

Support Department	Complete Reciprocated Costs	Budgeted Costs	Difference
Engineering and Production Control	$336,495	$300,000	$ 36,495
Materials Management	364,949	264,000	100,949
Total	$701,444	$564,000	$137,444

Each support department's complete reciprocated cost is greater than the budgeted amount because it takes into account that support costs are allocated to all departments using its services and not just to operating departments. This step ensures that the reciprocal method fully recognizes all interrelationships among support departments, as well as relationships between support and operating departments. The difference between complete reciprocated costs and budgeted costs for each support department reflects the costs allocated among support departments. The total costs allocated to the operating departments under the reciprocal method are still only $564,000 ($168,247 + $67,299 allocated from the Engineering and Production Control Department and $72,990 + $255,464 allocated from the Materials Management Department, see Exhibit 15-7).

[7] If there are n support departments, then Step 1 will yield n linear equations. Solving the equations to calculate the complete reciprocated costs then requires finding the inverse of an $n \times n$ matrix.

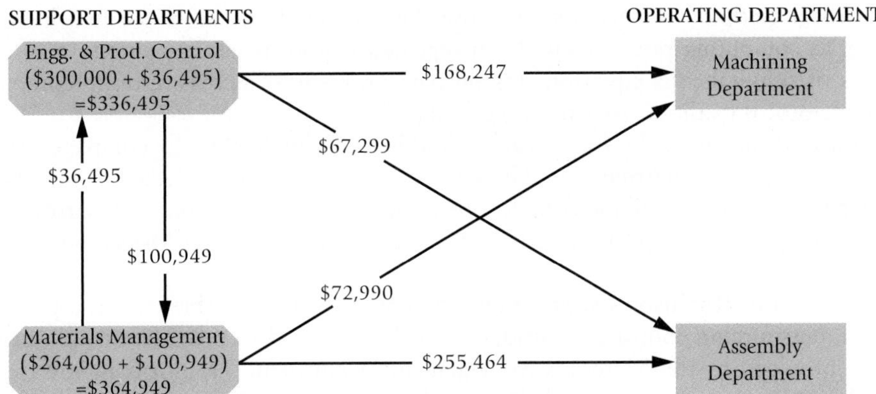

Exhibit 15-7

Reciprocal Method of Allocating Support-Department Costs Using Linear Equations at Robinson Company for 2013

	A	B	C	D	E	F	G
1		SUPPORT DEPARTMENTS			OPERATING DEPARTMENTS		
2		Engineering and Production Control	Materials Management		Machining	Assembly	Total
3	Budgeted overhead costs before any						
4	interdepartment cost allocations	$300,000	$264,000		$329,000	$227,000	$1,120,000
5	Allocation of Engg. & Prod. Control (3/10, 5/10, 2/10)[a]	(336,495)	100,949		168,247	67,299	
6	Allocation of Materials Management (1/10, 2/10, 7/10)[b]	36,495	(364,949)		72,990	255,464	
7							
8	Total budgeted overhead of operating departments	$ 0	$ 0		$570,237	$549,763	$1,120,000
9							
10	[a]Base is ($36,000 + $60,000 + $24,000), or $120,000 ; $36,000 ÷ $120,000 = 3/10; $60,000 ÷ $120,000 = 5/10; $24,000 ÷ $120,000 = 2/10.						
11	[b]Base is (400 + 800 + 2,800), or 4,000 hours; 400 ÷ 4,000 = 1/10; 800 ÷ 4,000 = 2/10; 2,800 ÷ 4,000 = 7/10.						

Overview of Methods

The amount of manufacturing overhead costs allocated to the Machining and Assembly Departments will differ depending on the method used to allocate support-department costs. Differences among the three methods' allocations increase (1) as the magnitude of the reciprocal allocations increases and (2) as the differences across operating departments' usage of each support department's services increase. Note that while the final allocations under the reciprocal method are in between those under the direct and step-down methods in our example (see page 610), in general, there is no relationship between the amount of costs allocated to the operating departments under the different methods. The method of allocation becomes particularly important in the case of cost-reimbursement contracts that require allocation of support-department costs. To avoid disputes, managers should always clarify the method to be used for allocation. For example, Medicare reimbursements and federal government research contracts with universities that pay for the recovery of indirect costs typically mandate use of the step-down method, with explicit requirements about the costs that can be included in the indirect cost pools.

The reciprocal method is conceptually the most precise method because it considers the mutual services provided among all support departments. The advantage of the direct and step-down methods is that they are simple for mangers to compute and understand relative to the reciprocal method. If the costs allocated to the operating departments using the direct or step-down methods closely approximate the costs allocated using the reciprocal method, managers should use the simpler direct or step-down methods. However, as computing power to perform repeated iterations (as in Exhibit 15-6) or to solve sets of simultaneous equations (as on pages 607–608) increases, more companies find the reciprocal method easier to implement.

Another advantage of the reciprocal method is that it highlights the complete reciprocated costs of support departments and how these costs differ from budgeted or actual costs of the departments. Knowing the complete reciprocated costs of a support department is a key input for decisions about whether to outsource all the services that the support department provides.

Suppose all of Robinson's support-department costs are variable over the period of a possible outsourcing contract. Consider a third party's bid to provide, say, all services currently provided by the Materials Management Department. Do not compare the bid to the \$264,000 costs reported for the Materials Management Department. The complete reciprocated costs of the Materials Management Department, which include the services the Engineering and Production Control Department provides the Materials Management Department, are \$364,949 to deliver 4,000 hours of material-handling labor to other departments at Robinson. The complete reciprocated costs for material-handling labor are \$91.24 per hour (\$364,949 ÷ 4,000 hours). Other things being equal, an external provider's bid to supply the same materials management services as Robinson's internal department at less than \$364,949, or \$91.24 per hour (even if much greater than \$264,000) would improve Robinson's operating income.

To see this point, note that the relevant savings from shutting down the Materials Management Department are \$264,000 of Materials Management Department costs *plus* \$100,949 of Engineering and Production Control Department costs. By closing down the Materials Management Department, Robinson will no longer incur the 30% of reciprocated Engineering and Production Control Department costs (equal to \$100,949) that were incurred to support the Materials Management Department. Therefore, the total cost savings are \$364,949 (\$264,000 + 100,949).[8] Neither the direct nor the step-down method can provide this relevant information for outsourcing decisions.

Calculating the Cost of Job WPP 298

Robinson uses the budgeted costs of each operating department (Machining and Assembly) to compute the rate per unit of each cost-allocation base used to allocate the indirect costs to a job (Step 5 in a job costing system, see Chapter 4). Robinson budgets 20,000 direct labor-hours for the Assembly Department (of the 28,000 total direct manufacturing labor-hours) and 10,000 machine-hours for the Machining Department.

The budgeted overhead allocation rates for each operating department by allocation method are:

Support Department Cost-Allocation Method	Total Budgeted Overhead Costs After Allocation of All Support-Department Costs: Machining	Assembly	Budgeted Overhead Rate per Hour for Product-Costing Purposes: Machining (10,000 machine-hours)	Assembly (20,000 labor-hours)
Direct	\$601,953	\$518,047	\$60.20	\$25.90
Step-down	557,667	562,333	55.77	28.12
Reciprocal	570,237	549,763	57.02	27.49

The next step in a job-costing system (Step 6, see Chapter 4) is to compute the indirect costs allocated to a job. For the WPP 298 job, Robinson uses 42 labor-hours in the Assembly Department (out of 88 direct manufacturing labor-hours) and 46 machine-hours in the

[8] Technical issues when using the reciprocal method in outsourcing decisions are discussed in Robert S. Kaplan and Anthony A. Atkinson, *Advanced Management Accounting*, 3rd ed. (Upper Saddle River, NJ: Prentice Hall, 1998, pp. 73–81).

Machining Department. The overhead costs allocated to the WPP 298 job under the three methods would be

Direct:	\$3,857 (46 × \$60.20 + 42 × \$25.90)
Step-down:	\$3,746 (46 × \$55.77 + 42 × \$28.12)
Reciprocal:	\$3,778 (46 × \$57.02 + 42 × \$27.49)

The manufacturing overhead costs allocated to WPP298 differ only a little under the three methods because the WPP 298 job requires roughly equal amounts of machine-hours and assembly labor-hours. These differences would be larger if a job required many more machine-hours than assembly hours or vice versa.

Using normal costing and multiple cost-allocation bases also results in higher indirect manufacturing costs allocated to Job WPP 298, \$3,778 (under the reciprocal method) compared to \$3,520 allocated using direct manufacturing labor-hours as the sole allocation base in Chapter 4 (page 115). Two cost-allocation bases—machine-hours and assembly labor-hours—are better able to model the drivers of manufacturing overhead costs.

The final step (Step 7, see Chapter 4) computes the total cost of the job by adding all direct and indirect costs assigned to the job. Under the reciprocal method, the total manufacturing costs of the WPP 298 job are as follows:

Direct manufacturing costs		
Direct materials	\$4,606	
Direct manufacturing labor	1,579	\$6,185
Manufacturing overhead costs		
Machining Department (\$57.02 per machine-hour × 46 machine-hours)	2,623	
Assembly Department (\$27.49 per labor-hour × 42 labor-hours)	1,155	3,778
Total manufacturing costs of job WPP 298		\$9,963

Note that the costs in Step 7 have four dollar amounts, each corresponding respectively to the two direct-cost and two indirect-cost categories in the costing system.

At the end of the year, actual manufacturing overhead costs of the Machining Department and the Assembly Department would be compared to the manufacturing overhead allocated for each department. To calculate the actual manufacturing overhead costs of the Machining and Assembly Departments, Robinson would need to allocate the actual costs of the Materials Management and Engineering and Production Control Departments to the Machining and Assembly Departments using the methods described in this chapter. Management accountants would then make end-of-year adjustments (pages 127–132) separately for each cost pool for under- or overallocated overhead costs.

We now consider common costs, another special class of costs for which management accountants have developed specific allocation methods.

Decision Point

What methods can managers use to allocate costs of multiple support departments to operating departments?

Allocating Common Costs

Learning Objective 4

Allocate common costs using the stand-alone method

...uses cost information of each user as a separate entity to allocate common costs

and the incremental method

...allocates common costs primarily to one user and the remainder to other users

A **common cost** is a cost of operating a facility, activity, or like cost object that is shared by two or more users. Common costs arise because each user obtains a lower cost by sharing than the separate cost that would result if each user operated independently.

The goal is to allocate common costs to each user in a reasonable way. Consider Jason Stevens, a graduating senior in Seattle who has been invited to a job interview with an employer in Albany. The round-trip Seattle–Albany airfare costs \$1,200. A week later, Stevens is also invited to an interview with an employer in Chicago. The Seattle–Chicago round-trip airfare costs \$800. Stevens decides to combine the two recruiting trips into a Seattle–Albany–Chicago–Seattle trip that will cost \$1,500 in airfare. The prospective employers will reimburse Stevens for the airfare. The \$1,500 is a common cost that benefits both prospective employers because it is less than the \$2,000 (\$1,200 + \$800) that the two employers would have to pay if they operated independently.

What is a reasonable way to allocate the common costs of $1,500? Two methods of allocating this common cost between the two prospective employers are the stand-alone method and the incremental method.

Stand-Alone Cost-Allocation Method

The **stand-alone cost-allocation method** determines the weights for cost allocation by considering each user of the cost as a separate entity. For the common-cost airfare of $1,500, information about the separate (stand-alone) round-trip airfares ($1,200 and $800) is used to determine the allocation weights:

$$\text{Albany employer: } \frac{\$1,200}{\$1,200 + \$800} \times \$1,500 = 0.60 \times \$1,500 = \$900$$

$$\text{Chicago employer: } \frac{\$800}{\$800 + \$1,200} \times \$1,500 = 0.40 \times \$1,500 = \$600$$

Advocates of this method often emphasize the fairness or equity criterion described in Exhibit 13-1 (page 519). The method is viewed as reasonable because each employer bears a proportionate share of total costs in relation to the individual stand-alone costs.

Incremental Cost-Allocation Method

The **incremental cost-allocation method** ranks the individual users of a cost object in the order of users most responsible for the common cost and then uses this ranking to allocate cost among those users. The first-ranked user of the cost object is the *primary user* (also called the *primary party*) and is allocated costs up to the costs of the primary user as a stand-alone user. The second-ranked user is the *first-incremental user* (*first-incremental party*) and is allocated the additional cost that arises from two users instead of only the primary user. The third-ranked user is the *second-incremental user* (*second-incremental party*) and is allocated the additional cost that arises from three users instead of two users, and so on.

To see how this method works, consider again Jason Stevens and his $1,500 airfare cost. Assume the Albany employer is viewed as the primary party. Stevens' rationale is that he had already committed to go to Albany before accepting the invitation to interview in Chicago. The cost allocations would be as follows:

Party	Costs Allocated	Cumulative Costs Allocated
Albany (primary)	$1,200	$1,200
Chicago (incremental)	300 ($1,500 − $1,200)	$1,500
Total	$1,500	

The Albany employer is allocated the full Seattle–Albany airfare. The unallocated part of the total airfare is then allocated to the Chicago employer. If the Chicago employer had been chosen as the primary party, the cost allocations would have been Chicago $800 (the stand-alone round-trip Seattle–Chicago airfare) and Albany $700 ($1,500 – $800). When there are more than two parties, this method requires them to be ranked from first to last (such as by the date on which each employer invited the candidate to interview).

Under the incremental method, the primary party typically receives the highest allocation of the common costs. If the incremental users are newly formed companies or subunits, such as a new product line or a new sales territory, the incremental method may enhance their chances for short-run survival by assigning them a low allocation of the common costs. The difficulty with the method is that, particularly if a large common cost is involved, every user would prefer to be viewed as the incremental party!

One approach managers can use to avoid disputes in such situations is to use the stand-alone cost-allocation method. Another approach is to use the *Shapley value*, which considers each party as first the primary party and then the incremental party. From the calculations shown earlier, the Albany employer is allocated $1,200 as the primary party and $700 as the incremental party, for an average of $950 [($1,200 + $700) ÷ 2]. The Chicago employer is allocated $800 as the primary party and $300 as the incremental party, for an average of $550 [($800 + 300) ÷ 2]. The Shapley value method allocates, to each employer, the average of the costs allocated as the primary party and as the incremental party: $950 to the Albany employer and $550 to the Chicago employer.[9]

As our discussion suggests, allocating common costs is not clear-cut and can generate disputes. Whenever feasible, managers should specify the rules for such allocations in advance. If this is not done, then, rather than blindly follow one method or another, managers should exercise judgment when allocating common costs by thinking carefully about allocation methods that appear fair to each party. For instance, Stevens must choose an allocation method for his airfare cost that is acceptable to each prospective employer. He cannot, for example, exceed the maximum reimbursable amount of airfare for either firm. The next section discusses the role of cost data in various types of contracts, another area where disputes about cost allocation frequently arise.

Decision Point

What methods can managers use to allocate common costs to two or more users?

Cost Allocations and Contract Disputes

Learning Objective 5

Explain the importance of explicit agreement between contracting parties when the reimbursement amount is based on costs incurred

...to avoid disputes regarding allowable cost items and how indirect costs should be allocated

Many commercial contracts include clauses based on cost accounting information. Examples include the following:

- A contract between the Department of Defense and a company designing and assembling a new fighter plane specifies that the price paid for the plane is to be based on the contractor's direct and overhead costs plus a fixed fee.
- A contract between a consulting firm and a hospital specifies that the consulting firm receive a fixed fee plus a share of the cost savings that arise from implementing the consulting firm's recommendations.

Contract disputes often arise over cost computations. Managers can reduce the areas of dispute between the contracting parties by making the "rules of the game" explicit and writing them into the contract that is signed. Such rules of the game include the definition of allowable cost items; the definitions of terms used, such as what constitutes direct labor; the permissible cost-allocation bases; and how to account for differences between budgeted and actual costs.

Contracting with the U.S. Government

The U.S. government reimburses most contractors in one of two main ways:

1. **The contractor is paid a set price without analysis of actual contract cost data.** This approach is used, for example, when there is competitive bidding, when there is adequate price competition, or when there is an established catalog with prices quoted for items sold in substantial quantities to the general public.
2. **The contractor is paid after analysis of actual contract cost data.** In some cases, when there is uncertainty about the cost to complete a job because of the nature of the task, for example, a new weapon system, the contract will explicitly state that the reimbursement amount is based on actual allocable costs plus a fixed fee.[10] This arrangement is called a *cost-plus contract*.

[9] For further discussion of the Shapley value, see Joel S. Demski, "Cost Allocation Games," in *Joint Cost Allocations*, ed. Shane Moriarity (University of Oklahoma Center for Economic and Management Research, 1981); Lech Kruś and Piotr Bronisz, "Cooperative Game Solution Concepts to a Cost Allocation Problem," *European Journal of Operational Research* 122:2 (April 16, 2000): 258–271.

[10] The Federal Acquisition Regulation (FAR), issued in March 2005 (see www.acquisition.gov/far/current/pdf/FAR.pdf) includes the following definition of *allocability* (in FAR 31.201-4): "A cost is allocable if it is assignable or chargeable to one or more cost objectives on the basis of relative benefits received or other equitable relationship. Subject to the foregoing, a cost is allocable to a Government contract if it:

(a) Is incurred specifically for the contract;

(b) Benefits both the contract and other work, and can be distributed to them in reasonable proportion to the benefits received; or

(c) Is necessary to the overall operation of the business, although a direct relationship to any particular cost objective cannot be shown."

All contracts with U.S. government agencies must comply with cost accounting standards issued by the **Cost Accounting Standards Board (CASB)**. For government contracts, the CASB has the exclusive authority to make, put into effect, amend, and rescind cost accounting standards and interpretations. The standards are designed to achieve *uniformity and consistency* in the measurement, assignment, and allocation of costs to government contracts within the United States.[11]

In government contracting, there is a complex interplay of political considerations and accounting principles. Terms such as *fairness* and *equity*, as well as cause and effect and benefits received, are often used in government contracts.

Fairness of Pricing

In many defense contracts, there is great uncertainty about the final cost to produce a new weapon or equipment. Such contracts are rarely subject to competitive bidding because no contractor is willing to assume all the risk of receiving a fixed price for the contract and subsequently incurring high costs to fulfill it. Therefore, setting a market-based fixed price for the contract fails to attract contractors or requires a contract price that is too high from the government's standpoint. To address this issue, the government typically assumes a major share of the risk of the potentially high costs of completing the contract. Rather than relying on selling prices as ordinarily set by suppliers in the marketplace, the government negotiates contracts on the basis of *costs plus a fixed fee*. In costs-plus-fixed-fee contracts, which often involve billions of dollars, the allocation of a specific cost, for example, general administration costs that support all contracts, may be difficult to defend on the basis of any cause-and-effect reasoning. Nonetheless, the contracting parties may still view it as a "reasonable" or "fair" means to help establish a contract amount.

Decision Point

How can contract disputes over reimbursement amounts based on costs be reduced?

Some costs are "allowable"; others are "unallowable." An **allowable cost** is a cost that the contract parties agree to include in the costs to be reimbursed. Some contracts specify how allowable costs are to be determined. For example, only economy-class airfares are allowable in many U.S. government contracts. Other contracts identify cost categories that are unallowable. For example, the costs of lobbying activities and alcoholic beverages are not allowable costs in U.S. government contracts. However, the set of allowable costs is not always clear-cut. Contract disputes and allegations about overcharging the government arise from time to time (see Concepts in Action: Contract Disputes over Reimbursable Costs for the U.S. Department of Defense).

Learning Objective 6

Understand how bundling of products

...two or more products sold for a single-price

causes revenue allocation issues

...allocating revenues to each product in the bundle to evaluate managers of individual products

and the methods managers use to allocate revenues

...using the stand-alone method or the incremental method

Bundled Products and Revenue Allocation Methods

Allocation issues can also arise when revenues from multiple products (for example, different software programs or cable and Internet packages) are bundled together and sold at a single price. The methods for revenue allocation parallel those described for common-cost allocations.

Bundling and Revenue Allocation

Revenues are inflows of assets (almost always cash or accounts receivable) companies receive for products or services provided to customers. Similar to cost allocation, **revenue allocation** occurs when revenues are related to a particular *revenue object* but cannot be traced to it in an economically feasible (cost-effective) way. A **revenue object** is anything for which a separate measurement of revenue is desired. Examples of revenue objects include products, customers, and divisions. We illustrate revenue-allocation

[11] Details on the Cost Accounting Standards Board are available at www.whitehouse.gov/omb/procurement/casb.html. The CASB is part of the Office of Federal Procurement Policy, U.S. Office of Management and Budget.

Concepts in Action

Contract Disputes over Reimbursable Costs for the U.S. Department of Defense

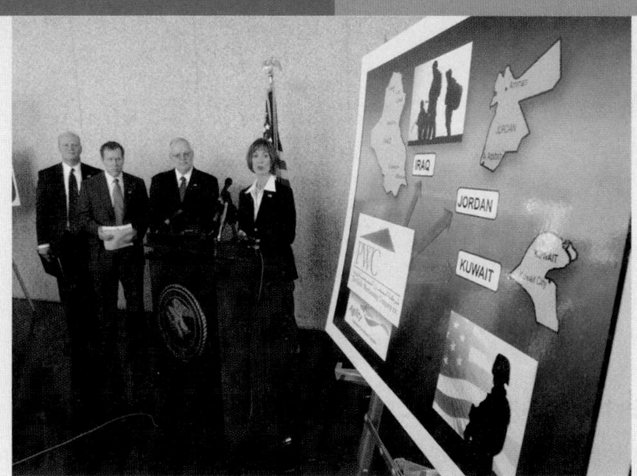

For 2013, the U.S. Department of Defense budget was more than $500 billion. A portion of this money was allocated to private companies to carry out specific contracted services. In recent years, the U.S. government has pursued cases against several contractors for overcharging for services. The following examples are from cases pursued by the U.S. Department of Justice's Civil Division on behalf of the federal government.

1. Maresk Line Limited paid $31.9 million to settle allegations of overcharging the U.S Department of Defense to ship thousands of cargo containers from Middle East ports to inland destinations in Iraq and Afghanistan. The company allegedly billed in excess of the contractual rate for refrigerated-container storage, late fees, and GPS cargo tracking.
2. United Technologies Corporation was found liable for more than $473 million arising out of a contract to provide the Air Force with F-15 and F-16 aircraft engines. The company excluded discounts that it received from suppliers in its proposed prices, which led to the Department of Defense paying more than it otherwise would have paid for the engines.
3. Lockheed Martin Corporation agreed to pay $15.8 million to settle charges that it overcharged the Department of Defense for tools used on multiple contracts. Specifically, the company was accused of inflating the cost of various tools and passing along those costs to the U.S. government for eight years.

Source: Press releases from the U.S. Department of Justice, Civil Division (2011–2013).

issues for Dynamic Software Corporation, which develops, sells, and supports three software programs:

1. WordMaster, a word-processing program, released 36 months ago
2. DataMaster, a spreadsheet program, released 18 months ago
3. FinanceMaster, a budgeting and cash-management program, released six months ago with a lot of favorable media attention

Dynamic Software sells these three products individually as well as together as bundled products.

A **bundled product** is a package of two or more products (or services) that is sold for a single price but whose individual components may be sold as separate items at their own "stand-alone" prices. The price of a bundled product is typically less than the sum of the prices of the individual products sold separately. For example, banks often provide individual customers with a bundle of services from different departments (checking, safety-deposit box, and investment advisory) for a single fee. A resort hotel may offer, for a single amount per customer, a weekend package that includes services from its lodging (the room), food (the restaurant), and recreational (golf and tennis) departments. When department managers have revenue or profit responsibilities for individual products, the bundled revenue must be allocated among the individual products in the bundle.

Dynamic Software allocates revenues from its bundled product sales (called "suite sales") to individual products. Individual-product profitability is used to compensate software engineers, developers, and product managers responsible for developing and managing each product.

How should Dynamic Software allocate suite revenues to individual products? Consider information pertaining to the three "stand-alone" and "suite" products in 2013:

	Selling Price	Manufacturing Cost per Unit
Stand-alone		
WordMaster	$125	$18
DataMaster	150	20
FinanceMaster	225	25
Suite		
Word + Data	$220	
Word + Finance	280	
Finance + Data	305	
Word + Finance + Data	380	

Just as we saw in the section on common-cost allocations, the two main revenue-allocation methods are the stand-alone method and the incremental method.

Stand-Alone Revenue-Allocation Method

The **stand-alone revenue-allocation method** uses product-specific information on the products in the bundle as weights for allocating the bundled revenues to the individual products. The term *stand-alone* refers to the product as a separate (nonsuite) item. Consider the Word + Finance suite, which sells for $280. Three types of weights for the stand-alone method are as follows:

1. **Selling prices.** Using the individual selling prices of $125 for WordMaster and $225 for FinanceMaster, the weights for allocating the $280 suite revenues between the products are as follows:

$$\text{WordMaster: } \frac{\$125}{\$125 + \$225} \times \$280 = 0.357 \times \$280 = \$100$$

$$\text{FinanceMaster: } \frac{\$225}{\$125 + \$225} \times \$280 = 0.643 \times \$280 = \$180$$

2. **Unit costs.** This method uses the costs of the individual products (in this case, manufacturing cost per unit) to determine the weights for the revenue allocations.

$$\text{WordMaster: } \frac{\$18}{\$18 + \$25} \times \$280 = 0.419 \times \$280 = \$117$$

$$\text{FinanceMaster: } \frac{\$25}{\$18 + \$25} \times \$280 = 0.581 \times \$280 = \$163$$

3. **Physical units.** This method gives each product unit in the suite the same weight when allocating suite revenue to individual products. Therefore, with two products in the Word + Finance suite, each product is allocated 50% of the suite revenues.

$$\text{WordMaster: } \frac{1}{1 + 1} \times \$280 = 0.50 \times \$280 = \$140$$

$$\text{FinanceMaster: } \frac{1}{1 + 1} \times \$280 = 0.50 \times \$280 = \$140$$

These three approaches to determining weights for the stand-alone method result in very different revenue allocations to the individual products:

Revenue-Allocation Weights	WordMaster	FinanceMaster
Selling prices	$100	$180
Unit costs	117	163
Physical units	140	140

Which method do managers prefer? The selling prices method is best because the weights explicitly consider the prices customers are willing to pay for the individual products. Weighting approaches that use revenue information better capture "benefits received" by customers than unit costs or physical units.[12] The physical-units revenue-allocation method is used when managers cannot use any of the other methods (such as when selling prices are unstable or unit costs are difficult to calculate for individual products).

Incremental Revenue-Allocation Method

The **incremental revenue-allocation method** ranks individual products in a bundle according to criteria determined by management—such as the product in the bundle with the most sales—and then uses this ranking to allocate bundled revenues to individual products. The first-ranked product is the *primary product* in the bundle. The second-ranked product is the *first-incremental product*, the third-ranked product is the *second-incremental product*, and so on.

How do companies decide on product rankings under the incremental revenue-allocation method? Some organizations survey customers about the importance of each of the individual products in their purchase decision. Others rank products on the basis of the recent stand-alone sales performance of the individual products in the bundle. A third approach is for top managers to use their knowledge or intuition to decide the rankings.

Consider again the Word + Finance suite. Assume WordMaster is designated as the primary product. If the suite selling price exceeds the stand-alone price of the primary product, the primary product is allocated 100% of its *stand-alone* revenue. Because the suite price of $280 exceeds the stand-alone price of $125 for WordMaster, WordMaster is allocated revenues of $125, with the remaining revenue of $155 ($280 − $125) allocated to FinanceMaster:

Product	Revenue Allocated	Cumulative Revenue Allocated
WordMaster	$125	$125
FinanceMaster	155 ($280 − $125)	$280
Total	$280	

If the suite price is less than or equal to the stand-alone price of the primary product, the primary product is allocated 100% of the *suite* revenue. All other products in the suite receive no allocation of revenue.

Now suppose FinanceMaster is designated as the primary product and WordMaster as the first-incremental product. Then the incremental revenue-allocation method allocates revenues of the Word + Finance suite as follows:

Product	Revenue Allocated	Cumulative Revenue Allocated
FinanceMaster	$225	$225
WordMaster	55 ($280 − $225)	$280
Total	$280	

If Dynamic Software sells equal quantities of WordMaster and FinanceMaster, then the Shapley value method allocates to each product the average of the revenues allocated as the primary and first-incremental products:

WordMaster:	($125 + $55) ÷ 2 = $180 ÷ 2 =	$ 90
FinanceMaster:	($225 + $155) ÷ 2 = $380 ÷ 2 =	190
Total		$280

[12] Revenue-allocation issues also arise in external reporting. The AICPA's Statement of Position 97-2 (Software Revenue Recognition) states that with bundled products, revenue allocation "based on vendor-specific objective evidence (VSOE) of fair value" is required. The "price charged when the element is sold separately" is said to be "objective evidence of fair value" (see "Statement of Position 97-2," Jersey City, NJ: AICPA, 1998). In September 2009, the FASB ratified Emerging Issues Task Force (EITF) Issue 08-1, specifying that with no VSOE or third-party evidence of selling price for all units of accounting in an arrangement, the consideration received for the arrangement should be allocated to the separate units based upon their estimated relative selling prices.

What happens if the firm sells 80,000 units of WordMaster and 20,000 units of FinanceMaster in the most recent quarter? Because Dynamic Software sells four times as many units of WordMaster, its managers believe that the sales of the Word + Finance suite are four times more likely to be driven by WordMaster as the primary product. The *weighted Shapley value method* takes this fact into account. It assigns four times as much weight to the revenue allocations when WordMaster is the primary product as when FinanceMaster is the primary product, resulting in the following allocations:

WordMaster:	(\$125 × 4 + \$55 × 1) ÷ (4 + 1) = \$555 ÷ 5 =	\$111
FinanceMaster:	(\$225 × 1 + \$155 × 4) ÷ (4 + 1) = \$845 ÷ 5 =	169
Total		\$280

When there are more than two products in the suite, the incremental revenue-allocation method allocates suite revenues sequentially. Assume WordMaster is the primary product in Dynamic Software's three-product suite (Word + Finance + Data). FinanceMaster is the first-incremental product, and DataMaster is the second-incremental product. This suite sells for \$380. The allocation of the \$380 suite revenues proceeds as follows:

Product	Revenue Allocated	Cumulative Revenue Allocated
WordMaster	\$125	\$125
FinanceMaster	155 (\$280 − \$125)	\$280 (price of Word + Finance suite)
DataMaster	100 (\$380 − \$280)	\$380 (price of Word + Finance + Data suite)
Total	\$380	

Now suppose WordMaster is the primary product, DataMaster is the first-incremental product, and FinanceMaster is the second-incremental product.

Product	Revenue Allocated	Cumulative Revenue Allocated
WordMaster	\$125	\$125
DataMaster	95 (\$220 − \$125)	\$220 (price of Word + Data suite)
FinanceMaster	160 (\$380 − \$220)	\$380 (price of Word + Data + Finance suite)
Total	\$380	

The ranking of the individual products in the suite determines the revenues allocated to them. Product managers at Dynamic Software likely would have different views of how their individual products contribute to sales of the suite products. In fact, each product manager would claim to be responsible for the primary product in the Word + Finance + Data suite![13] Because the stand-alone revenue-allocation method does not require rankings of individual products in the suite, this method is less likely to cause debates among product managers.

Decision Point

What is product bundling and how can managers allocate revenues of a bundled product to individual products in the package?

Revenue allocations are also important for tax reasons. For example, Verizon Communications Inc., the second-largest provider of telecommunications and cable services in the United States, sells each of its services—telephone, cable television, and broadband—separately and in bundled arrangements. State and local tax laws often stipulate that if a bundle is sold and the price for each line item is not split out on the consumer's bill, then all services are taxed as telephone services, which generally carries the highest tax rate. To preclude consumers from paying higher taxes on the entire package, Verizon allocates bundled service revenue to its telephone, cable television, and broadband services

[13] Calculating the Shapley value mitigates this problem because each product is considered as a primary, first-incremental, and second-incremental product. Assuming equal weights on all products, the revenue allocated to each product is an average of the revenues calculated for the product under these different assumptions. In the preceding example, the interested reader can verify that this will result in the following revenue assignments: FinanceMaster, \$180; WordMaster, \$87.50; and DataMaster, \$112.50.

based on the stand-alone selling prices of these services. Consumers then pay taxes on the amounts billed for each service. Specialized software packages, such as SureTax, help companies such as Verizon to properly recognize revenue according to the laws of each state.[14]

[14] SureTax, LLC, "SureTax Revenue Allocation Manager," http://www.suretax.com/solutions/suretax-revenue-allocation-manager/, accessed July 2013; Verizon Communication Inc., 2012 Annual Report (New York: Verizon Communications Inc., 2013).

Problem for Self-Study

This problem illustrates how costs of two corporate support departments are allocated to operating divisions using the dual-rate method. Fixed costs are allocated using budgeted costs and budgeted hours used by other departments. Variable costs are allocated using actual costs and actual hours used by other departments.

Computer Horizons reports the following budgeted and actual amounts for its two central corporate support departments (legal and personnel) for supporting each other and the two manufacturing divisions: the laptop division (LTD) and the work station division (WSD):

	A	B	C	D	E	F	G
1		SUPPORT			OPERATING		
2		Legal Department	Personnel Department		LTD	WSD	Total
3	**BUDGETED USAGE**						
4	Legal (hours)	—	250		1,500	750	2,500
5	(Percentages)	—	10%		60%	30%	100%
6	Personnel (hours)	2,500	—		22,500	25,000	50,000
7	(Percentages)	5%	—		45%	50%	100%
8							
9	**ACTUAL USAGE**						
10	Legal (hours)	—	400		400	1,200	2,000
11	(Percentages)	—	20%		20%	60%	100%
12	Personnel (hours)	2,000	—		26,600	11,400	40,000
13	(Percentages)	5%	—		66.5%	28.5%	100%
14	Budgeted fixed overhead costs before any						
15	interdepartment cost allocations	$360,000	$475,000		—	—	$835,000
16	Actual variable overhead costs before any						
17	interdepartment cost allocations	$200,000	$600,000		—	—	$800,000

Required

What amount of support-department costs for legal and personnel will be allocated to LTD and WSD using (a) the direct method, (b) the step-down method (allocating the legal department costs first), and (c) the reciprocal method using linear equations?

Solution

Exhibit 15-8 presents the computations for allocating the fixed and variable support-department costs. A summary of these costs follows:

	Laptop Division (LTD)	Work Station Division (WSD)
(a) Direct Method		
Fixed costs	$465,000	$370,000
Variable costs	470,000	330,000
	$935,000	$700,000

	Laptop Division (LTD)	Work Station Division (WSD)
(b) Step-Down Method		
Fixed costs	$458,053	$376,947
Variable costs	488,000	312,000
	$946,053	$688,947
(c) Reciprocal Method		
Fixed costs	$462,513	$372,487
Variable costs	476,364	323,636
	$938,877	$696,123

Exhibit 15-8 Alternative Methods of Allocating Corporate Support-Department Costs to Operating Divisions of Computer Horizons: Dual-Rate Method

	A	B	C	D	E	F	G
20		CORPORATE SUPPORT DEPARTMENTS			OPERATING DIVISIONS		
21	Allocation Method	Legal Department	Personnel Department		LTD	WSD	Total
22	**A. DIRECT METHOD**						
23	Fixed costs	$360,000	$475,000				
24	Legal (1,500 ÷ 2,250; 750 ÷ 2,250)	(360,000)			$240,000	$120,000	
25	Personnel (22,500 ÷ 47,500; 25,000 ÷ 47,500)		(475,000)		225,000	250,000	
26	Fixed support dept. cost allocated to operating divisions	$ 0	$ 0		$465,000	$370,000	$835,000
27	Variable costs	$200,000	$600,000				
28	Legal (400 ÷ 1,600; 1,200 ÷ 1,600)	(200,000)			$ 50,000	$150,000	
29	Personnel (26,600 ÷ 38,000; 11,400 ÷ 38,000)		(600,000)		420,000	180,000	
30	Variable support dept. cost allocated to operating divisions	$ 0	$ 0		$470,000	$330,000	$800,000
31	**B. STEP-DOWN METHOD**						
32	(Legal department first)						
33	Fixed costs	$360,000	$475,000				
34	Legal (250 ÷ 2,500; 1,500 ÷ 2,500; 750 ÷ 2,500)	(360,000)	36,000		$216,000	$108,000	
35	Personnel (22,500 ÷ 47,500; 25,000 ÷ 47,500)		(511,000)		242,053	268,947	
36	Fixed support dept. cost allocated to operating divisions	$ 0	$ 0		$458,053	$376,947	$835,000
37	Variable costs	$200,000	$600,000				
38	Legal (400 ÷ 2,000; 400 ÷ 2,000; 1,200 ÷ 2,000)	(200,000)	40,000		$ 40,000	$120,000	
39	Personnel (26,600 ÷ 38,000; 11,400 ÷ 38,000)		(640,000)		448,000	192,000	
40	Variable support dept. cost allocated to operating divisions	$ 0	$ 0		$488,000	$312,000	$800,000
41	**C. RECIPROCAL METHOD**						
42	Fixed costs	$360,000	$475,000				
43	Legal (250 ÷ 2,500; 1,500 ÷ 2,500; 750 ÷ 2,500)	(385,678)[a]	38,568		$231,407	$115,703	
44	Personnel (2,500 ÷ 50,000; 22,500 ÷ 50,000; 25,000 ÷ 50,000)	25,678	(513,568)[a]		231,106	256,784	
45	Fixed support dept. cost allocated to operating divisions	$ 0	$ 0		$462,513	$372,487	$835,000
46	Variable costs	$200,000	$600,000				
47	Legal (400 ÷ 2,000; 400 ÷ 2,000; 1,200 ÷ 2,000)	(232,323)[b]	46,465		$ 46,465	$139,393	
48	Personnel (2,000 ÷ 40,000; 26,600 ÷ 40,000; 11,400 ÷ 40,000)	32,323	(646,465)[b]		429,899	184,243	
49	Variable support dept. cost allocated to operating divisions	$ 0	$ 0		$476,364	$323,636	$800,000
50							

	A	B
51	[a] FIXED COSTS	[b] VARIABLE COSTS
52	Letting *LF* = Legal department fixed costs, and *PF* = Personnel department fixed costs, the simultaneous equations for the reciprocal method for fixed costs are	Letting *LV* = Legal department variable costs, and *PV* = Personnel department variable costs, the simultaneous equations for the reciprocal method for variable costs are
53	$LF = \$360{,}000 + 0.05\ PF$	$LV = \$200{,}000 + 0.05\ PV$
54	$PF = \$475{,}000 + 0.10\ LF$	$PV = \$600{,}000 + 0.20\ LV$
55	$LF = \$360{,}000 + 0.05\ (\$475{,}000 + 0.10\ LF)$	$LV = \$200{,}000 + 0.05\ (\$600{,}000 + 0.20\ LV)$
56	$LF = \$385{,}678$	$LV = \$232{,}323$
57	$PF = \$475{,}000 + 0.10\ (\$385{,}678) = \$513{,}568$	$PV = \$600{,}000 + 0.20\ (\$232{,}323) = \$646{,}465$

Decision Points

The following question-and-answer format summarizes the chapter's learning objectives. Each decision presents a key question related to a learning objective. The guidelines are the answer to that question.

Decision	Guidelines
1. When should managers use the dual-rate method over the single-rate method?	The single-rate method aggregates fixed and variable costs and allocates them to objects using a single allocation base and rate. Under the dual-rate method, costs are grouped into separate variable cost and fixed cost pools; each pool uses a different cost-allocation base and rate. If costs can be easily separated into variable and fixed costs, managers should use the dual-rate method because it provides better information for making decisions.
2. What factors should managers consider when deciding between allocation based on budgeted and actual rates and between budgeted and actual usage?	Using budgeted rates enables managers of user departments to have certainty about the costs allocated to them and insulates users from inefficiencies in the supplier department. Charging budgeted variable cost rates to users based on actual usage is causally appropriate and promotes control of resource consumption. Charging fixed cost rates on the basis of budgeted usage helps user divisions with planning and leads to goal congruence when considering outsourcing decisions.
3. What methods can managers use to allocate costs of multiple support departments to operating departments?	The three methods managers can use are the direct, the step-down, and the reciprocal methods. The direct method allocates each support department's costs to operating departments without allocating a support department's costs to other support departments. The step-down method allocates support-department costs to other support departments and to operating departments in a sequential manner that partially recognizes the mutual services provided among all support departments. The reciprocal method fully recognizes mutual services provided among all support departments.
4. What methods can managers use to allocate common costs to two or more users?	Common costs are the costs of a cost object (such as operating a facility or performing an activity) that are shared by two or more users. The stand-alone cost-allocation method uses information pertaining to each user of the cost object to determine cost-allocation weights. The incremental cost-allocation method ranks individual users of the cost object and allocates common costs first to the primary user and then to the other incremental users. The Shapley value method considers each user, in turn, as the primary and the incremental user.
5. How can contract disputes over reimbursement amounts based on costs be reduced?	Disputes can be reduced by making the cost-allocation rules as explicit as possible and including them in the contract. These rules should include details such as the allowable cost items, the acceptable cost-allocation bases, and how differences between budgeted and actual costs are to be accounted for.
6. What is product bundling, and how can managers allocate revenues of a bundled product to individual products in the package?	Bundling occurs when a package of two or more products (or services) is sold for a single price. Revenue allocation of the bundled price is required when managers of the individual products in the bundle are evaluated on product revenue or product operating income. Revenues can be allocated for a bundled product using the stand-alone method, the incremental method, or the Shapley value method.

Terms to Learn

This chapter and the Glossary at the end of the book contain definitions of the following important terms:

allowable cost **(p. 614)**
artificial costs **(p. 607)**
bundled product **(p. 615)**
common cost **(p. 611)**
complete reciprocated costs **(p. 607)**
Cost Accounting Standards Board (CASB) **(p. 614)**
direct method **(p. 604)**

dual-rate method **(p. 594)**
incremental cost-allocation method **(p. 612)**
incremental revenue-allocation method **(p. 617)**
matrix method **(p. 608)**
operating department **(p. 593)**
production department **(p. 593)**
reciprocal method **(p. 606)**
revenue allocation **(p. 614)**
revenue object **(p. 614)**
service department **(p. 593)**
single-rate method **(p. 594)**
sequential allocation method **(p. 605)**
stand-alone cost-allocation method **(p. 612)**
stand-alone revenue-allocation method **(p. 616)**
step-down method **(p. 605)**
support department **(p. 593)**

Assignment Material

MyAccountingLab

Questions

15-1 Distinguish between the single-rate and the dual-rate methods.

15-2 Describe how the dual-rate method is useful to division managers in decision making.

15-3 How do budgeted cost rates motivate the support-department manager to improve efficiency?

15-4 Give examples of allocation bases used to allocate support-department cost pools to operating departments.

15-5 Why might a manager prefer that budgeted rather than actual cost-allocation rates be used for costs being allocated to his or her department from another department?

15-6 "To ensure unbiased cost allocations, fixed costs should be allocated on the basis of estimated long-run use by user-department managers." Do you agree? Why?

15-7 Distinguish among the three methods of allocating the costs of support departments to operating departments.

15-8 What is conceptually the most defensible method for allocating support-department costs? Why?

15-9 Distinguish between two methods of allocating common costs.

15-10 What role does the Cost Accounting Standards Board play when companies contract with the U.S. government?

15-11 What is one key way to reduce cost-allocation disputes that arise with government contracts?

15-12 Describe how companies are increasingly facing revenue-allocation decisions.

15-13 Distinguish between the stand-alone and the incremental revenue-allocation methods.

15-14 Identify and discuss arguments that individual product managers may put forward to support their preferred revenue-allocation method.

15-15 How might a dispute over the allocation of revenues of a bundled product be resolved?

MyAccountingLab

Exercises

15-16 Single-rate versus dual-rate methods, support department. The Detroit power plant that services all manufacturing departments of MidWest Engineering has a budget for the coming year. This budget has been expressed in the following monthly terms:

Manufacturing Department	Needed at Practical Capacity Production Level (Kilowatt-Hours)	Average Expected Monthly Usage (Kilowatt-Hours)
Livonia	16,000	12,000
Warren	22,000	10,000
Dearborn	23,000	8,000
Westland	19,000	10,000
Total	80,000	40,000

The expected monthly costs for operating the power plant during the budget year are $21,600: $4,000 variable and $17,600 fixed.

Required

1. Assume that a single cost pool is used for the power plant costs. What budgeted amounts will be allocated to each manufacturing department if (a) the rate is calculated based on practical capacity and costs are allocated based on practical capacity and (b) the rate is calculated based on expected monthly usage and costs are allocated based on expected monthly usage?
2. Assume the dual-rate method is used with separate cost pools for the variable and fixed costs. Variable costs are allocated on the basis of expected monthly usage. Fixed costs are allocated on the

basis of practical capacity. What budgeted amounts will be allocated to each manufacturing department? Why might you prefer the dual-rate method?

15-17 Single-rate method, budgeted versus actual costs and quantities. Chocolat Inc. is a producer of premium chocolate based in Palo Alto. The company has a separate division for each of its two products: dark chocolate and milk chocolate. Chocolat purchases ingredients from Wisconsin for its dark chocolate division and from Louisiana for its milk chocolate division. Both locations are the same distance from Chocolat's Palo Alto plant.

Chocolat Inc. operates a fleet of trucks as a cost center that charges the divisions for variable costs (drivers and fuel) and fixed costs (vehicle depreciation, insurance, and registration fees) of operating the fleet. Each division is evaluated on the basis of its operating income. For 2013, the trucking fleet had a practical capacity of 50 round-trips between the Palo Alto plant and the two suppliers. It recorded the following information:

Home Insert Page Layout Formulas Data Review View

	A	B	C
1		**Budgeted**	**Actual**
2	Costs of truck fleet	$115,000	$96,750
3	Number of round-trips for dark chocolate division (Palo Alto plant—Wisconsin)	30	30
4	Number of round-trips for milk chocolate division (Palo Alto plant—Louisiana)	20	15

Required

1. Using the single-rate method, allocate costs to the dark chocolate division and the milk chocolate division in these three ways.
   a. Calculate the budgeted rate per round-trip and allocate costs based on round-trips budgeted for each division.
   b. Calculate the budgeted rate per round-trip and allocate costs based on actual round-trips used by each division.
   c. Calculate the actual rate per round-trip and allocate costs based on actual round-trips used by each division.
2. Describe the advantages and disadvantages of using each of the three methods in requirement 1. Would you encourage Chocolat Inc. to use one of these methods? Explain and indicate any assumptions you made.

15-18 Dual-rate method, budgeted versus actual costs and quantities (continuation of 15-17). Chocolat Inc. decides to examine the effect of using the dual-rate method for allocating truck costs to each round-trip. At the start of 2013, the budgeted costs were as follows:

Variable cost per round-trip	$ 1,350
Fixed costs	$47,500

The actual results for the 45 round-trips made in 2013 were as follows:

Variable costs	$58,500
Fixed costs	38,250
	$96,750

Assume all other information to be the same as in Exercise 15-17.

Required

1. Using the dual-rate method, what are the costs allocated to the dark chocolate division and the milk chocolate division when (a) variable costs are allocated using the budgeted rate per round-trip and actual round-trips used by each division and when (b) fixed costs are allocated based on the budgeted rate per round-trip and round-trips budgeted for each division?
2. From the viewpoint of the dark chocolate division, what are the effects of using the dual-rate method rather than the single-rate method?

15-19 Support-department cost allocation; direct and step-down methods. Phoenix Partners provides management consulting services to government and corporate clients. Phoenix has two support departments—administrative services (AS) and information systems (IS)—and two operating departments—government consulting (GOVT) and corporate consulting (CORP). For the first quarter of 2013, Phoenix's cost records indicate the following:

	A	B	C	D	E	F	G
1		SUPPORT			OPERATING		
2		AS	IS		GOVT	CORP	Total
3	Budgeted overhead costs before any						
4	interdepartment cost allocations	$600,000	$2,400,000		$8,756,000	$12,452,000	$24,208,000
5	Support work supplied by AS (budgeted head count)	—	25%		40%	35%	100%
6	Support work supplied by IS (budgeted computer time)	10%	—		30%	60%	100%

Required

1. Allocate the two support departments' costs to the two operating departments using the following methods:
   a. Direct method
   b. Step-down method (allocate AS first)
   c. Step-down method (allocate IS first)
2. Compare and explain differences in the support-department costs allocated to each operating department.
3. What approaches might be used to decide the sequence in which to allocate support departments when using the step-down method?

15-20 Support-department cost allocation, reciprocal method (continuation of 15-19). Refer to the data given in Exercise 15-19.

Required

1. Allocate the two support departments' costs to the two operating departments using the reciprocal method. Use (a) linear equations and (b) repeated iterations.
2. Compare and explain differences in requirement 1 with those in requirement 1 of Exercise 15-19. Which method do you prefer? Why?

15-21 Direct and step-down allocation. E-books, an online book retailer, has two operating departments—corporate sales and consumer sales—and two support departments—human resources and information systems. Each sales department conducts merchandising and marketing operations independently. E-books uses number of employees to allocate human resources costs and processing time to allocate information systems costs. The following data are available for September 2013:

	A	B	C	D	E	F
1		SUPPORT DEPARTMENTS			OPERATING DEPARTMENTS	
2		Human Resources	Information Systems		Corporate Sales	Consumer Sales
3	Budgeted costs incurred before any					
4	interdepartment cost allocations	$72,700	$234,400		$998,270	$489,860
5	Support work supplied by human resources department					
6	Budgeted number of employees	—	21		42	28
7	Support work supplied by information systems department					
8	Budgeted processing time (in minutes)	320	—		1,920	1,600

Required

1. Allocate the support departments' costs to the operating departments using the direct method.
2. Rank the support departments based on the percentage of their services provided to other support departments. Use this ranking to allocate the support departments' costs to the operating departments based on the step-down method.
3. How could you have ranked the support departments differently?

15-22 Reciprocal cost allocation (continuation of 15-21). Consider E-books again. The controller of E-books reads a widely used textbook that states that "the reciprocal method is conceptually the most defensible." He seeks your assistance.

Required

1. Describe the key features of the reciprocal method.
2. Allocate the support departments' costs (human resources and information systems) to the two operating departments using the reciprocal method.
3. In the case presented in this exercise, which method (direct, step-down, or reciprocal) would you recommend? Why?

15-23 Allocation of common costs. Evan and Brett are students at Berkeley College. They share an apartment that is owned by Brett. Brett is considering subscribing to an Internet provider that has the following packages available:

Package	Per Month
A. Internet access	$75
B. Phone services	25
C. Internet access + phone services	90

Evan spends most of his time on the Internet ("everything can be found online now"). Brett prefers to spend his time talking on the phone rather than using the Internet ("going online is a waste of time"). They agree that the purchase of the $90 total package is a "win–win" situation.

Required

1. Allocate the $90 between Evan and Brett using (a) the stand-alone cost-allocation method, (b) the incremental cost-allocation method, and (c) the Shapley value method.
2. Which method would you recommend they use and why?

15-24 Allocation of common costs. Barbara Richardson, a self-employed consultant near Sacramento, received an invitation to visit a prospective client in Baltimore. A few days later, she received an invitation to make a presentation to a prospective client in Chicago. She decided to combine her visits, traveling from Sacramento to Baltimore, Baltimore to Chicago, and Chicago to Sacramento.

Richardson received offers for her consulting services from both companies. Upon her return, she decided to accept the engagement in Chicago. She is puzzled over how to allocate her travel costs between the two clients. She has collected the following data for regular round-trip fares with no stopovers:

Sacramento to Baltimore	$900
Sacramento to Chicago	$600

Richardson paid $1,200 for her three-leg flight (Sacramento–Baltimore, Baltimore–Chicago, Chicago–Sacramento). In addition, she paid $30 each way for limousines from her home to Sacramento Airport and back when she returned.

Required

1. How should Richardson allocate the $1,600 airfare between the clients in Baltimore and Chicago using (a) the stand-alone cost-allocation method, (b) the incremental cost-allocation method, and (c) the Shapley value method?
2. Which method would you recommend Richardson use and why?
3. How should Richardson allocate the $60 limousine charges between the clients in Baltimore and Chicago?

15-25 Revenue allocation, bundled products. Essence Company blends and sells designer fragrances. It has a Men's Fragrances Division and a Women's Fragrances Division, each with different sales strategies, distribution channels, and product offerings. Essence is now considering the sale of a bundled product called Sync consisting of one bottle of Him, a men's cologne, and one bottle of Her, a women's perfume. For the most recent year, Essence reported the following:

Home Insert Page Layout Formulas

	A	B
1	**Product**	**Retail Price**
2	Him	$ 25.00
3	Her	$ 50.00
4	Sync (Him and Her)	$ 60.00

Required

1. Allocate revenue from the sale of each unit of Sync to Him and Her using the following:
   a. The stand-alone revenue-allocation method based on selling price of each product
   b. The incremental revenue-allocation method, with Him ranked as the primary product
   c. The incremental revenue-allocation method, with Her ranked as the primary product
   d. The Shapley value method, assuming equal unit sales of Him and Her
2. Of the four methods in requirement 1, which one would you recommend for allocating Sync's revenues to Him and Her? Explain.

15-26 Allocation of common costs. Doug Dandy Auto Sales uses all types of media to advertise its products (television, radio, newspaper, and so on). At the end of 2013, the company president, Doug Davenport, decided that all advertising costs would be incurred by corporate headquarters and allocated to each of the company's four sales locations based on number of vehicles sold. Doug was confident that his corporate purchasing manager could negotiate better advertising contracts on a corporate-wide basis than each of the sales managers could on their own. Davenport budgeted total advertising cost for 2014 to be $1.7 million. He introduced the new plan to his sales managers just before the New Year.

The manager of the east sales location, Mike Samson, was not happy. He complained that the new allocation method was unfair and would increase his advertising costs significantly over the prior year. The east location sold high volumes of low-priced used cars and most of the corporate advertising budget was related to new car sales.

Following Mike's complaint, Doug decided to take another hard look at what each of the divisions was paying for advertising before the new allocation plan. The results were as follows:

Sales Location	Actual Number of Cars Sold in 2013	Actual Advertising Cost Incurred in 2013
East	4,620	$ 261,600
West	1,120	392,400
North	3,220	697,600
South	5,040	828,400
	14,000	$2,180,000

Required

1. Using 2013 data as the cost bases, show the amount of the 2014 advertising cost ($1,700,000) that would be allocated to each of the divisions under the following criteria:
   a. Davenport's allocation method based on number of cars sold
   b. The stand-alone method
   c. The incremental-allocation method, with divisions ranked on the basis of dollars spent on advertising in 2013
2. Which method do you think is most equitable to the divisional sales managers? What other options might President Doug Davenport have for allocating the advertising costs?

MyAccountingLab

Problems

15-27 Single-rate, dual-rate, and practical capacity allocation. Preston Department Store has a new promotional program that offers a free gift-wrapping service for its customers. Preston's customer-service department has practical capacity to wrap 5,000 gifts at a budgeted fixed cost of $4,950 each month. The budgeted variable cost to gift-wrap an item is $0.35. During the most recent month, the department budgeted to wrap 4,500 gifts. Although the service is free to customers, a gift-wrapping service cost allocation is made to the department where the item was purchased. The customer-service department reported the following for the most recent month:

	A	B	C
1	Department	Budgeted Items Wrapped	Actual Items Wrapped
2	Giftware	1,000	1,200
3	Women's Apparel	850	650
4	Fragrances	1,000	900
5	Men's Apparel	750	450
6	Domestics	900	800
7	Total	4,500	4,000

Required

1. Using the single-rate method, allocate gift-wrapping costs to different departments in these three ways:
   a. Calculate the budgeted rate based on the budgeted number of gifts to be wrapped and allocate costs based on the budgeted use (of gift-wrapping services).
   b. Calculate the budgeted rate based on the budgeted number of gifts to be wrapped and allocate costs based on actual usage.
   c. Calculate the budgeted rate based on the practical gift-wrapping capacity available and allocate costs based on actual usage.
2. Using the dual-rate method, compute the amount allocated to each department when (a) the fixed-cost rate is calculated using budgeted costs and the practical gift-wrapping capacity, (b) fixed costs are allocated based on budgeted usage of gift-wrapping services, and (c) variable costs are allocated using the budgeted variable-cost rate and actual usage.
3. Comment on your results in requirements 1 and 2. Discuss the advantages of the dual-rate method.

15-28 Revenue allocation. Yang Inc. produces and sells DVDs to business people and students who are planning extended stays in China. It has been very successful with two DVDs: Beginning Mandarin and Conversational Mandarin. It is introducing a third DVD, Reading Chinese Characters. It has decided to market its new DVD in two different packages grouping the Reading Chinese Characters DVD with each of the other two language DVDs. Information about the separate DVDs and the packages follow.

DVD	Selling Price
Beginning Mandarin (BegM)	\$ 72
Conversational Mandarin (ConM)	\$112
Reading Chinese Characters (RCC)	\$ 48
BegM + RCC	\$100
ConM + RCC	\$140

Required

1. Using the selling prices, allocate revenues from the BegM + RCC package to each DVD in that package using (a) the stand-alone method; (b) the incremental method, in either order; and (c) the Shapley value method.
2. Using the selling prices, allocate revenues from the ConM + RCC package to each DVD in that package using (a) the stand-alone method; (b) the incremental method, in either order; and (c) the Shapley value method.
3. Which method is most appropriate for allocating revenues among the DVDs? Why?

15-29 Fixed-cost allocation. Baker University completed construction of its newest administrative building at the end of 2013. The University's first employees moved into the building on January 1, 2014. The building consists of office space, common meeting rooms (including a conference center), a cafeteria, and even a workout room for its exercise enthusiasts. The total 2014 building space of 250,000 square feet was utilized as follows:

Usage of Space	% of Total Building Space
Office space (occupied)	52%
Vacant office space	8%
Common meeting space	25%
Workout room	5%
Cafeteria	10%

The new building cost the university \$60 million and was depreciated using the straight-line method over 20 years. At the end of 2014 three departments occupied the building: executive offices of the president, accounting, and human resources. Each department's usage of its assigned space was as follows:

Department	Actual Office Space Used (sq. ft.)	Planned Office Space Used (sq. ft.)	Practical Capacity Office Space (sq. ft.)
Executive	32,500	24,800	36,000
Accounting	52,000	52,080	66,000
Human resources	45,500	47,120	48,000

Required

1. How much of the total building cost will be allocated in 2014 to each of the departments, if the total cost is allocated to each department on the basis of the following?
   a. Actual usage of the three departments
   b. Planned usage of the three departments
   c. Practical capacity of the three departments
2. Assume that Baker University allocates the total annual building cost in the following manner:
   a. All vacant office space is absorbed by the university and is not allocated to the departments.
   b. All occupied office space costs are allocated on the basis of actual square footage used.
   c. All common area costs are allocated on the basis of a department's practical capacity.

   Calculate the cost allocated to each department in 2014 under this plan. Do you think the allocation method used here is appropriate? Explain.

15-30 Allocating costs of support departments; step-down and direct methods. The Central Valley Company has prepared department overhead budgets for budgeted-volume levels before allocations as follows:

Support departments:		
Building and grounds	$45,000	
Personnel	300	
General plant administration	37,320	
Cafeteria: operating loss	970	
Storeroom	9,990	$ 93,580
Operating departments:		
Machining	$36,600	
Assembly	46,000	82,600
Total for support and operating departments		$176,180

Management has decided that the most appropriate inventory costs are achieved by using individual-department overhead rates. These rates are developed after support-department costs are allocated to operating departments.

Bases for allocation are to be selected from the following:

Department	Direct Manufacturing Labor-Hours	Number of Employees	Square Feet of Floor Space Occupied	Manufacturing Labor-Hours	Number of Requisitions
Building and grounds	0	0	0	0	0
Personnel[a]	0	0	2,500	0	0
General plant administration	0	40	12,000	0	0
Cafeteria: operating loss	0	10	5,000	3,000	0
Storeroom	0	5	6,000	2,000	0
Machining	8,000	55	22,000	13,000	6,000
Assembly	32,000	140	202,500	26,000	4,000
Total	40,000	250	250,000	44,000	10,000

[a]Basis used is number of employees.

Required

1. Using the step-down method, allocate support-department costs. Develop overhead rates per direct manufacturing labor-hour for machining and assembly. Allocate the costs of the support departments in the order given in this problem. Use the allocation base for each support department you think is most appropriate.
2. Using the direct method, rework requirement 1.
3. Based on the following information about two jobs, determine the total overhead costs for each job by using rates developed in (a) requirement 1 and (b) requirement 2.

	Direct Manufacturing Labor-Hours	
	Machining	Assembly
Job 88	17	7
Job 89	9	20

4. The company evaluates the performance of the operating department managers on the basis of how well they managed their total costs, including allocated costs. As the manager of the Machining Department, which allocation method would you prefer from the results obtained in requirements 1 and 2? Explain.

15-31 Support-department cost allocations; single-department cost pools; direct, step-down, and reciprocal methods. The Milton Company has two products. Product 1 is manufactured entirely in department X. Product 2 is manufactured entirely in department Y. To produce these two products, the Milton Company has two support departments: A (a materials-handling department) and B (a power-generating department).

An analysis of the work done by departments A and B in a typical period follows:

	Used by			
Supplied by	**A**	**B**	**X**	**Y**
A	—	200	500	300
B	750	—	125	375

The work done in department A is measured by the direct labor-hours of materials-handling time. The work done in department B is measured by the kilowatt-hours of power. The budgeted costs of the support departments for the coming year are as follows:

	Department A (Materials Handling)	Department B (Power Generation)
Variable indirect labor and indirect materials costs	$150,000	$15,000
Supervision	45,000	25,000
Depreciation	15,000	50,000
	$210,000	$90,000
	+Power costs	+Materials-handling costs

The budgeted costs of the operating departments for the coming year are $1,250,000 for department X and $950,000 for department Y.

Supervision costs are salary costs. Depreciation in department B is the straight-line depreciation of power-generation equipment in its 19th year of an estimated 25-year useful life; it is old, but well-maintained, equipment.

Required

1. What are the allocations of costs of support departments A and B to operating departments X and Y using (a) the direct method, (b) the step-down method (allocate department A first), (c) the step-down method (allocate department B first), and (d) the reciprocal method?
2. An outside company has offered to supply all the power needed by the Milton Company and to provide all the services of the present power department. The cost of this service will be $80 per kilowatt-hour of power. Should Milton accept? Explain.

15-32 Common costs. Taylor Inc. and Victor Inc. are two small clothing companies that are considering leasing a dyeing machine together. The companies estimated that in order to meet production, Taylor needs the machine for 600 hours and Victor needs it for 400 hours. If each company rents the machine on its own, the fee will be $60 per hour of usage. If they rent the machine together, the fee will decrease to $54 per hour of usage.

Required

1. Calculate Taylor's and Victor's respective share of fees under the stand-alone cost-allocation method.
2. Calculate Taylor's and Victor's respective share of fees using the incremental cost-allocation method. Assume Taylor to be the primary party.
3. Calculate Taylor's and Victor's respective share of fees using the Shapley value method.
4. Which method would you recommend Taylor and Victor use to share the fees?

15-33 Stand-alone revenue allocation. Office Magic, Inc., sells computer hardware to end consumers. Its most popular model, the CX30 is sold as a "bundle," which includes three hardware products: a personal computer (PC) tower, a 26-inch monitor, and a color laser printer. Each of these products is made in a separate manufacturing division of Office Magic and can be purchased individually as well as in a bundle. The individual selling prices and per unit costs are as follows:

Computer Component	Individual Selling Price per Unit	Cost per Unit
PC tower	$1,140	$376
Monitor	$ 260	$200
Color laser printer	$ 600	$224
Computer bundle purchase price	$1,500	

Required

1. Allocate the revenue from the computer bundle purchase to each of the hardware products using the stand-alone method based on the individual selling price per unit.
2. Allocate the revenue from the computer bundle purchase to each of the hardware products using the stand-alone method based on cost per unit.
3. Allocate the revenue from the computer bundle purchase to each of the hardware products using the stand-alone method based on physical units (that is, the number of individual units of product sold per bundle).
4. Which basis of allocation makes the most sense in this situation? Explain your answer.

15-34 Support-department cost allocations; single-department cost pools; direct, step-down, and reciprocal methods. Sportz, Inc., manufactures athletic shoes and athletic clothing for both amateur and professional athletes. The company has two product lines (clothing and shoes), which are produced in separate manufacturing facilities; however, both manufacturing facilities share the same support services for information technology and human resources. The following shows total costs for each manufacturing facility and for each support department.

	Variable Costs	Fixed Costs	Total Costs by Department (in thousands)
Information technology (IT)	$ 600	$ 2,000	$ 2,600
Human resources (HR)	$ 400	$ 1,000	$ 1,400
Clothing	$2,500	$ 8,000	$10,500
Shoes	$3,000	$ 4,500	$ 7,500
Total costs	$6,500	$15,500	$22,000

The total costs of the support departments (IT and HR) are allocated to the production departments (clothing and shoes) using a single rate based on the following:

Information technology:	Number of IT labor-hours worked by department
Human resources:	Number of employees supported by department

Data on the bases, by department, are given as follows:

Department	IT Hours Used	Number of Employees
Clothing	5,040	220
Shoes	3,960	88
Information technology	—	92
Human resources	3,000	—

Required

1. What are the total costs of the production departments (clothing and shoes) *after* the support department costs of information technology and human resources have been allocated using (a) the direct method, (b) the step-down method (allocate information technology first), (c) the step-down method (allocate human resources first), and (d) the reciprocal method?
2. Assume that all of the work of the IT department could be outsourced to an independent company for $97.50 per hour. If Sportz no longer operated its own IT department, 30% of the fixed costs of the IT department could be eliminated. Should Sportz outsource its IT services?

15-35 Revenue allocation, bundled products. Premier Resorts (PR) operates a five-star hotel with a championship golf course. PR has a decentralized management structure, with three divisions:

- Lodging (rooms, conference facilities)
- Food (restaurants and in-room service)
- Recreation (golf course, tennis courts, swimming pool, and so on)

Starting next month, PR will offer a two-day, two-person "getaway package" for $800.

This deal includes the following:

	As Priced Separately
Two nights' stay for two in an ocean-view room	$ 640 ($320 per night)
Two rounds of golf (can be used by either guest)	$ 300 ($150 per round)
Candlelight dinner for two at PR's finest restaurant	$ 160 ($80 per person)
Total package value	$1,100

Jenny Lee, president of the recreation division, recently asked the CEO of PR how her division would share in the $800 revenue from the getaway package. The golf course was operating at 100% capacity. Currently, anyone booking the package was guaranteed access to the golf course. Lee noted that every "getaway" booking would displace $300 of other golf bookings not related to the package. She emphasized that the high demand reflected the devotion of her team to keeping the golf course rated one of the "Best 10 Courses in the World" by *Golf Monthly*. As an aside, she also noted that the lodging and food divisions had to turn away customers during only "peak-season events such as the New Year's period."

Required

1. Using selling prices, allocate the $800 getaway-package revenue to the three divisions using:
   a. The stand-alone revenue-allocation method
   b. The incremental revenue-allocation method (with recreation first, then lodging, and then food)
2. What are the pros and cons of the two methods in requirement 1?
3. Because the recreation division is able to book the golf course at 100% capacity, the company CEO has decided to revise the getaway package to only include the lodging and food offerings shown previously. The new package will sell for $720. Allocate the revenue to the lodging and food divisions using the following:
   a. The Shapley value method
   b. The weighted Shapley value method, assuming that lodging is three times as likely to sell as the food

15-36 Support-department cost allocations; direct, step-down, and reciprocal methods. Montclair Tours provides guided educational tours to college alumni associations. The company is divided into two operating divisions: domestic tours and world tours. Each of the tour divisions uses the services of the company's two support departments: Administration and Information Technology. Additionally, the Administration and Information Technology departments use the services of each other. Data concerning the past year are as follows:

	Support Departments		Operating Departments		
	Administration	Information Technology	Domestic Tours	World Tours	Total
Budgeted overhead costs before any interdepartment cost allocations	$400,000	$250,000	$1,300,000	$1,840,000	$3,790,0000
Support work furnished:					
by Administration					
Budgeted administration salaries	—	$ 88,000	$ 55,000	$ 77,000	$ 220,000
Percentage	—	40%	25%	35%	100%
by Information Technology					
Budgeted IT service hours	600	—	2,200	1,200	4,000
Percentage	15%	—	55%	30%	100%

Required

1. What are the total overhead costs of the operating departments (domestic and world tours) *after* the support department costs of Administration and Information Technology have been allocated using (a) the direct method, (b) the step-down method (allocate Administration first), (c) the step-down method (allocate Information Technology first), and (d) the reciprocal method?
2. Which method would you recommend that Montclair Tours use to allocate service department costs? Why?

16 Cost Allocation: Joint Products and Byproducts

Learning Objectives

1. Identify the splitoff point in a joint-cost situation and distinguish joint products from byproducts
2. Explain why joint costs are allocated to individual products
3. Allocate joint costs using four methods
4. Identify situations when the sales value at splitoff method is preferred when allocating joint costs
5. Explain why joint costs are irrelevant in a sell-or-process-further decision
6. Account for byproducts using two methods

Many companies, such as petroleum refiners, produce and sell two or more products simultaneously.

For example, ExxonMobil sells petroleum, natural gas, and raw liquefied petroleum gas (LPG), which are produced when the company extracts crude oil and refines it. Similarly, some companies, such as health care providers, sell or provide multiple services. The question is, "How should these companies allocate costs to 'joint' products and services?" Knowing how to allocate joint product costs isn't something that only companies need to understand. It's something that farmers have to deal with, too, especially when it comes to the lucrative production of corn to make billions of gallons of ethanol fuel.

Joint Cost Allocation and the Production of Ethanol Fuel[1]

The increased global demand for oil has driven prices higher and forced countries to look for environmentally sustainable alternatives. In the United States, the largest source of alternative fuel comes from corn-based ethanol. In 2012, the U.S. produced 13.8 billion gallons of ethanol, up from 1.7 billion gallons per year in 2001. Producing ethanol requires a significant amount of corn. Forty percent of U.S. domestic corn production is used to create ethanol fuel, but not all of that corn winds up in the ethanol that gets blended into gasoline and sold at service stations.

Most biotechnology operations, such as making ethanol, produce two or more products. While distilling corn into ethanol, cell mass from the process—such as antibiotic and yeast fermentations—separates from the liquid and becomes a distinct product, which is often sold as animal feed. This separation point, where outputs become distinctly identifiable, is called the splitoff point. Similarly, the residues from corn processing plants create secondary products including distillers' dried grains and gluten.

Accountants refer to these secondary products as byproducts. Ethanol byproducts like animal feed and gluten are accounted for by deducting the income

---

[1] *Sources:* Hacking, Andrew. 1987. Economic aspects of biotechnology. Cambridge, United Kingdom: Cambridge University Press; Leber, Jessica. 2010. Economics improve for first commercial cellulosic ethanol plants. *New York Times,* February 16; PBS. 2006. Glut of ethanol byproducts coming. *The Environmental Report,* Spring; United States Department of Energy 2013. U.S. ethanol production and the renewable fuel standard RIN bank. Press Release, June 5; Meyer, Gregory. 2013. US ethanol lobby urges brake on biofuels. *Financial Times,* April 18.

from selling these products from the cost of ethanol fuel, the major product. Because the price of ethanol is about $2 per gallon, whereas the byproducts sell for just a few cents per pound, most of the costs of production are allocated to the ethanol fuel itself, the main product. Because ethanol producers would otherwise have to pay to dispose of the byproducts, the relatively small amount of revenue earned from them just helps the firms "break even" on their production.

In the coming years, however, this may change. With ethanol production growing, corn-based animal feed byproducts are becoming more plentiful. Some ethanol manufacturers are working together to create a market for ethanol feed, which is cheaper and higher in protein than plain corn. This allows ranchers' animals to gain weight faster and at a lower cost per pound.

This chapter examines methods for allocating costs to joint products. We also examine how cost numbers appropriate for one purpose, such as external reporting, may not be appropriate for other purposes, such as decisions about the further processing of joint products.

Joint-Cost Basics

Learning Objective 1

Identify the splitoff point in a joint-cost situation

...the point at which two or more products become separately identifiable

and distinguish joint products

...products with high sales values

from byproducts

...products with low sales values

Joint costs are the costs of a production process that yields multiple products simultaneously. Consider the distillation of coal, which yields coke, natural gas, and other products. The costs of this distillation are joint costs. The **splitoff point** is the juncture in a joint production process when two or more products become separately identifiable. An example is the point at which coal becomes coke, natural gas, and other products. **Separable costs** are all costs—manufacturing, marketing, distribution, and so on—incurred beyond the splitoff point that are assignable to each of the specific products identified at the splitoff point. At or beyond the splitoff point, decisions relating to the sale or further processing of each identifiable product can be made independently of decisions about the other products.

As the examples in Exhibit 16-1 show, the production processes in many industries simultaneously yield two or more products, either at the splitoff point or after further processing. In each of these examples, no individual product can be produced without the accompanying products appearing, although in some cases the proportions can be varied. Joint costing allocates the joint costs to the individual products that are eventually sold.

The outputs of a joint production process can be classified into two general categories: outputs with a positive sales value and outputs with a zero sales value.[2] For example, offshore processing of hydrocarbons yields oil and natural gas, which have positive sales value; the processing also yields water, which has zero sales value and is

[2] Some outputs of a joint production process have "negative" revenue when their disposal costs (such as the costs of handling nonsalable toxic substances that require special disposal procedures) are considered. These disposal costs should be added to the joint production costs that are allocated to joint or main products.

Exhibit 16-1 Examples of Joint-Cost Situations

Industry	Separable Products at the Splitoff Point
Agriculture and Food Processing Industries	
Cocoa beans	Cocoa butter, cocoa powder, cocoa drink mix, tanning cream
Lambs	Lamb cuts, tripe, hides, bones, fat
Hogs	Bacon, ham, spare ribs, pork roast
Raw milk	Cream, liquid skim
Lumber	Lumber of varying grades and shapes
Turkeys	Breast, wings, thighs, drumsticks, digest, feather meal, poultry meal
Extractive Industries	
Coal	Coke, gas, benzol, tar, ammonia
Copper ore	Copper, silver, lead, zinc
Petroleum	Crude oil, natural gas
Salt	Hydrogen, chlorine, caustic soda
Chemical Industries	
Raw LPG (liquefied petroleum gas)	Butane, ethane, propane
Crude oil	Gasoline, kerosene, benzene, naphtha
Semiconductor Industry	
Fabrication of silicon-wafer chips	Memory chips of different quality (as to capacity), speed, life expectancy, and temperature tolerance

recycled back into the ocean. The term **product** describes any output that has a positive total sales value (or an output that enables a company to avoid incurring costs, such as an intermediate chemical product used as input in another process). The total sales value can be high or low.

When a joint production process yields one product with a high total sales value, compared with the total sales values of other products of the process, that product is called a **main product**. When a joint production process yields two or more products with high total sales values relative to the total sales values of other products, those products are called **joint products**. In contrast, products of a joint production process that have low total sales values relative to the total sales value of the main product or of joint products are called **byproducts**.

Consider some examples. If timber (logs) is processed into standard lumber and wood chips, standard lumber is a main product and wood chips are the byproduct because standard lumber has a high total sales value compared with wood chips. If, however, the logs are processed into fine-grade lumber, standard lumber, and wood chips, fine-grade lumber and standard lumber are joint products and wood chips are the byproduct. That's because both fine-grade lumber and standard lumber have high total sales values relative to wood chips.

Decision Point

What do the terms joint cost and splitoff point mean, and how do joint products differ from byproducts?

Distinctions among main products, joint products, and byproducts are not so clear-cut in practice. Companies use different thresholds for determining whether the relative sales value of a product is high enough for it to be considered a joint product. Consider kerosene, obtained when refining crude oil. Based on a comparison of its sales value to the total sales values of gasoline and other products, some companies classify kerosene as a joint product whereas others classify it as a byproduct. Moreover, the classification of products—main, joint, or byproduct—can change over time, especially for products such as lower-grade semiconductor chips, whose market prices may increase or decrease by 30% or more in a year. When prices of lower-grade chips are high, they are considered joint products together with higher-grade chips; when prices of lower-grade chips fall considerably, they are considered byproducts. In practice, it is important to understand how a specific company chooses to classify its products.

Allocating Joint Costs

Learning Objective 2

Explain why joint costs are allocated to individual products

. . . to calculate cost of goods sold and inventory and for reimbursements under cost-plus contracts and other types of claims

Before a manager is able to allocate joint costs, she must first look at the context for doing so. Joint costs must be allocated to individual products or services for several purposes, including the following:

- Computing inventoriable costs and the cost of goods sold for external and internal reporting purposes. Recall from Chapter 9 that absorption costing is required for financial accounting and tax reporting. This necessitates the allocation of joint manufacturing or processing costs to products for calculating ending inventory values. In addition, many firms use internal accounting data based on joint cost allocations to analyze the profitability of their various divisions and evaluate the performance of division managers.
- Reimbursing companies that have some, but not all, of their products or services reimbursed under cost-plus contracts with, say, a government agency. For example, the joint costs incurred when multiple organs are removed from a single donor must be allocated to various organ centers in order to determine reimbursement rates for transplants into Medicare patients. In such cases, stringent rules typically specify the way in which joint costs are assigned to the products or services covered by the agreements. That said, fraud in defense contracting, which is often done via cost-plus contracts, remains one of the most active areas of false claim litigation under the Federal False Claims Act. A common practice is "cross-charging," where a contractor shifts joint costs from "fixed-price" defense contracts to those that are done on a cost-plus basis. Defense contractors have also attempted to secure contracts from private businesses or foreign governments by allocating an improper share of joint costs onto the cost-plus agreements they have with the U.S. government.[3]
- Regulating the rates or prices of one or more of the jointly produced products or services. This issue is critical in the extractive and energy industries, in which output prices are regulated to yield a fixed return on a cost basis that includes joint cost allocations. In telecommunications, a firm with significant market power has some products subject to price regulation (e.g., interconnection) and other activities that are unregulated (such as equipment rentals to end-users). In this case, joint costs must be allocated to ensure that costs are not transferred from unregulated services to regulated ones.
- For any commercial litigation or insurance settlement situation in which the costs of joint products or services are key inputs.

Decision Point

Why are joint costs allocated to individual products?

Concepts in Action: Are Charitable Organizations Allocating Joint Costs in a Misleading Way? outlines another scenario in which joint cost allocations are important and have also been the subject of some controversy.

Approaches to Allocating Joint Costs

Learning Objective 3

Allocate joint costs using four methods

. . . sales value at splitoff, physical measure, net realizable value (NRV), and constant gross-margin percentage NRV

Two approaches are used to allocate joint costs.

- **Approach 1.** Allocate joint costs using *market-based* data such as revenues. This chapter illustrates three methods that use this approach:
  1. Sales value at splitoff method
  2. Net realizable value (NRV) method
  3. Constant gross-margin percentage NRV method
- **Approach 2.** Allocate joint costs using *physical measures*, such as the weight, quantity (physical units), or volume of the joint products.

In preceding chapters, we used the cause-and-effect and benefits-received criteria for guiding cost-allocation decisions (see Exhibit 14-2, page 553). Joint costs do not have a cause-and-effect relationship with individual products because the production process simultaneously yields multiple products. Using the benefits-received criterion leads to a preference for

[3] See, for example, www.dodig.mil/iginformation/IGInformationReleases/3eSettlementPR.pdf.

Concepts in Action: Are Charitable Organizations Allocating Joint Costs in a Misleading Way?

Whether seeking to help children or eradicate disease, charities raise money from philanthropic donors to fulfill their public-interest missions. In the United States, charities that use direct mailings or other activities that combine a public education effort with fundraising appeals must allocate the joint costs related to these activities to programs, fundraising, and administration. Some critics say that joint-cost allocation can be used to mislead donors by disguising high fundraising costs and over-reporting funds used for an organization's mission.

According to the Financial Accounting Standards Board, charities are supposed to allocate joint costs only in certain circumstances. They must design the activity to get people to take a specific action to support their mission—for example, contact a public official, recycle waste, or reduce health risks. Additionally, they must select recipients because they are able to take that action or would benefit from it—not because they are likely donors. The main accounting issue is the following: for mailings, which are common for charities, to which category should the joint costs of the envelope and postage (usually the largest component of the total cost of the activity) be charged?

The American Heart Association, for example, allocated \$227.5 million out of total spending of almost \$596 million to joint costs and spent 78% on programs according to its 2012 tax form. If joint costs were discounted, program spending falls to 51%.

Many charities believe that joint costs, if used appropriately, reward efficiency because a charity can combine multiple goals in a single campaign and reflect that in its breakdown of costs. Others argue that joint costs allow charities to overstate the program portion of its work, thus misleading donors into believing that more is being done for the public than is really the case. With nonprofit watchdogs, including Charity Navigator and the Better Business Bureau, looking closely at the practices of U.S. charities, joint costs will likely remain in the nonprofit spotlight.

Source: Christopher Jones and Andrea Roberts, "Management of Financial Information in Charitable Organizations: The Case of Joint-Cost Allocations," *The Accounting Review* 81(1) (January 2006); Suzanne Perry, "Watchdog Cracks Down on Misleading Statements on Fundraising Costs," *The Chronicle of Philanthropy* (February 10, 2013); "Watchdog Barks Louder on Cost Allocation Issues," *The NonProfit Times* (October 1, 2012).

methods under approach 1 because revenues are, in general, a better indicator of benefits received than physical measures. Mining companies, for example, receive more benefit from 1 ton of gold than they do from 10 tons of coal.

In the simplest joint production process, the joint products are sold at the splitoff point without further processing. Example 1 illustrates the two methods that apply in this case: the sales value at splitoff method and the physical-measure method. Then we introduce joint production processes that yield products that require further processing beyond the splitoff point. Example 2 illustrates the NRV method and the constant-gross margin percentage NRV method. To help you focus on key concepts, we use numbers and amounts that are smaller than the numbers that are typically found in practice.

The exhibits in this chapter use the following symbols to distinguish a joint or main product from a byproduct:

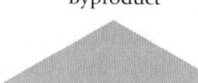

Joint Product or Main Product

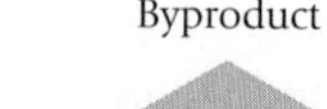

To compare the methods, we report gross-margin percentages for individual products under each method.

Example 1: Farmland Dairy purchases raw milk from individual farms and processes it until the splitoff point, when two products—cream and liquid skim—emerge. These two products are sold to an independent company, which markets and distributes them to supermarkets and other retail outlets.

In May 2014, Farmland Dairy processes 110,000 gallons of raw milk. During processing, 10,000 gallons are lost due to evaporation and spillage, yielding 25,000 gallons of cream and 75,000 gallons of liquid skim. The data are summarized as follows:

	A	B	C
1		**Joint Costs**	
2	Joint costs (costs of 110,000 gallons raw milk and processing to splitoff point)	$400,000	
3			
4		**Cream**	**Liquid Skim**
5	Beginning inventory (gallons)	0	0
6	Production (gallons)	25,000	75,000
7	Sales (gallons)	20,000	30,000
8	Ending inventory (gallons)	5,000	45,000
9	Selling price per gallon	$ 8	$ 4

Exhibit 16-2 depicts the basic relationships in this example.

How much of the $400,000 joint costs should be allocated to the cost of goods sold of 20,000 gallons of cream and 30,000 gallons of liquid skim, and how much should be allocated to the ending inventory of 5,000 gallons of cream and 45,000 gallons of liquid skim? We begin by illustrating the two methods that use the properties of the products at the splitoff point: the sales value at splitoff method and the physical-measure method.

Sales Value at Splitoff Method

The **sales value at splitoff method** allocates joint costs to joint products produced during the accounting period on the basis of the relative total sales value at the splitoff point.

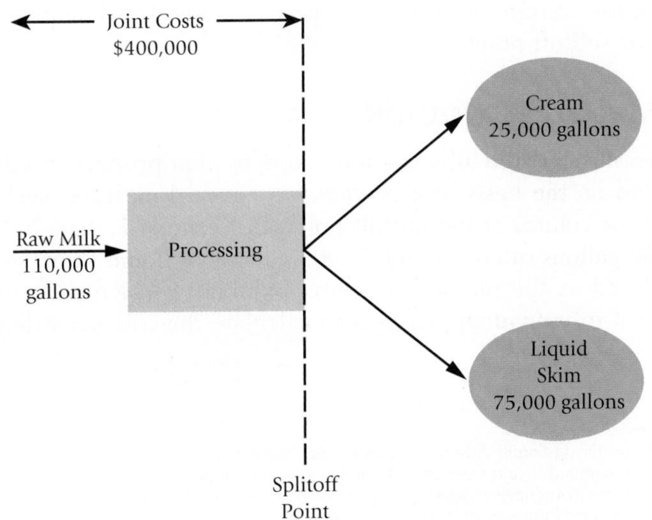

Exhibit 16-2

Example 1: Overview of Farmland Dairy

Exhibit 16-3 Joint-Cost Allocation and Product-Line Income Statement Using Sales Value at Splitoff Method: Farmland Dairy for May 2014

Home Insert Page Layout Formulas Data Review View

	A	B	C	D
1	**PANEL A: Allocation of Joint Costs Using Sales Value at Splitoff Method**	**Cream**	**Liquid Skim**	**Total**
2	Sales value of total production at splitoff point			
3	(25,000 gallons × $8 per gallon; 75,000 gallons × $4 per gallon)	$200,000	$300,000	$500,000
4	Weighting ($200,000 ÷ $500,000; $300,000 ÷ 500,000)	0.40	0.60	
5	Joint costs allocated (0.40 × $400,000; 0.60 × $400,000)	$160,000	$240,000	$400,000
6	Joint production cost per gallon			
7	($160,000 ÷ 25,000 gallons; $240,000 ÷ 75,000 gallons)	$ 6.40	$ 3.20	
8				
9	**PANEL B: Product-Line Income Statement Using Sales Value at Splitoff Method for May 2014**	**Cream**	**Liquid Skim**	**Total**
10	Revenues (20,000 gallons × $8 per gallon; 30,000 gallons × $4 per gallon)	$160,000	$120,000	$280,000
11	Cost of goods sold (joint costs)			
12	Production costs (0.40 × $400,000; 0.60 × $400,000)	160,000	240,000	400,000
13	Deduct ending inventory (5,000 gallons × $6.40 per gallon; 45,000 gallons × $3.20 per gallon)	32,000	144,000	176,000
14	Cost of goods sold (joint costs)	128,000	96,000	224,000
15	Gross margin	$ 32,000	$ 24,000	$ 56,000
16	Gross margin percentage ($32,000 ÷ $160,000; $24,000 ÷ $120,000; $56,000 ÷ $280,000)	20%	20%	20%

Using this method for Example 1, Exhibit 16-3, Panel A, shows how joint costs are allocated to individual products to calculate the cost per gallon of cream and liquid skim for valuing ending inventory. This method uses the sales value of the *entire production of the accounting period* (25,000 gallons of cream and 75,000 gallons of liquid skim), not just the quantity sold (20,000 gallons of cream and 30,000 gallons of liquid skim). The reason this method does not rely solely on the quantity sold is that the joint costs were incurred on all units produced, not just the portion sold during the current period. Exhibit 16-3, Panel B, presents the product-line income statement using the sales value at splitoff method. Note that the gross-margin percentage for each product is 20% because the sales value at splitoff method allocates joint costs to each product in proportion to the sales value of total production (cream: $160,000 ÷ $200,000 = 80%; liquid skim: $240,000 ÷ $300,000 = 80%). Therefore, the gross-margin percentage for each product manufactured in May 2014 is the same: 20%.[4]

Note how the sales value at splitoff method follows the benefits-received criterion of cost allocation: Costs are allocated to products in proportion to their revenue-generating power (their expected revenues). The cost-allocation base (total sales value at splitoff) is expressed in terms of a common denominator (the amount of revenues) that is systematically recorded in the accounting system. To use this method, selling prices must exist for all products at the splitoff point.

Physical-Measure Method

The **physical-measure method** allocates joint costs to joint products produced during the accounting period on the basis of a *comparable* physical measure, such as the relative weight, quantity, or volume at the splitoff point. In Example 1, the $400,000 joint costs produced 25,000 gallons of cream and 75,000 gallons of liquid skim. Using the number of gallons produced as the physical measure, Exhibit 16-4, Panel A, shows how joint costs are allocated to individual products to calculate the cost per gallon of cream and liquid skim.

[4] Suppose Farmland Dairy has beginning inventory of cream and liquid milk in May 2014 and when this inventory is sold, Farmland earns a gross margin different from 20%. Then the gross-margin percentage for cream and liquid skim will not be the same. The relative gross-margin percentages will depend on how much of the sales of each product came from beginning inventory and how much came from current-period production.

Exhibit 16-4 Joint-Cost Allocation and Product-Line Income Statement Using Physical-Measure Method: Farmland Dairy for May 2014

	A	B	C	D
1	**PANEL A: Allocation of Joint Costs Using Physical-Measure Method**	**Cream**	**Liquid Skim**	**Total**
2	Physical measure of total production (gallons)	25,000	75,000	100,000
3	Weighting (25,000 gallons ÷ 100,000 gallons; 75,000 gallons ÷ 100,000 gallons)	0.25	0.75	
4	Joint costs allocated (0.25 × $400,000; 0.75 × $400,000)	$100,000	$300,000	$400,000
5	Joint production cost per gallon ($100,000 ÷ 25,000 gallons; $300,000 ÷ 75,000 gallons)	$ 4.00	$ 4.00	
6				
7	**PANEL B: Product-Line Income Statement Using Physical-Measure Method for May 2014**	**Cream**	**Liquid Skim**	**Total**
8	Revenues (20,000 gallons × $8 per gallon; 30,000 gallons × $4 per gallon)	$160,000	$120,000	$280,000
9	Cost of goods sold (joint costs)			
10	Production costs (0.25 × $400,000; 0.75 × $400,000)	100,000	300,000	400,000
11	Deduct ending inventory (5,000 gallons × $4 per gallon; 45,000 gallons × $4 per gallon)	20,000	180,000	200,000
12	Cost of goods sold (joint costs)	80,000	120,000	200,000
13	Gross margin	$ 80,000	$ 0	$ 80,000
14	Gross margin percentage ($80,000 ÷ $160,000; $0 ÷ $120,000; $80,000 ÷ $280,000)	50%	0%	28.6%

Because the physical-measure method allocates joint costs on the basis of the number of gallons, the cost per gallon is the same for both products. Exhibit 16-4, Panel B, presents the product-line income statement using the physical-measure method. The gross-margin percentages are 50% for cream and 0% for liquid skim.

Under the benefits-received criterion, the physical-measure method is much less desirable than the sales value at splitoff method. Why? Because the physical measure of the individual products may have no relationship to their respective revenue-generating abilities. Consider a gold mine that extracts ore containing gold, silver, and lead. Using a common physical measure (tons) would result in almost all costs being allocated to lead, the product that weighs the most but has the lowest revenue-generating power. This method of cost allocation is inconsistent with the main reason the mining company is incurring mining costs—to earn revenues from gold and silver, not lead. When a company uses the physical-measure method in a product-line income statement, products that have a high sales value per ton, like gold and silver, would show a large "profit," and products that have a low sales value per ton, like lead, would show sizable losses.

Obtaining comparable physical measures for all products is not always straightforward. Consider the joint costs of producing oil and natural gas; oil is a liquid and gas is a vapor. To use a physical measure, the oil and gas need to be converted to the energy equivalent for oil and gas, British thermal units (BTUs). Using some physical measures to allocate joint costs may require assistance from technical personnel outside of accounting.

Determining which products of a joint process to include in a physical-measure computation can greatly affect the allocations to those products. Outputs with no sales value (such as dirt in gold mining) are always excluded. Although many more tons of dirt than gold are produced, costs are not incurred to produce outputs that have zero sales value. Byproducts are also often excluded from the denominator used in the physical-measure method because of their low sales values relative to the joint products or the main product. The general guideline for the physical-measure method is to include only the joint-product outputs in the weighting computations.

Net Realizable Value Method

In many cases, products are processed beyond the splitoff point to bring them to a marketable form or to increase their value above their selling price at the splitoff point. For example, when crude oil is refined, the gasoline, kerosene, benzene, and naphtha must be processed further before they can be sold. To illustrate, let's extend the Farmland Dairy example.

Example 2: Assume the same data as in Example 1 except that both cream and liquid skim can be processed further:

- Cream → Buttercream: 25,000 gallons of cream are further processed to yield 20,000 gallons of buttercream at additional processing costs of $280,000. Buttercream, which sells for $25 per gallon, is used in the manufacture of butter-based products.
- Liquid Skim → Condensed Milk: 75,000 gallons of liquid skim are further processed to yield 50,000 gallons of condensed milk at additional processing costs of $520,000. Condensed milk sells for $22 per gallon.
- Sales during May 2014 are 12,000 gallons of buttercream and 45,000 gallons of condensed milk.

Exhibit 16-5, Panel A, depicts how (a) raw milk is converted into cream and liquid skim in the joint production process and (b) how cream is separately processed into buttercream and liquid skim is separately processed into condensed milk. Panel B shows the data for Example 2.

Exhibit 16-5 Example 2: Overview of Farmland Dairy

PANEL A: Graphical Presentation of Process for Example 2

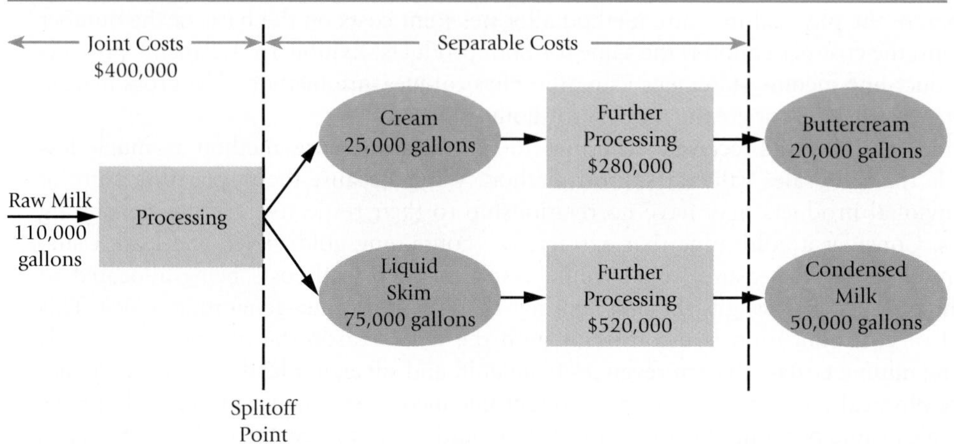

PANEL B: Data for Example 2

	A	B	C	D	E
1		Joint Costs		Buttercream	Condensed Milk
2	Joint costs (costs of 110,000 gallons raw milk and processing to splitoff point)	$400,000			
3	Separable cost of processing 25,000 gallons cream into 20,000 gallons buttercream			$280,000	
4	Separable cost of processing 75,000 gallons liquid skim into 50,000 gallons condensed milk				$520,000
5					
6		Cream	Liquid Skim	Buttercream	Condensed Milk
7	Beginning inventory (gallons)	0	0	0	0
8	Production (gallons)	25,000	75,000	20,000	50,000
9	Transfer for further processing (gallons)	25,000	75,000		
10	Sales (gallons)			12,000	45,000
11	Ending inventory (gallons)	0	0	8,000	5,000
12	Selling price per gallon	$ 8	$ 4	$ 25	$ 22

Exhibit 16-6 Joint-Cost Allocation and Product-Line Income Statement Using NRV Method: Farmland Dairy for May 2014

	A	B	C	D
1	**PANEL A: Allocation of Joint Costs Using Net Realizable Value Method**	**Buttercream**	**Condensed Milk**	**Total**
2	Final sales value of total production during accounting period			
3	(20,000 gallons × $25 per gallon; 50,000 gallons × $22 per gallon)	$500,000	$1,100,000	$1,600,000
4	Deduct separable costs	280,000	520,000	800,000
5	Net realizable value at splitoff point	$220,000	$ 580,000	$ 800,000
6	Weighting ($220,000 ÷ $800,000; $580,000 ÷ $800,000)	0.275	0.725	
7	Joint costs allocated (0.275 × $400,000; 0.725 × $400,000)	$110,000	$ 290,000	$ 400,000
8	Production cost per gallon			
9	([$110,000 + $280,000] ÷ 20,000 gallons; [$290,000 + $520,000] ÷ 50,000 gallons)	$ 19.50	$ 16.20	
10				
11	**PANEL B: Product-Line Income Statement Using Net Realizable Value Method for May 2014**	**Buttercream**	**Condensed Milk**	**Total**
12	Revenues (12,000 gallons × $25 per gallon; 45,000 gallons × $22 per gallon)	$300,000	$ 990,000	$1,290,000
13	Cost of goods sold			
14	Joint costs (0.275 × $400,000; 0.725 × $400,000)	110,000	290,000	400,000
15	Separable costs	280,000	520,000	800,000
16	Production costs	390,000	810,000	1,200,000
17	Deduct ending inventory (8,000 gallons × $19.50 per gallon; 5,000 gallons × $16.20 per gallon)	156,000	81,000	237,000
18	Cost of goods sold	234,000	729,000	963,000
19	Gross margin	$ 66,000	$ 261,000	$ 327,000
20	Gross margin percentage ($66,000 ÷ $300,000; $261,000 ÷ $990,000; $327,000 ÷ $1,290,000)	22.0%	26.4%	25.3%

The **net realizable value (NRV) method** allocates joint costs to joint products produced during the accounting period on the basis of their relative NRV—final sales value minus separable costs. The NRV method is typically used in preference to the sales value at splitoff method only when selling prices for one or more products at splitoff do not exist. Using this method for Example 2, Exhibit 16-6, Panel A, shows how joint costs are allocated to individual products to calculate cost per gallon of buttercream and condensed milk. Panel B presents the product-line income statement using the NRV method. The gross-margin percentages are 22.0% for buttercream and 26.4% for condensed milk.

The NRV method is often implemented using simplifying assumptions. For example, even when the selling prices of joint products vary frequently, companies implement the NRV method using a given set of selling prices throughout the accounting period. Similarly, even though companies may occasionally change the number or sequence of processing steps beyond the splitoff point in order to adjust to variations in input quality or local conditions, they assume a specific constant set of such steps when implementing the NRV method.

Constant Gross-Margin Percentage NRV Method

The **constant gross-margin percentage NRV method** allocates joint costs to joint products produced during the accounting period in such a way that each individual product achieves an identical gross-margin percentage. The method works backward in that the overall gross margin is computed first. Then, for each product, this gross-margin percentage and any separable costs are deducted from the final sales value of production in order to back into the joint cost allocation for that product. The method can be broken down into three discrete steps. Exhibit 16-7, Panel A, shows these steps for allocating the $400,000 joint costs between buttercream and condensed milk in the Farmland Dairy example. Refer to the panel for an illustration of each step as we describe it.

Step 1: **Compute the Overall Gross Margin Percentage.** The overall gross-margin percentage for all joint products together is calculated first. This is based on the final sales value of *total production* during the accounting period, not the *total revenues* of the period. Accordingly, Exhibit 16-7, Panel A, uses $1,600,000, the final expected sales value of the entire output of buttercream and condensed milk, not the $1,290,000 in actual sales revenue for the month of May.

Exhibit 16-7 Joint-Cost Allocation and Product-Line Income Statement Using Constant Gross-Margin Percentage NRV Method: Farmland Dairy for May 2014

	A	B	C	D
1	**PANEL A: Allocation of Joint Costs Using Constant Gross-Margin Percentage NRV Method**			
2	**Step 1**			
3	Final sales value of total production during accounting period: (20,000 gallons × $25 per gallon) + (50,000 gallons × $22 per gallon)	$1,600,000		
4	Deduct joint and separable costs ($400,000 + $280,000 + $520,000)	1,200,000		
5	Gross margin	$ 400,000		
6	Gross margin percentage ($400,000 ÷ $1,600,000)	25%		
7		**Buttercream**	**Condensed Milk**	**Total**
8	**Step 2**			
9	Final sales value of total production during accounting period: (20,000 gallons × $25 per gallon; 50,000 gallons × $22 per gallon)	$ 500,000	$1,100,000	$1,600,000
10	Deduct gross margin, using overall gross-margin percentage (25% × $500,000; 25% × $1,100,000)	125,000	275,000	400,000
11	Total production costs	375,000	825,000	1,200,000
12	**Step 3**			
13	Deduct separable costs	280,000	520,000	800,000
14	Joint costs allocated	$ 95,000	$ 305,000	$ 400,000
15				
16	**PANEL B: Product-Line Income Statement Using Constant Gross-Margin Percentage NRV Method for May 2014**	**Buttercream**	**Condensed Milk**	**Total**
17	Revenues (12,000 gallons × $25 per gallon; 45,000 gallons × $22 per gallon)	$ 300,000	$ 990,000	$1,290,000
18	Cost of goods sold			
19	Joint costs (from Panel A)	95,000	305,000	400,000
20	Separable costs	280,000	520,000	800,000
21	Production costs	375,000	825,000	1,200,000
22	Deduct ending inventory			
23	(8,000 gallons × $18.75 per gallon[a]; 5,000 gallons × $16.50 per gallon[b])	150,000	82,500	232,500
24	Cost of goods sold	225,000	742,500	967,500
25	Gross margin	$ 75,000	$ 247,500	$ 322,500
26	Gross margin percentage ($75,000 ÷ $300,000; $247,500 ÷ $990,000; $322,500 ÷ $1,290,000)	25%	25%	25%
27				
28	[a]Total production costs of buttercream ÷ Total production of buttercream = $375,000 ÷ 20,000 gallons = $18.75 per gallon.			
29	[b]Total production costs of condensed milk ÷ Total production of condensed milk = $825,000 ÷ 50,000 gallons = $16.50 per gallon.			

Step 2: **Compute the Total Production Costs for Each Product.** The gross margin (in dollars) for each product is computed by multiplying the overall gross-margin percentage by the product's final sales value of total production. The difference between the final sales value of total production and the gross margin then yields the total production costs that the product must bear.

Step 3: **Compute the Allocated Joint Costs.** As the final step, the separable costs for each product are deducted from the total production costs that the product must bear to obtain the joint-cost allocation for that product.

Exhibit 16-7, Panel B, presents the product-line income statement for the constant gross-margin percentage NRV method.

Decision Point

What methods can be used to allocate joint costs to individual products?

The constant gross-margin percentage NRV method is the only method whereby products can receive negative allocations. This may be required in order to bring the gross-margin percentages of relatively unprofitable products up to the overall average. The constant gross-margin percentage NRV method also differs from the other two market-based joint-cost-allocation methods described earlier in another fundamental way. Neither the sales value at splitoff method nor the NRV method takes account of profits earned either before or after the splitoff point when allocating the joint costs. In contrast, the constant gross-margin percentage NRV method allocates both joint costs and profits: The gross margin is allocated to the joint products in order to determine the joint-cost allocations so that the resulting gross-margin percentage for each product is the same.

Choosing an Allocation Method

Learning Objective 4

Identify situations when the sales value at splitoff method is preferred when allocating joint costs

. . . objectively measuring the benefits received by each product

Which method of allocating joint costs should be used? When selling-price data exist at the splitoff, the sales value at splitoff method is preferred, even if further processing is done. The following are reasons why:

1. **Measure of benefits received.** The sales value at splitoff is the best measure of the benefits received by joint products relative to all other methods of allocating joint costs. It is a meaningful basis for allocating joint costs because generating revenues is the reason why a company incurs joint costs in the first place. It is also sometimes possible to vary the physical mix of final output and thereby produce more or less market value by incurring more or less joint costs. In such cases, there is a clear causal link between total cost and total output value, thereby further validating the use of the sales value at splitoff method.[5]
2. **Independent of further processing decisions.** The sales value at splitoff method does not require information on the processing steps after the splitoff, if there are any. In contrast, the NRV and constant gross-margin percentage NRV methods require information on (a) the specific sequence of further processing decisions, (b) the separable costs of further processing, and (c) the point at which individual products will be sold.
3. **Common allocation basis.** As with other market-based approaches, the sales value at splitoff method provides a common basis for allocating joint costs to products, namely revenue. In contrast, the physical-measure at splitoff method may lack an easily identifiable common basis for cost allocation.
4. **Simplicity.** The sales value at splitoff method is simple. In contrast, the NRV and constant gross-margin percentage NRV methods can be complex for operations with multiple products and multiple splitoff points. This complexity increases when managers make frequent changes to the sequence of post-splitoff processing decisions or to the point at which individual products are sold.

When the selling prices of all products at the splitoff point are unavailable, the NRV method is the best alternative. It attempts to approximate the sales values at splitoff by subtracting from final selling prices the separable costs incurred after the splitoff point. The NRV method assumes that all the markup (the profit margin) is attributable to the joint process and none of the markup is attributable to the separable costs. This is unrealistic if, for example, a firm uses a special patented technology in its separable process or innovative marketing that enables it to generate significant profits. Despite this limitation, the NRV method is commonly used when selling prices at splitoff are not available as it provides a better measure of the benefits received than either the constant gross-margin percentage NRV method or the physical-measure method.

The constant gross-margin percentage NRV method treats the joint products as though they comprise a single product. This method calculates the aggregate gross-margin percentage, applies this percentage to each product, and views the residual after separable costs are accounted for as the amount of joint costs assigned to each product. Consequently, unlike the NRV method, the benefits received by each of the joint products at the splitoff point don't have to be measured. Also, the constant gross-margin percentage method recognizes that the profit margin is not just attributable to the joint process but is also derived from the costs incurred after splitoff. The drawback of the method is that it assumes that the profit margin is identical across products; that is, all products are assumed to have the same ratio of cost to sales value. Recall from our discussion of activity-based costing (ABC) in Chapter 5 that such a situation is uncommon when companies offer a diverse set of products.

Although there are difficulties in using the physical-measure method—such as lack of congruence with the benefits-received criterion—there are instances when it may be

[5] In the semiconductor industry, for example, the use of cleaner facilities, higher-quality silicon wafers, and more sophisticated equipment (all of which require higher joint costs) shifts the distribution of output to higher-quality memory devices with more market value. For details, see James F. Gatti and D. Jacque Grinnell, "Joint Cost Allocations: Measuring and Promoting Productivity and Quality Improvements," *Journal of Cost Management* (2000). The authors also demonstrate that joint cost allocations based on market value are preferable for promoting quality and productivity improvements.

preferred. In settings where end prices are volatile or the process after splitoff is long or uncertain, the presence of a comparable physical measure at splitoff would favor use of the method. This is true, for instance, in the chemical and oil refining industries. The physical-measure method is also useful when joint cost allocations are used as the basis for setting market prices, as in rate regulation. It avoids the circular reasoning of using selling prices to allocate the costs on which prices (rates) are based.

Not Allocating Joint Costs

Some companies choose to not allocate joint costs to products due to the complexity of their production or extraction processes and the difficulty of gathering a sufficient amount of data to allocate the costs correctly. For example, a survey of nine sawmills in Norway revealed that none of them allocated joint costs. The study's authors noted that the "interviewed sawmills considered the joint cost problem very interesting, but pointed out that the problem is not easily solved."[6]

Decision Point

When is the sales value at splitoff method considered preferable for allocating joint costs to individual products and why?

Rather than allocating joint costs, some firms simply subtract them directly from total revenues in the management accounts. If substantial inventories exist, the firms carry their product inventories at NRV. Companies in the meatpacking, canning, and mining industries often use variations of this approach. Accountants do not ordinarily record inventories at NRV because this practice recognizes the income on each product at the time it is completed but *before* it is sold. To deal with this problem, some of these companies carry their inventories at NRV minus an estimated operating income margin. When any end-of-period inventories are sold in the next period, the cost of goods sold then equals this carrying value. This approach is akin to the "production method" of accounting for byproducts, which we describe later in this chapter.

Learning Objective 5

Explain why joint costs are irrelevant in a sell-or-process-further decision

...because joint costs are the same whether or not further processing occurs

Why Joint Costs Are Irrelevant for Decision Making

Chapter 11 introduced the concepts of *relevant revenues*, expected future revenues that differ among alternative courses of action, and *relevant costs*, expected future costs that differ among alternative courses of action. These concepts can be applied to decisions on whether a joint product or main product should be sold at the splitoff point or processed further.

Sell-or-Process-Further Decisions

Consider Farmland Dairy's decision to either sell the joint products, cream and liquid skim, at the splitoff point or to further process them into buttercream and condensed milk. The decision to incur additional costs for further processing should be based on the incremental operating income attainable beyond the splitoff point. Example 2 assumed it was profitable for both cream and liquid skim to be further processed into buttercream and condensed milk, respectively. The incremental analysis for the decision to process further is as follows:

Further Processing Cream into Buttercream	
Incremental revenues	
(\$25/gallon × 20,000 gallons) − (\$8/gallon × 25,000 gallons)	\$300,000
Deduct incremental processing costs	280,000
Increase in operating income from buttercream	\$ 20,000
Further Processing Liquid Skim into Condensed Milk	
Incremental revenues	
(\$22/gallon × 50,000 gallons) − (\$4/gallon × 75,000 gallons)	\$800,000
Deduct incremental processing costs	520,000
Increase in operating income from condensed milk	\$280,000

[6] For further details, see Torgrim Tunes, Anders Q. Nyrud, and Birger Eikenes, "Cost and Performance Management in the Sawmill Industry," *Scandinavian Forest Economics* (2006).

In this example, the operating income increases for both products, so the manager decides to process cream into buttercream and liquid skim into condensed milk. *Note that the $400,000 joint costs incurred before the splitoff point are irrelevant in deciding whether to process further.* Why? Because the joint costs of $400,000 are the same whether the products are sold at the splitoff point or processed further. What matters is the incremental income from additional processing.

Incremental costs are the additional costs incurred for an activity, such as further processing. *Do not assume all separable costs in joint-cost allocations are incremental costs.* Some separable costs may be fixed costs, such as the lease cost on buildings where the further processing is done; some separable costs may be sunk costs, such as depreciation on the equipment that converts cream into buttercream; and some separable costs may be allocated costs, such as corporate costs allocated to the condensed milk operations. None of these costs will differ between the alternatives of selling products at the splitoff point or processing further; therefore, they are irrelevant.

Decision Making and Performance Evaluation

The potential conflict between cost concepts used for decision making and cost concepts used for evaluating the performance of managers often arises when sell-or-process-further decisions are being made. To see how, let us continue with Example 2. Suppose the *allocated* fixed corporate and administrative costs of further processing cream into buttercream equal $30,000 and that these costs will be allocated only to buttercream and to the manager's product-line income statement if buttercream is produced. How might this policy affect the decision to process further?

As we have seen, on the basis of incremental revenues and incremental costs, Farmland's operating income will increase by $20,000 if it processes cream into buttercream. However, producing the buttercream also results in an additional charge for allocated fixed costs of $30,000. If the manager is evaluated on a full-cost basis (that is, after allocating all costs), processing cream into buttercream will lower the manager's performance-evaluation measure by $10,000 (incremental operating income, $20,000 – allocated fixed costs, $30,000). Therefore, the manager may be tempted to sell the cream at the splitoff point and not process it into buttercream.

A similar conflict can also arise with joint products. Returning to Example 1, suppose Farmland Dairy has the option of selling raw milk at a profit of $20,000. From a decision-making standpoint, the company would maximize its operating income by processing raw milk into cream and liquid skim because the total revenues from selling both joint products ($500,000, see Exhibit 16-3, page 638) exceed the joint costs ($400,000, page 637) by $100,000, which is greater than the $20,000 profit from selling the raw milk. Suppose, however, the cream and liquid-skim product lines are managed by different managers, each of whom is evaluated based on a product-line income statement. If the physical-measure method of joint-cost allocation is used and the selling price per gallon of liquid skim falls below $4.00 per gallon, the liquid-skim product line will show a loss (from Exhibit 16-4, page 639, revenues will be less than $120,000, but cost of goods sold will be unchanged at $120,000). The manager of the liquid-skim line will therefore prefer, from a performance-evaluation standpoint, to not produce liquid skim but rather to sell the raw milk.

Farmland Dairy's performance-evaluation conflicts will be less severe if it uses any of the market-based methods of joint-cost allocations—sales value at splitoff, NRV, or constant gross-margin percentage NRV—because each of these methods allocates costs using revenues, which generally leads to a positive income for each joint product.

Pricing Decisions

Firms should be wary of using the full cost of a joint product (that is, the cost after joint costs are allocated) as the basis for making pricing decisions. Why? Because in many situations, there is no direct cause-and-effect relationship that identifies the resources demanded by each joint product that can then be used as a basis for pricing. In fact, the use of the sales value at splitoff or the net realizable value method to allocate joint costs

Decision Point

Are joint costs relevant in a sell-or-process-further decision?

results in a reverse effect: The selling prices of joint products drive joint-cost allocations, rather than cost allocations serving as the basis for the pricing of joint products! Of course, the principles of pricing covered in Chapter 13 apply to the joint process as a whole. Even if the firm cannot alter the mix of products generated by the joint process, it must ensure that the joint products generate a sufficient amount of combined revenue in the long run to cover the joint costs of processing.

Learning Objective 6

Account for byproducts using two methods

...recognize in financial statements at time of production or at time of sale

Accounting for Byproducts

Joint production processes can yield not only joint products and main products but also byproducts. Although their total sales values are relatively low, the byproducts in a joint production process can affect the allocation of joint costs. Moreover, byproducts can be quite profitable for a firm. Wendy's, the fast food chain, uses surplus hamburger patties in its "rich and meaty" chili and, because it cooks meat specifically for the chili only 10% of the time, makes great margins even at a price of $0.99 for an eight-ounce serving of chili.

Let's consider a two-product example consisting of a main product and a byproduct.

Example 3: The Westlake Corporation processes timber into fine-grade lumber and wood chips, which are used as mulch in gardens and lawns.

- Fine-grade lumber (the main product)—sells for $6 per board foot (b.f.)
- Wood chips (the byproduct)—sells for $1 per cubic foot (c.f.)

The data for July 2014 are as follows:

	Beginning Inventory	Production	Sales	Ending Inventory
Fine-grade lumber (b.f.)	0	50,000	40,000	10,000
Wood chips (c.f.)	0	4,000	1,200	2,800

The joint manufacturing costs for these products in July 2014 are $250,000. They consist of $150,000 for direct materials and $100,000 for conversion costs. Both products are sold at the splitoff point without further processing, as Exhibit 16-8 shows.

We present two byproduct accounting methods: the production method and the sales method. The production method recognizes byproducts in the financial statements when their production is completed. The sales method delays recognizing byproducts until they are sold.[7] Exhibit 16-9 presents the income statement of Westlake Corporation under both methods.

Exhibit 16-8

Example 3: Overview of Westlake Corporation

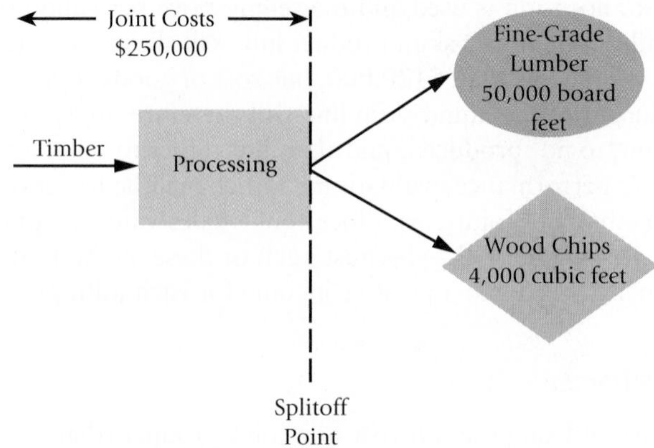

[7] For a discussion of joint cost allocation and byproduct accounting methods, see P. Douglas Marshall and Robert F. Dombrowski, "A Small Business Review of Accounting for Primary Products, Byproducts and Scrap," *The National Public Accountant* (February/March 2003): 10–13.

Exhibit 16-9 Income Statements of Westlake Corporation for July 2014 Using the Production and Sales Methods for Byproduct Accounting

	Production Method	Sales Method
Revenues		
Main product: Fine-grade lumber (40,000 b.f. × $6 per b.f.)	$240,000	$240,000
Byproduct: Wood chips (1,200 c.f. × $1 per c.f.)	—	1,200
Total revenues	240,000	241,200
Cost of goods sold		
Total manufacturing costs	250,000	250,000
Deduct byproduct revenue and inventory (4,000 c.f. × $1 per c.f.)	(4,000)	—
Net manufacturing costs	246,000	250,000
Deduct main-product inventory	(49,200)[a]	(50,000)[b]
Cost of goods sold	196,800	200,000
Gross margin	$ 43,200	$ 41,200
Gross-margin percentage ($43,200 ÷ $240,000; $41,200 ÷ $241,200)	18.00%	17.08%
Inventoriable costs (end of period):		
Main product: Fine-grade lumber	$ 49,200	$ 50,000
Byproduct: Wood chips (2,800 c.f. × $1 per c.f.)[c]	2,800	0

[a](10,000 ÷ 50,000) × net manufacturing cost = (10,000 ÷ 50,000) × $246,000 = $49,200

[b](10,000 ÷ 50,000) × total manufacturing cost = (10,000 ÷ 50,000) × $250,000 = $50,000

[c]Recorded at selling prices.

Production Method: Byproducts Recognized at Time Production Is Completed

This method recognizes the byproduct in the financial statements—the 4,000 cubic feet of wood chips—in the month it is produced, July 2014. The NRV from the byproduct produced is offset against the costs of the main product. The following journal entries illustrate the production method:

	Debit	Credit
1. Work in Process	150,000	
Accounts Payable		150,000
To record the direct materials purchased and used in production during July.		
2. Work in Process	100,000	
Various accounts such as Wages Payable and Accumulated Depreciation		100,000
To record the conversion costs in the production process during July; examples include energy, manufacturing supplies, all manufacturing labor, and plant depreciation.		
3. Byproduct Inventory—Wood Chips (4,000 c.f. × $1 per c.f.)	4,000	
Finished Goods—Fine-Grade Lumber ($250,000 − $4,000)	246,000	
Work in Process ($150,000 + $100,000)		250,000
To record the cost of goods completed during July.		
4a. Cost of Goods Sold [(40,000 b.f. ÷ 50,000 b.f.) × $246,000]	196,800	
Finished Goods—Fine-Grade Lumber		196,800
To record the cost of the main product sold during July.		
4b. Cash or Accounts Receivable (40,000 b.f. × $6 per b.f.)	240,000	
Revenues—Fine-Grade Lumber		240,000
To record the sales of the main product during July.		
5. Cash or Accounts Receivable (1,200 c.f. × $1 per c.f.)	1,200	
Byproduct Inventory—Wood Chips		1,200
To record the sales of the byproduct during July.		

The production method reports the byproduct inventory of wood chips in the balance sheet at its $1 per cubic foot selling price [(4,000 cubic feet − 1,200 cubic feet) × $1 per cubic foot = $2,800].

One variation of this method would be to report the byproduct inventory at its NRV reduced by a normal profit margin, say 20%: $2,800 − 20% × $2,800 = $2,240.[8] When the byproduct inventory is sold in a subsequent period, the income statement will match the selling price, $2,800, with the "cost" reported for the byproduct inventory, $2,240, resulting in a byproduct operating income of $560 ($2,800 − $2,240).

Sales Method: Byproducts Recognized at Time of Sale

With this method, no journal entries are made for byproducts until they are sold. At that time, the byproduct revenues are reported in the income statement. The revenues are either grouped with other sales, included as other income, or deducted from the cost of goods sold. In the Westlake Corporation example, byproduct revenues in July 2014 are $1,200 (1,200 cubic feet × $1 per cubic foot) because only 1,200 cubic feet of wood chips are sold in July (of the 4,000 cubic feet produced). The journal entries are as follows:

1. and 2.	*Same as for the production method.*		
	Work in Process	150,000	
	Accounts Payable		150,000
	Work in Process	100,000	
	Various accounts such as Wages Payable and Accumulated Depreciation		100,000
3.	Finished Goods—Fine-Grade Lumber	250,000	
	Work in Process		250,000
	To record the cost of the main product completed during July.		
4a.	Cost of Goods Sold [(40,000 b.f. ÷ 50,000 b.f.) × $250,000]	200,000	
	Finished Goods—Fine-Grade Lumber		200,000
	To record the cost of the main product sold during July.		
4b.	Same as for the production method.		
	Cash or Accounts Receivable (40,000 b.f. × $6 per b.f.)	240,000	
	Revenues—Fine-Grade Lumber		240,000
5.	Cash or Accounts Receivable	1,200	
	Revenues—Wood Chips		1,200
	To record the sales of the byproduct during July.		

Decision Point

What methods can be used to account for byproducts and which of them is preferable?

Which method should a company use? The production method for accounting for byproducts is consistent with the matching principle and is the preferred method. This method recognizes the byproduct inventory in the accounting period in which it is produced and simultaneously reduces the cost of manufacturing the main or joint products, thereby better matching the revenues and expenses from selling the main product. However, the sales method is simpler and is often used in practice, primarily because the dollar amounts of byproducts are immaterial. The drawback of the sales method is that it allows a firm to "manage" its reported earnings by timing the sale of byproducts. For example, to boost its revenues and income slightly, a firm might store the byproducts for several periods and then sell them when the revenues and profits from the main product or joint products are low.

[8] One way to make this calculation is to assume all products have the same "normal" profit margin, as in the constant gross-margin percentage NRV method. Alternatively, the company might allow products to have different profit margins based on an analysis of the margins earned by other companies that sell these products individually.

Problem for Self-Study

Inorganic Chemicals (IC) processes salt into various industrial products. In July 2014, IC incurred joint costs of $100,000 to purchase salt and convert it into two products: caustic soda and chlorine. Although there is an active outside market for chlorine, IC processes all 800 tons of chlorine it produces into 500 tons of PVC (polyvinyl chloride), which is then sold. There were no beginning or ending inventories of salt, caustic soda, chlorine, or PVC in July. Information for July 2014 production and sales follows:

	A	B	C	D
1		Joint Costs		PVC
2	Joint costs (costs of salt and processing to splitoff point)	$100,000		
3	Separable cost of processing 800 tons chlorine into 500 tons PVC			$20,000
4				
5		Caustic Soda	Chlorine	PVC
6	Beginning inventory (tons)	0	0	0
7	Production (tons)	1,200	800	500
8	Transfer for further processing (tons)		800	
9	Sales (tons)	1,200		500
10	Ending inventory (tons)	0	0	0
11	Selling price per ton in active outside market (for products not actually sold)		$ 75	
12	Selling price per ton for products sold	$ 50		$ 200

Required

1. Allocate the joint costs of $100,000 between caustic soda and PVC under (a) the sales value at splitoff method and (b) the physical-measure method.
2. Allocate the joint costs of $100,000 between caustic soda and PVC under the NRV method.
3. Under the three allocation methods in requirements 1 and 2, what is the gross-margin percentage of (a) caustic soda and (b) PVC?
4. Lifetime Swimming Pool Products offers to purchase 800 tons of chlorine in August 2014 at $75 per ton. Assume all other production and sales data are the same for August as they were for July. This sale of chlorine to Lifetime would mean that no PVC would be produced by IC in August. How would accepting this offer affect IC's August 2014 operating income?

Solution

The following picture provides a visual illustration of the main facts in this problem.

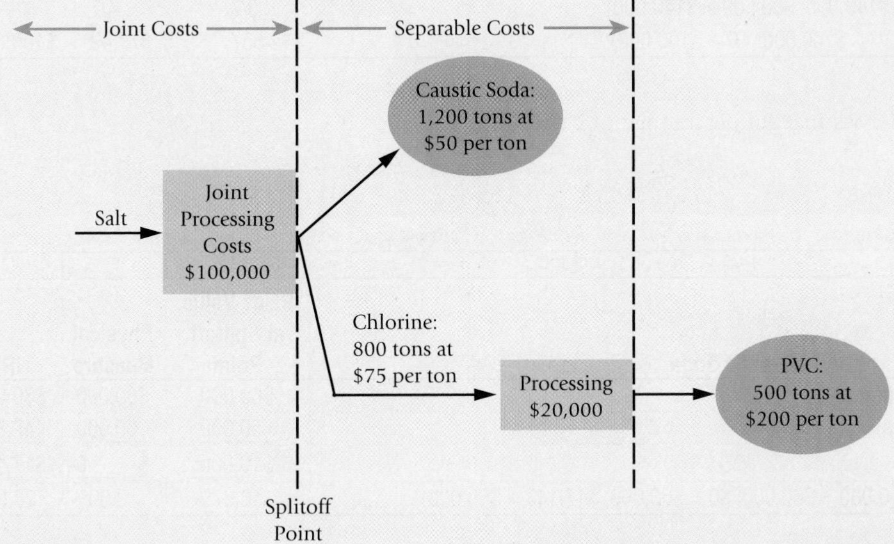

Note that caustic soda is sold as is while chlorine, despite having a market value at splitoff, is sold only in processed form as PVC. The goal is to allocate the joint costs of $100,000 to the final products—caustic soda and PVC. However, because PVC exists only in the form of chlorine at the splitoff point, we use chlorine's sales value and physical measure as the basis for allocating joint costs to PVC under the sales value at splitoff and physical measure at splitoff methods. Detailed calculations are shown next.

1a. Sales value at splitoff method

	A	B	C	D
1	**Allocation of Joint Costs Using Sales Value at Splitoff Method**	**Caustic Soda**	**PVC/Chlorine**	**Total**
2	Sales value of total production at splitoff point			
3	(1,200 tons × $50 per ton; 800 × $75 per ton)	$60,000	$60,000	$120,000
4	Weighting ($60,000 ÷ $120,000; $60,000 ÷ $120,000)	0.50	0.50	
5	Joint costs allocated (0.50 × $100,000; 0.50 × $100,000)	$50,000	$50,000	$100,000

1b. Physical-measure method

	A	B	C	D
8	**Allocation of Joint Costs Using Physical-Measure Method**	**Caustic Soda**	**PVC/Chlorine**	**Total**
9	Physical measure of total production (tons)	1,200	800	2,000
10	Weighting (1,200 tons ÷ 2,000 tons; 800 tons ÷ 2,000 tons)	0.60	0.40	
11	Joint cost allocated (0.60 × $100,000; 0.40 × $100,000)	$60,000	$40,000	$100,000

2. Net realizable value (NRV) method

	A	B	C	D
14	**Allocation of Joint Costs Using Net Realizable Value Method**	**Caustic Soda**	**PVC**	**Total**
15	Final sales value of total production during accounting period			
16	(1,200 tons × $50 per ton; 500 tons × $200 per ton)	$60,000	$100,000	$160,000
17	Deduct separable costs to complete and sell	0	20,000	20,000
18	Net realizable value at splitoff point	$60,000	$ 80,000	$140,000
19	Weighting ($60,000 ÷ $140,000; $80,000 ÷ $140,000)	3/7	4/7	
20	Joint costs allocated (3/7 × $100,000; 4/7 × $100,000)	$42,857	$ 57,143	$100,000

3a. Gross-margin percentage of caustic soda

	A	B	C	D
23	**Caustic Soda**	**Sales Value at Splitoff Point**	**Physical Measure**	**NRV**
24	Revenues (1,200 tons × $50 per ton)	$60,000	$60,000	$60,000
25	Cost of goods sold (joint costs)	50,000	60,000	42,857
26	Gross margin	$10,000	$ 0	$17,143
27	Gross margin percentage ($10,000 ÷ $60,000; $0 ÷ $60,000; $17,143 ÷ $60,000)	16.67%	0.00%	28.57%

3b. Gross-margin percentage of PVC

	A	B	C	D
30	PVC	Sales Value at Splitoff Point	Physical Measure	NRV
31	Revenues (500 tons × $200 per ton)	$100,000	$100,000	$100,000
32	Cost of goods sold			
33	Joint costs	50,000	40,000	57,143
34	Separable costs	20,000	20,000	20,000
35	Cost of goods sold	70,000	60,000	77,143
36	Gross margin	$ 30,000	$ 40,000	$ 22,857
37	Gross margin percentage ($30,000 ÷ $100,000; $40,000 ÷ $100,000; $22,857 ÷ $100,000)	30.00%	40.00%	22.86%

4. Sale of chlorine versus processing into PVC

	A	B
40	Incremental revenue from processing 800 tons of chlorine into 500 tons of PVC	
41	(500 tons × $200 per ton) – (800 tons × $75 per ton)	$40,000
42	Incremental cost of processing 800 tons of chlorine into 500 tons of PVC	20,000
43	Incremental operating income from further processing	$20,000

If IC sells 800 tons of chlorine to Lifetime Swimming Pool Products instead of further processing it into PVC, its August 2014 operating income will be reduced by $20,000.

Decision Points

The following question-and-answer format summarizes the chapter's learning objectives. Each decision presents a key question related to a learning objective. The guidelines are the answer to that question.

Decision	Guidelines
1. What do the terms joint cost and splitoff point mean, and how do joint products differ from byproducts?	A joint cost is the cost of a single production process that yields multiple products simultaneously. The splitoff point is the juncture in a joint production process when the products become separately identifiable. Joint products have high total sales values at the splitoff point. A byproduct has a low total sales value at the splitoff point relative to the total sales value of a joint or main product.
2. Why are joint costs allocated to individual products?	The purposes for allocating joint costs to products include inventory costing for financial accounting and internal reporting, cost reimbursement, insurance settlements, rate regulation, and product-cost litigation.
3. What methods can be used to allocate joint costs to individual products?	The methods to allocate joint costs to products are the sales value at splitoff, physical-measure, NRV, and constant gross-margin percentage NRV methods.

Decision	Guidelines
4. When is the sales value at splitoff method considered preferable for allocating joint costs to individual products and why?	The sales value at splitoff method is preferred when market prices exist at splitoff because using revenues is consistent with the benefits-received criterion; further, the method does not depend on subsequent decisions made about further processing and is simple.
5. Are joint costs relevant in a sell-or-process-further decision?	No, joint costs and how they are allocated are irrelevant because they are the same regardless of whether further processing occurs.
6. What methods can be used to account for byproducts, and which of them is preferable?	The production method recognizes byproducts in financial statements at the time of their production, whereas the sales method recognizes byproducts in financial statements at the time of their sale. The production method is conceptually superior, but the sales method is often used in practice because the dollar amounts of byproducts are immaterial.

Terms to Learn

This chapter and the Glossary at the end of the book contain definitions of the following important terms:

byproducts **(p. 634)**
constant gross-margin percentage NRV method **(p. 641)**
joint costs **(p. 633)**
joint products **(p. 634)**
main product **(p. 634)**
net realizable value (NRV) method **(p. 641)**
physical-measure method **(p. 638)**
product **(p. 634)**
sales value at splitoff method **(p. 637)**
separable costs **(p. 633)**
splitoff point **(p. 633)**

Assignment Material

MyAccountingLab

Questions

16-1 Give two examples of industries in which joint costs are found. For each example, what are the individual products at the splitoff point?

16-2 What is a joint cost? What is a separable cost?

16-3 Distinguish between a joint product and a byproduct.

16-4 Why might the number of products in a joint-cost situation differ from the number of outputs? Give an example.

16-5 Provide three reasons for allocating joint costs to individual products or services.

16-6 Why does the sales value at splitoff method use the sales value of the total production in the accounting period and not just the revenues from the products sold?

16-7 Describe a situation in which the sales value at splitoff method cannot be used but the NRV method can be used for joint-cost allocation.

16-8 Distinguish between the sales value at splitoff method and the NRV method.

16-9 Give two limitations of the physical-measure method of joint-cost allocation.

16-10 How might a company simplify its use of the NRV method when final selling prices can vary sizably in an accounting period and management frequently changes the point at which it sells individual products?

16-11 Why is the constant gross-margin percentage NRV method sometimes called a "joint-cost-allocation and a profit-allocation" method?

16-12 "Managers must decide whether a product should be sold at splitoff or processed further. The sales value at splitoff method of joint-cost allocation is the best method for generating the information managers need for this decision." Do you agree? Explain.

16-13 "Managers should consider only additional revenues and separable costs when making decisions about selling at splitoff or processing further." Do you agree? Explain.

16-14 Describe two major methods to account for byproducts.

16-15 Why might managers seeking a monthly bonus based on attaining a target operating income prefer the sales method of accounting for byproducts rather than the production method?

Exercises

MyAccountingLab

16-16 Joint-cost allocation, insurance settlement. Quality Chicken grows and processes chickens. Each chicken is disassembled into five main parts. Information pertaining to production in July 2014 is as follows:

Parts	Pounds of Product	Wholesale Selling Price per Pound When Production Is Complete
Breasts	100	$0.55
Wings	20	0.20
Thighs	40	0.35
Bones	80	0.10
Feathers	10	0.05

Joint cost of production in July 2014 was $50.

A special shipment of 40 pounds of breasts and 15 pounds of wings has been destroyed in a fire. Quality Chicken's insurance policy provides reimbursement for the cost of the items destroyed. The insurance company permits Quality Chicken to use a joint-cost-allocation method. The splitoff point is assumed to be at the end of the production process.

Required

1. Compute the cost of the special shipment destroyed using the following:
   a. Sales value at splitoff method
   b. Physical-measure method (pounds of finished product)
2. What joint-cost-allocation method would you recommend Quality Chicken use? Explain.

16-17 Joint products and byproducts (continuation of 16-16). Quality Chicken is computing the ending inventory values for its July 31, 2014, balance sheet. Ending inventory amounts on July 31 are 15 pounds of breasts, 4 pounds of wings, 6 pounds of thighs, 5 pounds of bones, and 2 pounds of feathers.

Quality Chicken's management wants to use the sales value at splitoff method. However, management wants you to explore the effect on ending inventory values of classifying one or more products as a byproduct rather than a joint product.

Required

1. Assume Quality Chicken classifies all five products as joint products. What are the ending inventory values of each product on July 31, 2014?
2. Assume Quality Chicken uses the production method of accounting for byproducts. What are the ending inventory values for each joint product on July 31, 2014, assuming breasts and thighs are the joint products and wings, bones, and feathers are byproducts?
3. Comment on differences in the results in requirements 1 and 2.

16-18 Net realizable value method. Stenback Company is one of the world's leading corn refiners. It produces two joint products—corn syrup and corn starch—using a common production process. In July 2014, Stenback reported the following production and selling-price information:

Home | Insert | Page Layout | Formulas | Data | Review | View

	A	B	C	D
1		Corn Syrup	Corn Starch	Joint Costs
2	Joint costs (costs of processing corn to splitoff point)			$329,000
3	Separable cost of processing beyond splitoff point	$406,340	$97,060	
4	Beginning inventory (cases)	0	0	
5	Production and Sales (cases)	13,000	5,900	
6	Ending inventory (cases)	0	0	
7	Selling price per case	$51	$26	

Required

Allocate the $329,000 joint costs using the NRV method.

16-19 Alternative joint-cost-allocation methods, further-process decision. The Wood Spirits Company produces two products—turpentine and methanol (wood alcohol)—by a joint process. Joint costs amount to $120,000 per batch of output. Each batch totals 10,000 gallons: 25% methanol and 75% turpentine. Both products are processed further without gain or loss in volume. Separable processing costs are methanol, $3 per gallon, and turpentine, $2 per gallon. Methanol sells for $21 per gallon. Turpentine sells for $14 per gallon.

Required

1. How much of the joint costs per batch will be allocated to turpentine and to methanol, assuming that joint costs are allocated based on the number of gallons at splitoff point?

2. If joint costs are allocated on an NRV basis, how much of the joint costs will be allocated to turpentine and to methanol?
3. Prepare product-line income statements per batch for requirements 1 and 2. Assume no beginning or ending inventories.
4. The company has discovered an additional process by which the methanol (wood alcohol) can be made into a pleasant-tasting alcoholic beverage. The selling price of this beverage would be $60 a gallon. Additional processing would increase separable costs $9 per gallon (in addition to the $3 per gallon separable cost required to yield methanol). The company would have to pay excise taxes of 20% on the selling price of the beverage. Assuming no other changes in cost, what is the joint cost applicable to the wood alcohol (using the NRV method)? Should the company produce the alcoholic beverage? Show your computations.

16-20 Alternative methods of joint-cost allocation, ending inventories. The Cook Company operates a simple chemical process to convert a single material into three separate items, referred to here as X, Y, and Z. All three end products are separated simultaneously at a single splitoff point.

Products X and Y are ready for sale immediately upon splitoff without further processing or any other additional costs. Product Z, however, is processed further before being sold. There is no available market price for Z at the splitoff point.

The selling prices quoted here are expected to remain the same in the coming year. During 2014, the selling prices of the items and the total amounts sold were as follows:

- X—68 tons sold for $1,200 per ton
- Y—480 tons sold for $900 per ton
- Z—672 tons sold for $600 per ton

The total joint manufacturing costs for the year were $580,000. Cook spent an additional $200,000 to finish product Z.

There were no beginning inventories of X, Y, or Z. At the end of the year, the following inventories of completed units were on hand: X, 132 tons; Y, 120 tons; Z, 28 tons. There was no beginning or ending work in process.

Required

1. Compute the cost of inventories of X, Y, and Z for balance sheet purposes and the cost of goods sold for income statement purposes as of December 31, 2014, using the following joint cost allocation methods:
   a. NRV method
   b. Constant gross-margin percentage NRV method
2. Compare the gross-margin percentages for X, Y, and Z using the two methods given in requirement 1.

16-21 Joint-cost allocation, process further. Sinclair Oil & Gas, a large energy conglomerate, jointly processes purchased hydrocarbons to generate three nonsalable intermediate products: ICR8, ING4, and XGE3. These intermediate products are further processed separately to produce crude oil, natural gas liquids (NGL), and natural gas (measured in liquid equivalents). An overview of the process and results for August 2014 are shown here. (Note: The numbers are small to keep the focus on key concepts.)

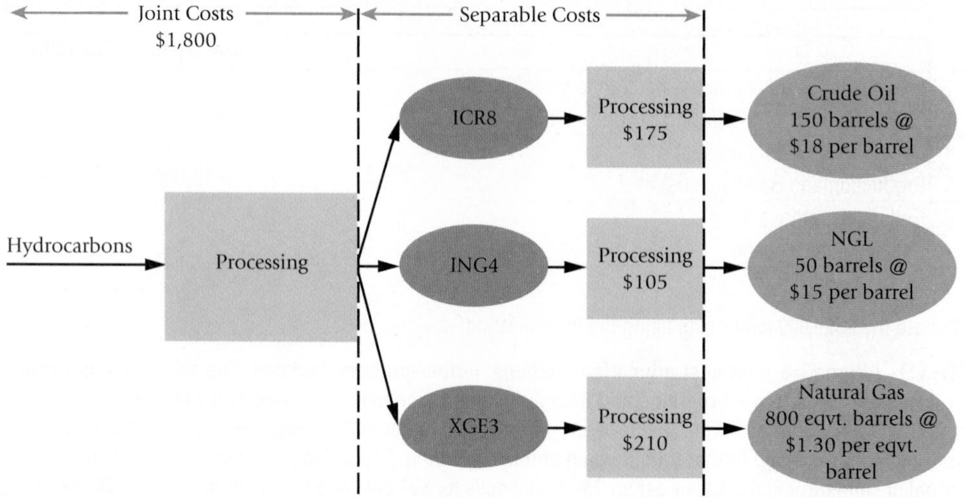

A new federal law has recently been passed that taxes crude oil at 30% of operating income. No new tax is to be paid on natural gas liquid or natural gas. Starting August 2014, Sinclair Oil & Gas must report a separate product-line income statement for crude oil. One challenge facing Sinclair Oil & Gas is how to allocate the joint cost of producing the three separate salable outputs. Assume no beginning or ending inventory.

Required

1. Allocate the August 2014 joint cost among the three products using the following:
   a. Physical-measure method
   b. NRV method
2. Show the operating income for each product using the methods in requirement 1.
3. Discuss the pros and cons of the two methods to Sinclair Oil & Gas for making decisions about product emphasis (pricing, sell-or-process-further decisions, and so on).
4. Draft a letter to the taxation authorities on behalf of Sinclair Oil & Gas that justifies the joint-cost-allocation method you recommend Sinclair use.

16-22 Joint-cost allocation, sales value, physical measure, NRV methods. Fancy Foods produces two types of microwavable products: beef-flavored ramen and shrimp-flavored ramen. The two products share common inputs such as noodle and spices. The production of ramen results in a waste product referred to as stock, which Fancy dumps at negligible costs in a local drainage area. In June 2014, the following data were reported for the production and sales of beef-flavored and shrimp-flavored ramen:

	A	B	C
1		Joint Costs	
2	Joint costs (costs of noodles, spices, and other inputs and processing to splitoff point)	$400,000	
3			
4		Beef Ramen	Shrimp Ramen
5	Beginning inventory (tons)	0	0
6	Production (tons)	20,000	28,000
7	Sales (tons)	20,000	28,000
8	Selling price per ton	$ 5	$ 20

Due to the popularity of its microwavable products, Fancy decides to add a new line of products that targets dieters. These new products are produced by adding a special ingredient to dilute the original ramen and are to be sold under the names Special B and Special S, respectively. Following are the monthly data for all the products:

	A	B	C	D	E
11		Joint Costs		Special B	Special S
12	Joint costs (costs of noodles, spices, and other inputs and processing to splitoff point)	$400,000			
13	Separable costs of processing 20,000 tons of Beef Ramen into 25,000 tons of Special B			$100,000	
14	Separable cost of processing 28,000 tons of Shrimp Ramen into 34,000 tons of Special S				$238,000
15					
16		Beef Ramen	Shrimp Ramen	Special B	Special S
17	Beginning inventory (tons)	0	0	0	0
18	Production (tons)	20,000	28,000	25,000	34,000
19	Transfer for further processing (tons)	20,000	28,000		
20	Sales (tons)			25,000	34,000
21	Selling price per ton	$ 5	$ 20	$ 17	$ 33

Required

1. Calculate Fancy's gross-margin percentage for Special B and Special S when joint costs are allocated using the following:
   a. Sales value at splitoff method
   b. Physical-measure method
   c. Net realizable value method
2. Recently, Fancy discovered that the stock it is dumping can be sold to cattle ranchers at $4 per ton. In a typical month with the production levels shown, 6,000 tons of stock are produced and can be sold by incurring marketing costs of $12,400. Sandra Dashel, a management accountant, points out that treating the stock as a joint product and using the sales value at splitoff method, the stock product would lose about $2,435 each month, so it should not be sold. How did Dashel arrive at that final number, and what do you think of her analysis? Should Fancy sell the stock?

16-23 Joint cost allocation: Sell immediately or process further. Illinois Soy Products (ISP) buys soybeans and processes them into other soy products. Each ton of soybeans that ISP purchases for $340 can be converted for an additional $190 into 575 pounds of soy meal and 160 gallons of soy oil. A pound of soy meal can be sold at splitoff for $1.24 and soy oil can be sold in bulk for $4.25 per gallon.

ISP can process the 575 pounds of soy meal into 725 pounds of soy cookies at an additional cost of $380. Each pound of soy cookies can be sold for $2.24 per pound. The 160 gallons of soy oil can be packaged at a cost of $240 and made into 640 quarts of Soyola. Each quart of Soyola can be sold for $1.35.

Required

1. Allocate the joint cost to the cookies and the Soyola using the following:
   a. Sales value at splitoff method
   b. NRV method
2. Should ISP have processed each of the products further? What effect does the allocation method have on this decision?

16-24 Accounting for a main product and a byproduct. (Cheatham and Green, adapted) Tasty, Inc., is a producer of potato chips. A single production process at Tasty, Inc., yields potato chips as the main product and a byproduct that can also be sold as a snack. Both products are fully processed by the splitoff point, and there are no separable costs.

For September 2014, the cost of operations is $500,000. Production and sales data are as follows:

	Production (in pounds)	Sales (in pounds)	Selling Price per Pound
Main Product:			
Potato Chips	52,000	42,640	$16
Byproduct	8,500	6,500	$10

There were no beginning inventories on September 1, 2014.

Required

1. What is the gross margin for Tasty, Inc., under the production method and the sales method of byproduct accounting?
2. What are the inventory costs reported in the balance sheet on September 30, 2014, for the main product and byproduct under the two methods of byproduct accounting in requirement 1?

16-25 Joint costs and decision making. Jack Bibby is a prospector in the Texas Panhandle. He has also been running a side business for the past couple of years. Based on the popularity of shows such as "Rattlesnake Nation," there has been a surge of interest from professionals and amateurs to visit the northern counties of Texas to capture snakes in the wild. Jack has set himself up as a purchaser of these captured snakes.

Jack purchases rattlesnakes in good condition from "snake hunters" for an average of $11 per snake. Jack produces canned snake meat, cured skins, and souvenir rattles, although he views snake meat as his primary product. At the end of the recent season, Jack Bibby evaluated his financial results:

	Meat	Skins	Rattles	Total
Sales revenues	$33,000	$8,800	$2,200	$44,000
Share of snake cost	19,800	5,280	1,320	26,400
Processing expenses	6,600	990	660	8,250
Allocated overhead	4,400	660	440	5,500
Income (loss)	$ 2,200	$1,870	($ 220)	$ 3,850

The cost of snakes is assigned to each product line using the *relative* sales value of meat, skins, and rattles (i.e., the percentage of total sales generated by each product). Processing expenses are directly traced to each product line. Overhead costs represent Jack's basic living expenses. These are allocated to each product line on the basis of processing expenses.

Jack has a philosophy of every product line paying for itself and is determined to cut his losses on rattles.

Required

1. Should Jack Bibby drop rattles from his product offerings? Support your answer with computations.
2. An old miner has offered to buy every rattle "as is" for $0.60 per rattle (note: "as is" refers to the situation where Jack only removes the rattle from the snake and no processing costs are incurred). Assume that Jack expects to process the same number of snakes each season. Should he sell rattles to the miner? Support your answer with computations.

16-26 Joint costs and byproducts. (W. Crum adapted) Royston, Inc., is a large food-processing company. It processes 150,000 pounds of peanuts in the peanuts department at a cost of $180,000 to yield 12,000 pounds of product A, 65,000 pounds of product B, and 16,000 pounds of product C.

- Product A is processed further in the salting department to yield 12,000 pounds of salted peanuts at a cost of $27,000 and sold for $12 per pound.
- Product B (raw peanuts) is sold without further processing at $3 per pound.
- Product C is considered a byproduct and is processed further in the paste department to yield 16,000 pounds of peanut butter at a cost of $12,000 and sold for $6 per pound.

The company wants to make a gross margin of 10% of revenues on product C and needs to allow 20% of revenues for marketing costs on product C. An overview of operations follows:

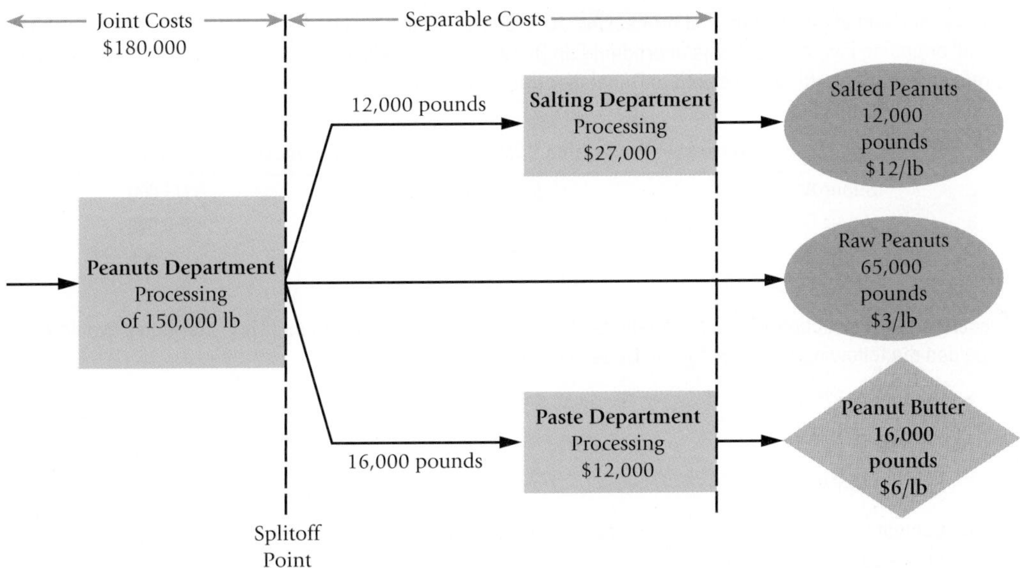

Required

1. Compute unit costs per pound for products A, B, and C, treating C as a byproduct. Use the NRV method for allocating joint costs. Deduct the NRV of the byproduct produced from the joint cost of products A and B.
2. Compute unit costs per pound for products A, B, and C, treating all three as joint products and allocating joint costs by the NRV method.

Problems

MyAccountingLab

16-27 Methods of joint-cost allocation, ending inventory. Tivoli Labs produces a drug used for the treatment of hypertension. The drug is produced in batches. Chemicals costing $60,000 are mixed and heated, creating a reaction; a unique separation process then extracts the drug from the mixture. A batch yields a total of 2,500 gallons of the chemicals. The first 2,000 gallons are sold for human use while the last 500 gallons, which contain impurities, are sold to veterinarians.

The costs of mixing, heating, and extracting the drug amount to $90,000 per batch. The output sold for human use is pasteurized at a total cost of $120,000 and is sold for $585 per gallon. The product sold to veterinarians is irradiated at a cost of $10 per gallon and is sold for $410 per gallon.

In March, Tivoli, which had no opening inventory, processed one batch of chemicals. It sold 1,700 gallons of product for human use and 300 gallons of the veterinarian product. Tivoli uses the net realizable value method for allocating joint production costs.

Required

1. How much in joint costs does Tivoli allocate to each product?
2. Compute the cost of ending inventory for each of Tivoli's products.
3. If Tivoli were to use the constant gross-margin percentage NRV method instead, how would it allocate its joint costs?
4. Calculate the gross margin on the sale of the product for human use in March under the constant gross-margin percentage NRV method.
5. Suppose that the separation process also yields 300 pints of a toxic byproduct. Tivoli currently pays a hauling company $5,000 to dispose of this byproduct. Tivoli is contacted by a firm interested in purchasing a modified form of this byproduct for a total price of $6,000. Tivoli estimates that it will cost about $30 per pint to do the required modification. Should Tivoli accept the offer?

16-28 Alternative methods of joint-cost allocation, product-mix decisions. The Eastern Oil Company buys crude vegetable oil. Refining this oil results in four products at the splitoff point: A, B, C, and D. Product C is fully processed by the splitoff point. Products A, B, and D can individually be further refined into Super A, Super B, and Super D. In the most recent month (December), the output at the splitoff point was as follows:

- Product A, 275,000 gallons
- Product B, 100,000 gallons
- Product C, 75,000 gallons
- Product D, 50,000 gallons

The joint costs of purchasing and processing the crude vegetable oil were $105,000. Eastern had no beginning or ending inventories. Sales of product C in December were $45,000. Products A, B, and D were further refined and then sold. Data related to December are as follows:

	Separable Processing Costs to Make Super Products	Revenues
Super A	$240,000	$375,000
Super B	60,000	150,000
Super D	45,000	75,000

Eastern had the option of selling products A, B, and D at the splitoff point. This alternative would have yielded the following revenues for the December production:

- Product A, $75,000
- Product B, $62,500
- Product D, $67,500

Required

1. Compute the gross-margin percentage for each product sold in December, using the following methods for allocating the $105,000 joint costs:
   a. Sales value at splitoff
   b. Physical-measure
   c. NRV
2. Could Eastern have increased its December operating income by making different decisions about the further processing of products A, B, or D? Show the effect on operating income of any changes you recommend.

16-29 Comparison of alternative joint-cost-allocation methods, further-processing decision, chocolate products. The Cocoa Factory manufactures and distributes chocolate products. It purchases cocoa beans and processes them into two intermediate products: chocolate-powder liquor base and milk-chocolate liquor base. These two intermediate products become separately identifiable at a single splitoff point. Every 2,000 pounds of cocoa beans yields 50 gallons of chocolate-powder liquor base and 50 gallons of milk-chocolate liquor base.

The chocolate-powder liquor base is further processed into chocolate powder. Every 50 gallons of chocolate-powder liquor base yield 650 pounds of chocolate powder. The milk-chocolate liquor base is further processed into milk chocolate. Every 50 gallons of milk-chocolate liquor base yield 1,070 pounds of milk chocolate.

Production and sales data for August 2014 are as follows (assume no beginning inventory):

- Cocoa beans processed, 28,000 pounds
- Costs of processing cocoa beans to splitoff point (including purchase of beans), $62,000

	Production	Sales	Selling Price	Separable Processing Costs
Chocolate powder	9,100 pounds	6,500 pounds	$ 9 per pound	$50,100
Milk chocolate	14,980 pounds	13,500 pounds	$10 per pound	$60,115

Cocoa Factory fully processes both of its intermediate products into chocolate powder or milk chocolate. There is an active market for these intermediate products. In August 2014, Cocoa Factory could have sold the chocolate-powder liquor base for $20 a gallon and the milk-chocolate liquor base for $60 a gallon.

Required

1. Calculate how the joint costs of $62,000 would be allocated between chocolate powder and milk chocolate under the following methods:
   a. Sales value at splitoff
   b. Physical-measure (gallons)
   c. NRV
   d. Constant gross-margin percentage NRV
2. What are the gross-margin percentages of chocolate powder and milk chocolate under each of the methods in requirement 1?
3. Could Cocoa Factory have increased its operating income by a change in its decision to fully process both of its intermediate products? Show your computations.

16-30 Joint-cost allocation, process further or sell. (CMA, adapted) Doughty Sawmill, Inc., (DSI) purchases logs from independent timber contractors and processes the logs into three types of lumber products:

- Studs for residential buildings (walls, ceilings)
- Decorative pieces (fireplace mantels, beams for cathedral ceilings)
- Posts used as support braces (mine support braces, braces for exterior fences on ranch properties)

These products are the result of a joint sawmill process that involves removal of bark from the logs, cutting the logs into a workable size (ranging from 8 to 16 feet in length), and then cutting the individual products from the logs.

The joint process results in the following costs of products for a typical month:

Direct materials (rough timber logs)	$ 485,000
Debarking (labor and overhead)	65,000
Sizing (labor and overhead)	215,000
Product cutting (labor and overhead)	255,000
Total joint costs	$1,020,000

Product yields and average sales values on a per-unit basis from the joint process are as follows:

Product	Monthly Output of Materials at Splitoff Point	Fully Processed Selling Price
Studs	82,000 units	$ 6
Decorative pieces	2,000 units	110
Posts	18,000 units	16

The studs are sold as rough-cut lumber after emerging from the sawmill operation without further processing by DSI. Also, the posts require no further processing beyond the splitoff point. The decorative pieces must be planed and further sized after emerging from the sawmill. This additional processing costs $110,000 per month and normally results in a loss of 10% of the units entering the process. Without this planing and sizing process, there is still an active intermediate market for the unfinished decorative pieces in which the selling price averages $70 per unit.

Required

1. Based on the information given for Doughty Sawmill, allocate the joint processing costs of $1,020,000 to the three products using:
   a. Sales value at splitoff method
   b. Physical-measure method (volume in units)
   c. NRV method

2. Prepare an analysis for Doughty Sawmill that compares processing the decorative pieces further, as it currently does, with selling them as a rough-cut product immediately at splitoff.
3. Assume Doughty Sawmill announced that in six months it will sell the unfinished decorative pieces at splitoff due to increasing competitive pressure. Identify at least three types of likely behavior that will be demonstrated by the skilled labor in the planing-and-sizing process as a result of this announcement. Include in your discussion how this behavior could be influenced by management.

16-31 Joint-cost allocation. Clover Dairy Products Corp. buys one input, full-cream milk, and refines it in a churning process. From each gallon of milk Clover produces three cups of butter and nine cups of buttermilk. During May 2014, Clover bought 12,000 gallons of milk for $44,500. Clover spent another $18,860 on the churning process to separate the milk into butter and buttermilk. Butter could be sold immediately for $4.40 per pound and buttermilk could be sold immediately for $2.40 per quart (note: two cups = one pound; four cups = one quart).

Clover chooses to process the butter further into spreadable butter by mixing it with canola oil, incurring an additional cost of $3.20 per pound. This process results in two tubs of spreadable butter for each pound of butter processed. Each tub of spreadable butter sells for $4.60.

Required

1. Allocate the $63,360 joint cost to the spreadable butter and the buttermilk using the following:
   a. Physical-measure method (using cups) of joint cost allocation
   b. Sales value at splitoff method of joint cost allocation
   c. NRV method of joint cost allocation
   d. Constant gross margin percentage NRV method of joint cost allocation
2. Each of these measures has advantages and disadvantages; what are they?
3. Some claim that the sales value at splitoff method is the best method to use. Discuss the logic behind this claim.

16-32 Further processing decision (continuation of 16-31). Clover has decided that buttermilk may sell better if it was marketed for baking and sold in pints. This would involve additional packaging at an incremental cost of $0.70 per pint. Each pint could be sold for $1.50 (note: one quart = two pints).

Required

1. If Clover uses the sales value at splitoff method, what combination of products should Clover sell to maximize profits?
2. If Clover uses the physical-measure method, what combination of products should Clover sell to maximize profits?
3. Explain the effect that the different cost allocation methods have on the decision to sell the products at splitoff or to process them further.

16-33 Joint-cost allocation with a byproduct. Mat Place purchases old tires and recycles them to produce rubber floor mats and car mats. The company washes, shreds, and molds the recycled tires into sheets. The floor and car mats are cut from these sheets. A small amount of rubber shred remains after the mats are cut. The rubber shreds can be sold to use as cover for paths and playgrounds. The company can produce 25 floor mats, 75 car mats, and 40 pounds of rubber shreds from 100 old tires.

In May, Mat Place, which had no beginning inventory, processed 125,000 tires and had joint production costs of $600,000. Mat Place sold 25,000 floor mats, 85,000 car mats, and 43,000 pounds of rubber shreds. The company sells each floor mat for $12 and each car mat for $6. The company treats the rubber shreds as a byproduct that can be sold for $0.70 per pound.

Required

1. Assume that Mat Place allocates the joint costs to floor mats and car mats using the sales value at splitoff method and accounts for the byproduct using the production method. What is the ending inventory cost for each product and gross margin for Mat Place?
2. Assume that Mat Place allocates the joint costs to floor mats and car mats using the sales value at splitoff method and accounts for the byproduct using the sales method. What is the ending inventory cost for each product and gross margin for Mat Place?
3. Discuss the difference between the two methods of accounting for byproducts, focusing on what conditions are necessary to use each method.

16-34 Byproduct-costing journal entries (continuation of 16-33). The Mat Place's accountant needs to record the information about the joint and byproducts in the general journal, but is not sure what the entries should be. The company has hired you as a consultant to help its accountant.

Required

1. Show journal entries at the time of production and at the time of sale assuming the Mat Place accounts for the byproduct using the production method.
2. Show journal entries at the time of production and at the time of sale assuming the Mat Place accounts for the byproduct using the sales method.

16-35 Process further or sell, byproduct. (CMA, adapted) Newcastle Mining Company (NMC) mines coal, puts it through a one-step crushing process, and loads the bulk raw coal onto river barges for shipment to customers.

NMC's management is currently evaluating the possibility of further processing the raw coal by sizing and cleaning it and selling it to an expanded set of customers at higher prices. The option of building a new sizing and cleaning plant is ruled out as being financially infeasible. Instead, Amy Kimbell, a mining engineer, is asked to explore outside-contracting arrangements for the cleaning and sizing process. Kimbell puts together the following summary:

Home | Insert | Page Layout | Formulas | Data | Review | View

	A	B	C
1	Selling price of raw coal	$30	per ton
2	Cost of producing raw coal	$21	per ton
3	Selling price of sized and cleaned coal	$34	per ton
4	Annual raw coal output	9,000,000	tons
5	Percentage of material weight loss in sizing/cleaning coal	6%	
6			
7		**Incremental Costs of Sizing & Cleaning Processes**	
8	Direct labor	$790,000	per year
9	Supervisory personnel	$190,000	per year
10	Heavy equipment: rental, operating, maintenance costs	$35,000	per month
11	Contract sizing and cleaning	$3.30	per ton of raw coal
12	Outbound rail freight	$250	per 600-ton rail car
13			
14	Percentage of sizing/cleaning waste that can be salvaged for coal fines	75%	
15	Range of costs per ton for preparing coal fine for sale	$3	$5
16	Range of coal fine selling prices (per ton)	$14	$25

Kimbell also learns that 75% of the material loss that occurs in the cleaning and sizing process can be salvaged as coal fines, which can be sold to steel manufacturers for their furnaces. The sale of coal fines is erratic and NMC may need to stockpile them in a protected area for up to one year. The selling price of coal fines ranges from $14 to $25 per ton and costs of preparing coal fines for sale range from $3 to $5 per ton.

Required

1. Prepare an analysis to show whether it is more profitable for NMC to continue selling raw bulk coal or to process it further through sizing and cleaning. (Ignore coal fines in your analysis.)
2. How would your analysis be affected if the cost of producing raw coal could be held down to $20 per ton?
3. Now consider the potential value of the coal fines and prepare an addendum that shows how their value affects the results of your analysis prepared in requirement 1.

16-36 Joint-cost allocation, process further or sell. Iridium Technologies manufactures a variety of flash memory chips at its main foundry in Anam, Korea. Some chips are sold by Iridium to makers of electronic equipment while others are embedded into consumer products for sale under Iridium's house label, Celeron. At Anam, Iridium produces three chips that arise from a common production process. The first chip, Apple, is sold to a maker of smartphones and personal computers. The second chip, Broadcom, is intended for a wireless and broadband communication firm. Iridium uses the third chip to manufacture and market a solid-state device under the Celeron name.

Data regarding these three products for the fiscal year ended June 30, 2014, are given below.

	Apple	Broadcom	Celeron
Units produced	510,000	990,000	1,500,000
Selling price per unit at splitoff	$ 7.00	$ 4.00	—
Separable costs	—	—	$8,400,000
Final selling price per unit	—	—	$ 10.00

Iridium incurred joint product costs up to the splitoff point of $10,800,000 during the fiscal year.

The head of Iridium, Amala Peterman, is considering a variety of alternatives that would potentially change the way the three products are processed and sold. Proposed changes for each product are as follows:

- Apple chips can be incorporated into Iridium's own memory stick. However, this additional processing causes a loss of 55,000 units of Apple. The separable costs to further process Apple chips are estimated to be $1,500,000 annually. The memory stick would sell for $11 per unit.
- Iridium's R&D unit has recommended that the company process Broadcom further into a 3D vertical chip and sell it to a high-end vendor of datacenter products. The additional processing would cost $2,000,000 annually and would result in 25% more units of product. The 3D vertical chip sells for $5.00 per unit.
- The third chip is currently incorporated into a solid-state device under the Celeron name. Galaxy Electronics has approached Iridium with an offer to purchase this chip at the splitoff point for $4.75 per unit.

Required

1. Allocate the $10,800,000 joint production cost to Apple, Broadcom, and Celeron using the NRV method.
2. Identify which of the three joint products Iridium should sell at the splitoff point in the future and which of the three the company should process further to maximize operating income. Support your decisions with appropriate computations.

16-37 Methods of joint-cost allocation, comprehensive. Kardash Cosmetics purchases flowers in bulk and processes them into perfume. From a certain mix of petals, the firm uses Process A to generate Seduction, its high-grade perfume, as well as a certain residue. The residue is then further treated, using Process B, to yield Romance, a medium-grade perfume. An ounce of residue typically yields an ounce of Romance.

In July, the company used 25,000 pounds of petals. Costs involved in Process A, i.e., reducing the petals to Seduction and the residue, were:

Direct Materials - $440,000; Direct Labor - $220,000; Overhead Costs - $110,000.

The additional costs of producing Romance in Process B were:

Direct Materials - $22,000; Direct Labor - $50,000; Overhead Costs - $40,000.

During July, Process A yielded 7,000 ounces of Seduction and 49,000 ounces of residue. From this, 5,000 ounces of Seduction were packaged and sold for $109.50 an ounce. Also, 28,000 ounces of Romance were processed in Process B and then packaged and sold for $31.50 an ounce. The other 21,000 ounces remained as residue. Packaging costs incurred were $137,500 for Seduction and $196,000 for Romance. The firm has no beginning inventory on July 1.

If it so desired, the firm could have sold unpackaged Seduction for $56 an ounce and the residue from Process A for $24 an ounce.

Required

1. What is the joint cost of the firm to be allocated to Seduction and Romance?
2. Under the physical measure method, how would the joint costs be allocated to Seduction and Romance?
3. Under the sales value at splitoff method, what portion of the joint costs would be allocated to Seduction and Romance, respectively?

4. What is the estimated net realizable value per ounce of Seduction and Romance?
5. Under the net realizable value method, what portion of the joint costs would be allocated to Seduction and Romance, respectively?
6. What is the gross margin percentage for the firm as a whole?
7. Allocate the joint costs to Seduction and Romance under the constant gross-margin percentage NRV method.
8. If you were the manager of Kardash Cosmetics, would you continue to process the petal residue into Romance perfume? Explain your answer.

17 Process Costing

Learning Objectives

1. Identify the situations in which process-costing systems are appropriate
2. Understand the basic concepts of process costing and compute average unit costs
3. Describe the five steps in process costing and calculate equivalent units
4. Use the weighted-average method and first-in, first-out (FIFO) method of process costing
5. Apply process-costing methods to situations with transferred-in costs
6. Understand the need for hybrid-costing systems such as operation costing

Many companies use mass-production techniques to produce identical or similar units of a product or service:

Apple (smartphones), Coca-Cola (soft drinks), ExxonMobil (gasoline), JP MorganChase (processing of checks), and Novartis (pharmaceuticals). Managerial accountants at companies like these use process costing because it helps them (1) determine how many units of the product the firm has on hand at the end of an accounting reporting period, (2) evaluate the units' stages of completion, and (3) assign costs to units produced and in inventory. There are different methods for process costing (for example, the FIFO or weighted-average methods) that are based on different assumptions about the flow of product costs. As you learned in your financial accounting class, the choice of method results in different operating income and affects the taxes a company pays and the performance evaluation of managers. At times, variations in international rules and customs also determine the method chosen. In the case of ExxonMobil, differences in inventory accounting rules for the United States versus Europe have a large impact on the company's profits and tax liability.

ExxonMobil and Accounting Differences in the Oil Patch[1]

In 2013, ExxonMobil was ranked second in the *Fortune* 500 annual ranking of the largest U.S. companies, with revenue of $453 billion and more than $44 billion in profits. Believe it or not, however, by one measure ExxonMobil's profits are *understated*.

ExxonMobil, like most U.S. energy companies, uses last-in, first-out (LIFO) accounting for financial reporting. Under LIFO, ExxonMobil records its cost of inventory at the latest price paid for crude oil in the open market, even though it is often selling oil produced at a much lower cost. This increases the company's cost of goods sold, which in turn reduces profit and tax payments.

Assigning costs to inventory is a critical part of process costing, and a company's choice of method can result in substantially different profits. For instance, ExxonMobil's 2012 net income would have been $4.3 billion lower under FIFO. However, if ExxonMobil had used FIFO accounting in prior years, its operating income over the years would have been higher by $21.3 billion. Assuming a marginal tax rate of 35%, this would have resulted in an incremental tax burden of almost $7.5 billion.

It is interesting to note that International Financial Reporting Standards (IFRS) do not permit the use of LIFO accounting. European oil companies such as Royal Dutch Shell and British Petroleum must use the first-in, first-out (FIFO) methodology instead

[1] *Source:* Exxon Mobil Corporation, 2012 Annual Report (Irving, TX: Exxon Mobil Corporation, 2013); Izabella Kaminska, "Shell, BP, and the Increasing Cost of Inventory," *Financial Times*. "FT Alphaville" blog (April 29, 2010); David Reilly, "Big Oil's Accounting Methods Fuel Criticism," *Wall Street Journal* (August 8, 2006).

when accounting for inventory, thereby preventing them from receiving the favorable inventory accounting treatment enjoyed by ExxonMobil.

Companies such as ExxonMobil, Kellogg (cereals), and AB InBev (beer) produce many identical or similar units of a product using mass-production techniques. The focus of these companies on individual production processes gives rise to process costing. This chapter describes how companies use process-costing methods to determine the costs of products or services and to value inventory and the cost of goods sold.

Illustrating Process Costing

Learning Objective 1

Identify the situations in which process-costing systems are appropriate

...when masses of identical or similar units are produced

Before examining process costing in more detail, let's briefly review the distinction between job costing and process costing explained in Chapter 4. Job-costing and process-costing systems are best viewed as ends of a continuum:

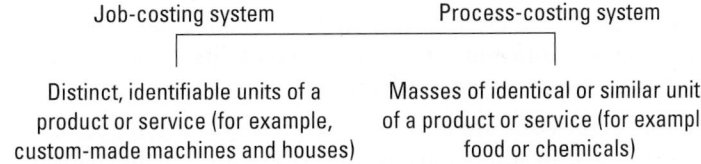

Job-costing system	Process-costing system
Distinct, identifiable units of a product or service (for example, custom-made machines and houses)	Masses of identical or similar units of a product or service (for example, food or chemicals)

In a *process-costing system*, the unit cost of a product or service is obtained by assigning total costs to many identical or similar units of output. In other words, unit costs are calculated by dividing total costs incurred by the number of units of output from the production process. In a manufacturing process-costing setting, each unit receives the same or similar amounts of direct material costs, direct manufacturing labor costs, and indirect manufacturing costs (manufacturing overhead).

The main difference between process costing and job costing is the *extent of averaging* used to compute the unit costs of products or services. In a job-costing system, individual jobs use different quantities of resources, so it would be incorrect to cost each job at the same average production cost. In contrast, when identical or similar units of products or services are mass-produced rather than processed as individual jobs, process costing is used to calculate an average production cost for all units produced. Some processes such as clothes manufacturing have aspects of both process costing (the cost per unit of each operation, such as cutting or sewing, is identical) and job costing (different materials are used in different batches of clothing, say, wool versus cotton). The final section in this chapter describes "hybrid" costing systems that combine elements of both job and process costing.

Consider the following example: Suppose that Pacific Electronics manufactures a variety of cell phone models. These models are assembled in the assembly department. Upon completion, units are transferred to the testing department. We focus on the assembly department process for one model, SG-40. All units of SG-40 are identical and must meet a set of demanding performance specifications. The process-costing system for SG-40 in the assembly department has a single direct-cost category—direct materials—and a single indirect-cost category—conversion costs. Conversion costs are all manufacturing costs other than direct material costs, including manufacturing labor, energy, plant depreciation, and so on. As the following figure shows, direct materials, such as a phone's circuit board, antenna, and microphone, are added at the beginning of the assembly process. Conversion costs are added evenly during assembly.

The following graphic represents these facts:

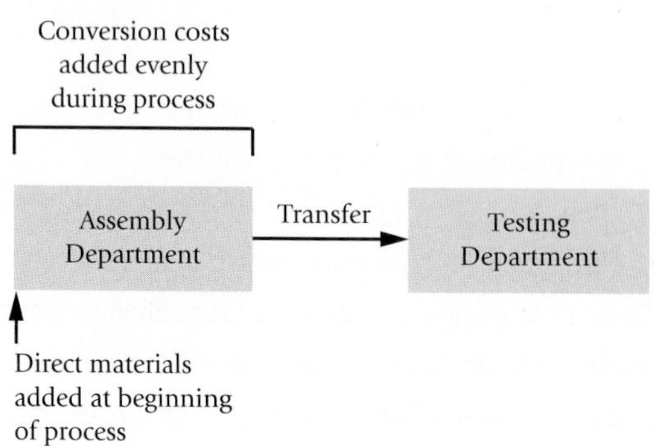

Process-costing systems separate costs into cost categories according to *when costs are introduced into the process*. Often, as in our Pacific Electronics example, only two cost classifications—direct materials and conversion costs—are necessary to assign costs to products. Why only two? Because *all* direct materials are added to the process at one time and all conversion costs generally are added to the process evenly through time. Sometimes the situation is different.

1. If two different direct materials—such as the circuit board and microphone—are added to the process at different times, two different direct-materials categories would be needed to assign these costs to products.
2. If manufacturing labor costs are added to the process at a different time compared to other conversion costs, an additional cost category—direct manufacturing labor costs—would be needed to assign these costs to products.

We illustrate process costing using three cases of increasing complexity:

- Case 1—Process costing with zero beginning and zero ending work-in-process inventory of SG-40. (That is, all units are started and fully completed within the accounting period.) *This case presents the most basic concepts of process costing and illustrates the averaging of costs.*
- Case 2—Process costing with zero beginning work-in-process inventory and some ending work-in-process inventory of SG-40. (That is, some units of SG-40 started during the accounting period are incomplete at the end of the period.) *This case introduces the five steps of process costing and the concept of equivalent units.*
- Case 3—Process costing with both some beginning and some ending work-in-process inventory of SG-40. *This case adds more complexity and illustrates the effects the weighted-average and first-in, first-out (FIFO) methods have on the cost of units completed and the cost of work-in-process inventory.*

Decision Point

Under what conditions is a process-costing system used?

Learning Objective 2

Understand the basic concepts of process-costing and compute average unit costs

...divide total costs by total units in a given accounting period

Case 1: Process Costing with No Beginning or Ending Work-in-Process Inventory

On January 1, 2014, there was no beginning inventory of SG-40 units in the assembly department. During the month of January, Pacific Electronics started, completely assembled, and transferred 400 units to the testing department.

Data for the assembly department for January 2014 are as follows:

Physical Units for January 2014	
Work in process, beginning inventory (January 1)	0 units
Started during January	400 units
Completed and transferred out during January	400 units
Work in process, ending inventory (January 31)	0 units

Physical units refer to the number of output units, whether complete or incomplete. In January 2014, all 400 physical units started were completed.

Total Costs for January 2014	
Direct materials costs added during January	$32,000
Conversion costs added during January	24,000
Total assembly department costs added during January	$56,000

Pacific Electronics records direct materials costs and conversion costs in the assembly department as these costs are incurred. The cost per unit is then calculated by dividing the total costs incurred in a given accounting period by the total units produced in that period. So, the assembly department cost of an SG-40 is $56,000 ÷ 400 units = $140 per unit:

Direct material cost per unit ($32,000 ÷ 400 units)	$ 80
Conversion cost per unit ($24,000 ÷ 400 units)	60
Assembly department cost per unit	$140

Decision Point

How are average unit costs computed when no inventories are present?

Case 1 applies whenever a company produces a homogeneous product or service but has no incomplete units when each accounting period ends, which is a common situation in service-sector organizations. For example, a bank can adopt this process-costing approach to compute the unit cost of processing 100,000 customer deposits made in a month because each deposit is processed in the same way regardless of the amount of the deposit.

Learning Objective 3

Describe the five steps in process costing

...to assign total costs to units completed and to units in work in process

and calculate equivalent units

...output units adjusted for incomplete units

Case 2: Process Costing with Zero Beginning and Some Ending Work-in-Process Inventory

In February 2014, Pacific Electronics places another 400 units of SG-40 into production. Because all units placed into production in January were completely assembled, there is no beginning inventory of partially completed units in the assembly department on February 1. Some customers order late, so not all units started in February are completed by the end of the month. Only 175 units are completed and transferred to the testing department.

Data for the assembly department for February 2014 are as follows:

Home Insert Page Layout Formulas Data Review View

	A	B	C	D	E
1		Physical Units (SG-40s) (1)	Direct Materials (2)	Conversion Costs (3)	Total Costs (4) = (2) + (3)
2	Work in process, beginning inventory (February 1)	0			
3	Started during February	400			
4	Completed and transferred out during February	175			
5	Work in process, ending inventory (February 28)	225			
6	Degree of completion of ending work in process		100%	60%	
7	Total costs added during February		$32,000	$18,600	$50,600

The 225 partially assembled units as of February 28, 2014, are fully processed for direct materials because all direct materials in the assembly department are added at the beginning of the assembly process. Conversion costs, however, are added evenly during assembly.

An assembly department supervisor estimates that the partially assembled units are, on average, 60% complete with respect to conversion costs.

The accuracy of the completion estimate of conversion costs depends on the care, skill, and experience of the estimator and the nature of the conversion process. Estimating the degree of completion is usually easier for direct material costs than for conversion costs because the quantity of direct materials needed for a completed unit and the quantity of direct materials in a partially completed unit can be measured more accurately. In contrast, the conversion sequence usually consists of a number of operations, each for a specified period of time, at various steps in the production process.[2] The degree of completion for conversion costs depends on the proportion of the total conversion costs needed to complete one unit (or a batch of production) that has already been incurred on the units still in process.

Department supervisors and line managers are most familiar with the conversion process, so they most often estimate completion rates for conversion costs. However, in some industries, such as semiconductor manufacturing, no exact estimate is possible because manufacturing occurs inside sealed environments that can be opened only when the process is complete. In other settings, such as the textile industry, vast quantities of unfinished products such as shirts and pants make the task of estimation too costly. In these cases, to calculate the conversion costs, managers assume that all work in process in a department is complete to some preset degree (for example, one-third, one-half, or two-thirds).

Because some units are fully assembled and some are only partially assembled, a common metric is needed to compare the work that's been done on them and, more importantly, obtain a total measure of the work done. The concept we will use in this regard is that of *equivalent units*. We will explain this concept in greater detail next as part of the set of five steps required to calculate (1) the cost of fully assembled units in February 2014 and (2) the cost of partially assembled units still in process at the end of that month, for Pacific Electronics. The five steps of process costing are as follows:

Step 1: Summarize the flow of physical units of output.

Step 2: Compute output in terms of equivalent units.

Step 3: Summarize the total costs to account for.

Step 4: Compute the cost per equivalent unit.

Step 5: Assign the total costs to the units completed and to the units in ending work-in-process inventory.

Summarizing the Physical Units and Equivalent Units (Steps 1 and 2)

In **Step 1**, managers track the physical units of output. Recall that physical units are the number of output units, whether complete or incomplete. The physical-units column of Exhibit 17-1 tracks where the physical units came from (400 units started) and where they went (175 units completed and transferred out and 225 units in ending inventory). Remember that when there is no beginning inventory, the number of units started must equal the sum of units transferred out and ending inventory.

Because not all 400 physical units are fully completed, in **Step 2**, managers compute the output in *equivalent units*, not in *physical units*. **Equivalent units** are a derived measure of output calculated by (1) taking the quantity of each input (factor of production) in units completed and in incomplete units of work in process and (2) converting the quantity of input into the amount of completed output units that could be produced with that quantity of input. To see what is meant by equivalent units, suppose that during a month, 50 physical units were started but not completed. Managers estimate that the 50 units in ending inventory are 70% complete for conversion costs. Now, suppose all the conversion costs represented in these units were used to make fully completed units instead. How many completed units would that have resulted in? The answer is 35 units.

[2] For example, consider the conventional tanning process for converting hide to leather. Obtaining 250–300 kg of leather requires putting one metric ton of raw hide through as many as 15 steps: from soaking, liming, and pickling to tanning, dyeing, and fatliquoring, the step in which oils are introduced into the skin before the leather is dried.

Exhibit 17-1

Summarize the Flow of Physical Units and Compute Output in Equivalent Units for the Assembly Department for February 2014

	A	B	C	D
1		(Step 1)	(Step 2)	
2			Equivalent Units	
3	Flow of Production	Physical Units	Direct Materials	Conversion Costs
4	Work in process, beginning	0		
5	Started during current period	400		
6	To account for	400		
7	Completed and transferred out during current period	175	175	175
8	Work in process, ending[a]	225		
9	(225 × 100%; 225 × 60%)		225	135
10	Accounted for	400		
11	Equivalent units of work done in current period		400	310
12				
13	[a]Degree of completion in this department; direct materials, 100%; conversion costs, 60%.			

Why? Because the conversion costs incurred to produce 50 units that are each 70% complete could have instead generated 35 (0.70 × 50) units that are 100% complete. The 35 units are referred to as *equivalent units* of output. That is, in terms of the work done on them, the 50 partially completed units are considered equivalent to 35 completed units.

Note that equivalent units are calculated separately for each input (such as direct materials and conversion costs). Moreover, every completed unit, by definition, is composed of one equivalent unit of each input required to make it. This chapter focuses on equivalent-unit calculations in manufacturing settings, but the calculations can be used in nonmanufacturing settings as well. For example, universities convert their part-time student enrollments into "full-time student equivalents" to get a better measure of faculty–student ratios over time. Without this adjustment, an increase in part-time students would lead to a lower faculty–student ratio. This would erroneously suggest a decline in the quality of instruction when, in fact, part-time students take fewer academic courses and do not need the same number of instructors as full-time students do.

When calculating the equivalent units in Step 2, focus on quantities. Disregard dollar amounts until after the equivalent units are computed. In the Pacific Electronics example, all 400 physical units—the 175 fully assembled units and the 225 partially assembled units—are 100% complete with respect to direct materials because all direct materials are added in the assembly department at the start of the process. Therefore, Exhibit 17-1 shows that the output is 400 *equivalent units* for direct materials: 175 equivalent units for the 175 physical units assembled and transferred out and 225 equivalent units for the 225 physical units in ending work-in-process inventory.

The 175 fully assembled units have also incurred all of their conversion costs. The 225 partially assembled units in ending work in process are 60% complete (on average). Therefore, their conversion costs are *equivalent* to the conversion costs incurred by 135 fully assembled units (225 × 60% = 135). Hence, Exhibit 17-1 shows that the output is a total of 310 *equivalent units* for the conversion costs: 175 equivalent units for the 175 physical units assembled and transferred out and 135 equivalent units for the 225 physical units in ending work-in-process inventory.

Calculating Product Costs (Steps 3, 4, and 5)

Exhibit 17-2 shows Steps 3, 4, and 5. Together, they are called the *production cost worksheet.*

In **Step 3**, managers summarize the total costs to account for. Because the beginning balance of work-in-process inventory is zero on February 1, the total costs to account for (that is, the total charges or debits to the Work in Process—Assembly account) consist only of costs added during February: $32,000 in direct materials and $18,600 in conversion costs, for a total of $50,600.

Exhibit 17-2 Summarize the Total Costs to Account For, Compute the Cost per Equivalent Unit, and Assign Costs to the Units Completed and Units in Ending Work-in-Process Inventory for the Assembly Department for February 2014

	A	B	C	D	E
1			**Total Production Costs**	**Direct Materials**	**Conversion Costs**
2	**(Step 3)**	Costs added during February	$50,600	$32,000	$18,600
3		Total costs to account for	$50,600	$32,000	$18,600
4					
5	**(Step 4)**	Costs added in current period	$50,600	$32,000	$18,600
6		Divide by equivalent units of work done in current period (Exhibit 17-1)		÷ 400	÷ 310
7		Cost per equivalent unit		$ 80	$ 60
8					
9	**(Step 5)**	Assignment of costs:			
10		Completed and transferred out (175 units)	$24,500	(175[a] × $80) +	(175[a] × $60)
11		Work in process, ending (225 units):	26,100	(225[b] × $80) +	(135[b] × $60)
12		Total costs accounted for	$50,600	$32,000 +	$18,600
13					
14	[a] Equivalent units completed and transferred out from Exhibit 17-1, step 2.				
15	[b] Equivalent units in ending work in process from Exhibit 17-1, step 2.				

In **Step 4**, managers calculate the cost per equivalent unit separately for the direct materials costs and conversion costs. This is done by dividing the direct material costs and conversion costs added during February by their related quantities of equivalent units of work done in February (as calculated in Exhibit 17-1).

To see why it is important to understand equivalent units in unit-cost calculations, compare the conversion costs for January and February 2014. The $18,600 in total conversion costs for the 400 units worked on during February are lower than the $24,000 in total conversion costs for the 400 units worked on in January. However, the conversion costs to fully assemble a unit are the same: $60 per unit in both January and February. Total conversion costs are lower in February because fewer equivalent units of conversion-costs work were completed in that month than in January (310 in February versus 400 in January). Note that using physical units instead of equivalent units would have resulted in a conversion cost per unit of just $46.50 ($18,600 ÷ 400 units) for February, which is down from $60 in January. This incorrect costing might lead the firm's managers to believe that the assembly department achieved efficiencies that lowered the conversion costs of the SG-40 when in fact the costs had not declined.

Once the cost per equivalent unit is calculated for both the direct materials and conversion costs, managers can move to **Step 5**: assigning the total direct materials and conversion costs to the units completed and transferred out and to the units still in process at the end of February 2014. As Exhibit 17-2 shows, this is done by multiplying the equivalent output units for each input by the cost per equivalent unit. For example, the total costs (direct materials and conversion costs assigned to the 225 physical units in ending work-in-process inventory are as follows:

Direct material costs of 225 equivalent units (calculated in Step 2) × $80 cost per equivalent unit of direct materials (calculated in Step 4)	$18,000
Conversion costs of 135 equivalent units (calculated in Step 2) × $60 cost per equivalent unit of conversion costs (calculated in Step 4)	8,100
Total cost of ending work-in-process inventory	$26,100

Note that the total costs to account for in Step 3 ($50,600) equal the total costs accounted for in Step 5.

Journal Entries

Journal entries in process-costing systems are similar to the entries made in job-costing systems with respect to direct materials and conversion costs. The main difference is that, when process costing is used, there is one Work in Process account for each process. In our example, there are accounts for (1) Work in Process—Assembly and (2) Work in Process—Testing. Pacific Electronics purchases direct materials as needed. These materials are delivered directly to the assembly department. Using the amounts from Exhibit 17-2, the summary journal entries for February are as follows:

1. Work in Process—Assembly	32,000	
Accounts Payable Control		32,000
To record the direct materials purchased and used in production during February.		
2. Work in Process—Assembly	18,600	
Various accounts such as Wages Payable Control and Accumulated Depreciation		18,600
To record the conversion costs for February; examples include energy, manufacturing supplies, all manufacturing labor, and plant depreciation.		
3. Work in Process—Testing	24,500	
Work in Process—Assembly		24,500
To record the cost of goods completed and transferred from assembly to testing during February.		

Exhibit 17-3 shows a general framework for the flow of costs through T-accounts. Notice how entry 3 for $24,500 follows the physical transfer of goods from the assembly to the testing department. The T-account Work in Process—Assembly shows February 2014's ending balance of $26,100, which is the beginning balance of Work in Process—Assembly in March 2014. It is important to ensure that all costs have been accounted for and that the ending inventory of the current month is the beginning inventory of the following month.

Earlier, we discussed the importance of accurately estimating the completion percentages for conversion costs. We can now calculate the effect of incorrect estimates of the degree of completion of units in ending work in process. Suppose, for example, that Pacific

Decision Point

What are the five steps in a process-costing system and how are equivalent units calculated?

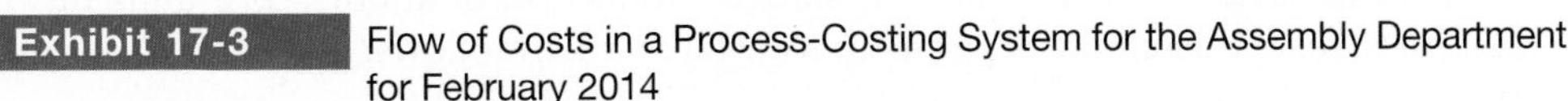
Exhibit 17-3 Flow of Costs in a Process-Costing System for the Assembly Department for February 2014

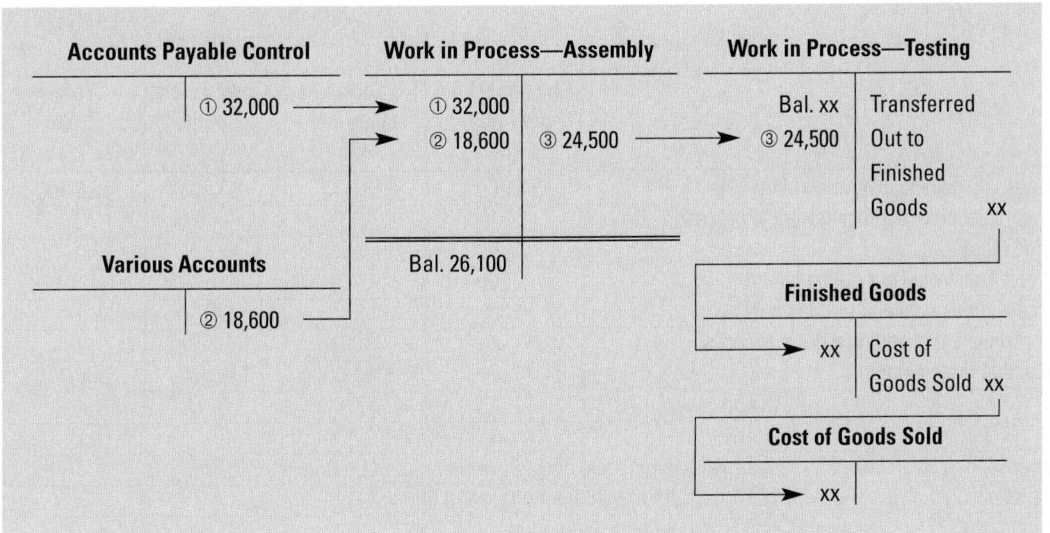

Electronics' managers overestimate the degree of completion for conversion costs at 80% instead of 60%. The computations would change as follows:

- Exhibit 17-1, Step 2
  Equivalent units of conversion costs in ending Work in Process—Assembly = 80% × 225 = 180
  Equivalent units of conversion costs for work done in the current period = 175 + 180 = 355
- Exhibit 17-2, Step 4
  Cost per equivalent unit of conversion costs = \$18,600 ÷ 355 = \$52.39
  Cost per equivalent unit of direct materials is the same, \$80
- Exhibit 17-2, Step 5
  Cost of 175 units of goods completed and transferred out = 175 × \$80 + 175 × \$52.39 = \$23,168.25

This amount is lower than the \$24,500 of costs assigned to goods completed and transferred out calculated in Exhibit 17-2. Overestimating the degree of completion decreases the costs assigned to goods transferred out and eventually to cost of goods sold and increases operating income.

Managers must ensure that department supervisors avoid introducing personal biases into estimates of degrees of completion. To show better performance, for example, a department supervisor might report a higher degree of completion resulting in overstated operating income. If performance for the period is very good, the department supervisor may be tempted to report a lower degree of completion, reducing income in the current period. This has the effect of reducing the costs carried in ending inventory and the costs carried to the following year in beginning inventory. In other words, estimates of degree of completion can help to smooth earnings from one period to the next.

To guard against the possibility of bias, managers should ask supervisors specific questions about the process they followed to prepare estimates. Top management should always emphasize obtaining the correct answer, regardless of how it affects reported performance. This emphasis drives ethical actions throughout the organization.

Learning Objective 4

Use the weighted-average method of process costing

...assigns costs based on total costs and equivalent units completed to date

and the first-in, first-out (FIFO) method of process costing

...to assign costs based on costs and equivalent units of work done in the current period

Case 3: Process Costing with Some Beginning and Some Ending Work-in-Process Inventory

At the beginning of March 2014, Pacific Electronics had 225 partially assembled SG-40 units in the assembly department. It started production of another 275 units in March. The data for the assembly department for March are as follows:

	A	B	C	D	E
1		Physical Units (SG-40s) (1)	Direct Materials (2)	Conversion Costs (3)	Total Costs (4) = (2) + (3)
2	Work in process, beginning inventory (March 1)	225	\$18,000[a]	\$8,100[a]	\$26,100
3	Degree of completion of beginning work in process		100%	60%	
4	Started during March	275			
5	Completed and transferred out during March	400			
6	Work in process, ending inventory (March 31)	100			
7	Degree of completion of ending work in process		100%	50%	
8	Total costs added during March		\$19,800	\$16,380	\$36,180
9					
10					
11	[a]Work in process, beginning inventory (equals work in process, ending inventory for February)				
12	Direct materials: 225 physical units × 100% completed × \$80 per unit = \$18,000				
13	Conversion costs: 225 physical units × 60% completed × \$60 per unit = \$8,100				

Pacific Electronics now has incomplete units in both beginning work-in-process inventory and ending work-in-process inventory for March 2014. We can still use the five steps described earlier to calculate (1) the cost of units completed and transferred out and (2) the cost of ending work-in-process inventory. To assign costs to each of these categories, however, we first need to choose an inventory-valuation method. We next describe the five-step approach for two key methods—the *weighted-average method* and the *first-in, first-out method.* These different valuation methods produce different costs for the units completed and for the ending work-in-process inventory when the unit cost of inputs changes from one period to the next.

Weighted-Average Method

The **weighted-average process-costing method** calculates the cost per equivalent unit of all *work done to date* (regardless of the accounting period in which it was done) and assigns this cost to equivalent units completed and transferred out of the process and to equivalent units in ending work-in-process inventory. The weighted-average cost is the total of all costs entering the Work in Process account (whether the costs are from beginning work in process or from work started during the current period) divided by total equivalent units of work done to date. We now describe the weighted-average method using the five-step procedure introduced on page 668.

Step 1: **Summarize the Flow of Physical Units of Output.** The physical-units column in Exhibit 17-4 shows where the units came from—225 units from beginning inventory and 275 units started during the current period—and where the units went—400 units completed and transferred out and 100 units in ending inventory.

Step 2: **Compute the Output in Terms of Equivalent Units.** We use the relationship shown in the following equation:

$$\begin{array}{c}\text{Equivalent units}\\\text{in beginning work}\\\text{in process}\end{array} + \begin{array}{c}\text{Equivalent units}\\\text{of work done in}\\\text{current period}\end{array} = \begin{array}{c}\text{Equivalent units}\\\text{completed and transferred}\\\text{out in current period}\end{array} + \begin{array}{c}\text{Equivalent units}\\\text{in ending work}\\\text{in process}\end{array}$$

Although we are interested in calculating the left side of the preceding equation, it is easier to calculate this sum using the equation's right side: (1) the equivalent units completed and transferred out in the current period plus (2) the equivalent units in ending work in process. *Note that the stage of completion of the current-period beginning work in process is not used in this computation.*

The equivalent-units columns in Exhibit 17-4 show the equivalent units of work done to date: 500 equivalent units of direct materials and 450 equivalent units of conversion

Exhibit 17-4

Summarize the Flow of Physical Units and Compute Output in Equivalent Units Using the Weighted-Average Method for the Assembly Department for March 2014

	A	B	C	D
1		**(Step 1)**	**(Step 2)**	
2			**Equivalent Units**	
3	**Flow of Production**	**Physical Units**	**Direct Materials**	**Conversion Costs**
4	Work in process, beginning (given)	225		
5	Started during current period (given)	275		
6	To account for	500		
7	Completed and transferred out during current period	400	400	400
8	Work in process, ending[a] (given)	100		
9	(100 × 100%; 100 × 50%)		100	50
10	Accounted for	500		
11	Equivalent units of work done to date		500	450
12				
13	[a]Degree of completion in this department; direct materials, 100%; conversion costs, 50%.			

Exhibit 17-5 Summarize the Total Costs to Account For, Compute the Cost per Equivalent Unit, and Assign Costs to the Units Completed and Units in Ending Work-in-Process Inventory Using the Weighted-Average Method for the Assembly Department for March 2014

Home Insert Page Layout Formulas Data Review View

	A	B	C	D		E
1			Total Production Costs	Direct Materials		Conversion Costs
2	(Step 3)	Work in process, beginning (given, p. 672)	$26,100	$18,000		$ 8,100
3		Costs added in current period (given, p. 672)	36,180	19,800		16,380
4		Total costs to account for	$62,280	$37,800		$24,480
5						
6	(Step 4)	Costs incurred to date		$37,800		$24,480
7		Divide by equivalent units of work done to date (Exhibit 17-4)		÷ 500		÷ 450
8		Cost per equivalent unit of work done to date		$ 75.60		$ 54.40
9						
10	(Step 5)	Assignment of costs:				
11		Completed and transferred out (400 units)	$52,000	(400[a] × $75.60)	+	(400[a] × $54.40)
12		Work in process, ending (100 units):	10,280	(100[b] × $75.60)	+	(50[b] × $54.40)
13		Total costs accounted for	$62,280	$37,800	+	$24,480
14						
15	[a]Equivalent units completed and transferred out from Exhibit 17-4, Step 2.					
16	[b]Equivalent units in ending work in process from Exhibit 17-4, Step 2.					

costs. All completed and transferred-out units are 100% complete with regard to both their direct materials and conversion costs. Partially completed units in ending work in process are 100% complete with regard to their direct materials costs (because the direct materials are introduced at the beginning of the process) and 50% complete with regard to their conversion costs, based on estimates from the assembly department manager.

Step 3: **Summarize the Total Costs to Account For.** Exhibit 17-5 presents Step 3. The total costs to account for in March 2014 are described in the example data on page 672:

Beginning work in process (direct materials, \$18,000 + conversion costs, \$8,100)	\$26,100
Costs added during March (direct materials, \$19,800 + conversion costs, \$16,380)	36,180
Total costs to account for in March	\$62,280

Step 4: **Compute the Cost per Equivalent Unit.** Exhibit 17-5, Step 4, shows how the weighted-average cost per equivalent unit for direct materials and conversion costs is computed. The weighted-average cost per equivalent unit is obtained by dividing the sum of the costs for beginning work in process plus the costs for work done in the current period by the total equivalent units of work done to date. For example, we calculate the weighted-average conversion cost per equivalent unit in Exhibit 17-5 as follows:

Total conversion costs (beginning work in process, \$8,100 + work done in current period, \$16,380)	\$24,480
Divided by the total equivalent units of work done to date (equivalent units of conversion costs in beginning work in process and in work done in current period)	÷ 450
Weighted-average cost per equivalent unit	\$ 54.40

Step 5: **Assign Costs to the Units Completed and to Units in Ending Work-in-Process Inventory.** Step 5 in Exhibit 17-5 takes the equivalent units completed and transferred out and the equivalent units in ending work in process (calculated in Exhibit 17-4, Step 2) and assigns dollar amounts to them using the weighted-average cost per equivalent unit for the direct materials and conversion costs calculated in Step 4. For example, the total costs of the 100 physical units in ending work in process are as follows:

Direct materials:	
100 equivalent units × weighted-average cost per equivalent unit of $75.60	$ 7,560
Conversion costs:	
50 equivalent units × weighted-average cost per equivalent unit of $54.40	2,720
Total costs of ending work in process	$10,280

The following table summarizes total costs to account for ($62,280) and how they are accounted for in Exhibit 17-5. The arrows indicate that the costs of units completed and transferred out and units in ending work in process are calculated using weighted-average total costs obtained after merging costs of beginning work in process and costs added in the current period.

Costs to Account For			Costs Accounted for Calculated on a Weighted-Average Basis	
Beginning work in process	$26,100	→	Completed and transferred out	$52,000
Costs added in current period	36,180	→	Ending work in process	10,280
Total costs to account for	$62,280		Total costs accounted for	$62,280

Before proceeding, review Exhibits 17-4 and 17-5 to check your understanding of the weighted-average method. Note: Exhibit 17-4 deals with only physical and equivalent units, not costs. Exhibit 17-5 shows the cost amounts.

Using amounts from Exhibit 17-5, the summary journal entries under the weighted-average method for March 2014 are as follows:

	Debit	Credit
1. Work in Process—Assembly	19,800	
Accounts Payable Control		19,800
To record the direct materials purchased and used in production during March.		
2. Work in Process—Assembly	16,380	
Various accounts such as Wages Payable Control and Accumulated Depreciation		16,380
To record the conversion costs for March; examples include energy, manufacturing supplies, all manufacturing labor, and plant depreciation.		
3. Work in Process—Testing	52,000	
Work in Process—Assembly		52,000
To record the cost of goods completed and transferred from assembly to testing during March.		

The T-account Work in Process—Assembly, under the weighted-average method, is as follows:

Work in Process—Assembly

Beginning inventory, March 1	26,100	③ Completed and transferred out to Work in Process—Testing	52,000
① Direct materials	19,800		
② Conversion costs	16,380		
Ending inventory, March 31	10,280		

First-In, First-Out Method

The **first-in, first-out (FIFO) process-costing method** (1) assigns the cost of the previous accounting period's equivalent units in beginning work-in-process inventory to the first units completed and transferred out of the process and (2) assigns the cost of equivalent units worked on during the *current* period first to complete the beginning inventory, next to start and complete new units, and finally to units in ending work-in-process inventory. The FIFO method assumes that the earliest equivalent units in work in process are completed first.

A distinctive feature of the FIFO process-costing method is that work done on the beginning inventory before the current period is kept separate from work done in the current period. The costs incurred and units produced in the current period are used to calculate the cost per equivalent unit of work done in the current period. In contrast, the equivalent-unit and cost-per-equivalent-unit calculations under the weighted-average method *merge* the units and costs in beginning inventory with the units and costs of work done in the current period.

We now describe the FIFO method using the five-step procedure introduced on page 668.

Step 1: **Summarize the Flow of Physical Units of Output.** Exhibit 17-6, Step 1, traces the flow of the physical units of production and explains how they are calculated under the FIFO method.

- The first physical units assumed to be completed and transferred out during the period are 225 units from beginning work-in-process inventory.
- The March data on page 672 indicate that 400 physical units were completed during March. The FIFO method assumes that of these 400 units, 175 units (400 units − 225 units from beginning work-in-process inventory) must have been started and completed during March.
- The ending work-in-process inventory consists of 100 physical units—the 275 physical units started minus the 175 units that were started and completed.
- The physical units "to account for" equal the physical units "accounted for" (500 units).

Step 2: **Compute the Output in Terms of Equivalent Units.** Exhibit 17-6 also presents the computations for Step 2 under the FIFO method. *The equivalent-unit calculations for each cost category focus on equivalent units of work done in the current period (March) only.*

Exhibit 17-6

Summarize the Flow of Physical Units and Compute Output in Equivalent Units Using the FIFO Method for the Assembly Department for March 2014

Home | Insert | Page Layout | Formulas | Data | Review | View

	A	B	C	D
1		(Step 1)	(Step 2)	
2			Equivalent Units	
3	Flow of Production	Physical Units	Direct Materials	Conversion Costs
4	Work in process, beginning (given, p. 673)	225	(work done before current period)	
5	Started during current period (given, p. 673)	275		
6	To account for	500		
7	Completed and transferred out during current period:			
8	From beginning work in process[a]	225		
9	[225 × (100% – 100%); 225 × (100% – 60%)]		0	90
10	Started and completed	175[b]		
11	(175 × 100%; 175 × 100%)		175	175
12	Work in process, ending[c] (given, p. 673)	100		
13	(100 × 100%; 100 × 50%)		100	50
14	Accounted for	500		
15	Equivalent units of work done in current period		275	315
16				
17	[a]Degree of completion in this department; direct materials, 100%; conversion costs, 60%.			
18	[b]400 physical units completed and transferred out minus 225 physical units completed and			
19	transferred out from beginning work-in-process inventory.			
20	[c]Degree of completion in this department: direct materials, 100%; conversion costs, 50%.			

Under the FIFO method, the equivalent units of work done in March on the beginning work-in-process inventory equal 225 physical units times *the percentage of work remaining to be done in March to complete these units*: 0% for direct materials, because the beginning work in process is 100% complete for direct materials, and 40% for conversion costs, because the beginning work in process is 60% complete for conversion costs. The results are 0 (0% × 225) equivalent units of work for direct materials and 90 (40% × 225) equivalent units of work for conversion costs.

The equivalent units of work done on the 175 physical units started and completed equals 175 units times 100% for both direct materials and conversion costs because all work on these units is done in the current period.

The equivalent units of work done on the 100 units of ending work in process equal 100 physical units times 100% for direct materials (because all direct materials for these units are added in the current period) and 50% for conversion costs (because 50% of the conversion-costs work on these units is done in the current period).

Step 3: **Summarize the Total Costs to Account For.** Exhibit 17-7 presents Step 3 and summarizes the $62,280 in total costs to account for in March 2014 (the costs of the beginning work in process, $26,100, and the costs added in the current period, $36,180).

Step 4: **Compute the Cost per Equivalent Unit.** Exhibit 17-7 shows the Step 4 computation of the cost per equivalent unit of *work done in the current period only* for the direct materials and conversion costs. For example, the conversion cost per equivalent

Exhibit 17-7 Summarize the Total Costs to Account For, Compute the Cost per Equivalent Unit, and Assign Costs to the Units Completed and Units in Ending Work-in-Process Inventory Using the FIFO Method for the Assembly Department for March 2014

Home | Insert | Page Layout | Formulas | Data | Review | View

	A	B	C	D	E
1			Total Production Costs	Direct Material	Conversion Costs
2	(Step 3)	Work in process, beginning (given, p. 672)	$26,100	$18,000	$ 8,100
3		Costs added in current period (given, p. 672)	36,180	19,800	16,380
4		Total costs to account for	$62,280	$37,800	$24,480
5					
6	(Step 4)	Costs added in current period		$19,800	$16,380
7		Divide by equivalent units of work done in current period (Exhibit 17-6)		÷ 275	÷ 315
8		Cost per equivalent unit of work done in current period		$ 72	$ 52
9					
10	(Step 5)	Assignment of costs:			
11		Completed and transferred out (400 units):			
12		Work in process, beginning (225 units)	$26,100	$18,000 +	$8,100
13		Costs added to beginning work in process in current period	4,680	(0[a] × $72) +	(90[a] × $52)
14		Total from beginning inventory	30,780		
15		Started and completed (175 units)	21,700	(175[b] × $72) +	(175[b] × $52)
16		Total costs of units completed and transferred out	52,480		
17		Work in process, ending (100 units):	9,800	(100[c] × $72) +	(50[c] × $52)
18		Total costs accounted for	$62,280	$37,800 +	$24,480
19					
20	[a]Equivalent units used to complete beginning work in process from Exhibit 17-6, Step 2.				
21	[b]Equivalent units started and completed from Exhibit 17-6, Step 2.				
22	[c]Equivalent units in ending work in process from Exhibit 17-6, Step 2.				

unit of $52 is obtained by dividing the current-period conversion costs of $16,380 by the current-period conversion-costs equivalent units of 315.

Step 5: **Assign Costs to the Units Completed and Units in Ending Work-in-Process Inventory.** Exhibit 17-7 shows the assignment of costs under the FIFO method. The costs of work done in the current period are assigned (1) first to the additional work done to complete the beginning work-in-process inventory, then (2) to work done on units started and completed during the current period, and finally (3) to ending work-in-process inventory. *Step 5 takes each quantity of equivalent units calculated in Exhibit 17-6, Step 2, and assigns dollar amounts to them (using the cost-per-equivalent-unit calculations in Step 4).* The goal is to use the cost of work done in the current period to determine the total costs of all units completed from beginning inventory and from work started and completed in the current period and the costs of ending work-in-process inventory.

Of the 400 completed units, 225 units are from beginning inventory and 175 units are started and completed during March. The FIFO method starts by assigning the costs of the beginning work-in-process inventory of $26,100 to the first units completed and transferred out. As we saw in Step 2, an additional 90 equivalent units of conversion costs are needed to complete these units in the current period. The current-period conversion cost per equivalent unit is $52, so $4,680 (90 equivalent units × $52 per equivalent unit) of additional costs are incurred to complete the beginning inventory. The total production costs for units in beginning inventory are $26,100 + $4,680 = $30,780. The 175 units started and completed in the current period consist of 175 equivalent units of direct materials and 175 equivalent units of conversion costs. These units are costed at the cost per equivalent unit in the current period (direct materials, $72, and conversion costs, $52) for a total production cost of $21,700 [175 × ($72 + $52)].

Under FIFO, the ending work-in-process inventory comes from units that were started but not fully completed during the current period. The total costs of the 100 partially assembled physical units in ending work in process are as follows:

Direct materials:	
100 equivalent units × $72 cost per equivalent unit in March	$7,200
Conversion costs:	
50 equivalent units × $52 cost per equivalent unit in March	2,600
Total cost of work in process on March 31	$9,800

The following table summarizes the total costs to account for and the costs accounted for under FIFO, which are $62,280 in Exhibit 17-7. Notice how the FIFO method keeps separate the layers of the beginning work-in-process costs and the costs added in the current period. The arrows indicate where the costs in each layer go—that is, to units completed and transferred out or to ending work in process. Be sure to include the costs of the beginning work-in-process inventory ($26,100) when calculating the costs of units completed.

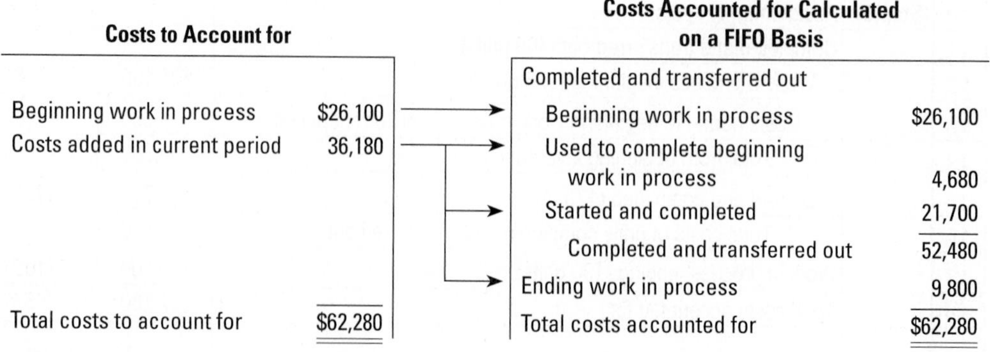

Costs to Account for		Costs Accounted for Calculated on a FIFO Basis	
		Completed and transferred out	
Beginning work in process	$26,100	Beginning work in process	$26,100
Costs added in current period	36,180	Used to complete beginning work in process	4,680
		Started and completed	21,700
		Completed and transferred out	52,480
		Ending work in process	9,800
Total costs to account for	$62,280	Total costs accounted for	$62,280

Before proceeding, review Exhibits 17-6 and 17-7 to check your understanding of the FIFO method. Note: Exhibit 17-6 deals with only physical and equivalent units, not costs. Exhibit 17-7 shows the cost amounts.

The journal entries under the FIFO method are identical to the journal entries under the weighted-average method except for one difference. The entry to record the cost of goods completed and transferred out would be \$52,480 under the FIFO method instead of \$52,000 under the weighted-average method.

Keep in mind that FIFO is applied within each department to compile the cost of units *transferred out*. As a practical matter, however, units *transferred in* during a given period usually are carried at a single average unit cost. For example, in the preceding example, the assembly department uses FIFO to distinguish between monthly batches of production. The resulting average cost of each SG-40 unit transferred out of the assembly department is \$52,480 ÷ 400 units = \$131.20. The testing department, however, costs these units (which consist of costs incurred in both February and March) at one average unit cost (\$131.20 in this example). If this averaging were not done, the attempt to track costs on a pure FIFO basis throughout a series of processes would be cumbersome. As a result, the FIFO method should really be called a *modified* or *department* FIFO method.

Comparing the Weighted-Average and FIFO Methods

Consider the summary of the costs assigned to units completed and to units still in process under the weighted-average and FIFO process-costing methods in our example for March 2014:

	Weighted Average (from Exhibit 17-5)	FIFO (from Exhibit 17-7)	Difference
Cost of units completed and transferred out	\$52,000	\$52,480	+ \$480
Work in process, ending	10,280	9,800	– \$480
Total costs accounted for	\$62,280	\$62,280	

The weighted-average ending inventory is higher than the FIFO ending inventory by \$480, or 4.9% (\$480 ÷ \$9,800 = 0.049, or 4.9%). This would be a significant difference when aggregated over the many thousands of products Pacific Electronics makes. When completed units are sold, the weighted-average method in our example leads to a lower cost of goods sold and, therefore, higher operating income than the FIFO method does. To see why, recall the data on page 672. For the beginning work-in-process inventory, the direct materials cost per equivalent unit is \$80 and the conversion cost per equivalent unit is \$60. These costs are greater, respectively, than the \$72 direct materials cost and the \$52 conversion cost per equivalent unit of work done during the current period. The current-period costs could be lower due to a decline in the prices of direct materials and conversion-cost inputs or as a result of Pacific Electronics becoming more efficient in its processes by using smaller quantities of inputs per unit of output or both.

FIFO assumes that (1) all the higher-cost units from the previous period in beginning work in process are the first to be completed and transferred out of the process and (2) the ending work in process consists of only the lower-cost current-period units. The weighted-average method, however, smooths out the cost per equivalent unit by assuming that (1) more of the lower-cost units are completed and transferred out and (2) some of the higher-cost units are placed in ending work in process. The decline in the current-period cost per equivalent unit results in a lower cost of units completed and transferred out and a higher ending work-in-process inventory under the weighted-average method relative to FIFO.

Managers use information from process-costing systems to make pricing and product-mix decisions and understand how well a firm's processes are performing. FIFO provides managers with information about changes in the costs per unit from one period to the next. Managers can use this data to adjust selling prices based on current conditions (for example, based on the \$72 direct material cost and \$52 conversion cost in March). The managers can also more easily evaluate the firm's cost performance relative to either a budget or the previous period (for example, both unit direct materials and conversion costs have declined relative to the prior period). By focusing on the work done and the costs of work done during the current period, the FIFO method provides valuable information for these planning and control purposes.

The weighted-average method merges unit costs from different accounting periods, obscuring period-to-period comparisons. For example, the weighted-average method would lead managers at Pacific Electronics to make decisions based on the $75.60 direct materials and $54.40 conversion costs, rather than the costs of $72 and $52 prevailing in the current period. However, costs are relatively easy to compute using the weighted-average method, and it results in a more-representative average unit cost when input prices fluctuate markedly from month to month.

The cost of units completed and, hence, a firm's operating income differ materially between the weighted-average and FIFO methods when (1) the direct materials or conversion cost per equivalent unit varies significantly from period to period and (2) the physical-inventory levels of the work in process are large relative to the total number of units transferred out of the process. As changes in unit costs and inventory levels across periods decrease, the difference in the costs of units completed under the weighted-average and FIFO methods also decreases.[3]

When the cost of units completed under the weighted-average and FIFO methods differs substantially, which method should a manager choose? In a period of falling prices, as in the Pacific Electronics case, the higher cost of goods sold under the FIFO method will lead to lower operating income and lower tax payments, saving the company cash and increasing the company's value. FIFO is the preferred choice, but managers may not make this choice. If the manager's compensation, for instance, is based on operating income, the manager may prefer the weighted-average method, which increases operating income even though it results in higher tax payments. Top managers must carefully design compensation plans to encourage managers to take actions that increase a company's value. For example, the compensation plan might reward after-tax cash flow metrics, in addition to operating income metrics, to align decision making and performance evaluation.

Occasionally, choosing a process-costing method can be more difficult. Suppose, for example, that by using FIFO a company would violate its debt covenants (agreements between a company and its creditors that the company will maintain certain financial ratios) resulting in its loans coming due. In this case, a manager may prefer the weighted-average method even though it results in higher taxes because the company does not have the liquidity to repay its loans.

In a period of rising prices, the weighted-average method will decrease taxes because cost of goods sold will be higher and operating income lower. Recall the vignette at the start of this chapter that describes how ExxonMobil uses the last-in, first-out (LIFO) method (not presented in this chapter) to save taxes.[4]

Decision Point

What are the weighted-average and first-in, first-out (FIFO) methods of process costing? Under what conditions will they yield different levels of operating income?

Finally, how is activity-based costing related to process costing? Like activity-based processing, each process—assembly, testing, and so on—can be considered a different (production) activity. However, no additional activities need to be identified within each process to use process costing. That's because products are homogeneous and use the resources of each process in a uniform way. The bottom line is that activity-based costing has less applicability in process-costing environments, especially when compared to the significant role it plays in job costing. *The appendix illustrates the use of the standard costing method for the assembly department.*

[3] For example, suppose the beginning work-in-process inventory for March was 125 physical units (instead of 225), and suppose the costs per equivalent unit of work done in the current period (March) were direct materials, $75, and conversion costs, $55. Assume that all other data for March are the same as in our example. In this case, the cost of units completed and transferred out would be $52,833 under the weighted-average method and $53,000 under the FIFO method. The work-in-process ending inventory would be $10,417 under the weighted-average method and $10,250 under the FIFO method (calculations not shown). These differences are much smaller than in the chapter example. The weighted-average ending inventory is higher than the FIFO ending inventory by only $167 ($10,417 − $10,250), or 1.6% ($167 ÷ $10,250 = 0.016), compared with 4.9% higher in the chapter example.

[4] Students not familiar with the LIFO method need only note that in a period of rising prices, the LIFO method reduces operating income and taxes even more than the weighted-average method.

Transferred-In Costs in Process Costing

Learning Objective 5

Apply process-costing methods to situations with transferred-in costs

...using weighted-average and FIFO methods

Many process-costing systems have two or more departments or processes in the production cycle. As units move from department to department, the related costs are also transferred by monthly journal entries. **Transferred-in costs** (also called **previous-department costs**) are costs incurred in previous departments that are carried forward as the product's cost when it moves to a subsequent process in the production cycle.

We now extend our Pacific Electronics example to the testing department. As the assembly process is completed, the assembly department of Pacific Electronics immediately transfers SG-40 units to the testing department. Conversion costs are added evenly during the testing department's process. At the *end of the testing process*, the units receive additional direct materials, including crating and other packing materials to prepare them for shipment. As units are completed in testing, they are immediately transferred to Finished Goods. The testing department costs consist of transferred-in costs, as well as direct materials and conversion costs added during testing.

The following diagram represents these facts:

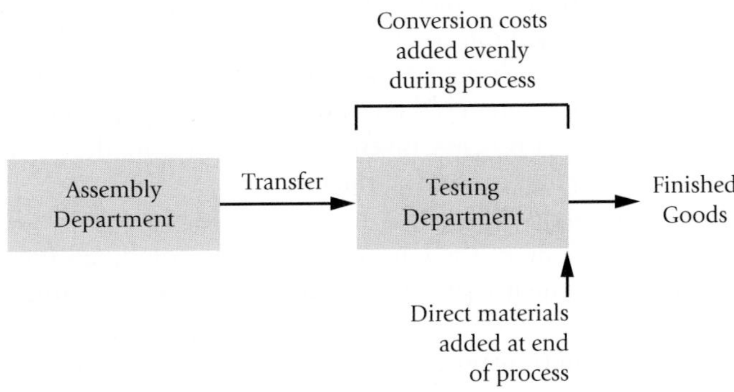

The data for the testing department for March 2014 are as follows:

	A	B	C	D	E
1		Physical Units (SG-40s)	Transferred-In Costs	Direct Materials	Conversion Costs
2	Work in process, beginning inventory (March 1)	240	$33,600	$ 0	$18,000
3	Degree of completion, beginning work in process		100%	0%	62.5%
4	Transferred in during March	400			
5	Completed and transferred out during March	440			
6	Work in process, ending inventory (March 31)	200			
7	Degree of completion, ending work in process		100%	0%	80%
8	Total costs added during March				
9	Direct materials and conversion costs			$13,200	$48,600
10	Transferred in (Weighted-average from Exhibit 17-5)[a]		$52,000		
11	Transferred in (FIFO from Exhibit 17-7)[a]		$52,480		
12					
13	[a]The transferred-in costs during March are different under the weighted-average method (Exhibit 17-5) and the FIFO method (Exhibit 17-7). In our example, beginning work-in-process inventory, $51,600 ($33,600 + $0 + $18,000), is the same under both the weighted-average and FIFO inventory methods because we assume costs per equivalent unit to be the same in both January and February. If costs per equivalent unit had been different in the two months, work-in-process inventory at the end of February (beginning of March) would be costed differently under the weighted-average and FIFO methods. The basic approach to process costing with transferred-in costs, however, would still be the same as what we describe in this section.				

Transferred-in costs are treated as if they are a separate type of direct material added at the beginning of the process. That is, the transferred-in costs are always 100% complete at the beginning of the process in the new department. When successive departments are involved, the transferred units from one department become all or a part of the direct materials of the next department; however, they are called transferred-in costs, not direct material costs.

Transferred-In Costs and the Weighted-Average Method

To examine the weighted-average process-costing method with transferred-in costs, we use the five-step procedure described earlier (page 668) to assign the costs of the testing department to units completed and transferred out and to the units in ending work in process.

Exhibit 17-8 shows Steps 1 and 2. The computations are similar to the calculations of equivalent units under the weighted-average method for the assembly department in Exhibit 17-4. The one difference here is that we have transferred-in costs as an additional input. All units, whether completed and transferred out during the period or in ending work in process, are always fully complete with respect to transferred-in costs. The reason is that the transferred-in costs are the costs incurred in the assembly department, and any units received in the testing department must have first been completed in the assembly department. However, the direct material costs have a zero degree of completion in both beginning and ending work-in-process inventories because, in the testing department, direct materials are introduced at the *end* of the process.

Exhibit 17-9 describes Steps 3, 4, and 5 for the weighted-average method. Beginning work in process and work done in the current period are combined for the purposes of computing the cost per equivalent unit for the transferred-in costs, direct materials costs, and conversion costs.

The journal entry for the transfer from testing to Finished Goods (see Exhibit 17-9) is as follows:

Finished Goods Control	120,890	
Work in Process—Testing		120,890
To record cost of goods completed and transferred from testing to Finished Goods.		

Exhibit 17-8 Summarize the Flow of Physical Units and Compute Output in Equivalent Units Using the Weighted-Average Method for the Testing Department for March 2014

Home Insert Page Layout Formulas Data Review View

	A	B	C	D	E
1		(Step 1)		(Step 2)	
2				Equivalent Units	
3	Flow of Production	Physical Units	Transferred-In Costs	Direct Materials	Conversion Costs
4	Work in process, beginning (given, p. 681)	240			
5	Transferred in during current period (given, p. 681)	400			
6	To account for	640			
7	Completed and transferred out during current period	440	440	440	440
8	Work in process, ending[a] (given, p. 681)	200			
9	(200 × 100%; 200 × 0%; 200 × 80%)		200	0	160
10	Accounted for	640			
11	Equivalent units of work done to date		640	440	600
12					
13	[a]Degree of completion in this department; transferred-in costs, 100%; direct materials, 0%; conversion costs, 80%.				

Exhibit 17-9 Summarize the Total Costs to Account For, Compute the Cost per Equivalent Unit, and Assign Costs to the Units Completed and Units in Ending Work-in-Process Inventory Using the Weighted-Average Method for the Testing Department for March 2014

	A	B	C	D		E		F
1			Total Production Costs	Transferred-In Costs		Direct Materials		Conversion Costs
2	(Step 3)	Work in process, beginning (given, p. 681)	$ 51,600	$33,600		$ 0		$18,000
3		Costs added in current period (given, p. 681)	113,800	52,000		13,200		48,600
4		Total costs to account for	$165,400	$85,600		$13,200		$66,600
5								
6	(Step 4)	Costs incurred to date		$85,600		$13,200		$66,600
7		Divide by equivalent units of work done to date (Exhibit 17-8)		÷ 640		÷ 440		÷ 600
8		Cost per equivalent unit of work done to date		$133.75		$ 30.00		$111.00
9								
10	(Step 5)	Assignment of costs:						
11		Completed and transferred out (440 units)	$120,890	(440[a] × $133.75)	+	(440[a] × $30)	+	(440[a] × $111)
12		Work in process, ending (200 units):	44,510	(200[b] × $133.75)	+	(0[b] × $30)	+	(160[b] × $111)
13		Total costs accounted for	$165,400	$85,600	+	$13,200	+	$66,600
14								
15	[a]Equivalent units completed and transferred out from Exhibit 17-8, Step 2.							
16	[b]Equivalent units in ending work in process from Exhibit 17-8, Step 2.							

Entries in the Work in Process—Testing account (see Exhibit 17-9) are as follows:

Work in Process—Testing

Beginning inventory, March 1	51,600	Transferred out	120,890
Transferred-in costs	52,000		
Direct materials	13,200		
Conversion costs	48,600		
Ending inventory, March 31	44,510		

Transferred-In Costs and the FIFO Method

To examine the FIFO process-costing method with transferred-in costs, we again use the five-step procedure. Exhibit 17-10 shows Steps 1 and 2. Other than accounting for transferred-in costs, computing the equivalent units is the same as under the FIFO method for the assembly department (see Exhibit 17-6).

Exhibit 17-11 describes Steps 3, 4, and 5. In Step 3, the $165,880 in total costs to account for under the FIFO method differ from the total costs under the weighted-average method, which are $165,400. This is because of the difference in the costs of completed units transferred in from the assembly department under the two methods—$52,480 under FIFO and $52,000 under the weighted-average method. The cost per equivalent unit for the current period in Step 4 is calculated on the basis of costs transferred in and work done in the current period only. Step 5 then accounts for the total costs of $165,880 by assigning them to the units transferred out and those in ending work-in-process inventory. Again, other than considering transferred-in costs, the calculations mirror those under the FIFO method for the assembly department (in Exhibit 17-7).

Exhibit 17-10 Summarize the Flow of Physical Units and Compute Output in Equivalent Units Using the FIFO Method for the Testing Department for March 2014

	A	B	C	D	E
1		(Step 1)		(Step 2)	
2				Equivalent Units	
3	Flow of Production	Physical Units	Transferred-In Costs	Direct Materials	Conversion Costs
4	Work in process, beginning (given, p. 681)	240	(work done before current period)		
5	Transferred in during current period (given, p. 681)	400			
6	To account for	640			
7	Completed and transferred out during current period:				
8	From beginning work in process[a]	240			
9	[240 × (100% – 100%); 240 × (100% – 0%); 240 × (100% – 62.5%)]		0	240	90
10	Started and completed	200[b]			
11	(200 × 100%; 200 × 100%; 200 × 100%)		200	200	200
12	Work in process, ending[c] (given, p. 681)	200			
13	(200 × 100%; 200 × 0%; 200 × 80%)		200	0	160
14	Accounted for	640			
15	Equivalent units of work done in current period		400	440	450
16					
17	[a]Degree of completion in this department: transferred-in costs, 100%; direct materials, 0%; conversion costs, 62.5%.				
18	[b]440 physical units completed and transferred out minus 240 physical units completed and transferred out from beginning				
19	work-in-process inventory.				
20	[c]Degree of completion in this department: transferred-in costs, 100%; direct materials, 0%; conversion costs, 80%.				

Remember that in a series of interdepartmental transfers, each department is regarded as separate and distinct for accounting purposes. The journal entry for the transfer from testing to Finished Goods (see Exhibit 17-11) is as follows:

Finished Goods Control	122,360	
Work in Process—Testing		122,360
To record the cost of goods completed and transferred from testing to Finished Goods.		

The entries in the Work in Process—Testing account (see Exhibit 17-11) are as follows:

Work in Process—Testing

Beginning inventory, March 1	51,600	Transferred out	122,360
Transferred-in costs	52,480		
Direct materials	13,200		
Conversion costs	48,600		
Ending inventory, March 31	43,520		

Points to Remember About Transferred-In Costs

Some points to remember when accounting for transferred-in costs are as follows:

1. Be sure to include the transferred-in costs from previous departments in your calculations.
2. When calculating the costs to be transferred using the FIFO method, do not overlook costs assigned in the previous period to units that were in process at the beginning of the current period but are now included in the units transferred. For example, do not overlook the $51,600 in Exhibit 17-11.

Exhibit 17-11 Summarize the Total Costs to Account For, Compute the Cost per Equivalent Unit, and Assign Costs to the Units Completed and Units in Ending Work-in-Process Inventory Using the FIFO Method for the Testing Department for March 2014

	A	B	C	D	E	F
1			Total Production Costs	Transferred-In Cost	Direct Material	Conversion Costs
2	(Step 3)	Work in process, beginning (given, p. 681)	$ 51,600	$33,600	$ 0	$18,000
3		Costs added in current period (given, p. 681)	114,280	52,480	13,200	48,600
4		Total costs to account for	$165,880	$86,080	$13,200	$66,600
5						
6	(Step 4)	Costs added in current period		$52,480	$13,200	$48,600
7		Divide by equivalent units of work done in current period (Exhibit 17-10)		÷ 400	÷ 440	÷ 450
8		Cost per equivalent unit of work done in current period		$131.20	$ 30	$ 108
9						
10	(Step 5)	Assignment of costs:				
11		Completed and transferred out (440 units)				
12		Work in process, beginning (240 units)	$ 51,600	$33,600 +	$0 +	$18,000
13		Costs added to beginning work in process in current period	16,920	(0^a × $131.20) +	(240^a × $30) +	(90^a × $108)
14		Total from beginning inventory	68,520			
15		Started and completed (200 units)	53,840	(200^b × $131.20) +	(200^b × $30) +	(200^b × $108)
16		Total costs of units completed and transferred out	122,360			
17		Work in process, ending (200 units):	43,520	(200^c × $131.20) +	(0^c × $30) +	(160^c × $108)
18		Total costs accounted for	$165,880	$86,080 +	$13,200 +	$66,600
19						
20	[a]Equivalent units used to complete beginning work in process from Exhibit 17-10, Step 2.					
21	[b]Equivalent units started and completed from Exhibit 17-10, Step 2.					
22	[c]Equivalent units in ending work in process from Exhibit 17-10, Step 2.					

3. Unit costs may fluctuate between periods. Therefore, transferred units may contain batches accumulated at different unit costs. For example, the 400 units transferred in at $52,480 in Exhibit 17-11 using the FIFO method consist of units that have different unit costs of direct materials and conversion costs when these units were worked on in the assembly department (see Exhibit 17-7). Remember, however, that when these units are transferred to the testing department, they are costed at *one average unit cost* of $131.20 ($52,480 ÷ 400 units), as in Exhibit 17-11.

4. Units may be measured in different denominations in different departments. Consider each department separately. For example, unit costs could be based on kilograms in the first department and liters in the second department. Accordingly, as units are received in the second department, their measurements must be converted to liters.

Decision Point

How are the weighted-average and FIFO process-costing methods applied to transferred-in costs?

Hybrid Costing Systems

Learning Objective 6

Understand the need for hybrid-costing systems such as operation costing

. . . when product-costing does not fall into job-costing or process-costing categories

Product-costing systems do not always fall neatly into either job-costing or process-costing categories. Many production systems are hybrid systems in which both mass production and customization occur. Consider Ford Motor Company. Automobiles are manufactured in a continuous flow (suited to process costing), but individual units may be customized with different engine sizes, transmissions, music systems, and so on (which requires job costing). A **hybrid-costing system** blends characteristics from both job-costing and process-costing systems. Managers must design product-costing systems to fit the particular characteristics of different production systems.

Firms that manufacture closely related standardized products (for example, various types of televisions, dishwashers, washing machines, and shoes) tend to use hybrid-costing

Concepts in Action: Hybrid Costing for Customized Shoes at Adidas

Adidas has been designing and manufacturing athletic footwear for nearly 90 years. Although shoemakers have long individually crafted shoes for professional athletes, Adidas took this concept a step further when it initiated the *mi adidas* program.

The mi adidas customization offering is available online and in retail stores around the world. Consumers can choose from more than 200 styles across seven sports and lifestyle categories. Along with competitors Nike and New Balance, mi adidas offers the opportunity to create individual, custom shoes for performance, fit, and design. Once the designs are created and purchased, the design and product data are transferred to manufacturing plants where the product is then built to order and shipped directly to the consumer.

Adidas uses a hybrid-costing system. Accounting for individual customization requires job costing, but the similar process used to make sneakers lends itself to process costing. The cost of making each pair of shoes is calculated by accumulating all production costs and dividing by the number of shoes made. In other words, even though each pair of shoes is different, the conversion cost is roughly the same.

The combination of customization with certain features of mass production is called mass customization. It is the consequence of being able to digitize information that individual customers indicate is important to them. Various products that companies can customize within a mass-production setting (including personal computers, jeans, and bicycles) still require job costing of materials and considerable human intervention. However, as manufacturing systems become flexible, companies are also using process costing to account for the standardized conversion costs.

Sources: Tien, Ellen. 2011. These (custom) colors do run. *New York Times*, April 7; Kamenev, Marina. 2006. Adidas' high tech footwear. *Bloomberg Businessweek*, November 3; Seifert, Ralf. 2003. The "mi adidas" mass customization initiative. IMD No. 159. Lausanne, Switzerland: International Institute for Management Development.

systems. They use process costing to account for the conversion costs and job costing for the material and customizable components. Consider Nike, which has a message for shoppers looking for the hottest new shoe design: Just do it … yourself! Athletic apparel manufacturers have long individually crafted shoes for professional athletes. Now, Nike is making it possible for other customers to design their own shoes and clothing. Using the Internet and mobile applications, Nike's customers can personalize with their own colors and patterns for Jordan-brand sneakers and other apparel. Concepts in Action: Hybrid Costing for Customized Shoes at Adidas describes customization and the use of a hybrid-costing system at Nike's main rival, Adidas. The next section explains *operation costing*, a common type of hybrid-costing system.

Overview of Operation-Costing Systems

An **operation** is a standardized method or technique performed repetitively, often on different materials, resulting in different finished goods. Multiple operations are usually conducted within a department. For instance, a suit maker may have a cutting operation and a hemming operation within a single department. The term *operation*, however, is often used loosely. It may be a synonym for a department or process. For example, some companies may call their finishing department a finishing process or a finishing operation.

An **operation-costing system** is a hybrid-costing system applied to batches of similar, but not identical, products. Each batch of products is often a variation of a single design, and it proceeds through a sequence of operations. Within each operation, all product units are treated exactly alike, using identical amounts of the operation's resources. A key point in the operation system is that each batch does not necessarily move through the same operations as other batches. Batches are also called production runs.

In a company that makes suits, managers may select a single basic design for every suit to be made, but depending on specifications, each batch of suits varies somewhat from other batches. Batches may vary with respect to the material used or the type of stitching. Semiconductors, textiles, and shoes are also manufactured in batches and may have similar variations from batch to batch.

An operation-costing system uses work orders that specify the needed direct materials and step-by-step operations. Product costs are compiled for each work order. Direct materials that are unique to different work orders are specifically identified with the appropriate work order, as in job costing. However, each unit is assumed to use an identical amount of conversion costs for a given operation, as in process costing. A single average conversion cost per unit is calculated for each operation. This is done by dividing the total conversion costs for that operation by the number of units that pass through it. This average cost is then assigned to each unit passing through the operation. Units that do not pass through an operation are not allocated any costs for that operation. There were only two cost categories—direct materials and conversion costs—in the examples we have discussed. However, operation costing can have more than two cost categories. The costs in each category are identified with specific work orders using job-costing or process-costing methods as appropriate.

Managers find operation costing useful in cost management because operation costing focuses on control of physical processes, or operations, of a given production system. For example, in clothing manufacturing, managers are concerned with fabric waste, how many fabric layers can be cut at one time, and so on. Operation costing measures, in financial terms, how well managers have controlled physical processes.

Illustrating an Operation-Costing System

The Baltimore Clothing Company, a clothing manufacturer, produces two lines of blazers for department stores: those made of wool and those made of polyester. Wool blazers use better-quality materials and undergo more operations than polyester blazers do. The operations information on work order 423 for 50 wool blazers and work order 424 for 100 polyester blazers is as follows:

	Work Order 423	**Work Order 424**
Direct materials	Wool	Polyester
	Satin full lining	Rayon partial lining
	Bone buttons	Plastic buttons
Operations		
1. Cutting cloth	Use	Use
2. Checking edges	Use	Do not use
3. Sewing body	Use	Use
4. Checking seams	Use	Do not use
5. Machine sewing of collars and lapels	Do not use	Use
6. Hand sewing of collars and lapels	Use	Do not use

The cost data for these work orders, started and completed in March 2014, are as follows:

	Work Order 423	**Work Order 424**
Number of blazers	50	100
Direct materials costs	$ 6,000	$3,000
Conversion costs allocated:		
Operation 1	580	1,160
Operation 2	400	—
Operation 3	1,900	3,800
Operation 4	500	—
Operation 5	—	875
Operation 6	700	—
Total manufacturing costs	$10,080	$8,835

As in process costing, all product units in any work order are assumed to consume identical amounts of conversion costs of a particular operation. Baltimore's operation-costing system uses a budgeted rate to calculate the conversion costs of each operation. The budgeted rate for Operation 1 (amounts assumed) is as follows:

$$\begin{aligned}\text{Operation 1 budgeted conversion-cost rate for 2014} &= \frac{\text{Operation 1 budgeted conversion costs for 2014}}{\text{Operation 1 budgeted product units for 2014}}\\ &= \frac{\$232{,}000}{20{,}000\text{ units}}\\ &= \$11.60\text{ per unit}\end{aligned}$$

The budgeted conversion costs of Operation 1 include labor, power, repairs, supplies, depreciation, and other overhead of this operation. If some units have not been completed (so all units in Operation 1 have not received the same amounts of conversion costs), the conversion-cost rate is computed by dividing the budgeted conversion costs by the *equivalent units* of the conversion costs, as in process costing.

As the company manufactures blazers, managers allocate the conversion costs to the work orders processed in Operation 1 by multiplying the $11.60 conversion cost per unit by the number of units processed. Conversion costs of Operation 1 for 50 wool blazers (Work Order 423) are $11.60 per blazer × 50 blazers = $580 and for 100 polyester blazers (Work Order 424) are $11.60 per blazer × 100 blazers = $1,160. When equivalent units are used to calculate the conversion-cost rate, costs are allocated to work orders by multiplying the conversion cost per equivalent unit by the number of equivalent units in the work order. The direct material costs of $6,000 for the 50 wool blazers (Work Order 423) and $3,000 for the 100 polyester blazers (Work Order 424) are specifically identified with each order, as in job costing. The basic point of operation costing is this: Operation unit costs are assumed to be the same regardless of the work order, but direct material costs vary across orders when the materials for each work order vary.

Journal Entries

The actual conversion costs for Operation 1 in March 2014—assumed to be $24,400, including the actual costs incurred for work order 423 and work order 424—are entered into a Conversion Costs Control account:

1. Conversion Costs Control	24,400	
Various accounts (such as Wages Payable Control and Accumulated Depreciation)		24,400

The summary journal entries for assigning the costs to polyester blazers (work order 424) follow. Entries for wool blazers would be similar. Of the $3,000 of direct materials for work order 424, $2,975 are used in Operation 1, and the remaining $25 of materials are used in another operation. The journal entry to record direct materials used for the 100 polyester blazers in March 2014 is as follows:

2. Work in Process, Operation 1	2,975	
Materials Inventory Control		2,975

The journal entry to record the allocation of conversion costs to products uses the budgeted rate of $11.60 per blazer times the 100 polyester blazers processed, or $1,160:

3. Work in Process, Operation 1	1,160	
Conversion Costs Allocated		1,160

The journal entry to record the transfer of the 100 polyester blazers (at a cost of $2,975 + $1,160) from Operation 1 to Operation 3 (polyester blazers do not go through Operation 2) is as follows:

4. Work in Process, Operation 3	4,135	
Work in Process, Operation 1		4,135

After posting these entries, the Work in Process, Operation 1, account appears as follows:

Work in Process, Operation 1

② Direct materials	2,975	④ Transferred to Operation 3	4,135
③ Conversion costs allocated	1,160		
Ending inventory, March 31	0		

The costs of the blazers are transferred through the operations in which blazers are worked on and then to finished goods in the usual manner. Costs are added throughout the fiscal year in the Conversion Costs Control account and the Conversion Costs Allocated account. Any overallocation or underallocation of conversion costs is disposed of in the same way as overallocated or underallocated manufacturing overhead in a job-costing system (see pages 127–132).

Decision Point

What is an operation-costing system and when is it a better approach to product costing?

Problem for Self-Study

Allied Chemicals operates a thermo-assembly process as the second of three processes at its plastics plant. Direct materials in thermo-assembly are added at the end of the process. Conversion costs are added evenly during the process. The following data pertain to the thermo-assembly department for June 2014:

	A	B	C	D	E
1		Physical Units	Transferred-In Costs	Direct Materials	Conversion Costs
2	Work in process, beginning inventory	50,000			
3	Degree of completion, beginning work in process		100%	0%	80%
4	Transferred in during current period	200,000			
5	Completed and transferred out during current period	210,000			
6	Work in process, ending inventory	?			
7	Degree of completion, ending work in process		100%	0%	40%

Required

Compute equivalent units under (1) the weighted-average method and (2) the FIFO method.

Solution

1. The weighted-average method uses equivalent units of work done to date to compute cost per equivalent unit. The calculations of equivalent units follow:

	A	B	C	D	E
1		(Step 1)	(Step 2)		
2			Equivalent Units		
3	Flow of Production	Physical Units	Transferred-In Costs	Direct Materials	Conversion Costs
4	Work in process, beginning (given)	50,000			
5	Transferred in during current period (given)	200,000			
6	To account for	250,000			
7	Completed and transferred out during current period	210,000	210,000	210,000	210,000
8	Work in process, ending[a]	40,000[b]			
9	(40,000 × 100%; 40,000 × 0%; 40,000 × 40%)		40,000	0	16,000
10	Accounted for	250,000			
11	Equivalent units of work done to date		250,000	210,000	226,000
12					
13	[a]Degree of completion in this department: transferred-in costs, 100%; direct materials, 0%; conversion costs, 40%.				
14	[b]250,000 physical units to account for minus 210,000 physical units completed and transferred out.				

2. The FIFO method uses equivalent units of work done in the current period only to compute cost per equivalent unit. The calculations of equivalent units follow:

	A	B	C	D	E
1		(Step 1)	(Step 2)		
2			Equivalent Units		
3	Flow of Production	Physical Units	Transferred-In Costs	Direct Materials	Conversion Costs
4	Work in process, beginning (given)	50,000			
5	Transferred in during current period (given)	200,000			
6	To account for	250,000			
7	Completed and transferred out during current period:				
8	From beginning work in process[a]	50,000			
9	[50,000 × (100% – 100%); 50,000 × (100% – 0%); 50,000 × (100% – 80%)]		0	50,000	10,000
10	Started and completed	160,000[b]			
11	(160,000 × 100%; 160,000 × 100%; 160,000 × 100%)		160,000	160,000	160,000
12	Work in process, ending[c]	40,000[d]			
13	(40,000 × 100%; 40,000 × 0%; 40,000 × 40%)		40,000	0	16,000
14	Accounted for	250,000			
15	Equivalent units of work done in current period		200,000	210,000	186,000
16					
17	[a]Degree of completion in this department: transferred-in costs, 100%; direct materials, 0%; conversion costs, 80%.				
18	[b]210,000 physical units completed and transferred out minus 50,000 physical units completed and transferred out from beginning work-in-process inventory.				
19	[c]Degree of completion in this department: transferred-in costs, 100%; direct materials, 0%; conversion costs, 40%.				
20	[d]250,000 physical units to account for minus 210,000 physical units completed and transferred out.				

Decision Points

The following question-and-answer format summarizes the chapter's learning objectives. Each decision presents a key question related to a learning objective. The guidelines are the answer to that question.

Decision	Guidelines
1. Under what conditions is a process-costing system used?	A process-costing system is used to determine cost of a product or service when masses of identical or similar units are produced. Industries using process-costing systems include the food, textiles, and oil-refining industries.
2. How are average unit costs computed when no inventories are present?	Average unit costs are computed by dividing the total costs in a given accounting period by the total units produced in that period.
3. What are the five steps in a process-costing system, and how are equivalent units calculated?	The five steps in a process-costing system are (1) summarize the flow of physical units of output, (2) compute the output in terms of equivalent units, (3) summarize the total costs to account for, (4) compute the cost per equivalent unit, and (5) assign the total costs to units completed and to units in ending work-in-process inventory. An equivalent unit is a derived measure of output that (a) takes the quantity of each input (factor of production) in units completed or in incomplete units in work in process and (b) converts the quantity of input into the amount of completed output units that could be made with that quantity of input.
4. What are the weighted-average and first-in, first-out (FIFO) methods of process costing? Under what conditions will they yield different levels of operating income?	The weighted-average method computes unit costs by dividing total costs in the Work in Process account by total equivalent units completed to date and assigns this average cost to units completed and to units in ending work-in-process inventory. The first-in, first-out (FIFO) method computes unit costs based on costs incurred during the current period and equivalent units of work done in the current period. Operating income can differ materially between the two methods when (1) direct material or conversion cost per equivalent unit varies significantly from period to period and (2) physical-inventory levels of work in process are large in relation to the total number of units transferred out of the process.
5. How are the weighted-average and FIFO process-costing methods applied to transferred-in costs?	The weighted-average method computes transferred-in costs per unit by dividing the total transferred-in costs to date by the total equivalent transferred-in units completed to date and assigns this average cost to units completed and to units in ending work-in-process inventory. The FIFO method computes the transferred-in costs per unit based on the costs transferred in during the current period and equivalent units of transferred-in costs of work done in the current period. The FIFO method assigns transferred-in costs in the beginning work-in-process inventory to units completed and costs transferred in during the current period first to complete the beginning inventory, next to start and complete new units, and finally to units in ending work-in-process inventory.
6. What is an operation-costing system, and when is it a better approach to product costing?	Operation costing is a hybrid-costing system that blends characteristics from both job-costing (for direct materials) and process-costing systems (for conversion costs). It is a better approach to product costing when production systems share some features of custom-order manufacturing and other features of mass-production manufacturing.

Appendix

Standard-Costing Method of Process Costing

Chapter 7 described accounting in a standard-costing system. Recall that this involves making entries using standard costs and then isolating variances from these standards in order to support management control. This appendix describes how the principles of standard costing can be employed in process-costing systems.

Benefits of Standard Costing

Companies that use process-costing systems produce masses of identical or similar units of output. In such companies, it is fairly easy to budget for the quantities of inputs needed to produce a unit of output. Standard cost per input unit can then be multiplied by input quantity standards to develop a standard cost per output unit.

The weighted-average and FIFO methods become very complicated when used in process industries, such as textiles, ceramics, paints, and packaged food, that produce a wide variety of similar products. For example, a steel-rolling mill uses various steel alloys and produces sheets of varying sizes and finishes. The different types of direct materials used and the operations performed are few, but used in various combinations, they yield a wide variety of products. In these cases, if the broad averaging procedure of *actual* process costing were used, the result would be inaccurate costs for each product. Therefore, managers in these industries typically use the standard-costing method of process costing.

Under the standard-costing method, teams of design and process engineers, operations personnel, and management accountants work together to determine *separate* standard costs per equivalent unit on the basis of different technical processing specifications for each product. Identifying standard costs for each product overcomes the disadvantage of costing all products at a single average amount, as under actual costing.

Computations Under Standard Costing

We return to the assembly department of Pacific Electronics, but this time we use standard costs. Assume the same standard costs apply in February and March 2014. Data for the assembly department are as follows:

	A	B	C	D	E
1		Physical Units (SG-40s) (1)	Direct Materials (2)	Conversion Costs (3)	Total Costs (4) = (2) + (3)
2	Standard cost per unit		$ 74	$ 54	
3	Work in process, beginning inventory (March 1)	225			
4	Degree of completion of beginning work in process		100%	60%	
5	Beginning work in process inventory at standard costs		$16,650[a]	$ 7,290[a]	$23,940
6	Started during March	275			
7	Completed and transferred out during March	400			
8	Work in process, ending inventory (March 31)	100			
9	Degree of completion of ending work in process		100%	50%	
10	Actual total costs added during March		$19,800	$16,380	$36,180
11					
12	[a]Work in process, beginning inventory at standard costs				
13	Direct materials: 225 physical units × 100% completed × $74 per unit = $16,650				
14	Conversion costs: 225 physical units × 60% completed × $54 per unit = $7,290				

We illustrate the standard-costing method of process costing using the five-step procedure introduced earlier (page 668).

Exhibit 17-12

Summarize the Flow of Physical Units and Compute Output in Equivalent Units Using the Standard-Costing Method for the Assembly Department for March 2014

	A	B	C	D
1		(Step 1)	(Step 2)	
2			Equivalent Units	
3	Flow of Production	Physical Units	Direct Materials	Conversion Costs
4	Work in process, beginning (given, p. 692)	225		
5	Started during current period (given, p. 692)	275		
6	To account for	500		
7	Completed and transferred out during current period:			
8	From beginning work in process[a]	225		
9	[225 × (100% – 100%); 225 × (100% – 60%)]		0	90
10	Started and completed	175[b]		
11	(175 × 100%; 175 × 100%)		175	175
12	Work in process, ending[c] (given, p. 692)	100		
13	(100 × 100%; 100 × 50%)		100	50
14	Accounted for	500		
15	Equivalent units of work done in current period		275	315
16				
17	[a]Degree of completion in this department: direct materials, 100%; conversion costs, 60%.			
18	[b]400 physical units completed and transferred out minus 225 physical units completed and transferred out from beginning work-in-process inventory.			
19	[c]Degree of completion in this department: direct materials, 100%; conversion costs, 50%.			

Exhibit 17-12 presents Steps 1 and 2. These steps are identical to the steps described for the FIFO method in Exhibit 17-6 because, as in FIFO, the standard-costing method also assumes that the earliest equivalent units in beginning work in process are completed first. Work done in the current period for direct materials is 275 equivalent units. Work done in the current period for conversion costs is 315 equivalent units.

Exhibit 17-13 describes Steps 3, 4, and 5. In Step 3, total costs to account for (that is, the total debits to Work in Process—Assembly) differ from total debits to Work in Process—Assembly under the actual-cost-based weighted-average and FIFO methods. That's because, as in all standard-costing systems, the debits to the Work in Process account are at standard costs, rather than actual costs. These standard costs total \$61,300 in Exhibit 17-13. In Step 4, costs per equivalent unit are standard costs: direct materials, \$74, and conversion costs, \$54. *Therefore, costs per equivalent unit do not have to be computed as they were for the weighted-average and FIFO methods.*

Exhibit 17-13, Step 5, assigns total costs to units completed and transferred out and to units in ending work-in-process inventory, as in the FIFO method. Step 5 assigns amounts of standard costs to equivalent units calculated in Exhibit 17-12. These costs are assigned (1) first to complete beginning work-in-process inventory, (2) next to start and complete new units, and (3) finally to start new units that are in ending work-in-process inventory. Note how the \$61,300 total costs accounted for in Step 5 of Exhibit 17-13 equal total costs to account for.

Accounting for Variances

Process-costing systems using standard costs record actual direct material costs in Direct Materials Control and actual conversion costs in Conversion Costs Control (similar to Variable and Fixed Overhead Control in Chapter 8). In the journal entries that follow, the first two record these *actual costs*. In entries 3 and 4a, the Work-in-Process—Assembly account accumulates direct material costs and conversion costs at *standard*

Exhibit 17-13 Summarize the Total Costs to Account For, Compute the Cost per Equivalent Unit, and Assign Costs to the Units Completed and Units in Ending Work-in-Process Inventory Using the Standard-Costing Method for the Assembly Department for March 2014

	A	B	C	D	E	F	G
1			Total Production Costs	Direct Materials		Conversion Costs	
2	(Step 3)	Work in process, beginning (given, p. 692)					
3		Direct materials, 225 × \$74; Conversion costs, 135 × \$54	\$23,940	\$16,650		\$ 7,290	
4		Costs added in current period at standard costs					
5		Direct materials, 275 × \$74; Conversion costs, 315 × \$54	37,360	20,350		17,010	
6		Total costs to account for	\$61,300	\$37,000		\$24,300	
7							
8	(Step 4)	Standard cost per equivalent unit (given, p. 692)		\$ 74		\$ 54	
9							
10	(Step 5)	Assignment of costs at standard costs:					
11		Completed and transferred out (400 units):					
12		Work in process, beginning (225 units)	\$23,940	\$16,650	+	\$ 7,290	
13		Costs added to beginning work in process in current period	4,860	(0[a] × \$74)	+	(90[a] × \$54)	
14		Total from beginning inventory	28,800				
15		Started and completed (175 units)	22,400	(175[b] × \$74)	+	(175[b] × \$54)	
16		Total costs of units completed and transferred out	51,200				
17		Work in process, ending (100 units):	10,100	(100[c] × \$74)	+	(50[c] × \$54)	
18		Total costs accounted for	\$61,300	\$37,000	+	\$24,300	
19							
20	Summary of variances for current performance:						
21	Costs added in current period at standard costs (see Step 3 above)			\$20,350		\$17,010	
22	Actual costs incurred (given, p. 692)			\$19,800		\$16,380	
23	Variance			\$ 550	F	\$ 630	F
24							
25	[a]Equivalent units used to complete beginning work in process from Exhibit 17-12, Step 2.						
26	[b]Equivalent units started and completed from Exhibit 17-12, Step 2.						
27	[c]Equivalent units in ending work in process from Exhibit 17-12, Step 2.						

costs. Entries 3 and 4b isolate total variances. The final entry transfers out completed goods at standard costs.

1. Assembly Department Direct Materials Control (at actual costs)	19,800	
Accounts Payable Control		19,800
To record the direct materials purchased and used in production during March. This cost control account is debited with actual costs.		
2. Assembly Department Conversion Costs Control (at actual costs)	16,380	
Various accounts such as Wages Payable Control and Accumulated Depreciation		16,380
To record the assembly department conversion costs for March. This cost control account is debited with actual costs.		
Entries 3, 4, and 5 use standard cost amounts from Exhibit 17-13.		
3. Work in Process—Assembly (at standard costs)	20,350	
Direct Materials Variances		550
Assembly Department Direct Materials Control		19,800
To record the standard costs of direct materials assigned to units worked on and total direct materials variances.		

		Debit	Credit
4a.	Work in Process—Assembly (at standard costs)	17,010	
	Assembly Department Conversion Costs Allocated		17,010
	To record the conversion costs allocated at standard rates to the units worked on during March.		
4b.	Assembly Department Conversion Costs Allocated	17,010	
	Conversion Costs Variances		630
	Assembly Department Conversion Costs Control		16,380
	To record the total conversion costs variances.		
5.	Work in Process—Testing (at standard costs)	51,200	
	Work in Process—Assembly (at standard costs)		51,200
	To record the standard costs of units completed and transferred out from assembly to testing.		

Variances arise under standard costing, as in entries 3 and 4b. That's because the standard costs assigned to products on the basis of work done in the current period do not equal actual costs incurred in the current period. Recall that variances that result in higher income than expected are termed favorable, while those that reduce income are unfavorable. From an accounting standpoint, favorable cost variances are credit entries, while unfavorable ones are debits. In the preceding example, both direct materials and conversion cost variances are favorable. This is also reflected in the "F" designations for both variances in Exhibit 17-13.

Variances can be analyzed in little or great detail for planning and control purposes, as described in Chapters 7 and 8. Sometimes direct materials price variances are isolated at the time direct materials are purchased and only efficiency variances are computed in entry 3. Exhibit 17-14 shows how the costs flow through the general-ledger accounts under standard costing.

Exhibit 17-14 Flow of Standard Costs in a Process-Costing System for the Assembly Department for March 2014

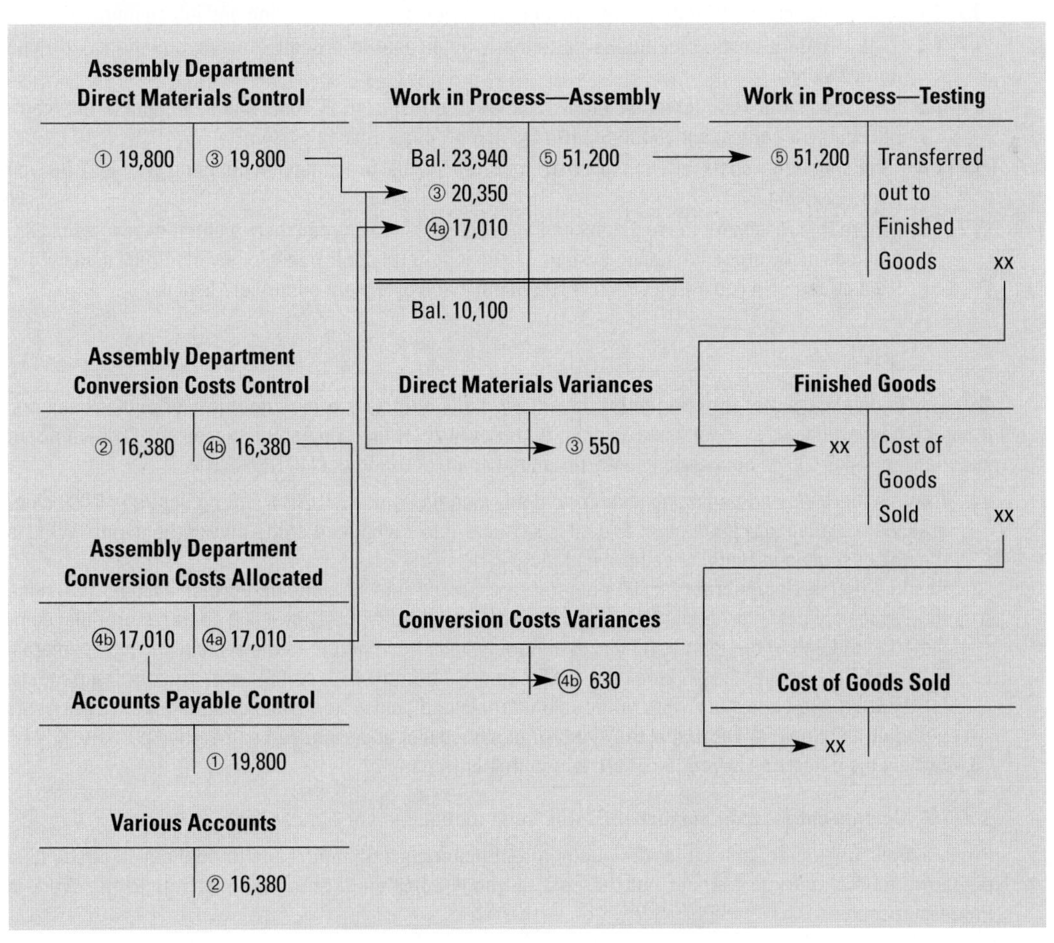

Terms to Learn

This chapter and the Glossary at the end of the book contain definitions of the following important terms:

equivalent units **(p. 668)**
first-in, first-out (FIFO) process-costing method **(p. 676)**
hybrid-costing system **(p. 685)**
operation **(p. 686)**
operation-costing system **(p. 686)**
previous-department costs **(p. 681)**
transferred-in costs **(p. 681)**
weighted-average process-costing method **(p. 673)**

Assignment Material

MyAccountingLab

Questions

17-1 Give three examples of industries that use process-costing systems.

17-2 In process costing, why are costs often divided into two main classifications?

17-3 Explain equivalent units. Why are equivalent-unit calculations necessary in process costing?

17-4 What problems might arise in estimating the degree of completion of semiconductor chips in a semiconductor plant?

17-5 Name the five steps in process costing when equivalent units are computed.

17-6 Name the three inventory methods commonly associated with process costing.

17-7 Describe the distinctive characteristic of weighted-average computations in assigning costs to units completed and to units in ending work in process.

17-8 Describe the distinctive characteristic of FIFO computations in assigning costs to units completed and to units in ending work in process.

17-9 Why should the FIFO method be called a modified or department FIFO method?

17-10 Identify a major advantage of the FIFO method for purposes of planning and control.

17-11 Identify the main difference between journal entries in process costing and job costing.

17-12 "The standard-costing method is particularly applicable to process-costing situations." Do you agree? Why?

17-13 Why should the accountant distinguish between transferred-in costs and additional direct material costs for each subsequent department in a process-costing system?

17-14 "Transferred-in costs are those costs incurred in the preceding accounting period." Do you agree? Explain.

17-15 "There's no reason for me to get excited about the choice between the weighted-average and FIFO methods in my process-costing system. I have long-term contracts with my materials suppliers at fixed prices." Do you agree with this statement made by a plant controller? Explain.

MyAccountingLab

Exercises

17-16 Equivalent units, zero beginning inventory. Candid, Inc., is a manufacturer of digital cameras. It has two departments: assembly and testing. In January 2014, the company incurred $800,000 on direct materials and $805,000 on conversion costs, for a total manufacturing cost of $1,605,000.

Required

1. Assume there was no beginning inventory of any kind on January 1, 2014. During January, 5,000 cameras were placed into production and all 5,000 were fully completed at the end of the month. What is the unit cost of an assembled camera in January?
2. Assume that during February 5,000 cameras are placed into production. Further assume the same total assembly costs for January are also incurred in February, but only 4,000 cameras are fully completed at the end of the month. All direct materials have been added to the remaining 1,000 cameras. However, on average, these remaining 1,000 cameras are only 60% complete as to conversion costs. (a) What are the equivalent units for direct materials and conversion costs and their respective costs per equivalent unit for February? (b) What is the unit cost of an assembled camera in February 2014?
3. Explain the difference in your answers to requirements 1 and 2.

17-17 Journal entries (continuation of 17-16). Refer to requirement 2 of Exercise 17-16.

Required

Prepare summary journal entries for the use of direct materials and incurrence of conversion costs. Also prepare a journal entry to transfer out the cost of goods completed. Show the postings to the Work in Process account.

17-18 Zero beginning inventory, materials introduced in middle of process. Pilar Chemicals has a mixing department and a refining department. Its process-costing system in the mixing department has two direct materials cost categories (chemical P and chemical Q) and one conversion costs pool. The following data pertain to the mixing department for July 2014:

Units	
Work in process, July 1	0
Units started	100,000
Completed and transferred to refining department	70,000
Costs	
Chemical P	$600,000
Chemical Q	140,000
Conversion costs	360,000

Chemical P is introduced at the start of operations in the mixing department, and chemical Q is added when the product is three-fourths completed in the mixing department. Conversion costs are added evenly during the process. The ending work in process in the mixing department is two-thirds complete.

Required

1. Compute the equivalent units in the mixing department for July 2014 for each cost category.
2. Compute (a) the cost of goods completed and transferred to the refining department during July and (b) the cost of work in process as of July 31, 2014.

17-19 Weighted-average method, equivalent units. The assembly division of Fenton Watches, Inc., uses the weighted-average method of process costing. Consider the following data for the month of May 2014:

	Physical Units (Watches)	Direct Materials	Conversion Costs
Beginning work in process (May 1)[a]	80	$ 493,360	$ 91,040
Started in May 2014	500		
Completed during May 2014	460		
Ending work in process (May 31)[b]	120		
Total costs added during May 2014		$3,220,000	$1,392,000

[a]Degree of completion: direct materials, 90%; conversion costs, 40%.
[b]Degree of completion: direct materials, 60%; conversion costs, 30%.

Required

Compute equivalent units for direct materials and conversion costs. Show physical units in the first column of your schedule.

17-20 Weighted-average method, assigning costs (continuation of 17-19).

Required

For the data in Exercise 17-19, summarize the total costs to account for, calculate the cost per equivalent unit for direct materials and conversion costs, and assign costs to the units completed (and transferred out) and units in ending work in process.

17-21 FIFO method, equivalent units. Refer to the information in Exercise 17-19. Suppose the assembly division at Fenton Watches, Inc., uses the FIFO method of process costing instead of the weighted-average method.

Required

Compute equivalent units for direct materials and conversion costs. Show physical units in the first column of your schedule.

17-22 FIFO method, assigning costs (continuation of 17-21).

Required

For the data in Exercise 17-19, use the FIFO method to summarize the total costs to account for, calculate the cost per equivalent unit for direct materials and conversion costs, and assign costs to units completed (and transferred out) and to units in ending work in process.

17-23 Operation costing. Whole Goodness Bakery needs to determine the cost of two work orders for the month of June. Work order 215 is for 2,400 packages of dinner rolls, and work order 216 is for 2,800 loaves of multigrain bread. Dinner rolls are mixed and cut into individual rolls before being baked and then packaged. Multigrain loaves are mixed and shaped before being baked, sliced, and packaged. The following information applies to work order 215 and work order 216:

	Work Order 215	Work Order 216
Quantity (packages)	2,400	2,800
Operations		
1. Mix	Use	Use
2. Shape loaves	Do not use	Use
3. Cut rolls	Use	Do not use
4. Bake	Use	Use
5. Slice loaves	Do not use	Use
6. Package	Use	Use

Selected budget information for June follows:

	Dinner Rolls	Multigrain Loaves	Total
Packages	9,600	13,000	22,600
Direct material costs	$5,280	$11,700	$ 16,980

Budgeted conversion costs for each operation for June follow:

Mixing	$18,080
Shaping	3,250
Cutting	1,440
Baking	14,690
Slicing	1,300
Packaging	16,950

Required

1. Using budgeted number of packages as the denominator, calculate the budgeted conversion-cost rates for each operation.
2. Using the information in requirement 1, calculate the budgeted cost of goods manufactured for the two June work orders.
3. Calculate the cost per package of dinner rolls and multigrain loaves for work order 215 and 216.

17-24 Weighted-average method, assigning costs. Tomlinson Corporation is a biotech company based in Milpitas. It makes a cancer-treatment drug in a single processing department. Direct materials are added at the start of the process. Conversion costs are added evenly during the process. Tomlinson uses the weighted-average method of process costing. The following information for July 2014 is available.

		Equivalent Units	
	Physical Units	Direct Materials	Conversion Costs
Work in process, July 1	8,700[a]	8,700	2,175
Started during July	34,500		
Completed and transferred out during July	32,000	32,000	32,000
Work in process, July 31	11,200[b]	11,200	7,840

[a]Degree of completion: direct materials, 100%; conversion costs, 25%.
[b]Degree of completion: direct materials, 100%; conversion costs, 70%.

Total Costs for July 2014		
Work in process, beginning		
Direct materials	$61,500	
Conversion costs	43,200	$104,700
Direct materials added during July		301,380
Conversion costs added during July		498,624
Total costs to account for		$904,704

1. Calculate the cost per equivalent unit for direct materials and conversion costs.
2. Summarize the total costs to account for, and assign them to units completed (and transferred out) and to units in ending work in process.

Required

17-25 FIFO method, assigning costs.

1. Do Exercise 17-24 using the FIFO method.
2. Tomlinson's management seeks to have a more consistent cost per equivalent unit. Which method of process costing should the company choose and why?

Required

17-26 Transferred-in costs, weighted-average method. Trendy Clothing, Inc., is a manufacturer of winter clothes. It has a knitting department and a finishing department. This exercise focuses on the finishing department. Direct materials are added at the end of the process. Conversion costs are added evenly during the process. Trendy uses the weighted-average method of process costing. The following information for June 2014 is available.

Home Insert Page Layout Formulas Data Review View

	A	B	C	D	E
1		Physical Units (tons)	Transferred-In Costs	Direct Materials	Conversion Costs
2	Work in process, beginning inventory (June 1)	60	$ 60,000	$ 0	$24,000
3	Degree of completion, beginning work in process		100%	0%	50%
4	Transferred in during June	100			
5	Completed and transferred out during June	120			
6	Work in process, ending inventory (June 30)	40			
7	Degree of completion, ending work in process		100%	0%	75%
8	Total costs added during June		$117,000	$27,000	$62,400

1. Calculate equivalent units of transferred-in costs, direct materials, and conversion costs.
2. Summarize the total costs to account for, and calculate the cost per equivalent unit for transferred-in costs, direct materials, and conversion costs.
3. Assign costs to units completed (and transferred out) and to units in ending work in process.

Required

17-27 Transferred-in costs, FIFO method. Refer to the information in Exercise 17-26. Suppose that Trendy uses the FIFO method instead of the weighted-average method in all of its departments. The only changes to Exercise 17-26 under the FIFO method are that total transferred-in costs of beginning work in process on June 1 are $45,000 (instead of $60,000) and total transferred-in costs added during June are $114,000 (instead of $117,000).

Do Exercise 17-26 using the FIFO method. Note that you first need to calculate equivalent units of work done in the current period (for transferred-in costs, direct materials, and conversion costs) to complete beginning work in process, to start and complete new units, and to produce ending work in process.

Required

17-28 Operation costing. Purex produces three different types of detergents: Breeze, Fresh, and Joy. The company uses four operations to manufacture the detergents: spray drying, mixing, blending, and packaging. Breeze and Fresh are produced in powder form in the mixing department, while Joy is produced in liquid form in the blending department. The powder detergents are packed in 50-ounce paperboard cartons, and the liquid detergent is packed in 50-ounce bottles made of recycled plastic.

Purex applies conversion costs based on labor-hours in the spray drying department. It takes 1½ minutes to mix the ingredients for a 50-ounce container for each product. Conversion costs are applied based on the number of containers in the mixing and blending departments and on the basis of machine-hours in the packaging department. It takes 0.3 minutes of machine time to fill a 50-ounce container, regardless of the product.

The budgeted number of containers and expected direct materials cost for each type of detergent are as follows:

	Breeze	Fresh	Joy
Number of 50-ounce containers	11,000	8,000	21,000
Direct materials cost	$21,450	$20,000	$52,500

The budgeted conversion costs for each department for July are as follows:

Department	Budgeted Conversion Cost
Spray Drying	$ 8,000
Mixing	22,800
Blending	30,450
Packaging	1,000

Required

1. Calculate the conversion cost rates for each department.
2. Calculate the budgeted cost of goods manufactured for Breeze, Fresh, and Joy for the month of July.
3. Calculate the cost per 50-ounce container for each type of detergent for the month of July.

17-29 Standard-costing with beginning and ending work in process. Priscilla's Pearls Company (PPC) is a manufacturer of knock-off jewelry. Priscilla attends Fashion Week in New York City every September and February to gauge the latest fashion trends in jewelry. She then makes jewelry at a fraction of the cost of those designers who participate in Fashion Week. This fall's biggest item is triple-stranded pearl necklaces. Because of her large volume, Priscilla uses process costing to account for her production. In October, she had started some of the triple strands. She continued to work on those in November. Costs and output figures are as follows:

Priscilla's Pearls Company Process Costing
For the Month Ended November 30, 2014

	Units	Direct Materials	Conversion Costs
Standard cost per unit		$ 2.40	$ 9.00
Work in process, beginning inventory (Nov. 1)	29,000	$ 69,600	$ 156,600
Degree of completion of beginning work in process		100%	60%
Started during November	124,200		
Completed and transferred out	127,000		
Work in process, ending inventory (Nov. 30)	26,200		
Degree of completion of ending work in process		100%	40%
Total costs added during November		$327,500	$1,222,000

Required

1. Compute equivalent units for direct materials and conversion costs. Show physical units in the first column of your schedule.
2. Compute the total standard costs of pearls transferred out in November and the total standard costs of the November 30 inventory of work in process.
3. Compute the total November variances for direct materials and conversion costs.

MyAccountingLab

Problems

17-30 Equivalent units, comprehensive. Louisville Sports manufactures baseball bats for use by players in the major leagues. A critical requirement for elite players is that each bat they use have an identical look and feel. As a result, Louisville uses a dedicated process to produce bats to each player's specifications.

One of Louisville's key clients is Ryan Brown of the Green Bay Brewers. Producing his bat involves the use of three materials—ash, cork, and ink—and a sequence of 20 standardized steps. Materials are added as follows:

Ash: This is the basic wood used in bats. Eighty percent of the ash content is added at the start of the process; the rest is added at the start of the 16th step of the process.

Cork: This is inserted into the bat in order to increase Ryan's bat speed. Half of the cork is introduced at the beginning of the seventh step of the process; the rest is added at the beginning of the 14th step.

Ink: This is used to stamp Ryan's name on the finished bat and is added at the end of the process.

Of the total conversion costs, 6% are added during each of the first 10 steps of the process, and 4% are added at each of the remaining 10 steps.

On May 1, 2014, Louisville had 100 bats in inventory. These bats had completed the ninth step of the process as of April 30, 2014. During May, Louisville put another 60 bats into production. At the end of May, Louisville was left with 40 bats that had completed the 12th step of the production process.

Required

1. Under the weighted-average method of process costing, compute equivalent units of work done for each relevant input for the month of May.
2. Under the FIFO method of process costing, compute equivalent units of work done for each relevant input for the month of May.

17-31 Weighted-average method. Larsen Company manufactures car seats in its San Antonio plant. Each car seat passes through the assembly department and the testing department. This problem focuses on the assembly department. The process-costing system at Larsen Company has a single direct-cost category (direct materials) and a single indirect-cost category (conversion costs). Direct materials are added at the beginning of the process. Conversion costs are added evenly during the process. When the assembly department finishes work on each car seat, it is immediately transferred to testing.

Larsen Company uses the weighted-average method of process costing. Data for the assembly department for October 2014 are as follows:

	Physical Units (Car Seats)	Direct Materials	Conversion Costs
Work in process, October 1[a]	5,000	$1,250,000	$ 402,750
Started during October 2014	20,000		
Completed during October 2014	22,500		
Work in process, October 31[b]	2,500		
Total costs added during October 2014		$4,500,000	$2,337,500

[a]Degree of completion: direct materials,?%; conversion costs, 60%.
[b]Degree of completion: direct materials,?%; conversion costs, 70%.

Required

1. For each cost category, compute equivalent units in the assembly department. Show physical units in the first column of your schedule.
2. What issues should the manager focus on when reviewing the equivalent units calculation?
3. For each cost category, summarize total assembly department costs for October 2014 and calculate the cost per equivalent unit.
4. Assign costs to units completed and transferred out and to units in ending work in process.

17-32 Journal entries (continuation of 17-31).

Required

Prepare a set of summarized journal entries for all October 2014 transactions affecting Work in Process—Assembly. Set up a T-account for Work in Process—Assembly and post your entries to it.

17-33 FIFO method (continuation of 17-31).

Required

1. Do Problem 17-31 using the FIFO method of process costing. Explain any difference between the cost per equivalent unit in the assembly department under the weighted-average method and the FIFO method.
2. Should Larsen's managers choose the weighted-average method or the FIFO method? Explain briefly.

17-34 Transferred-in costs, weighted-average method (related to 17-31 to 17-33). Larsen Company, as you know, is a manufacturer of car seats. Each car seat passes through the assembly department and testing department. This problem focuses on the testing department. Direct materials are added when the testing department process is 90% complete. Conversion costs are added evenly during the testing department's process. As work in assembly is completed, each unit is immediately transferred to testing. As each unit is completed in testing, it is immediately transferred to Finished Goods.

Larsen Company uses the weighted-average method of process costing. Data for the testing department for October 2014 are as follows:

	Physical Units (Car Seats)	Transferred-In Costs	Direct Materials	Conversion Costs
Work in process, October 1[a]	7,500	$2,932,500	$ 0	$ 835,460
Transferred in during October 2014	?			
Completed during October 2014	26,300			
Work in process, October 31[b]	3,700			
Total costs added during October 2014		$7,717,500	$9,704,700	$3,955,900

[a]Degree of completion: transferred-in costs,?%; direct materials,?%; conversion costs, 70%.
[b]Degree of completion: transferred-in costs,?%; direct materials,?%; conversion costs, 60%.

Required

1. What is the percentage of completion for (a) transferred-in costs and direct materials in beginning work-in-process inventory and (b) transferred-in costs and direct materials in ending work-in-process inventory?
2. For each cost category, compute equivalent units in the testing department. Show physical units in the first column of your schedule.
3. For each cost category, summarize total testing department costs for October 2014, calculate the cost per equivalent unit, and assign costs to units completed (and transferred out) and to units in ending work in process.
4. Prepare journal entries for October transfers from the assembly department to the testing department and from the testing department to Finished Goods.

17-35 Transferred-in costs, FIFO method (continuation of 17-34). Refer to the information in Problem 17-34. Suppose that Larsen Company uses the FIFO method instead of the weighted-average method in all of its departments. The only changes to Problem 17-34 under the FIFO method are that total transferred-in costs of beginning work in process on October 1 are $2,800,000 (instead of $2,932,500) and that total transferred-in costs added during October are $7,735,250 (instead of $7,717,500).

Required

Using the FIFO process-costing method, complete Problem 17-34.

17-36 Weighted-average method. McKnight Handcraft is a manufacturer of picture frames for large retailers. Every picture frame passes through two departments: the assembly department and the finishing department. This problem focuses on the assembly department. The process-costing system at McKnight has a single direct-cost category (direct materials) and a single indirect-cost category (conversion costs). Direct materials are added when the assembly department process is 10% complete. Conversion costs are added evenly during the assembly department's process.

McKnight uses the weighted-average method of process costing. Consider the following data for the assembly department in April 2014:

	Physical Unit (Frames)	Direct Materials	Conversion Costs
Work in process, April 1[a]	60	$ 1,530	$ 156
Started during April 2014	510		
Completed during April 2014	450		
Work in process, April 30[b]	120		
Total costs added during April 2014		$17,850	$11,544

[a]Degree of completion: direct materials, 100%; conversion costs, 40%.
[b]Degree of completion: direct materials, 100%; conversion costs, 15%.

Required

1. Summarize the total assembly department costs for April 2014, and assign them to units completed (and transferred out) and to units in ending work in process.
2. What issues should a manager focus on when reviewing the equivalent units calculation?

17-37 FIFO method (continuation of 17-36).

Required

1. Complete Problem 17-36 using the FIFO method of process costing.
2. If you did Problem 17-36, explain any difference between the cost of work completed and transferred out and the cost of ending work in process in the assembly department under the weighted-average method and the FIFO method. Should McKnight's managers choose the weighted-average method or the FIFO method? Explain briefly.

17-38 Transferred-in costs, weighted-average method. Publishers, Inc., has two departments: printing and binding. Each department has one direct-cost category (direct materials) and one indirect-cost category (conversion costs). This problem focuses on the binding department. Books that have undergone the printing process are immediately transferred to the binding department. Direct material is added when the binding process is 70% complete. Conversion costs are added evenly during binding operations. When those operations are done, the books are immediately transferred to Finished Goods. Publishers, Inc., uses the weighted-average method of process costing. The following is a summary of the April 2014 operations of the binding department.

	A	B	C	D	E
1		Physical Units (books)	Transferred-In Costs	Direct Materials	Conversion Costs
2	Beginning work in process	1,260	$ 39,060	$ 0	$16,380
3	Degree of completion, beginning work in process		100%	0%	50%
4	Transferred in during April 2014	2,880			
5	Completed and transferred out during April	3,240			
6	Ending work in process (April 30)	900			
7	Degree of completion, ending work in process		100%	0%	70%
8	Total costs added during April		$155,520	$28,188	$84,240

Required

1. Summarize total binding department costs for April 2014, and assign these costs to units completed (and transferred out) and to units in ending work in process.
2. Prepare journal entries for April transfers from the printing department to the binding department and from the binding department to Finished Goods.

17-39 Transferred-in costs, FIFO method. Refer to the information in Problem 17-38. Suppose that Publishers, Inc., uses the FIFO method instead of the weighted-average method in all of its departments. The only changes to Problem 17-38 under the FIFO method are that total transferred-in costs of beginning work in process on April 1 are $44,100 (instead of $39,060) and that total transferred-in costs added during April are $149,760 (instead of $155,520).

Required

1. Using the FIFO process-costing method, complete Problem 17-38.
2. If you did Problem 17-38, explain any difference between the cost of work completed and transferred out and the cost of ending work in process in the binding department under the weighted-average method and the FIFO method.

17-40 Transferred-in costs, weighted-average and FIFO methods. Portland Pale Ale, Inc., makes a variety of specialty beers at its main brewery in Oregon. Production of beer occurs in three main stages: mashing, boiling, and fermenting. Consider the fermenting department, where direct materials (bottles and other packaging) are added at the end of the process. Conversion costs are added evenly during the process.

Portland Pale Ale provides the following information related to its top-selling Gypsum Ale for the fermenting department for the month of July:

	Physical Units (Cases)	Transferred-In Costs	Direct Materials	Conversion Costs
Beginning work in process	2,500	$116,000	$ 0	$ 37,500
Transferred in during July from boiling department	10,000			
Completed during July	10,500			
Ending work in process, July 31	2,000			
Total costs added during July		$384,000	$110,775	$152,250

The units in beginning work in process are 25% complete for conversion costs, while the units in ending inventory are 50% complete for conversion costs.

Required

1. Using the weighted-average method, summarize the total fermenting department costs for July, and assign costs to units completed (and transferred out) and to units in ending work in process.
2. Assume that the FIFO method is used for the fermenting department. Under FIFO, the transferred-in costs for work-in-process beginning inventory in July are $115,680 (instead of $116,000 under the weighted-average method), and the transferred-in costs during July from the boiling department are $376,000 (instead of $384,000 under the weighted-average method). All other data are unchanged. Summarize the total fermenting department costs for July, and assign costs to units completed and transferred out and to units in ending work in process using the FIFO method.

17-41 Multiple processes or operations, costing. The Sedona Company is dedicated to making products that meet the needs of customers in a sustainable manner. Sedona is best known for its KLN water bottle, which is a BPA-free, dishwasher-safe, bubbly glass bottle in a soft silicone sleeve.

The production process consists of three basic operations. In the first operation, the glass is formed by remelting cullets (broken or refuse glass). In the second operation, the glass is assembled with the silicone gasket and sleeve. The resulting product is finished in the final operation with the addition of the polypropylene cap.

Consulting studies have indicated that of the total conversion costs required to complete a finished unit, the forming operation requires 60%, the assembly 30%, and the finishing 10%.

The following data are available for March 2014 (there is no opening inventory of any kind):

Cullets purchased	$67,500
Silicone purchased	$24,000
Polypropylene used	$ 6,000
Total conversion costs incurred	$68,850
Ending inventory, cullets	$ 4,500
Ending inventory, silicone	$ 3,000
Number of bottles completed and transferred	12,000
Inventory in process at the end of the month:	
Units formed but not assembled	4,000
Units assembled but not finished	2,000

Required

1. What is the cost per equivalent unit for conversion costs for KLN bottles in March 2014?
2. Compute the cost per equivalent unit with respect to each of the three materials: cullets, silicone, and polypropylene.
3. What is the cost of goods completed and transferred out?
4. What is the cost of goods formed but not assembled?
5. What is the cost of goods assembled but not finished?

17-42 Benchmarking, ethics. Amanda McNall is the corporate controller of Scott Quarry. Scott Quarry operates 12 rock-crushing plants in Scott County, Kentucky, that process huge chunks of limestone rock extracted from underground mines.

Given the competitive landscape for pricing, Scott's managers pay close attention to costs. Each plant uses a process-costing system, and at the end of every quarter, each plant manager submits a production report and a production-cost report. The production report includes the plant manager's estimate of the percentage of completion of the ending work in process as to direct materials and conversion costs, as well as the level of processed limestone inventory. McNall uses these estimates to compute the cost per equivalent unit of work done for each input for the quarter. Plants are ranked from 1 to 12, and the three plants with the lowest cost per equivalent unit for direct materials and conversion costs are each given a bonus and recognized in the company newsletter.

McNall has been pleased with the success of her benchmarking program. However, she has recently received anonymous emails that two plant managers have been manipulating their monthly estimates of percentage of completion in an attempt to obtain the bonus.

Required

1. Why and how might managers manipulate their monthly estimates of percentage of completion and level of inventory?
2. McNall's first reaction is to contact each plant controller and discuss the problem raised by the anonymous communications. Is that a good idea?
3. Assume that each plant controller's primary reporting responsibility is to the plant manager and that each plant controller receives the phone call from McNall mentioned in requirement 2. What is the ethical responsibility of each plant controller (a) to Amanda McNall and (b) to Scott Quarry in relation to the equivalent-unit and inventory information each plant provides?
4. How might McNall learn whether the data provided by particular plants are being manipulated?

17-43 Standard-costing method. Hi-sense Technologies produces stripped-down phones for sale to customers in frontier economies. The firm purchases used or obsolete models of specific smartphone models. It removes nonstandard applications, installs open source Android software, and unlocks the phone so it can operate on GSM networks. Hi-sense's most popular offering is the iZoom phone.

Given the importance of scaling and cost control for the success of its business model, Hi-sense uses a standard-costing system. The following information is available for the second quarter of 2014 (April 1–June 30):

Physical and Equivalent Units for iZoom
For the Second Quarter of 2014

		Equivalent Units	
	Physical Units	**Direct Materials**	**Conversion Costs**
Completion of beginning work in process	1,158,000	—	521,100
Started and completed	1,014,000	1,014,000	1,014,000
Work on ending work in process	2,180,400	2,180,400	1,308,240
Units to account for	4,352,400	3,194,400	2,843,340

	Costs
Cost of units completed from beginning work in process	$ 9,206,100
Cost of new units started and completed	8,061,300
Cost of units completed in the second quarter	17,267,400
Cost of ending work in process	14,630,484
Total costs accounted for	$31,897,884

Required

1. What are the completion percentages of iZoom phones in beginning work-in-process inventory with respect to the two inputs?
2. What are the completion percentages of iZoom phones in ending work-in-process inventory with respect to the two inputs?
3. What are the standard costs per unit for direct materials and conversion costs?
4. What is the total cost of work-in-process inventory as of April 1, 2014 (the start of the second quarter)?

18 Spoilage, Rework, and Scrap

Learning Objectives

1. Understand the definitions of spoilage, rework, and scrap
2. Identify the differences between normal and abnormal spoilage
3. Account for spoilage in process costing using the weighted-average method and the first-in, first-out (FIFO) method
4. Account for spoilage at various stages of completion in process costing
5. Account for spoilage in job costing
6. Account for rework in job costing
7. Account for scrap

When a product doesn't meet specification but is subsequently repaired and sold, it is called rework.

Firms try to minimize rework, as well as spoilage and scrap, during production. Why? Because higher-than-normal levels of spoilage and scrap can have a significant negative effect on a company's profits. Rework can also cause substantial production delays, as the following article about Boeing shows.

Rework and Delays on the Boeing Dreamliner[1]

In 2007, Boeing was scheduled to introduce its newest airplane, the Dreamliner 787. Engineered to be the most fuel-efficient commercial plane, the Dreamliner received more than 900 customer orders, making it the fastest-selling commercial airplane in history.

The first Dreamliner did not take flight, however, until late 2011. The design and assembly process was riddled with production snafus, parts shortages, and supply-chain bottlenecks. The Dreamliner was Boeing's first major attempt at giving suppliers and partners far-ranging responsibility for designing and building the wings, fuselage, and other critical components to be shipped to Boeing for final assembly. The problems continued after planes began rolling off the production line. In 2013, regulators grounded all 50 operational Dreamliners after batteries overheated on two separate aircraft—a Japan Airlines plane parked at the Boston airport and an All Nippon Airways jet forced to make an emergency landing in Japan.

The Boeing Dreamliner aircraft has required significant rework over the years. The company's engineers have redesigned structural flaws in the airplane's wings, repaired cracks in the composite materials used to construct the airplane, fixed faulty software, and reworked the plane's lithium-ion battery system. This rework has led to costly delays for Boeing. Many customers asked the company to compensate them for keeping less fuel-efficient planes in the air. Other customers canceled their orders. In 2012, Australia's Qantas Airways canceled an order for 35 airplanes and received $433 million from Boeing, which included returned deposits and compensation for delays. The company also lost an estimated $450 million in revenue

[1] *Sources:* "Boeing 787 Faces Limits on Extended Range," *CNBC.com* (March 27, 2013); "Dreamliner Ready for Phase II After Successful Test Flight," *Chicago Tribune* (March 26, 2013); Dominic Gates, "Boeing Dreamliner on Track, but Rework May Stretch to 2015," *Seattle Times* (November 26, 2012); Ross Kelly, "Qantas Deals New Blow to Boeing Dreamliner," *Wall Street Journal* (August 23, 2012); Peter Sanders, "At Boeing, Dreamliner Fix Turns Up New Glitch," *Wall Street Journal* (November 13, 2009); Karen West, "Boeing Has Much to Prove with 787," *MSNBC.com* (December 16, 2009).

and compensation payments to airlines while revamping the battery system. It appears that overall rework on the Dreamliner may stretch to 2015.

Like Boeing, companies are increasingly focused on improving the quality of, and reducing defects in, their products, services, and activities. A rate of defects regarded as normal in the past is no longer tolerable, and companies strive for ongoing improvements in quality. Firms in industries as varied as construction (Skanska), aeronautics (Lockheed Martin), product development software (Dassault Systemes), and specialty food (Tate & Lyle) have set zero-defects goals. In this chapter, we focus on three types of costs that arise as a result of defects—spoilage, rework, and scrap—and ways to account for them. We also describe how to determine (1) the cost of products, (2) cost of goods sold, and (3) inventory values when spoilage, rework, and scrap occur.

Defining Spoilage, Rework, and Scrap

Learning Objective 1

Understand the definitions of spoilage,

...unacceptable units of production

rework,

...unacceptable units of production subsequently repaired

and scrap

...leftover material

The following terms used in this chapter may seem familiar to you, but be sure you understand them in the context of management accounting.

Spoilage refers to units of production—whether fully or partially completed—that do not meet the specifications required by customers for good units and are discarded or sold at reduced prices. Some examples of spoilage are defective shirts, jeans, shoes, and carpeting sold as "seconds" and defective aluminum cans sold to aluminum manufacturers for remelting to produce other aluminum products.

Rework refers to units of production that do not meet the specifications required by customers but that are subsequently repaired and sold as good finished units. For example, defective units of products (such as smartphones, tablets, and laptops) detected during or after the production process but before the units are shipped to customers can sometimes be reworked and sold as good products.

Scrap is residual material that results from manufacturing a product. Examples are short lengths from woodworking operations, edges from plastic molding operations, and frayed cloth and end cuts from suit-making operations. Scrap can sometimes be sold for relatively small amounts. In that sense, scrap is similar to byproducts, which we studied in Chapter 16. The difference is that scrap arises as a residual from the manufacturing process and is not a product targeted for manufacture or sale by the firm.

A certain amount of spoilage, rework, or scrap is inherent in many production processes. For example, semiconductor manufacturing is so complex and delicate that some spoiled units are inevitable due to dust adhering to wafers in the wafer production process and crystal defects in the silicon substrate. Usually, the spoiled units cannot be reworked. In the manufacture of high-precision machine tools, spoiled units can be reworked to meet standards, but only at a considerable cost. And in the mining industry, companies process ore that contains varying amounts of valuable metals and rock. Some amount of rock, which is scrap, is inevitable.

Decision Point

What are spoilage, rework, and scrap?

Learning Objective 2

Identify the differences between normal spoilage

...spoilage inherent in an efficient production process

and abnormal spoilage

...spoilage that would not arise under efficient operation

Two Types of Spoilage

Accounting for spoilage includes determining the magnitude of spoilage costs and distinguishing between the costs of normal and abnormal spoilage.[2] To manage, control, and reduce spoilage costs, companies need to highlight them, not bury them as an unidentified part of the costs of good units manufactured.

To illustrate normal and abnormal spoilage, consider Mendoza Plastics, which uses plastic injection molding to make casings for the iMac desktop computer. In January 2014, Mendoza incurs costs of $3,075,000 to produce 20,500 units. Of these 20,500 units, 20,000 are good units and 500 are spoiled units. Mendoza has no beginning inventory and no ending inventory that month. Of the 500 spoiled units, 400 units are spoiled because the injection molding machines are unable to manufacture good casings 100% of the time. That is, these units are spoiled even though the machines were run carefully and efficiently. The remaining 100 units are spoiled because of machine breakdowns and operator errors.

Normal Spoilage

Normal spoilage is spoilage inherent in a particular production process. In particular, it arises even when the process is carried out in an efficient manner. The costs of normal spoilage are typically included as a component of the costs of good units manufactured because good units cannot be made without also making some defective units. For this reason, normal spoilage costs are inventoried, that is, they are included in the cost of the good units completed. The following calculations show how Mendoza Plastics accounts for the cost of the 400 units normal spoilage:

Manufacturing cost per unit, $3,075,000 ÷ 20,500 units = $150	
Manufacturing costs of good units alone, $150 per unit × 20,000 units	$3,000,000
Normal spoilage costs, $150 per unit × 400 units	60,000
Manufacturing costs of good units completed (includes normal spoilage)	$3,060,000

$$\text{Manufacturing cost per good unit} = \frac{\$3{,}060{,}000}{20{,}000 \text{ units}} = \$153$$

Normal spoilage rates are computed by dividing the units of normal spoilage by total *good units completed*, not total *actual units started* in production. At Mendoza Plastics, the normal spoilage rate is therefore computed as 400 ÷ 20,000 = 2%. There is a tradeoff between the speed of production and the normal spoilage rate. Managers make a conscious decision about how many units to produce per hour with the understanding that, at the chosen rate, a certain level of spoilage is unavoidable.

Abnormal Spoilage

Abnormal spoilage is spoilage that is not inherent in a particular production process and would not arise under efficient operating conditions. At Mendoza, the 100 units spoiled due to machine breakdowns and operator errors are abnormal spoilage. (If Mendoza had set 100% good units as its goal, then all 500 units of spoilage would be considered abnormal.) Abnormal spoilage is usually regarded as avoidable and controllable. Line operators and other plant personnel generally can decrease or eliminate abnormal spoilage by identifying the reasons for machine breakdowns, operator errors, and so forth, and by taking steps to prevent their recurrence. To highlight the effect of abnormal spoilage costs, companies calculate the units of abnormal spoilage and record the cost in the Loss from Abnormal Spoilage account, which appears as a separate line item in the income statement. That is, unlike normal spoilage, the costs of abnormal spoilage are not considered inventoriable and are written off as a period expense. At Mendoza, the loss from abnormal spoilage is $15,000 ($150 per unit × 100 units).

Decision Point

What is the distinction between normal and abnormal spoilage?

Issues about accounting for spoilage arise in both process-costing and job-costing systems. We discuss both instances next, beginning with spoilage when process costing is used.

[2] The helpful suggestions of Samuel Laimon, University of Saskatchewan, are gratefully acknowledged.

Spoilage in Process Costing Using Weighted-Average and FIFO

Learning Objective 3

Account for spoilage in process costing using the weighted-average method

...spoilage cost based on total costs and equivalent units completed to date

and the first-in, first-out (FIFO) method

...spoilage cost based on costs of current period and equivalent units of work done in current period

How do process-costing systems account for spoiled units? We have already said that units of abnormal spoilage should be counted and recorded separately in a Loss from Abnormal Spoilage account. But what about units of normal spoilage? The correct method is to count these units when computing both physical and equivalent output units in a process-costing system. The following example illustrates this approach.

Count All Spoilage

Example 1: Chipmakers, Inc., manufactures computer chips for television sets. All direct materials are added at the beginning of the production process. To highlight issues that arise with normal spoilage, we assume there's no beginning inventory and focus only on the direct materials costs. The following data are for May 2014.

	A	B	C
1		Physical Units	Direct Materials
2	Work in process, beginning inventory (May 1)	0	
3	Started during May	10,000	
4	Good units completed and transferred out during May	5,000	
5	Units spoiled (all normal spoilage)	1,000	
6	Work in process, ending inventory (May 31)	4,000	
7	Direct material costs added in May		$270,000

Spoilage is detected upon completion of the process and has zero net disposal value.

An **inspection point** is the stage of the production process at which products are examined to determine whether they are acceptable or unacceptable units. Spoilage is typically assumed to occur at the stage of completion where inspection takes place. As a result, the spoiled units in our example are assumed to be 100% complete for direct materials.

Exhibit 18-1 calculates and assigns the cost of the direct materials used to produce both good units and units of normal spoilage. Overall, Chipmakers generated 10,000 equivalent units of output: 5,000 equivalent units in good units completed (5,000 physical

Exhibit 18-1

Using Equivalent Units to Account for the Direct Materials Costs of Good and Spoiled Units for Chipmakers, Inc., for May 2014

	A	B
1		Approach Counting Spoiled Units When Computing Output in Equivalent Units
2	Costs to account for	$270,000
3	Divide by equivalent units of output	÷ 10,000
4	Cost per equivalent unit of output	$ 27
5	Assignment of costs:	
6	Good units completed (5,000 units × $27 per unit)	$135,000
7	Add normal spoilage (1,000 units × $27 per unit)	27,000
8	Total costs of good units completed and transferred out	162,000
9	Work in process, ending (4,000 units × $27 per unit)	108,000
10	Costs accounted for	$270,000

units × 100%), 4,000 units in ending work in process (4,000 physical units × 100%), and 1,000 equivalent units in normal spoilage (1,000 physical units × 100%). Given total direct material costs of $270,000 in May, this yields an equivalent-unit cost of $27. The total cost of good units completed and transferred out, which includes the cost of normal spoilage, is then $162,000 (6,000 equivalent units × $27). The ending work in process is assigned a cost of $108,000 (4,000 equivalent units × $27).

Notice that the 4,000 units in ending work in process are not assigned any of the costs of normal spoilage because they have not yet been inspected. Undoubtedly some of the units in ending work in process will be found to be spoiled after they are completed and inspected in the next accounting period. At that time, their costs will be assigned to the good units completed in that period. Notice too that Exhibit 18-1 delineates the cost of normal spoilage as $27,000. By highlighting the magnitude of this cost, the approach helps to focus management's attention on the potential economic benefits of reducing spoilage.

Five-Step Procedure for Process Costing with Spoilage

Example 2: Anzio Company manufactures a recycling container in its forming department. Direct materials are added at the beginning of the production process. Conversion costs are added evenly during the production process. Some units of this product are spoiled as a result of defects, which are detectable only upon inspection of finished units. Normally, spoiled units are 10% of the finished output of good units. That is, for every 10 good units produced, there is 1 unit of normal spoilage. Summary data for July 2014 are as follows:

Home Insert Page Layout Formulas Data Review View

	A	B	C	D	E
1		Physical Units (1)	Direct Materials (2)	Conversion Costs (3)	Total Costs (4) = (2) + (3)
2	Work in process, beginning inventory (July 1)	1,500	$12,000	$ 9,000	$ 21,000
3	Degree of completion of beginning work in process		100%	60%	
4	Started during July	8,500			
5	Good units completed and transferred out during July	7,000			
6	Work in process, ending inventory (July 31)	2,000			
7	Degree of completion of ending work in process		100%	50%	
8	Total costs added during July		$76,500	$89,100	$165,600
9	Normal spoilage as a percentage of good units	10%			
10	Degree of completion of normal spoilage		100%	100%	
11	Degree of completion of abnormal spoilage		100%	100%	

We can slightly modify the five-step procedure for process costing used in Chapter 17 to include the costs of Anzio Company's spoilage.

Step 1: **Summarize the Flow of Physical Units of Output.** Identify the number of units of both normal and abnormal spoilage.

$$\text{Total Spoilage} = \left(\text{Units in beginning work-in-process inventory} + \text{Units started}\right) - \left(\text{Good units completed and transferred out} + \text{Units in ending work-in-process inventory}\right)$$

$$= (1{,}500 + 8{,}500) - (7{,}000 + 2{,}000)$$

$$= 10{,}000 - 9{,}000$$

$$= 1{,}000 \text{ units}$$

Recall that Anzio Company's normal spoilage is 10% of good output. So, the number of units of normal spoilage equals 10% of the 7,000 units of *good* output, or 700 units. With this information, we can then calculate the number of units of abnormal spoilage:

$$\begin{aligned}\text{Abnormal spoilage} &= \text{Total spoilage} - \text{Normal spoilage}\\ &= 1{,}000 \text{ units} - 700 \text{ units}\\ &= 300 \text{ units}\end{aligned}$$

Step 2: **Compute the Output in Terms of Equivalent Units.** Managers compute the equivalent units for spoilage the same way they compute equivalent units for good units. All spoiled units are included in the computation of output units. Because Anzio's inspection point is at the completion of production, the same amount of work will have been done on each spoiled and each completed good unit.

Step 3: **Summarize the Total Costs to Account For.** The total costs to account for are all the costs debited to Work in Process. The details for this step are similar to Step 3 in Chapter 17.

Step 4: **Compute the Cost per Equivalent Unit.** This step is similar to Step 4 in Chapter 17.

Step 5: **Assign Costs to the Units Completed, Spoiled Units, and Units in Ending Work-in-Process Inventory.** This step now includes computing of the cost of spoiled units as well as the cost of good units.

We illustrate these five steps of process costing for the weighted-average and FIFO methods next. *The standard-costing method is illustrated in the appendix to this chapter.*

Weighted-Average Method and Spoilage

Exhibit 18-2, Panel A, presents Steps 1 and 2 to calculate the equivalent units of work done to date and includes calculations of equivalent units of normal and abnormal spoilage. Exhibit 18-2, Panel B, presents Steps 3, 4, and 5 (together called the production-cost worksheet).

In Step 3, managers summarize the total costs to account for. In Step 4, they calculate the cost per equivalent unit using the weighted-average method. Note how, for each cost category, the costs of beginning work in process and the costs of work done in the current period are totaled and divided by equivalent units of all work done to date to calculate the weighted-average cost per equivalent unit. In the final step, managers assign the total costs to completed units, normal and abnormal spoiled units, and ending inventory by multiplying the equivalent units calculated in Step 2 by the cost per equivalent unit calculated in Step 4. Also note that the $13,825 costs of normal spoilage are added to the costs of the good units completed and transferred out.

$$\begin{aligned}\text{Cost per good unit completed and transferred out of the process} &= \frac{\text{Total costs transferred out (including normal spoilage)}}{\text{Number of good units produced}}\\ &= \$152{,}075 \div 7{,}000 \text{ good units} = \$21.725 \text{ per good unit}\end{aligned}$$

This amount is not equal to $19.75 per good unit, the sum of the $8.85 cost per equivalent unit of direct materials plus the $10.90 cost per equivalent unit of conversion costs. That's because the cost per good unit equals the sum of the direct materials and conversion costs per equivalent unit, which is $19.75, plus a share of normal spoilage, $1.975 ($13,825 ÷ 7,000 good units), for a total of $21.725 per good unit. The $5,925 costs of abnormal spoilage are charged to the Loss from Abnormal Spoilage account and do not appear in the costs of good units.[3]

[3] The actual costs of spoilage (and rework) are often greater than the costs recorded in the accounting system because the opportunity costs of disruption of the production line, storage, and lost contribution margins are not recorded in accounting systems. Chapter 19 discusses these opportunity costs from the perspective of cost management.

Exhibit 18-2 Weighted-Average Method of Process Costing with Spoilage for the Forming Department for July 2014

PANEL A: Summarize the Flow of Physical Units and Compute Output in Equivalent Units

	A	B	C	D	E
1			(Step 1)	(Step 2)	
2				Equivalent Units	
3		Flow of Production	Physical Units	Direct Materials	Conversion Costs
4		Work in process, beginning (given, p. 710)	1,500		
5		Started during current period (given, p. 710)	8,500		
6		To account for	10,000		
7		Good units completed and transferred out during current period	7,000	7,000	7,000
8		Normal spoilage[a]	700		
9		(700 × 100%; 700 × 100%)		700	700
10		Abnormal spoilage[b]	300		
11		(300 × 100%; 300 × 100%)		300	300
12		Work in process, ending[c] (given, p. 710)	2,000		
13		(2,000 × 100%; 2,000 × 50%)		2,000	1,000
14		Accounted for	10,000		
15		Equivalent units of work done to date		10,000	9,000
16					
17	[a]Normal spoilage is 10% of good units transferred out: 10% × 7,000 = 700 units. Degree of completion of normal spoilage				
18	in this department: direct materials, 100%; conversion costs, 100%.				
19	[b]Abnormal spoilage = Total spoilage – Normal spoilage = 1,000 – 700 = 300 units. Degree of completion of abnormal spoilage				
20	in this department: direct materials, 100%; conversion costs, 100%.				
21	[c]Degree of completion in this department: direct materials, 100%; conversion costs, 50%.				

PANEL B: Summarize the Total Costs to Account For, Compute the Cost per Equivalent Unit, and Assign Costs to the Units Completed, Spoiled Units, and Units in Ending Work-in-Process Inventory

			Total Production Costs	Direct Materials		Conversion Costs
23						
24	(Step 3)	Work in process, beginning (given, p. 710)	$ 21,000	$12,000		$ 9,000
25		Costs added in current period (given, p. 710)	165,600	76,500		89,100
26		Total costs to account for	$186,600	$88,500		$98,100
27	(Step 4)	Costs incurred to date		$88,500		$98,100
28		Divide by equivalent units of work done to date (Panel A)		÷10,000		÷ 9,000
29		Cost per equivalent unit		$ 8.85		$ 10.90
30	(Step 5)	Assignment of costs:				
31		Good units completed and transferred out (7,000 units)				
32		Costs before adding normal spoilage	$138,250	(7,000[d] × $8.85)	+	(7,000[d] × $10.90)
33		Normal spoilage (700 units)	13,825	(700[d] × $8.85)	+	(700[d] × $10.90)
34	(A)	Total costs of good units completed and transferred out	152,075			
35	(B)	Abnormal spoilage (300 units)	5,925	(300[d] × $8.85)	+	(300[d] × $10.90)
36	(C)	Work in process, ending (2,000 units)	28,600	(2,000[d] × $8.85)	+	(1,000[d] × $10.90)
37	(A)+(B)+(C)	Total costs accounted for	$186,600	$88,500	+	$98,100
38						
39	[d]Equivalent units of direct materials and conversion costs calculated in Step 2 in Panel A.					

Exhibit 18-3 First-In, First-Out (FIFO) Method of Process Costing with Spoilage for the Forming Department for July 2014

PANEL A: Summarize the Flow of Physical Units and Compute Output in Equivalent Units

	A	B	C	D	E
1			(Step 1)	(Step 2)	
2				Equivalent Units	
3		Flow of Production	Physical Units	Direct Materials	Conversion Costs
4		Work in process, beginning (given, p. 710)	1,500		
5		Started during current period (given, p. 710)	8,500		
6		To account for	10,000		
7		Good units completed and transferred out during current period:			
8		From beginning work in process[a]	1,500		
9		[1,500 × (100% – 100%); 1,500 × (100% – 60%)]		0	600
10		Started and completed	5,500[b]		
11		(5,500 × 100%; 5,500 × 100%)		5,500	5,500
12		Normal spoilage[c]	700		
13		(700 × 100%; 700 × 100%)		700	700
14		Abnormal spoilage[d]	300		
15		(300 × 100%; 300 × 100%)		300	300
16		Work in process, ending[e] (given, p. 710)	2,000		
17		(2,000 × 100%; 2,000 × 50%)		2,000	1,000
18		Accounted for	10,000		
19		Equivalent units of work done in current period		8,500	8,100
20					
21	[a]Degree of completion in this department: direct materials, 100%; conversion costs, 60%.				
22	[b]7,000 physical units completed and transferred out minus 1,500 physical units completed and transferred out from beginning work-in-process inventory.				
23	[c]Normal spoilage is 10% of good units transferred out: 10% × 7,000 = 700 units. Degree of completion of normal spoilage in this department: direct materials, 100%; conversion costs, 100%.				
24	[d]Abnormal spoilage = Actual spoilage – Normal spoilage = 1,000 – 700 = 300 units. Degree of completion of abnormal spoilage in this department: direct materials, 100%; conversion costs, 100%.				
25	[e]Degree of completion in this department: direct materials, 100%; conversion costs, 50%.				

PANEL B: Summarize the Total Costs to Account For, Compute the Cost per Equivalent Unit, and Assign Costs to the Units Completed, Spoiled Units, and Units in Ending Work-in-Process Inventory

			Total Production Costs	Direct Materials		Conversion Costs
26						
27	(Step 3)	Work in process, beginning (given, p. 710)	$ 21,000	$12,000		$ 9,000
28		Costs added in current period (given, p. 710)	165,600	76,500		89,100
29		Total costs to account for	$186,600	$88,500		$98,100
30	(Step 4)	Costs added in current period		$76,500		$89,100
31		Divide by equivalent units of work done in current period (Panel A)		÷ 8,500		÷ 8,100
32		Cost per equivalent unit		$ 9.00		$ 11.00
33	(Step 5)	Assignment of costs:				
34		Good units completed and transferred out (7,000 units)				
35		Work in process, beginning (1,500 units)	$ 21,000	$12,000	+	$9,000
36		Costs added to beginning work in process in current period	6,600	(0[f] × $9)	+	(600[f] × $11)
37		Total from beginning inventory before normal spoilage	27,600			
38		Started and completed before normal spoilage (5,500 units)	110,000	(5,500[f] × $9)	+	(5,500[f] × $11)
39		Normal spoilage (700 units)	14,000	(700[f] × $9)	+	(700[f] × $11)
40	(A)	Total costs of good units completed and transferred out	151,600			
41	(B)	Abnormal spoilage (300 units)	6,000	(300[f] × $9)	+	(300[f] × $11)
42	(C)	Work in process, ending (2,000 units)	29,000	(2,000[f] × $9)	+	(1,000[f] × $11)
43	(A)+(B)+(C)	Total costs accounted for	$186,600	$88,500	+	$98,100
44						
45	[f]Equivalent units of direct materials and conversion costs calculated in Step 2 in Panel A.					

FIFO Method and Spoilage

Exhibit 18-3, Panel A, presents Steps 1 and 2 using the FIFO method, which focuses on equivalent units of work done in the current period. Exhibit 18-3, Panel B, presents Steps 3, 4, and 5. Note how when assigning costs, the FIFO method keeps the costs of the beginning work in process separate and distinct from the costs of the work done in the current period. All spoilage costs are assumed to be related to units completed during the period, using the unit costs of the current period.[4]

Chapter 17 highlighted taxes, performance evaluation, and accounting-based covenants as some of the elements managers must take into account when choosing between the FIFO and weighted-average methods. It also stressed the importance of making careful estimates of degrees of completion in order to avoid misstating operating income. All of these considerations apply equally well to the material in this chapter. In addition, a new issue that arises with spoilage is that of estimating the normal spoilage percentage in an unbiased manner. A supervisor who wishes to show better performance might categorize more of the spoilage as normal, thereby reducing the amount that must be written off against income as the loss from abnormal spoilage. Managers must stress the value of consistent and unbiased estimates of completion and normal spoilage percentages and drive home the importance of pursuing ethical actions and reporting the correct income figures, regardless of the short-term consequences of doing so.

Journal Entries

The information from Panel B in Exhibits 18-2 and 18-3 supports the following journal entries to transfer good units completed to finished goods and to recognize the loss from abnormal spoilage.

Decision Point

How do the weighted-average and FIFO methods of process costing calculate the costs of good units and spoilage?

	Weighted-Average		FIFO	
Finished Goods	152,075		151,600	
Work in Process—Forming		152,075		151,600
To record the transfer of good units completed in July.				
Loss from Abnormal Spoilage	5,925		6,000	
Work in Process—Forming		5,925		6,000
To record the abnormal spoilage detected in July.				

Learning Objective 4

Account for spoilage at various stages of completion in process costing

...spoilage costs vary based on the point at which inspection is carried out

Inspection Points and Allocating Costs of Normal Spoilage

Spoilage might occur at various stages of a production process, but it is typically detected only at one or more inspection points. The cost of spoiled units equals all costs incurred in producing them up to the point of inspection. When spoiled goods have a disposal value (for example, carpeting sold as "seconds"), we compute a net cost of the spoilage by deducting the disposal value from the costs of the spoiled goods.

The unit costs of normal and abnormal spoilage are the same when the two are detected at the same inspection point. This is the case in our Anzio Company example, where inspection occurs only upon completion of the units. However, situations may arise when abnormal spoilage is detected at a different point than normal spoilage. Consider shirt manufacturing. Normal spoilage in the form of defective shirts is identified upon inspection at the end of the production process. Now suppose a faulty machine causes many defective shirts to be produced at the halfway point of the production process. These defective shirts are abnormal spoilage and occur at a different point in the production process than normal spoilage. Then the per-unit cost of the abnormal spoilage, which is based on costs incurred up to the halfway point of the production process, differs from

[4] To simplify calculations under FIFO, spoiled units are accounted for as if they were started in the current period. Although some of the beginning work in process probably did spoil, all spoilage is treated as if it came from current production.

the per-unit cost of normal spoilage, which is based on costs incurred through the end of the production process.

The costs of abnormal spoilage are separately accounted for as losses of the accounting period in which they are detected. However, recall that normal spoilage costs are added to the costs of good units, which raises an additional issue: Should normal spoilage costs be allocated between completed units and ending work-in-process inventory? *The common approach is to presume that normal spoilage occurs at the inspection point in the production cycle and to allocate its cost over all units that have passed that point during the accounting period.*

Anzio Company inspects units only at the end of the production process. So, the units in ending work-in-process inventory are not assigned any costs of normal spoilage. Suppose Anzio were to inspect units at an earlier stage. Then, if the units in ending work in process have passed the inspection point, the costs of normal spoilage would be allocated to units in ending work in process as well as to completed units. For example, if the inspection point is at the halfway point of production, then any ending work in process that is at least 50% complete would be allocated a full measure of the normal spoilage costs, and those spoilage costs would be calculated on the basis of all costs incurred up to the inspection point. However, if the ending work-in-process inventory is less than 50% complete, no normal spoilage costs would be allocated to it.

To better understand these issues, assume Anzio Company inspects units at various stages in the production process. How does this affect the amount of normal and abnormal spoilage? As before, consider the forming department, and recall that direct materials are added at the start of production, whereas conversion costs are added evenly during the process.

Consider three different cases: Inspection occurs at (1) the 20%, (2) the 55%, or (3) the 100% completion stage. The last option is the one we have analyzed so far (see Exhibit 18-2). Assume that normal spoilage is 10% of the good units passing inspection. A total of 1,000 units are spoiled in all three cases. Normal spoilage is computed on the basis of the number of *good units* that pass the inspection point *during the current period*. The following data are for July 2014. Note how the number of units of normal and abnormal spoilage changes depending on when inspection occurs.

Home | Insert | Page Layout | Formulas | Data | Review | View

	A	B	C	D
1		**Physical Units: Stage of Completion at Which Inspection Occurs**		
2	**Flow of Production**	**20%**	**55%**	**100%**
3	Work in process, beginning[a]	1,500	1,500	1,500
4	Started during July	8,500	8,500	8,500
5	To account for	10,000	10,000	10,000
6	Good units completed and transferred out			
7	(10,000 – 1,000 spoiled – 2,000 ending)	7,000	7,000	7,000
8	Normal spoilage	750[c]	550[d]	700[e]
9	Abnormal spoilage (1,000 – normal spoilage)	250	450	300
10	Work in process, ending[b]	2,000	2,000	2,000
11	Accounted for	10,000	10,000	10,000
12				
13	[a]Degree of completion in this department: direct materials, 100%; conversion costs, 60%.			
14	[b]Degree of completion in this department: direct materials, 100%; conversion costs, 50%.			
15	[c]10% × (8,500 units started – 1,000 units spoiled), because only the units started passed the 20% completion			
16	inspection point in the current period. Beginning work in process is excluded from this calculation because,			
17	being 60% complete at the start of the period, it passed the inspection point in the previous period.			
18	[d]10% × (8,500 units started – 1,000 units spoiled – 2,000 units in ending work in process). Both beginning and			
19	ending work in process are excluded since neither was inspected this period.			
20	[e]10% × 7,000, because 7,000 units are fully completed and inspected in the current period.			

The following diagram shows the flow of physical units for July and illustrates the normal spoilage numbers in the table. Note that 7,000 good units are completed and transferred out—1,500 from beginning work in process and 5,500 started and completed during the period—while 2,000 units are in ending work in process.

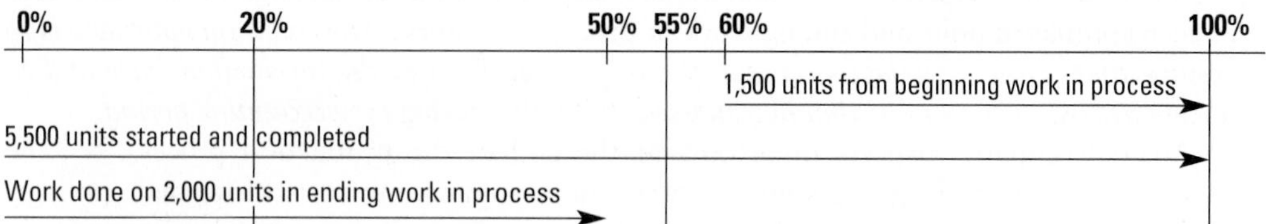

To see the number of units passing each inspection point, consider in the diagram the vertical lines at the 20%, 55%, and 100% inspection points. Note that the vertical line at 20% crosses two horizontal lines—5,500 good units started and completed and 2,000 units in ending work in process—for a total of 7,500 good units. (The 20% vertical line does not cross the line representing work done on the 1,500 good units completed from beginning work in process because these units are already 60% complete at the start of the period and, hence, are not inspected this period.) Normal spoilage equals 10% of 7,500 = 750 units. On the other hand, the vertical line at the 55% point crosses just the second horizontal line, indicating that only 5,500 good units pass this point. Normal spoilage in this case is 10% of 5,500 = 550 units. At the 100% point, the normal spoilage is 10% of 7,000 (1,500 + 5,500) good units = 700 units.

Exhibit 18-4 shows how equivalent units are computed under the weighted-average method if units are inspected at the 20% completion stage. The calculations depend on the direct materials and conversion costs incurred to get the units to this inspection point. The spoiled units have 100% of their direct materials costs and 20% of their conversion costs. Because the ending work-in-process inventory has passed the inspection point, these units are assigned the normal spoilage costs, just like the units that have been completed and transferred out. For example, the conversion costs of units completed and transferred out include the conversion costs for 7,000 good units produced plus

Exhibit 18-4

Computing Equivalent Units with Spoilage Using the Weighted-Average Method of Process Costing with Inspection at 20% of Completion for the Forming Department for July 2014

	A	B	C	D
1		(Step 1)	(Step 2)	
2			Equivalent Units	
3	Flow of Production	Physical Units	Direct Materials	Conversion Costs
4	Work in process, beginning[a]	1,500		
5	Started during current period	8,500		
6	To account for	10,000		
7	Good units completed and transferred out:	7,000	7,000	7,000
8	Normal spoilage	750		
9	(750 × 100%; 750 × 20%)		750	150
10	Abnormal spoilage	250		
11	(250 × 100%; 250 × 20%)		250	50
12	Work in process, ending[b]	2,000		
13	(2,000 × 100%; 2,000 × 50%)		2,000	1,000
14	Accounted for	10,000		
15	Equivalent units of work done to date		10,000	8,200
16				
17	[a]Degree of completion: direct materials, 100%; conversion costs, 60%.			
18	[b]Degree of completion: direct materials, 100%; conversion costs, 50%.			

20% × (10% × 5,500) = 110 equivalent units of normal spoilage. *We multiply by 20% to obtain the equivalent units of normal spoilage because the conversion costs are only 20% complete at the inspection point.* The conversion costs of the ending work-in-process inventory include the conversion costs of 50% of 2,000 = 1,000 equivalent good units plus 20% × (10% × 2,000) = 40 equivalent units of normal spoilage. Thus, the equivalent units of normal spoilage accounted for are 110 equivalent units related to the units completed and transferred out plus 40 equivalent units related to the units in ending work in process, for a total of 150 equivalent units, as Exhibit 18-4 shows.

Early inspections can help prevent any further costs being wasted on units that are already spoiled. For example, suppose the units can be inspected when they are 70% complete rather than 100% complete. If the spoilage occurs prior to the 70% point, a company can avoid incurring the final 30% of conversion costs on the spoiled units. While not applicable in the Anzio example, more generally a company can also save on the packaging or other direct materials that are added after the 70% stage. The downside to conducting inspections at too early a stage is that units spoiled at later stages of the process may go undetected. It is for these reasons that firms often conduct multiple inspections and also empower workers to identify and resolve defects on a timely basis.

Decision Point

How does inspection at various stages of completion affect the amount of normal and abnormal spoilage?

Job Costing and Spoilage

Learning Objective 5

Account for spoilage in job costing

...normal spoilage assigned directly or indirectly to job; abnormal spoilage written off as a loss of the period

The concepts of normal and abnormal spoilage also apply to job-costing systems. Companies attempt to identify abnormal spoilage separately so they can work to eliminate it altogether. The costs of abnormal spoilage are not considered to be inventoriable costs and are written off as costs of the accounting period in which the abnormal spoilage is detected. Normal spoilage costs in job-costing systems—as in process-costing systems—are inventoriable costs, although increasingly companies are tolerating only small amounts of spoilage as normal. When assigning costs, job-costing systems generally distinguish *normal spoilage attributable to a specific job from normal spoilage common to all jobs.*

We describe accounting for spoilage in job costing using the following example.

Example 3: In the Hull Machine Shop, 5 aircraft parts out of a job lot of 50 aircraft parts are spoiled. The costs assigned prior to the inspection point are $2,000 per part. When the spoilage is detected, the spoiled goods are inventoried at $600 per part, the net disposal value.

Our presentation here and in subsequent sections focuses on how the $2,000 cost per part is accounted for.

Normal Spoilage Attributable to a Specific Job

When normal spoilage occurs because of the specifications of a particular job, that job bears the cost of the spoilage minus the disposal value of the spoilage. The journal entry to recognize the disposal value is as follows (items in parentheses indicate subsidiary ledger postings):

Materials Control (spoiled goods at current net disposal value): 5 units × $600 per unit	3,000	
Work-in-Process Control (specific job): 5 units × $600 per unit		3,000

Note that the Work-in-Process Control (for the specific job) has already been debited (charged) $10,000 for the spoiled parts (5 spoiled parts × $2,000 per part). So, the net cost of the normal spoilage is $7,000 ($10,000 − $3,000), which is an additional cost of the 45 (50 − 5) good units produced. Therefore, total cost of the 45 good units is $97,000: $90,000 (45 units × $2,000 per unit) incurred to produce the good units plus the $7,000 net cost of normal spoilage. Cost per good unit is $2,155.56 ($97,000 ÷ 45 good units).

Normal Spoilage Common to All Jobs

In some cases, spoilage may be considered a normal characteristic of the production process. The spoilage inherent in production will, of course, occur when a specific job is being worked on. However, the spoilage is not attributable to, and hence is not charged directly to, the specific job. Instead, the spoilage is allocated indirectly to the job as manufacturing overhead because the spoilage is common to all jobs. The journal entry is as follows:

Materials Control (spoiled goods at current disposal value): 5 units × \$600 per unit	3,000	
Manufacturing Overhead Control (normal spoilage): (\$10,000 − \$3,000)	7,000	
Work-in-Process Control (specific job): 5 units × \$2,000 per unit		10,000

When normal spoilage is common to all jobs, the budgeted manufacturing overhead rate includes a provision for the normal spoilage cost. The normal spoilage cost is spread, through overhead allocation, over all jobs rather than being allocated to a specific job.[5] For example, if Hull produced 140 good units from all jobs in a given month, the \$7,000 of normal spoilage overhead costs would be allocated at the rate of \$50 per good unit (\$7,000 ÷ 140 good units). Normal spoilage overhead costs allocated to the 45 good units in the job would be \$2,250 (\$50 × 45 good units). The total cost of the 45 good units is \$92,250: \$90,000 (45 units × \$2,000 per unit) incurred to produce the good units plus \$2,250 of normal spoilage overhead costs. The cost per good unit is \$2,050 (\$92,250 ÷ 45 good units).

Abnormal Spoilage

If the spoilage is abnormal, the net loss is charged to the Loss from Abnormal Spoilage account. Unlike normal spoilage costs, abnormal spoilage costs are not included as a part of the cost of good units produced. The total cost of the 45 good units is \$90,000 (45 units × \$2,000 per unit). The cost per good unit is \$2,000 (\$90,000 ÷ 45 good units).

Materials Control (spoiled goods at current disposal value): 5 units × \$600 per unit	3,000	
Loss from Abnormal Spoilage (\$10,000 − \$3,000)	7,000	
Work-in-Process Control (specific job): 5 units × \$2,000 per unit		10,000

Even though, for external reporting purposes, abnormal spoilage costs are written off in the accounting period and are not linked to specific jobs or units, companies often identify the particular reasons for the abnormal spoilage and, when appropriate, link it with specific jobs or units for cost management purposes.

The accounting treatment described above highlights the potential impact of misclassifying the nature of the spoilage. Normal spoilage costs are inventoriable and are added to the cost of good units produced, while abnormal spoilage costs are expensed in the accounting period in which they occur. So, when inventories are present, classifying spoilage as normal rather than abnormal results in an increase in current operating income. In the above example, if the 45 parts remain unsold at the end of the period, such misclassification would boost income for that period by \$7,000. As with our discussion of completion percentages, it is important for managers to verify that spoilage rates and spoilage categories are not manipulated by department supervisors for short-term benefits.

Decision Point

How do job-costing systems account for spoilage?

Learning Objective 6

Account for rework in job costing

. . . normal rework assigned directly or indirectly to job; abnormal rework written off as a loss of the period

Job Costing and Rework

Rework refers to units of production that are inspected, determined to be unacceptable, repaired, and sold as acceptable finished goods. We again distinguish (1) normal rework attributable to a specific job, (2) normal rework common to all jobs, and (3) abnormal rework.

[5] Note that costs already assigned to products are charged back to Manufacturing Overhead Control, which generally accumulates only costs incurred, not both costs incurred and costs already assigned.

Consider the Hull Machine Shop data in Example 3 on page 717. Assume the five spoiled parts are reworked. The journal entry for the $10,000 of total costs (the details of these costs are assumed) assigned to the five spoiled units before considering rework costs is as follows:

Work-in-Process Control (specific job)	10,000	
Materials Control		4,000
Wages Payable Control		4,000
Manufacturing Overhead Allocated		2,000

Assume the rework costs equal $3,800 ($800 in direct materials, $2,000 in direct manufacturing labor, and $1,000 in manufacturing overhead).

Normal Rework Attributable to a Specific Job

If the rework is normal but occurs because of the requirements of a specific job, the rework costs are charged to that job. The journal entry is as follows:

Work-in-Process Control (specific job)	3,800	
Materials Control		800
Wages Payable Control		2,000
Manufacturing Overhead Allocated		1,000

Normal Rework Common to All Jobs

The costs of the rework when it is normal and not attributable to a specific job are charged to manufacturing overhead and are spread, through overhead allocation, over all jobs.

Manufacturing Overhead Control (rework costs)	3,800	
Materials Control		800
Wages Payable Control		2,000
Manufacturing Overhead Allocated		1,000

Abnormal Rework

If the rework is abnormal, it is charged to a loss account.

Loss from Abnormal Rework	3,800	
Materials Control		800
Wages Payable Control		2,000
Manufacturing Overhead Allocated		1,000

Accounting for rework in a process-costing system also requires abnormal rework to be distinguished from normal rework. Process costing accounts for abnormal rework in the same way as job costing. Accounting for normal rework follows the accounting described for normal rework common to all jobs (units) because masses of identical or similar units are being manufactured.

Costing rework focuses managers' attention on the resources wasted on activities that would not have to be undertaken if the product had been made correctly. The cost of rework prompts managers to seek ways to reduce rework, for example, by designing new products or processes, training workers, or investing in new machines. To eliminate rework and to simplify the accounting, some companies set a standard of zero rework. All rework is then treated as abnormal and is written off as a cost of the current period.

Decision Point

How do job-costing systems account for rework?

Learning Objective 7

Account for scrap

...reduces cost of job either at time of sale or at time of production

Accounting for Scrap

Scrap is residual material that results from manufacturing a product; it has low total sales value compared with the total sales value of the product. No distinction is made between normal and abnormal scrap because no cost is assigned to scrap. The only distinction made is between scrap attributable to a specific job and scrap common to all jobs.

There are two aspects of accounting for scrap:

1. Planning and control, including physical tracking
2. Inventory costing, including when and how scrap affects operating income

Initial entries to scrap records are commonly expressed in physical terms. In various industries, companies quantify items such as stamped-out metal sheets or edges of molded plastic parts by weighing, counting, or some other measure. Scrap records not only help measure efficiency, but also help keep track of scrap, and so reduce the chances of theft. Companies use scrap records to prepare periodic summaries of the amounts of actual scrap compared with budgeted or standard amounts. Scrap is either sold or disposed of quickly or it is stored for later sale, disposal, or reuse.

To carefully track their scrap, many companies maintain a distinct account for scrap costs somewhere in their accounting system. The issues here are similar to the issues in Chapter 16 regarding the accounting for byproducts:

- When should the value of scrap be recognized in the accounting records—at the time scrap is produced or at the time scrap is sold?
- How should the revenues from scrap be accounted for?

To illustrate, we extend our Hull example. Assume the manufacture of aircraft parts generates scrap and that the scrap from a job has a net sales value of $900.

Recognizing Scrap at the Time of Its Sale

When the dollar amount of the scrap is immaterial, it is simplest to record the physical quantity of scrap returned to the storeroom and to regard the revenues from the sale of scrap as a separate line item in the income statement. The only journal entry is as follows:

Sale of scrap:	Cash or Accounts Receivable	900	
	Scrap Revenues		900

When the dollar amount of the scrap is material and it is sold quickly after it is produced, the accounting depends on whether the scrap is attributable to a specific job or is common to all jobs.

Scrap Attributable to a Specific Job

Job-costing systems sometimes trace scrap revenues to the jobs that yielded the scrap. This method is used only when the tracing can be done in an economically feasible way. For example, the Hull Machine Shop and its customers, such as the U.S. Department of Defense, may reach an agreement that provides for charging specific jobs with all rework or spoilage costs and then crediting these jobs with all scrap revenues that arise from the jobs. The journal entry is as follows:

Scrap returned to storeroom:	No journal entry.		
	[Notation of quantity received and related job entered in the inventory record]		
Sale of scrap:	Cash or Accounts Receivable	900	
	Work-in-Process Control		900
	Posting made to specific job cost record.		

Unlike spoilage and rework, there is no cost assigned to the scrap, so no distinction is made between normal and abnormal scrap. All scrap revenues, whatever the amount, are credited to the specific job. Scrap revenues reduce the costs of the job.

Scrap Common to All Jobs

The journal entry in this case is as follows:

Scrap returned to storeroom:	No journal entry. [Notation of quantity received and related job entered in the inventory record]		
Sale of scrap:	Cash or Accounts Receivable	900	
	Manufacturing Overhead Control		900
	Posting made to subsidiary ledger—"Sales of Scrap" column on department cost record.		

Because the scrap is not linked with any particular job or product, all products bear its costs without any credit for scrap revenues except in an indirect manner: the expected scrap revenues are considered when setting the budgeted manufacturing overhead rate. Thus, the budgeted overhead rate is lower than it would be otherwise. This method of accounting for scrap is also used in process costing when the dollar amount of scrap is immaterial because the scrap in process costing is common to the manufacture of all the identical or similar units produced (and cannot be identified with specific units).

Recognizing Scrap at the Time of Its Production

Our preceding illustrations assume that scrap returned to the storeroom is sold quickly, so it is not assigned an inventory cost figure. Sometimes, as in the case with edges of molded plastic parts, the value of the scrap is not immaterial, and the time between storing it and selling or reusing it can be long and unpredictable. In these situations, the company assigns an inventory cost to scrap at a conservative estimate of its net realizable value so that production costs and related scrap revenues are recognized in the same accounting period. Some companies tend to delay selling scrap until its market price is attractive. Volatile price fluctuations are typical for scrap metal. In these cases, it's not easy to determine a "reasonable inventory value."

Scrap Attributable to a Specific Job

The journal entry in the Hull example is as follows:

Scrap returned to storeroom:	Materials Control	900	
	Work-in-Process Control		900

Scrap Common to All Jobs

The journal entry in this case is as follows:

Scrap returned to storeroom:	Materials Control	900	
	Manufacturing Overhead Control		900

Notice that the Materials Control account is debited in place of Cash or Accounts Receivable. When the scrap is sold, the journal entry is as follows:

Sale of scrap:	Cash or Accounts Receivable	900	
	Materials Control		900

Scrap is sometimes reused as direct material rather than sold as scrap. In this case, Materials Control is debited at its estimated net realizable value and then credited when the scrap is reused. For example, the entries when the scrap is common to all jobs are as follows:

Scrap returned to storeroom:	Materials Control	900	
	Manufacturing Overhead Control		900
Reuse of scrap:	Work-in-Process Control	900	
	Materials Control		900

Concepts in Action

American Apparel Turns Scrap into a Product for Sale

American Apparel is unique among clothing manufacturers in many ways. Known for its cutting-edge (and controversial!) advertising and product branding, the company employs a vertically integrated business model—American Apparel is its own manufacturer, wholesaler, and retailer, which minimizes the use of subcontractors. Knitting, dyeing, sewing, photography, marketing, distribution, and design all happen in the company's facilities in Los Angeles. American Apparel is also strongly committed to sustainability, with a goal of creating as little waste as it can.

One key way American Apparel reduces waste is by minimizing scrap, the residual material that results from manufacturing the company's clothing. As much as possible, the company minimizes the gaps between pattern pieces of cloth when cutting garments. Clothing styles are ranked by efficiency. For inefficient styles, American Apparel tries to find complementary styles that, when cut together, drastically reduce the amount of scrap generated. When the company has exhausted efficiency from the use of existing patterns, it turns much of the remaining material into yarn for new garments and, when possible, into smaller accessories. From these pattern gaps, American Apparel created its "Creative Reuse" line featuring 45 different items including scrunchies, hair bows, undergarments, and other accessories, with new products added regularly.

At this point, any scrap left over is...sold to American Apparel customers! In 2010, the company introduced its Bag-O-Scraps, a bag of scraps that sells for $8, along with a page of project suggestions. Overall, along with the traditional recycling of cutting and fiber scraps that are not reusable, American Apparel keeps more than 30,000 pounds of cotton cuttings per week out of landfills, or more than 1 million pounds annually.

Sources: Tice, Carol. 2010. American Apparel tries spinning straw into gold, sells scraps as econ-clothes. *CBS News*, May 11; American Apparel Inc., "Vertical Integration: Sustainability," http://www.americanapparel.net/verticalintegration/sustainability.html, accessed July 2013; "American Apparel takes environmental stand by recycling over 1 million pounds of cotton cuttings per year," American Apparel Inc. press release (Los Angeles, CA, August 13, 2002).

Accounting for scrap under process costing is similar to accounting under job costing when scrap is common to all jobs. That's because the scrap in process costing is common to the manufacture of masses of identical or similar units.

Managers focus their attention on ways to reduce scrap and to use it more profitably, especially when the cost of scrap is high. For example, General Motors has redesigned its plastic injection molding processes to reduce the scrap plastic that must be broken away from its molded products. General Motors also regrinds and reuses the plastic scrap as direct material, saving substantial input costs. Concepts in Action: American Apparel Turns Scrap into a Product for Sale shows how a firm that is deeply committed to principles of environmental sustainability minimizes the waste and scrap from its processes.

Decision Point

How is scrap accounted for?

Problem for Self-Study

Burlington Textiles has some spoiled goods that had an assigned cost of $40,000 and zero net disposal value.

Required

Prepare a journal entry for each of the following conditions under (a) process costing (department A) and (b) job costing:

1. Abnormal spoilage of $40,000
2. Normal spoilage of $40,000 regarded as common to all operations
3. Normal spoilage of $40,000 regarded as attributable to specifications of a particular job

Solution

	(a) Process Costing			(b) Job Costing		
1.	Loss from Abnormal Spoilage	40,000		Loss from Abnormal Spoilage	40,000	
	Work in Process—Dept. A		40,000	Work-in-Process Control (specific job)		40,000
2.	No entry until units are completed and transferred out. Then the normal spoilage costs are transferred as part of the cost of good units.			Manufacturing Overhead Control	40,000	
				Work-in-Process Control (specific job)		40,000
	Work in Process—Dept. B	40,000				
	Work in Process—Dept. A		40,000			
3.	Not applicable			No entry. Normal spoilage cost remains in Work-in-Process Control (specific job)		

▶ Decision Points

The following question-and-answer format summarizes the chapter's learning objectives. Each decision presents a key question related to a learning objective. The guidelines are the answer to that question.

Decision	Guidelines
1. What are spoilage, rework, and scrap?	Spoilage refers to units of production that do not meet the specifications required by customers for good units and that are discarded or sold at reduced prices. Spoilage is generally divided into normal spoilage, which is inherent to a particular production process, and abnormal spoilage, which arises because of operational inefficiency. Rework refers to unacceptable units that are subsequently repaired and sold as acceptable finished goods. Scrap is residual material that results from manufacturing a product; it has low total sales value compared with the total sales value of the product.
2. What is the distinction between normal and abnormal spoilage?	Normal spoilage is inherent in a particular production process and arises when the process is done in an efficient manner. Abnormal spoilage, on the other hand, is not inherent in a particular production process and would not arise under efficient operating conditions. Abnormal spoilage is usually regarded as avoidable and controllable.
3. How do the weighted-average and FIFO methods of process costing calculate the costs of good units and spoilage?	The weighted-average method combines the costs of beginning inventory with the costs of the current period when determining the costs of good units, which include normal spoilage, and the costs of abnormal spoilage, which are written off as a loss of the accounting period.

Decision	Guidelines
	The FIFO method keeps the costs of beginning inventory separate from the costs of the current period when determining the costs of good units (which include normal spoilage) and the costs of abnormal spoilage, which are written off as a loss of the accounting period.
4. How does inspecting at various stages of completion affect the amount of normal and abnormal spoilage?	The cost of spoiled units is assumed to equal all costs incurred in producing spoiled units up to the point of inspection. Spoilage costs therefore vary based on different inspection points.
5. How do job-costing systems account for spoilage?	Normal spoilage specific to a job is assigned to that job or, when common to all jobs, is allocated as part of manufacturing overhead. The cost of abnormal spoilage is written off as a loss in the accounting period.
6. How do job-costing systems account for rework?	Normal rework specific to a job is assigned to that job or, when common to all jobs, is allocated as part of manufacturing overhead. Cost of abnormal rework is written off as a loss of the accounting period.
7. How is scrap accounted for?	Scrap is recognized in a firm's accounting records either at the time of its sale or at the time of its production. If the scrap is immaterial, it is recognized as revenue when it's sold. If it's not immaterial, the net realizable value of the scrap when it's sold reduces the cost of a specific job or, when common to all jobs, reduces Manufacturing Overhead Control.

Appendix

Standard-Costing Method and Spoilage

The standard-costing method simplifies the computations for normal and abnormal spoilage. To illustrate, we return to the Anzio Company example in the chapter. Suppose Anzio develops the following standard costs per unit for work done in the forming department in July 2014:

Direct materials	$ 8.50
Conversion costs	10.50
Total manufacturing cost	$19.00

Assume the same standard costs per unit also apply to the beginning inventory: 1,500 (1,500 × 100%) equivalent units of direct materials and 900 (1,500 × 60%) equivalent units of conversion costs. Hence, the beginning inventory at standard costs is as follows:

Direct materials, 1,500 units × $8.50 per unit	$12,750
Conversion costs, 900 units × $10.50 per unit	9,450
Total manufacturing costs	$22,200

Exhibit 18-5, Panel A, presents Steps 1 and 2 for calculating physical and equivalent units. These steps are the same as for the FIFO method described in Exhibit 18-3. Exhibit 18-5, Panel B, presents Steps 3, 4, and 5.

The costs to account for in Step 3 are at standard costs and, hence, they differ from the costs to account for under the weighted-average and FIFO methods, which are at actual costs. In Step 4, cost per equivalent unit is simply the standard cost: $8.50 per unit for direct materials and $10.50 per unit for conversion costs. The standard-costing

Exhibit 18-5 Standard-Costing Method of Process Costing with Spoilage for the Forming Department for July 2014

PANEL A: Summarize the Flow of Physical Units and Compute Output in Equivalent Units

Home | Insert | Page Layout | Formulas | Data | Review | View

	A	B	C	D	E
1			(Step 1)	(Step 2)	
2				Equivalent Units	
3		Flow of Production	Physical Units	Direct Materials	Conversion Costs
4		Work in process, beginning (given, p. 710)	1,500		
5		Started during current period (given, p. 710)	8,500		
6		To account for	10,000		
7		Good units completed and transferred out during current period:			
8		From beginning work in process[a]	1,500		
9		[1,500 × (100% – 100%); 1,500 × (100% – 60%)]		0	600
10		Started and completed	5,500[b]		
11		(5,500 × 100%; 5,500 × 100%)		5,500	5,500
12		Normal spoilage[c]	700		
13		(700 × 100%; 700 × 100%)		700	700
14		Abnormal spoilage[d]	300		
15		(300 × 100%; 300 × 100%)		300	300
16		Work in process, ending[e] (given, p. 710)	2,000		
17		(2,000 × 100%; 2,000 × 50%)		2,000	1,000
18		Accounted for	10,000		
19		Equivalent units of work done in current period		8,500	8,100
20					
21	[a]Degree of completion in this department: direct materials, 100%; conversion costs, 60%.				
22	[b]7,000 physical units completed and transferred out minus 1,500 physical units completed and transferred out from beginning				
23	work-in-process inventory.				
24	[c]Normal spoilage is 10% of good units transferred out: 10% × 7,000 = 700 units. Degree of completion of normal spoilage in this				
25	department: direct materials, 100%; conversion costs, 100%.				
26	[d]Abnormal spoilage = Actual spoilage – Normal spoilage = 1,000 – 700 = 300 units. Degree of completion of abnormal spoilage in this				
27	department: direct materials, 100%; conversion costs, 100%.				
28	[e]Degree of completion in this department: direct materials, 100%; conversion costs, 50%.				

PANEL B: Summarize the Total Costs to Account For, Compute the Cost per Equivalent Unit, and Assign Costs to the Units Completed, Spoiled Units, and Units in Ending Work-in-Process Inventory

	A	B	C	D	E
30			Total Production Costs	Direct Materials	Conversion Costs
31	(Step 3)	Work in process, beginning (given, p. 724)	$ 22,200	(1,500 × $8.50)	(900 × $10.50)
32		Costs added in current period at standard prices	157,300	(8,500 × $8.50)	(8,100 × $10.50)
33		Total costs to account for	$179,500	$85,000	$94,500
34	(Step 4)	Standard costs per equivalent unit (given, p. 724)	$ 19.00	$ 8.50	$ 10.50
35	(Step 5)	Assignment of costs at standard costs:			
36		Good units completed and transferred out (7,000 units)			
37		Work in process, beginning (1,500 units)	$ 22,200	(1,500 × $8.50)	+ (900 × $10.50)
38		Costs added to beginning work in process in current period	6,300	(0[f] × $8.50)	+ (600[f] × $10.50)
39		Total from beginning inventory before normal spoilage	28,500		
40		Started and completed before normal spoilage (5,500 units)	104,500	(5,500[f] × $8.50)	+ (5,500[f] × $10.50)
41		Normal spoilage (700 units)	13,300	(700[f] × $8.50)	+ (700[f] × $10.50)
42	(A)	Total costs of good units completed and transferred out	146,300		
43	(B)	Abnormal spoilage (300 units)	5,700	(300[f] × $8.50)	+ (300[f] × $10.50)
44	(C)	Work in process, ending (2,000 units)	27,500	(2,000[f] × $8.50)	+ (1,000[f] × $10.50)
45	(A)+(B)+(C)	Total costs accounted for	$179,500	$85,000	+ $94,500
46					
47	[f]Equivalent units of direct materials and conversion costs calculated in Step 2 in Panel A.				

method makes calculating equivalent-unit costs unnecessary, so it simplifies process costing. In Step 5, managers assign standard costs to units completed (including normal spoilage), to abnormal spoilage, and to ending work-in-process inventory by multiplying the equivalent units calculated in Step 2 by the standard costs per equivalent unit presented in Step 4. This enables managers to measure and analyze variances in the manner described in the appendix to Chapter 17 (pages 693–695).[6]

Finally, note that the journal entries corresponding to the amounts calculated in Step 5 are as follows:

Finished Goods	146,300	
Work in Process—Forming		146,300
To record transfer of good units completed in July.		
Loss from Abnormal Spoilage	5,700	
Work in Process—Forming		5,700
To record abnormal spoilage detected in July.		

[6] For example, from Exhibit 18-5, Panel B, the standard costs for July are direct materials used, 8,500 × \$8.50 = \$72,250, and conversion costs, 8,100 × \$10.50 = \$85,050. From page 710, the actual costs added during July are direct materials, \$76,500, and conversion costs, \$89,100, resulting in a direct materials variance of \$72,250 − \$76,500 = \$4,250 U and a conversion costs variance of \$85,050 − \$89,100 = \$4,050 U. These variances could then be subdivided further as in Chapters 7 and 8; the abnormal spoilage would be part of the efficiency variance.

Terms to Learn

This chapter and the Glossary at the end of the book contain definitions of the following important terms:

abnormal spoilage **(p. 708)**
inspection point **(p. 709)**
normal spoilage **(p. 708)**
rework **(p. 707)**
scrap **(p. 707)**
spoilage **(p. 707)**

Assignment Material

MyAccountingLab

Questions

18-1 Why is there an unmistakable trend in manufacturing to improve quality?

18-2 Distinguish among spoilage, rework, and scrap.

18-3 "Normal spoilage is planned spoilage." Discuss.

18-4 "Costs of abnormal spoilage are losses." Explain.

18-5 "What has been regarded as normal spoilage in the past is not necessarily acceptable as normal spoilage in the present or future." Explain.

18-6 "Units of abnormal spoilage are inferred rather than identified." Explain.

18-7 "In accounting for spoiled units, we are dealing with cost assignment rather than cost incurrence." Explain.

18-8 "Total input includes abnormal as well as normal spoilage and is, therefore, inappropriate as a basis for computing normal spoilage." Do you agree? Explain.

18-9 "The inspection point is the key to the allocation of spoilage costs." Do you agree? Explain.

18-10 "The unit cost of normal spoilage is the same as the unit cost of abnormal spoilage." Do you agree? Explain.

18-11 "In job costing, the costs of normal spoilage that occur while a specific job is being done are charged to the specific job." Do you agree? Explain.

18-12 "The costs of rework are always charged to the specific jobs in which the defects were originally discovered." Do you agree? Explain.

18-13 "Abnormal rework costs should be charged to a loss account, not to manufacturing overhead." Do you agree? Explain.

18-14 When is a company justified in inventorying scrap?

18-15 How do managers use information about scrap?

Exercises

18-16 Normal and abnormal spoilage in units. The following data, in physical units, describe a grinding process for January:

Work in process, beginning	18,600
Started during current period	189,000
To account for	207,600
Spoiled units	12,600
Good units completed and transferred out	170,000
Work in process, ending	25,000
Accounted for	207,600

Inspection occurs at the 100% completion stage. Normal spoilage is 4% of the good units passing inspection.

Required

1. Compute the normal and abnormal spoilage in units.
2. Assume that the equivalent-unit cost of a spoiled unit is $11. Compute the amount of potential savings if all spoilage were eliminated, assuming that all other costs would be unaffected. Comment on your answer.

18-17 Weighted-average method, spoilage, equivalent units. (CMA, adapted) Consider the following data for November 2014 from Gray Manufacturing Company, which makes silk pennants and uses a process-costing system. All direct materials are added at the beginning of the process, and conversion costs are added evenly during the process. Spoilage is detected upon inspection at the completion of the process. Spoiled units are disposed of at zero net disposal value. Gray Manufacturing Company uses the weighted-average method of process costing.

	Physical Units (Pennants)	Direct Materials	Conversion Costs
Work in process, November 1[a]	1,000	$ 1,423	$ 1,110
Started in November 2014	?		
Good units completed and transferred out during November 2014	9,000		
Normal spoilage	100		
Abnormal spoilage	50		
Work in process, November 30[b]	2,000		
Total costs added during November 2014		$12,180	$27,750

[a]Degree of completion: direct materials, 100%; conversion costs, 50%.
[b]Degree of completion: direct materials, 100%; conversion costs, 30%.

Required

Compute equivalent units for direct materials and conversion costs. Show physical units in the first column of your schedule.

18-18 Weighted-average method, assigning costs (continuation of 18-17).

Required

For the data in Exercise 18-17, summarize the total costs to account for; calculate the cost per equivalent unit for direct materials and conversion costs; and assign costs to units completed and transferred out (including normal spoilage), to abnormal spoilage, and to units in ending work-in-process inventory.

18-19 FIFO method, spoilage, equivalent units. Refer to the information in Exercise 18-17. Suppose Gray Manufacturing Company uses the FIFO method of process costing instead of the weighted-average method.

Required

Compute equivalent units for direct materials and conversion costs. Show physical units in the first column of your schedule.

18-20 FIFO method, assigning costs (continuation of 18-19).

Required

For the data in Exercise 18-17, use the FIFO method to summarize the total costs to account for; calculate the cost per equivalent unit for direct materials and conversion costs; and assign costs to units completed and transferred out (including normal spoilage), to abnormal spoilage, and to units in ending work in process.

18-21 Weighted-average method, spoilage. LaCroix Company produces handbags from leather of moderate quality. It distributes the product through outlet stores and department store chains. At LaCroix's facility in northeast Ohio, direct materials (primarily leather hides) are added at the beginning of the process, while conversion costs are added evenly during the process. Given the importance of minimizing product returns, spoiled units are detected upon inspection at the end of the process and are discarded at a net disposal value of zero.

LaCroix uses the weighted-average method of process costing. Summary data for April 2014 are as follows:

	A	B	C	D
1		Physical Units	Direct Materials	Conversion Costs
2	Work in process, beginning inventory (April 1)	2,400	$21,240	$ 13,332
3	Degree of completion of beginning work in process		100%	50%
4	Started during April	12,000		
5	Good units completed and transferred out during April	10,800		
6	Work in process, ending inventory (April 30)	2,160		
7	Degree of completion of ending work in process		100%	75%
8	Total costs added during April		$97,560	$111,408
9	Normal spoilage as a percentage of good units	10%		
10	Degree of completion of normal spoilage		100%	100%
11	Degree of completion of abnormal spoilage		100%	100%

Required

1. For each cost category, calculate equivalent units. Show physical units in the first column of your schedule.
2. Summarize the total costs to account for; calculate the cost per equivalent unit for each cost category; and assign costs to units completed and transferred out (including normal spoilage), to abnormal spoilage, and to units in ending work in process.

18-22 FIFO method, spoilage.

Required

1. Do Exercise 18-21 using the FIFO method.
2. What are the managerial issues involved in selecting or reviewing the percentage of spoilage considered normal? How would your answer to requirement 1 differ if all spoilage were viewed as normal?

18-23 Spoilage, journal entries. Safeclear, Inc., is the leading manufacturer of automotive glass components such as windshields. The company uses a process-costing system to account for its work-in-process inventories. When Job 26, an order for windshields for the Chevy Malibu, was being processed, a piece of laminated sheet glass was off-center in the cutting machine and two windshields were spoiled. Because this problem occurs periodically, it is considered normal spoilage and is consequently recorded as an overhead cost. Because this step comes first in the process of making the windshields, the only costs incurred were $325 for direct materials. Assume the laminated glass cannot be sold, and its cost has been recorded in work-in-process inventory.

Required

Prepare the journal entries to record the spoilage incurred.

18-24 Recognition of loss from spoilage. Roku Electronics manufactures universal power adapters at its Desert Sands plant. The company provides you with the following information regarding operations for April 2014:

Total power adapters manufactured	10,000
Adapters rejected as spoiled units	375
Total manufacturing cost	$400,000

Assume the spoiled units have no disposal value.

Required

1. What is the unit cost of making the 10,000 universal power adapters?
2. What is the total cost of the 375 spoiled units?
3. If the spoilage is considered normal, what is the increase in the unit cost of good adapters manufactured as a result of the spoilage?
4. If the spoilage is considered abnormal, prepare the journal entries for the spoilage incurred.

18-25 Weighted-average method, spoilage. WaferCo is a fast-growing manufacturer of computer chips. Direct materials are added at the start of the production process. Conversion costs are added evenly during the process. Some units of this product are spoiled as a result of defects not detectable before inspection of finished goods. Spoiled units are disposed of at zero net disposal value. WaferCo uses the weighted-average method of process costing.

Summary data for September 2014 are as follows:

	A	B	C	D
1		Physical Units (Computer Chips)	Direct Materials	Conversion Costs
2	Work in process, beginning inventory (September 1)	1,200	$142,321	$ 16,314
3	Degree of completion of beginning work in process		100%	30%
4	Started during September	2,257		
5	Good units completed and transferred out during September	2,300		
6	Work in process, ending inventory (September 30)	520		
7	Degree of completion of ending work in process		100%	20%
8	Total costs added during September		$573,278	$257,376
9	Normal spoilage as a percentage of good units	15%		
10	Degree of completion of normal spoilage		100%	100%
11	Degree of completion of abnormal spoilage		100%	100%

Required

1. For each cost category, compute equivalent units. Show physical units in the first column of your schedule.
2. Summarize the total costs to account for; calculate the cost per equivalent unit for each cost category; and assign costs to units completed and transferred out (including normal spoilage), to abnormal spoilage, and to units in ending work in process.

18-26 FIFO method, spoilage. Refer to the information in Exercise 18-25.

Required

1. Do Exercise 18-25 using the FIFO method of process costing.
2. Should WaferCo's managers choose the weighted-average method or the FIFO method? Explain briefly.

18-27 Standard-costing method, spoilage. Refer to the information in Exercise 18-25. Suppose WaferCo determines standard costs of $240 per equivalent unit for direct materials and $100 per equivalent unit for conversion costs for both beginning work in process and work done in the current period.

Required

1. Do Exercise 18-25 using the standard-costing method.
2. What issues should the manager focus on when reviewing the equivalent units calculation?

18-28 Spoilage and job costing. (L. Bamber) Barrett Kitchens produces a variety of items in accordance with special job orders from hospitals, plant cafeterias, and university dormitories. An order for 2,100 cases of mixed vegetables costs $9 per case: direct materials, $4; direct manufacturing labor, $3; and manufacturing overhead allocated, $2. The manufacturing overhead rate includes a provision for normal spoilage. Consider each requirement independently.

Required

1. Assume that a laborer dropped 420 cases. Suppose part of the 420 cases could be sold to a nearby prison for $420 cash. Prepare a journal entry to record this event. Calculate and explain briefly the unit cost of the remaining 1,680 cases.
2. Refer to the original data. Tasters at the company reject 420 of the 2,100 cases. The 420 cases are disposed of for $840. Assume that this rejection rate is considered normal. Prepare a journal entry to record this event, and do the following:
   a. Calculate the unit cost if the rejection is attributable to exacting specifications of this particular job.
   b. Calculate the unit cost if the rejection is characteristic of the production process and is not attributable to this specific job.
   c. Are unit costs the same in requirements 2a and 2b? Explain your reasoning briefly.
3. Refer to the original data. Tasters rejected 420 cases that had insufficient salt. The product can be placed in a vat, salt can be added, and the product can be reprocessed into jars. This operation, which is considered normal, will cost $420. Prepare a journal entry to record this event and do the following:
   a. Calculate the unit cost of all the cases if this additional cost was incurred because of the exacting specifications of this particular job.

b. Calculate the unit cost of all the cases if this additional cost occurs regularly because of difficulty in seasoning.
c. Are unit costs the same in requirements 3a and 3b? Explain your reasoning briefly.

18-29 Reworked units, costs of rework. Heyer Appliances assembles dishwashers at its plant in Tuscaloosa, Alabama. In February 2014, 60 circulation motors that cost $110 each (from a new supplier who subsequently went bankrupt) were defective and had to be disposed of at zero net disposal value. Heyer Appliances was able to rework all 60 dishwashers by substituting new circulation motors purchased from one of its existing suppliers. Each replacement motor cost $125.

Required

1. What alternative approaches are there to account for the materials cost of reworked units?
2. Should Heyer Appliances use the $110 circulation motor or the $125 motor to calculate the cost of materials reworked? Explain.
3. What other costs might Heyer Appliances include in its analysis of the total costs of rework due to the circulation motors purchased from the (now) bankrupt supplier?

18-30 Scrap, job costing. The Russell Company has an extensive job-costing facility that uses a variety of metals. Consider each requirement independently.

Required

1. Job 372 uses a particular metal alloy that is not used for any other job. Assume that scrap is material in amount and sold for $480 quickly after it is produced. Prepare the journal entry.
2. The scrap from Job 372 consists of a metal used by many other jobs. No record is maintained of the scrap generated by individual jobs. Assume that scrap is accounted for at the time of its sale. Scrap totaling $4,500 is sold. Prepare two alternative journal entries that could be used to account for the sale of scrap.
3. Suppose the scrap generated in requirement 2 is returned to the storeroom for future use, and a journal entry is made to record the scrap. A month later, the scrap is reused as direct material on a subsequent job. Prepare the journal entries to record these transactions.

MyAccountingLab

Problems

18-31 Weighted-average method, spoilage. The Seafood Company is a food-processing firm based in Maine. It operates under the weighted-average method of process costing and has two departments: cleaning and packaging. For the cleaning department, conversion costs are added evenly during the process, and direct materials are added at the beginning of the process. Spoiled units are detected upon inspection at the end of the process and are disposed of at zero net disposal value. All completed work is transferred to the packaging department. Summary data for May follow:

	A	B	C	D
1	The Seafood Company: Cleaning Department	Physical Units	Direct Materials	Conversion Costs
2	Work in process, beginning inventory (May 1)	3,600	$ 5,316	$ 1,953
3	Degree of completion of beginning work in process		100%	60%
4	Started during May	30,000		
5	Good units completed and transferred out during May	24,600		
6	Work in process, ending inventory (May 31)	5,040		
7	Degree of completion of ending work in process		100%	30%
8	Total costs added during May		$55,500	$44,659
9	Normal spoilage as a percentage of good units	10%		
10	Degree of completion of normal spoilage		100%	100%
11	Degree of completion of abnormal spoilage		100%	100%

Required

For the cleaning department, summarize the total costs to account for and assign those costs to units completed and transferred out (including normal spoilage), to abnormal spoilage, and to units in ending work in process. (Problem 18-33 explores additional facets of this problem.)

18-32 FIFO method, spoilage. Refer to the information in Problem 18-31.

Required

Do Problem 18-31 using the FIFO method of process costing. (Problem 18-34 explores additional facets of this problem.)

18-33 Weighted-average method, packaging department (continuation of 18-31). In the Seafood Company's packaging department, conversion costs are added evenly during the process, and direct materials are added at the end of the process. Spoiled units are detected upon inspection at the end of the process and are disposed of at zero net disposal value. All completed work is transferred to the next department. The transferred-in costs for May equal the total cost of good units completed and transferred out in May from the cleaning department, which were calculated in Problem 18-31 using the weighted-average method of process costing. Summary data for May follow.

	A	B	C	D	E
1	The Seafood Company: Packaging Department	Physical Units	Transferred-In Costs	Direct Materials	Conversion Costs
2	Work in process, beginning inventory (May 1)	12,600	$33,698	$ 0	$23,475
3	Degree of completion of beginning work in process		100%	0%	70%
4	Started during May	24,600			
5	Good units completed and transferred out during May	26,400			
6	Work in process, ending inventory (May 31)	8,400			
7	Degree of completion of ending work in process		100%	0%	40%
8	Total costs added during May		?	$5,760	$40,845
9	Normal spoilage as a percentage of good units	8%			
10	Degree of completion of normal spoilage			100%	100%
11	Degree of completion of abnormal spoilage			100%	100%

Required

For the packaging department, use the weighted-average method to summarize the total costs to account for and assign those costs to units completed and transferred out (including normal spoilage), to abnormal spoilage, and to units in ending work in process.

18-34 FIFO method, packaging department (continuation of 18-32). Refer to the information in Problem 18-33 except that the transferred-in costs of beginning work in process on May 1 are $33,090 (instead of $33,698). Transferred-in costs for May equal the total cost of good units completed and transferred out in May from the cleaning department, as calculated in Problem 18-32 using the FIFO method of process costing.

Required

For the packaging department, use the FIFO method to summarize the total costs to account for and assign those costs to units completed and transferred out (including normal spoilage), to abnormal spoilage, and to units in ending work in process.

18-35 Physical units, inspection at various levels of completion, weighted-average process costing. SunEnergy produces solar panels. A key step in the conversion of raw silicon to a completed solar panel occurs in the assembly department, where lightweight photovoltaic cells are assembled into modules and connected on a frame. In this department, materials are added at the beginning of the process and conversion takes place uniformly.

At the start of November 2014, SunEnergy's assembly department had 2,400 panels in beginning work in process, which were 100% complete for materials and 40% complete for conversion costs. An additional 12,000 units were started in the department in November, and 3,600 units remain in work in process at the end of the month. These unfinished units are 100% complete for materials and 70% complete for conversion costs.

The assembly department had 1,800 spoiled units in November. Because of the difficulty of keeping moisture out of the modules and sealing the photovoltaic cells between layers of glass, normal spoilage is approximately 12% of good units. The department's costs for the month of November are as follows:

	Beginning WIP	Costs Incurred During Period
Direct materials costs	$ 76,800	$ 240,000
Conversion costs	123,000	1,200,000

Required

1. Using the format on page 715, compute the normal and abnormal spoilage in units for November, assuming the inspection point is at (a) the 30% stage of completion, (b) the 60% stage of completion, and (c) the 100% stage of completion.

2. Refer to your answer in requirement 1. Why are there different amounts of normal and abnormal spoilage at different inspection points?
3. Now assume that the assembly department inspects at the 60% stage of completion. Using the weighted-average method, calculate the cost of units transferred out, the cost of abnormal spoilage, and the cost of ending inventory for the assembly department in November.

18-36 Spoilage in job costing. Jellyfish Machine Shop is a manufacturer of motorized carts for vacation resorts.

Patrick Cullin, the plant manager of Jellyfish, obtains the following information for Job #10 in August 2014. A total of 46 units were started, and 6 spoiled units were detected and rejected at final inspection, yielding 40 good units. The spoiled units were considered to be normal spoilage. Costs assigned prior to the inspection point are $1,100 per unit. The current disposal price of the spoiled units is $235 per unit. When the spoilage is detected, the spoiled goods are inventoried at $235 per unit.

Required

1. What is the normal spoilage rate?
2. Prepare the journal entries to record the normal spoilage, assuming the following:
   a. The spoilage is related to a specific job.
   b. The spoilage is common to all jobs.
   c. The spoilage is considered to be abnormal spoilage.

18-37 Rework in job costing, journal entry (continuation of 18-36). Assume that the 6 spoiled units of Jellyfish Machine Shop's Job #10 can be reworked for a total cost of $1,800. A total cost of $6,600 associated with these units has already been assigned to Job #10 before the rework.

Required

Prepare the journal entries for the rework, assuming the following:

a. The rework is related to a specific job.
b. The rework is common to all jobs.
c. The rework is considered to be abnormal.

18-38 Scrap at time of sale or at time of production, journal entries (continuation of 18-36). Assume that Job #10 of Jellyfish Machine Shop generates normal scrap with a total sales value of $700 (it is assumed that the scrap returned to the storeroom is sold quickly).

Required

Prepare the journal entries for the recognition of scrap, assuming the following:

a. The value of scrap is immaterial and scrap is recognized at the time of sale.
b. The value of scrap is material, is related to a specific job, and is recognized at the time of sale.
c. The value of scrap is material, is common to all jobs, and is recognized at the time of sale.
d. The value of scrap is material, and scrap is recognized as inventory at the time of production and is recorded at its net realizable value.

18-39 Physical units, inspection at various stages of completion. Superb Furniture manufactures plastic lawn furniture in a continuous process. The company pours molten plastic into molds and then cools the plastic. Materials are added at the beginning of the process, and conversion is considered uniform through the period. Occasionally, the plastic does not completely fill a mold because of air pockets, and the chair is then considered spoiled. Normal spoilage is 6% of the good units that pass inspection. The following information pertains to March 2014:

Beginning inventory	2,200 units (100% complete for materials; 20% complete for conversion costs)
Units started	21,000
Units in ending work in process	1,900 (100% complete for materials; 70% complete for conversion costs)

Superb Furniture had 1,800 spoiled units in March 2014.

Required

Using the format on page 715, compute the normal and abnormal spoilage in units, assuming the inspection point is at (a) the 15% stage of completion, (b) the 40% stage of completion, and (c) the 100% stage of completion.

18-40 Job costing, rework. Avid Corporation manufactures a sophisticated controller that is compatible with a variety of gaming consoles. Excluding rework costs, the cost of manufacturing one controller is $220. This consists of $120 in direct materials, $24 in direct manufacturing labor, and $76 in manufacturing overhead. Maintaining a reputation for quality is critical to Avid. Any defective units identified at the inspection point are sent back for rework. It costs Avid $72 to rework each defective controller, including $24 in direct materials, $18 in direct manufacturing labor, and $30 in manufacturing overhead.

In August 2014, Avid manufactured 1,000 controllers, 80 of which required rework. Of these 80 controllers, 50 were considered normal rework common to all jobs and the other 30 were considered abnormal rework.

Required

1. Prepare journal entries to record the accounting for both the normal and abnormal rework.
2. What were the total rework costs of controllers in August 2014?
3. Suppose instead that the normal rework is attributable entirely to Job #9, for 200 controllers intended for Australia. In this case, what are the total and unit costs of the good units produced for that job in August 2014? Prepare journal entries for the manufacture of the 200 controllers, as well as the normal rework costs.

18-41 Weighted-average method, inspection at 80% completion. (A. Atkinson) The Horsheim Company is a furniture manufacturer with two departments: molding and finishing. The company uses the weighted-average method of process costing. In August, the following data were recorded for the finishing department:

Units of beginning work in process inventory	25,000
Percentage completion of beginning work in process units	25%
Cost of direct materials in beginning work in process	$ 0
Units started	175,000
Units completed	125,000
Units in ending inventory	50,000
Percentage completion of ending work in process units	95%
Spoiled units	25,000
Total costs added during current period:	
Direct materials	$1,638,000
Direct manufacturing labor	$1,589,000
Manufacturing overhead	$1,540,000
Work in process, beginning:	
Transferred-in costs	$ 207,250
Conversion costs	$ 105,000
Cost of units transferred in during current period	$1,618,750

Conversion costs are added evenly during the process. Direct material costs are added when production is 90% complete. The inspection point is at the 80% stage of production. Normal spoilage is 10% of all good units that pass inspection. Spoiled units are disposed of at zero net disposal value.

Required

1. For August, summarize total costs to account for and assign these costs to units completed and transferred out (including normal spoilage), to abnormal spoilage, and to units in ending work in process.
2. What are the managerial issues involved in determining the percentage of spoilage considered normal? How would your answer to requirement 1 differ if all spoilage were treated as normal?

19 Balanced Scorecard: Quality and Time

Learning Objectives

1. Explain the four cost categories in a costs-of-quality program
2. Develop nonfinancial measures and methods to improve quality
3. Use costs-of-quality measures to make decisions
4. Use financial and nonfinancial measures to evaluate quality
5. Describe customer-response time and on-time performance and why delays occur
6. Determine the costs of delays
7. Use financial and nonfinancial measures of time

To satisfy ever-increasing customer expectations, managers at companies such as Samsung, Sony, Texas Instruments, and Toyota find cost-effective ways to continuously improve the quality of their products and services and shorten response times.

They balance the costs of achieving these improvements against the benefits from higher performance. Improving quality and decreasing customer-response times are hard work, but when companies do not make these improvements, the losses can be substantial, as the following article about Toyota Motor Corporation shows.

Toyota Plans Changes After Millions of Defective Cars Are Recalled[1]

Toyota Motor Corporation, the Japanese automaker, built its reputation on manufacturing reliable cars. As part of an aggressive growth strategy, Toyota surpassed General Motors as the world's largest carmaker in 2008. But the company's focus on rapid growth came at a cost to its reputation for quality.

Between November 2009 and January 2010, Toyota was forced to recall 9 million vehicles worldwide because gas pedals began to stick and were causing unwanted acceleration on eight Toyota models. After months of disagreements with government safety officials, the company recalled 12 models and suspended the production and sales of eight new Toyota and Lexus models, including its popular Camry and Corolla sedans. Although most of the cars were quickly returned to the sales floor, Toyota lost an estimated $2 billion in sales due to the recall.

Beyond lost revenue, Toyota's once-vaunted image took a serious hit. As the crisis unfolded, the company was slow to take responsibility for the problems. It then faced the long and difficult task of restoring its credibility and assuring owners and new-car shoppers that it had fixed the problems. The company established a quality committee, added a brake override system, expanded quality training, and increased testing. It reduced engine types and product features to simplify work and focus on quality. By 2012, Toyota's sales had rebounded and the company reclaimed the title of world's largest automaker.

[1] *Sources:* "Can Toyota recover its reputation for quality?" Wendy Kaufman, *Morning Edition*, National Public Radio, February 9, 2010, http://www.npr.org/templates/story/story.php?storyId=123519027; Kate Linebaugh and Norihiko Shirouzu, "Toyota heir faces crisis at the wheel," *The Wall Street Journal* (January 27, 2010); Micheline Maynard and Hiroko Tabuchi, "Rapid growth has its perils, Toyota learns," *New York Times* (January 27, 2010); Mike Ramsey and Norihiko Shirouzu, "Toyota alters car development," *The Wall Street Journal* (July 6, 2010); and Chester Dawson, "Toyota again world's largest automaker," *The Wall Street Journal* (January 28, 2013).

The Toyota example vividly illustrates the importance of quality. The chapter covers two topics that give companies a competitive advantage. We first address quality as a competitive tool, looking at quality from the financial perspective, the customer perspective, the internal-business-process perspective, and the learning-and-growth perspective before discussing the evaluation of quality performance. We then address time as a competitive tool and focuses on customer-response time, on-time performance, time drivers, and financial and nonfinancial measures of time.

Quality as a Competitive Tool

Learning Objective 1

Explain the four cost categories in a costs-of-quality program

... prevention, appraisal, internal failure, and external failure costs

The American Society for Quality defines **quality** as the total features and characteristics of a product or a service made or performed according to specifications to satisfy customers at the time of purchase and during use. Many companies throughout the world—like Cisco Systems, Motorola, British Telecom, Fujitsu, Honda, Crysel, and Samsung—emphasize quality as an important strategic initiative. These companies have found that focusing on the quality of a product or service generally builds expertise in producing it, lowers the costs of providing it, creates higher satisfaction for customers using it, and generates higher future revenues for the company selling it. Several high-profile awards, such as the Malcolm Baldrige National Quality Award in the United States, the Deming Prize in Japan, and the Premio Nacional de Calidad in Mexico, are given to companies that produce high-quality products and services.

International quality standards have also emerged. ISO 9000, developed by the International Organization for Standardization, is a set of five international standards for quality management adopted by more than 85 countries. The standards help companies monitor, document, and certify the elements of their production processes that lead to quality. To ensure their suppliers deliver high-quality products at competitive costs, companies such as DuPont and General Electric require their suppliers to obtain ISO 9000 certification. ISO 9000 certification has become a necessary condition for competing in the global marketplace.

Companies are also using quality management and measurement practices to find cost-effective ways to reduce the environmental and economic costs of air pollution, wastewater, oil spills, and hazardous waste disposal. ISO 14000, also developed by the International Organization for Standardization, are standards designed to encourage organizations to develop (1) environmental management systems to reduce environmental costs and (2) environmental auditing and performance-evaluation systems to review and monitor their progress toward their environmental goals. Quality and environmental issues came together in a big way when British Petroleum's Deepwater Horizon platform exploded in the Gulf of Mexico in 2010 while drilling for oil. Eleven workers died as a result of the explosion, and over the course of approximately three months, nearly 5 million gallons of oil spilled out into the Gulf, causing an environmental catastrophe.

Product quality can also be an important engine for environmental progress. For example, Stonyfield Farm, the world's leading organic yogurt company, provides high-quality, all-natural products while educating customers and suppliers about sustainable farming and protecting the environment. As Stonyfield Farm transitioned to organic production, it developed quality control capabilities, performing more than 900 quality checks daily to ensure that its yogurt justified the higher costs of organic milk, fruit, and sugar. Automated systems accomplish quality compliance electronically. Plant processes are interlocked so elements of production cannot move forward unless the product passes inspection at every stage of the process. The quality focus has allowed Stonyfield to grow at a 23% annual rate for more than 18 years, while its use of organic ingredients has kept more than 180,000 farm acres free of pesticides and chemical fertilizers.

We focus on two basic aspects of quality: design quality and conformance quality. **Design quality** refers to how closely the characteristics of a product or service meet the needs and wants of customers. **Conformance quality** is the performance of a product or service relative to its design and product specifications. Apple Inc. has built a reputation for design quality by developing many innovative products such as the iPod, iPhone, and iPad that have uniquely met customers' music, telephone, entertainment, and business needs. Apple's products have also generally had excellent conformance quality; rarely do the products fail to do what they are supposed to do. In the case of the iPhone 5, however, the problems with the map application were an example of good design quality but poor conformance quality because maps were a feature desired by customers but the map application itself did not perform according to its specifications. The following diagram illustrates that actual performance can fall short of customer satisfaction because of design-quality failure and because of conformance-quality failure.

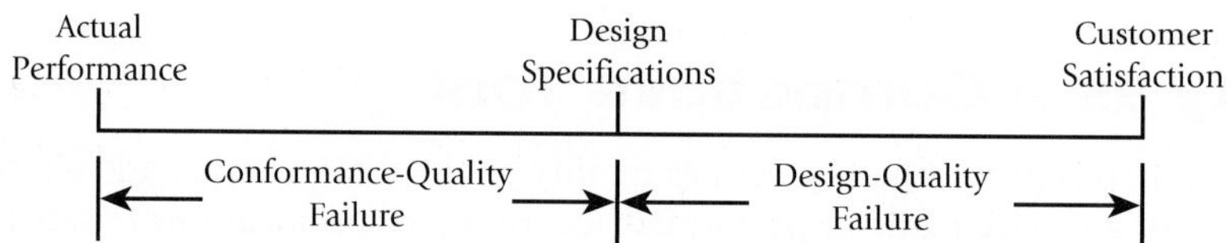

We illustrate the issues in managing quality—computing the costs of quality, identifying quality problems, and taking actions to improve quality—using Photon Corporation. While Photon makes many products, we focus only on Photon's photocopying machines, which earned an operating income of $24 million on revenues of $300 million (from sales of 20,000 copiers) in 2013.

Quality has both financial and nonfinancial components relating to customer satisfaction, improving internal quality processes, reducing defects, and the training and empowering of workers. To provide some structure, we discuss quality from the four perspectives of the balanced scorecard: financial in the next section and customer, internal-business-process, and learning-and-growth in the following section.

The Financial Perspective: The Costs of Quality

Financial measures include measures affected by quality, such as revenues and operating income growth. The most direct financial measure of quality, however, is the *costs of quality*. The **costs of quality** (COQ) are the costs incurred to prevent the production of a low-quality product or the costs arising as a result of such products. These costs are classified into the following four categories, and examples for each category are listed in Exhibit 19-1.

1. **Prevention costs**—costs incurred to prevent the production of products that do not conform to specifications
2. **Appraisal costs**—costs incurred to detect which of the individual units of products do not conform to specifications
3. **Internal failure costs**—costs incurred on defective products *before* they are shipped to customers
4. **External failure costs**—costs incurred on defective products *after* they have been shipped to customers

Exhibit 19-1 Items Pertaining to Costs-of-Quality Reports

Prevention Costs	Appraisal Costs	Internal Failure Costs	External Failure Costs
Design engineering Process engineering Supplier evaluations Preventive equipment maintenance Quality training Testing of new materials	Inspection Online product manufacturing and process inspection Product testing	Spoilage Rework Scrap Machine repairs Manufacturing/ process engineering on internal failures	Customer support Manufacturing/ process engineering for external failures Warranty repair costs Liability claims

The items in Exhibit 19-1 arise in all business functions of the value chain, and they are broader than the internal failure costs of spoilage, rework, and scrap described in Chapter 18.

Photon determines the COQ of its photocopying machines by adapting the seven-step activity-based costing approach described in Chapter 5.

Step 1: Identify the Chosen Cost Object. The cost object is the quality of the photocopying machine that Photon made and sold in 2013. Photon's goal is to calculate the total costs of quality of these 20,000 machines.

Step 2: Identify the Direct Costs of Quality of the Product. The photocopying machines have no direct costs of quality because there are no resources such as inspection or repair workers dedicated to managing the quality of the photocopying machines.

Step 3: Select the Activities and Cost-Allocation Bases to Use for Allocating the Indirect Costs of Quality to the Product. Column 1 of Exhibit 19-2, Panel A, classifies the activities that result in prevention, appraisal, and internal and external failure costs of quality at Photon Corporation and the business functions of the value chain in which these costs occur. For example, the quality-inspection activity results in appraisal costs and occurs in the manufacturing function. Photon identifies the total number of inspection-hours (across all products) as the cost-allocation base for the inspection activity. (To avoid details not needed to explain the concepts here, we do not show the total quantities of each cost-allocation base.)

Step 4: Identify the Indirect Costs of Quality Associated with Each Cost-Allocation Base. These are the total costs (variable and fixed) incurred for each of the costs-of-quality activities, such as inspections, across all of Photon's products. (To avoid details not needed to understand the points described here, we do not present these total costs.)

Step 5: Compute the Rate per Unit of Each Cost-Allocation Base. For each activity, the total costs (identified in Step 4) are divided by the total quantity of the cost-allocation base (calculated in Step 3) to compute the rate per unit of each cost-allocation base. Column 2 in Exhibit 19-2, Panel A, shows these rates (without supporting calculations).

Step 6: Compute the Indirect Costs of Quality Allocated to the Product. The indirect costs of quality of the photocopying machines, shown in Exhibit 19-2, Panel A, column 4, equal the cost-allocation rate from Step 5 (column 2) multiplied by the total quantity of the cost-allocation base used by the photocopying machines for each activity (column 3). For example, the inspection costs for ensuring the quality of the photocopying machines are $9,600,000 ($40 per hour × 240,000 inspection-hours).

Step 7: Compute the Total Costs of Quality by Adding All Direct and Indirect Costs of Quality Assigned to the Product. Photon's total costs of quality in the COQ report for photocopying machines is $40.02 million (Exhibit 19-2, Panel A, column 4), or 13.3% of current revenues (column 5).

Exhibit 19-2 Analysis of Activity-Based Costs of Quality (COQ) for Photocopying Machines at Photon Corporation

	A	B	C	D	E	F	G
1	**PANEL A: ACCOUNTING COQ REPORT**						**Percentage of**
2		**Cost Allocation**		**Quantity of Cost**		**Total**	**Revenues**
3	**Cost of Quality and Value-Chain Category**	**Rate[a]**		**Allocation Base**		**Costs**	**(5) = (4) ÷**
4	**(1)**	**(2)**		**(3)**		**(4) = (2) x (3)**	**$300,000,000**
5	*Prevention costs*						
6	Design engineering (R&D/Design)	$ 80	per hour	40,000	hours	$ 3,200,000	1.1%
7	Process engineering (R&D/Design)	$ 60	per hour	45,000	hours	2,700,000	0.9%
8	Total prevention costs					5,900,000	2.0%
9	*Appraisal costs*						
10	Inspection (Manufacturing)	$ 40	per hour	240,000	hours	9,600,000	3.2%
11	Total appraisal costs					9,600,000	3.2%
12	*Internal failure costs*						
13	Rework (Manufacturing)	$100	per hour	100,000	hours	10,000,000	3.3%
14	Total internal failure costs					10,000,000	3.3%
15	*External failure costs*						
16	Customer support (Marketing)	$ 50	per hour	12,000	hours	600,000	0.2%
17	Transportation (Distribution)	$240	per load	3,000	loads	720,000	0.2%
18	Warranty repair (Customer service)	$110	per hour	120,000	hours	13,200,000	4.4%
19	Total external failure costs					14,520,000	4.8%
20	Total costs of quality					$40,020,000	13.3%
21							
22	[a]Calculations not shown.						
23							
24	**PANEL B: OPPORTUNITY COST ANALYSIS**						
25						**Total Estimated**	**Percentage**
26						**Contribution**	**of Revenues**
27	**Cost of Quality Category**					**Margin Lost**	**(3) = (2) ÷**
28	**(1)**					**(2)**	**$300,000,000**
29	*External failure costs*						
30	Estimated forgone contribution margin						
31	and income on lost sales					$12,000,000[b]	4.0%
32	Total external failure costs					$12,000,000	4.0%
33							
34	[b]Calculated as total revenues minus all variable costs (whether output-unit, batch, product-sustaining, or facility-sustaining) on						
35	lost sales in 2013. If poor quality causes Photon to lose sales in subsequent years as well, the opportunity costs will be						
36	even greater.						

As we have seen in Chapter 11, opportunity costs are not recorded in financial accounting systems. Yet a significant component of costs of quality is the opportunity cost of the contribution margin and income forgone from lost sales, lost production, and lower prices resulting from poor design and conformance quality. Photon's market research department estimates that design and conformance quality problems experienced by some customers resulted in lost sales of 2,000 photocopying machines in 2013 and forgone contribution margin and operating income of $12 million (Exhibit 19-2, Panel B). The total costs of quality, including opportunity costs, therefore equal $52.02 million ($40.02 million recorded in the accounting system and shown in Panel A plus $12 million of opportunity costs shown in Panel B), or 17.3% of current revenues. Opportunity costs account for 23.1% ($12 million ÷ $52.02 million) of Photon's total costs of quality.

We turn next to the leading indicators of the costs of quality, the nonfinancial quality measures for Photon's photocopiers.

Decision Point

What are the four cost categories of a costs-of-quality program?

Using Nonfinancial Measures to Evaluate and Improve Quality

Learning Objective 2

Develop nonfinancial measures

...customer satisfaction measures such as number of customer complaints, internal-business process measures such as percentage of defective and reworked products, and learning-and-growth measures such as employee empowerment and training

and methods to improve quality

... control charts, Pareto diagrams, and cause-and-effect diagrams

Companies such as Unilever, FedEx, and TiVo use nonfinancial measures to manage quality. Almost always, the first step is to look at quality through the eyes of customers. Managers then turn their attention inward toward their organizations to develop processes that help improve quality and corporate cultures that help sustain it.

The Customer Perspective: Nonfinancial Measures of Customer Satisfaction

Photon's managers track the following measures of customer satisfaction:

- Market research information on customer preferences for and customer satisfaction with specific product features (to measure design quality)
- Market share
- Percentage of highly satisfied customers
- Number of defective units shipped to customers as a percentage of total units shipped
- Number of customer complaints (Companies estimate that for every customer who actually complains, there are 10 to 20 others who have had bad experiences with the product or service but did not complain.)
- Percentage of products that fail soon after delivery
- Average delivery delays (difference between the scheduled delivery date and the date requested by the customer)
- On-time delivery rate (percentage of shipments delivered on or before the scheduled delivery date)

Photon's managers monitor whether these numbers improve or deteriorate over time. Higher customer satisfaction should lead to lower external failure costs, lower costs of quality, and higher future revenues due to greater customer retention, loyalty, and positive word-of-mouth advertising. Lower customer satisfaction indicates that external failure costs and costs of quality will likely increase in the future. We next discuss internal business processes to identify and analyze quality problems that help to improve quality and increase customer satisfaction.

The Internal-Business-Process Perspective: Analyzing Quality Problems and Improving Quality

We present three techniques for identifying and analyzing quality problems: control charts, Pareto diagrams, and cause-and-effect diagrams.

Control Charts

Statistical quality control (SQC), also called statistical process control (SPC), is a formal means of distinguishing between random and nonrandom variations in an operating process. Random variations occur, for example, when chance fluctuations in the speed of equipment cause defective products to be produced, such as copiers that produce fuzzy and unclear copies or copies that are too light or too dark. Nonrandom variations occur when defective products are produced as a result of a systematic problem such as an incorrect speed setting, a flawed part design, or mishandling of a component part. A **control chart**, an important SQC tool, is a graph of a series of successive observations

Exhibit 19-3 Statistical Quality Control Charts: Daily Defect Rate for Photocopying Machines at Photon Corporation

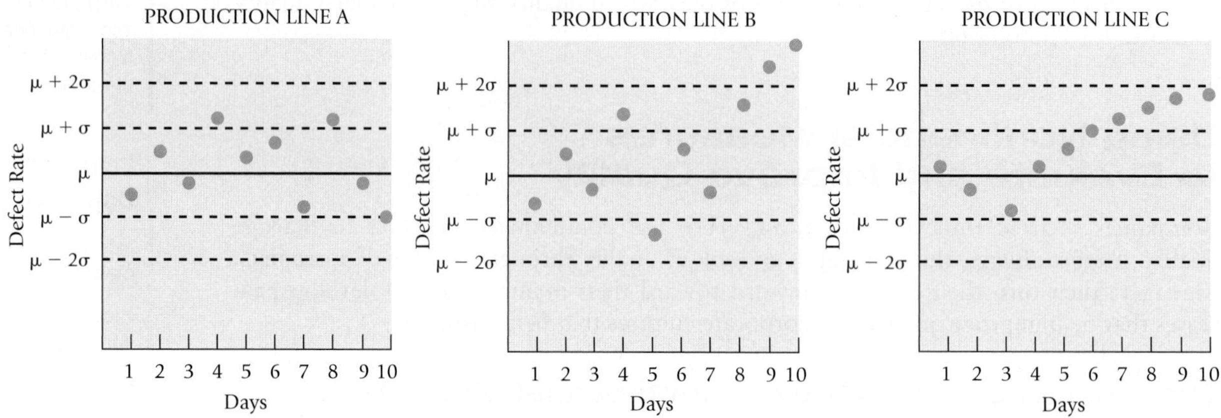

of a particular step, procedure, or operation taken at regular intervals of time. Each observation is plotted relative to specified ranges that represent the limits within which observations are expected to fall. Observations that fall outside the control limits are regarded as nonrandom and worth investigating.

Exhibit 19-3 presents control charts for the daily defect rates (defective copiers divided by the total number of copiers produced) observed at Photon's three photocopying-machine production lines. The defect rates in the prior 60 days for each production line provide a basis upon which to calculate the distribution of daily defect rates. The arithmetic mean (μ, read as "mu") and standard deviation (σ, read as "sigma," how much an observation deviates from the mean) are the two parameters of the distribution that are used in the control charts in Exhibit 19-3. On the basis of experience, the company decides that managers should investigate any observation outside the $\mu \pm 2\sigma$ range.

For production line A, all observations are within the range of $\mu \pm 2\sigma$, so managers believe no investigation is necessary. For production line B, the last two observations signal that a much higher percentage of copiers are not performing as they should, indicating that the problem is probably because of a nonrandom, out-of-control occurrence such as an incorrect speed setting or mishandling of a component part. Given the $\pm 2\sigma$ rule, both observations would be investigated. Production line C illustrates a process that would not prompt an investigation under the $\pm 2\sigma$ rule but that may well be out of control. Why? Because the last eight observations show a clear pattern: Over the last 6 days, the percentage of defective copiers increased and got further and further away from the mean. The pattern could be due, for example, to the tooling on a machine wearing out, resulting in poorly machined parts. As the tooling deteriorates further, the trend in producing defective copiers is likely to persist until the production line is no longer in statistical control. Statistical procedures have been developed using the trend as well as the variation to evaluate whether a process is out of control.

Pareto Diagrams

Observations outside control limits serve as inputs for Pareto diagrams. A **Pareto diagram** is a chart that indicates how frequently each type of defect occurs, ordered from the most frequent to the least frequent. Exhibit 19-4 presents a Pareto diagram of quality problems for all observations outside the control limits at the final inspection point in 2013. Copiers that produce fuzzy and unclear copies are the most frequently recurring problem, and they result in high rework costs. Sometimes problems such as these are detected at customer sites and result in high warranty and repair costs and low customer satisfaction.

Cause-and-Effect Diagrams

The most frequently recurring and costly problems identified by the Pareto diagram are analyzed using cause-and-effect diagrams. A **cause-and-effect diagram** identifies potential

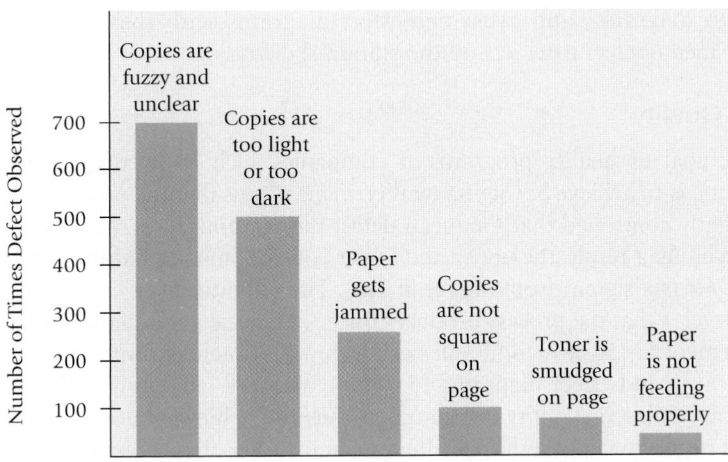

Exhibit 19-4

Pareto Diagram for Photocopying Machines at Photon Corporation

causes of defects using a diagram that resembles the bone structure of a fish (which is why the diagrams are also called *fishbone diagrams*).[2] Exhibit 19-5 presents the cause-and-effect diagram describing potential reasons for fuzzy and unclear copies. The "backbone" of the diagram represents the problem being examined. The large "bones" coming off the backbone represent the main categories of potential causes of failure. The exhibit identifies four of these: human factors, methods and design factors, machine-related factors, and materials and components factors. Photon's engineers identify the materials and components factor as an important reason for the fuzzy and unclear copies. Additional arrows, or bones, are added to provide more detailed reasons for each higher-level cause. For example, Photon's engineers determine that two potential causes of material and component problems are variations in purchased components and incorrect component specifications. The engineers quickly determine that Photon's component specifications are correct, so variations in the purchased components or mishandling of them is the likely cause. Further analysis leads Photon to conclude that mishandling of the steel frame that holds in place various components of the copier such as drums, mirrors, and lenses results in the misalignment of these components and causes fuzzy and unclear copies.

Manufacturers use automated equipment and computers to record the number and types of defects and the operating conditions that existed at the time the defects occurred. Using these inputs, computer programs simultaneously and iteratively prepare control

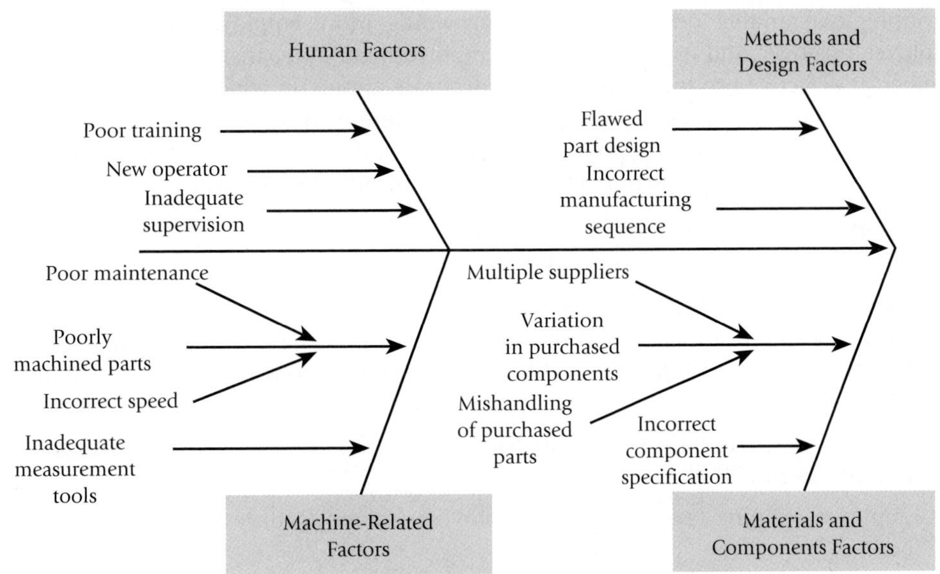

Exhibit 19-5

Cause-and-Effect Diagram for Fuzzy and Unclear Photocopies at Photon Corporation

[2] See Timothy J. Clark, "Getting the Most from Cause-and-Effect Diagrams," *Quality Progress* 33:6 (June 2000).

charts, Pareto diagrams, and cause-and-effect diagrams with the goal of continuously reducing the mean defect rate, μ, and the standard deviation, σ.

Six Sigma Quality

The ultimate goal of quality programs at companies such as Motorola, Honeywell, and General Electric is to achieve Six Sigma quality.[3] This means that the process is so well understood and tightly controlled that the mean defect rate, μ, and the standard deviation, σ, are both very small. As a result, the upper and lower control limits in Exhibit 19-3 can be set at a distance of 6σ (six sigma) from the mean (μ). The implication of controlling a process at a Six Sigma level is that the process produces only 3.4 defects per million products produced.

To implement Six Sigma, companies use techniques such as control charts, Pareto diagrams, and cause-and-effect diagrams to define, measure, analyze, improve, and control processes to minimize variability in manufacturing and achieve almost zero defects. Critics of Six Sigma argue that it emphasizes incremental rather than dramatic or disruptive innovation. Nevertheless, companies report substantial benefits from Six Sigma initiatives.

Nonfinancial Measures of Internal-Business-Process Quality

Companies routinely use nonfinancial measures to track the quality improvements they are making. Photon's managers use the following nonfinancial measures of internal-business-process quality:

- Percentage of defective products manufactured
- Percentage of reworked products
- Number of different types of defects analyzed using control charts, Pareto diagrams, and cause-and-effect diagrams
- Number of design and process changes made to improve design quality or reduce the costs of quality

Photon's managers believe that improving these measures will lead to greater customer satisfaction, lower costs of quality, and better financial performance.

The Learning-and-Growth Perspective: Quality Improvements

What are the drivers of internal-business-process quality? Photon's managers believe that recruiting outstanding design engineers, providing more employee training, lowering employee turnover, and greater employee empowerment and satisfaction will reduce the number of defective products. To create a corporate culture in which Photon's employees focus on quality, managers encourage them to continuously strive to improve quality by identifying and eliminating the root causes of defects. Photon measures the following factors in the learning-and-growth perspective in the balanced scorecard:

- The experience and qualifications of design engineers
- Employee turnover (ratio of number of employees who leave the company to the average total number of employees)
- Employee empowerment (ratio of the number of processes in which employees have the authority to make decisions without consulting supervisors to the total number of processes)
- Employee satisfaction (ratio of employees indicating high satisfaction ratings to the total number of employees surveyed)
- Employee training (percentage of employees trained in different quality-enhancing methods)

Decision Point

What nonfinancial measures and methods can managers use to improve quality?

[3] Six Sigma is a registered trademark of Motorola Inc.

Weighing the Costs and Benefits of Improving Quality

Learning Objective 3

Use costs of quality measures to make decisions

... identify relevant incremental costs and benefits and opportunity costs to evaluate tradeoffs

Recall that the cause-and-effect diagram reveals that the steel frame (or chassis) of the copier is often mishandled as it travels from a supplier's warehouse to Photon's warehouse and then to the production line. The frame must meet very precise specifications or else copier components (such as drums, mirrors, and lenses) will not fit exactly on the frame. Mishandling frames during transport causes misalignment and results in fuzzy and unclear copies.

A team of engineers offers two solutions: (1) electronically inspect and test the frames before production starts or (2) redesign and strengthen the frames and their shipping containers to withstand mishandling during transportation. The cost structure of the costs of quality for 2014 is expected to be the same as the cost structure for 2013 presented in Exhibit 19-2.

To evaluate each alternative versus the status quo, managers identify the relevant costs and benefits for each solution by focusing on *how total costs and total revenues will change under each alternative*. Relevant-cost and relevant-revenue analysis ignores allocated costs (see Chapter 11).

Photon uses only a 1-year time horizon (2014) for the analysis because it plans to introduce a completely new line of copiers at the end of 2014. The new line is so different that the choice of either the inspection or the redesign alternative will have no effect on the sales of copiers in future years.

Exhibit 19-6 shows the relevant costs and benefits for each alternative.

1. **Estimated incremental costs:** \$400,000 for the inspection alternative; \$660,000 for the redesign alternative (\$300,000 for process engineering, \$160,000 for design engineering, and \$200,000 for the frames).
2. **Cost savings from less rework, customer support, and repairs:** Exhibit 19-6, line 10, shows that reducing rework saves \$40 per hour of rework. However, Exhibit 19-2, Panel A, column 2, line 13, shows that the total rework cost per hour is \$100, not \$40. Why is there a difference? Because as it improves quality, Photon will save only the \$40 variable cost per rework-hour, not the \$60 in fixed cost per rework-hour. Exhibit 19-6, line 10, shows Photon will save a total of \$960,000 (\$40 per hour × 24,000 rework-hours saved) if it inspects the frames

Exhibit 19-6 Estimated Effects of Quality-Improvement Actions on Costs of Quality for Photocopying Machines at Photon Corporation

	A	B	C	D	E	F	G	H	I	J
1				Relevant Costs and Benefits of						
2				Further Inspecting Incoming Frames				Redesigning Frames		
3	Relevant Items	Relevant Benefit per Unit		Quantity		Total Benefits		Quantity		Total Benefits
4	(1)	(2)		(3)		(4)		(5)		(6)
5	Additional inspection and testing costs					\$ (400,000)				
6	Additional process engineering costs									\$ (300,000)
7	Additional design engineering costs									(160,000)
8	Additional cost of frames \$10 per frame × 20,000 frames									(200,000)
9						(2) × (3)				(2) × (5)
10	Savings in rework costs	\$ 40	per hour	24,000	hours	960,000		32,000	hours	1,280,000
11	Savings in customer-support costs	\$ 20	per hour	2,000	hours	40,000		2,800	hours	56,000
12	Savings in transportation costs for repair parts	\$ 180	per load	500	loads	90,000		700	loads	126,000
13	Savings in warranty repair costs	\$ 45	per hour	20,000	hours	900,000		28,000	hours	1,260,000
14	Total contribution margin from additional sales	\$6,000	per copier	250	copiers	1,500,000		300	copiers	1,800,000
15										
16	Net cost savings and additional contribution margin					\$3,090,000				\$3,862,000
17										
18	Difference in favor of redesigning frames **(J16) – (F16)**						\$772,000			

versus $1,280,000 ($40 per rework-hour × 32,000 rework-hours saved) if it redesigns the frames. The cost-benefit choice is clear for Photon's managers: Redesigning the frames and eliminating the root cause of the problem is better than trying to detect defective units later. Toyota has instituted a similar line of reasoning: Always emphasize defect prevention ("front of the pipe solutions") over defect inspection ("back of the pipe solutions"). Exhibit 19-6 also shows Photon's expected variable-cost savings for customer support (line 11), transportation (line 12), and warranty repair (line 13) for the two alternatives.

3. **Increased contribution margin from higher sales as a result of building a reputation for quality and performance:** Exhibit 19-6, line 14, shows $1,500,000 in higher contribution margins from selling 250 more copiers under the inspection alternative and $1,800,000 in higher contribution margin from selling 300 more copiers under the redesign alternative. Management should always look for opportunities to generate higher revenues, not just cost reductions, from quality improvements.

Exhibit 19-6 shows that both the inspection and the redesign alternatives yield net benefits relative to the status quo. However, consistent with value engineering, design for manufacturing, and Kaizen or continuous improvement that emphasize eliminating the root causes of defects, Photon expects the net benefits from the redesign alternative to be $772,000 greater.

Note how quality improvements affect the costs of quality. Redesigning the frame increases Photon's prevention costs (the costs of process engineering, design engineering, and frames increase), but decreases the firm's internal failure costs (rework) and external failure costs (customer support costs, transportation costs, and warranty repairs). Improving quality also results in greater sales and higher contribution margins. COQ reports provide more insight about quality improvements and allow managers to compare trends over time. In successful quality programs, companies decrease costs of quality and, in particular, internal and external failure costs as a percentage of revenues. Many companies, such as Hewlett-Packard, go further and believe they should eliminate all failure costs and have zero defects.

Decision Point

How do managers identify the relevant costs and benefits of quality-improvement programs?

Learning Objective 4

Use financial and nonfinancial measures to evaluate quality

... nonfinancial measures are leading indicators of future costs of quality

Evaluating a Company's Quality Performance

Because each offers different benefits, Photon's managers use both financial (COQ) and nonfinancial measures to evaluate the firm's quality performance.

Advantages of COQ Measures

- COQ measures focus managers' attention on how poor quality affects operating income.
- Total costs of quality help managers aggregate costs to evaluate the tradeoffs of incurring prevention costs and appraisal costs to eliminate internal and external failure costs.
- COQ measures assist in problem solving by comparing costs and benefits of different quality-improvement programs and by setting priorities for cost reduction.

Advantages of Nonfinancial Measures of Quality

- Nonfinancial measures of quality are often easy to quantify and understand.
- Nonfinancial measures direct attention to physical processes that help managers identify the precise problem areas that need improvement.
- Nonfinancial measures, such as number of defects, provide immediate short-run feedback on whether quality-improvement efforts are succeeding.
- Nonfinancial measures such as measures of customer satisfaction and employee satisfaction are useful indicators of long-run performance.

COQ measures and nonfinancial measures complement each other. Without financial quality measures, companies could be spending more money on improving nonfinancial quality measures than the effort is worth. Without nonfinancial quality measures, quality problems might not be identified until it is too late. Most organizations use both types of measures to gauge how well their firms are performing in terms of quality. McDonald's pays "mystery shoppers" to score individual restaurants on quality, cleanliness, service, and value measures. The company then evaluates each restaurant's performance across these dimensions over time and against other restaurants. In its balanced scorecard, Photon evaluates whether improvements in various nonfinancial quality measures eventually lead to improvements in financial measures.

Decision Point

How do managers use financial and nonfinancial measures to evaluate quality?

Time as a Competitive Tool

Learning Objective 5

Describe customer-response time

... time between receipt of customer order and product delivery

and on-time performance

...delivery of product at the time it is scheduled

and why delays occur

... uncertainty about the timing of customer orders and limited capacity

Companies increasingly view time as a driver of strategy. For example, Capital One has increased the business on its Web site by promising home-loan approval decisions in 30 minutes or less. Companies such as AT&T, General Electric, and Walmart attribute not only higher revenues but also lower costs to doing things faster and on time. These firms claim, for example, that they need to carry fewer inventories because they are able to respond rapidly to customer demands.

Managers need to measure time to manage it properly. In this section, we focus on two *operational measures of time*: *customer-response time*, which reveals how quickly companies respond to customers' demands for their products and services, and *on-time performance*, which indicates how reliably companies meet their scheduled delivery dates. We also show how managers measure the causes and costs of delays.

Customer-Response Time and On-Time Performance

Customer-response time is how long it takes from the time a customer places an order for a product or service to the time the product or service is delivered to the customer. Quickly responding to customers is strategically important in many industries, including the construction, banking, car-rental, and fast-food industries. Some companies, such as Airbus, have to pay penalties to compensate their customers (airline companies) for lost revenues and profits (from being unable to operate flights) as a result of delays in delivering aircraft to them.

Exhibit 19-7 describes the components of customer-response time. *Receipt time* is how long it takes the marketing department to specify to the manufacturing department the exact requirements of the customer's order. **Manufacturing cycle time** (also called **manufacturing lead time**) is how long it takes from the time an order is received by manufacturing to the time a finished good is produced. Manufacturing cycle time is the sum of waiting time and manufacturing time for an order. For example, an aircraft order received by Airbus' manufacturing department may need to wait for components before the plane can be assembled. *Delivery time* is how long it takes to deliver a completed order to a customer.

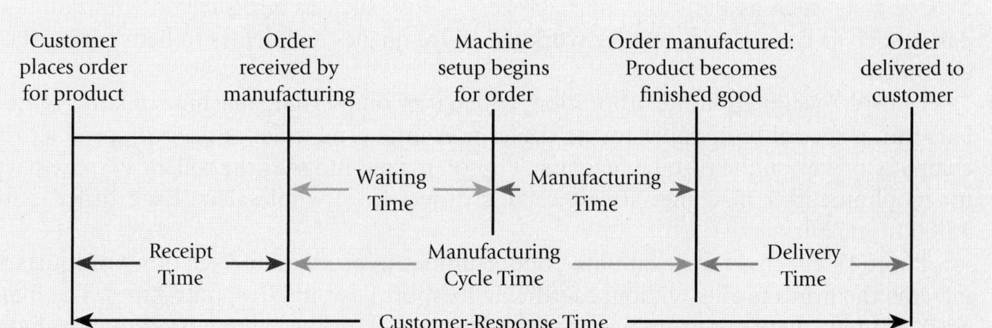

Exhibit 19-7

Components of Customer-Response Time

Some companies evaluate their response time improvement efforts using a measure called **manufacturing cycle efficiency (MCE)**:

$$\text{MCE} = (\text{Value-added manufacturing time} \div \text{Manufacturing cycle time})$$

Value-added manufacturing activities (see Chapter 13) are activities that customers perceive as adding value or utility to a product. The time spent efficiently assembling the product is value-added manufacturing time. The rest of the manufacturing cycle time, such as the time a product spends waiting for parts or for the next stage in the production process or being repaired, is non-value-added manufacturing time. Identifying and minimizing the sources of non-value-added manufacturing time increases a firm's responsiveness to its customers and reduces its costs.

Similar measures apply to service-sector companies. Consider a 40-minute doctor's office visit. Suppose a patient spends 9 of those minutes on administrative tasks such as filling out forms, 20 minutes waiting in the reception area and examination room, and 11 minutes with a nurse or doctor. The service cycle efficiency for this visit equals 11 ÷ 40, or 0.275. In other words, only 27.5% of the 40 minutes added value to the patient/customer. Minimizing their non-value-added service times has allowed hospitals such as Alle-Kiski Medical Center in Pennsylvania to treat more patients in less time.

On-time performance is the delivery of a product or service by the time it is scheduled to be delivered. Consider FedEx, which specifies a price per package and a next-day delivery time of 10:30 a.m. for its overnight courier service. FedEx measures the on-time performance of the service based on how often the firm meets that standard. Commercial airlines gain loyal passengers as a result of consistent on-time service. But there is a tradeoff between a customer's desire for a shorter response time and better on-time performance. Scheduling longer customer-response times, such as airlines lengthening scheduled arrival times, displeases customers on the one hand but increases customer satisfaction on the other hand by improving the airline's on-time performance.

Bottlenecks and Time Drivers

Managing customer-response time and on-time performance requires managers to understand the causes and costs of delays that occur, for example, at a machine in a manufacturing plant or at a checkout counter in a store. A **time driver** is any factor that causes a change in the speed of an activity when the factor changes. Two time drivers are:

1. **Uncertainty about when customers will order products or services.** For example, the more randomly Airbus receives orders for its airplanes, the more likely queues will form and delays will occur.
2. **Bottlenecks due to limited capacity.** A **bottleneck** occurs in an operation when the work to be performed approaches or exceeds the capacity available to do it. For example, a bottleneck results and causes delays when products that must be processed at a particular machine arrive while the machine is being used to process other products. Bottlenecks also occur on the Internet, for example, when many users try to operate wireless mobile devices at the same time (see Concepts in Action: Overcoming Wireless Data Bottlenecks).

Many banks, such as Bank of China; grocery stores, such as Kroger; and entertainment parks, such as Disneyland, actively work to reduce queues and delays to better serve their customers.

Consider again Photon Corporation, which uses one turning machine to convert steel bars into a special fuser roller for its copier machines. The roller is the only product the company makes on the turning machine. Photon makes and sells the rollers as spare parts for its photocopier machines after receiving orders from wholesalers. Each order is for 1,000 fuser rollers.

Photon's managers are examining opportunities to produce and sell other products to increase the firm's profits without sacrificing its short customer-response times. The managers examine these opportunities using the five-step decision-making process introduced in Chapter 1.

Step 1: Identify the Problem and Uncertainties. Photon's managers are considering introducing a second product, a fuser gear, which will use the same turning machine currently used to make fuser rollers. The primary uncertainty is how the introduction of a second product will affect the manufacturing cycle times for rollers. (We focus on Photon's manufacturing cycle time because the receipt time and delivery time for the rollers and gears are minimal.)

Step 2: Obtain Information. Managers gather data on the number of orders for rollers Photon has received in the past, the time it takes to manufacture them, the available capacity, and their average manufacturing cycle time. Photon typically receives 30 orders for rollers each year, but it could receive 10, 30, or 50 orders. Each order is for 1,000 units and takes 100 hours of manufacturing time (8 hours of setup time to clean and prepare the machine that makes the rollers and 92 hours of processing time). The annual capacity of the machine is 4,000 hours. If Photon receives the 30 orders it expects, the total amount of manufacturing time required on the machine is 3,000 hours (100 hours per order × 30 orders), which is less than the available machine capacity of 4,000 hours. Queues and delays still occur because wholesalers can place their orders at any time, even while the machine is processing an earlier order.

Average waiting time, the average amount of time that an order waits in line before the machine is set up and the order is processed, equals[4]

$$\frac{\begin{array}{c}\text{Annual average}\\ \text{number of}\\ \text{orders for rollers}\end{array} \times \left(\begin{array}{c}\text{Manufacturing}\\ \text{time per order}\\ \text{for rollers}\end{array}\right)^2}{2 \times \left[\begin{array}{c}\text{Annual machine}\\ \text{capacity}\end{array} - \left(\begin{array}{c}\text{Annual average number}\\ \text{of orders for rollers}\end{array} \times \begin{array}{c}\text{Manufacturing}\\ \text{time per order for rollers}\end{array}\right)\right]}$$

$$= \frac{30 \times (100)^2}{2 \times [4{,}000 - (30 \times 100)]} = \frac{30 \times 10{,}000}{2 \times (4{,}000 - 3{,}000)} = \frac{300{,}000}{2 \times 1{,}000} = \frac{300{,}000}{2{,}000}$$

$$= 150 \text{ hours per order (for rollers)}$$

Therefore, the average manufacturing cycle time for an order is 250 hours (150 hours of average waiting time + 100 hours of manufacturing time). Note that manufacturing time per order is a squared term in the numerator. The squared term indicates the disproportionately large impact the manufacturing time has on the waiting time. As the manufacturing time lengthens, there is a much greater chance that the machine will be in use when an order arrives, leading to longer delays. The denominator in this formula is a measure of the unused capacity, or cushion. As the unused capacity becomes smaller, the chance that the machine is processing an earlier order becomes more likely, leading to greater delays.

The formula describes only the *average* waiting time. A particular order might arrive when the machine is free, in which case manufacturing will start immediately. In another situation, Photon may receive an order while two other orders are waiting to be processed, which means the delay will be longer than 150 hours.

Step 3: Make Predictions About the Future. The manager makes the following predictions about gears: Photon expects to receive 10 orders for gears, each order for 1,600 units, in the coming year. Each order will take 50 hours of manufacturing time, composed of 3 hours for setup and 47 hours of processing. The expected demand for rollers will be unaffected by whether Photon produces and sells gears.

[4] The technical assumptions are (1) that customer orders for the product follow a Poisson distribution with a mean equal to the expected number of orders (30 in our example) and (2) that orders are processed on a first-in, first-out (FIFO) basis. The Poisson arrival pattern for customer orders has been found to be reasonable in many real-world settings. The FIFO assumption can be modified. Under the modified assumptions, the basic queuing and delay effects will still occur, but the precise formulas will be different.

The average waiting time *before* the machine setup begins is expected to be as follows (the formula is an extension of the preceding formula for the single-product case):

$$\frac{\left[\begin{matrix}\text{Annual average number}\\ \text{of orders for rollers}\end{matrix} \times \left(\begin{matrix}\text{Manufacturing}\\ \text{time per order}\\ \text{for rollers}\end{matrix}\right)^2\right] + \left[\begin{matrix}\text{Annual average number}\\ \text{of orders for gears}\end{matrix} \times \left(\begin{matrix}\text{Manufacturing}\\ \text{time per order}\\ \text{for gears}\end{matrix}\right)^2\right]}{2 \times \left[\begin{matrix}\text{Annual machine}\\ \text{capacity}\end{matrix} - \left(\begin{matrix}\text{Annual average number}\\ \text{of orders for rollers}\end{matrix} \times \begin{matrix}\text{Manufacturing}\\ \text{time per order}\\ \text{for rollers}\end{matrix}\right) - \left(\begin{matrix}\text{Annual average number}\\ \text{of orders for gears}\end{matrix} \times \begin{matrix}\text{Manufacturing}\\ \text{time per order}\\ \text{for gears}\end{matrix}\right)\right]}$$

$$= \frac{[30 \times (100)^2] + [10 \times (50)^2]}{2 \times [4{,}000 - (30 \times 100) - (10 \times 50)]} = \frac{(30 \times 10{,}000) + (10 \times 2{,}500)}{2 \times (4{,}000 - 3{,}000 - 500)}$$

$$= \frac{300{,}000 + 25{,}000}{2 \times 500} = \frac{325{,}000}{1{,}000} = 325 \text{ hours per order (for rollers and gears)}$$

Producing gears will cause the average waiting time for an order to more than double, from 150 hours to 325 hours. The waiting time increases because the production of gears will cause the machine's unused capacity to shrink, increasing the probability that new orders will arrive while current orders are being manufactured or waiting to be manufactured. The average waiting time is very sensitive to the shrinking of unused capacity.

Concepts in Action

Overcoming Wireless Data Bottlenecks

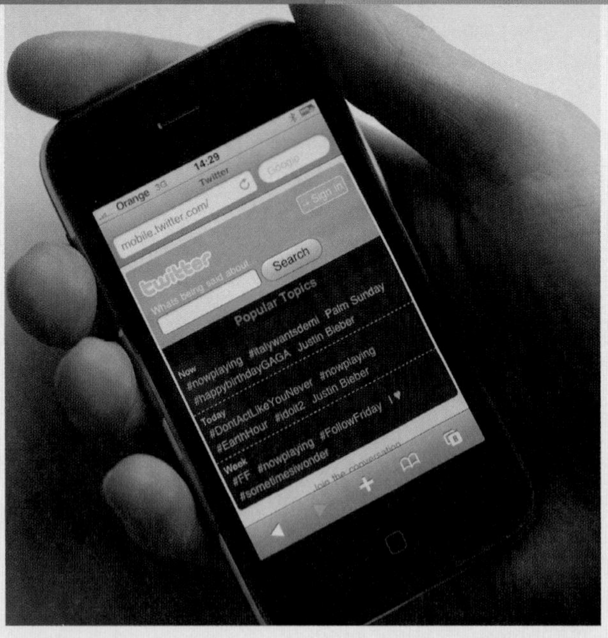

The wired world is quickly going wireless. In addition to the smartphone boom, emerging devices including e-book readers, iPads and other tablets, and machine-to-machine appliances (the so-called "Internet of things") will add to rapidly growing data traffic. Cisco recently forecast that data traffic will grow at a compound rate of 66% from 885 petabytes per month in 2012 to 11.2 exabytes per month by 2017 (an exabyte is one billion gigabytes).

This astronomical growth already causes many users to suffer from mobile bottlenecks caused by too many users trying to transfer mobile data at the same time in a given area. These bottlenecks are most harmful to companies, such as Amazon.com and eBay, buying and selling products and services over the mobile Internet. To relieve mobile bottlenecks, wireless providers and other high-tech companies are deploying more efficient mobile broadband networks, such as 4G LTE, and are working on complementary technologies that automatically choose the best available wireless network to increase capacity. Some technology providers also offer Wi-Fi direct, which allows mobile users to freely transfer video, music, and photos between mobile devices without choking up valuable bandwidth. Companies and government agencies around the world are also trying to increase the wireless broadband spectrum. In the United States, for example, current holders of spectrum—such as radio stations and government agencies—are being encouraged to sell or share their excess capacity to wireless providers in exchange for a share of the profits.

Sources: Cisco Systems, Inc., "Cisco Visual Networking Index: Global Mobile Data Traffic Forecast Update, 2012–2017" (February 6, 2013); Cliff Edwards, "Wifi Direct Seen as Way to Alleviate Network Congestion," *Bloomberg Businessweek* (January 7, 2010); John Morris, "CTIA: More Spectrum, and Other Ways to Break the Wireless Data Bottleneck," *ZDNet,* "Laptops & Desktops" blog (March 24, 2010); George Pyle, "Wireless Growth Leading to Bottlenecks," *Buffalo News* (May 9, 2010); Danny Yardon, "Federal Agencies Urged to Free Up Airwaves," *The Wall Street Journal* (June 14, 2013).

If Photon's managers decide to make gears as well as rollers, the average manufacturing cycle time will be 425 hours for a roller order (325 hours of average waiting time + 100 hours of manufacturing time) and 375 hours for a gear order (325 hours of average waiting time + 50 hours of manufacturing time). A roller order will spend 76.5% (325 hours ÷ 425 hours) of its manufacturing cycle time just waiting for its manufacturing to start!

Step 4: Make Decisions by Choosing Among Alternatives. Should Photon produce gears given how much it would slow down the manufacturing cycle time for rollers? To help the company's managers make a decision, the management accountant identifies and analyzes the relevant revenues and relevant costs of producing gears and, in particular, the cost of delays on all products. The next section focuses on this step.

Decision Point

What is customer response time and what are the reasons for delays?

Relevant Revenues and Costs of Delays

Learning Objective 6

Determine the costs of delays

...lower revenues and higher inventory carrying costs

To determine the relevant revenues and costs of producing gears under Step 4, the management accountant prepares the following additional information:

Product	Annual Average Number of Orders	Average Selling Price per Order If the Average Manufacturing Cycle Time per Order Is		Direct Materials Cost per Order	Inventory Carrying Cost per Order per Hour
		Less Than 300 Hours	More Than 300 Hours		
Rollers	30	$22,000	$21,500	$16,000	$1.00
Gears	10	10,000	9,600	8,000	0.50

Manufacturing cycle times affect both revenues and costs. Revenues are affected because customers are willing to pay a higher price for faster delivery. On the cost side, direct materials costs and inventory carrying costs are the only relevant costs of introducing gears (all other costs are unaffected and therefore irrelevant). Inventory carrying costs equal the opportunity costs of the investment tied up in inventory (see Chapter 11, pages 438–440) and the relevant costs of storage, such as space rental, spoilage, deterioration, and materials handling. Usually, companies calculate inventory carrying costs on a per-unit, per-year basis. To simplify the calculations, the management accountant calculates inventory carrying costs on a per-order, per-hour basis. Also, Photon acquires direct materials at the time the order is received by manufacturing and, therefore, calculates inventory carrying costs for the duration of the manufacturing cycle time.

Exhibit 19-8 presents relevant revenues and relevant costs for the "introduce gears" and "do not introduce gears" alternatives. Based on the analysis, Photon's managers decide not to introduce gears, even though they have a positive contribution margin of $1,600 ($9,600 − $8,000) per order and Photon has the capacity to make them. If it produces gears, Photon will, on average, use only 3,500 (Rollers: 100 hours per order × 30 orders + Gears: 50 hours per order × 10 orders) of the available 4,000 machine-hours. So why is Photon better off not introducing gears? *Because of the negative effects that producing them will have on the existing product, rollers.* The following table presents the *costs of time,* the expected loss in revenues and expected increase in carrying costs as a result of the delays that manufacturing the gears would cause.

Product	Effect of Increasing Average Manufacturing Cycle Time		Expected Loss in Revenues Plus Expected Increase in Carrying Costs of Introducing Gears (3) = (1) + (2)
	Expected Loss in Revenues for Rollers (1)	Expected Increase in Carrying Costs for All Products (2)	
Rollers	$15,000[a]	$5,250[b]	$20,250
Gears	—	1,875[c]	1,875
Total	$15,000	$7,125	$22,125

[a]($22,000 − $21,500) per order × 30 expected orders = $15,000.
[b](425 − 250) hours per order × $1.00 per hour × 30 expected orders = $5,250.
[c](375 − 0) hours per order × $0.50 per hour × 10 expected orders = $1,875.

Exhibit 19-8

Determining Expected Relevant Revenues and Relevant Costs for Photon's Decision to Introduce Gears

Relevant Items	Alternative 1: Introduce Gears (1)	Alternative 2: Do Not Introduce Gears (2)	Difference (3) = (1) − (2)
Expected revenues	$741,000[a]	$660,000[b]	$ 81,000
Expected variable costs	560,000[c]	480,000[d]	(80,000)
Expected inventory carrying costs	14,625[e]	7,500[f]	(7,125)
Expected total costs	574,625	487,500	(87,125)
Expected revenues minus expected costs	$166,375	$172,500	$ (6,125)

[a]($21,500 × 30) + ($9,600 × 10) = $741,000; average manufacturing cycle time will be more than 300 hours.

[b]($22,000 × 30) = $660,000; average manufacturing cycle time will be less than 300 hours.

[c]($16,000 × 30) + ($8,000 × 10) = $560,000.

[d]$16,000 × 30 = $480,000.

[e](Average manufacturing cycle time for rollers × Unit carrying cost per order for rollers × Expected number of orders for rollers) + (Average manufacturing cycle time for gears × Unit carrying cost per order for gears × Expected number of orders for gears) = (425 × $1.00 × 30) + (375 × $0.50 × 10) = $12,750 + $1,875 = $14,625.

[f]Average manufacturing cycle time for rollers × Unit carrying cost per order for rollers × Expected number of orders for rollers = 250 × $1.00 × 30 = $7,500.

Introducing gears causes the average manufacturing cycle time of rollers to increase from 250 hours to 425 hours. Longer manufacturing cycle times increase the inventory carrying costs of rollers and decrease roller revenues (the average manufacturing cycle time for rollers exceeds 300 hours so the average selling price per order decreases from $22,000 to $21,500). Together with the inventory carrying cost of the gears, the expected cost of introducing the gears, $22,125, exceeds the expected contribution margin of $16,000 ($1,600 per order × 10 expected orders) from selling gears by $6,125 (the difference calculated in Exhibit 19-8).

Decision Point

What are relevant revenues and costs of delays?

This example illustrates that when demand uncertainty is high, some unused capacity is desirable.[5] Increasing the capacity of a bottleneck resource reduces manufacturing cycle times and delays. One way to increase capacity is to reduce the time it takes for setups and processing. Another way to increase capacity is to invest in new equipment, such as flexible manufacturing systems that can be programmed to switch quickly from producing one product to producing another. Delays can also be reduced by carefully scheduling production, such as by batching similar jobs together for processing.

Learning Objective 7

Use financial and nonfinancial measures of time

...nonfinancial measures are leading indicators of future financial effects of delays

Balanced Scorecard and Time-Based Measures

In this section, we focus on the final step of the five-step decision-making process—**implement the decision, evaluate performance, and learn**—by tracking changes in time-based measures, evaluating and learning whether these changes affect financial performance, and modifying decisions and plans to achieve the company's goals. We use the structure of the balanced scorecard perspectives—financial, customer, internal business processes, and learning and growth—to summarize how financial and nonfinancial measures of time relate to one another, reduce delays, and increase the output of bottleneck operations.

Financial measures

Revenue gains or price increases from fewer delays
Carrying cost of inventories

[5] Other complexities, such as analyzing a network of machines, priority scheduling, and allowing for uncertainty in processing times, are beyond the scope of this book. In these cases, the basic queuing and delay effects persist, but the precise formulas are more complex.

Customer measures

Customer-response time (the time it takes to fulfill a customer order)

On-time performance (delivering a product or service by the scheduled time)

Internal-business-process measures

Average manufacturing time for key products

Manufacturing cycle efficiency for key processes

Defective units produced at bottleneck operations

Average reduction in setup time and processing time at bottleneck operations

Learning-and-growth measures

Employee satisfaction

Number of employees trained to manage bottlenecks

To see the cause-and-effect linkages across these balanced scorecard perspectives, consider the example of the Bell Group, a designer and manufacturer of equipment for the jewelry industry. A key financial measure was to achieve a higher profit margin on a specific product line. In the customer-measure category, the company set a goal of a 2-day turnaround time on all orders for the product. To achieve this goal, an internal-business-process measure required a bottleneck machine to be operated 22 hours per day, 6 days a week. Finally, in the learning-and-growth measures category, the company trained new employees to carry out nonbottleneck operations to free experienced employees to operate the bottleneck machine. The Bell Group's emphasis on time-related measures in its balanced scorecard has allowed the company to substantially increase manufacturing throughput and decrease customer-response times, leading to higher revenues and increased profits.

Decision Point

What financial and nonfinancial measures of time can managers use in the balanced scorecard?

Managers use both financial and nonfinancial measures to manage the performance of their firms along the time dimension. They use revenue and cost measures to evaluate the financial effects of increases or decreases in customer-response times. Nonfinancial measures help managers evaluate how well they have done on goals such as improving manufacturing cycle times and customer-response times.

Problem for Self-Study

The Sloan Moving Corporation transports household goods from one city to another within the continental United States. It measures quality of service in terms of (1) time required to transport goods, (2) on-time delivery (within 2 days of agreed-upon delivery date), and (3) number of lost or damaged items. Sloan is considering investing in a new scheduling-and-tracking system costing $160,000 per year, which should help it improve performance for items (2) and (3). The following information describes Sloan's current performance and the expected performance if the new system is implemented:

	Current Performance	Expected Future Performance
On-time delivery performance	85%	95%
Variable cost per carton lost or damaged	$60	$60
Fixed cost per carton lost or damaged	$40	$40
Number of cartons lost or damaged per year	3,000 cartons	1,000 cartons

Sloan expects each percentage point increase in on-time performance to increase revenue by $20,000 per year. Sloan's contribution margin percentage is 45%.

1. Should Sloan acquire the new system? Show your calculations.
2. Sloan is very confident about the cost savings from fewer lost or damaged cartons as a result of introducing the new system but unsure about the increase in revenues. Calculate the minimum amount of increase in revenues needed to make it worthwhile for Sloan to invest in the new system.

Solution

1. Additional costs of the new scheduling-and-tracking system are $160,000 per year. Additional annual benefits of the new scheduling-and-tracking system are as follows:

Additional annual revenues from a 10% improvement in on-time performance, from 85% to 95%, 20,000 per 1% × 10 percentage points	$200,000
45% contribution margin from additional annual revenues (0.45 × $200,000)	$ 90,000
Decrease in costs per year from fewer cartons lost or damaged (only variable costs are relevant) [$60 per carton × (3,000 − 1,000) cartons]	120,000
Total additional benefits	$210,000

Because the benefits of $210,000 exceed the costs of $160,000, Sloan should invest in the new system.

2. As long as Sloan earns a contribution margin of $40,000 (to cover incremental costs of $160,000 minus relevant variable-cost savings of $120,000) from additional annual revenues, investing in the new system is beneficial. This contribution margin corresponds to additional revenues of 40,000 ÷ 0.45 = 88,889.

▶ Decision Points

The following question-and-answer format summarizes the chapter's learning objectives. Each decision presents a key question related to a learning objective. The guidelines are the answer to that question.

Decision	Guidelines
1. What are the four cost categories of a costs-of-quality program?	Four cost categories in a costs-of-quality program are prevention costs (costs incurred to prevent the production of products that do not conform to specifications), appraisal costs (costs incurred to detect which of the individual units of products do not conform to specifications), internal failure costs (costs incurred on defective products before they are shipped to customers), and external failure costs (costs incurred on defective products after they are shipped to customers).
2. What nonfinancial measures and methods can managers use to improve quality?	Nonfinancial quality measures managers can use include customer satisfaction measures such as the number of customer complaints and percentage of defective units shipped to customers; internal-business-process measures such as the percentage of defective and reworked products; and learning-and-growth measures such as the percentage of employees trained in and empowered to use quality principles. Three methods to identify quality problems and to improve quality are (a) control charts to distinguish random from nonrandom variations in an operating process; (b) Pareto diagrams to indicate how frequently each type of failure occurs; and (c) cause-and-effect diagrams to identify and respond to potential causes of failure.

Decision	Guidelines
3. How do managers identify the relevant costs and benefits of quality-improvement programs?	The relevant costs of quality-improvement programs are the expected incremental costs to implement the program. The relevant benefits are the cost savings and the estimated increase in contribution margin from the higher revenues expected from quality improvements.
4. How do managers use financial and nonfinancial measures to evaluate quality?	Financial measures help managers evaluate the tradeoffs among prevention costs, appraisal costs, and failure costs. Nonfinancial measures identify problem areas that need improvement and serve as indicators of future financial performance.
5. What is customer-response time and what are the reasons for delays?	Customer-response time is how long it takes from the time a customer places an order for a product or service to the time the product or service is delivered to the customer. Delays occur because of (a) uncertainty about when customers will order products or services and (b) bottlenecks due to limited capacity. Bottlenecks are operations at which the work to be performed approaches or exceeds available capacity.
6. What are relevant revenues and costs of delays?	Relevant revenues and costs of delays include lower revenues and higher inventory carrying costs.
7. What financial and nonfinancial measures of time can managers use in the balanced scorecard?	Examples of financial and nonfinancial measures managers can use in the balanced scorecard to evaluate a company's performance related to time are revenue losses from delays, customer-response time, on-time performance, average manufacturing cycle time, and number of employees trained to manage bottleneck operations.

Terms to Learn

This chapter and the Glossary at the end of the book contain definitions of the following important terms:

appraisal costs **(p. 736)**
average waiting time **(p. 747)**
bottleneck **(p. 746)**
cause-and-effect diagram **(p. 740)**
conformance quality **(p. 736)**
control chart **(p. 739)**
costs of quality (COQ) **(p. 736)**
customer-response time **(p. 745)**
design quality **(p. 736)**
external failure costs **(p. 736)**
internal failure costs **(p. 736)**
manufacturing cycle efficiency (MCE) **(p. 746)**
manufacturing cycle time **(p. 745)**
manufacturing lead time **(p. 745)**
on-time performance **(p. 746)**
Pareto diagram **(p. 740)**
prevention costs **(p. 736)**
quality **(p. 735)**
time driver **(p. 746)**

Assignment Material

Questions

MyAccountingLab

19-1 Describe two benefits of improving quality.
19-2 How does conformance quality differ from design quality? Explain.
19-3 Name two items classified as prevention costs.
19-4 Give two examples of appraisal costs.
19-5 Distinguish between internal failure costs and external failure costs.
19-6 Describe three methods that companies use to identify quality problems.
19-7 "Companies should focus on financial measures of quality because these are the only measures of quality that can be linked to bottom-line performance." Do you agree? Explain.
19-8 Give two examples of nonfinancial measures of customer satisfaction relating to quality.

19-9 Give two examples of nonfinancial measures of internal-business-process quality.

19-10 "When evaluating alternative ways to improve quality, managers need to consider the fully allocated costs of quality." Do you agree? Explain.

19-11 Distinguish between customer-response time and manufacturing cycle time.

19-12 "There is no tradeoff between customer-response time and on-time performance." Do you agree? Explain.

19-13 Give two reasons why delays occur.

19-14 "Companies should always make and sell all products whose selling prices exceed variable costs." Assuming fixed costs are irrelevant, do you agree? Explain.

19-15 "When evaluating a company's performance on the time dimension, managers should only consider financial measures." Do you agree? Explain.

MyAccountingLab

Exercises

19-16 Costs of quality. (CMA, adapted) Osborn, Inc., produces cell phone equipment. Amanda Westerly, Osborn's president, decided to devote more resources to the improvement of product quality after learning that her company had been ranked fourth in product quality in a 2011 survey of cell phone users. Osborn's quality-improvement program has now been in operation for 2 years, and the cost report shown here has recently been issued.

Semi-Annual COQ Report, Osborn, Inc. (in thousands)

	6/30/2012	12/31/2012	6/30/2013	12/31/2013
Prevention costs				
Machine maintenance	$ 480	$ 480	$ 440	$ 290
Supplier training	21	90	45	35
Design reviews	30	218	198	196
Total prevention costs	531	788	683	521
Appraisal costs				
Incoming inspections	109	124	89	55
Final testing	327	327	302	202
Total appraisal costs	436	451	391	257
Internal failure costs				
Rework	226	206	166	115
Scrap	127	124	68	65
Total internal failure costs	353	330	234	180
External failure costs				
Warranty repairs	182	89	70	67
Customer returns	594	510	263	186
Total external failure costs	776	599	333	253
Total quality costs	$2,096	$2,168	$1,641	$1,211
Total revenues	$8,220	$9,180	$9,260	$9,050

Required

1. For each period, calculate the ratio of each COQ category to revenues and to total quality costs.
2. Based on the results of requirement 1, would you conclude that Osborn's quality program has been successful? Prepare a short report to present your case.
3. Based on the 2011 survey, Amanda Westerly believed that Osborn had to improve product quality. In making her case to Osborn management, how might Westerly have estimated the opportunity cost of not implementing the quality-improvement program?

19-17 Costs of quality analysis. Safe Travel produces car seats for children from newborn to 2 years old. The company is worried because one of its competitors has recently come under public scrutiny because of product failure. Historically, Safe Travel's only problem with its car seats was stitching in the straps. The problem can usually be detected and repaired during an internal inspection. The cost of the inspection is $5.00 per car seat, and the repair cost is $1.00 per car seat. All 200,000 car seats were inspected last year, and 5% were found to have problems with the stitching in the straps during the internal inspection. Another 1% of the 200,000 car seats had problems with the stitching, but the internal inspection did not discover them. Defective units that were sold and shipped to customers needed to be shipped back to Safe Travel and repaired. Shipping costs are $8.00 per car seat, and repair costs are $1.00 per car seat. However, the out-of-pocket costs (shipping and repair) are not the only costs of defects not discovered in the internal inspection. Negative publicity will result in a loss of future contribution margin of $100 for each external failure.

Required

1. Calculate appraisal cost.
2. Calculate internal failure cost.
3. Calculate out-of-pocket external failure cost.
4. Determine the opportunity cost associated with the external failures.
5. What are the total costs of quality?
6. Safe Travel is concerned with the high up-front cost of inspecting all 200,000 units. It is considering an alternative internal inspection plan that will cost only $3.00 per car seat inspected. During the internal inspection, the alternative technique will detect only 3.5% of the 200,000 car seats that have stitching problems. The other 2.5% will be detected after the car seats are sold and shipped. What are the total costs of quality for the alternative technique?
7. What factors other than cost should Safe Travel consider before changing inspection techniques?

19-18 Costs of quality, ethical considerations. Refer to information in Exercise 19-17 in answering this question. Safe Travel has discovered a more serious problem with the plastic core of its car seats. An accident can cause the plastic in some of the seats to crack and break, resulting in serious injuries to the occupant. It is estimated that this problem will affect about 200 car seats in the next year. This problem could be corrected by using a higher quality of plastic that would increase the cost of every car seat produced by $10. If this problem is not corrected, Safe Travel estimates that out of the 200 car seats affected, customers will realize that the problem is due to a defect in the seats in only three cases. Safe Travel's legal team has estimated that each of these three cases would result in a lawsuit that could be settled for about $500,000. All lawsuits settled would include a confidentiality clause, so Safe Travel's reputation would not be affected.

1. Assuming that Safe Travel expects to sell 200,000 car seats next year, what would be the cost of increasing the quality of all 200,000 car seats?
2. What will be the total cost of the lawsuits next year if the problem is not corrected?
3. Suppose Safe Travel has decided not to increase the quality of the plastic because the cost of increasing the quality exceeds the benefits (saving the cost of lawsuits). What do you think of this decision? (*Note:* Because of the confidentiality clause, the decision will have no effect on Safe Travel's reputation.)
4. Are there any other costs or benefits that Safe Travel should consider?

19-19 Costs of quality, quality improvement. Cell Design produces cell phone covers for all makes and models of cell phones. Cell Design sells 1,050,000 units each year at a price of $10 per unit and a contribution margin of 40%.

A survey of Cell Design customers over the past 12 months indicates that customers were very satisfied with the products but a disturbing number of customers were disappointed because the products they purchased did not fit their phones. They then had to hassle with returns and replacements.

Cell Design's managers want to modify their production processes to develop products that more closely match Cell Design's specifications because the quality control in place to prevent ill-fitting products from reaching customers is not working very well.

The current costs of quality are as follows:

Prevention costs	$210,000
Appraisal costs	$100,000
Internal failure costs	
Rework	$420,000
Scrap	$ 21,000
External failure costs	
Product replacements	$315,000
Lost sales from customer returns	$787,500
The QC manager and controller have forecast the following additional costs to modify the production process.	
CAD design improvement	$150,000
Improve machine calibration to specifications	$137,500

Required

1. Which cost of quality category are managers focusing on? Why?
2. If the improvements result in a 60% decrease in customer replacement cost and a 70% decrease in customer returns, what is the impact on the overall COQ and the company's operating income? What should Cell Design do? Explain.

3. Calculate prevention, appraisal, internal failure, and external failure costs as a percentage of total quality costs and as a percentage of sales before and after the change in the production process. Comment briefly on your results.

19-20 Quality improvement, relevant costs, relevant revenues. SpeedPrint manufactures and sells 18,000 high-technology printing presses each year. The variable and fixed costs of rework and repair are as follows:

	Variable Cost	Fixed Cost	Total Cost
Rework cost per hour	$79	$115	$194
Repair costs			
Customer support cost per hour	35	55	90
Transportation cost per load	350	115	465
Warranty repair cost per hour	89	150	239

SpeedPrint's current presses have a quality problem that causes variations in the shade of some colors. Its engineers suggest changing a key component in each press. The new component will cost $70 more than the old one. In the next year, however, SpeedPrint expects that with the new component it will (1) save 14,000 hours of rework, (2) save 850 hours of customer support, (3) move 225 fewer loads, (4) save 8,000 hours of warranty repairs, and (5) sell an additional 140 printing presses, for a total contribution margin of $1,680,000. SpeedPrint believes that even as it improves quality, it will not be able to save any of the fixed costs of rework or repair. SpeedPrint uses a 1-year time horizon for this decision because it plans to introduce a new press at the end of the year.

Required

1. Should SpeedPrint change to the new component? Show your calculations.
2. Suppose the estimate of 140 additional printing presses sold is uncertain. What is the minimum number of additional printing presses that SpeedPrint needs to sell to justify adopting the new component?
3. What other factors should managers at SpeedPrint consider when making their decision about changing to a new component?

19-21 Quality improvement, relevant costs, relevant revenues. Keswick Conference Center and Catering is a conference center and restaurant facility that hosts more than 300 national and international events each year attended by 50,000 professionals. Due to increased competition and soaring customer expectations, the company has been forced to revisit its quality standards. In the company's 25-year history, customer demand has never been greater for high-quality products and services. Keswick has the following budgeted fixed and variable costs for 2013:

	Total Conference Center Fixed Costs	Variable Cost per Conference Attendee
Building and facilities	$4,320,000	
Management salaries	$1,680,000	
Customer support and service personnel		$ 66
Food and drink		$120
Conference materials		$ 42
Incidental products and services		$ 18

The company's budgeted operating income is $4,200,000.

After conducting a survey of 3,000 conference attendees, the company has learned that its customers would most like to see the following changes in the quality of the company's products and services: (1) more menu options and faster service, (2) more incidental products and services (wireless access in all meeting rooms, computer stations for Internet use, free local calling, and so on), and (3) upscale and cleaner meeting facilities. To satisfy these customer demands, the company would be required to increase fixed costs by 50% per year and increase variable costs by $12 per attendee as follows:

Customer support and service personnel	$4
Food and drink	$5
Conference materials	$0
Incidental products and services	$3

Keswick believes that the preceding improvements in product and service quality would increase overall conference attendance by 40%.

Required

1. What is the budgeted revenue per conference attendee?
2. Assuming budgeted revenue per conference attendee is unchanged, should Keswick implement the proposed changes?
3. Assuming budgeted revenue per conference attendee is unchanged, what is the variable cost per conference attendee at which Keswick would be indifferent between implementing and not implementing the proposed changes?

19-22 Waiting time. Kitty Wonderland (KW) makes toys for cats and kittens. KW's managers have recently learned that they can calculate the average waiting time for an order from the time an order is received and the time it is manufactured. They have asked for your help and have provided the following information.

Expected number of orders for the product: 2,000

Manufacturing time per order: 4 hours

Annual machine capacity in hours: 10,000

1. Calculate the average waiting time per order.
2. After learning about the average waiting time, KW's managers are confused. They do not understand why, if annual machine capacity is greater than the average number of orders for the product, there would be any waiting time at all. Write a memo to clarify the situation.
3. The managers have asked for your suggestions on what they can do to minimize or eliminate waiting time. How would you respond?
4. Management is expecting sales to increase. Will average waiting time increase or decrease? Explain briefly.

19-23 Waiting time, service industry. The registration advisors at a small Midwestern university (SMU) help 4,200 students develop their class schedules and register for classes each semester. Each advisor works for 10 hours a day during the registration period. SMU currently has 10 advisors. While advising an individual student can take anywhere from 2 to 30 minutes, it takes an average of 12 minutes per student. During the registration period, the 10 advisors see an average of 300 students a day on a first-come, first-served basis.

Required

1. Using the formula on page 747, calculate how long the average student will have to wait in the advisor's office before being advised.
2. The head of the registration advisors would like to increase the number of students seen each day because at 300 students a day it would take 14 working days to see all of the students. This is a problem because the registration period lasts for only 2 weeks (10 working days). If the advisors could advise 420 students a day, it would take only 2 weeks (10 days). However, the head advisor wants to make sure that the waiting time is not excessive. What would be the average waiting time if 420 students were seen each day?
3. SMU wants to know the effect of reducing the average advising time on the average wait time. If SMU can reduce the average advising time to 10 minutes, what would be the average waiting time if 420 students were seen each day?

19-24 Waiting time, cost considerations, customer satisfaction. Refer to the information presented in Exercise 19-23. The head of the registration advisors at SMU has decided that the advisors must finish their advising in 2 weeks and therefore must advise 420 students a day. However, the average waiting time given a 12-minute advising period will result in student complaints, as will reducing the average advising time to 10 minutes. SMU is considering two alternatives:

a. Hire two more advisors for the 2-week (10-working day) advising period. This will increase the available number of advisors to 12 and therefore lower the average waiting time.
b. Increase the number of days that the advisors will work during the 2-week registration period to 6 days a week. If SMU increases the number of days worked to 6 per week, then the 10 advisors need only see 350 students a day to advise all of the students in 2 weeks.

Required

1. What would the average wait time be under alternative A and under alternative B?
2. If advisors earn $100 per day, which alternative would be cheaper for SMU (assume that if advisors work 6 days in a given work week, they will be paid time and a half for the sixth day)?
3. From a student satisfaction point of view, which of the two alternatives would be preferred? Why?

19-25 Nonfinancial measures of quality and time. Global Cell Phones (GCP) has developed a cell phone that can be used anywhere in the world (even countries like Japan that have a relatively unique cell phone system). GCP has been receiving complaints about the phone. For the past two years, GCP has been test-marketing the phones and gathering nonfinancial information related to actual and perceived aspects of the phone's quality. The company expects that, given the lack of competition in this market, increasing the quality of the phone will result in higher sales and thereby higher profits.

Quality data for 2012 and 2013 include the following:

	2012	2013
Cell phones produced and shipped	3,000	15,000
Number of defective units shipped	150	600
Number of customer complaints	225	375
Units reworked before shipping	180	1,050
Manufacturing cycle time	15 days	16 days
Average customer-response time	30 days	28 days

Required

1. For each year, 2012 and 2013, calculate the following:
   a. Percentage of defective units shipped
   b. Customer complaints as a percentage of units shipped
   c. Percentage of units reworked during production
   d. Manufacturing cycle time as a percentage of total time from order to delivery
2. Referring to the information computed in requirement 1, explain whether GCP's quality and timeliness have improved.
3. Why would manufacturing cycle time have increased while customer-response time decreased? (It may be useful to first describe what is included in each time measurement—see Exhibit 19-7, page 745.)

19-26 Nonfinancial measures of quality, manufacturing cycle efficiency. (CMA, adapted) Prescott Manufacturing evaluates the performance of its production managers based on a variety of factors, including cost, quality, and cycle time. The following are nonfinancial measures for quality and time for 2012 and 2013 for its only product:

Nonfinancial Quality Measures	2012	2013
Number of returned goods	750	915
Number of defective units reworked	2,200	1,640
Annual hours spent on quality training per employee	38	44
Number of units delivered on time	24,820	29,935
Annual Totals	**2012**	**2013**
Units of finished goods shipped	28,480	33,668
Average total hours worked per employee	2,000	2,000

The following information relates to the average amount of time needed to complete an order:

Time to Complete an Order	2012	2013
Wait time		
From customer placing order to order being received by production	15	14
From order received by production to machine being set up for production	13	12
Inspection time	4	2
Process time	8	8
Move time	4	4

Required

1. Compute the manufacturing cycle efficiency for an order for 2012 and 2013.
2. For each year 2012 and 2013, calculate the following:
   a. Percentage of goods returned
   b. Defective units reworked as a percentage of units shipped
   c. Percentage of on-time deliveries
   d. Percentage of hours spent by each employee on quality training
3. Evaluate management's performance on quality and timeliness in 2012 and 2013.

Problems

MyAccountingLab

19-27 Statistical quality control. Harvest Cereals produces a wide variety of breakfast products. The company's three best-selling breakfast cereals are Double Bran Bits, Honey Wheat Squares, and Sugar King Pops. Each box of a particular type of cereal is required to meet pre-determined weight specifications, so that no single box contains more or less cereal than another. The company measures the mean weight per production run to determine if there are variances over or under the company's specified upper- and lower-level control limits. A production run that falls outside of the specified control limit does not meet quality standards and is investigated further by management to determine the cause of the variance. The three Harvest breakfast cereals had the following weight standards and production run data for the month of March:

Quality Standard: Mean Weight per Production Run

Double Bran Bits	Honey Wheat Squares	Sugar King Pops
17.97 ounces	14 ounces	16.02 ounces

Actual Mean Weight per Production Run (Ounces)

Production Run	Double Bran Bits	Honey Wheat Squares	Sugar King Pops
1	18.23	14.11	15.83
2	18.14	14.13	16.11
3	18.22	13.98	16.24
4	18.30	13.89	15.69
5	18.10	13.91	15.95
6	18.05	14.01	15.50
7	17.84	13.94	15.86
8	17.66	13.99	16.23
9	17.60	14.03	16.15
10	17.52	13.97	16.60
Standard Deviation	**0.28**	**0.16**	**0.21**

Required

1. Using the $\pm 2\sigma$ rule, what variance investigation decisions would be made?
2. Present control charts for each of the three breakfast cereals for March. What inferences can you draw from the charts?
3. What are the costs of quality in this example? How could Harvest employ Six Sigma programs to improve quality?

19-28 Quality improvement, Pareto diagram, cause-and-effect diagram. Pauli's Pizza has recently begun collecting data on the quality of its customer order processing and delivery. Pauli's made 1,800 deliveries during the first quarter of 2013. The following quality data pertain to first-quarter deliveries:

Type of Quality Failure	Quality Failure Incidents, First Quarter 2013
Late delivery	50
Damaged or spoiled product delivered	5
Incorrect order delivered	12
Service complaints by customer of delivery personnel	8
Failure to deliver incidental items with order (drinks, side items, etc.)	18

Required

1. Draw a Pareto diagram of the quality failures experienced by Pauli's Pizza.
2. Give examples of prevention activities that could reduce the failures experienced by Pauli's.
3. Draw a cause-and-effect diagram of possible causes for late deliveries.

19-29 Quality improvement, relevant costs, and relevant revenues. The Tristan Corporation sells 250,000 V262 valves to the automobile and truck industry. Tristan has a capacity of 150,000 machine-hours and can produce two valves per machine-hour. V262's contribution margin per unit is $7. Tristan sells only 250,000 valves because 50,000 valves (20% of the good valves) need to be reworked. It takes 1 machine-hour to rework two valves, so 25,000 hours of capacity are used in the rework process. Tristan's rework costs are $550,000. Rework costs consist of the following:

- Direct materials and direct rework labor (variable costs): $5 per unit
- Fixed costs of equipment, rent, and overhead allocation: $6 per unit

Tristan's process designers have developed a modification that would maintain the speed of the process and ensure 100% quality and no rework. The new process would cost $538,000 per year. The following additional information is available:

- The demand for Tristan's V262 valves is 400,000 per year.
- The Colton Corporation has asked Tristan to supply 27,000 T971 valves (another product) if Tristan implements the new design. The contribution margin per T971 valve is $12. Tristan can make one T971 valve per machine-hour with 100% quality and no rework.

Required

1. Suppose Tristan's designers implement the new design. Should Tristan accept Colton's order for 27,000 T971 valves? Show your calculations.
2. Should Tristan implement the new design? Show your calculations.
3. What nonfinancial and qualitative factors should Tristan consider in deciding whether to implement the new design?

19-30 Quality improvement, relevant costs, and relevant revenues. The Harvest Corporation uses multicolored molding to make plastic lamps. The molding operation has a capacity of 100,000 units per year. The demand for lamps is very strong. Harvest will be able to sell whatever output quantities it can produce at $50 per lamp.

Harvest can start only 100,000 units into production in the molding department because of capacity constraints on the molding machines. If a defective unit is produced at the molding operation, it must be scrapped at a net disposal value of zero. Of the 100,000 units started at the molding operation, 10,000 defective units (10%) are produced. The cost of a defective unit, based on total (fixed and variable) manufacturing costs incurred up to the molding operation, equals $24 per unit, as follows:

Direct materials (variable)	$12 per unit
Direct manufacturing labor, setup labor, and materials-handling labor (variable)	2 per unit
Equipment, rent, and other allocated overhead, including inspection and testing costs on scrapped parts (fixed)	10 per unit
Total	$24 per unit

Harvest's designers have determined that adding a different type of material to the existing direct materials would result in no defective units being produced, but it would increase the variable costs by $3 per lamp in the molding department.

Required

1. Should Harvest use the new material? Show your calculations.
2. What nonfinancial and qualitative factors should Harvest consider in making the decision?

19-31 Waiting times, manufacturing cycle times. The Seawall Corporation uses an injection molding machine to make a plastic product, Z39, after receiving firm orders from its customers. Seawall estimates that it will receive 50 orders for Z39 during the coming year. Each order of Z39 will take 80 hours of machine time. The annual machine capacity is 5,000 hours.

Required

1. Calculate (a) the average amount of time that an order for Z39 will wait in line before it is processed and (b) the average manufacturing cycle time per order for Z39.
2. Seawall is considering introducing a new product, Y28. The company expects it will receive 25 orders of Y28 in the coming year. Each order of Y28 will take 20 hours of machine time. Assuming the demand for Z39 will not be affected by the introduction of Y28, calculate (a) the average waiting time for an order received and (b) the average manufacturing cycle time per order for each product, if Seawall introduces Y28.

19-32 Waiting times, relevant revenues, and relevant costs (continuation of 19-31). Seawall is still debating whether it should introduce Y28. The following table provides information on selling prices, variable costs, and inventory carrying costs for Z39 and Y28:

Product	Annual Average Number of Orders	Selling Price per Order If Average Manufacturing Cycle Time per Order Is		Variable Cost per Order	Inventory Carrying Cost per Order per Hour
		Less Than 320 Hours	More Than 320 Hours		
Z39	50	$27,000	$26,500	$15,000	$0.75
Y28	25	6,400	6,000	5,000	0.25

Using the average manufacturing cycle times calculated in Problem 19-31, requirement 2, should Seawall manufacture and sell Y28? Show your calculations and briefly explain your reasoning.

19-33 Manufacturing cycle times, relevant revenues, and relevant costs. The Brandt Corporation makes wire harnesses for the aircraft industry only upon receiving firm orders from its customers. Brandt has recently purchased a new machine to make two types of wire harnesses, one for Boeing airplanes (B7) and the other for Airbus Industries airplanes (A3). The annual capacity of the new machine is 6,000 hours. The following information is available for next year:

Customer	Annual Average Number of Orders	Manufacturing Time Required	Selling Price per Order If Average Manufacturing Cycle Time per Order Is		Variable Cost per Order	Inventory Carrying Cost per Order per Hour
			Less Than 200 Hours	More Than 200 Hours		
B7	125	40 hours	$15,000	$14,400	$10,000	$0.50
A3	10	50 hours	13,500	12,960	9,000	0.45

Required

1. Calculate the average manufacturing cycle times per order (a) if Brandt manufactures only B7 and (b) if Brandt manufactures both B7 and A3.
2. Even though A3 has a positive contribution margin, Brandt's managers are evaluating whether Brandt should (a) make and sell only B7 or (b) make and sell both B7 and A3. Which alternative will maximize Brandt's operating income? Show your calculations.
3. What other factors should Brandt consider in choosing between the alternatives in requirement 2?

19-34 Compensation linked with profitability, waiting time, and quality measures. Seashore Healthcare operates two medical groups, one in Philadelphia and one in Baltimore. The semiannual bonus plan for each medical group's president has three components:

a. Profitability performance. Add 1.50% of operating income.
b. Average patient waiting time. Add $30,000 if the average waiting time for a patient to see a doctor after the scheduled appointment time is less than 15 minutes. If average patient waiting time is more than 15 minutes, add nothing.
c. Patient satisfaction performance. Deduct $35,000 if patient satisfaction (measured using a survey asking patients about their satisfaction with their doctor and their overall satisfaction with Seashore Healthcare) falls below 65 on a scale from 0 (lowest) to 100 (highest). No additional bonus is awarded for satisfaction scores of 65 or more.

Semiannual data for 2013 for the Philadelphia and Baltimore groups are as follows:

	January–June	July–December
Philadelphia		
Operating income	$11,150,000	$10,000,000
Average waiting time	13 minutes	17 minutes
Patient satisfaction	72	66
Baltimore		
Operating income	$8,800,000	$7,500,000
Average waiting time	20 minutes	13 minutes
Patient satisfaction	59	68

Required

1. Compute the bonuses paid in each half year of 2013 to the Philadelphia and Baltimore medical group presidents.
2. Discuss the validity of the components of the bonus plan as measures of profitability, waiting time performance, and patient satisfaction. Suggest one shortcoming of each measure and how it might be overcome (by redesign of the plan or by another measure).
3. Why do you think Seashore Healthcare includes measures of both operating income and waiting time in its bonus plan for group presidents? Give one example of what might happen if waiting time was dropped as a performance measure.

19-35 Ethics and quality. Weston Corporation manufactures auto parts for two leading Japanese automakers. Nancy Evans is the management accountant for one of Weston's largest manufacturing plants. The plant's general manager, Chris Sheldon, has just returned from a meeting at corporate headquarters where quality expectations were outlined for 2014. Chris calls Nancy into his office to relay the corporate quality objective that total quality costs will not exceed 10% of total revenues by plant under any circumstances. Chris asks Nancy to provide him with a list of options for meeting corporate headquarters' quality objective. The plant's initial budgeted revenues and quality costs for 2014 are as follows:

Revenue	5,100,000
Quality costs:	
Testing of purchased materials	48,000
Quality control training for production staff	7,500
Warranty repairs	123,000
Quality design engineering	72,000
Customer support	55,500
Materials scrap	18,000
Product inspection	153,000
Engineering redesign of failed parts	31,500
Rework of failed parts	27,000

Prior to receiving the new corporate quality objective, Nancy had collected information for all of the plant's possible options for improving both product quality and costs of quality. She was planning to introduce the idea of reengineering the manufacturing process at a one-time cost of $112,500, which would decrease product inspection costs by approximately 25% per year and was expected to reduce warranty repairs and customer support by an estimated 40% per year. After seeing the new corporate objective, Nancy is reconsidering the reengineering idea.

Nancy returns to her office and crunches the numbers again to look for other alternatives. She concludes that by increasing the cost of quality control training for production staff by $22,500 per year, the company would reduce inspection costs by 10% annually and reduce warranty repairs and customer support costs by 20% per year as well. She is leaning toward only presenting this latter option to Chris because this is the only option that meets the new corporate quality objective.

Required

1. Calculate the ratio of each budgeted costs-of-quality category (prevention, appraisal, internal failure, and external failure) to budgeted revenues for 2014. Are the budgeted total costs of quality as a percentage of budgeted revenues currently less than 10%?
2. Which of the two quality options should Nancy propose to the general manager, Chris Sheldon? Show the 2-year outcome for each option: (a) reengineer the manufacturing process for $112,500 and (b) increase quality training expenditure by $22,500 per year.
3. Suppose Nancy decides not to present the reengineering option to Chris. Is Nancy's action unethical? Explain.

19-36 Quality improvement. Winchester Corporation makes printed cloth in two departments: weaving and printing. Currently, all product first moves through the weaving department and then through the printing department before it is sold to retail distributors for $2,500 per roll. Winchester provides the following information:

	Weaving	Printing
Monthly capacity	10,000 rolls	15,000 rolls
Monthly production	9,500 rolls	8,550 rolls
Direct material cost per roll of cloth processed at each operation	$1,000	$200
Fixed operating costs	$5,700,000	$855,000

Winchester can start only 10,000 rolls of cloth in the weaving department because of capacity constraints of the weaving machines. Of the 10,000 rolls of cloth started in the weaving department, 500 (5%) defective rolls are scrapped at zero net disposal value. The good rolls from the weaving department (called gray cloth) are sent to the printing department. Of the 9,500 good rolls started at the printing operation, 950 (10%) defective rolls are scrapped at zero net disposal value. The Winchester Corporation's total monthly sales of printed cloth equal the printing department's output.

Required

1. The printing department is considering buying 5,000 additional rolls of gray cloth from an outside supplier at $1,800 per roll, which is much higher than Winchester's cost to manufacture the roll. The printing department expects that 10% of the rolls obtained from the outside supplier will result in defective products. Should the printing department buy the gray cloth from the outside supplier? Show your calculations.
2. Winchester's engineers have developed a method that would lower the printing department's rate of defective products to 6% at the printing operation. Implementing the new method would cost $700,000 per month. Should Winchester implement the change? Show your calculations.
3. The design engineering team has proposed a modification that would lower the weaving department's rate of defective products to 3%. The modification would cost the company $350,000 per month. Should Winchester implement the change? Show your calculations.

20 Inventory Management, Just-in-Time, and Simplified Costing Methods

Learning Objectives

1. Identify six categories of costs associated with goods for sale
2. Balance ordering costs with carrying costs using the economic-order-quantity (EOQ) decision model
3. Identify the effect of errors that can arise when using the EOQ decision model and ways to reduce conflicts between the EOQ model and models used for performance evaluation
4. Describe why companies are using just-in-time (JIT) purchasing
5. Distinguish materials requirements planning (MRP) systems from just-in-time (JIT) systems for manufacturing
6. Identify the features and benefits of a just-in-time production system
7. Describe different ways backflush costing can simplify traditional inventory-costing systems
8. Understand the principles of lean accounting

Suppose you could receive a large quantity discount for a product that you regularly use, but the discount requires you to buy a year's supply of it and make a large up-front expenditure.

Would you take the quantity discount? Companies face similar decisions because firms pay a price for tying up money in inventory sitting on their shelves or elsewhere. Money tied up in inventory is a particularly serious problem when times are tough. Companies such as Costco work very hard to keep their inventories low.

Costco Aggressively Manages Its Inventory to Thrive in Tough Times[1]

Costco is widely known for its $55-a-year membership fee and its massive, austere warehouses stocked floor to ceiling with large portions of everything from soap to soda. With 627 Costco warehouses around the world, Costco stocks *fewer* items than its competitors and employs innovative inventory management practices that successfully reduce costs throughout its global operations.

The average grocery store carries around 40,000 items, but Costco limits its offerings to about 4,000 products or 90% less, reducing the costs of carrying inventory. Costco also employs a just-in-time inventory management system, which includes sharing data directly with many of its largest suppliers. Companies like PepsiCo and Kraft Foods can track sales performance of items on a warehouse-by-warehouse basis and ship products to replenish Costco's shelves only as needed. These inventory management techniques have allowed Costco to outperform its competitors. Costco turns its inventory more than 12 times a year, far more often than other retailers.

Occasionally, the company leverages its 87 million square feet of warehouse space to reduce its purchasing costs. For example, when Procter & Gamble recently announced a 6% price increase for its paper goods, Costco bought 258 truckloads of paper towels at the old rate and stored them in its distribution centers and warehouses.

Inventory management is important because materials costs often account for more than 40% of total costs of manufacturing companies and more than 70% of total

[1] *Source:* McGregor, Jena. 2008. Costco's artful discounts. *BusinessWeek*, October 20; Brad Stone, "Costco CEO Craig Jelinek Leads the Cheapest, Happiest Company in the World," *Bloomberg Businessweek* (June 6, 2013); Liz Parks, "Sharing the View," NRF Stores (February 2006); and Costco Wholesale Company, 2012 Annual Report (Issaquah, Washington: Costco Wholesale Company, 2012).

costs in merchandising companies. In this chapter, we describe the components of inventory costs, relevant costs for different inventory-related decisions, and how planning and control systems, such as just-in-time systems, can reduce inventory.

Inventory Management in Retail Organizations

Learning Objective 1

Identify six categories of costs associated with goods for sale

...purchasing, ordering, carrying, stockout, quality, and shrinkage

Inventory management includes planning, coordinating, and controlling activities related to the flow of inventory into, through, and out of an organization. Consider this breakdown of operations for three major retailers for which cost of goods sold constitutes their largest cost item.

	Kroger	Costco	Walmart
Revenues	100.0%	100.0%	100.0%
Deduct costs:			
Cost of goods sold	79.4%	87.6%	75.1%
Selling and administration costs	15.4%	9.6%	18.9%
Other costs, interest, and taxes	3.7%	1.1%	2.2%
Total costs	98.5%	98.3%	96.2%
Net income	1.5%	1.7%	3.8%

The low percentages of net income to revenues mean that improving the purchase and management of goods for sale can cause dramatic percentage increases in net income.

Costs Associated with Goods for Sale

There are a number of different types of costs associated with inventory other than the cost of the actual goods purchased. The costs associated with inventory fall into the following six categories:

1. **Purchasing costs** are the cost of goods acquired from suppliers, including incoming freight costs. These costs usually make up the largest cost category of goods in inventory. Discounts for various purchase-order sizes and supplier payment terms affect purchasing costs.
2. **Ordering costs** are the costs of preparing and issuing purchase orders, receiving and inspecting the items included in the orders, and matching invoices received, purchase orders, and delivery records to make payments. Ordering costs include the cost of obtaining purchase approvals, as well as other special processing costs.
3. **Carrying costs** are costs that arise while goods are being held in inventory. Carrying costs include the opportunity cost of the investment tied up in inventory (see Chapter 11, pages 438–440) and the costs associated with storage, such as space rental, insurance, and obsolescence.
4. **Stockout costs** are costs that arise when a company runs out of a particular item for which there is customer demand, a *stockout*. The company must act quickly to

replenish inventory to meet that demand or suffer the costs of not meeting it. A company may respond to a stockout by expediting an order from a supplier, which can be expensive because of additional ordering and manufacturing costs plus any associated transportation costs. Or the company may lose sales due to the stockout. In this case, the opportunity cost of the stockout includes the lost contribution margin on the sale not made plus any contribution margin lost on future sales due to customer ill will.

5. **Costs of quality** are the costs incurred to prevent and appraise, or the costs arising as a result of, quality issues. Quality problems arise, for example, because products get spoiled or broken or are mishandled while products are moved in and out of the warehouse. As discussed earlier in Chapter 19, there are four categories of quality costs: prevention costs, appraisal costs, internal failure costs, and external failure costs.
6. **Shrinkage costs** result from theft by outsiders, embezzlement by employees, misclassifications, and clerical errors. Shrinkage is measured by the difference between (a) the cost of inventory recorded on the books (after correcting errors) and (b) the cost of inventory when physically counted. Shrinkage can often be an important measure of management performance. Consider, for example, the grocery business, where operating income percentages hover around 2%. With such small margins, it is easy to see why one of a store manager's prime responsibilities is controlling inventory shrinkage. A \$1,000 increase in shrinkage will erase the operating income from sales of \$50,000 (2% × \$50,000 = \$1,000). Because shrinkage costs generally increase when a firm's inventory increases, most firms try not to hold more inventory than necessary.

Note that not all inventory costs are available in financial accounting systems. For example, opportunity costs are not recorded in these systems but are a significant component in several of these cost categories.

Decision Point

What are the six categories of costs associated with goods for sale?

Information-gathering technology increases the reliability and timeliness of inventory information and reduces the costs related to inventory. For example, barcoding technology allows a scanner to record individual units purchased and sold. As soon as a unit is scanned, a record of its movement is created, which helps a firm better manage its purchasing, carrying, and stockout costs. In the next several sections, we consider how relevant costs are computed for different inventory-related decisions in merchandising companies.

Learning Objective 2

Balance ordering costs with carrying costs using the economic-order-quantity (EOQ) decision model

...choose the inventory quantity per order to minimize these costs

The Economic-Order-Quantity Decision Model

How much should a firm order of a given product? The **economic order quantity** (EOQ) is a decision model that, under a given set of assumptions, calculates the optimal quantity of inventory to order.

- The simplest version of the EOQ model assumes there are only ordering and carrying costs because these are the most common costs of inventory.
- The same quantity is ordered at each reorder point.
- Demand, ordering costs, and carrying costs are known with certainty. The **purchase-order lead time**, the time between placing an order and its delivery, is also known with certainty.
- The purchasing cost per unit is unaffected by the order quantity. This assumption makes purchasing costs irrelevant to determining the EOQ because the purchase price is the same, whatever the order size.
- No stockouts occur. The basis for this assumption is that the costs of stockouts are so high that managers maintain adequate inventory to prevent them.
- When deciding on the size of a purchase order, managers consider the costs of quality and shrinkage costs only to the extent that these costs affect ordering or carrying costs.

Note that EOQ analysis ignores purchasing costs, stockout costs, costs of quality, and shrinkage costs. Also recall from Chapter 11 that managers only consider relevant costs when making decisions. In a later section we will discuss how to identify the relevant ordering and carrying costs. At this point, we simply note that EOQ is the order quantity that minimizes the sum of a company's relevant ordering and carrying costs. The sum of the costs is the firm's *relevant total ordering and carrying costs* of inventory. The relevant total costs are calculated as follows:

$$\text{Relevant total costs} = \text{Relevant ordering costs} + \text{Relevant carrying costs}$$

We use the following notations:

$$D = \text{Demand in units for a specified period (one year in this example)}$$

$$Q = \text{Size of each order (order quantity)}$$

$$\text{Number of purchase orders per period (one year)} = \frac{\text{Demand in units for a period (one year)}}{\text{Size of each order (order quantity)}} = \frac{D}{Q}$$

Average inventory in units $= \frac{Q}{2}$, because each time the inventory goes down to 0, an order for Q units is received. The inventory varies from Q to 0, so the average inventory is $\frac{0 + Q}{2}$.

$$P = \text{Relevant ordering cost per purchase order}$$

$$C = \text{Relevant carrying cost of one unit in stock for the time period used for } D \text{ (one year)}$$

For any order quantity, Q,

$$\text{Annual relevant ordering costs} = \left(\begin{array}{c}\text{Number of}\\ \text{purchase orders}\\ \text{per year}\end{array} \times \begin{array}{c}\text{Relevant ordering}\\ \text{cost per}\\ \text{purchase order}\end{array}\right) = \left(\frac{D}{Q} \times P\right)$$

$$\text{Annual relevant carrying costs} = \left(\begin{array}{c}\text{Average inventory}\\ \text{in units}\end{array} \times \begin{array}{c}\text{Annual}\\ \text{relevant carrying}\\ \text{cost per unit}\end{array}\right) = \left(\frac{Q}{2} \times C\right)$$

$$\text{Annual relevant total costs} = \begin{array}{c}\text{Annual}\\ \text{relevant ordering}\\ \text{costs}\end{array} + \begin{array}{c}\text{Annual}\\ \text{relevant carrying}\\ \text{costs}\end{array} = \left(\frac{D}{Q} \times P\right) + \left(\frac{Q}{2} \times C\right)$$

The order quantity that minimizes annual relevant total costs is

$$EOQ = \sqrt{\frac{2DP}{C}}$$

The EOQ model is solved using calculus, but the key intuition is that relevant total costs are minimized when relevant ordering costs equal relevant carrying costs. If carrying costs are less (greater) than ordering costs, the total costs can be reduced by increasing (decreasing) the order quantity. To solve for EOQ, we set

$$\left(\frac{Q}{2} \times C\right) = \left(\frac{D}{Q} \times P\right)$$

$$\text{Multiplying both sides by } \frac{2Q}{C}\text{, we get } Q^2 = \frac{2DP}{C}$$

$$Q = \sqrt{\frac{2DP}{C}}$$

The formula indicates that EOQ increases with higher demand and/or higher ordering costs and decreases with higher carrying costs.

Let's see how EOQ analysis works. Glare Shade sells sunglasses. This problem focuses on Glare Shade's basic sunglasses, UX1. Glare Shade purchases the UX1s from

Rytek at $14 a unit. Rytek pays for all incoming freight. No inspection is necessary at Glare Shade because Rytek supplies quality merchandise. Glare Shade's annual demand is 13,000 units of UX1s, at a rate of 250 units per week. Glare Shade requires a 15% annual rate of return on its investment. Relevant ordering cost per purchase order is $200.

The relevant carrying cost per unit per year is as follows:

Required annual return on investment, 0.15 × $14	$2.10
Relevant costs of insurance, materials handling, breakage, shrinkage, and so on, per year	3.10
Total	$5.20

What is the EOQ for ordering UX1 sunglasses?

Substituting $D = 13{,}000$ units per year, $P = \$200$ per order, and $C = \$5.20$ per unit per year, in the EOQ formula, we get

$$EOQ = \sqrt{\frac{2 \times 13{,}000 \times \$200}{\$5.20}} = \sqrt{1{,}000{,}000} = 1{,}000 \text{ units}$$

Purchasing 1,000 units per order minimizes total relevant ordering and carrying costs. Therefore, the number of deliveries each period (1 year in this example) is as follows:

$$\frac{D}{EOQ} = \frac{13{,}000}{1{,}000} = 13 \text{ deliveries}$$

Recall the annual relevant total costs (RTC) $= \left(\frac{D}{Q} \times P\right) + \left(\frac{Q}{2} \times C\right)$

For $Q = 1{,}000$ units,

$$RTC = \frac{13{,}000 \times \$200}{1{,}000} + \frac{1{,}000 \times \$5.20}{2}$$
$$= \$2{,}600 + \$2{,}600 = \$5{,}200$$

Exhibit 20-1 graphs the annual relevant total costs of ordering (DP/Q) and carrying inventory ($QC/2$) under various order sizes (Q), and it illustrates the tradeoff between these two types of costs. The larger the order quantity, the lower the annual relevant ordering

Exhibit 20-1 Graphic Analysis of Ordering Costs and Carrying Costs for UX1 Sunglasses at Glare Shade

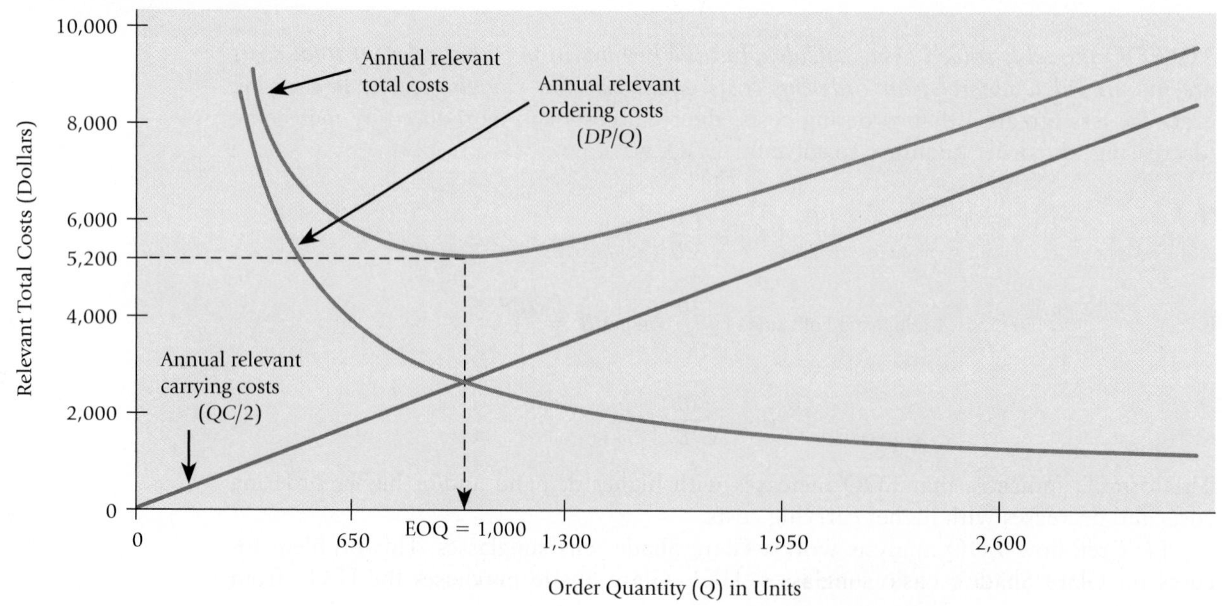

costs, but the higher the annual relevant carrying costs. *The annual relevant total costs are at a minimum at the EOQ at which the relevant ordering and carrying costs are equal.*

When to Order, Assuming Certainty

The second decision Glare Shade's managers face is *when to order* the units. The **reorder point** is the quantity level of inventory on hand that triggers a new purchase order. The reorder point is simplest to compute when both demand and the purchase-order lead time are known with certainty:

$$\text{Reorder point} = \frac{\text{Number of units sold}}{\text{per time period}} \times \frac{\text{Purchase-order}}{\text{lead time}}$$

Suppose the purchase-order lead time for UX1s is 2 weeks:

Economic order quantity	1,000 units
Number of units sold per week	250 units per week (13,000 units ÷ 52 weeks)
Purchase-order lead time	2 weeks

$$\text{Reorder point} = 250 \text{ units per week} \times 2 \text{ weeks} = 500 \text{ units}$$

Glare Shade will order 1,000 units of UX1s each time its inventory falls to 500 units.[2] Exhibit 20-2 shows the behavior of the inventory level of UX1 units, assuming demand occurs uniformly during each week. If the purchase-order lead time is 2 weeks, a new order will be placed when the inventory level falls to 500 units, so the 1,000 units ordered will be received at the precise time that inventory reaches zero.

Safety Stock

If Glare Shade's managers are uncertain about demand or the purchase-order lead time or if they are uncertain about the quantities of UX1s Rytek can provide, they will hold safety stock. **Safety stock** is inventory held at all times regardless of the quantity of inventory ordered using the EOQ model. Companies use safety stock as a buffer against unexpected increases in demand, uncertainty about lead time, and unavailability of stock from

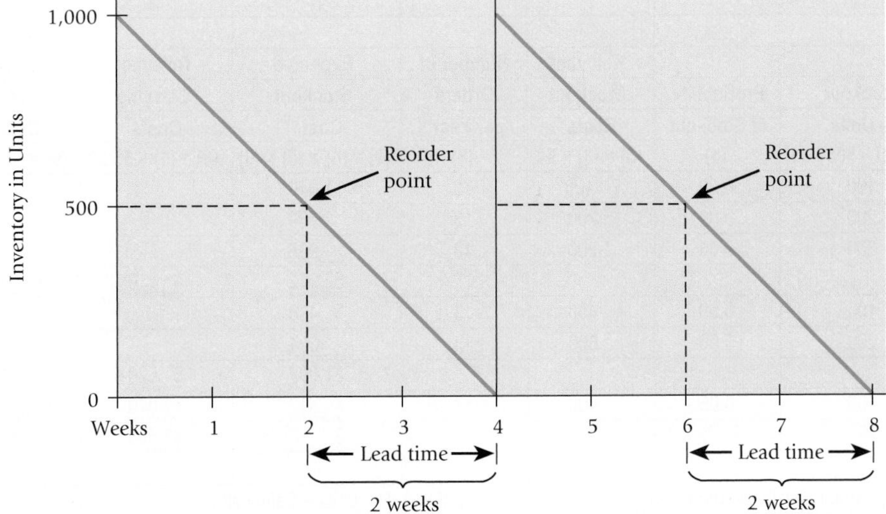

Exhibit 20-2

Inventory Level of UX1 Sunglasses at Glare Shade[a]

[a] This exhibit assumes that demand and purchase-order lead time are certain:
Demand = 250 UX1 sunglasses per week
Purchase-order lead time = 2 weeks

[2] This handy but special formula does not apply when receipt of the order fails to increase inventory to the reorder-point quantity (for example, when lead time is 3 weeks and the order is a 1-week supply). In these cases, orders will overlap.

suppliers. Suppose Glare Shade's managers are uncertain about demand. They expect the demand for UX1s to be 250 units per week, but it could be as high as 400 units per week or as low as 100 units per week. If stockout costs are very high, the managers will want to hold a safety stock of 300 units and incur higher carrying costs. The 300 units equal the maximum excess demand of 150(400 − 250) units per week times the 2 weeks of purchase-order lead time. If stockout costs are minimal, no safety stock will be held to avoid incurring the additional carrying costs.

Managers use a frequency distribution based on prior daily or weekly levels of demand to compute safety-stock levels. Assume that one of the following levels of demand for UX1s will occur over the 2-week purchase-order lead time.

Total Demand for 2 Weeks	**200 Units**	**300 Units**	**400 Units**	**500 Units**	**600 Units**	**700 Units**	**800 Units**
Probability (sums to 1.00)	0.06	0.09	0.20	0.30	0.20	0.09	0.06

We see that 500 units is the most likely level of demand for 2 weeks because it has the highest probability of occurrence. We see also a 0.35 probability that demand will be 600, 700, or 800 units (0.20 + 0.09 + 0.06 = 0.35).

If a customer wants to buy UX1s and the store has none in stock, Glare Shade can "rush" them to the customer at an additional cost to Glare Shade of $4 per unit. The relevant stockout costs in this case are $4 per unit. The optimal safety-stock level is the quantity of safety stock that minimizes the sum of annual relevant stockout and carrying costs. Note that Glare Shade will place 13 orders per year for UX1s and will incur the same ordering costs whatever level of safety stock it chooses. Therefore, ordering costs are irrelevant for the safety-stock decision. Recall that the relevant carrying cost for UX1s is $5.20 per unit per year.

Exhibit 20-3 tabulates the annual relevant total stockout and carrying costs when the reorder point is 500 units. Over the 2-week purchase-order lead time, stockouts can occur if demand is 600, 700, or 800 units because these levels exceed the 500 units in

Exhibit 20-3 Computation of Safety Stock for Glare Shade When Reorder Point Is 500 Units

Home Insert Page Layout Formulas Data Review View

	A	B	C	D	E	F	G	H	I
1	**Safety**	**Demand**							
2	**Stock**	**Levels**			**Relevant**	**Number of**	**Expected**	**Relevant**	**Relevant**
3	**Level**	**Resulting**	**Stockout**	**Probability**	**Stockout**	**Orders**	**Stockout**	**Carrying**	**Total**
4	**in Units**	**in Stockouts**	**in Units[a]**	**of Stockout**	**Costs[b]**	**per Year[c]**	**Costs[d]**	**Costs[e]**	**Costs**
5	**(1)**	**(2)**	**(3) = (2) – 500 – (1)**	**(4)**	**(5) = (3) × $4**	**(6)**	**(7) = (4) × (5) × (6)**	**(8) = (1) × $5.20**	**(9) = (7) + (8)**
6	0	600	100	0.20	$ 400	13	$1,040		
7		700	200	0.09	800	13	936		
8		800	300	0.06	1,200	13	936		
9							$2,912	$ 0	$2,912
10	100	700	100	0.09	400	13	$ 468		
11		800	200	0.06	800	13	624		
12							$1,092	$ 520	$1,612
13	200	800	100	0.06	400	13	$ 312	$1,040	$1,352
14	300	-	-	-	-	-	$ 0[f]	$1,560	$1,560
15									
16	[a]Demand level resulting in stockouts – Inventory available during lead time (excluding safety stock), 500 units – Safety stock.								
17	[b]Stockout in units × Relevant stockout costs of $4.00 per unit.								
18	[c]Annual demand, 13,000 ÷ 1,000 EOQ = 13 orders per year.								
19	[d]Probability of stockout × Relevant stockout costs × Number of orders per year.								
20	[e]Safety stock × Annual relevant carrying costs of $5.20 per unit (assumes that safety stock is on hand at all times and that there is no overstocking								
21	caused by decreases in expected usage).								
22	[f]At a safety stock level of 300 units, no stockout will occur and, hence, expected stockout costs = $0.								

stock at the time Glare Shade places the purchase orders. Consequently, Glare Shade only evaluates safety stock levels of 0, 100, 200, and 300 units of UX1s. If the safety stock is 0 units, Glare Shade will incur stockout costs if demand is 600, 700, or 800 units but will have no additional carrying costs. At the other extreme, if the safety stock is 300 units, Glare Shade will never incur stockout costs but will have higher carrying costs. As Exhibit 20-3 shows, the firm's annual relevant total stockout and carrying costs are lowest ($1,352) when a safety stock of 200 units of UX1s is maintained. Therefore, 200 units is the optimal safety-stock level. The 200 units of safety stock is the extra stock that Glare Shade always maintains. For example, Glare Shade's total inventory of UX1s at the time of reordering its EOQ of 1,000 units would be 700 units (the reorder point of 500 units plus safety stock of 200 units).

Decision Point

What does the EOQ decision model help managers do, and how do managers decide on the safety-stock levels?

Estimating Inventory-Related Relevant Costs and Their Effects

Learning Objective 3

Identify the effect of errors that can arise when using the EOQ decision model

...errors in predicting parameters have a small effect on costs

and ways to reduce conflicts between the EOQ model and models used for performance evaluation

...by making the two models congruent

How do Glare Shade's managers calculate the annual relevant inventory-related costs, such as the relevant carrying, stockout, and ordering costs?

We start by discussing the relevant inventory carrying costs of $5.20 per unit per year, which consist of the *relevant incremental costs* plus the *relevant opportunity cost of capital*. What are the *relevant incremental costs* of carrying inventory? Only those costs, such as warehouse rent, warehouse workers' salaries, costs of obsolescence, costs of shrinkage, costs of breakage, and costs of insurance, that change with the quantity of inventory held. The salaries paid to clerks, stock keepers, and materials handlers are irrelevant if they are unaffected by changes in inventory levels. Suppose, however, that as inventories increase (decrease), total salary costs increase (decrease) as clerks, stock keepers, and materials handlers are added (transferred to other activities or laid off). In this case, the salaries paid are relevant costs of carrying inventory. Similarly, costs of storage space owned that cannot be used for other profitable purposes when inventories decrease are irrelevant. But if the space has other profitable uses or if total rental cost is tied to the amount of space occupied, storage costs are relevant costs of carrying inventory.

What is the *relevant opportunity cost of capital*? It is the return forgone by investing capital in inventory rather than elsewhere. It is calculated as the required rate of return multiplied by the per-unit costs of acquiring inventory, such as the purchase price of units, incoming freight, and incoming inspection. Opportunity costs are also computed on investments (say, in equipment) if these investments are affected by changes in inventory levels.

In the case of stockouts, the relevant incremental cost is the cost of expediting an order from a supplier. The relevant opportunity cost is (1) the lost contribution margin on sales forgone because of the stockout and (2) the lost contribution margin on future sales forgone as a result of customer ill will.

The relevant ordering costs are only those ordering costs that change with the number of orders placed (for example, the costs of preparing and issuing purchase orders and receiving and inspecting materials).

Cost of a Prediction Error

Predicting relevant costs is difficult and seldom flawless, which raises the question, "What is the cost when actual relevant costs differ from the estimated relevant costs used for decision making?"

Suppose Glare Shade's relevant ordering costs per purchase order for UX1s are $100, but the manager predicts them to be $200 when calculating the order quantity. We can calculate the cost of this "prediction" error using a three-step approach.

Step 1: Compute the Monetary Outcome from the Best Action That Could Be Taken, Given the *Actual* Amount of the Cost Input (Cost per Purchase Order). This is the benchmark—that is, the decision the manager would have made if the manager had known the correct ordering cost against which actual performance can be measured. Using D = 13,000 units of UX1 per year, P = \$100, and C = \$5.20 per unit per year,

$$EOQ = \sqrt{\frac{2DP}{C}}$$

$$= \sqrt{\frac{2 \times 13{,}000 \times \$100}{\$5.20}} = \sqrt{500{,}000}$$

$$= 707 \text{ units (rounded)}$$

Glare Shade's annual relevant total costs when the EOQ = 707 units are as follows:

$$RTC = \frac{DP}{Q} + \frac{QC}{2}$$

$$= \frac{13{,}000 \times \$100}{707} + \frac{707 \times \$5.20}{2}$$

$$= \$1{,}839 + \$1{,}838 = \$3{,}677$$

Step 2: Compute the Monetary Outcome from the Best Action Based on the Incorrect *Predicted* Amount of the Cost Input (Cost per Purchase Order). In this step, the manager calculates the order quantity based on the prediction (that later proves to be wrong) that the ordering cost is \$200. When this is the case, the best action is to purchase 1,000 units in each order (page 768). However, the actual cost of the purchase order is only \$100. Consequently, the actual annual relevant total costs when D = 13,000 units per year, Q = 1,000 units, P = \$100, and C = \$5.20 per unit per year are as follows:

$$RTC = \frac{13{,}000 \times \$100}{1{,}000} + \frac{1{,}000 \times \$5.20}{2}$$

$$= \$1{,}300 + \$2{,}600 = \$3{,}900$$

Step 3: Compute the Difference Between the Monetary Outcomes from Step 1 and Step 2.

	Monetary Outcome
Step 1	\$3,677
Step 2	3,900
Difference	\$ (223)

The cost of the prediction error, \$223, is less than 7% of the relevant total costs of \$3,677. Note that the annual relevant-total-costs curve in Exhibit 20-1 is somewhat flat over the range of order quantities from 700 to 1,300 units. That is, the annual relevant cost is roughly the same even if misestimating the relevant carrying and ordering costs results in an EOQ quantity of 1,000 plus 30% (1,300) or 1,000 minus 30% (700). *The square root in the EOQ model diminishes the effect of estimation errors because it results in the effects of the incorrect numbers becoming smaller.*

In the next section, we consider a planning-and-control and performance-evaluation issue that frequently arises when managing inventory.

Conflicts Between the EOQ Decision Model and Managers' Performance Evaluation

What happens if the order quantity based on the EOQ decision model differs from the order quantity managers would choose to make their own performance look best? Consider, for example, opportunity costs. As we have seen, the EOQ model takes into account opportunity costs because these costs are relevant costs when calculating inventory carrying costs. However, managers evaluated on financial accounting numbers, which is often the case, will ignore opportunity costs. Why? Because financial accounting only records actual transactions, not the costs of opportunities forgone (see Chapter 11). Managers interested in making their own performance look better will only focus on measures used to evaluate their performance. Conflicts will then arise between the EOQ model's optimal order quantity and the order quantity that managers regard as optimal.

As a result of ignoring some of the carrying costs (the opportunity costs), managers will be inclined to purchase larger lot sizes of materials than the lot sizes calculated according to the EOQ model, particularly if larger lot sizes result in lower purchase prices. As we discussed in the previous section, the cost of these suboptimal choices is small if the quantities purchased are close to the EOQ. However, if the lot sizes become much greater, the cost to the company can be quite large. Moreover, if we consider other costs, such as costs of quality and shrinkage of holding large inventories, the cost to the company of purchasing in large lot sizes is even greater. To achieve congruence between the EOQ decision model and managers' performance evaluations, companies such as Walmart design performance-evaluation systems that charge managers responsible for managing inventory levels with carrying costs that include a required return on investment.

Decision Point

How do errors in predicting the parameters of the EOQ model affect costs? How can companies reduce the conflict between the EOQ decision model and models used for performance evaluation?

Just-in-Time Purchasing

Learning Objective 4

Describe why companies are using just-in-time (JIT) purchasing

. . . high carrying costs, costs of quality, and shrinkage costs, low ordering costs, high-quality suppliers, and reliable supply chains

Just-in-time (JIT) purchasing is the purchase of materials (or goods) so that they are delivered just as needed for production (or sales). Consider Hewlett-Packard's (HP's) JIT purchasing: HP has long-term agreements with suppliers of the major components of its printers. Each supplier is required to make frequent deliveries of small orders directly to the production floor, based on the production schedules HP provides them. The suppliers work hard to keep their commitments because any failure on their part will result in HP's assembly plant not meeting its scheduled deliveries of printers.

JIT Purchasing and EOQ Model Parameters

Suppose Glare Shade's managers believe that the current purchasing policies might result in the carrying costs of the firm's inventories (parameter *C* in the EOQ model) being much greater than what they had estimated because of higher warehousing, handling, insurance, and equipment costs. Suppose they also believe that the cost of placing a purchase order (parameter *P* in the EOQ model) is likely to decrease because of the following:

- Glare Shade is establishing long-term purchasing agreements that define the price and quality terms it has with its suppliers over an extended period. No additional negotiations need to take place before supplies can be ordered.
- New electronic systems allow Glare Shade to place purchase orders, tally delivery records, and make payments to suppliers more cost effectively.
- Glare Shade is using purchase-order cards (similar to consumer credit cards such as VISA and MasterCard). As long as purchasing personnel stay within preset total and individual-transaction dollar limits, traditional labor-intensive procurement-approval procedures are not required.

Exhibit 20-4 tabulates the sensitivity of the EOQ (page 768) to changes in carrying and ordering costs of UX1s. Exhibit 20-4 supports moving toward JIT purchasing because, as the company's relevant carrying costs increase and relevant ordering costs per purchase order decrease, the EOQ decreases and ordering frequency increases.

Relevant Costs of JIT Purchasing

JIT purchasing is not guided solely by the EOQ model because that model only emphasizes the tradeoff between relevant carrying and ordering costs. Inventory management, however, also includes accounting for a company's purchasing costs, stockout costs, costs of quality, and shrinkage costs. Glare Shade's managers are concerned that ordering and storing large quantities of UX1 units have contributed to defective and broken units and shrinkage. So, the company begins implementing JIT purchasing by asking the

Exhibit 20-4

Sensitivity of EOQ to Variations in Relevant Ordering and Carrying Costs for UX1 Sunglasses

	A	B	C	D	E	F	G
1				Economic Order Quantity in Units			
2				at Different Ordering and Carrying Costs			
3	Annual Demand (D) =	13,000	units				
4							
5	Relevant Carrying Costs			Relevant Ordering Costs per Purchase Order (P)			
6	Per unit per Year (C)			$ 200	$150	$100	$ 30
7	$ 5.20			1,000	866	707	387
8	7.00			862	746	609	334
9	10.00			721	624	510	279
10	15.00			589	510	416	228

supplier of UX1 units to make more frequent deliveries of smaller sizes. Glare Shade has recently established an Internet business-to-business purchase-order link with its supplier, Rytek. Glare Shade triggers a purchase order for UX1s by a single computer entry. Payments are made electronically for batches of deliveries, rather than for each individual delivery. These changes reduce the company's ordering costs from $200 to only $2 per purchase order! Glare Shade will use the Internet purchase-order link whether or not it shifts to JIT purchasing. We next evaluate the effect JIT purchasing has on quality and costs.

Description of Item	Current Purchasing Practice	JIT Purchasing Practice
Deliveries	1,000 units purchased 13 times per year	100 units purchased 130 times per year (5 times every 2 weeks)
Purchasing costs	$14 per unit	$14.02 per unit (Note: Many companies do not pay a higher price for more frequent deliveries.)
Inspection of units	Units inspected at the time of receipt at a cost of $0.05 per unit to identify units that need to be returned	Units not inspected because Rytek ensures that quality UX1 sunglasses are delivered to support Glare Shade's JIT purchasing.
Required rate of return on investment	15%	15%
Relevant carrying cost of insurance, materials handling, storage, etc.	$3.10 per unit of average inventory per year	$3.00 per unit of average inventory per year (lower insurance, materials handling, and storage rates)
Customer return costs	$10 for shipping and processing a defective unit returned by a customer. The high quality of units supplied by Rytek and Glare Shade's inspection procedures will result in no units being returned by customers.	$10 for shipping and processing a defective unit returned by a customer. The high quality of units supplied by Rytek will result in no units being returned by customers.
Stockout costs	No stockout costs because demand and purchase-order lead times during each 4-week period (52 weeks ÷ 13 deliveries) are known with certainty.	More stockouts because demand variations and delays in supplying units are more likely in the short time intervals between orders under JIT purchasing. Glare Shade expects to incur stockout costs on 150 units of UX1 per year under the JIT purchasing policy. When a stockout occurs, Glare Shade must rush-order units at an additional cost of $4 per unit.

Exhibit 20-5 Annual Relevant Costs of Current Purchasing Policy and JIT Purchasing Policy for UX1 Sunglasses

	A	B	C	D	E	F	G	H	I	J
1		Relevant Costs Under								
2		Current Purchasing Policy					JIT Purchasing Policy			
3	Relevant Items	Relevant Cost per Unit		Quantity per Year	Total Costs		Relevant Cost per Unit		Quantity per Year	Total Costs
4	(1)	(2)		(3)	(4) = (2) × (3)		(5)		(6)	(7) = (5) × (6)
5	Purchasing costs	$14.00	per unit	13,000	$182,000		$14.02	per unit	13,000	$182,260
6	Ordering costs	$ 2.00	per order	13	26		$ 2.00	per order	130	260
7	Inspection costs	$ 0.05	per unit	13,000	650		$ -	per unit	-	-
8	Opportunity carrying costs	$ 2.10[a]	per unit of average inventory per year	500[b]	1,050		$ 2.10[a]	per unit of average inventory per year	50[c]	105
9	Other carrying costs (insurance, materials handling, etc.)	$ 3.10	per unit of average inventory per year	500[b]	1,550		$ 3.00	per unit of average inventory per year	50[c]	150
10	Customer return costs	$10.00	per unit returned	0	0		$10.00	per unit returned	0	0
11	Stockout costs	$ 4.00	per unit	0	0		$ 4.00	per unit	150	600
12	Total annual relevant costs				$185,276					$183,375
13	Annual difference in favor of JIT Purchasing					$1,901				
14										
15	[a]Purchasing cost per unit × 0.15 per year									
16	[b]Order quantity/2 = 1,000/2 = 500 units									
17	[c]Order quantity/2 = 100/2 = 50 units									

Should Glare Shade implement the JIT purchasing option of 130 deliveries of UX1 per year? Exhibit 20-5 compares Glare Shade's relevant total costs under the current purchasing policy and the JIT policy. It shows net cost savings of $1,901 per year by shifting to a JIT purchasing policy. The benefits of JIT purchasing arise from lower carrying and inspection costs as a result of better quality. JIT purchasing gives Glare Shade's managers immediate feedback about quality problems by reducing the "safety net" large quantities of inventory afford.

Supplier Evaluation and Relevant Costs of Quality and Timely Deliveries

Companies that implement JIT purchasing choose their suppliers carefully and develop long-term supplier relationships. Some suppliers are better positioned than others to support JIT purchasing. For example, the corporate strategy of Frito-Lay, a supplier of potato chips and other snack foods, emphasizes service, consistency, freshness, and the quality of the products the company delivers. As a result, Frito-Lay makes deliveries to retail outlets more frequently than many of its competitors.

What are the relevant total costs when choosing suppliers? Consider again the UX1 units purchased by Glare Shade. Denton Corporation, another supplier of UX1 sunglasses, offers to supply all the units that Glare Shade needs. Glare Shade requires the supplier to deliver 100 units 130 times per year (5 times every 2 weeks). Glare Shade will establish an Internet-based purchase-order link with whichever supplier it chooses, trigger a purchase order for UX1 units by a single computer entry, and make payments electronically for batches of deliveries, rather than for each individual delivery. As discussed earlier, the company's ordering costs will be only $2 per purchase order. The following table provides information about Denton versus Rytek. Rytek charges a higher price than Denton but also supplies higher-quality UX1s. The information about Rytek is the same as that presented earlier under JIT purchasing in Exhibit 20-5.

Description of Item	Purchasing Terms from Rytek	Purchasing Terms from Denton
Purchasing costs	$14.02 per unit	$13.80 per unit
Inspection of UX1s	Glare Shade has bought UX1s from Rytek in the past and knows that it will deliver quality UX1s on time. UX1s supplied by Rytek require no inspection.	Denton does not enjoy a sterling reputation for quality, so Glare Shade plans to inspect UX1s at a cost of $0.05 per UX1.
Required rate of return on investment	15%	15%
Relevant carrying cost of insurance, materials handling, storage, etc.	$3.00 per unit per year	$2.90 per unit per year because of lower purchasing costs
Customer return costs	Glare Shade estimates $10 for shipping and processing a defective UX1 unit returned by a customer. Fortunately, the high quality of units supplied by Rytek will result in no units being returned by customers.	Glare Shade estimates $10 for shipping and processing a defective UX1 unit returned by a customer and product returns of 2.5% of all units sold.
Stockout costs	Glare Shade expects to incur stockout costs on 150 UX1 units each time resulting in a rush-order at a cost of $4 per unit.	Denton has less control over its processes, so Glare Shade expects to incur stockout costs on 360 UX1 units each time initiating rush orders at a cost of $4 per unit

Exhibit 20-6 shows the relevant total costs of purchasing from Rytek and Denton. Even though Denton is offering a lower price per unit, there is a net cost savings of $1,873 per year by purchasing UX1s from Rytek because of lower inspection, customer returns, and stockout costs. The benefit of purchasing from Rytek could be even greater if purchasing high-quality UX1s from Rytek enhances Glare Shade's reputation and increases customer goodwill, leading to higher sales and profitability in the future.

Exhibit 20-6 Annual Relevant Costs of JIT Purchasing for UX1 Sunglasses from Rytek and Denton

	A	B	C	D	E	F	G	H	I	J
1		Relevant Cost of JIT Purchasing From								
2		Rytek					Denton			
3	Relevant Items	Relevant Cost per Unit		Quantity per Year	Total Costs		Relevant Cost per Unit		Quantity per Year	Total Costs
4	(1)	(2)		(3)	(4) = (2) × (3)		(5)		(6)	(7) = (5) × (6)
5	Purchasing costs	$14.02	per unit	13,000	$182,260		$13.80	per unit	13,000	$179,400
6		$ 2.00	per order	130	260		2.00	per order	130	260
7	Inspection costs	-	per unit	-	-		0.05	per unit	13,000	650
8	Opportunity carrying costs	$ 2.10[a]	per unit of average inventory per year	50[b]	105		2.07[a]	per unit of average inventory per year	50[b]	103
9	Other carrying costs (insurance, materials handling, etc.)	$ 3.00	per unit of average inventory per year	50[b]	150		2.90	per unit of average inventory per year	50[b]	145
10	Customer return costs	$10.00	per unit returned	0	0		10.00	per unit returned	325[c]	3,250
11	Stockout costs	$ 4.00	per unit	150	600		4.00	per unit	360	1,440
12	Total annual relevant costs				$183,375					$185,248
13	Annual difference in favor of Rytek					$1,873				
14										
15	[a]Purchasing cost per unit × 0.15 per year									
16	[b]Order quantity ÷ 2 = 100 ÷ 2 = 50 units									
17	[c]2.5% of units returned × 13,000 units									

JIT Purchasing, Planning and Control, and Supply-Chain Analysis

Retailers' inventory levels depend on the demand patterns of their customers and supply relationships with their distributors and manufacturers, the suppliers to their manufacturers, and so on. The *supply chain* describes the flow of goods, services, and information from the initial sources of materials and services to the delivery of products to consumers, regardless of whether those activities occur in the same company or in other companies. Retailers can purchase inventories on a JIT basis only if activities throughout the supply chain are properly planned, coordinated, and controlled.

Procter and Gamble's (P&G's) experience with its Pampers product illustrates the gains from supply-chain coordination. Retailers selling Pampers found that the weekly demand for the product varied because families purchased disposable diapers randomly. Anticipating even more demand variability and lacking information about available inventory with P&G, retailers' orders to P&G became more variable. This, in turn, increased variability of orders at P&G's suppliers, resulting in high levels of inventory at all stages in the supply chain.

How did P&G respond to these problems? By sharing information and planning and coordinating activities throughout the supply chain among retailers, P&G, and P&G's suppliers. Sharing sales information reduced the level of uncertainty that P&G and its suppliers had about retail demand for the product and led to (1) fewer stockouts at the retail level, (2) reduced manufacturing of Pampers not immediately needed by retailers, (3) fewer manufacturing orders that had to be "rushed" or "expedited," and (4) lower inventories held by each company in the supply chain. The benefits of supply chain coordination at P&G have been so great that retailers such as Walmart have contracted with P&G to manage their inventories on a just-in-time basis. This practice is called *supplier- or vendor-managed inventory*. Coordinating supply chains, however, can be difficult because supply-chain partners don't always share accurate and timely information about their sales, inventory levels, and sales forecasts with one another. Some of the reasons for these challenges are communication problems, trust issues between the companies, incompatible information systems, and limited people and financial resources.

Decision Point

Why are companies using just-in-time (JIT) purchasing?

Inventory Management, MRP, and JIT Production

Learning Objective 5

Distinguish materials requirements planning (MRP) systems

...manufacturing products based on demand forecasts

from just-in-time (JIT) systems for manufacturing

...manufacturing products only upon receiving customer orders

We now turn our attention from purchasing to managing the production inventories of manufacturing companies. Two of the most widely used systems to plan and implement inventory activities within plants are materials requirements planning (MRP) and just-in-time (JIT) production.

Materials Requirements Planning

A **materials requirements planning (MRP) system** is a "push-through" system that manufactures finished goods for inventory on the basis of demand forecasts. Companies such as Guidant, which manufactures medical devices, and Philips, which makes consumer electronic products, use MRP systems. To determine outputs at each stage of production, MRP uses (1) the demand forecasts for final products; (2) a bill of materials detailing the materials, components, and subassemblies for each final product; and (3) information about a company's inventories of materials, components, and products. Taking into account the lead time required to purchase materials and to manufacture components and finished products, a master production schedule specifies the quantity and timing of each item to be produced. Once production starts as scheduled, the output of each department is pushed through the production line.

Maintaining accurate inventory records and costs is critical in an MRP system. For example, after becoming aware of the full costs of carrying finished goods inventory in its MRP system, National Semiconductor contracted with FedEx to airfreight its microchips from a central location in Singapore to customer sites worldwide instead of storing the chips at geographically dispersed warehouses.

Just-in-Time (JIT) Production

Decision Point

How do materials requirements planning (MRP) systems differ from just-in-time (JIT) production systems?

In contrast, JIT production is a "demand-pull" approach, which is used by companies such as Toyota in the automobile industry, Dell in the computer industry, and Braun in the appliance industry. **Just-in-time (JIT) production,** which is also called **lean production,** is a "demand-pull" manufacturing system that manufactures each component in a production line as soon as, and only when, needed by the next step in the production line. Demand triggers each step of the production process, starting with customer demand for a finished product at the end of the process and working all the way back to the demand for direct materials at the beginning of the process. In this way, demand pulls an order through the production line. The demand-pull feature of JIT production systems results in close coordination among workstations and smooths the flow of goods, despite low quantities of inventory. JIT production systems help companies meet the demand for high-quality products on time and at the lowest possible cost.

Learning Objective 6

Identify the features and benefits of a just-in-time production system

...for example, organizing work in manufacturing cells, improving quality, and reducing manufacturing lead time to reduce costs and earn higher margins

Features of JIT Production Systems

A JIT production system has these features:

- Production is organized in **manufacturing cells,** which are work areas with different types of equipment grouped together to make related products. Materials move from one machine to another, and various operations are performed in sequence, minimizing materials-handling costs.
- Workers are hired and trained to be multiskilled and capable of performing a variety of operations and tasks, including minor repairs and routine equipment maintenance.
- Defects are aggressively eliminated. Because of the tight links between workstations and the minimal inventories at each workstation, defects arising at one workstation quickly affect other workstations in the line. JIT creates an urgency for solving problems immediately and eliminating the root causes of defects as quickly as possible. Low levels of inventories allow workers to trace problems to and solve problems at earlier workstations in the production process, where the problems likely originated.
- The *setup time*, the time required to get equipment, tools, and materials ready to start the production of a component or product, and the *manufacturing cycle time*, the time from when an order is received by manufacturing until it becomes a finished good, are reduced. Setup costs correspond to the ordering costs P in the EOQ model. Reducing the setup time and its costs makes production in smaller batches economical, which in turn reduces inventory levels. Reducing the manufacturing cycle time enables a company to respond faster to changes in customer demand (see also Concepts in Action: After the Encore: Just-in-Time Live Concert Recordings).
- Suppliers are selected on the basis of their ability to deliver quality materials in a timely manner. Most companies implementing *JIT production* also implement *JIT purchasing*. JIT plants expect JIT suppliers to make timely deliveries of high-quality goods directly to the production floor.

We next present a relevant-cost analysis for deciding whether to implement a JIT production system.

Costs and Benefits of JIT Production

As we have seen, JIT production clearly lowers a company's carrying costs of inventory. But there are other benefits of lower inventories: heightened emphasis on improving quality by eliminating the specific causes of rework, scrap, and waste, and lower manufacturing cycle times. It is important, therefore, when computing the relevant benefits and costs of reducing inventories in JIT production systems for managers to take into account all benefits and all costs.

Consider Hudson Corporation, a manufacturer of brass fittings. Hudson is considering implementing a JIT production system. To implement JIT production, Hudson must incur $100,000 in annual tooling costs to reduce setup times. Hudson expects that JIT production will reduce its average inventory by $500,000 and that the relevant costs of insurance, storage, materials handling, and setups will decline by $30,000 per year. The company's required rate of return on its inventory investments is 10% per year. Should Hudson implement a JIT production system? On the basis of the information provided, we would be tempted to say "no" because the annual relevant total cost savings amount to $80,000 [(10% of $500,000) + $30,000)], which is less than the additional annual tooling costs of $100,000.

Our analysis, however, is incomplete. We have not considered the other benefits of lower inventories associated with JIT production. Hudson estimates that implementing JIT will improve quality and reduce rework on 500 units each year, resulting in savings of $50 per unit. Also, better quality and faster delivery will allow Hudson to charge $2 more per unit on the 20,000 units that it sells each year.

The annual relevant benefits and costs from implementing JIT equal the following:

Incremental savings in insurance, storage, materials handling, and set up	$ 30,000
Incremental savings in inventory carrying costs (10% × $500,000)	50,000
Incremental savings from reduced rework ($50 per unit × 500 units)	25,000
Additional contribution margin from better quality and faster delivery ($2 per unit × 20,000 units)	40,000
Incremental annual tooling costs	(100,000)
Net incremental benefit	$ 45,000

Therefore, Hudson *should* implement a JIT production system.

JIT in Service Industries

JIT purchasing and production methods can be used in service industries as well. For example, inventories and supplies, and the associated labor costs to manage them, represent more than a third of the costs in most hospitals. By implementing a JIT purchasing and distribution system, Eisenhower Memorial Hospital in Palm Springs, California, reduced its inventories and supplies by 90% in 18 months. McDonald's has adapted JIT production practices to making hamburgers.[3] Before, McDonald's precooked a batch of hamburgers that were placed under heat lamps to stay warm until ordered. If the hamburgers didn't sell within a specified period of time, they were discarded, resulting in high inventory holding costs and spoilage costs. Moreover, the quality of hamburgers deteriorated the longer they sat under the heat lamps. A customer placing a special order for a hamburger (such as a hamburger with no cheese) had to wait for it to be cooked. Now McDonald's cooks hamburgers only when they are ordered. By increasing the quality of hamburgers and reducing the time needed for special orders, JIT has led to greater customer satisfaction.

We next turn our attention to planning and control of production systems.

Enterprise Resource Planning (ERP) Systems[4]

Enterprise resource planning systems are frequently used in conjunction with JIT production. An **enterprise resource planning (ERP) system** is an integrated set of software modules covering a company's accounting, distribution, manufacturing, purchasing, human resources, and other functions. Real-time information is collected in a single database and simultaneously fed into all of the software applications, giving personnel greater visibility into the company's end-to-end business processes. For example, using an ERP system,

[3] Charles Atkinson, "McDonald's, A Guide to the Benefits of JIT," *Inventory Management Review* (November 8, 2005). http://www.inventorymanagementreview.org/2005/11/mcdonalds_a_gui.html.

[4] For an excellent discussion, see Thomas H. Davenport, "Putting the Enterprise into the Enterprise System," *Harvard Business Review* (July–August 1998); also see A. Cagilo, "Enterprise Resource Planning Systems and Accountants: Towards Hybridization?" *European Accounting Review* (May 2003).

Concepts in Action

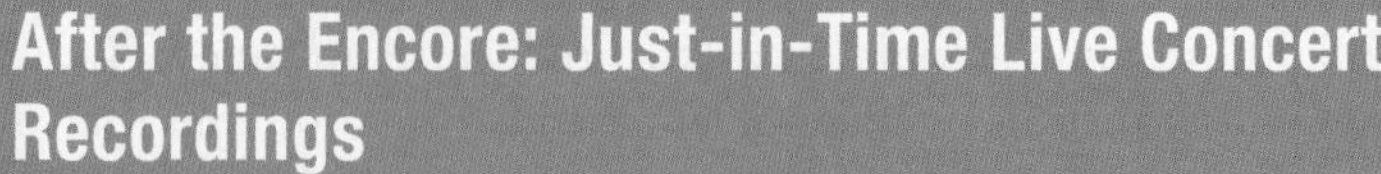

After the Encore: Just-in-Time Live Concert Recordings

Each year, millions of music fans flock to concerts to see artists ranging from Pearl Jam to the Dave Matthews Band. When fans stop by the merchandise stand to pick up a T-shirt or poster after the show ends, they often have another option: buying a professional recording of the concert they just saw! Just-in-time production, enabled by advances in technology, now allows fans to relive the live concert experience just a few minutes after the final chord is played.

Live concert recordings have long been hampered by production and distribution difficulties. Live albums typically sold few copies, and retail outlets that profit from volume-driven merchandise turnover, like Best Buy, were somewhat reluctant to carry them.

Several companies, including Live Nation and Nugs.net, now employ microphones, recording and audio mixing hardware and software, and an army of high-speed computers to produce concert recordings during the show. As soon as each song is complete, engineers burn that track onto hundreds of CDs or USB drives. At the end of the show, they have to burn only one last song. Once completed, the recordings are packaged and rushed to merchandise stands throughout the venue for instant sale.

Sources: Sabra Chartrand, "How to Take the Concert Home." *New York Times* (May 3, 2004); Stephen Humphries, "Get Your Official 'Bootleg' Here," *Christian Science Monitor* (November 21, 2003); Eliot Van Buskirk, "Apple Unveils 'Live Music' in iTunes," *Wired Business* (blog), November 24, 2009, http://www.wired.com/business/, accessed July 2013; and Clyde Smith, "Nugs.net Appetizer Puts Direct-to-Fan Download Sales In Facebook Newsfeed," Hypebot.com (blog), August 12, 2011, http://www.hypebot.com/, accessed July 2013.

a salesperson can generate a contract for a customer in Germany, verify the customer's credit limits, and place a production order. The system will then use this same information to schedule manufacturing in, say, Brazil, requisition materials from inventory, order components from suppliers, and schedule shipments. Simultaneously the system credits the salesperson with his or her commission and records all the costing and financial accounting information. An ERP system also allows a company to shift its manufacturing and distribution plans rapidly in response to changes in supply and demand.

Companies believe that an ERP system is essential to support JIT initiatives because of the effect it has on lead times. For example, using an ERP system, Autodesk, a maker of computer-aided design software, reduced order lead time from 2 weeks to 1 day. Fujitsu, an information technology company, reduced its lead time from 18 days to 1.5 days.

ERP systems are large and unwieldy. Because of their complexity, the suppliers of ERP systems such as SAP and Oracle provide software units that are standard but that can be customized at significant cost. Without some customization, unique and distinctive features that confer strategic advantage will not be available. The challenge when implementing ERP systems is to strike the proper balance between the lower cost and reliability of standardized systems and the strategic benefits that accrue from customization. Companies such as Netsuite are developing ERP systems for small and medium-sized enterprises that are easier to customize using cloud-based computing and providing the software as a service.

Performance Measures and Control in JIT Production

In addition to their personal observations, managers use financial and nonfinancial measures to evaluate and control JIT production. We now describe these measures and indicate the effect JIT systems are expected to have on these measures.

1. Financial performance measures, such as the inventory turnover ratio (cost of goods sold ÷ average inventory), which is expected to increase

2. Nonfinancial performance measures of inventory, quality, and time such as the following:
   - Number of days of inventory on hand, expected to decrease
   - Units produced per hour, expected to increase
   - $\frac{\text{Number of units scrapped or requiring rework}}{\text{Total number of units started and completed}}$, expected to decrease
   - Manufacturing cycle time, expected to decrease
   - $\frac{\text{Total setup time for machines}}{\text{Total manufacturing time}}$, expected to decrease

Personal observation and nonfinancial performance measures provide the most timely, intuitive, and easy-to-understand measures of manufacturing performance. Rapid, meaningful feedback is critical because the lack of inventories in a demand-pull system makes it urgent for managers to detect and solve problems quickly.

Effect of JIT Systems on Product Costing

By reducing materials handling, warehousing, and inspection, JIT systems reduce overhead costs. JIT systems also aid in the direct tracing of some costs usually classified as indirect. For example, the use of manufacturing cells makes it cost-effective to trace materials handling, machine operating, and inspection costs to specific products or product families made in these cells. These costs then become direct costs of those products. Also, the use of multiskilled workers in these cells allows the costs of setup, maintenance, and quality inspection to be traced as direct costs. These changes have prompted some companies using JIT to adopt simplified product-costing methods that dovetail with JIT production and that are less costly to operate than the traditional costing systems described in Chapters 4, 7, 8, and 17. We examine two of these methods next: backflush costing and lean accounting.

Decision Point

What are the features and benefits of a just-in-time (JIT) production system?

Backflush Costing

Learning Objective 7

Describe different ways backflush costing can simplify traditional inventory-costing systems

...for example, by not recording journal entries for work in process, purchase of materials, or production of finished goods

Organizing manufacturing in cells, reducing defects and manufacturing cycle times, and ensuring the timely delivery of materials enable a company's purchasing, production, and sales to occur in quick succession with minimal inventories. The absence of inventories makes choices about cost-flow assumptions (such as weighted average or first-in, first-out) or inventory-costing methods (such as absorption or variable costing) unimportant: All manufacturing costs of the accounting period flow directly into cost of goods sold. The rapid conversion of direct materials into finished goods that are immediately sold greatly simplifies the costing system.

Simplified Normal or Standard Costing Systems

Traditional normal or standard-costing systems (Chapters 4, 7, 8, and 17) use **sequential tracking**, which is a costing system in which the recording of the journal entries occurs in the same order as actual purchases and progress in production. Costs are tracked sequentially as products pass through each of the following four stages:

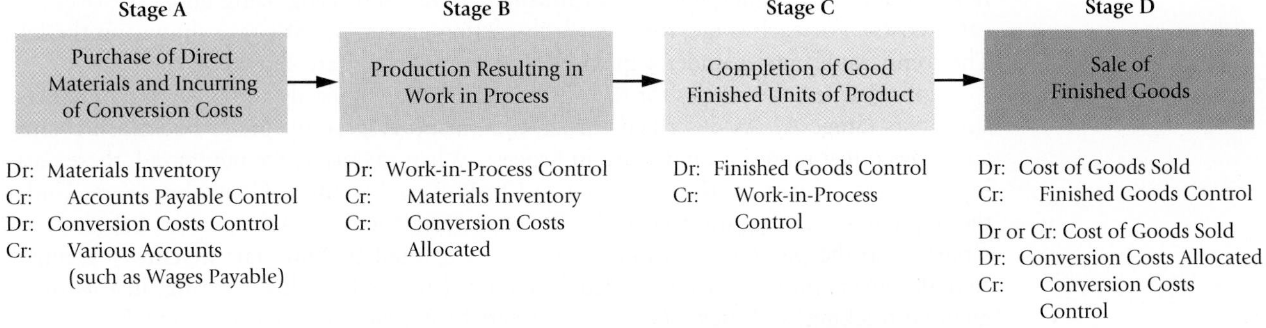

A sequential-tracking costing system has four *trigger points*, corresponding to Stages A, B, C, and D. A **trigger point** is a stage in the cycle, from the purchase of direct materials and incurring of conversion costs (Stage A) to the sale of finished goods (Stage D), at which journal entries are made in the accounting system. The journal entries (with Dr. representing debits and Cr. representing credits) for each stage are displayed below the box for that stage (as described in Chapter 4).

An alternative approach to sequential tracking is backflush costing. **Backflush costing** is a costing system that omits recording some of the journal entries relating to the stages from the purchase of direct materials to the sale of finished goods. When journal entries for one or more stages are omitted, the journal entries for a subsequent stage use normal or standard costs to work backward to "flush out" the costs in the cycle for which journal entries were *not* made. When inventories are minimal, as in JIT production systems, backflush costing simplifies costing systems without losing much information.

Consider the following data for the month of April for Silicon Valley Computer (SVC), which produces keyboards for personal computers.

- There are no beginning inventories of direct materials and no beginning or ending work-in-process inventories.
- SVC has only one direct manufacturing cost category (direct materials) and one indirect manufacturing cost category (conversion costs). All manufacturing labor costs are included in conversion costs.
- From its bill of materials and an operations list (description of operations to be undergone), SVC determines that the standard direct materials cost per keyboard unit is \$19 and the standard conversion cost is \$12.
- SVC purchases \$1,950,000 of direct materials. To focus on the basic concepts, we assume SVC has no direct materials variances. Actual conversion costs equal \$1,260,000. SVC produces 100,000 good keyboard units and sells 99,000 units.
- Any underallocated or overallocated conversion costs are written off to cost of goods sold at the end of April.

We use three examples to illustrate backflush costing. *They differ in the number and placement of trigger points.*

Example 1: The three trigger points for journal entries are Purchase of direct materials and incurring of conversion costs (Stage A), Completion of good finished units of product (Stage C), and Sale of finished goods (Stage D).

Note that there is no journal entry for Production resulting in work in process (Stage B) because this method is used when work-in-process inventory is minimal (units started are quickly converted to finished goods).

SVC records two inventory accounts:

Type	Account Title
Combined materials inventory and materials in work in process	Materials and In-Process Inventory Control
Finished goods	Finished Goods Control

Exhibit 20-7, Panel A, summarizes the journal entries for Example 1 with three trigger points: Purchase of direct materials and incurring of conversion costs, Completion of good finished units of product, and Sale of finished goods (and recognizing under- or overallocated costs). For each stage, the backflush costing entries for SVC are shown on the left. The comparable entries under sequential tracking (costing) are shown on the right.

Consider first the entries for the purchase of direct materials and incurring of conversion costs (Stage A). As described earlier, the inventory account under backflush costing combines direct materials and work in process. When materials are purchased, these costs increase (are debited to) the Materials and In-Process Inventory Control account. Under the sequential tracking approach, the direct materials and work-in-process accounts are separate, so the purchase of direct materials is debited to Materials Inventory Control. Actual conversion costs are recorded as incurred under backflush costing, just as in sequential tracking, and they increase (are debited to) Conversion Costs Control.

Exhibit 20-7 Journal Entries and General Ledger Overview for Backflush Costing and Journal Entries for Sequential Tracking with Three Trigger Points: Purchase of Direct Materials and Incurring of Conversion Costs, Completion of Good Finished Units of Product, and Sale of Finished Goods

PANEL A: Journal Entries

	Backflush Costing			Sequential Tracking		
Stage A: Record Purchase of Direct Materials and Incurring of Conversion Costs						
1. Record Direct Materials Purchased.						
Entry (A1)	Materials and In-Process Inventory Control	1,950,000		Materials Inventory Control	1,950,000	
	Accounts Payable Control		1,950,000	Accounts Payable Control		1,950,000
2. Record Conversion Costs Incurred.						
Entry (A2)	Conversion Costs Control	1,260,000		Conversion Costs Control	1,260,000	
	Various accounts (such as Wages Payable Control)		1,260,000	Various accounts (such as Wages Payable Control)		1,260,000
Stage B: Record Production Resulting in Work in Process.						
Entry (B1)	No Entry Recorded			Work-in-Process Control	3,100,000	
				Materials Inventory Control		1,900,000
				Conversion Costs Allocated		1,200,000
Stage C: Record Cost of Good Finished Units Completed.						
Entry (C1)	Finished Goods Control	3,100,000		Finished Goods Control	3,100,000	
	Materials and In-Process Inventory Control		1,900,000	Work-in-Process Control		3,100,000
	Conversion Costs Allocated		1,200,000			
Stage D: Record Cost of Finished Goods Sold (and Under- or Overallocated Conversion Costs).						
1. Record Cost of Finished Goods Sold.						
Entry (D1)	Cost of Goods Sold	3,069,000		Cost of Goods Sold	3,069,000	
	Finished Goods Control		3,069,000	Finished Goods Control		3,069,000
2. Record Underallocated or Overallocated Conversion Costs.						
Entry (D2)	Conversion Costs Allocated	1,200,000		Conversion Costs Allocated	1,200,000	
	Cost of Goods Sold	60,000		Cost of Goods Sold	60,000	
	Conversion Costs Control		1,260,000	Conversion Costs Control		1,260,000

PANEL B: General Ledger Overview for Backflush Costing

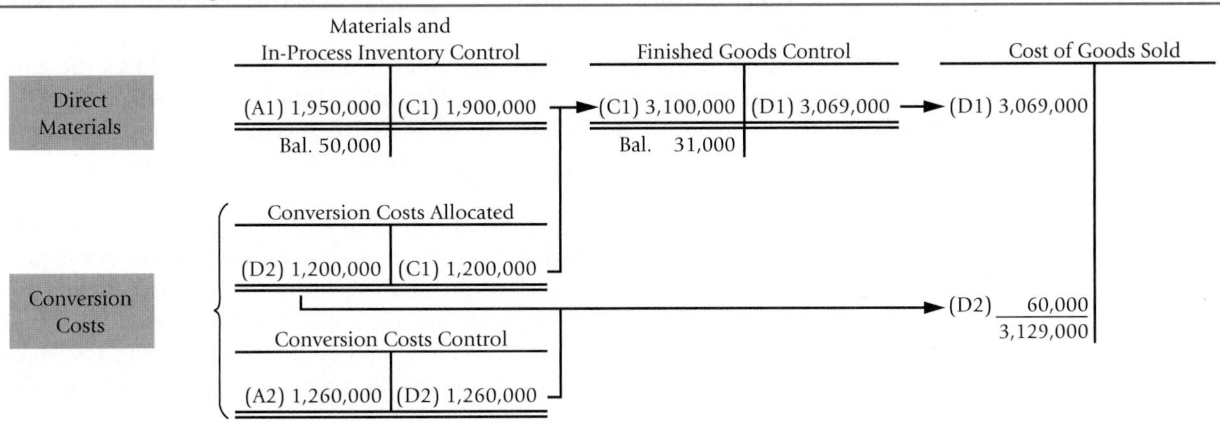

The coding that appears in parentheses for each entry indicates the stage in the production process that the entry relates to as presented in the text.

Next consider the entries for production resulting in work in process (Stage B). Recall that 100,000 units were started into production in April and that the standard cost for the units produced is $31 ($19 direct materials + $12 conversion costs) per unit. Under backflush costing, no entry is recorded in Stage B because work-in-process inventory is minimal and all units are quickly converted to finished goods. Under sequential tracking, work-in-process inventory is increased as manufacturing occurs and later decreased as manufacturing is completed and the product becomes a finished good.

The entries to record the completion of good finished units (Stage C) give backflush costing its name. The costs have not been recorded sequentially with the flow of the product along its production route through work in process and finished goods. Instead, the output trigger point reaches *back* and pulls ("*flushes*") the standard direct material costs from Materials and In-Process Inventory Control and the standard conversion costs for manufacturing the finished goods. Under the sequential tracking approach, Finished Goods Control is debited (increased) and Work-in-Process Control is credited (decreased) as manufacturing is completed and finished goods are produced. The net effect of Stages B and C under sequential tracking is the same as the effect under backflush costing (except for the name of the inventory account).

Finally consider the entries to record the sale of finished goods (and under- or overallocated conversion costs) (Stage D). The standard cost of 99,000 units sold in April equals $3,069,000 (99,000 units × $31 per unit). The entries to record the cost of finished goods sold are exactly the same under backflush costing and sequential tracking.

Actual conversion costs may be underallocated or overallocated in an accounting period. Chapter 4 (pages 127–132) discussed various ways to dispose of underallocated or overallocated manufacturing overhead costs. Companies that use backflush costing typically have low inventories, so prorating underallocated or overallocated conversion costs between work in process, finished goods, and cost of goods sold is seldom necessary. Generally, companies write off underallocated or overallocated conversion costs to cost of goods sold only at the end of the fiscal year. Other companies, like SVC, record the write-off monthly. The journal entry to dispose of the difference between actual conversion costs incurred and standard conversion costs allocated is exactly the same under backflush costing and sequential tracking.

The April 30 ending inventory balances under backflush costing are as follows:

Materials and In-Process Inventory Control ($1,950,000 − $1,900,000)	$50,000
Finished Goods Control, 1,000 units × $31/unit (or $3,100,000 − $3,069,000)	31,000
Total	$81,000

The April 30 ending inventory balances under sequential tracking would be exactly the same except that the inventory account would be Materials Inventory Control. Exhibit 20-7, Panel B (page 783), provides a general-ledger overview of this version of backflush costing.

The elimination of the typical Work-in-Process Control account reduces the amount of detail in the accounting system. Units on the production line may still be tracked in physical terms, but there is "no assignment of costs" to specific work orders while they are in the production cycle. In fact, there are no work orders or labor-time records in the accounting system.

The three trigger points to make journal entries in Example 1 will lead SVC's backflush costing system to report costs that are similar to the costs reported under sequential tracking when SVC has minimal work-in-process inventory. In Example 1, any inventories of direct materials or finished goods are recognized in SVC's backflush costing system when they are acquired or produced (as would be done in a costing system using sequential tracking). International Paper Company uses a method similar to Example 1 in its specialty papers plant.

Accounting for Variances

Accounting for variances between actual and standard costs is basically the same under all standard-costing systems. The procedures are described in Chapters 7 and 8. Suppose that in Example 1, SVC had an unfavorable direct materials price variance of $42,000. Then the journal entry would be as follows:

Materials and In-Process Inventory Control	1,950,000	
Direct Materials Price Variance	42,000	
Accounts Payable Control		1,992,000

Direct materials costs are often a large proportion of total manufacturing costs, sometimes as much as 60%. Consequently, many companies measure the direct materials efficiency variance in total by physically comparing what remains in direct materials inventory against what should remain based on the output of finished goods for the accounting period. In our example, suppose that such a comparison showed an unfavorable materials efficiency variance of $30,000. The journal entry would be as follows:

Direct Materials Efficiency Variance	30,000	
Materials and In-Process Inventory Control		30,000

The underallocated or overallocated conversion costs are split into various overhead variances (spending variance, efficiency variance, and production-volume variance), as explained in Chapter 8. Each variance is closed to the Cost of Goods Sold account, if it is immaterial in amount.

Example 2: The two trigger points are Purchase of direct materials and incurring of conversion costs (Stage A) and Sale of finished goods (Stage D).

This example uses the SVC data to illustrate a backflush costing that differs more from sequential tracking than the backflush costing in Example 1. This example and Example 1 have the same first trigger point, purchase of direct materials and incurring of conversion costs. But the second trigger point in Example 2 is the sale, not the completion, of finished goods. *Note that there is no journal entry for Production resulting in work in process (Stage B) and Completion of good finished units of product (Stage C) because this method is used when there are minimal work-in-process and finished goods inventories (units started are quickly converted into finished goods that are immediately sold).*
In this example, there is only one inventory account: direct materials, whether the materials are in storerooms, in process, or in finished goods.

Type	Account Title
Combines direct materials inventory and any direct materials in work-in-process and finished goods inventories	Inventory Control

Exhibit 20-8, Panel A, summarizes the journal entries for Example 2 with two trigger points: Purchase of direct materials and incurring of conversion costs and Sale of finished goods (and recognizing under- or overallocated costs). As in Example 1, for each stage, the backflush costing entries for SVC are shown on the left. The comparable entries under sequential tracking are shown on the right.

The entries for direct materials purchased and conversion costs incurred (Stage A) are the same as in Example 1, except that the inventory account is called Inventory Control. As in Example 1, no entry is made to record the production of work-in-process inventory (Stage B) because the work-in-process inventory is minimal. When finished goods are completed (Stage C), no entry is recorded because the completed units are expected to be sold quickly and the finished goods inventory is expected to be minimal. As finished goods are sold (Stage D), the cost of goods sold is calculated as 99,000 units sold × $31 per unit = $3,069,000, which is composed of direct materials costs (99,000 units × $19 per unit = $1,881,000) and conversion costs allocated (99,000 units × $12 per unit = $1,188,000). This is the same Cost of Goods Sold calculated under sequential tracking as described in Example 1.

Under this method of backflush costing, conversion costs are not inventoried because no entries are recorded when finished goods are produced in Stage C. That is, compared with sequential tracking, Example 2 does not assign $12,000 ($12 per unit × 1,000 units) of conversion costs to finished goods inventory produced but not sold. Of the $1,260,000 in conversion

Exhibit 20-8 Journal Entries and General Ledger Overview for Backflush Costing and Journal Entries for Sequential Tracking with Two Trigger Points: Purchase of Direct Materials and Incurring of Conversion Costs and Sale of Finished Goods

PANEL A: Journal Entries

	Backflush Costing			**Sequential Tracking**		
Stage A: Record Purchase of Direct Materials and Incurring of Conversion Costs						
1. Record Direct Materials Purchased.						
Entry (A1)	Inventory: Control	1,950,000		Materials Inventory Control	1,950,000	
	Accounts Payable Control		1,950,000	Accounts Payable Control		1,950,000
2. Record Conversion Costs Incurred.						
Entry (A2)	Conversion Costs Control	1,260,000		Conversion Costs Control	1,260,000	
	Various accounts (such as Wages Payable Control)		1,260,000	Various accounts (such as Wages Payable Control)		1,260,000
Stage B: Record Production Resulting in Work in Process.						
Entry (B1)	No Entry Recorded			Work-in-Process Control	3,100,000	
				Materials Inventory Control		1,900,000
				Conversion Costs Allocated		1,200,000
Stage C: Record Cost of Good Finished Units Completed.						
Entry (C1)	No Entry Recorded			Finished Goods Control	3,100,000	
				Work-in-Process Control		3,100,000
Stage D: Record Cost of Finished Goods Sold (and Under- or Overallocated Conversion Costs).						
1. Record Cost of Finished Goods Sold.						
Entry (D1)	Cost of Goods Sold	3,069,000		Cost of Goods Sold	3,069,000	
	Inventory Control		1,881,000	Finished Goods Control		3,069,000
	Conversion Costs Allocated		1,188,000			
2. Record Underallocated or Overallocated Conversion Costs.						
Entry (D2)	Conversion Costs Allocated	1,188,000		Conversion Costs Allocated	1,200,000	
	Cost of Goods Sold	72,000		Cost of Goods Sold	60,000	
	Conversion Costs Control		1,260,000	Conversion Costs Control		1,260,000

PANEL B: General Ledger Overview for Backflush Costing

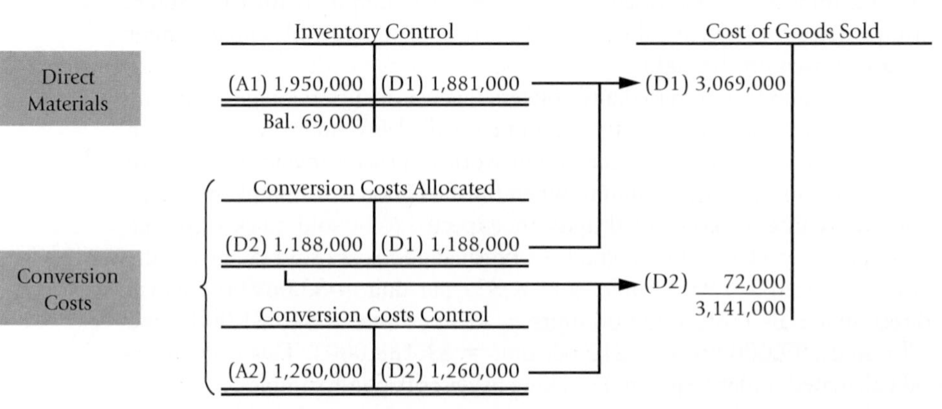

The coding that appears in parentheses for each entry indicates the stage in the production process that the entry relates to as presented in the text.

costs, \$1,188,000 is allocated at standard cost to the units sold. The remaining \$72,000 (\$1,260,000 − \$1,188,000) of conversion costs is underallocated compared to \$60,000 under sequential tracking. Entry (D2) presents the journal entry if SVC, like many companies, writes off these underallocated costs monthly as additions to the Cost of Goods Sold account.

The April 30 ending balance of the Inventory Control account is \$69,000 (\$1,950,000 − \$1,881,000). This balance represents the \$50,000 direct materials still on hand + \$19,000 direct materials embodied in the 1,000 finished units manufactured but not sold during the period. Finished goods inventory under sequential tracking is: direct materials, \$19,000 + conversion costs, \$12,000 for a total of \$31,000. Exhibit 20-8, Panel B, provides a general-ledger overview of Example 2. The approach described in Example 2 closely approximates the costs computed using sequential tracking when a company holds minimal work-in-process and finished goods inventories.

Toyota's cost accounting system at its Kentucky plant is similar to this example. Two advantages of this system are (1) it removes the incentive for managers to produce for inventory because conversion costs are recorded as period costs instead of inventoriable costs and (2) it focuses managers on sales.

Example 3: The two trigger points are Completion of good finished units of product (Stage C) and Sale of finished goods (Stage D).

This example has two trigger points. In contrast to Example 2, the first trigger point in Example 3 is delayed until Stage C, SVC's completion of good finished units of product. *Note that there are no journal entries for Purchase of direct materials and incurring of conversion costs (Stage A) and Production resulting in work in process (Stage B) because this method is used when there are minimal direct materials and work-in-process inventories (direct materials purchased are quickly placed into production and then quickly converted into finished goods).* Exhibit 20-9, Panel A, summarizes the journal entries for Example 3 with two trigger points: Completion of good finished units of product and Sale of finished goods (and recognizing under- or overallocated costs). As in Examples 1 and 2, for each stage, the backflush costing entries for SVC are shown on the left. The comparable entries under sequential tracking are shown on the right.

No entry is made for direct materials purchases of \$1,950,000 (Stage A) because the acquisition of direct materials is not a trigger point in this form of backflush costing. As in Examples 1 and 2, actual conversion costs are recorded as incurred and no entry is made to record production resulting in work-in-process inventory (Stage B). The cost of 100,000 good finished units completed (Stage C) is recorded at standard cost of \$31(\$19 direct materials + \$12 conversion costs) per unit as in Example 1 except that Accounts Payable Control is credited (instead of Materials and In-Process Inventory Control) because no entry had been made when direct materials were purchased in Stage A. Note that at the end of April, \$50,000 of direct materials purchased have not yet been placed into production (\$1,950,000 − \$1,900,000 = \$50,000), nor have the cost of those direct materials been entered into the inventory-costing system. The Example 3 version of backflush costing is suitable for a JIT production system in which both direct materials inventory and work-in-process inventory are minimal. As finished goods are sold (Stage D), the cost of goods sold is calculated as 99,000 units sold × \$31 per unit = \$3,069,000. This is the same Cost of Goods sold calculated under sequential tracking. The Finished Goods Control account has a balance of \$31,000 under both this form of backflush costing and sequential tracking. The journal entry to dispose of the difference between the actual conversion costs incurred and standard conversion costs allocated is the same under backflush costing and sequential tracking. The only difference between this form of backflush costing and sequential tracking is that direct materials inventory of \$50,000 (and the corresponding Accounts Payable Control) is not recorded, which is no problem if direct materials inventories are minimal. Exhibit 20-9, Panel B, provides a general-ledger overview of Example 3.

Extending Example 3, backflush costing systems could use the sale of finished goods as the only trigger point. This version of backflush costing is most suitable for a JIT production system with minimal direct materials, work-in-process, and finished goods inventories. That's because this backflush costing system maintains no inventory accounts.

Exhibit 20-9 Journal Entries and General Ledger Overview for Backflush Costing and Journal Entries for Sequential Tracking with Two Trigger Points: Completion of Good Finished Units of Product and Sale of Finished Goods

PANEL A: Journal Entries

Entry	Backflush Costing			Sequential Tracking		
Stage A: Record Purchase of Direct Materials and Incurring of Conversion Costs.						
1. Record Direct Materials Purchased.						
Entry (A1)	No Entry Recorded			Materials Inventory Control	1,950,000	
				Accounts Payable Control		1,950,000
2. Record Conversion Costs Incurred.						
Entry (A2)	Conversion Costs Control	1,260,000		Conversion Costs Control	1,260,000	
	Various accounts (such as Wages Payable Control)		1,260,000	Various accounts (such as Wages Payable Control)		1,260,000
Stage B: Record Production Resulting in Work in Process.						
Entry (B1)	No Entry Recorded			Work-in-Process Control	3,100,000	
				Materials Inventory Control		1,900,000
				Conversion Costs Allocated		1,200,000
Stage C: Record Cost of Good Finished Units Completed.						
Entry (C1)	Finished Goods Control	3,100,000		Finished Goods Control	3,100,000	
	Accounts Payable Control		1,900,000	Work-in-Process Control		3,100,000
	Conversion Costs Allocated		1,200,000			
Stage D: Record Cost of Finished Goods Sold (and Under- or Overallocated Conversion Costs).						
1. Record Cost of Finished Goods Sold.						
Entry (D1)	Cost of Goods Sold	3,069,000		Cost of Goods Sold	3,069,000	
	Finished Goods Control		3,069,000	Finished Goods Control		3,069,000
2. Record Underallocated or Overallocated Conversion Costs.						
Entry (D2)	Conversion Costs Allocated	1,200,000		Conversion Costs Allocated	1,200,000	
	Cost of Goods Sold	60,000		Cost of Goods Sold	60,000	
	Conversion Costs Control		1,260,000	Conversion Costs Control		1,260,000

PANEL B: General Ledger Overview for Backflush Costing

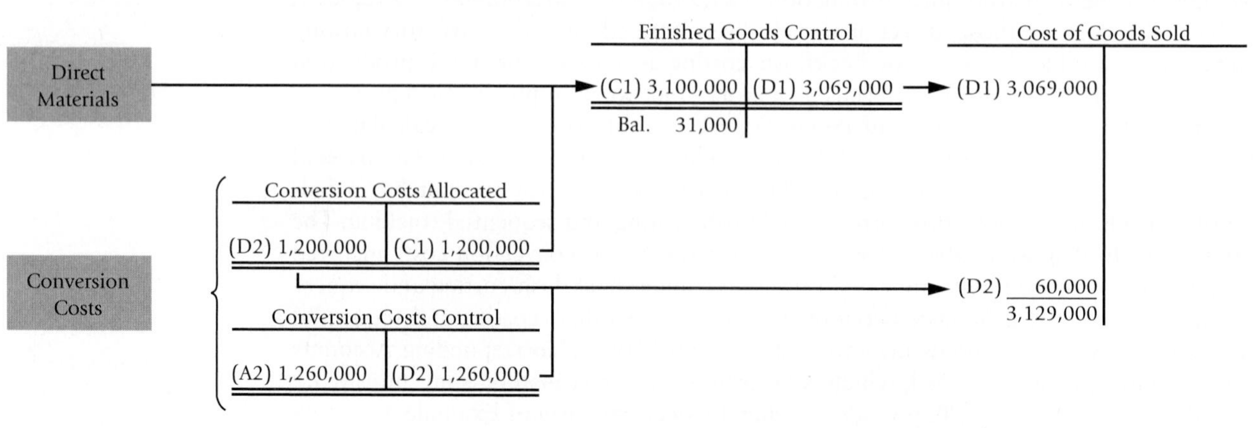

The coding that appears in parentheses for each entry indicates the stage in the production process that the entry relates to as presented in the text.

Special Considerations in Backflush Costing

The accounting procedures illustrated in Examples 1, 2, and 3 do not strictly adhere to Generally Accepted Accounting Principles (GAAP). For example, work-in-process inventory, which is an asset, exists but is not recognized in the financial accounting system. Advocates of backflush costing, however, cite the generally accepted accounting principle of materiality in support of the various versions of backflush costing. As the three examples illustrate, backflush costing can approximate the costs that would be reported under sequential tracking by varying the number of trigger points and where they are located. If significant amounts of direct materials inventory or finished goods inventory exist, adjusting entries can be incorporated (as explained next).

Suppose there are material differences in a company's operating income and inventories based on a backflush costing system and a conventional standard-costing system. A journal entry can be recorded to adjust the backflush number to comply with GAAP. For example, the backflush entries in Example 2 would result in expensing all conversion costs to the Cost of Goods Sold account ($1,188,000 at standard costs + $72,000 write-off of underallocated conversion costs = $1,260,000). But suppose conversion costs were regarded as sufficiently material in amount to be included in the Inventory Control account. Then entry (D2) in Example 2, closing the Conversion Costs accounts, would change as follows:

Original entry (D2)	Conversion Costs Allocated	1,188,000	
	Cost of Goods Sold	72,000	
	Conversion Costs Control		1,260,000
Revised entry (D2)	Conversion Costs Allocated	1,188,000	
	Inventory Control (1,000 units × $12)	12,000	
	Cost of Goods Sold	60,000	
	Conversion Costs Control		1,260,000

Critics say backflush costing leaves no audit trails—the ability of the accounting system to pinpoint the uses of resources at each step in the production process. However, the absence of sizable amounts of materials inventory, work-in-process inventory, and finished goods inventory means managers can keep track of operations by personal observations, computer monitoring, and nonfinancial measures.

What are the implications of JIT and backflush costing systems for activity-based costing (ABC) systems? Simplifying the production process, as a JIT system does, makes more of the costs direct and reduces the extent of overhead cost allocations. Simple ABC systems are often adequate for companies implementing JIT. These simple ABC systems work well with backflush costing. Costs from ABC systems yield a more accurate budgeted conversion cost per unit for different products in the backflush costing system. The activity-based cost information is also useful for product costing, decision making, and cost management.

Decision Point

How does backflush costing simplify traditional inventory costing?

Lean Accounting

Learning Objective 8

Understand the principles of lean accounting

...focus on costing value streams rather than products and limit arbitrary allocations

Another simplified product costing system that can be used with JIT (or lean production) systems is *lean accounting*. When a company utilizes JIT production, it has to focus on the entire value chain of business functions (from suppliers to manufacturing to customers) in order to reduce inventories, lead times, and waste. The improvements throughout the value chain that result have led some companies with JIT systems to develop organizational structures and costing systems that focus on **value streams,** which are all the value-added activities needed to design, manufacture, and deliver a given product or product line to customers. For example, a value stream can include the activities needed to develop and engineer products, advertise and market those products, process orders, purchase and receive materials, manufacture and ship orders, bill customers, and collect payments. The use of manufacturing cells in JIT systems helps keep a company focused on its value streams.

Lean accounting is a costing method that focuses on value streams, as distinguished from individual products or departments, thereby eliminating waste in the accounting process.[5] If a company makes multiple, related products in a single value stream, it does not compute product costs for the individual products. Instead, it traces many actual costs directly to the value stream. Tracing more costs as direct costs to value streams is possible because companies using lean accounting often dedicate resources to individual value streams. We now illustrate lean accounting for Manuela Corporation.

Manuela Corporation manufactures toner cartridges and ink cartridges for use with its printers. It makes two models of toner cartridges in one manufacturing cell and two models of ink cartridges in another manufacturing cell. The following table lists revenues, operating costs, operating income, and other information for the different products.

	Toner Cartridges		Ink Cartridges	
	Model A	**Model B**	**Model C**	**Model D**
Revenues	$600,000	$700,000	$800,000	$550,000
Direct materials	340,000	400,000	410,000	270,000
Direct manufacturing labor	70,000	78,000	105,000	82,000
Manufacturing overhead costs (e.g., equipment lease, supervision, and unused facility costs)	112,000	130,000	128,000	103,000
Rework costs	15,000	17,000	14,000	10,000
Design costs	20,000	21,000	24,000	18,000
Marketing and sales costs	30,000	33,000	40,000	28,000
Total costs	587,000	679,000	721,000	511,000
Operating income	$ 13,000	$ 21,000	$ 79,000	$ 39,000
Direct materials purchased	$350,000	$420,000	$430,000	$285,000
Unused facility costs	$ 22,000	$ 38,000	$ 18,000	$ 15,000

Using lean accounting principles, Manuela's managers calculate the value-stream operating costs and operating income for toner cartridges and ink cartridges, not individual models, as follows:

	Toner Cartridges	Ink Cartridges
Revenues ($600,000 + $700,000; $800,000 + $550,000)	$1,300,000	$1,350,000
Direct materials used ($340,000 + $400,000; $410,000 + $270,000)	740,000	680,000
Direct manufacturing labor ($70,000 + $78,000; $105,000 + $82,000)	148,000	187,000
Manufacturing overhead (after deducting unused facility costs) ($112,000 − $22,000) + ($130,000 − $38,000); ($128,000 − $18,000) + ($103,000 − $15,000)	182,000	198,000
Design costs ($20,000 + $21,000; $24,000 + $18,000)	41,000	42,000
Marketing and sales costs ($30,000 + $33,000; $40,000 + $28,000)	63,000	68,000
Total value stream operating costs	1,174,000	1,175,000
Value-stream operating income	$ 126,000	$ 175,000

[5] See Bruce L. Baggaley, "Costing by Value Stream," *Journal of Cost Management* (May–June 2003).

To gain insights, Manuela's lean accounting system, like many lean accounting systems, compares value-stream costs against costs that include costs of all purchased materials. Doing so keeps the company focused on reducing its direct materials and work-in-process inventory. In our example, the cost of direct material purchases exceeds the cost of direct materials used.

Manuela allocates its facility costs (such as depreciation, property taxes, and leases) to value streams based on the square footage each value stream uses. This encourages managers to use less space for production and for holding and moving inventory. Note that Manuela does not consider unused facility costs when calculating its manufacturing overhead costs of value streams. Instead, it treats these costs as plant or business unit expenses. Manuela excludes unused facility costs because it only includes in its value-stream costs those costs that add value. Increasing the visibility of unused capacity costs creates incentives to reduce these costs or to find alternative uses for the company's capacity. Manuela also excludes rework costs when calculating its value-stream costs and operating income because these costs are non-value-added costs. Companies also exclude from value-stream costs common costs such as corporate or support-department costs that cannot reasonably be assigned to value streams.

The analysis shows that although the total cost of the toner cartridges based on direct materials purchases rather than direct materials used is \$1,296,000 [\$587,000 + \$679,000 + (\$350,000 − \$340,000) + (\$420,000 − \$400,000)], the value-stream cost using lean accounting is \$1,174,000(90.6% × \$1,296,000). The difference between the two indicates that there are opportunities for improving the company's profitability by reducing unused facility and rework costs and by purchasing direct materials only as needed for production. Making improvements is particularly important because Manuela's value-stream operating income is only 9.7%(\$126,000 ÷ \$1,300,000) of its revenues. Manuela's ink cartridges portray a different picture. The total cost for ink cartridges based on direct materials purchases rather than direct materials used is \$1,267,000 [\$721,000 + \$511,000 + (\$430,000 − \$410,000) + (\$285,000 − \$270,000)], whereas the value-stream cost using lean accounting is \$1,175,000(92.7% × \$1,267,000). The ink cartridges value stream has low unused facility and rework costs and is more efficient. Moreover, the ink cartridges also have higher value-stream operating income profitability of 13%(\$175,000 ÷ \$1,350,000).

Lean accounting is much simpler than traditional product costing. Why? Because calculating actual product costs by value streams requires less overhead allocation. Consistent with JIT and lean production, lean accounting emphasizes improvements in the value chain from suppliers to customers. Lean accounting encourages practices—such as reducing direct materials and work-in-process inventories, improving quality, using less space, and eliminating unused capacity—that reflect the goals of JIT production.

Critics of lean accounting charge that it does not compute the costs of individual products, which makes it less useful for making decisions. Proponents of lean accounting argue that the lack of individual product costs is not a problem because most decisions are made at the product line level rather than the individual product level and that pricing decisions are based on the value created for the customer (market prices) and not product costs.

Another criticism of lean accounting is that it excludes certain support costs and unused capacity costs. As a result, the decisions based on only value-stream costs will look profitable because they do not consider all costs. Proponents of lean accounting argue that the method overcomes this problem by adding a larger markup on value-stream costs to compensate for some of these excluded costs. Moreover, in a competitive market, prices will eventually settle at a level that represents a reasonable markup above a product's value-stream costs because customers will be unwilling to pay for non-value-added costs. The goal must therefore be to eliminate non-value-added costs.

A final criticism of lean accounting is that, like backflush costing, it does not correctly account for inventories under Generally Accepted Accounting Principles (GAAP). However, the method's proponents are quick to point out that in lean accounting environments, work-in-process and finished goods inventories are immaterial from an accounting perspective.

Decision Point

How is lean accounting different from traditional costing systems?

Problems for Self-Study

Problem 1

Lee Company has a Singapore plant that manufactures MP3 players. One component is an XT chip. Expected demand is for 5,200 of these chips in March 2013. Lee estimates the ordering cost per purchase order to be $250. The monthly carrying cost for one unit of XT in stock is $5.

Required

1. Compute the EOQ for the XT chip.
2. Compute the number of deliveries of XT in March 2013.

Solution

$$EOQ = \sqrt{\frac{2 \times 5{,}200 \times \$250}{\$5}}$$

$$= 721 \text{ chips (rounded)}$$

$$\text{Number of deliveries} = \frac{5{,}200}{721}$$

$$= 8 \text{(rounded)}$$

Problem 2

Littlefield Company uses a backflush costing system with three trigger points:

- Purchase of direct materials
- Completion of good finished units of product
- Sale of finished goods

There are no beginning inventories. Information for April 2013 is as follows:

Direct materials purchased	$880,000	Conversion costs allocated	$ 400,000
Direct materials used	$850,000	Costs transferred to finished goods	$1,250,000
Conversion costs incurred	$422,000	Cost of goods sold	$1,190,000

Required

1. Prepare journal entries for April (without disposing of underallocated or overallocated conversion costs). Assume there are no direct materials variances.
2. Under an ideal JIT production system, how would the amounts in your journal entries differ from the journal entries in requirement 1?

Solution

1. Journal entries for April are as follows:

Entry (A1)	Materials and In-Process Inventory Control	880,000	
	Accounts Payable Control		880,000
	(direct materials purchased)		
Entry (A2)	Conversion Costs Control	422,000	
	Various accounts (such as Wages Payable Control)		422,000
	(conversion costs incurred)		
Entry (C1)	Finished Goods Control	1,250,000	
	Materials and In-Process Inventory Control		850,000
	Conversion Costs Allocated		400,000
	(standard cost of finished goods completed)		
Entry (D1)	Cost of Goods Sold	1,190,000	
	Finished Goods Control		1,190,000
	(standard costs of finished goods sold)		

2. Under an ideal JIT production system, if the manufacturing lead time per unit is very short, there would be zero inventories at the end of each day. Entry (C1) would be $1,190,000 finished goods production [to match finished goods sold in entry (D1)], not $1,250,000. If the marketing department could only sell goods costing $1,190,000, the JIT production system would call for direct materials purchases and conversion costs of lower than $880,000 and $422,000, respectively, in entries (A1) and (A2).

▶ Decision Points

The following question-and-answer format summarizes the chapter's learning objectives. Each decision presents a key question related to a learning objective. The guidelines are the answer to that question.

Decision	Guidelines
1. What are the six categories of costs associated with goods for sale?	The six categories are purchasing costs (costs of goods acquired from suppliers), ordering costs (costs of preparing a purchase order and receiving goods), carrying costs (costs of holding inventory of goods for sale), stockout costs (costs arising when a customer demands a unit of product and that unit is not on hand), costs of quality (prevention, appraisal, internal failure, and external failure costs), and shrinkage costs (the costs resulting from theft by outsiders, embezzlement by employees, misclassifications, and clerical errors).
2. What does the EOQ decision model help managers do, and how do managers decide on the safety-stock levels?	The economic-order-quantity (EOQ) decision model helps managers to calculate the optimal quantity of inventory to order by balancing ordering costs and carrying costs. The larger the order quantity, the higher are the annual carrying costs and the lower the annual ordering costs. The EOQ model includes costs recorded in the financial accounting system as well as opportunity costs of carrying inventory that are not recorded in the financial accounting system. Managers choose a level of safety stock to minimize the stockout costs and the carrying costs of holding more inventory.
3. How do errors in predicting the parameters of the EOQ model affect costs? How can companies reduce the conflict between the EOQ decision model and models used for performance evaluation?	The cost of prediction errors when using the EOQ model is small. To reduce the conflict between the EOQ decision model and the performance evaluation model, companies should include the opportunity cost of investment in inventory when evaluating managers. The opportunity cost of investment tied up in inventory is a key input in the EOQ decision model that is often ignored in the performance-evaluation model.
4. Why are companies using just-in-time (JIT) purchasing?	Just-in-time (JIT) purchasing is making purchases in small order quantities just as needed for production (or sales). JIT purchasing is a response to high carrying costs and low ordering costs. JIT purchasing increases the focus of companies and suppliers on quality and timely deliveries. Companies coordinate their activities and reduce inventories throughout the supply chain, from the initial sources of materials and services to the delivery of products to consumers.
5. How do materials requirements planning (MRP) systems differ from just-in-time (JIT) production systems?	Materials requirements planning (MRP) systems use a "push-through" approach whereby finished goods are manufactured on the basis of demand forecasts. Just-in-time (JIT) production systems use a "demand-pull" approach in which goods are manufactured only after receiving customer orders.

Decision	Guidelines
6. What are the features and benefits of a just-in-time (JIT) production system?	JIT production systems (a) organize production in manufacturing cells, (b) hire and train multiskilled workers, (c) emphasize total quality management, (d) reduce manufacturing lead time and setup time, and (e) build strong supplier relationships. The benefits of JIT production include lower costs and higher margins from better flow of information, higher quality, and faster delivery as well as simpler accounting systems.
7. How does backflush costing simplify traditional inventory costing?	Traditional inventory-costing systems use sequential tracking, in which recording of the journal entries occurs in the same order as actual purchases and progress in production. Most backflush costing systems do not record journal entries for the work-in-process stage of production. Some backflush costing systems also do not record entries for either the purchase of direct materials or the completion of finished goods.
8. How is lean accounting different from traditional costing systems?	Lean accounting assigns costs to value streams rather than to products. Non-value-added costs, unused capacity costs, and costs that cannot be easily traced to value streams are not allocated but instead expensed.

Terms to Learn

This chapter and the Glossary at the end of the book contain definitions of the following important terms:

backflush costing **(p. 782)**
carrying costs **(p. 765)**
economic order quantity (EOQ) **(p. 766)**
enterprise resource planning (ERP) system **(p. 779)**
inventory management **(p. 765)**
just-in-time (JIT) production **(p. 778)**
just-in-time (JIT) purchasing **(p. 773)**
lean accounting **(p. 790)**
lean production **(p. 778)**
manufacturing cells **(p. 778)**
materials requirements planning (MRP) system **(p. 777)**
ordering costs **(p. 765)**
purchase-order lead time **(p. 766)**
purchasing costs **(p. 765)**
reorder point **(p. 769)**
safety stock **(p. 769)**
sequential tracking **(p. 781)**
shrinkage costs **(p. 766)**
stockout costs **(p. 765)**
trigger point **(p. 782)**
value streams **(p. 789)**

Assignment Material

MyAccountingLab

Questions

20-1 Why do better decisions regarding the purchasing and managing of goods for sale frequently cause dramatic percentage increases in net income?

20-2 Name six cost categories that are important in managing goods for sale in a retail company.

20-3 What assumptions are made when using the simplest version of the economic-order-quantity (EOQ) decision model?

20-4 Give examples of costs included in annual carrying costs of inventory when using the EOQ decision model.

20-5 Give three examples of opportunity costs that typically are not recorded in accounting systems, although they are relevant when using the EOQ model in the presence of demand uncertainty.

20-6 What are the steps in computing the cost of a prediction error when using the EOQ decision model?

20-7 Why might goal-congruence issues arise when managers use an EOQ model to guide decisions on how much to order?

20-8 "JIT purchasing has many benefits but also some risks." Do you agree? Explain briefly.

20-9 What are three factors causing reductions in the cost to place purchase orders for materials?

20-10 "You should always choose the supplier who offers the lowest price per unit." Do you agree? Explain.

20-11 What is supply-chain analysis, and how can it benefit manufacturers and retailers?

20-12 What are the main features of JIT production, and what are its benefits and costs?

20-13 Distinguish inventory-costing systems using sequential tracking from those using backflush costing.

20-14 Describe three different versions of backflush costing.

20-15 Discuss the differences between lean accounting and traditional cost accounting.

Exercises

MyAccountingLab

20-16 Economic order quantity for retailer. Fan Base (FB) operates a megastore featuring sports merchandise. It uses an EOQ decision model to make inventory decisions. It is now considering inventory decisions for its Los Angeles Galaxy soccer jerseys product line. This is a highly popular item. Data for 2013 are as follows:

Expected annual demand for Galaxy jerseys	10,000
Ordering cost per purchase order	$200
Carrying cost per year	$7 per jersey

Each jersey costs FB $40 and sells for $80. The $7 carrying cost per jersey per year consists of the required return on investment of $4.80 (12% × $40 purchase price) plus $2.20 in relevant insurance, handling, and storage costs. The purchasing lead time is 7 days. FB is open 365 days a year.

Required

1. Calculate the EOQ.
2. Calculate the number of orders that will be placed each year.
3. Calculate the reorder point.

20-17 Economic order quantity, effect of parameter changes (continuation of 20-16). Athletic Textiles (AT) manufactures the Galaxy jerseys that Fan Base (FB) sells to its customers. AT has recently installed computer software that enables its customers to conduct "one-stop" purchasing using state-of-the-art Web site technology. FB's ordering cost per purchase order will be $30 using this new technology.

Required

1. Calculate the EOQ for the Galaxy jerseys using the revised ordering cost of $30 per purchase order. Assume all other data from Exercise 20-16 are the same. Comment on the result.
2. Suppose AT proposes to "assist" FB. AT will allow FB customers to order directly from the AT Web site. AT would ship directly to these customers. AT would pay $10 to FB for every Galaxy jersey purchased by one of FB's customers. Comment qualitatively on how this offer would affect inventory management at FB. What factors should FB consider in deciding whether to accept AT's proposal?

20-18 EOQ for a retailer. The Denim World sells fabrics to a wide range of industrial and consumer users. One of the products it carries is denim cloth, used in the manufacture of jeans and carrying bags. The supplier for the denim cloth pays all incoming freight. No incoming inspection of the denim is necessary because the supplier has a track record of delivering high-quality merchandise. The purchasing officer of the Denim World has collected the following information:

Annual demand for denim cloth	26,400 yards
Ordering cost per purchase order	$165
Carrying cost per year	20% of purchase costs
Safety-stock requirements	None
Cost of denim cloth	$9 per yard

The purchasing lead time is 2 weeks. The Denim World is open 250 days a year (50 weeks for 5 days a week).

Required

1. Calculate the EOQ for denim cloth.
2. Calculate the number of orders that will be placed each year.
3. Calculate the reorder point for denim cloth.

20-19 EOQ for manufacturer. Turfpro Company produces lawn mowers and purchases 4,500 units of a rotor blade part each year at a cost of $30 per unit. Turfpro requires a 15% annual rate of return on investment. In addition, the relevant carrying cost (for insurance, materials handling, breakage, etc.) is $3 per unit per year. The relevant ordering cost per purchase order is $75.

Required

1. Calculate Turfpro's EOQ for the rotor blade part.
2. Calculate Turfpro's annual relevant ordering costs for the EOQ calculated in requirement 1.
3. Calculate Turfpro's annual relevant carrying costs for the EOQ calculated in requirement 1.
4. Assume that demand is uniform throughout the year and known with certainty so there is no need for safety stocks. The purchase-order lead time is half a month. Calculate Turfpro's reorder point for the rotor blade part.

20-20 Sensitivity of EOQ to changes in relevant ordering and carrying costs, cost of prediction error. Alpha Company's annual demand for its only product, XT-590, is 10,000 units. Alpha is currently analyzing possible combinations of relevant carrying cost per unit per year and relevant ordering cost per purchase order, depending on the company's choice of supplier and average levels of inventory. This table presents three possible combinations of carrying and ordering costs.

Relevant Carrying Cost per Unit per Year	Relevant Ordering Cost per Purchase Order
$10	$400
$20	$200
$40	$100

Required

1. For each of the relevant ordering and carrying-cost alternatives, determine (a) EOQ and (b) annual relevant total costs.
2. How does your answer to requirement 1 give insight into the impact of changes in relevant ordering and carrying costs on EOQ and annual relevant total costs? Explain briefly.
3. Suppose the relevant carrying cost per unit per year was $20 and the relevant ordering cost per purchase order was $200. Suppose further that Alpha calculates EOQ after incorrectly estimating relevant carrying cost per unit per year to be $10 and relevant ordering cost per purchase order to be $400. Calculate the actual annual relevant total costs of Alpha's EOQ decision. Compare this cost to the annual relevant total costs that Alpha would have incurred if it had correctly estimated the relevant carrying cost per unit per year of $20 and the relevant ordering cost per purchase order of $200 that you have already calculated in requirement 1. Calculate and comment on the cost of the prediction error.

20-21 JIT production, relevant benefits, relevant costs. The Colonial Hardware Company manufactures specialty brass door handles at its Lynchburg plant. Colonial is considering implementing a JIT production system. The following are the estimated costs and benefits of JIT production:

a. Annual additional tooling costs would be $200,000.
b. Average inventory would decline by 80% from the current level of $2,000,000.
c. Insurance, space, materials-handling, and setup costs, which currently total $600,000 annually, would decline by 25%.
d. The emphasis on quality inherent in JIT production would reduce rework costs by 30%. Colonial currently incurs $400,000 in annual rework costs.
e. Improved product quality under JIT production would enable Colonial to raise the price of its product by $8 per unit. Colonial sells 40,000 units each year.

Colonial's required rate of return on inventory investment is 15% per year.

Required

1. Calculate the net benefit or cost to Colonial if it adopts JIT production at the Lynchburg plant.
2. What nonfinancial and qualitative factors should Colonial consider when making the decision to adopt JIT production?
3. Suppose Colonial implements JIT production at its Lynchburg plant. Give examples of performance measures Colonial could use to evaluate and control JIT production. What would be the benefit of Colonial implementing an enterprise resource planning (ERP) system?

20-22 Backflush costing and JIT production. Grand Devices Corporation assembles handheld computers that have scaled-down capabilities of laptop computers. Each handheld computer takes 6 hours to assemble. Grand Devices uses a JIT production system and a backflush costing system with three trigger points:

- Purchase of direct materials and incurring of conversion costs
- Completion of good finished units of product
- Sale of finished goods

There are no beginning inventories of materials or finished goods and no beginning or ending work-in-process inventories. The following data are for August 2013:

Direct materials purchased	$2,958,000	Conversion costs incurred	$777,600
Direct materials used	$2,937,600	Conversion costs allocated	$806,400

Grand Devices records direct materials purchased and conversion costs incurred at actual costs. It has no direct materials variances. When finished goods are sold, the backflush costing system "pulls through" standard direct material cost ($102 per unit) and standard conversion cost ($28 per unit). Grand Devices produced 28,800 finished units in August 2013 and sold 28,400 units. The actual direct material cost per unit in August 2013 was $102, and the actual conversion cost per unit was $27.

Required

1. Prepare summary journal entries for August 2013 (without disposing of under- or overallocated conversion costs).
2. Post the entries in requirement 1 to T-accounts for applicable Materials and In-Process Inventory Control, Finished Goods Control, Conversion Costs Control, Conversion Costs Allocated, and Cost of Goods Sold.
3. Under an ideal JIT production system, how would the amounts in your journal entries differ from those in requirement 1?

20-23 Backflush costing, two trigger points, materials purchase and sale (continuation of 20-22). Assume the same facts as in Exercise 20-22, except that Grand Devices now uses a backflush costing system with the following two trigger points:

- Purchase of direct materials and incurring of conversion costs
- Sale of finished goods

The Inventory Control account will include direct materials purchased but not yet in production, materials in work in process, and materials in finished goods but not sold. No conversion costs are inventoried. Any under- or overallocated conversion costs are written off monthly to Cost of Goods Sold.

Required

1. Prepare summary journal entries for August, including the disposition of under- or overallocated conversion costs.
2. Post the entries in requirement 1 to T-accounts for Inventory Control, Conversion Costs Control, Conversion Costs Allocated, and Cost of Goods Sold.

20-24 Backflush costing, two trigger points, completion of production and sale (continuation of 20-22). Assume the same facts as in Exercise 20-22, except now Grand Devices uses only two trigger points, Completion of good finished units of product and Sale of finished goods. Any under- or overallocated conversion costs are written off monthly to Cost of Goods Sold.

Required

1. Prepare summary journal entries for August, including the disposition of under- or overallocated conversion costs.
2. Post the entries in requirement 1 to T-accounts for Finished Goods Control, Conversion Costs Control, Conversion Costs Allocated, and Cost of Goods Sold.

Problems

MyAccountingLab

20-25 EOQ, uncertainty, safety stock, reorder point. Chadwick Shoe Co. produces and sells an excellent-quality walking shoe. After production, the shoes are distributed to 20 warehouses around the country. Each warehouse services approximately 100 stores in its region. Chadwick uses an EOQ model to determine the number of pairs of shoes to order for each warehouse from the factory. Annual demand for Warehouse OR2 is approximately 120,000 pairs of shoes. The ordering cost is $250 per order. The annual carrying cost of a pair of shoes is $2.40 per pair.

Required

1. Use the EOQ model to determine the optimal number of pairs of shoes per order.
2. Assume each month consists of approximately 4 weeks. If it takes 1 week to receive an order, at what point should warehouse OR2 reorder shoes?
3. Although OR2's average weekly demand is 2,500 pairs of shoes (120,000 ÷ 12 months ÷ 4 weeks), demand each week may vary with the following probability distribution:

Total demand for 1 week	2,000 pairs	2,250 pairs	2,500 pairs	2,750 pairs	3,000 pairs
Probability (sums to 1.00)	0.04	0.20	0.52	0.20	0.04

If a store wants shoes and OR2 has none in stock, OR2 can "rush" them to the store at an additional cost of $2 per pair. How much safety stock should Warehouse OR2 hold? How will this affect the reorder point and reorder quantity?

20-26 EOQ, uncertainty, safety stock, reorder point. Stewart Corporation is a major automobile manufacturer. It purchases steering wheels from Coase Corporation. Annual demand is 10,400 steering wheels per year or 200 steering wheels per week. The ordering cost is $100 per order. The annual carrying cost is $13 per steering wheel. It currently takes 1.5 weeks to supply an order to the assembly plant.

Required

1. What is the optimal number of steering wheels that Stewart's managers should order according to the EOQ model?
2. At what point should managers reorder the steering wheels, assuming that both demand and purchase-order lead time are known with certainty?

3. Now assume that demand can vary during the 1.5-week purchase-order lead time. The following table shows the probability distribution of various demand levels:

Total Demand for Steering Wheels for 1.5 Weeks	Probability of Demand (sums to 1)
100	0.15
200	0.20
300	0.40
400	0.20
500	0.05

If Stewart runs out of stock, it would have to rush order the steering wheels at an additional cost of $9 per steering wheel. How much safety stock should the assembly plant hold? How will this affect the reorder point and reorder quantity.

20-27 MRP, EOQ, and JIT. Tech Works Corp. produces J-Pods, music players that can download thousands of songs. Tech Works forecasts that demand in 2014 will be 48,000 J-Pods. The variable production cost of each J-Pod is $54. In its MRP system, due to the large $10,000 cost per setup, Tech Works plans to produce J-Pods once a month in batches of 4,000 each. The carrying cost of a unit in inventory is $17 per year.

Required

1. Using the MRP system, what is the annual cost of producing and carrying J-Pods in inventory? (Assume that, on average, half of the units produced in a month are in inventory.)
2. A new manager at Tech Works has suggested that the company use the EOQ model to determine the optimal batch size to produce. (To use the EOQ model, Tech Works needs to treat the setup cost in the same way it would treat ordering cost in a traditional EOQ model.) Determine the optimal batch size and number of batches. Round up the number of batches to the nearest whole number. What would be the annual cost of producing and carrying J-Pods in inventory if it uses the optimal batch size? Compare this cost to the cost calculated in requirement 1. Comment briefly.
3. Tech Works is also considering switching from its MRP system to a JIT system. This will result in producing J-Pods in batch sizes of 600 J-Pods and will reduce obsolescence, improve quality, and result in a higher selling price. The frequency of production batches will force Tech Works to reduce setup time and will result in a reduction in setup cost. The new setup cost will be $500 per setup. What is the annual cost of producing and carrying J-Pods in inventory under the JIT system?
4. Compare the models analyzed in the previous parts of the problem. What are the advantages and disadvantages of each?

20-28 Effect of management evaluation criteria on EOQ model. Computer Depot purchases one model of computer at a wholesale cost of $300 per unit and resells it to end consumers. The annual demand for the company's product is 600,000 units. Ordering costs are $1,200 per order and carrying costs are $75 per computer, including $30 in the opportunity cost of holding inventory.

Required

1. Compute the optimal order quantity using the EOQ model.
2. Compute (a) the number of orders per year and (b) the annual relevant total cost of ordering and carrying inventory.
3. Assume that when evaluating the manager, the company excludes the opportunity cost of carrying inventory. If the manager makes the EOQ decision excluding the opportunity cost of carrying inventory, the relevant carrying cost would be $45, not $75. How would this affect the EOQ amount and the actual annual relevant cost of ordering and carrying inventory?
4. What is the cost impact on the company of excluding the opportunity cost of carrying inventory when making EOQ decisions? Why do you think the company currently excludes the opportunity costs of carrying inventory when evaluating the manager's performance? What could the company do to encourage the manager to make decisions more congruent with the goal of reducing total inventory costs?

20-29 JIT purchasing, relevant benefits, relevant costs. (CMA, adapted) The Greene Corporation is an automotive supplier that uses automatic turning machines to manufacture precision parts from steel bars. Greene's inventory of raw steel averages $300,000. John Oates, president of Greene, and Helen Gorman, Greene's controller, are concerned about the costs of carrying inventory. The steel supplier is willing to supply steel in smaller lots at no additional charge. Gorman identifies the following effects of adopting a JIT inventory program to virtually eliminate steel inventory:

- Without scheduling any overtime, lost sales due to stockouts would increase by 35,000 units per year. However, by incurring overtime premiums of $20,000 per year, the increase in lost sales could be reduced to 20,000 units per year. This would be the maximum amount of overtime that would be feasible for Greene.
- Two warehouses currently used for steel bar storage would no longer be needed. Greene rents one warehouse from another company under a cancelable leasing arrangement at an annual cost of

$45,000. The other warehouse is owned by Greene and contains 12,000 square feet. Three-fourths of the space in the owned warehouse could be rented for $1.25 per square foot per year. Insurance and property tax costs totaling $7,000 per year would be eliminated.

Greene's required rate of return on investment is 20% per year. Greene's budgeted income statement for the year ending December 31, 2014, (in thousands) is:

Revenues (900,000 units)		$ 5,400
Cost of goods sold		
Variable costs	$2,025	
Fixed costs	725	
Total costs of goods sold		2,750
Gross margin		2,650
Marketing and distribution costs		
Variable costs	$ 450	
Fixed costs	750	
Total marketing and distribution costs		1,200
Operating income		$ 1,450

Required

1. Calculate the estimated dollar savings (loss) for the Greene Corporation that would result in 2014 from the adoption of JIT purchasing.
2. Identify and explain other factors that Greene should consider before deciding whether to adopt JIT purchasing.

20-30 Supply chain effects on total relevant inventory cost. Peach Computer Co. outsources the production of motherboards for its computers. It is currently deciding which of two suppliers to use: Alpha or Beta. Due to differences in the product failure rates in the two companies, 5% of motherboards purchased from Alpha will be inspected and 25% of motherboards purchased from Beta will be inspected. The following data refer to costs associated with Alpha and Beta:

	Alpha	Beta
Number of orders per year	50	50
Annual motherboards demanded	10,000	10,000
Price per motherboard	$108	$105
Ordering cost per order	$13	$10
Inspection cost per unit	$6	$6
Average inventory level	100 units	100 units
Expected number of stockouts	100	300
Stockout cost (cost of rush order) per stockout	$4	$6
Units returned by customers for replacing motherboards	50	500
Cost of replacing each motherboard	$30	$30
Required annual return on investment	10%	10%
Other carrying cost per unit per year	$3.50	$3.50

Required

1. What is the relevant cost of purchasing from Alpha and Beta?
2. What factors other than cost should Peach consider?

20-31 Supply chain effects on total relevant inventory cost. Joe's Deli orders specially-made sandwich buns from two different suppliers: Gold Star Breads and Grandma's Bakery. Joe's Deli would like to use only one of the suppliers in the future. Due to variations in quality, Joe's would need to inspect 30% of Gold Star's buns and 60% of Grandma's. The following data refer to costs associated with the two suppliers.

	Gold Star	Grandma's
Number of orders per year	100	100
Annual buns demanded	2,400	2,400
Price per bun	$ 2.50	$ 2.00
Ordering cost per order	$ 10.00	$ 12.00
Inspection cost per bun	$ 0.50	$ 0.50
Average inventory level	200	200

	Gold Star	Grandma's
Expected number of stockouts	10	10
Stockout cost of rush order	$ 10.00	$ 3.00
Estimated sandwiches returned by customers because of defective buns	60	100
Cost of fixing sandwiches returned by customers because of defective buns	$ 1.50	$ 1.50
Opportunity cost of investment	12%	12%
Other carrying costs per bun per year	$ 0.50	$ 0.50

Required

1. What is the relevant cost of purchasing from Gold Star and Grandma's?
2. What factors other than cost should Joe's Deli consider?

20-32 Backflush costing and JIT production. The Grand Meter Corporation manufactures electrical meters. For August, there were no beginning inventories of direct materials and no beginning or ending work in process. Grand Meter uses a JIT production system and backflush costing with three trigger points for making entries in the accounting system:

- Purchase of direct materials and incurring of conversion costs
- Completion of good finished units of product
- Sale of finished goods

Grand Meter's August standard cost per meter is direct materials, $25, and conversion cost, $20. Grand Meter has no direct materials variances. The following data apply to August manufacturing:

Direct materials purchased	$550,000	Number of finished units manufactured	21,000
Conversion costs incurred	$440,000	Number of finished units sold	20,000

Required

1. Prepare summary journal entries for August (without disposing of under- or overallocated conversion costs). Assume no direct materials variances.
2. Post the entries in requirement 1 to T-accounts for Materials and In-Process Inventory Control, Finished Goods Control, Conversion Costs Control, Conversion Costs Allocated, and Cost of Goods Sold.

20-33 Backflush, two trigger points, materials purchase and sale (continuation of 20-32). Assume that the second trigger point for Grand Meter Corporation is the sale—rather than the completion—of finished goods. Also, the inventory account is confined solely to direct materials, whether these materials are in a storeroom, in work in process, or in finished goods. No conversion costs are inventoried. They are allocated to the units sold at standard costs. Any under- or overallocated conversion costs are written off monthly to Cost of Goods Sold.

Required

1. Prepare summary journal entries for August, including the disposition of under- or overallocated conversion costs. Assume no direct materials variances.
2. Post the entries in requirement 1 to T-accounts for Inventory Control, Conversion Costs Control, Conversion Costs Allocated, and Cost of Goods Sold.

20-34 Backflush, two trigger points, completion of production and sale (continuation of 20-32). Assume the same facts as in Problem 20-33 except now there are only two trigger points: Completion of good finished units of product and Sale of finished goods.

Required

1. Prepare summary journal entries for August, including the disposition of under- or overallocated conversion costs. Assume no direct materials variances.
2. Post the entries in requirement 1 to T-accounts for Finished Goods Control, Conversion Costs Control, Conversion Costs Allocated, and Cost of Goods Sold.

20-35 Lean accounting. Reliable Security Devices (RSD) has introduced a just-in-time production process and is considering the adoption of lean accounting principles to support its new production philosophy. The company has two product lines: Mechanical Devices and Electronic Devices. Two individual products are made in each line. Product-line manufacturing overhead costs are traced directly to product lines and then allocated to the two individual products in each line. The company's traditional cost-accounting system allocates all plant-level facility costs and some corporate overhead costs to individual products. The latest accounting report using traditional cost accounting methods included the following information (in thousands of dollars):

	Mechanical Devices		Electronic Devices	
	Product A	Product B	Product C	Product D
Sales	$1,400	$1,000	$1,800	$900
Direct material (based on quantity used)	400	200	500	150
Direct manufacturing labor	300	150	400	120
Manufacturing overhead (equipment lease, supervision, production control)	180	240	400	190
Allocated plant-level facility costs	100	80	160	60
Design and marketing costs	190	100	210	84
Allocated corporate overhead costs	30	20	40	16
Operating income	$200	$210	$90	$280

RSD has determined that each of the two product lines represents a distinct value stream. It has also determined that out of the $400,000($100,000 + $80,000 + $160,000 + $60,000) plant-level facility costs, product A occupies 22% of the plant's square footage, product B occupies 18%, product C occupies 36%, and product D occupies 14%. The remaining 10% of square footage is not being used. Finally, RSD has decided that in order to identify inefficiencies, direct material should be expensed in the period it is purchased, rather than when the material is used. According to purchasing records, direct material purchase costs during the period were as follows:

	Mechanical Devices		Electronic Devices	
	Product A	Product B	Product C	Product D
Direct material (purchases)	$420	$240	$500	$180

Required

1. What are the cost objects in RSD's lean accounting system?
2. Compute operating income for the cost objects identified in requirement 1 using lean accounting principles. What would you compare this operating income against? Comment on your results.

20-36 JIT production, relevant benefits, relevant costs, ethics. Perez Container Corporation is considering implementing a JIT production system. The new system would reduce current average inventory levels of $4,000,000 by 75%, but it would require a much greater dependency on the company's core suppliers for on-time deliveries and high-quality inputs. The company's operations manager, Jim Ingram, is opposed to the idea of a new JIT system because he is concerned that the new system (a) will be too costly to manage; (b) will result in too many stockouts; and (c) will lead to the layoff of his employees, several of whom are currently managing inventory. He believes that these layoffs will affect the morale of his entire production department. The management accountant, Sue Winston, is in favor of the new system because of its likely cost savings. Jim wants Sue to rework the numbers because he is concerned that top management will give more weight to financial factors and not give due consideration to nonfinancial factors such as employee morale. In addition to the reduction in inventory described previously, Sue has gathered the following information for the upcoming year regarding the JIT system:

- Annual insurance and warehousing costs for inventory would be reduced by 60% of current budgeted level of $700,000.
- Payroll expenses for current inventory management staff would be reduced by 15% of the budgeted total of $1,200,000.
- Additional annual costs for JIT system implementation and management, including personnel costs, would equal $440,000.
- The additional number of stockouts under the new JIT system is estimated to be 5% of the total number of shipments annually. Ten thousand shipments are budgeted for the upcoming year. Each stockout would result in an average additional cost of $500.
- Perez's required rate of return on inventory investment is 10% per year.

Required

1. From a financial perspective, should Perez adopt the new JIT system?
2. Should Sue Winston rework the numbers?
3. How should she manage Jim Ingram's concerns?

21 Capital Budgeting and Cost Analysis

Learning Objectives

1. Understand the five stages of capital budgeting for a project
2. Use and evaluate the two main discounted cash flow (DCF) methods: the net present value (NPV) method and the internal rate-of-return (IRR) method
3. Use and evaluate the payback and discounted payback methods
4. Use and evaluate the accrual accounting rate-of-return (AARR) method
5. Identify relevant cash inflows and outflows for capital budgeting decisions
6. Understand issues involved in implementing capital budgeting decisions and evaluating managerial performance
7. Explain how managers can use capital budgeting to achieve their firms' strategic goals

Should Honda open a new plant in China or India?

Should Sony invest in developing the next generation of PlayStation consoles? Should the Gap discontinue its children's clothing line and expand its women's athletic clothing line? Working closely with accountants, top executives have to figure out how and when to best allocate the firm's financial resources among alternative opportunities to create future value for the company. Because it's hard to know what the future holds and how much projects will ultimately cost, this can be a challenging task, but it's one that managers must constantly confront. To meet this challenge, companies such as Target and Chevron have developed special groups to make project-related capital budgeting decisions. This chapter explains the different methods managers use to get the "biggest bang" for the firm's "buck" in terms of the projects they undertake.

Capital Budgeting Powers Decisions at the TVA[1]

The Tennessee Valley Authority (TVA) is the United States' largest public power provider and is wholly owned by the U.S. government. Although owned by the federal government, TVA is not financed with tax dollars; rather, the utility's funding comes from the sale of power to its customers. Recently, TVA faced a difficult strategic decision: ensuring sufficient power generation while at the same time continuing to provide affordable power to a growing number of customers in its service area.

At the same time, TVA was replacing a significant part of its existing power generation capability. TVA previously announced plans to retire multiple coal power plants by 2018 to reach its goal of becoming a clean energy leader. Potential sources of new power generation included the construction of nuclear, natural gas, coal, wind, and solar plants. The power generation options had differing costs, expected cash flows, and useful lives. Moreover, TVA's construction decisions were constrained by a limited capital budget. TVA turned to net present value (NPV) and internal rate-of-return (IRR) calculations to guide its decision making.

After extensive calculations, TVA discovered that the NPV and IRR of natural gas, nuclear, and wind plants were positive. The NPV of solar and coal plants was negative, and their IRR was below TVA's cost of capital (calculated as the current yield to maturity on 30-year government debt plus an added 1% premium). In 2012, four renewable wind-power sources located in Kansas, Illinois, and Iowa began delivery to the TVA power grid and construction began on a new gas-fired combustion turbine/combined

[1] *Sources:* Bob Wood, Steven Isbell, and Cass Larson, "The Tennessee Valley Authority: The Cost of Power." *IMA Educational Case Journal*, Volume 5, Number 4 (Montvale, NJ: Institute of Management Accountants, Inc., December 2012); and "TVA Releases Cost, Schedule Estimates for Watts Bar Nuclear Unit 2," Tennessee Valley Authority press release (Knoxville, TN, April 5, 2012).

cycle generating power plant. Additionally, the Watts Bar Unit 2 nuclear power generator is scheduled to begin operation in 2015. Construction on the unit, originally started in the mid-'80s, was resumed with updated technologies. TVA is also developing a smart grid deployment plan that will help customers better understand the costs and benefits of these new power sources.

Just as at the TVA, managers at companies such as Target, Honda, Sony, and the Gap face challenging investment decisions. In this chapter, we introduce several capital budgeting methods used to evaluate long-term investment projects. These methods help managers choose the projects that will contribute the most value to their organizations.

Stages of Capital Budgeting

Learning Objective 1

Understand the five stages of capital budgeting for a project

...identify projects; obtain information; make predictions; make decisions; and implement the decision, evaluate performance, and learn

Capital budgeting is the process of making long-run planning decisions for investments in projects. In much of accounting, income is calculated on a period-by-period basis. In choosing investments, however, managers make a selection from among multiple projects, each of which may span several periods. Exhibit 21-1 illustrates these two different yet intersecting dimensions of cost analysis: (1) horizontally across, as the *project dimension*, and (2) vertically upward, as the *accounting-period dimension*. Each project is represented as a horizontal rectangle starting and ending at different times and stretching over time spans longer than one year. The vertical rectangle for the 2015 accounting period, for example, represents the dimensions of income determination and routine annual planning and control that cut across all projects that are ongoing that year.

To make capital budgeting decisions, managers analyze each project by considering all the life-span cash flows from its initial investment through its termination. This process is analogous to life-cycle budgeting and costing (Chapter 13, pages 531–533). For example, when Honda considers producing a new model of automobile, it begins by estimating all potential revenues from the project as well as any costs that will be incurred during its life cycle, which may be as long as 10 years. Only after examining the potential costs and benefits across all of the business functions in the value chain, from research and development (R&D) to customer service, across the entire life span of the new-car project does Honda decide whether the new model is a wise investment.

Exhibit 21-1

The Project and Time Dimensions of Capital Budgeting

Managers use capital budgeting as a decision-making and a control tool. Like the five-step decision process that we have emphasized throughout this book, there are five stages to the capital budgeting process:

Stage 1: Identify Projects. *Identify potential capital investments that agree with the organization's strategy.* For example, Nike, an industry leader in product differentiation, makes significant investments in product innovation, engineering, and design, hoping to develop the next generation of high-quality sportswear. Alternatively, managers could promote products that improve productivity and efficiency as a cost-leadership strategy. For example, Dell's strategy of cost leadership includes outsourcing certain components to lower-cost contract manufacturing facilities located overseas. Identifying which types of capital projects to invest in is largely the responsibility of a firm's top managers.

Stage 2: Obtain Information. *Gather information from all parts of the value chain to evaluate alternative projects.* Returning to the new car example at Honda, in this stage, the firm's top managers ask the company's marketing managers for potential revenue numbers, plant managers for assembly times, and suppliers for prices and the availability of key components. Lower-level managers are asked to validate the data provided and to explain the assumptions underlying them. The goal is to encourage open and honest communication that results in accurate estimates so that the best investment decisions are made. Some projects will be rejected at this stage. For example, suppose Honda learns that the car cannot be built using existing plants. It may then opt to cancel the project altogether. At Akzo-Nobel, a global paints and coating company, the chief sustainability officer reviews projects against a set of environmental criteria and has the power to reject projects that do not meet the criteria or lack an acceptable explanation for why the company's sustainability factors were not considered.

Stage 3: Make Predictions. *Forecast all potential cash flows attributable to the alternative projects.* A new project generally requires a firm to make a substantial initial outlay of capital, which is recouped over time through annual cash inflows and the disposal value of the project's assets after it is terminated. Consequently, investing in a new project requires the firm to forecast its cash flows several years into the future. BMW, for example, estimates yearly cash flows and sets its investment budgets accordingly using a 12-year planning horizon. Because of the significant uncertainty associated with these predictions, firms typically analyze a wide range of alternate circumstances. In the case of BMW, the marketing group is asked to estimate a band of possible sales figures within a 90% confidence interval. Firms also attempt to ensure that estimates, especially for the later years of a project, are grounded in realistic scenarios. It is tempting for managers to introduce biases into these projections in order to drive the outcome of the capital budgeting process to their preferred choice. This effect is exacerbated by the fact that managers may not expect to be employed at the firm during those years and therefore cannot be held accountable for their estimates.

Stage 4: Make Decisions by Choosing Among Alternatives. *Determine which investment yields the greatest benefit and the least cost to the organization.* Using the quantitative information obtained in stage 3, the firm uses any one of several capital budgeting methodologies to determine which project best meets organizational goals. While capital budgeting calculations are typically limited to financial information, managers use their judgment and intuition to factor in qualitative information and strategic considerations as well. For example, even if a proposed new line of cars meets its financial targets on a standalone basis, Honda might decide not to pursue the line if it is not aligned with the strategic imperatives of the company on matters such as brand positioning, industry leadership in safety and technology, and fuel consumption. Considerations of environmental sustainability might also favor certain projects that currently appear unprofitable. For example, UPS relaxes the company's minimum rate of return on vehicles that have the potential to reduce fuel use and costs. Similarly, Sealed Air is willing to accept projects with a lower projected return if they look promising with regard to reducing greenhouse gas emissions. Finally, managers spend a significant amount of time assessing the risks of a project, in terms of both the uncertainty of the estimated cash flows as well as the potential downside risks of the project (as well as to the firm as a whole) if the worst-case scenario were to occur.

Stage 5: Implement the Decision, Evaluate Performance, and Learn. Given the complexities of capital investment decisions and their long-time horizons, this stage can be separated into two phases:

- *Obtain funding and make the investments selected in stage 4.* The sources of funding include internally generated cash as well as equity and debt securities sold in capital markets. Making capital investments is often an arduous task, laden with the purchase of many different goods and services. If Honda opts to build a new car, it must order steel, aluminum, paint, and so on. If some of the materials are unavailable, managers must determine the economic feasibility of using alternative inputs.
- *Track realized cash flows, compare against estimated numbers, and revise plans if necessary.* As the cash outflows and inflows begin to accumulate, managers can verify whether the predictions made in stage 3 agree with the actual flows of cash from the project. When the BMW group initially released the Mini Cooper in 2001, its sales were substantially higher than the original demand estimates. BMW responded by manufacturing more cars. It also expanded the Mini line to include convertibles and the larger Clubman model.

  It is equally important for a company to abandon projects that are performing poorly relative to expectations. A natural bias for managers is to escalate their commitment to a project they chose to implement for fear of revealing they made an incorrect capital budgeting decision. It is in the firm's and the managers' long-term interest, however, to acknowledge the mistake when it is clear that the project is not financially sustainable. For example, in April 2012, TransAlta, a Canadian electricity generator, halted a CA$1.4 billion project to capture carbon in the province of Alberta. After spending CA$30 million on engineering and design studies, the firm realized that the revenue from carbon sales and the costs of reducing emissions were insufficient to make the project economically viable.

To illustrate capital budgeting, consider Vector Transport. Vector operates bus lines throughout the United States, often providing transportation services on behalf of local transit authorities. Several of Vector's buses are nearing the end of their useful lives and are requiring increased operating and maintenance costs. Customers have also complained that the buses lack adequate storage, flexible seating configurations, and newer amenities such as wireless Internet access. The firm has made a commitment to act in an environmentally responsible manner and will only pursue projects that do minimal harm to the ecosystem. Accordingly, in stage 1, Vector's managers decide to look for replacement buses that generate low emissions. In the information-gathering stage (stage 2), the company learns that as early as 2014, it could feasibly begin purchasing and using diesel electric hybrid buses that have Wi-Fi and also offer greater comfort and storage. After collecting additional data, Vector begins to forecast its future cash flows if it invests in the new buses (stage 3). Vector estimates that it can purchase a hybrid bus with a useful life of 5 years for a net after-tax initial investment of $648,900, which is calculated as follows:[2]

Cost of new hybrid bus	$660,000
Investment in working capital	30,000
Cash flow from disposing of existing bus (after-tax)	(41,100)
Net initial investment for new bus	$648,900

Working capital refers to the difference between current assets and current liabilities. New projects often require additional investments in current assets such as inventories and receivables. In the case of Vector, the purchase of the new bus is accompanied by an incremental outlay of $30,000 for supplies, replacement batteries, and spare parts inventory. At the end of the project, the $30,000 in current assets is liquidated, resulting in a cash inflow. However, because of the rapid nature of improvements in hybrid technology, the bus itself is believed to have no terminal disposal value after 5 years.

[2] For the purposes of exposition, we study the capital budgeting problem for replacing one bus, rather than a fleet of buses.

Managers estimate that by introducing the new hybrid buses, operating cash inflows (cash revenues minus cash operating costs) will increase by \$180,000 (after tax) in the first 4 years and by \$150,000 in year 5. This arises from higher ticket prices and increases in ridership because of new customers who are drawn to the amenities of the hybrid bus, as well as savings in fuel, maintenance, and operating costs. To simplify the analysis, suppose that all cash flows occur at the end of each year. Note that cash flow at the end of the fifth year also increases by \$180,000—\$150,000 in operating cash inflows and \$30,000 in working capital. Management next calculates the costs and benefits of the proposed project (stage 4). This chapter discusses four capital budgeting methods to analyze financial information: (1) net present value (NPV), (2) internal rate-of-return (IRR), (3) payback, and (4) accrual accounting rate-of-return (AARR). Both the net present value (NPV) and internal rate-of-return (IRR) methods use *discounted cash flows,* which we discuss in the next section.

Decision Point

What are the five stages of capital budgeting?

Learning Objective 2

Use and evaluate the two main discounted cash flow (DCF) methods: the net present value (NPV) method and the internal rate-of-return (IRR) method

...to explicitly consider all project cash flows and the time value of money

Discounted Cash Flow

Discounted cash flow (DCF) methods measure all expected future cash inflows and outflows of a project discounted back to the present point in time. The key feature of DCF methods is the **time value of money**, which means that a dollar (or any other monetary unit) received today is worth more than a dollar received at any future time. The reason is that \$1 received today can be invested at, say, 10% per year so that it grows to \$1.10 at the end of one year. The time value of money is the opportunity cost (the return of \$0.10 forgone per year) from not having the money today. In this example, \$1 received 1 year from now is worth \$1 ÷ 1.10 = \$0.9091 today. Similarly, \$100 received 1 year from now will be weighted by 0.9091 to yield a discounted cash flow of \$90.91, which is today's value of that \$100 next year. In this way, discounted cash flow methods explicitly measure cash flows in terms of the time value of money. Note that DCF focuses exclusively on cash inflows and outflows rather than on operating income as calculated under accrual accounting.

The compound interest tables and formulas used in DCF analysis are in Appendix A, pages 909–916. If you are unfamiliar with compound interest, do not proceed until you have studied Appendix A, as the tables in Appendix A will be used frequently in this chapter.

The two DCF methods we describe are the net present value (NPV) method and the internal rate-of-return (IRR) method. Both DCF methods use the **required rate of return (RRR)**, the minimum acceptable annual rate of return on an investment. The RRR is internally set, usually by upper management, and typically represents the return that an organization could expect to receive elsewhere for an investment of comparable risk. The RRR is also called the **discount rate, hurdle rate, cost of capital,** or **opportunity cost of capital.** Let's suppose the CFO at Vector has set the required rate of return for the firm's investments at 8% per year.

Net Present Value Method

The **net present value (NPV) method** calculates the expected monetary gain or loss from a project by discounting all expected future cash inflows and outflows back to the present point in time using the required rate of return. To use the NPV method, apply the following three steps:

Step 1: Draw a Sketch of Relevant Cash Inflows and Outflows. The right side of Exhibit 21-2 shows arrows that depict the cash flows of the new hybrid bus. The sketch helps the decision maker visualize and organize the data in a systematic way. *Note that parentheses denote relevant cash outflows throughout all of the exhibits in this chapter.* Exhibit 21-2 includes the outflow for the acquisition of the new bus at the start of year 1 (also referred to as end of year 0) and the inflows over the subsequent 5 years. The NPV method specifies cash flows regardless of their source, such as operations, the purchase or sale of equipment, or an investment in or recovery of working capital. However, accrual-accounting

Exhibit 21-2 Net Present Value Method: Vector's Hybrid Bus

Home Insert Page Layout Formulas Data Review View

	A	B	C	D	E	F	G	H	I
1			Net initial investment	$648,900					
2			Useful life	5 years					
3			Annual cash flow	$180,000					
4			Required rate of return	8%					
5									
6		**Present Value**	**Present Value of**		**Sketch of Relevant Cash Flows at End of Each Year**				
7		**of Cash Flow**	**$1 Discounted at 8%**	**0**	**1**	**2**	**3**	**4**	**5**
8	**Approach 1: Discounting Each Year's Cash Flow Separately**[a]								
9	Net initial investment	$(648,900) ◄	1.000 ◄	$(648,900)					
10		166,680 ◄	0.926 ◄		$180,000				
11		154,260 ◄	0.857 ◄			$180,000			
12	Annual cash inflow	142,920 ◄	0.794 ◄				$180,000		
13		132,300 ◄	0.735 ◄					$180,000	
14		122,580 ◄	0.681 ◄						$180,000
15	NPV if new bus purchased	$ 69,840							
16									
17	**Approach 2: Using Annuity Table**[b]								
18	Net initial investment	$(648,900) ◄	1.000 ◄	$(648,900)					
19					$180,000	$180,000	$180,000	$180,000	$180,000
20									
21	Annual cash inflow	718,740 ◄	3.993 ◄						
22	NPV if new bus purchased	$ 69,840							
23									
24	*Note:* Parentheses denote relevant cash outflows throughout all exhibits in Chapter 21.								
25	[a] Present values from Table 2, Appendix A, at the end of the book. For example, $0.857 = 1 \div (1.08)^2$.								
26	[b] Annuity present value from Table 4, Appendix A. The annuity value of 3.993 is the sum of the individual discount rates 0.926 + 0.857 + 0.794 + 0.735 + 0.681.								

concepts such as sales made on credit or noncash expenses are not included because the focus is on *cash* inflows and outflows.

Step 2: Discount the Cash Flows Using the Correct Compound Interest Table from Appendix A and Sum Them. In the Vector example, we can discount each year's cash flow separately using Table 2, or we can compute the present value of an annuity, a series of equal cash flows at equal time intervals, using Table 4. (Both tables are in Appendix A.) If we use Table 2, we find the discount factors for periods 1–5 under the 8% column. Approach 1 in Exhibit 21-2 uses the five discount factors. To obtain the present value amount, multiply each discount factor by the corresponding amount represented by the arrow on the right in Exhibit 21-2 (−$648,900 × 1.000; $180,000 × 0.926; and so on to $180,000 × 0.681). Because the investment in the new bus produces an annuity, we may also use Table 4. Under Approach 2, we find that the annuity factor for five periods under the 8% column is 3.993, which is the sum of the five discount factors used in Approach 1. We multiply the uniform annual cash inflow by this factor to obtain the present value of the inflows ($718,740 = $180,000 × 3.993). Subtracting the initial investment then reveals the NPV of the project as $69,840 ($69,840 = $718,740 − $648,900).

Step 3: Make the Project Decision on the Basis of the Calculated NPV. An NPV that is zero or positive suggest that from a financial standpoint, the company should accept the project because its expected rate of return equals or exceeds the required rate of return. If the NPV is negative, the company should reject the project because its expected rate of return is below the required rate of return.

Exhibit 21-2 calculates an NPV of $69,840 at the required rate of return of 8% per year. The project is acceptable based on financial information. The cash flows from the project are adequate (1) to recover the net initial investment in the project and (2) to earn a return greater than 8% per year on the investment tied up in the project over its useful life.

Managers must also weigh nonfinancial factors such as the effect that purchasing the bus will have on Vector's brand. This is a nonfinancial factor because the financial benefits that accrue from Vector's brand are very difficult to estimate. Nevertheless, managers must consider brand effects before reaching a final decision. Suppose, for example, that the NPV of the hybrid bus is negative. Vector's managers might still decide to buy the bus if it maintains Vector's technological image and reputation for environmental responsibility. These are factors that could increase Vector's financial outcomes in the future, such as by attracting more riders or generating additional contracts from government transit agencies. For example, Alcoa, an aluminum producer, has found that its sustainability track record gives it better access to large markets such as Brazil, where a positive environmental record is becoming an important component in selecting products.

Pause here. Do not proceed until you understand what you see in Exhibit 21-2. Compare Approach 1 with Approach 2 in Exhibit 21-2 to see how Table 4 in Appendix A merely aggregates the present value factors of Table 2. That is, the fundamental table is Table 2. Table 4 simply reduces calculations when there is an annuity.

Internal Rate-of-Return Method

The **internal rate-of-return (IRR) method** calculates the discount rate at which an investment's present value of all expected cash inflows equals the present value of its expected cash outflows. That is, the IRR is the discount rate that makes NPV = $0. Exhibit 21-3 shows the cash flows and the NPV of Vector's hybrid project using a 12% annual

Exhibit 21-3 Internal Rate-of-Return Method: Vector's Hybrid Bus[a]

	A	B	C	D	E	F	G	H	I
1			Net initial investment	$648,900					
2			Useful life	5 years					
3			Annual cash flow	$180,000					
4			Annual discount rate	12%					
5									
6		Present Value	Present Value of		Sketch of Relevant Cash Flows at End of Each Year				
7		of Cash Flow	$1 Discounted at 12%	0	1	2	3	4	5
8	Approach 1: Discounting Each Year's Cash Flow Separately[b]								
9	Net initial investment	$(648,900)	1.000	$(648,900)					
10		160,740	0.893		$180,000				
11		143,460	0.797			$180,000			
12	Annual cash inflow	128,160	0.712				$180,000		
13		114,480	0.636					$180,000	
14		102,060	0.567						$180,000
15	NPV if new bus purchased	$ 0							
16	(the zero difference proves that								
17	the internal rate of return is 12%)								
18									
19	Approach 2: Using Annuity Table[c]								
20	Net initial investment	$(648,900)	1.000	$(648,900)					
21					$180,000	$180,000	$180,000	$180,000	$180,000
22									
23	Annual cash inflow	648,900	3.605						
24	NPV if new bus purchased	$ 0							
25									
26	*Note*: Parentheses denote relevant cash outflows throughout all exhibits in Chapter 21.								
27	[a]The internal rate of return is computed by methods explained on pp. 808–809.								
28	[b]Present values from Table 2, Appendix A, at the end of the book.								
29	[c]Annuity present value from Table 4, Appendix A. The annuity table value of 3.605 is the sum of the individual discount rates 0.893 + 0.797 + 0.712 + 0.636 + 0.567.								

discount rate. At a 12% discount rate, the NPV of the project is $0. Therefore, the IRR is 12% per year.

Managers or analysts solving capital budgeting problems typically use a calculator or computer program to provide the internal rate of return. The following trial-and-error approach can also provide the answer.

Step 1: Use a discount rate and calculate the project's NPV.

Step 2: If the calculated NPV is less than zero, use a lower discount rate. (A *lower* discount rate will *increase* the NPV. Remember that we are trying to find a discount rate for which the NPV = $0.) If the NPV exceeds zero, use a higher discount rate to lower the NPV. Keep adjusting the discount rate until the NPV does equal $0. In the Vector example, a discount rate of 8% yields an NPV of +$69,840 (see Exhibit 21-2). A discount rate of 14% yields an NPV of −$30,960 (3.433, the present value annuity factor from Table 4, × $180,000 minus $648,900). Therefore, the discount rate that makes the NPV equal $0 must lie between 8% and 14%. We use 12% and get NPV = $0. Hence, the IRR is 12% per year.

Computing the IRR is easier when the cash inflows are constant, as in our Vector example. Information from Exhibit 21-3 can be expressed as follows:

$$\$648{,}900 = \text{Present value of annuity of } \$180{,}000 \text{ at } X\% \text{ per year for 5 years}$$

Or what factor F in Table 4 (in Appendix A) will satisfy this equation?

$$\$648{,}900 = \$180{,}000F$$

$$F = \$648{,}900 \div \$180{,}000 = 3.605$$

On the five-period line of Table 4, find the percentage column that is closest to 3.605. It is exactly 12%. If the factor (F) falls between the factors in two columns, straight-line interpolation is used to approximate the IRR. This interpolation is illustrated in the Problem for Self-Study (pages 824–825).

Managers accept a project only if its IRR equals or exceeds the firm's RRR (required rate of return). In the Vector example, the hybrid bus has an IRR of 12%, which is greater than the RRR of 8%. On the basis of financial factors, Vector should invest in the new bus. In general, the NPV and IRR decision rules result in consistent project acceptance or rejection decisions. If the IRR exceeds the RRR, then the project has a positive NPV (favoring acceptance). If the IRR equals the RRR, then NPV equals $0, so the company is indifferent between accepting and rejecting the project. If the IRR is less than the RRR, the NPV is negative (favoring rejection). Obviously, managers prefer projects with higher IRRs to projects with lower IRRs, if all other things are equal. The IRR of 12% means the cash inflows from the project are adequate to (1) recover the net initial investment in the project and (2) earn a return of exactly 12% on the investment tied up in the project over its useful life.

Comparing the Net Present Value and Internal Rate-of-Return Methods

The NPV method is the preferred method for selecting projects because its use leads to shareholder value maximization. At an intuitive level, this occurs because the NPV measure captures the value, in today's dollars, of the surplus the project generates for the firm's shareholders over and above the required rate of return.[3] Next, we highlight some of the limitations of the IRR method relative to the NPV technique.

One advantage of the NPV method is that it's expressed in dollars, not in percentages. Therefore, we can sum NPVs of individual projects to calculate an NPV of a combination or portfolio of projects. In contrast, the IRRs of individual projects cannot be added or averaged to represent the IRR of a combination of projects.

[3] More detailed explanations of the preeminence of the NPV criterion can be found in corporate finance texts.

A second advantage of NPV is that it can be expressed as a unique number. From the sign and magnitude of this number, the firm can then make an accurate assessment of the financial consequences of accepting or rejecting the project. Under the IRR method, it is possible that more than one IRR may exist for a given project. In other words, there may be multiple discount rates that equate the NPV of a set of cash flows to zero. This is especially true when the signs of the cash flows switch over time; that is, when there are outflows, followed by inflows, followed by additional outflows, and so forth. In such cases, it is difficult to know which of the IRR estimates should be compared to the firm's required rate of return.

A third advantage of the NPV method is that it can be used when the RRR varies over the life of a project. Suppose Vector's management sets an RRR of 10% per year in years 1 and 2 and 14% per year in years 3, 4, and 5. Total present value of the cash inflows can be calculated as $633,780 (computations not shown). It is not possible to use the IRR method in this case. That's because different RRRs in different years mean there is no single RRR that the IRR (a single figure) can be compared against to decide if the project should be accepted or rejected.

Finally, in some situations, the IRR method is prone to indicating erroneous decisions. This can occur when mutually exclusive projects with unequal lives or unequal levels of initial investment are being compared to one another. The reason is that the IRR method implicitly assumes that project cash flows can be reinvested at the *project's* rate of return. The NPV method, in contrast, accurately assumes that project cash flows can only be reinvested at the *company's* required rate of return.

Despite its limitations, the IRR method is widely used.[4] Why? Probably because managers find the percentage return computed under the IRR method easy to understand and compare. Moreover, in most instances where a single project is being evaluated, their decisions would likely be unaffected by using IRR or NPV.

Sensitivity Analysis

To present the basics of the NPV and IRR methods, we have assumed that the expected values of cash flows will occur *for certain*. In reality, there is much uncertainty associated with predicting future cash flows. To examine how a result will change if the predicted financial outcomes are not achieved or if an underlying assumption changes, managers use *sensitivity analysis*, or "what-if" technique, introduced in Chapter 3.

A common way to apply sensitivity analysis for capital budgeting decisions is to vary each of the inputs to the NPV calculation by a certain percentage and assess the effect on the project's NPV. Sensitivity analysis can take on other forms as well. Suppose a manager at Vector believes the firm's forecasted cash flows are difficult to predict. She asks, "What are the minimum annual cash inflows that make the investment in a new hybrid bus acceptable—that is, what inflows lead to an $NPV = \$0$?" For the data in Exhibit 21-2, let A = annual cash flow and let the NPV = $0. The net initial investment is $648,900, and the present value factor at the 8% required annual rate of return for a 5-year annuity of $1 is 3.993. Then

$$\begin{aligned} NPV &= \$0 \\ 3.993A - \$648{,}900 &= \$0 \\ 3.993A &= \$648{,}900 \\ A &= \$162{,}509 \end{aligned}$$

At the discount rate of 8% per year, the annual (after tax) cash inflows can decrease to $162,509 (a decline of $180,000 − $162,509 = $17,491) before the NPV falls to $0. If the manager believes she can attain annual cash inflows of at least $162,509, she can justify investing in the hybrid bus on financial grounds.

[4] In a survey, John Graham and Campbell Harvey found that 75.7% of CFOs always or almost always used IRR for capital budgeting decisions, while a slightly smaller number, 74.9%, always or almost always used the NPV criterion.

	A	B	C	D	E	F
1	Required	Annual Cash Flows				
2	Rate of Return	$ 140,000	$160,000	$180,000	$200,000	$220,000
3	8%	$ (89,880)	$ (10,020)	$ 69,840	$149,700	$229,560
4	10%	$(118,160)	$ (42,340)	$ 33,480	$109,300	$185,120
5	12%	$(144,200)	$ (72,100)	$ 0	$ 72,100	$144,200
6						
7	[a]All calculated amounts assume the project's useful life is 5 years.					

Exhibit 21-4

Net Present Value Calculations for Vector's Hybrid Bus Under Different Assumptions of Annual Cash Flows and Required Rates of Return[a]

Exhibit 21-4 shows that variations in the annual cash inflows or the RRR significantly affect the NPV of the hybrid bus project. NPVs can also vary with different useful lives of a project. Sensitivity analysis helps managers to focus on decisions that are most sensitive to different assumptions and to worry less about decisions that are not so sensitive. It is also an important risk-management tool because it provides information to managers about the downside risks of projects as well as their potential impact on the health of the overall firm.

Decision Point

What are the two primary discounted cash flow (DCF) methods for project evaluation?

Payback Method

Learning Objective 3

Use and evaluate the payback and discounted payback methods

...to calculate the time it takes to recoup the investment

We now consider the third method for analyzing the financial aspects of projects. The **payback method** measures the time it will take to recoup, in the form of expected future cash flows, the net initial investment in a project. Like the NPV and IRR methods, the payback method does not distinguish among the sources of cash flows, such as those from operations, purchase or sale of equipment, or investment or recovery of working capital. As you will see, the payback method is simpler to calculate when a project has uniform cash flows than when cash flows are uneven over time.

Uniform Cash Flows

The hybrid bus Vector is considering buying costs $648,900 and generates a *uniform* $180,000 in cash flow every year of its 5-year expected useful life. The payback period is calculated as follows:

$$\text{Payback period} = \frac{\text{Net initial investment}}{\text{Uniform increase in annual future cash flows}}$$

$$= \frac{\$648{,}900}{\$180{,}000} = 3.6 \text{ years}^{5}$$

The payback method highlights liquidity, a factor that often plays a role in capital budgeting decisions, particularly when the investments are large. Managers prefer projects with shorter payback periods (projects that are more liquid) to projects with longer payback periods, if all other things are equal. Projects with shorter payback periods give an organization more flexibility because funds for other projects become available sooner. Also, managers are less confident about cash flow predictions that stretch far into the future, again favoring shorter payback periods.

Unlike the NPV and IRR methods where managers select the RRR, under the payback method, managers choose a cutoff period for the project. Projects with payback

[5] Cash inflows from the new hybrid bus occur uniformly *throughout* the year, but for simplicity in calculating NPV and IRR, we assume they occur at the *end* of each year. A literal interpretation of this assumption would imply a payback of 4 years because Vector will only recover its investment when cash inflows occur at the end of year 4. The calculations shown in the chapter, however, better approximate Vector's payback on the basis of uniform cash flows throughout the year.

periods that are shorter than the cutoff period are considered acceptable, and those with payback periods that are longer than the cutoff period are rejected. Japanese companies favor the payback method over other methods and use cutoff periods ranging from 3 to 5 years depending on the risks involved with the project.[6] In general, modern risk management calls for using shorter cutoff periods for riskier projects. If Vector's cutoff period under the payback method is 3 years, it will reject the new bus.

The payback method is easy to understand. As in DCF methods, the payback method is not affected by accrual accounting conventions such as depreciation. Payback is a useful measure when (1) preliminary screening of many proposals is necessary, (2) interest rates are high, and (3) the expected cash flows in later years of a project are highly uncertain. Under these conditions, companies give much more weight to cash flows in early periods of a capital budgeting project and to recovering the investments they have made, thereby making the payback criterion especially relevant.

Two weaknesses of the payback method are that (1) it fails to explicitly incorporate the time value of money and (2) it does not consider a project's cash flows after the payback period. Consider an alternative to the $648,900 hybrid bus. Another hybrid bus, one with a 3-year useful life and no terminal disposal value, requires only a $540,000 net initial investment and will also result in cash inflows of $180,000 per year. First, compare the payback periods:

$$\text{Bus 1} = \frac{\$648{,}900}{\$180{,}000} = 3.6 \text{ years}$$

$$\text{Bus 2} = \frac{\$540{,}000}{\$180{,}000} = 3.0 \text{ years}$$

The payback criterion favors bus 2, which has a shorter payback. If the cutoff period were 3 years, bus 1 would fail to meet the payback criterion.

Consider next the NPV of the two investment options using Vector's 8% required rate of return for the hybrid bus investment. At a discount rate of 8%, the NPV of bus 2 is −$76,140 (2.577, the present value annuity factor for 3 years at 8% per year from Table 4, times $180,000 = $463,860 minus net initial investment of $540,000). Bus 1, as we know, has a positive NPV of $69,840 (from Exhibit 21-2). The NPV criterion suggests Vector should acquire bus 1. Bus 2, which has a negative NPV, would fail to meet the NPV criterion.

The payback method gives a different answer from the NPV method in this example because the payback method ignores cash flows after the payback period and ignores the time value of money. Another problem with the payback method is that choosing too short a cutoff period can lead to projects with high short-run cash flows being selected. Projects with long-run, positive NPVs will tend to be rejected. Despite these differences, companies find it useful to look at both NPV and payback when making capital investment decisions.

Nonuniform Cash Flows

When cash flows are not uniform, the payback computation takes a cumulative form: The cash flows over successive years are accumulated until the amount of net initial investment is recovered. Suppose Venture Law Group is considering purchasing videoconferencing equipment for $150,000. The equipment is expected to provide a total cash savings of $340,000 over the next 5 years, due to reduced travel costs and more effective use of associates' time. The cash savings occur uniformly throughout each year but are not uniform across years.

---

[6] A 2010 survey of Japanese firms found that 50.2% of them often or always used the payback method to make capital budgeting decisions. The NPV method came in a distant second at 30.5% (see Tomonari Shinoda, "Capital Budgeting Management Practices in Japan," *Economic Journal of Hokkaido University* 39 (2010): 39–50).

Year	Cash Savings	Cumulative Cash Savings	Net Initial Investment Unrecovered at End of Year
0	—	—	$150,000
1	$50,000	$ 50,000	100,000
2	55,000	105,000	45,000
3	60,000	165,000	—
4	85,000	250,000	—
5	90,000	340,000	—

The chart shows that payback occurs during the third year. Straight-line interpolation within the third year reveals that the final \$45,000 needed to recover the \$150,000 investment (that is, \$150,000 − \$105,000 recovered by the end of year 2) will be achieved three-quarters of the way through year 3 (in which \$60,000 of cash savings occur):

$$\text{Payback period} = 2 \text{ years} + \left(\frac{\$45{,}000}{\$60{,}000} \times 1 \text{ year}\right) = 2.75 \text{ years}$$

It is relatively simple to adjust the payback method to incorporate the time value of money by using a similar cumulative approach. The **discounted payback method** calculates the amount of time required for the discounted expected future cash flows to recoup the net initial investment in a project. For the videoconferencing example, we can modify the preceding chart by discounting the cash flows at the 8% required rate of return.

Year (1)	Cash Savings (2)	Present Value of \$1 Discounted at 8% (3)	Discounted Cash Savings (4) = (2) × (3)	Cumulative Discounted Cash Savings (5)	Net Initial Investment Unrecovered at End of Year (6)
0	—	1.000	—	—	$150,000
1	$50,000	0.926	$46,300	$ 46,300	103,700
2	55,000	0.857	47,135	93,435	56,565
3	60,000	0.794	47,640	141,075	8,925
4	85,000	0.735	62,475	203,550	—
5	90,000	0.681	61,290	264,840	—

The fourth column shows the present values of the future cash savings. It is evident from the chart that discounted payback occurs between years 3 and 4. At the end of the third year, \$8,925 of the initial investment is still unrecovered. Comparing this to the \$62,475 in present value of savings achieved in the fourth year, straight-line interpolation then reveals that the discounted payback period is exactly one-seventh of the way into the fourth year:

$$\text{Discounted payback period} = 3 \text{ years} + \left(\frac{\$8{,}925}{\$62{,}475} \times 1 \text{ year}\right) = 3.14 \text{ years}$$

The discounted payback does incorporate the time value of money, but is still subject to the other criticism of the payback method—that cash flows beyond the discounted payback period are ignored, resulting in a bias toward projects with high short-run cash flows. Companies such as Hewlett-Packard value the discounted payback method (HP refers to it as "breakeven time") because they view longer-term cash flows as inherently unpredictable in high-growth industries, such as technology.

Finally, the videoconferencing example has a single cash outflow of \$150,000 in year 0. When a project has multiple cash outflows occurring at different points in time, these outflows are first aggregated to obtain a total cash-outflow figure for the project. For computing the payback period, the cash flows are simply added, with no adjustment for the time value of money. For calculating the discounted payback period, the present values of the outflows are added instead.

Decision Point

What are the payback and discounted payback methods? What are their main weaknesses?

Learning Objective 4

Use and evaluate the accrual accounting rate-of-return (AARR) method

. . . after-tax operating income divided by investment

Accrual Accounting Rate-of-Return Method

We now consider a fourth method for analyzing the financial aspects of capital budgeting projects. The **accrual accounting rate-of-return (AARR) method** divides the average annual (accrual accounting) income of a project by a measure of the investment in it. We illustrate this method for Vector using the project's net initial investment as the amount in the denominator:

$$\text{Accrual accounting rate of return} = \frac{\text{Increase in expected average annual after-tax operating income}}{\text{Net initial investment}}$$

If Vector purchases the new hybrid bus, its net initial investment is \$648,900. The increase in the expected average annual after-tax operating cash inflows is \$174,000. This amount is the expected after-tax total operating cash inflows of \$870,000 (\$180,000 for 4 years and \$150,000 in year 5), divided by the time horizon of 5 years. Suppose that the new bus results in additional depreciation deductions of \$120,000 per year (\$132,000 in annual depreciation for the new bus, relative to \$12,000 per year on the existing bus).[7] The increase in the expected average annual after-tax income is therefore \$54,000 (the difference between the cash flow increase of \$174,000 and the depreciation increase of \$120,000). The AARR on net initial investment is computed as:

$$AARR = \frac{\$174{,}000 - \$120{,}000}{\$648{,}900} = \frac{\$54{,}000 \text{ per year}}{\$648{,}900} = 0.083, \text{ or } 8.3\% \text{ per year}$$

The 8.3% figure for AARR indicates the average rate at which a dollar of investment generates after-tax operating income. The new hybrid bus has a low AARR for two reasons: (1) the use of the net initial investment as the denominator and (2) the use of income as the numerator, which necessitates deducting depreciation charges from the annual operating cash flows. To mitigate the first issue, many companies calculate AARR using an average level of investment. This alternative procedure recognizes that the book value of the investment declines over time. In its simplest form, average investment for Vector is calculated as the arithmetic mean of the net initial investment of \$648,900 and the net terminal cash flow of \$30,000 (terminal disposal value of hybrid bus of \$0, plus the terminal recovery of working capital of \$30,000):

$$\text{Average investment over 5 years} = \frac{\text{Net initial investment} + \text{Net terminal cash flow}}{2}$$

$$= \frac{\$648{,}900 + \$30{,}000}{2} = \$339{,}450$$

The AARR on average investment is then calculated as follows:

$$AARR = \frac{\$54{,}000}{\$339{,}450} = 0.159, \text{ or } 15.9\% \text{ per year}$$

Our point here is that companies vary in how they calculate the AARR. There is no uniformly preferred approach. Be sure you understand how the AARR is defined in each individual situation. Projects with AARRs that exceed a specific required rate of return are regarded as acceptable (the higher the AARR, the better the project is considered to be).

The AARR method is similar to the IRR method in that both calculate a rate-of-return percentage. The AARR method calculates the return using operating-income numbers after considering accruals and taxes, whereas the IRR method calculates the return using after-tax cash flows and the time value of money. Because cash flows and time value of money are central to capital budgeting decisions, the IRR method is regarded as better than the AARR method.

---

[7] We provide further details on these numbers in the next section; see page 815.

AARR computations are easy to understand, and they use numbers reported in the financial statements. The AARR gives managers an idea of how the accounting numbers they will report in the future will be affected if a project is accepted. Unlike the payback method, which ignores cash flows after the payback period, the AARR method considers income earned *throughout* a project's expected useful life. Unlike the NPV method, the AARR method uses accrual accounting income numbers, it does not track cash flows, and it ignores the time value of money. Critics of the AARR method argue that these are its drawbacks.

Overall, keep in mind that companies frequently use multiple methods for evaluating capital investment decisions. When different methods lead to different rankings of projects, more weight should be given to the NPV method because the assumptions made by the NPV method are most consistent with making decisions that maximize a company's value.

Decision Point

What are the strengths and weaknesses of the accrual accounting rate-of-return (AARR) method for evaluating long-term projects?

Relevant Cash Flows in Discounted Cash Flow Analysis

Learning Objective 5

Identify relevant cash inflows and outflows for capital budgeting decisions

...the differences in expected future cash flows resulting from the investment

So far, we have examined methods for evaluating long-term projects in settings where the expected future cash flows of interest were assumed to be known. One of the biggest challenges in capital budgeting, particularly DCF analysis, however, is determining which cash flows are relevant in making an investment selection. Relevant cash flows are the differences in expected future cash flows as a result of making the investment. In the Vector example, the relevant cash flows are the differences in expected future cash flows that will result from continuing to use one of the firm's old buses versus purchasing a new hybrid bus. *When reading this section, focus on identifying expected future cash flows and the differences in expected future cash flows.*

To illustrate relevant cash flow analysis, consider a more complex version of the Vector example with these additional assumptions:

- Vector is a profitable company. The income tax rate is 40% of operating income each year.
- The before-tax additional operating cash inflows from the hybrid bus are \$220,000 in years 1–4 and \$170,000 in year 5.
- For tax purposes, Vector uses the straight-line depreciation method and assumes there is no terminal disposal value of the bus.
- Gains or losses on the sale of depreciable assets are taxed at the same rate as ordinary income.
- The tax effects of cash inflows and outflows occur at the same time that the cash inflows and outflows occur.
- Vector uses an 8% required rate of return for discounting after-tax cash flows.

The data for the buses follow:

	Old Bus	New Hybrid Bus
Purchase price	—	\$660,000
Current book value	\$60,000	—
Current disposal value	28,500	Not applicable
Terminal disposal value five years from now	0	0
Annual depreciation	12,000[a]	132,000[b]
Working capital required	6,000	36,000

[a]\$60,000 ÷ 5 years = \$12,000 annual depreciation.
[b]\$660,000 ÷ 5 years = \$132,000 annual depreciation.

Relevant After-Tax Flows

We use the concepts of differential cost and differential revenue introduced in Chapter 11. We compare (1) the after-tax cash outflows as a result of replacing the old bus with (2) the additional after-tax cash inflows generated from using the new bus rather than the old bus.

Exhibit 21-5

Effect on Cash Flow from Operations, Net of Income Taxes, in Year 1 for Vector's Investment in the New Hybrid Bus

PANEL A: Two Methods Based on the Income Statement

C	Operating cash inflows from investment in bus	\$220,000
D	Additional depreciation deduction	120,000
OI	Increase in operating income	100,000
T	Income taxes (Income tax rate $t \times OI$) = 40% × \$100,000	40,000
NI	Increase in net income	\$ 60,000
	Increase in cash flow from operations, net of income taxes	
	Method 1: $C - T$ = \$220,000 − \$40,000 = \$180,000; or	
	Method 2: $NI + D$ = \$60,000 + \$120,000 = \$180,000	

PANEL B: Item-by-Item Method

	Effect of cash operating flows	
C	Operating cash inflows from investment in bus	\$220,000
$t \times C$	Deduct income tax cash outflow at 40%	88,000
$C \times (1 - t)$	After-tax cash flow from operations (excluding the depreciation effect)	\$132,000
	Effect of depreciation	
D	Additional depreciation deduction, \$120,000	
$t \times D$	Income tax cash savings from additional depreciation deduction at 40% × \$120,000	48,000
$C \times (1 - t) + t \times D$	Cash flow from operations, net of income taxes	\$180,000

As Benjamin Franklin said, "Two things in life are certain: death and taxes." Income taxes are a fact of life for most corporations and individuals. It is important first to understand how income taxes affect cash flows in each year. Exhibit 21-5 shows how investing in the new bus will affect Vector's cash flow from operations and its income taxes in year 1. Recall that Vector will generate \$220,000 in before-tax additional operating cash inflows by investing in the new bus (page 815), but it will record additional depreciation of \$120,000 (\$132,000 − \$12,000) for tax purposes.

Panel A shows, using two methods based on the income statement, that the year 1 cash flow from operations, net of income taxes, equals \$180,000. The first method focuses on cash items only, the \$220,000 operating cash inflows minus income taxes of \$40,000. The second method starts with the \$60,000 increase in net income (calculated after subtracting the \$120,000 additional depreciation deductions for income tax purposes) and adds back the \$120,000 because depreciation is an operating cost that reduces net income but is a noncash item itself.

Panel B of Exhibit 21-5 describes a third method frequently used to compute the cash flow from operations, net of income taxes. The easiest way to interpret the third method is to think of the government as a 40% (equal to the tax rate) partner in Vector. Each time Vector obtains operating cash inflows, C, its income is higher by C, so it will pay 40% of the operating cash inflows (0.40C) in taxes. This results in additional after-tax cash operating flows of C − 0.40C, which in this example is \$220,000 − (0.40 × \$220,000) = \$132,000, or \$220,000 × (1 − 0.40) = \$132,000.

To achieve the higher operating cash inflows, C, Vector incurs higher depreciation charges, *D*, from investing in the new bus. Depreciation costs do not directly affect cash flows because depreciation is a noncash cost, but higher depreciation cost *lowers* Vector's taxable income by *D*, saving income tax cash outflows of 0.40*D*, which in this example is 0.40 × \$120,000 = \$48,000.

Letting t = tax rate, cash flow from operations, net of income taxes, in this example equals the operating cash inflows, C, minus the tax payments on these inflows, $t \times C$, plus the tax savings on depreciation deductions, $t \times D$: \$220,000 − (0.40 × \$220,000) + (0.40 × \$120,000) = \$220,000 − \$88,000 + \$48,000 = \$180,000.

By the same logic, each time Vector has a gain on the sale of assets, *G*, it will show tax outflows, $t \times G$; and each time Vector has a loss on the sale of assets, *L*, it will show tax benefits or savings of $t \times L$.

Categories of Cash Flows

A capital investment project typically has three categories of cash flows: (1) the net initial investment in the project, which includes the acquisition of assets and any associated additions to working capital, minus the after-tax cash flow from the disposal of existing assets; (2) the after-tax cash flow from operations (including income tax cash savings from annual depreciation deductions) each year; and (3) the after-tax cash flow from disposing of an asset and recovering any working capital invested at the termination of the project. We use the Vector example to discuss these three categories.

As you work through the cash flows in each category, refer to Exhibit 21-6. This exhibit sketches the relevant cash flows for Vector's decision to purchase the new bus as described in items 1–3 here. Note that the total relevant cash flows for each year equal the relevant cash flows used in Exhibits 21-2 and 21-3 to illustrate the NPV and IRR methods.

1. **Net Initial Investment.** Three components of net-initial-investment cash flows are (a) the cash outflow to purchase the hybrid bus, (b) the cash outflow for working capital, and (c) the after-tax cash inflow from the current disposal of the old bus.

1a. *Initial bus investment.* These outflows, made for purchasing plant and equipment, occur at the beginning of the project's life and include cash outflows for transporting and installing the equipment. In the Vector example, the $660,000 cost (including transportation and initial preparation) of the hybrid bus is an outflow in year 0. These cash flows are relevant to the capital budgeting decision because they will be incurred only if Vector decides to purchase the new bus.

1b. *Initial working-capital investment.* Initial investments in plant and equipment are usually accompanied by additional investments in working capital. These additional investments take the form of current assets, such as accounts receivable and inventories, minus current liabilities, such as accounts payable. Working-capital investments are similar to plant and equipment investments in that they require

Exhibit 21-6 Relevant Cash Inflows and Outflows for Vector's Hybrid Bus

	A	B	C	D	E	F	G	H
1			Sketch of Relevant Cash Flows at End of Each Year					
2			0	1	2	3	4	5
3	1a.	Initial hybrid bus investment	$(660,000)					
4	1b.	Initial working-capital investment	(30,000)					
5	1c.	After-tax cash inflow from current disposal						
6		of old bus	41,100					
7	Net initial investment		(648,900)					
8	2a.	Annual after-tax cash flow from operations						
9		(excluding the depreciation effect)		$ 132,000	$ 132,000	$ 132,000	$ 132,000	$ 102,000
10	2b.	Income tax savings from annual						
11		depreciation deductions		48,000	48,000	48,000	48,000	48,000
12	3a.	After-tax cash flow from terminal disposal						
13		of bus						0
14	3b.	After-tax cash flow from recovery of						
15		working capital						30,000
16	Total relevant cash flows,							
17		as shown in Exhibits 21-2 and 21-3	$(648,900)	$ 180,000	$180,000	$180,000	$180,000	$180,000
18								

cash. The magnitude of the investment generally increases as a function of the level of additional sales generated by the project. However, the exact relationship varies based on the nature of the project and the operating cycle of the industry. For a given dollar of sales, a maker of heavy equipment, for example, would require more working capital support than Vector, which in turn has to invest more in working capital than a retail grocery store.

The Vector example assumes a $30,000 additional investment in working capital if the hybrid bus is acquired. The additional working-capital investment is the difference between the working capital required to operate the new bus ($36,000) and that required to operate the old bus ($6,000). The $30,000 additional investment, a consequence of the higher cost of replacement batteries and spare parts for the technologically advanced new bus, is a cash outflow in year 0 and is returned, that is, becomes a cash inflow, at the end of year 5.

1c. *After-tax cash flow from current disposal of old bus.* Any cash received from disposal of the old bus is a relevant cash inflow (in year 0) because it is a cash flow that differs between the alternatives of investing and not investing in the new bus. Vector will dispose of the old bus for $28,500 only if it invests in the new hybrid bus. Recall from Chapter 11 (page 449) that the book value (which is original cost minus accumulated depreciation) of the old equipment is generally irrelevant to the decision because it is a past, or sunk, cost. However, when tax considerations are included, the book value does play a role because it determines the gain or loss on the sale of the bus and, therefore, the taxes paid (or saved) on the transaction.

Consider the tax consequences of disposing of the old bus. We first have to compute the gain or loss on disposal:

Current disposal value of old bus (given, page 815)	$ 28,500
Deduct current book value of old bus (given, page 815)	60,000
Loss on disposal of bus	$(31,500)

Any loss on the sale of assets lowers taxable income and results in tax savings. The after-tax cash flow from disposal of the old bus is as follows:

Current disposal value of old bus	$28,500
Tax savings on loss (0.40 × $31,500)	12,600
After-tax cash inflow from current disposal of old bus	$41,100

The sum of items **1a, 1b,** and **1c** appears in Exhibit 21-6 as the year 0 net initial investment for the new hybrid bus. It equals $648,900 (initial bus investment, $660,000, plus additional working-capital investment, $30,000, minus the after-tax cash inflow from current disposal of the old bus, $41,100).[8]

2. **Cash Flow from Operations.** This category includes the difference between each year's cash flow from operations under the two alternatives. Organizations make capital investments to generate future cash inflows. These inflows may result from producing and selling additional goods or, as for Vector, from savings in fuel, maintenance, and operating costs and the additional revenue from higher ticket prices as well as new customers who wish to take advantage of the greater comfort and accessibility of the hybrid bus. The annual cash flow from operations can be net outflows in some years. For example, Chevron periodically upgrades its oil extraction equipment, and when it does, the cash flow from operations tends to be negative for the site being upgraded. However, in the long run, the upgrades are NPV positive. Always focus on the cash flow from operations, not on revenues and expenses under accrual accounting.

Vector's additional operating cash inflows—$220,000 in each of the first 4 years and $170,000 in the fifth year—are relevant because they are expected future cash flows that will differ depending on whether the firm purchases the new bus. The after-tax effects of these cash flows follow.

[8] To illustrate the case when there is a gain on disposal, suppose that the old bus could be sold now for $70,000 instead. Then the firm would record a gain on disposal of $10,000 ($70,000 less the book value of $60,000), resulting in additional tax payments of $4,000 (0.40 tax rate × $10,000 gain). The after-tax cash inflow from current disposal would therefore equal $66,000 (the disposal value of $70,000, less the tax payment of $4,000).

2a. *Annual after-tax cash flow from operations (excluding the depreciation effect).* The 40% tax rate reduces the benefit of the $220,000 additional operating cash inflows for years 1–4 with the new hybrid bus. The after-tax cash flow (excluding the depreciation effect) is:

Annual cash flow from operations with new bus	$220,000
Deduct income tax payments (0.40 × $220,000)	88,000
Annual after-tax cash flow from operations	$132,000

For year 5, the after-tax cash flow (excluding the depreciation effect) is as follows:

Annual cash flow from operations with new bus	$170,000
Deduct income tax payments (0.40 × $170,000)	68,000
Annual after-tax cash flow from operations	$102,000

Exhibit 21-6, item **2a**, shows that the after-tax cash flows are $132,000 in each of years 1 through 4 and $102,000 for year 5.

To reinforce the idea about focusing on cash flows, consider the following additional fact about Vector. Suppose its total administrative costs will not change whether the company purchases a new bus or keeps the old one. The administrative costs are allocated to individual buses—Vector has several—on the basis of the costs for operating each bus. Because the new hybrid bus would have lower operating costs, the administrative costs allocated to it would be $30,000 less than the amount allocated to the bus it would replace. How should Vector incorporate the $30,000 decrease in allocated administrative costs in the relevant cash flow analysis?

To answer that question, we need to ask, "Do *total* administrative costs decrease at Vector Transport as a result of acquiring the new bus?" In our example, they do not. They remain the same whether or not the new bus is acquired. *Only the administrative costs allocated to individual buses change.* The administrative costs allocated to the new bus are $30,000 less than the amount allocated to the bus it would replace. This $30,000 difference in costs would be allocated to *other* buses in the company. That is, no cash flow savings in total costs would occur. Therefore, the $30,000 should not be included as part of the annual cash savings from operations.

Next consider the effects of depreciation. *The depreciation line item is itself irrelevant in a DCF analysis.* That's because depreciation is a noncash allocation of costs, whereas DCF is based on inflows and outflows of *cash*. If a DCF method is used, the initial cost of equipment is regarded as a *lump-sum* outflow of cash in year 0. Deducting depreciation expenses from operating cash inflows would result in counting the lump-sum amount twice. *However, depreciation results in income tax cash savings. These tax savings are a relevant cash flow.*

2b. *Income tax cash savings from annual depreciation deductions.* Tax deductions for depreciation, in effect, partially offset the cost of acquiring the new hybrid bus. By purchasing the new bus, Vector is able to deduct $132,000 in depreciation each year, relative to the $12,000 depreciation on the old bus. The additional annual depreciation deduction of $120,000 results in incremental income tax cash savings of $120,000 × 0.4, or $48,000 annually. Exhibit 21-6, item **2b**, shows these $48,000 amounts for years 1 through 5.[9]

For economic-policy reasons, usually to encourage (or in some cases, discourage) investments, tax laws specify which depreciation methods and which depreciable lives are permitted. Suppose the government permitted accelerated depreciation to be used, allowing for higher depreciation deductions in earlier years. Should Vector then use accelerated depreciation? Yes, because there is a general rule in tax planning for profitable companies such as Vector: When there

[9] If Vector were a nonprofit foundation not subject to income taxes, cash flow from operations would equal $220,000 in years 1 through 4 and $170,000 in year 5. The revenues would not be reduced by 40% nor would there be income tax cash savings from the depreciation deduction.

is a legal choice, take the depreciation (or any other deduction) sooner rather than later. Doing so causes the (cash) income tax savings to occur earlier, which increases a project's NPV.

3. **Terminal Disposal of Investment.** The disposal of an investment generally increases cash inflow of a project at its termination. An error in forecasting the disposal value is seldom critical for a long-duration project because the present value of the amounts to be received in the distant future is usually small. For Vector, the two components of the terminal disposal value of an investment are (a) the after-tax cash flow from the terminal disposal of buses and (b) the after-tax cash flow from recovery of working capital.

3a. *After-tax cash flow from terminal disposal of buses.* At the end of the useful life of the project, the bus's terminal disposal value is usually considerably less than the net initial investment (and sometimes zero). The relevant cash inflow is the difference in the expected after-tax cash inflow from terminal disposal at the end of 5 years under the two alternatives. Disposing of both the existing and the new bus will result in a zero after-tax cash inflow in year 5. Hence, there is no difference in the disposal-related after-tax cash inflows of the two alternatives.

Because both the existing and new bus have disposal values that equal their book values at the time of their disposal (in each case, this value is $0), there are no tax effects for either alternative. What if either the existing or the new bus had a terminal value that differed from its book value at the time of disposal? In that case, the approach for computing the terminal inflow is identical to that for calculating the after-tax cash flow from current disposal illustrated earlier in part 1c.

3b. *After-tax cash flow from terminal recovery of working-capital investment.* The initial investment in working capital is usually fully recouped when the project is terminated. At that time, inventories and accounts receivable necessary to support the project are no longer needed. Vector receives cash equal to the book value of its working capital. Thus, there is no gain or loss on working capital and, hence, no tax consequences. The relevant cash inflow is the difference in the expected working capital recovered under the two alternatives. At the end of year 5, Vector recovers $36,000 cash from working capital if it invests in the new hybrid bus versus $6,000 if it continues to use the old bus. The relevant cash inflow at the end of year 5 if Vector invests in the new bus is thus $30,000 ($36,000 − $6,000).

Some capital investment projects *reduce* working capital. Assume that a computer-integrated manufacturing (CIM) project with a 7-year life will reduce inventories and, hence, working capital by $20 million from, say, $50 million to $30 million. This reduction will be represented as a $20 million cash *inflow* for the project in year 0. At the end of 7 years, the recovery of working capital will show a relevant incremental cash *outflow* of $20 million. That's because, at the end of year 7, the company recovers only $30 million of working capital under CIM, rather than the $50 million of working capital it would have recovered had it not implemented CIM.

Decision Point

What are the relevant cash inflows and outflows for capital budgeting decisions? How should accrual accounting concepts be considered?

Exhibit 21-6 shows items **3a** and **3b** in the "year 5" column. The relevant cash flows in Exhibit 21-6 serve as inputs for the four capital budgeting methods described earlier in the chapter.

Learning Objective 6

Understand issues involved in implementing capital budgeting decisions and evaluating managerial performance

...the importance of post-investment audits and the correct choice of performance measures

Project Management and Performance Evaluation

We have so far looked at ways to identify relevant cash flows and techniques for analyzing them. The final stage (stage 5) of capital budgeting begins with implementing the decision and managing the project.[10] This includes management control of the investment activity itself, as well as the project as a whole.

[10] In this section, we do not consider the different options for financing a project (refer to a text on corporate finance for details).

Capital budgeting projects, such as purchasing a hybrid bus or videoconferencing equipment, are easier to implement than projects involving building shopping malls or manufacturing plants. The building projects are more complex, so monitoring and controlling the investment schedules and budgets are critical to successfully completing the investment activity. This leads to the second dimension of stage 5 in the capital budgeting process: evaluate performance and learn.

Post-Investment Audits

A post-investment audit provides managers with feedback about the performance of a project so they can compare the actual results to the costs and benefits expected at the time the project was selected. Suppose the actual outcomes (such as the additional operating cash flows from Vector's purchase of a new hybrid bus) are much lower than expected. Managers must then determine if this result occurred because the original estimates were overly optimistic or because of implementation problems. Either of these explanations is a concern.

Optimistic estimates can result in managers accepting a project they should reject. To discourage unrealistic forecasts, companies such as DuPont maintain records comparing the actual results of the firm's projects to the estimates individual managers either made or signed off on when seeking approval for capital investments. Post-investment audits prevent managers from overstating the expected cash inflows from projects and accepting projects they should reject. Implementation problems, such as weak project management, poor quality control, or inadequate marketing, are also a concern. Post-investment audits help to alert senior management to these problems so they can be quickly corrected.

Companies should perform post-investment audits with thought and care, and only after the outcomes of projects are fully known. Performing audits too early can be misleading. In addition, obtaining actual results to compare against estimates is often difficult. For example, in any particular period, macroeconomic factors, such as the weather and changes in fuel prices, can greatly affect the ridership on buses and the costs of running them. Consequently, the overall additional net revenues from Vector's new hybrid bus may not be immediately comparable to the estimated revenues. A better evaluation would look at the average revenues across a couple of seasons.

Performance Evaluation

As the preceding discussion suggests, ideally one should evaluate managers on a project-by-project basis and look at how well managers achieve the amounts and timing of forecasted cash flows. In practice, however, companies often evaluate managers based on aggregate information, especially when multiple projects are under way at any point in time. It is important then for companies to ensure that the method of evaluation does not conflict with the use of the NPV method for making capital budgeting decisions. For example, suppose Vector uses the accrual accounting rate of return generated in each period to assess its managers. We know the managers should purchase the hybrid bus because it has a positive NPV of $69,840. However, they may reject the project if the AARR of 8.3% on the net initial investment is lower than the minimum accounting rate of return Vector requires them to achieve.

There is an inconsistency between promoting the NPV method as best for capital budgeting decisions and then using a different method to evaluate performance. Even though the NPV method is best for capital budgeting decisions, managers will be tempted to make those decisions based on the method on which they are being evaluated. The temptation becomes more pronounced if managers are frequently transferred (or promoted) or if their bonuses are affected by the level of year-to-year income earned under accrual accounting.

Decision Point

What conflicts can arise between using DCF methods for capital budgeting decisions and accrual accounting for performance evaluation? How can these conflicts be reduced?

Other conflicts between decision making and performance evaluation persist even if a company uses similar measures for both purposes. If the AARR on the hybrid bus exceeds the minimum required AARR but is below Vector's current AARR in the region, the manager may still be tempted to reject purchase of the hybrid bus because the lower AARR of the hybrid bus will reduce the AARR of the entire region and hurt the manager's reported performance. Or consider an example where the cash inflows from the hybrid bus occur mostly in the later years of the project. Then, even if the project's AARR exceeds the current AARR of the projects overseen by the manager (as well as the minimum required return), the manager may still reject the purchase because for the first few years it will have a negative effect on the rate of return earned under accrual accounting. In Chapter 23, we study these conflicts in greater depth and describe how performance evaluation models such as economic value added (EVA®) help lessen these conflicts.

Learning Objective 7

Explain how managers can use capital budgeting to achieve their firms' strategic goals

...make critical investments aligned with the firm's objectives but whose benefits are uncertain or difficult to estimate

Strategic Considerations in Capital Budgeting

Managers consider a company's strategic goals when making capital budgeting decisions. Strategic decisions by United Airlines, Westin Hotels, FedEx, and Pizza Hut to expand in Europe and Asia required capital investments in several countries (also see Concepts in Action: International Capital Budgeting at Disney). The strategic decision by Barnes & Noble to support book sales over the Internet required capital investments creating barnesandnoble.com and an Internet infrastructure. AOL's desire to create an enhanced digital destination with greater appeal for consumers and advertisers led to its purchase of *The Huffington Post*, as well as increased investment in editorial staff and sales representatives and higher marketing expenses. AstraZeneca's decision to develop Nexium as a patented replacement drug for its blockbuster Prilosec to prevent the formation of gastric acid led to major investments in R&D and marketing. Toyota's decision to offer a line of hybrids across both its Toyota and Lexus platforms required start-up investments to form a hybrid division and ongoing investments to fund the division's continuing research efforts.

Concepts in Action: International Capital Budgeting at Disney

The Walt Disney Company, one of the world's leading entertainment producers with $42 billion in 2012 revenue, spends about $1 billion annually in capital investments on its theme park business. These funds are invested in new theme parks, rides and attractions, and other park construction and improvements.

Years ago, Disney developed a robust capital budgeting approval process. Project approval relied heavily on projected returns on capital investment as measured by net present value (NPV) and internal rate-of-return (IRR) calculations. This worked well for Disney's investments in its domestic theme park business, but the company experienced challenges when it considered building the DisneySea theme park near Tokyo, Japan.

While capital budgeting in the United States relies on discounted cash flow analysis, Japanese firms frequently use the average accounting return (AAR) method instead. AAR is analogous to an accrual accounting rate-of-return (AARR) measure based on average investment. However, it focuses on the first few years of a project (5 years, in the case of DisneySea) and ignores terminal values.

Disney discovered that the difference in capital budgeting techniques between U.S. and Japanese firms reflected the difference in corporate governance in the two countries. The use of NPV and IRR in the United States underlined a focus on shareholder-value maximization. On the other hand, the preference for AAR in Japan reflected the importance of achieving complete consensus among all parties affected by the investment decision.

When the DisneySea project was evaluated, it was found to have a positive NPV but a negative AAR. To account for the differences in philosophies and capital budgeting techniques, managers at Disney introduced a third calculation method called average cash flow return (ACFR). This hybrid method measured the average cash flow over the first 5 years, with the asset assumed to be sold for book value at the end of that period as a fraction of the initial investment in the project. The resulting ratio was found to exceed the return on Japanese government bonds and hence to yield a positive return for DisneySea. As a result, the park was constructed next to Tokyo Disneyland and has since become a profitable addition to Disney's Japanese operations.

Sources: Misawa, Mitsuru. 2006. Tokyo Disneyland and the DisneySea Park: Corporate governance and differences in capital budgeting concepts and methods between American and Japanese companies. University of Hong Kong No. HKU568, Hong Kong: University of Hong Kong Asia Case Research Center; and The Walt Disney Company. 2013. 2012 annual report. Burbank, CA: The Walt Disney Company.

Capital investment decisions that are strategic in nature require managers to consider a broad range of factors that may be difficult to estimate. Consider some of the difficulties of justifying investments made by companies such as Mitsubishi, Sony, and Audi in computer-integrated manufacturing (CIM) technology. In CIM, computers give instructions that quickly and automatically set up and run equipment to manufacture many different products. Quantifying these benefits requires some notion of how quickly consumer demand will change in the future. CIM technology also increases worker knowledge of and experience with automation; however, the benefit of this knowledge and experience is difficult to measure. Managers must develop judgment and intuition to make these decisions.

Investment in Research and Development

Companies such as GlaxoSmithKline, in the pharmaceutical industry, and Intel, in the semiconductor industry, regard R&D projects as important strategic investments. The distant payoffs from R&D investments, however, are more uncertain than other investments such as new equipment purchases. On the positive side, R&D investments are often staged: As time unfolds, companies can increase or decrease the resources committed to a project based on how successful it has been up to that point. This option feature of R&D investments, called real options, is an important aspect of R&D investments and increases the NPV of these investments because a company can limit its losses when things are going badly and take advantage of new opportunities when things are going well. As an example, a pharmaceutical company can increase or decrease its investment in an R&D joint venture based on the progress of the clinical trials of new drugs being developed by the venture.

Customer Value and Capital Budgeting

Finally, note that managers can use the framework described in this chapter to both evaluate investment projects and to make strategic decisions regarding which customers to invest in. Consider Potato Supreme, which makes potato products for sale to retail outlets. It is currently analyzing two of its customers: Shine Stores and Always Open. Potato Supreme predicts the following cash flow from operations, net of income taxes (in thousands), from each customer account for the next 5 years:

	2014	2015	2016	2017	2018
Shine Stores	$1,450	$1,305	$1,175	$1,058	$ 950
Always Open	690	1,160	1,900	2,950	4,160

Which customer is more valuable to Potato Supreme? Looking at only the current period, 2014, Shine Stores provides more than double the cash flow compared to Always Open ($1,450 versus $690). A different picture emerges, however, if you look at the entire 5-year horizon. Potato Supreme anticipates Always Open's orders to increase; meanwhile, it expects Shine Stores' orders to decline. Using Potato Supreme's 10% RRR, the NPV of the Always Open customer is $7,610, compared with $4,591 for Shine Stores (computations not shown). Note how NPV captures in its estimate of customer value the future growth of Always Open. Potato Supreme uses this information to allocate more resources and salespeople to service the Always Open account. Potato Supreme can also use NPV calculations to examine the effects of alternative ways of increasing customer loyalty and retention, such as introducing frequent-purchaser cards.

A comparison of year-to-year changes in customer NPV estimates highlights whether managers have been successful in maintaining long-run profitable relationships with their customers. Suppose the NPV of Potato Supreme's customer accounts declines by 15% in a year. The firm's managers can then examine the reasons for the decline, such as aggressive pricing by competitors, and devise new-product development and marketing strategies for the future.

Capital One, a financial-services company, uses NPV to estimate the value of different credit-card customers. Cellular telephone companies such as Sprint and Verizon Wireless attempt to sign up customers for multiple years of service. The objective is to prevent "customer churn"—that is, customers switching frequently from one company to another. The higher the probability is of a customer switching, the lower the customer's NPV.

Decision Point

How can managers use capital budgeting to achieve strategic goals?

Problem for Self-Study

Part A

Returning to the Vector hybrid bus project, assume that Vector is a *nonprofit organization* and that the expected additional operating cash inflows are \$240,000 in years 1 through 4 and \$210,000 in year 5. Using data from page 815, the net initial investment is \$661,500 (new bus, \$660,000, plus additional working capital, \$30,000, minus terminal disposal value of old bus, \$28,500). All other facts are unchanged: a 5-year useful life, no terminal disposal value, and an 8% RRR. Year 5 cash inflows are \$240,000, which includes a \$30,000 recovery of working capital.

Required

Calculate the following:

1. Net present value
2. Internal rate of return
3. Payback
4. Accrual accounting rate of return on net initial investment

Solution

1. $NPV = (\$240{,}000 \times 3.993) - \$661{,}500$

   $= \$958{,}320 - \$661{,}500 = \$296{,}820$

2. There are several approaches to computing IRR. One is to use a calculator with an IRR function. This approach gives an IRR of 23.8%. Another approach is to use Table 4 in Appendix A at the end of the text:

$$\$661{,}500 = \$240{,}000F$$

$$F = \frac{\$661{,}500}{\$240{,}000} = 2.756$$

On the five-period line of Table 4, the column closest to 2.756 is 24%. To obtain a more-accurate number, use straight-line interpolation:

	Present Value Factors	
22%	2.864	2.864
IRR	—	2.756
24%	2.745	—
Difference	0.119	0.108

$$IRR = 22\% + \frac{0.108}{0.119}(2\%) = 23.8\% \text{ per year}$$

3. $$\text{Payback period} = \frac{\text{Net initial investment}}{\text{Uniform increase in annual future cash flows}}$$

$$= \$661{,}500 \div \$240{,}000 = 2.76 \text{ years}$$

4. $$AARR = \frac{\text{Increase in expected average annual operating income}}{\text{Net initial investment}}$$

$$\text{Increase in expected average annual operating cash inflows} = [(\$240{,}000 \times 4) + \$210{,}000] \div 5 \text{ years}$$

$$= \$1{,}170{,}000 \div 5 = \$234{,}000$$

$$\text{Increase in annual depreciation} = \$120{,}000 (\$132{,}000 - \$12{,}000, \text{ see p. } 814)$$

$$\text{Increase in expected average annual operating income} = \$234{,}000 - \$120{,}000 = \$114{,}000$$

$$AARR = \frac{\$114{,}000}{\$661{,}500} = 17.2\% \text{ per year}$$

Part B

Assume that Vector is subject to income tax at a 40% rate. All other information from Part A is unchanged. Compute the NPV of the new hybrid bus project.

Solution

To save space, Exhibit 21-7 shows the calculations using a format slightly different from the format used in this chapter. Item **2a** is where the new cash flow assumptions affect the NPV analysis (compared with Exhibit 21-6). All other amounts in Exhibit 21-7 are identical to the corresponding amounts in Exhibit 21-6. For years 1 through 4, after-tax cash flow (excluding the depreciation effect) is as follows:

Annual cash flow from operations with new bus	$240,000
Deduct income tax payments (0.40 × $240,000)	96,000
Annual after-tax cash flow from operations	$144,000

For year 5, after-tax cash flow (excluding the depreciation effect) is as follows:

Annual cash flow from operations with new bus	$210,000
Deduct income tax payments (0.40 × $210,000)	84,000
Annual after-tax cash flow from operations	$126,000

NPV in Exhibit 21-7 is $125,928. As computed in Part A, NPV when there are no income taxes is $296,820. The difference in these two NPVs illustrates the impact of income taxes in capital budgeting analysis.

Exhibit 21-7 Net Present Value Method Incorporating Income Taxes: Vector's Hybrid Bus with Revised Annual Cash Flow from Operations

Home | Insert | Page Layout | Formulas | Data | Review | View

	A	B	C	D	E	F	G	H	I	J
1			Present Value	Present Value of		Sketch of Relevant Cash Flows at End of Year				
2			of Cash Flow	$1 Discounted at 8%	0	1	2	3	4	5
3	1a.	Initial hybrid bus investment	$(660,000)	1.000	$(660,000)					
4										
5	1b.	Initial working-capital investment	(30,000)	1.000	$ (30,000)					
6	1c.	After-tax cash inflow from current disposal								
7		of old bus	41,100	1.000	$ 41,100					
8	Net initial investment		(648,900)							
9	2a.	Annual after-tax cash flow from operations								
10		(excluding the depreciation effect)								
11		Year 1	133,344	0.926		$144,000				
12		Year 2	123,408	0.857			$144,000			
13		Year 3	114,336	0.794				$144,000		
14		Year 4	105,840	0.735					$144,000	
15		Year 5	85,806	0.681						$126,000
16	2b.	Income tax cash savings from annual								
17		depreciation deductions								
18		Year 1	44,448	0.926		$ 48,000				
19		Year 2	41,136	0.857			$ 48,000			
20		Year 3	38,112	0.794				$ 48,000		
21		Year 4	35,280	0.735					$ 48,000	
22		Year 5	32,688	0.681						$ 48,000
23	3.	After-tax cash flow from recovery of								
24		a. Terminal disposal of bus	0	0.681						$ 0
25		b. Recovery of working capital	20,430	0.681						$ 30,000
26	NPV if new hybrid bus purchased		$ 125,928							
27										

▶ Decision Points

The following question-and-answer format summarizes the chapter's learning objectives. Each decision presents a key question related to a learning objective. The guidelines are the answer to that question.

Decision	Guidelines
1. What are the five stages of capital budgeting?	Capital budgeting is long-run planning for proposed investment projects. The five stages of capital budgeting are as follows: (1) Identify projects: Identify potential capital investments aligned with the organization's strategy; (2) Obtain information: Gather information from all parts of the value chain to evaluate alternative projects; (3) Make predictions: Forecast all potential cash flows attributable to the alternative projects; (4) Choose among alternatives: Determine which investment yields the greatest benefit and the least cost to the organization; and (5) Implement the decision, evaluate performance, and learn: Obtain funding and make the investments selected in stage 4; track the realized cash flows, compare them against estimated numbers, and revise plans if necessary.
2. What are the two primary discounted cash flow (DCF) methods for project evaluation?	The two main DCF methods are the net present value (NPV) method and the internal rate-of-return (IRR) method. The NPV method calculates the expected net monetary gain or loss from a project by discounting to the present all expected future cash inflows and outflows, using the required rate of return. A project is acceptable in financial terms if it has a positive NPV. The IRR method computes the rate of return (also called the discount rate) at which a project's present value of expected cash inflows equals the present value of its expected cash outflows. A project is acceptable in financial terms if its IRR exceeds the required rate of return. DCF is the best approach to capital budgeting. It explicitly includes all project cash flows and recognizes the time value of money. The NPV method is the preferred DCF method.
3. What are the payback and discounted payback methods? What are their main weaknesses?	The payback method measures the time it will take to recoup, in the form of cash inflows, the total cash amount invested in a project. The payback method neglects the time value of money and ignores cash flows beyond the payback period. The discounted payback method measures the time taken for the present value of cash inflows to equal the present value of cash outflows. It adjusts for the time value of money but overlooks cash flows after the discounted payback period.
4. What are the strengths and weaknesses of the accrual accounting rate-of-return (AARR) method for evaluating long-term projects?	The accrual accounting rate of return (AARR) divides an accrual accounting measure of average annual income from a project by an accrual accounting measure of its investment. AARR gives managers an idea of how accepting a project will affect a firm's future reported accounting profitability. However, AARR uses accrual accounting income numbers, does not track cash flows, and ignores the time value of money.
5. What are the relevant cash inflows and outflows for capital budgeting decisions? How should accrual accounting concepts be considered?	Relevant cash inflows and outflows in a DCF analysis are the differences in expected future cash flows as a result of making the investment. Only cash inflows and outflows matter; accrual accounting concepts are irrelevant for DCF methods. For example, the income taxes saved as a result of depreciation deductions are relevant because they decrease cash outflows, but the depreciation itself is a noncash item.

Decision	Guidelines
6. What conflicts can arise between using DCF methods for capital budgeting decisions and accrual accounting for performance evaluation? How can these conflicts be reduced?	Using accrual accounting to evaluate the performance of a manager may create conflicts with the use of DCF methods for capital budgeting. Frequently, the decision made using a DCF method will not report good "operating income" results in the project's early years under accrual accounting. For this reason, managers are tempted to not use DCF methods even though the decisions based on them would be in the best interests of the company as a whole over the long run. This conflict can be reduced by evaluating managers on a project-by-project basis and by looking at their ability to achieve the amounts and timing of forecasted cash flows.
7. How can managers use capital budgeting to achieve strategic goals?	A company's strategy is the source of its strategic capital budgeting decisions. Such decisions require managers to consider a broad range of factors that may be difficult to estimate. Managers must develop judgment and intuition to make these decisions. R&D projects, for example, are important strategic investments, with distant and usually highly uncertain payoffs.

Appendix

Capital Budgeting and Inflation

The Vector example (Exhibits 21-2 to 21-6) does not include adjustments for inflation in the relevant revenues and costs. **Inflation** is the decline in the general purchasing power of the monetary unit, such as dollars. An inflation rate of 10% per year means that an item bought for $100 at the beginning of the year will cost $110 at the end of the year.

Why is it important to account for inflation in capital budgeting? Because declines in the general purchasing power of the monetary unit will inflate future cash flows above what they would have been in the absence of inflation. These inflated cash flows will cause the project to look better than it really is unless the analyst recognizes that the inflated cash flows are measured in dollars that have less purchasing power than the dollars that were initially invested. When analyzing inflation, distinguish real rate of return from nominal rate of return:

Real rate of return is the rate of return demanded to cover investment risk if there is no inflation. The real rate is made up of two elements: (1) a risk-free element (the pure rate of return on risk-free long-term government bonds when there is no expected inflation) and (2) a business-risk element (that's the risk premium demanded for bearing risk).

Nominal rate of return is the rate of return demanded to cover investment risk and the decline in general purchasing power of the monetary unit as a result of expected inflation. The nominal rate is made up of three elements: (a) a risk-free element when there is no expected inflation, (b) a business-risk element, and (c) an inflation element. Items (a) and (b) make up the real rate of return to cover investment risk. The inflation element is the premium above the real rate. The rates of return earned in the financial markets are nominal rates because investors want to be compensated both for the investment risks they take and for the expected decline in the general purchasing power, as a result of inflation, of the money they get back.

Assume that the real rate of return for investments in high-risk cellular data-transmission equipment at Network Communications is 20% per year and that the expected inflation rate is 10% per year. Nominal rate of return is as follows:

$$\begin{aligned}\text{Nominal rate} &= (1 + \text{Real rate})(1 + \text{Inflation rate}) - 1\\ &= (1 + 0.20)(1 + 0.10) - 1\\ &= (1.20 \times 1.10) - 1 = 1.32 - 1 = 0.32, \text{ or } 32\%\end{aligned}$$

Nominal rate of return is related to the real rate of return and the inflation rate:

Real rate of return	0.20
Inflation rate	0.10
Combination (0.20 × 0.10)	0.02
Nominal rate of return	0.32

Note the nominal rate, 0.32, is slightly higher than 0.30, the real rate (0.20) plus the inflation rate (0.10). That's because the nominal rate recognizes that inflation of 10% also decreases the purchasing power of the real rate of return of 20% earned during the year. The combination component represents the additional compensation investors seek for the decrease in the purchasing power of the real return earned during the year because of inflation.[11]

Net Present Value Method and Inflation

When incorporating inflation into the NPV method, the key is *internal consistency*. There are two internally consistent approaches:

1. **Nominal approach**—predicts cash inflows and outflows in nominal monetary units *and* uses a nominal rate as the required rate of return
2. **Real approach**—predicts cash inflows and outflows in real monetary units *and* uses a real rate as the required rate of return

We will limit our discussion to the simpler nominal approach. Consider an investment that is expected to generate sales of 100 units and a net cash inflow of $1,000 ($10 per unit) each year for 2 years *absent inflation*. Assume cash flows occur at the end of each year. If inflation of 10% is expected each year, net cash inflows from the sale of each unit would be $11 ($10 × 1.10) in year 1 and $12.10 ($11 × 1.10, or $10 × $(1.10)^2$) in year 2, resulting in net cash inflows of $1,100 in year 1 and $1,210 in year 2. The net cash inflows of $1,100 and $1,210 are nominal cash inflows because they include the effects of inflation. *Nominal cash flows are the cash flows that are recorded in the accounting system.* The cash inflows of $1,000 each year are real cash flows. The accounting system does not record these cash flows. The nominal approach is easier to understand and apply because it uses nominal cash flows from accounting systems and nominal rates of return from financial markets.

Assume that Network Communications can purchase equipment to make and sell a cellular data-transmission product at a net initial investment of $750,000. It is expected to have a 4-year useful life and no terminal disposal value. An annual inflation rate of 10% is expected over this 4-year period. Network Communications requires an after-tax nominal rate of return of 32% (see page 827). The following table presents the predicted amounts of real (that's assuming no inflation) and nominal (that's after considering cumulative inflation) net cash inflows from the equipment over the next 4 years (excluding the $750,000 investment in the equipment and before any income tax payments):

Year (1)	Before-Tax Cash Inflows in Real Dollars (2)	Cumulative Inflation Rate Factor[a] (3)	Before-Tax Cash Inflows in Nominal Dollars (4) = (2) × (3)
1	$500,000	$(1.10)^1 = 1.1000$	$550,000
2	600,000	$(1.10)^2 = 1.2100$	726,000
3	600,000	$(1.10)^3 = 1.3310$	798,600
4	300,000	$(1.10)^4 = 1.4641$	439,230

[a]1.10 = 1.00 + 0.10 inflation rate.

[11] The real rate of return can be expressed in terms of the nominal rate of return as follows:

$$\text{Real rate} = \frac{1 + \text{Nominal rate}}{1 + \text{Inflation rate}} - 1 = \frac{1 + 0.32}{1 + 0.10} - 1 = 0.20, \text{ or } 20\%$$

Exhibit 21-8 Net Present Value Method Using Nominal Approach to Inflation for Network Communication's New Equipment

	A	B	C	D	E	F	G	H	I	J	K	L
1						Present	Present Value					
2						Value of	Discount Factor[a] at	Sketch of Relevant Cash Flows at End of Each Year				
3						Cash Flow	32%	0	1	2	3	4
4	1.	Net initial investment										
5		Year	Investment Outflows									
6		0	$(750,000)			$(750,000)	← 1.000 ←	$(750,000)				
7	2a.	Annual after-tax cash flow from										
8		operations (excluding the depreciation effect)										
9			Annual		Annual							
10			Before-Tax	Income	After-Tax							
11			Cash Flow	Tax	Cash Flow							
12		Year	from Operations	Outflows	from Operations							
13		(1)	(2)	(3) = 0.40 x (2)	(4) = (2) - (3)							
14		1	$550,000	$220,000	$330,000	250,140	← 0.758 ←		$330,000			
15		2	726,000	290,400	435,600	250,034	← 0.574 ←			$435,600		
16		3	798,600	319,440	479,160	208,435	← 0.435 ←				$479,160	
17		4	439,230	175,692	263,538	86,704	← 0.329 ←					$263,538
18						795,313						
19	2b.	Income tax cash savings from annual										
20		depreciation deductions										
21		Year	Depreciation	Tax Cash Savings								
22		(1)	(2)	(3) = 0.40 x (2)								
23		1	$187,500[b]	$75,000		56,850	← 0.758 ←		$ 75,000			
24		2	187,500	75,000		43,050	← 0.574 ←			$ 75,000		
25		3	187,500	75,000		32,625	← 0.435 ←				$ 75,000	
26		4	187,500	75,000		24,675	← 0.329 ←					$ 75,000
27						157,200						
28	NPV if new equipment purchased					$ 202,513						
29												
30												
31	[a]The nominal discount rate of 32% is made up of the real rate of return of 20% and the inflation rate of 10% [(1 + 0.20) (1 + 1.10)] – 1 = 0.32.											
32	[b]$750,000 ÷ 4 = $187,500											

We continue to make the simplifying assumption that cash flows occur at the end of each year. The income tax rate is 40%. For tax purposes, the cost of the equipment will be depreciated using the straight-line method.

Exhibit 21-8 shows the calculation of NPV using cash flows in nominal dollars and using a nominal discount rate. The calculations in Exhibit 21-8 include the net initial bus investment, annual after-tax cash flows from operations (excluding the depreciation effect), and income tax cash savings from annual depreciation deductions. The NPV is $202,513, and, based on financial considerations alone, Network Communications should purchase the equipment.

Terms to Learn

This chapter and the Glossary at the end of the book contain definitions of the following important terms:

accrual accounting rate-of-return (AARR) method **(p. 814)**
capital budgeting **(p. 803)**
cost of capital **(p. 806)**
discount rate **(p. 806)**
discounted cash flow (DCF) methods **(p. 806)**
discounted payback method **(p. 813)**
hurdle rate **(p. 806)**
inflation **(p. 827)**
internal rate-of-return (IRR) method **(p. 808)**
net present value (NPV) method **(p. 806)**
nominal rate of return **(p. 827)**
opportunity cost of capital **(p. 806)**
payback method **(p. 811)**
real rate of return **(p. 827)**
required rate of return (RRR) **(p. 806)**
time value of money **(p. 806)**

Assignment Material

MyAccountingLab

Questions

21-1 "Capital budgeting has the same focus as accrual accounting." Do you agree? Explain.

21-2 List and briefly describe each of the five stages in capital budgeting.

21-3 What is the essence of the discounted cash flow methods?

21-4 "Only quantitative outcomes are relevant in capital budgeting analyses." Do you agree? Explain.

21-5 How can sensitivity analysis be incorporated in DCF analysis?

21-6 What is the payback method? What are its main strengths and weaknesses?

21-7 Describe the accrual accounting rate-of-return method. What are its main strengths and weaknesses?

21-8 "The trouble with discounted cash flow methods is that they ignore depreciation." Do you agree? Explain.

21-9 "Let's be more practical. DCF is not the gospel. Managers should not become so enchanted with DCF that strategic considerations are overlooked." Do you agree? Explain.

21-10 "All overhead costs are relevant in NPV analysis." Do you agree? Explain.

21-11 Bill Watts, president of Western Publications, accepts a capital budgeting project proposed by division X. This is the division in which the president spent his first 10 years with the company. On the same day, the president rejects a capital budgeting project proposal from division Y. The manager of division Y is incensed. She believes that the division Y project has an internal rate of return at least 10 percentage points higher than the division X project. She comments, "What is the point of all our detailed DCF analysis? If Watts is panting over a project, he can arrange to have the proponents of that project massage the numbers so that it looks like a winner." What advice would you give the manager of division Y?

21-12 Distinguish different categories of cash flows to be considered in an equipment-replacement decision by a taxpaying company.

21-13 Describe three ways income taxes can affect the cash inflows or outflows in a motor-vehicle-replacement decision by a taxpaying company.

21-14 How can capital budgeting tools assist in evaluating a manager who is responsible for retaining customers of a cellular telephone company?

21-15 Distinguish the nominal rate of return from the real rate of return.

MyAccountingLab

Exercises

21-16 Exercises in compound interest, no income taxes. To be sure that you understand how to use the tables in Appendix A at the end of this book, solve the following exercises. Ignore income tax considerations. The correct answers, rounded to the nearest dollar, appear on pages 838–839.

Required

1. You have just won $10,000. How much money will you accumulate at the end of 10 years if you invest it at 8% compounded annually? At 10%?
2. Ten years from now, the unpaid principal of the mortgage on your house will be $154,900. How much do you need to invest today at 4% interest compounded annually to accumulate the $154,900 in 10 years?
3. If the unpaid mortgage on your house in 10 years will be $154,900, how much money do you need to invest at the end of each year at 10% to accumulate exactly this amount at the end of the 10th year?
4. You plan to save $7,500 of your earnings at the end of each year for the next 10 years. How much money will you accumulate at the end of the 10th year if you invest your savings compounded at 8% per year?
5. You have just turned 65 and an endowment insurance policy has paid you a lump sum of $250,000. If you invest the sum at 8%, how much money can you withdraw from your account in equal amounts at the end of each year so that at the end of 10 years (age 75) there will be nothing left?
6. You have estimated that for the first 10 years after you retire you will need a cash inflow of $65,000 at the end of each year. How much money do you need to invest at 8% at your retirement age to obtain this annual cash inflow? At 12%?

7. The following table shows two schedules of prospective operating cash inflows, each of which requires the same net initial investment of $10,000 now:

	Annual Cash Inflows	
Year	**Plan A**	**Plan B**
1	$ 3,000	$ 1,000
2	5,000	2,000
3	2,000	3,000
4	3,000	4,000
5	2,000	5,000
Total	$15,000	$15,000

The required rate of return is 8% compounded annually. All cash inflows occur at the end of each year. In terms of net present value, which plan is more desirable? Show your computations.

21-17 Capital budgeting methods, no income taxes. Riverbend Company runs hardware stores in a tristate area. Riverbend's management estimates that if it invests $250,000 in a new computer system, it can save $65,000 in annual cash operating costs. The system has an expected useful life of 8 years and no terminal disposal value. The required rate of return is 8%. Ignore income tax issues in your answers. Assume all cash flows occur at year-end except for initial investment amounts.

Required

1. Calculate the following for the new computer system:
   a. Net present value
   b. Payback period
   c. Discounted payback period
   d. Internal rate of return (using the interpolation method)
   e. Accrual accounting rate of return based on the net initial investment (assume straight-line depreciation)
2. What other factors should Riverbend consider in deciding whether to purchase the new computer system?

21-18 Capital budgeting methods, no income taxes. City Hospital, a nonprofit organization, estimates that it can save $28,000 a year in cash operating costs for the next 10 years if it buys a special-purpose eye-testing machine at a cost of $110,000. No terminal disposal value is expected. City Hospital's required rate of return is 14%. Assume all cash flows occur at year-end except for initial investment amounts. City Hospital uses straight-line depreciation.

Required

1. Calculate the following for the special-purpose eye-testing machine:
   a. Net present value
   b. Payback period
   c. Internal rate of return
   d. Accrual accounting rate of return based on net initial investment
   e. Accrual accounting rate of return based on average investment
2. What other factors should City Hospital consider in deciding whether to purchase the special-purpose eye-testing machine?

21-19 Capital budgeting, income taxes. Assume the same facts as in Exercise 21-18 except that City Hospital is a taxpaying entity. The income tax rate is 30% for all transactions that affect income taxes.

Required

1. Do requirement 1 of Exercise 21-18.
2. How would your computations in requirement 1 be affected if the special-purpose machine had a $10,000 terminal disposal value at the end of 10 years? Assume depreciation deductions are based on the $110,000 purchase cost and zero terminal disposal value using the straight-line method. Answer briefly in words without further calculations.

21-20 Capital budgeting with uneven cash flows, no income taxes. America Cola is considering the purchase of a special-purpose bottling machine for $65,000. It is expected to have a useful life of 4 years with no terminal disposal value. The plant manager estimates the following savings in cash operating costs:

Year	Amount
1	$25,000
2	22,000
3	21,000
4	20,000
Total	$88,000

Southern Cola uses a required rate of return of 18% in its capital budgeting decisions. Ignore income taxes in your analysis. Assume all cash flows occur at year-end except for initial investment amounts.

Calculate the following for the special-purpose bottling machine:

Required

1. Net present value
2. Payback period
3. Discounted payback period
4. Internal rate of return (using the interpolation method)
5. Accrual accounting rate of return based on net initial investment (Assume straight-line depreciation. Use the average annual savings in cash operating costs when computing the numerator of the accrual accounting rate of return.)

21-21 Comparison of projects, no income taxes. (CMA, adapted) New Tech Corporation is a rapidly growing biotech company that has a required rate of return of 8%. It plans to build a new facility in Santa Clara County. The building will take 2 years to complete. The building contractor offered New Bio a choice of three payment plans, as follows:

- **Plan I:** Payment of $325,000 at the time of signing the contract and $4,825,000 upon completion of the building. The end of the second year is the completion date.
- **Plan II:** Payment of $1,675,000 at the time of signing the contract and $1,675,000 at the end of each of the 2 succeeding years.
- **Plan III:** Payment of $425,000 at the time of signing the contract and $1,650,000 at the end of each of the 3 succeeding years.

Required

1. Using the net present value method, calculate the comparative cost of each of the three payment plans being considered by New Tech.
2. Which payment plan should New Tech choose? Explain.
3. Discuss the financial factors, other than the cost of the plan, and the nonfinancial factors that should be considered in selecting an appropriate payment plan.

21-22 Payback and NPV methods, no income taxes. (CMA, adapted) Andrews Construction is analyzing its capital expenditure proposals for the purchase of equipment in the coming year. The capital budget is limited to $5,000,000 for the year. Lori Bart, staff analyst at Andrews, is preparing an analysis of the three projects under consideration by Corey Andrews, the company's owner.

Home Insert Page Layout Formulas Data Review View

	A	B	C	D
1		**Project A**	**Project B**	**Project C**
2	**Projected cash outflow**			
3	Net initial investment	$3,000,000	$1,500,000	$4,000,000
4				
5	**Projected cash inflows**			
6	Year 1	$1,000,000	$ 400,000	$2,000,000
7	Year 2	1,000,000	900,000	2,000,000
8	Year 3	1,000,000	800,000	200,000
9	Year 4	1,000,000		100,000
10				
11	Required rate of return	10%	10%	10%

Required

1. Because the company's cash is limited, Andrews thinks the payback method should be used to choose between the capital budgeting projects.
   a. What are the benefits and limitations of using the payback method to choose between projects?
   b. Calculate the payback period for each of the three projects. Ignore income taxes. Using the payback method, which projects should Andrews choose?
2. Bart thinks that projects should be selected based on their NPVs. Assume all cash flows occur at the end of the year except for initial investment amounts. Calculate the NPV for each project. Ignore income taxes.
3. Which projects, if any, would you recommend funding? Briefly explain why.

21-23 DCF, accrual accounting rate of return, working capital, evaluation of performance, no income taxes. Century Lab plans to purchase a new centrifuge machine for its New Hampshire facility. The machine costs $137,500 and is expected to have a useful life of 8 years, with a terminal disposal value of $37,500. Savings in cash operating costs are expected to be $31,250 per year. However, additional working capital is needed to keep the machine running efficiently. The working capital must continually be replaced, so an investment of $10,000 needs to be maintained at all times, but this investment is fully recoverable (will be "cashed in") at the end of the useful life. Century Lab's required rate of return is 14%. Ignore income taxes in your analysis. Assume all cash flows occur at year-end except for initial investment amounts. Century Lab uses straight-line depreciation for its machines.

Required

1. Calculate net present value.
2. Calculate internal rate of return.
3. Calculate accrual accounting rate of return based on net initial investment.
4. Calculate accrual accounting rate of return based on average investment.
5. You have the authority to make the purchase decision. Why might you be reluctant to base your decision on the DCF methods?

21-24 New equipment purchase, income taxes. Ella's Bakery plans to purchase a new oven for its store. The oven has an estimated useful life of 4 years. The estimated pretax cash flows for the oven are as shown in the table that follows, with no anticipated change in working capital. Ella's Bakery has a 14% after-tax required rate of return and a 35% income tax rate. Assume depreciation is calculated on a straight-line basis for tax purposes using the initial oven investment and estimated terminal disposal value of the oven. Assume all cash flows occur at year-end except for initial investment amounts.

Home | Insert | Page Layout | Formulas | Data | Review | View

	A	B	C	D	E	F
1		Relevant Cash Flows at End of Each Year				
2		0	1	2	3	4
3	Initial machine investment	$(186,000)				
4	Annual cash flow from operations (excluding the depreciation effect)		$77,000	$77,000	$77,000	$77,000
5	Cash flow from terminal disposal of over					$ 6,000

Required

1. Calculate (a) net present value, (b) payback period, and (c) internal rate of return.
2. Calculate accrual accounting rate of return based on net initial investment.

21-25 New equipment purchase, income taxes. Nikola Inc. is considering the purchase of a new industrial electric motor to improve efficiency at its Rochester plant. The motor has an estimated useful life of 5 years. The estimated pretax cash flows for the motor are shown in the table that follows, with no anticipated change in working capital. Nikola has a 10% after-tax required rate of return and a 30% income tax rate. Assume depreciation is calculated on a straight-line basis for tax purposes. Assume all cash flows occur at year-end except for initial investment amounts.

Home | Insert | Page Layout | Formulas | Data | Review | View

	A	B	C	D	E	F	G
1		Relevant Cash Flows at End of Each Year					
2		0	1	2	3	4	5
3	Initial motor investment	$(75,000)					
4	Annual cash flow from operations (excluding the depreciation effect)		$25,000	$25,000	$25,000	$25,000	$25,000
5	Cash flow from terminal disposal of motor						$ 0

Required

1. Calculate (a) net present value, (b) payback period, (c) discounted payback period, and (d) internal rate of return.
2. Compare and contrast the capital budgeting methods in requirement 1.

21-26 Project choice, taxes. Harrison Ventures has invested in a variety of retail outlets in key mall locations. Harrison is contemplating an investment in upgrading the furnishings and fittings of these properties. The upgrades will require an up-front investment of $100,000. Harrison estimates that they will yield incremental margins of $43,000 annually due to higher foot traffic and sales and require incremental cash maintenance costs of $15,000 annually. Harrison expects the life span of these improvements at 5 years and estimates a terminal disposal value of $20,000.

Harrison faces a 30% income tax rate. It depreciates assets on a straight-line basis (to terminal value) for tax purposes. The required rate of return on investments is 12%.

Required

1. What is the expected increase in annual net income from investing in the improvements?
2. Calculate the accrual accounting rate of return based on average investment.
3. Is the project worth investing in from an NPV standpoint?
4. Suppose the tax authorities are willing to let Harrison depreciate the project down to zero over its useful life. If Harrison plans to liquidate the project in 5 years, should it take this option? Quantify the impact of this choice on the NPV of the project.

21-27 Customer value. Ortel Telecom sells telecommunication products and services to a variety of small businesses. Two of Ortel's key clients are Square and Cloudburst, both fast-growing technology start-ups located in New York City. Ortel has compiled information regarding its transactions with Square and Cloudburst for 2014, as well as its expectations regarding their interactions for the next 3 years:

Home Insert Page Layout Formulas Data Review

	A	B	C	D	E
1		Expected Annual percentage increase		2014	
2		Square	Cloudburst	Square	Cloudburst
3	Sales revenues	6%	5.5%	$567,000	$3,510,000
4	Cost of sales	5%	4.5%	$364,800	$3,060,000
5	Net cash flow			$202,200	$450,000

Ortel's transactions with Square and Cloudburst are in cash. Assume that they occur at year-end. Ortel is headquartered in the Cayman Islands and pays no income taxes. The owners of Ortel insist on a required rate of return of 12%.

Required

1. What is the expected net cash flow from Square and Cloudburst for the next 3 years?
2. Based on the net present value from cash flows over the next 3 years, is Cloudburst or Square a more valuable customer for Ortel?
3. Cloudburst threatens to switch to another supplier unless Ortel gives a 10% price reduction on all sales starting in 2015. Calculate the 3-year NPV of Cloudburst after incorporating the 10% discount. Should Ortel continue to transact with Cloudburst? What other factors should it consider before making its final decision?

21-28 Selling a plant, income taxes. (CMA, adapted) The Lucky Seven Company is an international clothing manufacturer. Its Redmond plant will become idle on December 31, 2014. Peter Laney, the corporate controller, has been asked to look at three options regarding the plant:

- **Option 1:** The plant, which has been fully depreciated for tax purposes, can be sold immediately for $900,000.
- **Option 2:** The plant can be leased to the Preston Corporation, one of Lucky Seven's suppliers, for 4 years. Under the lease terms, Preston would pay Lucky Seven $220,000 rent per year (payable at year-end) and would grant Lucky Seven a $40,000 annual discount off the normal price of fabric purchased by Lucky Seven. (Assume that the discount is received at year-end for each of the 4 years.) Preston would bear all of the plant's ownership costs. Lucky Seven expects to sell this plant for $150,000 at the end of the 4-year lease.

- **Option 3:** The plant could be used for 4 years to make souvenir jackets for the Olympics. Fixed overhead costs (a cash outflow) before any equipment upgrades are estimated to be $20,000 annually for the 4-year period. The jackets are expected to sell for $55 each. Variable cost per unit is expected to be $43. The following production and sales of jackets are expected: 2015, 18,000 units; 2016, 26,000 units; 2017, 30,000 units; 2018, 10,000 units. In order to manufacture the jackets, some of the plant equipment would need to be upgraded at an immediate cost of $160,000. The equipment would be depreciated using the straight-line depreciation method and zero terminal disposal value over the 4 years it would be in use. Because of the equipment upgrades, Lucky Seven could sell the plant for $270,000 at the end of 4 years. No change in working capital would be required.

Lucky Seven treats all cash flows as if they occur at the end of the year, and it uses an after-tax required rate of return of 10%. Lucky Seven is subject to a 35% tax rate on all income, including capital gains.

Required

1. Calculate net present value of each of the options and determine which option Lucky Seven should select using the NPV criterion.
2. What nonfinancial factors should Lucky Seven consider before making its choice?

Problems

MyAccountingLab

21-29 Equipment replacement, no income taxes. Clean Chips is a manufacturer of prototype chips based in Dublin, Ireland. Next year, in 2015, Clean Chips expects to deliver 535 prototype chips at an average price of $55,000. Clean Chips' marketing vice president forecasts growth of 65 prototype chips per year through 2021. That is, demand will be 535 in 2015, 600 in 2016, 665 in 2017, and so on.

The plant cannot produce more than 525 prototype chips annually. To meet future demand, Clean Chips must either modernize the plant or replace it. The old equipment is fully depreciated and can be sold for $4,300,000 if the plant is replaced. If the plant is modernized, the costs to modernize it are to be capitalized and depreciated over the useful life of the updated plant. The old equipment is retained as part of the modernize alternative. The following data on the two options are available:

	Modernize	Replace
Initial investment in 2015	$36,800,000	$61,700,000
Terminal disposal value in 2021	$7,000,000	$17,000,000
Useful life	7 years	7 years
Total annual cash operating costs per prototype chip	$35,500	$26,000

Clean Chips uses straight-line depreciation, assuming zero terminal disposal value. For simplicity, we assume no change in prices or costs in future years. The investment will be made at the beginning of 2015, and all transactions thereafter occur on the last day of the year. Clean Chips' required rate of return is 10%.

There is no difference between the modernize and replace alternatives in terms of required working capital. Clean Chips has a special waiver on income taxes until 2021.

Required

1. Sketch the cash inflows and outflows of the modernize and replace alternatives over the 2015–2021 period.
2. Calculate payback period for the modernize and replace alternatives.
3. Calculate net present value of the modernize and replace alternatives.
4. What factors should Clean Chips consider in choosing between the alternatives?

21-30 Equipment replacement, income taxes (continuation of 21-29). Assume the same facts as in Problem 21-29, except that the plant is located in Austin, Texas. Clean Chips has no special waiver on income taxes. It pays a 30% tax rate on all income. Proceeds from sales of equipment above book value are taxed at the same 30% rate.

Required

1. Sketch the after-tax cash inflows and outflows of the modernize and replace alternatives over the 2015–2021 period.
2. Calculate the net present value of the modernize and replace alternatives.
3. Suppose Clean Chips is planning to build several more plants. It wants to have the most advantageous tax position possible. Clean Chips has been approached by Spain, Malaysia, and Australia to construct plants in their countries. Use the data in Problem 21-29 and this problem to briefly describe in qualitative terms the income tax features that would be advantageous to Clean Chips.

21-31 DCF, sensitivity analysis, no income taxes. (CMA, adapted) Invigor Corporation is an international manufacturer of fragrances for women. Management at Invigor is considering expanding the product line to men's fragrances. From the best estimates of the marketing and production managers, annual sales (all for cash) for this new line are 1,200,000 units at $50 per unit; cash variable cost is $20 per unit; and cash fixed costs are $8,000,000 per year. The investment project requires $70,000,000 of cash outflow and has a project life of 8 years.

At the end of the 8-year useful life, there will be no terminal disposal value. Assume all cash flows occur at year-end except for initial investment amounts.

Men's fragrance is a new market for Invigor, and management is concerned about the reliability of the estimates. The controller has proposed applying sensitivity analysis to selected factors. Ignore income taxes in your computations. Invigor's required rate of return on this project is 12%.

Required

1. Calculate the net present value of this investment proposal.
2. Calculate the effect on the net present value of the following two changes in assumptions. (Treat each item independently of the other.)
   a. 10% reduction in the selling price
   b. 10% increase in the variable cost per unit
3. Discuss how management would use the data developed in requirements 1 and 2 in its consideration of the proposed capital investment.

21-32 NPV and AARR, goal-congruence issues. Eric Ishton, a manager of the Plate Division for the Stone Ware Manufacturing company, has the opportunity to expand the division by investing in additional machinery costing $430,000. He would depreciate the equipment using the straight-line method and expects it to have no residual value. It has a useful life of 8 years. The firm mandates a required after-tax rate of return of 12% on investments. Eric estimates annual net cash inflows for this investment of $110,000 before taxes and an investment in working capital of $7,500. The tax rate is 30%.

Required

1. Calculate the net present value of this investment.
2. Calculate the accrual accounting rate of return based on net initial investment for this project.
3. Should Eric accept the project? Will Eric accept the project if his bonus depends on achieving an accrual accounting rate of return of 12%? How can this conflict be resolved?

21-33 Payback methods, even and uneven cash flows. Cardinal Laundromat is trying to enhance the services it provides to customers, mostly college students. It is looking into the purchase of new high-efficiency washing machines that will allow for the laundry's status to be checked via smartphone.

Cardinal estimates the cost of the new equipment at $186,000. The equipment has a useful life of 9 years. Cardinal expects cash fixed costs of $82,000 per year to operate the new machines, as well as cash variable costs in the amount of 5% of revenues. Cardinal evaluates investments using a cost of capital of 6%.

Required

1. Calculate the payback period and the discounted payback period for this investment, assuming Cardinal expects to generate $180,000 in revenues every year from the new machines.
2. Assume instead that Cardinal expects the following uneven stream of cash revenues from installing the new washing machines:

Home Insert Page Layout Formulas Data Review View

	A	B	C	D	E	F	G	H	I	J
1	**Year**	**1**	**2**	**3**	**4**	**5**	**6**	**7**	**8**	**9**
2	**Projected revenue**	$110,000	$100,000	$150,000	$95,000	$165,000	$205,000	$150,000	$165,000	$170,000

Based on this estimated revenue stream, what are the payback and discounted payback periods for the investment?

21-34 Replacement of a machine, income taxes, sensitivity. (CMA, adapted) The Frooty Company is a family-owned business that produces fruit jam. The company has a grinding machine that has been in use for 3 years. On January 1, 2014, Frooty is considering the purchase of a new grinding machine. Frooty has two options: (1) continue using the old machine or (2) sell the old machine and purchase a new machine. The seller of the new machine isn't offering a trade-in. The following information has been obtained:

	A	B	C
1		**Old Machine**	**New Machine**
2	Initial purchase cost of machines	\$150,000	\$190,000
3	Useful life from acquisition date (years)	8	5
4	Terminal disposal value at the end of useful life on Dec. 31, 2018, assumed for depreciation purposes	\$ 20,000	\$ 25,000
5	Expected annual cash operating costs:		
6	Variable cost per can of jam	\$ 0.25	\$ 0.19
7	Total fixed costs	\$ 25,000	\$ 24,000
8	Depreciation method for tax purposes	Straight line	Straight line
9	Estimated disposal value of machines:		
10	January 1, 2014	\$ 68,000	\$190,000
11	December 31, 2018	\$ 12,000	\$ 22,000
12	Expected cans of jam made and sold each year	475,000	475,000

Frooty is subject to a 34% income tax rate. Assume that any gain or loss on the sale of machines is treated as an ordinary tax item and will affect the taxes paid by Frooty in the year in which it occurs. Frooty's after-tax required rate of return is 12%. Assume all cash flows occur at year-end except for initial investment amounts.

Required

1. A manager at Frooty asks you whether it should buy the new machine. To help in your analysis, calculate the following:
   a. One-time after-tax cash effect of disposing of the old machine on January 1, 2014
   b. Annual recurring after-tax cash operating savings from using the new machine (variable and fixed)
   c. Cash tax savings due to differences in annual depreciation of the old machine and the new machine
   d. Difference in after-tax cash flow from terminal disposal of new machine and old machine
2. Use your calculations in requirement 1 and the net present value method to determine whether Frooty should use the old machine or acquire the new machine.
3. How much more or less would the recurring after-tax cash operating savings of the new machine need to be for Frooty to earn exactly the 12% after-tax required rate of return? Assume that all other data about the investment do not change.

21-35 Recognizing cash flows for capital investment projects. Johnny Buster owns Entertainment World, a place that combines fast food, innovative beverages, and arcade games. Worried about the shifting tastes of younger audiences, Johnny contemplates bringing in new simulators and virtual reality games to maintain customer interest.

As part of this overhaul, Johnny is also looking at replacing his old Guitar Hero equipment with a Rock Band Pro machine. The Guitar Hero setup was purchased for \$25,200 and has accumulated depreciation of \$23,000, with a current trade-in value of \$2,700. It currently costs Johnny \$600 per month in utilities and another \$5,000 a year in maintenance to run the Guitar Hero equipment. Johnny feels that the equipment could be kept in service for another 11 years, after which it would have no salvage value.

The Rock Band Pro machine is more energy-efficient and durable. It would reduce the utilities costs by 30% and cut the maintenance cost in half. The Rock Band Pro costs \$49,000 and has an expected disposal value of \$5,000 at the end of its useful life of 11 years.

Johnny charges an entrance fee of \$5 per hour for customers to play an unlimited number of games. He does not believe that replacing Guitar Hero with Rock Band Pro will have an impact on this charge or materially change the number of customers who will visit Entertainment World.

Required

1. Johnny wants to evaluate the Rock Band Pro project using capital budgeting techniques. To help him, read through the problem and separate the cash flows into four groups: (1) net initial investment cash flows, (2) cash flow savings from operations, (3) cash flows from terminal disposal of investment, and (4) cash flows not relevant to the capital budgeting problem.
2. Assuming a tax rate of 40%, a required rate of return of 8%, and straight-line depreciation over the remaining useful life of equipment, should Johnny purchase Rock Band Pro?

21-36 NPV, inflation and taxes. Cheap-O Foods is considering replacing all 10 of its old cash registers with new ones. The old registers are fully depreciated and have no disposal value. The new registers cost \$899,640 (in total). Because the new registers are more efficient than the old registers, Cheap-O will have annual incremental cash savings from using the new registers in the amount of \$192,000 per year. The registers have a 7-year useful life and no terminal disposal value and are depreciated using the straight-line method. Cheap-O requires an 8% real rate of return.

Required

1. Given the preceding information, what is the net present value of the project? Ignore taxes.
2. Assume the \$192,000 cost savings are in current real dollars and the inflation rate is 5.5%. Recalculate the NPV of the project.
3. Based on your answers to requirements 1 and 2, should Cheap-O buy the new cash registers?
4. Now assume that the company's tax rate is 30%. Calculate the NPV of the project assuming no inflation.
5. Again assuming that the company faces a 30% tax rate, calculate the NPV of the project under an inflation rate of 5.5%.
6. Based on your answers to requirements 4 and 5, should Cheap-O buy the new cash registers?

21-37 NPV of information system, income taxes. Saina Supplies leases and sells materials, tools, and equipment and also provides add-on services such as ground maintenance and waterproofing to construction and mining sites. The company has grown rapidly over the past few years. The owner, Saina Torrance, feels that for the company to continue to scale, it needs to install a professional information system rather than relying on intuition and Excel analyses. After some research, Saina's CFO reports back with the following data about a data warehousing and analytics system that she views as promising:

- The system will cost \$750,000. For tax purposes, it can be depreciated straight-line to a zero terminal value over a 5-year useful life. However, the CFO expects that the system will still be worth \$50,000 at that time.
- There is an additional \$75,000 annual fee for software upgrades and technical support from the vendor.
- The ability to provide better services and to target and reach more clients as a result of the new system will directly result in a \$500,000 increase in revenues for Saina in the first year after installation. Revenues will grow by 5% each year thereafter. Saina's contribution margin is 60%.
- Due to greater efficiency in ordering and dispatching supplies, as well as in collecting receivables, the firm's working-capital requirements will decrease by \$100,000.
- Saina will also be able to reduce the amount of warehouse space it currently leases, saving \$40,000 annually in the process.
- Saina Supplies pays an income tax of 30% and requires an after-tax rate of return of 12%.

Assume that all cash flows occur at year-end except for initial investment amounts.

Required

1. If Saina decides to purchase and install the new information system, what is the expected incremental after-tax cash flow from operations during each of the 5 years?
2. Compute the net present value of installing the information system at Saina Supplies.
3. In addition to the analysis in requirement 2, what nonfinancial factors you would consider in making the decision about the information system?

Answers to Exercises in Compound Interest (Exercise 21-16)

The general approach to these exercises centers on a key question: Which of the four basic tables in Appendix A should be used? No computations should be made until this basic question has been answered with confidence.

1. **From Table 1.** The \$10,000 is the present value P of your winnings. Their future value S in 10 years will be as follows:

$$S = P(1 + r)^n$$

The conversion factor, $(1 + r)^n$, is on line 10 of Table 1.

$$\text{Substituting at 8\%: } S = \$10{,}000(2.159) = \$21{,}590$$

$$\text{Substituting at 10\%: } S = \$10{,}000(2.594) = \$25{,}940$$

2. **From Table 2.** The \$154,900 is a future value. You want the present value of that amount. $P = S \div (1 + r)^n$. The conversion factor, $1 \div (1 + r)^n$, is on line 10 of Table 2. Substituting,

$$P = \$154{,}900(.676) = \$104{,}712.40$$

3. **From Table 3.** The $154,900 is a future value. You are seeking the uniform amount (annuity) to set aside annually. Note that $1 invested each year for 10 years at 10% has a future value of $15.937 after 10 years, from line 10 of Table 3.

$$\$154{,}900/15.937 = \$9{,}719.52$$

4. **From Table 3.** You need to find the future value of an annuity of $7,500 per year. Note that $1 invested each year for 10 years at 8% has a future value of $14.487 after 10 years.

$$\$7{,}500(14.487) = \$108{,}652.50$$

5. **From Table 4.** When you reach age 65, you will get $250,000, a present value at that time. You need to find the annuity that will exactly exhaust the invested principal in 10 years. To pay yourself $1 each year for 10 years when the interest rate is 8% requires you to have $6.710 today, from line 10 of Table 4.

$$\$250{,}000/6.710 = \$37{,}257.82$$

6. **From Table 4.** You need to find the present value of an annuity for 10 years at 8% and at 12%:

$$8\%\text{: } \$65{,}000(6.710) = \$436{,}150.00$$

$$12\%\text{: } \$65{,}000(5.650) = \$367{,}250.00$$

7. Plan A is preferable. The NPV of plan A exceeds that of plan B by $851.

		Plan A		Plan B	
Year	**PV Factor at 8%**	**Cash Inflows**	**PV of Cash Inflows**	**Cash Inflows**	**PV of Cash Inflows**
0	1.000	$(10,000)	$ (10,000)	$(10,000)	$ (10,000)
1	0.926	3,000	2,778	1,000	926
2	0.857	5,000	4,285	2,000	1,714
3	0.794	2,000	1,588	3,000	2,382
4	0.735	3,000	2,205	4,000	2,940
5	0.681	2,000	1,362	5,000	3,405
			$ 2,218		$ 1,367

Even though plans A and B have the same total cash inflows over the 5 years, plan A is preferred because it has greater cash inflows occurring earlier.

22 Management Control Systems, Transfer Pricing, and Multinational Considerations

Learning Objectives

1. Describe a management control system and its three key properties
2. Describe the benefits and costs of decentralization
3. Explain transfer prices and the four criteria managers use to evaluate them
4. Calculate transfer prices using three methods
5. Illustrate how market-based transfer prices promote goal congruence in perfectly competitive markets
6. Understand how to avoid making suboptimal decisions when transfer prices are based on full cost plus a markup
7. Describe the range of feasible transfer prices when there is unused capacity and alternative methods for arriving at the eventual hybrid price
8. Apply a general guideline for determining a minimum transfer price
9. Incorporate income tax considerations in multinational transfer pricing

Transfer pricing is the price one subunit of a company charges for the services it provides another subunit of the same company.

At Ford, for example, automotive components, vehicles, and assembly services are bought and sold internally across divisions. The intellectual property patents of many pharmaceutical companies, such as Merck, are usually held by foreign subsidiaries, making the transfer price to these subsidiaries a critical factor in how much income is recognized in various tax jurisdictions.

Firms use transfer prices (1) to focus managers' attention on the performance of their own subunits and (2) to plan and coordinate the actions of different subunits to maximize the company's income as a whole. Transfer prices can lead to disagreements, however, because managers of different subunits often have very different preferences about how transfer prices should be set. For example, some managers prefer the prices be based on market prices. Others prefer the prices be based on costs alone. Controversies also arise when multinational corporations seek to reduce their overall income tax burden by charging high transfer prices to units located in countries with high tax rates. Many countries, including the United States, attempt to restrict this practice, as the following article shows.

Symantec Wins $545 Million Opinion in Transfer Pricing Dispute with the IRS[1]

Symantec Corp., a large U.S. software company, won a significant court decision in December 2009, saving it $545 million in contested back taxes. The Internal Revenue Service (IRS) had been seeking back taxes it alleged were owed by Veritas Software Corp., a company acquired by Symantec in 2005. The dispute was over the company's formula for "transfer pricing," a complex set of rules determining how companies set prices, fees, and cost-allocation arrangements between their operations in different tax jurisdictions.

[1] *Sources:* Cabell Chinnis Jr. et al., "Tax Court Upends IRS's Billion Dollar Buy-in Valuation Adjustment in Veritas," *Mondaq Business Briefing* (December 17, 2009); Kelly Phillips Erb, "IRS Brings 'A Team' to Crush Transfer Pricing Abuses," *Forbes* blog (March 27, 2012); John Letzing, "Symantec Wins $545M Opinion in Tax Case," *Dow Jones News Service* (December 11, 2009).

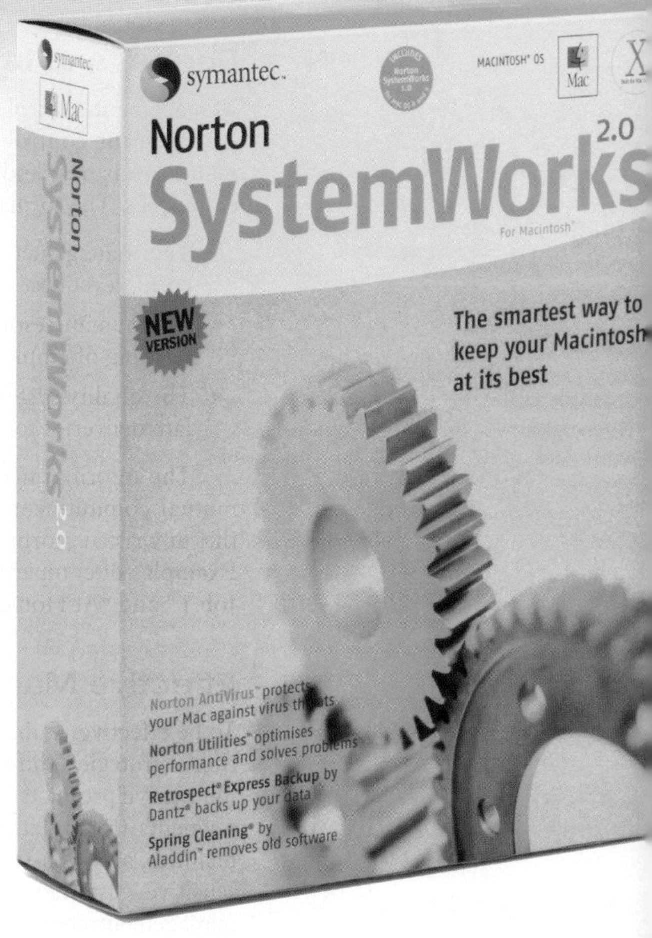

At issue were the fees and cost-allocation arrangements between Veritas and its Irish subsidiary, which was granted rights to conduct research and development on various intangibles (such as computer programs and manufacturing process technologies) related to data storage software and related devices. Under the agreement, Veritas Ireland paid $160 million for this grant of rights from 1999 to 2001. Based on a discounted cash flow analysis, the IRS contended that the true value of the transferred rights was closer to $1.675 billion. As a consequence, the IRS claimed that the transaction artificially increased the income of Veritas Ireland at the expense of income in the U.S. parent corporation, consequently lowering the company's U.S. tax bills.

Veritas, however, maintained that it acted appropriately. Veritas testified that the $160 million figure was based on royalty rates it had received from seven original equipment manufacturers for rights to incorporate the company's U.S. software and technologies into an operating system, with adjustments made for purposes of comparability. At trial, the United States Tax Court supported this position and called the IRS's valuation of the intangibles "arbitrary, capricious, and unreasonable." While it lost the Symantec case, the IRS continues to aggressively pursue transfer-pricing cases. In 2011, Western Union paid $1.2 billion to settle a transfer-pricing dispute with the IRS, and AstraZeneca agreed to pay $1.1 billion to settle two long-running disputes.

Though not all companies face multinational tax concerns, transfer-pricing issues are common to many companies. In these companies, transfer pricing is part of the larger management control system. This chapter discusses the links among a firm's strategy, organizational structure, management control systems, and accounting information. We'll examine the benefits and costs of centralized and decentralized organizational structures and look at the pricing of products or services transferred between subunits of the same company. We emphasize how accounting data, such as costs, budgets, and prices, help in planning and coordinating actions of subunits.

Learning Objective 1

Describe a management control system

...gathers information for planning and control decisions

and its three key properties

...aligns with strategy, supports organizational responsibility of managers, and motivates employees

Management Control Systems

A **management control system** is a means of gathering and using information to aid and coordinate the planning and control decisions throughout an organization and to guide the behavior of its managers and other employees. Some companies design their management control system around the concept of the balanced scorecard. For example, ExxonMobil's management control system contains financial and nonfinancial information in each of the four perspectives of the balanced scorecard (see Chapter 12 for details). Well-designed management control systems use information both from within the company, such as its net income and levels of employee satisfaction, and from outside the company, such as its stock price and customer-satisfaction data.

Formal and Informal Systems

Management control systems consist of formal and informal control systems. The formal management control system of a company includes explicit rules, procedures, performance measures, and incentive plans that guide the behavior of its managers and other employees. The formal control system is composed of several systems, such as:

- The management accounting systems, which provide information about the firm's costs, revenues, and income
- The human resources systems, which provide information about the recruiting and training of employees, absenteeism, and accidents
- The quality system, which provides information about yields, defective products, and late deliveries to customers

The informal management control system includes the shared values, loyalties, and mutual commitments among members of the organization, the company's culture, and the unwritten norms about acceptable behavior for managers and other employees. Examples of company slogans that reinforce values and loyalties are "At Ford, Quality Is Job 1" and "At Home Depot, Low Prices Are Just the Beginning."

Effective Management Control

To be effective, management control systems should be closely aligned with the organization's strategies and goals. Two examples of strategies at ExxonMobil are (1) providing innovative products and services to increase the company's market share in key customer segments (by targeting customers who are willing to pay more for faster service, better facilities, and well-stocked convenience stores) and (2) reducing costs and targeting price-sensitive customers. Suppose ExxonMobil decides to pursue the former strategy. The management control system must then reinforce this goal, and ExxonMobil should tie managers' rewards to achieving the targeted measures.

Management control systems should also be designed to support the organizational responsibilities of individual managers. Different levels of management at ExxonMobil need different kinds of information to perform their tasks. For example, top managers needs stock-price information to evaluate how much shareholder value the company has created. The stock price, however, is less important for line managers supervising individual refineries. Those managers are more concerned with obtaining information about the firm's on-time delivery of gasoline, equipment downtime, product quality, number of days lost to accidents and environmental problems, cost per gallon of gasoline, and employee satisfaction. Similarly, marketing managers are more concerned with information about the service at gas stations, customer satisfaction, and market share.

Effective management control systems should also motivate managers and other employees. **Motivation** is the desire to attain a selected goal (the *goal-congruence* aspect) combined with the resulting pursuit of that goal (the *effort* aspect).

Goal congruence exists when individuals and groups work toward achieving the organization's goals—that is, managers working in their own best interest take actions that align with the overall goals of top management. Suppose the goal of ExxonMobil's top management is to maximize operating income. If the management control system evaluates refinery managers *only* on the basis of costs, the managers may be tempted to make decisions that minimize costs but overlook product quality or timely delivery to retail stations. This oversight probably won't maximize the operating income of the company as a whole. In this case, the management control system will not achieve goal congruence.

Decision Point

What is a management control system and how should it be designed?

Effort is the extent to which managers strive or endeavor in order to achieve a goal. Effort goes beyond physical exertion, such as a worker producing at a faster rate, to include mental actions as well. For example, effort includes the diligence or acumen with which a manager gathers and analyzes data before authorizing a new investment. It is impossible to directly observe or reward effort. As a result, management control systems motivate employees to exert effort by rewarding them for the achievement of tangible goals, such as profit targets or stock returns. This induces managers to exert effort because higher levels of effort increase the likelihood that the goals are achieved. The rewards can be monetary (such as cash, shares of company stock, use of a company car, or membership in a club) or nonmonetary (such as a better title, greater responsibility, or authority over a larger number of employees). Management control systems must be aligned with an organization's structure. An organization with a decentralized structure will have different issues to consider when designing its management control system than a firm with a centralized structure.

Decentralization

Learning Objective 2

Describe the benefits of decentralization

...responsiveness to customers, faster decision making, management development

and the costs of decentralization

...loss of control, duplication of activities

Until the mid-20th century, many firms were organized in a centralized, hierarchical fashion. Centralization is an organizational structure in which power is concentrated at the top and there is relatively little freedom for managers at the lower levels to make decisions. Perhaps the most famous example of a highly centralized structure is the Soviet Union, prior to its collapse in the late 1980s.

Today, organizations are far more decentralized and many companies have pushed decision-making authority down to subunit managers. **Decentralization** is an organizational structure that gives managers at lower levels the freedom to make decisions. **Autonomy** is the degree of freedom to make decisions. The greater the freedom, the greater the autonomy. As we discuss the issues of decentralization and autonomy, we use the term *subunit* to refer to any part of an organization. A subunit may be a large division, such as the refining division of ExxonMobil, or a small group, such as a two-person advertising department of a local clothing chain.

Examples of firms with decentralized structures include Nucor, the U.S. steel giant, which gives the general managers of its plants a substantial amount of operational autonomy, and Tesco, Britain's largest retailer, which offers great latitude to its store managers. Of course, no firm is completely decentralized. Nucor's top managers are still responsible for the firm's overall strategic planning, financing, setting of base salary levels and bonus targets, and so on. How much decentralization is optimal? Companies try to choose the degree of decentralization that maximizes benefits over costs. We next discuss the key benefits and costs of decentralization.

Benefits of Decentralization

Supporters of decentralizing decision making claim the following benefits from granting responsibilities to managers of subunits:

1. **Creates greater responsiveness to the needs of a subunit's customers, suppliers, and employees.** Good decisions cannot be made without good information. Compared with top managers, subunit managers are better informed about their competitors, suppliers, and employees, as well as about local factors that affect performance, such as ways to decrease costs, improve quality, and better respond to customers. Flextronics, a global supply chain solutions company, uses decentralization to reduce bureaucracy and increase responsiveness. Managers can use the company's worldwide information technology to solve a local customer's problem or send a project to other managers without going through red tape.
2. **Leads to gains from faster decision making by subunit managers.** Decentralization speeds decision making, creating a competitive advantage over centralized organizations. Centralization slows down decision making because the decisions must be pushed upward through layer after layer of management before they are finalized. Interlake Mecalux, a leading provider of materials-handling solutions and storage products, cites this benefit of decentralization: "We have distributed decision-making powers more broadly to the cutting edge of product and market opportunity." Interlake's storage system solutions must often be customized to fit the needs of customers. Delegating decision making to the sales force allows Interlake to respond faster to changing customer requirements.

3. **Assists management development and learning.** Subunit managers are more motivated and committed when they can exercise initiative. Moreover, giving managers more responsibility helps a company develop an experienced pool of talent to fill higher-level management positions and weed out people unlikely to be successful top managers. According to Tektronix, an electronics company based in Oregon, "Decentralized units provide a training ground for general managers and a visible field of combat where product champions can fight for their ideas."
4. **Sharpens the focus of subunit managers and broadens the reach of top management.** In a decentralized setting, the manager of a subunit has a concentrated focus. The head of Yahoo Japan, for example, can develop country-specific knowledge and expertise (about local advertising trends, cultural norms, payment forms, and so on) and focus on maximizing Yahoo's profits in Japan. At the same time, this relieves Yahoo's senior managers at its Sunnyvale, California, headquarters from the burden of controlling day-to-day operating decisions in Japan. They can spend more time and effort on strategic planning for the entire organization.

Costs of Decentralization

Advocates of more-centralized decision making believe decentralizing is costly because it does the following:

1. **Leads to suboptimal decision making.** If the subunit managers do not have the necessary expertise or talent to make major decisions, the company, as a whole, is worse off because its top managers have relinquished their responsibility for doing so. Even if subunit managers are sufficiently skilled, **suboptimal decision making**—also called **incongruent decision making** or **dysfunctional decision making**—occurs when a decision's benefit to one subunit is more than offset by the costs to the organization as a whole. This is most prevalent when the subunits of the company are highly interdependent, such as when the end product of one subunit is used or sold by another subunit. For example, suppose Nintendo's marketing group receives a rush order for additional Wii consoles in Australia following the release of some popular new games. A manufacturing manager in Japan who is evaluated on the basis of costs may be unwilling to arrange this rush order because altering production schedules invariably increases manufacturing costs. From Nintendo's viewpoint, however, supplying the consoles may be optimal, both because the Australian customers are willing to pay a premium price and because the current shipment is expected to stimulate future orders for other Nintendo games and consoles.
2. **Leads to unhealthy competition.** In a decentralized setting, subunit managers may regard themselves as competing with managers of other subunits in the same company as if they were external rivals. This pushes them to view the relative performance of the subunit as more important than the goals of the company. Consequently, managers may be unwilling to assist other subunits (as in the Nintendo example) or share important information. The 2010 Congressional hearings on the recall of Toyota vehicles revealed that it was common for Toyota's Japan unit to not share information about engineering problems or reported defects between its United States, Asian, and European operations. Toyota has since asserted that it will change this dysfunctional behavior.
3. **Results in duplication of output.** If subunits provide similar products or services, their internal competition could lead to failure in the external markets. The reason is that divisions may find it easier to steal market share from one another, by mimicking each other's successful products, rather than those of competing firms. Eventually, this leads to confusion in the minds of customers and the loss of each division's distinctive strengths. A classic example is General Motors, which eventually dissolved its Oldsmobile, Pontiac, and Saturn divisions. Similarly, Condé Nast Publishing's initially distinct food magazines *Bon Appétit* and *Gourmet* eventually ended up chasing the

same readers and advertisers, to the detriment of both. *Gourmet* magazine stopped publication in November 2009.[2]

4. **Results in duplication of activities.** Even if the subunits operate in distinct markets, several individual subunits of the company may undertake the same activity separately. In a highly decentralized company, each subunit may have personnel to carry out staff functions such as human resources or information technology. Centralizing these functions helps to streamline and use fewer resources for these activities and eliminates wasteful duplication. For example, ABB of Switzerland, a global leader in power and automation technology, is decentralized but has generated significant cost savings of late by centralizing its sourcing decisions across business units for parts, such as pipe pumps and fittings, as well as engineering and erection services. Having subunits share services such as information technology and human resources is becoming popular with companies because it saves 30–40% of the cost of having each subunit purchase these services on its own.

Comparing Benefits and Costs

Top managers must compare the benefits and costs of decentralization, often on a function-by-function basis, when choosing an organizational structure. Surveys of U.S. and European companies report that the decisions made most frequently at the decentralized level are related to product mix and advertising. In these areas, subunit managers develop their own operating plans and performance reports and make faster decisions based on local information. Decisions related to the type and source of long-term financing are made least frequently at the decentralized level. Corporate managers have better information about financing terms in different markets and can obtain the best terms. Likewise, centralizing its income tax strategies allows the organization to optimize across subunits, for example by offsetting the income in one subunit with losses in others.

Decentralization in Multinational Companies

Multinational companies—companies that operate in multiple countries—are often decentralized because centralizing the control of their subunits around the world can be physically and practically impossible. Also, language, customs, cultures, business practices, rules, laws, and regulations vary significantly across countries. Decentralization enables managers in different countries to make decisions that exploit their knowledge of local business and political conditions and enables them to deal with uncertainties in their individual environments. For example, Philips, a global electronics company headquartered in the Netherlands, delegates marketing and pricing decisions for its television businesses in India and Singapore to the managers in those countries. Multinational corporations often rotate managers between foreign locations and corporate headquarters. Job rotation combined with decentralization helps develop the ability of managers to operate in the global environment.

There are drawbacks to decentralizing multinational companies. One of the most important is the lack of control and the resulting risks. In 1995, Barings PLC, a British investment banking firm, went bankrupt and had to be sold when one of its traders in Singapore caused the firm to lose more than £1 billion on unauthorized trades that went undetected. Similarly, in 2011, a London trader working for UBS, Switzerland's largest bank, circumvented the bank's risk controls and made unauthorized trades that resulted in a $2.3 billion loss for the company. UBS's CEO and other top managers resigned because of the scandal. Multinational corporations that implement decentralized decision making usually design their management control systems to measure and monitor the performance of divisions. Information and communications technology helps the flow of information for reporting and control.

---

[2] For an intriguing comparison of the failure of decentralization in these disparate settings, see Jack Shafer's article, "How Condé Nast Is Like General Motors: The Magazine Empire as Car Wreck," *Slate* (October 5, 2009). http://www.slate.com/id/2231177/.

Choices About Responsibility Centers

Recall (from Chapter 6) that a responsibility center is a segment or subunit of the organization whose manager is accountable for a specified set of activities. To measure the performance of subunits in centralized or decentralized companies, the management control system uses one or a mix of the four types of responsibility centers:

1. *Cost center*—the manager is accountable for costs only.
2. *Revenue center*—the manager is accountable for revenues only.
3. *Profit center*—the manager is accountable for revenues and costs.
4. *Investment center*—the manager is accountable for investments, revenues, and costs.

Each type of responsibility center can be found in either centralized or decentralized companies.

Decision Point

What are the benefits and costs of decentralization?

A common misconception is that *profit center*—and, in some cases, *investment center*—is a synonym for a decentralized subunit and *cost center* is a synonym for a centralized subunit. *Profit centers can be coupled with a highly centralized organization, and cost centers can be coupled with a highly decentralized organization.* For example, managers in a division organized as a profit center may have little freedom in making decisions. They may need to obtain approval from corporate headquarters for introducing new products and services or to make expenditures over some preset limit. When Michael Eisner ran Walt Disney Company, the giant media and entertainment conglomerate, from 1984 until 2005, the firm's strategic-planning division scrutinized business proposals so closely that managers were reluctant to pitch new ideas.[3] In other companies, divisions such as information technology may be organized as cost centers, but their managers may have great latitude to make capital expenditures and purchase materials and services. In short, the labels *profit center* and *cost center* are independent of the degree of centralization or decentralization in a company.

Learning Objective 3

Explain transfer prices

...price one subunit charges another for product

and the four criteria managers use to evaluate them

...goal congruence, management effort, subunit performance evaluation, and subunit autonomy

Transfer Pricing

In a decentralized organization, much of the decision-making power resides in its individual subunits. Often, the subunits interact by supplying goods or services to one another. In these cases, top management uses *transfer prices* to coordinate the actions of the subunits and to evaluate the performance of their managers.

A **transfer price** is the price one subunit (department or division) charges for a product or service supplied to another subunit of the same organization. If, for example, a car manufacturer like BMW or Ford has a separate division that manufactures engines, the transfer price is the price the engine division charges when it transfers engines to the car assembly division. The transfer price creates revenues for the selling subunit (the engine division in our example) and costs for the buying subunit (the assembly division in our example), affecting each subunit's operating income. These operating incomes can be used to evaluate the subunits' performances and to motivate their managers. The product or service transferred between subunits of an organization is called an **intermediate product.** The receiving unit (the assembly division in the engine example) may work on the product further or the product may be transferred from production to marketing and sold directly to an external customer.

In one sense, transfer pricing is a curious phenomenon. Activities within an organization are clearly nonmarket in nature; products and services are not bought and sold as they are in open-market transactions. Yet establishing prices for transfers among subunits of a company has a distinctly market flavor. The rationale for transfer prices is that when subunit managers (such as the manager of the engine division) make decisions, they need only focus on how their decisions will affect their subunit's performance without evaluating how their decisions affect company-wide performance. In this sense, transfer prices

[3] When Robert Iger replaced Eisner as CEO in 2005, one of his first acts was to disassemble the strategic-planning division, thereby giving more authority to Disney's business units (parks and resorts, consumer products, and media networks).

ease the subunit managers' information-processing and decision-making tasks. In a well-designed transfer-pricing system, managers focus on maximizing the performance of their subunits and in doing so optimize the performance of the company as a whole.

Criteria for Evaluating Transfer Prices

To help a company achieve its goals, transfer prices should meet four key criteria:

1. Promote goal congruence, so that division managers acting in their own interest will take actions that are aligned with the objectives of top management.
2. Induce managers to exert a high level of effort. Subunits selling a product or service should be motivated to hold down their costs; subunits buying the product or service should be motivated to acquire and use inputs efficiently.
3. Help top managers evaluate the performance of individual subunits.
4. Preserve autonomy of subunits if top managers favor a high degree of decentralization. A subunit manager seeking to maximize the operating income of the subunit should have the freedom to transact with other subunits of the company (on the basis of transfer prices) or to transact with external parties.

Decision Point

What are transfer prices, and what criteria do managers use to evaluate them?

Calculating Transfer Prices

Learning Objective 4

Calculate transfer prices using three methods

...(a) market-based, (b) cost-based, or (c) hybrid, each of which yields different operating incomes for the subunits

There are three broad categories of methods top managers can use to determine transfer prices. They are as follows:

1. **Market-based transfer prices.** Top managers may choose to use the price of a similar product or service publicly listed on, say, a trade association's Web site. Or they may select the external price a subunit charges outside customers.
2. **Cost-based transfer prices.** Top managers may choose a transfer price based on the cost of producing the product being transferred. Examples include the variable production cost, variable and fixed production costs, and full cost of the product. The full cost of the product includes all production costs plus costs from other business functions (R&D, design, marketing, distribution, and customer service). The cost used in cost-based transfer prices can be actual cost or budgeted cost. Sometimes, the cost-based transfer price includes a markup or profit margin that represents a return on subunit investment.
3. **Hybrid transfer prices.** Hybrid transfer prices take into account both cost and market information. Top managers may set the prices by specifying a transfer price that is an average of the cost of producing and transporting the product internally and the market price for comparable products. At other times, a hybrid transfer price may allow for the revenue recognized by the selling unit to differ from the cost recognized by the buying unit. The most common form of hybrid prices arises via negotiation—the subunit managers are asked to negotiate the transfer price between them and to decide whether to buy and sell internally or deal with external parties. Negotiated transfer prices are often employed when market prices are volatile. Thus, managers need current information about the costs and prices of products to participate in the bargaining process.

Under what circumstances should each of these options be used? To answer this question, we next demonstrate how each of the three transfer-pricing methods works and highlight the differences among them. We examine transfer pricing at Horizon Petroleum against the four criteria of promoting goal congruence, motivating management effort, evaluating subunit performance, and preserving subunit autonomy.

An Illustration of Transfer Pricing

Horizon Petroleum has two divisions, each operating as a profit center. The transportation division purchases crude oil in Matamoros, Mexico, and transports it from Matamoros to Houston, Texas. The refining division processes crude oil into gasoline.

For simplicity, we assume gasoline is the only salable product the Houston refinery makes and that it takes two barrels of crude oil to yield one barrel of gasoline.

The variable costs of each division are associated with a single cost driver: barrels of crude oil transported by the transportation division and barrels of gasoline produced by the refining division. The fixed cost per unit is based on the budgeted annual fixed costs and practical capacity of crude oil that can be transported by the transportation division, as well as the budgeted annual fixed costs and practical capacity of gasoline that can be produced by the refining division. Horizon Petroleum reports all costs and revenues of its non-U.S. operations in U.S. dollars using the prevailing exchange rate.

- The transportation division has obtained rights to certain oil fields in the Matamoros area. It has a long-term contract to purchase crude oil extracted from these fields at \$72 per barrel. The division transports the oil to Houston and then "sells" it to the refining division. The pipeline from Matamoros to Houston can transport 40,000 barrels of crude oil per day.
- The refining division has been operating at capacity (30,000 barrels of crude oil a day), using oil supplied by Horizon's transportation division (an average of 10,000 barrels per day) and oil bought from another producer and delivered to the Houston refinery (an average of 20,000 barrels per day at \$85 per barrel).
- The refining division sells the gasoline it produces to outside parties at \$190 per barrel.

Exhibit 22-1 summarizes Horizon Petroleum's variable and fixed costs per barrel of crude oil in the transportation division and variable and fixed costs per barrel of gasoline in the refining division, the external market prices of buying crude oil, and the external market price of selling gasoline. What's missing in the exhibit is the actual transfer price from the transportation division to the refining division. This transfer price will vary depending on the transfer-pricing method used. The transfer prices from the transportation division to the refining division under each of the three methods are as follows:

1. A market-based transfer price of \$85 per barrel of crude oil based on the competitive market price in Houston.
2. A cost-based transfer price at, say, 105% of full cost, where the full cost is the cost of the crude oil purchased in Matamoros plus the transportation division's own variable and fixed costs (from Exhibit 22-1): $1.05 \times (\$72 + \$1 + \$3) = \$79.80$.
3. A hybrid transfer price of, say, \$82 per barrel of crude oil, which is between the market-based and cost-based transfer prices. We describe later in this section the various ways in which hybrid prices can be determined.

Exhibit 22-1 Operating Data for Horizon Petroleum

Home Insert Page Layout Formulas Data Review View

	A	B	C	D	E	F	G	H
1								
2				**Transportation Division**				
3				Variable cost per barrel of crude oil	\$1			
4	Contract price per barrel of crude oil supplied in Matamoros	= \$72	⟶	Fixed cost per barrel of crude oil	3			
5				Full cost per barrel of crude oil	\$4			
6				↓				
7								
8				Barrels of crude oil transferred				
9				↓				
10								
11				**Refining Division**				
12				Variable cost per barrel of gasoline	\$ 8			
13	Market price per barrel of crude oil supplied to Houston refinery	= \$85	⟶	Fixed cost per barrel of gasoline	6	⟶	Market price per barrel of gasoline sold to external parties =	\$190
14				Full cost per barrel of gasoline	\$14			
15								

Exhibit 22-2 Division Operating Income of Horizon Petroleum for 100 Barrels of Crude Oil Under Alternative Transfer-Pricing Methods

	A	B	C	D	E	F	G	H
1	**Production and Sales Data**							
2	Barrels of crude oil transferred = 100							
3	Barrels of gasoline sold = 50							
4								
5		**Internal Transfers at**			**Internal Transfers at**		**Internal Transfers at**	
6		**Market Price =**			**105% of Full Cost =**		**Hybrid Price =**	
7		**$85 per Barrel**			**$79.80 per Barrel**		**$82 per Barrel**	
8	**Transportation Division**							
9	Revenues, $85, $79.80, $82 × 100 barrels of crude oil	$8,500			$7,980		$8,200	
10	Costs							
11	Crude oil purchase costs, $72 × 100 barrels of crude oil	7,200			7,200		7,200	
12	Division variable costs, $1 × 100 barrels of crude oil	100			100		100	
13	Division fixed costs, $3 × 100 barrels of crude oil	300			300		300	
14	Total division costs	7,600			7,600		7,600	
15	Division operating income	$ 900			$ 380		$ 600	
16								
17	**Refining Division**							
18	Revenues, $190 × 50 barrels of gasoline	$9,500			$9,500		$9,500	
19	Costs							
20	Transferred-in costs, $85, $79.80, $82							
21	× 100 barrels of crude oil	8,500			7,980		8,200	
22	Division variable costs, $8 × 50 barrels of gasoline	400			400		400	
23	Division fixed costs, $6 × 50 barrels of gasoline	300			300		300	
24	Total division costs	9,200			8,680		8,900	
25	Division operating income	$ 300			$ 820		$ 600	
26	Operating income of both divisions together	$1,200			$1,200		$1,200	

Exhibit 22-2 presents division operating incomes per 100 barrels of crude oil purchased under each transfer-pricing method. Transfer prices create income for the selling division and corresponding costs for the buying division that cancel out when divisional results are consolidated for the company as a whole. The exhibit assumes all three transfer-pricing methods yield transfer prices that are in a range that does not cause division managers to change the business relationships shown in Exhibit 22-1. That is, Horizon Petroleum's total operating income from purchasing, transporting, and refining the 100 barrels of crude oil and selling the 50 barrels of gasoline is the same ($1,200) *regardless of the internal transfer prices used.*

$$\begin{aligned}\text{Operating income} &= \text{Revenues} - \text{Cost of crude oil purchases in Matamoros} - \text{Transportation Division costs} - \text{Refining Division costs}\\ &= (\$190 \times 50 \text{ barrels of gasoline}) - (\$72 \times 100 \text{ barrels of crude oil})\\ &\quad - (\$4 \times 100 \text{ barrels of crude oil}) - (\$14 \times 50 \text{ barrels of gasoline})\\ &= \$9{,}500 - \$7{,}200 - \$400 - \$700 = \$1{,}200\end{aligned}$$

Note further that under all three methods, summing the two division operating incomes equals Horizon Petroleum's total operating income of $1,200. By keeping the total operating income the same, we focus attention on the effects different transfer-pricing methods have on the operating income of each division. Subsequent sections of this chapter show that different transfer-pricing methods can cause managers to take different actions leading to different total operating incomes.

Consider the two methods in the first two columns in Exhibit 22-2. The operating income of the transportation division is $520 more ($900 − $380) if transfer prices are based on market prices rather than on 105% of the full cost. The operating income of the refining division is $520 more ($820 − $300) if transfer prices are based on 105% of the full cost rather than market prices. If the transportation division's sole criterion were to maximize its own operating income, it would favor transfer prices at market prices. In contrast, the refining division would prefer transfer prices at 105% of full cost to maximize its own operating income. The hybrid transfer price of $82 is between the 105% of full cost and market-based transfer prices. It splits the $1,200 of operating income equally between the divisions. This price could arise as a result of negotiations between the transportation and refining division managers.

It's not surprising that subunit managers, especially those whose compensation or promotion directly depends on subunit operating income, take considerable interest in setting transfer prices. To reduce the excessive focus of subunit managers on their own subunits, many companies compensate subunit managers on the basis of both the operating income earned by their respective subunits and the company as a whole.

Decision Point

What are alternative ways of calculating transfer prices?

We next examine market-based, cost-based, and hybrid transfer prices in more detail. We show how the choice of transfer-pricing method combined with managers' sourcing decisions can determine the size of the company-wide operating-income pie itself.

Learning Objective 5

Illustrate how market-based transfer prices promote goal congruence in perfectly competitive markets

...division managers transacting internally are motivated to take the same actions as if they were transacting externally

Market-Based Transfer Prices

Transferring products or services at market prices generally leads to optimal decisions when three conditions are satisfied: (1) The market for the intermediate product is perfectly competitive, (2) the interdependencies of subunits are minimal, and (3) there are no additional costs or benefits to the company as a whole from buying or selling in the external market instead of transacting internally.

Perfectly-Competitive-Market Case

A **perfectly competitive market** exists when there is a homogeneous product with buying prices equal to selling prices and no individual buyers or sellers can affect those prices by their own actions. By using market-based transfer prices in perfectly competitive markets, a company can (1) promote goal congruence, (2) motivate management effort, (3) evaluate the performance of subunits, and (4) preserve their autonomy.

Consider Horizon Petroleum again. Assume there is a perfectly competitive market for crude oil in the Houston area. As a result, the transportation division can sell and the refining division can buy as much crude oil as each wants at $85 per barrel. Horizon would prefer its managers to buy or sell crude oil internally. Think about the decisions that Horizon's division managers would make if each had the autonomy to sell or buy crude oil externally. If the transfer price between Horizon's transportation and refining divisions is set below $85, the manager of the transportation division will be motivated to sell all crude oil to external buyers in the Houston area at $85 per barrel. If the transfer price is set above $85, the manager of the refining division will be motivated to purchase all crude oil from external suppliers. Only an $85 transfer price will motivate the transportation division and the refining division to buy and sell internally. That's because neither division profits by buying or selling in the external market.

Suppose Horizon evaluates its division managers on the basis of their individual division's operating income. The transportation division will sell, either internally or externally, as much crude oil as it can profitably transport, and the refining division will buy, either internally or externally, as much crude oil as it can profitably refine. An $85-per-barrel transfer price results in goal congruence—the actions that maximize each division's operating income are also the actions that maximize the operating income of Horizon Petroleum as a whole. Furthermore, because the transfer price is not based on costs, it motivates each division manager to maximize his or her own division's operating income. Market prices also serve to evaluate the economic viability and profitability of each division individually. For example,

Koch Industries, the second-largest private company in the United States, uses market-based pricing for all internal transfers. As its CFO, Steve Feilmeier, notes, "We believe that the alternative for any given asset should always be considered in order to best optimize the profitability of the asset. If you simply transfer price between two different divisions at cost, then you may be subsidizing your whole operation and not know it." Returning to our Horizon example, suppose that under market-based transfer prices, the refining division consistently shows small or negative profits. Then Horizon may consider shutting down the refining division and simply transport and sell the oil to other refineries in the Houston area.

Distress Prices

When supply outstrips demand, market prices may drop well below their historical averages. If the drop in prices is expected to be temporary, these low market prices are called "distress prices." Deciding whether a current market price is a distress price is often difficult. Prior to the worldwide spike in commodity prices in the 2006–2008 period, the market prices of several mineral and agricultural commodities, including nickel, uranium, and wheat, stayed for many years at what people initially believed were temporary distress levels!

Which transfer price should be used for judging performance if distress prices prevail? Some companies use the distress prices themselves, but others use long-run average prices, or "normal" market prices. In the short run, the manager of the selling subunit should supply the product or service at the distress price as long as it exceeds the *incremental costs* of supplying the product or service. If the distress price is used as the transfer price, the selling division will show a loss because the distress price will not exceed the *full cost* of the division. If the long-run average market price is used, forcing the manager to buy internally at a price above the current market price will hurt the buying division's short-run operating income. But the long-run average market price will provide a better measure of the long-run profitability and viability of the supplier division. Of course, if the price remains low in the long run, the company should use the low market price as the transfer price. If this price is lower than the variable and fixed costs that can be saved if manufacturing facilities are shut down, the production facilities of the selling subunit should be sold and the buying subunit should purchase the product from an external supplier.

Imperfect Competition

If markets are not perfectly competitive, selling prices affect the quantity of product sold. Consider an auto dealer: In order to move more new or used cars off the lot, the dealer has to reduce the price of the vehicles. A similar situation applies to industries ranging from toilet paper and toothpaste to software. Faced with an imperfectly competitive market, the manager of the selling division will choose a price and quantity combination for the intermediate product that maximizes the division's operating income. If the transfer price is set at this price, the buying division may find that acquiring the product is too costly and results in a loss and decide not to purchase the product. Yet, from the point of view of the company as a whole, it may well be that profits are maximized if the selling division transfers the product to the buying division for further processing and sale. For this reason, when the market for the intermediate good is imperfectly competitive, the transfer price must generally be set below the external market price (but above the selling division's variable cost) in order to induce efficient transfers.[4]

Decision Point

Under what market conditions do market-based transfer prices promote goal congruence?

[4] Consider a firm where division S produces the intermediate product. S has a capacity of 15 units and a variable cost per unit of \$2. The imperfect competition is reflected in a downward-sloping demand curve for the intermediate product—if S wants to sell Q units, it has to lower the market price to $P = 20 - Q$. The division's profit function is therefore given by $Q \times (20 - Q) - 2Q = 18Q - Q^2$. Simple calculus reveals that it is optimal for S to sell 9 units of the intermediate product at a price of \$11, thereby making a profit of \$81. Now, suppose that division B in the same firm can take the intermediate product, incur an additional variable cost of \$4, and sell it in the external market for \$12. Because S has surplus capacity (it only uses 9 of its 15 units of capacity), it is clearly in the firm's interest to have S make additional units and transfer them to B. The firm makes an incremental profit of \$12 − \$2 − \$4 = \$6 for each transferred unit. However, if the transfer price for the intermediate product were set equal to the market price of \$11, B would reject the transaction because it would lose money on it (\$12 − \$11 − \$4 = −\$3 per unit).

To resolve this conflict, the transfer price should be set at a suitable *discount* to the external price in order to induce the buying division to seek internal transfers. In our example, the selling price must be greater than S's variable cost of \$2, but less than B's contribution margin of \$8. That is, the transfer price has to be discounted relative to the market price (\$11) by a minimum of \$3. We explore the issue of feasible transfer pricing ranges further in the section on hybrid transfer prices.

Learning Objective 6

Understand how to avoid making suboptimal decisions when transfer prices are based on full cost plus a markup

...buying divisions should not regard the fixed costs and the markup as variable costs

Cost-Based Transfer Prices

Cost-based transfer prices are helpful when market prices are unavailable, inappropriate, or too costly to obtain, such as when markets are not perfectly competitive, when the product is specialized, or when the internal product is different from the products available externally in terms of its quality and the customer service provided for it.

Full-Cost Bases

In practice, many companies use transfer prices based on a product's full cost. To approximate market prices, cost-based transfer prices are sometimes set at the full cost plus a margin. These transfer prices, however, can lead to suboptimal decisions. Suppose Horizon Petroleum makes internal transfers at 105% of the full cost. Recall that the refining division purchases, on average, 20,000 barrels of crude oil per day from a local Houston supplier, who delivers the crude oil to the refinery at a price of $85 per barrel. To reduce its crude oil costs, the refining division has located an independent producer in Matamoros—Gulfmex Corporation—that is willing to sell 20,000 barrels of crude oil per day at $79 per barrel, delivered to Horizon's pipeline in Matamoros. Given Horizon's organizational structure, the transportation division would purchase the 20,000 barrels of crude oil in Matamoros from Gulfmex, transport it to Houston, and then sell it to the refining division. The pipeline has unused capacity and can ship the 20,000 barrels per day at its variable cost of $1 per barrel without affecting the shipment of the 10,000 barrels of crude oil per day acquired under its existing long-term contract arrangement. Will Horizon Petroleum incur lower costs by purchasing crude oil from Gulfmex in Matamoros or by purchasing crude oil from the Houston supplier? Will the refining division show lower crude oil purchasing costs by acquiring oil from Gulfmex or by acquiring oil from its current Houston supplier?

The following analysis shows that Horizon Petroleum's operating income would be maximized by purchasing oil from Gulfmex. The analysis compares the incremental costs in both divisions under the two alternatives. The analysis assumes the fixed costs of the transportation division will be the same regardless of the alternative chosen. That is, the transportation division cannot save any of its fixed costs if it does not transport Gulfmex's 20,000 barrels of crude oil per day.

- **Alternative 1:** Buy 20,000 barrels from the Houston supplier at $85 per barrel. The total costs to Horizon Petroleum are 20,000 barrels × $85 per barrel = $1,700,000.
- **Alternative 2:** Buy 20,000 barrels in Matamoros at $79 per barrel and transport them to Houston at a variable cost of $1 per barrel. The total costs to Horizon Petroleum are 20,000 barrels × ($79 + $1) per barrel = $1,600,000.

There is a reduction in total costs to Horizon Petroleum of $100,000 ($1,700,000 − $1,600,000) by acquiring oil from Gulfmex.

Suppose the transportation division's transfer price to the refining division is 105% of the full cost. The refining division will see its reported division costs increase if the crude oil is purchased from Gulfmex:

$$\text{Transfer price} = 1.05 \times \left(\begin{array}{c}\text{Purchase price}\\ \text{from}\\ \text{Gulfmex}\end{array} + \begin{array}{c}\text{Variable cost per unit}\\ \text{of Transportation}\\ \text{Division}\end{array} + \begin{array}{c}\text{Fixed cost per unit}\\ \text{of Transportation}\\ \text{Division}\end{array} \right)$$

$$= 1.05 \times (\$79 + \$1 + \$3) = 1.05 \times \$83 = \$87.15 \text{ per barrel}$$

- **Alternative 1:** Buy 20,000 barrels from Houston supplier at $85 per barrel. The total costs to the refining division are 20,000 barrels × $85 per barrel = $1,700,000.
- **Alternative 2:** Buy 20,000 barrels from the transportation division of Horizon Petroleum that were purchased from Gulfmex. The total costs to the refining division are 20,000 barrels × $87.15 per barrel = $1,743,000.

As a profit center, the refining division can maximize its short-run division operating income by purchasing from the Houston supplier.

The refining division looks at each barrel that it obtains from the transportation division as a variable cost of $87.15 per barrel; if 10 barrels are transferred, it costs the refining division $871.50; if 100 barrels are transferred, it costs $8,715. In fact, the variable cost per barrel is $80 ($79 to purchase the oil from Gulfmex plus $1 to transport it to Houston). The remaining $7.15 ($87.15 − $80) per barrel is the transportation division's fixed cost and markup. *The full cost plus a markup transfer-pricing method causes the refining division to regard the fixed cost (and the 5% markup) of the transportation division as a variable cost and leads to goal incongruence.*

Should Horizon's top managers interfere and force the refining division to buy from the transportation division? Doing so would undercut the philosophy of decentralization, so Horizon's top managers would probably view the decision by the refining division to purchase crude oil from external suppliers as an inevitable cost of decentralization and not interfere. Of course, some interference may occasionally be necessary to prevent costly blunders. But recurring interference would simply transform Horizon from a decentralized company into a centralized company.

What transfer price will promote goal congruence for both the transportation and refining divisions? The minimum transfer price is $80 per barrel. A transfer price below $80 does not provide the transportation division with an incentive to purchase crude oil from Gulfmex in Matamoros because it is below the transportation division's incremental costs. The maximum transfer price is $85 per barrel. A transfer price above $85 will cause the refining division to purchase crude oil from the external market in Houston rather than from the transportation division. A transfer price between the minimum and maximum transfer prices of $80 and $85 will promote goal congruence: Each division will increase its own reported operating income while increasing Horizon Petroleum's operating income if the refining division purchases crude oil from Gulfmex in Matamoros.

In the absence of a market-based transfer price, Horizon's top managers cannot easily determine the profitability of the investment made in the transportation division and hence whether Horizon should keep or sell the pipeline. Furthermore, if the transfer price had been based on the actual costs of the transportation division, it would provide the division with no incentive to control costs. That's because all cost inefficiencies of the transportation division would get passed along as part of the actual full-cost transfer price. In fact, every additional dollar of cost arising from wastefulness in the transportation division would generate an additional 5 cents in profit for the division under the "105% of full cost" rule!

Surveys by accounting firms and researchers indicate that, despite its limitations, managers generally prefer to use full-cost-based transfer prices because (1) they represent relevant costs for long-run decisions, (2) they facilitate external pricing based on variable and fixed costs, and (3) they are the least costly to administer. However, full-cost transfer pricing does raise many issues. How are each subunit's indirect costs allocated to products? Have the correct activities, cost pools, and cost-allocation bases been identified? Should the chosen fixed-cost rates be actual or budgeted? The issues here are similar to the issues related to allocating fixed costs, discussed in Chapter 14. Many companies determine the transfer price based on budgeted rates and practical capacity because it overcomes the problem of inefficiencies in actual costs and costs of unused capacity getting passed along to the buying division.

Variable-Cost Bases

Transferring 20,000 barrels of crude oil from the transportation division to the refining division at the variable cost of $80 per barrel achieves goal congruence, as shown in the preceding section. The refining division would buy from the transportation division because the transportation division's variable cost is less than the $85 price charged by external suppliers. Setting the transfer price equal to the variable cost has other benefits. Knowing the variable cost per barrel of crude oil helps the refining division make many decisions such as the short-run pricing decisions discussed in Chapter 11. However, at the $80-per-barrel transfer price, the transportation division would record an operating loss

Decision Point

What problems can arise when full cost plus a markup is used as the transfer price?

and the refining division would show large profits because it would be charged only for the variable costs of the transportation division. One approach to addressing this problem is to have the refining division make a lump-sum transfer payment to cover the fixed costs and generate some operating income for the transportation division while the transportation division continues to make transfers at the variable cost. The fixed payment is the price the refining division pays for using the capacity of the transportation division. The income earned by each division can then be used to evaluate the performance of each division and its manager.

Learning Objective 7

Describe the range of feasible transfer prices when there is unused capacity

...from variable cost to market price of the product transferred

and alternative methods for arriving at the eventual hybrid price

...proration, negotiation between divisions, and dual pricing

Hybrid Transfer Prices

Consider again Horizon Petroleum. As we saw earlier, the transportation division has unused capacity it can use to transport oil from Matamoros to Houston at an incremental cost of $80 per barrel. Horizon Petroleum, as a whole, maximizes its operating income if the refining division purchases crude oil from the transportation division rather than from the Houston market (the incremental cost per barrel is $80 versus the price per barrel of $85). Both divisions would be interested in transacting with each other (and the firm achieves goal congruence) if the transfer price is between $80 and $85.

For any internal transaction, there is generally a minimum transfer price the selling division will not go below, based on its cost structure. In the Horizon Petroleum example, the minimum price acceptable to the transportation division is $80. There is also a maximum price the buying division will not wish to exceed, which is determined by the lower of two quantities—the eventual contribution the division generates from an internal transaction and the price of purchasing a comparable intermediate product from an outside party. For the refining division, each barrel of gasoline sold to external parties generates $182 in contribution (the $190 price less the $8 variable cost of refining). Because it takes two barrels of crude oil to generate a barrel of gasoline, this is equivalent to a contribution of $91 per barrel of crude. For any price higher than $91, the refining division would lose money for each barrel of crude it buys from the transportation division. On the other hand, the refining division can purchase crude oil on the open market for $85 rather than having it transported internally. The maximum feasible transfer price is thus the lower of $91 and $85, or $85 in this instance. We saw previously that a transfer price between the minimum price ($80) and the maximum ($85) would promote goal congruence. We now describe three different ways in which firms attempt to determine the specific transfer price within these bounds.

Prorating the Difference Between Maximum and Minimum Transfer Prices

One approach that Horizon Petroleum could pursue is to choose a transfer price that splits, on some fair basis, the $5 difference between the $85-per-barrel market-based maximum price the refining division is willing to pay and the $80-per-barrel variable cost-based minimum price the transportation division wants to receive. An easy solution is to split the difference equally, resulting in a transfer price of $82.50. However, this solution ignores the relative costs incurred by the two divisions and might lead to disparate profit margins on the work contributed by each division to the final product. As an alternative approach, Horizon Petroleum could allocate the $5 difference on the basis of the variable costs of the two divisions. Using the data in Exhibit 22-1 (page 848), variable costs are as follows:

Transportation division's variable costs to transport 100 barrels of crude oil ($1 × 100)	$100
Refining division's variable costs to refine 100 barrels of crude oil and produce 50 barrels of gasoline ($8 × 50)	400
Total variable costs	$500

Of the \$5 difference, the transportation division gets to keep (\$100 ÷ \$500) × \$5.00 = \$1.00, and the refining division gets to keep (\$400 ÷ \$500) × \$5.00 = \$4.00. That is, the transfer price is \$81 per barrel of crude oil (\$79 purchase cost + \$1 variable cost + \$1 that the transportation division gets to keep). In effect, this approach results in a budgeted variable-cost-plus transfer price. The "plus" indicates the setting of a transfer price above variable cost.

To decide on the \$1 and \$4 allocations of the \$5 incremental benefit to the company's total operating income per barrel, the divisions must share information about their variable costs. In effect, each division does not operate (at least for this transaction) in a totally decentralized manner. Furthermore, each division has an incentive to overstate its variable costs to receive a more-favorable transfer price. In the preceding example, suppose the transportation division claims it costs \$2 per barrel to ship crude oil from Gulfmex to Houston. This increased cost raises the variable cost-based minimum price to \$79 + \$2 = \$81 per barrel; the maximum price remains \$85. Of the \$4 difference between the minimum and maximum, the transportation division now gets to keep (\$200 ÷ (\$200 + \$400)) × \$4.00 = \$1.33, resulting in a higher transfer price of \$82.33. The refining division similarly benefits from asserting that its variable cost to refine 100 barrels of crude oil is greater than \$400. As a consequence, proration methods either require a high degree of trust and exchange of information among divisions or include provisions for objective audits of cost information in order to be successful.

Negotiated Pricing

Negotiated pricing is the most common hybrid method. Under this approach, top managers do not administer a specific split of the eventual profits across the transacting divisions. Rather, the eventual transfer price results from a bargaining process between the selling and buying subunits. In Horizon Petroleum's case, for example, the transportation division and the refining division would be free to negotiate a price that is mutually acceptable to both.

Recall that the minimum and maximum feasible transfer prices are \$80 and \$85, respectively, per barrel of crude oil. Where between \$80 and \$85 will the transfer price per barrel be set? Under a negotiated transfer price, the answer depends on several things: the bargaining strengths of the two divisions; information the transportation division has about the price minus the incremental marketing costs of supplying crude oil to outside refineries; and the information the refining division has about its other available sources of crude oil. The negotiations become particularly sensitive because Horizon Petroleum can now evaluate each division's performance on the basis of its operating income. The price negotiated by the two divisions will, in general, have no specific relationship to either costs or the market price. But the cost and price information is often the starting point in the negotiation process.

Consider the following situation: Suppose the refining division receives an order to supply specially processed gasoline. The incremental cost to purchase and supply crude oil is still \$80 per barrel. However, suppose the refining division will profit from this order only if the transportation division can supply crude oil at a price not exceeding \$82 per barrel.[5] In this case, the transfer price that would benefit both divisions must be greater than \$80 but less than \$82. Negotiations would allow the two divisions to achieve an acceptable transfer price. By contrast, a rule-based transfer price, such as a market-based price of \$85 or a 105% of full-cost-based price of \$87.15, would result in Horizon passing up a profitable opportunity.

A negotiated transfer price strongly preserves the autonomy of divisions, and the division managers are motivated to put forth effort to increase the operating income of their respective divisions. Surveys have found that approximately 15–20% of firms set transfer

[5] For example, suppose a barrel of specially processed gasoline could be sold for \$200 but also required a higher variable cost of refining of \$36 per barrel. In this setting, the incremental contribution to the refining division is \$164 per barrel of gasoline, which implies that it will pay at most \$82 for a barrel of crude oil (because two barrels of crude are required for one barrel of gasoline).

prices based on negotiation. Firms that do not use negotiated prices believe the time and energy spent by managers haggling over transfer prices make the method too costly.

Dual Pricing

There is seldom a single transfer price that simultaneously meets all the criteria we have discussed (achieving goal congruence, motivating managerial effort, evaluating the performance of subunits, and preserving their autonomy). As a result, some companies choose **dual pricing,** which uses two separate transfer-pricing methods to price each transfer from one subunit to another. An example of dual pricing arises when the selling division receives a full-cost-based price and the buying division pays the market price for the internally transferred products. Assume Horizon Petroleum purchases crude oil from Gulfmex in Matamoros at $79 per barrel. One way to record the journal entry for the transfer between the transportation division and the refining division is as follows:

1. Debit the refining division (the buying division) with the market-based transfer price of $85 per barrel of crude oil.
2. Credit the transportation division (the selling division) with the 105%-of-full-cost transfer price of $87.15 per barrel of crude oil.
3. Debit a corporate cost account for the $2.15 ($87.15 − $85) per barrel difference between the two transfer prices.

The dual-pricing system promotes goal congruence because it makes the refining division no worse off if it purchases the crude oil from the transportation division rather than from the external supplier at $85 per barrel. The transportation division receives a corporate subsidy. As a result, the operating income for Horizon Petroleum as a whole under dual pricing is less than the sum of the operating incomes of the divisions.

Decision Point

Within a range of feasible transfer prices, what are alternative ways for firms to arrive at the eventual hybrid price?

Dual pricing is not widely used. One concern with dual pricing is that it leads to disputes about which price should be used when computing the taxable income of subunits located in different tax jurisdictions, such as in our example, where the transportation division is taxed in Mexico while the refining division is taxed in the United States. A second concern is that dual pricing insulates managers from the realities of the marketplace because costs, not market prices, affect the revenues of the supplying division.

Learning Objective 8

Apply a general guideline for determining a minimum transfer price

...incremental cost plus opportunity cost of supplying division

A General Guideline for Transfer-Pricing Situations

Exhibit 22-3 summarizes the properties of market-based, cost-based, and negotiated transfer-pricing methods using the criteria we have described in this chapter. As the exhibit indicates, it is difficult for a transfer-pricing method to meet all the criteria. The transfer price a company will eventually choose depends on the economic circumstances and the decision being made. Surveys by Ernst & Young as well as those sponsored by the Institute of Management Accountants indicate that the full-cost-based transfer price is generally the most frequently used method around the world, followed by market-based transfer price and negotiated transfer price.[6]

Our discussion so far highlights that, barring settings in which a perfectly competitive market exists for the intermediate product, there is generally a range of possible transfer prices that would promote goal congruence. The following formula provides a general guideline for determining the minimum price in that range:

$$\text{Minimum transfer price} = \begin{array}{c}\text{Incremental cost}\\ \text{per unit}\\ \text{incurred up}\\ \text{to the point of transfer}\end{array} + \begin{array}{c}\text{Opportunity cost}\\ \text{per unit}\\ \text{to the selling subunit}\end{array}$$

[6]See, for example, *Current Trends and Corporate Cases in Transfer Pricing* by Roger Tang with IMA Foundation for Applied Research, Institute of Management Accountants (Westport, CT: Quorum Books, 2002).

Criteria	Market-Based	Cost-Based	Negotiated
Achieves goal congruence	Yes, when markets are competitive	Often, but not always	Yes
Motivates management effort	Yes	Yes, when based on budgeted costs; less incentive to control costs if transfers are based on actual costs	Yes
Useful for evaluating subunit performance	Yes, when markets are competitive	Difficult unless transfer price exceeds full cost and even then is somewhat arbitrary	Yes, but transfer prices are affected by bargaining strengths of the buying and selling divisions
Preserves subunit autonomy	Yes, when markets are competitive	No, because it is rule-based	Yes, because it is based on negotiations between subunits
Other factors	Market may not exist, or markets may be imperfect or in distress	Useful for determining full cost of products and services; easy to implement	Bargaining and negotiations take time and may need to be reviewed repeatedly as conditions change

Exhibit 22-3

Comparison of Different Transfer-Pricing Methods

The incremental cost in the formula is the additional cost of producing and transferring the product or service. The opportunity cost is the maximum contribution margin forgone by the selling subunit if the product or service is transferred internally. For example, if the selling subunit is operating at capacity, the opportunity cost of transferring a unit internally rather than selling it externally is equal to the market price minus the variable cost. That's because by transferring a unit internally, the subunit forgoes the contribution margin it could have obtained by selling the unit in the external market. We distinguish the incremental cost from the opportunity cost because financial accounting systems record incremental cost but do not record opportunity cost. The guideline measures a *minimum* transfer price because it represents the selling unit's cost of transferring the product. We illustrate the general guideline in some specific situations using data from Horizon Petroleum.

1. **A perfectly competitive market for the intermediate product exists, and the selling division has no unused capacity.** If the market for crude oil in Houston is perfectly competitive, the transportation division can sell all the crude oil it transports to the external market at \$85 per barrel, and it will have no unused capacity. The transportation division's incremental cost (as shown in Exhibit 22-1, page 848) is \$73 per barrel (the purchase cost of \$72 per barrel plus the variable transportation cost of \$1 per barrel) for oil purchased under the long-term contract or \$80 per barrel (the purchase cost of \$79 plus the variable transportation cost of \$1) for oil purchased at current market prices from Gulfmex. The transportation division's opportunity cost per barrel of transferring the oil internally is the contribution margin per barrel forgone by not selling the crude oil in the external market: \$12 for oil purchased under the long-term contract (the market price, \$85, minus the variable cost, \$73) and \$5 for oil purchased from Gulfmex (the market price, \$85, minus the variable cost, \$80). In either case,

$$\frac{\text{Minimum transfer price}}{\text{per barrel}} = \frac{\text{Incremental cost}}{\text{per barrel}} + \frac{\text{Opportunity cost}}{\text{per barrel}}$$

$$= \$73 + \$12 = \$85$$

or

$$= \$80 + \$5 = \$85$$

2. **An intermediate market exists that is not perfectly competitive, and the selling division has unused capacity.** In markets that are not perfectly competitive, companies can increase their capacity utilization only by decreasing their prices. Unused capacity exists because decreasing prices is often not worthwhile—it decreases operating income.

   If the transportation division at Horizon Petroleum has unused capacity, its opportunity cost of transferring the oil internally is zero because the division does not forgo any external sales or contribution margin from internal transfers. In this case,

$$\text{Minimum transfer price per barrel} = \text{Incremental cost per barrel} = \text{\$73 per barrel for oil purchased under the long-term contract or \$80 per barrel for oil purchased from Gulfmax in Matamoros}$$

   In general, when markets are not perfectly competitive, the impact of prices on demand (and operating income) complicates the measurement of opportunity costs. The transfer price depends on constantly changing levels of supply and demand. There is not just one transfer price. Rather, the transfer prices for various quantities supplied and demanded depend on the incremental costs and opportunity costs of the units transferred.

Decision Point

What is the general guideline for determining a minimum transfer price?

3. **No market exists for the intermediate product.** This situation would occur if the crude oil transported by the transportation division could be used only by the Houston refinery (due to, say, its high tar content) and would not be wanted by external parties. Here the opportunity cost of supplying crude oil internally is zero because it can't be sold externally, so no contribution margin is forgone. For the transportation division, the minimum transfer price under the general guideline is the incremental cost per barrel (either \$73 or \$80). As in the previous case, any transfer price between the incremental cost and \$85 will achieve goal congruence.

Learning Objective 9

Incorporate income tax considerations in multinational transfer pricing

...set transfer prices to minimize tax payments to the extent permitted by tax authorities

How Multinationals Use Transfer Pricing to Minimize their Taxes

Transfer pricing is an important accounting priority for managers around the world. A 2010 Ernst & Young survey of multinational enterprises in 25 countries found that 74% of parent firms and 76% of subsidiary respondents believed that transfer pricing was "absolutely critical" or "very important" to their organizations. The reason is that parent companies can save large sums of money in taxes depending on the transfer pricing methods they use. Consider Google, which earned £6 billion in advertising revenues in the United Kingdom from 2004 to 2010. The UK's corporate income tax rate is 28%, yet Google UK paid just £8 million in taxes during that time. How is that possible? To start with, Google has licensed the offshore rights to its intellectual property to Google Ireland Holdings, an Irish company that is managed from Bermuda, thereby exempting it from Irish taxes. When Google earns revenue from a customer in Britain, that amount is credited to a different Irish entity, Google Ireland Limited, located in Dublin. About 88% of Google's non-U.S. revenues flow through this entity. However, it records almost no pretax profit because it pays a royalty fee to the Bermuda/Irish company for the use of Google's intellectual property. Rather than pay the amount directly, which would trigger an Irish withholding tax, the money is routed through Google Netherlands Holdings BV (Amsterdam).[7] These techniques are estimated to have saved Google about \$1 billion a year. Facebook, Microsoft, and Forest Laboratories, a pharmaceutical company

[7] Netherlands Holdings BV has no employees—it is simply a legal entity through which money is routed. This arrangement, which involves transfers between two Irish entities via the Netherlands, is referred to by tax planners as "Double Irish" or "Dutch Sandwich." For a detailed description of Apple's use of this structure, see http://www.nytimes.com/interactive/2012/04/28/business/Double-Irish-With-A-Dutch-Sandwich.html?ref=business.

headquartered in New York City, have used similar transfer-pricing practices. Such profit-shifting arrangements are estimated to save companies as much as $60 billion annually.[8]

Transfer prices affect not just income taxes, but also payroll taxes, customs duties, tariffs, sales taxes, value-added taxes, environment-related taxes, and other government levies. Our aim here is to highlight tax factors, and in particular income taxes, as important considerations for managers when determining transfer prices.

Consider the Horizon Petroleum data in Exhibit 22-2 (page 849). Assume that the transportation division based in Mexico pays a Mexican tax rate of 30% on its operating income and that the refining division based in the United States pays a U.S. income tax rate of 20% on its operating income. Horizon Petroleum would minimize its total income tax payments with the 105%-of-full-cost transfer-pricing method, as shown in the following table, because this method minimizes the income reported in Mexico, where income is taxed at a higher rate than in the United States.

	Operating Income for 100 Barrels of Crude Oil			Income Tax on 100 Barrels of Crude Oil		
Transfer-Pricing Method	Transportation Division (Mexico) (1)	Refining Division (United States) (2)	Total (3) = (1) + (2)	Transportation Division (Mexico) (4) = 0.30 × (1)	Refining Division (United States) (5) = 0.20 × (2)	Total (6) = (4) + (5)
Market price	$900	$300	$1,200	$270	$ 60	$330
105% of full costs	380	820	1,200	114	164	278
Hybrid price	600	600	1,200	180	120	300

Minimizing a firm's income taxes can sometimes conflict with the other objectives the firm's top managers hope to achieve via transfer pricing. Suppose the market for crude oil in Houston is perfectly competitive. In this case, the market-based transfer price achieves goal congruence, provides incentives for management effort, and helps Horizon to evaluate the economic profitability of the transportation division. But it is costly from the perspective of income taxes. To minimize its income taxes, Horizon would favor using 105% of the full cost for tax reporting. But the tax laws in the United States and Mexico limit this option. Mexico's tax authorities would challenge any attempt by Horizon to shift income to the refining division through an unreasonably low transfer price (see also Concepts in Action: Transfer Pricing Dispute Temporarily Stops the Flow of Fiji Water).

Section 482 of the U.S. Internal Revenue Code governs how multinationals can set transfer prices for tax purposes. Section 482 requires that transfer prices between a company and its foreign division or subsidiary, for both tangible and intangible property, equal the price that would be charged by an unrelated third party in a comparable transaction. Regulations related to Section 482 recognize that transfer prices can be market-based or cost-plus-based, where the plus represents margins on comparable transactions.[9]

Consequently, if the market for crude oil in Houston is perfectly competitive, Horizon would be required to calculate its taxes using the market price of $85 for transfers from the transportation division to the refining division. Horizon might successfully argue that the transfer price should be set below the market price because the transportation division incurs no marketing and distribution costs when selling crude oil to the refining division. For example, if marketing and distribution costs equal $2 per barrel, Horizon could set the transfer price at $83 ($85 − $2) per barrel, the selling price net of

[8] It is important to understand that U.S. companies pay no taxes to the IRS until profits are repatriated back to the United States. As a result, the incentive for top management is to keep and reinvest cash overseas rather than in the United States. According to Apple CFO Peter Oppenheimer, "We think that the current tax laws provide a considerable economic disincentive to U.S. companies that might otherwise repatriate." As of April 2013, Apple had $145 billion in cash, but chose to borrow $17 billion in order to finance a payout to shareholders. The reason—about $102 billion of Apple's cash sits overseas, and bringing that "home" would trigger close to a 35% repatriation tax. Such actions led to the recent bipartisan Senate probe that resulted in Apple CEO Tim Cook testifying to Congress on allegations that Apple had used transfer pricing and other loopholes to avoid paying U.S. taxes on $44 billion in offshore income between 2009 and 2012.

[9] Robert Feinschreiber (Ed.), *Transfer Pricing Handbook*, 3rd ed. (New York: John Wiley & Sons, 2002); W. Joey Styron, "Transfer Pricing and Tax Planning: Opportunities for US Corporations Operating Abroad," *CPA Journal Online* (November 2007).

Concepts in Action

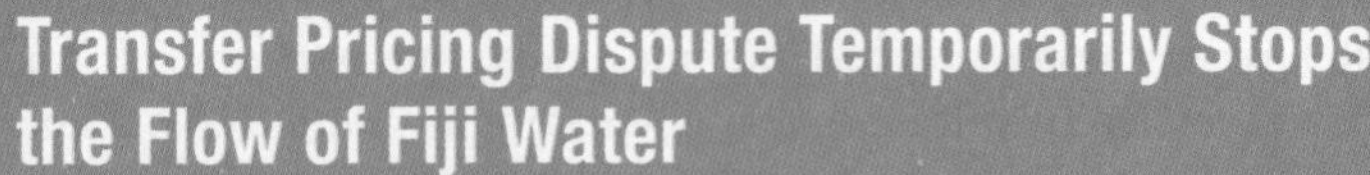

From 2008 until 2010, Fiji Water, LLC, a U.S.-based company, was engaged in a fierce transfer-pricing dispute with the government of the Fiji Islands, where its water bottling plant is located. While Fiji Water is produced in the Fiji Islands and accounts for 20% of the country's exports, all other activities in the company's value chain—importing, distributing, and retailing—occur in the 40 countries where Fiji Water is sold. Over time, the Fiji Islands government became concerned that Fiji Water was engaging in transfer-price manipulations, selling the water shipments produced in the Fiji Islands at a very low price to the company's U.S. headquarters.

As a result, the Fiji Islands Revenue and Customs Authority (FIRCA) halted Fuji Water exports in January 2008 and accused Fiji Water of transfer-price manipulations. FIRCA's chief executive, Jitoko Tikolevu, said, "The wholly U.S.-owned Fijian subsidiary sold its water exclusively to its U.S. parent at the declared rate, in Fiji, of $4 a carton. In the U.S., though, the same company then sold it for up to $50 a carton." Fiji Water immediately filed a lawsuit against FIRCA with the High Court of Fiji arguing that on a global basis it sold each carton of water for $20 to $28 and did not make a profit due to "heavy investments in assets, employees, and marketing necessary to aggressively grow a successful branded product."

The transfer-pricing dispute between FICRA and Fiji Water was ultimately resolved through taxation. While Fiji Water maintained its previous transfer price of $4 for water produced at its bottling plant in the Fiji Islands, the Fijian government implemented a new 15-cents-per-liter excise tax—up from one-third of one cent—on water extracted by Fiji Water. While the company disputed the new tax, in late 2010 the company agreed to pay the new levy. As this high-profile case demonstrates, transfer pricing formulas and taxation details remain a contentious issue for governments and countries around the globe.

Sources: Bloxham, Andy. 2011. Fiji Water accused of environmentally misleading claims. *The Telegraph*, June 20; Chapman, Paul. 2010. Fiji Water reopens Pacific bottling plant. *The Telegraph*, December 1; Matau, Robert. 2008. Fiji Water explains saga. *Fiji Times*, February 9; McMaster, James and Jan Novak. 2009. Fiji Water and corporate social responsibility—Green makeover or 'green-washing'? The University of Western Ontario Richard Ivey School of Business No. 909A08, London, Ontario: Ivey Publishing.

marketing and distribution costs. Under the U.S. Internal Revenue Code, Horizon could obtain advanced approval of the transfer-pricing arrangements from the tax authorities, called an *advanced pricing agreement* (*APA*). The APA is a binding agreement for a specified number of years. The goal of the APA program is to avoid costly transfer-pricing disputes between taxpayers and tax authorities. As of the end of 2012, the APA program had completed 1,155 APAs since inception and had pending requests for another 391 new APAs. In 2012 alone, there were a record 140 APAs executed, of which 103 were bilateral agreements with other tax treaty countries. Walmart, for example, signed the first bilateral APA between the United States and China in 2007.

The number of countries that have imposed transfer-pricing regulations approximately quadrupled from 1995 to 2007, according to a 2008 KPMG report. The last global recession pushed even more governments around the world to impose tighter trading rules and aggressively pursue tax revenues. Foreign businesses formerly enjoyed favorable treatment in China. But officials there recently issued new rules requiring multinationals to submit extensive transfer-pricing documentation. Countries such as India, Canada, Turkey, and Greece have brought greater scrutiny to bear on transfer pricing, focusing in particular on intellectual-property values, the costs of back-office functions, and losses of any type. In the United States, the Obama administration plans to shrink a "tax gap" the IRS estimates may be as high as $345 billion by restricting or closing several widely used tax loopholes. While the plan does not directly address transfer-pricing practice, the IRS has become more aggressive with enforcement. The agency has added hundreds of additional people to its international staff. In 2011, the IRS named its first director of transfer pricing and, in early 2012, raised inquiries or disputes with a variety of technology firms, including Amazon, Adobe, Juniper Networks, and Yahoo. The IRS has proposed Amazon pay a $1.5 billion tax increase related to transfer pricing for the period 2005–2012. In 2006, the agency won the largest settlement ever in a transfer-pricing dispute, getting GlaxoSmithKline, a UK-based pharmaceutical and health care company, to pay $3.4 billion to cover back taxes and interest for the period 1989–2005.

The tariffs and customs duties governments levy on imports of products into a country also affect the transfer pricing practices of multinationals. The issues here are similar to income tax considerations. Companies will have incentives to lower the transfer prices of products they are exporting into a country to reduce the tariffs and customs duties charged on those products. The restrictions some countries place on dividend- or income-related payments to parties outside their national borders also affect how firms set their transfer prices. By increasing the prices of goods or services transferred into divisions in these countries, companies can increase the cash paid out of these countries without violating dividend- or income-related restrictions.

Transfer Prices Designed for Multiple Objectives

At times, one transfer price will not satisfy all of a firm's objectives, such as minimizing its income taxes, achieving goal congruence, and motivating managers' effort. As a result, a company may choose to keep one set of accounting records for tax reporting and a second set for internal management reporting. Of course, it is costly to maintain two sets of books. Some companies, such as Case New Holland, a world leader in the agricultural and construction equipment business, oppose doing so based on the principle that statutory and internal reporting systems must reflect the same information. However, a survey by the AnswerThink Consulting Group of large companies (more than $2 billion in revenues) found that 77% of companies considered to follow "best practices" used separate reporting systems to track internal pricing information, compared with about 25% of companies outside that group.

Microsoft, for example, believes in "delinking" transfer prices and employs an internal measurement system (Microsoft Accounting Principles, or MAPs) that uses a separate set of company-designed rules and accounts.[10] A key aspect of management control at Microsoft is holding product and division managers accountable for the profitability of products and establishing appropriate sales and marketing spending levels for every product line. To establish these sales and spending levels, the firm creates a profitability statement for every product in every region and allocates R&D and administrative costs across sales divisions in ways that aren't necessarily the most tax efficient.

Even if a company does not have separated reporting systems, a firm can still informally adjust its transfer prices to satisfy the tradeoff between minimizing its taxes and incentivizing its managers. Consider a multinational firm that makes semiconductor products that it sells through its sales organization in a higher-tax country. To minimize the firm's taxes, the parent company sets a high transfer price, thereby lowering the operating income of the foreign sales organization. It would be inappropriate to penalize the country sales manager for this low income because the sales organization has no say in determining the transfer price. As an alternative, the company can evaluate the sales manager on the direct contribution (revenues minus marketing costs) incurred in the country. That is, the transfer price incurred to acquire the semiconductor products is omitted for performance-evaluation purposes. Of course, this is not a perfect solution. By ignoring the cost of acquiring the products, the sales manager has an incentive to overspend on local marketing relative to what would be optimal from the firm's perspective. If the dysfunctional effects are suitably large, corporate managers must then step in, evaluate

Decision Point

How do income tax considerations affect transfer pricing in multinationals?

[10] For further details, see I. Springsteel, "Separate but Unequal," *CFO Magazine* (August 1999).

the situation, and dictate specific operational decisions and goals for the manager. More generally, when a firm adopts a tax-compliant transfer pricing policy, it needs nonfinancial performance indicators (such as production yields, number of on-time deliveries, or customer response times) at lower management levels in order to better evaluate and reward performance.[11]

Problem for Self-Study

The Pillercat Corporation is a highly decentralized company. Each division manager has full authority for sourcing decisions and selling decisions. The machining division of Pillercat has been the major supplier of the 2,000 crankshafts the tractor division needs each year.

The tractor division, however, has just announced that it plans to purchase all its crankshafts in the forthcoming year from two external suppliers at $200 per crankshaft. The machining division of Pillercat recently increased its selling price for the forthcoming year to $220 per unit (from $200 per unit in the current year).

Juan Gomez, manager of the machining division, feels that the 10% price increase is justified. It results from a higher depreciation charge on some new specialized equipment used to manufacture crankshafts and an increase in labor costs. Gomez wants the president of Pillercat Corporation to force the tractor division to buy all its crankshafts from the machining division at the price of $220. The following table summarizes the key data.

	A	B
1	Number of crankshafts purchased by Tractor Division	2,000
2	External supplier's market price per crankshaft	$ 200
3	Variable cost per crankshaft in Machining Division	$ 190
4	Fixed cost per crankshaft in Machining Division	$ 20

Required

1. Compute the advantage or disadvantage in terms of annual operating income to the Pillercat Corporation as a whole if the tractor division buys crankshafts internally from the machining division under each of the following cases:
   a. The machining division has no alternative use for the facilities used to manufacture crankshafts.
   b. The machining division can use the facilities for other production operations, which will result in annual cash operating savings of $29,000.
   c. The machining division has no alternative use for its facilities, and the external supplier drops the price to $185 per crankshaft.
2. As the president of Pillercat, how would you respond to Juan Gomez's request that you force the tractor division to purchase all of its crankshafts from the machining division? Would your response differ according to the three cases described in requirement 1? Explain.

[11] Cools, M. et al., "Management Control in the Transfer Pricing Tax Compliant Multinational Enterprise," *Accounting, Organizations and Society* (August 2008) provides an illustrative case study of this issue in the context of a semiconductor product division of a multinational firm.

Solution

1. Computations for the tractor division buying crankshafts internally for one year under cases **a**, **b**, and **c** are as follows:

	A	B	C	D
1			Case	
2		a	b	c
3	Number of crankshafts purchased by Tractor Division	2,000	2,000	2,000
4	External supplier's market price per crankshaft	$ 200	$ 200	$ 185
5	Variable cost per crankshaft in Machining Division	$ 190	$ 190	$ 190
6	Opportunity costs of the Machining Division supplying crankshafts to the Tractor Division	-	$ 29,000	-
7				
8	Total purchase costs if buying from an external supplier			
9	(2,000 shafts × $200, $200, $185 per shaft)	$400,000	$400,000	$370,000
10	Incremental cost of buying from the Machining Division			
11	(2,000 shafts × $190 per shaft)	380,000	380,000	380,000
12	Total opportunity costs of the Machining Division	-	29,000	-
13	Total relevant costs	380,000	409,000	380,000
14	Annual operating income advantage (disadvantage)			
15	to Pillercat of buying from the Machining Division	$ 20,000	$ (9,000)	$ (10,000)

The general guideline that was introduced in the chapter (page 856) as a first step in setting a transfer price can be used to highlight the alternatives:

	A	B	C	D	E	F	G
1	Case	Incremental Cost per Unit Incurred to Point of Transfer	+	Opportunity Cost per Unit to the Supplying Division	=	Transfer Price	External Market Price
2	a	$190	+	$0	=	$190.00	$200
3	b	$190	+	$14.50[a]	=	$204.50	$200
4	c	$190	+	$0	=	$190.00	$185
5							
6	[a]Opportunity cost per unit = Total opportunity costs ($29,000) ÷ Number of crankshafts (2,000) = $14.50						

Comparing transfer price to external-market price, the tractor division will maximize annual operating income of Pillercat Corporation as a whole by purchasing from the machining division in case **a** and by purchasing from the external supplier in cases **b** and **c**.

2. Pillercat Corporation is a highly decentralized company. If no forced transfer were made, the tractor division would use an external supplier, a decision that would be in the best interest of the company as a whole in cases **b** and **c** of requirement 1 but not in case **a**.

   Suppose in case **a**, the machining division refuses to meet the price of $200. This decision means that the company will be $20,000 worse off in the short run. Should top management interfere and force a transfer at $200? This interference would undercut the philosophy of decentralization. Many top managers would not interfere because they would view the $20,000 as an inevitable cost of a suboptimal decision that can occur under decentralization. But how high must this cost be before the temptation to interfere would be irresistible? $30,000? $40,000?

Any top management interference with lower-level decision making weakens decentralization. Of course, Pillercat's management may occasionally interfere to prevent costly mistakes. But recurring interference and constraints would hurt Pillercat's attempts to operate as a decentralized company.

▶ Decision Points

The following question-and-answer format summarizes the chapter's learning objectives. Each decision presents a key question related to a learning objective. The guidelines are the answer to that question.

Decision	Guidelines
1. What is a management control system, and how should it be designed?	A management control system is a means of gathering and using information to aid and coordinate the planning and control decisions throughout the organization and to guide the behavior of managers and other employees. Effective management control systems (a) are closely aligned to the organization's strategy, (b) support the organizational responsibilities of individual managers, and (c) motivate managers and other employees to give effort to achieve the organization's goals.
2. What are the benefits and costs of decentralization?	The benefits of decentralization include (a) greater responsiveness to local needs, (b) gains from faster decision making, (c) greater management development and learning, and (d) sharpened focus of subunit managers. The costs of decentralization include (a) suboptimal decision making, (b) excessive focus on the subunit rather than the company as a whole, (c) increased costs of information gathering, and (d) duplication of activities.
3. What are transfer prices, and what criteria do managers use to evaluate them?	A transfer price is the price one subunit charges for a product or service supplied to another subunit of the same organization. Transfer prices seek to (a) promote goal congruence, (b) motivate management effort, (c) help evaluate subunit performance, and (d) preserve subunit autonomy (if desired).
4. What are alternative ways of calculating transfer prices?	Transfer prices can be (a) market-based, (b) cost-based, or (c) hybrid. Different transfer-pricing methods produce different revenues and costs for individual subunits and, so, different operating incomes for the subunits.
5. Under what market conditions do market-based transfer prices promote goal congruence?	In perfectly competitive markets, there is no unused capacity, and division managers can buy and sell as much of a product or service as they want at the market price. In such settings, using the market price as the transfer price motivates division managers to transact internally and to take exactly the same actions as they would if they were transacting in the external market.
6. What problems can arise when full cost plus a markup is used as the transfer price?	A transfer price based on the full cost plus a markup may lead to suboptimal decisions because it leads the buying division to regard the fixed costs and the markup of the selling division as a variable cost. The buying division may then purchase products from an external supplier and expect cost savings that will not occur.
7. Within a range of feasible transfer prices, what are alternative ways for firms to arrive at the eventual hybrid price?	When there is unused capacity, the transfer-price range lies between the minimum price at which the selling division is willing to sell (its variable cost per unit) and the maximum price the buying division is willing to pay (the lower of its contribution or price at which the product is available from external suppliers). Methods for arriving at a price in this range include proration (such as splitting the difference equally or on the basis of relative variable costs), negotiation between divisions, and dual pricing.

Decision	Guidelines
8. What is the general guideline for determining a minimum transfer price?	The general guideline states that the minimum transfer price equals the incremental cost per unit incurred up to the point of transfer plus the opportunity cost per unit to the selling division.
9. How do income tax considerations affect transfer pricing in multinationals?	A firm can use transfer pricing to lower its income tax payments by reporting more income in low-tax-rate countries and less income in high-tax-rate countries. However, the tax regulations of different countries restrict the transfer prices that companies can use.

Terms to Learn

This chapter and the Glossary at the end of the book contain definitions of the following important terms:

autonomy **(p. 843)**
decentralization **(p. 843)**
dual pricing **(p. 856)**
dysfunctional decision making **(p. 844)**
effort **(p. 842)**
goal congruence **(p. 842)**
incongruent decision making **(p. 844)**
intermediate product **(p. 846)**
management control system **(p. 841)**
motivation **(p. 842)**
perfectly competitive market **(p. 850)**
suboptimal decision making **(p. 844)**
transfer price **(p. 846)**

Assignment Material

Questions

MyAccountingLab

22-1 What is a management control system?

22-2 Describe three criteria you would use to evaluate whether a management control system is effective.

22-3 What is the relationship among motivation, goal congruence, and effort?

22-4 Name three benefits and two costs of decentralization.

22-5 "Organizations typically adopt a consistent decentralization or centralization philosophy across all their business functions." Do you agree? Explain.

22-6 "Transfer pricing is confined to profit centers." Do you agree? Explain.

22-7 What are the three methods for determining transfer prices?

22-8 What properties should transfer-pricing systems have?

22-9 "All transfer-pricing methods give the same division operating income." Do you agree? Explain.

22-10 Under what conditions is a market-based transfer price optimal?

22-11 What is one potential limitation of full-cost-based transfer prices?

22-12 Give two reasons why the dual-pricing system of transfer pricing is not widely used.

22-13 "Cost and price information play no role in negotiated transfer prices." Do you agree? Explain.

22-14 "Under the general guideline for transfer pricing, the minimum transfer price will vary depending on whether the supplying division has unused capacity or not." Do you agree? Explain.

22-15 How should managers consider income tax issues when choosing a transfer-pricing method?

Exercises

MyAccountingLab

22-16 Evaluating management control systems, balanced scorecard. Adventure Parks Inc. (API) operates 10 theme parks throughout the United States. The company's slogan is "Name Your Adventure," and its mission is to offer an exciting theme park experience to visitors of all ages. API's corporate strategy supports this mission by stressing the importance of sparkling clean surroundings, efficient crowd management, and, above all, cheerful employees. Of course, improved shareholder value drives this strategy.

Required

1. Assume that API uses a balanced scorecard approach (see Chapter 12) to formulating its management control system. List three measures that API might use to evaluate each of the four balanced scorecard perspectives: financial perspective, customer perspective, internal-business-process perspective, and learning-and-growth perspective.

2. How would the management controls related to financial and customer perspectives at API differ between the following three managers: a souvenir shop manager, a park general manager, and the corporation's CEO?

22-17 Cost centers, profit centers, decentralization, transfer prices. Fenster Corporation manufactures windows with wood and metal frames. Fenster has three departments: glass, wood, and metal. The glass department makes the window glass and sends it to either the wood or metal department where the glass is framed. The window is then sold. Upper management sets the production schedules for the three departments and evaluates them on output quantity, cost variances, and product quality.

Required

1. Are the three departments cost centers, revenue centers, or profit centers?
2. Are the three departments centralized or decentralized?
3. Can a centralized department be a profit center? Why or why not?
4. Suppose the upper management of Fenster Corporation decides to let the three departments set their own production schedules, buy and sell products in the external market, and have the wood and metal departments negotiate with the glass department for the glass panes using a transfer price.
   a. Will this change your answers to requirements 1 and 2?
   b. How would you recommend upper management evaluate the three departments if this change is made?

22-18 Benefits and costs of decentralization. Jackson Markets, a chain of traditional supermarkets, is interested in gaining access to the organic and health food retail market by acquiring a regional company in that sector. Jackson intends to operate the newly acquired stores independently from its supermarkets.

One of the prospects is Health Source, a chain of 20 stores in the mid-Atlantic region. Buying for all 20 stores is done by the company's central office. Store managers must follow strict guidelines for all aspects of store management in an attempt to maintain consistency among stores. Store managers are evaluated on the basis of achieving profit goals developed by the central office.

The other prospect is Harvest Moon, a chain of 30 stores in the Northeast. Harvest Moon managers are given significant flexibility in product offerings, allowing them to negotiate purchases with local organic farmers. Store managers are rewarded for exceeding self-developed return-on-investment goals with company stock options. Some managers have become significant shareholders in the company and have even decided on their own to open additional store locations to improve market penetration. However, the increased autonomy has led to competition and price cutting among Harvest Moon stores within the same geographic market, resulting in lower margins.

Required

1. Would you describe Health Source as having a centralized or a decentralized structure? Explain.
2. Would you describe Harvest Moon as having a centralized or a decentralized structure? Discuss some of the benefits and costs of that type of structure.
3. Would stores in each chain be considered cost centers, revenue centers, profit centers, or investment centers? How does that tie into the evaluation of store managers?
4. Assume that Jackson chooses to acquire Harvest Moon. What steps can Jackson take to improve goal congruence between store managers and the larger company?

22-19 Transfer-pricing methods, goal congruence. British Columbia Lumber has a raw lumber division and a finished lumber division. The variable costs are as follows:

- Raw lumber division: $100 per 100 board-feet of raw lumber
- Finished lumber division: $125 per 100 board-feet of finished lumber

Assume that there is no board-feet loss in processing raw lumber into finished lumber. Raw lumber can be sold at $200 per 100 board-feet. Finished lumber can be sold at $275 per 100 board-feet.

Required

1. Should British Columbia Lumber process raw lumber into its finished form? Show your calculations.
2. Assume that internal transfers are made at 110% of variable cost. Will each division maximize its division operating-income contribution by adopting the action that is in the best interest of British Columbia Lumber as a whole? Explain.
3. Assume that internal transfers are made at market prices. Will each division maximize its division operating-income contribution by adopting the action that is in the best interest of British Columbia Lumber as a whole? Explain.

22-20 Multinational transfer pricing, effect of alternative transfer-pricing methods, global income tax minimization. Tech Friendly Computer, Inc., with headquarters in San Francisco, manufactures and sells a desktop computer. Tech Friendly has three divisions, each of which is located in a different country:

a. China division—manufactures memory devices and keyboards

b. South Korea division—assembles desktop computers using locally manufactured parts, along with memory devices and keyboards from the China division

c. U.S. division—packages and distributes desktop computers

Each division is run as a profit center. The costs for the work done in each division for a single desktop computer are as follows:

China division:	Variable cost = 900 yuan
	Fixed cost = 1,980 yuan
South Korea division:	Variable cost = 350,000 won
	Fixed cost = 470,000 won
U.S. division:	Variable cost = $125
	Fixed cost = $325

- Chinese income tax rate on the China division's operating income: 40%
- South Korean income tax rate on the South Korea division's operating income: 20%
- U.S. income tax rate on the U.S. division's operating income: 30%

Each desktop computer is sold to retail outlets in the United States for $3,800. Assume that the current foreign exchange rates are as follows:

9 yuan = $1 U.S.
1,000 won = $1 U.S.

Both the China and the South Korea divisions sell part of their production under a private label. The China division sells the comparable memory/keyboard package used in each Tech Friendly desktop computer to a Chinese manufacturer for 4,500 yuan. The South Korea division sells the comparable desktop computer to a South Korean distributor for 1,340,000 won.

Required

1. Calculate the after-tax operating income per unit earned by each division under the following transfer-pricing methods: (a) market price, (b) 200% of full cost, and (c) 350% of variable cost. (Income taxes are not included in the computation of the cost-based transfer prices.)
2. Which transfer-pricing method(s) will maximize the after-tax operating income per unit of Tech Friendly Computer?

22-21 Effect of alternative transfer-pricing methods on division operating income. (CMA, adapted) Ajax Corporation has two divisions. The mining division makes toldine, which is then transferred to the metals division. The toldine is further processed by the metals division and is sold to customers at a price of $150 per unit. The mining division is currently required by Ajax to transfer its total yearly output of 200,000 units of toldine to the metals division at 110% of full manufacturing cost. Unlimited quantities of toldine can be purchased and sold on the outside market at $90 per unit.

The following table gives the manufacturing cost per unit in the mining and metals divisions for 2014:

	Mining Division	Metals Division
Direct material cost	$12	$ 6
Direct manufacturing labor cost	16	20
Manufacturing overhead cost	32[a]	25[b]
Total manufacturing cost per unit	$60	$51

[a]Manufacturing overhead costs in the mining division are 25% fixed and 75% variable.
[b]Manufacturing overhead costs in the metals division are 60% fixed and 40% variable.

Required

1. Calculate the operating incomes for the mining and metals divisions for the 200,000 units of toldine transferred under the following transfer-pricing methods: (a) market price and (b) 110% of full manufacturing cost.
2. Suppose Ajax rewards each division manager with a bonus, calculated as 1% of division operating income (if positive). What is the amount of bonus that will be paid to each division manager under the transfer-pricing methods in requirement 1? Which transfer-pricing method will each division manager prefer to use?
3. What arguments would Brian Jones, manager of the mining division, make to support the transfer-pricing method that he prefers?

22-22 Transfer pricing, general guideline, goal congruence. (CMA, adapted). Quest Motors, Inc., operates as a decentralized multidivision company. The Vivo division of Quest Motors purchases most of its airbags from the airbag division. The airbag division's incremental cost for manufacturing the airbags is $90 per unit. The airbag division is currently working at 80% of capacity. The current market price of the airbags is $125 per unit.

Required

1. Using the general guideline presented in the chapter, what is the minimum price at which the airbag division would sell airbags to the Vivo division?
2. Suppose that Quest Motors requires that whenever divisions with unused capacity sell products internally, they must do so at the incremental cost. Evaluate this transfer-pricing policy using the criteria of goal congruence, evaluating division performance, motivating management effort, and preserving division autonomy.
3. If the two divisions were to negotiate a transfer price, what is the range of possible transfer prices? Evaluate this negotiated transfer-pricing policy using the criteria of goal congruence, evaluating division performance, motivating management effort, and preserving division autonomy.
4. Instead of allowing negotiation, suppose that Quest specifies a hybrid transfer price that "splits the difference" between the minimum and maximum prices from the divisions' standpoint. What would be the resulting transfer price for airbags?

22-23 Multinational transfer pricing, global tax minimization. The Questron Company manufactures telecommunications equipment at its plant in Scranton, Pennsylvania. The company has marketing divisions throughout the world. A Questron marketing division in Hamburg, Germany, imports 100,000 broadband routers from the United States. The following information is available:

U.S. income tax rate on the U.S. division's operating income	35%
German income tax rate on the German division's operating income	40%
German import duty	15%
Variable manufacturing cost per router	$275
Full manufacturing cost per router	$400
Selling price (net of marketing and distribution costs) in Germany	$575

Suppose the United States and German tax authorities only allow transfer prices that are between the full manufacturing cost per unit of $400 and a market price of $475, based on comparable imports into Germany. The German import duty is charged on the price at which the product is transferred into Germany. Any import duty paid to the German authorities is a deductible expense for calculating German income taxes.

Required

1. Calculate the after-tax operating income earned by the United States and German divisions from transferring 100,000 broadband routers (a) at full manufacturing cost per unit and (b) at market price of comparable imports. (Income taxes are not included in the computation of the cost-based transfer prices.)
2. Which transfer price should the Questron Company select to minimize the total of company import duties and income taxes? Remember that the transfer price must be between the full manufacturing cost per unit of $400 and the market price of $475 of comparable imports into Germany. Explain your reasoning.

22-24 Multinational transfer pricing, goal congruence (continuation of 22-23). Suppose that the U.S. division could sell as many broadband routers as it makes at $450 per unit in the U.S. market, net of all marketing and distribution costs.

Required

1. From the viewpoint of the Questron Company as a whole, would after-tax operating income be maximized if it sold the 100,000 routers in the United States or in Germany? Show your computations.
2. Suppose division managers act autonomously to maximize their division's after-tax operating income. Will the transfer price calculated in requirement 2 in Exercise 22-23 result in the U.S. division manager taking the actions determined to be optimal in requirement 1 of this exercise? Explain.
3. What is the minimum transfer price that the U.S. division manager would agree to? Does this transfer price result in the Questron Company as a whole paying more import duty and taxes than the answer to requirement 2 in Exercise 22-23? If so, by how much?

22-25 Transfer-pricing dispute. The Kelly-Elias Corporation, manufacturer of tractors and other heavy farm equipment, is organized along decentralized product lines, with each manufacturing division operating as a separate profit center. Each division manager has been delegated full authority on all decisions involving the sale of that division's output both to outsiders and to other divisions of Kelly-Elias. Division C has in the past always purchased its requirement of a particular tractor-engine component from division A.

However, when informed that division A is increasing its selling price to $135, division C's manager decides to purchase the engine component from external suppliers.

Division C can purchase the component for $115 per unit in the open market. Division A insists that, because of the recent installation of some highly specialized equipment and the resulting high depreciation charges, it will not be able to earn an adequate return on its investment unless it raises its price. Division A's manager appeals to top management of Kelly-Elias for support in the dispute with division C and supplies the following operating data:

C's annual purchases of the tractor-engine component	1,900 units
A's variable cost per unit of the tractor-engine component	$ 105
A's fixed cost per unit of the tractor-engine component	$ 25

Required

1. Assume that there are no alternative uses for internal facilities of division A. Determine whether the company as a whole will benefit if division C purchases the component from external suppliers for $115 per unit. What should the transfer price for the component be set at so that division managers acting in their own divisions' best interests take actions that are also in the best interest of the company as a whole?
2. Assume that internal facilities of division A would not otherwise be idle. By not producing the 1,900 units for division C, division A's equipment and other facilities would be used for other production operations that would result in annual cash-operating savings of $22,800. Should division C purchase from external suppliers? Show your computations.
3. Assume that there are no alternative uses for division A's internal facilities and that the price from outsiders drops $15. Should division C purchase from external suppliers? What should the transfer price for the component be set at so that division managers acting in their own divisions' best interests take actions that are also in the best interest of the company as a whole?

22-26 Transfer-pricing problem (continuation of 22-25). Refer to Exercise 22-25. Assume that division A can sell the 1,900 units to other customers at $137 per unit, with variable marketing cost of $2 per unit.

Required

Determine whether Kelly-Elias will benefit if division C purchases the 1,900 units from external suppliers at $115 per unit. Show your computations.

Problems

MyAccountingLab

22-27 General guideline, transfer pricing. The Slate Company manufactures and sells television sets. Its assembly division (AD) buys television screens from the screen division (SD) and assembles the TV sets. The SD, which is operating at capacity, incurs an incremental manufacturing cost of $65 per screen. The SD can sell all its output to the outside market at a price of $100 per screen, after incurring a variable marketing and distribution cost of $8 per screen. If the AD purchases screens from outside suppliers at a price of $100 per screen, it will incur a variable purchasing cost of $7 per screen. Slate's division managers can act autonomously to maximize their own division's operating income.

Required

1. What is the minimum transfer price at which the SD manager would be willing to sell screens to the AD?
2. What is the maximum transfer price at which the AD manager would be willing to purchase screens from the SD?
3. Now suppose that the SD can sell only 70% of its output capacity of 20,000 screens per month on the open market. Capacity cannot be reduced in the short run. The AD can assemble and sell more than 20,000 TV sets per month.
   a. What is the minimum transfer price at which the SD manager would be willing to sell screens to the AD?
   b. From the point of view of Slate's management, how much of the SD output should be transferred to the AD?
   c. If Slate mandates the SD and AD managers to "split the difference" on the minimum and maximum transfer prices they would be willing to negotiate over, what would be the resulting transfer price? Does this price achieve the outcome desired in requirement 3b?

22-28 Pertinent transfer price, perfect and imperfect markets. Wheely, Inc., has two divisions, A and B, that manufacture expensive bicycles. Division A produces the bicycle frame, and division B assembles the rest of the bicycle onto the frame. There is a market for both the subassembly and the final product. Each division has been designated as a profit center. The transfer price for the subassembly has been set at the long-run average market price. The following data are available for each division:

Selling price for final product	$360
Long-run average selling price for intermediate product	275
Incremental cost per unit for completion in division B	120
Incremental cost per unit in division A	90

The manager of division B has made the following calculation:

Selling price for final product		$360
Transferred-in cost per unit (market)	$275	
Incremental cost per unit for completion	120	395
Contribution (loss) on product		$ (35)

Required

1. Should transfers be made to division B if there is no unused capacity in division A? Is the market price the correct transfer price? Show your computations.
2. Assume that division A's maximum capacity for this product is 1,200 units per month and sales to the intermediate market are now 900 units. Should 300 units be transferred to division B? At what transfer price? Assume that for a variety of reasons, division A will maintain the $275 selling price indefinitely. That is, division A is not considering lowering the price to outsiders even if idle capacity exists.
3. Suppose division A quoted a transfer price of $240 for up to 300 units. What would be the contribution to the company as a whole if a transfer were made? As manager of division B, would you be inclined to buy at $240? Explain.
4. Suppose the manager of division A has the option of (a) cutting the external price to $270, with the certainty that sales will rise to 1,200 units, or (b) maintaining the external price of $275 for the 900 units and transferring the 300 units to division B at a price that would produce the same operating income for division A. What transfer price would produce the same operating income for division A? Is that price consistent with that recommended by the general guideline in the chapter so that the resulting decision would be desirable for the company as a whole?

22-29 Effect of alternative transfer-pricing methods on division operating income. Cranergy Products is a cranberry cooperative that operates two divisions, a harvesting division and a processing division. Currently, all of harvesting's output is converted into cranberry juice by the processing division, and the juice is sold to large beverage companies that produce cranberry juice blends. The processing division has a yield of 500 gallons of juice per 1,000 pounds of cranberries. Cost and market price data for the two divisions are as follows:

	A	B	C	D	E
1	**Harvesting Division**			**Processing Division**	
2	Variable cost per pound of cranberries	$0.14		Variable processing cost per gallon of juice produced	$0.32
3	Fixed cost per pound of cranberries	$0.26		Fixed cost per gallon of juice produced	$0.50
4	Selling price per pound of cranberries in outside market	$0.58		Selling price per gallon of juice	$2.15

Required

1. Compute Cranergy's operating income from harvesting 420,000 pounds of cranberries during June 2014 and processing them into juice.
2. Cranergy rewards its division managers with a bonus equal to 3% of operating income. Compute the bonus earned by each division manager in June 2014 for each of the following transfer pricing methods:
   a. 150% of full cost
   b. Market price
3. Which transfer-pricing method will each division manager prefer? How might Cranergy resolve any conflicts that may arise on the issue of transfer pricing?

22-30 Goal-congruence problems with cost-plus transfer-pricing methods, dual-pricing system (continuation of 22-29). Assume that Pat Borges, CEO of Cranergy, had mandated a transfer price equal to 150% of full cost. Now he decides to decentralize some management decisions and sends around a memo that states the following: "Effective immediately, each division of Cranergy is free to make its own decisions regarding the purchase of direct materials and the sale of finished products."

Required

1. Give an example of a goal-congruence problem that will arise if Cranergy continues to use a transfer price of 150% of full cost and Borges's decentralization policy is adopted.
2. Borges feels that a dual transfer-pricing policy will improve goal congruence. He suggests that transfers out of the harvesting division be made at 150% of full cost and transfers into the processing division be made at market price. Compute the operating income of each division under this dual transfer-pricing method when 420,000 pounds of cranberries are harvested during June 2014 and processed into juice.
3. Why is the sum of the division operating incomes computed in requirement 2 different from Cranergy's operating income from harvesting and processing 420,000 pounds of cranberries?
4. Suggest two problems that may arise if Cranergy implements the dual transfer prices described in requirement 2.

22-31 Multinational transfer pricing, global tax minimization. Supergrow, Inc., based in Des Moines, Iowa, sells high-end fertilizers. Supergrow has two divisions:

- North Italy mining division, which mines potash in northern Italy
- U.S. processing division, which uses potash in manufacturing top-grade fertilizer

The processing division's yield is 50%: It takes 2 tons of raw potash to produce 1 ton of top-grade fertilizer. Although all of the mining division's output of 12,000 tons of potash is sent for processing in the United States, there is also an active market for potash in Italy. The foreign exchange rate is 0.80 Euro = $1 U.S. The following information is known about the two divisions:

	A	B	C	D	F	G
1	**North Italy Mining Division**					
2	Variable cost per ton of raw potash				72	EURO
3	Fixed cost per ton of raw potash				112	EURO
4	Market price per ton of raw potash				296	EURO
5	Tax rate				30%	
6						
7	**U.S. Processing Division**					
8	Variable cost per ton of fertilizer				48	U.S. dollars
9	Fixed cost per ton of fertilizer				120	U.S. dollars
10	Market price per ton of fertilizer				1,150	U.S. dollars
11	Tax rate				35%	

Required

1. Compute the annual pretax operating income, in U.S. dollars, of each division under the following transfer-pricing methods: (a) 150% of full cost and (b) market price.
2. Compute the after-tax operating income, in U.S. dollars, for each division under the transfer-pricing methods in requirement 1. (Income taxes are not included in the computation of cost-based transfer price, and Supergrow does not pay U.S. income tax on income already taxed in Italy.)
3. If the two division managers are compensated based on after-tax division operating income, which transfer-pricing method will each prefer? Which transfer-pricing method will maximize the total after-tax operating income of Supergrow?
4. In addition to tax minimization, what other factors might Supergrow consider in choosing a transfer-pricing method?

22-32 Transfer pricing, external market, goal congruence. Baldenius Corp. produces and sells high-quality scissors made of stainless steel. The firm consists of two divisions, UP and DOWN. The UP division manufactures 30,000 pairs of scissors per year. It incurs variable manufacturing costs of $9 per unit and total annual fixed manufacturing costs of $60,000. The UP division sells 10,000 units externally at a price of $16 each, mostly to office supplies stores. It transfers the remaining 20,000 units internally to the DOWN division, which modifies the units, adds a titanium plasma coating, and sells them for use by salon professionals in the United States.

Baldenius Corp. has adopted a market-based transfer pricing policy. For each pair of scissors it receives from the UP division, the DOWN division pays the weighted-average external price the UP division charges its customers outside the company. The current transfer price is accordingly set at $16.

Kathleen Bono, the manager of the UP division, receives an offer from Jean-Georges, an international hair salon supplier. Jean-Georges offers to buy 4,000 pairs of scissors at a price of $12.50 each, knowing that the entire scissors industry (including Baldenius Corp.) has excess capacity at this time. The variable manufacturing cost to UP for the units Jean-Georges is requesting is $9, and there are no additional costs associated with this offer. Accepting Jean-Georges' offer would not affect the current price of $16 charged to existing external customers.

Required

1. Calculate the UP division's current annual level of profit (without the new order).
2. Compute the change in the UP division's profit if it accepts Jean-Georges' offer. Will Kathleen Bono accept this offer if her aim is to maximize the UP division's profit?
3. Would the top management of Baldenius Corp. want the UP division to accept the offer? Compute the change in firmwide profit associated with Jean-Georges' offer.
4. Baldenius Corp. is considering changing its policy. Henceforth, the transfer price will be set at a fixed percentage discount from the weighted-average price charged by UP on external sales. At what percentage discount would the goal incongruence identified in your answer to requirements 2 and 3 no longer be a problem?

22-33 International transfer pricing, taxes, goal congruence. Castor, a division of Gemini Corporation, is located in the United States. Its effective income tax rate is 30%. Another division of Gemini, Pollux, is located in Canada, where the income tax rate is 40%. Pollux manufactures, among other things, an intermediate product for Castor called IP-2014. Pollux operates at capacity and makes 15,000 units of IP-2014 for Castor each period, at a variable cost of $56 per unit. Assume that there are no outside customers for IP-2014. Because the IP-2014 must be shipped from Canada to the United States, it costs Pollux an additional $8 per unit to ship the IP-2014 to Castor. There are no direct fixed costs for IP-2014. Pollux also manufactures other products.

A product similar to IP-2014 that Castor could use as a substitute is available in the United States for $77 per unit.

Required

1. What is the minimum and maximum transfer price that would be acceptable to Castor and Pollux for IP-2014, and why?
2. What transfer price would minimize income taxes for Gemini Corporation as a whole? Would Castor and Pollux want to be evaluated on operating income using this transfer price?
3. Suppose Gemini uses the transfer price from requirement 2 and each division is evaluated on its own after-tax division operating income. Now suppose Pollux has an opportunity to sell 8,000 units of IP-2014 to an outside customer for $62 each. Pollux will not incur shipping costs because the customer is nearby and offers to pay for shipping. Assume that if Pollux accepts the special order, Castor will have to buy 8,000 units of the substitute product in the United States at $77 per unit.
   a. Will accepting the special order maximize after-tax operating income for Gemini Corporation as a whole?
   b. Will Castor want Pollux to accept this special order? Why or why not?
   c. Will Pollux want to accept this special order? Explain.
   d. Suppose Gemini Corporation wants to operate in a decentralized manner. What transfer price should Gemini set for IP-2014 so that each division acting in its own best interest takes actions with respect to the special order that are in the best interests of Gemini Corporation as a whole?

22-34 Transfer pricing, goal congruence, ethics. Sustainable Industries manufactures cardboard containers (boxes) made from recycled paper products. The company operates two divisions, paper recycling and box manufacturing, as decentralized entities. The recycling division is free to sell recycled paper to outside buyers, and the box manufacturing division is free to purchase recycled paper from other sources. Currently, however, the recycling division sells all of its output to the manufacturing division, and the manufacturing division does not purchase materials from outside suppliers.

The recycled paper is transferred from the recycling division to the manufacturing division at 110% of full cost. The recycling division purchases recyclable paper products for $0.075 per pound. The recycling division uses 100 pounds of recyclable paper products to produce one roll of recycled paper. The division's other variable costs equal $6.35 per roll, and fixed costs at a monthly production level of 10,000 rolls are $2.15 per roll. During the most recent month, 10,000 rolls of recycled paper were transferred between the two divisions. The recycling division's capacity is 15,000 rolls.

With the increase in demand for sustainably made products, the manufacturing division expects to use 12,000 rolls of paper next month. Ecofree Corporation has offered to sell 2,000 rolls of recycled paper next month to the manufacturing division for $17.00 per roll.

Required

1. Compute the transfer price per roll of recycled paper. If each division is considered a profit center, would the manufacturing manager choose to purchase 2,000 rolls next month from Ecofree Corporation?
2. Is the purchase in the best interest of Sustainable Industries? Show your calculations. What is the cause of this goal incongruence?
3. The manufacturing division manager suggests that $17.00 is now the market price for recycled paper rolls and that this should be the new transfer price. Sustainable's corporate management tends to agree. The paper recycling manager is suspicious. Ecofree's prices have always been much higher than $17.00 per roll. Why the sudden price cut? After further investigation by the recycling division manager, it is revealed that the $17.00 per roll price was a one-time-only offer made to the manufacturing division due to excess inventory at Ecofree. Future orders would be priced at $18.50 per roll. Comment on the validity of the $17.00 per roll market price and the ethics of the manufacturing manager. Would changing the transfer price to $17.00 matter to Sustainable Industries?

22-35 Transfer pricing, goal congruence. The Croydon Division of CC Industries supplies the Hauser Division with 100,000 units per month of an infrared LED that Hauser uses in a remote control device it sells. The transfer price of the LED is $8, which is the market price. However, Croydon does not operate at or near capacity. The variable cost to Croydon of the LED is $4.80, while Hauser incurs variable costs (excluding the transfer price) of $12 for each remote control. Hauser's selling price is $32.

Hauser's manager is considering a promotional campaign. The market research department of Hauser has developed the following estimates of additional monthly volume associated with additional monthly promotional expenses.

Additional Monthly Promotional Expenses:	$80,000	$120,000	$160,000
Additional Monthly Volume (Units)	10,000	15,000	18,000

Required

1. What level of additional promotional expenses would the Hauser division manager choose?
2. As the manager of the Croydon division, what level of additional promotional expenses would you like to see the Hauser division manager select?
3. As the president of CC Industries, what level of spending would you like the Hauser division manager to select?
4. What is the maximum transfer price that would induce the Hauser division to spend the optimal additional promotional expense from the standpoint of the firm as a whole?

22-36 Transfer pricing, perfect and imperfect markets. Letang Company has three divisions (R, S, and T), organized as decentralized profit centers. Division R produces the basic chemical Ranbax (in multiples of 1,000 pounds) and transfers it to Divisions S and T. Division S processes Ranbax into the final product Syntex, and Division T processes Ranbax into the final product Termix. No material is lost during processing.

Division R has no fixed costs. The variable cost per pound of Ranbax is $0.18. Division R has a capacity limit of 10,000 pounds. Divisions S and T have capacity limits of 4,000 and 6,000 pounds, respectively. Divisions S and T sell their final product in separate markets. The company keeps no inventories of any kind.

The *cumulative* net revenues (i.e., total revenues – total processing costs) for divisions S and T at various output levels are summarized below.

Division S

Pounds of Ranbax processed in S	1,000	2,000	3,000	4,000
Total net revenues ($) from sale of Syntex	$ 500	$ 850	$1,100	$1,200

Division T

Pounds of Ranbax processed in T	1,000	2,000	3,000	4,000	5,000	6,000
Total net revenues ($) from sale of Termix	$ 600	$1,200	$1,800	$2,100	$2,250	$2,350

Required

1. Suppose there is no external market for Ranbax. What quantity of Ranbax should the Letang Company produce to maximize overall income? How should this quantity be allocated between the two processing divisions?
2. What range of transfer prices will motivate Divisions S and T to demand the quantities that maximize overall income (as determined in requirement 1), as well as motivate Division R to produce the sum of those quantities?
3. Suppose that Division R can sell any quantity of Ranbax in a perfectly competitive market for $0.33 a pound. To maximize Letang's income, how many pounds of Ranbax should Division R transfer to Divisions S and T, and how much should it sell in the external market?
4. What range of transfer prices will result in Divisions R, S, and T taking the actions determined as optimal in requirement 3? Explain your answer.

23 Performance Measurement, Compensation, and Multinational Considerations

Learning Objectives

1. Select financial and nonfinancial performance measures to use in a balanced scorecard
2. Examine accounting-based measures for evaluating a business unit's performance, including return on investment (ROI), residual income (RI), and economic value added (EVA®)
3. Analyze the key measurement choices in the design of each performance measure
4. Study the choice of performance targets and design of feedback mechanisms
5. Indicate the difficulties that occur when the performance of divisions operating in different countries is compared
6. Understand the roles of salaries and incentives when rewarding managers
7. Describe the four levers of control and why they are necessary

When you complete this course, you'll receive a grade that represents a measure of your performance in it.

Your grade will likely consist of four elements—homework, quizzes, exams, and class participation. Do some of these elements better reflect your knowledge of the material than others? Would the relative weights placed on the various elements when determining your final grade influence how much effort you expend to improve your performance on the different elements? Would it be fair if you received a good grade regardless of your performance? The following article about former AIG chief executive Martin Sullivan examines that very situation in a corporate context. Sullivan continued to receive performance bonuses despite pushing AIG to the brink of bankruptcy. By failing to link pay to performance, AIG's board of directors rewarded behavior that led to a government takeover of the firm.

Misalignment Between CEO Compensation and Performance at AIG[1]

After the collapse and government takeover of AIG, many shareholders and observers focused on the company's executive compensation. Experts argued that the incentive structures for executives helped fuel the real estate bubble. Though people were placing long-term bets on mortgage-backed securities, much of their compensation was in the form of short-term bonuses. This encouraged excessive risk without the fear of significant repercussions.

Judging solely by financial measures, AIG's results in 2007—the year before the crisis—were a failure. Driven by the write-down of $11.1 billion in fixed income guarantees, the company's revenue was down 56% from 2006 results. Despite this, AIG chief executive Martin Sullivan earned $14.3 million in salary, bonus, stock options, and other

[1] *Sources:* Nathan Blair, "AIG—Blame for the Bailout," Stanford Graduate School of Business No. A-203 (Stanford, CA: Stanford Graduate School of Business, 2009); Hugh Son and Erik Holm, "AIG's Former Chief Sullivan's Gets $47 Million Package, *Bloomberg.com* (July 1, 2008); Zachary Tracer, "Benmosche Gets 24% Pay Boost in 2013 After AIG Bailout Repaid," *Bloomberg.com* (April 4, 2013).

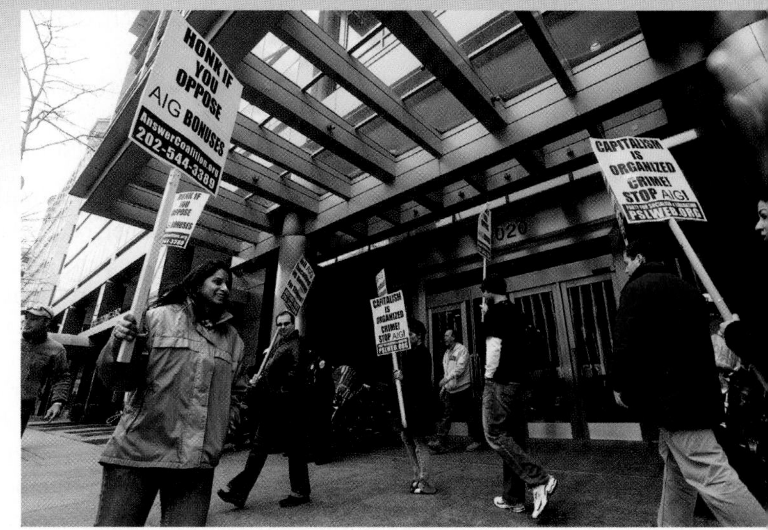

incentives. In June 2008, AIG replaced Sullivan. By then, AIG reported cumulative losses totaling $20 billion. During Sullivan's three-year tenure at the helm, AIG lost 46% of its market value. At the time of his dismissal, the AIG board of directors gave the ousted CEO about $47 million in severance pay, bonus, and long-term compensation. At a Congressional hearing in the aftermath of AIG's failure, one witness testified on Sullivan's compensation stating, "I think it is fair to say by any standard of measurement that this pay plan is as uncorrelated to performance as it is possible to be."

While under government control, executive compensation at AIG was subject to restrictions. Once the U.S. bailout was repaid in early 2013, AIG announced a 24% raise for current CEO Robert Benmosche. Benmosche was eligible for $13 million in 2013, including a $2 million salary, a $4 million annual bonus, and $7 million in multiyear incentive pay. Going forward, pay for AIG's top five officers will be based mostly on results. Executives will be eligible for bonuses based on AIG's performance relative to peers in terms of total shareholder return and growth in tangible net book value over a three-year period.

Companies measure and reward performance to motivate managers to work toward organizational goals. As the AIG example illustrates, if rewards are inappropriate or not connected to sustained performance, managers can increase their compensation without supporting the company's objectives. This chapter discusses the general design, implementation, and uses of performance measures, which are part of the final step in the decision-making process.

Financial and Nonfinancial Performance Measures

Learning Objective 1

Select financial performance measures

...such as return on investment and residual income

and nonfinancial performance measures to use in a balanced scorecard

...such as customer satisfaction and number of defects

As you have learned, many organizations record financial and nonfinancial performance measures for their subunits on a *balanced scorecard*. The scorecards of different organizations emphasize different measures, but the measures are always derived from a company's strategy. Consider the case of Hospitality Inns, a chain of hotels. Hospitality Inns' strategy is to provide excellent customer service and to charge a higher room rate than its competitors. Hospitality Inns uses the following measures in its balanced scorecard:

1. **Financial perspective**—the firm's stock price, net income, return on sales, return on investment, and economic value added
2. **Customer perspective**—market share in different geographic locations, customer satisfaction, brand image, and average number of repeat visits
3. **Internal-business-process perspective**—customer-service time for making reservations, check-in, and restaurant services; cleanliness of the hotels and rooms and room-service and restaurant quality; time taken to clean rooms; reductions in waste output and energy and water consumption; number of new services provided to customers (wireless Internet, video games, and so on); and the time taken to plan and build new hotels

4. **Learning-and-growth perspective**—the education, skills, and satisfaction levels of the firm's employees; employee turnover and hours of employee training; and the company's achievement of ISO 14001:2004 certification for environment management

As in all balanced scorecard implementations, the goal is to make improvements in the learning-and-growth perspective that will lead to enhancements in the internal-business-process perspective that, in turn, will result in improvements in the customer and financial perspectives. Hospitality Inns also uses balanced scorecard measures to evaluate and reward the performance of its managers.

Some performance measures, such as the time it takes to plan and build new hotels, have a long time horizon. Other measures, such as time taken to check in or quality of room service, have a short time horizon. In this chapter, we focus on *organization subunits'* most widely used performance measures that cover an intermediate-to-long time horizon. These are internal financial measures based on accounting numbers routinely reported by organizations. In later sections, we describe why companies use both financial and nonfinancial measures to evaluate performance.

Designing accounting-based performance measures requires several steps:

Step 1: Choose Performance Measures That Align with the Firm's Financial Goals. For example, is operating income, net income, return on assets, or revenues the best measure of a subunit's financial performance?

Step 2: Choose the Details of Each Performance Measure in Step 1. Once a firm has chosen a specific performance measure, it must make a variety of decisions about the precise way in which various components of the measure are to be calculated. For example, if the chosen performance measure is return on assets, should it be calculated for one year or for a multiyear period? Should assets be defined as total assets or net assets (total assets minus total liabilities)? Should assets be measured at historical cost or current cost?

Decision Point

What financial and nonfinancial performance measures do companies use in their balanced scorecards?

Step 3: Choose a Target Level of Performance and Feedback Mechanism for Each Performance Measure in Step 1. For example, should all subunits have identical targets, such as the same required rate of return on assets? Should performance reports be sent to top managers daily, weekly, or monthly?

The decisions made in these steps don't have to be sequential. The issues considered in each step are interdependent, and top managers will often proceed through these steps several times before deciding on one or more accounting-based performance measures. At each step, the answers to the questions raised depend on top management's beliefs about how well each measure fulfills the behavioral criteria of promoting goal congruence, motivating management effort, evaluating subunit performance, and preserving subunit autonomy (see Chapter 22).

Learning Objective 2

Examine accounting-based measures for evaluating a business unit's performance, including return on investment (ROI),

...return on sales times investment turnover

residual income (RI),

...income minus a dollar amount for required return on investment

and economic value added (EVA®)

...a variation of residual income

Accounting-Based Measures for Business Units

Companies commonly use four measures to evaluate the economic performance of their subunits. We illustrate these measures for Hospitality Inns.

Hospitality Inns owns and operates three hotels: one each in San Francisco, Chicago, and New Orleans. Exhibit 23-1 summarizes data for each hotel for 2014. At present, Hospitality Inns does not allocate the total long-term debt of the company to the three separate hotels. The exhibit indicates that the New Orleans hotel generates the highest operating income, $510,000, compared with Chicago's $300,000 and San Francisco's $240,000. But does this comparison mean the New Orleans hotel is the most "successful"? The main weakness of comparing operating incomes alone is that it ignores the differences in *the size of the investment* in each hotel. **Investment** refers to the resources or assets used to generate income. The real question is whether a division generates sufficient operating income relative to the investment made to earn it.

Exhibit 23-1

Financial Data for Hospitality Inns for 2014 (in thousands)

	A	B	C	D	E
1		San Francisco Hotel	Chicago Hotel	New Orleans Hotel	Total
2	Hotel revenues	$1,200,000	$1,400,000	$3,185,000	$5,785,000
3	Hotel variable costs	310,000	375,000	995,000	1,680,000
4	Hotel fixed costs	650,000	725,000	1,680,000	3,055,000
5	Hotel operating income	$ 240,000	$ 300,000	$ 510,000	1,050,000
6	Interest costs on long-term debt at 10%				450,000
7	Income before income taxes				600,000
8	Income taxes at 30%				180,000
9	Net income				$ 420,000
10	Net book value at the end of 2014:				
11	Current assets	$ 400,000	$ 500,000	$ 660,000	$1,560,000
12	Long-term assets	600,000	1,500,000	2,340,000	4,440,000
13	Total assets	$1,000,000	$2,000,000	$3,000,000	$6,000,000
14	Current liabilities	$ 50,000	$ 150,000	$ 300,000	$ 500,000
15	Long-term debt				4,500,000
16	Stockholders' equity				1,000,000
17	Total liabilities and stockholders' equity				$6,000,000
18					

Three of the approaches to measuring performance include a measure of investment: return on investment, residual income, and economic value added. A fourth approach, return on sales, does not measure investment.

Return on Investment

Return on investment (ROI) is an accounting measure of income divided by an accounting measure of investment.

$$\text{Return on investment} = \frac{\text{Income}}{\text{Investment}}$$

Return on investment is the most popular approach to measure performance for two reasons: (1) It blends all the ingredients of profitability—revenues, costs, and investment—into a single percentage and (2) it can be compared with the rate of return on opportunities elsewhere, inside or outside the company. As with any single performance measure, however, managers should use ROI cautiously and in conjunction with other measures.

ROI is also called the *accounting rate of return* or the *accrual accounting rate of return* (Chapter 21, pages 814–815). Managers usually use the term *ROI* when evaluating the performance of an organization's subunit and the term *accrual accounting rate of return* when using an ROI measure to evaluate a project. Companies vary in the way they define income in the numerator and investment in the denominator of the ROI calculation. Some companies use operating income for the numerator; others prefer to calculate ROI on an after-tax basis and use net income. Some companies use total assets in the denominator; others prefer to focus on only those assets financed by long-term debt and stockholders' equity and use total assets minus current liabilities.

Consider the ROIs of each of the three Hospitality hotels in Exhibit 23-1. For our calculations, we use the operating income of each hotel for the numerator and the total assets of each hotel for the denominator.

Using these ROI figures, the San Francisco hotel appears to make the best use of its total assets.

Hotel	Operating Income	÷	Total Assets	=	ROI
San Francisco	$240,000	÷	$1,000,000	=	24%
Chicago	$300,000	÷	$2,000,000	=	15%
New Orleans	$510,000	÷	$3,000,000	=	17%

Each manager can increase his or her hotel's ROI by increasing its revenues or decreasing its costs (each of which increases the numerator) or by decreasing the investment in the hotel (which decreases the denominator). Even when a hotel's operating income falls, the manager can increase its ROI by reducing its total assets by a greater percentage. Suppose, for example, that the operating income of the Chicago hotel decreases by 4% from \$300,000 to \$288,000 [\$300,000 × (1 − 0.04)] and its total assets decrease by 10% from \$2,000,000 to \$1,800,000 [\$2,000,000 × (1 − 0.10)]. The ROI of the Chicago hotel would then increase from 15% to 16% (\$288,000 ÷ \$1,800,000).

ROI can provide more insight into performance when it is represented as two components:

$$\frac{\text{Income}}{\text{Investment}} = \frac{\text{Income}}{\text{Revenues}} \times \frac{\text{Revenues}}{\text{Investment}}$$

which is also written as

$$ROI = \text{Return on sales} \times \text{Investment turnover}$$

This approach is known as the *DuPont method of profitability analysis*. The DuPont method recognizes the two basic ingredients in profit making: increasing the income per dollar of revenues and using assets to generate more revenues. An improvement in either ingredient without changing the other increases the ROI.

Assume Hospitality Inns' top managers adopt a 30% target ROI for the San Francisco hotel. How can this return be attained? Using the DuPont method, the following example shows three ways the managers of the hotel can increase its ROI from 24% to 30%.

	Operating Income (1)	Revenues (2)	Total Assets (3)	Operating Income / Revenues (4) = (1) ÷ (2)	×	Revenues / Total Assets (5) = (2) ÷ (3)	=	Operating Income / Total Assets (6) = (4) × (5)
Current ROI	$240,000	$1,200,000	$1,000,000	20%	×	1.2	=	24%
Alternatives								
A. Decrease assets (such as receivables), keeping revenues and operating income per dollar of revenue constant	$240,000	$1,200,000	$ 800,000	20%	×	1.5	=	30%
B. Increase revenues (via higher occupancy rate), keeping assets and operating income per dollar of revenue constant	$300,000	$1,500,000	$1,000,000	20%	×	1.5	=	30%
C. Decrease costs (via, say, efficient maintenance) to increase operating income per dollar of revenue, keeping revenue and assets constant	$300,000	$1,200,000	$1,000,000	25%	×	1.2	=	30%

Other alternatives, such as increasing the selling price per room, could increase both the revenues per dollar of total assets and the operating income per dollar of revenues.

ROI makes clear the benefits managers can obtain by reducing their investment in current or long-term assets. Most managers know they need to boost revenues and control costs, but pay less attention to reducing their investment base. Reducing the investment base involves decreasing idle cash, managing credit judiciously, determining proper inventory levels, and spending carefully on long-term assets.

Residual Income

Residual income (RI) is an accounting measure of income minus a dollar amount for required return on an accounting measure of investment.

$$\text{Residual income } (RI) = \text{Income} - (\text{Required rate of return} \times \text{Investment})$$

The required rate of return multiplied by the investment is the *imputed cost of the investment*. The **imputed cost** of the investment is a cost recognized in particular situations but not recorded in financial accounting systems because it is an opportunity cost. In this situation, the imputed cost refers to the return Hospitality Inns could have obtained by making an alternative investment with similar risk characteristics.

Assume that each hotel faces similar risks and that Hospitality Inns has a required rate of return of 12%. The RI for each hotel is calculated as the operating income minus the required rate of return of 12% of total assets:

Hotel	Operating Income	−	Required Rate of Return	×	Investment	=	Residual Income
San Francisco	$240,000	−	(12%	×	$1,000,000)	=	$120,000
Chicago	$300,000	−	(12%	×	$2,000,000)	=	$ 60,000
New Orleans	$510,000	−	(12%	×	$3,000,000)	=	$150,000

Note that the New Orleans hotel has the best RI. In general, RI is influenced by size: For a given level of performance, larger divisions generate higher RI.

Some companies favor the RI measure because managers will concentrate on maximizing an absolute amount, such as dollars of RI, rather than a percentage, such as ROI. The objective of maximizing RI means that as long as a subunit earns a return in excess of the required return for investments, that subunit should continue to invest.

The objective of maximizing ROI may give managers of highly profitable subunits the incentive to reject projects that, from the viewpoint of the company as a whole, should be accepted. Suppose Hospitality Inns is considering upgrading room features and furnishings at the San Francisco hotel. The upgrade will increase the operating income of the San Francisco hotel by $70,000 and increase its total assets by $400,000. The ROI for the expansion is 17.5% ($70,000 ÷ $400,000), which is attractive to Hospitality Inns because it exceeds the required rate of return of 12%. By making this expansion, however, the San Francisco hotel's ROI will decrease:

$$\text{Pre-upgrade } ROI = \frac{\$240{,}000}{\$1{,}000{,}000} = 0.24, \text{ or } 24\%$$

$$\text{Post-upgrade } ROI = \frac{\$240{,}000 + \$70{,}000}{\$1{,}000{,}000 + \$400{,}000} = \frac{\$310{,}000}{\$1{,}400{,}000} = 0.221, \text{ or } 22.1\%$$

The annual bonus paid to the San Francisco manager may decrease if ROI affects the bonus calculation and the upgrading option is selected. Consequently, the manager may shun the expansion. In contrast, if the annual bonus is a function of RI, the San Francisco manager will favor the expansion:

$$\text{Pre-upgrade } RI = \$240{,}000 - (0.12 \times \$1{,}000{,}000) = \$120{,}000$$

$$\text{Post-upgrade } RI = \$310{,}000 - (0.12 \times \$1{,}400{,}000) = \$142{,}000$$

So, it is more likely that a firm will achieve goal congruence if it uses RI rather than ROI to measure the subunit manager's performance.

To see that this is a general result, notice that the post-upgrade ROI is a weighted average of the pre-upgrade ROI and the ROI of the project under consideration. Therefore, whenever a new project has a return higher than the required rate of return (12% in our example) but below the current ROI of the division (24% in our example), the division manager is tempted to reject it even though it is a project shareholders would like to pursue.[2] On the other hand, RI is a measure that aggregates linearly, that is, the post-upgrade RI always equals the pre-upgrade RI plus the RI of the project under consideration. To verify this in the preceding example, observe that the project's RI is \$70,000 − (12% × \$400,000) = \$22,000, which is the difference between the post-upgrade and pre-upgrade RI amounts. As a result, a manager who is evaluated on residual income will choose a new project only if it has a positive RI. But this is exactly the criterion shareholders want the manager to employ; in other words, RI achieves goal congruence.

Economic Value Added

Economic value added (EVA®) is a variation of RI used by many companies.[3] It is calculated as follows:

$$\text{Economic value added (EVA)} = \text{After-tax operating income} - \left[\text{Weighted-average cost of capital} \times \left(\text{Total assets} - \text{Current liabilities}\right)\right]$$

That is, EVA substitutes the following numbers in the RI calculation:

1. Income: After-tax operating income,
2. Required rate of return: (After-tax) weighted-average cost of capital, and
3. Investment: Total assets minus current liabilities.[4]

We use the Hospitality Inns data in Exhibit 23-1 to illustrate the basic EVA calculations. The weighted-average cost of capital (WACC) equals the *after-tax* average cost of all the long-term funds Hospitality Inns uses. The company has two sources of long-term funds: (a) long-term debt with a market value and book value of \$4.5 million issued at an interest rate of 10%, and (b) equity capital that also has a market value of \$4.5 million (but a book value of \$1 million).[5] Because interest costs are tax-deductible and the income tax rate is 30%, the after-tax cost of debt financing is 0.10 × (1 − Tax rate) = 0.10 × (1 − 0.30) = 0.07, or 7%. The cost of equity capital is the opportunity cost to investors of not investing their capital in another investment that is similar in risk to Hospitality Inns. Hospitality Inns' cost of equity capital is 14%.[6] The WACC computation, which uses market values of debt and equity, is as follows:

---

[2] Analogously, the manager of an underperforming division with an ROI of 7%, say, may wish to accept projects with returns between 7% and 12% even though these opportunities do not meet the shareholders' required rate of return.

[3] Stephen F. O'Byrne and S. David Young, *EVA and Value-Based Management: A Practical Guide to Implementation* (New York: McGraw-Hill, 2000); Joel M. Stern, John S. Shiely, and Irwin Ross, *The EVA Challenge: Implementing Value Added Change in an Organization* (New York: John Wiley and Sons, 2001).

[4] When implementing EVA, companies make several adjustments to the operating income and asset numbers reported under Generally Accepted Accounting Principles (GAAP). For example, when calculating EVA, costs such as R&D, restructuring costs, and leases that have long-run benefits are recorded as assets (which are then amortized), rather than as current operating costs. The goal of these adjustments is to obtain a better representation of the economic assets, particularly intangible assets, used to earn income. Of course, the specific adjustments applicable to a company will depend on its individual circumstances.

[5] The market value of Hospitality Inns' equity exceeds book value because book value, based on historical cost, does not measure the current value of the company's assets and because various intangible assets, such as the company's brand name, are not shown at current value in the balance sheet under GAAP.

[6] In practice, the most common method of calculating the cost of equity capital is by applying the capital asset pricing model (CAPM). For details, see Jonathan Berk and Peter DeMarzo, *Corporate Finance*, 3rd ed. (Upper Saddle River, NJ: Prentice Hall, 2013).

$$WACC = \frac{(7\% \times \text{Market value of debt}) + (14\% \times \text{Market value of equity})}{\text{Market value of debt} + \text{Market value of equity}}$$

$$= \frac{(0.07 \times \$4{,}500{,}000) + (0.14 \times \$4{,}500{,}000)}{\$4{,}500{,}000 + \$4{,}500{,}000}$$

$$= \frac{\$945{,}000}{\$9{,}000{,}000} = 0.105, \text{ or } 10.5\%$$

The company applies the same WACC to all its hotels because each hotel faces similar risks.

Total assets minus current liabilities (see Exhibit 23-1) can also be computed as follows:

$$\begin{aligned}\text{Total assets} - \text{Current liabilities} &= \text{Long-term assets} + \text{Current assets} - \text{Current liabilities}\\ &= \text{Long-term assets} + \text{Working capital}\end{aligned}$$

where

$$\text{Working capital} = \text{Current assets} - \text{Current liabilities}$$

After-tax hotel operating income is:

$$\text{Hotel operating income} \times (1 - \text{Tax rate}) = \text{Hotel operating income} \times (1 - 0.30) = \text{Hotel operating income} \times 0.70$$

EVA calculations for Hospitality Inns are as follows:

Hotel	After-Tax Operating Income	–	[WACC × (Total Assets – Current Liabilities)]	=	EVA
San Francisco	$240,000 × 0.70	–	[10.50% × ($1,000,000 – $50,000)]	=	$68,250
Chicago	$300,000 × 0.70	–	[10.50% × ($2,000,000 – $150,000)]	=	$15,750
New Orleans	$510,000 × 0.70	–	[10.50% × ($3,000,000 – $300,000)]	=	$73,500

The New Orleans hotel has the highest EVA. Economic value added, like residual income, charges managers for the cost of their investments in long-term assets and working capital. Value is created only if the subunit's after-tax operating income exceeds the cost of investing the capital. To improve EVA, managers can, for example, (a) earn more after-tax operating income with the same amount of capital, (b) use less capital to earn the same after-tax operating income, or (c) invest capital in high-return projects.[7]

Companies such as Briggs and Stratton (a leading producer of gasoline engines), Coca-Cola, Equifax, and FMC, a specialty chemical company, use EVA to guide their decisions. CSX, a railroad company, credits EVA for decisions such as to run trains with three locomotives instead of four and to schedule arrivals just in time for unloading rather than having trains arrive at their destination several hours in advance. The result? Higher income because of lower fuel costs and lower capital investments in locomotives. Division managers find EVA helpful because it allows them to incorporate the cost of capital, which is generally only available at the company-wide level, into the decisions they make. Comparing the actual EVA achieved to the estimated EVA is useful for evaluating the performance of subunits and their managers.

Return on Sales

The income-to-revenues ratio (or sales ratio), often called the *return on sales* (*ROS*), is a frequently used financial performance measure. As we have seen, ROS is one component

[7] Observe that the sum of the divisional after-tax operating incomes used in the EVA calculation, ($240,000 + $300,000 + $510,000) × 0.7 = $735,000, exceeds the firm's net income of $420,000. The difference is due to the firm's after-tax interest expense on its long-term debt, which amounts to $450,000 × 0.7 = $315,000. Because the EVA measure includes a charge for the weighted-average cost of capital, which includes the after-tax cost of debt, the income figure used to compute EVA should reflect the after-tax profit before interest payments on debt are considered. The after-tax operating income (often referred to in practice as NOPAT, or net operating profit after taxes) is thus the relevant measure of divisional profit for EVA calculations.

of ROI in the DuPont method of profitability analysis. To calculate the ROS for each of Hospitality's hotels, we divide operating income by revenues:

Hotel	Operating Income	÷	Revenues (Sales)	=	ROS
San Francisco	$240,000	÷	$1,200,000	=	20.0%
Chicago	$300,000	÷	$1,400,000	=	21.4%
New Orleans	$510,000	÷	$3,185,000	=	16.0%

The Chicago hotel has the highest ROS, but its performance is rated worse than the other hotels using measures such as ROI, RI, and EVA.

Comparing Performance Measures

The following table summarizes the performance of each hotel and ranks it (in parentheses) under each of the four performance measures:

Hotel	ROI	RI	EVA	ROS
San Francisco	24% (1)	$120,000 (2)	$68,250 (2)	20.0% (2)
Chicago	15% (3)	$ 60,000 (3)	$15,750 (3)	21.4% (1)
New Orleans	17% (2)	$150,000 (1)	$73,500 (1)	16.0% (3)

The RI and EVA rankings are the same. They differ from the ROI and ROS rankings. Consider the ROI and RI rankings for the San Francisco and New Orleans hotels. The New Orleans hotel has a smaller ROI. Although its operating income is only slightly more than twice the operating income of the San Francisco hotel—$510,000 versus $240,000—its total assets are three times as large—$3 million versus $1 million. The New Orleans hotel has a higher RI because it earns a higher income after covering the required rate of return on investment of 12%. The high ROI of the San Francisco hotel indicates that its assets are being used efficiently. Even though each dollar invested in the New Orleans hotel does not yield the same return as the San Francisco hotel, this large investment creates considerable value because its return exceeds the required rate of return. The Chicago hotel has the highest ROS but the lowest ROI. The high ROS indicates that the Chicago hotel has the lowest cost structure per dollar of revenues of all of Hospitality Inns' hotels. Chicago has a low ROI because it generates very low revenues per dollar of assets invested. Is any method better than the others for measuring performance? No, because each evaluates a different aspect of performance.

Decision Point

What are the relative merits of return on investment (ROI), residual income (RI), and economic value added (EVA) as performance measures for subunit managers?

ROS measures how effectively costs are managed. To evaluate a unit's overall aggregate performance, however, ROI, RI, or EVA measures are more appropriate than ROS because they consider both income and investment. ROI indicates which investment yields the highest return. RI and EVA overcome some of the goal-congruence problems of ROI. Some managers favor EVA because of the accounting adjustments related to the capitalization of investments in intangibles. Other managers favor RI because it is easier to calculate and because, in most cases, it leads to the same conclusions as EVA does. Generally, companies use multiple financial measures to evaluate performance.

Learning Objective 3

Analyze the key measurement choices in the design of each performance measure

...choice of time horizon, alternative definitions, and measurement of assets

Choosing the Details of the Performance Measures

It is not sufficient for a company to identify the set of performance measures it wishes to use. The company has to decide how to compute the measures. This includes deciding on the time frame over which the measures are computed, defining key terms such as *investment*, and agreeing on how to calculate the components of each performance measure.

Alternative Time Horizons

An important element in designing accounting-based performance measures is choosing the time horizon of the performance measures. The ROI, RI, EVA, and ROS calculations represent the results for a single period, one year in our example. Managers could take actions that cause short-run increases in these measures but that conflict with the long-run interest of the company. For example, managers might curtail R&D and plant maintenance spending in the last three months of a fiscal year to achieve a target level of annual operating income. For this reason, many companies evaluate subunits on the basis of ROI, RI, EVA, and ROS over multiple years.

Another reason to evaluate subunits over multiple years is that the benefits of actions taken in the current period may not show up in short-run performance measures, such as the current year's ROI or RI. For example, an investment in a new hotel may adversely affect ROI and RI in the short run but positively affect them in the long run.

A multiyear analysis highlights another advantage of the RI measure: The net present value of all cash flows over the life of an investment equals the net present value of the RIs.[8] This means that if managers use the net present value method to make investment decisions (as Chapter 21 advocates), then using a multiyear RI to evaluate managers' performances achieves goal congruence.

Another way to motivate managers to take a long-run perspective is by compensating them on the basis of changes in the market price of the company's stock because stock prices incorporate the expected future effects of a firm's current decisions.

Alternative Definitions of Investment

Companies use a variety of definitions to measure the investments made in their divisions. Four common alternative definitions used in the construction of accounting-based performance measures are:

1. **Total assets available**—includes all assets, regardless of their intended purpose
2. **Total assets employed**—total assets available minus the sum of idle assets and assets purchased for future expansion. For example, if the New Orleans hotel in Exhibit 23-1 has unused land set aside for potential expansion, the total assets employed by the hotel would exclude the cost of that land.
3. **Total assets employed minus current liabilities**—total assets employed, excluding assets financed by short-term creditors. One negative feature of defining investment in this way is that it may encourage subunit managers to use an excessive amount of short-term debt because short-term debt reduces the amount of investment.
4. **Stockholders' equity**—calculated by assigning liabilities among subunits and deducting these amounts from the total assets of each subunit. One drawback of this method is that it combines the operating decisions made by hotel managers with the financing decisions made by top management.

Companies that use ROI or RI generally define investment as the total assets available. When a firm directs a subunit manager to carry extra or idle assets, the total assets

[8] This equivalence, often referred to as the "conservation property" of residual income, was originally articulated by Gabriel Preinreich in 1938. To see the equivalence, suppose the $400,000 investment in the San Francisco hotel increases its operating income by $70,000 per year as follows: Increase in operating cash flows of $150,000 each year for 5 years minus depreciation of $80,000 ($400,000 ÷ 5) per year, assuming straight-line depreciation and $0 terminal disposal value. Depreciation reduces the investment amount by $80,000 each year. Assuming a required rate of return of 12%, the net present values of cash flows and residual incomes are as follows:

Year		0	1	2	3	4	5	Net Present Value
(1)	Cash flow	–$400,000	$150,000	$150,000	$150,000	$150,000	$150,000	
(2)	Present value of $1 discounted at 12%	1	0.89286	0.79719	0.71178	0.63552	0.56743	
(3)	Present value: (1) × (2)	–$400,000	$133,929	$119,578	$106,767	$ 95,328	$ 85,114	$140,716
(4)	Operating income		$ 70,000	$ 70,000	$ 70,000	$ 70,000	$ 70,000	
(5)	Assets at start of year		$400,000	$320,000	$240,000	$160,000	$ 80,000	
(6)	Capital charge: (5) × 12%		$ 48,000	$ 38,400	$ 28,800	$ 19,200	$ 9,600	
(7)	Residual income: (4)–(6)		$ 22,000	$ 31,600	$ 41,200	$ 50,800	$ 60,400	
(8)	Present value of RI: (7) × (2)		$ 19,643	$ 25,191	$ 29,325	$ 32,284	$ 34,273	$140,716

employed (used) can be more informative than total assets available. Companies that use EVA define investment as the total assets employed minus current liabilities. The rationale for using this definition is that it captures total investment as measured by the sum of working capital (current assets minus current liabilities) and the long-term assets employed in the subunit. Managers are responsible for generating an adequate return on both components.

Alternative Asset Measurements

To design accounting-based performance measures, we must consider different ways to measure the assets included in the investment calculations. Should the assets be measured at historical cost or current cost? Should gross book value (that is, original cost) or net book value (original cost minus accumulated depreciation) be used for depreciable assets?

Current Cost

Current cost is the cost of purchasing an asset today identical to the one currently held or the cost of purchasing an asset that provides services like the one currently held if an identical asset cannot be purchased. Of course, measuring assets at current costs will result in different ROIs than the ROIs calculated on the basis of historical costs.

We illustrate the current-cost ROI calculations using the data for Hospitality Inns (Exhibit 23-1) and then compare current-cost-based ROIs and historical-cost-based ROIs. Consider the following additional information about the long-term assets of each hotel:

	San Francisco	Chicago	New Orleans
Age of facility in years (at end of 2014)	8	4	2
Gross book value (original cost)	$1,400,000	$2,100,000	$2,730,000
Accumulated depreciation	$ 800,000	$ 600,000	$ 390,000
Net book value (at end of 2014)	$ 600,000	$1,500,000	$2,340,000
Depreciation for 2014	$ 100,000	$ 150,000	$ 195,000

Hospitality Inns assumes its facilities have a 14-year estimated useful life and zero terminal disposal value and uses straight-line depreciation.

An index of construction costs indicating how the cost of construction has changed over the eight-year period Hospitality Inns has been operating (2006 year-end = 100) is as follows:

Year	2007	2008	2009	2010	2011	2012	2013	2014
Construction cost index	110	122	136	144	152	160	174	180

Earlier in this chapter, we computed an ROI of 24% for San Francisco, 15% for Chicago, and 17% for New Orleans (page 878). One possible explanation for the high ROI for the San Francisco hotel is that its long-term assets are expressed in 2006 construction-price levels—prices that prevailed eight years ago—and the long-term assets for the Chicago and New Orleans hotels are expressed in terms of higher, more recent construction-price levels, which depress ROIs for these two hotels.

Exhibit 23-2 illustrates a step-by-step approach for incorporating current-cost estimates of long-term assets and depreciation expense into the ROI calculation. We make these calculations to approximate what it would cost today to obtain assets that would produce the same expected operating income the subunits currently earn. (For RI and EVA calculations, similar adjustments to represent the current costs of capital and depreciation expense can be made.) The current-cost adjustment reduces the ROI of the San Francisco hotel by more than half.

	Historical-Cost ROI	Current-Cost ROI
San Francisco	24%	10.8%
Chicago	15%	11.1%
New Orleans	17%	14.7%

Exhibit 23-2 ROI for Hospitality Inns: Computed Using Current-Cost Estimates as of the End of 2014 for Depreciation Expense and Long-Term Assets

Home Insert Page Layout Formulas Data Review View

	A	B	C	D	E	F	G	H	I	J
1	**Step 1:** Restate long-term assets from gross book value at historical cost to gross book value at current cost as of the end of 2014.									
2		**Gross book value of long-term assets at historical cost**	**×**	**(Construction cost index in 2014**	÷	**Construction cost index in year of construction)**	=	**Gross book value of long-term assets at current cost at end of 2014**		
3	San Francisco	$1,400,000	×	(180	÷	100)	=	$2,520,000		
4	Chicago	$2,100,000	×	(180	÷	144)	=	$2,625,000		
5	New Orleans	$2,730,000	×	(180	÷	160)	=	$3,071,250		
6										
7	**Step 2:** Derive net book value of long-term assets at current cost as of the end of 2014. (Assume estimated useful life of each hotel is 14 years.)									
8		**Gross book value of long-term assets at current cost at end of 2014**	**×**	**(Estimated remaining useful life**	÷	**Estimated total useful life)**	=	**Net book value of long-term assets at current cost at end of 2014**		
9	San Francisco	$2,520,000	×	(6	÷	14)	=	$1,080,000		
10	Chicago	$2,625,000	×	(10	÷	14)	=	$1,875,000		
11	New Orleans	$3,071,250	×	(12	÷	14)	=	$2,632,500		
12										
13	**Step 3:** Compute current cost of total assets in 2014. (Assume current assets of each hotel are expressed in 2014 dollars.)									
14		**Current assets at end of 2014 (from Exhibit 23-1)**	+	**Long-term assets from Step 2**	=	**Current cost of total assets at end of 2014**				
15	San Francisco	$400,000	+	$1,080,000	=	$1,480,000				
16	Chicago	$500,000	+	$1,875,000	=	$2,375,000				
17	New Orleans	$660,000	+	$2,632,500	=	$3,292,500				
18										
19	**Step 4:** Compute current-cost depreciation expense in 2014 dollars.									
20		**Gross book value of long-term assets at current cost at end of 2014 (from Step 1)**	÷	**Estimated total useful life**	=	**Current-cost depreciation expense in 2014 dollars**				
21	San Francisco	$2,520,000	÷	14	=	$180,000				
22	Chicago	$2,625,000	÷	14	=	$187,500				
23	New Orleans	$3,071,250	÷	14	=	$219,375				
24										
25	**Step 5:** Compute 2014 operating income using 2014 current-cost depreciation expense.									
26		**Historical-cost operating income**	–	**(Current-cost depreciation expense in 2014 dollars (from Step 4)**	–	**Historical-cost depreciation expense)**	=	**Operating income for 2014 using current-cost depreciation expense in 2014 dollars**		
27	San Francisco	$240,000	–	($180,000	–	$100,000)	=	$160,000		
28	Chicago	$300,000	–	($187,500	–	$150,000)	=	$262,500		
29	New Orleans	$510,000	–	($219,375	–	$195,000)	=	$485,625		
30										
31	**Step 6:** Compute ROI using current-cost estimates for long-term assets and depreciation expense.									
32		**Operating income for 2014 using current-cost depreciation expense in 2014 dollars (from Step 5)**	÷	**Current cost of total assets at end of 2014 (from Step 3)**	=	**ROI using current-cost estimate**				
33	San Francisco	$160,000	÷	$1,480,000	=	10.8%				
34	Chicago	$262,500	÷	$2,375,000	=	11.1%				
35	New Orleans	$485,625	÷	$3,292,500	=	14.7%				

Adjusting assets to recognize current costs negates differences in the investment base caused solely by differences in construction-price levels. The current-cost ROI better measures the current economic returns from the investment than the historical-cost ROI does. If Hospitality Inns were to invest in a new hotel today, investing in one like the New Orleans hotel offers the best ROI.

Current-cost estimates can be difficult to obtain for some assets. Why? Because the estimate requires a company to consider, in addition to increases in price levels, technological advances and process improvements that could reduce the current cost of assets needed to earn today's operating income.

Long-Term Assets: Gross or Net Book Value?

The historical cost of assets is often used to calculate ROI. There has been much discussion about whether managers should use gross book value or net book value of assets. Using the data in Exhibit 23-1 (page 877), we calculate ROI using net and gross book values of plant and equipment:

	Operating Income (from Exhibit 23-1) (1)	Net Book Value of Total Assets (from Exhibit 23-1) (2)	Accumulated Depreciation (from page 884) (3)	Gross Book Value of Total Assets (4) = (2) + (3)	2014 ROI Using Net Book Value of Total Assets calculated earlier (5) = (1) ÷ (2)	2014 ROI Using Gross Book Value of Total Assets (6) = (1) ÷ (4)
San Francisco	$240,000	$1,000,000	$800,000	$1,800,000	24%	13.3%
Chicago	$300,000	$2,000,000	$600,000	$2,600,000	15%	11.5%
New Orleans	$510,000	$3,000,000	$390,000	$3,390,000	17%	15.0%

Using gross book value, the 13.3% ROI of the older San Francisco hotel is lower than the 15.0% ROI of the newer New Orleans hotel. Those who favor using gross book value claim it enables a firm to compare ROI across its subunits more accurately. For example, when using gross-book-value calculations, the return on the original plant-and-equipment investment is higher for the newer New Orleans hotel than for the older San Francisco hotel. This difference probably reflects the decline in earning power of the San Francisco hotel. Using the net book value masks this decline in earning power because the constantly decreasing investment base results in a higher ROI for the San Francisco hotel—24% in this example. This higher rate may mislead decision makers into thinking that the earning power of the San Francisco hotel has not decreased.

Decision Point

Over what time frame should companies measure performance, and what are the alternative choices for calculating the components of each performance measure?

The proponents of using net book value as an investment base maintain that it is less confusing because (1) it is consistent with the amount of total assets shown in the conventional balance sheet and (2) it is consistent with income computations that include deductions for depreciation expense. Surveys report that the net book value is the measure of assets most commonly used by companies for internal performance evaluation.

Learning Objective 4

Study the choice of performance targets and design of feedback mechanisms

...carefully crafted budgets and sufficient feedback for timely corrective action

Target Levels of Performance and Feedback

Now that we have covered the different types of measures and how to choose them, let us turn our attention to how mangers set and measure target levels of performance.

Choosing Target Levels of Performance

Historical-cost-based accounting measures are usually inadequate for evaluating economic returns on new investments and, in some cases, create disincentives for expansion. Despite these problems, managers can use historical-cost ROIs to evaluate current performance by establishing *target* ROIs. For Hospitality Inns, we need to recognize that the hotels were built in different years, which means they were built at different construction-price levels. The firm could adjust the target historical-cost-based ROIs accordingly, say, by setting San Francisco's ROI at 26%, Chicago's at 21%, and New Orleans' at 19%.

This useful alternative of comparing actual results with targeted, or budgeted, results is often overlooked, but should not be. *Companies should tailor and negotiate a budget for a particular subunit, a particular accounting system, and a particular performance measure while keeping in mind the pitfalls of using historical-cost accounting.* For example, many problems related to valuing assets and measuring income can be resolved if top managers can get subunit managers to focus on what is attainable in the forthcoming budget period—whether ROI, RI, or EVA is used and whether the financial measures are based on historical costs or some other measure, such as current costs.

A popular way to establish targets is to set continuous improvement targets. If a company is using EVA as a performance measure, the firm can evaluate operations on the year-to-year changes in EVA, rather than on absolute measures of EVA. Evaluating performance on the basis of *improvements* in EVA makes the initial method of calculating it less important.

Companies using balanced scorecards establish targets for financial performance measures, while simultaneously setting targets in the customer, internal-business-process, and learning-and-growth perspectives. For example, Hospitality Inns will establish targets for employee training and satisfaction, customer-service times for reservations and check-in, the quality of room service, and customer satisfaction levels that each hotel must reach to achieve its ROI and EVA targets.

Choosing the Timing of Feedback

A final step in designing accounting-based performance measures is the timing of performance feedback, which depends largely on (1) how critical the information is for the success of the organization, (2) the management level receiving the feedback, and (3) the sophistication of the organization's information technology. For example, hotel managers responsible for room sales want information on the number of rooms sold (rented) on a daily or weekly basis because a large percentage of hotel costs are fixed costs. Achieving high room sales and taking quick action to reverse any declining sales trends are critical to the financial success of each hotel. Supplying managers with daily information about room sales is much easier if Hospitality Inns has a computerized room-reservation and check-in system. The company's top managers, however, might look at information about daily room sales only on a monthly basis unless there is a problem, like the low sales-to-total-assets ratio the Chicago hotel has. In this case, the managers might want the information weekly.

Similarly, human resources managers at each hotel measure employee satisfaction annually because satisfaction is best measured over a longer horizon. However, housekeeping department managers measure the quality of room service over much shorter time horizons, such as a week, because poor levels of performance in these areas for even a short period of time can harm a hotel's reputation for a long period. Moreover, managers can detect and resolve housekeeping problems over a short time period.

Decision Point

What targets should companies use and when should they give feedback to managers regarding their performance relative to these targets?

Performance Measurement in Multinational Companies

Learning Objective 5

Indicate the difficulties that occur when the performance of divisions operating in different countries is compared

...adjustments needed for differences in inflation rates and changes in exchange rates

Our discussion so far has focused on performance evaluation of different divisions of a company operating within a single country. We next discuss the additional difficulties created when managers compare the performance of divisions of a company operating in different countries. Several issues arise.[9]

- The economic, legal, political, social, and cultural environments differ significantly across countries. Operating a division in an open economy like Singapore is very different from operating in a closed economy such as Venezuela, where many prices are controlled and there is a constant threat of nationalization.

[9] See M. Zafar Iqbal, *International Accounting: A Global Perspective* (Cincinnati: South-Western College Publishing, 2002).

- Import quotas and tariffs range widely from country to country, and it's not unusual for countries to impose tariffs and custom duties to restrict the imports of certain goods.
- The availability of materials and skilled labor as well as the costs of materials, labor, and infrastructure (power, transportation, and communication) also differ significantly across countries. Companies operating in Indonesia, for example, must spend 30% of their total production costs on transportation, whereas these costs account for just 12% of total spending in China.
- Divisions operating in different countries account for their performance in different currencies, and inflation and fluctuations in foreign-currency exchange rates affect performance measurement. For example, fast-growing economies such as Paraguay, Nigeria, and Vietnam suffer from double-digit inflation, which dampens the performance of divisions in those countries when their results are measured in dollars.

As a result of these differences, adjustments need to be made to accurately compare the performance of divisions in different countries.

Calculating a Foreign Division's ROI in the Foreign Currency

Suppose Hospitality Inns invests in a hotel in Mexico City. The investment consists mainly of the costs of buildings and furnishings. Also assume the following:

- The exchange rate at the time of Hospitality's investment on December 31, 2013, is 10 pesos = \$1.
- During 2014, the Mexican peso suffers a steady decline in its value. The exchange rate on December 31, 2014, is 15 pesos = \$1.
- The average exchange rate during 2014 is [(10 + 15) ÷ 2] = 12.5 pesos = \$1.
- The investment (total assets) in the Mexico City hotel is 30,000,000 pesos.
- The operating income of the Mexico City hotel in 2014 is 6,000,000 pesos.

What is the historical-cost-based ROI for the Mexico City hotel in 2014?

To answer this question, Hospitality Inns' managers first have to determine if they should calculate the ROI in pesos or in dollars. If they calculate the ROI in dollars, what exchange rate should they use? The managers may also be interested in how the ROI of Hospitality Inns Mexico City (HIMC) compares with the ROI of Hospitality Inns New Orleans (HINO), which is also a relatively new hotel of approximately the same size. The answers to these questions yield information that will be helpful when making future investment decisions.

$$\text{HIMC's } ROI \text{ (calculated using pesos)} = \frac{\text{Operating income}}{\text{Total assets}} = \frac{6{,}000{,}000 \text{ pesos}}{30{,}000{,}000 \text{ pesos}} = 0.20, \text{ or } 20\%$$

HIMC's ROI of 20% is higher than HINO's ROI of 17% (page 878). Does this mean that HIMC outperformed HINO based on the ROI criterion? Not necessarily. That's because HIMC operates in a very different economic environment than HINO.

The peso has declined in value relative to the dollar in 2014. This decline has led to higher inflation in Mexico than in the United States. As a result of the higher inflation in Mexico, HIMC will charge higher prices for its hotel rooms, which will increase HIMC's operating income and lead to a higher ROI. Inflation clouds the real economic returns on an asset and makes historical-cost-based ROI higher. Differences in inflation rates between the two countries make a direct comparison of HIMC's peso-denominated ROI with HINO's dollar-denominated ROI misleading.

Calculating the Foreign Division's ROI in U.S. Dollars

One way to make a comparison of historical-cost-based ROIs more meaningful is to restate HIMC's performance in U.S. dollars. But what exchange rate should the managers use to make the comparison meaningful? Assume HIMC's operating income was earned evenly throughout 2014. Hospitality Inns' managers should use the average exchange rate of 12.5 pesos = $1 to convert the operating income from pesos to dollars: 6,000,000 pesos ÷ 12.5 pesos per dollar = $480,000. The effect of dividing the operating income in pesos by the higher pesos-to-dollar exchange rate prevailing during 2014, rather than the 10 pesos = $1 exchange rate on December 31, 2013, is that any increase in operating income in pesos as a result of inflation during 2014 is eliminated when converting back to dollars.

At what rate should HIMC's total assets of 30,000,000 pesos be converted? They should be converted at the 10 pesos = $1 exchange rate, which was the exchange rate when the assets were acquired on December 31, 2013. Why? Because HIMC's assets are recorded in pesos at the December 31, 2013, cost, and the assets are not revalued as a result of inflation in Mexico in 2014. Because subsequent inflation does not affect the cost of assets in HIMC's financial accounting records, managers should use the exchange rate prevailing on the date the assets were acquired to convert the assets into dollars. Using exchange rates after December 31, 2013, would be incorrect because these exchange rates incorporate the higher inflation in Mexico in 2014. HIMC's total assets are therefore $3,000,000 (30,000,000 pesos ÷ 10 pesos per dollar).

Then

$$\text{HIMC's } ROI \text{ (calculated using dollars)} = \frac{\text{Operating income}}{\text{Total assets}} = \frac{\$480{,}000}{\$3{,}000{,}000} = 0.16, \text{ or } 16\%$$

As we have discussed, these adjustments make the historical-cost-based ROIs of the Mexico City and New Orleans hotels comparable because they negate the effects of any differences in inflation rates between the two countries. Now HIMC's ROI is less than HINO's (16% versus HINO's ROI of 17%).

Calculating residual income in pesos poses the same problems as calculating the ROI does. Calculating HIMC's RI in dollars adjusts for changes in exchange rates and makes for more-meaningful comparisons with Hospitality's other hotels:

$$\begin{aligned}\text{HIMC's } RI &= \$480{,}000 - (0.12 \times \$3{,}000{,}000)\\ &= \$480{,}000 - \$360{,}000 = \$120{,}000\end{aligned}$$

which is also less than HINO's RI of $150,000.

Keep in mind that HIMC's and HINO's ROIs and RIs are historical-cost-based calculations. However, both hotels are relatively new, so this is less of a concern.

Decision Point

How can companies compare the performance of divisions operating in different countries?

Distinguishing the Performance of Managers From the Performance of Their Subunits[10]

Learning Objective 6

Understand the roles of salaries and incentives when rewarding managers

...balancing risk and performance-based rewards

Our focus has been on how to evaluate the performance of a subunit of a company, such as a division. However, is evaluating the performance of a subunit manager the same as evaluating the performance of the subunit? If the subunit performed well, does it mean the manager performed well? In this section, we argue that a company should distinguish between the performance evaluation of a *manager* and the performance evaluation of that manager's *subunit*. For example, companies often put the most skillful division manager in charge of the division producing the poorest economic return in an attempt to improve it. But this may take years and the relative underperformance of the division during that time is no reflection of the performance of the manager.

As another example, consider again the Hospitality Inns Mexico City (HIMC) hotel. Suppose, despite the high inflation in Mexico, HIMC could not increase its room prices because of price-control regulations imposed by the government. HIMC's performance in dollar terms would be poor because of the decline in the value of the peso. But should top managers conclude the HIMC manager performed poorly? Probably not. The poor

[10] The presentations here draw (in part) from teaching notes prepared by S. Huddart, N. Melumad, and S. Reichelstein.

performance of HIMC is largely the result of regulatory and economic factors beyond the manager's control.

In the following sections, we show the basic principles for evaluating the performance of an individual subunit manager. These principles apply to managers at all organization levels. Later sections consider the principles that apply to rank-and-file employees and those that apply to top executives. We illustrate these principles using the RI performance measure.

The Basic Tradeoff: Creating Incentives Versus Imposing Risk

How companies measure and evaluate the performance of managers and other employees affects their rewards. Compensation arrangements range from a flat salary with no performance-based incentive (or bonus), as in the case of many government employees, to rewards based solely on performance, as in the case of real estate agents who are compensated only via commissions paid on the properties they sell. The total compensation for most managers includes some combination of salary and performance-based incentive. In designing compensation arrangements, we need to consider the *tradeoff between creating incentives and imposing risk*. We illustrate this tradeoff in the context of our Hospitality Inns example.

Indra Chungi owns the Hospitality Inns chain of hotels. Roger Brett manages the Hospitality Inns San Francisco (HISF) hotel. Assume Chungi uses RI to measure performance. To improve the hotel's RI, Chungi would like Brett to increase its sales, control its costs, provide prompt and courteous customer service, and reduce the hotel's working capital. But even if Brett did all those things, a high RI is not guaranteed. HISF's RI is affected by many factors beyond Chungi's and Brett's control, such as a downturn in San Francisco's economy or road construction near the hotel that would make it difficult for customers to get to it.

As an entrepreneur, Chungi expects to bear risk. But Brett does not like being subject to risk. One way of "insuring" Brett against risk is to pay him a flat salary, regardless of the actual amount of RI the hotel earns. Chungi would then bear all of the risk. This arrangement creates a problem, however, because Brett's effort is difficult to monitor. The absence of performance-based compensation means that Brett has no direct incentive to work harder or to undertake extra physical and mental effort beyond what is necessary to hold onto his job.

Moral hazard describes a situation in which an employee prefers to exert less effort compared with the effort the owner desires because the owner cannot accurately monitor and enforce the employee's effort.[11] Moral hazard also occurs when an employee reports inaccurate or distorted information for personal benefit because the owner cannot monitor the validity of the reported information. Repetitive jobs, as in electronic assembly, are relatively straightforward to monitor and so are less subject to moral hazard. However, a manager's job, which is to gather and interpret information and exercise judgment on the basis of the information obtained, is more difficult to monitor.

Paying no salary and rewarding Brett *only* on the basis of some performance measure—RI in our example—raises different concerns. In this case, Brett would be motivated to strive to increase the hotel's RI because his rewards would increase. But compensating Brett on RI also subjects him to risk because HISF's RI depends not only on Brett's effort, but also on factors such as local economic conditions over which Brett has no control.

Brett does not like being subject to risk. To compensate Brett for taking risk, Chungi must pay him extra compensation. That is, using performance-based bonuses will cost Chungi more money, *on average*, than paying Brett a flat salary. Why "on average"? Because Chungi's compensation payment to Brett will vary with RI outcomes. When averaged over these outcomes, the RI-based compensation will cost Chungi more than

[11] The term *moral hazard* originated in insurance contracts to represent situations in which insurance coverage caused insured parties to take less care of their properties than they might otherwise. One response to moral hazard in insurance contracts is the system of deductibles (that is, the insured parties pay for damages below a specified amount).

paying Brett a flat salary. The motivation for having some salary and some performance-based compensation is to balance the benefit of incentives against the extra cost of imposing risk on a manager.

Intensity of Incentives and Financial and Nonfinancial Measurements

What affects the intensity of incentives? That is, how large should the incentive component of a manager's compensation be relative to the salary component? To answer these questions, we need to understand how much the performance measure is affected by the actions the manager takes to further the owner's objectives.

Preferred performance measures are those that are sensitive to or that change significantly with the manager's performance. They do not change much with changes in factors that are beyond the manager's control. Sensitive performance measures motivate the manager as well as limit the manager's exposure to risk, reducing the cost of providing incentives. Less-sensitive performance measures are not affected by the manager's performance and fail to induce the manager to improve. The more owners have access to sensitive performance measures, the more they can rely on incentive compensation for their managers.

The salary component of compensation dominates when performance measures that are sensitive to managers' actions are not available. This is the case, for example, for some corporate staff and government employees. A high salary component, however, does not mean incentives are completely absent. Promotions and salary increases do depend on some overall measure of performance, but the incentives are less direct. The incentive component of compensation is high when sensitive performance measures are available and when monitoring the employee's effort is difficult, such as in real estate agencies.

To evaluate Brett, Chungi uses measures from multiple perspectives of the balanced scorecard because nonfinancial measures on the balanced scorecard—employee satisfaction and the time taken for check-in, cleaning rooms, and providing room service—are more sensitive to Brett's actions. Financial measures such as RI are less sensitive to Brett's actions because they are affected by external factors such as local economic conditions beyond Brett's control. Residual income may be a very good measure of the economic viability of the hotel, but it is only a partial measure of Brett's performance.

In addition to considerations of sensitivity and risk, another reason for using nonfinancial measures is that these measures follow Hospitality Inns' strategy and are drivers of future performance. Evaluating managers on these nonfinancial measures motivates them to take actions that will sustain the long-run performance of the firm's hotels while meeting the company's environmental and social goals. Therefore, evaluating performance in all four perspectives of the balanced scorecard promotes both short- and long-run actions. The relative weight placed on the various measures in the scorecard is ideally aimed at achieving congruence between the extent to which the manager is motivated to maximize each performance metric and its importance in generating the long-run objective the firm wishes to achieve. The tradeoff between considerations of sensitivity and risk, on the one hand, and the congruence of goals, on the other, determines the effective intensity of incentives placed on each measure of performance.

Benchmarks and Relative Performance Evaluation

Owners often use financial and nonfinancial benchmarks to evaluate the performance of their managers. The benchmarks, which are metrics that correspond to the best practices of organizations, may be available inside or outside of the organization. For HISF, the benchmarks could be from similar hotels, either within or outside of the Hospitality Inns chain. Suppose Brett is responsible for HISF's revenues, costs, and investments. To evaluate Brett's performance, Chungi would want to benchmark a similar-sized hotel—one affected by the same uncontrollable factors, such as location, demographic trends, or economic conditions, that affect HISF. If all these factors were the same or very similar, the *differences* in the performances of the two hotels could, for the most part, be attributed to the differences in the two managers' performances. Benchmarking, which is also called *relative performance evaluation*, filters out the effects of the common uncontrollable factors.

Can the performance of two managers responsible for running similar operations within a company be benchmarked against each other? Yes, but this approach could create a problem: It could reduce the managers' incentives to help one another. When managers do not cooperate, the company suffers. In this case, using internal benchmarks for performance evaluation may not lead to goal congruence (also see Concepts in Action: Avoiding Performance-Measurement Silos at Staples).

Performance Measures at the Individual Activity Level

Managers need to do two things when designing the measures used to evaluate the performance of individual employees: (1) design performance measures for activities that require multiple tasks and (2) design performance measures for activities done in teams.

Performing Multiple Tasks

Most employees perform more than one task as part of their jobs. Marketing representatives sell products, provide customer support, and gather market information. Manufacturing workers are responsible for both the quantity and quality of their output. Employers want employees to allocate their time and effort intelligently among various tasks or aspects of their jobs.

Consider mechanics at an auto repair shop. Their jobs have two distinct aspects: repair work—performing more repair work generates more revenues for the shop—and customer satisfaction—the higher the quality of the job, the more likely the customer will be pleased. If the employer wants an employee to focus on both aspects, then the employer must measure and compensate performance on both aspects.

Concepts in Action

To effectively measure company performance, organizations should not allow hierarchical boundaries and concerns to dictate performance metrics. While it is natural for organizations to measure managers on the performance of their functional departments, measuring too narrowly leads to suboptimization and conflict within companies. To improve performance, organizations need to understand and measure the key company-wide drivers of success and profitability.

At Staples, the $24 billion office-supply retailer, the leading performance measurement metric is customer satisfaction. Highly satisfied Staples customers are more profitable than other customers, and they are more likely to recommend the company to other potential customers. Previously, Staples' leaders focused on departmental or functional expense metrics (for example, warehouse operating expense as a percent of sales). As a result, many functional managers built careers as expert cost managers, but it created an environment where many individuals could be "successful" reaching their numbers while Staples only succeeded marginally.

To overcome this performance-measurement problem, Staples created incentives for functional managers to provide enhanced service to customers, even if it means exceeding their budget targets. The company was able to demonstrate how investments in service translated into faster sales growth of higher-margin products. As a result, the company rewarded managers who "failed" in the expense measures related to their own units but who, in doing so, delivered substantially more profits in other shared measures. The effects have been impressive: Staples is the largest office-supply retailer in the United States with growth far outpacing Office Depot, its leading competitor.

Sources: Based on Michael Hammer, "The Seven Deadly Sins of Performance Measurement and How To Avoid Them." *MIT Sloan Management Review* 48 (Spring 2007): 19-28; Staples, Inc. *2012 Annual Report*. Framingham, Massachusetts: Staples, Inc., 2013; and Office Depot, Inc., *2012 Annual Report*. Boca Raton, Florida: Office Depot, Inc., 2013.

Suppose the employer can easily measure the quantity, but not the quality, of auto repairs. If the employer rewards workers on a by-the-job rate, which pays workers only on the basis of the number of repairs actually performed, mechanics will likely increase the number of repairs they make and quality will suffer. Sears Auto Center experienced this problem when it introduced by-the-job rates for its mechanics. To resolve the problem, Sears took three steps to motivate workers to balance both quantity and quality: (1) The company dropped the by-the-job rate system and paid mechanics an hourly salary, a step that deemphasized the quantity of repairs. Managers determined mechanics' bonuses, promotions, and pay increases on the basis of an assessment of each mechanic's overall quantity and quality of repairs. (2) Sears evaluated employees, in part, using the number of dissatisfied customers, the number of customer complaints, and data gathered from customer satisfaction surveys. (3) Finally, Sears used staff from an independent outside agency to randomly monitor whether the repairs performed were of high quality.

Team-Based Compensation Arrangements

Many manufacturing, marketing, and design problems can be resolved when employees with multiple skills, knowledge, experiences, and perceptions pool their talents. A team achieves better results than individual employees acting alone.[12] Many companies reward employees on teams based on how well their teams perform. Team-based incentives encourage individuals to help one another as they strive toward a common goal.

The specific forms of team-based compensation vary across companies. Colgate-Palmolive rewards teams based on each team's performance. Novartis, the Swiss pharmaceutical company, rewards teams based on the company's overall performance; some team-based bonuses are paid only if the company reaches certain goals. Eastman Chemical Company rewards team members using a checklist of team-based skills, such as communication and the willingness to help one another. Whether team-based compensation is desirable depends, to a large extent, on the culture and management style of a particular organization. One criticism of team-based compensation is that it diminishes the incentives of individual employees, which can harm a firm's overall performance. Another problem is how to manage team members who are not productive contributors to the team's success but who, nevertheless, share in the team's rewards.

Executive Performance Measures and Compensation

The principles of performance evaluation described in the previous sections also apply to executive compensation plans. These plans are based on both financial and nonfinancial performance measures and consist of a mix of (1) base salary; (2) annual incentives, such as a cash bonus based on achieving a target annual RI; (3) long-run incentives, such as stock options (described later in this section) based on a stock's performance over, say, a five-year period; and (4) other benefits, such as medical benefits, pensions plans, and life insurance.

Well-designed plans use a compensation mix that balances risk (the effect of uncontrollable factors on the performance measure and hence compensation) with short-run and long-run incentives. For example, an evaluation based on a firm's annual EVA sharpens an executive's short-run focus. Using EVA and stock option plans over, say, five years motivates the executive to take a long-run view as well.

Stock options give executives the right to buy company stock at a specified price (called the exercise price) within a specified period. Suppose that on September 16, 2014, Hospitality Inns gave its CEO the option to buy 200,000 shares of the company's stock at any time before June 30, 2019, at the September 16, 2014, market price of $49 per share. Let's say Hospitality Inns' stock price rises to $69 per share on March 24, 2019, and the CEO exercises his options on all 200,000 shares. The CEO would earn $20($69 − $49) per share on 200,000 shares, or $4 million. If Hospitality Inns' stock

---

[12] *Teams That Click: The Results-Driven Manager Series* (Boston: Harvard Business School Press, 2004).

price stays below $49 during the entire period, the CEO will simply forgo his right to buy the shares. By linking CEO compensation to increases in the company's stock price, the stock option plan motivates the CEO to improve the company's long-run performance and stock price.

The Securities and Exchange Commission (SEC) requires detailed disclosures of the compensation arrangements of top-level executives. In 2012, Starwood Hotels and Resorts, for example, disclosed a compensation table showing the salaries, bonuses, stock options, other stock awards, and other compensation earned by its top five executives during the 2009, 2010, and 2011 fiscal years. Starwood, whose brands include Sheraton, Westin, and the W Hotels, also disclosed the peer companies it uses to set the pay for its executives and conduct performance comparisons. These companies include competitors in the hotel and hospitality industry (such as Hyatt, Marriott, and Wyndham), as well as companies with similar revenues in other industries that have comparable talent and recruitment needs (including Avon, Kellogg, Nike, and Starbucks). Investors use this information to evaluate the relationship between compensation and performance across companies generally and across companies operating in similar industries.

SEC rules also require companies to disclose the principles underlying their executive compensation plans. In its financial statements, Starwood describes some of its compensation principles. They include improving the company's competitive position, providing a balanced approach to incentivizing and retaining employees, and aligning senior management's interests with those of shareholders. In addition, the SEC requires companies to disclose the performance criteria—such as a firm's profitability, revenue growth, and market share—used to reward executives. Starwood uses earnings per share and EBITDA to determine the annual incentives for all of its executives. Moreover, each executive has an individual scorecard of financial and nonfinancial performance measures. The company's board of directors establishes the individual strategic, operational, and leadership goals for executives that support the company's overall goals and are tailored to each executive's area of control.

Decision Point

Why are managers compensated based on a mix of salary and incentives?

The Dodd-Frank law passed in 2010 in response to the financial crisis requires companies to provide shareholders with an advisory (nonbinding) vote on executive compensation. These "say-on-pay" votes must be held at least once every three years. The votes have reshaped the way companies create, disclose, and communicate their executive compensation policies. To date, however, they have done little to slow down the rapid growth in executive pay. Further, the results have indicated overwhelming shareholder approval of executive pay in public companies. Only 2% of say-on-pay votes failed in 2012 and 2013, while 75% of companies received greater than 90% support.

Learning Objective 7

Describe the four levers of control and why they are necessary

...boundary, belief, and interactive control systems counterbalance diagnostic control systems

Strategy and Levers of Control[13]

Financial and nonfinancial performance-evaluation measures help managers track their progress toward achieving a company's strategic goals. Because these measures help diagnose whether a company is performing to expectations, they are collectively called **diagnostic control systems.** Companies motivate managers by holding them accountable for and by rewarding them for meeting these goals. It's not unusual for managers to cut corners and misreport numbers to make their performance look better than it is, as happened at companies such as Enron, WorldCom, Tyco, and Health South. To prevent unethical and outright fraudulent behavior, companies need to balance the push for performance resulting from diagnostic control systems, the first of four levers of control, with three other levers: *boundary systems*, *belief systems*, and *interactive control systems*. This will ensure that proper business ethics, inspirational values, and attention to future threats and opportunities are not sacrificed while achieving business results.

[13] For a more detailed discussion, see Robert Simons, *Levers of Control: How Managers Use Innovative Control Systems to Drive Strategic Renewal* (Boston: Harvard Business School Press, 1995).

Boundary Systems

Boundary systems describe standards of behavior and codes of conduct expected of all employees, especially actions that are off-limits. Ethical behavior on the part of managers is paramount. In particular, numbers that subunit managers report should not be tainted by "cooking the books." The books should be free of, for example, overstated assets, understated liabilities, fictitious revenues, and understated costs.

Codes of business conduct signal appropriate and inappropriate individual behaviors. The following are excerpts from Caterpillar's "Worldwide Code of Conduct":

> While we conduct our business within the framework of applicable laws and regulations, for us, mere compliance with the law is not enough. We strive for more than that.... We must not engage in activities that create, or even appear to create, conflict between our personal interests and the interests of the company.

Division managers who fail to adhere to legal or ethical accounting policies and procedures often rationalize their behavior by claiming they were under enormous pressure from top managers "to make the budget." A healthy amount of motivational pressure is desirable, as long as the "tone from the top" and the firm's code of conduct simultaneously communicate the absolute need for all managers to behave ethically at all times. Managers should also train employees to behave ethically. They should promptly and severely reprimand unethical conduct, regardless of the benefits that might accrue to the company from unethical actions. Some companies, such as Lockheed Martin, emphasize ethical behavior by routinely evaluating employees against the firm's code of ethics.

Many organizations also set explicit boundaries precluding actions that harm the environment. Environmental violations (such as water and air pollution) carry heavy fines and prison terms under the laws of the United States and other countries.

In many companies, the environmental responsibilities of employees extend beyond legal requirements. Some companies, such as DuPont, make environmental performance a line item on every employee's salary appraisal report. Duke Power Company appraises employees on measures such as reducing solid waste, cutting emissions and discharges, and implementing environmental plans. Socially responsible companies such as Best Buy, Campbell Soup, and Intel set aggressive environmental goals and measure and report their performance against them. German, Swiss, and Scandinavian companies report on environmental performance as part of a larger set of social responsibility disclosures (such as employee welfare and community development activities). In 2012, Dutch financial services giant ING began incorporating social, ethical, and environmental objectives as part of its top management's pay structure. Other firms in the Netherlands—including chemical company Akzo Nobel, life sciences group DSM, and mail operator TNT—also tie executive compensation to environmental improvement.

Belief Systems

Belief systems articulate the mission, purpose, and core values of a company. They describe the accepted norms and patterns of behavior expected of all managers and other employees when interacting with one another, shareholders, customers, and communities. For example, Johnson & Johnson describes its values and norms in a credo statement that is intended to inspire all managers and other employees to do their best.[14] Belief systems play to employees' *intrinsic motivation*, the desire to achieve self-satisfaction for performing well regardless of external rewards such as bonuses or promotion. Intrinsic motivation comes from being given greater responsibility, doing

[14] A full statement of the credo can be accessed at www.jnj.com/about-jnj/jnj-credo.

interesting and creative work, having pride in doing that work, making a commitment to the organization, and developing personal bonds with one's coworkers. High intrinsic motivation enhances a firm's performance because managers and workers feel a sense of achievement in doing something important, feel satisfied with their jobs, and see opportunities for personal growth.

Interactive Control Systems

Interactive control systems are formal information systems managers use to focus the company's attention and learning on key strategic issues. Managers use interactive control systems to create an ongoing dialogue around these key issues and to personally involve themselves in the decision-making activities of subordinates. An excessive focus on diagnostic control systems and critical performance variables can cause an organization to ignore emerging threats and opportunities—changes in technology, customer preferences, regulations, and competitors that can undercut a business. Interactive control systems help prevent this problem by highlighting and tracking strategic uncertainties businesses face, such as the emergence of digital imaging in the case of Kodak and Fujifilm, airline deregulation in the case of American Airlines, and the shift in customer preferences toward open-source Android operating systems in the case of BlackBerry. The key to this control lever is frequent face-to-face communications among managers and employees regarding these critical uncertainties. The result is ongoing discussion and debate about assumptions and action plans. New strategies emerge from the dialogue and debate surrounding the interactive process. Interactive control systems force busy managers to step back from the actions needed to manage the business today and to shift their focus forward to positioning the organization for the opportunities and threats of tomorrow.

Decision Point

What are the four levers of control, and why does a company need to implement them?

Problems for Self-Study

The baseball division of Home Run Sports manufactures and sells baseballs. Assume production equals sales. Budgeted data for February 2014 are as follows:

Current assets	$ 400,000
Long-term assets	600,000
Total assets	$1,000,000
Production output	200,000 baseballs per month
Target ROI (Operating income ÷ Total assets)	30%
Fixed costs	$400,000 per month
Variable cost	$4 per baseball

Required

1. Compute the minimum selling price per baseball necessary to achieve the target ROI of 30%.
2. Using the selling price from requirement 1, separate the target ROI into its two components using the DuPont method.
3. Compute the RI of the baseball division for February 2014, using the selling price from requirement 1. Home Run Sports uses a required rate of return of 12% on total division assets when computing division RI.
4. In addition to her salary, Amanda Kelly, the division manager, receives 3% of the monthly RI of the baseball division as a bonus. Compute Kelly's bonus. Why do you think Kelly is rewarded using both salary and a performance-based bonus? Kelly does not like bearing risk.

Solution

1.

$$\text{Target operating income} = 30\% \text{ of } \$1{,}000{,}000 \text{ of total assets}$$
$$= \$300{,}000$$
$$\text{Let } P = \text{Selling price}$$
$$\text{Revenues} - \text{Variable costs} - \text{Fixed costs} = \text{Operating income}$$
$$200{,}000P - (200{,}000 \times \$4) - \$400{,}000 = \$300{,}000$$
$$200{,}000P = \$300{,}000 + \$800{,}000 + \$400{,}000$$
$$= \$1{,}500{,}000$$
$$P = \$7.50 \text{ per baseball}$$

Proof:		
	Revenues, 200,000 baseballs × $7.50/baseball	$1,500,000
	Variable costs, 200,000 baseballs × $4/baseball	800,000
	Contribution margin	700,000
	Fixed costs	400,000
	Operating income	$ 300,000

2. The DuPont method describes ROI as the product of two components: return on sales (income ÷ revenues) and investment turnover (revenues ÷ investment).

$$\frac{\text{Income}}{\text{Revenues}} \times \frac{\text{Revenues}}{\text{Investment}} = \frac{\text{Income}}{\text{Investment}}$$
$$\frac{\$300{,}000}{\$1{,}500{,}000} \times \frac{\$1{,}500{,}000}{\$1{,}000{,}000} = \frac{\$300{,}000}{\$1{,}000{,}000}$$
$$0.2 \times 1.5 = 0.30, \text{ or } 30\%$$

3.
$$RI = \text{Operating income} - \text{Required return on investment}$$
$$= \$300{,}000 - (0.12 \times \$1{,}000{,}000)$$
$$= \$300{,}000 - \$120{,}000$$
$$= \$180{,}000$$

4.
$$\text{Kelly's bonus} = 3\% \text{ of } RI$$
$$= 0.03 \times \$180{,}000 = \$5{,}400$$

The baseball division's RI is affected by many factors, such as general economic conditions, beyond Kelly's control. These uncontrollable factors make the baseball division's profitability uncertain and risky. Because Kelly does not like bearing risk, paying her a flat salary, regardless of RI, would shield her from this risk. But there is a moral-hazard problem with this compensation arrangement. Because Kelly's effort is difficult to monitor, the absence of performance-based compensation will provide her with no incentive to undertake extra physical and mental effort beyond what is necessary to retain her job or to uphold her personal values.

Paying no salary and rewarding Kelly only on the basis of RI provides her with incentives to work hard but also subjects her to excessive risk because of uncontrollable factors that will affect RI and hence Kelly's compensation. A compensation arrangement based only on RI would be more costly for Home Run Sports because it would have to compensate Kelly for taking on uncontrollable risk. A compensation arrangement that consists of both a salary and an RI-based performance bonus balances the benefits of incentives against the extra costs of imposing uncontrollable risk.

▶ Decision Points

The following question-and-answer format summarizes the chapter's learning objectives. Each decision presents a key question related to a learning objective. The guidelines are the answer to that question.

Decision	Guidelines
1. What financial and nonfinancial performance measures do companies use in their balanced scorecards?	Financial measures such as the return on investment and residual income measure aspects of the performance of organizations, their subunits, managers, and employees. In many cases, financial measures are supplemented with nonfinancial measures of performance based on the customer, internal-business-process, and learning-and-growth perspectives of the balanced scorecard—for example, customer satisfaction, quality of products and services, employee satisfaction, and the achievement of environmental objectives.
2. What are the relative merits of return on investment (ROI), residual income (RI), and economic value added (EVA) as performance measures for subunit managers?	Return on investment (ROI) is the product of two components: income divided by revenues (return on sales) and revenues divided by investment (investment turnover). Managers can increase ROI by increasing revenues, decreasing costs, and decreasing the investment. But ROI may induce the managers of highly profitable divisions to reject projects in the firm's best interest because accepting the project reduces the ROI for their divisions. Residual income (RI) is income minus a dollar amount of required return on investment. RI is more likely than ROI to promote goal congruence. Evaluating managers on RI is also consistent with using the net present value method to choose long-term projects. Economic value added (EVA) is a variation of the RI calculation. It equals after-tax operating income minus the product of the (after-tax) weighted-average cost of capital and total assets minus current liabilities.
3. Over what time frame should companies measure performance, and what are the alternative choices for calculating the components of each performance measure?	A multiyear measure gives managers the incentive to consider the long-term consequences of their actions and prevents a myopic focus on short-run profits. When constructing accounting-based performance measures, firms must first define what constitutes investment. They must also choose whether the assets included in the investment calculations are measured at historical cost or current cost and whether depreciable assets are calculated at gross or net book value.
4. What targets should companies use, and when should they give feedback to managers regarding their performance relative to the targets?	Companies should tailor a budget to a particular subunit, a particular accounting system, and a particular performance measure. In general, asset valuation and income measurement problems can be overcome by emphasizing budgets and targets that stress continuous improvement. Timely feedback enables managers to implement actions that correct deviations from the target performance.
5. How can companies compare the performance of divisions operating in different countries?	Comparing the performance of divisions operating in different countries is difficult because of legal, political, social, economic, and currency differences. ROI and RI calculations for subunits operating in different countries need to be adjusted for differences in inflation between the two countries and changes in exchange rates.

Decision	Guidelines
6. Why are managers compensated based on a mix of salary and incentives?	Companies create incentives by rewarding managers on the basis of performance. But managers face risk because factors beyond their control may also affect their performance. Owners choose a mix of salary and incentive compensation to trade off the incentive benefit against the cost of imposing risk.
7. What are the four levers of control, and why does a company need to implement them?	The four levers of control are diagnostic control systems, boundary systems, belief systems, and interactive control systems. Implementing the four levers of control helps a company simultaneously strive for performance, behave ethically, inspire employees, and respond to strategic threats and opportunities.

Terms to Learn

This chapter and the Glossary at the end of the book contain definitions of the following important terms:

belief systems **(p. 895)**
boundary systems **(p. 895)**
current cost **(p. 884)**
diagnostic control systems **(p. 894)**
economic value added (EVA®) **(p. 880)**
imputed cost **(p. 879)**
interactive control systems **(p. 896)**
investment **(p. 876)**
moral hazard **(p. 890)**
residual income (RI) **(p. 879)**
return on investment (ROI) **(p. 877)**

Assignment Material

Questions

MyAccountingLab

23-1 Give examples of financial and nonfinancial performance measures that can be found in each of the four perspectives of the balanced scorecard.

23-2 What are the three steps in designing accounting-based performance measures?

23-3 What factors affecting ROI does the DuPont method of profitability analysis highlight?

23-4 "RI is not identical to ROI, although both measures incorporate income and investment into their computations." Do you agree? Explain.

23-5 Describe EVA.

23-6 Give three definitions of investment used in practice when computing ROI.

23-7 Distinguish between measuring assets based on current cost and historical cost.

23-8 What special problems arise when evaluating performance in multinational companies?

23-9 Why is it important to distinguish between the performance of a manager and the performance of the organization subunit for which the manager is responsible? Give an example.

23-10 Describe moral hazard.

23-11 "Managers should be rewarded only on the basis of their performance measures. They should be paid no salary." Do you agree? Explain.

23-12 Explain the role of benchmarking in evaluating managers.

23-13 Explain the incentive problems that can arise when employees must perform multiple tasks as part of their jobs.

23-14 Describe two disclosures required by the SEC with respect to executive compensation.

23-15 Describe the four levers of control.

Exercises

MyAccountingLab

23-16 **ROI, comparisons of three companies.** (CMA, adapted) Return on investment (ROI) is often expressed as follows:

$$\frac{\text{Income}}{\text{Investment}} = \frac{\text{Income}}{\text{Revenues}} \times \frac{\text{Revenues}}{\text{Investment}}$$

Required

1. What advantages are there in the breakdown of the computation into two separate components?
2. Fill in the following blanks:

	Companies in Same Industry		
	A	B	C
Revenues	$ 500,000	$200,000	?
Income	$ 150,000	$ 60,000	?
Investment	$ 250,000	?	$1,000,000
Income as a percentage of revenues	?	?	3.0%
Investment turnover	?	?	2
ROI	?	6%	?

After filling in the blanks, comment on the relative performance of these companies as thoroughly as the data permit.

23-17 Analysis of return on invested assets, comparison of two divisions, DuPont method. Global Data, Inc., has two divisions: Test Preparation and Language Arts. Results (in millions) for the past three years are partially displayed here:

	A	B	C	D	E	F	G
1		Operating Income	Operating Revenues	Total Assets	Operating Income/ Operating Revenues	Operating Revenues/ Total Assets	Operating Income/ Total Assets
2	Test Preparation Division						
3	2012	$ 720	$ 9,000	$1,800	?	?	?
4	2013	920	?	?	11.5%	?	46%
5	2014	1,140	?	?	9.5%	6	?
6	Language Arts Division						
7	2012	$ 660	$ 3,000	$2,000	?	?	?
8	2013	?	3,525	2,350	20%	?	?
9	2014	?	?	2,900	?	1.6	20%
10	Global Data, Inc.						
11	2012	$1,380	$12,000	$3,800	?	?	?
12	2013	?	?	?	?	?	?
13	2014	?	?	?	?	?	?

Required

1. Complete the table by filling in the blanks.
2. Use the DuPont method of profitability analysis to explain changes in the operating-income-to-total-assets ratios over the 2012–2014 period for each division and for Global Data as a whole. Comment on the results.

23-18 ROI and RI. (D. Kleespie, adapted) The Outdoor Sports Company produces a wide variety of outdoor sports equipment. Its newest division, Golf Technology, manufactures and sells a single product—AccuDriver, a golf club that uses global positioning satellite technology to improve the accuracy of golfers' shots. The demand for AccuDriver is relatively insensitive to price changes. The following data are available for Golf Technology, which is an investment center for Outdoor Sports:

Total annual fixed costs	$30,000,000
Variable cost per AccuDriver	$ 500
Number of AccuDrivers sold each year	150,000
Average operating assets invested in the division	$48,000,000

Required

1. Compute Golf Technology's ROI if the selling price of AccuDrivers is $720 per club.
2. If management requires an ROI of at least 25% from the division, what is the minimum selling price that the Golf Technology Division should charge per AccuDriver club?

3. Assume that Outdoor Sports judges the performance of its investment centers on the basis of RI rather than ROI. What is the minimum selling price that Golf Technology should charge per AccuDriver if the company's required rate of return is 20%?

23-19 ROI and RI with manufacturing costs. Fabulous Motor Company makes electric cars and has two products, the Simplegreen and the Fabulousgreen. To produce the Simplegreen, Fabulous Motor employed assets of $24,500,000 at the beginning of the period and $30,000,000 of assets at the end of the period. Other costs to manufacture the Simplegreen include the following:

Direct materials	$1,000 per unit
Setup	$1,600 per setup-hour
Production	$470 per machine-hour

General administration and selling costs total $8,940,000 for the period. In the current period, Fabulous Motor produced 9,000 Simplegreen cars using 7,000 setup-hours and 176,500 machine-hours. Fabulous Motor sold these cars for $13,000 each.

Required

1. Assuming that Fabulous Motor defines investment as average assets during the period, what is the return on investment for the Simplegreen division?
2. Calculate the residual income for Simplegreen if Fabulous Motor has a required rate of return of 8% on investments.

23-20 ROI, RI, EVA. Hamilton Corp. is a reinsurance and financial services company. Hamilton strongly believes in evaluating the performance of its standalone divisions using financial metrics such as ROI and residual income. For the year ended December 31, 2013, Hamilton's CFO received the following information about the performance of the property/casualty division:

Sales revenues	$1,200,000
Operating income	200,000
Total assets	1,250,000
Current liabilities	250,000
Debt (interest rate: 6.25%)	600,000
Common equity	400,000

For the purposes of divisional performance evaluation, Hamilton defines investment as total assets and income as operating income (that is, income before interest and taxes). The firm pays a flat rate of 20% in taxes on its income.

Required

1. What was the net income after taxes of the property/casualty division?
2. What was the division's ROI for the year?
3. Based on Hamilton's required rate of return of 10%, what was the property/casualty division's residual income for 2013?
4. Hamilton's CFO has heard about EVA and is curious about whether it might be a better measure to use for evaluating division managers. Hamilton's four divisions have similar risk characteristics. Hamilton's debt trades at book value while its equity has a market value approximately twice that of its book value. The company's cost of equity capital is 12%. Calculate each of the following components of EVA for the property/casualty division, as well as the final EVA figure:
   a. Net operating profit after taxes
   b. Weighted-average cost of capital
   c. Investment, as measured for EVA calculations

23-21 Goal incongruence and ROI. McCall Corporation manufactures furniture in several divisions, including the patio furniture division. The manager of the patio furniture division plans to retire in two years. The manager receives a bonus based on the division's ROI, which is currently 10%.

One of the machines that the patio furniture division uses to manufacture the furniture is rather old, and the manager must decide whether to replace it. The new machine would cost $50,000 and would last 10 years. It would have no salvage value. The old machine is fully depreciated and has no trade-in value. McCall uses straight-line depreciation for all assets. The new machine, being new and more efficient, would save the company $8,000 per year in cash operating costs. The only difference between cash flow and net income is depreciation. The internal rate of return of the project is approximately 10%. McCall Corporation's weighted-average cost of capital is 4%. McCall is not subject to any income taxes.

Required

1. Should McCall Corporation replace the machine? Why or why not?
2. Assume that "investment" is defined as average net long-term assets after depreciation. Compute the project's ROI for each of its first five years. If the patio furniture manager is interested in maximizing his bonus, would he replace the machine before he retires? Why or why not?
3. What can McCall do to entice the manager to replace the machine before retiring?

23-22 ROI, RI, EVA. Performance Auto Company operates a new car division (that sells high-performance sports cars) and a performance parts division (that sells performance-improvement parts for family cars). Some division financial measures for 2014 are as follows:

	A	B	C
1		**New Car Division**	**Performance Parts Division**
2	Total assets	$33,000,000	$28,500,000
3	Current liabilities	$ 6,600,000	$ 8,400,000
4	Operating income	$ 2,475,000	$ 2,565,000
5	Required rate of return	12%	12%

Required

1. Calculate return on investment (ROI) for each division using operating income as a measure of income and total assets as a measure of investment.
2. Calculate residual income (RI) for each division using operating income as a measure of income and total assets minus current liabilities as a measure of investment.
3. William Abraham, the new car division manager, argues that the performance parts division has "loaded up on a lot of short-term debt" to boost its RI. Calculate an alternative RI for each division that is not sensitive to the amount of short-term debt taken on by the performance parts division. Comment on the result.
4. Performance Auto Company, whose tax rate is 40%, has two sources of funds: long-term debt with a market value of $18,000,000 at an interest rate of 10% and equity capital with a market value of $12,000,000 and a cost of equity of 15%. Applying the same weighted-average cost of capital (WACC) to each division, calculate EVA for each division.
5. Use your preceding calculations to comment on the relative performance of each division.

23-23 Capital budgeting, RI. Samantha Shiells, a new associate at Hansen Partners, has compiled the following data for a potential venture:

Investment: $200,000

5-year useful life, with no salvage value

Annual sales revenues = $100,000

Annual cash costs = $42,000

Hansen faces a 20% tax rate on income and knows that the tax authorities will only permit straight-line depreciation for tax purposes. Hansen imposes an after-tax required rate of return of 10%.

Required

1. Based on net present value considerations, is this a project Hansen Partners would want to take?
2. Hansen Partners use straight-line depreciation for internal accounting and measure investment as the net book value of assets at the start of the year. Calculate the residual income in each year if the project were adopted.
3. Demonstrate that the conservation property of residual income, as described on page 883, holds in this example.
4. If Samantha Shiells is evaluated on the residual income of the projects she undertakes, would she take this project? Explain.

23-24 Multinational performance measurement, ROI, RI. The Mountainside Corporation manufactures similar products in the United States and Norway. The U.S. and Norwegian operations are organized as decentralized divisions. The following information is available for 2014; ROI is calculated as operating income divided by total assets:

	U.S. Division	Norwegian Division
Operating income	?	7,560,000 kroner
Total assets	$8,000,000	54,000,000 kroner
ROI	13.75%	?

Both investments were made on December 31, 2013. The exchange rate at the time of Mountainside's investment in Norway on December 31, 2013, was 6 kroner = $1. During 2014, the Norwegian kroner decreased steadily in value so that the exchange rate on December 31, 2014, is 8 kroner = $1. The average exchange rate during 2014 is [(6 + 8) ÷ 2] = 7 kroner = $1.

Required

1. **a.** Calculate the U.S. division's operating income for 2014.
   b. Calculate the Norwegian division's ROI for 2014 in kroner.
2. Top management wants to know which division earned a better ROI in 2014. What would you tell them? Explain your answer.
3. Which division do you think had the better RI performance? Explain your answer. The required rate of return on investment (calculated in U.S. dollars) is 13%.

23-25 ROI, RI, EVA, and performance evaluation. Lucy Manufacturing makes fashion products and competes on the basis of quality and leading-edge designs. The company has $3,200,000 invested in assets in its clothing manufacturing division. After-tax operating income from sales of clothing this year is $800,000. The cosmetics division has $7,500,000 invested in assets and an after-tax operating income this year of $1,800,000. Income for the clothing division has grown steadily over the past few years. The weighted-average cost of capital for Lucy is 11%. The CEO of Lucy has told the manager of each division that the division that "performs best" this year will get a bonus.

Required

1. Calculate the ROI and residual income for each division of Lucy Manufacturing, and briefly explain which manager will get the bonus. What are the advantages and disadvantages of each measure?
2. The CEO of Lucy Manufacturing has recently heard of another measure similar to residual income called EVA. The CEO has the accountant calculate EVA adjusted incomes of clothing and cosmetics and finds that the adjusted after-tax operating incomes are $938,000 and $1,147,200, respectively. Also, the clothing division has $520,000 of current liabilities, while the cosmetics division has only $330,000 of current liabilities. Using the preceding information, calculate EVA and discuss which division manager will get the bonus.
3. What nonfinancial measures could Lucy use to evaluate divisional performances?

23-26 Risk sharing, incentives, benchmarking, multiple tasks. The Dexter division of AMCO sells car batteries. AMCO's corporate management gives Dexter management considerable operating and investment autonomy in running the division. AMCO is considering how it should compensate Jim Marks, the general manager of the Dexter division. Proposal 1 calls for paying Marks a fixed salary. Proposal 2 calls for paying Marks no salary and compensating him only on the basis of the division's ROI, calculated based on operating income before any bonus payments. Proposal 3 calls for paying Marks some salary and some bonus based on ROI. Assume that Marks does not like bearing risk.

Required

1. Evaluate the three proposals, specifying the advantages and disadvantages of each.
2. Suppose that AMCO competes against Tiara Industries in the car battery business. Tiara is approximately the same size as the Dexter division and operates in a business environment that is similar to Dexter's. The top management of AMCO is considering evaluating Marks on the basis of Dexter's ROI minus Tiara's ROI. Marks complains that this approach is unfair because the performance of another company, over which he has no control, is included in his performance-evaluation measure. Is Marks's complaint valid? Why or why not?
3. Now suppose that Marks has no authority for making capital-investment decisions. Corporate management makes these decisions. Is ROI a good performance measure to use to evaluate Marks? Is ROI a good measure to evaluate the economic viability of the Dexter division? Explain.
4. Dexter's salespeople are responsible for selling and providing customer service and support. Sales are easy to measure. Although customer service is important to Dexter in the long run, it has not yet implemented customer-service measures. Marks wants to compensate his sales force only on the basis of sales commissions paid for each unit of product sold. He cites two advantages to this plan: (a) It creates strong incentives for the sales force to work hard, and (b) the company pays salespeople only when the company itself is earning revenues. Do you like his plan? Why or why not?

23-27 Residual income and EVA; timing issues. Doorharmony Company makes doorbells. It has a weighted-average cost of capital of 5% and total assets of $5,900,000. Doorharmony has current liabilities of $750,000. Its operating income for the year was $690,000. Doorharmony does not have to pay any income taxes. One of the expenses for accounting purposes was a $120,000 advertising campaign. The entire amount was deducted this year, although the Doorharmony CEO believes the beneficial effects of this advertising will last 4 years.

Required

1. Calculate residual income, assuming Doorharmony defines investment as total assets.
2. Calculate EVA for the year. Adjust both the assets and operating income for advertising assuming that for the purposes of economic value added the advertising is capitalized and amortized on a straight-line basis over 4 years.
3. Discuss the difference between the outcomes of requirements 1 and 2 and which measure is preferred.

MyAccountingLab

Problems

23-28 ROI performance measures based on historical cost and current cost. Nature's Juice Corporation operates three divisions that process and bottle natural fruit juices. The historical-cost accounting system reports the following information for 2014:

	Passion Fruit Division	Kiwi Fruit Division	Mango Fruit Division
Revenues	$1,300,000	$1,800,000	$2,400,000
Operating costs			
(excluding plant depreciation)	550,000	1,050,000	900,000
Plant depreciation	270,000	175,000	290,000
Operating income	$ 480,000	$ 575,000	$1,210,000
Current assets	$ 425,000	$ 600,000	$ 700,000
Long-term assets—plant	540,000	1,575,000	3,190,000
Total assets	$ 965,000	$2,175,000	$3,890,000

Nature's Juice estimates the useful life of each plant to be 12 years, with no terminal disposal value. The straight-line depreciation method is used. At the end of 2014, the passion fruit plant is 10 years old, the kiwi fruit plant is 3 years old, and the mango fruit plant is 1 year old. An index of construction costs over the 10-year period that Nature's Juice has been operating (2004 year-end =100) is as follows:

2004	2011	2013	2014
100	120	185	200

Given the high turnover of current assets, management believes that the historical-cost and current-cost measures of current assets are approximately the same.

Required

1. Compute the ROI ratio (operating income to total assets) of each division using historical-cost measures. Comment on the results.
2. Use the approach in Exhibit 23-2 (page 885) to compute the ROI of each division, incorporating current-cost estimates as of 2014 for depreciation expense and long-term assets. Comment on the results.
3. What advantages might arise from using current-cost asset measures as compared with historical-cost measures for evaluating the performance of the managers of the three divisions?

23-29 ROI, measurement alternatives for performance measures Appleton's owns and operates a variety of casual dining restaurants in three cities: St. Louis, Memphis, and New Orleans. Each geographic market is considered a separate division. The St. Louis division includes four restaurants, each built in early 2004. The Memphis division consists of three restaurants, each built in January 2008. The New Orleans division is the newest, consisting of three restaurants built 4 years ago. Division managers at Appleton's are evaluated on the basis of ROI. The following information refers to the three divisions at the end of 2014:

	A	B	C	D	E
1		St. Louis	Memphis	New Orleans	Total
2	Division revenues	$17,336,000	$12,050,000	$10,890,000	$40,276,000
3	Division expenses	15,890,000	11,042,000	9,958,000	36,890,000
4	Division operating income	1,446,000	1,008,000	932,000	3,386,000
5	Gross book value of long-term assets	9,000,000	7,500,000	8,100,000	24,600,000
6	Accumulated depreciation	6,600,000	3,500,000	2,160,000	12,260,000
7	Current assets	1,999,600	1,536,400	1,649,200	5,185,200
8	Depreciation expense	600,000	500,000	540,000	1,640,000
9	Construction cost index for year of construction	100	110	118	

Required

1. Calculate ROI for each division using net book value of total assets.
2. Using the technique in Exhibit 23-2, compute ROI using current-cost estimates for long-term assets and depreciation expense. The construction cost index for 2014 is 122. Estimated useful life of operational assets is 15 years.
3. How does the choice of long-term asset valuation affect management decisions regarding new capital investments? Why might this choice be more significant to the St. Louis division manager than to the New Orleans division manager?

23-30 Multinational firms, differing risk, comparison of profit, ROI, and RI. Zeiss Multinational, Inc., has divisions in the United States, Germany, and New Zealand. The U.S. division is the oldest and most established of the three and has a cost of capital of 6.5%. The German division was started 3 years ago when the exchange rate for the euro was 1 euro = \$1.40. The German division is a large and powerful division of Zeiss, Inc., with a cost of capital of 10%. The New Zealand division was started this year, when the exchange rate was 1 New Zealand Dollar (NZD) = \$0.75. Its cost of capital is 13%. Average exchange rates for the current year are 1 euro = \$1.50 and 1 NZD = \$0.60. Other information for the three divisions includes:

	United States	Germany	New Zealand
Long-term assets	\$24,214,700	11,897,321 euros	7,343,744 NZD
Operating revenues	\$23,362,940	6,250,000 euros	5,718,750 NZD
Operating expenses	\$18,520,000	4,200,000 euros	4,250,000 NZD
Income-tax rate	40%	35%	25%

Required

1. Translate the German and New Zealand information into dollars to make the divisions comparable. Find the after-tax operating income for each division and compare the profits.
2. Calculate ROI using after-tax operating income. Compare among divisions.
3. Use after-tax operating income and the individual cost of capital of each division to calculate residual income and compare.
4. Redo requirement 2 using pretax operating income instead of net income. Why is there a big difference, and what does it mean for performance evaluation?

23-31 ROI, RI, DuPont method, investment decisions, balanced scorecard. News Report Group has two major divisions: Print and Internet. Summary financial data (in millions) for 2013 and 2014 are as follows:

	A	B	C	D	E	F	G	H	I
1		Operating Income			Revenues			Total Assets	
2		2013	2014		2013	2014		2013	2014
3	Print	\$3,720	\$4,500		\$18,700	\$22,500		\$18,200	\$25,000
4	Internet	525	690		25,000	23,000		11,150	10,000

The two division managers' annual bonuses are based on division ROI (defined as operating income divided by total assets). If a division reports an increase in ROI from the previous year, its management is automatically eligible for a bonus; however, the management of a division reporting a decline in ROI has to present an explanation to the News Report Group board and is unlikely to get any bonus.

Carol Mays, manager of the Print division, is considering a proposal to invest \$2,580 million in a new computerized news reporting and printing system. It is estimated that the new system's state-of-the-art graphics and ability to quickly incorporate late-breaking news into papers will increase 2015 division operating income by \$360 million. News Report Group uses a 10% required rate of return on investment for each division.

Required

1. Use the DuPont method of profitability analysis to explain differences in 2014 ROIs between the two divisions. Use 2014 total assets as the investment base.
2. Why might Mays be less than enthusiastic about accepting the investment proposal for the new system despite her belief in the benefits of the new technology?
3. John Mendenhall, CEO of News Report Group, is considering a proposal to base division executive compensation on division RI.
   a. Compute the 2014 RI of each division.
   b. Would adoption of an RI measure reduce Mays' reluctance to adopt the new computerized system investment proposal?
4. Mendenhall is concerned that the focus on annual ROI could have an adverse long-run effect on News Report Group's customers. What other measurements, if any, do you recommend that Mendenhall use? Explain briefly.

23-32 Division managers' compensation, levers of control (continuation of 23-31). John Mendenhall seeks your advice on revising the existing bonus plan for division managers of News Report Group. Assume division managers do not like bearing risk. Mendenhall is considering three ideas:

- Make each division manager's compensation depend on division RI.
- Make each division manager's compensation depend on company-wide RI.
- Use benchmarking and compensate division managers on the basis of their division's RI minus the RI of the other division.

Required

1. Evaluate the three ideas Mendenhall has put forth using performance-evaluation concepts described in this chapter. Indicate the positive and negative features of each proposal.
2. Mendenhall is concerned that the pressure for short-run performance may cause managers to cut corners. What systems might Mendenhall introduce to avoid this problem? Explain briefly.
3. Mendenhall is also concerned that the pressure for short-run performance might cause managers to ignore emerging threats and opportunities. What system might Mendenhall introduce to prevent this problem? Explain briefly.

23-33 Executive compensation, balanced scorecard. Mercantile Bank recently introduced a new bonus plan for its business unit executives. The company believes that current profitability and customer satisfaction levels are equally important to the bank's long-term success. As a result, the new plan awards a bonus equal to 1% of salary for each 1% increase in business unit net income or 1% increase in the business unit's customer satisfaction index. For example, increasing net income from $3 million to $3.3 million (or 10% from its initial value) leads to a bonus of 10% of salary, while increasing the business unit's customer satisfaction index from 70 to 73.5 (or 5% from its initial value) leads to a bonus of 5% of salary. There is no bonus penalty when net income or customer satisfaction declines. In 2013 and 2014, Mercantile Bank's three business units reported the following performance results:

	Retail Banking		Business Banking		Credit Cards	
	2013	2014	2013	2014	2013	2014
Net income	$3,600,000	$3,912,000	$3,800,000	$3,940,000	$3,550,000	$3,499,000
Customer satisfaction	73	75.48	68	75.9	67	78.88

Required

1. Compute the bonus as a percent of salary earned by each business unit executive in 2014.
2. What factors might explain the differences between improvement rates for net income and those for customer satisfaction in the three units? Are increases in customer satisfaction likely to result in increased net income right away?
3. Mercantile Bank's board of directors is concerned that the 2014 bonus awards may not actually reflect the executives' overall performance. In particular, the bank is concerned that executives can earn large bonuses by doing well on one performance dimension but underperforming on the other. What changes can it make to the bonus plan to prevent this from happening in the future? Explain briefly.

23-34 Financial and nonfinancial performance measures, goal congruence. (CMA, adapted) Precision Equipment specializes in the manufacture of medical equipment, a field that has become increasingly competitive. Approximately 2 years ago, Pedro Mendez, president of Precision, decided to revise the bonus plan (based, at the time, entirely on operating income) to encourage division managers to focus on areas that were important to customers and that added value without increasing cost. In addition to a profitability incentive, the revised plan includes incentives for reduced rework costs, reduced sales returns, and on-time deliveries. The company calculates and rewards bonuses semiannually on the following basis: A base bonus is calculated at 2% of operating income; this amount is then adjusted as:

a. (i) Reduced by excess of rework costs over and above 2% of operating income
   (ii) No adjustment if rework costs are less than or equal to 2% of operating income
b. (i) Increased by $4,000 if more than 98% of deliveries are on time and by $1,500 if 96–98% of deliveries are on time
   (ii) No adjustment if on-time deliveries are below 96%
c. (i) Increased by $2,500 if sales returns are less than or equal to 1.5% of sales
   (ii) Decreased by 50% of excess of sales returns over 1.5% of sales

Note: If the calculation of the bonus results in a negative amount for a particular period, the manager simply receives no bonus, and the negative amount is not carried forward to the next period.

Results for Precision's Central division and Western division for 2014, the first year under the new bonus plan, follow. In 2013, under the old bonus plan, the Central division manager earned a bonus of $20,295 and the Western division manager a bonus of $15,830.

	Central Division		Western Division	
	Jan, 1, 2014, to June 30, 2014	July 1, 2014, to Dec 31, 2014	Jan. 1, 2014, to June 30, 2014	July 1, 2014, to Dec. 31, 2014
Revenues	$3,150,000	$3,300,000	$2,137,500	$2,175,000
Operating income	$346,500	$330,000	$256,500	$304,500
On-time delivery	95.4%	97.3%	98.2%	94.6%
Rework costs	$8,625	$8,250	$4,500	$6,000
Sales returns	$63,000	$52,500	$33,560	$31,875

Required

1. Why did Mendez need to introduce these new performance measures? That is, why does Mendez need to use these performance measures in addition to the operating-income numbers for the period?
2. Calculate the bonus earned by each manager for each 6-month period and for 2014.
3. What effect did the change in the bonus plan have on each manager's behavior? Did the new bonus plan achieve what Mendez wanted? What changes, if any, would you make to the new bonus plan?

23-35 ROI, RI, decision making. The following data refer to the successful Munger division of Buffett, Inc. Munger makes and sells high-end cordless drills. The drills sell for $80 each, and Munger expects sales of 300,000 units in 2014. Munger's annual fixed costs are $4 million. The variable cost per drill is $48.

Buffett evaluates Munger based on residual income. The total investment attributed to Munger is $16 million, and Buffett has a required rate of return on investment of 20%.

Ignore taxes and depreciation expense. Answer each of the following parts *independently*, unless otherwise stated.

Required

1. What is the expected residual income in 2014?
2. Munger receives an external special order for 100,000 units at $60 each. If the order is accepted, Munger will have to incur incremental fixed costs of $850,000 and invest an additional $2 million in various assets.

   What is the effect on Munger's residual income of accepting the order?
3. One of the components Munger manufactures for its drill has a variable cost of $4. An outside vendor has offered to supply the 300,000 units required at a cost of $5.25 per unit. If the component is purchased outside, fixed costs will decline by $200,000 and assets with a book value of $760,000 will be sold at book value.

   Will Munger decide to make or buy the component? Explain your answer.
4. One of Munger's regular customers asks for a special drill made of tempered steel. The customer requires 15,000 drills. Munger estimates its variable cost for these special units at $54 apiece. Munger will also have to undertake new investment of $1,500,000 to produce the drills.

   What is the minimum selling price that will make the deal acceptable to Munger?
5. Assume the same facts as in requirement 4. Also suppose that the customer has offered $82 for each special drill. In addition, the customer has indicated that its purchases of the existing product will drop by 6,000 units.
   a. What is the net change in Munger's residual income from taking the offer, relative to its planned 2014 situation?
   b. At what drop in unit sales of the regular drill would Munger be indifferent to the offer?

23-36 Ethics, levers of control. Best Moulding is a large manufacturer of wood picture frame moulding. The company operates distribution centers in Dallas and Philadelphia. The distribution centers cut frames to size (called "chops") and ship them to custom picture framers. Because of the exacting standards and natural flaws of wood picture frame moulding, the company typically produces a large amount of waste in cutting chops. In recent years, the company's average yield has been 78% of length moulding. The remaining 22% is sent to a wood recycler. Best's performance-evaluation system pays its distribution center managers substantial bonuses if the company achieves annual budgeted profit numbers. In the last quarter of 2014, Stuart Brown, Best's controller, noted a significant increase in yield percentage of the Dallas distribution center, from 76% to 87%. This increase resulted in a 6% increase in the center's profits.

During a recent trip to the Dallas center, Brown wandered into the moulding warehouse. He noticed that much of the scrap moulding was being returned to the inventory bins rather than being placed in the discard pile. Upon further inspection, he determined that the moulding was in fact unusable. When he asked one of the workers, he was told that the center's manager had directed workers to stop scrapping all but the very shortest pieces. This practice resulted in the center overreporting both yield and ending inventory. The overstatement of Dallas inventory will have a significant impact on Best's financial statements.

Required

1. What should Brown do? You may want to refer to the *IMA Statement of Ethical Professional Practice*, page 18.
2. Which lever of control is Best emphasizing? What changes, if any, should be made?

23-37 RI, EVA, measurement alternatives, goal congruence. Refresh Resorts, Inc., operates health spas in Key West, Florida; Phoenix, Arizona; and Carmel, California. The Key West spa was the company's first and opened in 1988. The Phoenix spa opened in 2001, and the Carmel spa opened in 2010. Refresh Resorts has previously evaluated divisions based on RI, but the company is considering changing to an EVA approach. All spas are assumed to face similar risks. Data for 2014 are:

	A	B	C	D	E
1		**Key West**	**Phoenix**	**Carmel**	**Total**
2	Revenues	$4,100,000	$4,380,000	$3,230,000	$11,710,000
3	Variable costs	1,600,000	1,630,000	955,000	4,185,000
4	Fixed costs	1,280,000	1,560,000	980,000	3,820,000
5	Operating income	1,220,000	1,190,000	1,295,000	3,705,000
6	Interest costs on long-term debt at 8%	368,000	416,000	440,000	1,224,000
7	Income before taxes	852,000	774,000	855,000	2,481,000
8	Net income after 35% taxes	553,800	503,100	555,750	1,612,650
9					
10	Net book value at 2014 year-end:				
11	Current assets	$1,280,000	$ 850,000	$ 600,000	$ 2,730,000
12	Long-term assets	4,875,000	5,462,000	6,835,000	17,172,000
13	Total assets	6,155,000	6,312,000	7,435,000	19,902,000
14					
15	Current liabilities	330,000	265,000	84,000	679,000
16	Long-term debt	4,600,000	5,200,000	5,500,000	15,300,000
17	Stockholders' equity	1,225,000	847,000	1,851,000	3,923,000
18	Total liabilities and stockholders' equity	6,155,000	6,312,000	7,435,000	19,902,000
19					
20	Market value of debt	$4,600,000	$5,200,000	$5,500,000	$15,300,000
21	Market value of equity	2,400,000	2,660,000	2,590,000	7,650,000
22	Cost of equity capital				14%
23	Required rate of return				11%
24	Accumulated depreciation on long-term assets	$2,200,000	$1,510,000	$220,000	

Required

1. Calculate RI for each of the spas based on operating income and using total assets as the measure of investment. Suppose that the Key West spa is considering adding a new group of saunas from Finland that will cost $225,000. The saunas are expected to bring in operating income of $22,000. What effect would this project have on the RI of the Key West spa? Based on RI, would the Key West manager accept or reject this project? Why? Without resorting to calculations, would the other managers accept or reject the project? Why?
2. Why might Refresh Resorts want to use EVA instead of RI for evaluating the performance of the three spas?
3. Refer back to the original data. Calculate the WACC for Refresh Resorts.
4. Refer back to the original data. Calculate EVA for each of the spas, using net book value of long-term assets. Calculate EVA again, this time using gross book value of long-term assets. Comment on the differences between the two methods.
5. How does the selection of asset measurement method affect goal congruence?

Appendix A

Notes on Compound Interest and Interest Tables

Interest is the cost of using money. It is the rental charge for funds, just as renting a building and equipment entails a rental charge. When the funds are used for a period of time, it is necessary to recognize interest as a cost of using the borrowed ("rented") funds. This requirement applies even if the funds represent ownership capital and if interest does not entail an outlay of cash. Why must interest be considered? Because the selection of one alternative automatically commits a given amount of funds that could otherwise be invested in some other alternative.

Interest is generally important, even when short-term projects are under consideration. Interest looms correspondingly larger when long-run plans are studied. The rate of interest has significant enough impact to influence decisions regarding borrowing and investing funds. For example, $100,000 invested now and compounded annually for 10 years at 8% will accumulate to $215,900; at 20%, the $100,000 will accumulate to $619,200.

Interest Tables

Many computer programs and pocket calculators are available that handle computations involving the time value of money. You may also turn to the following four basic tables to compute interest.

Table 1—Future Amount of $1

Table 1 shows how much $1 invested now will accumulate in a given number of periods at a given compounded interest rate per period. Consider investing $1,000 now for three years at 8% compound interest. A tabular presentation of how this $1,000 would accumulate to $1,259.70 follows:

Year	Interest per Year	Cumulative Interest Called Compound Interest	Total at End of Year
0	$—	$—	$1,000.00
1	80.00 (0.08 × $1,000)	80.00	1,080.00
2	86.40 (0.08 × $1,080)	166.40	1,166.40
3	93.30 (0.08 × $1,166.40)	259.70	1,259.70

This tabular presentation is a series of computations that could appear as follows, where *S* is the future amount and the subscripts 1, 2, and 3 indicate the number of time periods.

$$S_1 = \$1{,}000(1.08)^1 = \$1{,}080$$

$$S_2 = \$1{,}080(1.08) = \$1{,}000(1.08)^2 = \$1{,}166.40$$

$$S_3 = \$1{,}166.40 \times (1.08) = \$1{,}000(1.08)^3 = \$1{,}259.70$$

The formula for the "future amount of \$P," often called the "future value of \$P," or "compound amount of \$P," can be written as follows:

$$S = P(1 + r)^n$$

S is the future value amount; P is the present value, r is the rate of interest; and n is the number of time periods.

When $P = \$1,000$, $n = 3$, $r = 0.08$, $S = \$1,000(1 + .08)^3 = \$1,259.70$.

Fortunately, tables make key computations readily available. A facility in selecting the *proper* table will minimize computations. Check the accuracy of the preceding answer using Table 1, page 913.

Table 2—Present Value of \$1

In the previous example, if \$1,000 compounded at 8% per year will accumulate to \$1,259.70 in three years, then \$1,000 must be the present value of \$1,259.70 due at the end of three years. The formula for the present value can be derived by reversing the process of *accumulation* (finding the future amount) that we just finished.

If

$$S = P(1 + r)^n$$

then

$$P = \frac{S}{(1 + r)^n}$$

In our example, $S = \$1,259.70$, $n = 3$, $r = 0.08$, so

$$P = \frac{\$1,259.70}{(1.08)^3} = \$1,000$$

Use Table 2, page 914, to check this calculation.

When accumulating, we advance or roll forward in time. The difference between our original amount and our accumulated amount is called *compound interest*. When discounting, we retreat or roll back in time. The difference between the future amount and the present value is called *compound discount*. Note the following formulas:

$$\text{Compound interest} = P[(1 + r)^n - 1]$$

In our example, $P = \$1,000$, $n = 3$, $r = 0.08$, so

$$\text{Compound interest} = \$1,000[(1.08)^3 - 1] = \$259.70$$

$$\text{Compound discount} = S\left[1 - \frac{1}{(1 + r)^n}\right]$$

In our example, $S = \$1,259.70$, $n = 3$, $r = 0.08$, so

$$\text{Compound discount} = \$1,259.70\left[1 - \frac{1}{(1.08)^3}\right] = \$259.70$$

Table 3—Compound Amount (Future Value) of Annuity of $1

An (ordinary) *annuity* is a series of equal payments (receipts) to be paid (or received) at the end of successive periods of equal length. Assume that $1,000 is invested at the end of each of three years at 8%:

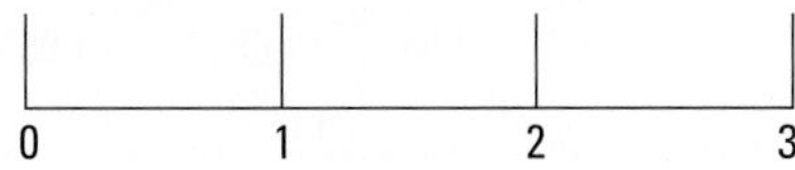

End of Year			Amount
1st payment	$1,000.00 ⟶	$1,080.00 ⟶	$1,166.40, which is $1,000(1.08)^2
2nd payment		$1,000.00 ⟶	1,080.00, which is $1,000(1.08)^1
3rd payment			1,000.00
Accumulation (compound amount)			$3,246.40

The preceding arithmetic may be expressed algebraically as the future value of an ordinary annuity of $1,000 for 3 years = $\$1{,}000(1 + r)^2 + \$1{,}000(1 + r)^1 + \$1{,}000$.

We can develop the general formula for S_n, the future value of an ordinary annuity of $1, by using the preceding example as a basis where $n = 3$ and $r = 0.08$:

1. $S_3 = 1 + (1 + r)^1 + (1 + r)^2$
2. Substitute $r = 0.08$: $S_3 = 1 + (1.08)^1 + (1.08)^2$
3. Multiply (2) by $(1 + r)$: $(1.08)S_3 = (1.08)^1 + (1.08)^2 + (1.08)^3$
4. Subtract (2) from (3): Note that all terms on the right-hand side are removed except $(1.08)^3$ in equation (3) and 1 in equation (2). $1.08S_3 - S_3 = (1.08)^3 - 1$
5. Factor (4): $S_3(1.08 - 1) = (1.08)^3 - 1$
6. Divide (5) by $(1.08 - 1)$: $S_3 = \frac{(1.08)^3 - 1}{1.08 - 1} = \frac{(1.08)^3 - 1}{0.08} = \frac{0.2597}{0.08} = 3.246$
7. The general formula for the future value of an ordinary annuity of $1 becomes: $S_n = \frac{(1 + r)^n - 1}{r}$ or $\frac{\text{Compound interest}}{\text{Rate}}$

This formula is the basis for Table 3, page 915. Check the answer in the table.

Table 4—Present Value of an Ordinary Annuity of $1

Using the same example as for Table 3, we can show how the formula of P_n, *the present value of an ordinary annuity*, is developed.

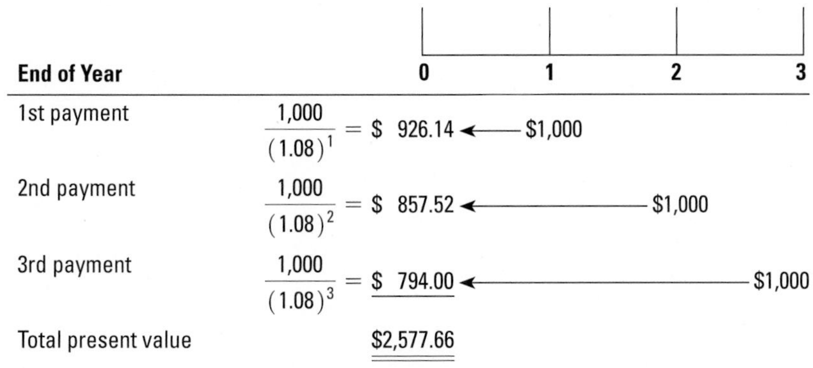

End of Year
0
1
2
3
1st payment
$\frac{1,000}{(1.08)^1}$ = $ 926.14 ⟵ $1,000
2nd payment
$\frac{1,000}{(1.08)^2}$ = $ 857.52 ⟵ $1,000
3rd payment
$\frac{1,000}{(1.08)^3}$ = $ 794.00 ⟵ $1,000
Total present value
$2,577.66

We can develop the general formula for P_n by using the preceding example as a basis where $n = 3$ and $r = 0.08$:

1. $$P_3 = \frac{1}{1+r} + \frac{1}{(1+r)^2} + \frac{1}{(1+r)^3}$$

2. Substitute $r = 0.08$: $$P_3 = \frac{1}{1.08} + \frac{1}{(1.08)^2} + \frac{1}{(1.08)^3}$$

3. Multiply (2) by $\frac{1}{1.08}$: $$P_3\frac{1}{1.08} = \frac{1}{(1.08)^2} + \frac{1}{(1.08)^3} + \frac{1}{(1.08)^4}$$

4. Subtract (3) from (2): $$P_3 - P_3\frac{1}{1.08} = \frac{1}{1.08} - \frac{1}{(1.08)^4}$$

5. Factor (4): $$P_3\left(1 - \frac{1}{(1.08)}\right) = \frac{1}{1.08}\left[1 - \frac{1}{(1.08)^3}\right]$$

6. or $$P_3\left(\frac{0.08}{1.08}\right) = \frac{1}{1.08}\left[1 - \frac{1}{(1.08)^3}\right]$$

7. Multiply (6) by $\frac{1.08}{0.08}$: $$P_3 = \frac{1}{0.08}\left[1 - \frac{1}{(1.08)^3}\right] = \frac{0.2062}{0.08} = 2.577$$

The general formula for the present value of an annuity of \$1.00 is as follows:

$$P_n = \frac{1}{r}\left[1 - \frac{1}{(1+r)^n}\right] = \frac{\text{Compound discount}}{\text{Rate}}$$

The formula is the basis for Table 4, page 916. Check the answer in the table. The present value tables, Tables 2 and 4, are used most frequently in capital budgeting.

The tables for annuities are not essential. With Tables 1 and 2, compound interest and compound discount can readily be computed. It is simply a matter of dividing either of these by the rate to get values equivalent to those shown in Tables 3 and 4.

Table 1

Compound Amount of \$1.00 (The Future Value of \$1.00)

$S = P(1 + r)^n$. In this table $P = \$1.00$

Periods	2%	4%	6%	8%	10%	12%	14%	16%	18%	20%	22%	24%	26%	28%	30%	32%	40%	Periods
1	1.020	1.040	1.060	1.080	1.100	1.120	1.140	1.160	1.180	1.200	1.220	1.240	1.260	1.280	1.300	1.320	1.400	1
2	1.040	1.082	1.124	1.166	1.210	1.254	1.300	1.346	1.392	1.440	1.488	1.538	1.588	1.638	1.690	1.742	1.960	2
3	1.061	1.125	1.191	1.260	1.331	1.405	1.482	1.561	1.643	1.728	1.816	1.907	2.000	2.097	2.197	2.300	2.744	3
4	1.082	1.170	1.262	1.360	1.464	1.574	1.689	1.811	1.939	2.074	2.215	2.364	2.520	2.684	2.856	3.036	3.842	4
5	1.104	1.217	1.338	1.469	1.611	1.762	1.925	2.100	2.288	2.488	2.703	2.932	3.176	3.436	3.713	4.007	5.378	5
6	1.126	1.265	1.419	1.587	1.772	1.974	2.195	2.436	2.700	2.986	3.297	3.635	4.002	4.398	4.827	5.290	7.530	6
7	1.149	1.316	1.504	1.714	1.949	2.211	2.502	2.826	3.185	3.583	4.023	4.508	5.042	5.629	6.275	6.983	10.541	7
8	1.172	1.369	1.594	1.851	2.144	2.476	2.853	3.278	3.759	4.300	4.908	5.590	6.353	7.206	8.157	9.217	14.758	8
9	1.195	1.423	1.689	1.999	2.358	2.773	3.252	3.803	4.435	5.160	5.987	6.931	8.005	9.223	10.604	12.166	20.661	9
10	1.219	1.480	1.791	2.159	2.594	3.106	3.707	4.411	5.234	6.192	7.305	8.594	10.086	11.806	13.786	16.060	28.925	10
11	1.243	1.539	1.898	2.332	2.853	3.479	4.226	5.117	6.176	7.430	8.912	10.657	12.708	15.112	17.922	21.199	40.496	11
12	1.268	1.601	2.012	2.518	3.138	3.896	4.818	5.936	7.288	8.916	10.872	13.215	16.012	19.343	23.298	27.983	56.694	12
13	1.294	1.665	2.133	2.720	3.452	4.363	5.492	6.886	8.599	10.699	13.264	16.386	20.175	24.759	30.288	36.937	79.371	13
14	1.319	1.732	2.261	2.937	3.797	4.887	6.261	7.988	10.147	12.839	16.182	20.319	25.421	31.691	39.374	48.757	111.120	14
15	1.346	1.801	2.397	3.172	4.177	5.474	7.138	9.266	11.974	15.407	19.742	25.196	32.030	40.565	51.186	64.359	155.568	15
16	1.373	1.873	2.540	3.426	4.595	6.130	8.137	10.748	14.129	18.488	24.086	31.243	40.358	51.923	66.542	84.954	217.795	16
17	1.400	1.948	2.693	3.700	5.054	6.866	9.276	12.468	16.672	22.186	29.384	38.741	50.851	66.461	86.504	112.139	304.913	17
18	1.428	2.026	2.854	3.996	5.560	7.690	10.575	14.463	19.673	26.623	35.849	48.039	64.072	85.071	112.455	148.024	426.879	18
19	1.457	2.107	3.026	4.316	6.116	8.613	12.056	16.777	23.214	31.948	43.736	59.568	80.731	108.890	146.192	195.391	597.630	19
20	1.486	2.191	3.207	4.661	6.727	9.646	13.743	19.461	27.393	38.338	53.358	73.864	101.721	139.380	190.050	257.916	836.683	20
21	1.516	2.279	3.400	5.034	7.400	10.804	15.668	22.574	32.324	46.005	65.096	91.592	128.169	178.406	247.065	340.449	1171.356	21
22	1.546	2.370	3.604	5.437	8.140	12.100	17.861	26.186	38.142	55.206	79.418	113.574	161.492	228.360	321.184	449.393	1639.898	22
23	1.577	2.465	3.820	5.871	8.954	13.552	20.362	30.376	45.008	66.247	96.889	140.831	203.480	292.300	417.539	593.199	2295.857	23
24	1.608	2.563	4.049	6.341	9.850	15.179	23.212	35.236	53.109	79.497	118.205	174.631	256.385	374.144	542.801	783.023	3214.200	24
25	1.641	2.666	4.292	6.848	10.835	17.000	26.462	40.874	62.669	95.396	144.210	216.542	323.045	478.905	705.641	1033.590	4499.880	25
26	1.673	2.772	4.549	7.396	11.918	19.040	30.167	47.414	73.949	114.475	175.936	268.512	407.037	612.998	917.333	1364.339	6299.831	26
27	1.707	2.883	4.822	7.988	13.110	21.325	34.390	55.000	87.260	137.371	214.642	332.955	512.867	784.638	1192.533	1800.927	8819.764	27
28	1.741	2.999	5.112	8.627	14.421	23.884	39.204	63.800	102.967	164.845	261.864	412.864	646.212	1004.336	1550.293	2377.224	12347.670	28
29	1.776	3.119	5.418	9.317	15.863	26.750	44.693	74.009	121.501	197.814	319.474	511.952	814.228	1285.550	2015.381	3137.935	17286.737	29
30	1.811	3.243	5.743	10.063	17.449	29.960	50.950	85.850	143.371	237.376	389.758	634.820	1025.927	1645.505	2619.996	4142.075	24201.432	30
35	2.000	3.946	7.686	14.785	28.102	52.800	98.100	180.314	327.997	590.668	1053.402	1861.054	3258.135	5653.911	9727.860	16599.217	130161.112	35
40	2.208	4.801	10.286	21.725	45.259	93.051	188.884	378.721	750.378	1469.772	2847.038	5455.913	10347.175	19426.689	36118.865	66520.767	700037.697	40

Table 2 *(Place a clip on this page for your reference.)*

Present Value of $1.00

$P = \frac{S}{(1 + r)^n}$. In this table $S = \$1.00$.

Periods	2%	4%	6%	8%	10%	12%	14%	16%	18%	20%	22%	24%	26%	28%	30%	32%	40%	Periods
1	0.980	0.962	0.943	0.926	0.909	0.893	0.877	0.862	0.847	0.833	0.820	0.806	0.794	0.781	0.769	0.758	0.714	1
2	0.961	0.925	0.890	0.857	0.826	0.797	0.769	0.743	0.718	0.694	0.672	0.650	0.630	0.610	0.592	0.574	0.510	2
3	0.942	0.889	0.840	0.794	0.751	0.712	0.675	0.641	0.609	0.579	0.551	0.524	0.500	0.477	0.455	0.435	0.364	3
4	0.924	0.855	0.792	0.735	0.683	0.636	0.592	0.552	0.516	0.482	0.451	0.423	0.397	0.373	0.350	0.329	0.260	4
5	0.906	0.822	0.747	0.681	0.621	0.567	0.519	0.476	0.437	0.402	0.370	0.341	0.315	0.291	0.269	0.250	0.186	5
6	0.888	0.790	0.705	0.630	0.564	0.507	0.456	0.410	0.370	0.335	0.303	0.275	0.250	0.227	0.207	0.189	0.133	6
7	0.871	0.760	0.665	0.583	0.513	0.452	0.400	0.354	0.314	0.279	0.249	0.222	0.198	0.178	0.159	0.143	0.095	7
8	0.853	0.731	0.627	0.540	0.467	0.404	0.351	0.305	0.266	0.233	0.204	0.179	0.157	0.139	0.123	0.108	0.068	8
9	0.837	0.703	0.592	0.500	0.424	0.361	0.308	0.263	0.225	0.194	0.167	0.144	0.125	0.108	0.094	0.082	0.048	9
10	0.820	0.676	0.558	0.463	0.386	0.322	0.270	0.227	0.191	0.162	0.137	0.116	0.099	0.085	0.073	0.062	0.035	10
11	0.804	0.650	0.527	0.429	0.350	0.287	0.237	0.195	0.162	0.135	0.112	0.094	0.079	0.066	0.056	0.047	0.025	11
12	0.788	0.625	0.497	0.397	0.319	0.257	0.208	0.168	0.137	0.112	0.092	0.076	0.062	0.052	0.043	0.036	0.018	12
13	0.773	0.601	0.469	0.368	0.290	0.229	0.182	0.145	0.116	0.093	0.075	0.061	0.050	0.040	0.033	0.027	0.013	13
14	0.758	0.577	0.442	0.340	0.263	0.205	0.160	0.125	0.099	0.078	0.062	0.049	0.039	0.032	0.025	0.021	0.009	14
15	0.743	0.555	0.417	0.315	0.239	0.183	0.140	0.108	0.084	0.065	0.051	0.040	0.031	0.025	0.020	0.016	0.006	15
16	0.728	0.534	0.394	0.292	0.218	0.163	0.123	0.093	0.071	0.054	0.042	0.032	0.025	0.019	0.015	0.012	0.005	16
17	0.714	0.513	0.371	0.270	0.198	0.146	0.108	0.080	0.060	0.045	0.034	0.026	0.020	0.015	0.012	0.009	0.003	17
18	0.700	0.494	0.350	0.250	0.180	0.130	0.095	0.069	0.051	0.038	0.028	0.021	0.016	0.012	0.009	0.007	0.002	18
19	0.686	0.475	0.331	0.232	0.164	0.116	0.083	0.060	0.043	0.031	0.023	0.017	0.012	0.009	0.007	0.005	0.002	19
20	0.673	0.456	0.312	0.215	0.149	0.104	0.073	0.051	0.037	0.026	0.019	0.014	0.010	0.007	0.005	0.004	0.001	20
21	0.660	0.439	0.294	0.199	0.135	0.093	0.064	0.044	0.031	0.022	0.015	0.011	0.008	0.006	0.004	0.003	0.001	21
22	0.647	0.422	0.278	0.184	0.123	0.083	0.056	0.038	0.026	0.018	0.013	0.009	0.006	0.004	0.003	0.002	0.001	22
23	0.634	0.406	0.262	0.170	0.112	0.074	0.049	0.033	0.022	0.015	0.010	0.007	0.005	0.003	0.002	0.002	0.000	23
24	0.622	0.390	0.247	0.158	0.102	0.066	0.043	0.028	0.019	0.013	0.008	0.006	0.004	0.003	0.002	0.001	0.000	24
25	0.610	0.375	0.233	0.146	0.092	0.059	0.038	0.024	0.016	0.010	0.007	0.005	0.003	0.002	0.001	0.001	0.000	25
26	0.598	0.361	0.220	0.135	0.084	0.053	0.033	0.021	0.014	0.009	0.006	0.004	0.002	0.002	0.001	0.001	0.000	26
27	0.586	0.347	0.207	0.125	0.076	0.047	0.029	0.018	0.011	0.007	0.005	0.003	0.002	0.001	0.001	0.001	0.000	27
28	0.574	0.333	0.196	0.116	0.069	0.042	0.026	0.016	0.010	0.006	0.004	0.002	0.002	0.001	0.001	0.000	0.000	28
29	0.563	0.321	0.185	0.107	0.063	0.037	0.022	0.014	0.008	0.005	0.003	0.002	0.001	0.001	0.000	0.000	0.000	29
30	0.552	0.308	0.174	0.099	0.057	0.033	0.020	0.012	0.007	0.004	0.003	0.002	0.001	0.001	0.000	0.000	0.000	30
35	0.500	0.253	0.130	0.068	0.036	0.019	0.010	0.006	0.003	0.002	0.001	0.001	0.000	0.000	0.000	0.000	0.000	35
40	0.453	0.208	0.097	0.046	0.022	0.011	0.005	0.003	0.001	0.001	0.000	0.000	0.000	0.000	0.000	0.000	0.000	40

Table 3

Compound Amount of Annuity of $1.00 in Arrears* (Future Value of Annuity)

$$S_n = \frac{(1 + r)^n - 1}{r}$$

Periods	2%	4%	6%	8%	10%	12%	14%	16%	18%	20%	22%	24%	26%	28%	30%	32%	40%	Periods
1	1.000	1.000	1.000	1.000	1.000	1.000	1.000	1.000	1.000	1.000	1.000	1.000	1.000	1.000	1.000	1.000	1.000	1
2	2.020	2.040	2.060	2.080	2.100	2.120	2.140	2.160	2.180	2.200	2.220	2.240	2.260	2.280	2.300	2.320	2.400	2
3	3.060	3.122	3.184	3.246	3.310	3.374	3.440	3.506	3.572	3.640	3.708	3.778	3.848	3.918	3.990	4.062	4.360	3
4	4.122	4.246	4.375	4.506	4.641	4.779	4.921	5.066	5.215	5.368	5.524	5.684	5.848	6.016	6.187	6.362	7.104	4
5	5.204	5.416	5.637	5.867	6.105	6.353	6.610	6.877	7.154	7.442	7.740	8.048	8.368	8.700	9.043	9.398	10.946	5
6	6.308	6.633	6.975	7.336	7.716	8.115	8.536	8.977	9.442	9.930	10.442	10.980	11.544	12.136	12.756	13.406	16.324	6
7	7.434	7.898	8.394	8.923	9.487	10.089	10.730	11.414	12.142	12.916	13.740	14.615	15.546	16.534	17.583	18.696	23.853	7
8	8.583	9.214	9.897	10.637	11.436	12.300	13.233	14.240	15.327	16.499	17.762	19.123	20.588	22.163	23.858	25.678	34.395	8
9	9.755	10.583	11.491	12.488	13.579	14.776	16.085	17.519	19.086	20.799	22.670	24.712	26.940	29.369	32.015	34.895	49.153	9
10	10.950	12.006	13.181	14.487	15.937	17.549	19.337	21.321	23.521	25.959	28.657	31.643	34.945	38.593	42.619	47.062	69.814	10
11	12.169	13.486	14.972	16.645	18.531	20.655	23.045	25.733	28.755	32.150	35.962	40.238	45.031	50.398	56.405	63.122	98.739	11
12	13.412	15.026	16.870	18.977	21.384	24.133	27.271	30.850	34.931	39.581	44.874	50.895	57.739	65.510	74.327	84.320	139.235	12
13	14.680	16.627	18.882	21.495	24.523	28.029	32.089	36.786	42.219	48.497	55.746	64.110	73.751	84.853	97.625	112.303	195.929	13
14	15.974	18.292	21.015	24.215	27.975	32.393	37.581	43.672	50.818	59.196	69.010	80.496	93.926	109.612	127.913	149.240	275.300	14
15	17.293	20.024	23.276	27.152	31.772	37.280	43.842	51.660	60.965	72.035	85.192	100.815	119.347	141.303	167.286	197.997	386.420	15
16	18.639	21.825	25.673	30.324	35.950	42.753	50.980	60.925	72.939	87.442	104.935	126.011	151.377	181.868	218.472	262.356	541.988	16
17	20.012	23.698	28.213	33.750	40.545	48.884	59.118	71.673	87.068	105.931	129.020	157.253	191.735	233.791	285.014	347.309	759.784	17
18	21.412	25.645	30.906	37.450	45.599	55.750	68.394	84.141	103.740	128.117	158.405	195.994	242.585	300.252	371.518	459.449	1064.697	18
19	22.841	27.671	33.760	41.446	51.159	63.440	78.969	98.603	123.414	154.740	194.254	244.033	306.658	385.323	483.973	607.472	1491.576	19
20	24.297	29.778	36.786	45.762	57.275	72.052	91.025	115.380	146.628	186.688	237.989	303.601	387.389	494.213	630.165	802.863	2089.206	20
21	25.783	31.969	39.993	50.423	64.002	81.699	104.768	134.841	174.021	225.026	291.347	377.465	489.110	633.593	820.215	1060.779	2925.889	21
22	27.299	34.248	43.392	55.457	71.403	92.503	120.436	157.415	206.345	271.031	356.443	469.056	617.278	811.999	1067.280	1401.229	4097.245	22
23	28.845	36.618	46.996	60.893	79.543	104.603	138.297	183.601	244.487	326.237	435.861	582.630	778.771	1040.358	1388.464	1850.622	5737.142	23
24	30.422	39.083	50.816	66.765	88.497	118.155	158.659	213.978	289.494	392.484	532.750	723.461	982.251	1332.659	1806.003	2443.821	8032.999	24
25	32.030	41.646	54.865	73.106	98.347	133.334	181.871	249.214	342.603	471.981	650.955	898.092	1238.636	1706.803	2348.803	3226.844	11247.199	25
26	33.671	44.312	59.156	79.954	109.182	150.334	208.333	290.088	405.272	567.377	795.165	1114.634	1561.682	2185.708	3054.444	4260.434	15747.079	26
27	35.344	47.084	63.706	87.351	121.100	169.374	238.499	337.502	479.221	681.853	971.102	1383.146	1968.719	2798.706	3971.778	5624.772	22046.910	27
28	37.051	49.968	68.528	95.339	134.210	190.699	272.889	392.503	566.481	819.223	1185.744	1716.101	2481.586	3583.344	5164.311	7425.699	30866.674	28
29	38.792	52.966	73.640	103.966	148.631	214.583	312.094	456.303	669.447	984.068	1447.608	2128.965	3127.798	4587.680	6714.604	9802.923	43214.343	29
30	40.568	56.085	79.058	113.263	164.494	241.333	356.787	530.312	790.948	1181.882	1767.081	2640.916	3942.026	5873.231	8729.985	12940.859	60501.081	30
35	49.994	73.652	111.435	172.317	271.024	431.663	693.573	1120.713	1816.652	2948.341	4783.645	7750.225	12527.442	20188.966	32422.868	51869.427	325400.279	35
40	60.402	95.026	154.762	259.057	442.593	767.091	1342.025	2360.757	4163.213	7343.858	12936.535	22728.803	39792.982	69377.460	120392.883	207874.272	1750091.741	40

*Payments (or receipts) at the end of each period.

Table 4 *(Place a clip on this page for your reference.)*

Present Value of Annuity $1.00 in Arrears*

$$P_n = \frac{1}{r}\left[1 - \frac{1}{(1+r)^n}\right]$$

Periods	2%	4%	6%	8%	10%	12%	14%	16%	18%	20%	22%	24%	26%	28%	30%	32%	40%	Periods
1	0.980	0.962	0.943	0.926	0.909	0.893	0.877	0.862	0.847	0.833	0.820	0.806	0.794	0.781	0.769	0.758	0.714	1
2	1.942	1.886	1.833	1.783	1.736	1.690	1.647	1.605	1.566	1.528	1.492	1.457	1.424	1.392	1.361	1.331	1.224	2
3	2.884	2.775	2.673	2.577	2.487	2.402	2.322	2.246	2.174	2.106	2.042	1.981	1.923	1.868	1.816	1.766	1.589	3
4	3.808	3.630	3.465	3.312	3.170	3.037	2.914	2.798	2.690	2.589	2.494	2.404	2.320	2.241	2.166	2.096	1.849	4
5	4.713	4.452	4.212	3.993	3.791	3.605	3.433	3.274	3.127	2.991	2.864	2.745	2.635	2.532	2.436	2.345	2.035	5
6	5.601	5.242	4.917	4.623	4.355	4.111	3.889	3.685	3.498	3.326	3.167	3.020	2.885	2.759	2.643	2.534	2.168	6
7	6.472	6.002	5.582	5.206	4.868	4.564	4.288	4.039	3.812	3.605	3.416	3.242	3.083	2.937	2.802	2.677	2.263	7
8	7.325	6.733	6.210	5.747	5.335	4.968	4.639	4.344	4.078	3.837	3.619	3.421	3.241	3.076	2.925	2.786	2.331	8
9	8.162	7.435	6.802	6.247	5.759	5.328	4.946	4.607	4.303	4.031	3.786	3.566	3.366	3.184	3.019	2.868	2.379	9
10	8.983	8.111	7.360	6.710	6.145	5.650	5.216	4.833	4.494	4.192	3.923	3.682	3.465	3.269	3.092	2.930	2.414	10
11	9.787	8.760	7.887	7.139	6.495	5.938	5.453	5.029	4.656	4.327	4.035	3.776	3.543	3.335	3.147	2.978	2.438	11
12	10.575	9.385	8.384	7.536	6.814	6.194	5.660	5.197	4.793	4.439	4.127	3.851	3.606	3.387	3.190	3.013	2.456	12
13	11.348	9.986	8.853	7.904	7.103	6.424	5.842	5.342	4.910	4.533	4.203	3.912	3.656	3.427	3.223	3.040	2.469	13
14	12.106	10.563	9.295	8.244	7.367	6.628	6.002	5.468	5.008	4.611	4.265	3.962	3.695	3.459	3.249	3.061	2.478	14
15	12.849	11.118	9.712	8.559	7.606	6.811	6.142	5.575	5.092	4.675	4.315	4.001	3.726	3.483	3.268	3.076	2.484	15
16	13.578	11.652	10.106	8.851	7.824	6.974	6.265	5.668	5.162	4.730	4.357	4.033	3.751	3.503	3.283	3.088	2.489	16
17	14.292	12.166	10.477	9.122	8.022	7.120	6.373	5.749	5.222	4.775	4.391	4.059	3.771	3.518	3.295	3.097	2.492	17
18	14.992	12.659	10.828	9.372	8.201	7.250	6.467	5.818	5.273	4.812	4.419	4.080	3.786	3.529	3.304	3.104	2.494	18
19	15.678	13.134	11.158	9.604	8.365	7.366	6.550	5.877	5.316	4.843	4.442	4.097	3.799	3.539	3.311	3.109	2.496	19
20	16.351	13.590	11.470	9.818	8.514	7.469	6.623	5.929	5.353	4.870	4.460	4.110	3.808	3.546	3.316	3.113	2.497	20
21	17.011	14.029	11.764	10.017	8.649	7.562	6.687	5.973	5.384	4.891	4.476	4.121	3.816	3.551	3.320	3.116	2.498	21
22	17.658	14.451	12.042	10.201	8.772	7.645	6.743	6.011	5.410	4.909	4.488	4.130	3.822	3.556	3.323	3.118	2.498	22
23	18.292	14.857	12.303	10.371	8.883	7.718	6.792	6.044	5.432	4.925	4.499	4.137	3.827	3.559	3.325	3.120	2.499	23
24	18.914	15.247	12.550	10.529	8.985	7.784	6.835	6.073	5.451	4.937	4.507	4.143	3.831	3.562	3.327	3.121	2.499	24
25	19.523	15.622	12.783	10.675	9.077	7.843	6.873	6.097	5.467	4.948	4.514	4.147	3.834	3.564	3.329	3.122	2.499	25
26	20.121	15.983	13.003	10.810	9.161	7.896	6.906	6.118	5.480	4.956	4.520	4.151	3.837	3.566	3.330	3.123	2.500	26
27	20.707	16.330	13.211	10.935	9.237	7.943	6.935	6.136	5.492	4.964	4.524	4.154	3.839	3.567	3.331	3.123	2.500	27
28	21.281	16.663	13.406	11.051	9.307	7.984	6.961	6.152	5.502	4.970	4.528	4.157	3.840	3.568	3.331	3.124	2.500	28
29	21.844	16.984	13.591	11.158	9.370	8.022	6.983	6.166	5.510	4.975	4.531	4.159	3.841	3.569	3.332	3.124	2.500	29
30	22.396	17.292	13.765	11.258	9.427	8.055	7.003	6.177	5.517	4.979	4.534	4.160	3.842	3.569	3.332	3.124	2.500	30
35	24.999	18.665	14.498	11.655	9.644	8.176	7.070	6.215	5.539	4.992	4.541	4.164	3.845	3.571	3.333	3.125	2.500	35
40	27.355	19.793	15.046	11.925	9.779	8.244	7.105	6.233	5.548	4.997	4.544	4.166	3.846	3.571	3.333	3.125	2.500	40

*Payments (or receipts) at the end of each period.

Glossary

Abnormal spoilage. Spoilage that would not arise under efficient operating conditions; it is not inherent in a particular production process. (708)

Absorption costing. Method of inventory costing in which all variable manufacturing costs and all fixed manufacturing costs are included as inventoriable costs. (330)

Account analysis method. Approach to cost function estimation that classifies various cost accounts as variable, fixed, or mixed with respect to the identified level of activity. Typically, qualitative rather than quantitative analysis is used when making these cost-classification decisions. (377)

Accrual accounting rate-of-return (AARR) method. Capital budgeting method that divides an accrual accounting measure of average annual income of a project by an accrual accounting measure of its investment. See also *return on investment (ROI)*. (814)

Activity. An event, task, or unit of work with a specified purpose. (158)

Activity-based budgeting (ABB). Budgeting approach that focuses on the budgeted cost of the activities necessary to produce and sell products and services. (209)

Activity-based costing (ABC). Approach to costing that focuses on individual activities as the fundamental cost objects. It uses the costs of these activities as the basis for assigning costs to other cost objects such as products or services. (158)

Activity-based management (ABM). Method of management decision-making that uses activity-based costing information to improve customer satisfaction and profitability. (169)

Actual cost. Cost incurred (a historical or past cost), as distinguished from a budgeted or forecasted cost. (29)

Actual costing. A costing system that traces direct costs to a cost object by using the actual direct-cost rates times the actual quantities of the direct-cost inputs and allocates indirect costs based on the actual indirect-cost rates times the actual quantities of the cost allocation bases. (110)

Actual indirect-cost rate. Actual total indirect costs in a cost pool divided by the actual total quantity of the cost-allocation base for that cost pool. (119)

Adjusted allocation-rate approach. Restates all overhead entries in the general ledger and subsidiary ledgers using actual cost rates rather than budgeted cost rates. (128)

Allowable cost. Cost that the contract parties agree to include in the costs to be reimbursed. (614)

Appraisal costs. Costs incurred to detect which of the individual units of products do not conform to specifications. (736)

Artificial costs. See *complete reciprocated costs*. (607)

Autonomy. The degree of freedom to make decisions. (843)

Average cost. See *unit cost*. (36)

Average waiting time. The average amount of time that an order will wait in line before the machine is set up and the order is processed. (747)

Backflush costing. Costing system that omits recording some of the journal entries relating to the stages from purchase of direct materials to the sale of finished goods. (782)

Balanced scorecard. A framework for implementing strategy that translates an organization's mission and strategy into a set of performance measures. (476)

Batch-level costs. The costs of activities related to a group of units of products or services rather than to each individual unit of product or service. (161)

Belief systems. Lever of control that articulates the mission, purpose, norms of behaviors, and core values of a company intended to inspire managers and other employees to do their best. (895)

Benchmarking. The continuous process of comparing the levels of performance in producing products and services and executing activities against the best levels of performance in competing companies or in companies having similar processes. (267)

Book value. The original cost minus accumulated depreciation of an asset. (448)

Bottleneck. An operation where the work to be performed approaches or exceeds the capacity available to do it. (746)

Boundary systems. Lever of control that describes standards of behavior and codes of conduct expected of all employees, especially actions that are off-limits. (895)

Breakeven point (BEP). Quantity of output sold at which total revenues equal total costs, that is where the operating income is zero. (73)

Budget. Quantitative expression of a proposed plan of action by management for a specified period and an aid to coordinating what needs to be done to implement that plan. (11)

Budgetary slack. The practice of underestimating budgeted revenues, or overestimating budgeted costs, to make budgeted targets more easily achievable. (218)

Budgeted cost. Predicted or forecasted cost (future cost) as distinguished from an actual or historical cost. (29)

Budgeted indirect-cost rate. Budgeted annual indirect costs in a cost pool divided by the budgeted annual quantity of the cost allocation base. (112)

Budgeted performance. Expected performance or a point of reference to compare actual results. (249)

Bundled product. A package of two or more products (or services) that is sold for a single price, but whose individual components may be sold as separate items at their own "standalone" prices. (615)

Business function costs. The sum of all costs (variable and fixed) in a particular business function of the value chain. (429)

Byproducts. Products from a joint production process that have low total sales values compared with the total sales value of the main product or of joint products. (634)

Capital budgeting. The making of long-run planning decisions for investments in projects. (803)

Carrying costs. Costs that arise while holding inventory of goods for sale. (765)

Cash budget. Schedule of expected cash receipts and disbursements. (225)

Cause-and-effect diagram. Diagram that identifies potential causes of defects. Four categories of potential causes of failure are human factors, methods and design factors, machine-related factors, and materials and components factors. Also called a *fishbone diagram*. (740)

Chief financial officer (CFO). Executive responsible for overseeing the financial operations of an organization. Also called *finance director*. (14)

Choice criterion. Objective that can be quantified in a decision model. (90)

Coefficient of determination (r^2). Measures the percentage of variation in a dependent variable explained by one or more independent variables. (399)

Collusive pricing. Companies in an industry conspire in their pricing and production decisions to achieve a price above the competitive price and so restrain trade. (536)

Common cost. Cost of operating a facility, activity, or like cost object that is shared by two or more users. (611)

Complete reciprocated costs. The support department's own costs plus any interdepartmental cost allocations. Also called the *artificial costs* of the support department. (607)

Composite unit. Hypothetical unit with weights based on the mix of individual units. (572)

Conference method. Approach to cost function estimation on the basis of analysis and opinions about costs and their drivers gathered from various departments of a company (purchasing, process engineering, manufacturing, employee relations, and so on). (377)

Conformance quality. Refers to the performance of a product or service relative to its design and product specifications. (736)

Constant. The component of total cost that, within the relevant range, does not vary with changes in the level of the activity. Also called *intercept*. (372)

Constant gross-margin percentage NRV method. Method that allocates joint costs to joint products in such a way that the overall gross-margin percentage is identical for the individual products. (641)

Constraint. A mathematical inequality or equality that must be satisfied by the variables in a mathematical model. (455)

Continuous budget. See *rolling budget*. (202)

Contribution income statement. Income statement that groups costs into variable costs and fixed costs to highlight the contribution margin. (69)

Contribution margin. Total revenues minus total variable costs. (68)

Contribution margin per unit. Selling price minus the variable cost per unit. (69)

Contribution margin percentage. Contribution margin per unit divided by selling price. Also called *contribution margin ratio*. (69)

Contribution margin ratio. See *contribution margin percentage*. (69)

Control. Taking actions that implement the planning decisions, deciding how to evaluate performance, and providing feedback and learning that will help future decision making. (11)

Control chart. Graph of a series of successive observations of a particular step, procedure, or operation taken at regular intervals of time. Each observation is plotted relative to specified ranges that represent the limits within which observations are expected to fall. (739)

Controllability. Degree of influence that a specific manager has over costs, revenues, or related items for which he or she is responsible. (217)

Controllable cost. Any cost that is primarily subject to the influence of a given responsibility center manager for a given period. (217)

Controller. The financial executive primarily responsible for management accounting and financial accounting. Also called *chief accounting officer*. (14)

Conversion costs. All manufacturing costs other than direct material costs. (46)

Cost. Resource sacrificed or forgone to achieve a specific objective. (29)

Cost accounting. Measures, analyzes, and reports financial and nonfinancial information relating to the costs of acquiring or using resources in an organization. It provides information for both management accounting and financial accounting. (4)

Cost Accounting Standards Board (CASB). Government agency that has the exclusive authority to make, put into effect, amend, and rescind cost accounting standards and interpretations thereof designed to achieve uniformity and consistency in regard to measurement, assignment, and allocation of costs to government contracts within the United States. (614)

Cost accumulation. Collection of cost data in some organized way by means of an accounting system. (29)

Cost allocation. Assignment of indirect costs to a particular cost object. (30)

Cost-allocation base. A factor that links in a systematic way an indirect cost or group of indirect costs to a cost object. (108)

Cost-application base. Cost-allocation base when the cost object is a job, product, or customer. (108)

Cost assignment. General term that encompasses both (1) tracing accumulated costs that have a direct relationship to a cost object and (2) allocating accumulated costs that have an indirect relationship to a cost object. (30)

Cost–benefit approach. Approach to decision-making and resource allocation based on a comparison of the expected benefits from attaining company goals and the expected costs. (13)

Cost center. Responsibility center where the manager is accountable for costs only. (216)

Cost driver. A variable, such as the level of activity or volume, that causally affects costs over a given time span. (34)

Cost estimation. The attempt to measure a past relationship based on data from past costs and the related level of an activity. (374)

Cost function. Mathematical description of how a cost changes with changes in the level of an activity relating to that cost. (371)

Cost hierarchy. Categorization of indirect costs into different cost pools on the basis of the different types of cost drivers, or cost-allocation bases, or different degrees of difficulty in determining cause-and-effect (or benefits received) relationships. (161)

Cost incurrence. Describes when a resource is consumed (or benefit forgone) to meet a specific objective. (525)

Cost leadership. Organization's ability to achieve lower costs relative to competitors through productivity and efficiency improvements, elimination of waste, and tight cost control. (474)

Cost management. The approaches and activities of managers to use resources to increase value to customers and to achieve organizational goals. (4)

Cost object. Anything for which a measurement of costs is desired. (29)

Cost of capital. See *required rate of return (RRR)*. (806)

Cost of goods manufactured. Cost of goods brought to completion, whether they were started before or during the current accounting period. (43)

Cost pool. A grouping of individual cost items. (108)

Cost predictions. Forecasts about future costs. (374)

Cost tracing. Describes the assignment of direct costs to a particular cost object. (30)

Costs of quality (COQ). Costs incurred to prevent, or the costs arising as a result of, the production of a low-quality product. (736)

Cost–volume–profit (CVP) analysis. Examines the behavior of total revenues, total costs, and operating income as changes occur in the units sold, the selling price, the variable cost per unit, or the fixed costs of a product. (67)

Cumulative average-time learning model. Learning curve model in which the cumulative average time per unit declines by a constant percentage each time the cumulative quantity of units produced doubles. (390)

Current cost. Asset measure based on the cost of purchasing an asset today identical to the one currently held, or the cost of purchasing an asset that provides services like the one currently held if an identical asset cannot be purchased. (884)

Customer-cost hierarchy. Hierarchy that categorizes costs related to customers into different cost pools on the basis of different types of cost drivers, or cost-allocation bases, or different degrees of difficulty in determining cause-and-effect or benefits-received relationships. (552)

Customer life-cycle costs. Focuses on the total costs incurred by a customer to acquire, use, maintain, and dispose of a product or service. (533)

Customer-profitability analysis. The reporting and analysis of revenues earned from customers and the costs incurred to earn those revenues. (551)

Customer relationship management (CRM). A strategy that integrates people and technology in all business functions to deepen relationships with customers, partners, and distributors. (7)

Customer-response time. Duration from the time a customer places an order for a product or service to the time the product or service is delivered to the customer. (745)

Customer service. Providing after-sale support to customers. (6)

Decentralization. The freedom for managers at lower levels of the organization to make decisions. (843)

Decision model. Formal method for making a choice, often involving both quantitative and qualitative analyses. (425)

Decision table. Summary of the alternative actions, events, outcomes, and probabilities of events in a decision model. (91)

Degree of operating leverage. Contribution margin divided by operating income at any given level of sales. (82)

Denominator level. The denominator in the budgeted fixed overhead rate computation. (292)

Denominator-level variance. See *production-volume variance*. (298)

Dependent variable. The cost to be predicted. (379)

Design of products and processes. The detailed planning and engineering of products and processes. (6)

Design quality. Refers to how closely the characteristics of a product or service meet the needs and wants of customers. (736)

Designed-in costs. See *locked-in costs*. (525)

Diagnostic control systems. Lever of control that monitors critical performance variables that help managers track progress toward achieving a company's strategic goals. Managers are held accountable for meeting these goals. (894)

Differential cost. Difference in total cost between two alternatives. (433)

Differential revenue. Difference in total revenue between two alternatives. (434)

Direct costing. See *variable costing*. (329)

Direct costs of a cost object. Costs related to the particular cost object that can be traced to that object in an economically feasible (cost-effective) way. (30)

Direct manufacturing labor costs. Include the compensation of all manufacturing labor that can be traced to the cost object (work in process and then finished goods) in an economically feasible way. (39)

Direct materials costs. Acquisition costs of all materials that eventually become part of the cost object (work in process and then finished goods), and that can be traced to the cost object in an economically feasible way. (39)

Direct materials inventory. Direct materials in stock and awaiting use in the manufacturing process. (38)

Direct materials mix variance. The difference between (1) budgeted cost for actual mix of the actual total quantity of direct materials used and (2) budgeted cost of budgeted mix of the actual total quantity of direct materials used. (272)

Direct materials yield variance. The difference between (1) budgeted cost of direct materials based on the actual total quantity of direct materials used and (2) flexible-budget cost of direct materials based on the budgeted total quantity of direct materials allowed for the actual output produced. (272)

Direct method. Cost allocation method that allocates each support department's costs to operating departments only. (604)

Discount rate. See *required rate of return (RRR)*. (806)

Discounted cash flow (DCF) methods. Capital budgeting methods that measure all expected future cash inflows and outflows of a project as if they occurred at the present point in time. (806)

Discounted payback method. Capital budgeting method that calculates the amount of time required for the discounted expected future cash flows to recoup the net initial investment in a project. (813)

Discretionary costs. Arise from periodic (usually annual) decisions regarding the maximum amount to be incurred and have no measurable cause-and-effect relationship between output and resources used. (496)

Distribution. Delivering products or services to customers. (6)

Downsizing. An integrated approach of configuring processes, products, and people to match costs to the activities that need to be performed to operate effectively and efficiently in the present and future. Also called *rightsizing*. (497)

Downward demand spiral. Pricing context where prices are raised to spread capacity costs over a smaller number of output units. Continuing reduction in the demand for products that occurs when the prices of competitors' products are not met and, as demand drops further, higher and higher unit costs result in more and more reluctance to meet competitors' prices. (346)

Dual pricing. Approach to transfer pricing using two separate transfer-pricing methods to price each transfer from one subunit to another. (856)

Dual-rate method. Allocation method that classifies costs in each cost pool into two pools (a variable-cost pool and a fixed-cost pool) with each pool using a different cost-allocation base. (594)

Dumping. Under U.S. laws, it occurs when a non-U.S. company sells a product in the United States at a price below the market value in the country where it is produced, and this lower price materially injures or threatens to materially injure an industry in the United States. (536)

Dysfunctional decision making. See *suboptimal decision making*. (844)

Economic order quantity (EOQ). Decision model that calculates the optimal quantity of inventory to order under a set of assumptions. (766)

Economic value added (EVA®). After-tax operating income minus the (after-tax) weighted-average cost of capital multiplied by total assets minus current liabilities. (880)

Effectiveness. The degree to which a predetermined objective or target is met. (265)

Efficiency. The relative amount of inputs used to achieve a given output level. (265)

Efficiency variance. The difference between actual input quantity used and budgeted input quantity allowed for actual output, multiplied by budgeted price. Also called *usage variance*. (258)

Effort. Exertion toward achieving a goal. (842)

Engineered costs. Costs that result from a cause-and-effect relationship between the cost driver, output, and the (direct or indirect) resources used to produce that output. (496)

Enterprise resource planning (ERP) system. An integrated set of software modules covering a company's accounting, distribution, manufacturing, purchasing, human resources, and other functions. (779)

Equivalent units. Derived amount of output units that (a) takes the quantity of each input (factor of production) in units completed and in incomplete units of work in process and (b) converts the quantity of input into the amount of completed output units that could be produced with that quantity of input. (668)

Event. A possible relevant occurrence in a decision model. (90)

Expected monetary value. See *expected value*. (91)

Expected value. Weighted average of the outcomes of a decision with the probability of each outcome serving as the weight. Also called *expected monetary value*. (91)

Experience curve. Function that measures the decline in cost per unit in various business functions of the value chain, such as manufacturing, marketing, distribution, and so on, as the amount of these activities increases. (389)

External failure costs. Costs incurred on defective products after they are shipped to customers. (736)

Facility-sustaining costs. The costs of activities that cannot be traced to individual products or services but support the organization as a whole. (161)

Factory overhead costs. See *indirect manufacturing costs*. (39)

Favorable variance. Variance that has the effect of increasing operating income relative to the budgeted amount. Denoted F. (251)

Finance director. See *chief financial officer (CFO)*. (14)

Financial accounting. Measures and records business transactions and provides financial statements that are based on generally accepted accounting principles. It focuses on reporting to external parties such as investors and banks. (3)

Financial budget. Part of the master budget that focuses on how operations and planned capital outlays affect cash. It is made up of the capital expenditures budget, the cash budget, the budgeted balance sheet, and the budgeted statement of cash flows. (203)

Financial planning models. Mathematical representations of the relationships among operating activities, financial activities, and other factors that affect the master budget. (213)

Finished goods inventory. Goods completed but not yet sold. (38)

First-in, first-out (FIFO) process-costing method. Method of process costing that assigns the cost of the previous accounting period's equivalent units in beginning work-in-process inventory to the first units completed and transferred out of the process, and assigns the cost of equivalent units worked on during the current period first to complete beginning inventory, next to start and complete new units, and finally to units in ending work-in-process inventory. (676)

Fixed cost. Cost that remains unchanged in total for a given time period, despite wide changes in the related level of total activity or volume. (32)

Fixed overhead flexible-budget variance. The difference between actual fixed overhead costs and fixed overhead costs in the flexible budget. (297)

Fixed overhead spending variance. Same as the fixed overhead flexible-budget variance. The difference between actual fixed overhead costs and fixed overhead costs in the flexible budget. (297)

Flexible budget. Budget developed using budgeted revenues and budgeted costs based on the actual output in the budget period. (252)

Flexible-budget variance. The difference between an actual result and the corresponding flexible-budget amount based on the actual output level in the budget period. (253)

Full costs of the product. The sum of all variable and fixed costs in all business functions of the value chain (R&D, design, production, marketing, distribution, and customer service). (429)

Goal congruence. Exists when individuals and groups work toward achieving the organization's goals. Managers working in their own best interest take actions that align with the overall goals of top management. (842)

Gross margin percentage. Gross margin divided by revenues. (88)

Growth component. Change in operating income attributable solely to the change in the quantity of output sold between one period and the next. (489)

High-low method. Method used to estimate a cost function that uses only the highest and lowest observed values of the cost driver within the relevant range and their respective costs. (381)

Homogeneous cost pool. Cost pool in which all the costs have the same or a similar cause-and-effect or benefits-received relationship with the cost-allocation base. (569)

Hurdle rate. See *required rate of return (RRR)*. (806)

Hybrid-costing system. Costing system that blends characteristics from both job-costing systems and process-costing systems. (685)

Idle time. Wages paid for unproductive time caused by lack of orders, machine breakdowns, material shortages, poor scheduling, and the like. (47)

Imputed costs. Costs recognized in particular situations but not incorporated in financial accounting records. (879)

Incongruent decision making. See *suboptimal decision making*. (844)

Incremental cost. Additional total cost incurred for an activity. (433)

Incremental cost-allocation method. Method that ranks the individual users of a cost object in the order of users most responsible for the common cost and then uses this ranking to allocate cost among those users. (617)

Incremental revenue. Additional total revenue from an activity. (434)

Incremental revenue-allocation method. Method that ranks individual products in a bundle according to criteria determined by management (for example, sales), and then uses this ranking to allocate bundled revenues to the individual products. (617)

Incremental unit-time learning model. Learning curve model in which the incremental time needed to produce the last unit declines by a constant percentage each time the cumulative quantity of units produced doubles. (391)

Independent variable. Level of activity or cost driver used to predict the dependent variable (costs) in a cost estimation or prediction model. (379)

Indirect costs of a cost object. Costs related to the particular cost object that cannot be traced to that object in an economically feasible (cost-effective) way. (30)

Indirect manufacturing costs. All manufacturing costs that are related to the cost object (work in process and then finished goods) but that cannot be traced to that cost object in an economically feasible way. Also called *manufacturing overhead costs* and *factory overhead costs*. (39)

Industrial engineering method. Approach to cost function estimation that analyzes the relationship between inputs and outputs in physical terms. Also called *work measurement method*. (376)

Inflation. The decline in the general purchasing power of the monetary unit, such as dollars. (827)

Insourcing. Process of producing goods or providing services within the organization rather than purchasing those same goods or services from outside vendors. (432)

Inspection point. Stage of the production process at which products are examined to determine whether they are acceptable or unacceptable units. (709)

Interactive control systems. Formal information systems that managers use to focus organization attention and learning on key strategic issues. (896)

Intercept. See *constant*. (372)

Intermediate product. Product transferred from one subunit to another subunit of an organization. This product may either be further worked on by the receiving subunit or sold to an external customer. (846)

Internal failure costs. Costs incurred on defective products before they are shipped to customers. (736)

Internal rate-of-return (IRR) method. Capital budgeting discounted cash flow (DCF) method that calculates the discount rate at which the present value of expected cash inflows from a project equals the present value of its expected cash outflows. (808)

Inventoriable costs. All costs of a product that are considered as assets in the balance sheet when they are incurred and that become cost of goods sold only when the product is sold. (39)

Inventory management. Planning, coordinating, and controlling activities related to the flow of inventory into, through, and out of an organization. (765)

Investment. Resources or assets used to generate income. (876)

Investment center. Responsibility center where the manager is accountable for investments, revenues, and costs. (216)

Job. A unit or multiple units of a distinct product or service. (108)

Job-cost record. Source document that records and accumulates all the costs assigned to a specific job, starting when work begins. Also called *job-cost sheet*. (113)

Job-cost sheet. See *job-cost record*. (113)

Job-costing system. Costing system in which the cost object is a unit or multiple units of a distinct product or service called a job. (108)

Joint costs. Costs of a production process that yields multiple products simultaneously. (633)

Joint products. Two or more products that have high total sales values compared with the total sales values of other products yielded by a joint production process. (634)

Just-in-time (JIT) production. Demand-pull manufacturing system in which each component in a production line is produced as soon as, and only when, needed by the next step in the production line. Also called *lean production*. (778)

Just-in-time (JIT) purchasing. The purchase of materials (or goods) so that they are delivered just as needed for production (or sales). (773)

Kaizen budgeting. Budgetary approach that explicitly incorporates continuous improvement anticipated during the budget period into the budget numbers. (220)

Labor-time sheet. Source document that contains information about the amount of labor time used for a specific job in a specific department. (114)

Lean accounting. Costing method that supports creating value for the customer by costing the entire value stream, not individual products or departments, thereby eliminating waste in the accounting process. (790)

Lean production. See *just-in-time (JIT) production*. (778)

Learning. Involves managers examining past performance and systematically exploring alternative ways to make better-informed decisions and plans in the future. (12)

Learning curve. Function that measures how labor-hours per unit decline as units of production increase because workers are learning and becoming better at their jobs. (389)

Life-cycle budgeting. Budget that estimates the revenues and business function costs of the value chain attributable to each product from initial R&D to final customer service and support. (531)

Life-cycle costing. System that tracks and accumulates business function costs of the value chain attributable to each product from initial R&D to final customer service and support. (531)

Line management. Managers (for example, in production, marketing, or distribution) who are directly responsible for attaining the goals of the organization. (14)

Linear cost function. Cost function in which the graph of total costs versus the level of a single activity related to that cost is a straight line within the relevant range. (371)

Linear programming (LP). Optimization technique used to maximize an objective function (for example, contribution margin of a mix of products), when there are multiple constraints. (456)

Locked-in costs. Costs that have not yet been incurred but, based on decisions that have already been made, will be incurred in the future. Also called *designed-in costs*. (525)

Main product. Product from a joint production process that has a high total sales value compared with the total sales values of all other products of the joint production process. (634)

Make-or-buy decisions. Decisions about whether a producer of goods or services will insource (produce goods or services within the firm) or outsource (purchase them from outside vendors). (432)

Management accounting. Measures, analyzes, and reports financial and nonfinancial information that helps managers make decisions to fulfill the goals of an organization. It focuses on internal reporting. (4)

Management by exception. Practice of focusing management attention on areas not operating as expected and giving less attention to areas operating as expected. (249)

Management control system. Means of gathering and using information to aid and coordinate the planning and control decisions throughout an organization and to guide the behavior of its managers and employees. (841)

Manufacturing cells. Grouping of all the different types of equipment used to make a given product. (778)

Manufacturing cycle efficiency (MCE). Value-added manufacturing time divided by manufacturing cycle time. (746)

Manufacturing cycle time. See *manufacturing lead time*. (745)

Manufacturing lead time. Duration between the time an order is received by manufacturing to the time a finished good is produced. Also called *manufacturing cycle time*. (745)

Manufacturing overhead allocated. Amount of manufacturing overhead costs allocated to individual jobs, products, or services based on the budgeted rate multiplied by the actual quantity used of the cost-allocation base. Also called *manufacturing overhead applied*. (122)

Manufacturing overhead applied. See *manufacturing overhead allocated*. (122)

Manufacturing overhead costs. See *indirect manufacturing costs*. (39)

Manufacturing-sector companies. Companies that purchase materials and components and convert them into various finished goods. (38)

Margin of safety. Amount by which budgeted (or actual) revenues exceed breakeven revenues. (79)

Marketing. Promoting and selling products or services to customers or prospective customers. (6)

Market-share variance. The difference in budgeted contribution margin for actual market size in units caused solely by actual market share being different from budgeted market share. (574)

Market-size variance. The difference in budgeted contribution margin at the budgeted market share caused solely by actual market size in units being different from budgeted market size in units. (574)

Master budget. Expression of management's operating and financial plans for a specified period (usually a fiscal year) including a set of budgeted financial statements. Also called *pro forma statements*. (199)

Master-budget capacity utilization. The expected level of capacity utilization for the current budget period (typically one year). (344)

Materials requirements planning (MRP). Push-through system that manufactures finished goods for inventory on the basis of demand forecasts. (777)

Materials-requisition record. Source document that contains information about the cost of direct materials used on a specific job and in a specific department. (114)

Matrix method. See *reciprocal method*. (608)

Merchandising-sector companies. Companies that purchase and then sell tangible products without changing their basic form. (38)

Mixed cost. A cost that has both fixed and variable elements. Also called a *semivariable cost*. (372)

Moral hazard. Describes situations in which an employee prefers to exert less effort (or to report distorted information) compared with the effort (or accurate information) desired by the owner because the employee's effort (or validity of the reported information) cannot be accurately monitored and enforced. (890)

Motivation. The desire to attain a selected goal (the goal-congruence aspect) combined with the resulting pursuit of that goal (the effort aspect). (842)

Multicollinearity. Exists when two or more independent variables in a multiple regression model are highly correlated with each other. (406)

Multiple regression. Regression model that estimates the relationship between the dependent variable and two or more independent variables. (383)

Net income. Operating income plus nonoperating revenues (such as interest revenue) minus nonoperating costs (such as interest cost) minus income taxes. (76)

Net present value (NPV) method. Capital budgeting discounted cash flow (DCF) method that calculates the expected monetary gain or loss from a project by discounting all expected future cash inflows and outflows to the present point in time, using the required rate of return. (806)

Net realizable value (NRV) method. Method that allocates joint costs to joint products on the basis of final sales value minus separable costs of total production of the joint products during the accounting period. (641)

Nominal rate of return. Made up of three elements: (a) a risk-free element when there is no expected inflation, (b) a business-risk element, and (c) an inflation element. (827)

Nonlinear cost function. Cost function in which the graph of total costs based on the level of a single activity is not a straight line within the relevant range. (388)

Non-value-added cost. A cost that, if eliminated, would not reduce the actual or perceived value or utility (usefulness) customers obtain from using the product or service. (525)

Normal capacity utilization. The level of capacity utilization that satisfies average customer demand over a period (say, two to three years) that includes seasonal, cyclical, and trend factors. (344)

Normal costing. A costing system that traces direct costs to a cost object by using the actual direct-cost rates times the actual quantities of the direct-cost inputs and that allocates indirect costs based on the budgeted indirect-cost rates times the actual quantities of the cost-allocation bases. (112)

Normal spoilage. Spoilage inherent in a particular production process that arises even under efficient operating conditions. (708)

Objective function. Expresses the objective to be maximized (for example, operating income) or minimized (for example, operating costs) in a decision model (for example, a linear programming model). (455)

On-time performance. Delivering a product or service by the time it is scheduled to be delivered. (746)

One-time-only special order. Orders that have no long-run implications. (428)

Operating budget. Budgeted income statement and its supporting budget schedules. (203)

Operating department. Department that directly adds value to a product or service. Also called a *production department* in manufacturing companies. (593)

Operating income. Total revenues from operations minus cost of goods sold and operating costs (excluding interest expense and income taxes). (44)

Operating-income volume variance. The difference between static-budget operating income and the operating income based on budgeted profit per unit and actual units of output. (307)

Operating leverage. Effects that fixed costs have on changes in operating income as changes occur in units sold and hence in contribution margin. (82)

Operation. A standardized method or technique that is performed repetitively, often on different materials, resulting in different finished goods. (686)

Operation-costing system. Hybrid-costing system applied to batches of similar, but not identical, products. Each batch of products is often a variation of a single design, and it proceeds through a sequence of operations, but each batch does not necessarily move through the same operations as other batches. Within each operation, all product units use identical amounts of the operation's resources. (686)

Opportunity cost. The contribution to operating income that is forgone or rejected by not using a limited resource in its next-best alternative use. (436)

Opportunity cost of capital. See *required rate of return (RRR)*. (806)

Ordering costs. Costs of preparing, issuing, and paying purchase orders, plus receiving and inspecting the items included in the orders. (765)

Organization structure. Arrangement of lines of responsibility within the organization. (216)

Outcomes. Predicted economic results of the various possible combinations of actions and events in a decision model. (91)

Output unit–level costs. The costs of activities performed on each individual unit of a product or service. (161)

Outsourcing. Process of purchasing goods and services from outside vendors rather than producing the same goods or providing the same services within the organization. (432)

Overabsorbed indirect costs. See *overallocated indirect costs*. (127)

Overallocated indirect costs. Allocated amount of indirect costs in an accounting period is greater than the actual (incurred) amount in that period. Also called *overapplied indirect costs* and *overabsorbed indirect costs*. (127)

Overapplied indirect costs. See *overallocated indirect costs*. (127)

Overtime premium. Wage rate paid to workers (for both direct labor and indirect labor) in excess of their straight-time wage rates. (47)

Pareto diagram. Chart that indicates how frequently each type of defect occurs, ordered from the most frequent to the least frequent. (740)

Partial productivity. Measures the quantity of output produced divided by the quantity of an individual input used. (503)

Payback method. Capital budgeting method that measures the time it will take to recoup, in the form of expected future cash flows, the net initial investment in a project. (811)

Peak-load pricing. Practice of charging a higher price for the same product or service when the demand for it approaches the physical limit of the capacity to produce that product or service. (534)

Perfectly competitive market. Exists when there is a homogeneous product with buying prices equal to selling prices and no individual buyers or sellers can affect those prices by their own actions. (850)

Period costs. All costs in the income statement other than cost of goods sold. (39)

Physical-measure method. Method that allocates joint costs to joint products on the basis of the relative weight, volume, or other physical measure at the splitoff point of total production of these products during the accounting period. (638)

Planning. Selecting organization goals, predicting results under various alternative ways of achieving those goals, deciding how to attain the desired goals, and communicating the goals and how to attain them to the entire organization. (11)

Practical capacity. The level of capacity that reduces theoretical capacity by unavoidable operating interruptions such as scheduled maintenance time, shutdowns for holidays, and so on. (344)

Predatory pricing. Company deliberately prices below its costs in an effort to drive out competitors and restrict supply and then raises prices rather than enlarge demand. (535)

Prevention costs. Costs incurred to preclude the production of products that do not conform to specifications. (673)

Previous-department costs. See *transferred-in costs*. (681)

Price discount. Reduction in selling price below list selling price to encourage increases in customer purchases. (552)

Price discrimination. Practice of charging different customers different prices for the same product or service. (534)

Price-recovery component. Change in operating income attributable solely to changes in prices of inputs and outputs between one period and the next. (489)

Price variance. The difference between actual price and budgeted price multiplied by actual quantity of input. Also called *rate variance*. (258)

Prime costs. All direct manufacturing costs. (45)

Pro forma statements. Budgeted financial statements. (199)

Probability. Likelihood or chance that an event will occur. (90)

Probability distribution. Describes the likelihood (or the probability) that each of the mutually exclusive and collectively exhaustive set of events will occur. (90)

Process-costing system. Costing system in which the cost object is masses of identical or similar units of a product or service. (109)

Product. Any output that has a positive total sales value (or an output that enables an organization to avoid incurring costs). (634)

Product cost. Sum of the costs assigned to a product for a specific purpose. (48)

Product-cost cross-subsidization. Costing outcome where one undercosted (overcosted) product results in at least one other product being overcosted (undercosted). (152)

Product differentiation. Organization's ability to offer products or services perceived by its customers to be superior and unique relative to the products or services of its competitors. (474)

Product life cycle. Spans the time from initial R&D on a product to when customer service and support is no longer offered for that product. (531)

Product-mix decisions. Decisions about which products to sell and in what quantities. (440)

Product overcosting. A product consumes a low level of resources but is reported to have a high cost per unit. (152)

Product-sustaining costs. The costs of activities undertaken to support individual products regardless of the number of units or batches in which the units are produced. (161)

Product undercosting. A product consumes a high level of resources but is reported to have a low cost per unit. (152)

Production. Acquiring, coordinating, and assembling resources to produce a product or deliver a service. (6)

Production department. See *operating department*. (593)

Production-volume variance. The difference between budgeted fixed overhead and fixed overhead allocated on the basis of actual output produced. Also called *denominator-level variance*. (298)

Productivity. Measures the relationship between actual inputs used (both quantities and costs) and actual outputs produced; the lower the inputs for a given quantity of outputs or the higher the outputs for a given quantity of inputs, the higher the productivity. (503)

Productivity component. Change in costs attributable to a change in the quantity of inputs used in the current period relative to the quantity of inputs that would have been used in the prior period to produce the quantity of current period output. (489)

Profit center. Responsibility center where the manager is accountable for revenues and costs. (216)

Proration. The spreading of underallocated manufacturing overhead or overallocated manufacturing overhead among ending work in process, finished goods, and cost of goods sold. (128)

Purchase-order lead time. The time between placing an order and its delivery. (766)

Purchasing costs. Cost of goods acquired from suppliers including incoming freight or transportation costs. (765)

PV graph. Shows how changes in the quantity of units sold affect operating income. (75)

Qualitative factors. Outcomes that are difficult to measure accurately in numerical terms. (428)

Quality. The total features and characteristics of a product made or a service performed according to specifications to satisfy customers at the time of purchase and during use. (735)

Quantitative factors. Outcomes that are measured in numerical terms. (427)

Rate variance. See *price variance*. (258)

Real rate of return. The rate of return demanded to cover investment risk (with no inflation). It has a risk-free element and a business-risk element. (827)

Reciprocal method. Cost allocation method that fully recognizes the mutual services provided among all support departments. Also called *matrix method*. (606)

Reengineering. The fundamental rethinking and redesign of business processes to achieve improvements in critical measures of performance, such as cost, quality, service, speed, and customer satisfaction. (475)

Refined costing system. Costing system that reduces the use of broad averages for assigning the cost of resources to cost objects (jobs, products, services) and provides better measurement of the costs of indirect resources used by different cost objects—no matter how differently various cost objects use indirect resources. (157)

Regression analysis. Statistical method that measures the average amount of change in the dependent variable associated with a unit change in one or more independent variables. (383)

Relevant costs. Expected future costs that differ among alternative courses of action being considered. (426)

Relevant range. Band of normal activity level or volume in which there is a specific relationship between the level of activity or volume and the cost in question. (35)

Relevant revenues. Expected future revenues that differ among alternative courses of action being considered. (426)

Reorder point. The quantity level of inventory on hand that triggers a new purchase order. (769)

Required rate of return (RRR). The minimum acceptable annual rate of return on an investment. Also called the *discount rate*, *hurdle rate*, *cost of capital*, or *opportunity cost of capital*. (806)

Research and development (R&D). Generating and experimenting with ideas related to new products, services, or processes. (6)

Residual income (RI). Accounting measure of income minus a dollar amount for required return on an accounting measure of investment. (879)

Residual term. The vertical difference or distance between actual cost and estimated cost for each observation in a regression model. (383)

Responsibility accounting. System that measures the plans, budgets, actions, and actual results of each responsibility center. (216)

Responsibility center. Part, segment, or subunit of an organization whose manager is accountable for a specified set of activities. (216)

Return on investment (ROI). An accounting measure of income divided by an accounting measure of investment. See also *accrual accounting rate of return method*. (877)

Revenue allocation. The allocation of revenues that are related to a particular revenue object but cannot be traced to it in an economically feasible (cost-effective) way. (614)

Revenue center. Responsibility center where the manager is accountable for revenues only. (216)

Revenue driver. A variable, such as volume, that causally affects revenues. (72)

Revenue object. Anything for which a separate measurement of revenue is desired. (614)

Revenues. Inflows of assets (usually cash or accounts receivable) received for products or services provided to customers. (39)

Rework. Units of production that do not meet the specifications required by customers for finished units that are subsequently repaired and sold as good finished units. (707)

Rightsizing. See *downsizing*. (497)

Rolling budget. Budget or plan that is always available for a specified future period by adding a period (month, quarter, or year) to the period that just ended. Also called *continuous budget or rolling forecast*. (202)

Safety stock. Inventory held at all times regardless of the quantity of inventory ordered using the EOQ model. (769)

Sales mix. Quantities of various products or services that constitute total unit sales. (84)

Sales-mix variance. The difference between (1) budgeted contribution margin for the actual sales mix, and (2) budgeted contribution margin for the budgeted sales mix. (572)

Sales-quantity variance. The difference between (1) budgeted contribution margin based on actual units sold of all products at the budgeted mix and (2) contribution margin in the static budget (which is based on the budgeted units of all products to be sold at the budgeted mix). (572)

Sales value at splitoff method. Method that allocates joint costs to joint products on the basis of the relative total sales value at the splitoff point of the total production of these products during the accounting period. (637)

Sales-volume variance. The difference between a flexible-budget amount and the corresponding static-budget amount. (253)

Scrap. Residual material left over when making a product. (707)

Selling-price variance. The difference between the actual selling price and the budgeted selling price multiplied by the actual units sold. (255)

Semivariable cost. See *mixed cost*. (372)

Sensitivity analysis. A what-if technique that managers use to calculate how an outcome will change if the original predicted data are not achieved or if an underlying assumption changes. (79)

Separable costs. All costs (manufacturing, marketing, distribution, and so on) incurred beyond the splitoff point that are assignable to each of the specific products identified at the splitoff point. (633)

Sequential allocation method. See *step-down method*. (605)

Sequential tracking. Approach in a product-costing system in which recording of the journal entries occurs in the same order as actual purchases and progress in production. (781)

Service department. See *support department*. (593)

Service-sector companies. Companies that provide services or intangible products to their customers. (38)

Service-sustaining costs. The costs of activities undertaken to support individual services. (161)

Shrinkage costs. Costs that result from theft by outsiders, embezzlement by employees, misclassifications, and clerical errors. (766)

Simple regression. Regression model that estimates the relationship between the dependent variable and one independent variable. (383)

Single-rate method. Allocation method that allocates costs in each cost pool to cost objects using the same rate per unit of a single allocation base. (594)

Slope coefficient. Coefficient term in a cost estimation model that indicates the amount by which total cost changes when a one-unit change occurs in the level of activity within the relevant range. (372)

Source document. An original record that supports journal entries in an accounting system. (113)

Specification analysis. Testing of the assumptions of regression analysis. (401)

Splitoff point. The juncture in a joint-production process when two or more products become separately identifiable. (633)

Spoilage. Units of production that do not meet the specifications required by customers for good units and that are discarded or sold at reduced prices. (707)

Staff management. Staff (such as management accountants and human resources managers) who provide advice and assistance to line management. (14)

Stand-alone cost-allocation method. Method that uses information pertaining to each user of a cost object as a separate entity to determine the cost-allocation weights. (612)

Stand-alone revenue-allocation method. Method that uses product-specific information on the products in the bundle as weights for allocating the bundled revenues to the individual products. (616)

Standard. A carefully determined price, cost, or quantity that is used as a benchmark for judging performance. It is usually expressed on a per unit basis. (257)

Standard cost. A carefully determined cost of a unit of output. (257)

Standard costing. Costing system that traces direct costs to output produced by multiplying the standard prices or rates by the standard quantities of inputs allowed for actual outputs produced and allocates overhead costs on the basis of the standard overhead-cost rates times the standard quantities of the allocation bases allowed for the actual outputs produced. (290)

Standard error of the estimated coefficient. Regression statistic that indicates how much the estimated value of the coefficient is likely to be affected by random factors. (400)

Standard error of the regression. Statistic that measures the variance of residuals in a regression analysis. (399)

Standard input. A carefully determined quantity of input required for one unit of output. (257)

Standard price. A carefully determined price that a company expects to pay for a unit of input. (257)

Static budget. Budget based on the level of output planned at the start of the budget period. (251)

Static-budget variance. Difference between an actual result and the corresponding budgeted amount in the static budget. (251)

Step cost function. A cost function in which the cost remains the same over various ranges of the level of activity, but the cost increases by discrete amounts (that is, increases in steps) as the level of activity changes from one range to the next. (388)

Step-down method. Cost allocation method that partially recognizes the mutual services provided among all support departments. Also called *sequential allocation method*. (605)

Stockout costs. Costs that result when a company runs out of a particular item for which there is customer demand. The company must act to meet that demand or suffer the costs of not meeting it. (765)

Strategic cost management. Describes cost management that specifically focuses on strategic issues. (5)

Strategy. Specifies how an organization matches its own capabilities with the opportunities in the marketplace to accomplish its objectives. (5)

Strategy map. A diagram that describes how an organization creates value by connecting strategic objectives in explicit cause-and-effect relationships with each other in the financial, customer, internal business process, and learning and growth perspectives. (477)

Suboptimal decision making. Decisions in which the benefit to one subunit is more than offset by the costs or loss of benefits to the organization as a whole. Also called *incongruent decision making* or *dysfunctional decision making*. (844)

Sunk costs. Past costs that are unavoidable because they cannot be changed no matter what action is taken. (427)

Super-variable costing. See *throughput costing*. (341)

Supply chain. Describes the flow of goods, services, and information from the initial sources of materials and services to the delivery of products to consumers, regardless of whether those activities occur in the same organization or in other organizations. (7)

Support department. Department that provides the services that assist other internal departments (operating departments and other support departments) in the company. Also called a *service department*. (593)

Sustainability. The development and implementation of strategies to achieve long-term financial, social, and environmental goals. (8)

Target cost per unit. Estimated long-run cost per unit of a product or service that enables the company to achieve its target operating income per unit when selling at the target price. Target cost per unit is derived by subtracting the target operating income per unit from the target price. (523)

Target operating income per unit. Operating income that a company aims to earn per unit of a product or service sold. (523)

Target price. Estimated price for a product or service that potential customers will pay. (522)

Target rate of return on investment. The target annual operating income that an organization aims to achieve divided by invested capital. (529)

Theoretical capacity. The level of capacity based on producing at full efficiency all the time. (343)

Theory of constraints (TOC). Describes methods to maximize operating income when faced with some bottleneck and some nonbottleneck operations. (441)

Throughput costing. Method of inventory costing in which only variable direct material costs are included as inventoriable costs. Also called *super-variable costing*. (341)

Throughput margin. Revenues minus the direct material costs of the goods sold. (441)

Time driver. Any factor in which a change in the factor causes a change in the speed of an activity. (746)

Time value of money. Takes into account that a dollar (or any other monetary unit) received today is worth more than a dollar received at any future time. (806)

Total factor productivity (TFP). The ratio of the quantity of output produced to the costs of all inputs used, based on current period prices. (504)

Total-overhead variance. The sum of the flexible-budget variance and the production-volume variance. (305)

Total quality management (TQM). An integrative philosophy of management for continuously improving the quality of products and processes. (8)

Transfer price. Price one subunit (department or division) charges for a product or service supplied to another subunit of the same organization. (846)

Transferred-in costs. Costs incurred in previous departments that are carried forward as the product's costs when it moves to a subsequent process in the production cycle. Also called *previous department costs*. (681)

Trigger point. Refers to a stage in the cycle from purchase of direct materials to sale of finished goods at which journal entries are made in the accounting system. (782)

Uncertainty. The possibility that an actual amount will deviate from an expected amount. (80)

Underabsorbed indirect costs. See *underallocated indirect costs*. (127)

Underallocated indirect costs. Allocated amount of indirect costs in an accounting period is less than the actual (incurred) amount in that period. Also called *underapplied indirect costs* or *underabsorbed indirect costs*. (127)

Underapplied indirect costs. See *underallocated indirect costs*. (127)

Unfavorable variance. Variance that has the effect of decreasing operating income relative to the budgeted amount. Denoted U. (251)

Unit cost. Cost computed by dividing total cost by the number of units. Also called *average cost*. (36)

Unused capacity. The amount of productive capacity available over and above the productive capacity employed to meet consumer demand in the current period. (496)

Usage variance. See *efficiency variance*. (258)

Value-added cost. A cost that, if eliminated, would reduce the actual or perceived value or utility (usefulness) customers obtain from using the product or service. (525)

Value chain. The sequence of business functions in which customer usefulness is added to products or services of a company. (6)

Value engineering. Systematic evaluation of all aspects of the value chain, with the objective of reducing costs and achieving a quality level that satisfies customers. (525)

Value streams. All valued-added activities needed to design, manufacture, and deliver a given product or product line to customers. (789)

Variable cost. Cost that changes in total in proportion to changes in the related level of total activity or volume. (32)

Variable costing. Method of inventory costing in which only all variable manufacturing costs are included as inventoriable costs. Also called *direct costing*. (329)

Variable overhead efficiency variance. The difference between the actual quantity of variable overhead cost-allocation base used and budgeted quantity of variable overhead cost-allocation base that should have been used to produce actual output, multiplied by budgeted variable overhead cost per unit of cost-allocation base. (293)

Variable overhead flexible-budget variance. The difference between actual variable overhead costs incurred and flexible-budget variable overhead amounts. (293)

Variable overhead spending variance. The difference between actual variable overhead cost per unit and budgeted variable overhead cost per unit of the cost-allocation base, multiplied by actual quantity of variable overhead cost-allocation base used for actual output. (295)

Variance. The difference between actual result and expected performance. (249)

Weighted-average process-costing method. Method of process costing that assigns the equivalent-unit cost of the work done to date (regardless of the accounting period in which it was done) to equivalent units completed and transferred out of the process and to equivalent units in ending work-in-process inventory. (673)

Whale curve. A typically backward-bending curve that represents the results from customer profitability analysis by first ranking customers from best to worst and then plotting their cumulative profitability level. (558)

Work-in-process inventory. Goods partially worked on but not yet completed. Also called *work in progress*. (38)

Work in progress. See *work-in-process inventory*. (38)

Work-measurement method. See *industrial engineering method*. (376)

Index

Author

Company

Subject

Photo Credits

Chapter 1
Page 3: FocusDigital/Alamy;
Page 9: BirchTree/Alamy

Chapter 2
Page 29: Rachel Youdelman/Pearson Education, Inc.;
Page 34: Jim Wilson/The New York Times/Redux Pictures;
Page 45: Kristoffer Tripplaar/Alamy

Chapter 3
Page 67: Lyle A. Waisman/Getty Images;
Page 83: Steve Skjold/Alamy

Chapter 4
Page 107: Ludinko/Shutterstock;
Page 116: Tony Gutierrez/AP Images;
Page 118: Joe Raedle/Staff/Getty Images

Chapter 5
Page 151: Wolfgang Kumm/Picture-Alliance/DPA/AP Images;
Page 173: Fuse/Getty Images

Chapter 6
Page 197: Suzanne Porter/Rough Guides/Pearson Education, Inc.;
Page 215: ZUMA Press, Inc./Alamy

Chapter 7
Page 249: Alexandru Magurean/Getty Images;
Page 255: Rachel Youdelman/Pearson Education, Inc;
Page 264: Soultana Koleska/Alamy

Chapter 8
Page 289: MShieldsPhotos/Alamy;
Page 301: Liaison/Getty Images

Chapter 9
Page 329: Bloomberg/Getty Images;
Page 338: Paul Sakuma/AP Images

Chapter 10
Page 371: Terry Smith Images/Alamy;
Page 378: Rachel Youdelman/Pearson Education, Inc.;
Page 387: Jan Woitas/DPA/Landov

Chapter 11
Page 425: Fred Prouser/Reuters/Landov;
Page 435: Jirasaki/Shutterstock

Chapter 12
Page 473: Michael Kappeler/Staff/AFP/Getty Images;
Page 495: Roberta Sherman/Pearson Education, Inc.

Chapter 13
Page 517: Roberta Sherman/Pearson Education, Inc.;
Page 524: Steve Sheppard/AP Images

Chapter 14
Page 551: Rachel Youdelman/Pearson Education, Inc.;
Page 559: Pearson Education, Inc.

Chapter 15
Page 593: M. Spencer Green/AP Images;
Page 615: Erik S. Lesser/AP Images

Chapter 16
Page 633: Jim Parkin/Alamy;
Page 636: Klaus Eppele/Fotolia

Chapter 17
Page 665: Roberta Sherman/Pearson Education, Inc.;
Page 686: AP Images

Chapter 18
Page 707: Bloomberg/Contributor/Getty Images;
Page 722: Rachel Youdelman/Pearson Education, Inc.

Chapter 19
Page 735: Sandy Huffaker/Corbis;
Page 748: Daniel Heighton/Alamy

Chapter 20
Page 765: Roberta Sherman/Pearson Education, Inc.;
Page 780: Diane Bondareff/AP Images

Chapter 21
Page 803: Wade Payne/AP Images;
Page 822: Yoshikazu Tsuno/AFP/Getty Images/Newscom

Chapter 22
Page 841: Jeff Morgan 16/Alamy;
Page 860: Lenscap/Alamy

Chapter 23
Page 875: Olivier Douliery/ABACA/Newscom;
Page 892: Jeff Greenberg/Alamy